Collins

Collins
Spanish
Dictionary

HarperCollins Publishers
Westerhill Road
Bishopbriggs
Glasgow
G64 2QT
Great Britain

This edition 2012

Reprint 10 9 8 7 6 5 4 3 2 1 0

© HarperCollins Publishers 2012

ISBN 978-0-00-791702-0

www.collinslanguage.com

A catalogue record for this book is
available from the British Library

Typeset by Wordcraft, Glasgow

Printed and bound in Great Britain by
Clays Ltd, St Ives plc

Acknowledgements
We would like to thank those
authors and publishers who kindly
gave permission for copyright
material to be used in the Collins
Word Web. We would also like to
thank Times Newspapers Ltd for
providing valuable data.

MANAGING EDITOR
Gaëlle Amiot-Cadey

CONTRIBUTORS
José Martín Calera
Wendy Lee
José María Ruiz Vaca
Cordelia Lilly

EDITORIAL COORDINATION
Susie Beattie

SERIES EDITOR
Rob Scriven

ÍNDICE

CONTENTS

William Collins' dream of knowledge for all began with the publication of his first book in 1819. A self-educated mill worker, he not only enriched millions of lives, but also founded a flourishing publishing house. Today, staying true to this spirit, Collins books are packed with inspiration, innovation, and practical expertise. They place you at the centre of a world of possibility and give you exactly what you need to explore it.

Language is the key to this exploration, and at the heart of Collins Dictionaries is language as it is really used. New words, phrases, and meanings spring up every day, and all of them are captured and analysed by the Collins Word Web. Constantly updated, and with over 2.5 billion entries, this living language resource is unique to our dictionaries.

Words are tools for life. And a Collins Dictionary makes them work for you.

Collins. Do more

INTRODUCCIÓN

Estamos muy satisfechos de que hayas decidido comprar este diccionario y esperamos que lo disfrutes y que te sirva de gran ayuda ya sea en el colegio, en el trabajo, en tus vacaciones o en casa.

INTRODUCTION

We are delighted that you have decided to buy this Spanish dictionary and hope you will enjoy and benefit from using it at school, at home, on holiday or at work.

ABREVIATURAS

ABBREVIATIONS

abreviatura	*ab(b)r*	abbreviation
adjetivo, locución adjetiva	*adj*	adjective, adjectival phrase
administración	*Admin*	administration
adverbio, locución adverbial	*adv*	adverb, adverbial phrase
agricultura	*Agr*	agriculture
anatomía	*Anat*	anatomy
Argentina	*Arg*	Argentina
arquitectura	*Arq, Arch*	architecture
el automóvil	*Aut(o)*	the motor car and motoring
aviación, viajes aéreos	*Aviac, Aviat*	flying, air travel
biología	*Bio(l)*	biology
botánica, flores	*Bot*	botany
inglés británico	BRIT	British English
Centroamérica	CAM	Central America
química	*Chem*	chemistry
comercio, finanzas, banca	*Com(m)*	commerce, finance, banking
informática	*Comput*	computing
conjunción	*conj*	conjunction
construcción	*Constr*	building
compuesto	*cpd*	compound element
Cono Sur	CS	Southern Cone
cocina	*Culin*	cookery
economía	*Econ*	economics
eletricidad, electrónica	*Elec*	electricity, electronics
enseñanza, sistema escolar y universitario	*Escol*	schooling, schools and universities
España	ESP	Spain
especialmente	*esp*	especially
exclamación, interjección	*excl*	exclamation, interjection
femenino	*f*	feminine
lengua familiar (! vulgar)	*fam(!)*	colloquial usage (! particularly offensive)
ferrocarril	*Ferro*	railways
uso figurado	*fig*	figurative use
fotografía	*Foto*	photography
(verbo inglés) del cual la partícula es inseparable	*fus*	(phrasal verb) where the particle is inseparable
generalmente	*gen*	generally
geografía, geología	*Geo*	geography, geology
geometría	*Geom*	geometry
historia	*Hist*	history
uso familiar (! vulgar)	*inf(!)*	colloquial usage (! particularly offensive)
infinitivo	*infin*	infinitive
informática	*Inform*	computing
invariable	*inv*	invariable
irregular	*irreg*	irregular
lo jurídico	*Jur*	law
América Latina	LAM	Latin America
gramática, lingüística	*Ling*	grammar, linguistics

ABREVIATURAS

ABBREVIATIONS

masculino	*m*	masculine
matemáticas	*Mat(h)*	mathematics
masculino/femenino	*m/f*	masculine/feminine
medicina	*Med*	medicine
México	*MÉX, MEX*	Mexico
lo militar, ejército	*Mil*	military matters
música	*Mús, Mus*	music
substantivo, nombre	*n*	noun
navegación, náutica	*Náut, Naut*	sailing, navigation
sustantivo numérico	*num*	numeral noun
complemento	*obj*	(grammatical) object
	o.s.	oneself
peyorativo	*pey, pej*	derogatory, pejorative
fotografía	*Phot*	photography
fisiología	*Physiol*	physiology
plural	*pl*	plural
política	*Pol*	politics
participio de pasado	*pp*	past participle
preposición	*prep*	preposition
pronombre	*pron*	pronoun
psicología, psiquiatría	*Psico, Psych*	psychology, psychiatry
tiempo pasado	*pt*	past tense
química	*Quím*	chemistry
ferrocarril	*Rail*	railways
religión	*Rel*	religion
Río de la Plata	*RPL*	River Plate
	sb	somebody
Cono Sur	*SC*	Southern Cone
enseñanza, sistema escolar y universitario	*Scol*	schooling, schools and universities
singular	*sg*	singular
España	*SP*	Spain
	sth	something
sujeto	*su(b)j*	(grammatical) subject
subjuntivo	*subjun*	subjunctive
tauromaquia	*Taur*	bullfighting
también	*tb*	also
técnica, tecnología	*Tec(h)*	technical term, technology
telecomunicaciones	*Telec, Tel*	telecommunications
imprenta, tipografía	*Tip, Typ*	typography, printing
televisión	*TV*	television
universidad	*Univ*	university
inglés norteamericano	*US*	American English
verbo	*vb*	verb
verbo intransitivo	*vi*	intransitive verb
verbo pronominal	*vr*	reflexive verb
verbo transitivo	*vt*	transitive verb
zoología	*Zool*	zoology
marca registrada	®	registered trademark
indica un equivalente cultural	≈	introduces a cultural equivalent

SPANISH PRONUNCIATION

VOWELS

a	[a]	pata	not as long as *a* in f*a*r. When followed by a consonant in the same syllable (i.e. in a closed syllable), as in *a*mante, the *a* is short, as in b*a*t
e	[e]	m**e**	like *e* in th*e*y. In a closed syllable, as in g*e*nte, the *e* is short as in p*e*t
i	[i]	pino	as in m*ea*n or mach*i*ne
o	[o]	lo	as in l*o*cal. In a closed syllable, as in c*o*ntrol, the *o* is short as in c*o*t
u	[u]	lunes	as in r*u*le. It is silent after q, and in g*ue*, g*ui*, unless marked g*üe*, g*üi* e.g. antig*üe*dad, when it is pronounced like *w* in *w*olf

SEMIVOWELS

i, y	[j]	bien hielo yunta	pronounced like *y* in *y*es
u	[w]	huevo fuento antigüedad	unstressed *u* between consonant and vowel is pronounced like *w* in *w*ell. See notes on *u* above.

DIPHTHONGS

ai, ay	[ai]	baile	as *i* in r*i*de
au	[au]	auto	as *ou* in sh*ou*t
ei, ey	[ei]	buey	as *ey* in gr*ey*
eu	[eu]	deuda	both elements pronounced independently [e] + [u]
oi, oy	[oi]	hoy	as *oy* in t*oy*

CONSONANTS

b	[b,β]	boda bomba labor	see notes on *v* below
c	[k]	caja	*c* before *a, o, u* is pronounced as in *c*at
ce, ci	[θe,θi]	cero cielo	*c* before *e* or *i* is pronounced as in *th*in
ch	[tʃ]	chiste	*ch* is pronounced as *ch* in *ch*air
d	[d,ð]	danés ciudad	at the beginning of a phrase or after *l* or *n*, *d* is pronounced as in English. In any other position it is pronounced like *th* in *th*e

g	[g, ɣ]	**g**afas	*g* before *a*, *o* or *u* is pronounced as in
		pa**g**a	*g*ap, if at the beginning of a phrase
			or after *n*. In other positions the sound
			is softened
ge, gi	[xe, xi]	**g**ente	*g* before *e* or *i* is pronounced similar
		girar	to *ch* in Scottish lo*ch*
h		**h**aber	*h* is always silent in Spanish
j	[x]	**j**ugar	*j* is pronounced similar to *ch* in
			Scottish lo*ch*
ll	[ʎ]	ta**ll**e	*ll* is pronounced like the *y* in *y*et or the
			lli in mi*lli*on
ñ	[ʃ]	ni**ñ**o	*ñ* is pronounced like the *ni* in o*ni*on
q	[k]	**q**ue	*q* is pronounced as *k* in *k*ing
r, rr	[r, rr]	quita**r**	*r* is always pronounced in Spanish,
		ga**rr**a	unlike the silent *r* in dance*r*. *rr* is trilled,
			like a Scottish *r*
s	[s]	quizá**s**	*s* is usually pronounced as in pa*ss*,
		i**s**la	but before *b*, *d*, *g*, *l*, *m* or *n* it is
			pronounced as in ro*s*e
v	[b, β]	**v**ía	*v* is pronounced something like *b*.
			At the beginning of a phrase or after
			m or *n* it is pronounced as *b* in *b*oy.
			In any other position the sound is
			softened
z	[θ]	tena**z**	*z* is pronounced as *th* in *th*in

f, k, l, m, n, p, t and x are pronounced as in English.

STRESS

The rules of stress in Spanish are as follows:

(a) when a word ends in a vowel or in *n* or *s*, the second last syllable is stressed:
   pa*ta*ta, pa*ta*tas; *co*me, *co*men
(b) when a word ends in a consonant other than *n* or *s*, the stress falls on the last syllable:
   pa*red*, ha*blar*
(c) when the rules set out in (a) and (b) are not applied, an acute accent appears over the stressed vowel:
   co*mún*, geogra*fía*, in*glés*

In the phonetic transcription, the symbol [¹] precedes the syllable on which the stress falls.

LA PRONUNCIACIÓN INGLESA

VOCALES

	Ejemplo inglés	*Explicación*
[ɑː]	father	Entre *a* de p*a*dre y *o* de n*o*che
[ʌ]	but, come	*a* muy breve
[æ]	man, cat	Con los labios en la posición de *e* en p*e*na y luego se pronuncia el sonido *a* parecido a la *a* de c*a*rro
[ə]	father, ago	Vocal neutra parecida a una *e* u *o* casi muda
[əː]	bird, heard	Entre *e* abierta y *o* cerrada, sonido alargado
[ɛ]	get, bed	Como en p*e*rro
[ɪ]	it, big	Más breve que en s*i*
[iː]	tea, see	Como en f*i*no
[ɔ]	hot, wash	Como en t*o*rre
[ɔː]	saw, all	Como en p*o*r
[u]	put, book	Sonido breve, más cerrado que b*u*rro
[uː]	too, you	Sonido largo, como en *u*no

DIPTONGOS

	Ejemplo inglés	*Explicación*
[aɪ]	fly, high	Como en fr*ai*le
[au]	how, house	Como en p*au*sa
[ɛə]	there, bear	Casi como en v*ea*, pero el sonido *a* se mezcla con el indistinto [ə]
[eɪ]	day, obey	*e* cerrada seguida por una *i* débil
[ɪə]	here, hear	Como en man*ía*, mezclándose el sonido *a* con el indistinto [ə]
[əu]	go, note	[ə] seguido por una breve *u*
[ɔɪ]	boy, oil	Como en v*oy*
[uə]	poor, sure	*u* bastante larga más el sonido indistinto [ə]

CONSONANTES

	Ejemplo inglés	Explicación
[b]	big, lobby	Como en tumban
[d]	mended	Como en conde, andar
[g]	go, get, big	Como en grande, gol
[dʒ]	gin, judge	Como en la ll andaluza y en Generalitat (catalán)
[ŋ]	sing	Como en vínculo
[h]	house, he	Como la jota hispanoamericana
[j]	young, yes	Como en ya
[k]	come, mock	Como en caña, Escocia
[r]	red, tread	Se pronuncia con la punta de la lengua hacia atrás y sin hacerla vibrar
[s]	sand, yes	Como en casa, sesión
[z]	rose, zebra	Como en desde, mismo
[ʃ]	she, machine	Como en chambre (francés), roxo (portugués)
[tʃ]	chin, rich	Como en chocolate
[v]	valley	Como f, pero se retiran los dientes superiores vibrándolos contra el labio inferior
[w]	water, which	Como la u de huevo, puede
[ʒ]	vision	Como en journal (francés)
[θ]	think, myth	Como en receta, zapato
[ð]	this, the	Como en hablado, verdad

f, l, m, n, p, t y x iguales que en español.

El signo [*] indica que la r final escrita apenas se pronuncia en inglés británico cuando la palabra siguiente empieza con vocal.
El signo ['] indica la sílaba acentuada.

SPANISH VERB TABLES

1 Gerund 2 Imperative 3 Present 4 Preterite 5 Future 6 Present subjunctive 7 Imperfect subjunctive 8 Past participle 9 Imperfect

Etc indicates that the irregular root is used for all persons of the tense, e.g. **oír**: 6 oiga, oigas, oigamos, oigáis, oigan

agradecer 3 agradezco 6 agradezca *etc*

aprobar 2 aprueba 3 apruebo, apruebas, aprueba, aprueban 6 apruebe, apruebes, apruebe, aprueben

atravesar 2 atraviesa 3 atravieso, atraviesas, atraviesa, atraviesan 6 atraviese, atravieses, atraviese, atraviesen

caber 3 quepo 4 cupe, cupiste, cupo, cupimos, cupisteis, cupieron 5 cabré *etc* 6 quepa *etc* 7 cupiera *etc*

caer 1 cayendo 3 caigo 4 cayó, cayeron 6 caiga *etc* 7 cayera *etc*

cerrar 2 cierra 3 cierro, cierras, cierra, cierran 6 cierre, cierres, cierre, cierren

COMER 1 comiendo 2 come, comed 3 como, comes, come, comemos, coméis, comen 4 comí, comiste, comió, comimos, comisteis, comieron 5 comeré, comerás, comerá, comeremos, comeréis, comerán 6 coma, comas, coma, comamos, comáis, coman 7 comiera, comieras, comiera, comiéramos, comierais, comieran 8 comido 9 comía, comías, comía, comíamos, comíais, comían

conocer 3 conozco 6 conozca *etc*

contar 2 cuenta 3 cuento, cuentas, cuenta, cuentan 6 cuente, cuentes, cuente, cuenten

dar 3 doy 4 di, diste, dio, dimos, disteis, dieron 7 diera *etc*

decir 2 di 3 digo 4 dije, dijiste, dijo, dijimos, dijisteis, dijeron 5 diré *etc* 6 diga *etc* 7 dijera *etc* 8 dicho

despertar 2 despierta 3 despierto, despiertas, despierta, despiertan 6 despierte, despiertes, despierte, despierten

divertir 1 divirtiendo 2 divierte 3 divierto, diviertes, divierte, divierten 4 divirtió, divirtieron 6 divierta, diviertas, divierta, divirtamos, divirtáis, diviertan 7 divirtiera *etc*

dormir 1 durmiendo 2 duerme 3 duermo, duermes, duerme, duermen 4 durmió, durmieron 6 duerma, duermas, duerma, durmamos, durmáis, duerman 7 durmiera *etc*

empezar 2 empieza 3 empiezo, empiezas, empieza, empiezan 4 empecé 6 empiece, empieces, empiece, empecemos, empecéis, empiecen

entender 2 entiende 3 entiendo, entiendes, entiende, entienden 6 entienda, entiendas, entienda, entiendan

ESTAR 2 está 3 estoy, estás, está, están 4 estuve, estuviste, estuvo, estuvimos, estuvisteis, estuvieron **6** esté, estés, esté, estén **7** estuviera *etc*

HABER 3 he, has, ha, hemos, han **4** hube, hubiste, hubo, hubimos, hubisteis, hubieron **5** habré *etc* **6** haya *etc* **7** hubiera *etc*

HABLAR 1 hablando **2** habla, hablad **3** hablo, hablas, habla, hablamos, habláis, hablan **4** hablé, hablaste, habló, hablamos, hablasteis, hablaron **5** hablaré, hablarás, hablará, hablaremos, hablaréis, hablarán **6** hable, hables, hable, hablemos, habléis, hablen **7** hablara, hablaras, hablara, habláramos, hablarais, hablaran **8** hablado **9** hablaba, hablabas, hablaba, hablábamos, hablabais, hablaban

hacer 2 haz **3** hago **4** hice, hiciste, hizo, hicimos, hicisteis, hicieron **5** haré *etc* **6** haga *etc* **7** hiciera *etc* **8** hecho

instruir 1 instruyendo **2** instruye **3** instruyo, instruyes, instruye, instruyen **4** instruyó, instruyeron **6** instruya *etc* **7** instruyera *etc*

ir 1 yendo **2** ve **3** voy, vas, va, vamos, vais, van **4** fui, fuiste, fue, fuimos, fuisteis, fueron **6** vaya, vayas, vaya, vayamos, vayáis, vayan **7** fuera *etc* **9** iba, ibas, iba, íbamos, ibais, iban

jugar 2 juega **3** juego, juegas, juega, juegan **4** jugué **6** juegue *etc*

leer 1 leyendo **4** leyó, leyeron **7** leyera *etc*

morir 1 muriendo **2** muere **3** muero, mueres, muere, mueren **4** murió, murieron

6 muera, mueras, muera, muramos, muráis, mueran **7** muriera *etc* **8** muerto

mover 2 mueve **3** muevo, mueves, mueve, mueven **6** mueva, muevas, mueva, muevan

negar 2 niega **3** niego, niegas, niega, niegan **4** negué **6** niegue, niegües, niegue, neguemos, neguéis, nieguen

ofrecer 3 ofrezco **6** ofrezca *etc*

oír 1 oyendo **2** oye **3** oigo, oyes, oye, oyen **4** oyó, oyeron **6** oiga *etc* **7** oyera *etc*

oler 2 huele **3** huelo, hueles, huele, huelen **6** huela, huelas, huela, huelan

parecer 3 parezco **6** parezca *etc*

pedir 1 pidiendo **2** pide **3** pido, pides, pide, piden **4** pidió, pidieron **6** pida *etc* **7** pidiera *etc*

pensar 2 piensa **3** pienso, piensas, piensa, piensan **6** piense, pienses, piense, piensen

perder 2 pierde **3** pierdo, pierdes, pierde, pierden **6** pierda, pierdas, pierda, pierdan

poder 1 pudiendo **2** puede **3** puedo, puedes, puede, pueden **4** pude, pudiste, pudo, pudimos, pudisteis, pudieron **5** podré *etc* **6** pueda, puedas, pueda, puedan **7** pudiera *etc*

poner 2 pon **3** pongo **4** puse, pusiste, puso, pusimos, pusisteis, pusieron **5** pondré *etc* **6** ponga *etc* **7** pusiera *etc* **8** puesto

preferir 1 prefiriendo **2** prefiere **3** prefiero, prefieres, prefiere, prefieren **4** prefirió, prefirieron **6** prefiera, prefieras, prefiera, prefiramos, prefiráis, prefieran **7** prefiriera *etc*

querer 2 quiere **3** quiero, quieres, quiere, quieren **4** quise, quisiste, quiso, quisimos, quisisteis, quisieron **5** querré *etc* **6** quiera, quieras, quiera, quieran **7** quisiera *etc*

reír 2 ríe **3** río, ríes, ríe, ríen **4** reí, rieron **6** ría, rías, ría, riamos, riáis, rían **7** riera *etc*

repetir 1 repitiendo **2** repite **3** repito, repites, repite, repiten **4** repitió, repitieron **6** repita *etc* **7** repitiera *etc*

rogar 2 ruega **3** ruego, ruegas, ruega, ruegan **4** rogué **6** ruegue, ruegues, ruegue, roguemos, roguéis, rueguen

saber 3 sé **4** supe, supiste, supo, supimos, supisteis, supieron **5** sabré *etc* **6** sepa *etc* **7** supiera *etc*

salir 2 sal **3** salgo **5** saldré *etc* **6** salga *etc*

seguir 1 siguiendo **2** sigue **3** sigo, sigues, sigue, siguen **4** siguió, siguieron **6** siga *etc* **7** siguiera *etc*

sentar 2 sienta **3** siento, sientas, sienta, sientan **6** siente, sientes, siente, sienten

sentir 1 sintiendo **2** siente **3** siento, sientes, siente, sienten **4** sintió, sintieron **6** sienta, sientas, sienta, sintamos, sintáis, sientan **7** sintiera *etc*

SER 2 sé **3** soy, eres, es, somos, sois, son **4** fui, fuiste, fue, fuimos, fuisteis, fueron **6** sea *etc* **7** fuera *etc* **9** era, eras, era, éramos, erais, eran

servir 1 sirviendo **2** sirve **3** sirvo, sirves, sirve, sirven **4** sirvió, sirvieron **6** sirva *etc* **7** sirviera *etc*

soñar 2 sueña **3** sueño, sueñas, sueña, sueñan **6** sueñe, sueñes, sueñe, sueñen

tener 2 ten **3** tengo, tienes, tiene, tienen **4** tuve, tuviste, tuvo, tuvimos, tuvisteis, tuvieron **5** tendré *etc* **6** tenga *etc* **7** tuviera *etc*

traer 1 trayendo **3** traigo **4** traje, trajiste, trajo, trajimos, trajisteis, trajeron **6** traiga *etc* **7** trajera *etc*

valer 2 vale **3** valgo **5** valdré *etc* **6** valga *etc*

venir 2 ven **3** vengo, vienes, viene, vienen **4** vine, viniste, vino, vinimos, vinisteis, vinieron **5** vendré *etc* **6** venga *etc* **7** viniera *etc*

ver 3 veo **6** vea *etc* **8** visto **9** veía *etc*

vestir 1 vistiendo **2** viste **3** visto, vistes, viste, visten **4** vistió, vistieron **6** vista *etc* **7** vistiera *etc*

VIVIR 1 viviendo **2** vive, vivid **3** vivo, vives, vive, vivimos, vivís, viven **4** viví, viviste, vivió, vivimos, vivisteis, vivieron **5** viviré, vivirás, vivirá, viviremos, viviréis, vivirán **6** viva, vivas, viva, vivamos, viváis, vivan **7** viviera, vivieras, viviera, viviéramos, vivierais, vivieran **8** vivido **9** vivía, vivías, vivía, vivíamos, vivías, vivían

volver 2 vuelve **3** vuelvo, vuelves, vuelve, vuelven **6** vuelva, vuelvas, vuelva, vuelvan **8** vuelto

VERBOS IRREGULARES EN INGLÉS

PRESENTE	PASADO	PARTICIPIO	PRESENTE	PASADO	PARTICIPIO
arise	arose	arisen	fall	fell	fallen
awake	awoke	awoken	feed	fed	fed
be (am, is, are; being)	was, were	been	feel	felt	felt
			fight	fought	fought
bear	bore	born(e)	find	found	found
beat	beat	beaten	flee	fled	fled
become	became	become	fling	flung	flung
begin	began	begun	fly	flew	flown
bend	bent	bent	forbid	forbad(e)	forbidden
bet	bet, betted	bet, betted	forecast	forecast	forecast
			forget	forgot	forgotten
bid (at auction, cards)	bid	bid	forgive	forgave	forgiven
			forsake	forsook	forsaken
bid (say)	bade	bidden	freeze	froze	frozen
bind	bound	bound	get	got	got, (us) gotten
bite	bit	bitten			
bleed	bled	bled	give	gave	given
blow	blew	blown	go (goes)	went	gone
break	broke	broken	grind	ground	ground
breed	bred	bred	grow	grew	grown
bring	brought	brought	hang	hung	hung
build	built	built	hang (suspend) (execute)	hanged	hanged
burn	burnt, burned	burnt, burned	have	had	had
burst	burst	burst	hear	heard	heard
buy	bought	bought	hide	hid	hidden
can	could	(been able)	hit	hit	hit
cast	cast	cast	hold	held	held
catch	caught	caught	hurt	hurt	hurt
choose	chose	chosen	keep	kept	kept
cling	clung	clung	kneel	knelt, kneeled	knelt, kneeled
come	came	come			
cost (be valued at)	cost	cost	know	knew	known
			lay	laid	laid
cost (work out price of)	costed	costed	lead	led	led
			lean	leant, leaned	leant, leaned
creep	crept	crept			
cut	cut	cut	leap	leapt, leaped	leapt, leaped
deal	dealt	dealt			
dig	dug	dug	learn	learnt, learned	learnt, learned
do (does)	did	done			
draw	drew	drawn	leave	left	left
dream	dreamed, dreamt	dreamed, dreamt	lend	lent	lent
			let	let	let
drink	drank	drunk	lie (lying)	lay	lain
drive	drove	driven	light	lit, lighted	lit, lighted
dwell	dwelt	dwelt			
eat	ate	eaten	lose	lost	lost

PRESENTE	PASADO	PARTICIPIO	PRESENTE	PASADO	PARTICIPIO
make	made	made	speed	sped,	sped,
may	might	–		speeded	speeded
mean	meant	meant	spell	spelt,	spelt,
meet	met	met		spelled	spelled
mistake	mistook	mistaken	spend	spent	spent
mow	mowed	mown,	spill	spilt,	spilt,
		mowed		spilled	spilled
must	(had to)	(had to)	spin	spun	spun
pay	paid	paid	spit	spat	spat
put	put	put	spoil	spoiled,	spoiled,
quit	quit,	quit,		spoilt	spoilt
	quitted	quitted	spread	spread	spread
read	read	read	spring	sprang	sprung
rid	rid	rid	stand	stood	stood
ride	rode	ridden	steal	stole	stolen
ring	rang	rung	stick	stuck	stuck
rise	rose	risen	sting	stung	stung
run	ran	run	stink	stank	stunk
saw	sawed	sawed,	stride	strode	stridden
		sawn	strike	struck	struck
say	said	said	strive	strove	striven
see	saw	seen	swear	swore	sworn
seek	sought	sought	sweep	swept	swept
sell	sold	sold	swell	swelled	swollen,
send	sent	sent			swelled
set	set	set	swim	swam	swum
sew	sewed	sewn	swing	swung	swung
shake	shook	shaken	take	took	taken
shear	sheared	shorn,	teach	taught	taught
		sheared	tear	tore	torn
shed	shed	shed	tell	told	told
shine	shone	shone	think	thought	thought
shoot	shot	shot	throw	threw	thrown
show	showed	shown	thrust	thrust	thrust
shrink	shrank	shrunk	tread	trod	trodden
shut	shut	shut	wake	woke,	woken,
sing	sang	sung		waked	waked
sink	sank	sunk	wear	wore	worn
sit	sat	sat	weave (on	wove	woven
slay	slew	slain	loom)		
sleep	slept	slept	weave (wind)	weaved	weaved
slide	slid	slid	wed	wedded,	wedded,
sling	slung	slung		wed	wed
slit	slit	slit	weep	wept	wept
smell	smelt,	smelt,	win	won	won
	smelled	smelled	wind	wound	wound
sow	sowed	sown,	wring	wrung	wrung
		sowed	write	wrote	written
speak	spoke	spoken			

the government!; **cuesta/río ~** downhill/ downstream; **de arriba ~** from top to bottom; **el ~ firmante** the undersigned; **más ~** lower o further down

abalanzarse [aβalan'θarse] *vr*: **~ sobre** o **contra** to throw o.s. at

abanderado, -a [aβande'raðo] *nm/f* (*portaestandarte*) standard bearer; (*de un movimiento*) champion, leader; (MÉX: *linier*) linesman, assistant referee

abandonado, -a [aβando'naðo, a] *adj* derelict; (*desatendido*) abandoned; (*desierto*) deserted; (*descuidado*) neglected

abandonar [aβando'nar] *vt* to leave; (*persona*) to abandon, desert; (*cosa*) to abandon, leave behind; (*descuidar*) to neglect; (*renunciar a*) to give up; (*Inform*) to quit; **abandonarse** *vr*: **~se a** to abandon o.s. to; **abandono** *nm* (*acto*) desertion, abandonment; (*estado*) abandon, neglect; (*renuncia*) withdrawal, retirement; **ganar por abandono** to win by default

abanico [aβa'niko] *nm* fan; (*Náut*) derrick

abarcar [aβar'kar] *vt* to include, embrace; (LAM: *acaparar*) to monopolize

abarrotado, -a [aβarro'taðo, a] *adj* packed

abarrotar [aβarro'tar] *vt* (*local, estadio, teatro*) to fill, pack

abarrotero, -a [aβarro'tero, a] (MÉX) *nm/f* grocer; **abarrotes** (MÉX) *nmpl* groceries; **tienda de abarrotes** (MÉX, CAM) grocery store

abastecer [aβaste'θer] *vt*: **~ (de)** to supply (with); **abastecimiento** *nm* supply

abasto [a'βasto] *nm* supply; **no dar ~ a** to be unable to cope with

abatible [aβa'tiβle] *adj*: **asiento ~** tip-up seat; (*Auto*) reclining seat

abatido, -a [aβa'tiðo, a] *adj* dejected, downcast

abatir [aβa'tir] *vt* (*muro*) to demolish; (*pájaro*) to shoot o bring down; (*fig*) to depress

abdicar [aβði'kar] *vi* to abdicate

abdomen [aβ'ðomen] *nm* abdomen; **abdominales** *nmpl* (*tb*: **ejercicios abdominales**) sit-ups

abecedario [aβeθe'ðarjo] *nm* alphabet

abedul [aβe'ðul] *nm* birch

abeja [a'βexa] *nf* bee

abejorro [aβe'xorro] *nm* bumblebee

abertura [aβer'tura] *nf* = **apertura**

abeto [a'βeto] *nm* fir

abierto, -a [a'βjerto, a] *pp de* **abrir** ▷ *adj* open

abismal [aβis'mal] *adj* (*fig*) vast, enormous

○ **PALABRA CLAVE**

a [a] (*a + el = al*) *prep* **1** (*dirección*) to; **fueron a Madrid/Grecia** they went to Madrid/ Greece; **me voy a casa** I'm going home

2 (*distancia*): **está a 15 km de aquí** it's 15 kms from here

3 (*posición*): **estar a la mesa** to be at table; **al lado de** next to, beside; *V tb* **puerta**

4 (*tiempo*): **a las 10/a medianoche** at 10/ midnight; **a la mañana siguiente** the following morning; **a los pocos días** after a few days; **estamos a 9 de julio** it's the ninth of July; **a los 24 años** at the age of 24; **al año/a la semana** a year/week later

5 (*manera*): **a la francesa** the French way; **a caballo** on horseback; **a oscuras** in the dark

6 (*medio, instrumento*): **a lápiz** in pencil; **a mano** by hand; **cocina a gas** gas stove

7 (*razón*): **a 30 céntimos el kilo** at 30 cents a kilo; **a más de 50 km/h** at more than 50 kms per hour

8 (*dativo*): **se lo di a él** I gave it to him; **vi al policía** I saw the policeman; **se lo compré a él** I bought it from him

9 (*tras ciertos verbos*): **voy a verle** I'm going to see him; **empezó a trabajar** he started working o to work

10 (*+ infin*): **al verlo, lo reconocí inmediatamente** when I saw him I recognized him at once; **el camino a recorrer** the distance we *etc* have to travel; **¡a callar!** keep quiet!; **¡a comer!** let's eat!

abad, esa [a'βað, 'ðesa] *nm/f* abbot/ abbess; **abadía** *nf* abbey

abajo [a'βaxo] *adv* (*situación*) (down) below, underneath; (*en edificio*) downstairs; (*dirección*) down, downwards; **el piso de ~** the downstairs flat; **la parte de ~** the lower part; **¡~ el gobierno!** down with

abismo [a'βismo] nm abyss

ablandar [aβlan'dar] vt to soften;
ablandarse vr to get softer

abocado, -a [aβo'kaðo, a] adj (vino)
smooth, pleasant

abochornar [aβotʃor'nar] vt to
embarrass

abofetear [aβofete'ar] vt to slap (in the
face)

abogado, -a [aβo'ɤaðo, a] nm/f lawyer;
(notario) solicitor; (en tribunal) barrister
(BRIT), attorney (US); **abogado defensor**
defence lawyer o (US) attorney

abogar [aβo'ɤar] vi: ~ **por** to plead for; (fig)
to advocate

abolir [aβo'lir] vt to abolish; (cancelar) to
cancel

abolladura [aβoʎa'ðura] nf dent

abollar [aβo'ʎar] vt to dent

abombarse [aβom'barse] (LAM) vr to
go bad

abominable [aβomi'naβle] adj
abominable

abonado, -a [aβo'naðo, a] adj (deuda)
paid(-up) ▷ nm/f subscriber

abonar [aβo'nar] vt (deuda) to settle;
(terreno) to fertilize; (idea) to endorse;
abonarse vr to subscribe; **abono** nm
payment; fertilizer; subscription

abordar [aβor'ðar] vt (barco) to board;
(asunto) to broach

aborigen [aβo'rixen] nmf aborigine

aborrecer [aβorre'θer] vt to hate, loathe

abortar [aβor'tar] vi (malparir) to have
a miscarriage; (deliberadamente) to have
an abortion; **aborto** nm miscarriage;
abortion

abovedado, -a [aβoβe'ðaðo, a] adj
vaulted, domed

abrasar [aβra'sar] vt to burn (up); (Agr) to
dry up, parch

abrazar [aβra'θar] vt to embrace, hug

abrazo [a'βraθo] nm embrace, hug; **un ~**
(en carta) with best wishes

abrebotellas [aβreβo'teʎas] nm inv bottle
opener

abrecartas [aβre'kartas] nm inv letter
opener

abrelatas [aβre'latas] nm inv tin (BRIT) o
can opener

abreviatura [aβreβja'tura] nf
abbreviation

abridor [aβri'ðor] nm bottle opener; (de
latas) tin (BRIT) o can opener

abrigador, a [aβriga'ðor, a] (MÉX) adj
warm

abrigar [aβri'ɤar] vt (proteger) to shelter;
(ropa) to keep warm; (fig) to cherish

abrigo [a'βriɤo] nm (prenda) coat,
overcoat; (lugar protegido) shelter

abril [a'βril] nm April

abrillantador [aβriʎanta'ðor] nm polish

abrillantar [aβriʎan'tar] vt to polish

abrir [a'βrir] vt to open (up) ▷ vi to open;
abrirse vr to open (up); (extenderse) to open
out; (cielo) to clear; **~se paso** to find o force
a way through

abrochar [aβro'tʃar] vt (con botones) to
button (up); (zapato, con broche) to do up

abrupto, -a [a'βrupto, a] adj abrupt;
(empinado) steep

absoluto, -a [aβso'luto, a] adj absolute;
en ~ adv not at all

absolver [aβsol'βer] vt to absolve; (Jur) to
pardon; (: acusado) to acquit

absorbente [aβsor'βente] adj absorbent;
(interesante) absorbing

absorber [aβsor'βer] vt to absorb;
(embeber) to soak up

absorción [aβsor'θjon] nf absorption;
(Com) takeover

abstemio, -a [aβs'temjo, a] adj teetotal

abstención [aβsten'θjon] nf abstention

abstenerse [aβste'nerse] vr: ~ **(de)** to
abstain o refrain (from)

abstinencia [aβsti'nenθja] nf
abstinence; (ayuno) fasting

abstracto, -a [aβs'trakto, a] adj abstract

abstraer [aβstra'er] vt to abstract;
abstraerse vr to be o become absorbed

abstraído, -a [aβstra'iðo, a] adj absent-
minded

absuelto [aβ'swelto] pp de **absolver**

absurdo, -a [aβ'surðo, a] adj absurd

abuchear [aβutʃe'ar] vt to boo

abuelo, -a [a'βwelo, a] nm/f
grandfather(-mother); **abuelos** nmpl
grandparents

abultado, -a [aβul'taðo, a] adj bulky

abultar [aβul'tar] vi to be bulky

abundancia [aβun'danθja] nf: **una ~
de** plenty of; **abundante** adj abundant,
plentiful

abundar [aβun'dar] vi to abound, be
plentiful

aburrido, -a [aβu'rriðo, a] adj (hastiado)
bored; (que aburre) boring; **aburrimiento**
nm boredom, tedium

aburrir [aβu'rrir] vt to bore; **aburrirse** vr
to be bored, get bored

abusado, -a [aβu'saðo, a] (MÉX: fam) adj
(astuto) sharp, cunning ▷ excl: **¡~!** (inv) look
out!, careful!

abusar [aβu'sar] vi to go too far; ~ **de** to
abuse

abusivo, -a [aβu'siβo, a] adj (precio)

exorbitant

abuso [a'βuso] *nm* abuse

acá [a'ka] *adv* (*lugar*) here

acabado, -a [aka'βaðo, a] *adj* finished, complete; (*perfecto*) perfect; (*agotado*) worn out; (*fig*) masterly ▷ *nm* finish

acabar [aka'βar] *vt* (*llevar a su fin*) to finish, complete; (*consumir*) to use up; (*rematar*) to finish off ▷ *vi* to finish, end; **acabarse** *vr* to finish, stop; (*terminarse*) to be over; (*agotarse*) to run out; **~ con** to put an end to; **~ de llegar** to have just arrived; **~ por hacer** to end (up) by doing; **¡se acabó!** it's all over!; (*¡basta!*) that's enough!

acabóse [aka'βose] *nm*: **esto es el ~** this is the last straw

academia [aka'ðemja] *nf* academy; **academia de idiomas** language school; **académico, -a** *adj* academic

acalorado, -a [akalo'raðo, a] *adj* (*discusión*) heated

acampar [akam'par] *vi* to camp

acantilado [akanti'laðo] *nm* cliff

acaparar [akapa'rar] *vt* to monopolize; (*acumular*) to hoard

acariciar [akari'θjar] *vt* to caress; (*esperanza*) to cherish

acarrear [akarre'ar] *vt* to transport; (*fig*) to cause, result in

acaso [a'kaso] *adv* perhaps, maybe; **(por) si ~** (just) in case

acatar [aka'tar] *vt* to respect; (*ley*) obey

acatarrarse [akata'rrarse] *vr* to catch a cold

acceder [akθe'ðer] *vi*: **~ a** (*petición etc*) to agree to; (*tener acceso a*) to have access to; (*Inform*) to access

accesible [akθe'siβle] *adj* accessible

acceso [ak'θeso] *nm* access, entry; (*camino*) access, approach; (*Med*) attack, fit

accesorio, -a [akθe'sorjo, a] *adj, nm* accessory

accidentado, -a [akθiðen'taðo, a] *adj* uneven; (*montañoso*) hilly; (*azaroso*) eventful ▷ *nm/f* accident victim

accidental [akθiðen'tal] *adj* accidental

accidente [akθi'ðente] *nm* accident; **accidentes** *nmpl* (*de terreno*) unevenness *sg*; **accidente laboral** o **de trabajo/de tráfico** industrial/road o traffic accident

acción [ak'θjon] *nf* action; (*acto*) action, act; (*Com*) share; (*Jur*) action, lawsuit; **accionar** *vt* to work, operate; (*Inform*) to drive

accionista [akθjo'nista] *nmf* shareholder, stockholder

acebo [a'θeβo] *nm* holly; (*árbol*) holly tree

acechar [aθe'tʃar] *vt* to spy on; (*aguardar*) to lie in wait for; **acecho** *nm*: **estar al acecho (de)** to lie in wait (for)

aceite [a'θeite] *nm* oil; **aceite de girasol/ oliva** olive/sunflower oil; **aceitera** *nf* oilcan; **aceitoso, -a** *adj* oily

aceituna [aθei'tuna] *nf* olive; **aceituna rellena** stuffed olive

acelerador [aθelera'ðor] *nm* accelerator

acelerar [aθele'rar] *vt* to accelerate

acelga [a'θelxa] *nf* chard, beet

acento [a'θento] *nm* accent; (*acentuación*) stress

acentuar [aθen'twar] *vt* to accent; to stress; (*fig*) to accentuate

acepción [aθep'θjon] *nf* meaning

aceptable [aθep'taβle] *adj* acceptable

aceptación [aθepta'θjon] *nf* acceptance; (*aprobación*) approval

aceptar [aθep'tar] *vt* to accept; (*aprobar*) to approve; **~ hacer algo** to agree to do sth

acequia [a'θekja] *nf* irrigation ditch

acera [a'θera] *nf* pavement (BRIT), sidewalk (US)

acerca [a'θerka]: **~ de** *prep* about, concerning

acercar [aθer'kar] *vt* to bring o move nearer; **acercarse** *vr* to approach, come near

acero [a'θero] *nm* steel

acérrimo, -a [a'θerrimo, a] *adj* (*partidario*) staunch; (*enemigo*) bitter

acertado, -a [aθer'taðo, a] *adj* correct; (*apropiado*) apt; (*sensato*) sensible

acertar [aθer'tar] *vt* (*blanco*) to hit; (*solución*) to get right; (*adivinar*) to guess ▷ *vi* to get it right, be right; **~ a** to manage to; **~ con** to happen o hit on

acertijo [aθer'tixo] *nm* riddle, puzzle

achacar [atʃa'kar] *vt* to attribute

achacoso, -a [atʃa'koso, a] *adj* sickly

achicar [atʃi'kar] *vt* to reduce; (*Náut*) to bale out

achicharrar [atʃitʃa'rrar] *vt* to scorch, burn

achichincle [atʃi'tʃinkle] (MÉX: *fam*) *nmf* minion

achicoria [atʃi'korja] *nf* chicory

achuras [a'tʃuras] (RPL) *nfpl* offal *sg*

acicate [aθi'kate] *nm* spur

acidez [aθi'ðeθ] *nf* acidity

ácido, -a ['aθiðo, a] *adj* sour, acid ▷ *nm* acid

acierto *etc* [a'θjerto] *vb* V **acertar** ▷ *nm* success; (*buen paso*) wise move; (*solución*) solution; (*habilidad*) skill, ability

acitronar [aθitro'nar] (MÉX: *fam*) *vt* to brown

aclamar [akla'mar] *vt* to acclaim;

(*aplaudir*) to applaud

aclaración [aklara'θjon] *nf* clarification, explanation

aclarar [akla'rar] *vt* to clarify, explain; (*ropa*) to rinse ▷ *vi* to clear up; **aclararse** *vr* (*explicarse*) to understand; **~se la garganta** to clear one's throat

aclimatación [aklimata'θjon] *nf* acclimatization

aclimatar [aklima'tar] *vt* to acclimatize; **aclimatarse** *vr* to become acclimatized

acné [ak'ne] *nm* acne

acobardar [akoβar'ðar] *vt* to intimidate

acogedor, a [akoxe'ðor, a] *adj* welcoming; (*hospitalario*) hospitable

acoger [ako'xer] *vt* to welcome; (*abrigar*) to shelter

acogida [ako'xiða] *nf* reception; refuge

acomedido, -a [akome'ðiðo, a] (*MÉX*) *adj* helpful, obliging

acometer [akome'ter] *vt* to attack; (*emprender*) to undertake; **acometida** *nf* attack, assault

acomodado, -a [akomo'ðaðo, a] *adj* (*persona*) well-to-do

acomodador, a [akomoða'ðor, a] *nm/f* usher(ette)

acomodar [akomo'ðar] *vt* to adjust; (*alojar*) to accommodate; **acomodarse** *vr* to conform; (*instalarse*) to install o.s.; (*adaptarse*): **~se (a)** to adapt (to)

acompañar [akompa'ɲar] *vt* to accompany; (*documentos*) to enclose

acondicionar [akondiθjo'nar] *vt* to arrange, prepare; (*pelo*) to condition

aconsejar [akonse'xar] *vt* to advise, counsel; **~ a algn hacer** *o* **que haga algo** to advise sb to do sth

acontecer [akonte'θer] *vi* to happen, occur; **acontecimiento** *nm* event

acopio [a'kopjo] *nm* store, stock

acoplar [ako'plar] *vt* to fit; (*Elec*) to connect; (*vagones*) to couple

acorazado, -a [akora'θaðo, a] *adj* armour-plated, armoured ▷ *nm* battleship

acordar [akor'ðar] *vt* (*resolver*) to agree, resolve; (*recordar*) to remind; **acordarse** *vr* to agree; **~ hacer algo** to agree to do sth; **~se (de algo)** to remember (sth); **acorde** *adj* (*Mús*) harmonious; **acorde con** (*medidas etc*) in keeping with ▷ *nm* chord

acordeón [akorðe'on] *nm* accordion

acordonado, -a [akorðo'naðo, a] *adj* (*calle*) cordoned-off

acorralar [akorra'lar] *vt* to round up, corral

acortar [akor'tar] *vt* to shorten; (*duración*) to cut short; (*cantidad*) to reduce; **acortarse** *vr* to become shorter

acosar [ako'sar] *vt* to pursue relentlessly; (*fig*) to hound, pester; **acoso** *nm* harassment; **acoso sexual** sexual harassment

acostar [akos'tar] *vt* (*en cama*) to put to bed; (*en suelo*) to lay down; **acostarse** *vr* to go to bed; to lie down; **~se con algn** to sleep with sb

acostumbrado, -a [akostum'braðo, a] *adj* usual; **~ a** used to

acostumbrar [akostum'brar] *vt*: **~ a algn a algo** to get sb used to sth ▷ *vi*: **~ (a) hacer** to be in the habit of doing; **acostumbrarse** *vr*: **~se a** to get used to

acotación [akota'θjon] *nf* marginal note; (*Geo*) elevation mark; (*de límite*) boundary mark; (*Teatro*) stage direction

acotamiento [akota'mjento] (*MÉX*) *nm* hard shoulder (*BRIT*), berm (*US*)

acre ['akre] *adj* (*olor*) acrid; (*fig*) biting ▷ *nm* acre

acreditar [akreði'tar] *vt* (*garantizar*) to vouch for, guarantee; (*autorizar*) to authorize; (*dar prueba de*) to prove; (*Com: abonar*) to credit; (*embajador*) to accredit

acreedor, a [akree'ðor, a] *nm/f* creditor

acribillar [akriβi'ʎar] *vt*: **~ a balazos** to riddle with bullets

acróbata [a'kroβata] *nmf* acrobat

acta ['akta] *nf* certificate; (*de comisión*) minutes *pl*, record; **acta de matrimonio/nacimiento** (*MÉX*) marriage/birth certificate; **acta notarial** affidavit

actitud [akti'tuð] *nf* attitude; (*postura*) posture

activar [akti'βar] *vt* to activate; (*acelerar*) to speed up

actividad [aktiβi'ðað] *nf* activity

activo, -a [ak'tiβo, a] *adj* active; (*vivo*) lively ▷ *nm* (*Com*) assets *pl*

acto ['akto] *nm* act, action; (*ceremonia*) ceremony; (*Teatro*) act; **en el ~** immediately

actor [ak'tor] *nm* actor; (*Jur*) plaintiff ▷ *adj*: **parte ~a** prosecution

actriz [ak'triθ] *nf* actress

actuación [aktwa'θjon] *nf* action; (*comportamiento*) conduct, behaviour; (*Jur*) proceedings *pl*; (*desempeño*) performance

actual [ak'twal] *adj* present(-day), current

▌No confundir **actual** con la palabra inglesa *actual*.

actualidad *nf* present; **actualidades** *nfpl* (*noticias*) news *sg*; **en la actualidad** at present; (*hoy día*) nowadays; **actualizar** [aktwali'θar] *vt* to update, modernize; **actualmente** [aktwal'mente] *adv* at present; (*hoy día*) nowadays

▌No confundir **actualmente** con la palabra inglesa *actually*.

actuar [ak'twar] *vi* (*obrar*) to work, operate; (*actor*) to act, perform ▷ *vt* to work, operate; **~ de** to act as

acuarela [akwa'rela] *nf* watercolour

acuario [a'kwarjo] *nm* aquarium; (*Astrología*): **A~** Aquarius

acuático, -a [a'kwatiko, a] *adj* aquatic

acudir [aku'ðir] *vi* (*asistir*) to attend; (*ir*) to go; **~ a** (*fig*) to turn to; **~ a una cita** to keep an appointment; **~ en ayuda de** to go to the aid of

acuerdo *etc* [a'kwerðo] *vb* V **acordar** ▷ *nm* agreement; **¡de ~!** agreed!; **de ~ con** (*persona*) in agreement with; (*acción, documento*) in accordance with; **estar de ~** to be agreed, agree

acumular [akumu'lar] *vt* to accumulate, collect

acuñar [aku'nar] *vt* (*moneda*) to mint; (*frase*) to coin

acupuntura [akupun'tura] *nf* acupuncture

acurrucarse [akurru'karse] *vr* to crouch; (*ovillarse*) to curl up

acusación [akusa'θjon] *nf* accusation

acusar [aku'sar] *vt* to accuse; (*revelar*) to reveal; (*denunciar*) to denounce

acuse [a'kuse] *nm*: **~ de recibo** acknowledgement of receipt

acústica [a'kustika] *nf* acoustics *pl*

acústico, -a [a'kustiko, a] *adj* acoustic

adaptación [aðapta'θjon] *nf* adaptation

adaptador [aðapta'ðor] *nm* (*Elec*) adapter, adaptor; **adaptador universal** universal adapter *o* adaptor

adaptar [aðap'tar] *vt* to adapt; (*acomodar*) to fit

adecuado, -a [aðe'kwaðo, a] *adj* (*apto*) suitable; (*oportuno*) appropriate

a. de J.C. *abr* (= *antes de Jesucristo*) B.C.

adelantado, -a [aðelan'taðo, a] *adj* advanced; (*reloj*) fast; **pagar por ~** to pay in advance

adelantamiento [aðelanta'mjento] *nm* (*Auto*) overtaking

adelantar [aðelan'tar] *vt* to move forward; (*avanzar*) to advance; (*acelerar*) to speed up; (*Auto*) to overtake ▷ *vi* to go forward, advance; **adelantarse** *vr* to go forward, advance

adelante [aðe'lante] *adv* forward(s), ahead ▷ *excl* come in!; **de hoy en ~** from now on; **más ~** later on; (*más allá*) further on

adelanto [aðe'lanto] *nm* advance; (*mejora*) improvement; (*progreso*) progress

adelgazar [aðelɣa'θar] *vt* to thin (down) ▷ *vi* to get thin; (*con régimen*) to slim down, lose weight

ademán [aðe'man] *nm* gesture; **ademanes** *nmpl* manners

además [aðe'mas] *adv* besides; (*por otra parte*) moreover; (*también*) also; **~ de** besides, in addition to

adentrarse [aðen'trarse] *vr*: **~ en** to go into, get inside; (*penetrar*) to penetrate (into)

adentro [a'ðentro] *adv* inside, in; **mar ~** out at sea; **tierra ~** inland

adepto, -a [a'ðepto, a] *nm/f* supporter

aderezar [aðere'θar] *vt* (*ensalada*) to dress; (*comida*) to season; **aderezo** *nm* dressing; seasoning

adeudar [aðeu'ðar] *vt* to owe

adherirse [aðe'rirse] *vr*: **~ a** to adhere to; (*partido*) to join

adhesión [aðe'sjon] *nf* adhesion; (*fig*) adherence

adicción [aðik'θjon] *nf* addiction

adición [aði'θjon] *nf* addition

adicto, -a [a'ðikto, a] *adj*: **~ a** addicted to; (*dedicado*) devoted to ▷ *nm/f* supporter, follower; (*toxicómano*) addict

adiestrar [aðjes'trar] *vt* to train, teach; (*conducir*) to guide, lead

adinerado, -a [aðine'raðo, a] *adj* wealthy

adiós [a'ðjos] *excl* (*para despedirse*) goodbye!, cheerio!; (*al pasar*) hello!

aditivo [aði'tiβo] *nm* additive

adivinanza [aðiβi'nanθa] *nf* riddle

adivinar [aðiβi'nar] *vt* to prophesy; (*conjeturar*) to guess; **adivino, -a** *nm/f* fortune-teller

adj *abr* (= *adjunto*) encl

adjetivo [aðxe'tiβo] *nm* adjective

adjudicar [aðxuði'kar] *vt* to award; **adjudicarse** *vr*: **~se algo** to appropriate sth

adjuntar [aðxun'tar] *vt* to attach, enclose; **adjunto, -a** *adj* attached, enclosed ▷ *nm/f* assistant

administración [aðministra'θjon] *nf* administration; (*dirección*) management; **administrador, a** *nm/f* administrator, manager(ess)

administrar [aðminis'trar] *vt* to administer; **administrativo, -a** *adj* administrative

admirable [aðmi'raβle] *adj* admirable

admiración [aðmira'θjon] *nf* admiration; (*asombro*) wonder; (*Ling*) exclamation mark

admirar [aðmi'rar] *vt* to admire; (*extrañar*) to surprise

admisible [aðmi'siβle] *adj* admissible

admisión [aðmi'sjon] *nf* admission;
(*reconocimiento*) acceptance
admitir [aðmi'tir] *vt* to admit; (*aceptar*)
to accept
adobar [aðo'βar] *vt* (*Culin*) to season
adobe [a'ðoβe] *nm* adobe, sun-dried brick
adolecer [aðole'θer] *vi*: ~ **de** to suffer from
adolescente [aðoles'θente] *nmf*
adolescent, teenager
adonde [a'ðonðe] *conj* (to) where
adónde [a'ðonðe] *adv* = **dónde**
adopción [aðop'θjon] *nf* adoption
adoptar [aðop'tar] *vt* to adopt
adoptivo, -a [aðop'tiβo, a] *adj* (*padres*)
adoptive; (*hijo*) adopted
adoquín [aðo'kin] *nm* paving stone
adorar [aðo'rar] *vt* to adore
adornar [aðor'nar] *vt* to adorn
adorno [a'ðorno] *nm* ornament;
(*decoración*) decoration
adosado, -a [aðo'saðo, a] *adj*: **casa**
adosada semi-detached house
adosar [aðo'sar] (*MÉX*) *vt* (*adjuntar*) to
attach, enclose (*with a letter*)
adquiero *etc vb* V **adquirir**
adquirir [aðki'rir] *vt* to acquire, obtain
adquisición [aðkisi'θjon] *nf* acquisition
adrede [a'ðreðe] *adv* on purpose
ADSL *nm abr* broadband
aduana [a'ðwana] *nf* customs *pl*
aduanero, -a [aðwa'nero, a] *adj* customs
cpd ▷ *nm/f* customs officer
adueñarse [aðwe'ɲarse] *vr*: ~ **de** to take
possession of
adular [aðu'lar] *vt* to flatter
adulterar [aðulte'rar] *vt* to adulterate
adulterio [aðul'terjo] *nm* adultery
adúltero, -a [a'ðultero, a] *adj* adulterous
▷ *nm/f* adulterer/adulteress
adulto, -a [a'ðulto, a] *adj, nm/f* adult
adverbio [að'βerβjo] *nm* adverb
adversario, -a [aðβer'sarjo, a] *nm/f*
adversary
adversidad [aðβersi'ðað] *nf* adversity;
(*contratiempo*) setback
adverso, -a [að'βerso, a] *adj* adverse
advertencia [aðβer'tenθja] *nf* warning;
(*prefacio*) preface, foreword
advertir [aðβer'tir] *vt* to notice; (*avisar*): ~
a algn de to warn sb about o of
Adviento [að'βjento] *nm* Advent
advierto *etc vb* V **advertir**
aéreo, -a [a'ereo, a] *adj* aerial
aerobic [ae'roβik] *nm* aerobics *sg*;
aerobics (*MÉX*) *nmpl* aerobics *sg*
aeromozo, -a [aero'moθo, a] (*LAM*) *nm/f*
air steward(ess)
aeronáutica [aero'nautika] *nf*

aeronautics *sg*
aeronave [aero'naβe] *nm* spaceship
aeroplano [aero'plano] *nm* aeroplane
aeropuerto [aero'pwerto] *nm* airport
aerosol [aero'sol] *nm* aerosol
afamado, -a [afa'maðo, a] *adj* famous
afán [a'fan] *nm* hard work; (*deseo*) desire
afanador, a [afana'ðor, a] (*MÉX*) *nm/f* (*de*
limpieza) cleaner
afanar [afa'nar] *vt* to harass; (*fam*) to
pinch
afear [afe'ar] *vt* to disfigure
afección [afek'θjon] *nf* (*Med*) disease
afectado, -a [afek'taðo, a] *adj* affected
afectar [afek'tar] *vt* to affect
afectísimo, -a [afek'tisimo, a] *adj*
affectionate; **suyo ~** yours truly
afectivo, -a [afek'tiβo, a] *adj* (*problema*
etc) emotional
afecto [a'fekto] *nm* affection; **tenerle ~ a**
algn to be fond of sb
afectuoso, -a [afek'twoso, a] *adj*
affectionate
afeitar [afei'tar] *vt* to shave; **afeitarse**
vr to shave
afeminado, -a [afemi'naðo, a] *adj*
effeminate
Afganistán [afɣanis'tan] *nm*
Afghanistan
afianzar [afjan'θar] *vt* to strengthen;
to secure; **afianzarse** *vr* to become
established
afiche [a'fitʃe] (*RPL*) *nm* poster
afición [afi'θjon] *nf* fondness, liking; **la ~**
the fans *pl*; **pinto por ~** I paint as a hobby;
aficionado, -a *adj* keen, enthusiastic; (*no*
profesional) amateur ▷ *nm/f* enthusiast, fan;
amateur; **ser aficionado a algo** to be very
keen on o fond of sth
aficionar [afiθjo'nar] *vt*: ~ **a algn a algo** to
make sb like sth; **aficionarse** *vr*: **~se a algo**
to grow fond of sth
afilado, -a [afi'laðo, a] *adj* sharp
afilar [afi'lar] *vt* to sharpen
afiliarse [afi'ljarse] *vr* to affiliate
afín [a'fin] *adj* (*parecido*) similar; (*conexo*)
related
afinar [afi'nar] *vt* (*Tec*) to refine; (*Mús*) to
tune ▷ *vi* (*tocar*) to play in tune; (*cantar*) to
sing in tune
afincarse [afin'karse] *vr* to settle
afinidad [afini'ðað] *nf* affinity;
(*parentesco*) relationship; **por ~** by marriage
afirmación [afirma'θjon] *nf* affirmation
afirmar [afir'mar] *vt* to affirm, state;
afirmativo, -a *adj* affirmative
afligir [afli'xir] *vt* to afflict; (*apenar*) to
distress

aflojar [aflo'xar] *vt* to slacken; (*desatar*) to loosen, undo; (*relajar*) to relax ▷ *vi* to drop; (*bajar*) to go down; **aflojarse** *vr* to relax

afluente [aflu'ente] *adj* flowing ▷ *nm* tributary

afmo, -a *abr* (= *afectísimo(a) suyo(a)*) Yours

afónico, -a [a'foniko, a] *adj*: **estar ~** to have a sore throat; to have lost one's voice

aforo [a'foro] *nm* (*de teatro etc*) capacity

afortunado, -a [afortu'naðo, a] *adj* fortunate, lucky

África ['afrika] *nf* Africa; **África del Sur** South Africa; **africano, -a** *adj*, *nm/f* African

afrontar [afron'tar] *vt* to confront; (*poner cara a cara*) to bring face to face

afrutado, -a [afru'taðo, a] *adj* fruity

after ['after] (*pl* **~s**) *nm* after-hours club; **afterhours** [after'aurs] *nm inv* = **after**

afuera [a'fwera] *adv* out, outside; **afueras** *nfpl* outskirts

agachar [aɣa'tʃar] *vt* to bend, bow; **agacharse** *vr* to stoop, bend

agalla [a'ɣaʎa] *nf* (*Zool*) gill; **tener ~s** (*fam*) to have guts

agarradera [aɣarra'ðera] (*MÉX*) *nf* handle

agarrado, -a [aɣa'rraðo, a] *adj* mean, stingy

agarrar [aɣa'rrar] *vt* to grasp, grab; (*LAM: tomar*) to take, catch; (*recoger*) to pick up ▷ *vi* (*planta*) to take root; **agarrarse** *vr* to hold on (tightly)

agencia [a'xenθja] *nf* agency; **agencia de viajes** travel agency; **agencia inmobiliaria** estate (*BRIT*) o real estate (*US*) agent's (office)

agenciarse [axen'θjarse] *vr* to obtain, procure

agenda [a'xenda] *nf* diary; **~ electronica** PDA

▌ No confundir **agenda** con la palabra inglesa *agenda*.

agente [a'xente] *nmf* agent; (*tb*: **~ de policía**) policeman/policewoman; **agente de seguros** insurance agent; **agente de tránsito** (*MÉX*) traffic cop; **agente inmobiliario** estate agent (*BRIT*), realtor (*US*)

ágil ['axil] *adj* agile, nimble; **agilidad** *nf* agility, nimbleness

agilizar [axili'θar] *vt* (*trámites*) to speed up

agiotista [axjo'tista] (*MÉX*) *nmf* (*usurero*) usurer

agitación [axita'θjon] *nf* (*de mano etc*) shaking, waving; (*de líquido etc*) stirring; (*fig*) agitation

agitado, -a [axi'aðo, a] *adj* hectic; (*viaje*) bumpy

agitar [axi'tar] *vt* to wave, shake; (*líquido*) to stir; (*fig*) to stir up, excite; **agitarse** *vr*

to get excited; (*inquietarse*) to get worried o upset

aglomeración [aɣlomera'θjon] *nf* agglomeration; **aglomeración de gente/ tráfico** mass of people/traffic jam

agnóstico, -a [aɣ'nostiko, a] *adj*, *nm/f* agnostic

agobiar [aɣo'βjar] *vt* to weigh down; (*oprimir*) to oppress; (*cargar*) to burden

agolparse [aɣol'parse] *vr* to crowd together

agonía [aɣo'nia] *nf* death throes *pl*; (*fig*) agony, anguish

agonizante [aɣoni'θante] *adj* dying

agonizar [aɣoni'θar] *vi* to be dying

agosto [a'ɣosto] *nm* August

agotado, -a [aɣo'taðo, a] *adj* (*persona*) exhausted; (*libros*) out of print; (*acabado*) finished; (*Com*) sold out; **agotador, a** [aɣota'ðor, a] *adj* exhausting

agotamiento [aɣota'mjento] *nm* exhaustion

agotar [aɣo'tar] *vt* to exhaust; (*consumir*) to drain; (*recursos*) to use up, deplete; **agotarse** *vr* to be exhausted; (*acabarse*) to run out; (*libro*) to go out of print

agraciado, -a [aɣra'θjaðo, a] *adj* (*atractivo*) attractive; (*en sorteo etc*) lucky

agradable [aɣra'ðaβle] *adj* pleasant, nice

agradar [aɣra'ðar] *vt*: **él me agrada** I like him

agradecer [aɣraðe'θer] *vt* to thank; (*favor etc*) to be grateful for; **agradecido, -a** *adj* grateful; **¡muy agradecido!** thanks a lot!; **agradecimiento** *nm* thanks *pl*; gratitude

agradezco *etc vb* V **agradecer**

agrado [a'ɣraðo] *nm*: **ser de tu** *etc* **~** to be to your *etc* liking

agrandar [aɣran'dar] *vt* to enlarge; (*fig*) to exaggerate; **agrandarse** *vr* to get bigger

agrario, -a [a'ɣrarjo, a] *adj* agrarian, land *cpd*; (*política*) agricultural, farming

agravante [aɣra'βante] *adj* aggravating ▷ *nm*: **con el ~ de que ...** with the further difficulty that ...

agravar [aɣra'βar] *vt* (*pesar sobre*) to make heavier; (*irritar*) to aggravate; **agravarse** *vr* to worsen, get worse

agraviar [aɣra'βjar] *vt* to offend; (*ser injusto con*) to wrong

agredir [aɣre'ðir] *vt* to attack

agregado, -a [aɣre'ɣaðo, a] *nm/f*: **A~ ≈** teacher (*who is not head of department*) ▷ *nm* aggregate; (*persona*) attaché

agregar [aɣre'ɣar] *vt* to gather; (*añadir*) to add; (*persona*) to appoint

agresión [aɣre'sjon] *nf* aggression

agresivo, -a [aɣre'siβo, a] *adj* aggressive

agriar [a'ɣrjar] vt to (turn) sour
agrícola [a'ɣrikola] adj farming cpd, agricultural
agricultor, a [aɣrikul'tor, a] nm/f farmer
agricultura [aɣrikul'tura] nf agriculture, farming
agridulce [aɣri'ðulθe] adj bittersweet; (Culin) sweet and sour
agrietarse [aɣrje'tarse] vr to crack; (piel) to chap
agrio, -a ['aɣrjo, a] adj bitter
agrupación [aɣrupa'θjon] nf group; (acto) grouping
agrupar [aɣru'par] vt to group
agua ['aɣwa] nf water; (Náut) wake; (Arq) slope of a roof; **aguas** nfpl (de piedra) water sg, sparkle sg; (Med) water sg, urine sg; (Náut) waters; **agua bendita/destilada/potable** holy/distilled/drinking water; **agua caliente** hot water; **agua corriente** running water; **agua de colonia** eau de cologne; **agua mineral (con/sin gas)** (sparkling/still) mineral water; **agua oxigenada** hydrogen peroxide; **aguas abajo/arriba** downstream/upstream; **aguas jurisdiccionales** territorial waters
aguacate [aɣwa'kate] nm avocado (pear)
aguacero [aɣwa'θero] nm (heavy) shower, downpour
aguado, -a [a'ɣwaðo, a] adj watery, watered down
aguafiestas [aɣwa'fjestas] nmf inv spoilsport, killjoy
aguamiel [aɣwa'mjel] (MÉX) nf fermented maguey o agave juice
aguanieve [aɣwa'njeβe] nf sleet
aguantar [aɣwan'tar] vt to bear, put up with; (sostener) to hold up ▷ vi to last; **aguantarse** vr to restrain o.s.; **aguante** nm (paciencia) patience; (resistencia) endurance
aguar [a'ɣwar] vt to water down
aguardar [aɣwar'ðar] vt to wait for
aguardiente [aɣwar'ðjente] nm brandy, liquor
aguarrás [aɣwa'rras] nm turpentine
aguaviva [aɣwa'βiβa] (RPL) nf jellyfish
agudeza [aɣu'ðeθa] nf sharpness; (ingenio) wit
agudo, -a [a'ɣuðo, a] adj sharp; (voz) high-pitched, piercing; (dolor, enfermedad) acute
agüero [a'ɣwero] nm: **buen/mal ~** good/bad omen
aguijón [aɣi'xon] nm sting; (fig) spur
águila ['aɣila] nf eagle; (fig) genius
aguileño, -a [aɣi'leɲo, a] adj (nariz) aquiline; (rostro) sharp-featured

aguinaldo [aɣi'naldo] nm Christmas box
aguja [a'ɣuxa] nf needle; (de reloj) hand; (Arq) spire; (Tec) firing-pin; **agujas** nfpl (Zool) ribs; (Ferro) points
agujerear [aɣuxere'ar] vt to make holes in
agujero [aɣu'xero] nm hole
agujetas [aɣu'xetas] nfpl stitch sg; (rigidez) stiffness sg
ahí [a'i] adv there; **de ~ que** so that, with the result that; **~ llega** here he comes; **por ~ that** way; (allá) over there; **200 o por ~** 200 or so
ahijado, -a [ai'xaðo, a] nm/f godson/daughter
ahogar [ao'ɣar] vt to drown; (asfixiar) to suffocate, smother; (fuego) to put out; **ahogarse** vr (en el agua) to drown; (por asfixia) to suffocate
ahogo [a'oɣo] nm breathlessness; (fig) financial difficulty
ahondar [aon'dar] vt to deepen, make deeper; (fig) to study thoroughly ▷ vi: **~ en** to study thoroughly
ahora [a'ora] adv now; (hace poco) a moment ago, just now; (dentro de poco) in a moment; **~ voy** I'm coming; **~ mismo** right now; **~ bien** now then; **por ~** for the present
ahorcar [aor'kar] vt to hang
ahorita [ao'rita] (fam) adv (LAM: en este momento) right now; (MÉX: hace poco) just now; (: dentro de poco) in a minute
ahorrar [ao'rrar] vt (dinero) to save; (esfuerzos) to save, avoid; **ahorro** nm (acto) saving; **ahorros** nmpl (dinero) savings
ahuecar [awe'kar] vt to hollow (out); (voz) to deepen; **ahuecarse** vr to give o.s. airs
ahumar [au'mar] vt to smoke, cure; (llenar de humo) to fill with smoke ▷ vi to smoke; **ahumarse** vr to fill with smoke
ahuyentar [aujen'tar] vt to drive off, frighten off; (fig) to dispel
aire ['aire] nm air; (viento) wind; (corriente) draught; (Mús) tune; **al ~ libre** in the open air; **aire acondicionado** air conditioning; **airear** vt to air; **airearse** vr (persona) to go out for a breath of fresh air; **airoso, -a** adj windy; draughty; (fig) graceful
aislado, -a [ais'laðo, a] adj isolated; (incomunicado) cut-off; (Elec) insulated
aislar [ais'lar] vt to isolate; (Elec) to insulate
ajardinado, -a [axarði'naðo, a] adj landscaped
ajedrez [axe'ðreθ] nm chess
ajeno, -a [a'xeno, a] adj (que pertenece a otro) somebody else's; **~ a** foreign to
ajetreado, -a [axetre'aðo, a] adj busy

ajetreo [axe'treo] *nm* bustle

ají [a'xi] (CS) *nm* chil(l)i, red pepper; (*salsa*) chil(l)i sauce

ajillo [a'xiʎo] *nm*: **gambas al ~** garlic prawns

ajo ['axo] *nm* garlic

ajuar [a'xwar] *nm* household furnishings *pl*; (*de novia*) trousseau; (*de niño*) layette

ajustado, -a [axus'taðo, a] *adj* (*tornillo*) tight; (*cálculo*) right; (*ropa*) tight(-fitting); (*resultado*) close

ajustar [axus'tar] *vt* (*adaptar*) to adjust; (*encajar*) to fit; (*Tec*) to engage; (*Imprenta*) to make up; (*apretar*) to tighten; (*concertar*) to agree (on); (*reconciliar*) to reconcile; (*cuentas, deudas*) to settle ▷ *vi* to fit; **ajustarse** *vr*: **~se a** (*precio etc*) to be in keeping with, fit in with; **~ las cuentas a algn** to get even with sb

ajuste [a'xuste] *nm* adjustment; (*Costura*) fitting; (*acuerdo*) compromise; (*de cuenta*) settlement

al [al] = **a + el**; V **a**

ala ['ala] *nf* wing; (*de sombrero*) brim; winger; **ala delta** *nf* hang-glider

alabanza [ala'βanθa] *nf* praise

alabar [ala'βar] *vt* to praise

alacena [ala'θena] *nf* kitchen cupboard (BRIT) o closet (US)

alacrán [ala'kran] *nm* scorpion

alambrada [alam'braða] *nf* wire fence; (*red*) wire netting

alambre [a'lambre] *nm* wire; **alambre de púas** barbed wire

alameda [ala'meða] *nf* (*plantío*) poplar grove; (*lugar de paseo*) avenue, boulevard

álamo ['alamo] *nm* poplar

alarde [a'larðe] *nm* show, display; **hacer ~ de** to boast of

alargador [alarxa'ðor] *nm* (*Elec*) extension lead

alargar [alar'xar] *vt* to lengthen, extend; (*paso*) to hasten; (*brazo*) to stretch out; (*cuerda*) to pay out; (*conversación*) to spin out; **alargarse** *vr* to get longer

alarma [a'larma] *nf* alarm; **alarma de incendios** fire alarm; **alarmar** *vt* to alarm; **alarmarse** to get alarmed; **alarmante** [alar'mante] *adj* alarming

alba ['alβa] *nf* dawn

albahaca [al'βaka] *nf* basil

Albania [al'βanja] *nf* Albania

albañil [alβa'ɲil] *nm* bricklayer; (*cantero*) mason

albarán [alβa'ran] *nm* (*Com*) delivery note, invoice

albaricoque [alβari'koke] *nm* apricot

albedrío [alβe'ðrio] *nm*: **libre ~** free will

alberca [al'βerka] *nf* reservoir; (MÉX: *piscina*) swimming pool

albergar [alβer'xar] *vt* to shelter

albergue *etc* [al'βerxe] *vb* V **albergar** ▷ *nm* shelter, refuge; **albergue juvenil** youth hostel

albóndiga [al'βondixa] *nf* meatball

albornoz [alβor'noθ] *nm* (*de los árabes*) burnous; (*para el baño*) bathrobe

alborotar [alβoro'tar] *vi* to make a row ▷ *vt* to agitate, stir up; **alborotarse** *vr* to get excited; (*mar*) to get rough; **alboroto** *nm* row, uproar

álbum ['alβum] (*pl* **-s, -es**) *nm* album; **álbum de recortes** scrapbook

albur [al'βur] (MÉX) *nm* (*juego de palabras*) pun; (*doble sentido*) double entendre

alcachofa [alka'tʃofa] *nf* artichoke

alcalde, -esa [al'kalde, esa] *nm/f* mayor(ess)

alcaldía [alkal'dia] *nf* mayoralty; (*lugar*) mayor's office

alcance *etc* [al'kanθe] *vb* V **alcanzar** ▷ *nm* reach; (*Com*) adverse balance; **al ~ de algn** available to sb

alcancía [alkan'θia] (LAM) *nf* (*para ahorrar*) money box; (*para colectas*) collection box

alcantarilla [alkanta'riʎa] *nf* (*de aguas cloacales*) sewer; (*en la calle*) gutter

alcanzar [alkan'θar] *vt* (*algo: con la mano, el pie*) to reach; (*alguien: en el camino etc*) to catch up (with); (*autobús*) to catch; (*bala*) to hit, strike ▷ *vi* (*ser suficiente*) to be enough; **~ a hacer** to manage to do

alcaparra [alka'parra] *nf* caper

alcayata [alka'jata] *nf* hook

alcázar [al'kaθar] *nm* fortress; (*Náut*) quarter-deck

alcoba [al'koβa] *nf* bedroom

alcohol [al'kol] *nm* alcohol; **alcohol metílico** methylated spirits *pl* (BRIT), wood alcohol (US); **alcohólico, -a** *adj, nm/f* alcoholic; **alcoholímetro** [alko'limetro] *nm* Breathalyser® (BRIT), drunkometer (US); **alcoholismo** [alko'lismo] *nm* alcoholism

alcornoque [alkor'noke] *nm* cork tree; (*fam*) idiot

aldea [al'dea] *nf* village; **aldeano, -a** *adj* village *cpd* ▷ *nm/f* villager

aleación [alea'θjon] *nf* alloy

aleatorio, -a [alea'torjo, a] *adj* random

aleccionar [alekθjo'nar] *vt* to instruct; (*adiestrar*) to train

alegar [ale'xar] *vt* to claim; (*Jur*) to plead ▷ *vi* (LAM: *discutir*) to argue

alegoría [alexo'ria] *nf* allegory

alegrar [ale'xrar] *vt* (*causar alegría*) to cheer (up); (*fuego*) to poke; (*fiesta*) to liven

up; **alegrarse** *vr* (*fam*) to get merry o tight; **~se de** to be glad about
alegre [a'leɣre] *adj* happy, cheerful; (*fam*) merry, tight; (*chiste*) risqué, blue; **alegría** *nf* happiness; merriment
alejar [ale'xar] *vt* to remove; (*fig*) to estrange; **alejarse** *vr* to move away
alemán, -ana [ale'man, ana] *adj, nm/f* German ▷ *nm* (*Ling*) German
Alemania [ale'manja] *nf* Germany
alentador, a [alenta'ðor, a] *adj* encouraging
alentar [alen'tar] *vt* to encourage
alergia [a'lerxja] *nf* allergy
alero [a'lero] *nm* (*de tejado*) eaves *pl*; (*guardabarros*) mudguard
alerta [a'lerta] *adj, nm* alert
aleta [a'leta] *nf* (*de pez*) fin; (*ala*) wing; (*de foca, Deporte*) flipper; (*Auto*) mudguard
aletear [alete'ar] *vi* to flutter
alevín [ale'βin] *nm* fry, young fish
alevosía [aleβo'sia] *nf* treachery
alfabeto [alfa'βeto] *nm* alphabet
alfalfa [al'falfa] *nf* alfalfa, lucerne
alfarería [alfare'ria] *nf* pottery; (*tienda*) pottery shop; **alfarero, -a** *nm/f* potter
alféizar [al'feiðar] *nm* window-sill
alférez [al'fereθ] *nm* (*Mil*) second lieutenant; (*Náut*) ensign
alfil [al'fil] *nm* (*Ajedrez*) bishop
alfiler [alfi'ler] *nm* pin; (*broche*) clip
alfombra [al'fombra] *nf* carpet; (*más pequeña*) rug; **alfombrilla** *nf* rug, mat; (*Inform*) mouse mat o pad
alforja [al'forxa] *nf* saddlebag
algas [ˈalɣas] *nfpl* seaweed
álgebra [ˈalxeβra] *nf* algebra
algo [ˈalɣo] *pron* something; anything ▷ *adv* somewhat, rather; **¿~ más?** anything else?; (*en tienda*) is that all?; **por ~ será** there must be some reason for it
algodón [alɣo'ðon] *nm* cotton; (*planta*) cotton plant; **algodón de azúcar** candy floss (*BRIT*), cotton candy (*US*); **algodón hidrófilo** cotton wool (*BRIT*), absorbent cotton (*US*)
alguien [ˈalɣjen] *pron* someone, somebody; (*en frases interrogativas*) anyone, anybody
alguno, -a [al'ɣuno, a] *adj* (*delante de nm*): **algún** some; (*después de n*): **no tiene talento ~** he has no talent, he doesn't have any talent ▷ *pron* (*alguien*) someone, somebody; **algún que otro libro** some book or other; **algún día iré** I'll go one o some day; **sin interés ~** without the slightest interest; **~ que otro** an occasional one; **~s piensan** some (people) think

alhaja [a'laxa] *nf* jewel; (*tesoro*) precious object, treasure
alhelí [ale'li] *nm* wallflower, stock
aliado, -a [a'ljaðo, a] *adj* allied
alianza [a'ljanθa] *nf* alliance; (*anillo*) wedding ring
aliar [a'ljar] *vt* to ally; **aliarse** *vr* to form an alliance
alias [ˈaljas] *adv* alias
alicatado [alika'taðo] (*ESP*) *nm* tiling
alicates [ali'kates] *nmpl* pliers
aliciente [ali'θjente] *nm* incentive; (*atracción*) attraction
alienación [aljena'θjon] *nf* alienation
aliento [a'ljento] *nm* breath; (*respiración*) breathing; **sin ~** breathless
aligerar [alixe'rar] *vt* to lighten; (*reducir*) to shorten; (*aliviar*) to alleviate; (*mitigar*) to ease; (*paso*) to quicken
alijo [a'lixo] *nm* consignment
alimaña [ali'maɲa] *nf* pest
alimentación [alimenta'θjon] *nf* (*comida*) food; (*acción*) feeding; (*tienda*) grocer's (shop)
alimentar [alimen'tar] *vt* to feed; (*nutrir*) to nourish; **alimentarse** *vr* to feed
alimenticio, -a [alimen'tiθjo, a] *adj* food *cpd*; (*nutritivo*) nourishing, nutritious
alimento [ali'mento] *nm* food; (*nutrición*) nourishment
alineación [alinea'θjon] *nf* alignment; (*Deporte*) line-up
alinear [aline'ar] *vt* to align; (*Deporte*) to select, pick
aliñar [ali'ɲar] *vt* (*Culin*) to season; **aliño** *nm* (*Culin*) dressing
alioli [ali'oli] *nm* garlic mayonnaise
alisar [ali'sar] *vt* to smooth
alistarse [alis'tarse] *vr* to enlist; (*inscribirse*) to enrol
aliviar [ali'βjar] *vt* (*carga*) to lighten; (*persona*) to relieve; (*dolor*) to relieve, alleviate
alivio [a'liβjo] *nm* alleviation, relief
aljibe [al'xiβe] *nm* cistern
allá [a'ʎa] *adv* (*lugar*) there; (*por ahí*) over there; (*tiempo*) then; **~ abajo** down there; **más ~** further on; **más ~ de** beyond; **¡~ tú!** that's your problem!; **¡~ voy!** I'm coming!
allanamiento [aʎana'mjento] *nm* (*LAM*: *de policía*) raid; **allanamiento de morada** burglary
allanar [aʎa'nar] *vt* to flatten, level (out); (*igualar*) to smooth (out); (*fig*) to subdue; (*Jur*) to burgle, break into
allegado, -a [aʎe'ɣaðo, a] *adj* near, close ▷ *nm/f* relation
allí [a'ʎi] *adv* there; **~ mismo** right there;

por ~ over there; (*por ese camino*) that way
alma ['alma] *nf* soul; (*persona*) person
almacén [alma'θen] *nm* (*depósito*)
warehouse, store; (*Mil*) magazine; (*cs: de
comestibles*) grocer's (shop); **grandes
almacenes** department store *sg*;
almacenaje *nm* storage
almacenar [almaθe'nar] *vt* to store, put
in storage; (*proveerse*) to stock up with
almanaque [alma'nake] *nm* almanac
almeja [al'mexa] *nf* clam
almendra [al'mendra] *nf* almond;
almendro *nm* almond tree
almíbar [al'miβar] *nm* syrup
almidón [almi'ðon] *nm* starch
almirante [almi'rante] *nm* admiral
almohada [almo'aða] *nf* pillow; (*funda*)
pillowcase; **almohadilla** *nf* cushion; (*para
alfileres*) pincushion; (*Tec*) pad
almohadón [almoa'ðon] *nm* large pillow;
bolster
almorranas [almo'rranas] *nfpl* piles,
haemorrhoids
almorzar [almor'θar] *vt:* **~ una tortilla** to
have an omelette for lunch ▷ *vi* to (have)
lunch
almuerzo *etc* [al'mwerθo] *vb* V **almorzar**
▷ *nm* lunch
alocado, -a [alo'kaðo, a] *adj* crazy
alojamiento [aloxa'mjento] *nm*
lodging(s) *pl*; (*viviendas*) housing
alojar [alo'xar] *vt* to lodge; **alojarse** *vr* to
lodge, stay
alondra [a'londra] *nf* lark, skylark
alpargata [alpar'ɣata] *nf* rope-soled
sandal, espadrille
Alpes ['alpes] *nmpl:* **los ~** the Alps
alpinismo [alpi'nismo] *nm*
mountaineering, climbing; **alpinista** *nmf*
mountaineer, climber
alpiste [al'piste] *nm* birdseed
alquilar [alki'lar] *vt* (*propietario: inmuebles*)
to let, rent (out); (: *coche*) to hire out; (: *TV*) to
rent (out); (*alquilador: inmuebles, TV*) to rent;
(: *coche*) to hire; **"se alquila casa"** "house to
let (*BRIT*) o for rent (*US*)"
alquiler [alki'ler] *nm* renting; letting;
hiring; (*arriendo*) rent; hire charge; **de ~** for
hire; **alquiler de automóviles** *o* **coches**
car hire
alquimia [al'kimja] *nf* alchemy
alquitrán [alki'tran] *nm* tar
alrededor [alreðe'ðor] *adv* around,
about; **~ de** around, about; **mirar a su ~** to
look (round) about one; **alrededores** *nmpl*
surroundings
alta ['alta] *nf* (certificate of) discharge
altar [al'tar] *nm* altar

altavoz [alta'βoθ] *nm* loudspeaker;
(*amplificador*) amplifier
alteración [altera'θjon] *nf* alteration;
(*alboroto*) disturbance
alterar [alte'rar] *vt* to alter; to disturb;
alterarse *vr* (*persona*) to get upset
altercado [alter'kaðo] *nm* argument
alternar [alter'nar] *vt* to alternate ▷ *vi* to
alternate; (*turnar*) to take turns; **alternarse**
vr to alternate; to take turns; **~ con** to mix
with; **alternativa** *nf* alternative; (*elección*)
choice; **alternativo, -a** *adj* alternative;
(*alterno*) alternating; **alterno, -a** *adj*
alternate; (*Elec*) alternating
Alteza [al'teθa] *nf* (*tratamiento*) Highness
altibajos [alti'βaxos] *nmpl* ups and downs
altiplano [alti'plano] *nm* = **altiplanicie**
altisonante [altiso'nante] *adj* high-
flown, high-sounding
altitud [alti'tuð] *nf* height; (*Aviac, Geo*)
altitude
altivo, -a [al'tiβo, a] *adj* haughty,
arrogant
alto, -a ['alto, a] *adj* high; (*persona*) tall;
(*sonido*) high, sharp; (*noble*) high, lofty ▷ *nm*
halt; (*Mús*) alto; (*Geo*) hill ▷ *adv* (*de sitio*)
high; (*de sonido*) loud, loudly ▷ *excl* halt!;
la pared tiene 2 metros de ~ the wall is 2
metres high; **en alta mar** on the high seas;
en voz alta in a loud voice; **las altas horas
de la noche** the small o wee hours; **en lo ~
de** at the top of; **pasar por ~** to overlook;
altoparlante [altopar'lante] (*LAM*) *nm*
loudspeaker
altura [al'tura] *nf* height; (*Náut*) depth;
(*Geo*) latitude; **la pared tiene 1.80 de ~** the
wall is 1 metre 80cm high; **a estas ~s** at
this stage; **a estas ~s del año** at this time
of the year
alubia [a'luβja] *nf* bean
alucinación [aluθina'θjon] *nf*
hallucination
alucinar [aluθi'nar] *vi* to hallucinate ▷ *vt*
to deceive; (*fascinar*) to fascinate
alud [a'luð] *nm* avalanche; (*fig*) flood
aludir [alu'ðir] *vi:* **~ a** to allude to; **darse
por aludido** to take the hint
alumbrado [alum'braðo] *nm* lighting
alumbrar [alum'brar] *vt* to light (up) ▷ *vi*
(*Med*) to give birth
aluminio [alu'minjo] *nm* aluminium
(*BRIT*), aluminum (*US*)
alumno, -a [a'lumno, a] *nm/f* pupil,
student
alusión [alu'sjon] *nf* allusion
alusivo, -a [alu'siβo, a] *adj* allusive
aluvión [alu'βjon] *nm* alluvium; (*fig*) flood
alverja [al'βerxa] (*LAM*) *nf* pea

alza ['alθa] *nf* rise; (*Mil*) sight
alzamiento [alθa'mjento] *nm* (*rebelión*)
rising
alzar [al'θar] *vt* to lift (up); (*precio, muro*)
to raise; (*cuello de abrigo*) to turn up; (*Agr*) to
gather in; (*Imprenta*) to gather; **alzarse** *vr*
to get up, rise; (*rebelarse*) to revolt; (*Com*) to
go fraudulently bankrupt; (*Jur*) to appeal
ama ['ama] *nf* lady of the house; (*dueña*)
owner; (*institutriz*) governess; (*madre
adoptiva*) foster mother; **ama de casa**
housewife; **ama de llaves** housekeeper
amabilidad [amaβili'ðað] *nf* kindness;
(*simpatía*) niceness; **amable** *adj* kind; nice;
es usted muy amable that's very kind of
you
amaestrado, -a [amaes'traðo, a] *adj*
(*animal: en circo etc*) performing
amaestrar [amaes'trar] *vt* to train
amago [a'maɣo] *nm* threat; (*gesto*)
threatening gesture; (*Med*) symptom
amainar [amai'nar] *vi* (*viento*) to die
down
amamantar [amaman'tar] *vt* to suckle,
nurse
amanecer [amane'θer] *vi* to dawn ▷ *nm*
dawn; **~ afiebrado** to wake up with a fever
amanerado, -a [amane'raðo, a] *adj*
affected
amante [a'mante] *adj*: **~ de** fond of ▷ *nmf*
lover
amapola [ama'pola] *nf* poppy
amar [a'mar] *vt* to love
amargado, -a [amar'ɣaðo, a] *adj* bitter
amargar [amar'ɣar] *vt* to make bitter;
(*fig*) to embitter; **amargarse** *vr* to become
embittered
amargo, -a [a'marɣo, a] *adj* bitter
amarillento, -a [amari'ʎento, a] *adj*
yellowish; (*tez*) sallow; **amarillo, -a** *adj*,
nm yellow
amarrado, -a [ama'rraðo, a] (*MÉx: fam*)
adj mean, stingy
amarrar [ama'rrar] *vt* to moor; (*sujetar*)
to tie up
amarras [a'marras] *nfpl*: **soltar ~** to set
sail
amasar [ama'sar] *vt* (*masa*) to knead;
(*mezclar*) to mix, prepare; (*confeccionar*) to
concoct
amateur [ama'ter] *nmf* amateur
amazona [ama'θona] *nf* horsewoman;
Amazonas *nm*: **el Amazonas** the Amazon
ámbar ['ambar] *nm* amber
ambición [ambi'θjon] *nf* ambition;
ambicionar *vt* to aspire to; **ambicioso, -a**
adj ambitious
ambidextro, -a [ambi'ðekstro, a] *adj*
ambidextrous
ambientación [ambjenta'θjon] *nf* (*Cine,
Teatro etc*) setting; (*Radio*) sound effects
ambiente [am'bjente] *nm* atmosphere;
(*medio*) environment
ambigüedad [ambiɣwe'ðað] *nf*
ambiguity; **ambiguo, -a** *adj* ambiguous
ámbito ['ambito] *nm* (*campo*) field; (*fig*)
scope
ambos, -as ['ambos, as] *adj pl, pron pl*
both
ambulancia [ambu'lanθja] *nf*
ambulance
ambulante [ambu'lante] *adj* travelling
cpd, itinerant
ambulatorio [ambula'torio] *nm* state
health-service clinic
amén [a'men] *excl* amen; **~ de** besides
amenaza [ame'naθa] *nf* threat;
amenazar [amena'θar] *vt* to threaten
▷ *vi*: **amenazar con hacer** to threaten to do
ameno, -a [a'meno, a] *adj* pleasant
América [a'merika] *nf* America; **América
Central/Latina** Central/Latin America;
América del Norte/del Sur North/South
America; **americana** *nf* coat, jacket; V
tb **americano**; **americano, -a** *adj*, *nm/f*
American
ametralladora [ametraʎa'ðora] *nf*
machine gun
amigable [ami'ɣaβle] *adj* friendly
amígdala [a'miɣðala] *nf* tonsil;
amigdalitis *nf* tonsillitis
amigo, -a [a'miɣo, a] *adj* friendly ▷ *nm/f*
friend; (*amante*) lover; **ser ~ de algo** to be
fond of sth; **ser muy ~s** to be close friends
aminorar [amino'rar] *vt* to diminish;
(*reducir*) to reduce; **~ la marcha** to slow
down
amistad [amis'tað] *nf* friendship;
amistades *nfpl* (*amigos*) friends; **amistoso,
-a** *adj* friendly
amnesia [am'nesja] *nf* amnesia
amnistía [amnis'tia] *nf* amnesty
amo ['amo] *nm* owner; (*jefe*) boss
amolar [amo'lar] (*MÉx: fam*) *vt* to ruin,
damage
amoldar [amol'dar] *vt* to mould; (*adaptar*)
to adapt
amonestación [amonesta'θjon] *nf*
warning; **amonestaciones** *nfpl* (*Rel*)
marriage banns
amonestar [amones'tar] *vt* to warn; (*Rel*)
to publish the banns of
amontonar [amonto'nar] *vt* to collect,
pile up; **amontonarse** *vr* to crowd
together; (*acumularse*) to pile up
amor [a'mor] *nm* love; (*amante*) lover;

hacer el ~ to make love; **amor propio**
self-respect
amoratado, -a [amora'taðo, a] adj
purple
amordazar [amorða'θar] vt to muzzle;
(fig) to gag
amorfo, -a [a'morfo, a] adj amorphous,
shapeless
amoroso, -a [amo'roso, a] adj
affectionate, loving
amortiguador [amortigwa'ðor] nm
shock absorber; (parachoques) bumper;
amortiguadores nmpl (Auto) suspension
sg
amortiguar [amorti'ɣwar] vt to deaden;
(ruido) to muffle; (color) to soften
amotinar [amoti'nar] vt to stir up, incite
(to riot); **amotinarse** vr to mutiny
amparar [ampa'rar] vt to protect;
ampararse vr to seek protection; (de la
lluvia etc) to shelter; **amparo** nm help,
protection; **al amparo de** under the
protection of
amperio [am'perjo] nm ampère, amp
ampliación [amplja'θjon] nf
enlargement; (extensión) extension
ampliar [am'pljar] vt to enlarge; to
extend
amplificador [amplifika'ðor] nm
amplifier
amplificar [amplifi'kar] vt to amplify
amplio, -a ['ampljo, a] adj spacious; (de
falda etc) full; (extenso) extensive; (ancho)
wide; **amplitud** nf spaciousness; extent;
(fig) amplitude
ampolla [am'poʎa] nf blister; (Med)
ampoule
amputar [ampu'tar] vt to cut off,
amputate
amueblar [amwe'βlar] vt to furnish
anales [a'nales] nmpl annals
analfabetismo [analfaβe'tismo]
nm illiteracy; **analfabeto, -a** adj, nm/f
illiterate
analgésico [anal'xesiko] nm painkiller,
analgesic
análisis [a'nalisis] nm inv analysis
analista [ana'lista] nmf (gen) analyst
analizar [anali'θar] vt to analyse
analógico, -a [ana'loxiko, a] adj (Inform)
analog; (reloj) analogue (BRIT), analog (US)
análogo, -a [a'naloɣo, a] adj analogous,
similar
ananá [ana'na] (RPL) nm pineapple
anarquía [anar'kia] nf anarchy;
anarquista nmf anarchist
anatomía [anato'mia] nf anatomy
anca ['anka] nf rump, haunch; **ancas** nfpl

(fam) behind sg
ancho, -a ['antʃo, a] adj wide; (falda)
full; (fig) liberal ▷ nm width; (Ferro) gauge;
ponerse ~ to get conceited; **estar a sus
anchas** to be at one's ease
anchoa [an'tʃoa] nf anchovy
anchura [an'tʃura] nf width; (extensión)
wideness
anciano, -a [an'θjano, a] adj old, aged
▷ nm/f old man/woman; elder
ancla ['ankla] nf anchor
Andalucía [andalu'θia] nf Andalusia;
andaluz, -a adj, nm/f Andalusian
andamio [an'damjo] nm scaffold(ing)
andar [an'dar] vt to go, cover, travel
▷ vi to go, walk, travel; (funcionar) to go,
work; (estar) to be ▷ nm walk, gait, pace;
andarse vr to go away; **~ a pie/a caballo/
en bicicleta** to go on foot/on horseback/
by bicycle; **~ haciendo algo** to be doing sth;
¡**anda**! (sorpresa) go on!; **anda por o en los
40** he's about 40
andén [an'den] nm (Ferro) platform; (Náut)
quayside; (CAM: de la calle) pavement (BRIT),
sidewalk (US)
Andes ['andes] nmpl: **los ~** the Andes
andinismo [andi'nismo] (LAM) nm
mountaineering, climbing
Andorra [an'dorra] nf Andorra
andrajoso, -a [andra'xoso, a] adj ragged
anduve etc vb V **andar**
anécdota [a'nekðota] nf anecdote, story
anegar [ane'ɣar] vt to flood; (ahogar) to
drown
anemia [a'nemja] nf anaemia
anestesia [anes'tesja] nf (sustancia)
anaesthetic; (proceso) anaesthesia;
anestesia general/local general/local
anaesthetic
anexar [anek'sar] vt to annex; (documento)
to attach; **anexión** nf annexation; **anexo,
-a** adj attached ▷ nm annexe
anfibio, -a [an'fiβjo, a] adj amphibious
▷ nm amphibian
anfiteatro [anfite'atro] nm
amphitheatre; (Teatro) dress circle
anfitrión, -ona [anfi'trjon, ona] nm/f
host(ess)
ánfora ['anfora] nf (cántaro) amphora;
(MÉX Pol) ballot box
ángel ['anxel] nm angel; **ángel de la
guarda** guardian angel
angina [an'xina] nf (Med) inflammation
of the throat; **tener ~s** to have tonsillitis;
angina de pecho angina
anglicano, -a [angli'kano, a] adj, nm/f
Anglican
anglosajón, -ona [anglosa'xon, ona] adj

Anglo-Saxon

anguila [an'gila] *nf* eel

angula [an'gula] *nf* elver, baby eel

ángulo ['angulo] *nm* angle; (*esquina*) corner; (*curva*) bend

angustia [an'gustja] *nf* anguish

anhelar [ane'lar] *vt* to be eager for; (*desear*) to long for, desire ▷ *vi* to pant, gasp; **anhelo** *nm* eagerness; desire

anidar [ani'ðar] *vi* to nest

anillo [a'niʎo] *nm* ring; **anillo de boda/ compromiso** wedding/engagement ring

animación [anima'θjon] *nf* liveliness; (*vitalidad*) life; (*actividad*) activity; bustle

animado, -a [ani'maðo, a] *adj* lively; (*vivaz*) animated; **animador, a** *nm/f* (*TV*) host(ess), compère; (*Deporte*) cheerleader

animal [ani'mal] *adj* animal; (*fig*) stupid ▷ *nm* animal; (*fig*) fool; (*bestia*) brute

animar [ani'mar] *vt* (*Bio*) to animate, give life to; (*fig*) to liven up, brighten up, cheer up; (*estimular*) to stimulate; **animarse** *vr* to cheer up; to feel encouraged; (*decidirse*) to make up one's mind

ánimo ['animo] *nm* (*alma*) soul; (*mente*) mind; (*valentía*) courage ▷ *excl* cheer up!

animoso, -a [ani'moso, a] *adj* brave; (*vivo*) lively

aniquilar [aniki'lar] *vt* to annihilate, destroy

anís [a'nis] *nm* aniseed; (*licor*) anisette

aniversario [aniβer'sarjo] *nm* anniversary

anoche [a'notʃe] *adv* last night; **antes de ~** the night before last

anochecer [anotʃe'θer] *vi* to get dark ▷ *nm* nightfall, dark; **al ~** at nightfall

anodino, -a [ano'ðino, a] *adj* dull, anodyne

anomalía [anoma'lia] *nf* anomaly

anonadado, -a [anona'ðaðo, a] *adj*: **estar ~** to be overwhelmed *o* amazed

anonimato [anoni'mato] *nm* anonymity

anónimo, -a [a'nonimo, a] *adj* anonymous; (*Com*) limited ▷ *nm* (*carta anónima*) anonymous letter; (: *maliciosa*) poison-pen letter

anormal [anor'mal] *adj* abnormal

anotación [anota'θjon] *nf* note; annotation

anotar [ano'tar] *vt* to note down; (*comentar*) to annotate

ansia ['ansja] *nf* anxiety; (*añoranza*) yearning; **ansiar** *vt* to long for

ansiedad [ansje'ðað] *nf* anxiety

ansioso, -a [an'sjoso, a] *adj* anxious; (*anhelante*) eager; **~ de** *o* **por algo** greedy for sth

antaño [an'taɲo] *adv* long ago, formerly

Antártico [an'tartiko] *nm*: **el ~** the Antarctic

ante ['ante] *prep* before, in the presence of; (*problema etc*) faced with ▷ *nm* (*piel*) suede; **~ todo** above all

anteanoche [antea'notʃe] *adv* the night before last

anteayer [antea'jer] *adv* the day before yesterday

antebrazo [ante'βraθo] *nm* forearm

antecedente [anteθe'ðente] *adj* previous ▷ *nm* antecedent; **antecedentes** *nmpl* (*historial*) record *sg*; **antecedentes penales** criminal record

anteceder [anteθe'ðer] *vt* to precede, go before

antecesor, a [anteθe'sor, a] *nm/f* predecessor

antelación [antela'θjon] *nf*: **con ~** in advance

antemano [ante'mano]: **de ~** *adv* beforehand, in advance

antena [an'tena] *nf* antenna; (*de televisión etc*) aerial; **antena parabólica** satellite dish

antenoche [ante'notʃe] (*LAM*) *adv* the night before last

anteojo [ante'oxo] *nm* eyeglass; **anteojos** *nmpl* (*LAM*: *gafas*) glasses, spectacles

antepasados [antepa'saðos] *nmpl* ancestors

anteponer [antepo'ner] *vt* to place in front; (*fig*) to prefer

anterior [ante'rjor] *adj* preceding, previous; **anterioridad** *nf*: **con anterioridad a** prior to, before

antes ['antes] *adv* (*con prioridad*) before ▷ *prep*: **~ de** before ▷ *conj*: **~ ir/de que te vayas** before going/before you go; **~ bien** (but) rather; **dos días ~** two days before *o* previously; **no quiso venir ~** she didn't want to come any earlier; **tomo el avión ~ que el barco** I take the plane rather than the boat; **~ de** *o* **que nada** (*en el tiempo*) first of all; (*indicando preferencia*) above all; **~ que yo** before me; **lo ~ posible** as soon as possible; **cuanto ~ mejor** the sooner the better

antibalas [anti'βalas] *adj inv*: **chaleco ~** bullet-proof jacket

antibiótico [anti'βjotiko] *nm* antibiotic

anticaspa [anti'kaspa] *adj inv* anti-dandruff *cpd*

anticipación [antiθipa'θjon] *nf* anticipation; **con 10 minutos de ~** 10 minutes early

anticipado, -a [antiθi'paðo, a] *adj* (*pago*) advance; **por ~** in advance

anticipar [antiθi'par] *vt* to anticipate;

(*adelantar*) to bring forward; (*Com*) to advance; **anticiparse** *vr*: **~se a su época** to be ahead of one's time

anticipo [anti'θipo] *nm* (*Com*) advance

anticonceptivo, -a [antikonθep'tiβo, a] *adj, nm* contraceptive

anticongelante [antikonxe'lante] *nm* antifreeze

anticuado, -a [anti'kwaðo, a] *adj* out-of-date, old-fashioned; (*desusado*) obsolete

anticuario [anti'kwarjo] *nm* antique dealer

anticuerpo [anti'kwerpo] *nm* (*Med*) antibody

antidepresivo [antiðepre'siβo] *nm* antidepressant

antidóping [anti'dopin] *adj inv*: **control ~** drugs test

antídoto [an'tiðoto] *nm* antidote

antiestético, -a [anties'tetiko, a] *adj* unsightly

antifaz [anti'faθ] *nm* mask; (*velo*) veil

antiglobalización [antiɣloβaliθa'θjon] *nf* anti-globalization; **antiglobalizador, a** *adj* anti-globalization *cpd*

antiguamente [antiɣwa'mente] *adv* formerly; (*hace mucho tiempo*) long ago

antigüedad [antiɣwe'ðað] *nf* antiquity; (*artículo*) antique; (*rango*) seniority

antiguo, -a [an'tiɣwo, a] *adj* old, ancient; (*que fue*) former

Antillas [an'tiʎas] *nfpl*: **las ~** the West Indies

antílope [an'tilope] *nm* antelope

antinatural [antinatu'ral] *adj* unnatural

antipatía [antipa'tia] *nf* antipathy, dislike; **antipático, -a** *adj* disagreeable, unpleasant

antirrobo [anti'rroβo] *adj inv* (*alarma etc*) anti-theft

antisemita [antise'mita] *adj* anti-Semitic ▷ *nmf* anti-Semite

antiséptico, -a [anti'septiko, a] *adj* antiseptic ▷ *nm* antiseptic

antivirus [anti'birus] *nm inv* (*Comput*) antivirus program

antojarse [anto'xarse] *vr* (*desear*): **se me antoja comprarlo** I have a mind to buy it; (*pensar*): **se me antoja que ...** I have a feeling that ...

antojitos [anto'xitos] (*MÉX*) *nmpl* snacks, nibbles

antojo [an'toxo] *nm* caprice, whim; (*rosa*) birthmark; (*lunar*) mole

antología [antolo'xia] *nf* anthology

antorcha [an'tortʃa] *nf* torch

antro ['antro] *nm* cavern

antropología [antropolo'xia] *nf* anthropology

anual [a'nwal] *adj* annual

anuario [a'nwarjo] *nm* yearbook

anulación [anula'θjon] *nf* annulment; (*cancelación*) cancellation

anular [anu'lar] *vt* (*contrato*) to annul, cancel; (*ley*) to revoke, repeal; (*suscripción*) to cancel ▷ *nm* ring finger

anunciar [anun'θjar] *vt* to announce; (*proclamar*) to proclaim; (*Com*) to advertise

anuncio [a'nunθjo] *nm* announcement; (*señal*) sign; (*Com*) advertisement; (*cartel*) poster

anzuelo [an'θwelo] *nm* hook; (*para pescar*) fish hook

añadidura [aɲaði'ðura] *nf* addition, extra; **por ~** besides, in addition

añadir [aɲa'ðir] *vt* to add

añejo, -a [a'ɲexo, a] *adj* old; (*vino*) mellow

añicos [a'ɲikos] *nmpl*: **hacer ~** to smash, shatter

año ['aɲo] *nm* year; **¡Feliz A~ Nuevo!** Happy New Year!; **tener 15 ~s** to be 15 (years old); **los ~s 90** the nineties; **el ~ que viene** next year; **año bisiesto/escolar/fiscal/sabático** leap/school/tax/sabbatical year

añoranza [aɲo'ranθa] *nf* nostalgia; (*anhelo*) longing

apa ['apa] (*MÉX*) *excl* goodness me!, good gracious!

apabullar [apaβu'ʎar] *vt* to crush, squash

apacible [apa'θiβle] *adj* gentle, mild

apaciguar [apaθi'ɣwar] *vt* to pacify, calm (down)

apadrinar [apaðri'nar] *vt* to sponsor, support; (*Rel*) to be godfather to

apagado, -a [apa'ɣaðo, a] *adj* (*volcán*) extinct; (*color*) dull; (*voz*) quiet; (*sonido*) muted, muffled; (*persona: apático*) listless; **estar ~** (*fuego, luz*) to be out; (*Radio, TV etc*) to be off

apagar [apa'ɣar] *vt* to put out; (*Elec, Radio, TV*) to turn off; (*sonido*) to silence, muffle; (*sed*) to quench

apagón [apa'ɣon] *nm* blackout; power cut

apalabrar [apala'βrar] *vt* to agree to; (*contratar*) to engage

apalear [apale'ar] *vt* to beat, thrash

apantallar [apanta'ʎar] (*MÉX*) *vt* to impress

apañar [apa'ɲar] *vt* to pick up; (*asir*) to take hold of, grasp; (*reparar*) to mend, patch up; **apañarse** *vr* to manage, get along

apapachar [apapa'tʃar] (*MÉX: fam*) *vt* to cuddle, hug

aparador [apara'ðor] *nm* sideboard; (*MÉX: escaparate*) shop window

aparato [apa'rato] *nm* apparatus;

(*máquina*) machine; (*doméstico*) appliance; (*boato*) ostentation; **aparato digestivo** (*Anat*) digestive system; **aparatoso, -a** *adj* showy, ostentatious

aparcamiento [aparka'mjento] *nm* car park (*BRIT*), parking lot (*US*)

aparcar [apar'kar] *vt, vi* to park

aparear [apare'ar] *vt* (*objetos*) to pair, match; (*animales*) to mate; **aparearse** *vr* to make a pair; to mate

aparecer [apare'θer] *vi* to appear; **aparecerse** *vr* to appear

aparejador, a [aparexa'ðor, a] *nm/f* (*Arq*) master builder

aparejo [apa'rexo] *nm* harness; rigging; (*de poleas*) block and tackle

aparentar [aparen'tar] *vt* (*edad*) to look; (*fingir*): ~ **tristeza** to pretend to be sad

aparente [apa'rente] *adj* apparent; (*adecuado*) suitable

aparezco *etc vb* V **aparecer**

aparición [apari'θjon] *nf* appearance; (*de libro*) publication; (*espectro*) apparition

apariencia [apa'rjenθja] *nf* (outward) appearance; **en ~** outwardly, seemingly

apartado, -a [apar'taðo, a] *adj* separate; (*lejano*) remote ▷ *nm* (*tipográfico*) paragraph; **apartado de correos** (*ESP*) post office box; **apartado postal** (*LAM*) post office box

apartamento [aparta'mento] *nm* apartment, flat (*BRIT*)

apartar [apar'tar] *vt* to separate; (*quitar*) to remove; **apartarse** *vr* to separate, part; (*irse*) to move away; to keep away

aparte [a'parte] *adv* (*separadamente*) separately; (*además*) besides ▷ *nm* aside; (*tipográfico*) new paragraph

aparthotel [aparto'tel] *nm* serviced apartments

apasionado, -a [apasjo'naðo, a] *adj* passionate

apasionar [apasjo'nar] *vt* to excite; **le apasiona el fútbol** she's crazy about football; **apasionarse** *vr* to get excited

apatía [apa'tia] *nf* apathy

apático, -a [a'patiko, a] *adj* apathetic

Apdo *abr* (= *Apartado (de Correos)*) PO Box

apeadero [apea'ðero] *nm* halt, stop, stopping place

apearse [ape'arse] *vr* (*jinete*) to dismount; (*bajarse*) to get down o out; (*Auto, Ferro*) to get off o out

apechugar [apetʃu'ɣar] *vr*: ~ **con algo** to face up to sth

apegarse [ape'ɣarse] *vr*: ~ **a** to become attached to; **apego** *nm* attachment, devotion

apelar [ape'lar] *vi* to appeal; ~ **a** (*fig*) to resort to

apellidar [apeʎi'ðar] *vt* to call, name; **apellidarse** *vr*: **se apellida Pérez** her (sur)name's Pérez

apellido [ape'ʎiðo] *nm* surname

apenar [ape'nar] *vt* to grieve, trouble; (*LAM: avergonzar*) to embarrass; **apenarse** *vr* to grieve; (*LAM: avergonzarse*) to be embarrassed

apenas [a'penas] *adv* scarcely, hardly ▷ *conj* as soon as, no sooner

apéndice [a'pendiθe] *nm* appendix; **apendicitis** *nf* appendicitis

aperitivo [aperi'tiβo] *nm* (*bebida*) aperitif; (*comida*) appetizer

apertura [aper'tura] *nf* opening; (*Pol*) liberalization

apestar [apes'tar] *vt* to infect ▷ *vi*: ~ **(a)** to stink (of)

apetecer [apete'θer] *vt*: ¿**te apetece un café?** do you fancy a (cup of) coffee?; **apetecible** *adj* desirable; (*comida*) appetizing

apetito [ape'tito] *nm* appetite; **apetitoso, -a** *adj* appetizing; (*fig*) tempting

apiadarse [apja'ðarse] *vr*: ~ **de** to take pity on

ápice ['apiθe] *nm* whit, iota

apilar [api'lar] *vt* to pile o heap up

apiñarse [api'ɲarse] *vr* to crowd o press together

apio ['apjo] *nm* celery

apisonadora [apisona'ðora] *nf* steamroller

aplacar [apla'kar] *vt* to placate

aplastante [aplas'tante] *adj* overwhelming; (*lógica*) compelling

aplastar [aplas'tar] *vt* to squash (flat); (*fig*) to crush

aplaudir [aplau'ðir] *vt* to applaud

aplauso [a'plauso] *nm* applause; (*fig*) approval, acclaim

aplazamiento [aplaθa'mjento] *nm* postponement

aplazar [apla'θar] *vt* to postpone, defer

aplicación [aplika'θjon] *nf* application; (*esfuerzo*) effort

aplicado, -a [apli'kaðo, a] *adj* diligent, hard-working

aplicar [apli'kar] *vt* (*ejecutar*) to apply; **aplicarse** *vr* to apply o.s.

aplique *etc* [a'plike] *vb* V **aplicar** ▷ *nm* wall light

aplomo [a'plomo] *nm* aplomb, self-assurance

apodar [apo'ðar] *vt* to nickname

apoderado [apoðe'raðo] *nm* agent,

representative

apoderarse [apoðe'rrarse] *vr*: **~ de** to take possession of

apodo [a'poðo] *nm* nickname

apogeo [apo'xeo] *nm* peak, summit

apoquinar [apoki'nar] (*fam*) *vt* to fork out, cough up

aporrear [aporre'ar] *vt* to beat (up)

aportar [apor'tar] *vt* to contribute ▷ *vi* to reach port; **aportarse** *vr* (*LAM*: *llegar*) to arrive, come

aposta [a'posta] *adv* deliberately, on purpose

apostar [apos'tar] *vt* to bet, stake; (*tropas etc*) to station, post ▷ *vi* to bet

apóstol [a'postol] *nm* apostle

apóstrofo [a'postrofo] *nm* apostrophe

apoyar [apo'jar] *vt* to lean, rest; (*fig*) to support, back; **apoyarse** *vr*: **~se en** to lean on; **apoyo** *nm* (*gen*) support; backing, help

apreciable [apre'θjaβle] *adj* considerable; (*fig*) esteemed

apreciar [apre'θjar] *vt* to evaluate, assess; (*Com*) to appreciate, value; (*persona*) to respect; (*tamaño*) to gauge, assess; (*detalles*) to notice

aprecio [a'preθjo] *nm* valuation, estimate; (*fig*) appreciation

aprehender [apreen'der] *vt* to apprehend, detain

apremio [a'premjo] *nm* urgency

aprender [apren'der] *vt, vi* to learn; **~ algo de memoria** to learn sth (off) by heart

aprendiz, a [apren'diθ, a] *nm/f* apprentice; (*principiante*) learner; **aprendizaje** *nm* apprenticeship

aprensión [apren'sjon] *nm* apprehension, fear; **aprensivo, -a** *adj* apprehensive

apresar [apre'sar] *vt* to seize; (*capturar*) to capture

apresurado, -a [apresu'raðo, a] *adj* hurried, hasty

apresurar [apresu'rar] *vt* to hurry, accelerate; **apresurarse** *vr* to hurry, make haste

apretado, -a [apre'taðo, a] *adj* tight; (*escritura*) cramped

apretar [apre'tar] *vt* to squeeze; (*Tec*) to tighten; (*presionar*) to press together, pack ▷ *vi* to be too tight

apretón [apre'ton] *nm* squeeze; **apretón de manos** handshake

aprieto [a'prjeto] *nm* squeeze; (*dificultad*) difficulty; **estar en un ~** to be in a fix

aprisa [a'prisa] *adv* quickly, hurriedly

aprisionar [aprisjo'nar] *vt* to imprison

aprobación [aproβa'θjon] *nf* approval

aprobar [apro'βar] *vt* to approve (of); (*examen, materia*) to pass ▷ *vi* to pass

apropiado, -a [apro'pjaðo, a] *adj* suitable

apropiarse [apro'pjarse] *vr*: **~ de** to appropriate

aprovechado, -a [aproβe'tʃaðo, a] *adj* industrious, hard-working; (*económico*) thrifty; (*pey*) unscrupulous

aprovechar [aproβe'tʃar] *vt* to use; (*explotar*) to exploit; (*experiencia*) to profit from; (*oferta, oportunidad*) to take advantage of ▷ *vi* to progress, improve; **aprovecharse** *vr*: **~se de** to make use of; to take advantage of; **¡que aproveche!** enjoy your meal!

aproximación [aproksima'θjon] *nf* approximation; (*de lotería*) consolation prize

aproximar [aproksi'mar] *vt* to bring nearer; **aproximarse** *vr* to come near, approach

apruebo *etc vb* V **aprobar**

aptitud [apti'tuð] *nf* aptitude

apto, -a ['apto, a] *adj* suitable

apuesta [a'pwesta] *nf* bet, wager

apuesto, -a [a'pwesto, a] *adj* neat, elegant

apuntar [apun'tar] *vt* (*con arma*) to aim at; (*con dedo*) to point at o to; (*anotar*) to note (down); (*Teatro*) to prompt; **apuntarse** *vr* (*Deporte: tanto, victoria*) to score; (*Escol*) to enrol

> No confundir **apuntar** con la palabra inglesa *appoint*.

apunte [a'punte] *nm* note

apuñalar [apuɲa'lar] *vt* to stab

apurado, -a [apu'raðo, a] *adj* needy; (*difícil*) difficult; (*peligroso*) dangerous; (*LAM: con prisa*) hurried, rushed

apurar [apu'rar] *vt* (*agotar*) to drain; (*recursos*) to use up; (*molestar*) to annoy; **apurarse** *vr* (*preocuparse*) to worry; (*LAM: darse prisa*) to hurry

apuro [a'puro] *nm* (*aprieto*) fix, jam; (*escasez*) want, hardship; (*vergüenza*) embarrassment; (*LAM: prisa*) haste, urgency

aquejado, -a [ake'xaðo, a] *adj*: **~ de** (*Med*) afflicted by

aquel, aquella [a'kel, a'keʎa] *adj* that; **~los(as)** those

aquél, aquélla [a'kel, a'keʎa] *pron* that (one); **~los(as)** those (ones)

aquello [a'keʎo] *pron* that, that business

aquí [a'ki] *adv* (*lugar*) here; (*tiempo*) now; **~ arriba** up here; **~ mismo** right here; **~ yace** here lies; **de ~ a siete días** a week from now

ara ['ara] *nf*: **en ~s de** for the sake of

árabe ['araβe] *adj, nmf* Arab ▷ *nm* (*Ling*) Arabic

Arabia [a'raβja] *nf* Arabia; **Arabia Saudí** *o* **Saudita** Saudi Arabia

arado [a'raðo] *nm* plough

Aragón [ara'ɣon] *nm* Aragon; **aragonés, -esa** *adj, nm/f* Aragonese

arancel [aran'θel] *nm* tariff, duty

arandela [aran'dela] *nf* (*Tec*) washer

araña [a'raɲa] *nf* (*Zool*) spider; (*lámpara*) chandelier

arañar [ara'ɲar] *vt* to scratch

arañazo [ara'ɲaθo] *nm* scratch

arbitrar [arβi'trar] *vt* to arbitrate in; (*Deporte*) to referee ▷ *vi* to arbitrate

arbitrario, -a [arβi'trarjo, a] *adj* arbitrary

árbitro ['arβitro] *nm* arbitrator; (*Deporte*) referee; (*Tenis*) umpire

árbol ['arβol] *nm* (*Bot*) tree; (*Náut*) mast; (*Tec*) axle, shaft; **árbol de Navidad** Christmas tree

arboleda [arβo'leða] *nf* grove, plantation

arbusto [ar'βusto] *nm* bush, shrub

arca ['arka] *nf* chest, box

arcada [ar'kaða] *nf* arcade; (*de puente*) arch, span; **arcadas** *nfpl* (*náuseas*) retching *sg*

arcaico, -a [ar'kaiko, a] *adj* archaic

arce ['arθe] *nm* maple tree

arcén [ar'θen] *nm* (*de autopista*) hard shoulder; (*de carretera*) verge

archipiélago [artʃi'pjelaɣo] *nm* archipelago

archivador [artʃiβa'ðor] *nm* filing cabinet

archivar [artʃi'βar] *vt* to file (away); **archivo** *nm* file, archive(s) *pl*; **archivo adjunto** (*Inform*) attachment; **archivo de seguridad** (*Inform*) backup file

arcilla [ar'θiʎa] *nf* clay

arco ['arko] *nm* arch; (*Mat*) arc; (*Mil, Mús*) bow; **arco iris** rainbow

arder [ar'ðer] *vi* to burn; **estar que arde** (*persona*) to fume

ardid [ar'ðið] *nm* ploy, trick

ardiente [ar'ðjente] *adj* burning, ardent

ardilla [ar'ðiʎa] *nf* squirrel

ardor [ar'ðor] *nm* (*calor*) heat; (*fig*) ardour; **ardor de estómago** heartburn

arduo, -a ['arðwo, a] *adj* arduous

área ['area] *nf* area; (*Deporte*) penalty area

arena [a'rena] *nf* sand; (*de una lucha*) arena; **arenas movedizas** quicksand *sg*; **arenal** [are'nal] *nm* (*terreno arenoso*) sandy spot

arenisca [are'niska] *nf* sandstone; (*cascajo*) grit

arenoso, -a [are'noso, a] *adj* sandy

arenque [a'renke] *nm* herring

arete [a'rete] (*MÉX*) *nm* earring

Argel [ar'xel] *n* Algiers; **Argelia** *nf* Algeria; **argelino, -a** *adj, nm/f* Algerian

Argentina [arxen'tina] *nf* (*tb*: **la ~**) Argentina

argentino, -a [arxen'tino, a] *adj* Argentinian; (*de plata*) silvery ▷ *nm/f* Argentinian

argolla [ar'ɣoʎa] *nf* (large) ring

argot [ar'ɣo] (*pl* **~s**) *nm* slang

argucia [ar'ɣuθja] *nf* subtlety, sophistry

argumentar [arɣumen'tar] *vt, vi* to argue

argumento [arɣu'mento] *nm* argument; (*razonamiento*) reasoning; (*de novela etc*) plot; (*Cine, TV*) storyline

aria ['arja] *nf* aria

aridez [ari'ðeθ] *nf* aridity, dryness

árido, -a ['ariðo, a] *adj* arid, dry

Aries ['arjes] *nm* Aries

arisco, -a [a'risko, a] *adj* surly; (*insociable*) unsociable

aristócrata [aris'tokrata] *nmf* aristocrat

arma ['arma] *nf* arm; **armas** *nfpl* arms; **arma blanca** blade, knife; **arma de doble filo** double-edged sword; **arma de fuego** firearm; **armas de destrucción masiva** weapons of mass destruction

armada [ar'maða] *nf* armada; (*flota*) fleet

armadillo [arma'ðiʎo] *nm* armadillo

armado, -a [ar'maðo, a] *adj* armed; (*Tec*) reinforced

armadura [arma'ðura] *nf* (*Mil*) armour; (*Tec*) framework; (*Zool*) skeleton; (*Física*) armature

armamento [arma'mento] *nm* armament; (*Náut*) fitting-out

armar [ar'mar] *vt* (*soldado*) to arm; (*máquina*) to assemble; (*navío*) to fit out; **~la, ~ un lío** to start a row, kick up a fuss

armario [ar'marjo] *nm* wardrobe; (*de cocina, baño*) cupboard; **armario empotrado** built-in cupboard

armatoste [arma'toste] *nm* (*mueble*) monstrosity; (*máquina*) contraption

armazón [arma'θon] *nf o m* body, chassis; (*de mueble etc*) frame; (*Arq*) skeleton

armiño [ar'miɲo] *nm* stoat; (*piel*) ermine

armisticio [armis'tiθjo] *nm* armistice

armonía [armo'nia] *nf* harmony

armónica [ar'monika] *nf* harmonica

armonizar [armoni'θar] *vt* to harmonize; (*diferencias*) to reconcile

aro ['aro] *nm* ring; (*tejo*) quoit; (*cs: pendiente*) earring

aroma [a'roma] *nm* aroma, scent; **aromaterapia** *n* aromatherapy; **aromático, -a** [aro'matiko, a] *adj* aromatic

arpa ['arpa] *nf* harp

arpía [ar'pia] nf shrew

arpón [ar'pon] nm harpoon

arqueología [arkeolo'xia] nf archaeology; **arqueólogo, -a** nm/f archaeologist

arquetipo [arke'tipo] nm archetype

arquitecto [arki'tekto] nm architect; **arquitectura** nf architecture

arrabal [arra'βal] nm poor suburb, slum; **arrabales** nmpl (afueras) outskirts

arraigar [arrai'xar] vt to establish ▷ vi to take root

arrancar [arran'kar] vt (sacar) to extract, pull out; (arrebatar) to snatch (away); (Inform) to boot; (fig) to extract ▷ vi (Auto, máquina) to start; (ponerse en marcha) to get going; **~ de** to stem from

arranque etc [a'rranke] vb V **arrancar** ▷ nm sudden start; (Auto) start; (fig) fit, outburst

arrasar [arra'sar] vt (aplanar) to level, flatten; (destruir) to demolish

arrastrar [arras'trar] vt to drag (along); (fig) to drag down, degrade; (agua, viento) to carry away ▷ vi to drag, trail on the ground; **arrastrarse** vr to crawl; (fig) to grovel; **llevar algo arrastrado** to drag sth along

arrear [arre'ar] vt to drive on, urge on ▷ vi to hurry along

arrebatar [arreβa'tar] vt to snatch (away), seize; (fig) to captivate

arrebato [arre'βato] nm fit of rage, fury; (éxtasis) rapture

arrecife [arre'θife] nm reef

arreglado, -a [arre'xlaðo, a] adj (ordenado) neat, orderly; (moderado) moderate, reasonable

arreglar [arre'xlar] vt (poner orden) to tidy up; (algo roto) to fix, repair; (problema) to solve; **arreglarse** vr to reach an understanding; **arreglárselas** (fam) to get by, manage

arreglo [a'rrexlo] nm settlement; (orden) order; (acuerdo) agreement; (Mús) arrangement, setting

arremangar [arreman'gar] vt to roll up, turn up; **arremangarse** vr to roll up one's sleeves

arremeter [arreme'ter] vi: **~ contra** to attack, rush at

arrendamiento [arrenda'mjento] nm letting; (alquilar) hiring; (contrato) lease; (alquiler) rent; **arrendar** vt to let, lease; to rent; **arrendatario, -a** nm/f tenant

arreos [a'rreos] nmpl (de caballo) harness sg, trappings

arrepentimiento [arrepenti'mjento] nm regret, repentance

arrepentirse [arrepen'tirse] vr to repent; **~ de** to regret

arresto [a'rresto] nm arrest; (Mil) detention; (audacia) boldness, daring; **arresto domiciliario** house arrest

arriar [a'rrjar] vt (velas) to haul down; (bandera) to lower, strike; (cable) to pay out

O **PALABRA CLAVE**

arriba [a'rriβa] adv 1 (posición) above; **desde arriba** from above; **arriba de todo** at the very top, right on top; **Juan está arriba** Juan is upstairs; **lo arriba mencionado** the aforementioned

2 (dirección): **calle arriba** up the street

3 **de arriba abajo** from top to bottom; **mirar a algn de arriba abajo** to look sb up and down

4 **para arriba: de 5000 euros para arriba** from 5000 euros up(wards)

▷ adj: **de arriba: el piso de arriba** the upstairs (BRIT) flat o apartment; **la parte de arriba** the top o upper part

▷ prep: **arriba de** (LAM: por encima de) above; **arriba de 200 dólares** more than 200 dollars

▷ excl: **¡arriba!** up!; **¡manos arriba!** hands up!; **¡arriba España!** long live Spain!

arribar [arri'βar] vi to put into port; (llegar) to arrive

arriendo etc [a'rrjendo] vb V **arrendar** ▷ nm = **arrendamiento**

arriesgado, -a [arrjes'xaðo, a] adj (peligroso) risky; (audaz) bold, daring

arriesgar [arrjes'xar] vt to risk; (poner en peligro) to endanger; **arriesgarse** vr to take a risk

arrimar [arri'mar] vt (acercar) to bring close; (poner de lado) to set aside; **arrimarse** vr to come close o closer; **~se a** to lean on

arrinconar [arrinko'nar] vt (colocar) to put in a corner; (enemigo) to corner; (fig) to put on one side; (abandonar) to push aside

arroba [a'rroβa] nf (Internet) at (sign)

arrodillarse [arroði'ʎarse] vr to kneel (down)

arrogante [arro'xante] adj arrogant

arrojar [arro'xar] vt to throw, hurl; (humo) to emit, give out; (Com) to yield, produce; **arrojarse** vr to throw o hurl o.s.

arrojo [a'rroxo] nm daring

arrollador, a [arroʎa'ðor, a] adj overwhelming

arrollar [arro'ʎar] vt (Auto etc) to run over, knock down; (Deporte) to crush

arropar [arro'par] vt to cover, wrap up;

arroparse *vr* to wrap o.s. up

arroyo [a'rrojo] *nm* stream; (*de la calle*) gutter

arroz [a'rroθ] *nm* rice; **arroz con leche** rice pudding

arruga [a'rruxa] *nf* (*de cara*) wrinkle; (*de vestido*) crease; **arrugar** [arru'xar] *vt* to wrinkle; to crease; **arrugarse** *vr* to get creased

arruinar [arrwi'nar] *vt* to ruin, wreck; **arruinarse** *vr* to be ruined, go bankrupt

arsenal [arse'nal] *nm* naval dockyard; (*Mil*) arsenal

arte ['arte] (*gen m en sg y siempre f en pl*) *nm* art; (*maña*) skill, guile; **artes** *nfpl* (*bellas artes*) arts

artefacto [arte'fakto] *nm* appliance

arteria [ar'terja] *nf* artery

artesanía [artesa'nia] *nf* craftsmanship; (*artículos*) handicrafts *pl*; **artesano, -a** *nm/f* artisan, craftsman(-woman)

ártico, -a ['artiko, a] *adj* Arctic ▷ *nm*: **el Á~** the Arctic

articulación [artikula'θjon] *nf* articulation; (*Med, Tec*) joint

artículo [ar'tikulo] *nm* article; (*cosa*) thing, article; **artículos** *nmpl* (*Com*) goods; **artículos de escritorio** stationery

artífice [ar'tifiθe] *nmf* (*fig*) architect

artificial [artifi'θjal] *adj* artificial

artillería [artiʎe'ria] *nf* artillery

artilugio [arti'luxjo] *nm* gadget

artimaña [arti'maɲa] *nf* trap, snare; (*astucia*) cunning

artista [ar'tista] *nmf* (*pintor*) artist, painter; (*Teatro*) artist, artiste; **artista de cine** film actor/actress; **artístico, -a** *adj* artistic

artritis [ar'tritis] *nf* arthritis

arveja [ar'βexa] (*LAM*) *nf* pea

arzobispo [arθo'βispo] *nm* archbishop

as [as] *nm* ace

asa ['asa] *nf* handle; (*fig*) lever

asado [a'saðo] *nm* roast (meat); (*LAM: barbacoa*) barbecue

● **ASADO**
●
● Traditional Latin American barbecues,
● especially in the River Plate area, are
● celebrated in the open air around a large
● grill which is used to grill mainly beef
● and various kinds of spicy pork sausage.
● They are usually very common during
● the summer and can go on for several
● days. The head cook is nearly always
● a man.

asador [asa'ðor] *nm* spit

asadura [asa'ðura] *nf* entrails *pl*, offal

asalariado, -a [asala'rjaðo, a] *adj* paid, salaried ▷ *nm/f* wage earner

asaltar [asal'tar] *vt* to attack, assault; (*fig*) to assail; **asalto** *nm* attack, assault; (*Deporte*) round

asamblea [asam'blea] *nf* assembly; (*reunión*) meeting

asar [a'sar] *vt* to roast

ascendencia [asθen'denθja] *nf* ancestry; (*LAM: influencia*) ascendancy; **de ~ francesa** of French origin

ascender [asθen'der] *vi* (*subir*) to ascend, rise; (*ser promovido*) to gain promotion ▷ *vt* to promote; **~ a** to amount to; **ascendiente** *nm* influence ▷ *nmf* ancestor

ascensión [asθen'sjon] *nf* ascent; (*Rel*): **la A~** the Ascension

ascenso [as'θenso] *nm* ascent; (*promoción*) promotion

ascensor [asθen'sor] *nm* lift (*BRIT*), elevator (*US*)

asco ['asko] *nm*: **¡qué ~!** how revolting *o* disgusting; **el ajo me da ~** I hate *o* loathe garlic; **estar hecho un ~** to be filthy

ascua ['askwa] *nf* ember

aseado, -a [ase'aðo, a] *adj* clean; (*arreglado*) tidy; (*pulcro*) smart

asear [ase'ar] *vt* to clean, wash; to tidy (up)

asediar [ase'ðjar] *vt* (*Mil*) to besiege, lay siege to; (*fig*) to chase, pester; **asedio** *nm* siege; (*Com*) run

asegurado, -a [aseɣu'raðo, a] *adj* insured

asegurador, a [aseɣura'ðor, a] *nm/f* insurer

asegurar [aseɣu'rar] *vt* (*consolidar*) to secure, fasten; (*dar garantía de*) to guarantee; (*preservar*) to safeguard; (*afirmar, dar por cierto*) to assure, affirm; (*tranquilizar*) to reassure; (*tomar un seguro*) to insure; **asegurarse** *vr* to assure o.s., make sure

asemejarse [aseme'xarse] *vr* to be alike; **~ a** to be like, resemble

asentado, -a [asen'taðo, a] *adj* established, settled

asentar [asen'tar] *vt* (*sentar*) to seat, sit down; (*poner*) to place, establish; (*alisar*) to level, smooth down *o* out; (*anotar*) to note down ▷ *vi* to be suitable, suit

asentir [asen'tir] *vi* to assent, agree; **~ con la cabeza** to nod (one's head)

aseo [a'seo] *nm* cleanliness; **aseos** *nmpl* (*servicios*) toilet *sg* (*BRIT*), cloakroom *sg* (*BRIT*), restroom *sg* (*US*)

aséptico, -a [a'septiko, a] *adj* germ-free,

free from infection

asequible [ase'kiβle] adj (precio) reasonable; (meta) attainable; (persona) approachable

asesinar [asesi'nar] vt to murder; (Pol) to assassinate; **asesinato** nm murder; assassination

asesino, -a [ase'sino, a] nm/f murderer, killer; (Pol) assassin

asesor, a [ase'sor, a] nm/f adviser, consultant; **asesorar** [aseso'rar] vt (Jur) to advise, give legal advice to; (Com) to act as consultant to; **asesorarse** vr: **asesorarse con** o **de** to take advice from, consult; **asesoría** nf (cargo) consultancy; (oficina) consultant's office

asestar [ases'tar] vt (golpe) to deal, strike

asfalto [as'falto] nm asphalt

asfixia [as'fiksja] nf asphyxia, suffocation; **asfixiar** [asfik'sjar] vt to asphyxiate, suffocate; **asfixiarse** vr to be asphyxiated, suffocate

así [a'si] adv (de esta manera) in this way, like this, thus; (aunque) although; (tan pronto como) as soon as; **~ que** so; **~ como** as well as; **~ y todo** even so; **¿no es ~?** isn't it?, didn't you? etc; **~ de grande** this big

Asia ['asja] nf Asia; **asiático, -a** adj, nm/f Asian, Asiatic

asiduo, -a [a'siðwo, a] adj assiduous; (frecuente) frequent ▷ nm/f regular (customer)

asiento [a'sjento] nm (mueble) seat, chair; (de coche, en tribunal etc) seat; (localidad) seat, place; (fundamento) site; **asiento delantero/trasero** front/back seat

asignación [asiɣna'θjon] nf (atribución) assignment; (reparto) allocation; (sueldo) salary; **asignación (semanal)** pocket money

asignar [asiɣ'nar] vt to assign, allocate

asignatura [asiɣna'tura] nf subject; course

asilo [a'silo] nm (refugio) asylum, refuge; (establecimiento) home, institution; **asilo político** political asylum

asimilar [asimi'lar] vt to assimilate

asimismo [asi'mismo] adv in the same way, likewise

asistencia [asis'tenθja] nf audience; (Med) attendance; (ayuda) assistance; **asistencia en carretera** roadside assistance; **asistente** nmf assistant; **los asistentes** those present; **asistente social** social worker

asistido, -a [asis'tiðo, a] adj: **~ por ordenador** computer-assisted

asistir [asis'tir] vt to assist, help ▷ vi: **~ a** to attend, be present at

asma ['asma] nf asthma

asno ['asno] nm donkey; (fig) ass

asociación [asoθja'θjon] nf association; (Com) partnership; **asociado, -a** adj associate ▷ nm/f associate; (Com) partner

asociar [aso'θjar] vt to associate

asomar [aso'mar] vt to show, stick out ▷ vi to appear; **asomarse** vr to appear, show up; **~ la cabeza por la ventana** to put one's head out of the window

asombrar [asom'brar] vt to amaze, astonish; **asombrarse** vr (sorprenderse) to be amazed; (asustarse) to get a fright; **asombro** nm amazement, astonishment; (susto) fright; **asombroso, -a** adj astonishing, amazing

asomo [a'somo] nm hint, sign

aspa ['aspa] nf (cruz) cross; (de molino) sail; **en ~** X-shaped

aspaviento [aspa'βjento] nm exaggerated display of feeling; (fam) fuss

aspecto [as'pekto] nm (apariencia) look, appearance; (fig) aspect

áspero, -a ['aspero, a] adj rough; bitter; sour; harsh

aspersión [asper'sjon] nf sprinkling

aspiración [aspira'θjon] nf breath, inhalation; (Mús) short pause; **aspiraciones** nfpl (ambiciones) aspirations

aspirador [aspira'ðor] nm = **aspiradora**

aspiradora [aspira'ðora] nf vacuum cleaner, Hoover®

aspirante [aspi'rante] nmf (candidato) candidate; (Deporte) contender

aspirar [aspi'rar] vt to breathe in ▷ vi: **~ a** to aspire to

aspirina [aspi'rina] nf aspirin

asqueroso, -a [aske'roso, a] adj disgusting, sickening

asta ['asta] nf lance; (arpón) spear; (mango) shaft, handle; (Zool) horn; **a media ~** at half mast

asterisco [aste'risko] nm asterisk

astilla [as'tiʎa] nf splinter; (pedacito) chip; **astillas** nfpl (leña) firewood sg

astillero [asti'ʎero] nm shipyard

astro ['astro] nm star

astrología [astrolo'xia] nf astrology; **astrólogo, -a** nm/f astrologer

astronauta [astro'nauta] nmf astronaut

astronomía [astrono'mia] nf astronomy

astucia [as'tuθja] nf astuteness; (ardid) clever trick

asturiano, -a [astu'rjano, a] adj, nm/f Asturian

astuto, -a [as'tuto, a] adj astute; (taimado) cunning

asumir [asu'mir] vt to assume
asunción [asun'θjon] nf assumption;
(Rel): **A~** Assumption
asunto [a'sunto] nm (tema) matter,
subject; (negocio) business
asustar [asus'tar] vt to frighten;
asustarse vr to be (o become) frightened
atacar [ata'kar] vt to attack
atadura [ata'ðura] nf bond, tie
atajar [ata'xar] vt (enfermedad, mal) to stop
▷ vi (persona) to take a short cut
atajo [a'taxo] nm short cut
atañer [ata'ɲer] vi: **~ a** to concern
ataque etc [a'take] vb V **atacar** ▷ nm
attack; **ataque cardíaco** heart attack
atar [a'tar] vt to tie, tie up
atarantado, -a [ataran'taðo, a] (MÉX)
adj (aturdido) dazed
atardecer [atarðe'θer] vi to get dark ▷ nm
evening; (crepúsculo) dusk
atareado, -a [atare'aðo, a] adj busy
atascar [atas'kar] vt to clog up; (obstruir)
to jam; (fig) to hinder; **atascarse** vr to
stall; (cañería) to get blocked up; **atasco** nm
obstruction; (Auto) traffic jam
ataúd [ata'uð] nm coffin
ataviar [ata'βjar] vt to deck, array
atemorizar [atemori'θar] vt to frighten,
scare
Atenas [a'tenas] n Athens
atención [aten'θjon] nf attention;
(bondad) kindness ▷ excl (be) careful!, look
out!
atender [aten'der] vt to attend to, look
after; (Tel) to answer ▷ vi to pay attention
atenerse [ate'nerse] vr: **~ a** to abide by,
adhere to
atentado [aten'taðo] nm crime, illegal
act; (asalto) assault; (tb: **~ terrorista**)
terrorist attack; **~ contra la vida de algn**
attempt on sb's life; **atentado suicida**
suicide bombing
atentamente [atenta'mente] adv: **Le
saluda ~** Yours faithfully
atentar [aten'tar] vi: **~ a o contra** to
commit an outrage against
atento, -a [a'tento, a] adj attentive,
observant; (cortés) polite, thoughtful; **estar
~ a** (explicación) to pay attention to
atenuar [ate'nwar] vt (disminuir) to
lessen, minimize
ateo, -a [a'teo, a] adj atheistic ▷ nm/f
atheist
aterrador, a [aterra'ðor, a] adj
frightening
aterrizaje [aterri'θaxe] nm landing;
aterrizaje forzoso emergency o forced
landing

aterrizar [aterri'θar] vi to land
aterrorizar [aterrori'θar] vt to terrify
atesorar [ateso'rar] vt to hoard
atestar [ates'tar] vt to pack, stuff; (Jur) to
attest, testify to
atestiguar [atesti'ɣwar] vt to testify to,
bear witness to
atiborrar [atiβo'rrar] vt to fill, stuff;
atiborrarse vr to stuff o.s.
ático ['atiko] nm (desván) attic;
(apartamento) penthouse
atinado, -a [ati'naðo, a] adj (sensato)
wise; (correcto) right, correct
atinar [ati'nar] vi (al disparar): **~ al blanco**
to hit the target; (fig) to be right
atizar [ati'θar] vt to poke; (horno etc) to
stoke; (fig) to stir up, rouse
atlántico, -a [at'lantiko, a] adj Atlantic
▷ nm: **el (océano) A~** the Atlantic (Ocean)
atlas ['atlas] nm inv atlas
atleta [at'leta] nm athlete; **atlético, -a** adj
athletic; **atletismo** nm athletics sg
atmósfera [at'mosfera] nf atmosphere
atolladero [atoʎa'ðero] nm (fig) jam, fix
atómico, -a [a'tomiko, a] adj atomic
átomo ['atomo] nm atom
atónito, -a [a'tonito, a] adj astonished,
amazed
atontado, -a [aton'taðo, a] adj stunned;
(bobo) silly, daft
atormentar [atormen'tar] vt to torture;
(molestar) to torment; (acosar) to plague,
harass
atornillar [atorni'ʎar] vt to screw on o
down
atosigar [atosi'ɣar] vt to harass, pester
atracador, a [ataka'ðor, a] nm/f robber
atracar [atra'kar] vt (Náut) to moor;
(robar) to hold up, rob ▷ vi to moor;
atracarse vr: **~se (de)** to stuff o.s. (with)
atracción [atrak'θjon] nf attraction
atraco [a'trako] nm holdup, robbery
atracón [atra'kon] nm: **darse o pegarse
un ~ (de)** (fam) to stuff o.s. (with)
atractivo, -a [atrak'tiβo, a] adj
attractive ▷ nm appeal
atraer [atra'er] vt to attract
atragantarse [atraɣan'tarse] vr: **~ (con)**
to choke (on); **se me ha atragantado el
chico** I can't stand the boy
atrancar [atran'kar] vt (puerta) to bar, bolt
atrapar [atra'par] vt to trap; (resfriado etc)
to catch
atrás [a'tras] adv (movimiento) back(-
wards); (lugar) behind; (tiempo) previously; **ir
hacia ~** to go back(wards), to go to the rear;
estar ~ to be behind o at the back
atrasado, -a [atra'saðo, a] adj slow;

(*pago*) overdue, late; (*país*) backward
atrasar [atra'sar] *vi* to be slow; **atrasarse** *vr* to remain behind; (*tren*) to be o run late; **atraso** *nm* slowness; lateness, delay; (*de país*) backwardness; **atrasos** *nmpl* (Com) arrears
atravesar [atraβe'sar] *vt* (*cruzar*) to cross (over); (*traspasar*) to pierce; to go through; (*poner al través*) to lay o put across; **atravesarse** *vr* to come in between; (*intervenir*) to interfere
atravieso etc *vb* V **atravesar**
atreverse [atre'βerse] *vr* to dare; (*insolentarse*) to be insolent; **atrevido, -a** *adj* daring; insolent; **atrevimiento** *nm* daring; insolence
atribución [atriβu'θjon] *nf* attribution; **atribuciones** *nfpl* (Pol) powers; (*Admin*) responsibilities
atribuir [atriβu'ir] *vt* to attribute; (*funciones*) to confer
atributo [atri'βuto] *nm* attribute
atril [a'tril] *nm* (*para libro*) lectern; (*Mús*) music stand
atropellar [atrope'ʎar] *vt* (*derribar*) to knock over o down; (*empujar*) to push (aside); (*Auto*) to run over, run down; (*agraviar*) to insult; **atropello** *nm* (Auto) accident; (*empujón*) push; (*agravio*) wrong; (*atrocidad*) outrage
atroz [a'troθ] *adj* atrocious, awful
ATS *nmf abr* (= *Ayudante Técnico Sanitario*) nurse
atuendo [a'twendo] *nm* attire
atún [a'tun] *nm* tuna
aturdir [atur'ðir] *vt* to stun; (*de ruido*) to deafen; (*fig*) to dumbfound, bewilder
audacia [au'ðaθja] *nf* boldness, audacity; **audaz** *adj* bold, audacious
audición [auði'θjon] *nf* hearing; (Teatro) audition
audiencia [au'ðjenθja] *nf* audience; (*Jur: tribunal*) court
audífono [au'ðifono] *nm* (*para sordos*) hearing aid
auditor [auði'tor] *nm* (Jur) judge advocate; (*Com*) auditor
auditorio [auði'torjo] *nm* audience; (*sala*) auditorium
auge ['auxe] *nm* boom; (*clímax*) climax
augurar [auxu'rar] *vt* to predict; (*presagiar*) to portend
augurio [au'xurjo] *nm* omen
aula ['aula] *nf* classroom; (*en universidad etc*) lecture room
aullar [au'ʎar] *vi* to howl, yell
aullido [au'ʎiðo] *nm* howl, yell
aumentar [aumen'tar] *vt* to increase;

(*precios*) to put up; (*producción*) to step up; (*con microscopio, anteojos*) to magnify ▷ *vi* to increase, be on the increase; **aumentarse** *vr* to increase, be on the increase; **aumento** *nm* increase; rise
aun [a'un] *adv* even; ~ **así** even so; ~ **más** even o yet more
aún [a'un] *adv*: ~ **está aquí** he's still here; ~ **no lo sabemos** we don't know yet; **¿no ha venido ~?** hasn't she come yet?
aunque [a'unke] *conj* though, although, even though
aúpa [a'upa] *excl* come on!
auricular [auriku'lar] *nm* (Tel) receiver; **auriculares** *nmpl* (*cascos*) headphones
aurora [au'rora] *nf* dawn
ausencia [au'senθja] *nf* absence
ausentarse [ausen'tarse] *vr* to go away; (*por poco tiempo*) to go out
ausente [au'sente] *adj* absent
austero, -a [aus'tero, a] *adj* austere
austral [aus'tral] *adj* southern ▷ *nm* monetary unit of Argentina
Australia [aus'tralja] *nf* Australia; **australiano, -a** *adj, nm/f* Australian
Austria ['austrja] *nf* Austria; **austríaco, -a** *adj, nm/f* Austrian
auténtico, -a [au'tentiko, a] *adj* authentic
auto ['auto] *nm* (Jur) edict, decree; (*: orden*) writ; (*Auto*) car; **autos** *nmpl* (Jur) proceedings; (*: acta*) court record *sg*
autoadhesivo [autoaðe'siβo] *adj* self-adhesive; (*sobre*) self-sealing
autobiografía [autoβjoɣra'fia] *nf* autobiography
autobomba [auto'bomba] (RPL) *nm* fire engine
autobronceador [autoβronθea'ðor] *adj* self-tanning
autobús [auto'βus] *nm* bus; **autobús de línea** long-distance coach
autocar [auto'kar] *nm* coach (BRIT), (passenger) bus (US)
autóctono, -a [au'toktono, a] *adj* native, indigenous
autodefensa [autoðe'fensa] *nf* self-defence
autodidacta [autoði'ðakta] *adj* self-taught
autoescuela [autoes'kwela] (ESP) *nf* driving school
autógrafo [au'toɣrafo] *nm* autograph
autómata [au'tomata] *nm* automaton
automático, -a [auto'matiko, a] *adj* automatic ▷ *nm* press stud
automóvil [auto'moβil] *nm* (motor) car (BRIT), automobile (US); **automovilismo** *nm*

(*actividad*) motoring; (*Deporte*) motor racing;
automovilista *nmf* motorist, driver
autonomía [autono'mia] *nf* autonomy;
autónomo, -a (*ESP*), **autonómico, -a** (*ESP*)
adj (*Pol*) autonomous
autopista [auto'pista] *nf* motorway
(*BRIT*), freeway (*US*); **autopista de cuota**
(*ESP*) *o* **peaje** (*MÉX*) toll (*BRIT*) *o* turnpike
(*US*) road
autopsia [au'topsja] *nf* autopsy,
postmortem
autor, a [au'tor, a] *nm/f* author
autoridad [autori'ðað] *nf* authority;
autoritario, -a *adj* authoritarian
autorización [autoriθa'θjon] *nf*
authorization; **autorizado, -a** *adj*
authorized; (*aprobado*) approved
autorizar [autori'θar] *vt* to authorize;
(*aprobar*) to approve
autoservicio [autoser'βiθjo] *nm* (*tienda*)
self-service shop (*BRIT*) *o* store (*US*);
(*restaurante*) self-service restaurant
autostop [auto'stop] *nm* hitch-hiking;
hacer ~ to hitch-hike; **autostopista** *nmf*
hitch-hiker
autovía [auto'βia] *nf* ≈ A-road (*BRIT*), dual
carriageway (*BRIT*), ≈ state highway (*US*)
auxiliar [auksi'ljar] *vt* to help ▷ *nmf*
assistant; **auxilio** *nm* assistance, help;
primeros auxilios first aid *sg*
Av *abr* (= *Avenida*) Av(e)
aval [a'βal] *nm* guarantee; (*persona*)
guarantor
avalancha [aβa'lantʃa] *nf* avalanche
avance [a'βanθe] *nm* advance; (*pago*)
advance payment; (*Cine*) trailer
avanzar [aβan'θar] *vt, vi* to advance
avaricia [aβa'riθja] *nf* avarice, greed;
avaricioso, -a *adj* avaricious, greedy
avaro, -a [a'βaro, a] *adj* miserly, mean
▷ *nm/f* miser
Avda *abr* (= *Avenida*) Av(e)
AVE ['aβe] *nm abr* (= *Alta Velocidad Española*)
≈ bullet train
ave ['aβe] *nf* bird; **ave de rapiña** bird of
prey
avecinarse [aβeθi'narse] *vr* (*tormenta: fig*)
to be on the way
avellana [aβe'ʎana] *nf* hazelnut;
avellano *nm* hazel tree
avemaría [aβema'ria] *nm* Hail Mary,
Ave Maria
avena [a'βena] *nf* oats *pl*
avenida [aβe'niða] *nf* (*calle*) avenue
aventajar [aβenta'xar] *vt* (*sobrepasar*) to
surpass, outstrip
aventón [aβen'ton] (*MÉX: fam*) *nm* ride;
dar ~ a algn to give sb a ride

aventura [aβen'tura] *nf* adventure;
aventurero, -a *adj* adventurous
avergonzar [aβerxon'θar] *vt* to shame;
(*desconcertar*) to embarrass; **avergonzarse**
vr to be ashamed; to be embarrassed
avería [aβe'ria] *nf* (*Tec*) breakdown, fault
averiado, -a [aβe'rjaðo, a] *adj* broken
down; "**~**" "out of order"
averiguar [aβeri'xwar] *vt* to investigate;
(*descubrir*) to find out, ascertain
avestruz [aβes'truθ] *nm* ostrich
aviación [aβja'θjon] *nf* aviation; (*fuerzas
aéreas*) air force
aviador, a [aβja'ðor, a] *nm/f* aviator,
airman(-woman)
ávido, -a ['aβiðo, a] *adj* avid, eager
avinagrado, -a [aβina'xraðo, a] *adj*
sour, acid
avión [a'βjon] *nm* aeroplane; (*ave*) martin;
avión de reacción jet (plane)
avioneta [aβjo'neta] *nf* light aircraft
avisar [aβi'sar] *vt* (*advertir*) to warn,
notify; (*informar*) to tell; (*aconsejar*) to advise,
counsel; **aviso** *nm* warning; (*noticia*) notice
avispa [a'βispa] *nf* wasp
avispado, -a [aβis'paðo, a] *adj* sharp,
clever
avivar [aβi'βar] *vt* to strengthen, intensify
axila [ak'sila] *nf* armpit
ay [ai] *excl* (*dolor*) ow!, ouch!; (*aflicción*) oh!,
oh dear!; **¡~ de mí!** poor me!
ayer [a'jer] *adv, nm* yesterday; **antes de
~** the day before yesterday; **~ mismo** only
yesterday
ayote [a'jote] (*CAM*) *nm* pumpkin
ayuda [a'juða] *nf* help, assistance ▷ *nm*
page; **ayudante** *nmf* assistant, helper;
(*Escol*) assistant; (*Mil*) adjutant
ayudar [aju'ðar] *vt* to help, assist
ayunar [aju'nar] *vi* to fast; **ayunas**
nfpl: **estar en ayunas** to be fasting; **ayuno**
nm fast; fasting
ayuntamiento [ajunta'mjento] *nm*
(*consejo*) town (*o* city) council; (*edificio*) town
(*o* city) hall
azafata [aθa'fata] *nf* air stewardess
azafrán [aθa'fran] *nm* saffron
azahar [aθa'ar] *nm* orange/lemon
blossom
azar [a'θar] *nm* (*casualidad*) chance, fate;
(*desgracia*) misfortune, accident; **por ~** by
chance; **al ~** at random
Azores [a'θores] *nfpl*: **las ~** the Azores
azotar [aθo'tar] *vt* to whip, beat; (*pegar*)
to spank; **azote** *nm* (*látigo*) whip; (*latigazo*)
lash, stroke; (*en las nalgas*) spank; (*calamidad*)
calamity
azotea [aθo'tea] *nf* (flat) roof

azteca [aθ'teka] *adj, nmf* Aztec
azúcar [a'θukar] *nm* sugar; **azucarado, -a**
  adj sugary, sweet
azucarero, -a [aθuka'rero, a] *adj* sugar
  cpd ▷ *nm* sugar bowl
azucena [aθu'θena] *nf* white lily
azufre [a'θufre] *nm* sulphur
azul [a'θul] *adj, nm* blue; **azul celeste/
  marino** sky/navy blue
azulejo [aθu'lexo] *nm* tile
azuzar [aθu'θar] *vt* to incite, egg on

B.A. *abr* (= *Buenos Aires*) B.A.
baba ['baβa] *nf* spittle, saliva; **babear** *vi*
  to drool, slaver
babero [ba'βero] *nm* bib
babor [ba'βor] *nm* port (side)
babosada [baβo'saða] (*MÉX, CAM: fam*) *nf*
  drivel; **baboso, -a** [ba'βoso, a] (*LAM: fam*)
  adj silly
baca ['baka] *nf* (*Auto*) luggage o roof rack
bacalao [baka'lao] *nm* cod (fish)
bache ['batʃe] *nm* pothole, rut; (*fig*) bad
  patch
bachillerato [batʃiʎe'rato] *nm* higher
  secondary school course
bacinica [baθi'nika] (*LAM*) *nf* potty
bacteria [bak'terja] *nf* bacterium, germ
Bahama [ba'ama]: **las (Islas) ~** *nfpl* the
  Bahamas
bahía [ba'ia] *nf* bay
bailar [bai'lar] *vt, vi* to dance; **bailarín,
  -ina** *nm/f* (ballet) dancer; **baile** *nm* dance;
  (*formal*) ball
baja ['baxa] *nf* drop, fall; (*Mil*) casualty;
  dar de ~ (*soldado*) to discharge; (*empleado*)
  to dismiss
bajada [ba'xaða] *nf* descent; (*camino*)
  slope; (*de aguas*) ebb
bajar [ba'xar] *vi* to go down, come down;
  (*temperatura, precios*) to drop, fall ▷ *vt*
  (*cabeza*) to bow; (*escalera*) to go down, come
  down; (*precio, voz*) to lower; (*llevar abajo*) to
  take down; **bajarse** *vr* (*de coche*) to get out;
  (*de autobús, tren*) to get off; **~ de** (*coche*) to get
  out of; (*autobús, tren*) to get off; **~se algo de
  Internet** to download sth from the Internet
bajío [ba'xio] (*LAM*) *nm* lowlands *pl*
bajo, -a ['baxo] *adj* (*mueble, número, precio*)
  low; (*piso*) ground; (*de estatura*) small, short;
  (*color*) pale; (*sonido*) faint, soft, low; (*voz: en
  tono*) deep; (*metal*) base; (*humilde*) low,
  humble ▷ *adv* (*hablar*) softly, quietly; (*volar*)

low ▷ *prep* under, below, underneath ▷ *nm*
(*Mús*) bass; **~ la lluvia** in the rain
bajón [ba'xon] *nm* fall, drop
bakalao [baka'lao] (*ESP: fam*) *nm* rave
(music)
bala ['bala] *nf* bullet
balacear [balaθe'ar] (*MÉX, CAM*) *vt* to
shoot
balance [ba'lanθe] *nm* (*Com*) balance;
(: *libro*) balance sheet; (: *cuenta general*)
stocktaking
balancear [balanθe'ar] *vt* to balance ▷ *vi*
to swing (to and fro); (*vacilar*) to hesitate;
balancearse *vr* to swing (to and fro), to
hesitate
balanza [ba'lanθa] *nf* scales *pl*, balance;
balanza comercial balance of trade;
balanza de pagos balance of payments
balaustrada [balaus'traða] *nf*
balustrade; (*pasamanos*) banisters *pl*
balazo [ba'laθo] *nm* (*golpe*) shot; (*herida*)
bullet wound
balbucear [balβuθe'ar] *vi, vt* to stammer,
stutter
balcón [bal'kon] *nm* balcony
balde ['balde] *nm* bucket, pail; **de ~** (for)
free, for nothing; **en ~** in vain
baldosa [bal'dosa] *nf* (*azulejo*) floor tile;
(*grande*) flagstone; **baldosín** *nm* (small) tile
Baleares [bale'ares] *nfpl*: **las (Islas) ~** the
Balearic Islands
balero [ba'lero] (*LAM*) *nm* (*juguete*) cup-
and-ball toy
baliza [ba'liθa] *nf* (*Aviac*) beacon; (*Náut*)
buoy
ballena [ba'ʎena] *nf* whale
ballet [ba'le] (*pl* **~s**) *nm* ballet
balneario [balne'arjo] *nm* spa; (*cs: en la
costa*) seaside resort
balón [ba'lon] *nm* ball
baloncesto [balon'θesto] *nm* basketball
balonmano [balon'mano] *nm* handball
balsa ['balsa] *nf* raft; (*Bot*) balsa wood
bálsamo ['balsamo] *nm* balsam, balm
baluarte [ba'lwarte] *nm* bastion, bulwark
bambú [bam'bu] *nm* bamboo
banana [ba'nana] (*LAM*) *nf* banana;
banano *nm* (*LAM: árbol*) banana tree;
(*CAM: fruta*) banana
banca ['banka] *nf* (*Com*) banking
bancario, -a [ban'karjo, a] *adj* banking
cpd, bank *cpd*
bancarrota [banka'rrota] *nf* bankruptcy;
hacer ~ to go bankrupt
banco ['banko] *nm* bench; (*Escol*) desk;
(*Com*) bank; (*Geo*) stratum; **banco de arena**
sandbank; **banco de crédito** credit bank;
banco de datos databank

banda ['banda] *nf* band; (*pandilla*) gang;
(*Náut*) side, edge; **banda ancha** broadband;
banda sonora soundtrack
bandada [ban'daða] *nf* (*de pájaros*) flock;
(*de peces*) shoal
bandazo [ban'daθo] *nm*: **dar ~s** to sway
from side to side
bandeja [ban'dexa] *nf* tray
bandera [ban'dera] *nf* flag
banderilla [bande'riʎa] *nf* banderilla
bandido [ban'diðo] *nm* bandit
bando ['bando] *nm* (*edicto*) edict,
proclamation; (*facción*) faction; **bandos**
nmpl (*Rel*) banns
bandolera [bando'lera] *nf*: **llevar en ~** to
wear across one's chest
banquero [ban'kero] *nm* banker
banqueta [ban'keta] *nf* stool; (*MÉX: en
calle*) pavement (*BRIT*), sidewalk (*US*)
banquete [ban'kete] *nm* banquet; (*para
convidados*) formal dinner; **banquete de
boda(s)** wedding reception
banquillo [ban'kiʎo] *nm* (*Jur*) dock,
prisoner's bench; (*banco*) bench; (*para los
pies*) footstool
banquina [ban'kina] (*RPL*) *nf* hard
shoulder (*BRIT*), berm (*US*)
bañadera [baɲa'ðera] (*RPL*) *nf* bathtub
bañador [baɲa'ðor] (*ESP*) *nm* swimming
costume (*BRIT*), bathing suit (*US*)
bañar [ba'ɲar] *vt* to bath, bathe; (*objeto*)
to dip; (*de barniz*) to coat; **bañarse** *vr* (*en el
mar*) to bathe, swim; (*en la bañera*) to have
a bath
bañera [ba'ɲera] (*ESP*) *nf* bath(tub)
bañero, -a [ba'ɲero, a] (*cs*) *nm/f* lifeguard
bañista [ba'ɲista] *nmf* bather
baño ['baɲo] *nm* (*en bañera*) bath; (*en río*)
dip, swim; (*cuarto*) bathroom; (*bañera*)
bath(tub); (*capa*) coating; **darse** *o* **tomar
un ~** (*en bañera*) to have *o* take a bath; (*en
mar, piscina*) to have a swim; **baño María**
bain-marie
bar [bar] *nm* bar
barahúnda [bara'unda] *nf* uproar,
hubbub
baraja [ba'raxa] *nf* pack (of cards); **barajar**
vt (*naipes*) to shuffle; (*fig*) to jumble up
baranda [ba'randa] *nf* = **barandilla**
barandilla [baran'diʎa] *nf* rail, railing
barata [ba'rata] (*MÉX*) *nf* (*bargain*) sale
baratillo [bara'tiʎo] *nm* (*tienda*) junkshop;
(*subasta*) bargain sale; (*conjunto de cosas*)
secondhand goods *pl*
barato, -a [ba'rato, a] *adj* cheap ▷ *adv*
cheap, cheaply
barba ['barβa] *nf* (*mentón*) chin; (*pelo*)
beard

barbacoa [bar'βa'koa] *nf* (*parrilla*)
barbecue; (*carne*) barbecued meat
barbaridad [barβari'ðað] *nf* barbarity;
(*acto*) barbarism; (*atrocidad*) outrage; **una ~**
(*fam*) loads; **¡qué ~!** (*fam*) how awful!
barbarie [bar'βarje] *nf* barbarism,
savagery; (*crueldad*) barbarity
bárbaro, -a ['barβaro, a] *adj* barbarous,
cruel; (*grosero*) rough, uncouth ▷ *nm/f*
barbarian ▷ *adv*: **lo pasamos ~** (*fam*) we had
a great time; **¡qué ~!** (*fam*) how marvellous!;
un éxito ~ (*fam*) a terrific success; **es un**
tipo ~ (*fam*) he's a great bloke
barbero [bar'βero] *nm* barber, hairdresser
barbilla [bar'βiʎa] *nf* chin, tip of the chin
barbudo, -a [bar'βuðo, a] *adj* bearded
barca ['barka] *nf* (small) boat; **barcaza**
nf barge
Barcelona [barθe'lona] *n* Barcelona
barco ['barko] *nm* boat; (*grande*) ship;
barco de carga/pesca cargo/fishing boat;
barco de vela sailing ship
barda ['barða] (*MÉX*) *nf* (*de madera*) fence
baremo [ba'remo] *nm* (*Mat: fig*) scale
barítono [ba'ritono] *nm* baritone
barman ['barman] *nm* barman
barniz [bar'niθ] *nm* varnish; (*en loza*) glaze;
(*fig*) veneer; **barnizar** *vt* to varnish; (*loza*)
to glaze
barómetro [ba'rometro] *nm* barometer
barquillo [bar'kiʎo] *nm* cone, cornet
barra ['barra] *nf* bar, rod; (*de un bar, café*)
bar; (*de pan*) French stick; (*palanca*) lever;
barra de labios lipstick; **barra libre** free bar
barraca [ba'rraka] *nf* hut, cabin
barranco [ba'rranko] *nm* ravine; (*fig*)
difficulty
barrena [ba'rrena] *nf* drill
barrer [ba'rrer] *vt* to sweep; (*quitar*) to
sweep away
barrera [ba'rrera] *nf* barrier
barriada [ba'rrjaða] *nf* quarter, district
barricada [barri'kaða] *nf* barricade
barrida [ba'rriða] *nf* sweep, sweeping
barriga [ba'rriɣa] *nf* belly; (*panza*) paunch;
barrigón, -ona *adj* potbellied; **barrigudo,**
-a *adj* potbellied
barril [ba'rril] *nm* barrel, cask
barrio ['barrjo] *nm* (*vecindad*) area,
neighborhood (*us*); (*en afueras*) suburb;
barrio chino (*ESP*) red-light district
barro ['barro] *nm* (*lodo*) mud; (*objetos*)
earthenware; (*Med*) pimple
barroco, -a [ba'rroko, a] *adj, nm* baroque
barrote [ba'rrote] *nm* (*de ventana*) bar
bartola [bar'tola] *nf*: **tirarse** *o* **tumbarse a**
la ~ to take it easy, be lazy
bártulos ['bartulos] *nmpl* things,

belongings
barullo [ba'ruʎo] *nm* row, uproar
basar [ba'sar] *vt* to base; **basarse** *vr*: **~se**
en to be based on
báscula ['baskula] *nf* (platform) scales
base ['base] *nf* base; **~ de** on the basis
. of; (*mediante*) by means of; **base de datos**
(*Inform*) database
básico, -a ['basiko, a] *adj* basic
basílica [ba'silika] *nf* basilica
básquetbol ['basketbol] (*LAM*) *nm*
basketball

○ **PALABRA CLAVE**

bastante [bas'tante] *adj* **1** (*suficiente*)
enough; **bastante dinero** enough *o*
sufficient money; **bastantes libros** enough
books
2 (*valor intensivo*): **bastante gente** quite a
lot of people; **tener bastante calor** to be
rather hot
▷ *adv*: **bastante bueno/malo** quite good/
rather bad; **bastante rico** pretty rich; **(lo)**
bastante inteligente (como) para hacer
algo clever enough *o* sufficiently clever to
do sth

bastar [bas'tar] *vi* to be enough *o*
sufficient; **bastarse** *vr* to be self-sufficient;
~ para to be enough to; **¡basta!** (that's)
enough!
bastardo, -a [bas'tarðo, a] *adj, nm/f*
bastard
bastidor [basti'ðor] *nm* frame; (*de coche*)
chassis; (*Teatro*) wing; **entre ~es** (*fig*) behind
the scenes
basto, -a ['basto, a] *adj* coarse, rough;
bastos *nmpl* (*Naipes*) ≈ clubs
bastón [bas'ton] *nm* stick, staff; (*para*
pasear) walking stick
bastoncillo [baston'θiʎo] *nm* cotton bud
basura [ba'sura] *nf* rubbish (*BRIT*),
garbage (*US*) ▷ *adj*: **comida/televisión ~**
junk food/TV
basurero [basu'rero] *nm* (*hombre*)
dustman (*BRIT*), garbage man (*US*); (*lugar*)
dump; (*cubo*) (rubbish) bin (*BRIT*), trash
can (*US*)
bata ['bata] *nf* (*gen*) dressing gown;
(*cubretodo*) smock, overall; (*Med, Tec etc*)
lab(oratory) coat
batalla [ba'taʎa] *nf* battle; **de ~** (*fig*) for
everyday use; **batalla campal** pitched
battle
batallón [bata'ʎon] *nm* battalion
batata [ba'tata] *nf* sweet potato
batería [bate'ria] *nf* battery; (*Mús*) drums;

batería de cocina kitchen utensils
batido, -a [ba'tiðo, a] *adj* (*camino*) beaten, well-trodden ▷ *nm* (*Culin: de leche*) milk shake
batidora [bati'ðora] *nf* beater, mixer; **batidora eléctrica** food mixer, blender
batir [ba'tir] *vt* to beat, strike; (*vencer*) to beat, defeat; (*revolver*) to beat, mix; **batirse** *vr* to fight; **~ palmas** to applaud
batuta [ba'tuta] *nf* baton; **llevar la ~** (*fig*) to be the boss, be in charge
baúl [ba'ul] *nm* trunk; (*Auto*) boot (*BRIT*), trunk (*US*)
bautismo [bau'tismo] *nm* baptism, christening
bautizar [bauti'θar] *vt* to baptize, christen; (*fam: diluir*) to water down; **bautizo** *nm* baptism, christening
bayeta [ba'jeta] *nf* floorcloth
baza ['baθa] *nf* trick; **meter ~** to butt in
bazar [ba'θar] *nm* bazaar
bazofia [ba'θofja] *nf* trash
be [be] *nf* name of the letter B; **be chica/grande** (*MÉX*) V/B; **be larga** (*LAM*) B
beato, -a [be'ato, a] *adj* blessed; (*piadoso*) pious
bebé [be'βe] (*pl* **~s**) *nm* baby
bebedero [beβe'ðero, a] (*MÉX, CS*) *nm* drinking fountain
bebedor, a [beβe'ðor, a] *adj* hard-drinking
beber [be'βer] *vt, vi* to drink
bebida [be'βiða] *nf* drink; **bebido, -a** *adj* drunk
beca ['beka] *nf* grant, scholarship; **becario, -a** [be'karjo, a] *nm/f* scholarship holder, grant holder
bedel [be'ðel] *nm* (*Escol*) janitor; (*Univ*) porter
béisbol ['beisβol] *nm* baseball
Belén [be'len] *nm* Bethlehem; **belén** *nm* (*de Navidad*) nativity scene, crib
belga ['belγa] *adj, nmf* Belgian
Bélgica ['belxika] *nf* Belgium
bélico, -a ['beliko, a] *adj* (*actitud*) warlike
belleza [be'ʎeθa] *nf* beauty
bello, -a ['beʎo, a] *adj* beautiful, lovely; **Bellas Artes** Fine Art
bellota [be'ʎota] *nf* acorn
bemol [be'mol] *nm* (*Mús*) flat; **esto tiene ~es** (*fam*) this is a tough one
bencina [ben'θina] *nf* (*Quím*) benzine
bendecir [bende'θir] *vt* to bless
bendición [bendi'θjon] *nf* blessing
bendito, -a [ben'dito, a] *pp de* **bendecir** ▷ *adj* holy; (*afortunado*) lucky; (*feliz*) happy; (*sencillo*) simple ▷ *nm/f* simple soul
beneficencia [benefi'θenθja] *nf* charity

beneficiario, -a [benefi'θjarjo, a] *nm/f* beneficiary
beneficio [bene'fiθjo] *nm* (*bien*) benefit, advantage; (*ganancia*) profit, gain; **a ~ de algn** in aid of sb; **beneficioso, -a** *adj* beneficial
benéfico, -a [be'nefiko, a] *adj* charitable
beneplácito [bene'plaθito] *nm* approval, consent
benévolo, -a [be'neβolo, a] *adj* benevolent, kind
benigno, -a [be'nixno, a] *adj* kind; (*suave*) mild; (*Med: tumor*) benign, non-malignant
berberecho [berβe'retʃo] *nm* (*Zool, Culin*) cockle
berenjena [beren'xena] *nf* aubergine (*BRIT*), eggplant (*US*)
Berlín [ber'lin] *n* Berlin
berlinesa [berli'nesa] (*RPL*) *nf* doughnut, donut (*US*)
bermudas [ber'muðas] *nfpl* Bermuda shorts
berrido [be'rriðo] *nm* bellow(ing)
berrinche [be'rrintʃe] (*fam*) *nm* temper, tantrum
berro ['berro] *nm* watercress
berza ['berθa] *nf* cabbage
besamel [besa'mel] *nf* (*Culin*) white sauce, bechamel sauce
besar [be'sar] *vt* to kiss; (*fig: tocar*) to graze; **besarse** *vr* to kiss (one another); **beso** *nm* kiss
bestia ['bestja] *nf* beast, animal; (*fig*) idiot; **bestia de carga** beast of burden; **bestial** [bes'tjal] *adj* bestial; (*fam*) terrific; **bestialidad** *nf* bestiality; (*fam*) stupidity
besugo [be'suxo] *nm* sea bream; (*fam*) idiot
besuquear [besuke'ar] *vt* to cover with kisses; **besuquearse** *vr* to kiss and cuddle
betabel [beta'bel] (*MÉX*) *nm* beetroot (*BRIT*), beet (*US*)
betún [be'tun] *nm* shoe polish; (*Quím*) bitumen
biberón [biβe'ron] *nm* feeding bottle
Biblia ['biβlja] *nf* Bible
bibliografía [biβljoxra'fia] *nf* bibliography
biblioteca [biβljo'teka] *nf* library; (*mueble*) bookshelves; **biblioteca de consulta** reference library; **bibliotecario, -a** *nm/f* librarian
bicarbonato [bikarβo'nato] *nm* bicarbonate
bicho ['bitʃo] *nm* (*animal*) small animal; (*sabandija*) bug, insect; (*Taur*) bull
bici ['biθi] (*fam*) *nf* bike
bicicleta [biθi'kleta] *nf* bicycle, cycle; **ir**

en ~ to cycle

bidé [bi'ðe] (*pl* **~s**) *nm* bidet

bidón [bi'ðon] *nm* (*de aceite*) drum; (*de gasolina*) can

○ **PALABRA CLAVE**

bien [bjen] *nm* **1** (*bienestar*) good; **te lo digo por tu bien** I'm telling you for your own good; **el bien y el mal** good and evil
2 (*posesión*): **bienes** goods; **bienes de consumo** consumer goods; **bienes inmuebles** *o* **raíces/bienes muebles** real estate *sg*/personal property *sg* ▷ *adv*
1 (*de manera satisfactoria, correcta etc*) well; **trabaja/come bien** she works/eats well; **contestó bien** he answered correctly; **me siento bien** I feel fine; **no me siento bien** I don't feel very well; **se está bien aquí** it's nice here
2 (*frases*): **hiciste bien en llamarme** you were right to call me
3 (*valor intensivo*) very; **un cuarto bien caliente** a nice warm room; **bien se ve que ...** it's quite clear that ...
4 estar bien: estoy muy bien aquí I feel very happy here; **está bien que vengan** it's all right for them to come; **¡está bien! lo haré** oh all right, I'll do it
5 (*de buena gana*): **yo bien que iría pero ...** I'd gladly go but ... ▷ *excl*: **¡bien!** (*aprobación*) O.K.!; **¡muy bien!** well done! ▷ *adj inv* (*matiz despectivo*): **gente bien** posh people ▷ *conj*
1 bien ... bien: bien en coche bien en tren either by car or by train
2 (*LAM*): **no bien: no bien llegue te llamaré** as soon as I arrive I'll call you
3 si bien even though; V *tb* **más**

bienal [bje'nal] *adj* biennial

bienestar [bjenes'tar] *nm* well-being, welfare

bienvenida [bjembe'niða] *nf* welcome; **dar la ~ a algn** to welcome sb

bienvenido [bjembe'niðo] *excl* welcome!

bife ['bife] (*cs*) *nm* steak

bifurcación [bifurka'θjon] *nf* fork

bígamo, -a ['biɣamo, a] *adj* bigamous ▷ *nm/f* bigamist

bigote [bi'ɣote] *nm* moustache; **bigotudo, -a** *adj* with a big moustache

bikini [bi'kini] *nm* bikini; (*Culin*) toasted ham and cheese sandwich

bilingüe [bi'lingwe] *adj* bilingual

billar [bi'ʎar] *nm* billiards *sg*; **billares** *nmpl* (*lugar*) billiard hall; (*sala de juegos*) amusement arcade; **billar americano** pool

billete [bi'ʎete] *nm* ticket; (*de banco*) (bank)note (*BRIT*), bill (*US*); (*carta*) note; **~ de 20 libras** £20 note; **billete de ida y vuelta** return (*BRIT*) *o* round-trip (*US*) ticket; **billete sencillo** *o* **de ida** single (*BRIT*) *o* one-way (*US*) ticket; **billete electrónico** e-ticket

billetera [biʎe'tera] *nf* wallet

billón [bi'ʎon] *nm* billion

bimensual [bimen'swal] *adj* twice monthly

bingo ['bingo] *nm* bingo

biodegradable [bioðeɣra'ðaβle] *adj* biodegradable

biografía [bjoɣra'fia] *nf* biography

biología [bjolo'xia] *nf* biology; **biológico, -a** *adj* biological; (*cultivo, producto*) organic; **biólogo, -a** *nm/f* biologist

biombo ['bjombo] *nm* (folding) screen

bioterrorismo [bjoterro'rismo] *nm* bioterrorism

biquini [bi'kini] *nm o* (*RPL*) *f* bikini

birlar [bir'lar] (*fam*) *vt* to pinch

Birmania [bir'manja] *nf* Burma

birome [bi'rome] (*RPL*) *nf* ballpoint (pen)

birria ['birrja] *nf*: **ser una ~** (*película, libro*) to be rubbish

bis [bis] *excl* encore!

bisabuelo, -a [bisa'βwelo, a] *nm/f* great-grandfather(-mother)

bisagra [bi'saɣra] *nf* hinge

bisiesto [bi'sjesto] *adj*: **año ~** leap year

bisnieto, -a [bis'njeto, a] *nm/f* great-grandson/daughter

bisonte [bi'sonte] *nm* bison

bisté [bis'te] *nm* = **bistec**

bistec [bis'tek] *nm* steak

bisturí [bistu'ri] *nm* scalpel

bisutería [bisute'ria] *nf* imitation *o* costume jewellery

bit [bit] *nm* (*Inform*) bit

bizco, -a ['biθko, a] *adj* cross-eyed

bizcocho [biθ'kotʃo] *nm* (*Culin*) sponge cake

blanca ['blanka] *nf* (*Mús*) minim; **estar sin ~** (*ESP: fam*) to be broke; V *tb* **blanco**

blanco, -a ['blanko, a] *adj* white ▷ *nm/f* white man/woman, white ▷ *nm* (*color*) white; (*en texto*) blank; (*Mil, fig*) target; **en ~** blank; **noche en ~** sleepless night

blandir [blan'dir] *vt* to brandish

blando, -a ['blando, a] *adj* soft; (*tierno*) tender, gentle; (*carácter*) mild; (*fam*) cowardly

blanqueador [blankea'ðor] (*MÉX*) *nm* bleach

blanquear [blanke'ar] *vt* to whiten; (*fachada*) to whitewash; (*paño*) to bleach ▷ *vi* to turn white

blanquillo [blan'kiʎo] (*MÉX, CAM*) *nm* egg

blasfemar [blasfe'mar] *vi* to blaspheme, curse

bledo ['bleðo] *nm*: **me importa un ~** I couldn't care less

blindado, -a [blin'daðo, a] *adj* (*Mil*) armour-plated; (*antibala*) bullet-proof; **coche** (*ESP*) *o* **carro** (*LAM*) ~ armoured car

bloc [blok] (*pl* ~**s**) *nm* writing pad

blof [blof] (*MÉX*) *nm* bluff; **blofear** (*MÉX*) *vi* to bluff

blog [bloɣ] (*pl* ~**s**) *nm* blog

bloque ['bloke] *nm* block; (*Pol*) bloc

bloquear [bloke'ar] *vt* to blockade; **bloqueo** *nm* blockade; (*Com*) freezing, blocking; **bloqueo mental** mental block

blusa ['blusa] *nf* blouse

bobada [bo'βaða] *nf* foolish action; foolish statement; **decir ~s** to talk nonsense

bobina [bo'βina] *nf* (*Tec*) bobbin; (*Foto*) spool; (*Elec*) coil

bobo, -a ['boβo, a] *adj* (*tonto*) daft, silly; (*cándido*) naõve ▷ *nm/f* fool, idiot ▷ *nm* (*Teatro*) clown, funny man

boca ['boka] *nf* mouth; (*de crustáceo*) pincer; (*de cañón*) muzzle; (*entrada*) mouth, entrance; **bocas** *nfpl* (*de río*) mouth *sg*; ~ **abajo/arriba** face down/up; **se me hace la ~ agua** my mouth is watering; **boca de incendios** hydrant; **boca del estómago** pit of the stomach; **boca de metro** underground (*BRIT*) *o* subway (*US*) entrance

bocacalle [boka'kaʎe] *nf* (entrance to a) street; **la primera ~** the first turning *o* street

bocadillo [boka'ðiʎo] *nm* sandwich

bocado [bo'kaðo] *nm* mouthful, bite; (*de caballo*) bridle

bocajarro [boka'xarro]: **a ~** *adv* (*disparar*) point-blank

bocanada [boka'naða] *nf* (*de vino*) mouthful, swallow; (*de aire*) gust, puff

bocata [bo'kata] (*fam*) *nm* sandwich

bocazas [bo'kaθas] (*fam*) *nm inv* bigmouth

boceto [bo'θeto] *nm* sketch, outline

bochorno [bo'tʃorno] *nm* (*vergüenza*) embarrassment; (*calor*): **hace ~** it's very muggy

bocina [bo'θina] *nf* (*Mús*) trumpet; (*Auto*) horn; (*para hablar*) megaphone

boda ['boða] *nf* (*tb*: ~**s**) wedding, marriage; (*fiesta*) wedding reception; **bodas de oro/plata** golden/silver wedding *sg*

bodega [bo'ðexa] *nf* (*de vino*) (wine) cellar; (*depósito*) storeroom; (*de barco*) hold

bodegón [boðe'ɣon] *nm* (*Arte*) still life

bofetada [bofe'taða] *nf* slap (in the face)

boga ['boɣa] *nf*: **en ~** (*fig*) in vogue

Bogotá [boɣo'ta] *n* Bogotá

bohemio, -a [bo'emjo, a] *adj*, *nm/f* Bohemian

bohío [bo'io] (*CAM*) *nm* shack, hut

boicot [boi'kot] (*pl* ~**s**) *nm* boycott; **boicotear** *vt* to boycott

bóiler ['boiler] (*MÉX*) *nm* boiler

boina ['boina] *nf* beret

bola ['bola] *nf* ball; (*canica*) marble; (*Naipes*) (grand) slam; (*betún*) shoe polish; (*mentira*) tale, story; **bolas** *nfpl* (*LAM*: *caza*) bolas *sg*; **bola de billar** billiard ball; **bola de nieve** snowball

boleadoras [bolea'ðoras] *nfpl* bolas *sg*

bolear [bole'ar] (*MÉX*) *vt* (*zapatos*) to polish, shine

bolera [bo'lera] *nf* skittle *o* bowling alley

bolero, -a (*MÉX*) [bo'lero] *nm/f* (*limpiabotas*) shoeshine boy/girl

boleta [bo'leta] (*LAM*) *nf* (*de rifa*) ticket; (*CS*: *recibo*) receipt; **boleta de calificaciones** (*MÉX*) report card

boletería [bolete'ria] (*LAM*) *nf* ticket office

boletín [bole'tin] *nm* bulletin; (*periódico*) journal, review; **boletín de noticias** news bulletin

boleto [bo'leto] *nm* (*LAM*) ticket; **boleto de ida y vuelta** (*LAM*) round trip ticket; **boleto electrónico** (*LAM*) e-ticket; **boleto redondo** (*MÉX*) round trip ticket

boli ['boli] (*fam*) *nm* Biro®

bolígrafo [bo'liɣrafo] *nm* ball-point pen, Biro®

bolilla [bo'liʎa] (*RPL*) *nf* topic

bolillo [bo'liʎo] (*MÉX*) *nm* (bread) roll

bolita [bo'lita] (*CS*) *nf* marble

bolívar [bo'liβar] *nm* monetary unit of Venezuela

Bolivia [bo'liβja] *nf* Bolivia; **boliviano, -a** *adj*, *nm/f* Bolivian

bollería [boʎe'ria] *nf* cakes *pl* and pastries *pl*

bollo ['boʎo] *nm* (*pan*) roll; (*bulto*) bump, lump; (*abolladura*) dent

bolo ['bolo] *nm* skittle; (*píldora*) (large) pill; **(juego de) bolos** *nmpl* skittles *sg*

bolsa ['bolsa] *nf* (*para llevar algo*) bag; (*MÉX*, *CAM*: *bolsillo*) pocket; (*MÉX*: *de mujer*) handbag; (*Anat*) cavity, sac; (*Com*) stock exchange; (*Minería*) pocket; **de ~** pocket *cpd*; **bolsa de agua caliente** hot water bottle; **bolsa de aire** air pocket; **bolsa de dormir** (*MÉX*, *RPL*) sleeping bag; **bolsa de la compra** shopping bag; **bolsa de papel/plástico** paper/plastic bag

bolsear [bolse'ar] (*MÉX*, *CAM*) *vt*: ~ **a algn** to pick sb's pocket

bolsillo [bol'siʎo] *nm* pocket; (*cartera*) purse; **de ~** pocket(-size)

bolso ['bolso] *nm* (*bolsa*) bag; (*de mujer*)

handbag
bomba ['bomba] nf (Mil) bomb; (Tec) pump ▷ adj (fam): **noticia ~** bombshell ▷ adv (fam): **pasarlo ~** to have a great time; **bomba atómica/de efecto retardado/de humo** atomic/time/smoke bomb
bombacha [bom'batʃa] (RPL) nf panties pl
bombardear [bombarðe'ar] vt to bombard; (Mil) to bomb; **bombardeo** nm bombardment; bombing
bombazo [bom'baθo] (MÉX) nm (explosión) explosion; (fam: notición) bombshell; (: éxito) smash hit
bombear [bombe'ar] vt (agua) to pump (out o up)
bombero [bom'bero] nm fireman
bombilla [bom'biʎa] (ESP) nf (light) bulb
bombita [bom'bita] (RPL) nf (light) bulb
bombo ['bombo] nm (Mús) bass drum; (Tec) drum
bombón [bom'bon] nm chocolate; (MÉX: de caramelo) marshmallow
bombona [bom'bona] (ESP) nf (de butano, oxígeno) cylinder
bonachón, -ona [bona'tʃon, ona] adj good-natured, easy-going
bonanza [bo'nanθa] nf (Náut) fair weather; (fig) bonanza; (Minería) rich pocket o vein
bondad [bon'dað] nf goodness, kindness; **tenga la ~ de** (please) be good enough to
bonito, -a [bo'nito, a] adj pretty; (agradable) nice ▷ nm (atún) tuna (fish)
bono ['bono] nm voucher; (Finanzas) bond
bonobús [bono'βus] (ESP) nm bus pass
bonoloto [bono'loto] nf state-run weekly lottery
boquerón [boke'ron] nm (pez) (kind of) anchovy; (agujero) large hole
boquete [bo'kete] nm gap, hole
boquiabierto, -a [bokia'βjerto, a] adj: **quedarse ~** to be amazed o flabbergasted
boquilla [bo'kiʎa] nf (para riego) nozzle; (para cigarro) cigarette holder; (Mús) mouthpiece
borbotón [borβo'ton] nm: **salir a borbotones** to gush out
borda ['borða] nf (Náut) (ship's) rail; **tirar algo/caerse por la ~** to throw sth/fall overboard
bordado [bor'ðaðo] nm embroidery
bordar [bor'ðar] vt to embroider
borde ['borðe] nm edge, border; (de camino etc) side; (en la costura) hem; **al ~ de** (fig) on the verge o brink of; **ser ~** (ESP: fam) to be rude; **bordear** vt to border
bordillo [bor'ðiʎo] nm kerb (BRIT), curb (US)

bordo ['borðo] nm (Náut) side; **a ~** on board
borlote [bor'lote] (MÉX) nm row, uproar
borrachera [borra'tʃera] nf (ebriedad) drunkenness; (orgía) spree, binge
borracho, -a [bo'rratʃo, a] adj drunk ▷ nm/f (habitual) drunkard, drunk; (temporal) drunk, drunk man/woman
borrador [borra'ðor] nm (escritura) first draft, rough sketch; (goma) rubber (BRIT), eraser
borrar [bo'rrar] vt to erase, rub out
borrasca [bo'rraska] nf storm
borrego, -a [bo'rreɣo, a] nm/f (Zool: joven) (yearling) lamb; (adulto) sheep ▷ nm (MÉX: fam) false rumour
borrico, -a [bo'rriko, a] nm/f donkey/she-donkey; (fig) stupid man/woman
borrón [bo'rron] nm (mancha) stain
borroso, -a [bo'rroso, a] adj vague, unclear; (escritura) illegible
bosque ['boske] nm wood; (grande) forest
bostezar [boste'θar] vi to yawn; **bostezo** nm yawn
bota ['bota] nf (calzado) boot; (para vino) leather wine bottle; **botas de agua** o **goma** Wellingtons
botana [bo'tana] (MÉX) nf snack, appetizer
botánica [bo'tanika] nf (ciencia) botany; V tb **botánico**
botánico, -a [bo'taniko, a] adj botanical ▷ nm/f botanist
botar [bo'tar] vt to throw, hurl; (Náut) to launch; (LAM: echar) to throw out ▷ vi (ESP: saltar) to bounce
bote ['bote] nm (salto) bounce; (golpe) thrust; (ESP: envase) tin, can; (embarcación) boat; (MÉX, CAM: pey: cárcel) jail; **de ~ en ~** packed, jammed full; **bote de la basura** (MÉX) dustbin (BRIT), trashcan (US); **bote salvavidas** lifeboat
botella [bo'teʎa] nf bottle; **botellín** nm small bottle; **botellón** nm (ESP: fam) outdoor drinking session
botijo [bo'tixo] nm (earthenware) jug
botín [bo'tin] nm (calzado) half boot; (polaina) spat; (Mil) booty
botiquín [boti'kin] nm (armario) medicine cabinet; (portátil) first-aid kit
botón [bo'ton] nm button; (Bot) bud
botones [bo'tones] nm inv bellboy (BRIT), bellhop (US)
bóveda ['boβeða] nf (Arq) vault
boxeador [boksea'ðor] nm boxer
boxeo [bok'seo] nm boxing
boya ['boja] nf (Náut) buoy; (de caña) float
boyante [bo'jante] adj prosperous
bozal [bo'θal] nm (para caballos) halter; (de

perro) muzzle

bragas ['braxas] *nfpl* (*de mujer*) panties, knickers (BRIT)

bragueta [bra'xeta] *nf* fly, flies *pl*

braille [breil] *nm* braille

brasa ['brasa] *nf* live o hot coal

brasero [bra'sero] *nm* brazier

brasier [bra'sjer] (MÉX) *nm* bra

Brasil [bra'sil] *nm* (*tb*: **el ~**) Brazil; **brasileño, -a** *adj, nm/f* Brazilian

brassier [bra'sjer] (MÉX) *nm* V **brasier**

bravo, -a ['braβo, a] *adj* (*valiente*) brave; (*feroz*) ferocious; (*salvaje*) wild; (*mar etc*) rough, stormy ▷ *excl* bravo!; **bravura** *nf* bravery; ferocity

braza ['braθa] *nf* fathom; **nadar a ~** to swim breast-stroke

brazalete [braθa'lete] *nm* (*pulsera*) bracelet; (*banda*) armband

brazo ['braθo] *nm* arm; (*Zool*) foreleg; (*Bot*) limb, branch; **luchar a ~ partido** to fight hand-to-hand; **ir cogidos del ~** to walk arm in arm

brebaje [bre'βaxe] *nm* potion

brecha ['bretʃa] *nf* (*hoyo, vacío*) gap, opening; (*Mil, fig*) breach

brega ['breɣa] *nf* (*lucha*) struggle; (*trabajo*) hard work

breva ['breβa] *nf* early fig

breve ['breβe] *adj* short, brief ▷ *nf* (*Mús*) breve; **en ~** (*pronto*) shortly, before long; **brevedad** *nf* brevity, shortness

bribón, -ona [bri'βon, ona] *adj* idle, lazy ▷ *nm/f* (*pícaro*) rascal, rogue

bricolaje [briko'laxe] *nm* do-it-yourself, DIY

brida ['briða] *nf* bridle, rein; (*Tec*) clamp

bridge [britʃ] *nm* bridge

brigada [bri'ɣaða] *nf* (*unidad*) brigade; (*de trabajadores*) squad, gang ▷ *nm* ≈ staff-sergeant, sergeant-major

brillante [bri'ʎante] *adj* brilliant ▷ *nm* diamond

brillar [bri'ʎar] *vi* to shine; (*joyas*) to sparkle

brillo ['briʎo] *nm* shine; (*brillantez*) brilliance; (*fig*) splendour; **sacar ~ a** to polish

brincar [brin'kar] *vi* to skip about, hop about, jump about

brinco ['brinko] *nm* jump, leap

brindar [brin'dar] *vi*: **~ a o por** to drink (a toast) to ▷ *vt* to offer, present

brindis ['brindis] *nm inv* toast

brío ['brio] *nm* spirit, dash

brisa ['brisa] *nf* breeze

británico, -a [bri'taniko, a] *adj* British ▷ *nm/f* Briton, British person

brizna ['briθna] *nf* (*de hierba, paja*) blade; (*de tabaco*) leaf

broca ['broka] *nf* (*Tec*) drill, bit

brocha ['brotʃa] *nf* (large) paintbrush; **brocha de afeitar** shaving brush

broche ['brotʃe] *nm* brooch

broma ['broma] *nf* joke; **de o en ~** in fun, as a joke; **broma pesada** practical joke; **bromear** *vi* to joke

bromista [bro'mista] *adj* fond of joking ▷ *nmf* joker, wag

bronca ['bronka] *nf* row; **echar una ~ a algn** to tick sb off

bronce ['bronθe] *nm* bronze; **bronceado, -a** *adj* bronze; (*por el sol*) tanned ▷ *nm* (sun) tan; (*Tec*) bronzing

bronceador [bronθea'ðor] *nm* suntan lotion

broncearse [bronθe'arse] *vr* to get a suntan

bronquio ['bronkjo] *nm* (*Anat*) bronchial tube

bronquitis [bron'kitis] *nf inv* bronchitis

brotar [bro'tar] *vi* (*Bot*) to sprout; (*aguas*) to gush (forth); (*Med*) to break out

brote ['brote] *nm* (*Bot*) shoot; (*Med, fig*) outbreak

bruces ['bruθes]: **de bruces** *adv*: **caer o dar de ~** to fall headlong, fall flat

bruja ['bruxa] *nf* witch; **brujería** *nf* witchcraft

brujo ['bruxo] *nm* wizard, magician

brújula ['bruxula] *nf* compass

bruma ['bruma] *nf* mist

brusco, -a ['brusko, a] *adj* (*súbito*) sudden; (*áspero*) brusque

Bruselas [bru'selas] *n* Brussels

brutal [bru'tal] *adj* brutal; **brutalidad** [brutali'ðað] *nf* brutality

bruto, -a ['bruto, a] *adj* (*idiota*) stupid; (*bestial*) brutish; (*peso*) gross; **en ~** raw, unworked

Bs.As. *abr* (= *Buenos Aires*) B.A.

bucal [bu'kal] *adj* oral; **por vía ~** orally

bucear [buθe'ar] *vi* to dive ▷ *vt* to explore; **buceo** *nm* diving

bucle ['bukle] *nm* curl

budismo [bu'ðismo] *nm* Buddhism

buen [bwen] *adj m* V **bueno**

buenamente [bwena'mente] *adv* (*fácilmente*) easily; (*voluntariamente*) willingly

buenaventura [bwenaβen'tura] *nf* (*suerte*) good luck; (*adivinación*) fortune

buenmozo [bwen'moθo] (MÉX) *adj* handsome

○ **PALABRA CLAVE**

bueno, -a ['bweno, a] (*antes de nmsg*: **buen**) *adj* **1** (*excelente etc*) good; **es un libro bueno, es un buen libro** it's a good book; **hace bueno, hace buen tiempo** the weather is fine, it is fine; **el bueno de Paco** good old Paco; **fue muy bueno conmigo** he was very nice o kind to me

2 (*apropiado*): **ser bueno para** to be good for; **creo que vamos por buen camino** I think we're on the right track

3 (*irónico*): **le di un buen rapapolvo** I gave him a good o real ticking off; **¡buen conductor estás hecho!** some o a fine driver you are!; **¡estaría bueno que …!** a fine thing it would be if …!

4 (*atractivo, sabroso*): **está bueno este bizcocho** this sponge is delicious; **Carmen está muy buena** Carmen is gorgeous

5 (*saludos*): **¡buen día!, ¡buenos días!** (good) morning!; **¡buenas (tardes)!** (good) afternoon!; (*más tarde*) (good) evening!; **¡buenas noches!** good night!

6 (*otras locuciones*): **estar de buenas** to be in a good mood; **por las buenas o por las malas** by hook or by crook; **de buenas a primeras** all of a sudden ▷ *excl*: **¡bueno!** all right!; **bueno, ¿y qué?** well, so what?

Buenos Aires [bweno'saires] *nm* Buenos Aires

buey [bwei] *nm* ox

búfalo ['bufalo] *nm* buffalo

bufanda [bu'fanda] *nf* scarf

bufete [bu'fete] *nm* (*despacho de abogado*) lawyer's office

bufón [bu'fon] *nm* clown

buhardilla [buar'ðiʎa] *nf* attic

búho ['buo] *nm* owl; (*fig*) hermit, recluse

buitre ['bwitre] *nm* vulture

bujía [bu'xia] *nf* (*vela*) candle; (*Elec*) candle (power); (*Auto*) spark plug

bula ['bula] *nf* (*papal*) bull

bulbo ['bulβo] *nm* bulb

bulevar [bule'βar] *nm* boulevard

Bulgaria [bul'ɣarja] *nf* Bulgaria; **búlgaro, -a** *adj, nm/f* Bulgarian

bulla ['buʎa] *nf* (*ruido*) uproar; (*de gente*) crowd

bullicio [bu'ʎiθjo] *nm* (*ruido*) uproar; (*movimiento*) bustle

bulto ['bulto] *nm* (*paquete*) package; (*fardo*) bundle; (*tamaño*) size, bulkiness; (*Med*) swelling, lump; (*silueta*) vague shape

buñuelo [bu'ɲwelo] *nm* ≈ doughnut (*BRIT*), ≈ donut (*US*); (*fruta de sartén*) fritter

buque ['buke] *nm* ship, vessel; **buque de guerra** warship

burbuja [bur'βuxa] *nf* bubble

burdel [bur'ðel] *nm* brothel

burgués, -esa [bur'ɣes, esa] *adj* middle-class, bourgeois; **burguesía** *nf* middle class, bourgeoisie

burla ['burla] *nf* (*mofa*) gibe; (*broma*) joke; (*engaño*) trick; **burlar** [bur'lar] *vt* (*engañar*) to deceive ▷ *vi* to joke; **burlarse** *vr* to joke; **burlarse de** to make fun of

burlón, -ona [bur'lon, ona] *adj* mocking

buró [bu'ro] (*MÉX*) *nm* bedside table

burocracia [buro'kraθja] *nf* civil service

burrada [bu'rraða] *nf*: **decir o soltar ~s** to talk nonsense; **hacer ~s** to act stupid; **una ~** (*ESP: mucho*) a (hell of a) lot

burro, -a ['burro, a] *nm/f* donkey/she-donkey; (*fig*) ass, idiot

bursátil [bur'satil] *adj* stock-exchange *cpd*

bus [bus] *nm* bus

busca ['buska] *nf* search, hunt ▷ *nm* (*Tel*) bleeper; **en ~ de** in search of

buscador [buska'ðor] *nm* (*Internet*) search engine

buscar [bus'kar] *vt* to look for, search for, seek ▷ *vi* to look, search, seek; **se busca secretaria** secretary wanted

busque *etc vb* V **buscar**

búsqueda ['buskeða] *nf* = **busca**

busto ['busto] *nm* (*Anat, Arte*) bust

butaca [bu'taka] *nf* armchair; (*de cine, teatro*) stall, seat

butano [bu'tano] *nm* butane (gas)

buzo ['buθo] *nm* diver

buzón [bu'θon] *nm* (*en puerta*) letter box; (*en calle*) pillar box

C

C. abr (= centígrado) C; (compañía) Co.

C/ abr (= calle) St

cabal [ka'βal] adj (exacto) exact; (correcto) right, proper; (acabado) finished, complete; **cabales** nmpl: **no está en sus cabales** she isn't in her right mind

cábalas ['kaβalas] nfpl: **hacer ~** to guess

cabalgar [kaβal'ɣar] vt, vi to ride

cabalgata [kaβal'ɣata] nf procession

caballa [ka'βaʎa] nf mackerel

caballería [kaβaʎe'ria] nf mount; (Mil) cavalry

caballero [kaβa'ʎero] nm gentleman; (de la orden de caballería) knight; (trato directo) sir

caballete [kaβa'ʎete] nm (Arte) easel; (Tec) trestle

caballito [kaβa'ʎito] nm (caballo pequeño) small horse, pony; **caballitos** nmpl (en verbena) roundabout, merry-go-round

caballo [ka'βaʎo] nm horse; (Ajedrez) knight; (Naipes) queen; **ir en ~** to ride; **caballo de carreras** racehorse; **caballo de fuerza** o **vapor** horsepower

cabaña [ka'βaɲa] nf (casita) hut, cabin

cabecear [kaβeθe'ar] vt, vi to nod

cabecera [kaβe'θera] nf head; (Imprenta) headline

cabecilla [kaβe'θiʎa] nm ringleader

cabellera [kaβe'ʎera] nf (head of) hair; (de cometa) tail

cabello [ka'βeʎo] nm (tb: ~s) hair; **cabello de ángel** confectionery and pastry filling made of pumpkin and syrup

caber [ka'βer] vi (entrar) to fit, go; **caben 3 más** there's room for 3 more

cabestrillo [kaβes'triʎo] nm sling

cabeza [ka'βeθa] nf head; (Pol) chief, leader; **cabeza de ajo** bulb of garlic; **cabeza de familia** head of the household; **cabeza rapada** skinhead; **cabezada** nf (golpe) butt; **dar cabezadas** to nod off; **cabezón, -ona**

adj (vino) heady; (fam: persona) pig-headed

cabida [ka'βiða] nf space

cabina [ka'βina] nf cabin; (de avión) cockpit; (de camión) cab; **cabina telefónica** telephone (BRIT) box o booth

cabizbajo, -a [kaβiθ'βaxo, a] adj crestfallen, dejected

cable ['kaβle] nm cable

cabo ['kaβo] nm (de objeto) end, extremity; (Mil) corporal; (Náut) rope, cable; (Geo) cape; **al ~ de 3 días** after 3 days; **llevar a ~** to carry out

cabra ['kaβra] nf goat

cabré etc vb V **caber**

cabrear [kaβre'ar] (fam) vt to bug; **cabrearse** vr (enfadarse) to fly off the handle

cabrito [ka'βrito] nm kid

cabrón [ka'βron] nm cuckold; (fam!) bastard (!)

caca ['kaka] (fam) nf pooh

cacahuete [kaka'wete] (ESP) nm peanut

cacao [ka'kao] nm cocoa; (Bot) cacao

cacarear [kakare'ar] vi (persona) to boast; (gallina) to crow

cacería [kaθe'ria] nf hunt

cacarizo, -a [kaka'riθo, a] (MÉX) adj pockmarked

cacerola [kaθe'rola] nf pan, saucepan

cachalote [katʃa'lote] nm (Zool) sperm whale

cacharro [ka'tʃarro] nm earthenware pot; **cacharros** nmpl pots and pans

cachear [katʃe'ar] vt to search, frisk

cachemir [katʃe'mir] nm cashmere

cachetada [katʃe'taða] (LAM: fam) nf (bofetada) slap

cachete [ka'tʃete] nm (Anat) cheek; (ESP: bofetada) slap (in the face)

cachivache [katʃi'βatʃe] nm (trasto) piece of junk; **cachivaches** nmpl junk sg

cacho ['katʃo] nm (small) bit; (LAM: cuerno) horn

cachondeo [katʃon'deo] (ESP: fam) nm farce, joke

cachondo, -a [ka'tʃondo, a] adj (Zool) on heat; (fam: sexualmente) randy; (: gracioso) funny

cachorro, -a [ka'tʃorro, a] nm/f (perro) pup, puppy; (león) cub

cachucha [ka'tʃuka] (MÉX: fam) nf cap

cacique [ka'θike] nm chief, local ruler; (Pol) local party boss

cactus ['kaktus] nm inv cactus

cada ['kaða] adj inv each; (antes de número) every; **~ día** each day, every day; **~ dos días** every other day; **~ uno/a** each one, every one; **~ vez más/menos** more and more/less and less; **~ vez que ...** whenever, every

time (that) ...; **uno de ~ diez** one out of every ten

cadáver [ka'ðaβer] nm (dead) body, corpse

cadena [ka'ðena] nf chain; (TV) channel; **trabajo en ~** assembly line work; **cadena montañosa** mountain range; **cadena perpetua** (Jur) life imprisonment

cadera [ka'ðera] nf hip

cadete [ka'ðete] nm cadet

caducar [kaðu'kar] vi to expire; **caduco, -a** adj expired; (persona) very old

caer [ka'er] vi to fall (down); **caerse** vr to fall (down); **me cae bien/mal** I get on well with him/I can't stand him; **~ en la cuenta** to realize; **dejar ~** to drop; **su cumpleaños cae en viernes** her birthday falls on a Friday

café [ka'fe] (pl **~s**) nm (bebida, planta) coffee; (lugar) café ⊳ adj (MÉX: color) brown, tan; **café con leche** white coffee; **café negro** (LAM) black coffee; **café solo** (ESP) black coffee

cafetera [kafe'tera] nf coffee pot

cafetería [kafete'ria] nf (gen) café

cafetero, -a [kafe'tero, a] adj coffee cpd; **ser muy ~** to be a coffee addict

cafishio [ka'fiʃjo] (CS) nm pimp

cagar [ka'ɣar] (fam!) vt to bungle, mess up ⊳ vi to have a shit (!)

caída [ka'iða] nf fall; (declive) slope; (disminución) fall, drop

caído, -a [ka'iðo, a] adj drooping

caiga etc vb V **caer**

caimán [kai'man] nm alligator

caja ['kaxa] nf box; (para reloj) case; (de ascensor) shaft; (Com) cashbox; (donde se hacen los pagos) cashdesk; (: en supermercado) checkout, till; **caja de ahorros** savings bank; **caja de cambios** gearbox; **caja de fusibles** fuse box; **caja fuerte** o **de caudales** safe, strongbox

cajero, -a [ka'xero, a] nm/f cashier; **cajero automático** cash dispenser

cajetilla [kaxe'tiʎa] nf (de cigarrillos) packet

cajón [ka'xon] nm big box; (de mueble) drawer

cajuela (MÉX) nf (Auto) boot (BRIT), trunk (US)

cal [kal] nf lime

cala ['kala] nf (Geo) cove, inlet; (de barco) hold

calabacín [kalaβa'θin] nm (Bot) baby marrow; (: más pequeño) courgette (BRIT), zucchini (US)

calabacita [kalaβa'θita] (MÉX) nf courgette (BRIT), zucchini (US)

calabaza [kala'βaθa] nf (Bot) pumpkin

calabozo [kala'βoθo] nm (cárcel) prison; (celda) cell

calada [ka'laða] (ESP) nf (de cigarrillo) puff

calado, -a [ka'laðo, a] adj (prenda) lace cpd ⊳ nm (Náut) draught

calamar [kala'mar] nm squid no pl

calambre [ka'lambre] nm (Elec) shock

calar [ka'lar] vt to soak, drench; (penetrar) to pierce, penetrate; (comprender) to see through; (vela) to lower; **calarse** vr (Auto) to stall; **~se las gafas** to stick one's glasses on

calavera [kala'βera] nf skull

calcar [kal'kar] vt (reproducir) to trace; (imitar) to copy

calcetín [kalθe'tin] nm sock

calcio ['kalθjo] nm calcium

calcomanía [kalkoma'nia] nf transfer

calculador, a [kalkula'ðor, a] adj (persona) calculating; **calculadora** [kalkula'ðora] nf calculator

calcular [kalku'lar] vt (Mat) to calculate, compute; **~ que ...** to reckon that ...

caldera [kal'dera] nf boiler

calderilla [kalde'riʎa] nf (moneda) small change

caldo ['kaldo] nm stock; (consomé) consommé

calefacción [kalefak'θjon] nf heating; **calefacción central** central heating

calefón [kale'fon] (RPL) nm boiler

calendario [kalen'darjo] nm calendar

calentador [kalenta'ðor] nm heater

calentamiento [kalenta'mjento] nm (Deporte) warm-up; **calentamiento global** global warming

calentar [kalen'tar] vt to heat (up); **calentarse** vr to heat up, warm up; (fig: discusión etc) to get heated

calentón [kalen'ton] (RPL: fam) adj (sexualmente) horny, randy (BRIT)

calentura [kalen'tura] nf (Med) fever, (high) temperature

calesita [kale'sita] (RPL) nf merry-go-round, carousel

calibre [ka'liβre] nm (de cañón) calibre, bore; (diámetro) diameter; (fig) calibre

calidad [kali'ðað] nf quality; **de ~** quality cpd; **en ~ de** in the capacity of, as

cálido, -a ['kaliðo, a] adj hot; (fig) warm

caliente etc [ka'ljente] vb V **calentar** ⊳ adj hot; (fig) fiery; (disputa) heated; (fam: cachondo) randy

calificación [kalifika'θjon] nf qualification; (de alumno) grade, mark

calificado, -a [kalifi'kaðo, a] (LAM) adj (competente) qualified; (obrero) skilled

calificar [kalifi'kar] vt to qualify; (alumno) to grade, mark; **~ de** to describe as

calima [ka'lima] nf (cerca del mar) mist
cáliz ['kaliθ] nm chalice
caliza [ka'liθa] nf limestone
callado, -a [ka'ʎaðo, a] adj quiet
callar [ka'ʎar] vt (asunto delicado) to keep
quiet about, say nothing about; (persona,
opinión) to silence ▷ vi to keep quiet, be
silent; **callarse** vr to keep quiet, be silent;
¡**cállate!** be quiet!, shut up!
calle ['kaʎe] nf street; (Deporte) lane; **~
arriba/abajo** up/down the street; **calle
de sentido único** one-way street; **calle
mayor** (ESP) high (BRIT) o main (US) street;
calle peatonal pedestrianized o pedestrian
street; **calle principal** (LAM) high (BRIT) o
main (US) street; **callejear** vi to wander
(about) the streets; **callejero, -a** adj street
cpd ▷ nm street map; **callejón** nm alley,
passage; **callejón sin salida** cul-de-sac;
callejuela nf side-street, alley
callista [ka'ʎista] nmf chiropodist
callo ['kaʎo] nm callus; (en el pie) corn;
callos nmpl (Culin) tripe sg
calma ['kalma] nf calm
calmante [kal'mante] nm sedative,
tranquillizer
calmar [kal'mar] vt to calm, calm down
▷ vi (tempestad) to abate; (mente etc) to
become calm
calor [ka'lor] nm heat; (agradable) warmth;
hace ~ it's hot; **tener ~** to be hot
caloría [kalo'ria] nf calorie
calumnia [ka'lumnja] nf calumny,
slander
caluroso, -a [kalu'roso, a] adj hot; (sin
exceso) warm; (fig) enthusiastic
calva ['kalβa] nf bald patch; (en bosque)
clearing
calvario [kal'βarjo] nm stations pl of the
cross
calvicie [kal'βiθje] nf baldness
calvo, -a ['kalβo, a] adj bald; (terreno)
bare, barren; (tejido) threadbare
calza ['kalθa] nf wedge, chock
calzada [kal'θaða] nf roadway, highway
calzado, -a [kal'θaðo, a] adj shod ▷ nm
footwear
calzador [kalθa'ðor] nm shoehorn
calzar [kal'θar] vt (zapatos etc) to wear;
(mueble) to put a wedge under; **calzarse**
vr: **~se los zapatos** to put on one's shoes;
¿**qué (número) calza?** what size do you
take?
calzón [kal'θon] nm (ESP: pantalón corto)
shorts; (LAM: ropa interior: de hombre)
underpants, pants (BRIT), shorts (US); (: de
mujer) panties, knickers (BRIT)
calzoncillos [kalθon'θiʎos] nmpl
underpants

cama ['kama] nf bed; **hacer la ~** to make
the bed; **cama individual/de matrimonio**
single/double bed
camaleón [kamale'on] nm chameleon
cámara ['kamara] nf chamber;
(habitación) room; (sala) hall; (Cine) cine
camera; (fotográfica) camera; **cámara de
aire** (ESP) inner tube; **cámara de comercio**
chamber of commerce; **cámara de gas** gas
chamber; **cámara digital** digital camera;
cámara frigorífica cold-storage room
camarada [kama'raða] nmf comrade,
companion
camarera [kama'rera] nf (en restaurante)
waitress; (en casa, hotel) maid
camarero [kama'rero] nm waiter
camarógrafo, -a [kama'rografo, a] (LAM)
nm/f cameraman/camerawoman
camarón [kama'ron] nm shrimp
camarote [kama'rote] nm cabin
cambiable [kam'bjaβle] adj (variable)
changeable, variable; (intercambiable)
interchangeable
cambiante [kam'bjante] adj variable
cambiar [kam'bjar] vt to change; (dinero)
to exchange ▷ vi to change; **cambiarse** vr
(mudarse) to move; (de ropa) to change; **~ de
idea** u **opinión** to change one's mind; **~se
de ropa** to change one's clothes)
cambio ['kambjo] nm change; (trueque)
exchange; (Com) rate of exchange; (oficina)
bureau de change; (dinero menudo) small
change; **a ~ de** in return o exchange for; **en
~** on the other hand; (en lugar de) instead;
cambio climático climate change; **cambio
de divisas** foreign exchange; **cambio de
marchas** o **velocidades** gear lever
camelar [kame'lar] vt to sweet-talk
camello [ka'meʎo] nm camel;
(fam: traficante) pusher
camerino [kame'rino] nm dressing room
camilla [ka'miʎa] nf (Med) stretcher
caminar [kami'nar] vi (marchar) to walk,
go ▷ vt (recorrer) to cover, travel
caminata [kami'nata] nf long walk; (por
el campo) hike
camino [ka'mino] nm way, road; (sendero)
track; **a medio ~** halfway (there); **en el ~**
on the way, en route; **~ de** on the way to;
Camino de Santiago Way of St James;
camino particular private road

⬤ **CAMINO DE SANTIAGO**
⬤
⬤ The **Camino de Santiago** is a medieval
⬤ pilgrim route stretching from the
⬤ Pyrenees to Santiago de Compostela

● in north-west Spain, where tradition
● has it the body of the Apostle James is
● buried. Nowadays it is a popular tourist
● route as well as a religious one.

camión [ka'mjon] *nm* lorry (BRIT), truck
(US); (MÉX: *autobús*) bus; **camión cisterna**
tanker; **camión de la basura** dustcart,
refuse lorry; **camión de mudanzas** removal
(BRIT) o moving (US) van; **camionero, -a**
nm/f lorry o truck driver
camioneta [kamjo'neta] *nf* van, light
truck
camisa [ka'misa] *nf* shirt; (Bot) skin;
camisa de fuerza straitjacket
camiseta [kami'seta] *nf* (*prenda*) tee-
shirt; (*ropa interior*) vest; (*de deportista*) top
camisón [kami'son] *nm* nightdress,
nightgown
camorra [ka'morra] *nf*: **buscar ~** to look
for trouble
camote [ka'mote] *nm* (MÉX, cs: *batata*)
sweet potato, yam; (MÉX: *bulbo*) tuber, bulb;
(cs: *fam: enamoramiento*) crush
campamento [kampa'mento] *nm* camp
campana [kam'pana] *nf* bell;
campanada *nf* peal; **campanario** *nm* belfry
campanilla [kampa'niʎa] *nf* small bell
campaña [kam'paɲa] *nf* (Mil, Pol)
campaign; **campaña electoral** election
campaign
campechano, -a [kampe'tʃano, a] *adj*
(*franco*) open
campeón, -ona [kampe'on, ona]
nm/f champion; **campeonato** *nm*
championship
cámper ['kamper] (LAM) *nm* o *f* caravan
(BRIT), trailer (US)
campera [kam'pera] (RPL) *nf* anorak
campesino, -a [kampe'sino, a] *adj*
country *cpd*, rural; (*gente*) peasant *cpd*
▷ *nm/f* countryman/woman; (*agricultor*)
farmer
campestre [kam'pestre] *adj* country
cpd, rural
camping ['kampin] (*pl* ~**s**) *nm* camping;
(*lugar*) campsite; **ir** o **estar de ~** to go
camping
campo ['kampo] *nm* (*fuera de la ciudad*)
country, countryside; (Agr, Elec) field; (*de
fútbol*) pitch; (*de golf*) course; (Mil) camp;
campo de batalla battlefield; **campo
de concentración** concentration camp;
campo de deportes sports ground, playing
field; **campo visual** field of vision, visual
field
camuflaje [kamu'flaxe] *nm* camouflage
cana ['kana] *nf* white o grey hair; **tener ~s**

to be going grey
Canadá [kana'ða] *nm* Canada;
canadiense *adj, nmf* Canadian ▷ *nf* fur-
lined jacket
canal [ka'nal] *nm* canal; (Geo) channel,
strait; (*de televisión*) channel; (*de tejado*)
gutter; **canal de Panamá** Panama Canal
canaleta [kana'leta] (LAM) *nf* (*de tejado*)
gutter
canalizar [kanali'θar] *vt* to channel
canalla [ka'naʎa] *nf* rabble, mob ▷ *nm*
swine
canapé [kana'pe] (*pl* ~**s**) *nm* sofa, settee;
(Culin) canapé
Canarias [ka'narjas] *nfpl* (tb: **las Islas ~**)
the Canary Islands, the Canaries
canario, -a [ka'narjo, a] *adj, nm/f*
(native) of the Canary Isles ▷ *nm* (Zool)
canary
canasta [ka'nasta] *nf* (round) basket
canasto [ka'nasto] *nm* large basket
cancela [kan'θela] *nf* gate
cancelación [kanθela'θjon] *nf*
cancellation
cancelar [kanθe'lar] *vt* to cancel; (*una
deuda*) to write off
cáncer ['kanθer] *nm* (Med) cancer; **C~**
(Astrología) Cancer
cancha ['kantʃa] *nf* (*de baloncesto*) court;
(LAM: *campo*) pitch; **cancha de tenis** (LAM)
tennis court
canciller [kanθi'ʎer] *nm* chancellor
canción [kan'θjon] *nf* song; **canción de
cuna** lullaby
candado [kan'daðo] *nm* padlock
candente [kan'dente] *adj* red-hot;
(*fig: tema*) burning
candidato, -a [kandi'ðato, a] *nm/f*
candidate
cándido, -a ['kandiðo, a] *adj* simple;
naive

▌ No confundir **cándido** con la palabra
inglesa *candid*.

candil [kan'dil] *nm* oil lamp; **candilejas**
nfpl (Teatro) footlights
canela [ka'nela] *nf* cinnamon
canelones [kane'lones] *nmpl* cannelloni
cangrejo [kan'grexo] *nm* crab
canguro [kan'guro] *nm* kangaroo; **hacer
de ~** to babysit
caníbal [ka'niβal] *adj, nmf* cannibal
canica [ka'nika] *nf* marble
canijo, -a [ka'nixo, a] *adj* frail, sickly
canilla [ka'niʎa] (RPL) *nf* tap (BRIT), faucet
(US)
canjear [kanxe'ar] *vt* to exchange
canoa [ka'noa] *nf* canoe
canon ['kanon] *nm* canon; (*pensión*) rent;

(Com) tax

canonizar [kanoni'θar] *vt* to canonize

canoso, -a [ka'noso, a] *adj* grey-haired

cansado, -a [kan'saðo, a] *adj* tired, weary; *(tedioso)* tedious, boring

cansancio [kan'sanθjo] *nm* tiredness, fatigue

cansar [kan'sar] *vt (fatigar)* to tire, tire out; *(aburrir)* to bore; *(fastidiar)* to bother; **cansarse** *vr* to tire, get tired; *(aburrirse)* to get bored

cantábrico, -a [kan'taβriko, a] *adj* Cantabrian

cantante [kan'tante] *adj* singing ▷ *nmf* singer

cantar [kan'tar] *vt* to sing ▷ *vi* to sing; *(insecto)* to chirp ▷ *nm (acción)* singing; *(canción)* song; *(poema)* poem

cántaro ['kantaro] *nm* pitcher, jug; **llover a ~s** to rain cats and dogs

cante ['kante] *nm (Mús)* Andalusian folk song; **cante jondo** flamenco singing

cantera [kan'tera] *nf* quarry

cantero [kan'tero] *(RPL) nm (arriate)* border

cantidad [kanti'ðað] *nf* quantity, amount; **~ de** lots of

cantimplora [kantim'plora] *nf (frasco)* water bottle, canteen

cantina [kan'tina] *nf* canteen; *(de estación)* buffet; *(LAM: bar)* bar

cantinero, -a [kanti'nero, a] *(MÉX) nm/f* barman/barmaid, bartender *(US)*

canto ['kanto] *nm* singing; *(canción)* song; *(borde)* edge, rim; *(de cuchillo)* back; **canto rodado** boulder

cantor, a [kan'tor, a] *nm/f* singer

canturrear [kanturre'ar] *vi* to sing softly

canuto [ka'nuto] *nm (tubo)* small tube; *(fam: droga)* joint

caña ['kaɲa] *nf (Bot: tallo)* stem, stalk; *(carrizo)* reed; *(vaso)* tumbler; *(de cerveza)* glass of beer; *(Anat)* shinbone; **caña de azúcar** sugar cane; **caña de pescar** fishing rod

cañada [ka'ɲaða] *nf (entre dos montañas)* gully, ravine; *(camino)* cattle track

cáñamo ['kaɲamo] *nm* hemp

cañería [kaɲe'ria] *nf (tubo)* pipe

caño ['kaɲo] *nm (tubo)* tube, pipe; *(de albañal)* sewer; *(Mús)* pipe; *(de fuente)* jet

cañón [ka'ɲon] *nm (Mil)* cannon; *(de fusil)* barrel; *(Geo)* canyon, gorge

caoba [ka'oβa] *nf* mahogany

caos ['kaos] *nm* chaos

capa ['kapa] *nf* cloak, cape; *(Geo)* layer, stratum; **capa de ozono** ozone layer

capacidad [kapaθi'ðað] *nf (medida)* capacity; *(aptitud)* capacity, ability

caparazón [kapara'θon] *nm* shell

capataz [kapa'taθ] *nm* foreman

capaz [ka'paθ] *adj* able, capable; *(amplio)* capacious, roomy

capellán [kape'ʎan] *nm* chaplain; *(sacerdote)* priest

capicúa [kapi'kua] *adj inv (número, fecha)* reversible

capilla [ka'piʎa] *nf* chapel

capital [kapi'tal] *adj* capital ▷ *nm (Com)* capital ▷ *nf (ciudad)* capital; **capital social** share o authorized capital

capitalismo [kapita'lismo] *nm* capitalism; **capitalista** *adj, nmf* capitalist

capitán [kapi'tan] *nm* captain

capítulo [ka'pitulo] *nm* chapter

capó [ka'po] *nm (Auto)* bonnet

capón [ka'pon] *nm (gallo)* capon

capota [ka'pota] *nf (de mujer)* bonnet; *(Auto)* hood *(BRIT)*, top *(US)*

capote [ka'pote] *nm (abrigo: de militar)* greatcoat; *(de torero)* cloak

capricho [ka'pritʃo] *nm* whim, caprice; **caprichoso, -a** *adj* capricious

Capricornio [kapri'kornjo] *nm* Capricorn

cápsula ['kapsula] *nf* capsule

captar [kap'tar] *vt (comprender)* to understand; *(Radio)* to pick up; *(atención, apoyo)* to attract

captura [kap'tura] *nf* capture; *(Jur)* arrest; **capturar** *vt* to capture; to arrest

capucha [ka'putʃa] *nf* hood, cowl

capuchón [kapu'tʃon] *(ESP) nm (de bolígrafo)* cap

capullo [ka'puʎo] *nm (Bot)* bud; *(Zool)* cocoon; *(fam)* idiot

caqui ['kaki] *nm* khaki

cara ['kara] *nf (Anat: de moneda)* face; *(de disco)* side; *(descaro)* boldness; **~ a** facing; **de ~** opposite, facing; **dar la ~** to face the consequences; **¿~ o cruz?** heads or tails?; **¡qué ~ (más dura)!** what a nerve!

Caracas [ka'rakas] *n* Caracas

caracol [kara'kol] *nm (Zool)* snail; *(concha)* (sea) shell

carácter [ka'rakter] *(pl* **caracteres***) nm* character; **tener buen/mal ~** to be good natured/bad tempered

característica [karakte'ristika] *nf* characteristic

característico, -a [karakte'ristiko, a] *adj* characteristic

caracterizar [karakteri'θar] *vt* to characterize, typify

caradura [kara'ðura] *nmf:* **es un ~** he's got a nerve

carajillo [kara'xiʎo] *nm* coffee with a dash

of brandy
carajo [ka'raxo] *(fam!)* *nm*: ¡~! shit! *(!)*
caramba [ka'ramba] *excl* good gracious!
caramelo [kara'melo] *nm (dulce)* sweet;
 (azúcar fundida) caramel
caravana [kara'βana] *nf* caravan; *(fig)*
 group; *(Auto)* tailback
carbón [kar'βon] *nm* coal; **papel ~** carbon
 paper
carbono [kar'βono] *nm* carbon
carburador [karβura'ðor] *nm* carburettor
carburante [karβu'rante] *nm (para
 motor)* fuel
carcajada [karka'xaða] *nf* (loud) laugh,
 guffaw
cárcel ['karθel] *nf* prison, jail; *(Tec)* clamp
carcoma [kar'koma] *nf* woodworm
cardar [kar'ðar] *vt (pelo)* to backcomb
cardenal [karðe'nal] *nm (Rel)* cardinal;
 (Med) bruise
cardíaco, -a [kar'ðiako, a] *adj* cardiac,
 heart *cpd*
cardinal [karði'nal] *adj* cardinal
cardo ['karðo] *nm* thistle
carecer [kare'θer] *vi*: **~ de** to lack, be in
 need of
carencia [ka'renθja] *nf* lack; *(escasez)*
 shortage; *(Med)* deficiency
careta [ka'reta] *nf* mask
carga ['karɣa] *nf (peso, Elec)* load; *(de barco)*
 cargo, freight; *(Mil)* charge; *(responsabilidad)*
 duty, obligation
cargado, -a [kar'ɣaðo, a] *adj* loaded;
 (Elec) live; *(café, té)* strong; *(cielo)* overcast
cargamento [karɣa'mento] *nm (acción)*
 loading; *(mercancías)* load, cargo
cargar [kar'ɣar] *vt (barco, arma)* to load;
 (Elec) to charge; *(Com: algo en cuenta)* to
 charge; *(Inform)* to load ▷ *vi (Mil)* to charge;
 (Auto) to load (up); **~ con** to pick up, carry
 away; *(peso: fig)* to shoulder, bear; **cargarse**
 vr (fam: estropear) to break; *(: matar)* to
 bump off
cargo ['karɣo] *nm (puesto)* post, office;
 (responsabilidad) duty, obligation; *(Jur)*
 charge; **hacerse ~ de** to take charge of *o*
 responsibility for
carguero [kar'ɣero] *nm* freighter, cargo
 boat; *(avión)* freight plane
Caribe [ka'riβe] *nm*: **el ~** the Caribbean; **del
 ~** Caribbean; **caribeño, -a** [kari'βeɲo, a]
 adj Caribbean
caricatura [karika'tura] *nf* caricature
caricia [ka'riθja] *nf* caress
caridad [kari'ðað] *nf* charity
caries ['karjes] *nf inv* tooth decay
cariño [ka'riɲo] *nm* affection, love; *(caricia)*
 caress; *(en carta)* love ...; **tener ~ a** to be fond

of; **cariñoso, -a** *adj* affectionate
carisma [ka'risma] *nm* charisma
caritativo, -a [karita'tiβo, a] *adj*
 charitable
cariz [ka'riθ] *nm*: **tener** *o* **tomar buen/mal
 ~** to look good/bad
carmín [kar'min] *nm* lipstick
carnal [kar'nal] *adj* carnal; **primo ~** first
 cousin
carnaval [karna'βal] *nm* carnival

> **CARNAVAL**
>
> **Carnaval** is the traditional period of
> fun, feasting and partying which takes
> place in the three days before the start of
> Lent ("Cuaresma"). Although in decline
> during the Franco years the carnival has
> grown in popularity recently in Spain.
> Cádiz and Tenerife are particularly
> well-known for their flamboyant
> celebrations with fancy-dress parties,
> parades and firework displays being the
> order of the day.

carne ['karne] *nf* flesh; *(Culin)* meat; **se
 me pone la ~ de gallina sólo verlo** I get
 the creeps just seeing it; **carne de cerdo/
 cordero/ternera/vaca** pork/lamb/veal/
 beef; **carne de gallina** *(fig)* gooseflesh;
 carne molida *(LAM)* mince *(BRIT)*, ground
 meat *(US)*; **carne picada** *(ESP, RPL)* mince
 (BRIT), ground meat *(US)*
carné [kar'ne] *(ESP) (pl ~s)* *nm*: **~ de
 conducir** driving licence *(BRIT)*, driver's
 license *(US)*; **~ de identidad** identity card; **~
 de socio** membership card
carnero [kar'nero] *nm* sheep, ram; *(carne)*
 mutton
carnet [kar'ne] *(ESP) (pl ~s)* *nm* = **carné**
carnicería [karniθe'ria] *nf* butcher's
 (shop); *(fig: matanza)* carnage, slaughter
carnicero, -a [karni'θero, a] *adj*
 carnivorous ▷ *nm/f* butcher; *(carnívoro)*
 carnivore
carnívoro, -a [kar'niβoro, a] *adj*
 carnivorous
caro, -a ['karo, a] *adj* dear; *(Com)* dear,
 expensive ▷ *adv* dear, dearly
carpa ['karpa] *nf (pez)* carp; *(de circo)* big
 top; *(LAM: tienda de campaña)* tent
carpeta [kar'peta] *nf* folder, file; **carpeta
 de anillas** ring binder
carpintería [karpinte'ria] *nf* carpentry,
 joinery; **carpintero** *nm* carpenter
carraspear [karraspe'ar] *vi* to clear one's
 throat
carraspera [karras'pera] *nf* hoarseness

carrera [ka'rrera] nf (acción) run(ning); (espacio recorrido) run; (competición) race; (trayecto) course; (profesión) career; (licenciatura) degree; **a la ~** at (full) speed; **carrera de obstáculos** (Deporte) steeplechase

carrete [ka'rrete] nm reel, spool; (Tec) coil

carretera [karre'tera] nf (main) road, highway; **carretera de circunvalación** ring road; **carretera nacional** ≈ A road (BRIT), ≈ state highway (US)

carretilla [karre'tiʎa] nf trolley; (Agr) (wheel)barrow

carril [ka'rril] nm furrow; (de autopista) lane; (Ferro) rail; **carril-bici** cycle lane

carrito [ka'rrito] nm trolley

carro ['karro] nm cart, wagon; (Mil) tank; (LAM: coche) car; **carro patrulla** (LAM) patrol o panda (BRIT) car

carrocería [karroθe'ria] nf bodywork, coachwork

carroña [ka'rroɲa] nf carrion no pl

carroza [ka'rroθa] nf (carruaje) coach

carrusel [karru'sel] nm merry-go-round, roundabout

carta ['karta] nf letter; (Culin) menu; (naipe) card; (mapa) map; (Jur) document; **carta certificada/urgente** registered/special-delivery letter

cartabón [karta'βon] nm set square

cartel [kar'tel] nm (anuncio) poster, placard; (Escol) wall chart; (Com) cartel; **cartelera** nf hoarding, billboard; (en periódico etc) entertainments guide; **"en cartelera"** "showing"

cartera [kar'tera] nf (de bolsillo) wallet; (de colegial, cobrador) satchel; (de señora) handbag; (para documentos) briefcase; (Com) portfolio; **ocupa la ~ de Agricultura** she is Minister of Agriculture

carterista [karte'rista] nmf pickpocket

cartero [kar'tero] nm postman

cartilla [kar'tiʎa] nf primer, first reading book; **cartilla de ahorros** savings book

cartón [kar'ton] nm cardboard; **cartón piedra** papier-mâché

cartucho [kar'tutʃo] nm (Mil) cartridge

cartulina [kartu'lina] nf card

casa ['kasa] nf house; (hogar) home; (Com) firm, company; **en ~** at home; **casa consistorial** town hall; **casa de campo** country house; **casa de huéspedes** boarding house; **casa de socorro** first aid post; **casa rodante** (CS) caravan (BRIT), trailer (US)

casado, -a [ka'saðo, a] adj married ▷ nm/f married man/woman

casar [ka'sar] vt to marry; (Jur) to quash,

annul; **casarse** vr to marry, get married

cascabel [kaska'βel] nm (small) bell

cascada [kas'kaða] nf waterfall

cascanueces [kaska'nweθes] nm inv nutcrackers pl

cascar [kas'kar] vt to crack, split, break (open); **cascarse** vr to crack, split, break (open)

cáscara ['kaskara] nf (de huevo, fruta seca) shell; (de fruta) skin; (de limón) peel

casco ['kasko] nm (de bombero, soldado) helmet; (Náut: de barco) hull; (Zool: de caballo) hoof; (botella) empty bottle; (de ciudad) **el ~ antiguo** the old part; **el ~ urbano** the town centre; **los ~s azules** the UN peace-keeping force, the blue berets

cascote [kas'kote] nm rubble

caserío [kase'rio] (ESP) nm farmhouse; (casa) country mansion

casero, -a [ka'sero, a] adj (pan etc) home-made ▷ nm/f (propietario) landlord/lady; **ser muy ~** to be home-loving; **"comida casera"** "home cooking"

caseta [ka'seta] nf hut; (para bañista) cubicle; (de feria) stall

casete [ka'sete] nm o f cassette

casi ['kasi] adv almost, nearly; **~ nada** hardly anything; **~ nunca** hardly ever, almost never; **~ te caes** you almost fell

casilla [ka'siʎa] nf (casita) hut, cabin; (Ajedrez) square; (para cartas) pigeonhole; **casilla de correo** (CS) P.O. Box; **casillero** nm (para cartas) pigeonholes pl

casino [ka'sino] nm club; (de juego) casino

caso ['kaso] nm case; **en ~ de** in case of; **en ~ de que ...** in case ...; **el ~ es que ...** the fact is that ...; **en ese/todo ~** in that/any case; **hacer ~ a** to pay attention to; **venir al ~** to be relevant

caspa ['kaspa] nf dandruff

cassette [ka'sete] nm o f = **casete**

castaña [kas'taɲa] nf chestnut

castaño, -a [kas'taɲo, a] adj chestnut(-coloured), brown ▷ nm chestnut tree

castañuelas [kasta'ɲwelas] nfpl castanets

castellano, -a [kaste'ʎano, a] adj, nm/f Castilian ▷ nm (Ling) Castilian, Spanish

castigar [kasti'ɣar] vt to punish; (Deporte) to penalize; **castigo** nm punishment; (Deporte) penalty

Castilla [kas'tiʎa] nf Castille

castillo [kas'tiʎo] nm castle

castizo, -a [kas'tiθo, a] adj (Ling) pure

casto, -a ['kasto, a] adj chaste, pure

castor [kas'tor] nm beaver

castrar [kas'trar] vt to castrate

casual [ka'swal] *adj* chance, accidental

▌No confundir **casual** con la palabra inglesa *casual*.

casualidad *nf* chance, accident; (*combinación de circunstancias*) coincidence; **da la casualidad de que ...** it (just) so happens that ...; **¡qué casualidad!** what a coincidence!

cataclismo [kata'klismo] *nm* cataclysm

catador, a [kata'ðor, a] *nm/f* wine taster

catalán, -ana [kata'lan, ana] *adj, nm/f* Catalan ▷ *nm* (*Ling*) Catalan

catalizador [kataliθa'ðor] *nm* catalyst; (*Auto*) catalytic convertor

catalogar [katalo'xar] *vt* to catalogue; **~ a algn (de)** (*fig*) to categorize sb (as)

catálogo [ka'taloxo] *nm* catalogue

Cataluña [kata'luɲa] *nf* Catalonia

catar [ka'tar] *vt* to taste, sample

catarata [kata'rata] *nf* (*Geo*) waterfall; (*Med*) cataract

catarro [ka'tarro] *nm* catarrh; (*constipado*) cold

catástrofe [ka'tastrofe] *nf* catastrophe

catear [kate'ar] (*fam*) *vt* (*examen, alumno*) to fail

cátedra ['kateðra] *nf* (*Univ*) chair, professorship

catedral [kate'ðral] *nf* cathedral

catedrático, -a [kate'ðratiko, a] *nm/f* professor

categoría [katexo'ria] *nf* category; (*rango*) rank, standing; (*calidad*) quality; **de ~** (*hotel*) top-class

cateto, -a ['kateto, a] (*ESP: pey*) *nm/f* peasant

catolicismo [katoli'θismo] *nm* Catholicism

católico, -a [ka'toliko, a] *adj, nm/f* Catholic

catorce [ka'torθe] *num* fourteen

cauce ['kauθe] *nm* (*de río*) riverbed; (*fig*) channel

caucho ['kautʃo] (*ESP*) *nm* rubber

caudal [kau'ðal] *nm* (*de río*) volume, flow; (*fortuna*) wealth; (*abundancia*) abundance

caudillo [kau'ðiʎo] *nm* leader, chief

causa ['kausa] *nf* cause; (*razón*) reason; (*Jur*) lawsuit, case; **a ~ de** because of; **causar** [kau'sar] *vt* to cause

cautela [kau'tela] *nf* caution, cautiousness; **cauteloso, -a** *adj* cautious, wary

cautivar [kauti'βar] *vt* to capture; (*atraer*) to captivate

cautiverio [kauti'βerjo] *nm* captivity

cautividad [kautiβi'ðað] *nf* = **cautiverio**

cautivo, -a [kau'tiβo, a] *adj, nm/f* captive

cauto, -a ['kauto, a] *adj* cautious, careful

cava ['kaβa] *nm* champagne-type wine

cavar [ka'βar] *vt* to dig

caverna [ka'βerna] *nf* cave, cavern

cavidad [kaβi'ðað] *nf* cavity

cavilar [kaβi'lar] *vt* to ponder

cayendo *etc vb* V **caer**

caza ['kaθa] *nf* (*acción: gen*) hunting; (: *con fusil*) shooting; (*una caza*) hunt, chase; (*de animales*) game ▷ *nm* (*Aviac*) fighter; **ir de ~** to go hunting; **caza mayor** game hunting; **cazador, a** [kaθa'ðor, a] *nm/f* hunter; **cazadora** *nf* jacket; **cazar** [ka'θar] *vt* to hunt; (*perseguir*) to chase; (*prender*) to catch

cazo ['kaθo] *nm* saucepan

cazuela [ka'θwela] *nf* (*vasija*) pan; (*guisado*) casserole

CD *nm abr* (= *compact disc*) CD

CD-ROM [θeðe'rom] *nm abr* CD-ROM

CE *nf abr* (= *Comunidad Europea*) EC

cebada [θe'βaða] *nf* barley

cebar [θe'βar] *vt* (*animal*) to fatten (up); (*anzuelo*) to bait; (*Mil, Tec*) to prime

cebo ['θeβo] *nm* (*para animales*) feed, food; (*para peces, fig*) bait; (*de arma*) charge

cebolla [θe'βoʎa] *nf* onion; **cebolleta** *nf* spring onion

cebra ['θeβra] *nf* zebra

cecear [θeθe'ar] *vi* to lisp

ceder [θe'ðer] *vt* to hand over, give up, part with ▷ *vi* (*renunciar*) to give in, yield; (*disminuir*) to diminish, decline; (*romperse*) to give way

cedro ['θeðro] *nm* cedar

cédula ['θeðula] *nf* certificate, document; **cédula de identidad** (*LAM*) identity card; **cédula electoral** (*LAM*) ballot

cegar [θe'xar] *vt* to blind; (*tubería etc*) to block up, stop up ▷ *vi* to go blind; **cegarse** *vr*: **~se (de)** to be blinded (by)

ceguera [θe'xera] *nf* blindness

ceja ['θexa] *nf* eyebrow

cejar [θe'xar] *vi* (*fig*) to back down

celador, a [θela'ðor, a] *nm/f* (*de edificio*) watchman; (*de museo etc*) attendant

celda ['θelda] *nf* cell

celebración [θeleβra'θjon] *nf* celebration

celebrar [θele'βrar] *vt* to celebrate; (*alabar*) to praise ▷ *vi* to be glad; **celebrarse** *vr* to occur, take place

célebre ['θelebre] *adj* famous

celebridad [θeleβri'ðað] *nf* fame; (*persona*) celebrity

celeste [θe'leste] *adj* (*azul*) sky-blue

celestial [θeles'tjal] *adj* celestial, heavenly

celo¹ ['θelo] *nm* zeal; (*Rel*) fervour; (*Zool*): **en ~** on heat; **celos** *nmpl* jealousy *sg*; **dar ~s a algn** to make sb jealous; **tener ~s** to be jealous

celo²® ['θelo] *nm* Sellotape®

celofán [θelo'fan] *nm* cellophane

celoso, -a [θe'loso, a] *adj* jealous; *(trabajador)* zealous

celta ['θelta] *adj* Celtic ▷ *nmf* Celt

célula ['θelula] *nf* cell

celulitis [θelu'litis] *nf* cellulite

cementerio [θemen'terjo] *nm* cemetery, graveyard

cemento [θe'mento] *nm* cement; *(hormigón)* concrete; *(LAM: cola)* glue

cena ['θena] *nf* evening meal, dinner; **cenar** [θe'nar] *vt* to have for dinner ▷ *vi* to have dinner

cenicero [θeni'θero] *nm* ashtray

ceniza [θe'niθa] *nf* ash, ashes *pl*

censo ['θenso] *nm* census; **censo electoral** electoral roll

censura [θen'sura] *nf* (*Pol*) censorship; **censurar** [θensu'rar] *vt* (*idea*) to censure; *(cortar: película)* to censor

centella [θen'teʎa] *nf* spark

centenar [θente'nar] *nm* hundred

centenario, -a [θente'narjo, a] *adj* centenary; hundred-year-old ▷ *nm* centenary

centeno [θen'teno] *nm* (*Bot*) rye

centésimo, -a [θen'tesimo, a] *adj* hundredth

centígrado [θen'tiɣraðo] *adj* centigrade

centímetro [θen'timetro] *nm* centimetre (*BRIT*), centimeter (*US*)

céntimo ['θentimo] *nm* cent

centinela [θenti'nela] *nm* sentry, guard

centollo [θen'toʎo] *nm* spider crab

central [θen'tral] *adj* central ▷ *nf* head office; *(Tec)* plant; *(Tel)* exchange; **central eléctrica** power station; **central nuclear** nuclear power station; **central telefónica** telephone exchange

centralita [θentra'lita] *nf* switchboard

centralizar [θentrali'θar] *vt* to centralize

centrar [θen'trar] *vt* to centre

céntrico, -a ['θentriko, a] *adj* central

centrifugar [θentrifu'ɣar] *vt* to spin-dry

centro ['θentro] *nm* centre; **centro comercial** shopping centre; **centro de atención al cliente** call centre; **centro de salud** health centre; **centro escolar** school; **centro juvenil** youth club; **centro turístico** *(lugar muy visitado)* tourist centre; **centro urbano** urban area, city

centroamericano, -a [θentroameri'kano, a] *adj, nm/f* Central American

ceñido, -a [θe'ɲiðo, a] *adj* (*chaqueta, pantalón*) tight(-fitting)

ceñir [θe'ɲir] *vt* (*rodear*) to encircle, surround; *(ajustar)* to fit (tightly)

ceño ['θeɲo] *nm* frown, scowl; **fruncir el ~** to frown, knit one's brow

cepillar [θepi'ʎar] *vt* to brush; *(madera)* to plane (down)

cepillo [θe'piʎo] *nm* brush; *(para madera)* plane; **cepillo de dientes** toothbrush

cera ['θera] *nf* wax

cerámica [θe'ramika] *nf* pottery; *(arte)* ceramics

cerca ['θerka] *nf* fence ▷ *adv* near, nearby, close; **~ de** near, close to

cercanías [θerka'nias] *nfpl* (*afueras*) outskirts, suburbs

cercano, -a [θer'kano, a] *adj* close, near

cercar [θer'kar] *vt* to fence in; *(rodear)* to surround

cerco ['θerko] *nm* (*Agr*) enclosure; (*LAM: valla*) fence; (*Mil*) siege

cerdo, -a [θerðo, a] *nm/f* pig/sow

cereal [θere'al] *nm* cereal; **cereales** *nmpl* cereals, grain *sg*

cerebro [θe'reβro] *nm* brain; *(fig)* brains *pl*

ceremonia [θere'monja] *nf* ceremony; **ceremonioso, -a** *adj* ceremonious

cereza [θe'reθa] *nf* cherry

cerilla [θe'riʎa] *nf* (*fósforo*) match

cerillo [θe'riʎo] (*MÉX*) *nm* match

cero ['θero] *nm* nothing, zero

cerquillo [θer'kiʎo] (*CAM, RPL*) *nm* fringe (*BRIT*), bangs *pl* (*US*)

cerrado, -a [θe'rraðo, a] *adj* closed, shut; *(con llave)* locked; *(tiempo)* cloudy, overcast; *(curva)* sharp; *(acento)* thick, broad

cerradura [θerra'ðura] *nf* (*acción*) closing; *(mecanismo)* lock

cerrajero [θerra'xero] *nm* locksmith

cerrar [θe'rrar] *vt* to close, shut; *(paso, carretera)* to close; *(grifo)* to turn off; *(cuenta, negocio)* to close ▷ *vi* to close, shut; *(noche)* to come down; **cerrarse** *vr* to close, shut; **~ con llave** to lock; **~ un trato** to strike a bargain

cerro ['θerro] *nm* hill

cerrojo [θe'rroxo] *nm* (*herramienta*) bolt; *(de puerta)* latch

certamen [θer'tamen] *nm* competition, contest

certero, -a [θer'tero, a] *adj* (*gen*) accurate

certeza [θer'teθa] *nf* certainty

certidumbre [θerti'ðumβre] *nf* = **certeza**

certificado, -a [θertifi'kaðo, a] *adj* (*carta, paquete*) registered; *(aprobado)* certified ▷ *nm* certificate; **certificado médico** medical certificate

certificar [θertifi'kar] *vt* (*asegurar, atestar*) to certify

cervatillo [θerβa'tiʎo] *nm* fawn

cervecería [θerβeθe'ria] *nf (fábrica)* brewery; *(bar)* public house, pub

cerveza [θer'βeθa] *nf* beer

cesar [θe'sar] *vi* to cease, stop ▷ *vt (funcionario)* to remove from office

cesárea [θe'sarea] *nf (Med)* Caesarean operation *o* section

cese ['θese] *nm (de trabajo)* dismissal; *(de pago)* suspension

césped ['θespeð] *nm* grass, lawn

cesta ['θesta] *nf* basket

cesto ['θesto] *nm* (large) basket, hamper

cfr *abr (= confróntese)* cf.

chabacano, -a [tʃaβa'kano, a] *adj* vulgar, coarse

chabola [tʃa'βola] *(ESP) nf* shack; **barrio de chabolas** shanty town

chacal [tʃa'kal] *nm* jackal

chacha ['tʃatʃa] *(fam) nf* maid

cháchara ['tʃatʃara] *nf* chatter; **estar de ~** to chatter away

chacra ['tʃakra] *(CS) nf* smallholding

chafa ['tʃafa] *(MÉX: fam) adj* useless, dud

chafar [tʃa'far] *vt (aplastar)* to crush; *(plan etc)* to ruin

chal [tʃal] *nm* shawl

chalado, -a [tʃa'lado, a] *(fam) adj* crazy

chalé [tʃa'le] *(pl ~s) nm* villa, ≈ detached house

chaleco [tʃa'leko] *nm* waistcoat, vest *(US)*; **chaleco de seguridad** *(Aut)* reflective safety vest; **chaleco salvavidas** life jacket

chalet [tʃa'le] *(pl ~s) nm* = **chalé**

chamaco, -a *(MÉX)* [tʃa'mako, a] *nm/f (niño)* kid

chambear [tʃambe'ar] *(MÉX: fam) vi* to earn one's living

champán [tʃam'pan] *nm* champagne

champiñón [tʃampi'ɲon] *nm* mushroom

champú [tʃam'pu] *(pl ~es, ~s) nm* shampoo

chamuscar [tʃamus'kar] *vt* to scorch, sear, singe

chance ['tʃanθe] *(LAM) nm* chance

chancho, -a ['tʃantʃo, a] *(LAM) nm/f* pig

chanchullo [tʃan'tʃuʎo] *(fam) nm* fiddle

chandal [tʃan'dal] *nm* tracksuit

chantaje [tʃan'taxe] *nm* blackmail

chapa ['tʃapa] *nf (de metal)* plate, sheet; *(de madera)* board, panel; *(RPL Auto)* number *(BRIT) o* license *(US)* plate; **chapado, -a** *adj*: **chapado en oro** gold-plated

chaparrón [tʃapa'rron] *nm* downpour, cloudburst

chaperón [tʃape'ron] *(MÉX) nm*: **hacer de ~** to play gooseberry; **chaperona** *(LAM) nf*: **hacer de chaperona** to play gooseberry

chapopote [tʃapo'pote] *(MÉX) nm* tar

chapulín [tʃapu'lin] *(MÉX, CAM) nm* grasshopper

chapurrear [tʃapurre'ar] *vt (idioma)* to speak badly

chapuza [tʃa'puθa] *nf* botched job

chapuzón [tʃapu'θon] *nm*: **darse un ~** to go for a dip

chaqueta [tʃa'keta] *nf* jacket

chaquetón [tʃake'ton] *nm* long jacket

charca ['tʃarka] *nf* pond, pool

charco ['tʃarko] *nm* pool, puddle

charcutería [tʃarkute'ria] *nf (tienda)* shop selling chiefly pork meat products; *(productos)* cooked pork meats *pl*

charla ['tʃarla] *nf* talk, chat; *(conferencia)* lecture; **charlar** [tʃar'lar] *vi* to talk, chat; **charlatán, -ana** [tʃarla'tan, ana] *nm/f (hablador)* chatterbox; *(estafador)* trickster

charol [tʃa'rol] *nm* varnish; *(cuero)* patent leather

charola [tʃa'rola] *(MÉX) nf* tray

charro ['tʃarro, a] *(MÉX) nm* typical Mexican

chasco ['tʃasko] *nm (desengaño)* disappointment

chasis ['tʃasis] *nm inv* chassis

chasquido [tʃas'kiðo] *nm* crack; click

chat [tʃat] *nm (Internet)* chat room

chatarra [tʃa'tarra] *nf* scrap (metal)

chatear [tʃate'ar] *vi (Internet)* to chat

chato, -a ['tʃato, a] *adj* flat; *(nariz)* snub

chaucha ['tʃautʃa] *(RPL) nf* runner *(BRIT) o* pole *(US)* bean

chaval, a [tʃa'βal, a] *(ESP) nm/f* kid, lad/lass

chavo, -a ['tʃaβo] *(MÉX: fam) nm/f* guy/girl

checar [tʃe'kar] *(MÉX) vt*: **~ tarjeta** *(al entrar)* to clock in o on; *(: al salir)* to clock off o out

checo, -a ['tʃeko, a] *adj, nm/f* Czech ▷ *nm (Ling)* Czech

checoslovaco, -a [tʃekoslo'βako, a] *adj, nm/f* Czech, Czechoslovak

Checoslovaquia [tʃekoslo'βakja] *nf (Hist)* Czechoslovakia

cheque ['tʃeke] *nm* cheque *(BRIT)*, check *(US)*; **cobrar un ~** to cash a cheque; **cheque al portador** cheque payable to bearer; **cheque de viaje** traveller's cheque *(BRIT)*, traveler's check *(US)*; **cheque en blanco** blank cheque

chequeo [tʃe'keo] *nm (Med)* check-up; *(Auto)* service

chequera [tʃe'kera] *(LAM) nf* chequebook *(BRIT)*, checkbook *(US)*

chévere ['tʃeβere] *(LAM: fam) adj* great

chícharo ['tʃitʃaro] *(MÉX, CAM) nm* pea

chichón [tʃi'tʃon] nm bump, lump

chicle ['tʃikle] nm chewing gum

chico, -a ['tʃiko, a] adj small, little ⊳ nm/f (niño) child; (muchacho) boy/girl

chiflado, -a [tʃi'flaðo, a] adj crazy

chiflar [tʃi'flar] vt to hiss, boo

chilango, -a [tʃi'lango, a] (MÉX) adj of o from Mexico City

Chile ['tʃile] nm Chile; **chileno, -a** adj, nm/f Chilean

chile ['tʃile] nm chilli pepper

chillar [tʃi'ʎar] vi (persona) to yell, scream; (animal salvaje) to howl; (cerdo) to squeal

chillido [tʃi'ʎiðo] nm (de persona) yell, scream; (de animal) howl

chimenea [tʃime'nea] nf chimney; (hogar) fireplace

China ['tʃina] nf (tb: **la ~**) China

chinche ['tʃintʃe] nf (insecto) (bed)bug; (Tec) drawing pin (BRIT), thumbtack (US) ⊳ nmf nuisance, pest

chincheta [tʃin'tʃeta] nf drawing pin (BRIT), thumbtack (US)

chingada [tʃin'gaða] (MÉX: fam!) nf: **hijo de la ~** bastard

chino, -a ['tʃino, a] adj, nm/f Chinese ⊳ nm (Ling) Chinese

chipirón [tʃipi'ron] nm (Zool, Culin) squid

Chipre ['tʃipre] nf Cyprus; **chipriota** adj, nmf Cypriot

chiquillo, -a [tʃi'kiʎo, a] nm/f (fam) kid

chirimoya [tʃiri'moja] nf custard apple

chiringuito [tʃirin'ɣito] nm small open-air bar

chiripa [tʃi'ripa] nf fluke

chirriar [tʃi'rrjar] vi to creak, squeak

chirrido [tʃi'rriðo] nm creak(ing), squeak(ing)

chisme ['tʃisme] nm (habladurías) piece of gossip; (objeto) thingummyjig

chismoso, -a [tʃis'moso, a] adj gossiping ⊳ nm/f gossip

chispa ['tʃispa] nf spark; (fig) sparkle; (ingenio) wit; (fam) drunkenness

chispear [tʃispe'ar] vi (lloviznar) to drizzle

chiste ['tʃiste] nm joke, funny story

chistoso, -a [tʃis'toso, a] adj funny, amusing

chivo, -a ['tʃiβo, a] nm/f (billy-/nanny-)goat; **chivo expiatorio** scapegoat

chocante [tʃo'kante] adj startling; (extraño) odd; (ofensivo) shocking

chocar [tʃo'kar] vi (coches etc) to collide, crash ⊳ vt to shock; (sorprender) to startle; **~ con** to collide with; (fig) to run into, run up against; **¡chócala!** (fam) put it there!

chochear [tʃotʃe'ar] vi to be senile

chocho, -a ['tʃotʃo, a] adj doddering, senile; (fig) soft, doting

choclo ['tʃoklo] (CS) nm (grano) sweet corn; (mazorca) corn on the cob

chocolate [tʃoko'late] adj, nm chocolate; **chocolatina** nf chocolate

chofer [tʃo'fer] nm = **chófer**

chófer ['tʃofer] nm driver

chollo ['tʃoʎo] (ESP: fam) nm bargain, snip

choque etc ['tʃoke] vb V **chocar** ⊳ nm (impacto) impact; (golpe) jolt; (Auto) crash; (fig) conflict; **choque frontal** head-on collision

chorizo [tʃo'riθo] nm hard pork sausage, (type of) salami

chorrada [tʃo'rraða] (ESP: fam) nf: **¡es una ~!** that's crap! (!); **decir ~s** to talk crap (!)

chorrear [tʃorre'ar] vi to gush (out), spout (out); (gotear) to drip, trickle

chorro ['tʃorro] nm jet; (fig) stream

choza ['tʃoθa] nf hut, shack

chubasco [tʃu'βasko] nm squall

chubasquero [tʃuβas'kero] nm lightweight raincoat

chuchería [tʃutʃe'ria] nf trinket

chuleta [tʃu'leta] nf chop, cutlet

chulo ['tʃulo] nm (de prostituta) pimp

chupaleta [tʃupa'leta] (MÉX) nf lollipop

chupar [tʃu'par] vt to suck; (absorber) to absorb; **chuparse** vr to grow thin

chupete [tʃu'pete] (ESP, CS) nm dummy (BRIT), pacifier (US)

chupetín [tʃupe'tin] (RPL) nf lollipop

chupito [tʃu'pito] (fam) nm shot

chupón [tʃu'pon] nm (piruleta) lollipop; (LAM: chupete) dummy (BRIT), pacifier (US)

churro ['tʃurro] nm (type of) fritter

chusma ['tʃusma] nf rabble, mob

chutar [tʃu'tar] vi to shoot (at goal)

Cía abr (= compañía) Co.

cianuro [θja'nuro] nm cyanide

cibercafé [θiβerka'fe] nm cybercafé

cibernauta [θiβer'nauta] nmf web surfer, Internet user

ciberterrorista [θiβerterro'rista] nmf cyberterrorist

cicatriz [θika'triθ] nf scar; **cicatrizarse** vr to heal (up), form a scar

ciclismo [θi'klismo] nm cycling

ciclista [θi'klista] adj cycle cpd ⊳ nmf cyclist

ciclo ['θiklo] nm cycle; **cicloturismo** nm touring by bicycle

ciclón [θi'klon] nm cyclone

ciego, -a ['θjeɣo, a] adj blind ⊳ nm/f blind man/woman

cielo ['θjelo] nm sky; (Rel) heaven; **¡~s!** good heavens!

ciempiés [θjem'pjes] nm inv centipede

cien [θjen] *num* V **ciento**

ciencia ['θjenθja] *nf* science; **ciencias** *nfpl* (*Escol*) science *sg*; **ciencia-ficción** *nf* science fiction

científico, -a [θjen'tifiko, a] *adj* scientific ▷ *nm/f* scientist

ciento ['θjento] *num* hundred; **pagar al 10 por ~** to pay at 10 per cent; V *tb* **cien**

cierre *etc* ['θjerre] *vb* V **cerrar** ▷ *nm* closing, shutting; (*con llave*) locking; (*LAM*: *cremallera*) zip (fastener)

cierro *etc vb* V **cerrar**

cierto, -a ['θjerto, a] *adj* sure, certain; (*un tal*) a certain; (*correcto*) right, correct; **por ~** by the way; **~ hombre** a certain man; **ciertas personas** certain *o* some people; **sí, es ~** yes, that's correct

ciervo ['θjerβo] *nm* deer; (*macho*) stag

cifra ['θifra] *nf* number; (*secreta*) code; **cifrar** [θi'frar] *vt* to code, write in code

cigala [θi'xala] *nf* Norway lobster

cigarra [θi'xarra] *nf* cicada

cigarrillo [θixa'rriʎo] *nm* cigarette

cigarro [θi'xarro] *nm* cigarette; (*puro*) cigar

cigüeña [θi'xweɲa] *nf* stork

cilíndrico, -a [θi'lindriko, a] *adj* cylindrical

cilindro [θi'lindro] *nm* cylinder

cima ['θima] *nf* (*de montaña*) top, peak; (*de árbol*) top; (*fig*) height

cimentar [θimen'tar] *vt* to lay the foundations of; (*fig: fundar*) to found

cimiento [θi'mjento] *nm* foundation

cincel [θin'θel] *nm* chisel

cinco ['θinko] *num* five

cincuenta [θin'kwenta] *num* fifty

cine ['θine] *nm* cinema; **cinematográfico, -a** [θinemato'xrafiko, a] *adj* cine-, film *cpd*

cínico, -a ['θiniko, a] *adj* cynical ▷ *nm/f* cynic

cinismo [θi'nismo] *nm* cynicism

cinta ['θinta] *nf* band, strip; (*de tela*) ribbon; (*película*) reel; (*de máquina de escribir*) ribbon; **cinta adhesiva/aislante** sticky/insulating tape; **cinta de vídeo** videotape; **cinta magnetofónica** tape; **cinta métrica** tape measure

cintura [θin'tura] *nf* waist

cinturón [θintu'ron] *nm* belt; **cinturón de seguridad** safety belt

ciprés [θi'pres] *nm* cypress (tree)

circo ['θirko] *nm* circus

circuito [θir'kwito] *nm* circuit

circulación [θirkula'θjon] *nf* circulation; (*Auto*) traffic

circular [θirku'lar] *adj, nf* circular ▷ *vi, vt* to circulate ▷ *vi* (*Auto*) to drive; **"circule por la derecha"** "keep (to the) right"

círculo ['θirkulo] *nm* circle; **círculo vicioso** vicious circle

circunferencia [θirkunfe'renθja] *nf* circumference

circunstancia [θirkuns'tanθja] *nf* circumstance

cirio ['θirjo] *nm* (wax) candle

ciruela [θi'rwela] *nf* plum; **ciruela pasa** prune

cirugía [θiru'xia] *nf* surgery; **cirugía estética** *o* **plástica** plastic surgery

cirujano [θiru'xano] *nm* surgeon

cisne ['θisne] *nm* swan

cisterna [θis'terna] *nf* cistern, tank

cita ['θita] *nf* appointment, meeting; (*de novios*) date; (*referencia*) quotation

citación [θita'θjon] *nf* (*Jur*) summons *sg*

citar [θi'tar] *vt* (*gen*) to make an appointment with; (*Jur*) to summons; (*un autor, texto*) to quote; **citarse** *vr*: **se ~on en el cine** they arranged to meet at the cinema

cítricos ['θitrikos] *nmpl* citrus fruit(s)

ciudad [θju'ðað] *nf* town; (*más grande*) city; **ciudadano, -a** *nm/f* citizen

cívico, -a ['θiβiko, a] *adj* civic

civil [θi'βil] *adj* civil ▷ *nm* (*guardia*) policeman; **civilización** [θiβiliθa'θjon] *nf* civilization; **civilizar** [θiβili'θar] *vt* to civilize

cizaña [θi'θaɲa] *nf* (*fig*) discord

cl. *abr* (= *centilitro*) cl.

clamor [kla'mor] *nm* clamour, protest

clandestino, -a [klandes'tino, a] *adj* clandestine; (*Pol*) underground

clara ['klara] *nf* (*de huevo*) egg white

claraboya [klara'βoja] *nf* skylight

clarear [klare'ar] *vi* (*el día*) to dawn; (*el cielo*) to clear up, brighten up; **clarearse** *vr* to be transparent

claridad [klari'ðað] *nf* (*de día*) brightness; (*de estilo*) clarity

clarificar [klarifi'kar] *vt* to clarify

clarinete [klari'nete] *nm* clarinet

claro, -a ['klaro, a] *adj* clear; (*luminoso*) bright; (*color*) light; (*evidente*) clear, evident; (*poco espeso*) thin ▷ *nm* (*en bosque*) clearing ▷ *adv* clearly ▷ *excl*: **¡~ que sí!** of course!; **¡~ que no!** of course not!

clase ['klase] *nf* class; **dar ~(s)** to teach; **clase alta/media/obrera** upper/middle/working class; **clases particulares** private lessons *o* tuition *sg*

clásico, -a ['klasiko, a] *adj* classical

clasificación [klasifika'θjon] *nf* classification; (*Deporte*) league (table)

clasificar [klasifi'kar] *vt* to classify

claustro ['klaustro] *nm* cloister

cláusula ['klausula] nf clause
clausura [klau'sura] nf closing, closure
clavar [kla'βar] vt (clavo) to hammer in; (cuchillo) to stick, thrust
clave ['klaβe] nf key; (Mús) clef; **clave de acceso** password; **clave lada** (MÉX) dialling (BRIT) o area (US) code
clavel [kla'βel] nm carnation
clavícula [kla'βikula] nf collar bone
clavija [kla'βixa] nf peg, dowel, pin; (Elec) plug
clavo ['klaβo] nm (de metal) nail; (Bot) clove
claxon ['klakson] (pl ~s) nm horn
clérigo ['klerixo] nm priest
clero ['klero] nm clergy
clicar [kli'kar] vi (Internet) to click; ~ **en el icono** to click on an icon; ~ **dos veces** to double-click
cliché [kli'tʃe] nm cliché; (Foto) negative
cliente, -a ['kljente, a] nm/f client, customer; **clientela** [kljen'tela] nf clientele, customers pl
clima ['klima] nm climate; **climatizado, -a** [klimati'θaðo, a] adj air-conditioned
clímax ['klimaks] nm inv climax
clínica ['klinika] nf clinic; (particular) private hospital
clip [klip] (pl ~s) nm paper clip
clítoris ['klitoris] nm inv (Anat) clitoris
cloaca [klo'aka] nf sewer
clonar [klo'nar] vt to clone
cloro ['kloro] nm chlorine
clóset ['kloset] (MÉX) nm cupboard
club [klub] (pl ~s o ~es) nm club; **club nocturno** night club
cm abr (= centímetro, centímetros) cm
coágulo [ko'aɣulo] nm clot
coalición [koali'θjon] nf coalition
coartada [koar'taða] nf alibi
coartar [koar'tar] vt to limit, restrict
coba ['koβa] nf: **dar ~ a algn** (adular) to suck up to sb
cobarde [ko'βarðe] adj cowardly ▷ nm coward; **cobardía** nf cowardice
cobaya [ko'βaja] nf guinea pig
cobertizo [koβer'tiθo] nm shelter
cobertura [koβer'tura] nf cover; **aquí no hay ~** (Tel) I can't get a signal
cobija [ko'βixa] (LAM) nf blanket; **cobijar** [koβi'xar] vt (cubrir) to cover; (proteger) to shelter; **cobijo** nm shelter
cobra ['koβra] nf cobra
cobrador, a [koβra'ðor, a] nm/f (de autobús) conductor/conductress; (de impuestos, gas) collector
cobrar [ko'βrar] vt (cheque) to cash; (sueldo) to collect, draw; (objeto) to recover; (precio) to charge; (deuda) to collect ▷ vi to be paid;

cóbrese al entregar cash on delivery; **¿me cobra, por favor?** how much do I owe you?, can I have the bill, please?
cobre ['koβre] nm copper; **cobres** nmpl (Mús) brass instruments
cobro ['koβro] nm (de cheque) cashing; **presentar al ~** to cash
cocaína [koka'ina] nf cocaine
cocción [kok'θjon] nf (Culin) cooking; (en agua) boiling
cocer [ko'θer] vt, vi to cook; (en agua) to boil; (en horno) to bake
coche ['kotʃe] nm (Auto) car (BRIT), automobile (US); (de tren, de caballos) coach, carriage; (para niños) pram (BRIT), baby carriage (US); **ir en ~** to drive; **coche celular** police van; **coche de bomberos** fire engine; **coche de carreras** racing car; **coche fúnebre** hearse; **coche-cama** (pl **coches-cama**) nm (Ferro) sleeping car, sleeper
cochera [ko'tʃera] nf garage; (de autobuses, trenes) depot
coche restaurante (pl **coches restaurante**) nm (Ferro) dining car, diner
cochinillo [kotʃi'niʎo] nm (Culin) suckling pig, sucking pig
cochino, -a [ko'tʃino, a] adj filthy, dirty ▷ nm/f pig
cocido [ko'θiðo] nm stew
cocina [ko'θina] nf kitchen; (aparato) cooker, stove; (acto) cookery; **cocina eléctrica/de gas** electric/gas cooker; **cocina francesa** French cuisine; **cocinar** vt, vi to cook
cocinero, -a [koθi'nero, a] nm/f cook
coco ['koko] nm coconut
cocodrilo [koko'ðrilo] nm crocodile
cocotero [koko'tero] nm coconut palm
cóctel ['koktel] nm cocktail; **cóctel molotov** petrol bomb, Molotov cocktail
codazo [ko'ðaθo] nm: **dar un ~ a algn** to nudge sb
codicia [ko'ðiθja] nf greed; **codiciar** vt to covet
código ['koðixo] nm code; **código civil** common law; **código de barras** bar code; **código de circulación** highway code; **código de la zona** (LAM) dialling (BRIT) o area (US) code; **código postal** postcode
codillo [ko'ðiʎo] nm (Zool) knee; (Tec) elbow (joint)
codo ['koðo] nm (Anat, de tubo) elbow; (Zool) knee
codorniz [koðor'niθ] nf quail
coexistir [koe(k)sis'tir] vi to coexist
cofradía [kofra'ðia] nf brotherhood, fraternity
cofre ['kofre] nm (de joyas) case; (de dinero)

chest

coger [ko'xer] (ESP) vt to take (hold of);
(objeto caído) to pick up; (frutas) to pick,
harvest; (resfriado, ladrón, pelota) to catch
▷ vi: ~ por el buen camino to take the right
road; cogerse vr (el dedo) to catch; ~se a
algo to get hold of sth
cogollo [ko'ɣoʎo] nm (de lechuga) heart
cogote [ko'ɣote] nm back o nape of the
neck
cohabitar [koaβi'tar] vi to live together,
cohabit
coherente [koe'rente] adj coherent
cohesión [koe'sjon] nm cohesion
cohete [ko'ete] nm rocket
cohibido, -a [koi'βiðo, a] adj (Psico)
inhibited; (tímido) shy
coincidencia [koinθi'ðenθja] nf
coincidence
coincidir [koinθi'ðir] vi (en idea) to
coincide, agree; (en lugar) to coincide
coito ['koito] nm intercourse, coitus
coja etc vb V coger
cojear [koxe'ar] vi (persona) to limp,
hobble; (mueble) to wobble, rock
cojera [ko'xera] nf limp
cojín [ko'xin] nm cushion
cojo, -a etc ['koxo, a] vb V coger ▷ adj
(que no puede andar) lame, crippled; (mueble)
wobbly ▷ nm/f lame person, cripple
cojón [ko'xon] (fam!) nm: ¡cojones! shit! (!);
cojonudo, -a (fam) adj great, fantastic
col [kol] nf cabbage; coles de Bruselas
Brussels sprouts
cola ['kola] nf tail; (de gente) queue; (lugar)
end, last place; (para pegar) glue, gum; hacer
~ to queue (up)
colaborador, a [kolaβora'ðor, a] nm/f
collaborator
colaborar [kolaβo'rar] vi to collaborate
colada [ko'laða] (ESP) nf: hacer la ~ to do
the washing
colador [kola'ðor] nm (para líquidos)
strainer; (para verduras etc) colander
colapso [ko'lapso] nm collapse
colar [ko'lar] vt (líquido) to strain off;
(metal) to cast ▷ vi to ooze, seep (through);
colarse vr to jump the queue; ~se en to get
into without paying; (fiesta) to gatecrash
colcha ['koltʃa] nf bedspread
colchón [kol'tʃon] nm mattress; colchón
inflable air bed o mattress
colchoneta [koltʃo'neta] nf (en gimnasio)
mat; (de playa) air bed
colección [kolek'θjon] nf collection;
coleccionar vt to collect; coleccionista
nmf collector
colecta [ko'lekta] nf collection

47 | coloquio

colectivo, -a [kolek'tiβo, a] adj
collective, joint ▷ nm (ARG: autobús) (small)
bus
colega [ko'leɣa] nmf colleague;
(ESP: amigo) mate
colegial, a [kole'xjal, a] nm/f
schoolboy(-girl)
colegio [ko'lexjo] nm college; (escuela)
school; (de abogados etc) association;
colegio electoral polling station; colegio
mayor (ESP) hall of residence

  COLEGIO

  A colegio is normally a private primary
  or secondary school. In the state system
  it means a primary school although
  these are also called escuelas. State
  secondary schools are called institutos.

cólera ['kolera] nf (ira) anger; (Med)
cholera
colesterol [koleste'rol] nm cholesterol
coleta [ko'leta] nf pigtail
colgante [kol'ɣante] adj hanging ▷ nm
(joya) pendant
colgar [kol'ɣar] vt to hang (up); (ropa) to
hang out ▷ vi to hang; (Tel) to hang up
cólico ['koliko] nm colic
coliflor [koli'flor] nf cauliflower
colilla [ko'liʎa] nf cigarette end, butt
colina [ko'lina] nf hill
colisión [koli'sjon] nf collision; colisión
frontal head-on crash
collar [ko'ʎar] nm necklace; (de perro) collar
colmar [kol'mar] vt to fill to the brim; (fig)
to fulfil, realize
colmena [kol'mena] nf beehive
colmillo [kol'miʎo] nm (diente) eye tooth;
(de elefante) tusk; (de perro) fang
colmo ['kolmo] nm: ¡es el ~! it's the limit!
colocación [koloka'θjon] nf (acto)
placing; (empleo) job, position
colocar [kolo'kar] vt to place, put,
position; (dinero) to invest; (poner en empleo)
to find a job for; colocarse vr to get a job
Colombia [ko'lombja] nf Colombia;
colombiano, -a adj, nm/f Colombian
colonia [ko'lonja] nf colony; (agua de
colonia) cologne; (MÉX: de casas) residential
area; colonia proletaria (MÉX) shantytown
colonización [koloniθa'θjon]
nf colonization; colonizador, a
[koloniθa'ðor, a] adj colonizing ▷ nm/f
colonist, settler
colonizar [koloni'θar] vt to colonize
coloquio [ko'lokjo] nm conversation;
(congreso) conference

color [ko'lor] *nm* colour
colorado, -a [kolo'raðo, a] *adj* (*rojo*) red; (*MÉX: chiste*) smutty, rude
colorante [kolo'rante] *nm* colouring
colorear [kolore'ar] *vt* to colour
colorete [kolo'rete] *nm* blusher
colorido [kolo'riðo] *nm* colouring
columna [ko'lumna] *nf* column; (*pilar*) pillar; (*apoyo*) support; (*tb:* **~ vertebral**) spine, spinal column; (*fig*) backbone
columpiar [kolum'pjar] *vt* to swing; **columpiarse** *vr* to swing; **columpio** *nm* swing
coma ['koma] *nf* comma ▷ *nm* (*Med*) coma
comadre [ko'maðre] *nf* (*madrina*) godmother; (*chismosa*) gossip; **comadrona** *nf* midwife
comal [ko'mal] (*MÉX, CAM*) *nm* griddle
comandante [koman'dante] *nm* commandant
comarca [ko'marka] *nf* region
comba ['komba] (*ESP*) *nf* (*cuerda*) skipping rope; **saltar a la ~** to skip
combate [kom'bate] *nm* fight
combatir [komba'tir] *vt* to fight, combat
combinación [kombina'θjon] *nf* combination; (*Quím*) compound; (*prenda*) slip
combinar [kombi'nar] *vt* to combine
combustible [kombus'tiβle] *nm* fuel
comedia [ko'meðja] *nf* comedy; (*Teatro*) play, drama; **comediante** [kome'ðjante] *nmf* (*comic*) actor/actress
comedido, -a [kome'ðiðo, a] *adj* moderate
comedor, a [kome'ðor, a] *nm* (*habitación*) dining room; (*cantina*) canteen
comensal [komen'sal] *nmf* fellow guest (*o diner*)
comentar [komen'tar] *vt* to comment on; **comentario** [komen'tarjo] *nm* comment, remark; (*literario*) commentary; **comentarios** *nmpl* (*chismes*) gossip *sg*; **comentarista** [komenta'rista] *nmf* commentator
comenzar [komen'θar] *vt, vi* to begin, start; **~ a hacer algo** to begin *o* start doing sth
comer [ko'mer] *vt* to eat; (*Damas, Ajedrez*) to take, capture ▷ *vi* to eat; (*ESP, MÉX: almorzar*) to have lunch; **comerse** *vr* to eat up
comercial [komer'θjal] *adj* commercial; (*relativo al negocio*) business *cpd*; **comercializar** *vt* (*producto*) to market; (*pey*) to commercialize
comerciante [komer'θjante] *nmf* trader, merchant
comerciar [komer'θjar] *vi* to trade, do business
comercio [ko'merθjo] *nm* commerce, trade; (*tienda*) shop, store; (*negocio*) business; (*fig*) dealings *pl*; **comercio electrónico** e-commerce; **comercio exterior/interior** foreign/domestic trade
comestible [komes'tiβle] *adj* eatable, edible; **comestibles** *nmpl* food *sg*, foodstuffs
cometa [ko'meta] *nm* comet ▷ *nf* kite
cometer [kome'ter] *vt* to commit
cometido [kome'tiðo] *nm* task, assignment
cómic ['komik] *nm* comic
comicios [ko'miθjos] *nmpl* elections
cómico, -a ['komiko, a] *adj* comic(al) ▷ *nm/f* comedian
comida [ko'miða] *nf* (*alimento*) food; (*almuerzo, cena*) meal; (*de mediodía*) lunch; **comida basura** junk food; **comida chatarra** (*MÉX*) junk food
comidilla [komi'ðiʎa] *nf*: **ser la ~ del barrio** *o* **pueblo** to be the talk of the town
comienzo *etc* [ko'mjenθo] *vb* V **comenzar** ▷ *nm* beginning, start
comillas [ko'miʎas] *nfpl* quotation marks
comilona [komi'lona] (*fam*) *nf* blow-out
comino [ko'mino] *nm*: **(no) me importa un ~** I don't give a damn
comisaría [komisa'ria] *nf* (*de policía*) police station; (*Mil*) commissariat
comisario [komi'sarjo] *nm* (*Mil etc*) commissary; (*Pol*) commissar
comisión [komi'sjon] *nf* commission; **Comisiones Obreras** (*ESP*) Communist trade union
comité [komi'te] (*pl* **~s**) *nm* committee
comitiva [komi'tiβa] *nf* retinue
como ['komo] *adv* as; (*tal* **~**) like; (*aproximadamente*) about, approximately ▷ *conj* (*ya que, puesto que*) as, since; **¡~ no!** of course!; **~ no lo haga hoy** unless he does it today; **~ si** as if; **es tan alto ~ ancho** it is as high as it is wide
cómo ['komo] *adv* how?, why? ▷ *excl* what?, I beg your pardon? ▷ *nm*: **el ~ y el porqué** the whys and wherefores
cómoda ['komoða] *nf* chest of drawers
comodidad [komoði'ðað] *nf* comfort
comodín [komo'ðin] *nm* joker
cómodo, -a ['komoðo, a] *adj* comfortable; (*práctico, de fácil uso*) convenient
compact [kom'pakt] (*pl* **~s**) *nm* (*tb:* **~ disc**) compact disk player
compacto, -a [kom'pakto, a] *adj*

compact

compadecer [kompaðe'θer] vt to pity, be sorry for; **compadecerse** vr: **~se de** to pity, be o feel sorry for

compadre [kom'paðre] nm (padrino) godfather; (amigo) friend, pal

compañero, -a [kompa'ɲero, a] nm/f companion; (novio) boy/girlfriend; **compañero de clase** classmate

compañía [kompa'ɲia] nf company; **hacer ~ a algn** to keep sb company

comparación [kompara'θjon] nf comparison; **en ~ con** in comparison with

comparar [kompa'rar] vt to compare

comparecer [kompare'θer] vi to appear (in court)

comparsa [kom'parsa] nmf (Teatro) extra

compartimiento [komparti'mjento] nm (Ferro) compartment

compartir [kompar'tir] vt to share; (dinero, comida etc) to divide (up), share (out)

compás [kom'pas] nm (Mús) beat, rhythm; (Mat) compasses pl; (Náut etc) compass

compasión [kompa'sjon] nf compassion, pity

compasivo, -a [kompa'siβo, a] adj compassionate

compatible [kompa'tiβle] adj compatible

compatriota [kompa'trjota] nmf compatriot, fellow countryman/woman

compenetrarse [kompene'trarse] vr to be in tune

compensación [kompensa'θjon] nf compensation

compensar [kompen'sar] vt to compensate

competencia [kompe'tenθja] nf (incumbencia) domain, field; (Jur, habilidad) competence; (rivalidad) competition

competente [kompe'tente] adj competent

competición [kompeti'θjon] nf competition

competir [kompe'tir] vi to compete

compinche [kom'pintʃe] nmf (LAM) mate, buddy (US)

complacer [kompla'θer] vt to please; **complacerse** vr to be pleased

complaciente [kompla'θjente] adj kind, obliging, helpful

complejo, -a [kom'plexo, a] adj, nm complex

complementario, -a [komplemen'tarjo, a] adj complementary

completar [komple'tar] vt to complete

completo, -a [kom'pleto, a] adj complete; (perfecto) perfect; (lleno) full ▷ nm

full complement

complicado, -a [kompli'kaðo, a] adj complicated; **estar ~ en** to be mixed up in

cómplice ['kompliθe] nmf accomplice

complot [kom'plo(t)] (pl **~s**) nm plot

componer [kompo'ner] vt (Mús, Literatura, Imprenta) to compose; (algo roto) to mend, repair; (arreglar) to arrange; **componerse** vr: **~se de** to consist of

comportamiento [komporta'mjento] nm behaviour, conduct

comportarse [kompor'tarse] vr to behave

composición [komposi'θjon] nf composition

compositor, a [komposi'tor, a] nm/f composer

compostura [kompos'tura] nf (actitud) composure

compra ['kompra] nf purchase; **hacer la ~** to do the shopping; **ir de ~s** to go shopping; **comprador, a** nm/f buyer, purchaser; **comprar** [kom'prar] vt to buy, purchase

comprender [kompren'der] vt to understand; (incluir) to comprise, include

comprensión [kompren'sjon] nf understanding; **comprensivo, -a** adj (actitud) understanding

compresa [kom'presa] nf (para mujer) sanitary towel (BRIT) o napkin (US)

comprimido, -a [kompri'miðo, a] adj compressed ▷ nm (Med) pill, tablet

comprimir [kompri'mir] vt to compress; (Internet) to zip

comprobante [kompro'βante] nm proof; (Com) voucher; **comprobante de compra** proof of purchase

comprobar [kompro'βar] vt to check; (probar) to prove; (Tec) to check, test

comprometer [komprome'ter] vt to compromise; (poner en peligro) to endanger; **comprometerse** vr (involucrarse) to get involved

compromiso [kompro'miso] nm (obligación) obligation; (cometido) commitment; (convenio) agreement; (apuro) awkward situation

compuesto, -a [kom'pwesto, a] adj: **~ de** composed of, made up of ▷ nm compound

computadora [komputa'ðora] (LAM) nf computer; **computadora central** mainframe (computer); **computadora personal** personal computer

cómputo ['komputo] nm calculation

comulgar [komul'ɣar] vi to receive communion

común [ko'mun] adj common ▷ nm: **el ~** the community

comunicación [komunika'θjon] *nf*
communication; (*informe*) report
comunicado [komuni'kaðo] *nm*
announcement; **comunicado de prensa**
press release
comunicar [komuni'kar] *vt, vi* to
communicate; **comunicarse** *vr* to
communicate; **está comunicando** (*Tel*)
the line's engaged (*BRIT*) o busy (*US*);
comunicativo, -a *adj* communicative
comunidad [komuni'ðað] *nf*
community; **comunidad autónoma**
(*ESP*) autonomous region; **Comunidad
(Económica) Europea** European
(Economic) Community; **comunidad de
vecinos** residents' association
comunión [komu'njon] *nf* communion
comunismo [komu'nismo] *nm*
communism; **comunista** *adj, nmf*
communist

○ **PALABRA CLAVE**

con [kon] *prep* **1** (*medio, compañía*) with;
comer con cuchara to eat with a spoon;
pasear con algn to go for a walk with sb
2 (*a pesar de*): **con todo, merece nuestros
respetos** all the same, he deserves our
respect
3 (*para con*): **es muy bueno para con los
niños** he's very good with (the) children
4 (+ *infin*): **con llegar a las seis estará bien**
if you come by six it will be fine ▷ *conj*: **con
que: será suficiente con que le escribas** it
will be sufficient if you write to her

concebir [konθe'βir] *vt, vi* to conceive
conceder [konθe'ðer] *vt* to concede
concejal, a [konθe'xal, a] *nm/f* town
councillor
concentración [konθentra'θjon] *nf*
concentration
concentrar [konθen'trar] *vt* to
concentrate; **concentrarse** *vr* to
concentrate
concepto [kon'θepto] *nm* concept
concernir [konθer'nir] *vi* to concern;
en lo que concierne a ... as far as ... is
concerned; **en lo que a mí concierne** as far
as I'm concerned
concertar [konθer'tar] *vt* (*Mús*) to
harmonize; (*acordar: precio*) to agree;
(: *tratado*) to conclude; (*trato*) to arrange, fix
up; (*combinar: esfuerzos*) to coordinate ▷ *vi*
to harmonize, be in tune
concesión [konθe'sjon] *nf* concession
concesionario [konθesjo'narjo] *nm*
(licensed) dealer, agent

concha ['kontʃa] *nf* shell
conciencia [kon'θjenθja] *nf* conscience;
tomar ~ de to become aware of; **tener la ~
tranquila** to have a clear conscience
concienciar [konθjen'θjar] *vt* to make
aware; **concienciarse** *vr* to become aware
concienzudo, -a [konθjen'θuðo, a] *adj*
conscientious
concierto *etc* [kon'θjerto] *vb* V **concertar**
▷ *nm* concert; (*obra*) concerto
conciliar [konθi'ljar] *vt* to reconcile; **~ el
sueño** to get to sleep
concilio [kon'θiljo] *nm* council
conciso, -a [kon'θiso, a] *adj* concise
concluir [konklu'ir] *vt, vi* to conclude;
concluirse *vr* to conclude
conclusión [konklu'sjon] *nf* conclusion
concordar [konkor'ðar] *vt* to reconcile
▷ *vi* to agree, tally
concordia [kon'korðja] *nf* harmony
concretar [konkre'tar] *vt* to make
concrete, make more specific; **concretarse**
vr to become more definite
concreto, -a [kon'kreto, a] *adj, nm*
(*LAM: hormigón*) concrete; **en ~** (*en resumen*)
to sum up; (*específicamente*) specifically; **no
hay nada en ~** there's nothing definite
concurrido, -a [konku'rriðo, a] *adj* (*calle*)
busy; (*local, reunión*) crowded
concursante [konkur'sante] *nmf*
competitor
concurso [kon'kurso] *nm* (*de público*)
crowd; (*Escol, Deporte, competencia*)
competition; (*ayuda*) help,
cooperation
condal [kon'dal] *adj*: **la Ciudad C~**
Barcelona
conde ['konde] *nm* count
condecoración [kondekora'θjon] *nf*
(*Mil*) medal
condena [kon'dena] *nf* sentence;
condenación [kondena'θjon] *nf*
condemnation; (*Rel*) damnation; **condenar**
[konde'nar] *vt* to condemn; (*Jur*) to convict;
condenarse *vr* (*Rel*) to be damned
condesa [kon'desa] *nf* countess
condición [kondi'θjon] *nf* condition; **a ~
de que ...** on condition that ...; **condicional**
adj conditional
condimento [kondi'mento] *nm*
seasoning
condominio [kondo'minjo] (*LAM*) *nm*
condominium
condón [kon'don] *nm* condom
conducir [kondu'θir] *vt* to take, convey;
(*Auto*) to drive ▷ *vi* to drive; (*fig*) to lead;
conducirse *vr* to behave
conducta [kon'dukta] *nf* conduct,

behaviour

conducto [kon'dukto] *nm* pipe, tube; (*fig*) channel

conductor, a [konduk'tor, a] *adj* leading, guiding ▷ *nm* (*Física*) conductor; (*de vehículo*) driver

conduje *etc vb* V **conducir**

conduzco *etc vb* V **conducir**

conectado, -a [konek'taðo, a] *adj* (*Inform*) on-line

conectar [konek'tar] *vt* to connect (up); (*enchufar*) plug in

conejillo [kone'xiʎo] *nm:* **~ de Indias** guinea pig

conejo [ko'nexo] *nm* rabbit

conexión [konek'sjon] *nf* connection

confección [konfe(k)'θjon] *nf* preparation; (*industria*) clothing industry

confeccionar [konfekθjo'nar] *vt* to make (up)

conferencia [konfe'renθja] *nf* conference; (*lección*) lecture; (*ESP Tel*) call; **conferencia de prensa** press conference

conferir [konfe'rir] *vt* to award

confesar [konfe'sar] *vt* to confess, admit

confesión [konfe'sjon] *nf* confession

confesionario [konfesjo'narjo] *nm* confessional

confeti [kon'feti] *nm* confetti

confiado, -a [kon'fjaðo, a] *adj* (*crédulo*) trusting; (*seguro*) confident

confianza [kon'fjanθa] *nf* trust; (*seguridad*) confidence; (*familiaridad*) intimacy, familiarity

confiar [kon'fjar] *vt* to entrust ▷ *vi* to trust; **~ en algn** to trust sb; **~ en que ...** to hope that ...

confidencial [konfiðen'θjal] *adj* confidential

confidente [konfi'ðente] *nmf* confidant/e; (*policial*) informer

configurar [konfiɣu'rar] *vt* to shape, form

confín [kon'fin] *nm* limit; **confines** *nmpl* confines, limits

confirmar [konfir'mar] *vt* to confirm

confiscar [konfis'kar] *vt* to confiscate

confite [kon'fite] *nm* sweet (BRIT), candy (US); **confitería** [konfite'ria] *nf* (*tienda*) confectioner's (shop)

confitura [konfi'tura] *nf* jam

conflictivo, -a [konflik'tiβo, a] *adj* (*asunto, propuesta*) controversial; (*país, situación*) troubled

conflicto [kon'flikto] *nm* conflict; (*fig*) clash

confluir [kon'flwir] *vi* (*ríos*) to meet; (*gente*) to gather

conformar [konfor'mar] *vt* to shape, fashion ▷ *vi* to agree; **conformarse** *vr* to conform; (*resignarse*) to resign o.s.; **~se con algo** to be happy with sth

conforme [kon'forme] *adj* (*correspondiente*): **~ con** in line with; (*de acuerdo*): **estar ~s (con algo)** to be in agreement (with sth) ▷ *adv* as ▷ *excl* agreed! ▷ *prep:* **~ a** in accordance with; **quedarse ~ (con algo)** to be satisfied (with sth)

confortable [konfor'taβle] *adj* comfortable

confortar [konfor'tar] *vt* to comfort

confrontar [konfron'tar] *vt* to confront; (*dos personas*) to bring face to face; (*cotejar*) to compare

confundir [konfun'dir] *vt* (*equivocar*) to mistake, confuse; (*turbar*) to confuse; **confundirse** *vr* (*turbarse*) to get confused; (*equivocarse*) to make a mistake; (*mezclarse*) to mix

confusión [konfu'sjon] *nf* confusion

confuso, -a [kon'fuso, a] *adj* confused

congelado, -a [konxe'laðo, a] *adj* frozen; **congelados** *nmpl* frozen food(s); **congelador** *nm* (*aparato*) freezer, deep freeze

congelar [konxe'lar] *vt* to freeze; **congelarse** *vr* (*sangre, grasa*) to congeal

congeniar [konxe'njar] *vi* to get on (BRIT) o along (US) well

congestión [konxes'tjon] *nf* congestion

congestionar [konxestjo'nar] *vt* to congest

congraciarse [kongra'θjarse] *vr* to ingratiate o.s.

congratular [kongratu'lar] *vt* to congratulate

congregar [kongre'ɣar] *vt* to gather together; **congregarse** *vr* to gather together

congresista [kongre'sista] *nmf* delegate, congressman/woman

congreso [kon'greso] *nm* congress

conjetura [konxe'tura] *nf* guess; **conjeturar** *vt* to guess

conjugar [konxu'ɣar] *vt* to combine, fit together; (*Ling*) to conjugate

conjunción [konxun'θjon] *nf* conjunction

conjunto, -a [kon'xunto, a] *adj* joint, united ▷ *nm* whole; (*Mús*) band; **en ~** as a whole

conmemoración [konmemora'θjon] *nf* commemoration

conmemorar [konmemo'rar] *vt* to commemorate

conmigo [kon'miɣo] *pron* with me

conmoción [konmo'θjon] *nf* shock; (*fig*) upheaval; **conmoción cerebral** (*Med*) concussion

conmovedor, a [konmoβe'ðor, a] *adj* touching, moving; (*emocionante*) exciting

conmover [konmo'βer] *vt* to shake, disturb; (*fig*) to move

conmutador [konmuta'ðor] *nm* switch; (*LAM: centralita*) switchboard; (: *central*) telephone exchange

cono ['kono] *nm* cone; **Cono Sur** Southern Cone

conocedor, a [konoθe'ðor, a] *adj* expert, knowledgeable ▷ *nm/f* expert

conocer [kono'θer] *vt* to know; (*por primera vez*) to meet, get to know; (*entender*) to know about; (*reconocer*) to recognize; **conocerse** *vr* (*una persona*) to know o.s.; (*dos personas*) to (get to) know each other; **~ a algn de vista** to know sb by sight

conocido, -a [kono'θiðo, a] *adj* (well-) known ▷ *nm/f* acquaintance

conocimiento [konoθi'mjento] *nm* knowledge; (*Med*) consciousness; **conocimientos** *nmpl* (*saber*) knowledge *sg*

conozco *etc vb* V **conocer**

conque ['konke] *conj* and so, so then

conquista [kon'kista] *nf* conquest; **conquistador, a** *adj* conquering ▷ *nm* conqueror; **conquistar** [konkis'tar] *vt* to conquer

consagrar [konsa'ɣrar] *vt* (*Rel*) to consecrate; (*fig*) to devote

consciente [kons'θjente] *adj* conscious

consecución [konseku'θjon] *nf* acquisition; (*de fin*) attainment

consecuencia [konse'kwenθja] *nf* consequence, outcome; (*coherencia*) consistency

consecuente [konse'kwente] *adj* consistent

consecutivo, -a [konseku'tiβo, a] *adj* consecutive

conseguir [konse'ɣir] *vt* to get, obtain; (*objetivo*) to attain

consejero, -a [konse'xero, a] *nm/f* adviser, consultant; (*Pol*) councillor

consejo [kon'sexo] *nm* advice; (*Pol*) council; **consejo de administración** (*Com*) board of directors; **consejo de guerra** court martial; **consejo de ministros** cabinet meeting

consenso [kon'senso] *nm* consensus

consentimiento [konsenti'mjento] *nm* consent

consentir [konsen'tir] *vt* (*permitir, tolerar*) to consent to; (*mimar*) to pamper, spoil;

(*aguantar*) to put up with ▷ *vi* to agree, consent; **~ que algn haga algo** to allow sb to do sth

conserje [kon'serxe] *nm* caretaker; (*portero*) porter

conservación [konserβa'θjon] *nf* conservation; (*de alimentos, vida*) preservation

conservador, a [konserβa'ðor, a] *adj* (*Pol*) conservative ▷ *nm/f* conservative

conservante [konser'βante] *nm* preservative

conservar [konser'βar] *vt* to conserve, keep; (*alimentos, vida*) to preserve; **conservarse** *vr* to survive

conservas [kon'serβas] *nfpl* canned food(s) *pl*

conservatorio [konserβa'torjo] *nm* (*Mús*) conservatoire, conservatory

considerable [konsiðe'raβle] *adj* considerable

consideración [konsiðera'θjon] *nf* consideration; (*estimación*) respect

considerado, -a [konsiðe'raðo, a] *adj* (*atento*) considerate; (*respetado*) respected

considerar [konsiðe'rar] *vt* to consider

consigna [kon'siɣna] *nf* (*orden*) order, instruction; (*para equipajes*) left-luggage office

consigo *etc* [kon'siɣo] *vb* V **conseguir** ▷ *pron* (*m*) with him; (*f*) with her; (*Vd*) with you; (*reflexivo*) with o.s.

consiguiendo *etc vb* V **conseguir**

consiguiente [konsi'ɣjente] *adj* consequent; **por ~** and so, therefore, consequently

consistente [konsis'tente] *adj* consistent; (*sólido*) solid, firm; (*válido*) sound

consistir [konsis'tir] *vi*: **~ en** (*componerse de*) to consist of

consola [kon'sola] *nf* (*mueble*) console table; (*de videojuegos*) console

consolación [konsola'θjon] *nf* consolation

consolar [konso'lar] *vt* to console

consolidar [konsoli'ðar] *vt* to consolidate

consomé [konso'me] (*pl* **~s**) *nm* consommé, clear soup

consonante [konso'nante] *adj* consonant, harmonious ▷ *nf* consonant

consorcio [kon'sorθjo] *nm* consortium

conspiración [konspira'θjon] *nf* conspiracy

conspirar [konspi'rar] *vi* to conspire

constancia [kons'tanθja] *nf* constancy; **dejar ~ de** to put on record

constante [kons'tante] *adj, nf* constant

constar [kons'tar] *vi* (*evidenciarse*) to be

clear o evident; **~ de** to consist of

constipado, -a [konsti'paðo, a]
adj: **estar ~** to have a cold ▷ nm cold
▌ No confundir **constipado** con la palabra
inglesa *constipated*.

constitución [konstitu'θjon] nf
constitution

constituir [konstitu'ir] vt (*formar,
componer*) to constitute, make up; (*fundar,
erigir, ordenar*) to constitute, establish

construcción [konstruk'θjon] nf
construction, building

constructor, a [konstruk'tor, a] nm/f
builder

construir [konstru'ir] vt to build,
construct

construyendo etc vb V **construir**

consuelo [kon'swelo] nm consolation,
solace

cónsul ['konsul] nm consul; **consulado**
nm consulate

consulta [kon'sulta] nf consultation;
(*Med*): **horas de ~** surgery hours; **consultar**
[konsul'tar] vt to consult; **consultar
algo con algn** to discuss sth with sb;
consultorio [konsul'torjo] nm (*Med*)
surgery

consumición [konsumi'θjon] nf
consumption; (*bebida*) drink; (*comida*) food;
consumición mínima cover charge

consumidor, a [konsumi'ðor, a] nm/f
consumer

consumir [konsu'mir] vt to consume;
consumirse vr to be consumed; (*persona*)
to waste away

consumismo [konsu'mismo] nm
consumerism

consumo [kon'sumo] nm consumption

contabilidad [kontaβili'ðað] nf
accounting, book-keeping; (*profesión*)
accountancy; **contable** nmf accountant

contacto [kon'takto] nm contact; (*Auto*)
ignition; **estar/ponerse en ~ con algn** to
be/to get in touch with sb

contado, -a [kon'taðo, a] adj: **~s** (*escasos*)
numbered, scarce, few ▷ nm: **pagar al ~** to
pay (in) cash

contador [konta'ðor] nm (*ESP: aparato*)
meter ▷ nmf (*LAM Com*) accountant

contagiar [konta'xjar] vt (*enfermedad*)
to pass on, transmit; (*persona*) to infect;
contagiarse vr to become infected

contagio [kon'taxjo] nm infection;
contagioso, -a adj infectious; (*fig*)
catching

contaminación [kontamina'θjon] nf
contamination; (*polución*) pollution

contaminar [kontami'nar] vt to
contaminate; (*aire, agua*) to pollute

contante [kon'tante] adj: **dinero ~ (y
sonante)** cash

contar [kon'tar] vt (*páginas, dinero*) to
count; (*anécdota, chiste etc*) to tell ▷ vi to
count; **~ con** to rely on, count on

contemplar [kontem'plar] vt to
contemplate; (*mirar*) to look at

contemporáneo, -a [kontempo'raneo,
a] adj, nm/f contemporary

contenedor [kontene'ðor] nm container

contener [konte'ner] vt to contain, hold;
(*retener*) to hold back, contain; **contenerse**
vr to control o restrain o.s.

contenido, -a [konte'niðo, a] adj
(*moderado*) restrained; (*risa etc*) suppressed
▷ nm contents pl, content

contentar [konten'tar] vt (*satisfacer*) to
satisfy; (*complacer*) to please; **contentarse**
vr to be satisfied

contento, -a [kon'tento, a] adj (*alegre*)
pleased; (*feliz*) happy

contestación [kontesta'θjon] nf answer,
reply

contestador [kontesta'ðor] nm (*tb: ~
automático*) answering machine

contestar [kontes'tar] vt to answer, reply;
(*Jur*) to corroborate, confirm
▌ No confundir **contestar** con la palabra
inglesa *contest*.

contexto [kon'te(k)sto] nm context

contigo [kon'tixo] pron with you

contiguo, -a [kon'tixwo, a] adj adjacent,
adjoining

continente [konti'nente] adj, nm
continent

continuación [kontinwa'θjon] nf
continuation; **a ~** then, next

continuar [konti'nwar] vt to continue,
go on with ▷ vi to continue, go on; **~
hablando** to continue talking o to talk

continuidad [kontinwi'ðað] nf
continuity

continuo, -a [kon'tinwo, a] adj (*sin
interrupción*) continuous; (*acción perseverante*)
continual

contorno [kon'torno] nm outline; (*Geo*)
contour; **contornos** nmpl neighbourhood
sg, surrounding area sg

contra ['kontra] prep, adv against ▷ nm inv
con ▷ nf: **la C~** (*de Nicaragua*) the Contras pl

contraataque [kontraa'take] nm
counter-attack

contrabajo [kontra'βaxo] nm double
bass

contrabandista [kontraβan'dista] nmf
smuggler

contrabando [kontra'βando] nm (*acción*)

smuggling; (*mercancías*) contraband

contracción [kontrak'θjon] *nf* contraction

contracorriente [kontrako'rrjente] *nf* cross-current

contradecir [kontraðe'θir] *vt* to contradict

contradicción [kontraðik'θjon] *nf* contradiction

contradictorio, -a [kontraðik'torjo, a] *adj* contradictory

contraer [kontra'er] *vt* to contract; (*limitar*) to restrict; **contraerse** *vr* to contract; (*limitarse*) to limit o.s.

contraluz [kontra'luθ] *nm* view against the light

contrapartida [kontrapar'tiða] *nf*: **como ~ (de)** in return (for)

contrapelo [kontra'pelo]: **a ~** *adv* the wrong way

contrapeso [kontra'peso] *nm* counterweight

contraportada [kontrapor'taða] *nf* (*de revista*) back cover

contraproducente [kontraproðu'θente] *adj* counterproductive

contrario, -a [kon'trarjo, a] *adj* contrary; (*persona*) opposed; (*sentido, lado*) opposite ▷ *nm/f* enemy, adversary; (*Deporte*) opponent; **al** *o* **por el ~** on the contrary; **de lo ~** otherwise

contrarreloj [kontrarre'lo] *nf* (*tb*: **prueba ~**) time trial

contrarrestar [kontrarres'tar] *vt* to counteract

contrasentido [kontrasen'tiðo] *nm* (*contradicción*) contradiction

contraseña [kontra'seɲa] *nf* (*Inform*) password

contrastar [kontras'tar] *vt, vi* to contrast

contraste [kon'traste] *nm* contrast

contratar [kontra'tar] *vt firmar un acuerdo para*, to contract for; (*empleados, obreros*) to hire, engage

contratiempo [kontra'tjempo] *nm* setback

contratista [kontra'tista] *nmf* contractor

contrato [kon'trato] *nm* contract

contraventana [kontraβen'tana] *nf* shutter

contribución [kontriβu'θjon] *nf* (*municipal etc*) tax; (*ayuda*) contribution

contribuir [kontriβu'ir] *vt, vi* to contribute; (*Com*) to pay (in taxes)

contribuyente [kontriβu'jente] *nmf* (*Com*) taxpayer; (*que ayuda*) contributor

contrincante [kontrin'kante] *nmf* opponent

control [kon'trol] *nm* control; (*inspección*) inspection, check; **control de pasaportes** passport inspection; **controlador, a** *nm/f* controller; **controlador aéreo** air-traffic controller; **controlar** [kontro'lar] *vt* to control; (*inspeccionar*) to inspect, check

contundente [kontun'dente] *adj* (*instrumento*) blunt; (*argumento, derrota*) overwhelming

contusión [kontu'sjon] *nf* bruise

convalecencia [kombale'θenθja] *nf* convalescence

convalecer [kombale'θer] *vi* to convalesce, get better

convalidar [kombali'ðar] *vt* (*título*) to recognize

convencer [komben'θer] *vt* to convince; **~ a algn (de** *o* **para hacer algo)** to persuade sb (to do sth)

convención [komben'θjon] *nf* convention

conveniente [kombe'njente] *adj* suitable; (*útil*) useful

convenio [kom'benjo] *nm* agreement, treaty

convenir [kombe'nir] *vi* (*estar de acuerdo*) to agree; (*venir bien*) to suit, be suitable

▌ No confundir **convenir** con la palabra inglesa *convene*.

convento [kom'bento] *nm* convent

convenza *etc vb* V **convencer**

convergir [komber'xir] *vi* = **converger**

conversación [kombersa'θjon] *nf* conversation

conversar [komber'sar] *vi* to talk, converse

conversión [komber'sjon] *nf* conversion

convertir [komber'tir] *vt* to convert

convidar [kombi'ðar] *vt* to invite; **~ a algn a una cerveza** to buy sb a beer

convincente [kombin'θente] *adj* convincing

convite [kom'bite] *nm* invitation; (*banquete*) banquet

convivencia [kombi'βenθja] *nf* coexistence, living together

convivir [kombi'βir] *vi* to live together

convocar [kombo'kar] *vt* to summon, call (together)

convocatoria [komboka'torja] *nf* (*de oposiciones, elecciones*) notice; (*de huelga*) call

cónyuge ['konjuxe] *nmf* spouse

coñac [ko'na(k)] (*pl* **~s**) *nm* cognac, brandy

coño ['koɲo] (*fam!*) *excl* (*enfado*) shit! (*!*); (*sorpresa*) bloody hell! (*!*)

cool [kul] *adj* (*fam*) cool

cooperación [koopera'θjon] *nf* cooperation

cooperar [koope'rar] *vi* to cooperate

cooperativa [koopera'tiβa] *nf* cooperative

coordinadora [koorðina'ðora] *nf* (*comité*) coordinating committee

coordinar [koorði'nar] *vt* to coordinate

copa ['kopa] *nf* cup; (*vaso*) glass; (*bebida*): **tomar una ~** (to have a) drink; (*de árbol*) top; (*de sombrero*) crown; **copas** *nfpl* (*Naipes*) ≈ hearts

copia ['kopja] *nf* copy; **copia de respaldo** *o* **seguridad** (*Inform*) back-up copy; **copiar** *vt* to copy

copla ['kopla] *nf* verse; (*canción*) (popular) song

copo ['kopo] *nm*: **~ de nieve** snowflake; **~s de maíz** cornflakes

coqueta [ko'keta] *adj* flirtatious, coquettish; **coquetear** *vi* to flirt

coraje [ko'raxe] *nm* courage; (*ánimo*) spirit; (*ira*) anger

coral [ko'ral] *adj* choral ▷ *nf* (*Mús*) choir ▷ *nm* (*Zool*) coral

coraza [ko'raθa] *nf* (*armadura*) armour; (*blindaje*) armour-plating

corazón [kora'θon] *nm* heart

corazonada [koraθo'naða] *nf* impulse; (*presentimiento*) hunch

corbata [kor'βata] *nf* tie

corchete [kor'tʃete] *nm* catch, clasp

corcho ['kortʃo] *nm* cork; (*Pesca*) float

cordel [kor'ðel] *nm* cord, line

cordero [kor'ðero] *nm* lamb

cordial [kor'ðjal] *adj* cordial

cordillera [korði'ʎera] *nf* range (of mountains)

Córdoba ['korðoβa] *n* Cordova

cordón [kor'ðon] *nm* (*cuerda*) cord, string; (*de zapatos*) lace; (*Mil etc*) cordon; **cordón umbilical** umbilical cord

cordura [kor'ðura] *nf*: **con ~** (*obrar, hablar*) sensibly

corneta [kor'neta] *nf* bugle

cornisa [kor'nisa] *nf* (*Arq*) cornice

coro ['koro] *nm* chorus; (*conjunto de cantores*) choir

corona [ko'rona] *nf* crown; (*de flores*) garland

coronel [koro'nel] *nm* colonel

coronilla [koro'niʎa] *nf* (*Anat*) crown (of the head)

corporal [korpo'ral] *adj* corporal, bodily

corpulento, -a [korpu'lento, a] *adj* (*persona*) heavily-built

corral [ko'rral] *nm* farmyard

correa [ko'rrea] *nf* strap; (*cinturón*) belt; (*de perro*) lead, leash; **correa del ventilador** (*Auto*) fan belt

corrección [korrek'θjon] *nf* correction; (*reprensión*) rebuke; **correccional** *nm* reformatory

correcto, -a [ko'rrekto, a] *adj* correct; (*persona*) well-mannered

corredizo, -a [korre'ðiθo, a] *adj* (*puerta etc*) sliding

corredor, a [korre'ðor, a] *nm* (*pasillo*) corridor; (*balcón corrido*) gallery; (*Com*) agent, broker ▷ *nm/f* (*Deporte*) runner

corregir [korre'xir] *vt* (*error*) to correct; **corregirse** *vr* to reform

correo [ko'rreo] *nm* post, mail; (*persona*) courier; **Correos** *nmpl* (*ESP*) Post Office *sg*; **correo aéreo** airmail; **correo basura** (*Inform*) spam; **correo electrónico** e-mail, electronic mail; **correo web** webmail

correr [ko'rrer] *vt* to run; (*cortinas*) to draw; (*cerrojo*) to shoot ▷ *vi* to run; (*líquido*) to run, flow; **correrse** *vr* to slide, move; (*colores*) to run

correspondencia [korrespon'denθja] *nf* correspondence; (*Ferro*) connection

corresponder [korrespon'der] *vi* to correspond; (*convenir*) to be suitable; (*pertenecer*) to belong; (*concernir*) to concern; **corresponderse** *vr* (*por escrito*) to correspond; (*amarse*) to love one another

correspondiente [korrespon'djente] *adj* corresponding

corresponsal [korrespon'sal] *nmf* correspondent

corrida [ko'rriða] *nf* (*de toros*) bullfight

corrido, -a [ko'rriðo, a] *adj* (*avergonzado*) abashed; **un kilo ~** a good kilo

corriente [ko'rrjente] *adj* (*agua*) running; (*dinero etc*) current; (*común*) ordinary, normal ▷ *nf* current ▷ *nm* current month; **estar al ~ de** to be informed about; **corriente eléctrica** electric current

corrija *etc vb* V **corregir**

corro ['korro] *nm* ring, circle (of people)

corromper [korrom'per] *vt* (*madera*) to rot; (*fig*) to corrupt

corrosivo, -a [korro'siβo, a] *adj* corrosive

corrupción [korrup'θjon] *nf* rot, decay; (*fig*) corruption

corsé [kor'se] *nm* corset

cortacésped [korta'θespeð] *nm* lawn mower

cortado, -a [kor'taðo, a] *adj* (*gen*) cut; (*leche*) sour; (*tímido*) shy; (*avergonzado*) embarrassed ▷ *nm* coffee (with a little milk)

cortafuegos [korta'fweɣos] *nm inv* (*en el bosque*) firebreak, fire lane (*US*); (*Internet*) firewall

cortar [kor'tar] *vt* to cut; (*suministro*) to

cut off; (*un pasaje*) to cut out ▷ *vi* to cut;
cortarse *vr* (*avergonzarse*) to become
embarrassed; (*leche*) to turn, curdle; **~se el
pelo** to have one's hair cut
cortauñas [korta'uɲas] *nm inv* nail
clippers *pl*
corte ['korte] *nm* cut, cutting; (*de tela*)
piece, length ▷ *nf*: **las C~s** the Spanish
Parliament; **corte de luz** power cut; **corte y
confección** dressmaking
cortejo [kor'texo] *nm* entourage; **cortejo
fúnebre** funeral procession
cortés [kor'tes] *adj* courteous, polite
cortesía [korte'sia] *nf* courtesy
corteza [kor'teθa] *nf* (*de árbol*) bark; (*de
pan*) crust
cortijo [kor'tixo] (*ESP*) *nm* farm,
farmhouse
cortina [kor'tina] *nf* curtain
corto, -a ['korto, a] *adj* (*breve*) short;
(*tímido*) bashful; **~ de luces** not very bright;
~ de vista short-sighted; **estar ~ de fondos**
to be short of funds; **cortocircuito** *nm*
short circuit; **cortometraje** *nm* (*Cine*) short
cosa ['kosa] *nf* thing; **~ de** about; **eso es ~
mía** that's my business
coscorrón [kosko'rron] *nm* bump on
the head
cosecha [ko'setʃa] *nf* (*Agr*) harvest; (*de
vino*) vintage; **cosechar** [kose'tʃar] *vt* to
harvest, gather (in)
coser [ko'ser] *vt* to sew
cosmético, -a [kos'metiko, a] *adj, nm*
cosmetic
cosquillas [kos'kiʎas] *nfpl*: **hacer ~** to
tickle; **tener ~** to be ticklish
costa ['kosta] *nf* (*Geo*) coast; **a toda ~** at
all costs; **Costa Brava** Costa Brava; **Costa
Cantábrica** Cantabrian Coast; **Costa del
Sol** Costa del Sol
costado [kos'taðo] *nm* side
costanera [kosta'nera] (*cs*) *nf*
promenade, sea front
costar [kos'tar] *vt* (*valer*) to cost; **me
cuesta hablarle** I find it hard to talk to him
Costa Rica [kosta'rika] *nf* Costa Rica;
costarricense *adj, nmf* Costa Rican;
costarriqueño, -a *adj, nm/f* Costa Rican
coste ['koste] *nm* = **costo**
costear [koste'ar] *vt* to pay for
costero, -a [kos'tero, a] *adj* (*pueblecito,
camino*) coastal
costilla [kos'tiʎa] *nf* rib; (*Culin*) cutlet
costo ['kosto] *nm* cost, price; **costo de (la)
vida** cost of living; **costoso, -a** *adj* costly,
expensive
costra ['kostra] *nf* (*corteza*) crust; (*Med*)
scab

costumbre [kos'tumbre] *nf* custom,
habit
costura [kos'tura] *nf* sewing, needlework;
(*zurcido*) seam
costurera [kostu'rera] *nf* dressmaker
costurero [kostu'rero] *nm* sewing box
o case
cotidiano, -a [koti'ðjano, a] *adj* daily,
day to day
cotilla [ko'tiʎa] (*ESP: fam*) *nmf* gossip;
cotillear (*ESP*) *vi* to gossip; **cotilleo** (*ESP*)
nm gossip(ing)
cotizar [koti'θar] *vt* (*Com*) to quote, price;
cotizarse *vr*: **~se a** to sell at, fetch; (*Bolsa*) to
stand at, be quoted at
coto ['koto] *nm* (*terreno cercado*) enclosure;
(*de caza*) reserve
cotorra [ko'torra] *nf* parrot
coyote [ko'jote] *nm* coyote, prairie wolf
coz [koθ] *nf* kick
crack [krak] *nm* (*droga*) crack
cráneo ['kraneo] *nm* skull, cranium
cráter ['krater] *nm* crater
crayón [kra'jon] (*MÉX, RPL*) *nm* crayon,
chalk
creación [krea'θjon] *nf* creation
creador, a [krea'ðor, a] *adj* creative
▷ *nm/f* creator
crear [kre'ar] *vt* to create, make
crecer [kre'θer] *vi* to grow; (*precio*) to rise
creces ['kreθes]: **con ~** *adv* amply, fully
crecido, -a [kre'θiðo, a] *adj* (*persona,
planta*) full-grown; (*cantidad*) large
crecimiento [kreθi'mjento] *nm* growth;
(*aumento*) increase
credencial [kreðen'θjal] *nf* (*LAM: tarjeta*)
card; **credenciales** *nfpl* credentials;
credencial de socio (*LAM*) membership card
crédito ['kreðito] *nm* credit
credo ['kreðo] *nm* creed
creencia [kre'enθja] *nf* belief
creer [kre'er] *vt, vi* to think, believe;
creerse *vr* to believe o.s. (to be); **~ en** to
believe in; **creo que sí/no** I think/don't
think so; **¡ya lo creo!** I should think so!
creído, -a [kre'iðo, a] *adj* (*engreído*)
conceited
crema ['krema] *nf* cream; **crema batida**
(*LAM*) whipped cream; **crema pastelera**
(confectioner's) custard
cremallera [krema'ʎera] *nf* zip (fastener)
crepe ['krepe] (*ESP*) *nf* pancake
cresta ['kresta] *nf* (*Geo, Zool*) crest
creyendo *etc vb* V **creer**
creyente [kre'jente] *nmf* believer
creyó *etc vb* V **creer**
crezco *etc vb* V **crecer**
cría *etc* ['kria] *vb* V **criar** ▷ *nf* (*de animales*)

rearing, breeding; (*animal*) young; V tb **crío**

criadero [kria'ðero] nm (*Zool*) breeding place

criado, -a [kri'aðo, a] nm servant ▷ nf servant, maid

criador [kria'ðor] nm breeder

crianza [kri'anθa] nf rearing, breeding; (*fig*) breeding

criar [kri'ar] vt (*educar*) to bring up; (*producir*) to grow, produce; (*animales*) to breed

criatura [kria'tura] nf creature; (*niño*) baby, (small) child

cribar [kri'βar] vt to sieve

crimen ['krimen] nm crime

criminal [krimi'nal] adj, nmf criminal

crines ['krines] nfpl mane

crío, -a ['krio, a] (*fam*) nm/f (*niño*) kid

crisis ['krisis] nf inv crisis; **crisis nerviosa** nervous breakdown

crismas ['krismas] (*ESP*) nm inv Christmas card

cristal [kris'tal] nm crystal; (*de ventana*) glass, pane; (*lente*) lens; **cristalino, -a** adj crystalline; (*fig*) clear ▷ nm lens (of the eye)

cristianismo [kristja'nismo] nm Christianity

cristiano, -a [kris'tjano, a] adj, nm/f Christian

Cristo ['kristo] nm Christ; (*crucifijo*) crucifix

criterio [kri'terjo] nm criterion; (*juicio*) judgement

crítica ['kritika] nf criticism; V tb **crítico**

criticar [kriti'kar] vt to criticize

crítico, -a ['kritiko, a] adj critical ▷ nm/f critic

Croacia [kro'aθja] nf Croatia

cromo ['kromo] nm chrome

crónica ['kronika] nf chronicle, account

crónico, -a ['kroniko, a] adj chronic

cronómetro [kro'nometro] nm stopwatch

croqueta [kro'keta] nf croquette

cruce etc ['kruθe] vb V **cruzar** ▷ nm (*para peatones*) crossing; (*de carreteras*) crossroads

crucero [kru'θero] nm (*viaje*) cruise

crucificar [kruθifi'kar] vt to crucify

crucifijo [kruθi'fixo] nm crucifix

crucigrama [kruθi'ɣrama] nm crossword (puzzle)

cruda ['kruða] (*MÉX, CAM: fam*) nf hangover

crudo, -a ['kruðo, a] adj raw; (*no maduro*) unripe; (*petróleo*) crude; (*rudo, cruel*) cruel ▷ nm crude (oil)

cruel [krwel] adj cruel; **crueldad** nf cruelty

crujiente [kru'xjente] adj (*galleta etc*) crunchy

crujir [kru'xir] vi (*madera etc*) to creak; (*dedos*) to crack; (*dientes*) to grind; (*nieve, arena*) to crunch

cruz [kruθ] nf cross; (*de moneda*) tails sg; **cruz gamada** swastika

cruzada [kru'θaða] nf crusade

cruzado, -a [kru'θaðo, a] adj crossed ▷ nm crusader

cruzar [kru'θar] vt to cross; **cruzarse** vr (*líneas etc*) to cross; (*personas*) to pass each other

Cruz Roja nf Red Cross

cuaderno [kwa'ðerno] nm notebook; (*de escuela*) exercise book; (*Náut*) logbook

cuadra ['kwaðra] nf (*caballeriza*) stable; (*LAM: entre calles*) block

cuadrado, -a [kwa'ðraðo, a] adj square ▷ nm (*Mat*) square

cuadrar [kwa'ðrar] vt to square ▷ vi: ~ **con** to square with, tally with; **cuadrarse** vr (*soldado*) to stand to attention

cuadrilátero [kwaðri'latero] nm (*Deporte*) boxing ring; (*Geom*) quadrilateral

cuadrilla [kwa'ðriʎa] nf party, group

cuadro ['kwaðro] nm square; (*Arte*) painting; (*Teatro*) scene; (*diagrama*) chart; (*Deporte, Med*) team; **tela a ~s** checked (*BRIT*) o chequered (*US*) material

cuajar [kwa'xar] vt (*leche*) to curdle; (*sangre*) to congeal; (*Culin*) to set; **cuajarse** vr to curdle; to congeal; to set; (*llenarse*) to fill up

cuajo ['kwaxo] nm: **de ~** (*arrancar*) by the roots; (*cortar*) completely

cual [kwal] adv like, as ▷ pron: **el** etc ~ which; (*persona sujeto*) who; (: *objeto*) whom ▷ adj such as; **cada ~** each one; **déjalo tal ~** leave it just as it is

cuál [kwal] pron interr which (one)

cualesquier, a [kwales'kjer(a)] pl de **cualquier(a)**

cualidad [kwali'ðað] nf quality

cualquier [kwal'kjer] adj V **cualquiera**

cualquiera [kwal'kjera] (pl **cualesquiera**) adj (*delante de nm y f* **cualquier**) any ▷ pron anybody; **un coche ~ servirá** any car will do; **no es un hombre ~** he isn't just anybody; **cualquier día/libro** any day/ book; **eso ~ lo sabe hacer** anybody can do that; **es un ~** he's a nobody

cuando ['kwando] adv when; (*aún si*) if, even if ▷ conj (*puesto que*) since ▷ prep: **yo, ~ niño ...** when I was a child ...; **~ no sea así** even if it is not so; **~ más** at (the) most; **~ menos** at least; **~ no** if not, otherwise; **de ~ en ~** from time to time

cuándo ['kwando] adv when; **¿desde ~?**

since when?
cuantía [kwan'tia] *nf* extent

○ **PALABRA CLAVE**

cuanto, -a ['kwanto, a] *adj* **1**(*todo*):
tiene todo cuanto desea he's got
everything he wants; **le daremos cuantos
ejemplares necesite** we'll give him as many
copies as o all the copies he needs; **cuantos
hombres la ven** all the men who see her
**2 unos cuantos: había unos cuantos
periodistas** there were a few journalists
3 (+ *más*): **cuanto más vino bebes peor te
sentirás** the more wine you drink the worse
you'll feel
▷ *pron*: **tiene cuanto desea** he has
everything he wants; **tome cuanto/
cuantos quiera** take as much/many as
you want
▷ *adv*: **en cuanto: en cuanto profesor** as
a teacher; **en cuanto a mí** as for me; V *tb*
antes
▷ *conj* **1 cuanto más gana menos gasta**
the more he earns the less he spends;
cuanto más joven más confiado the
younger you are the more trusting you are
2 en cuanto: en cuanto llegue/llegué as
soon as I arrive/arrived

cuánto, -a ['kwanto, a] *adj* (*exclamación*)
what a lot of; (*interr: sg*) how much?; (: *pl*)
how many? ▷ *pron, adv* how; (: *interr: sg*)
how much?; (: *pl*) how many?; **¡cuánta
gente!** what a lot of people!; **¿~ cuesta?**
how much does it cost?; **¿a ~s estamos?**
what's the date?
cuarenta [kwa'renta] *num* forty
cuarentena [kwaren'tena] *nf* quarantine
cuaresma [kwa'resma] *nf* Lent
cuarta ['kwarta] *nf* (*Mat*) quarter, fourth;
(*palmo*) span
cuartel [kwar'tel] *nm* (*Mil*) barracks *pl*;
cuartel de bomberos (*RPL*) fire station;
cuartel general headquarters *pl*
cuarteto [kwar'teto] *nm* quartet
cuarto, -a ['kwarto, a] *adj* fourth ▷ *nm*
(*Mat*) quarter, fourth; (*habitación*) room;
cuarto de baño bathroom; **cuarto de estar**
living room; **cuarto de hora** quarter (of an)
hour; **cuarto de kilo** quarter kilo; **cuartos
de final** quarter finals
cuatro ['kwatro] *num* four
Cuba ['kuβa] *nf* Cuba
cuba ['kuβa] *nf* cask, barrel
cubano, -a [ku'βano, a] *adj, nm/f* Cuban
cubata [ku'βata] *nm* (*fam*) large drink (*of
rum and coke etc*)

cubeta [ku'βeta] (*ESP, MÉX*) *nf* (*balde*)
bucket, tub
cúbico, -a ['kuβiko, a] *adj* cubic
cubierta [ku'βjerta] *nf* cover, covering;
(*neumático*) tyre; (*Náut*) deck
cubierto, -a [ku'βjerto, a] *pp de* **cubrir**
▷ *adj* covered ▷ *nm* cover; (*lugar en la mesa*)
place; **cubiertos** *nmpl* cutlery *sg*; **a ~** under
cover
cubilete [kuβi'lete] *nm* (*en juegos*) cup
cubito [ku'βito] *nm* (*tb*: **~ de hielo**)
ice-cube
cubo ['kuβo] *nm* (*Mat*) cube; (*ESP: balde*)
bucket, tub; (*Tec*) drum; **cubo de (la) basura**
dustbin (*BRIT*), trash can (*US*)
cubrir [ku'βrir] *vt* to cover; **cubrirse** *vr*
(*cielo*) to become overcast
cucaracha [kuka'ratʃa] *nf* cockroach
cuchara [ku'tʃara] *nf* spoon; (*Tec*) scoop;
cucharada *nf* spoonful; **cucharadita** *nf*
teaspoonful
cucharilla [kutʃa'riʎa] *nf* teaspoon
cucharón [kutʃa'ron] *nm* ladle
cuchilla [ku'tʃiʎa] *nf* (large) knife; (*de
arma blanca*) blade; **cuchilla de afeitar**
razor blade
cuchillo [ku'tʃiʎo] *nm* knife
cuchitril [kutʃi'tril] *nm* hovel
cuclillas [ku'kliʎas] *nfpl*: **en ~** squatting
cuco, -a ['kuko, a] *adj* pretty; (*astuto*)
sharp ▷ *nm* cuckoo
cucurucho [kuku'rutʃo] *nm* cornet
cueca ['kweka] *nf* Chilean national dance
cuello ['kweʎo] *nm* (*Anat*) neck; (*de vestido,
camisa*) collar
cuenca ['kwenka] *nf* (*Anat*) eye socket;
(*Geo*) bowl, deep valley
cuenco ['kwenko] *nm* bowl
cuenta *etc* ['kwenta] *vb* V **contar**
▷ *nf* (*cálculo*) count, counting; (*en café,
restaurante*) bill; (*de collar*) bead; **a fin de ~s** in the
end; **caer en la ~** to catch on; **darse ~ de** to
realize; **tener en ~** to bear in mind; **echar
~s** to take stock; **cuenta atrás** countdown;
cuenta corriente/de ahorros current/
savings account; **cuenta de correo
(electrónica)** (*Inform*) email account;
cuentakilómetros *nm inv* ≈ milometer; (*de
velocidad*) speedometer
cuento *etc* ['kwento] *vb* V **contar** ▷ *nm*
story; **cuento chino** tall story; **cuento de
hadas** a fairy tale
cuerda ['kwerða] *nf* rope; (*fina*) string;
(*de reloj*) spring; **dar ~ a un reloj** to wind up
a clock; **cuerda floja** tightrope; **cuerdas
vocales** vocal cords
cuerdo, -a ['kwerðo, a] *adj* sane;

(*prudente*) wise, sensible
cuerno ['kwerno] *nm* horn
cuero ['kwero] *nm* leather; **en ~s** stark naked; **cuero cabelludo** scalp
cuerpo ['kwerpo] *nm* body
cuervo ['kwerβo] *nm* crow
cuesta *etc* ['kwesta] *vb* V **costar** ▷ *nf* slope; (*en camino etc*) hill; **~ arriba/abajo** uphill/downhill; **a ~s** on one's back
cueste *etc vb* V **costar**
cuestión [kwes'tjon] *nf* matter, question
cuete ['kwete] *adj* (*MÉX: fam*) drunk ▷ *nm* (*LAM: cohete*) rocket; (*MÉX,RPL: fam: embriaguez*) drunkenness; (*MÉX: Culin*) steak
cueva ['kweβa] *nf* cave
cuidado [kwi'ðaðo] *nm* care, carefulness; (*preocupación*) care, worry ▷ *excl* careful!, look out!; **eso me tiene sin ~** I'm not worried about that
cuidadoso, -a [kwiða'ðoso, a] *adj* careful; (*preocupado*) anxious
cuidar [kwi'ðar] *vt* (*Med*) to care for; (*ocuparse de*) to take care of, look after ▷ *vi*: **~ de** to take care of, look after; **cuidarse** *vr* to look after o.s.; **~se de hacer algo** to take care to do sth
culata [ku'lata] *nf* (*de fusil*) butt
culebra [ku'leβra] *nf* snake
culebrón [kule'βron] (*fam*) *nm* (TV) soap(-opera)
culo ['kulo] *nm* bottom, backside; (*de vaso, botella*) bottom
culpa ['kulpa] *nf* fault; (*Jur*) guilt; **por ~ de** because of; **echar la ~ a algn** to blame sb for sth; **tener la ~ (de)** to be to blame (for); **culpable** *adj* guilty ▷ *nmf* culprit; **culpar** [kul'par] *vt* to blame; (*acusar*) to accuse
cultivar [kulti'βar] *vt* to cultivate
cultivo [kul'tiβo] *nm* (*acto*) cultivation; (*plantas*) crop
culto, -a ['kulto, a] *adj* (*que tiene cultura*) cultured, educated ▷ *nm* (*homenaje*) worship; (*religión*) cult
cultura [kul'tura] *nf* culture
culturismo [kultu'rismo] *nm* body-building
cumbia ['kumbja] *nf* popular Colombian dance
cumbre ['kumbre] *nf* summit, top
cumpleaños [kumple'aɲos] *nm inv* birthday
cumplido, -a [kum'pliðo, a] *adj* (*abundante*) plentiful; (*cortés*) courteous ▷ *nm* compliment; **visita de ~** courtesy call
cumplidor, a [kumpli'ðor, a] *adj* reliable
cumplimiento [kumpli'mjento] *nm* (*de un deber*) fulfilment; (*acabamiento*) completion

cumplir [kum'plir] *vt* (*orden*) to carry out, obey; (*promesa*) to carry out, fulfil; (*condena*) to serve ▷ *vi*: **~ con** (*deber*) to carry out, fulfil; **cumplirse** *vr* (*plazo*) to expire; **hoy cumple dieciocho años** he is eighteen today
cuna ['kuna] *nf* cradle, cot
cundir [kun'dir] *vi* (*noticia, rumor, pánico*) to spread; (*rendir*) to go a long way
cuneta [ku'neta] *nf* ditch
cuña ['kuɲa] *nf* wedge
cuñado, -a [ku'ɲaðo, a] *nm/f* brother-/sister-in-law
cuota ['kwota] *nf* (*parte proporcional*) share; (*cotización*) fee, dues *pl*
cupe *etc vb* V **caber**
cupiera *etc vb* V **caber**
cupo ['kupo] *vb* V **caber** ▷ *nm* quota
cupón [ku'pon] *nm* coupon
cúpula ['kupula] *nf* dome
cura ['kura] *nf* (*curación*) cure; (*método curativo*) treatment ▷ *nm* priest
curación [kura'θjon] *nf* cure
curandero, -a [kuran'dero, a] *nm/f* quack
curar [ku'rar] *vt* (*Med: herida*) to treat, dress; (: *enfermo*) to cure; (*Culin*) to cure, salt; (*cuero*) to tan; **curarse** *vr* to get well, recover
curiosear [kurjose'ar] *vt* to glance at, look over ▷ *vi* to look round, wander round; (*explorar*) to poke about
curiosidad [kurjosi'ðað] *nf* curiosity
curioso, -a [ku'rjoso, a] *adj* curious ▷ *nm/f* bystander, onlooker
curita [ku'rita] (*LAM*) *nf* (sticking) plaster (*BRIT*), Bandaid® (*US*)
currante [ku'rrante] (*ESP: fam*) *nmf* worker
currar [ku'rrar] (*ESP: fam*) *vi* to work
currículo [ku'rrikulo] = **curriculum**
curriculum [ku'rrikulum] *nm* curriculum vitae
cursi ['kursi] (*fam*) *adj* affected
cursillo [kur'siʎo] *nm* short course
cursiva [kur'siβa] *nf* italics *pl*
curso ['kurso] *nm* course; **en ~** (*año*) current; (*proceso*) going on, under way
cursor [kur'sor] *nm* (*Inform*) cursor
curul [ku'rul] (*MÉX*) *nm* (*escaño*) seat
curva ['kurβa] *nf* curve, bend
custodia [kus'toðja] *nf* safekeeping; custody
cutis ['kutis] *nm inv* skin, complexion
cutre ['kutre] (*ESP: fam*) *adj* (*lugar*) grotty
cuyo, -a ['kujo, a] *pron* (*de quien*) whose; (*de que*) whose, of which; **en ~ caso** in which case
C.V. *abr* (= *caballos de vapor*) H.P.

d

más tarde we came across him two hours later; **al final di con la solución** I eventually came up with the answer
2: **dar en** (*blanco, suelo*) to hit; **el sol me da en la cara** the sun is shining (right) on my face
3: **dar de sí** (*zapatos etc*) to stretch, give
darse *vr* **1**: **darse por vencido** to give up
2 (*ocurrir*): **se han dado muchos casos** there have been a lot of cases
3: **darse a: se ha dado a la bebida** he's taken to drinking
4: **se me dan bien/mal las ciencias** I'm good/bad at science
5: **dárselas de: se las da de experto** he fancies himself o poses as an expert

D. *abr* (= *Don*) Esq
dado, -a ['daðo, a] *pp de* **dar** ▷ *nm* die; **dados** *nmpl* dice; **~ que** given that
daltónico, -a [dal'toniko, a] *adj* colour-blind
dama ['dama] *nf* (*gen*) lady; (*Ajedrez*) queen; **damas** *nfpl* (*juego*) draughts *sg*; **dama de honor** bridesmaid
damasco [da'masko] (*RPL*) *nm* apricot
danés, -esa [da'nes, esa] *adj* Danish ▷ *nm/f* Dane
dañar [da'ɲar] *vt* (*objeto*) to damage; (*persona*) to hurt; **dañarse** *vr* (*objeto*) to get damaged
dañino, -a [da'ɲino, a] *adj* harmful
daño ['daɲo] *nm* (*objeto*) damage; (*persona*) harm, injury; **~s y perjuicios** (*Jur*) damages; **hacer ~ a** to damage; (*persona*) to hurt, injure; **hacerse ~** to hurt o.s.

○ **PALABRA CLAVE**

dar [dar] *vt* **1** (*gen*) to give; (*obra de teatro*) to put on; (*film*) to show; (*fiesta*) to hold; **dar algo a algn** to give sb sth o sth to sb; **dar de beber a algn** to give sb a drink
2 (*producir: intereses*) to yield; (*fruta*) to produce
3 (*locuciones + n*): **da gusto escucharle** it's a pleasure to listen to him; *V tb* **paseo**
4 (+ *n.* = *perífrasis de verbo*): **me da asco** it sickens me
5 (*considerar*): **dar algo por descontado/entendido** to take sth for granted/as read; **dar algo por concluido** to consider sth finished
6 (*hora*): **el reloj dio las 6** the clock struck 6 (o'clock)
7: **me da lo mismo** it's all the same to me; *V tb* **igual, más**
▷ *vi* **1** **dar con: dimos con él dos horas**

dardo ['darðo] *nm* dart
dátil ['datil] *nm* date
dato ['dato] *nm* fact, piece of information; **datos personales** personal details
dcha. *abr* (= *derecha*) r.h.
d. de C. *abr* (= *después de Cristo*) A.D.

○ **PALABRA CLAVE**

de [de] (*de* + *el* = *del*) *prep* **1** (*posesión*) of; **la casa de Isabel/mis padres** Isabel's/my parents' house; **es de ellos** it's theirs
2 (*origen, distancia, con números*) from; **soy de Gijón** I'm from Gijón; **de 8 a 20** from 8 to 20; **salir del cine** to go out o leave the cinema; **de 2 en 2** 2 by 2, 2 at a time
3 (*valor descriptivo*): **una copa de vino** a glass of wine; **la mesa de la cocina** the kitchen table; **un billete de 10 euros** a 10 euro note; **un niño de tres años** a three-year-old (child); **una máquina de coser** a sewing machine; **ir vestido de gris** to be dressed in grey; **la niña del vestido azul** the girl in the blue dress; **trabaja de profesora** she works as a teacher; **de lado** sideways; **de atrás/delante** rear/front
4 (*hora, tiempo*): **a las 8 de la mañana** at 8 o'clock in the morning; **de día/noche** by day/night; **de hoy en ocho días** a week from now; **de niño era gordo** as a child he was fat
5 (*comparaciones*): **más/menos de cien personas** more/less than a hundred people; **el más caro de la tienda** the most expensive in the shop; **menos/más de lo pensado** less/more than expected
6 (*causa*): **del calor** from the heat
7 (*tema*) about; **clases de inglés** English classes; **¿sabes algo de él?** do you know anything about him?; **un libro de física** a physics book

8 (adj + de + infin): **fácil de entender** easy to understand

9 (oraciones pasivas): **fue respetado de todos** he was loved by all

10 (condicional + infin) if; **de ser posible** if possible; **de no terminarlo hoy** if I etc don't finish it today

dé [de] vb V **dar**

debajo [de'βaxo] adv underneath; **~ de** below, under; **por ~ de** beneath

debate [de'βate] nm debate; **debatir** vt to debate

deber [de'βer] nm duty ▷vt to owe ▷vi: **debe (de)** it must, it should; **deberes** nmpl (Escol) homework; **deberse** vr: **~se a** to be owing o due to; **debo hacerlo** I must do it; **debe de ir** he should go

debido, -a [de'βiðo, a] adj proper, just; **~ a** due to, because of

débil ['deβil] adj (persona, carácter) weak; (luz) dim; **debilidad** nf weakness; dimness

debilitar [deβili'tar] vt to weaken; **debilitarse** vr to grow weak

débito ['deβito] nm debit; **débito bancario** (LAM) direct debit (BRIT) o billing (US)

debutar [deβu'tar] vi to make one's debut

década ['dekaða] nf decade

decadencia [deka'ðenθja] nf (estado) decadence; (proceso) decline, decay

decaído, -a [deka'iðo, a] adj: **estar ~** (abatido) to be down

decano, -a [de'kano, a] nm/f (de universidad etc) dean

decena [de'θena] nf: **una ~** ten (or so)

decente [de'θente] adj decent

decepción [deθep'θjon] nf disappointment

No confundir **decepción** con la palabra inglesa deception.

decepcionar [deθepθjo'nar] vt to disappoint

decidir [deθi'ðir] vt, vi to decide; **decidirse** vr: **~se a** to make up one's mind to

décimo, -a ['deθimo, a] adj tenth ▷nm tenth

decir [de'θir] vt to say; (contar) to tell; (hablar) to speak ▷nm saying; **decirse** vr: **se dice que** it is said that; **es ~** that is (to say); **~ para sí** to say to o.s.; **querer ~** to mean; **¡dígame!** (Tel) hello!; (en tienda) can I help you?

decisión [deθi'sjon] nf (resolución) decision; (firmeza) decisiveness

decisivo, -a [deθi'siβo, a] adj decisive

declaración [deklara'θjon] nf (manifestación) statement; (de amor) declaration; **declaración fiscal** o **de la**

renta income-tax return

declarar [dekla'rar] vt to declare ▷vi to declare; (Jur) to testify; **declararse** vr to propose

decoración [dekora'θjon] nf decoration

decorado [deko'raðo] nm (Cine, Teatro) scenery, set

decorar [deko'rar] vt to decorate; **decorativo, -a** adj ornamental, decorative

decreto [de'kreto] nm decree

dedal [de'ðal] nm thimble

dedicación [deðika'θjon] nf dedication

dedicar [deði'kar] vt (libro) to dedicate; (tiempo, dinero) to devote; (palabras: decir, consagrar) to dedicate, devote; **dedicatoria** nf (de libro) dedication

dedo ['deðo] nm finger; **hacer ~** (fam) to hitch (a lift); **dedo anular** ring finger; **dedo corazón** middle finger; **dedo (del pie)** toe; **dedo gordo** (de la mano) thumb; (del pie) big toe; **dedo índice** index finger; **dedo meñique** little finger; **dedo pulgar** thumb

deducción [deðuk'θjon] nf deduction

deducir [deðu'θir] vt (concluir) to deduce, infer; (Com) to deduct

defecto [de'fekto] nm defect, flaw; **defectuoso, -a** adj defective, faulty

defender [defen'der] vt to defend; **defenderse** vr (desenvolverse) to get by

defensa [de'fensa] nf defence ▷nm (Deporte) defender, back; **defensivo, -a** adj defensive; **a la defensiva** on the defensive

defensor, a [defen'sor, a] adj defending ▷nm/f (abogado defensor) defending counsel; (protector) protector

deficiencia [defi'θjenθja] nf deficiency

deficiente [defi'θjente] adj (defectuoso) defective; **~ en** lacking o deficient in; **ser un ~ mental** to be mentally handicapped

déficit ['defiθit] (pl **~s**) nm deficit

definición [defini'θjon] nf definition

definir [defi'nir] vt (determinar) to determine, establish; (decidir) to define; (aclarar) to clarify; **definitivo, -a** adj definitive; **en definitiva** definitively; (en resumen) in short

deformación [deforma'θjon] nf (alteración) deformation; (Radio etc) distortion

deformar [defor'mar] vt (gen) to deform; **deformarse** vr to become deformed; **deforme** adj (informe) deformed; (feo) ugly; (malhecho) misshapen

defraudar [defrau'ðar] vt (decepcionar) to disappoint; (estafar) to defraud

defunción [defun'θjon] nf death, demise

degenerar [dexene'rar] vi to degenerate

degradar [dexra'ðar] vt to debase,

degrade; **degradarse** vr to demean o.s.
degustación [deɣusta'θjon] nf sampling, tasting
dejar [de'xar] vt to leave; (permitir) to allow, let; (abandonar) to abandon, forsake; (beneficios) to produce, yield ▷ vi: **~ de** (parar) to stop; (no hacer) to fail to; **~ a un lado** to leave o set aside; **~ entrar/salir** to let in/out; **~ pasar** to let through
del [del] (= **de** + **el**) ∨ **de**
delantal [delan'tal] nm apron
delante [de'lante] adv in front; (enfrente) opposite; (adelante) ahead; **~ de** in front of, before
delantera [delan'tera] nf (de vestido, casa etc) front part; (Deporte) forward line; **llevar la ~ (a algn)** to be ahead (of sb)
delantero, -a [delan'tero, a] adj front ▷ nm (Deporte) forward, striker
delatar [dela'tar] vt to inform on o against, betray; **delator, a** nm/f informer
delegación [deleɣa'θjon] nf (acción, delegados) delegation; (Com: oficina) office, branch; **delegación de policía** (MÉX) police station
delegado, -a [dele'ɣaðo, a] nm/f delegate; (Com) agent
delegar [dele'ɣar] vt to delegate
deletrear [deletre'ar] vt to spell (out)
delfín [del'fin] nm dolphin
delgado, -a [del'ɣaðo, a] adj thin; (persona) slim, thin; (tela etc) light, delicate
deliberar [deliβe'rar] vt to debate, discuss
delicadeza [delika'ðeθa] nf (gen) delicacy; (refinamiento, sutileza) refinement
delicado, -a [deli'kaðo, a] adj (gen) delicate; (sensible) sensitive; (quisquilloso) touchy
delicia [de'liθja] nf delight
delicioso, -a [deli'θjoso, a] adj (gracioso) delightful; (exquisito) delicious
delimitar [delimi'tar] vt (función, responsabilidades) to define
delincuencia [delin'kwenθja] nf delinquency; **delincuente** nmf delinquent; (criminal) criminal
delineante [deline'ante] nmf draughtsman/woman
delirante [deli'rante] adj delirious
delirar [deli'rar] vi to be delirious, rave
delirio [de'lirjo] nm (Med) delirium; (palabras insensatas) ravings pl
delito [de'lito] nm (gen) crime; (infracción) offence
delta ['delta] nm delta
demacrado, -a [dema'kraðo, a] adj: **estar ~** to look pale and drawn, be wasted away

demanda [de'manda] nf (pedido, Com) demand; (petición) request; (Jur) action, lawsuit; **demandar** [deman'dar] vt (gen) to demand; (Jur) to sue, file a lawsuit against
demás [de'mas] adj: **los ~ niños** the other o remaining children ▷ pron: **los/las ~** the others, the rest (of them); **lo ~** the rest (of it)
demasía [dema'sia] nf (exceso) excess, surplus; **comer en ~** to eat to excess
demasiado, -a [dema'sjaðo, a] adj: **~ vino** too much wine ▷ adv (antes de adj, adv) too; **~s libros** too many books; **¡esto es ~!** that's the limit!; **hace ~ calor** it's too hot; **~ despacio** too slowly; **~s** too many
demencia [de'menθja] nf (locura) madness
democracia [demo'kraθja] nf democracy
demócrata [de'mokrata] nmf democrat; **democrático, -a** adj democratic
demoler [demo'ler] vt to demolish; **demolición** nf demolition
demonio [de'monjo] nm devil, demon; **¡~s!** hell!, damn!; **¿cómo ~s?** how the hell?
demora [de'mora] nf delay
demos ['demos] vb ∨ **dar**
demostración [demostra'θjon] nf (Mat) proof; (de afecto) show, display
demostrar [demos'trar] vt (probar) to prove; (mostrar) to show; (manifestar) to demonstrate
den [den] vb ∨ **dar**
denegar [dene'ɣar] vt (rechazar) to refuse; (Jur) to reject
denominación [denomina'θjon] nf (acto) naming; **Denominación de Origen** see below

⬤ **DENOMINACIÓN DE ORIGEN**
⬤
⬤ The **Denominación de Origen**,
⬤ abbreviated to **D.O.**, is a prestigious
⬤ classification awarded to food products
⬤ such as wines, cheeses, sausages
⬤ and hams which meet the stringent
⬤ quality and production standards of the
⬤ designated region. **D.O.** labels serve as a
⬤ guarantee of quality.

densidad [densi'ðað] nf density; (fig) thickness
denso, -a ['denso, a] adj dense; (espeso, pastoso) thick; (fig) heavy
dentadura [denta'ðura] nf (set of) teeth pl; **dentadura postiza** false teeth pl
dentera [den'tera] nf (grima): **dar ~ a algn** to set sb's teeth on edge
dentífrico, -a [den'tifriko, a] adj dental ▷ nm toothpaste

dentista [den'tista] *nmf* dentist

dentro ['dentro] *adv* inside ▷ *prep*: **~ de** in, inside, within; **por ~** (on the) inside; **mirar por ~** to look inside; **~ de tres meses** within three months

denuncia [de'nunθja] *nf* (*delación*) denunciation; (*acusación*) accusation; (*de accidente*) report; **denunciar** *vt* to report; (*delatar*) to inform on o against

departamento [departa'mento] *nm* *sección administrativa*, department, section; (LAM: *apartamento*) flat (BRIT), apartment

depender [depen'der] *vi*: **~ de** to depend on; **depende** it (all) depends

dependienta [depen'djenta] *nf* saleswoman, shop assistant

dependiente [depen'djente] *adj* dependent ▷ *nm* salesman, shop assistant

depilar [depi'lar] *vt* (*con cera*) to wax; (*cejas*) to pluck

deportar [depor'tar] *vt* to deport

deporte [de'porte] *nm* sport; **hacer ~** to play sports; **deportista** *adj* sports *cpd* ▷ *nmf* sportsman/woman; **deportivo, -a** *adj* (*club, periódico*) sports *cpd* ▷ *nm* sports car

depositar [deposi'tar] *vt* (*dinero*) to deposit; (*mercancías*) to put away, store; **depositarse** *vr* to settle

depósito [de'posito] *nm* (*gen*) deposit; (*almacén*) warehouse, store; (*de agua, gasolina etc*) tank; **depósito de cadáveres** mortuary

depredador, a [depreða'ðor, a] *adj* predatory ▷ *nm* predator

depresión [depre'sjon] *nf* depression; **depresión nerviosa** nervous breakdown

deprimido, -a [depri'miðo, a] *adj* depressed

deprimir [depri'mir] *vt* to depress; **deprimirse** *vr* (*persona*) to become depressed

deprisa [de'prisa] *adv* quickly, hurriedly

depurar [depu'rar] *vt* to purify; (*purgar*) to purge

derecha [de'retʃa] *nf* right(-hand) side; (Pol) right; **a la ~** (*estar*) on the right; (*torcer etc*) (to the) right

derecho, -a [de'retʃo, a] *adj* right, right-hand ▷ *nm* (*privilegio*) right; (*lado*) right(-hand) side; (*leyes*) law ▷ *adv* straight, directly; **derechos** *nmpl* (*de aduana*) duty *sg*; (*de autor*) royalties; **tener ~ a** to have a right to; **derechos de autor** royalties

deriva [de'riβa] *nf*: **ir** o **estar a la ~** to drift, be adrift

derivado [deri'βaðo] *nm* (Com) by-product

derivar [deri'βar] *vt* to derive; (*desviar*) to direct ▷ *vi* to derive, be derived; (Náut) to drift; **derivarse** *vr* to derive, be derived; to drift

derramamiento [derrama'mjento] *nm* (*dispersión*) spilling; **derramamiento de sangre** bloodshed

derramar [derra'mar] *vt* to spill; (*verter*) to pour out; (*esparcir*) to scatter; **derramarse** *vr* to pour out

derrame [de'rrame] *nm* (*de líquido*) spilling; (*de sangre*) shedding; (*de tubo etc*) overflow; (*pérdida*) leakage; **derrame cerebral** brain haemorrhage

derredor [derre'ðor] *adv*: **al** o **en ~ de** around, about

derretir [derre'tir] *vt* (*gen*) to melt; (*nieve*) to thaw; **derretirse** *vr* to melt

derribar [derri'βar] *vt* to knock down; (*construcción*) to demolish; (*persona, gobierno, político*) to bring down

derrocar [derro'kar] *vt* (*gobierno*) to bring down, overthrow

derrochar [derro'tʃar] *vt* to squander; **derroche** *nm* (*despilfarro*) waste, squandering

derrota [de'rrota] *nf* (Náut) course; (Mil, Deporte etc) defeat, rout; **derrotar** *vt* (*gen*) to defeat; **derrotero** *nm* (*rumbo*) course

derrumbar [derrum'bar] *vt* (*edificio*) to knock down; **derrumbarse** *vr* to collapse

des *etc vb* V **dar**

desabrochar [desaβro'tʃar] *vt* (*botónes, broches*) to undo, unfasten; **desabrocharse** *vr* (*ropa etc*) to come undone

desacato [desa'kato] *nm* (*falta de respeto*) disrespect; (Jur) contempt

desacertado, -a [desaθer'taðo, a] *adj* (*equivocado*) mistaken; (*inoportuno*) unwise

desacierto [desa'θjerto] *nm* mistake, error

desaconsejar [desakonse'xar] *vt* to advise against

desacreditar [desakreði'tar] *vt* (*desprestigiar*) to discredit, bring into disrepute; (*denigrar*) to run down

desacuerdo [desa'kwerðo] *nm* disagreement, discord

desafiar [desa'fjar] *vt* (*retar*) to challenge; (*enfrentarse a*) to defy

desafilado, -a [desafi'laðo, a] *adj* blunt

desafinado, -a [desafi'naðo, a] *adj*: **estar ~** to be out of tune

desafinar [desafi'nar] *vi* (*al cantar*) to be o go out of tune

desafío *etc* [desa'fio] *vb* V **desafiar** ▷ *nm* (*reto*) challenge; (*combate*) duel; (*resistencia*) defiance

desafortunado, -a [desafortu'naðo, a]

consentir) to reject

desgraciado) unfortunate, unlucky

desagradable [desaɣraˈðaβle] *adj (fastidioso, enojoso)* unpleasant; *(irritante)* disagreeable

desagradar [desaɣraˈðar] *vi (disgustar)* to displease; *(molestar)* to bother

desagradecido, -a [desaɣraðeˈθiðo, a] *adj* ungrateful

desagrado [desaˈɣraðo] *nm (disgusto)* displeasure; *(contrariedad)* dissatisfaction

desagüe [desˈaɣwe] *nm (de un líquido)* drainage; *(cañería)* drainpipe; *(salida)* outlet, drain

desahogar [desaoˈɣar] *vt (aliviar)* to ease, relieve; *(ira)* to vent; **desahogarse** *vr (relajarse)* to relax; *(desfogarse)* to let off steam

desahogo [desaˈoɣo] *nm (alivio)* relief; *(comodidad)* comfort, ease

desahuciar [desauˈθjar] *vt (enfermo)* to give up hope for; *(inquilino)* to evict

desairar [desaiˈrar] *vt (menospreciar)* to slight, snub

desalentador, a [desalentaˈðor, a] *adj* discouraging

desaliño [desaˈliɲo] *nm* slovenliness

desalmado, -a [desalˈmaðo, a] *adj (cruel)* cruel, heartless

desalojar [desaloˈxar] *vt (expulsar, echar)* to eject; *(abandonar)* to move out of ▷ *vi* to move out

desamor [desaˈmor] *nm (frialdad)* indifference; *(odio)* dislike

desamparado, -a [desampaˈraðo, a] *adj (persona)* helpless; *(lugar: expuesto)* exposed; *(desierto)* deserted

desangrar [desanˈgrar] *vt* to bleed; *(fig: persona)* to bleed dry; **desangrarse** *vr* to lose a lot of blood

desanimado, -a [desaniˈmaðo, a] *adj (persona)* downhearted; *(espectáculo, fiesta)* dull

desanimar [desaniˈmar] *vt (desalentar)* to discourage; *(deprimir)* to depress; **desanimarse** *vr* to lose heart

desapacible [desapaˈθiβle] *adj (gen)* unpleasant

desaparecer [desapareˈθer] *vi (gen)* to disappear; *(el sol, el luz)* to vanish; **desaparecido, -a** *adj* missing; **desaparición** *nf* disappearance

desapercibido, -a [desaperθiˈβiðo, a] *adj (desprevenido)* unprepared; **pasar ~** to go unnoticed

desaprensivo, -a [desaprenˈsiβo, a] *adj* unscrupulous

desaprobar [desaproˈβar] *vt (reprobar)* to disapprove of; *(condenar)* to condemn; *(no*

desaprovechado, -a [desaproβeˈtʃaðo, a] *adj (oportunidad, tiempo)* wasted; *(estudiante)* slack

desaprovechar [desaproβeˈtʃar] *vt* to waste

desarmador [desarmaˈðor] *(MÉX) nm* screwdriver

desarmar [desarˈmar] *vt (Mil, fig)* to disarm; *(Tec)* to take apart, dismantle; **desarme** *nm* disarmament

desarraigar [desarraiˈxar] *vt* to uproot; **desarraigo** *nm* uprooting

desarreglar [desarreˈxlar] *vt (desordenar)* to disarrange; *(trastocar)* to upset, disturb

desarrollar [desarroˈʎar] *vt (gen)* to develop; **desarrollarse** *vr* to develop; *(ocurrir)* to take place; *(Foto)* to develop; **desarrollo** *nm* development

desarticular [desartikuˈlar] *vt (hueso)* to dislocate; *(objeto)* to take apart; *(fig)* to break up

desasosegar [desasoseˈɣar] *vt (inquietar)* to disturb, make uneasy

desasosiego *etc* [desasoˈsjeɣo] *vb* V **desasosegar** ▷ *nm (intranquilidad)* uneasiness, restlessness; *(ansiedad)* anxiety

desastre [deˈsastre] *nm* disaster; **desastroso, -a** *adj* disastrous

desatar [desaˈtar] *vt (nudo)* to untie; *(paquete)* to undo; *(separar)* to detach; **desatarse** *vr (zapatos)* to come untied; *(tormenta)* to break

desatascar [desatasˈkar] *vt (cañería)* to unblock, clear

desatender [desatenˈder] *vt no prestar atención a,* to disregard; *(abandonar)* to neglect

desatino [desaˈtino] *nm (idiotez)* foolishness, folly; *(error)* blunder

desatornillar [desatorniˈʎar] *vt* to unscrew

desatrancar [desatranˈkar] *vt (puerta)* to unbolt; *(cañería)* to clear, unblock

desautorizado, -a [desautoriˈθaðo, a] *adj* unauthorized

desautorizar [desautoriˈθar] *vt (oficial)* to deprive of authority; *(informe)* to deny

desayunar [desajuˈnar] *vi* to have breakfast ▷ *vt* to have for breakfast; **desayuno** *nm* breakfast

desazón [desaˈθon] *nf* anxiety

desbarajuste [desβaraˈxuste] *nm* confusion, disorder

desbaratar [desβaraˈtar] *vt (deshacer, destruir)* to ruin

desbloquear [desβlokeˈar] *vt (negociaciónes, tráfico)* to get going again;

(*Com: cuenta*) to unfreeze

desbordar [desβor'ðar] *vt* (*sobrepasar*) to go beyond; (*exceder*) to exceed; **desbordarse** *vr* (*río*) to overflow; (*entusiasmo*) to erupt

descabellado, -a [deskaβe'ʎaðo, a] *adj* (*disparatado*) wild, crazy

descafeinado, -a [deskafei'naðo, a] *adj* decaffeinated ▷ *nm* decaffeinated coffee

descalabro [deska'laβro] *nm* blow; (*desgracia*) misfortune

descalificar [deskalifi'kar] *vt* to disqualify; (*desacreditar*) to discredit

descalzar [deskal'θar] *vt* (*zapato*) to take off; **descalzo, -a** *adj* barefoot(ed)

descambiar [deskam'bjar] *vt* to exchange

descaminado, -a [deskami'naðo, a] *adj* (*equivocado*) on the wrong road; (*fig*) misguided

descampado [deskam'paðo] *nm* open space

descansado, -a [deskan'saðo, a] *adj* (*gen*) rested; (*que tranquiliza*) restful

descansar [deskan'sar] *vt* (*gen*) to rest ▷ *vi* to rest, have a rest; (*echarse*) to lie down

descansillo [deskan'siʎo] *nm* (*de escalera*) landing

descanso [des'kanso] *nm* (*reposo*) rest; (*alivio*) relief; (*pausa*) break; (*Deporte*) interval, half time

descapotable [deskapo'taβle] *nm* (*tb*: **coche ~**) convertible

descarado, -a [deska'raðo, a] *adj* shameless; (*insolente*) cheeky

descarga [des'karɣa] *nf* (*Arq, Elec, Mil*) discharge; (*Náut*) unloading; **descargar** [deskar'ɣar] *vt* to unload; (*golpe*) to let fly; **descargarse** *vr* to unburden o.s.; **descargarse algo de Internet** to download sth from the Internet

descaro [des'karo] *nm* nerve

descarriar [deska'rrjar] *vt* (*descaminar*) to misdirect; (*fig*) to lead astray; **descarriarse** *vr* (*perderse*) to lose one's way; (*separarse*) to stray; (*pervertirse*) to err, go astray

descarrilamiento [deskarrila'mjento] *nm* (*de tren*) derailment

descarrilar [deskarri'lar] *vi* to be derailed

descartar [deskar'tar] *vt* (*rechazar*) to reject; (*eliminar*) to rule out; **descartarse** *vr* (*Naipes*) to discard; **~se de** to shirk

descendencia [desθen'denθja] *nf* (*origen*) origin, descent; (*hijos*) offspring

descender [desθen'der] *vt* (*bajar: escalera*) to go down ▷ *vi* to descend; (*temperatura, nivel*) to fall, drop; **~ de** to be descended from

descendiente [desθen'djente] *nmf* descendant

descenso [des'θenso] *nm* descent; (*de temperatura*) drop

descifrar [desθi'frar] *vt* to decipher; (*mensaje*) to decode

descolgar [deskol'ɣar] *vt* (*bajar*) to take down; (*teléfono*) to pick up; **descolgarse** *vr* to let o.s. down

descolorido, -a [deskolo'riðo, a] *adj* faded; (*pálido*) pale

descompasado, -a [deskompa'saðo, a] *adj* (*sin proporción*) out of all proportion; (*excesivo*) excessive

descomponer [deskompo'ner] *vt* (*desordenar*) to disarrange, disturb; (*Tec*) to put out of order; (*dividir*) to break down (into parts); (*fig*) to provoke; **descomponerse** *vr* (*corromperse*) to rot, decompose; (*LAM Tec*) to break down

descomposición [deskomposi'θjon] *nf* (*de un objeto*) breakdown; (*de fruta etc*) decomposition; **descomposición de vientre** (*ESP*) stomach upset, diarrhoea

descompostura [deskompos'tura] *nf* (*MÉX: avería*) breakdown, fault; (*LAM: diarrea*) diarrhoea

descomprimir [deskompri'mir] (*Internet*) to unzip

descompuesto, -a [deskom'pwesto, a] *adj* (*corrompido*) decomposed; (*roto*) broken

desconcertado, -a [deskonθer'taðo, a] *adj* disconcerted, bewildered

desconcertar [deskonθer'tar] *vt* (*confundir*) to baffle; (*incomodar*) to upset, put out; **desconcertarse** *vr* (*turbarse*) to be upset

desconchado, -a [deskon'tʃaðo, a] *adj* (*pintura*) peeling

desconcierto *etc* [deskon'θjerto] *vb* V **desconcertar** ▷ *nm* (*gen*) disorder; (*desorientación*) uncertainty; (*inquietud*) uneasiness

desconectar [deskonek'tar] *vt* to disconnect

desconfianza [deskon'fjanθa] *nf* distrust

desconfiar [deskon'fjar] *vi* to be distrustful; **~ de** to distrust, suspect

descongelar [deskonxe'lar] *vt* to defrost; (*Com, Pol*) to unfreeze

descongestionar [deskonxestjo'nar] *vt* (*cabeza, tráfico*) to clear

desconocer [deskono'θer] *vt* (*ignorar*) not to know, be ignorant of

desconocido, -a [deskono'θiðo, a] *adj* unknown ▷ *nm/f* stranger

desconocimiento [deskonoθi'mjento]

nm *falta de conocimientos,* ignorance
desconsiderado, -a [deskonsiðe'raðo, a]
  adj inconsiderate; (*insensible*)
  thoughtless
desconsuelo *etc* [deskon'swelo] *vb* V
  desconsolar ▷ *nm* (*tristeza*) distress;
  (*desesperación*) despair
descontado, -a [deskon'taðo, a] *adj*:
  dar por ~ (que) to take (it) for granted
  (that)
descontar [deskon'tar] *vt* (*deducir*) to take
  away, deduct; (*rebajar*) to discount
descontento, -a [deskon'tento, a]
  adj dissatisfied ▷ *nm* dissatisfaction,
  discontent
descorchar [deskor'tʃar] *vt* to uncork
descorrer [desko'rrer] *vt* (*cortinas, cerrojo*)
  to draw back
descortés [deskor'tes] *adj* (*mal educado*)
  discourteous; (*grosero*) rude
descoser [desko'ser] *vt* to unstitch;
  descoserse *vr* to come apart (at the
  seams)
descosido, -a [desko'siðo, a] *adj*
  (*Costura*) unstitched
descreído, -a [deskre'iðo, a] *adj*
  (*incrédulo*) incredulous; (*falto de fe*)
  unbelieving
descremado, -a [deskre'maðo, a] *adj*
  skimmed
describir [deskri'βir] *vt* to describe;
  descripción [deskrip'θjon] *nf* description
descrito [des'krito] *pp de* **describir**
descuartizar [deskwarti'θar] *vt* (*animal*)
  to cut up
descubierto, -a [desku'βjerto, a] *pp de*
  descubrir ▷ *adj* uncovered, bare; (*persona*)
  bareheaded ▷ *nm* (*bancario*) overdraft; **al ~**
  in the open
descubrimiento [deskuβri'mjento] *nm*
  (*hallazgo*) discovery; (*revelación*) revelation
descubrir [desku'βrir] *vt* to discover,
  find; (*inaugurar*) to unveil; (*vislumbrar*) to
  detect; (*revelar*) to reveal, show; (*destapar*)
  to uncover; **descubrirse** *vr* to reveal o.s.;
  (*quitarse sombrero*) to take off one's hat;
  (*confesar*) to confess
descuento *etc* [des'kwento] *vb* V
  descontar ▷ *nm* discount
descuidado, -a [deskwi'ðaðo, a] *adj*
  (*sin cuidado*) careless; (*desordenado*) untidy;
  (*olvidadizo*) forgetful; (*dejado*) neglected;
  (*desprevenido*) unprepared
descuidar [deskwi'ðar] *vt* (*dejar*) to
  neglect; (*olvidar*) to overlook; **descuidarse**
  vr (*distraerse*) to be careless; (*abandonarse*) to
  let o.s. go; (*desprevenirse*) to drop one's guard;
  ¡descuida! don't worry!; **descuido** *nm*

(*dejadez*) carelessness; (*olvido*) negligence

○ **PALABRA CLAVE**

desde ['desðe] *prep* **1** (*lugar*) from; **desde
  Burgos hasta mi casa hay 30 km** it's 30 km
  from Burgos to my house
  2 (*posición*): **hablaba desde el balcón** she
  was speaking from the balcony
  3 (*tiempo:* + *adv, n*): **desde ahora** from now
  on; **desde la boda** since the wedding;
  desde niño since I *etc* was a child; **desde 3
  años atrás** since 3 years ago
  4 (*tiempo:* + *vb, fecha*) since; for; **nos
  conocemos desde 1992/desde hace 20
  años** we've known each other since 1992/
  for 20 years; **no le veo desde 1997/desde
  hace 5 años** I haven't seen him since 1997/
  for 5 years
  5 (*gama*): **desde los más lujosos hasta los
  más económicos** from the most luxurious
  to the most reasonably priced
  6: **desde luego (que no)** of course (not)
  ▷ *conj*: **desde que: desde que recuerdo**
  for as long as I can remember; **desde que
  llegó no ha salido** he hasn't been out since
  he arrived

desdén [des'ðen] *nm* scorn
desdeñar [desðe'ɲar] *vt* (*despreciar*) to
  scorn
desdicha [des'ðitʃa] *nf* (*desgracia*)
  misfortune; (*infelicidad*) unhappiness;
  desdichado, -a *adj* (*sin suerte*) unlucky;
  (*infeliz*) unhappy
desear [dese'ar] *vt* to want, desire, wish
  for
desechar [dese'tʃar] *vt* (*basura*) to throw
  out o away; (*ideas*) to reject, discard;
  desechos *nmpl* rubbish *sg*, waste *sg*
desembalar [desemba'lar] *vt* to unpack
desembarazar [desembara'θar] *vt*
  (*desocupar*) to clear; (*desenredar*) to free;
  desembarazarse *vr*: **~se de** to free o.s. of,
  get rid of
desembarcar [desembar'kar] *vt*
  (*mercancías etc*) to unload ▷ *vi* to disembark
desembocadura [desemboka'ðura] *nf*
  (*de río*) mouth; (*de calle*) opening
desembocar [desembo'kar] *vi* (*río*) to
  flow into; (*fig*) to result in
desembolso [desem'bolso] *nm* payment
desembrollar [desembro'ʎar] *vt* (*madeja*)
  to unravel; (*asunto, malentendido*) to sort out
desemejanza [deseme'xanθa] *nf*
  dissimilarity
desempaquetar [desempake'tar] *vt*
  (*regalo*) to unwrap; (*mercancía*) to unpack

desempate [desem'pate] nm (Fútbol)
replay, play-off; (Tenis) tie-break(er)

desempeñar [desempe'ɲar] vt (cargo)
to hold; (papel) to perform; (lo empeñado) to
redeem; ~ **un papel** (fig) to play (a role)

desempleado, -a [desemple'aðo, a]
nm/f unemployed person; **desempleo** nm
unemployment

desencadenar [desenkaðe'nar] vt to
unchain; (ira) to unleash; **desencadenarse**
vr to break loose; (tormenta) to burst;
(guerra) to break out

desencajar [desenka'xar] vt (hueso) to
dislocate; (mecanismo, pieza) to disconnect,
disengage

desencanto [desen'kanto] nm
disillusionment

desenchufar [desentʃu'far] vt to unplug

desenfadado, -a [desenfa'ðaðo, a]
adj (desenvuelto) uninhibited; (descarado)
forward; **desenfado** nm (libertad) freedom;
(comportamiento) free and easy manner;
(descaro) forwardness

desenfocado, -a [desenfo'kaðo, a] adj
(Foto) out of focus

desenfreno [desen'freno] nm wildness;
(de las pasiones) lack of self-control

desenganchar [desengan'tʃar] vt (gen)
to unhook; (Ferro) to uncouple

desengañar [desenga'ɲar] vt to
disillusion; **desengañarse** vr to
become disillusioned; **desengaño**
nm disillusionment; (decepción)
disappointment

desenlace [desen'laθe] nm outcome

desenmascarar [desenmaska'rar] vt to
unmask

desenredar [desenre'ðar] vt (pelo) to
untangle; (problema) to sort out

desenroscar [desenros'kar] vt to
unscrew

desentenderse [desenten'derse] vr: ~ **de**
to pretend not to know about; (apartarse) to
have nothing to do with

desenterrar [desente'rrar] vt to exhume;
(tesoro, fig) to unearth, dig up

desentonar [desento'nar] vi (Mús) to sing
(o play) out of tune; (color) to clash

desentrañar [desentra'ɲar] vt (misterio)
to unravel

desenvoltura [desenβol'tura] nf ease

desenvolver [desenβol'βer] vt (paquete)
to unwrap; (fig) to develop; **desenvolverse**
vr (desarrollarse) to unfold, develop;
(arreglárselas) to cope

deseo [de'seo] nm desire, wish; **deseoso,
-a** adj: **estar deseoso de** to be anxious to

desequilibrado, -a [desekili'βraðo, a]
adj unbalanced

desertar [deser'tar] vi to desert

desértico, -a [de'sertiko, a] adj desert
cpd

desesperación [desespera'θjon]
nf (impaciencia) desperation, despair;
(irritación) fury

desesperar [desespe'rar] vt to drive to
despair; (exasperar) to drive to distraction
▷ vi: ~ **de** to despair of; **desesperarse** vr to
despair, lose hope

desestabilizar [desestaβili'θar] vt to
destabilize

desestimar [desesti'mar] vt
(menospreciar) to have a low opinion of;
(rechazar) to reject

desfachatez [desfatʃa'teθ] nf (insolencia)
impudence; (descaro) rudeness

desfalco [des'falko] nm embezzlement

desfallecer [desfaʎe'θer] vi (perder las
fuerzas) to become weak; (desvanecerse) to
faint

desfasado, -a [desfa'saðo, a] adj
(anticuado) old-fashioned; **desfase** nm
(diferencia) gap

desfavorable [desfaβo'raβle] adj
unfavourable

desfigurar [desfiɣu'rar] vt (cara) to
disfigure; (cuerpo) to deform

desfiladero [desfila'ðero] nm gorge

desfilar [desfi'lar] vi to parade; **desfile**
nm procession; **desfile de modelos** fashion
show

desgana [des'ɣana] nf (falta de apetito)
loss of appetite; (apatía) unwillingness;
desganado, -a adj: **estar desganado** (sin
apetito) to have no appetite; (sin entusiasmo)
to have lost interest

desgarrar [desɣa'rrar] vt to tear (up);
(fig) to shatter; **desgarro** nm (en tela) tear;
(aflicción) grief

desgastar [desɣas'tar] vt (deteriorar)
to wear away o down; (estropear) to spoil;
desgastarse vr to get worn out; **desgaste**
nm wear (and tear)

desglosar [desɣlo'sar] vt (factura) to
break down

desgracia [des'ɣraθja] nf misfortune;
(accidente) accident; (vergüenza) disgrace;
(contratiempo) setback; **por ~** unfortunately;
desgraciado, -a [desɣra'θjaðo, a] adj (sin
suerte) unlucky, unfortunate; (miserable)
wretched; (infeliz) miserable

desgravar [desɣra'βar] vt (impuestos) to
reduce the tax o duty on

desguace [des'ɣwaθe] (ESP) nm junkyard

deshabitado, -a [desaβi'taðo, a] adj
uninhabited

deshacer [desa'θer] vt (casa) to break up; (Tec) to take apart; (enemigo) to defeat; (diluir) to melt; (contrato) to break; (intriga) to solve; **deshacerse** vr (disolverse) to melt; (despedazarse) to come apart o undone; **~se de** to get rid of; **~se en lágrimas** to burst into tears

deshecho, -a [des'etʃo, a] adj undone; (roto) smashed; (persona): **estar ~** to be shattered

desheredar [desere'ðar] vt to disinherit

deshidratar [desiðra'tar] vt to dehydrate

deshielo [des'jelo] nm thaw

deshonesto, -a [deso'nesto, a] adj indecent

deshonra [des'onra] nf (deshonor) dishonour; (vergüenza) shame

deshora [des'ora]: **a ~** adv at the wrong time

deshuesadero [deswesa'ðero] (MÉX) nm junkyard

deshuesar [deswe'sar] vt (carne) to bone; (fruta) to stone

desierto, -a [de'sjerto, a] adj (casa, calle, negocio) deserted ▷ nm desert

designar [desiɣ'nar] vt (nombrar) to designate; (indicar) to fix

desigual [desi'ɣwal] adj (terreno) uneven; (lucha etc) unequal

desilusión [desilu'sjon] nf disillusionment; (decepción) disappointment; **desilusionar** vt to disillusion; to disappoint; **desilusionarse** vr to become disillusioned

desinfectar [desinfek'tar] vt to disinfect

desinflar [desin'flar] vt to deflate

desintegración [desinteɣra'θjon] nf disintegration

desinterés [desinte'res] nm (desgana) lack of interest; (altruismo) unselfishness

desintoxicarse [desintoksi'karse] vr (drogadicto) to undergo detoxification

desistir [desis'tir] vi (renunciar) to stop, desist

desleal [desle'al] adj (infiel) disloyal; (Com: competencia) unfair; **deslealtad** nf disloyalty

desligar [desli'ɣar] vt (desatar) to untie, undo; (separar) to separate; **desligarse** vr (de un compromiso) to extricate o.s.

desliz [des'liθ] nm (fig) lapse; **deslizar** vt to slip, slide

deslumbrar [deslum'brar] vt to dazzle

desmadrarse [desma'ðrarse] (fam) vr (descontrolarse) to run wild; (divertirse) to let one's hair down; **desmadre** (fam) nm (desorganización) chaos; (jaleo) commotion

desmán [des'man] nm (exceso) outrage; (abuso de poder) abuse

desmantelar [desmante'lar] vt (deshacer) to dismantle; (casa) to strip

desmaquillador [desmakiʎa'ðor] nm make-up remover

desmayar [desma'jar] vi to lose heart; **desmayarse** vr (Med) to faint; **desmayo** nm (Med: acto) faint; (: estado) unconsciousness

desmemoriado, -a [desmemo'rjado, a] adj forgetful

desmentir [desmen'tir] vt (contradecir) to contradict; (refutar) to deny

desmenuzar [desmenu'θar] vt (deshacer) to crumble; (carne) to chop; (examinar) to examine closely

desmesurado, -a [desmesu'raðo, a] adj disproportionate

desmontable [desmon'taβle] adj (que se quita: pieza) detachable; (plegable) collapsible, folding

desmontar [desmon'tar] vt (deshacer) to dismantle; (tierra) to level ▷ vi to dismount

desmoralizar [desmorali'θar] vt to demoralize

desmoronar [desmoro'nar] vt to wear away, erode; **desmoronarse** vr (edificio, dique) to collapse; (economía) to decline

desnatado, -a [desna'taðo, a] adj skimmed

desnivel [desni'βel] nm (de terreno) unevenness

desnudar [desnu'ðar] vt (desvestir) to undress; (despojar) to strip; **desnudarse** vr (desvestirse) to get undressed; **desnudo, -a** adj naked ▷ nm/f nude; **desnudo de** devoid o bereft of

desnutrición [desnutri'θjon] nf malnutrition; **desnutrido, -a** adj undernourished

desobedecer [desoβeðe'θer] vt, vi to disobey; **desobediencia** nf disobedience

desocupado, -a [desoku'paðo, a] adj at leisure; (desempleado) unemployed; (deshabitado) empty, vacant

desodorante [desoðo'rante]·nm deodorant

desolación [desola'θjon] nf (de lugar) desolation; (fig) grief

desolar [deso'lar] vt to ruin, lay waste

desorbitado, -a [desorβi'taðo, a] adj (excesivo: ambición) boundless; (deseos) excessive; (: precio) exorbitant

desorden [des'orðen] nm confusion; (político) disorder, unrest

desorganización [desorɣaniθa'θjon] nf (de persona) disorganization; (en empresa, oficina) disorder, chaos

desorientar [desorjen'tar] vt (extraviar) to mislead; (confundir, desconcertar) to confuse; **desorientarse** vr (perderse) to lose one's way

despabilado, -a [despaβi'laðo, a] adj (despierto) wide-awake; (fig) alert, sharp

despachar [despa'tʃar] vt (negocio) to do, complete; (enviar) to send, dispatch; (vender) to sell, deal in; (billete) to issue; (mandar ir) to send away

despacho [des'patʃo] nm (oficina) office; (de paquetes) dispatch; (venta) sale; (comunicación) message

despacio [des'paθjo] adv slowly

desparpajo [despar'paxo] nm self-confidence; (pey) nerve

desparramar [desparra'mar] vt (esparcir) to scatter; (líquido) to spill

despecho [des'petʃo] nm spite

despectivo, -a [despek'tiβo, a] adj (despreciativo) derogatory; (Ling) pejorative

despedida [despe'ðiða] nf (adiós) farewell; (de obrero) sacking

despedir [despe'ðir] vt (visita) to see off, show out; (empleado) to dismiss; (inquilino) to evict; (objeto) to hurl; (olor etc) to give out o off; **despedirse** vr: ~se de to say goodbye to

despegar [despe'xar] vt to unstick ▷ vi (avión) to take off; **despegarse** vr to come loose, come unstuck; **despego** nm detachment

despegue etc [des'pexe] vb V **despegar** ▷ nm takeoff

despeinado, -a [despei'naðo, a] adj dishevelled, unkempt

despejado, -a [despe'xaðo, a] adj (lugar) clear, free; (cielo) clear; (persona) wide-awake, bright

despejar [despe'xar] vt (gen) to clear; (misterio) to clear up ▷ vi (el tiempo) to clear; **despejarse** vr (tiempo, cielo) to clear (up); (misterio) to become clearer; (cabeza) to clear

despensa [des'pensa] nf larder

despeñarse [despe'ɲarse] vr to hurl o.s. down; (coche) to tumble over

desperdicio [desper'ðiθjo] nm (despilfarro) squandering; **desperdicios** nmpl (basura) rubbish sg (BRIT), garbage sg (US); (residuos) waste sg

desperezarse [despere'θarse] vr to stretch

desperfecto [desper'fekto] nm (deterioro) slight damage; (defecto) flaw, imperfection

despertador [desperta'ðor] nm alarm clock

despertar [desper'tar] nm awakening ▷ vt (persona) to wake up; (recuerdos) to revive; (sentimiento) to arouse ▷ vi to awaken, wake up; **despertarse** vr to awaken, wake up

despido etc [des'piðo] vb V **despedir** ▷ nm dismissal, sacking

despierto, -a etc [des'pjerto, a] vb V **despertar** ▷ adj awake; (fig) sharp, alert

despilfarro [despil'farro] nm (derroche) squandering; (lujo desmedido) extravagance

despistar [despis'tar] vt to throw off the track o scent; (confundir) to mislead, confuse; **despistarse** vr to take the wrong road; (confundirse) to become confused

despiste [des'piste] nm absent-mindedness; **un ~** a mistake o slip

desplazamiento [desplaθa'mjento] nm displacement

desplazar [despla'θar] vt to move; (Náut) to displace; (Inform) to scroll; (fig) to oust; **desplazarse** vr (persona) to travel

desplegar [desple'xar] vt (tela, papel) to unfold, open out; (bandera) to unfurl; **despliegue** etc [des'plexe] vb V **desplegar** ▷ nm display

desplomarse [desplo'marse] vr (edificio, gobierno, persona) to collapse

desplumar [desplu'mar] vt (ave) to pluck; (fam: estafar) to fleece

despoblado, -a [despo'βlaðo, a] adj (sin habitantes) uninhabited

despojar [despo'xar] vt (alguien: de sus bienes) to divest of, deprive of; (casa) to strip, leave bare; (alguien: de su cargo) to strip of

despojo [des'poxo] nm (acto) plundering; (objetos) plunder, loot; **despojos** nmpl (de ave, res) offal sg

desposado, -a [despo'saðo, a] adj, nm/f newly-wed

despreciar [despre'θjar] vt (desdeñar) to despise, scorn; (afrentar) to slight; **desprecio** nm scorn, contempt; slight

desprender [despren'der] vt (broche) to unfasten; (olor) to give off; **desprenderse** vr (botón: caerse) to fall off; (broche) to come unfastened; (olor, perfume) to be given off; ~se de algo que ... to draw from sth that ...

desprendimiento [desprendi'mjento] nm (gen) loosening; (generosidad) disinterestedness; (de tierra, rocas) landslide; **desprendimiento de retina** detachment of the retina

despreocupado, -a [despreoku'paðo, a] adj (sin preocupación) unworried, nonchalant; (negligente) careless

despreocuparse [despreoku'parse] vr not to worry; ~ **de** to have no interest in

desprestigiar [despresti'xjar] vt (criticar) to run down; (desacreditar) to discredit

desprevenido, -a [despreβe'niðo, a] *adj*
(*no preparado*) unprepared, unready
desproporcionado, -a
[desproporθjo'naðo, a] *adj*
disproportionate, out of proportion
desprovisto, -a [despro'βisto, a] *adj*: ~
de devoid of
después [des'pwes] *adv* afterwards,
later; (*próximo paso*) next; ~ **de comer** after
lunch; **un año** ~ a year later; ~ **se debatió el
tema** next the matter was discussed; ~ **de
corregido el texto** after the text had been
corrected; ~ **de todo** after all
desquiciado, -a [deski'θjaðo, a] *adj*
deranged
destacar [desta'kar] *vt* to emphasize,
point up; (*Mil*) to detach, detail ▷ *vi*
(*resaltarse*) to stand out; (*persona*) to be
outstanding *o* exceptional; **destacarse**
vr to stand out; to be outstanding *o*
exceptional
destajo [des'taxo] *nm*: **trabajar a** ~ to do
piecework
destapar [desta'par] *vt* (*botella*) to open;
(*cacerola*) to take the lid off; (*descubrir*) to
uncover; **destaparse** *vr* (*revelarse*) to reveal
one's true character
destartalado, -a [destarta'laðo, a] *adj*
(*desordenado*) untidy; (*ruinoso*) tumbledown
destello [des'teʎo] *nm* (*de estrella*) twinkle;
(*de faro*) signal light
destemplado, -a [destem'plaðo, a] *adj*
(*Mús*) out of tune; (*voz*) harsh; (*Med*) out of
sorts; (*tiempo*) unpleasant, nasty
desteñir [deste'ɲir] *vt* to fade ▷ *vi* to
fade; **desteñirse** *vr* to fade; **esta tela no
destiñe** this fabric will not run
desternillarse [desterni'ʎarse] *vr*: ~ **de
risa** to split one's sides laughing
desterrar [deste'rrar] *vt* (*exiliar*) to exile;
(*fig*) to banish, dismiss
destiempo [des'tjempo]: **a** ~ *adv* out of
turn
destierro *etc* [des'tjerro] *vb* V **desterrar**
▷ *nm* exile
destilar [desti'lar] *vt* to distil; **destilería**
nf distillery
destinar [desti'nar] *vt* (*funcionario*) to
appoint, assign; (*fondos*): ~ **(a)** to set aside
(for)
destinatario, -a [destina'tarjo, a] *nm/f*
addressee
destino [des'tino] *nm* (*suerte*) destiny; (*de
avión, viajero*) destination; **con ~ a Londres**
(*barco*) (bound) for London; (*avión, carta*) to
London
destituir [destitu'ir] *vt* to dismiss
destornillador [destorniʎa'ðor] *nm*

screwdriver
destornillar [destorni'ʎar] *vt* (*tornillo*) to
unscrew; **destornillarse** *vr* to unscrew
destreza [des'treθa] *nf* (*habilidad*) skill;
(*maña*) dexterity
destrozar [destro'θar] *vt* (*romper*) to
smash, break (up); (*estropear*) to ruin;
(*nervios*) to shatter
destrozo [des'troθo] *nm* (*acción*)
destruction; (*desastre*) smashing; **destrozos**
nmpl (*pedazos*) pieces; (*daños*) havoc *sg*
destrucción [destruk'θjon] *nf*
destruction
destruir [destru'ir] *vt* to destroy
desuso [des'uso] *nm* disuse; **caer en** ~ to
become obsolete
desvalijar [desvali'xar] *vt* (*persona*) to rob;
(*casa, tienda*) to burgle; (*coche*) to break into
desván [des'βan] *nm* attic
desvanecer [desβane'θer] *vt* (*disipar*) to
dispel; (*borrar*) to blur; **desvanecerse** *vr*
(*humo etc*) to vanish, disappear; (*color*) to
fade; (*recuerdo, sonido*) to fade away; (*Med*) to
pass out; (*duda*) to be dispelled
desvariar [desβa'rjar] *vi* (*enfermo*) to be
delirious
desvelar [desβe'lar] *vt* to keep awake;
desvelarse *vr* (*no poder dormir*) to stay
awake; (*preocuparse*) to be vigilant *o*
watchful
desventaja [desβen'taxa] *nf*
disadvantage
desvergonzado, -a [desβerɣon'θaðo, a]
adj shameless
desvestir [desβes'tir] *vt* to undress;
desvestirse *vr* to undress
desviación [desβja'θjon] *nf* deviation;
(*Auto*) diversion, detour
desviar [des'βjar] *vt* to turn aside; (*río*)
to alter the course of; (*navío*) to divert, re-
route; (*conversación*) to sidetrack; **desviarse**
vr (*apartarse del camino*) to turn aside;
(: *barco*) to go off course
desvío *etc* [des'βio] *vb* V **desviar**
▷ *nm* (*desviación*) detour, diversion; (*fig*)
indifference
desvivirse [desβi'βirse] *vr*: ~ **por** (*anhelar*)
to long for, crave for; (*hacer lo posible por*) to
do one's utmost for
detallar [deta'ʎar] *vt* to detail
detalle [de'taʎe] *nm* detail; (*gesto*) gesture,
token; **al** ~ in detail; (*Com*) retail
detallista [deta'ʎista] *nmf* (*Com*) retailer
detective [detek'tiβe] *nmf* detective;
detective privado private detective
detener [dete'ner] *vt* (*gen*) to stop; (*Jur*)
to arrest; (*objeto*) to keep; **detenerse** *vr*
to stop; (*demorarse*): ~**se en** to delay over,

linger over

detenidamente [deteniða'mente] *adv*
(*minuciosamente*) carefully; (*extensamente*) at
great length

detenido, -a [dete'niðo, a] *adj* (*arrestado*)
under arrest ▷ *nm/f* person under arrest,
prisoner

detenimiento [deteni'mjento] *nm*: **con ~**
thoroughly; (*observar, considerar*) carefully

detergente [deter'xente] *nm* detergent

deteriorar [deterjo'rar] *vt* to spoil,
damage; **deteriorarse** *vr* to deteriorate;
deterioro *nm* deterioration

determinación [determina'θjon] *nf*
(*empeño*) determination; (*decisión*) decision;
determinado, -a *adj* specific

determinar [determi'nar] *vt* (*plazo*) to
fix; (*precio*) to settle; **determinarse** *vr* to
decide

detestar [detes'tar] *vt* to detest

detractor, a [detrak'tor, a] *nm/f*
slanderer, libeller

detrás [de'tras] *adv* (*tb:* **por ~**) behind;
(*atrás*) at the back; **~ de** behind

detrimento [detri'mento] *nm*: **en ~ de** to
the detriment of

deuda ['deuða] *nf* debt; **deuda exterior/
pública** foreign/national debt

devaluación [deβalwa'θjon] *nf*
devaluation

devastar [deβas'tar] *vt* (*destruir*) to
devastate

deveras [de'βeras] (*MÉX*) *nf inv*: **un amigo
de (a) ~** a true *o* real friend

devoción [deβo'θjon] *nf* devotion

devolución [deβolu'θjon] *nf* (*reenvío*)
return, sending back; (*reembolso*)
repayment; (*Jur*) devolution

devolver [deβol'βer] *vt* to return; (*lo
extraviado, lo prestado*) to give back; (*carta al
correo*) to send back; (*Com*) to repay, refund
▷ *vi* (*vomitar*) to be sick

devorar [deβo'rar] *vt* to devour

devoto, -a [de'βoto, a] *adj* devout ▷ *nm/f*
admirer

devuelto *pp de* **devolver**

devuelva *etc vb V* **devolver**

di *etc vb V* **dar; decir**

día ['dia] *nm* day; **¿qué ~ es?** what's the
date?; **estar/poner al ~** to be/keep up
to date; **el ~ de hoy/de mañana** today/
tomorrow; **al ~ siguiente** (on) the following
day; **vivir al ~** to live from hand to mouth;
de ~ by day, in daylight; **en pleno ~** in
full daylight; **Día de la Independencia**
Independence Day; **Día de los Muertos**
(*MÉX*) All Souls' Day; **Día de Reyes** Epiphany;
día feriado (*LAM*) holiday; **día festivo** (*ESP*)

holiday; **día lectivo** teaching day; **día libre**
day off

diabetes [dja'βetes] *nf* diabetes

diablo ['djaβlo] *nm* devil; **diablura** *nf*
prank

diadema [dja'ðema] *nf* tiara

diafragma [dja'fraɣma] *nm* diaphragm

diagnóstico [djaɣ'nostiko] *nm* =
diagnosis

diagonal [djaɣo'nal] *adj* diagonal

diagrama [dja'ɣrama] *nm* diagram

dial [djal] *nm* dial

dialecto [dja'lekto] *nm* dialect

dialogar [djalo'ɣar] *vi*: **~ con** (*Pol*) to hold
talks with

diálogo ['djaloɣo] *nm* dialogue

diamante [dja'mante] *nm* diamond

diana ['djana] *nf* (*Mil*) reveille; (*de blanco*)
centre, bull's-eye

diapositiva [djaposi'tiβa] *nf* (*Foto*) slide,
transparency

diario, -a ['djarjo, a] *adj* daily ▷ *nm*
newspaper; **a ~** daily; **de ~** everyday

diarrea [dja'rrea] *nf* diarrhoea

dibujar [diβu'xar] *vt* to draw, sketch;
dibujo *nm* drawing; **dibujos animados**
cartoons

diccionario [dikθjo'narjo] *nm* dictionary

dice *etc vb V* **decir**

dicho, -a ['ditʃo, a] *pp de* **decir** ▷ *adj*: **en
~s países** in the aforementioned countries
▷ *nm* saying

dichoso, -a [di'tʃoso, a] *adj* happy

diciembre [di'θjembre] *nm* December

dictado [dik'taðo] *nm* dictation

dictador [dikta'ðor] *nm* dictator;
dictadura *nf* dictatorship

dictar [dik'tar] *vt* (*carta*) to dictate;
(*Jur: sentencia*) to pronounce; (*decreto*) to
issue; (*LAM: clase*) to give

didáctico, -a [di'ðaktiko, a] *adj*
educational

diecinueve [djeθi'nweβe] *num* nineteen

dieciocho [djeθi'otʃo] *num* eighteen

dieciséis [djeθi'seis] *num* sixteen

diecisiete [djeθi'sjete] *num* seventeen

diente ['djente] *nm* (*Anat, Tec*) tooth; (*Zool*)
fang; (*: de elefante*) tusk; (*de ajo*) clove

diera *etc vb V* **dar**

diesel ['disel] *adj*: **motor ~** diesel engine

diestro, -a ['djestro, a] *adj* (*derecho*) right;
(*hábil*) skilful

dieta ['djeta] *nf* diet; **estar a ~** to be on
a diet

diez [djeθ] *num* ten

diferencia [dife'renθja] *nf* difference; **a
~ de** unlike; **diferenciar** *vt* to differentiate
between ▷ *vi* to differ; **diferenciarse**

vr to differ, be different; (*distinguirse*) to distinguish o.s.

diferente [dife'rente] *adj* different

diferido [dife'riðo] *nm*: **en ~** (*TV etc*) recorded

difícil [di'fiθil] *adj* difficult

dificultad [difikul'tað] *nf* difficulty; (*problema*) trouble

dificultar [difikul'tar] *vt* (*complicar*) to complicate, make difficult; (*estorbar*) to obstruct

difundir [difun'dir] *vt* (*calor, luz*) to diffuse; (*Radio, TV*) to broadcast; **~ una noticia** to spread a piece of news; **difundirse** *vr* to spread (out)

difunto, -a [di'funto, a] *adj* dead, deceased ▷ *nm/f* deceased (person)

difusión [difu'sjon] *nf* (*Radio, TV*) broadcasting

diga *etc vb* V **decir**

digerir [dixe'rir] *vt* to digest; (*fig*) to absorb; **digestión** *nf* digestion; **digestivo, -a** *adj* digestive

digital [dixi'tal] *adj* digital

dignarse [diɣ'narse] *vr* to deign to

dignidad [diɣni'ðað] *nf* dignity

digno, -a ['diɣno, a] *adj* worthy

digo *etc vb* V **decir**

dije *etc vb* V **decir**

dilatar [dila'tar] *vt* (*cuerpo*) to dilate; (*prolongar*) to prolong

dilema [di'lema] *nm* dilemma

diluir [dilu'ir] *vt* to dilute

diluvio [di'luβjo] *nm* deluge, flood

dimensión [dimen'sjon] *nf* dimension

diminuto, -a [dimi'nuto, a] *adj* tiny, diminutive

dimitir [dimi'tir] *vi* to resign

dimos *vb* V **dar**

Dinamarca [dina'marka] *nf* Denmark

dinámico, -a [di'namiko, a] *adj* dynamic

dinamita [dina'mita] *nf* dynamite

dínamo ['dinamo] *nf* dynamo

dineral [dine'ral] *nm* large sum of money, fortune

dinero [di'nero] *nm* money; **dinero en efectivo** *o* **metálico** cash; **dinero suelto** (loose) change

dio *vb* V **dar**

dios [djos] *nm* god; **¡D~ mío!** (oh,) my God!; **¡por D~!** for heaven's sake!; **diosa** ['djosa] *nf* goddess

diploma [di'ploma] *nm* diploma

diplomacia [diplo'maθja] *nf* diplomacy; (*fig*) tact

diplomado, -a [diplo'mado, a] *adj* qualified

diplomático, -a [diplo'matiko, a] *adj*

diplomatic ▷ *nm/f* diplomat

diputación [diputa'θjon] *nf* (*tb*: **~ provincial**) ≈ county council

diputado, -a [dipu'tado, a] *nm/f* delegate; (*Pol*) ≈ member of parliament (*BRIT*) ≈ representative (*US*)

dique ['dike] *nm* dyke

diré *etc vb* V **decir**

dirección [direk'θjon] *nf* direction; (*señas*) address; (*Auto*) steering; (*gerencia*) management; (*Pol*) leadership; **dirección única/prohibida** one-way street/no entry

direccional [direkθjo'nal] (*MÉX*) *nf* (*Auto*) indicator

directa [di'rekta] *nf* (*Auto*) top gear

directiva [direk'tiβa] *nf* (*tb*: **junta ~**) board of directors

directo, -a [di'rekto, a] *adj* direct; (*Radio, TV*) live; **transmitir en ~** to broadcast live

director, a [direk'tor, a] *adj* leading ▷ *nm/f* director; (*Escol*) head(teacher) (*BRIT*), principal (*US*); (*gerente*) manager/ ess; (*Prensa*) editor; **director de cine** film director; **director general** managing director

directorio [direk'torjo] (*MÉX*) *nm* (*telefónico*) phone book

dirigente [diri'xente] *nmf* (*Pol*) leader

dirigir [diri'xir] *vt* to direct; (*carta*) to address; (*obra de teatro, film*) to direct; (*Mús*) to conduct; (*negocio*) to manage; **dirigirse** *vr*: **~se a** to go towards, make one's way towards; (*hablar con*) to speak to

dirija *etc vb* V **dirigir**

disciplina [disθi'plina] *nf* discipline

discípulo, -a [dis'θipulo, a] *nm/f* disciple

Discman® ['diskman] *nm* Discman®

disco ['disko] *nm* disc; (*Deporte*) discus; (*Tel*) dial; (*Auto: semáforo*) light; (*Mús*) record; **disco compacto/de larga duración** compact disc/long-playing record; **disco de freno** brake disc; **disco flexible/duro** *o* **rígido** (*Inform*) floppy/hard disk

disconforme [diskon'forme] *adj* differing; **estar ~ (con)** to be in disagreement (with)

discordia [dis'korðja] *nf* discord

discoteca [disko'teka] *nf* disco(theque)

discreción [diskre'θjon] *nf* discretion; (*reserva*) prudence; **comer a ~** to eat as much as one wishes

discreto, -a [dis'kreto, a] *adj* discreet

discriminación [diskrimina'θjon] *nf* discrimination

disculpa [dis'kulpa] *nf* excuse; (*pedir perdón*) apology; **pedir ~s a/por** to apologize to/for; **disculpar** *vt* to excuse, pardon; **disculparse** *vr* to excuse o.s.; to apologize

discurso [dis'kurso] *nm* speech

discusión [disku'sjon] *nf* (*diálogo*) discussion; (*riña*) argument

discutir [disku'tir] *vt* (*debatir*) to discuss; (*pelear*) to argue about; (*contradecir*) to argue against ▷ *vi* (*debatir*) to discuss; (*pelearse*) to argue

disecar [dise'kar] *vt* (*conservar: animal*) to stuff; (: *planta*) to dry

diseñar [dise'ɲar] *vt*, *vi* to design

diseño [di'seɲo] *nm* design

disfraz [dis'fraθ] *nm* (*máscara*) disguise; (*excusa*) pretext; **disfrazar** *vt* to disguise; **disfrazarse** *vr*: **disfrazarse de** to disguise o.s. as

disfrutar [disfru'tar] *vt* to enjoy ▷ *vi* to enjoy o.s.; **~ de** to enjoy, possess

disgustar [disɣus'tar] *vt* (*no gustar*) to displease; (*contrariar, enojar*) to annoy, upset; **disgustarse** *vr* (*enfadarse*) to get upset; (*dos personas*) to fall out

❚ No confundir **disgustar** con la palabra inglesa *disgust*.

disgusto [dis'ɣusto] *nm* (*contrariedad*) annoyance; (*tristeza*) grief; (*riña*) quarrel

disimular [disimu'lar] *vt* (*ocultar*) to hide, conceal ▷ *vi* to dissemble

dislocarse [dislo'karse] *vr* (*articulación*) to sprain, dislocate

disminución [disminu'θjon] *nf* decrease, reduction

disminuido, -a [disminu'iðo, a] *nm/f*: **~ mental/físico** mentally/physically handicapped person

disminuir [disminu'ir] *vt* to decrease, diminish

disolver [disol'βer] *vt* (*gen*) to dissolve; **disolverse** *vr* to dissolve; (*Com*) to go into liquidation

dispar [dis'par] *adj* different

disparar [dispa'rar] *vt*, *vi* to shoot, fire

disparate [dispa'rate] *nm* (*tontería*) foolish remark; (*error*) blunder; **decir ~s** to talk nonsense

disparo [dis'paro] *nm* shot

dispersar [disper'sar] *vt* to disperse; **dispersarse** *vr* to scatter

disponer [dispo'ner] *vt* (*arreglar*) to arrange; (*ordenar*) to put in order; (*preparar*) to prepare, get ready ▷ *vi*: **~ de** to have, own; **disponerse** *vr*: **~se a** o **para hacer** to prepare to do

disponible [dispo'niβle] *adj* available

disposición [disposi'θjon] *nf* arrangement, disposition; (*voluntad*) willingness; (*Inform*) layout; **a su ~** at your service

dispositivo [disposi'tiβo] *nm* device, mechanism

dispuesto, -a [dis'pwesto, a] *pp de* **disponer** ▷ *adj* (*arreglado*) arranged; (*preparado*) disposed

disputar [dispu'tar] *vt* (*carrera*) to compete in

disquete [dis'kete] *nm* floppy disk, diskette

distancia [dis'tanθja] *nf* distance; **distanciar** [distan'θjar] *vt* to space out; **distanciarse** *vr* to become estranged; **distante** [dis'tante] *adj* distant

diste *vb* V **dar**

disteis *vb* V **dar**

distinción [distin'θjon] *nf* distinction; (*elegancia*) elegance; (*honor*) honour

distinguido, -a [distin'giðo, a] *adj* distinguished

distinguir [distin'gir] *vt* to distinguish; (*escoger*) to single out; **distinguirse** *vr* to be distinguished

distintivo [distin'tiβo] *nm* badge; (*fig*) characteristic

distinto, -a [dis'tinto, a] *adj* different; (*claro*) clear

distracción [distrak'θjon] *nf* distraction; (*pasatiempo*) hobby, pastime; (*olvido*) absent-mindedness, distraction

distraer [distra'er] *vt* (*atención*) to distract; (*divertir*) to amuse; (*fondos*) to embezzle; **distraerse** *vr* (*entretenerse*) to amuse o.s.; (*perder la concentración*) to allow one's attention to wander

distraído, -a [distra'iðo, a] *adj* (*gen*) absent-minded; (*entretenido*) amusing

distribuidor, a [distriβui'ðor, a] *nm/f* distributor; **distribuidora** *nf* (*Com*) dealer, agent; (*Cine*) distributor

distribuir [distriβu'ir] *vt* to distribute

distrito [dis'trito] *nm* (*sector, territorio*) region; (*barrio*) district; **Distrito Federal** (*MÉX*) Federal District; **distrito postal** postal district

disturbio [dis'turβjo] *nm* disturbance; (*desorden*) riot

disuadir [diswa'ðir] *vt* to dissuade

disuelto [di'swelto] *pp de* **disolver**

DIU *nm abr* (= *dispositivo intrauterino*) IUD

diurno, -a ['djurno, a] *adj* day *cpd*

divagar [diβa'ɣar] *vi* (*desviarse*) to digress

diván [di'βan] *nm* divan

diversidad [diβersi'ðað] *nf* diversity, variety

diversión [diβer'sjon] *nf* (*gen*) entertainment; (*actividad*) hobby, pastime

diverso, -a [di'βerso, a] *adj* diverse; **~s libros** several books; **diversos** *nmpl*

sundries
divertido, -a [diβer'tiðo, a] adj (chiste)
amusing; (fiesta etc) enjoyable
divertir [diβer'tir] vt (entretener, recrear) to
amuse; **divertirse** vr (pasarlo bien) to have a
good time; (distraerse) to amuse o.s.
dividendos [diβi'ðendos] nmpl (Com)
dividends
dividir [diβi'ðir] vt (gen) to divide;
(distribuir) to distribute, share out
divierta etc vb V **divertir**
divino, -a [di'βino, a] adj divine
divirtiendo etc vb V **divertir**
divisa [di'βisa] nf (emblema) emblem,
badge; **divisas** nfpl foreign exchange sg
divisar [diβi'sar] vt to make out,
distinguish
división [diβi'sjon] nf (gen) division; (de
partido) split; (de país) partition
divorciar [diβor'θjar] vt to divorce;
divorciarse vr to get divorced; **divorcio**
nm divorce
divulgar [diβul'xar] vt (ideas) to spread;
(secreto) to divulge
DNI (ESP) nm abr (= Documento Nacional de
Identidad) national identity card

● **DNI**
●
● The **Documento Nacional de**
● **Identidad** is a Spanish ID card
● which must be carried at all times
● and produced on request for the
● police. It contains the holder's photo,
● fingerprints and personal details. It
● is also known as the **DNI** or "carnet de
● identidad".

Dña. abr (= doña) Mrs
do [do] nm (Mús) do, C
dobladillo [doβla'ðiʎo] nm (de vestido)
hem; (de pantalón: vuelta) turn-up (BRIT),
cuff (US)
doblar [do'βlar] vt to double; (papel) to
fold; (caño) to bend; (la esquina) to turn, go
round; (film) to dub ▷ vi to turn; (campana)
to toll; **doblarse** vr (plegarse) to fold (up),
crease; (encorvarse) to bend; **~ a la derecha/
izquierda** to turn right/left
doble ['doβle] adj double; (de dos aspectos)
dual; (fig) two-faced ▷ nm double ▷ nmf
(Teatro) double, stand-in; **dobles** nmpl
(Deporte) doubles sg; **con ~ sentido** with a
double meaning
doce ['doθe] num twelve; **docena** nf
dozen
docente [do'θente] adj: **centro/personal
~** teaching establishment/staff

dócil ['doθil] adj (pasivo) docile; (obediente)
obedient
doctor, a [dok'tor, a] nm/f doctor
doctorado [dokto'raðo] nm doctorate
doctrina [dok'trina] nf doctrine, teaching
documentación [dokumenta'θjon] nf
documentation, papers pl
documental [dokumen'tal] adj, nm
documentary
documento [doku'mento] nm (certificado)
document; **documento adjunto** (Inform)
attachment; **documento nacional de
identidad** identity card
dólar ['dolar] nm dollar
doler [do'ler] vt, vi to hurt; (fig) to grieve;
dolerse vr (de su situación) to grieve,
feel sorry; (de las desgracias ajenas) to
sympathize; **me duele el brazo** my arm
hurts
dolor [do'lor] nm pain; (fig) grief,
sorrow; **dolor de cabeza/estómago/
muelas** headache/stomachache/
toothache
domar [do'mar] vt to tame
domesticar [domesti'kar] vt = **domar**
doméstico, -a [do'mestiko, a] adj (vida,
servicio) home; (tareas) household; (animal)
tame, pet
domicilio [domi'θiljo] nm home; **servicio
a ~** home delivery service; **sin ~ fijo** of no
fixed abode; **domicilio particular** private
residence
dominante [domi'nante] adj dominant;
(persona) domineering
dominar [domi'nar] vt (gen) to dominate;
(idiomas) to be fluent in ▷ vi to dominate,
prevail
domingo [do'mingo] nm Sunday;
Domingo de Ramos/Resurrección Palm/
Easter Sunday
dominio [do'minjo] nm (tierras) domain;
(autoridad) power, authority; (de las pasiones)
grip, hold; (de idiomas) command
don [don] nm (talento) gift; **~ Juan Gómez**
Mr Juan Gómez, Juan Gómez Esq (BRIT)

● **DON/DOÑA**
●
● The term **don/doña** often abbreviated
● to **D./Dña** is placed before the first
● name as a mark of respect to an older
● or more senior person – eg Don Diego,
● Doña Inés. Although becoming rarer
● in Spain it is still used with names and
● surnames on official documents and
● formal correspondence – eg "Sr. D. Pedro
● Rodríguez Hernández", "Sra. Dña. Inés
● Rodríguez Hernández".

dona ['dona] (MÉX) nf doughnut, donut (US)

donar [do'nar] vt to donate

donativo [dona'tiβo] nm donation

donde ['donde] adv where ▷ prep: **el coche está allí ~ el farol** the car is over there by the lamppost o where the lamppost is; **en ~** where, in which

dónde ['donde] adv where?; **¿a ~ vas?** where are you going (to)?; **¿de ~ vienes?** where have you been?; **¿por ~?** where?, whereabouts?

dondequiera [donde'kjera] adv anywhere; **por ~** everywhere, all over the place ▷ conj: **~ que** wherever

donut® [do'nut] (ESP) nm doughnut, donut (US)

doña ['dona] nf: **~ Alicia** Alicia; **~ Victoria Benito** Mrs Victoria Benito

dorado, -a [do'raðo, a] adj (color) golden; (Tec) gilt

dormir [dor'mir] vt: **~ la siesta** to have an afternoon nap ▷ vi to sleep; **dormirse** vr to fall asleep

dormitorio [dormi'torjo] nm bedroom

dorsal [dor'sal] nm (Deporte) number

dorso ['dorso] nm (de mano) back; (de hoja) other side

dos [dos] num two

dosis ['dosis] nf inv dose, dosage

dotado, -a [do'taðo, a] adj gifted; **~ de** endowed with

dotar [do'tar] vt to endow; **dote** nf dowry; **dotes** nfpl (talentos) gifts

doy [doj] vb V **dar**

drama ['drama] nm drama; **dramaturgo** [drama'turɣo] nm dramatist, playwright

drástico, -a ['drastiko, a] adj drastic

drenaje [dre'naxe] nm drainage

droga ['droɣa] nf drug; **drogadicto, -a** [droɣa'ðikto, a] nm/f drug addict

droguería [droɣe'ria] nf hardware shop (BRIT) o store (US)

ducha ['dutʃa] nf (baño) shower; (Med) douche; **ducharse** vr to take a shower

duda ['duða] nf doubt; **no cabe ~** there is no doubt about it; **dudar** vt, vi to doubt; **dudoso, -a** [du'ðoso, a] adj (incierto) hesitant; (sospechoso) doubtful

duela etc vb V **doler**

duelo ['dwelo] vb V **doler** ▷ nm (combate) duel; (luto) mourning

duende ['dwende] nm imp, goblin

dueño, -a ['dweɲo, a] nm/f (propietario) owner; (de pensión, taberna) landlord/lady; (empresario) employer

duermo etc vb V **dormir**

dulce ['dulθe] adj sweet ▷ adv gently, softly ▷ nm sweet

dulcería [dulθe'ria] (LAM) nf confectioner's (shop)

dulzura [dul'θura] nf sweetness; (ternura) gentleness

dúo ['duo] nm duet

duplicar [dupli'kar] vt (hacer el doble de) to duplicate

duque ['duke] nm duke; **duquesa** nf duchess

duración [dura'θjon] nf (de película, disco etc) length; (de pila etc) life; (curso: de acontecimientos etc) duration

duradero, -a [dura'ðero, a] adj (tela etc) hard-wearing; (fe, paz) lasting

durante [du'rante] prep during

durar [du'rar] vi to last; (recuerdo) to remain

durazno [du'raθno] (LAM) nm (fruta) peach; (árbol) peach tree

durex ['dureks] (MÉX, ARG) nm (tira adhesiva) Sellotape® (BRIT), Scotch tape® (US)

dureza [du'reθa] nf (calidad) hardness

duro, -a ['duro, a] adj hard; (carácter) tough ▷ adv hard ▷ nm (moneda) five-peseta coin o piece

DVD nm abr (= disco de vídeo digital) DVD

E *abr* (= *este*) E

e [e] *conj* and

ébano ['eβano] *nm* ebony

ebrio, -a ['eβrjo, a] *adj* drunk

ebullición [eβuʎi'θjon] *nf* boiling

echar [e'tʃar] *vt* to throw; (*agua, vino*) to pour (out); (*empleado*: *despedir*) to fire, sack; (*hojas*) to sprout; (*cartas*) to post; (*humo*) to emit, give out ▷ *vi*: **~ a correr** to run off; **echarse** *vr* to lie down; **~ llave a** to lock (up); **~ abajo** (*gobierno*) to overthrow; (*edificio*) to demolish; **~ mano a** to lay hands on; **~ una mano a algn** (*ayudar*) to give sb a hand; **~ de menos** to miss; **~se atrás** (*fig*) to back out

eclesiástico, -a [ekle'sjastiko, a] *adj* ecclesiastical

eco ['eko] *nm* echo; **tener ~** to catch on

ecología [ekolo'xia] *nf* ecology; **ecológico, -a** *adj* (*producto, método*) environmentally-friendly; (*agricultura*) organic; **ecologista** *adj* ecological, environmental ▷ *nmf* environmentalist

economía [ekono'mia] *nf* (*sistema*) economy; (*carrera*) economics

económico, -a [eko'nomiko, a] *adj* (*barato*) cheap, economical; (*ahorrativo*) thrifty; (*Com*: *año etc*) financial; (: *situación*) economic

economista [ekono'mista] *nmf* economist

Ecuador [ekwa'ðor] *nm* Ecuador; **ecuador** *nm* (*Geo*) equator

ecuatoriano, -a [ekwato'rjano, a] *adj*, *nm/f* Ecuadorian

ecuestre [e'kwestre] *adj* equestrian

edad [e'ðað] *nf* age; **¿qué ~ tienes?** how old are you?; **tiene ocho años de ~** he's eight (years old); **de ~ mediana/avanzada** middle-aged/advanced in years; **la E~ Media** the Middle Ages

edición [eði'θjon] *nf* (*acto*) publication; (*ejemplar*) edition

edificar [edifi'kar] *vt, vi* to build

edificio [eði'fiθjo] *nm* building; (*fig*) edifice, structure

Edimburgo [eðim'burxo] *nm* Edinburgh

editar [eði'tar] *vt* (*publicar*) to publish; (*preparar textos*) to edit

editor, a [eði'tor, a] *nm/f* (*que publica*) publisher; (*redactor*) editor ▷ *adj* publishing *cpd*; **editorial** *adj* editorial ▷ *nm* leading article, editorial; **casa editorial** publisher

edredón [eðre'ðon] *nm* duvet

educación [eðuka'θjon] *nf* education; (*crianza*) upbringing; (*modales*) (good) manners *pl*

educado, -a [eðu'kaðo, a] *adj*: **bien/mal ~** well/badly behaved

educar [eðu'kar] *vt* to educate; (*criar*) to bring up; (*voz*) to train

EE. UU. *nmpl abr* (= *Estados Unidos*) US(A)

efectivamente [efectiβa'mente] *adv* (*como respuesta*) exactly, precisely; (*verdaderamente*) really; (*de hecho*) in fact

efectivo, -a [efek'tiβo, a] *adj* effective; (*real*) actual, real ▷ *nm*: **pagar en ~** to pay (in) cash; **hacer ~ un cheque** to cash a cheque

efecto [e'fekto] *nm* effect, result; **efectos** *nmpl* (*efectos personales*) effects; (*bienes*) goods; (*Com*) assets; **en ~** in fact; (*respuesta*) exactly, indeed; **efecto invernadero** greenhouse effect; **efectos especiales/secundarios/sonoros** special/side/sound effects

efectuar [efek'twar] *vt* to carry out; (*viaje*) to make

eficacia [efi'kaθja] *nf* (*de persona*) efficiency; (*de medicamento etc*) effectiveness

eficaz [efi'kaθ] *adj* (*persona*) efficient; (*acción*) effective

eficiente [efi'θjente] *adj* efficient

egipcio, -a [e'xipθjo, a] *adj*, *nm/f* Egyptian

Egipto [e'xipto] *nm* Egypt

egoísmo [exo'ismo] *nm* egoism

egoísta [exo'ista] *adj* egoistical, selfish ▷ *nmf* egoist

Eire ['eire] *nm* Eire

ej. *abr* (= *ejemplo*) eg

eje ['exe] *nm* (*Geo, Mat*) axis; (*de rueda*) axle; (*de máquina*) shaft, spindle

ejecución [exeku'θjon] *nf* execution; (*cumplimiento*) fulfilment; (*Mús*) performance; (*Jur*: *embargo de deudor*) attachment

ejecutar [exeku'tar] *vt* to execute, carry out; (*matar*) to execute; (*cumplir*) to fulfil;

(*Mús*) to perform; (*Jur: embargar*) to attach, distrain (on)

ejecutivo, -a [exeku'tiβo, a] *adj* executive; **el (poder) ~** the executive (power)

ejemplar [exem'plar] *adj* exemplary ▷ *nm* example; (*Zool*) specimen; (*de libro*) copy; (*de periódico*) number, issue

ejemplo [e'xemplo] *nm* example; **por ~** for example

ejercer [exer'θer] *vt* to exercise; (*influencia*) to exert; (*un oficio*) to practise ▷ *vi* (*practicar*): **~ (de)** to practise (as)

ejercicio [exer'θiθjo] *nm* exercise; (*período*) tenure; **hacer ~** to take exercise; **ejercicio comercial** financial year

ejército [e'xerθito] *nm* army; **entrar en el ~** to join the army, join up; **ejército del aire/ de tierra** Air Force/Army

ejote [e'xote] (*MÉX*) *nm* green bean

○ **PALABRA CLAVE**

el [el] (*f* **la**, *pl* **los, las**, *neutro* **lo**) *art def* **1** the; **el libro/la mesa/los estudiantes** the book/table/students

2 (*con n abstracto: no se traduce*): **el amor/la juventud** love/youth

3 (*posesión: se traduce a menudo por adj posesivo*): **romperse el brazo** to break one's arm; **levantó la mano** he put his hand up; **se puso el sombrero** she put her hat on

4 (*valor descriptivo*): **tener la boca grande/ los ojos azules** to have a big mouth/blue eyes

5 (*con días*) on; **me iré el viernes** I'll leave on Friday; **los domingos suelo ir a nadar** on Sundays I generally go swimming

6 (*lo +adj*): **lo difícil/caro** what is difficult/ expensive; (*cuán*) **no se da cuenta de lo pesado que es** he doesn't realise how boring he is

▷ *pron demos* **1**: **mi libro y el de usted** my book and yours; **las de Pepe son mejores** Pepe's are better; **no la(s) blanca(s) sino la(s) gris(es)** not the white one(s) but the grey one(s)

2: **lo de: lo de ayer** what happened yesterday; **lo de las facturas** that business about the invoices

▷ *pron relativo* **1** (*indef*): **el que: el (los) que quiera(n) que se vaya(n)** anyone who wants to can leave; **llévese el que más le guste** take the one you like best

2 (*def*): **el que: el que compré ayer** the one I bought yesterday; **los que se van** those who leave

3: **lo que: lo que pienso yo/más me gusta** what I think/like most

▷ *conj*: **el que: el que lo diga** the fact that he says so; **el que sea tan vago me molesta** his being so lazy bothers me

▷ *excl*: **¡el susto que me diste!** what a fright you gave me!

▷ *pron personal* **1** (*persona: m*) him; (*: f*) her; (*: pl*) them; **lo/las veo** I can see him/them

2 (*animal, cosa: sg*) it; (*: pl*) them; **lo (o la) veo** I can see it; **los (o las) veo** I can see them

3 (*como sustituto de frase*): **lo: no lo sabía** I didn't know; **ya lo entiendo** I understand now

él [el] *pron* (*persona*) he; (*cosa*) it; (*después de prep: persona*) him; (*: cosa*) it; **de ~** his

elaborar [elaβo'rar] *vt* (*producto*) to make, manufacture; (*preparar*) to prepare; (*madera, metal etc*) to work; (*proyecto etc*) to work on o out

elástico, -a [e'lastiko, a] *adj* elastic; (*flexible*) flexible ▷ *nm* elastic; (*un elástico*) elastic band

elección [elek'θjon] *nf* election; (*selección*) choice, selection; **elecciones generales** general election *sg*

electorado [elekto'raðo] *nm* electorate, voters *pl*

electricidad [elektriθi'ðað] *nf* electricity

electricista [elektri'θista] *nmf* electrician

eléctrico, -a [e'lektriko, a] *adj* electric

electro... [elektro] *prefijo* electro...; **electrocardiograma** *nm* electrocardiogram; **electrocutar** *vt* to electrocute; **electrodo** *nm* electrode; **electrodomésticos** *nmpl* (electrical) household appliances

electrónica [elek'tronika] *nf* electronics *sg*

electrónico, -a [elek'troniko, a] *adj* electronic

elefante [ele'fante] *nm* elephant

elegancia [ele'ɣanθja] *nf* elegance, grace; (*estilo*) stylishness

elegante [ele'ɣante] *adj* elegant, graceful; (*estiloso*) stylish, fashionable

elegir [ele'xir] *vt* (*escoger*) to choose, select; (*optar*) to opt for; (*presidente*) to elect

elemental [elemen'tal] *adj* (*claro, obvio*) elementary; (*fundamental*) elemental, fundamental

elemento [ele'mento] *nm* element; (*fig*) ingredient; **elementos** *nmpl* elements, rudiments

elevación [eleβa'θjon] *nf* elevation; (*acto*) raising, lifting; (*de precios*) rise; (*Geo etc*) height, altitude

elevar [ele'βar] *vt* to raise, lift (up); (*precio*)

to put up; **elevarse** *vr* (*edificio*) to rise; (*precios*) to go up

eligiendo *etc vb* V **elegir**

elija *etc vb* V **elegir**

eliminar [elimi'nar] *vt* to eliminate, remove

eliminatoria [elimina'torja] *nf* heat, preliminary (round)

élite ['elite] *nf* elite

ella ['eʎa] *pron* (*persona*) she; (*cosa*) it; (*después de prep: persona*) her; (: *cosa*) it; **de ~** hers

ellas ['eʎas] *pron* (*personas y cosas*) they; (*después de prep*) them; **de ~** theirs

ello ['eʎo] *pron* it

ellos ['eʎos] *pron* they; (*después de prep*) them; **de ~** theirs

elogiar [elo'xjar] *vt* to praise; **elogio** *nm* praise

elote [e'lote] (*MÉX*) *nm* corn on the cob

eludir [elu'ðir] *vt* to avoid

email [i'mel] *nm* email; (*dirección*) email address; **mandar un ~ a** algn to email sb, send sb an email

embajada [emba'xaða] *nf* embassy

embajador, a [embaxa'ðor, a] *nm/f* ambassador/ambassadress

embalar [emba'lar] *vt* to parcel, wrap (up); **embalarse** *vr* to go fast

embalse [em'balse] *nm* (*presa*) dam; (*lago*) reservoir

embarazada [embara'θaða] *adj* pregnant ▷ *nf* pregnant woman

┃ No confundir **embarazada** con la palabra inglesa *embarrassed*.

embarazo [emba'raθo] *nm* (*de mujer*) pregnancy; (*impedimento*) obstacle, obstruction; (*timidez*) embarrassment; **embarazoso, -a** *adj* awkward, embarrassing

embarcación [embarka'θjon] *nf* (*barco*) boat, craft; (*acto*) embarkation, boarding

embarcadero [embarka'ðero] *nm* pier, landing stage

embarcar [embar'kar] *vt* (*cargamento*) to ship, stow; (*persona*) to embark, put on board; **embarcarse** *vr* to embark, go on board

embargar [embar'ɣar] *vt* (*Jur*) to seize, impound

embargo [em'barɣo] *nm* (*Jur*) seizure; (*Com, Pol*) embargo

embargue *etc vb* V **embargar**

embarque *etc* [em'barke] *vb* V **embarcar** ▷ *nm* shipment, loading

embellecer [embeʎe'θer] *vt* to embellish, beautify

embestida [embes'tiða] *nf* attack, onslaught; (*carga*) charge

embestir [embes'tir] *vt* to attack, assault; to charge, attack ▷ *vi* to attack

emblema [em'blema] *nm* emblem

embobado, -a [embo'βaðo, a] *adj* (*atontado*) stunned, bewildered

embolia [em'bolja] *nf* (*Med*) clot

émbolo ['embolo] *nm* (*Auto*) piston

emborrachar [emborra'tʃar] *vt* to make drunk, intoxicate; **emborracharse** *vr* to get drunk

emboscada [embos'kaða] *nf* ambush

embotar [embo'tar] *vt* to blunt, dull

embotellamiento [emboteʎa'mjento] *nm* (*Auto*) traffic jam

embotellar [embote'ʎar] *vt* to bottle

embrague [em'braxe] *nm* (*tb*: **pedal de ~**) clutch

embrión [em'brjon] *nm* embryo

embrollo [em'broʎo] *nm* (*enredo*) muddle, confusion; (*aprieto*) fix, jam

embrujado, -a [embru'xado, a] *adj* bewitched; **casa embrujada** haunted house

embrutecer [embrute'θer] *vt* (*atontar*) to stupefy

embudo [em'buðo] *nm* funnel

embuste [em'buste] *nm* (*mentira*) lie; **embustero, -a** *adj* lying, deceitful ▷ *nm/f* (*mentiroso*) liar

embutido [embu'tiðo] *nm* (*Culin*) sausage; (*Tec*) inlay

emergencia [emer'xenθja] *nf* emergency; (*surgimiento*) emergence

emerger [emer'xer] *vi* to emerge, appear

emigración [emiɣra'θjon] *nf* emigration; (*de pájaros*) migration

emigrar [emi'ɣrar] *vi* (*personas*) to emigrate; (*pájaros*) to migrate

eminente [emi'nente] *adj* eminent, distinguished; (*elevado*) high

emisión [emi'sjon] *nf* (*acto*) emission; (*Com etc*) issue; (*Radio, TV: acto*) broadcasting; (: *programa*) broadcast, programme (*BRIT*), program (*US*)

emisora [emi'sora] *nf* radio o broadcasting station

emitir [emi'tir] *vt* (*olor etc*) to emit, give off; (*moneda etc*) to issue; (*opinión*) to express; (*Radio*) to broadcast

emoción [emo'θjon] *nf* emotion; (*excitación*) excitement; (*sentimiento*) feeling

emocionante [emoθjo'nante] *adj* (*excitante*) exciting, thrilling

emocionar [emoθjo'nar] *vt* (*excitar*) to excite, thrill; (*conmover*) to move, touch; (*impresionar*) to impress

emoticón [emoti'kon], **emoticono**

[emoti'kono] *nm* smiley

emotivo, -a [emo'tiβo, a] *adj* emotional

empacho [em'patʃo] *nm* (*Med*) indigestion; (*fig*) embarrassment

empalagoso, -a [empala'ɣoso, a] *adj* cloying; (*fig*) tiresome

empalmar [empal'mar] *vt* to join, connect ▷ *vi* (*dos caminos*) to meet, join; **empalme** *nm* joint, connection; junction; (*de trenes*) connection

empanada [empa'naða] *nf* pie, pasty

empañarse [empa'ɲarse] *vr* (*cristales etc*) to steam up

empapar [empa'par] *vt* (*mojar*) to soak, saturate; (*absorber*) to soak up, absorb; **empaparse** *vr:* ~**se de** to soak up

empapelar [empape'lar] *vt* (*paredes*) to paper

empaquetar [empake'tar] *vt* to pack, parcel up

empastar [empas'tar] *vt* (*embadurnar*) to paste; (*diente*) to fill

empaste [em'paste] *nm* (*de diente*) filling

empatar [empa'tar] *vi* to draw, tie; ~**on a dos** they drew two-all; **empate** *nm* draw, tie

empecé *etc vb* V **empezar**

empedernido, -a [empeðer'niðo, a] *adj* hard, heartless; (*fumador*) inveterate

empeine [em'peine] *nm* (*de pie, zapato*) instep

empeñado, -a [empe'ɲaðo, a] *adj* (*persona*) determined; (*objeto*) pawned

empeñar [empe'ɲar] *vt* (*objeto*) to pawn, pledge; (*persona*) to compel; **empeñarse** *vr* (*endeudarse*) to get into debt; ~**se en** to be set on, be determined to

empeño [em'peɲo] *nm* (*determinación, insistencia*) determination, insistence; **casa de ~s** pawnshop

empeorar [empeo'rar] *vt* to make worse, worsen ▷ *vi* to get worse, deteriorate

empezar [empe'θar] *vt, vi* to begin, start

empiece *etc vb* V **empezar**

empiezo *etc vb* V **empezar**

emplasto [em'plasto] *nm* (*Med*) plaster

emplazar [empla'θar] *vt* (*ubicar*) to site, place, locate; (*Jur*) to summons; (*convocar*) to summon

empleado, -a [emple'aðo, a] *nm/f* (*gen*) employee; (*de banco etc*) clerk

emplear [emple'ar] *vt* (*usar*) to use, employ; (*dar trabajo a*) to employ; **emplearse** *vr* (*conseguir trabajo*) to be employed; (*ocuparse*) to occupy o.s.

empleo [em'pleo] *nm* (*puesto*) job; (*puestos: colectivamente*) employment; (*uso*) use, employment

empollar [empo'ʎar] (*ESP: fam*) *vt, vi* to swot (up); **empollón, -ona** (*ESP: fam*) *nm/f* swot

emporio [em'porjo] (*LAM*) *nm* (*gran almacén*) department store

empotrado, -a [empo'traðo, a] *adj* (*armario etc*) built-in

emprender [empren'der] *vt* (*empezar*) to begin, embark on; (*acometer*) to tackle, take on

empresa [em'presa] *nf* (*de espíritu etc*) enterprise; (*Com*) company, firm; **empresariales** *nfpl* business studies; **empresario, -a** *nm/f* (*Com*) businessman(-woman)

empujar [empu'xar] *vt* to push, shove

empujón [empu'xon] *nm* push, shove

empuñar [empu'ɲar] *vt* (*asir*) to grasp, take (firm) hold of

○ **PALABRA CLAVE**

en [en] *prep* **1** (*posición*) in; (: *sobre*) on; **está en el cajón** it's in the drawer; **en Argentina/La Paz** in Argentina/La Paz; **en la oficina/el colegio** at the office/school; **está en el suelo/quinto piso** it's on the floor/the fifth floor

2 (*dirección*) into; **entró en el aula** she went into the classroom; **meter algo en el bolso** to put sth into one's bag

3 (*tiempo*) in; on; **en 1605/3 semanas/invierno** in 1605/3 weeks/winter; **en (el mes de) enero** in (the month of) January; **en aquella ocasión/época** on that occasion/at that time

4 (*precio*) for; **lo vendió en 20 dólares** he sold it for 20 dollars

5 (*diferencia*) by; **reducir/aumentar en una tercera parte/un 20 por ciento** to reduce/increase by a third/20 per cent

6 (*manera*): **en avión/autobús** by plane/bus; **escrito en inglés** written in English

7 (*después de vb que indica gastar etc*) on; **han cobrado demasiado en dietas** they've charged too much to expenses; **se le va la mitad del sueldo en comida** he spends half his salary on food

8 (*tema, ocupación*): **experto en la materia** expert on the subject; **trabaja en la construcción** he works in the building industry

9 (*adj + en + infin*): **lento en reaccionar** slow to react

enaguas [e'naɣwas] *nfpl* petticoat *sg*, underskirt *sg*

enajenación [enaxena'θjon] *nf* (*Psico: tb:*

~ mental) mental derangement

enamorado, -a [enamo'raðo, a] *adj* in
love ▷ *nm/f* lover; **estar ~ (de)** to be in love
(with)

enamorar [enamo'rar] *vt* to win the love
of; **enamorarse** *vr*: **~se de algn** to fall in
love with sb

enano, -a [e'nano, a] *adj* tiny ▷ *nm/f*
dwarf

encabezamiento [enkaβeθa'mjento] *nm*
(*de carta*) heading; (*de periódico*) headline

encabezar [enkaβe'θar] *vt* (*movimiento*,
revolución) to lead, head; (*lista*) to head, be at
the top of; (*carta*) to put a heading to

encadenar [enkaðe'nar] *vt* to chain
(together); (*poner grilletes a*) to shackle

encajar [enka'xar] *vt* (*ajustar*): **~ (en)** to fit
(into); (*fam: golpe*) to take ▷ *vi* to fit (well);
(*fig: corresponder a*) to match

encaje [en'kaxe] *nm* (*labor*) lace

encallar [enka'ʎar] *vi* (*Náut*) to run
aground

encaminar [enkami'nar] *vt* to direct,
send

encantado, -a [enkan'taðo, a] *adj*
(*hechizado*) bewitched; (*muy contento*)
delighted; **¡~!** how do you do, pleased to
meet you

encantador, a [enkanta'ðor, a] *adj*
charming, lovely ▷ *nm/f* magician,
enchanter/enchantress

encantar [enkan'tar] *vt* (*agradar*) to
charm, delight; (*hechizar*) to bewitch, cast
a spell on; **me encanta eso** I love that;
encanto *nm* (*hechizo*) spell, charm; (*fig*)
charm, delight

encarcelar [enkarθe'lar] *vt* to imprison,
jail

encarecer [enkare'θer] *vt* to put up the
price of; **encarecerse** *vr* to get dearer

encargado, -a [enkar'xaðo, a] *adj* in
charge ▷ *nm/f* agent, representative;
(*responsable*) person in charge

encargar [enkar'xar] *vt* to entrust;
(*recomendar*) to urge, recommend;
encargarse *vr*: **~se de** to look after, take
charge of; **~ algo a algn** to put sb in charge
of sth; **~ a algn que haga algo** to ask sb
to do sth

encargo [en'karxo] *nm* (*tarea*)
assignment, job; (*responsabilidad*)
responsibility; (*Com*) order

encariñarse [enkari'ɲarse] *vr*: **~ con** to
grow fond of, get attached to

encarnación [enkarna'θjon] *nf*
incarnation, embodiment

encarrilar [enkarri'lar] *vt* (*tren*) to put
back on the rails; (*fig*) to correct, put on the
right track

encasillar [enkasi'ʎar] *vt* (*fig*) to
pigeonhole; (*actor*) to typecast

encendedor [enθende'ðor] *nm* lighter

encender [enθen'der] *vt* (*con fuego*)
to light; (*luz, radio*) to put on, switch on;
(*avivar: pasión*) to inflame; **encenderse** *vr*
to catch fire; (*excitarse*) to get excited; (*de
cólera*) to flare up; (*el rostro*) to blush

encendido [enθen'diðo] *nm* (*Auto*)
ignition

encerado [enθe'raðo] *nm* (*Escol*)
blackboard

encerrar [enθe'rrar] *vt* (*confinar*) to shut
in, shut up; (*comprender, incluir*) to include,
contain

encharcado, -a [entʃar'kaðo, a] *adj*
(*terreno*) flooded

encharcarse [entʃar'karse] *vr* to get
flooded

enchufado, -a [entʃu'faðo, a] (*fam*) *nm/f*
well-connected person

enchufar [entʃu'far] *vt* (*Elec*) to plug in;
(*Tec*) to connect, fit together; **enchufe** *nm*
(*Elec: clavija*) plug; (: *toma*) socket; (*do dos
tubos*) joint, connection; (*fam: influencia*)
contact, connection; (: *puesto*) cushy job

encía [en'θia] *nf* gum

encienda *etc vb* V **encender**

encierro *etc* [en'θjerro] *vb* V **encerrar**
▷ *nm* shutting in, shutting up; (*calabozo*)
prison

encima [en'θima] *adv* (*sobre*) above, over;
(*además*) besides; **~ de** (*en*) on, on top of;
(*sobre*) above, over; (*además de*) besides, on
top of; **por ~ de** over; **¿llevas dinero ~?** have
you (got) any money on you?; **se me vino ~**
it took me by surprise

encina [en'θina] *nf* holm oak

encinta [en'θinta] *adj* pregnant

enclenque [en'klenke] *adj* weak, sickly

encoger [enko'xer] *vt* to shrink, contract;
encogerse *vr* to shrink, contract; (*fig*) to
cringe; **~se de hombros** to shrug one's
shoulders

encomendar [enkomen'dar] *vt* to
entrust, commend; **encomendarse** *vr*: **~se
a** to put one's trust in

encomienda *etc* [enko'mjenda] *vb* V
encomendar ▷ *nf* (*encargo*) charge,
commission; (*elogio*) tribute; **encomienda
postal** (LAM) package

encontrar [enkon'trar] *vt* (*hallar*) to
find; (*inesperadamente*) to meet, run into;
encontrarse *vr* to meet (each other);
(*situarse*) to be (situated); **~se con** to meet;
~se bien (de salud) to feel well

encrucijada [enkruθi'xaða] *nf*

crossroads *sg*

encuadernación [enkwaðerna'θjon] *nf* binding

encuadrar [enkwa'ðrar] *vt* (*retrato*) to frame; (*ajustar*) to fit, insert; (*contener*) to contain

encubrir [enku'βrir] *vt* (*ocultar*) to hide, conceal; (*criminal*) to harbour, shelter

encuentro *etc* [en'kwentro] *vb* V **encontrar** ▷ *nm* (*de personas*) meeting; (*Auto etc*) collision, crash; (*Deporte*) match, game; (*Mil*) encounter

encuerado, -a (*MÉX*) [enkwe'raðo, a] *adj* nude, naked

encuesta [en'kwesta] *nf* inquiry, investigation; (*sondeo*) (public) opinion poll

encumbrar [enkum'brar] *vt* (*persona*) to exalt

endeble [en'deβle] *adj* (*persona*) weak; (*argumento, excusa, persona*) weak

endemoniado, -a [endemo'njaðo, a] *adj* possessed (of the devil); (*travieso*) devilish

enderezar [endere'θar] *vt* (*poner derecho*) to straighten (out); (: *verticalmente*) to set upright; (*situación*) to straighten o sort out; (*dirigir*) to direct; **enderezarse** *vr* (*persona sentada*) to straighten up

endeudarse [endeu'ðarse] *vr* to get into debt

endiablado, -a [endja'βlaðo, a] *adj* devilish, diabolical; (*travieso*) mischievous

endilgar [endil'ɣar] (*fam*) *vt*: **~le algo a algn** to lumber sb with sth

endiñar [endi'ɲar] (*ESP: fam*) *vt* (*bofetón*) to land, belt

endosar [endo'sar] *vt* (*cheque etc*) to endorse

endulzar [endul'θar] *vt* to sweeten; (*suavizar*) to soften

endurecer [endure'θer] *vt* to harden; **endurecerse** *vr* to harden, grow hard

enema [e'nema] *nm* (*Med*) enema

enemigo, -a [ene'miɣo, a] *adj* enemy, hostile ▷ *nm/f* enemy

enemistad [enemis'tað] *nf* enmity

enemistar [enemis'tar] *vt* to make enemies of, cause a rift between; **enemistarse** *vr* to become enemies; (*amigos*) to fall out

energía [ener'xia] *nf* (*vigor*) energy, drive; (*empuje*) push; (*Tec, Elec*) energy, power; **energía eólica** wind power; **energía solar** solar energy o power

enérgico, -a [e'nerxiko, a] *adj* (*gen*) energetic; (*voz, modales*) forceful

energúmeno, -a [ener'ɣumeno, a] (*fam*) *nm/f* (*fig*) madman(-woman)

enero [e'nero] *nm* January

enfadado, -a [enfa'ðaðo, a] *adj* angry, annoyed

enfadar [enfa'ðar] *vt* to anger, annoy; **enfadarse** *vr* to get angry o annoyed

enfado [en'faðo] *nm* (*enojo*) anger, annoyance; (*disgusto*) trouble, bother

énfasis ['enfasis] *nm* emphasis, stress

enfático, -a [en'fatiko, a] *adj* emphatic

enfermar [enfer'mar] *vt* to make ill ▷ *vi* to fall ill, be taken ill

enfermedad [enferme'ðað] *nf* illness; **enfermedad venérea** venereal disease

enfermera [enfer'mera] *nf* nurse

enfermería [enferme'ria] *nf* infirmary; (*de colegio etc*) sick bay

enfermero [enfer'mero] *nm* (male) nurse

enfermizo, -a [enfer'miθo, a] *adj* (*persona*) sickly, unhealthy; (*fig*) unhealthy

enfermo, -a [en'fermo, a] *adj* ill, sick ▷ *nm/f* invalid, sick person; (*en hospital*) patient; **caer** o **ponerse ~** to fall ill

enfocar [enfo'kar] *vt* (*foto etc*) to focus; (*problema etc*) to approach

enfoque *etc* [en'foke] *vb* V **enfocar** ▷ *nm* focus

enfrentar [enfren'tar] *vt* (*peligro*) to face (up to), confront; (*oponer*) to bring face to face; **enfrentarse** *vr* (*dos personas*) to face o confront each other; (*Deporte: dos equipos*) to meet; **~se** a o **con** to face up to, confront

enfrente [en'frente] *adv* opposite; **la casa de ~** the house opposite, the house across the street; **~ de** opposite, facing

enfriamiento [enfria'mjento] *nm* chilling, refrigeration; (*Med*) cold, chill

enfriar [enfri'ar] *vt* (*alimentos*) to cool, chill; (*algo caliente*) to cool down; **enfriarse** *vr* to cool down; (*Med*) to catch a chill; (*amistad*) to cool

enfurecer [enfure'θer] *vt* to enrage, madden; **enfurecerse** *vr* to become furious, fly into a rage; (*mar*) to get rough

enganchar [engan'tʃar] *vt* to hook; (*dos vagones*) to hitch up; (*Tec*) to couple, connect; (*Mil*) to recruit; **engancharse** *vr* (*Mil*) to enlist, join up

enganche [en'gantʃe] *nm* hook; (*ESP Tec*) coupling, connection; (*acto*) hooking (up); (*Mil*) recruitment, enlistment; (*MÉX: depósito*) deposit

engañar [enga'ɲar] *vt* to deceive; (*estafar*) to cheat, swindle; **engañarse** *vr* (*equivocarse*) to be wrong; (*disimular la verdad*) to deceive o.s.

engaño [en'gaɲo] *nm* deceit; (*estafa*) trick, swindle; (*error*) mistake, misunderstanding; (*ilusión*) delusion; **engañoso, -a** *adj* (*tramposo*) crooked; (*mentiroso*) dishonest, deceitful; (aspecto) deceptive; (consejo) misleading

engatusar [engatu'sar] (fam) vt to coax

engendro [en'xendro] nm (Bio) foetus; (fig) monstrosity

englobar [englo'βar] vt to include, comprise

engordar [engor'ðar] vt to fatten ▷ vi to get fat, put on weight

engorroso, -a [engo'rroso, a] adj bothersome, trying

engranaje [engra'naxe] nm (Auto) gear

engrasar [engra'sar] vt (Tec: poner grasa) to grease; (: lubricar) to lubricate, oil; (manchar) to make greasy

engreído, -a [engre'iðo, a] adj vain, conceited

enhebrar [ene'βrar] vt to thread

enhorabuena [enora'βwena] excl: ¡~! congratulations! ▷ nf: **dar la ~ a** to congratulate

enigma [e'niɣma] nm enigma; (problema) puzzle; (misterio) mystery

enjambre [en'xambre] nm swarm

enjaular [enxau'lar] vt to (put in a) cage; (fam) to jail, lock up

enjuagar [enxwa'ɣar] vt (ropa) to rinse (out)

enjuague etc [en'xwaxe] vb V **enjuagar** ▷ nm (Med) mouthwash; (de ropa) rinse, rinsing

enlace [en'laθe] nm link, connection; (relación) relationship; (tb: ~ **matrimonial**) marriage; (de carretera, trenes) connection; **enlace sindical** shop steward

enlatado, -a [enla'taðo, a] adj (alimentos, productos) tinned, canned

enlazar [enla'θar] vt (unir con lazos) to bind together; (atar) to tie; (conectar) to link, connect; (LAM: caballo) to lasso

enloquecer [enloke'θer] vt to drive mad ▷ vi to go mad

enmarañar [enmara'nar] vt (enredar) to tangle (up), entangle; (complicar) to complicate; (confundir) to confuse

enmarcar [enmar'kar] vt (cuadro) to frame

enmascarar [enmaska'rar] vt to mask; **enmascararse** vr to put on a mask

enmendar [enmen'dar] vt to emend, correct; (constitución etc) to amend; (comportamiento) to reform; **enmendarse** vr to reform, mend one's ways; **enmienda** nf correction; amendment; reform

enmudecer [enmuðe'θer] vi (perder el habla) to fall silent; (guardar silencio) to remain silent

ennoblecer [ennoβle'θer] vt to ennoble

enojado, -a [eno'xaðo, a] (LAM) adj angry

enojar [eno'xar] vt (encolerizar) to anger; (disgustar) to annoy, upset; **enojarse** vr to get angry; to get annoyed

enojo [e'noxo] nm (cólera) anger; (irritación) annoyance

enorme [e'norme] adj enormous, huge; (fig) monstrous

enredadera [enreða'ðera] nf (Bot) creeper, climbing plant

enredar [enre'ðar] vt (cables, hilos etc) to tangle (up), entangle; (situación) to complicate, confuse; (meter cizaña) to sow discord among o between; (implicar) to embroil, implicate; **enredarse** vr to get entangled, get tangled (up); (situación) to get complicated; (persona) to get embroiled; (LAM: fam) to meddle

enredo [en'reðo] nm (maraña) tangle; (confusión) mix-up, confusion; (intriga) intrigue

enriquecer [enrike'θer] vt to make rich, enrich; **enriquecerse** vr to get rich

enrojecer [enroxe'θer] vt to redden ▷ vi (persona) to blush; **enrojecerse** vr to blush

enrollar [enro'ʎar] vt to roll (up), wind (up)

ensalada [ensa'laða] nf salad; **ensaladilla (rusa)** nf Russian salad

ensanchar [ensan'tʃar] vt (hacer más ancho) to widen; (agrandar) to enlarge, expand; (Costura) to let out; **ensancharse** vr to get wider, expand

ensayar [ensa'jar] vt to test, try (out); (Teatro) to rehearse

ensayo [en'sajo] nm test, trial; (Quím) experiment; (Teatro) rehearsal; (Deporte) try; (Escol, Literatura) essay

enseguida [ense'ɣiða] adv at once, right away

ensenada [ense'naða] nf inlet, cove

enseñanza [ense'nanθa] nf (educación) education; (acción) teaching; (doctrina) teaching, doctrine; **enseñanza (de) primaria/secundaria** elementary/ secondary education

enseñar [ense'nar] vt (educar) to teach; (mostrar, señalar) to show

enseres [en'seres] nmpl belongings

ensuciar [ensu'θjar] vt (manchar) to dirty, soil; (fig) to defile; **ensuciarse** vr to get dirty; (bebé) to dirty one's nappy

entablar [enta'βlar] vt (recubrir) to board (up); (Ajedrez, Damas) to set up; (conversación) to strike up; (Jur) to file ▷ vi to draw

ente ['ente] nm (organización) body, organization; (fam: persona) odd character

entender [enten'der] vt (comprender) to

understand; (*darse cuenta*) to realize ▷ *vi* to understand; (*creer*) to think, believe; **entenderse** *vr* (*comprenderse*) to be understood; (*ponerse de acuerdo*) to agree, reach an agreement; **~ de** to know all about; **~ algo de** to know a little about; **~ en** to deal with, have to do with; **~ mal** to misunderstand; **~se con algn** (*llevarse bien*) to get on *o* along with sb; **~se mal** (*dos personas*) to get on badly

entendido, -a [enten'diðo, a] *adj* (*comprendido*) understood; (*hábil*) skilled; (*inteligente*) knowledgeable ▷ *nm/f* (*experto*) expert ▷ *excl* agreed!; **entendimiento** *nm* (*comprensión*) understanding; (*inteligencia*) mind, intellect; (*juicio*) judgement

enterado, -a [ente'raðo, a] *adj* well-informed; **estar ~ de** to know about, be aware of

enteramente [entera'mente] *adv* entirely, completely

enterar [ente'rar] *vt* (*informar*) to inform, tell; **enterarse** *vr* to find out, get to know

enterito [ente'rito] (RPL) *nm* boiler suit (BRIT), overalls (US)

entero, -a [en'tero, a] *adj* (*total*) whole, entire; (*fig: honesto*) honest; (: *firme*) firm, resolute ▷ *nm* (Com: *punto*) point

enterrar [ente'rrar] *vt* to bury

entidad [enti'ðað] *nf* (*empresa*) firm, company; (*organismo*) body; (*sociedad*) society; (*Filosofía*) entity

entiendo *etc vb* V **entender**

entierro [en'tjerro] *nm* (*acción*) burial; (*funeral*) funeral

entonación [entona'θjon] *nf* (Ling) intonation

entonar [ento'nar] *vt* (*canción*) to intone; (*colores*) to tone; (Med) to tone up ▷ *vi* to be in tune

entonces [en'tonθes] *adv* then, at that time; **desde ~** since then; **en aquel ~** at that time; **(pues) ~** and so

entornar [entor'nar] *vt* (*puerta, ventana*) to half-close, leave ajar; (*los ojos*) to screw up

entorpecer [entorpe'θer] *vt* (*entendimiento*) to dull; (*impedir*) to obstruct, hinder; (: *tránsito*) to slow down, delay

entrada [en'traða] *nf* (*acción*) entry, access; (*sitio*) entrance, way in; (Inform) input; (Com) receipts *pl*, takings *pl*; (Culin) starter; (Deporte) innings *sg*; (Teatro) house, audience; (*billete*) ticket; **~s y salidas** (Com) income and expenditure; **de ~** from the outset; **entrada de aire** (Tec) air intake *o* inlet

entrado, -a [en'traðo, a] *adj*: **~ en años** elderly; **una vez ~ el verano** in the summer(time), when summer comes

entramparse [entram'parse] *vr* to get into debt

entrante [en'trante] *adj* next, coming; **mes/año ~** next month/year; **entrantes** *nmpl* starters

entraña [en'traɲa] *nf* (fig: *centro*) heart, core; (*raíz*) root; **entrañas** *nfpl* (Anat) entrails; (fig) heart *sg*; **entrañable** *adj* close, intimate; **entrañar** *vt* to entail

entrar [en'trar] *vt* (*introducir*) to bring in; (Inform) to input ▷ *vi* (*meterse*) to go in, come in, enter; (*comenzar*): **~ diciendo** to begin by saying; **hacer ~** to show in; **me entró sed/sueño** I started to feel thirsty/sleepy; **no me entra** I can't get the hang of it

entre ['entre] *prep* (*dos*) between; (*más de dos*) among(st)

entreabrir [entrea'ßrir] *vt* to half-open, open halfway

entrecejo [entre'θexo] *nm*: **fruncir el ~** to frown

entredicho [entre'ðitʃo] *nm* (Jur) injunction; **poner en ~** to cast doubt on; **estar en ~** to be in doubt

entrega [en'treɣa] *nf* (*de mercancías*) delivery; (*de novela etc*) instalment; **entregar** [entre'ɣar] *vt* (*dar*) to hand (over), deliver; **entregarse** *vr* (*rendirse*) to surrender, give in, submit; (*dedicarse*) to devote o.s.

entremeses [entre'meses] *nmpl* hors d'œuvres

entremeter [entreme'ter] *vt* to insert, put in; **entremeterse** *vr* to meddle, interfere; **entremetido, -a** *adj* meddling, interfering

entremezclar [entremeθ'klar] *vt* to intermingle; **entremezclarse** *vr* to intermingle

entrenador, a [entrena'ðor, a] *nm/f* trainer, coach

entrenarse [entre'narse] *vr* to train

entrepierna [entre'pjerna] *nf* crotch

entresuelo [entre'swelo] *nm* mezzanine

entretanto [entre'tanto] *adv* meanwhile, meantime

entretecho [entre'tetʃo] (CS) *nm* attic

entretejer [entrete'xer] *vt* to interweave

entretener [entrete'ner] *vt* (*divertir*) to entertain, amuse; (*detener*) to hold up, delay; **entretenerse** *vr* (*divertirse*) to amuse o.s.; (*retrasarse*) to delay, linger; **entretenido, -a** *adj* entertaining, amusing; **entretenimiento** *nm* entertainment, amusement

entrever [entre'ßer] *vt* to glimpse, catch a glimpse of

entrevista [entre'ßista] *nf* interview;

entrevistar vt to interview; **entrevistarse** vr to have an interview

entristecer [entriste'θer] vt to sadden, grieve; **entristecerse** vr to grow sad

entrometerse [entrome'terse] vr: **~ (en)** to interfere (in o with)

entumecer [entume'θer] vt to numb, benumb; **entumecerse** vr (por el frío) to go o become numb

enturbiar [entur'βjar] vt (el agua) to make cloudy; (fig) to confuse; **enturbiarse** vr (oscurecerse) to become cloudy; (fig) to get confused, become obscure

entusiasmar [entusjas'mar] vt to excite, fill with enthusiasm; (gustar mucho) to delight; **entusiasmarse** vr: **~se con** o **por** to get enthusiastic o excited about

entusiasmo [entu'sjasmo] nm enthusiasm; (excitación) excitement

entusiasta [entu'sjasta] adj enthusiastic ▷ nmf enthusiast

enumerar [enume'rar] vt to enumerate

envainar [embai'nar] vt to sheathe

envalentonar [embalento'nar] vt to give courage to; **envalentonarse** vr (pey: jactarse) to boast, brag

envasar [emba'sar] vt (empaquetar) to pack, wrap; (enfrascar) to bottle; (enlatar) to can; (embolsar) to pocket

envase [em'base] nm (en paquete) packing, wrapping; (en botella) bottling; (en lata) canning; (recipiente) container; (paquete) package; (botella) bottle; (lata) tin (BRIT), can

envejecer [embexe'θer] vt to make old, age ▷ vi (volverse viejo) to grow old; (parecer viejo) to age

envenenar [embene'nar] vt to poison; (fig) to embitter

envergadura [emberɣa'ðura] nf (fig) scope, compass

enviar [em'bjar] vt to send; **~ un mensaje a algn** (por movil) to text sb, to send sb a text message

enviciarse [embi'θjarse] vr: **~ (con)** to get addicted (to)

envidia [em'biðja] nf envy; **tener ~ a** to envy, be jealous of; **envidiar** vt to envy

envío [em'bio] nm (acción) sending; (de mercancías) consignment; (de dinero) remittance

enviudar [embju'ðar] vi to be widowed

envoltura [embol'tura] nf (cobertura) cover; (embalaje) wrapper, wrapping; **envoltorio** nm package

envolver [embol'βer] vt to wrap (up); (cubrir) to cover; (enemigo) to surround; (implicar) to involve, implicate

envuelto [em'bwelto] pp de **envolver**

enyesar [enje'sar] vt (pared) to plaster; (Med) to put in plaster

enzarzarse [enθar'θarse] vr: **~ en** (pelea) to get mixed up in; (disputa) to get involved in

épica ['epika] nf epic

epidemia [epi'ðemja] nf epidemic

epilepsia [epi'lepsja] nf epilepsy

episodio [epi'soðjo] nm episode

época ['epoka] nf period, time; (Hist) age, epoch; **hacer ~** to be epoch-making

equilibrar [ekili'βrar] vt to balance; **equilibrio** nm balance, equilibrium; **mantener/perder el equilibrio** to keep/ lose one's balance; **equilibrista** nmf (funámbulo) tightrope walker; (acróbata) acrobat

equipaje [eki'paxe] nm luggage; (avíos): **hacer el ~** to pack; **equipaje de mano** hand luggage

equipar [eki'par] vt (proveer) to equip

equipararse [ekipa'rarse] vr: **~ con** to be on a level with

equipo [e'kipo] nm (conjunto de cosas) equipment; (Deporte) team; (de obreros) shift

equis ['ekis] nf inv (the letter) X

equitación [ekita'θjon] nf horse riding

equivalente [ekiβa'lente] adj, nm equivalent

equivaler [ekiβa'ler] vi to be equivalent o equal

equivocación [ekiβoka'θjon] nf mistake, error

equivocado, -a [ekiβo'kaðo, a] adj wrong, mistaken

equivocarse [ekiβo'karse] vr to be wrong, make a mistake; **~ de camino** to take the wrong road

era ['era] vb V **ser** ▷ nf era, age

erais vb V **ser**

éramos vb V **ser**

eran vb V **ser**

eras vb V **ser**

erección [erek'θjon] nf erection

eres vb V **ser**

erigir [eri'xir] vt to erect, build; **erigirse** vr: **~se en** to set o.s. up as

erizo [e'riθo] nm (Zool) hedgehog; **erizo de mar** sea-urchin

ermita [er'mita] nf hermitage; **ermitaño, -a** [ermi'taɲo, a] nm/f hermit

erosión [ero'sjon] nf erosion

erosionar [erosjo'nar] vt to erode

erótico, -a [e'rotiko, a] adj erotic; **erotismo** nm eroticism

errante [e'rrante] adj wandering, errant

erróneo, -a [e'rroneo, a] adj (equivocado) wrong, mistaken

error [e'rror] nm error, mistake; (Inform)

bug; **error de imprenta** misprint

eructar [eruk'tar] vt to belch, burp

erudito, -a [eru'ðito, a] adj erudite, learned

erupción [erup'θjon] nf eruption; (Med) rash

es vb V **ser**

esa ['esa] (pl **~s**) adj demos V **ese**

ésa ['esa] (pl **~s**) pron V **ése**

esbelto, -a [es'βelto, a] adj slim, slender

esbozo [es'βoθo] nm sketch, outline

escabeche [eska'βetʃe] nm brine; (de aceitunas etc) pickle; **en ~** pickled

escabullirse [eskaβu'ʎirse] vr to slip away, to clear out

escafandra [eska'fandra] nf (buzo) diving suit; (escafandra espacial) space suit

escala [es'kala] nf (proporción, Mús) scale; (de mano) ladder; (Aviac) stopover; **hacer ~ en** to stop o call in at

escalafón [eskala'fon] nm (escala de salarios) salary scale, wage scale

escalar [eska'lar] vt to climb, scale

escalera [eska'lera] nf stairs pl, staircase; (escala) ladder; (Naipes) run; **escalera de caracol** spiral staircase; **escalera de incendios** fire escape; **escalera mecánica** escalator

escalfar [eskal'far] vt (huevos) to poach

escalinata [eskali'nata] nf staircase

escalofriante [eskalo'frjante] adj chilling

escalofrío [eskalo'frio] nm (Med) chill; **escalofríos** nmpl (fig) shivers

escalón [eska'lon] nm step, stair; (de escalera) rung

escalope [eska'lope] nm (Culin) escalope

escama [es'kama] nf (de pez, serpiente) scale; (de jabón) flake; (fig) resentment

escampar [eskam'par] vb impers to stop raining

escandalizar [eskandali'θar] vt to scandalize, shock; **escandalizarse** vr to be shocked; (ofenderse) to be offended

escándalo [es'kandalo] nm scandal; (alboroto, tumulto) row, uproar; **escandaloso, -a** adj scandalous, shocking

escandinavo, -a [eskandi'naβo, a] adj, nm/f Scandinavian

escanear [eskane'ar] vt to scan

escaño [es'kaɲo] nm bench; (Pol) seat

escapar [eska'par] vi (gen) to escape, run away; (Deporte) to break away; **escaparse** vr to escape, get away; (agua, gas) to leak (out)

escaparate [eskapa'rate] nm shop window

escape [es'kape] nm (de agua, gas) leak; (de motor) exhaust

escarabajo [eskara'βaxo] nm beetle

escaramuza [eskara'muθa] nf skirmish

escarbar [eskar'βar] vt (tierra) to scratch

escarceos [eskar'θeos] nmpl: **en mis ~ con la política ...** in my dealings with politics ...; **escarceos amorosos** love affairs

escarcha [es'kartʃa] nf frost; **escarchado, -a** [eskar'tʃaðo, a] adj (Culin: fruta) crystallized

escarlatina [eskarla'tina] nf scarlet fever

escarmentar [eskarmen'tar] vt to punish severely ▷ vi to learn one's lesson

escarmiento etc [eskar'mjento] vb V **escarmentar** ▷ nm (ejemplo) lesson; (castigo) punishment

escarola [eska'rola] nf endive

escarpado, -a [eskar'paðo, a] adj (pendiente) sheer, steep; (rocas) craggy

escasear [eskase'ar] vi to be scarce

escasez [eska'seθ] nf (falta) shortage, scarcity; (pobreza) poverty

escaso, -a [es'kaso, a] adj (poco) scarce; (raro) rare; (ralo) thin, sparse; (limitado) limited

escatimar [eskati'mar] vt to skimp (on), be sparing with

escayola [eska'jola] nf plaster

escena [es'θena] nf scene; **escenario** [esθe'narjo] nm (Teatro) stage; (Cine) set; (fig) scene

> No confundir **escenario** con la palabra inglesa scenery.

escenografía nf set design

escéptico, -a [es'θeptiko, a] adj sceptical ▷ nm/f sceptic

esclarecer [esklare'θer] vt (misterio, problema) to shed light on

esclavitud [esklaβi'tuð] nf slavery

esclavizar [esklaβi'θar] vt to enslave

esclavo, -a [es'klaβo, a] nm/f slave

escoba [es'koβa] nf broom; **escobilla** nf brush

escocer [esko'θer] vi to burn, sting; **escocerse** vr to chafe, get chafed

escocés, -esa [esko'θes, esa] adj Scottish ▷ nm/f Scotsman(-woman), Scot

Escocia [es'koθja] nf Scotland

escoger [esko'xer] vt to choose, pick, select; **escogido, -a** adj chosen, selected

escolar [esko'lar] adj school cpd ▷ nmf schoolboy(-girl), pupil

escollo [es'koʎo] nm (obstáculo) pitfall

escolta [es'kolta] nf escort; **escoltar** vt to escort

escombros [es'kombros] nmpl (basura) rubbish sg; (restos) debris sg

esconder [eskon'der] vt to hide, conceal; **esconderse** vr to hide; **escondidas** (LAM) *nfpl*: **a escondidas** secretly; **escondite** *nm* hiding place; (ESP: *juego*) hide-and-seek; **escondrijo** *nm* hiding place, hideout

escopeta [esko'peta] *nf* shotgun

escoria [es'korja] *nf* (*de alto horno*) slag; (*fig*) scum, dregs *pl*

Escorpio [es'korpjo] *nm* Scorpio

escorpión [eskor'pjon] *nm* scorpion

escotado, -a [esko'taðo, a] *adj* low-cut

escote [es'kote] *nm* (*de vestido*) low neck; **pagar a ~** to share the expenses

escotilla [esko'tiʎa] *nf* (*Náut*) hatch(way)

escozor [esko'θor] *nm* (*dolor*) sting(ing)

escribible [eskri'βiβle] *adj* writable

escribir [eskri'βir] *vt, vi* to write; **~ a máquina** to type; **¿cómo se escribe?** how do you spell it?

escrito, -a [es'krito, a] *pp de* **escribir** ▷ *nm* (*documento*) document; (*manuscrito*) text, manuscript; **por ~** in writing

escritor, a [eskri'tor, a] *nm/f* writer

escritorio [eskri'torjo] *nm* desk

escritura [eskri'tura] *nf* (*acción*) writing; (*caligrafía*) (hand)writing; (*Jur: documento*) deed

escrúpulo [es'krupulo] *nm* scruple; (*minuciosidad*) scrupulousness; **escrupuloso, -a** *adj* scrupulous

escrutinio [eskru'tinjo] *nm* (*examen atento*) scrutiny; (*Pol: recuento de votos*) count(ing)

escuadra [es'kwaðra] *nf* (*Mil etc*) squad; (*Náut*) squadron; (*flota: de coches etc*) fleet; **escuadrilla** *nf* (*de aviones*) squadron; (LAM: *de obreros*) gang

escuadrón [eskwa'ðron] *nm* squadron

escuálido, -a [es'kwaliðo, a] *adj* skinny, scraggy; (*sucio*) squalid

escuchar [esku'tʃar] *vt* to listen to ▷ *vi* to listen

escudo [es'kuðo] *nm* shield

escuela [es'kwela] *nf* school; **escuela de artes y oficios** (ESP) ≈ technical college; **escuela de choferes** (LAM) driving school; **escuela de manejo** (MÉX) driving school

escueto, -a [es'kweto, a] *adj* plain; (*estilo*) simple

escuincle, -a [es'kwinkle, a] (MÉX: *fam*) *nm/f* kid

esculpir [eskul'pir] *vt* to sculpt; (*grabar*) to engrave; (*tallar*) to carve; **escultor, a** *nm/f* sculptor(-tress); **escultura** *nf* sculpture

escupidera [eskupi'ðera] *nf* spittoon

escupir [esku'pir] *vt, vi* to spit (out)

escurreplatos [eskurre'platos] (ESP) *nm inv* draining board (BRIT), drainboard (US)

escurridero [eskurri'ðero] (LAM) *nm* draining board (BRIT), drainboard (US)

escurridizo, -a [eskurri'ðiθo, a] *adj* slippery

escurridor [eskurri'ðor] *nm* colander

escurrir [esku'rrir] *vt* (*ropa*) to wring out; (*verduras, platos*) to drain ▷ *vi* (*líquidos*) to drip; **escurrirse** *vr* (*secarse*) to drain; (*resbalarse*) to slip, slide; (*escaparse*) to slip away

ese ['ese] (*f* **esa**, *pl* **esos, esas**) *adj demos* (*sg*) that; (*pl*) those

ése ['ese] (*f* **ésa**, *pl* **ésos, ésas**) *pron* (*sg*) that (one); (*pl*) those (ones); **~ ... éste ...** the former ... the latter ...; **no me vengas con ésas** don't give me any more of that nonsense

esencia [e'senθja] *nf* essence; **esencial** *adj* essential

esfera [es'fera] *nf* sphere; (*de reloj*) face; **esférico, -a** *adj* spherical

esforzarse [esfor'θarse] *vr* to exert o.s., make an effort

esfuerzo *etc* [es'fwerθo] *vb V* **esforzarse** ▷ *nm* effort

esfumarse [esfu'marse] *vr* (*apoyo, esperanzas*) to fade away

esgrima [es'ɣrima] *nf* fencing

esguince [es'ɣinθe] *nm* (*Med*) sprain

eslabón [esla'βon] *nm* link

eslip [ez'lip] *nm* pants *pl* (BRIT), briefs *pl*

eslovaco, -a [eslo'βako, a] *adj, nm/f* Slovak, Slovakian ▷ *nm* (*Ling*) Slovak, Slovakian

Eslovaquia [eslo'βakja] *nf* Slovakia

esmalte [es'malte] *nm* enamel; **esmalte de uñas** nail varnish o polish

esmeralda [esme'ralda] *nf* emerald

esmerarse [esme'rarse] *vr* (*aplicarse*) to take great pains, exercise great care; (*afanarse*) to work hard

esmero [es'mero] *nm* (great) care

esnob [es'nob] (*pl* **~s**) *adj* (*persona*) snobbish ▷ *nmf* snob

eso ['eso] *pron* that, that thing o matter; **~ de su coche** that business about his car; **~ de ir al cine** all that about going to the cinema; **a ~ de las cinco** at about five o'clock; **en ~** thereupon, at that point; **~ es** that's it; **¡~ sí que es vida!** now that is really living!; **por ~ te lo dije** that's why I told you; **y ~ que llovía** in spite of the fact it was raining

esos *adj demos V* **ese**

ésos *pron V* **ése**

espabilar *etc* [espaβi'lar] = **despabilar** *etc*

espacial [espa'θjal] *adj* (*del espacio*) space *cpd*

espaciar [espa'θjar] *vt* to space (out)

espacio [es'paθjo] *nm* space; (*Mús*)

interval; (*Radio, TV*) programme (*BRIT*), program (*US*); **el ~** space; **espacio aéreo/ exterior** air/outer space; **espacioso, -a** *adj* spacious, roomy

espada [es'paða] *nf* sword; **espadas** *nfpl* (*Naipes*) spades

espaguetis [espa'ɣetis] *nmpl* spaghetti *sg*

espalda [es'palda] *nf* (*gen*) back; **espaldas** *nfpl* (*hombros*) shoulders; **a ~s de algn** behind sb's back; **estar de ~s** to have one's back turned; **tenderse de ~s** to lie (down) on one's back; **volver la ~ a algn** to cold-shoulder sb

espantajo [espan'taxo] *nm* = **espantapájaros**

espantapájaros [espanta'paxaros] *nm inv* scarecrow

espantar [espan'tar] *vt* (*asustar*) to frighten, scare; (*ahuyentar*) to frighten off; (*asombrar*) to horrify, appal; **espantarse** *vr* to get frightened *o* scared; to be appalled

espanto [es'panto] *nm* (*susto*) fright; (*terror*) terror; (*asombro*) astonishment; **espantoso, -a** *adj* frightening; terrifying; astonishing

España [es'paɲa] *nf* Spain; **español, a** *adj* Spanish ▷ *nm/f* Spaniard ▷ *nm* (*Ling*) Spanish

esparadrapo [espara'ðrapo] *nm* (sticking) plaster (*BRIT*), adhesive tape (*US*)

esparcir [espar'θir] *vt* to spread; (*diseminar*) to scatter; **esparcirse** *vr* to spread (out), to scatter; (*divertirse*) to enjoy o.s.

espárrago [es'parraɣo] *nm* asparagus

esparto [es'parto] *nm* esparto (grass)

espasmo [es'pasmo] *nm* spasm

espátula [es'patula] *nf* spatula

especia [es'peθja] *nf* spice

especial [espe'θjal] *adj* special; **especialidad** *nf* speciality (*BRIT*), specialty (*US*)

especie [es'peθje] *nf* (*Bio*) species; (*clase*) kind, sort; **en ~** in kind

especificar [espeθifi'kar] *vt* to specify; **específico, -a** *adj* specific

espécimen [es'peθimen] (*pl* **especímenes**) *nm* specimen

espectáculo [espek'takulo] *nm* (*gen*) spectacle; (*Teatro etc*) show

espectador, a [espekta'ðor, a] *nm/f* spectator

especular [espeku'lar] *vt, vi* to speculate

espejismo [espe'xismo] *nm* mirage

espejo [es'pexo] *nm* mirror; **(espejo) retrovisor** rear-view mirror

espeluznante [espeluθ'nante] *adj* horrifying, hair-raising

espera [es'pera] *nf* (*pausa, intervalo*) wait; (*Jur: plazo*) respite; **en ~ de** waiting for; (*con expectativa*) expecting

esperanza [espe'ranθa] *nf* (*confianza*) hope; (*expectativa*) expectation; **hay pocas ~s de que venga** there is little prospect of his coming; **esperanza de vida** life expectancy

esperar [espe'rar] *vt* (*aguardar*) to wait for; (*tener expectativa de*) to expect; (*desear*) to hope for ▷ *vi* to wait; to expect; to hope; **hacer ~ a algn** to keep sb waiting; **~ un bebé** to be expecting (a baby)

esperma [es'perma] *nf* sperm

espeso, -a [es'peso, a] *adj* thick; **espesor** *nm* thickness

espía [es'pia] *nmf* spy; **espiar** *vt* (*observar*) to spy on

espiga [es'piɣa] *nf* (*Bot: de trigo etc*) ear

espigón [espi'ɣon] *nm* (*Bot*) ear; (*Náut*) breakwater

espina [es'pina] *nf* thorn; (*de pez*) bone; **espina dorsal** (*Anat*) spine

espinaca [espi'naka] *nf* spinach

espinazo [espi'naθo] *nm* spine, backbone

espinilla [espi'niʎa] *nf* (*Anat: tibia*) shin(bone); (*grano*) blackhead

espinoso, -a [espi'noso, a] *adj* (*planta*) thorny, prickly; (*asunto*) difficult

espionaje [espjo'naxe] *nm* spying, espionage

espiral [espi'ral] *adj, nf* spiral

espirar [espi'rar] *vt* to breathe out, exhale

espiritista [espiri'tista] *adj, nmf* spiritualist

espíritu [es'piritu] *nm* spirit; **Espíritu Santo** Holy Ghost *o* Spirit; **espiritual** *adj* spiritual

espléndido, -a [es'plendiðo, a] *adj* (*magnífico*) magnificent, splendid; (*generoso*) generous

esplendor [esplen'dor] *nm* splendour

espolvorear [espolβore'ar] *vt* to dust, sprinkle

esponja [es'ponxa] *nf* sponge; (*fig*) sponger; **esponjoso, -a** *adj* spongy

espontaneidad [espontanei'ðað] *nf* spontaneity; **espontáneo, -a** *adj* spontaneous

esposa [es'posa] *nf* wife; **esposas** *nfpl* handcuffs; **esposar** *vt* to handcuff

esposo [es'poso] *nm* husband

espray [es'prai] *nm* spray

espuela [es'pwela] *nf* spur

espuma [es'puma] *nf* foam; (*de cerveza*) froth, head; (*de jabón*) lather; **espuma de afeitar** shaving foam; **espumadera** *nf* (*utensilio*) skimmer; **espumoso, -a** *adj*

frothy, foamy; (vino) sparkling
esqueleto [eske'leto] nm skeleton
esquema [es'kema] nm (diagrama)
diagram; (dibujo) plan; (Filosofía) schema
esquí [es'ki] (pl **~s**) nm (objeto) ski; (Deporte)
skiing; **esquí acuático** water-skiing;
esquiar vi to ski
esquilar [eski'lar] vt to shear
esquimal [eski'mal] adj, nmf Eskimo
esquina [es'kina] nf corner; **esquinazo**
[eski'naθo] nm: **dar esquinazo a algn** to
give sb the slip
esquirol [eski'rol] (ESP) nm strikebreaker,
scab
esquivar [eski'βar] vt to avoid
esta ['esta] adj demos V **este²**
está vb V **estar**
ésta pron V **éste**
estabilidad [estaβili'ðað] nf stability;
estable adj stable
establecer [estaβle'θer] vt to establish;
establecerse vr to establish o.s.; (echar
raíces) to settle (down); **establecimiento**
nm establishment
establo [es'taβlo] nm (Agr) stable
estaca [es'taka] nf stake, post; (de tienda de
campaña) peg
estacada [esta'kaða] nf (cerca) fence,
fencing; (palenque) stockade
estación [esta'θjon] nf station; (del
año) season; **estación balnearia** seaside
resort; **estación de autobuses** bus station;
estación de servicio service station
estacionamiento [estaθjona'mjento]
nm (Auto) parking; (Mil) stationing
estacionar [estaθjo'nar] vt (Auto) to park;
(Mil) to station
estadía [esta'ðia] (LAM) nf stay
estadio [es'taðjo] nm (fase) stage, phase;
(Deporte) stadium
estadista [esta'ðista] nm (Pol) statesman;
(Mat) statistician
estadística [esta'ðistika] nf figure,
statistic; (ciencia) statistics sg
estado [es'taðo] nm (Pol: condición) state;
estar en ~ to be pregnant; **estado civil**
marital status; **estado de ánimo** state of
mind; **estado de cuenta** bank statement;
estado de sitio state of siege; **estado
mayor** staff; **Estados Unidos** United States
(of America)
estadounidense [estaðouni'ðense]
adj United States cpd, American ▷ nmf
American
estafa [es'tafa] nf swindle, trick; **estafar**
vt to swindle, defraud
estáis vb V **estar**
estallar [esta'ʎar] vi to burst; (bomba) to

explode, go off; (epidemia, guerra, rebelión) to
break out; **~ en llanto** to burst into tears;
estallido nm explosion; (fig) outbreak
estampa [es'tampa] nf print, engraving;
estampado, -a [estam'paðo, a] adj
printed ▷ nm (impresión: acción) printing;
(: efecto) print; (marca) stamping
estampar [estam'par] vt (imprimir) to
print; (marcar) to stamp; (metal) to engrave;
(poner sello en) to stamp; (fig) to stamp,
imprint
estampida [estam'piða] nf stampede
estampido [estam'piðo] nm bang, report
estampilla [estam'piʎa] (LAM) nf
(postage) stamp
están vb V **estar**
estancado, -a [estan'kaðo, a] adj
stagnant
estancar [estan'kar] vt (aguas) to hold
up, hold back; (Com) to monopolize; (fig) to
block, hold up; **estancarse** vr to stagnate
estancia [es'tanθja] nf (ESP,
MÉX: permanencia) stay; (sala) room; (RPL: de
ganado) farm, ranch; **estanciero** (RPL) nm
farmer, rancher
estanco, -a [es'tanko, a] adj watertight
▷ nm tobacconist's (shop), cigar store (US)

ESTANCO

Cigarettes, tobacco, postage stamps
and official forms are all sold under state
monopoly in shops called **estancos**.
Although tobacco products can also be
bought in bars and quioscos they are
generally more expensive.

estándar [es'tandar] adj, nm standard
estandarte [estan'darte] nm banner,
standard
estanque [es'tanke] nm (lago) pool, pond;
(Agr) reservoir
estanquero, -a [estan'kero, a] nm/f
tobacconist
estante [es'tante] nm (armario) rack,
stand; (biblioteca) bookcase; (anaquel) shelf;
estantería nf shelving, shelves pl

○ **PALABRA CLAVE**

estar [es'tar] vi 1 (posición) to be; **está en la
plaza** it's in the square; **¿está Juan?** is Juan
in?; **estamos a 30 km de Junín** we're 30 kms
from Junín
2 (+ adj: estado) to be; **estar enfermo** to be ill;
está muy elegante he's looking very smart;
¿cómo estás? how are you keeping?
3 (+ gerundio) to be; **estoy leyendo** I'm

4 (*uso pasivo*): **está condenado a muerte** he's been condemned to death; **está envasado en ...** it's packed in ...

5 (*con fechas*): **¿a cuántos estamos?** what's the date today?; **estamos a 5 de mayo** it's the 5th of May

6 (*locuciones*): **¿estamos?** (*¿de acuerdo?*) okay?; (*¿listo?*) ready?

7: **estar de: estar de vacaciones/viaje** to be on holiday/away *o* on a trip; **está de camarero** he's working as a waiter

8: **estar para: está para salir** he's about to leave; **no estoy para bromas** I'm not in the mood for jokes

9: **estar por** (*propuesta etc*) to be in favour of; (*persona etc*) to support, side with; **está por limpiar** it still has to be cleaned

10: **estar sin: estar sin dinero** to have no money; **está sin terminar** it isn't finished yet

estarse *vr*: **se estuvo en la cama toda la tarde** he stayed in bed all afternoon

estas ['estas] *adj demos* V **este²**
éstas *pron* V **éste**
estatal [esta'tal] *adj* state *cpd*
estático, -a [es'tatiko, a] *adj* static
estatua [es'tatwa] *nf* statue
estatura [esta'tura] *nf* stature, height
este¹ ['este] *nm* east
este² ['este] (*f* **esta**, *pl* **estos, estas**) *adj demos* (*sg*) this; (*pl*) these
esté *etc vb* V **estar**
éste ['este] (*f* **ésta**, *pl* **éstos, éstas**) *pron* (*sg*) this (one); (*pl*) these (ones); **ése ... ~ ...** the former ... the latter ...
estén *etc vb* V **estar**
estepa [es'tepa] *nf* (*Geo*) steppe
estera [es'tera] *nf* mat(ting)
estéreo [es'tereo] *adj inv, nm* stereo; **estereotipo** *nm* stereotype
estéril [es'teril] *adj* sterile, barren; (*fig*) vain, futile; **esterilizar** *vt* to sterilize
esterlina [ester'lina] *adj*: **libra ~** pound sterling
estés *etc vb* V **estar**
estética [es'tetika] *nf* aesthetics *sg*
estético, -a [es'tetiko, a] *adj* aesthetic
estiércol [es'tjerkol] *nm* dung, manure
estigma [es'tiɣma] *nm* stigma
estilo [es'tilo] *nm* style; (*Tec*) stylus; (*Natación*) stroke; **algo por el ~** something along those lines
estima [es'tima] *nf* esteem, respect; **estimación** [estima'θjon] *nf* (*evaluación*) estimation; (*aprecio, afecto*) esteem, regard; **estimado, a** *adj* esteemed; **E~ señor** Dear

Sir

estimar [esti'mar] *vt* (*evaluar*) to estimate; (*valorar*) to value; (*apreciar*) to esteem, respect; (*pensar, considerar*) to think, reckon
estimulante [estimu'lante] *adj* stimulating ▷ *nm* stimulant
estimular [estimu'lar] *vt* to stimulate; (*excitar*) to excite
estímulo [es'timulo] *nm* stimulus; (*ánimo*) encouragement
estirar [esti'rar] *vt* to stretch; (*dinero, suma etc*) to stretch out; **estirarse** *vr* to stretch
estirón [esti'ron] *nm* pull, tug; (*crecimiento*) spurt, sudden growth; **dar** *o* **pegar un ~** (*fam: niño*) to shoot up (*inf*)
estirpe [es'tirpe] *nf* stock, lineage
estival [esti'βal] *adj* summer *cpd*
esto ['esto] *pron* this, this thing *o* matter; **~ de la boda** this business about the wedding
Estocolmo [esto'kolmo] *nm* Stockholm
estofado [esto'faðo] *nm* stew
estómago [es'tomaxo] *nm* stomach; **tener ~** to be thick-skinned
estorbar [estor'βar] *vt* to hinder, obstruct; (*molestar*) to bother, disturb ▷ *vi* to be in the way; **estorbo** *nm* (*molestia*) bother, nuisance; (*obstáculo*) hindrance, obstacle
estornudar [estornu'ðar] *vi* to sneeze
estos ['estos] *adj demos* V **este²**
éstos *pron* V **éste**
estoy *vb* V **estar**
estrado [es'traðo] *nm* platform
estrafalario, -a [estrafa'larjo, a] *adj* odd, eccentric
estrago [es'traxo] *nm* ruin, destruction; **hacer ~s en** to wreak havoc among
estragón [estra'xon] *nm* tarragon
estrambótico, -a [estram'botiko, a] *adj* (*persona*) eccentric; (*peinado, ropa*) outlandish
estrangular [estrangu'lar] *vt* (*persona*) to strangle; (*Med*) to strangulate
estratagema [estrata'xema] *nf* (*Mil*) stratagem; (*astucia*) cunning
estrategia [estra'texja] *nf* strategy; **estratégico, -a** *adj* strategic
estrato [es'trato] *nm* stratum, layer
estrechar [estre'tʃar] *vt* (*reducir*) to narrow; (*Costura*) to take in; (*abrazar*) to hug, embrace; **estrecharse** *vr* (*reducirse*) to narrow, grow narrow; (*abrazarse*) to embrace; **~ la mano** to shake hands
estrechez [estre'tʃeθ] *nf* narrowness; (*de ropa*) tightness; **estrecheces** *nfpl* (*dificultades económicas*) financial difficulties
estrecho, -a [es'tretʃo, a] *adj* narrow; (*apretado*) tight; (*íntimo*) close, intimate; (*miserable*) mean ▷ *nm* strait; **~ de miras**

89 | **estrecho**

narrow-minded

estrella [es'treʎa] nf star; **estrella de mar**
(Zool) starfish; **estrella fugaz** shooting star

estrellar [estre'ʎar] vt (hacer añicos)
to smash (to pieces); (huevos) to fry;
estrellarse vr to smash; (chocarse) to crash;
(fracasar) to fail

estremecer [estreme'θer] vt to shake;
estremecerse vr to shake, tremble

estrenar [estre'nar] vt (vestido) to wear for
the first time; (casa) to move into; (película,
obra de teatro) to première; **estrenarse** vr
(persona) to make one's début; **estreno** nm
(Cine etc) première

estreñido, -a [estre'ɲiðo, a] adj
constipated

estreñimiento [estreɲi'mjento] nm
constipation

estrepitoso, -a [estrepi'toso, a] adj
noisy; (fiesta) rowdy

estría [es'tria] nf groove

estribar [estri'βar] vi: ~ **en** to lie on

estribillo [estri'βiʎo] nm (Literatura)
refrain; (Mús) chorus

estribo [es'triβo] nm (de jinete) stirrup; (de
coche, tren) step; (de puente) support; (Geo)
spur; **perder los ~s** to fly off the handle

estribor [estri'βor] nm (Náut) starboard

estricto, -a [es'trikto, a] adj (riguroso)
strict; (severo) severe

estridente [estri'ðente] adj (color) loud;
(voz) raucous

estropajo [estro'paxo] nm scourer

estropear [estrope'ar] vt to spoil; (dañar)
to damage; **estropearse** vr (objeto) to get
damaged; (persona, piel) to be ruined

estructura [estruk'tura] nf structure

estrujar [estru'xar] vt (apretar) to squeeze;
(aplastar) to crush; (fig) to drain, bleed

estuario [es'twarjo] nm estuary

estuche [es'tutʃe] nm box, case

estudiante [estu'ðjante] nmf student;
estudiantil adj student cpd

estudiar [estu'ðjar] vt to study

estudio [es'tuðjo] nm study; (Cine, Arte,
Radio) studio; **estudios** nmpl studies;
(erudición) learning sg; **estudioso, -a** adj
studious

estufa [es'tufa] nf heater, fire

estupefaciente [estupefa'θjente] nm
drug, narcotic

estupefacto, -a [estupe'fakto, a] adj
speechless, thunderstruck

estupendo, -a [estu'pendo, a] adj
wonderful, terrific; (fam) great; ¡~! that's
great!, fantastic!

estupidez [estupi'ðeθ] nf (torpeza)
stupidity; (acto) stupid thing (to do)

estúpido, -a [es'tupiðo, a] adj stupid,
silly

estuve etc vb V **estar**

ETA ['eta] (ESP) nf abr (= Euskadi ta
Askatasuna) ETA

etapa [e'tapa] nf (de viaje) stage; (Deporte)
leg; (parada) stopping place; (fase) stage,
phase

etarra [e'tarra] nmf member of ETA

etc. abr (= etcétera) etc

etcétera [et'θetera] adv etcetera

eternidad [eterni'ðað] nf eternity;
eterno, -a adj eternal, everlasting

ética ['etika] nf ethics pl

ético, -a ['etiko, a] adj ethical

etiqueta [eti'keta] nf (modales) etiquette;
(rótulo) label, tag

Eucaristía [eukaris'tia] nf Eucharist

euforia [eu'forja] nf euphoria

euro ['euro] nm (moneda) euro

eurodiputado, -a [eurodipu'taðo, a]
nm/f Euro MP, MEP

Europa [eu'ropa] nf Europe; **europeo, -a**
adj, nm/f European

Euskadi [eus'kaði] nm the Basque
Country o Provinces pl

euskera [eus'kera] nm (Ling) Basque

evacuación [eβakwa'θjon] nf evacuation

evacuar [eβa'kwar] vt to evacuate

evadir [eβa'ðir] vt to evade, avoid;
evadirse vr to escape

evaluar [eβa'lwar] vt to evaluate

evangelio [eβan'xeljo] nm gospel

evaporar [eβapo'rar] vt to evaporate;
evaporarse vr to vanish

evasión [eβa'sjon] nf escape, flight; (fig)
evasion; **evasión de capitales** flight of
capital

evasiva [eβa'siβa] nf (pretexto) excuse

evento [e'βento] nm event

eventual [eβen'twal] adj possible,
conditional (upon circumstances);
(trabajador) casual, temporary

▌No confundir **eventual** con la palabra
inglesa eventual.

evidencia [eβi'ðenθja] nf evidence, proof

evidente [eβi'ðente] adj obvious, clear,
evident

evitar [eβi'tar] vt (evadir) to avoid; (impedir)
to prevent; ~ **hacer algo** to avoid doing sth

evocar [eβo'kar] vt to evoke, call forth

evolución [eβolu'θjon] nf (desarrollo)
evolution, development; (cambio) change;
(Mil) manoeuvre; **evolucionar** vi to evolve;
to manoeuvre

ex [eks] adj ex-; **el ~ ministro** the former
minister, the ex-minister

exactitud [eksakti'tuð] nf exactness;

(*precisión*) accuracy; (*puntualidad*) punctuality; **exacto, -a** *adj* exact; accurate; punctual; **¡exacto!** exactly!

exageración [eksaxera'θjon] *nf* exaggeration

exagerar [eksaxe'rar] *vt, vi* to exaggerate

exaltar [eksal'tar] *vt* to exalt, glorify; **exaltarse** *vr* (*excitarse*) to get excited o worked up

examen [ek'samen] *nm* examination; **examen de conducir** driving test; **examen de ingreso** entrance examination

examinar [eksami'nar] *vt* to examine; **examinarse** *vr* to be examined, take an examination

excavadora [ekskaβa'ðora] *nf* excavator

excavar [ekska'βar] *vt* to excavate

excedencia [eksθe'ðenθja] *nf:* **estar en ~** to be on leave; **pedir** o **solicitar la ~** to ask for leave

excedente [eksθe'ðente] *adj, nm* excess, surplus

exceder [eksθe'ðer] *vt* to exceed, surpass; **excederse** *vr* (*extralimitarse*) to go too far

excelencia [eksθe'lenθja] *nf* excellence; **su E~** his Excellency; **excelente** *adj* excellent

excéntrico, -a [eks'θentriko, a] *adj, nm/f* eccentric

excepción [eksθep'θjon] *nf* exception; **a ~ de** with the exception of, except for; **excepcional** *adj* exceptional

excepto [eks'θepto] *adv* excepting, except (for)

exceptuar [eksθep'twar] *vt* to except, exclude

excesivo, -a [eksθe'siβo, a] *adj* excessive

exceso [eks'θeso] *nm* (*gen*) excess; (*Com*) surplus; **exceso de equipaje/peso** excess luggage/weight; **exceso de velocidad** speeding

excitado, -a [eksθi'taðo, a] *adj* excited; (*emociones*) aroused

excitar [eksθi'tar] *vt* to excite; (*incitar*) to urge; **excitarse** *vr* to get excited

exclamación [eksklama'θjon] *nf* exclamation

exclamar [ekskla'mar] *vi* to exclaim

excluir [eksklu'ir] *vt* to exclude; (*dejar fuera*) to shut out; (*descartar*) to reject

exclusiva [eksklu'siβa] *nf* (*Prensa*) exclusive, scoop; (*Com*) sole right

exclusivo, -a [eksklu'siβo, a] *adj* exclusive; **derecho ~** sole o exclusive right

Excmo. *abr* = **excelentísmo**

excomulgar [ekskomul'ɣar] *vt* (*Rel*) to excommunicate

excomunión [ekskomu'njon] *nf* excommunication

excursión [ekskur'sjon] *nf* excursion, outing; **excursionista** *nmf* (*turista*) sightseer

excusa [eks'kusa] *nf* excuse; (*disculpa*) apology; **excusar** [eksku'sar] *vt* to excuse

exhaustivo, -a [eksaus'tiβo, a] *adj* (*análisis*) thorough; (*estudio*) exhaustive

exhausto, -a [ek'sausto, a] *adj* exhausted

exhibición [eksiβi'θjon] *nf* exhibition, display, show

exhibir [eksi'βir] *vt* to exhibit, display, show

exigencia [eksi'xenθja] *nf* demand, requirement; **exigente** *adj* demanding

exigir [eksi'xir] *vt* (*gen*) to demand, require; **~ el pago** to demand payment

exiliado, -a [eksi'ljaðo, a] *adj* exiled ▷ *nm/f* exile

exilio [ek'siljo] *nm* exile

eximir [eksi'mir] *vt* to exempt

existencia [eksis'tenθja] *nf* existence; **existencias** *nfpl* stock(s) *pl*

existir [eksis'tir] *vi* to exist, be

éxito ['eksito] *nm* (*triunfo*) success; (*Mús etc*) hit; **tener ~** to be successful

▌ No confundir **éxito** con la palabra inglesa *exit*.

exorbitante [eksorβi'tante] *adj* (*precio*) exorbitant; (*cantidad*) excessive

exótico, -a [ek'sotiko, a] *adj* exotic

expandir [ekspan'dir] *vt* to expand

expansión [ekspan'sjon] *nf* expansion

expansivo, -a [ekspan'siβo, a] *adj:* **onda expansiva** shock wave

expatriarse [ekspa'trjarse] *vr* to emigrate; (*Pol*) to go into exile

expectativa [ekspekta'tiβa] *nf* (*espera*) expectation; (*perspectiva*) prospect

expedición [ekspeði'θjon] *nf* (*excursión*) expedition

expediente [ekspe'ðjente] *nm* expedient; (*Jur: procedimento*) action, proceedings *pl*; (*: papeles*) dossier, file, record

expedir [ekspe'ðir] *vt* (*despachar*) to send, forward; (*pasaporte*) to issue

expensas [eks'pensas] *nfpl:* **a ~ de** at the expense of

experiencia [ekspe'rjenθja] *nf* experience

experimentado, -a [eksperimen'taðo, a] *adj* experienced

experimentar [eksperimen'tar] *vt* (*en laboratorio*) to experiment with; (*probar*) to test, try out; (*notar, observar*) to experience; (*deterioro, pérdida*) to suffer; **experimento** *nm* experiment

experto, -a [eks'perto, a] *adj* expert, skilled ▷ *nm/f* expert

expirar [ekspi'rar] *vi* to expire

explanada [ekspla'naða] *nf (llano)* plain

explayarse [ekspla'jarse] *vr (en discurso)* to speak at length; **~ con algn** to confide in sb

explicación [eksplika'θjon] *nf* explanation

explicar [ekspli'kar] *vt* to explain; **explicarse** *vr* to explain (o.s.)

explícito, -a [eks'pliθito, a] *adj* explicit

explique *etc vb* V **explicar**

explorador, a [eksplora'ðor, a] *nm/f (pionero)* explorer; *(Mil)* scout ▷ *nm (Med)* probe; *(Tec)* (radar) scanner

explorar [eksplo'rar] *vt* to explore; *(Med)* to probe; *(radar)* to scan

explosión [eksplo'sjon] *nf* explosion; **explosivo, -a** *adj* explosive

explotación [eksplota'θjon] *nf* exploitation; *(de planta etc)* running

explotar [eksplo'tar] *vt* to exploit to run, operate ▷ *vi* to explode

exponer [ekspo'ner] *vt* to expose; *(cuadro)* to display; *(vida)* to risk; *(idea)* to explain; **exponerse** *vr:* **~se a (hacer) algo** to run the risk of (doing) sth

exportación [eksporta'θjon] *nf (acción)* export; *(mercancías)* exports *pl*

exportar [ekspor'tar] *vt* to export

exposición [eksposi'θjon] *nf (gen)* exposure; *(de arte)* show, exhibition; *(explicación)* explanation; *(declaración)* account, statement

expresamente [ekspresa'mente] *adv (decir)* clearly; *(a propósito)* expressly

expresar [ekspre'sar] *vt* to express; **expresión** *nf* expression

expresivo, -a [ekspre'siβo, a] *adj (persona, gesto, palabras)* expressive; *(cariñoso)* affectionate

expreso, -a [eks'preso, a] *pp de* **expresar** ▷ *adj (explícito)* express; *(claro)* specific, clear; *(tren)* fast ▷ *adv:* **enviar ~** to send by express (delivery)

express [eks'pres] (LAM) *adv:* **enviar algo ~** to send sth special delivery

exprimidor [eksprimi'ðor] *nm* squeezer

exprimir [ekspri'mir] *vt (fruta)* to squeeze; *(zumo)* to squeeze out

expuesto, -a [eks'pwesto, a] *pp de* **exponer** ▷ *adj* exposed; *(cuadro etc)* on show, on display

expulsar [ekspul'sar] *vt (echar)* to eject, throw out; *(alumno)* to expel; *(despedir)* to sack, fire; *(Deporte)* to send off; **expulsión** *nf* expulsion; sending-off

exquisito, -a [ekski'sito, a] *adj* exquisite; *(comida)* delicious

éxtasis ['ekstasis] *nm* ecstasy

extender [eksten'der] *vt* to extend; *(los brazos)* to stretch out, hold out; *(mapa, tela)* to spread (out), open (out); *(mantequilla)* to spread; *(certificado)* to issue; *(cheque, recibo)* to make out; *(documento)* to draw up; **extenderse** *vr (gen)* to extend; *(persona: en el suelo)* to stretch out; *(epidemia)* to spread; **extendido, -a** *adj (abierto)* spread out, open; *(brazos)* outstretched; *(costumbre)* widespread

extensión [eksten'sjon] *nf (de terreno, mar)* expanse, stretch; *(de tiempo)* length, duration; *(Tel)* extension; **en toda la ~ de la palabra** in every sense of the word

extenso, -a [eks'tenso, a] *adj* extensive

exterior [ekste'rjor] *adj (de fuera)* external; *(afuera)* outside, exterior; *(apariencia)* outward; *(deuda, relaciones)* foreign ▷ *nm (gen)* exterior, outside; *(aspecto)* outward appearance; *(Deporte)* wing(er); *(países extranjeros)* abroad; **en el ~** abroad; **al ~** outwardly, on the surface

exterminar [ekstermi'nar] *vt* to exterminate

externo, -a [eks'terno, a] *adj (exterior)* external, outside; *(superficial)* outward ▷ *nm/f* day pupil

extinguir [ekstin'gir] *vt (fuego)* to extinguish, put out; *(raza, población)* to wipe out; **extinguirse** *vr (fuego)* to go out; *(Bio)* to die out, become extinct

extintor [ekstin'tor] *nm* (fire) extinguisher

extirpar [ekstir'par] *vt (Med)* to remove (surgically)

extra ['ekstra] *adj inv (tiempo)* extra; *(chocolate, vino)* good-quality ▷ *nmf* extra ▷ *nm* extra; *(bono)* bonus

extracción [ekstrak'θjon] *nf* extraction; *(en lotería)* draw

extracto [eks'trakto] *nm* extract

extradición [ekstraði'θjon] *nf* extradition

extraer [ekstra'er] *vt* to extract, take out

extraescolar [ekstraesko'lar] *adj:* **actividad ~** extracurricular activity

extranjero, -a [ekstran'xero, a] *adj* foreign ▷ *nm/f* foreigner ▷ *nm* foreign countries *pl*; **en el ~** abroad

> No confundir **extranjero** con la palabra inglesa *stranger*.

extrañar [ekstra'nar] *vt (sorprender)* to find strange o odd; *(echar de menos)* to miss; **extrañarse** *vr (sorprenderse)* to be amazed, be surprised; **me extraña** I'm surprised

extraño, -a [eks'traɲo, a] *adj* (*extranjero*) foreign; (*raro, sorprendente*) strange, odd

extraordinario, -a [ekstraorði'narjo, a] *adj* extraordinary; (*edición, número*) special ▷ *nm* (*de periódico*) special edition; **horas extraordinarias** overtime *sg*

extrarradio [ekstra'rraðjo] *nm* suburbs

extravagante [ekstraβa'ɣante] *adj* (*excéntrico*) eccentric; (*estrafalario*) outlandish

extraviado, -a [ekstra'βjaðo, a] *adj* lost, missing

extraviar [ekstra'βjar] *vt* (*persona: desorientar*) to mislead, misdirect; (*perder*) to lose, misplace; **extraviarse** *vr* to lose one's way, get lost

extremar [ekstre'mar] *vt* to carry to extremes

extremaunción [ekstremaun'θjon] *nf* extreme unction

extremidad [ekstremi'ðað] *nf* (*punta*) extremity; **extremidades** *nfpl* (Anat) extremities

extremo, -a [eks'tremo, a] *adj* extreme; (*último*) last ▷ *nm* end; (*límite, grado sumo*) extreme; **en último ~** as a last resort

extrovertido, -a [ekstroβer'tiðo, a] *adj, nm/f* extrovert

exuberante [eksuβe'rante] *adj* exuberant; (*fig*) luxuriant, lush

eyacular [ejaku'lar] *vt, vi* to ejaculate

fa [fa] *nm* (Mús) fa, F

fabada [fa'βaða] *nf* bean and sausage stew

fábrica ['faβrika] *nf* factory; **marca de ~** trademark; **precio de ~** factory price

❚ No confundir **fábrica** con la palabra inglesa *fabric*.

fabricación [faβrika'θjon] *nf* (*manufactura*) manufacture; (*producción*) production; **de ~ casera** home-made; **fabricación en serie** mass production

fabricante [faβri'kante] *nmf* manufacturer

fabricar [faβri'kar] *vt* (*manufacturar*) to manufacture, make; (*construir*) to build; (*cuento*) to fabricate, devise

fábula ['faβula] *nf* (*cuento*) fable; (*chisme*) rumour; (*mentira*) fib

fabuloso, -a [faβu'loso, a] *adj* (*oportunidad, tiempo*) fabulous, great

facción [fak'θjon] *nf* (Pol) faction; **facciones** *nfpl* (*de rostro*) features

faceta [fa'θeta] *nf* facet

facha ['fatʃa] (fam) *nf* (*aspecto*) look; (*cara*) face

fachada [fa'tʃaða] *nf* (Arq) façade, front

fácil ['faθil] *adj* (*simple*) easy; (*probable*) likely

facilidad [faθili'ðað] *nf* (*capacidad*) ease; (*sencillez*) simplicity; (*de palabra*) fluency; **facilidades** *nfpl* facilities; **facilidades de pago** credit facilities

facilitar [faθili'tar] *vt* (*hacer fácil*) to make easy; (*proporcionar*) to provide

factor [fak'tor] *nm* factor

factura [fak'tura] *nf* (*cuenta*) bill; **facturación** *nf* (*de equipaje*) check-in; **facturar** *vt* (Com) to invoice, charge for; (*equipaje*) to check in

facultad [fakul'tað] *nf* (*aptitud, Escol etc*) faculty; (*poder*) power

faena [fa'ena] nf (trabajo) work; (quehacer) task, job

faisán [fai'san] nm pheasant

faja ['faxa] nf (para la cintura) sash; (de mujer) corset; (de tierra) strip

fajo ['faxo] nm (de papeles) bundle; (de billetes) wad

falda ['falda] nf (prenda de vestir) skirt; **falda pantalón** culottes pl, split skirt

falla ['faʎa] nf (defecto) fault, flaw; **falla humana** (LAM) human error

fallar [fa'ʎar] vt (Jur) to pronounce sentence on ▷ vi (memoria) to fail; (motor) to miss

Fallas ['faʎas] nfpl Valencian celebration of the feast of St Joseph

● **FALLAS**
●
● In the week of 19 March (the feast
● of San José), Valencia honours its
● patron saint with a spectacular fiesta
● called **Las Fallas**. The **Fallas** are huge
● papier-mâché, cardboard and wooden
● sculptures which are built by competing
● teams throughout the year. They depict
● politicians and well-known public
● figures and are thrown onto bonfires
● and set alight once a jury has judged
● them – only the best sculpture escapes
● the flames.

fallecer [faʎe'θer] vi to pass away, die; **fallecimiento** nm decease, demise

fallido, -a [fa'ʎiðo, a] adj (gen) frustrated, unsuccessful

fallo ['faʎo] nm (Jur) verdict, ruling; (fracaso) failure; **fallo cardíaco** heart failure; **fallo humano** (ESP) human error

falsificar [falsifi'kar] vt (firma etc) to forge; (moneda) to counterfeit

falso, -a ['falso, a] adj false; (documento, moneda etc) fake; **en ~** falsely

falta ['falta] nf (defecto) fault, flaw; (privación) lack, want; (ausencia) absence; (carencia) shortage; (equivocación) mistake; (Deporte) foul; **echar en ~** to miss; **hacer ~ hacer algo** to be necessary to do sth; **me hace ~ una pluma** I need a pen; **falta de educación** bad manners pl; **falta de ortografía** spelling mistake

faltar [fal'tar] vi (escasear) to be lacking, be wanting; (ausentarse) to be absent, be missing; **faltan 2 horas para llegar** there are 2 hours to go till arrival; **~ al respeto a algn** to be disrespectful to sb; **¡no faltaba más!** (no hay de qué) don't mention it

fama ['fama] nf (renombre) fame; (reputación) reputation

familia [fa'milja] nf family; **familia numerosa** large family; **familia política** in-laws pl

familiar [fami'ljar] adj (relativo a la familia) family cpd; (conocido, informal) familiar ▷ nm relative, relation

famoso, -a [fa'moso, a] adj (renombrado) famous

fan [fan] (pl **~s**) nmf fan

fanático, -a [fa'natiko, a] adj fanatical ▷ nm/f fanatic; (Cine, Deporte) fan

fanfarrón, -ona [fanfa'rron, ona] adj boastful

fango ['fango] nm mud

fantasía [fanta'sia] nf fantasy, imagination; **joyas de ~** imitation jewellery sg

fantasma [fan'tasma] nm (espectro) ghost, apparition; (fanfarrón) show-off

fantástico, -a [fan'tastiko, a] adj fantastic

farmacéutico, -a [farma'θeutiko, a] adj pharmaceutical ▷ nm/f chemist (BRIT), pharmacist

farmacia [far'maθja] nf chemist's (shop) (BRIT), pharmacy; **farmacia de guardia** all-night chemist

fármaco ['farmako] nm drug

faro ['faro] nm (Náut: torre) lighthouse; (Auto) headlamp; **faros antiniebla** fog lamps; **faros delanteros/traseros** headlights/rear lights

farol [fa'rol] nm lantern, lamp

farola [fa'rola] nf street lamp (BRIT) o light (US)

farra ['farra] (LAM: fam) nf party; **ir de ~** to go on a binge

farsa ['farsa] nf (gen) farce

farsante [far'sante] nmf fraud, fake

fascículo [fas'θikulo] nm (de revista) part, instalment

fascinar [fasθi'nar] vt (gen) to fascinate

fascismo [fas'θismo] nm fascism; **fascista** adj, nmf fascist

fase ['fase] nf phase

fashion ['faʃon] adj (fam) trendy

fastidiar [fasti'ðjar] vt (molestar) to annoy, bother; (estropear) to spoil; **fastidiarse** vr: **¡que se fastidie!** (fam) he'll just have to put up with it!

fastidio [fas'tiðjo] nm (molestia) annoyance; **fastidioso, -a** adj (molesto) annoying

fatal [fa'tal] adj (gen) fatal; (desgraciado) ill-fated; (fam: malo, pésimo) awful; **fatalidad** nf (destino) fate; (mala suerte) misfortune

fatiga [fa'tixa] nf (cansancio) fatigue,

weariness

fatigar [fati'ɣar] vt to tire, weary

fatigoso, -a [fati'ɣoso, a] adj (cansador) tiring

fauna ['fauna] nf fauna

favor [fa'βor] nm favour; **estar a ~ de** to be in favour of; **haga el ~ de ...** would you be so good as to ...; kindly ...; **por ~** please; **favorable** adj favourable

favorecer [faβore'θer] vt to favour; (vestido etc) to become, flatter; **este peinado le favorece** this hairstyle suits him

favorito, -a [faβo'rito, a] adj, nm/f favourite

fax [faks] nm inv fax; **mandar por ~** to fax

fe [fe] nf (Rel) faith; (documento) certificate; **actuar con buena/mala ~** to act in good/bad faith

febrero [fe'βrero] nm February

fecha ['fetʃa] nf date; **con ~ adelantada** postdated; **en ~ próxima** soon; **hasta la ~** to date, so far; **poner ~** to date; **fecha de caducidad** (de producto alimenticio) sell-by date; (de contrato etc) expiry date; **fecha de nacimiento** date of birth; **fecha límite** o **tope** deadline

fecundo, -a [fe'kundo, a] adj (fértil) fertile; (fig) prolific; (productivo) productive

federación [feðera'θjon] nf federation

felicidad [feliθi'ðað] nf happiness; **¡~es!** (deseos) best wishes, congratulations!; (en cumpleaños) happy birthday!

felicitación [feliθita'θjon] nf (tarjeta) greeting(s) card

felicitar [feliθi'tar] vt to congratulate

feliz [fe'liθ] adj happy

felpudo [fel'puðo] nm doormat

femenino, -a [feme'nino, a] adj, nm feminine

feminista [femi'nista] adj, nmf feminist

fenómeno [fe'nomeno] nm phenomenon; (fig) freak, accident ▷ adj great ▷ excl great!, marvellous!; **fenomenal** adj = **fenómeno**

feo, -a ['feo, a] adj (gen) ugly; (desagradable) bad, nasty

féretro ['feretro] nm (ataúd) coffin; (sarcófago) bier

feria ['ferja] nf (gen) fair; (descanso) holiday, rest day; (MÉX: cambio) small o loose change; (cs: mercado) village market

feriado [fe'rjaðo] (LAM) nm holiday

fermentar [fermen'tar] vi to ferment

feroz [fe'roθ] adj (cruel) cruel; (salvaje) fierce

férreo, -a ['ferreo, a] adj iron

ferretería [ferrete'ria] nf (tienda) ironmonger's (shop) (BRIT), hardware store (US)

ferrocarril [ferroka'rril] nm railway

ferroviario, -a [ferro'βjarjo, a] adj rail cpd

ferry ['ferri] (pl **~s** o **ferries**) nm ferry

fértil ['fertil] adj (productivo) fertile; (rico) rich; **fertilidad** nf (gen) fertility; (productividad) fruitfulness

fervor [fer'βor] nm fervour

festejar [feste'xar] vt (celebrar) to celebrate

festejo [fes'texo] nm celebration; **festejos** nmpl (fiestas) festivals

festín [fes'tin] nm feast, banquet

festival [festi'βal] nm festival

festividad [festiβi'ðað] nf festivity

festivo, -a [fes'tiβo, a] adj (de fiesta) festive; (Cine, Literatura) humorous; **día ~** holiday

feto ['feto] nm foetus

fiable ['fjaβle] adj (persona) trustworthy; (máquina) reliable

fiambre ['fjambre] nm cold meat

fiambrera [fjam'brera] nf (para almuerzo) lunch box

fianza ['fjanθa] nf surety; (Jur): **libertad bajo ~** release on bail

fiar [fi'ar] vt (salir garante de) to guarantee; (vender a crédito) to sell on credit ▷ vi to trust; **fiarse** vr to trust (in), rely on; **~ a** (secreto) to confide (to); **~se de algn** to rely on sb

fibra ['fiβra] nf fibre; **fibra óptica** optical fibre

ficción [fik'θjon] nf fiction

ficha ['fitʃa] nf (Tel) token; (en juegos) counter, marker; (tarjeta) (index) card; **fichaje** nm (Deporte) signing; **fichar** vt (archivar) to file, index; (Deporte) to sign; **estar fichado** to have a record; **fichero** nm box file; (Inform) file

ficticio, -a [fik'tiθjo, a] adj (imaginario) fictitious; (falso) fabricated

fidelidad [fiðeli'ðað] nf (lealtad) fidelity, loyalty; **alta ~** high fidelity, hi-fi

fideos [fi'ðeos] nmpl noodles

fiebre ['fjeβre] nf (Med) fever; (fig) fever, excitement; **tener ~** to have a temperature; **fiebre aftosa** foot-and-mouth disease

fiel [fjel] adj (leal) faithful, loyal; (fiable) reliable; (exacto) accurate, faithful ▷ nm: **los ~es** the faithful

fieltro ['fjeltro] nm felt

fiera ['fjera] nf (animal feroz) wild animal o beast; (fig) dragon; V tb **fiero**

fiero, -a ['fjero, a] adj (cruel) cruel; (feroz) fierce; (duro) harsh

fierro ['fjerro] (LAM) nm (hierro) iron

fiesta ['fjesta] *nf* party; (*de pueblo*) festival; (*vacaciones*: tb: **~s**) holiday *sg*; **fiesta mayor** annual festival; **fiesta patria** (*LAM*) independence day

● **FIESTAS**
●
● **Fiestas** can be official public holidays
● or holidays set by each autonomous
● region, many of which coincide with
● religious festivals. There are also
● many **fiestas** all over Spain for a local
● patron saint or the Virgin Mary. These
● often last several days and can include
● religious processions, carnival parades,
● bullfights and dancing.

figura [fi'ɣura] *nf* (*gen*) figure; (*forma, imagen*) shape, form; (*Naipes*) face card
figurar [fiɣu'rar] *vt* (*representar*) to represent; (*fingir*) to figure ▷ *vi* to figure; **figurarse** *vr* (*imaginarse*) to imagine; (*suponer*) to suppose
fijador [fixa'ðor] *nm* (*Foto etc*) fixative; (*de pelo*) gel
fijar [fi'xar] *vt* (*gen*) to fix; (*estampilla*) to affix, stick (on); **fijarse** *vr*: **~se en** to notice
fijo, -a ['fixo, a] *adj* (*gen*) fixed; (*firme*) firm; (*permanente*) permanent ▷ *adv*: **mirar ~** to stare
fila ['fila] *nf* row; (*Mil*) rank; **ponerse en ~** to line up, get into line; **fila india** single file
filatelia [fila'telja] *nf* philately, stamp collecting
filete [fi'lete] *nm* (*de carne*) fillet steak; (*de pescado*) fillet
filiación [filja'θjon] *nf* (*Pol*) affiliation
filial [fi'ljal] *adj* filial ▷ *nf* subsidiary
Filipinas [fili'pinas] *nfpl*: **las (Islas) ~** the Philippines; **filipino, -a** *adj, nm/f* Philippine
filmar [fil'mar] *vt* to film, shoot
filo ['filo] *nm* (*gen*) edge; **sacar ~ a** to sharpen; **al ~ del mediodía** at about midday; **de doble ~** double-edged
filología [filolo'ɣia] *nf* philology; **filología inglesa** (*Univ*) English Studies
filón [fi'lon] *nm* (*Minería*) vein, lode; (*fig*) goldmine
filosofía [filoso'fia] *nf* philosophy; **filósofo, -a** *nm/f* philosopher
filtrar [fil'trar] *vt, vi* to filter, strain; **filtrarse** *vr* to filter; **filtro** *nm* (*Tec, utensilio*) filter
fin [fin] *nm* end; (*objetivo*) aim, purpose; **al ~ y al cabo** when all's said and done; **a ~ de** in order to; **por ~** finally; **en ~** in short; **fin de semana** weekend

final [fi'nal] *adj* final ▷ *nm* end, conclusion ▷ *nf* final; **al ~** in the end; **a ~es de** at the end of; **finalidad** *nf* (*propósito*) purpose, intention; **finalista** *nmf* finalist; **finalizar** *vt* to end, finish; (*Inform*) to log out o off ▷ *vi* to end, come to an end
financiar [finan'θjar] *vt* to finance; **financiero, -a** *adj* financial ▷ *nm/f* financier
finca ['finka] *nf* (*casa de campo*) country house; (*ESP: bien inmueble*) property, land; (*LAM: granja*) farm
finde ['finde] *nm abr* (*fam: fin de semana*) weekend
fingir [fin'xir] *vt* (*simular*) to simulate, feign ▷ *vi* (*aparentar*) to pretend
finlandés, -esa [finlan'des, esa] *adj* Finnish ▷ *nm/f* Finn ▷ *nm* (*Ling*) Finnish
Finlandia [fin'landja] *nf* Finland
fino, -a ['fino, a] *adj* fine; (*delgado*) slender; (*de buenas maneras*) polite, refined; (*jerez*) fino, dry
firma ['firma] *nf* signature; (*Com*) firm, company
firmamento [firma'mento] *nm* firmament
firmar [fir'mar] *vt* to sign
firme ['firme] *adj* firm; (*estable*) stable; (*sólido*) solid; (*constante*) steady; (*decidido*) resolute ▷ *nm* road (surface); **firmeza** *nf* firmness; (*constancia*) steadiness; (*solidez*) solidity
fiscal [fis'kal] *adj* fiscal ▷ *nmf* public prosecutor; **año ~** tax o fiscal year
fisgonear [fisɣone'ar] *vt* to poke one's nose into ▷ *vi* to pry, spy
física ['fisika] *nf* physics *sg*; V tb **físico**
físico, -a ['fisiko, a] *adj* physical ▷ *nm* physique ▷ *nm/f* physicist
fisura [fi'sura] *nf* crack; (*Med*) fracture
flác(c)ido, -a ['fla(k)θiðo, a] *adj* flabby
flaco, -a ['flako, a] *adj* (*muy delgado*) skinny, thin; (*débil*) weak, feeble
flagrante [fla'ɣrante] *adj* flagrant
flama ['flama] (*MÉX*) *nf* flame; **flamable** (*MÉX*) *adj* flammable
flamante [fla'mante] (*fam*) *adj* brilliant; (*nuevo*) brand-new
flamenco, -a [fla'menko, a] *adj* (*de Flandes*) Flemish; (*baile, música*) flamenco ▷ *nm* (*baile, música*) flamenco; (*Zool*) flamingo
flamingo [fla'mingo] (*MÉX*) *nm* flamingo
flan [flan] *nm* creme caramel
▌No confundir **flan** con la palabra inglesa *flan*.
flash [flaʃ] (*pl ~o ~es*) *nm* (*Foto*) flash
flauta ['flauta] *nf* (*Mús*) flute

flecha ['fletʃa] nf arrow
flechazo [fle'tʃaθo] nm love at first sight
fleco ['fleko] nm fringe
flema ['flema] nm phlegm
flequillo [fle'kiʎo] nm (pelo) fringe
flexible [flek'siβle] adj flexible
flexión [flek'sjon] nf press-up
flexo ['flekso] nm adjustable table-lamp
flirtear [flirte'ar] vi to flirt
flojera [flo'xera] (LAM: fam) nf: **me da ~** I can't be bothered
flojo, -a ['floxo, a] adj (gen) loose; (sin fuerzas) limp; (débil) weak
flor [flor] nf flower; **a ~ de** on the surface of; **flora** nf flora; **florecer** vi (Bot) to flower, bloom; (fig) to flourish; **florería** (LAM) nf florist's (shop); **florero** nm vase; **floristería** nf florist's (shop)
flota ['flota] nf fleet
flotador [flota'ðor] nm (gen) float; (para nadar) rubber ring
flotar [flo'tar] vi (gen) to float; **flote** nm: **a flote** afloat; **salir a flote** (fig) to get back on one's feet
fluidez [flui'ðeθ] nf fluidity; (fig) fluency
fluido, -a ['fluiðo, a] adj, nm fluid
fluir [flu'ir] vi to flow
flujo ['fluxo] nm flow; **flujo y reflujo** ebb and flow
flúor ['fluor] nm fluoride
fluorescente [flwores'θente] adj fluorescent ▷ nm fluorescent light
fluvial [fluβi'al] adj (navegación, cuenca) fluvial, river cpd
fobia ['fobja] nf phobia; **fobia a las alturas** fear of heights
foca ['foka] nf seal
foco ['foko] nm focus; (Elec) floodlight; (MÉX: bombilla) (light) bulb
fofo, -a ['fofo, a] adj soft, spongy; (carnes) flabby
fogata [fo'ɣata] nf bonfire
fogón [fo'ɣon] nm (de cocina) ring, burner
folio ['foljo] nm folio, page
follaje [fo'ʎaxe] nm foliage
folleto [fo'ʎeto] nm (Pol) pamphlet
follón [fo'ʎon] (ESP: fam) nm (lío) mess; (conmoción) fuss; **armar un ~** to kick up a row
fomentar [fomen'tar] vt (Med) to foment
fonda ['fonda] nf inn
fondo ['fondo] nm (de mar) bottom; (de coche, sala) back; (Arte etc) background; (reserva) fund; **fondos** nmpl (Com) funds, resources; **una investigación a ~** a thorough investigation; **en el ~** at bottom, deep down
fonobuzón [fonoβu'θon] nm voice mail

fontanería [fontane'ria] nf plumbing; **fontanero, -a** nm/f plumber
footing ['futɪn] nm jogging; **hacer ~** to jog, go jogging
forastero, -a [foras'tero, a] nm/f stranger
forcejear [forθexe'ar] vi (luchar) to struggle
forense [fo'rense] nmf pathologist
forma ['forma] nf (figura) form, shape; (Med) fitness; (método) way, means; **las ~s** the conventions; **estar en ~** to be fit; **de ~ que ...** so that ...; **de todas ~s** in any case
formación [forma'θjon] nf (gen) formation; (educación) education; **formación profesional** vocational training
formal [for'mal] adj (gen) formal; (fig: serio) serious; (: de fiar) reliable; **formalidad** nf formality; seriousness; **formalizar** vt (Jur) to formalize; (situación) to put in order, regularize; **formalizarse** vr (situación) to be put in order, be regularized
formar [for'mar] vt (componer) to form, shape; (constituir) to make up, constitute; (Escol) to train, educate; **formarse** vr (Escol) to be trained, educated; (cobrar forma) to form, take form; (desarrollarse) to develop
formatear [formate'ar] vt to format
formato [for'mato] nm format
formidable [formi'ðaβle] adj (temible) formidable; (estupendo) tremendous
fórmula ['formula] nf formula
formulario [formu'larjo] nm form
fornido, -a [for'niðo, a] adj well-built
foro ['foro] nm (Pol, Inform etc) forum
forrar [fo'rrar] vt (abrigo) to line; (libro) to cover; **forro** nm (de cuaderno) cover; (Costura) lining; (de sillón) upholstery; **forro polar** fleece
fortalecer [fortale'θer] vt to strengthen
fortaleza [forta'leθa] nf (Mil) fortress, stronghold; (fuerza) strength; (determinación) resolution
fortuito, -a [for'twito, a] adj accidental
fortuna [for'tuna] nf (suerte) fortune, (good) luck; (riqueza) fortune, wealth
forzar [for'θar] vt (puerta) to force (open); (compeler) to compel
forzoso, -a [for'θoso, a] adj necessary
fosa ['fosa] nf (sepultura) grave; (en tierra) pit; **fosas nasales** nostrils
fósforo ['fosforo] nm (Quím) phosphorus; (cerilla) match
fósil ['fosil] nm fossil
foso ['foso] nm ditch; (Teatro) pit; (Auto) inspection pit
foto ['foto] nf photo, snap(shot); **sacar una ~** to take a photo o picture; **foto (de)**

carné passport(-size) photo
fotocopia [foto'kopja] nf photocopy;
fotocopiadora nf photocopier; **fotocopiar**
vt to photocopy
fotografía [fotoɣra'fia] nf (Arte)
photography; (una fotografía) photograph;
fotografiar vt to photograph
fotógrafo, -a [fo'toɣrafo, a] nm/f
photographer
fotomatón [fotoma'ton] nm photo booth
FP (ESP) nf abr (= Formación Profesional)
vocational courses for 14- to 18-year-olds
fracasar [fraka'sar] vi (gen) to fail
fracaso [fra'kaso] nm failure
fracción [frak'θjon] nf fraction
fractura [frak'tura] nf fracture, break
fragancia [fra'ɣanθja] nf (olor) fragrance,
perfume
frágil ['fraxil] adj (débil) fragile; (Com)
breakable
fragmento [fraɣ'mento] nm (pedazo)
fragment
fraile ['fraile] nm (Rel) friar; (: monje) monk
frambuesa [fram'bwesa] nf raspberry
francés, -esa [fran'θes, esa] adj French
▷ nm/f Frenchman(-woman) ▷ nm (Ling)
French
Francia ['franθja] nf France
franco, -a ['franko, a] adj (cándido) frank,
open; (Com: exento) free ▷ nm (moneda) franc
francotirador, a [frankotira'ðor, a] nm/f
sniper
franela [fra'nela] nf flannel
franja ['franxa] nf fringe
franquear [franke'ar] vt (camino) to
clear; (carta, paquete postal) to frank, stamp;
(obstáculo) to overcome
franqueo [fran'keo] nm postage
franqueza [fran'keθa] nf (candor)
frankness
frasco ['frasko] nm bottle, flask
frase ['frase] nf sentence; **frase hecha** set
phrase; (pey) stock phrase
fraterno, -a [fra'terno, a] adj brotherly,
fraternal
fraude ['frauðe] nm (cualidad) dishonesty;
(acto) fraud
frazada [fra'saða] (LAM) nf blanket
frecuencia [fre'kwenθja] nf frequency;
con ~ frequently, often
frecuentar [frekwen'tar] vt to frequent
frecuente [fre'kwente] adj (gen) frequent
fregadero [freɣa'ðero] nm (kitchen) sink
fregar [fre'ɣar] vt (frotar) to scrub; (platos)
to wash (up); (LAM: fam: fastidiar) to annoy;
(: malograr) to screw up
fregona [fre'ɣona] nf mop
freír [fre'ir] vt to fry

frenar [fre'nar] vt to brake; (fig) to check
frenazo [fre'naθo] nm: **dar un ~** to brake
sharply
frenesí [frene'si] nm frenzy
freno ['freno] nm (Tec, Auto) brake; (de
cabalgadura) bit; (fig) check; **freno de mano**
handbrake
frente ['frente] nm (Arq, Pol) front; (de
objeto) front part ▷ nf forehead, brow; **~ a** in
front of; (en situación opuesta de) opposite; **al**
~ de (fig) at the head of; **chocar de ~** to crash
head-on; **hacer ~ a** to face up to
fresa ['fresa] (ESP) nf strawberry
fresco, -a ['fresko, a] adj (nuevo) fresh;
(frío) cool; (descarado) cheeky ▷ nm (aire)
fresh air; (Arte) fresco; (LAM: jugo) fruit drink
▷ nm/f (fam): **ser un ~** to have a nerve;
tomar el ~ to get some fresh air; **frescura**
nf freshness; (descaro) cheek, nerve
frialdad [frial'daθ] nf (gen) coldness;
(indiferencia) indifference
frigidez [frixi'θeθ] nf frigidity
frigorífico [friɣo'rifiko] nm refrigerator
frijol [fri'xol] nm kidney bean
frío, -a etc ['frio, a] vb V **freír** ▷ adj
cold; (indiferente) indifferent ▷ nm cold;
indifference; **hace ~** it's cold; **tener ~** to
be cold
frito, -a ['frito, a] adj fried; **me trae ~**
ese hombre I'm sick and tired of that man;
fritos nmpl fried food
frívolo, -a ['friβolo, a] adj frivolous
frontal [fron'tal] adj frontal; **choque ~**
head-on collision
frontera [fron'tera] nf frontier;
fronterizo, -a adj frontier cpd; (contiguo)
bordering
frontón [fron'ton] nm (Deporte: cancha)
pelota court; (: juego) pelota
frotar [fro'tar] vt to rub; **frotarse** vr: **~se**
las manos to rub one's hands
fructífero, -a [fruk'tifero, a] adj fruitful
fruncir [frun'θir] vt to pucker; (Costura) to
pleat; **~ el ceño** to knit one's brow
frustrar [frus'trar] vt to frustrate
fruta ['fruta] nf fruit; **frutería** nf fruit
shop; **frutero, -a** adj fruit cpd ▷ nm/f
fruiterer ▷ nm fruit bowl
frutilla [fru'tiʎa] (CS) nf strawberry
fruto ['fruto] nm fruit; (fig: resultado) result;
(: beneficio) benefit; **frutos secos** nuts and
dried fruit pl
fucsia ['fuksja] nf fuchsia
fue [fwe] vb V **ser; ir**
fuego ['fweɣo] nm (gen) fire; **a ~ lento**
on a low heat; **¿tienes ~?** have you (got) a
light?; **fuego amigo** friendly fire; **fuegos**
artificiales fireworks

fuente ['fwente] nf fountain; (manantial: fig) spring; (origen) source; (plato) large dish

fuera etc ['fwera] vb V **ser; ir** ▷ adv out(side); (en otra parte) away; (excepto, salvo) except, save ▷ prep: **~ de** outside; (fig) besides; **~ de sí** beside o.s.; **por ~** (on the) outside

fuera-borda [fwera'βorða] nm speedboat

fuerte ['fwerte] adj strong; (golpe) hard; (ruido) loud; (comida) rich; (lluvia) heavy; (dolor) intense ▷ adv strongly; hard; loud(ly)

fuerza etc ['fwerθa] vb V **forzar** ▷ nf (fortaleza) strength; (Tec, Elec) power; (coacción) force; (Mil, Pol) force; **a ~ de** by dint of; **cobrar ~s** to recover one's strength; **tener ~s para** to have the strength to; **a la ~** forcibly, by force; **por ~** of necessity; **fuerza de voluntad** willpower; **fuerzas aéreas** air force sg; **fuerzas armadas** armed forces

fuga ['fuxa] nf (huida) flight, escape; (de gas etc) leak

fugarse [fu'xarse] vr to flee, escape

fugaz [fu'xaθ] adj fleeting

fugitivo, a [fuxi'tiβo, a] adj, nm/f fugitive

fui [fwi] vb V **ser; ir**

fulano, -a [fu'lano, a] nm/f so-and-so, what's-his-name/what's-her-name

fulminante [fulmi'nante] adj (fig: mirada) fierce; (Med: enfermedad, ataque) sudden; (fam: éxito, golpe) sudden

fumador, a [fuma'ðor, a] nm/f smoker

fumar [fu'mar] vt, vi to smoke; **~ en pipa** to smoke a pipe

función [fun'θjon] nf function; (en trabajo) duties pl; (espectáculo) show; **entrar en funciones** to take up one's duties

funcionar [funθjo'nar] vi (gen) to function; (máquina) to work; **"no funciona"** "out of order"

funcionario, -a [funθjo'narjo, a] nm/f civil servant

funda ['funda] nf (gen) cover; (de almohada) pillowcase

fundación [funda'θjon] nf foundation

fundamental [fundamen'tal] adj fundamental, basic

fundamento [funda'mento] nm (base) foundation

fundar [fun'dar] vt to found; **fundarse** vr: **~se en** to be founded on

fundición [fundi'θjon] nf fusing; (fábrica) foundry

fundir [fun'dir] vt (gen) to fuse; (metal) to smelt, melt down; (nieve etc) to melt; (Com) to merge; (estatua) to cast; **fundirse** vr (colores etc) to merge, blend; (unirse) to fuse together; (Elec: fusible, lámpara etc) to fuse, blow; (nieve etc) to melt

fúnebre ['funeβre] adj funeral cpd, funereal

funeral [fune'ral] nm funeral; **funeraria** nf undertaker's

funicular [funiku'lar] nm (tren) funicular; (teleférico) cable car

furgón [fur'xon] nm wagon; **furgoneta** nf (Auto, Com) (transit) van (BRIT), pick-up (truck) (US)

furia ['furja] nf (ira) fury; (violencia) violence; **furioso, -a** adj (iracundo) furious; (violento) violent

furtivo, -a [fur'tiβo, a] adj furtive ▷ nm poacher

fusible [fu'siβle] nm fuse

fusil [fu'sil] nm rifle; **fusilar** vt to shoot

fusión [fu'sjon] nf (gen) melting; (unión) fusion; (Com) merger

fútbol ['futβol] nm football (BRIT), soccer (US); **fútbol americano** American football (BRIT), football (US); **fútbol sala** indoor football (BRIT) o soccer (US); **futbolín** nm table football; **futbolista** nmf footballer

futuro, -a [fu'turo, a] adj, nm future

g

gabardina [gaβar'ðina] nf raincoat, gabardine

gabinete [gaβi'nete] nm (Pol) cabinet; (estudio) study; (de abogados etc) office

gachas ['gatʃas] nfpl porridge sg

gafas ['gafas] nfpl glasses; **gafas de sol** sunglasses

gafe ['gafe] (ESP) nmf jinx

gaita ['gaita] nf bagpipes pl

gajes ['gaxes] nmpl: ~ **del oficio** occupational hazards

gajo ['gaxo] nm (de naranja) segment

gala ['gala] nf (traje de etiqueta) full dress; **galas** nfpl (ropa) finery sg; **estar de ~** to be in one's best clothes; **hacer ~ de** to display

galápago [ga'lapaxo] nm (Zool) turtle

galardón [galar'ðon] nm award, prize

galaxia [ga'laksja] nf galaxy

galera [ga'lera] nf (nave) galley; (carro) wagon; (Imprenta) galley

galería [gale'ria] nf (gen) gallery; (balcón) veranda(h); (pasillo) corridor; **galería comercial** shopping mall

Gales ['gales] nm (tb: **País de ~**) Wales; **galés, -esa** adj Welsh ⊳ nm/f Welshman(-woman) ⊳ nm (Ling) Welsh

galgo, -a ['galxo, a] nm/f greyhound

gallego, -a [ga'ʎexo, a] adj, nm/f Galician

galleta [ga'ʎeta] nf biscuit (BRIT), cookie (US)

gallina [ga'ʎina] nf hen ⊳ nmf (fam: cobarde) chicken; **gallinero** nm henhouse; (Teatro) top gallery

gallo ['gaʎo] nm cock, rooster

galopar [galo'par] vi to gallop

gama ['gama] nf (fig) range

gamba ['gamba] nf prawn (BRIT), shrimp (US)

gamberro, -a [gam'berro, a] (ESP) nm/f hooligan, lout

gamuza [ga'muθa] nf chamois

gana ['gana] nf (deseo) desire, wish; (apetito) appetite; (voluntad) will; (añoranza) longing; **de buena ~** willingly; **de mala ~** reluctantly; **me da ~s de** I feel like, I want to; **no me da la ~** I don't feel like it; **tener ~s de** to feel like

ganadería [ganaðe'ria] nf (ganado) livestock; (ganado vacuno) cattle pl; (cría, comercio) cattle raising

ganadero, -a [gana'ðero, a] (ESP) nm/f (hacendado) rancher

ganado [ga'naðo] nm livestock; **ganado porcino** pigs pl

ganador, a [gana'ðor, a] adj winning ⊳ nm/f winner

ganancia [ga'nanθja] nf (lo ganado) gain; (aumento) increase; (beneficio) profit; **ganancias** nfpl (ingresos) earnings; (beneficios) profit sg, winnings

ganar [ga'nar] vt (obtener) to get, obtain; (sacar ventaja) to gain; (salario etc) to earn; (Deporte, premio) to win; (derrotar a) to beat; (alcanzar) to reach ⊳ vi (Deporte) to win; **ganarse** vr: **~se la vida** to earn one's living

ganchillo [gan'tʃiʎo] nm crochet

gancho ['gantʃo] nm (gen) hook; (colgador) hanger

gandul, a [gan'dul, a] adj, nm/f good-for-nothing, layabout

ganga ['ganga] nf bargain

gangrena [gan'grena] nf gangrene

ganso, -a ['ganso, a] nm/f (Zool) goose; (fam) idiot

ganzúa [gan'θua] nf skeleton key

garabato [gara'βato] nm (escritura) scrawl, scribble

garaje [ga'raxe] nm garage

garantía [garan'tia] nf guarantee

garantizar [garanti'θar] vt to guarantee

garbanzo [gar'βanθo] nm chickpea (BRIT), garbanzo (US)

garfio ['garfjo] nm grappling iron

garganta [gar'xanta] nf (Anat) throat; (de botella) neck; **gargantilla** nf necklace

gárgaras ['garxaras] nfpl: **hacer ~** to gargle

gargarear [garxare'ar] (LAM) vi to gargle

garita [ga'rita] nf cabin, hut; (Mil) sentry box

garra ['garra] nf (de gato, Tec) claw; (de ave) talon; (fam: mano) hand, paw

garrafa [ga'rrafa] nf carafe, decanter

garrapata [garra'pata] nf tick

gas [gas] nm gas; **gases lacrimógenos** tear gas sg

gasa ['gasa] nf gauze

gaseosa [gase'osa] nf lemonade

gaseoso, -a [gase'oso, a] adj gassy, fizzy

gasoil [ga'soil] *nm* diesel (oil)
gasóleo [ga'soleo] *nm* = **gasoil**
gasolina [gaso'lina] *nf* petrol (BRIT),
 gas(oline) (US); **gasolinera** *nf* petrol (BRIT) o
 gas (US) station
gastado, -a [gas'taðo, a] *adj* (*dinero*)
 spent; (*ropa*) worn out; (*usado: frase etc*) trite
gastar [gas'tar] *vt* (*dinero, tiempo*) to
 spend; (*fuerzas*) to use up; (*desperdiciar*) to
 waste; (*llevar*) to wear; **gastarse** *vr* to wear
 out; (*estropearse*) to waste; **~ en** to spend
 on; **~ bromas** to crack jokes; **¿qué número
 gastas?** what size (shoe) do you take?
gasto ['gasto] *nm* (*desembolso*)
 expenditure, spending; (*consumo, uso*)
 use; **gastos** *nmpl* (*desembolsos*) expenses;
 (*cargos*) charges, costs
gastronomía [gastrono'mia] *nf*
 gastronomy
gatear [gate'ar] *vi* (*andar a gatas*) to go on
 all fours
gatillo [ga'tiʎo] *nm* (*de arma de fuego*)
 trigger; (*de dentista*) forceps
gato, -a ['gato, a] *nm/f* cat ▷ *nm* (*Tec*)
 jack; **andar a gatas** to go on all fours
gaucho ['gautʃo] *nm* gaucho

● **GAUCHO**
●
● **Gauchos** are the herdsmen or riders of
● the Southern Cone plains. Although
● popularly associated with Argentine
● folklore, **gauchos** belong equally to the
● cattle-raising areas of Southern Brazil
● and Uruguay. **Gauchos'** traditions and
● clothing reflect their mixed ancestry
● and cultural roots. Their baggy trousers
● are Arabic in origin, while the horse and
● guitar are inherited from the Spanish
● conquistadors; the poncho, maté and
● **boleadoras** (strips of leather weighted
● at either end with stones) form part of
● the Indian tradition.

gaviota [ga'βjota] *nf* seagull
gay [ge] *adj inv, nm* gay, homosexual
gazpacho [gaθ'patʃo] *nm* gazpacho
gel [xel] *nm*: **~ de baño/ducha** bath/
 shower gel
gelatina [xela'tina] *nf* jelly; (*polvos etc*)
 gelatine
gema ['xema] *nf* gem
gemelo, -a [xe'melo, a] *adj, nm/f* twin;
 gemelos *nmpl* (*de camisa*) cufflinks;
 (*prismáticos*) field glasses, binoculars
gemido [xe'miðo] *nm* (*quejido*) moan,
 groan; (*aullido*) howl
Géminis ['xeminis] *nm* Gemini

gemir [xe'mir] *vi* (*quejarse*) to moan,
 groan; (*aullar*) to howl
generación [xenera'θjon] *nf* generation
general [xene'ral] *adj* general ▷ *nm*
 general; **por lo** o **en ~** in general;
 Generalitat *nf* Catalan parliament;
 generalizar *vt* to generalize;
 generalizarse *vr* to become generalized,
 spread
generar [xene'rar] *vt* to generate
género ['xenero] *nm* (*clase*) kind, sort;
 (*tipo*) type; (*Bio*) genus; (*Ling*) gender; (*Com*)
 material; **género humano** human race
generosidad [xenerosi'ðað] *nf*
 generosity; **generoso, -a** *adj* generous
genial [xe'njal] *adj* inspired; (*idea*)
 brilliant; (*estupendo*) wonderful
genio ['xenjo] *nm* (*carácter*) nature,
 disposition; (*humor*) temper; (*facultad
 creadora*) genius; **de mal ~** bad-tempered
genital [xeni'tal] *adj* genital; **genitales**
 nmpl genitals
genoma [xe'noma] *nm* genome
gente ['xente] *nf* (*personas*) people *pl*;
 (*parientes*) relatives *pl*
gentil [xen'til] *adj* (*elegante*) graceful;
 (*encantador*) charming

▌ No confundir **gentil** con la palabra
▌ inglesa *gentle*.

genuino, -a [xe'nwino, a] *adj* genuine
geografía [xeoɣra'fia] *nf* geography
geología [xeolo'xia] *nf* geology
geometría [xeome'tria] *nf* geometry
gerente [xe'rente] *nmf* (*supervisor*)
 manager; (*jefe*) director
geriatría [xeria'tria] *nf* (*Med*) geriatrics *sg*
germen ['xermen] *nm* germ
gesticular [xestiku'lar] *vi* to gesticulate;
 (*hacer muecas*) to grimace; **gesticulación** *nf*
 gesticulation; (*mueca*) grimace
gestión [xes'tjon] *nf* management;
 (*diligencia, acción*) negotiation
gesto ['xesto] *nm* (*mueca*) grimace;
 (*ademán*) gesture
Gibraltar [xiβral'tar] *nm* Gibraltar;
 gibraltareño, -a *adj, nm/f* Gibraltarian
gigante [xi'ɣante] *adj, nmf* giant;
 gigantesco, -a *adj* gigantic
gilipollas [xili'poʎas] (*fam*) *adj inv* daft
 ▷ *nmf inv* wally
gimnasia [xim'nasja] *nf* gymnastics *pl*;
 gimnasio *nm* gymnasium; **gimnasta** *nmf*
 gymnast
ginebra [xi'neβra] *nf* gin
ginecólogo, -a [xine'koloɣo, a] *nm/f*
 gynaecologist
gira ['xira] *nf* tour, trip
girar [xi'rar] *vt* (*dar la vuelta*) to turn

(around); (: *rápidamente*) to spin; (*Com*: *giro postal*) to draw; (: *letra de cambio*) to issue ▷ *vi* to turn (round); (*rápido*) to spin

girasol [xira'sol] *nm* sunflower

giratorio, -a [xira'torjo, a] *adj* revolving

giro ['xiro] *nm* (*movimiento*) turn, revolution; (*Ling*) expression; (*Com*) draft; **giro bancario/postal** bank draft/money order

gis [xis] (*MÉX*) *nm* chalk

gitano, -a [xi'tano, a] *adj, nm/f* gypsy

glacial [gla'θjal] *adj* icy, freezing

glaciar [gla'θjar] *nm* glacier

glándula ['glandula] *nf* gland

global [glo'βal] *adj* global; **globalización** *nf* globalization

globo ['gloβo] *nm* (*esfera*) globe, sphere; (*aerostato, juguete*) balloon

glóbulo ['gloβulo] *nm* globule; (*Anat*) corpuscle

gloria ['glorja] *nf* glory

glorieta [glo'rjeta] *nf* (*de jardín*) bower, arbour; (*plazoleta*) roundabout (*BRIT*), traffic circle (*US*)

glorioso, -a [glo'rjoso, a] *adj* glorious

glotón, -ona [glo'ton, ona] *adj* gluttonous, greedy ▷ *nm/f* glutton

glucosa [glu'kosa] *nf* glucose

gobernador, a [goβerna'ðor, a] *adj* governing ▷ *nm/f* governor; **gobernante** *adj* governing

gobernar [goβer'nar] *vt* (*dirigir*) to guide, direct; (*Pol*) to rule, govern ▷ *vi* to govern; (*Náut*) to steer

gobierno *etc* [go'βjerno] *vb* V **gobernar** ▷ *nm* (*Pol*) government; (*dirección*) guidance, direction; (*Náut*) steering

goce *etc* ['goθe] *vb* V **gozar** ▷ *nm* enjoyment

gol [gol] *nm* goal

golf [golf] *nm* golf

golfa ['golfa] (*fam!*) *nf* (*mujer*) slut, whore

golfo, -a ['golfo, a] *nm* (*Geo*) gulf ▷ *nm/f* (*fam*: *niño*) urchin; (*gamberro*) lout

golondrina [golon'drina] *nf* swallow

golosina [golo'sina] *nf* (*dulce*) sweet; **goloso, -a** *adj* sweet-toothed

golpe ['golpe] *nm* blow; (*de puño*) punch; (*de mano*) smack; (*de remo*) stroke; (*fig*: *choque*) clash; **no dar ~** to be bone idle; **de un ~** with one blow; **de ~** suddenly; **golpe (de estado)** coup (d'état); **golpear** *vt, vi* to strike, knock; (*asestar*) to beat; (*de puño*) to punch; (*golpetear*) to tap

goma ['goma] *nf* (*caucho*) rubber; (*elástico*) elastic; (*una goma*) elastic band; **goma de borrar** eraser, rubber (*BRIT*); **goma espuma** foam rubber

gomina [go'mina] *nf* hair gel

gomita [go'mita] (*RPL*) *nf* rubber band

gordo, -a ['gorðo, a] *adj* (*gen*) fat; (*fam*) enormous; **el (premio) ~** (*en lotería*) first prize

gorila [go'rila] *nm* gorilla

gorra ['gorra] *nf* cap; (*de bebé*) bonnet; (*militar*) bearskin; **entrar de ~** (*fam*) to gatecrash; **ir de ~** to sponge

gorrión [go'rrjon] *nm* sparrow

gorro ['gorro] *nm* (*gen*) cap; (*de bebé, mujer*) bonnet

gorrón, -ona [go'rron, ona] *nm/f* scrounger; **gorronear** (*fam*) *vi* to scrounge

gota ['gota] *nf* (*gen*) drop; (*de sudor*) bead; (*Med*) gout; **gotear** *vi* to drip; (*lloviznar*) to drizzle; **gotera** *nf* leak

gozar [go'θar] *vi* to enjoy o.s.; **~ de** (*disfrutar*) to enjoy; (*poseer*) to possess

gr. *abr* (= *gramo, gramos*) g

grabación [graβa'θjon] *nf* recording

grabado [gra'βaðo] *nm* print, engraving

grabadora [graβa'ðora] *nf* tape-recorder; **grabadora de CD/DVD** CD/DVD writer

grabar [gra'βar] *vt* to engrave; (*discos, cintas*) to record

gracia [gra'θja] *nf* (*encanto*) grace, gracefulness; (*humor*) humour, wit; **¡(muchas) ~s!** thanks (very much)!; **~s a** thanks to; **dar las ~s a algn por algo** to thank sb for sth; **tener ~** (*chiste etc*) to be funny; **no me hace ~** I am not keen; **gracioso, -a** *adj* (*divertido*) funny, amusing; (*cómico*) comical ▷ *nm/f* (*Teatro*) comic character

grada ['graða] *nf* (*de escalera*) step; (*de anfiteatro*) tier, row; **gradas** *nfpl* (*Deporte: de estadio*) terraces

grado ['graðo] *nm* degree; (*de aceite, vino*) grade; (*grada*) step; (*Mil*) rank; **de buen ~** willingly; **grado centígrado/Fahrenheit** degree centigrade/Fahrenheit

graduación [graðwa'θjon] *nf* (*del alcohol*) proof, strength; (*Escol*) graduation; (*Mil*) rank

gradual [gra'ðwal] *adj* gradual

graduar [gra'ðwar] *vt* (*gen*) to graduate; (*Mil*) to commission; **graduarse** *vr* to graduate; **~se la vista** to have one's eyes tested

gráfica ['grafika] *nf* graph

gráfico, -a ['grafiko, a] *adj* graphic ▷ *nm* diagram; **gráficos** *nmpl* (*Inform*) graphics

grajo ['graxo] *nm* rook

gramática [gra'matika] *nf* grammar

gramo ['gramo] *nm* gramme (*BRIT*), gram (*US*)

gran [gran] *adj* V **grande**

grana ['grana] *nf* (*color, tela*) scarlet
granada [gra'naða] *nf* pomegranate; (*Mil*) grenade
granate [gra'nate] *adj* deep red
Gran Bretaña [-bre'taɲa] *nf* Great Britain
grande ['grande] (*antes de nmsg* **gran**) *adj* (*de tamaño*) big, large; (*alto*) tall; (*distinguido*) great; (*impresionante*) grand ▷ *nm* grandee
granel [gra'nel]: **a ~** *adv* (*Com*) in bulk
granero [gra'nero] *nm* granary, barn
granito [gra'nito] *nm* (*Agr*) small grain; (*roca*) granite
granizado [graniˈθaðo] *nm* iced drink
granizar [graniˈθar] *vi* to hail; **granizo** *nm* hail
granja ['granxa] *nf* (*gen*) farm; **granjero, -a** *nm/f* farmer
grano ['grano] *nm* grain; (*semilla*) seed; (*de café*) bean; (*Med*) pimple, spot
granuja [gra'nuxa] *nmf* rogue; (*golfillo*) urchin
grapa ['grapa] *nf* staple; (*Tec*) clamp; **grapadora** *nf* stapler
grasa ['grasa] *nf* (*gen*) grease; (*de cocinar*) fat, lard; (*sebo*) suet; (*mugre*) filth; **grasiento, -a** *adj* greasy; (*de aceite*) oily; **graso, -a** *adj* (*leche, queso, carne*) fatty; (*pelo, piel*) greasy
gratinar [grati'nar] *vt* to cook au gratin
gratis ['gratis] *adv* free
grato, -a ['grato, a] *adj* (*agradable*) pleasant, agreeable
gratuito, -a [gra'twito, a] *adj* (*gratis*) free; (*sin razón*) gratuitous
grave ['graβe] *adj* heavy; (*serio*) grave, serious; **gravedad** *nf* gravity
Grecia ['greθja] *nf* Greece
gremio ['gremjo] *nm* trade, industry
griego, -a ['grjexo, a] *adj, nm/f* Greek
grieta ['grjeta] *nf* crack
grifo ['grifo] (*ESP*) *nm* tap (*BRIT*), faucet (*US*)
grillo ['griʎo] *nm* (*Zool*) cricket
gripa ['gripa] (*MÉX*) *nf* flu, influenza
gripe ['gripe] *nf* flu, influenza; **gripe aviar** bird flu
gris [gris] *adj* (*color*) grey
gritar [gri'tar] *vt, vi* to shout, yell; **grito** *nm* shout, yell; (*de horror*) scream
grosella [gro'seʎa] *nf* (red)currant
grosero, -a [gro'sero, a] *adj* (*poco cortés*) rude, bad-mannered; (*ordinario*) vulgar, crude
grosor [gro'sor] *nm* thickness
grúa ['grua] *nf* (*Tec*) crane; (*de petróleo*) derrick
grueso, -a ['grweso, a] *adj* thick; (*persona*) stout ▷ *nm* bulk; **el ~ de** the bulk of
grulla ['gruʎa] *nf* crane
grumo ['grumo] *nm* clot, lump

gruñido [gru'ɲiðo] *nm* grunt; (*de persona*) grumble
gruñir [gru'ɲir] *vi* (*animal*) to growl; (*persona*) to grumble
grupo ['grupo] *nm* group; (*Tec*) unit, set; **grupo de presión** pressure group; **grupo sanguíneo** blood group
gruta ['gruta] *nf* grotto
guacho, -a ['gwatʃo, a] (*cs*) *nm/f* homeless child
guajolote [gwaxo'lote] (*MÉX*) *nm* turkey
guante ['gwante] *nm* glove; **guantes de goma** rubber gloves; **guantera** *nf* glove compartment
guapo, -a ['gwapo, a] *adj* good-looking, attractive; (*elegante*) smart
guarda ['gwarða] *nmf* (*persona*) guard, keeper ▷ *nf* (*acto*) guarding; (*custodia*) custody; **guarda jurado** (armed) security guard; **guardabarros** *nm inv* mudguard (*BRIT*), fender (*US*); **guardabosques** *nm inv* gamekeeper; **guardacostas** *nm inv* coastguard vessel ▷ *nmf* guardian, protector; **guardaespaldas** *nmf inv* bodyguard; **guardameta** *nmf* goalkeeper; **guardar** *vt* (*gen*) to keep; (*vigilar*) to guard, watch over; (*dinero: ahorrar*) to save; **guardarse** *vr* (*preservarse*) to protect o.s.; (*evitar*) to avoid; **guardar cama** to stay in bed; **guardarropa** *nm* (*armario*) wardrobe; (*en establecimiento público*) cloakroom
guardería [gwarðe'ria] *nf* nursery
guardia ['gwarðja] *nf* (*Mil*) guard; (*cuidado*) care, custody ▷ *nmf* guard; (*policía*) policeman(-woman); **estar de ~** to be on guard; **montar ~** to mount guard; **Guardia Civil** Civil Guard
guardián, -ana [gwar'ðjan, ana] *nm/f* (*gen*) guardian, keeper
guarida [gwa'riða] *nf* (*de animal*) den, lair; (*refugio*) refuge
guarnición [gwarni'θjon] *nf* (*de vestimenta*) trimming; (*de piedra*) mount; (*Culin*) garnish; (*arneses*) harness; (*Mil*) garrison
guarro, -a ['gwarro, a] *nm/f* pig
guasa ['gwasa] *nf* joke; **guasón, -ona** *adj* (*bromista*) joking ▷ *nm/f* wit; joker
Guatemala [gwate'mala] *nf* Guatemala
guay [gwai] (*fam*) *adj* super, great
güero, -a ['gwero, a] (*MÉX*) *adj* blond(e)
guerra ['gerra] *nf* war; **dar ~** to annoy; **guerra civil** civil war; **guerra fría** cold war; **guerrero, -a** *adj* fighting; (*carácter*) warlike ▷ *nm/f* warrior
guerrilla [ge'rriʎa] *nf* guerrilla warfare; (*tropas*) guerrilla band o group
guía *etc* ['gia] *vb* V **guiar** ▷ *nmf* (*persona*)

guide; (*nf: libro*) guidebook; **guía telefónica**
telephone directory; **guía turística** tourist
guide
guiar [gi'ar] *vt* to guide, direct; (*Auto*) to
steer; **guiarse** *vr*: **~se por** to be guided by
guinda ['ginda] *nf* morello cherry
guindilla [gin'diʎa] *nf* chilli pepper
guiñar [gi'ɲar] *vt* to wink
guión [gi'on] *nm* (*Ling*) hyphen, dash; (*Cine*)
script; **guionista** *nmf* scriptwriter
guiri ['giri] (*ESP: fam, pey*) *nmf* foreigner
guirnalda [gir'nalda] *nf* garland
guisado [gi'saðo] *nm* stew
guisante [gi'sante] *nm* pea
guisar [gi'sar] *vt, vi* to cook; **guiso** *nm*
cooked dish
guitarra [gi'tarra] *nf* guitar
gula ['gula] *nf* gluttony, greed
gusano [gu'sano] *nm* worm; (*lombriz*)
earthworm
gustar [gus'tar] *vt* to taste, sample ▷ *vi* to
please, be pleasing; **~ de algo** to like o enjoy
sth; **me gustan las uvas** I like grapes; **le
gusta nadar** she likes o enjoys swimming
gusto ['gusto] *nm* (*sentido, sabor*) taste;
(*placer*) pleasure; **tiene ~ a menta** it tastes
of mint; **tener buen ~** to have good taste;
coger el o **tomar ~ a algo** to take a liking
to sth; **sentirse a ~** to feel at ease; **mucho
~ (en conocerle)** pleased to meet you; **el ~
es mío** the pleasure is mine; **con ~** willingly,
gladly

ha *vb* V **haber**
haba ['aβa] *nf* bean
Habana [a'βana] *nf*: **la ~** Havana
habano [a'βano] *nm* Havana cigar
habéis *vb* V **haber**

○ **PALABRA CLAVE**

haber [a'βer] *vb aux* **1** (*tiempos compuestos*)
to have; **había comido** I had eaten; **antes/
después de haberlo visto** before seeing/
after seeing o having seen it
2: **¡haberlo dicho antes!** you should have
said so before!
3: **haber de: he de hacerlo** I have to do
it; **ha de llegar mañana** it should arrive
tomorrow
▷ *vb impers* **1** (*existencia: sg*) there is; (: *pl*)
there are; **hay un hermano/dos hermanos**
there is one brother/there are two brothers;
¿cuánto hay de aquí a Sucre? how far is it
from here to Sucre?
2 (*obligación*): **hay que hacer algo**
something must be done; **hay que
apuntarlo para acordarse** you have to
write it down to remember
3: **¡hay que ver!** well I never!
4: **¡no hay de** o **por** (*LAM*) **qué!** don't
mention it!, not at all!
5: **¿qué hay?** (*¿qué pasa?*) what's up?, what's
the matter?; (*¿qué tal?*) how's it going?
▷ *vt*: **he aquí unas sugerencias** here are
some suggestions; **no hay cintas blancas
pero sí las hay rojas** there aren't any white
ribbons but there are some red ones
▷ *nm* (*en cuenta*) credit side; **haberes** *nmpl*
assets; **¿cuánto tengo en el haber?** how
much do I have in my account?; **tiene varias
novelas en su haber** he has several novels
to his credit
haberse *vr*: **habérselas con algn** to have

it out with sb

habichuela [aβi'tʃwela] *nf* kidney bean
hábil ['aβil] *adj* (*listo*) clever, smart; (*capaz*)
fit, capable; (*experto*) expert; **día ~** working
day; **habilidad** *nf* skill, ability
habitación [aβita'θjon] *nf* (*cuarto*) room;
(*Bio: morada*) habitat; **habitación doble** *o*
de matrimonio double room; **habitación**
individual *o* **sencilla** single room
habitante [aβi'tante] *nmf* inhabitant
habitar [aβi'tar] *vt* (*residir en*) to inhabit;
(*ocupar*) to occupy ▷ *vi* to live
hábito ['aβito] *nm* habit
habitual [aβi'twal] *adj* usual
habituar [aβi'twar] *vt* to accustom;
habituarse *vr*: **~se a** to get used to
habla ['aβla] *nf* (*capacidad de hablar*)
speech; (*idioma*) language; (*dialecto*) dialect;
perder el ~ to become speechless; **de ~**
francesa French-speaking; **estar al ~** to be
in contact; (*Tel*) to be on the line; **¡González**
al ~! (*Tel*) González speaking!
hablador, a [aβla'ðor, a] *adj* talkative
▷ *nm/f* chatterbox
habladuría [aβlaðu'ria] *nf* rumour;
habladurías *nfpl* gossip *sg*
hablante [a'βlante] *adj* speaking ▷ *nmf*
speaker
hablar [a'βlar] *vt* to speak, talk ▷ *vi* to
speak; **hablarse** *vr* to speak to each other;
~ con to speak to; **~ de** to speak of *o* about;
¡ni ~! it's out of the question!; **"se habla**
inglés" "English spoken here"
habré *etc* [a'βre] *vb* V **haber**
hacendado [aθen'daðo] (*LAM*) *nm*
rancher, farmer
hacendoso, -a [aθen'doso, a] *adj*
industrious

○ **PALABRA CLAVE**

hacer [a'θer] *vt* **1** (*fabricar, producir*) to
make; (*construir*) to build; **hacer una**
película/un ruido to make a film/noise;
el guisado lo hice yo I made *o* cooked the
stew
2 (*ejecutar: trabajo etc*) to do; **hacer la colada**
to do the washing; **hacer la comida** to do
the cooking; **¿qué haces?** what are you
doing?; **hacer el malo** *o* **el papel del malo**
(*Teatro*) to play the villain
3 (*estudios, algunos deportes*) to do; **hacer**
español/económicas to do *o* study
Spanish/economics; **hacer yoga/**
gimnasia to do yoga/go to gym
4 (*transformar, incidir en*): **esto lo hará más**
difícil this will make it more difficult; **salir**

te hará sentir mejor going out will make
you feel better
5 (*cálculo*): **2 y 2 hacen 4** 2 and 2 make 4; **éste**
hace 100 this one makes 100
6 (+ *sub*): **esto hará que ganemos** this will
make us win; **harás que no quiera venir**
you'll stop him wanting to come
7 (*como sustituto de vb*) to do; **él bebió y yo**
hice lo mismo he drank and I did likewise
8 no hace más que criticar all he does is
criticize
▷ *vb semi-aux* (*directo*): **hacer +** *infin*: **les**
hice venir I made *o* had them come; **hacer**
trabajar a los demás to get others to work
▷ *vi* **1 haz como que no lo sabes** act as if
you don't know
2 (*ser apropiado*): **si os hace** if it's alright
with you
3 hacer de: hacer de Otelo to play Othello
▷ *vb impers* **1 hace calor/frío** it's hot/cold;
V *tb* **bueno, sol, tiempo**
2 (*tiempo*): **hace 3 años** 3 years ago; **hace**
un mes que voy/no voy I've been going/I
haven't been for a month
3 ¿cómo has hecho para llegar tan
rápido? how did you manage to get here
so quickly?
hacerse *vr* **1** (*volverse*) to become; **se**
hicieron amigos they became friends
2 (*acostumbrarse*): **hacerse a** to get used to
3 se hace con huevos y leche it's made
out of eggs and milk; **eso no se hace** that's
not done
4 (*obtener*): **hacerse de** *o* **con algo** to get
hold of sth
5 (*fingirse*): **hacerse el sueco** to turn a deaf
ear

hacha ['atʃa] *nf* axe; (*antorcha*) torch
hachís [a'tʃis] *nm* hashish
hacia ['aθja] *prep* (*en dirección de*)
towards; (*cerca de*) near; (*actitud*) towards;
~ adelante/atrás forwards/backwards; **~**
arriba/abajo up(wards)/down(wards); **~**
mediodía/las cinco about noon/five
hacienda [a'θjenda] *nf* (*propiedad*)
property; (*finca*) farm; (*LAM: rancho*) ranch;
(Ministerio de) H~ Exchequer (*BRIT*),
Treasury Department (*US*); **hacienda**
pública public finance
hada ['aða] *nf* fairy
hago *etc* *vb* V **hacer**
Haití [ai'ti] *nm* Haiti
halagar [ala'ɣar] *vt* to flatter
halago [a'laɣo] *nm* flattery
halcón [al'kon] *nm* falcon, hawk
hallar [a'ʎar] *vt* (*gen*) to find; (*descubrir*) to
discover; (*toparse con*) to run into; **hallarse**

h

vr to be (situated)
halterofilia [altero'filja] *nf* weightlifting
hamaca [a'maka] *nf* hammock
hambre ['ambre] *nf* hunger; (*plaga*)
famine; (*deseo*) longing; **tener ~** to be
hungry; **¡me muero de ~!** I'm starving!;
hambriento, -a *adj* hungry, starving
hamburguesa [ambur'ɣesa] *nf*
hamburger; **hamburguesería** *nf* burger
bar
han *vb* V **haber**
harapos [a'rapos] *nmpl* rags
haré *vb* V **hacer**
harina [a'rina] *nf* flour; **harina de maíz**
cornflour (BRIT), cornstarch (US); **harina de
trigo** wheat flour
hartar [ar'tar] *vt* to satiate, glut; (*fig*) to
tire, sicken; **hartarse** *vr* (*de comida*) to fill
o.s., gorge o.s.; (*cansarse*): **~se (de)** to get fed
up (with); **harto, -a** *adj* (*lleno*) full; (*cansado*)
fed up ⊳ *adv* (*bastante*) enough; (*muy*) very;
estar harto de hacer algo/de algn to be
fed up of doing sth/with sb
has *vb* V **haber**
hasta ['asta] *adv* even ⊳ *prep* (*alcanzando
a*) as far as; up to; down to; (*de tiempo: a tal
hora*) until; (*antes de*) before ⊳ *conj*: **~ que**
... until; **~ luego/el sábado** see you soon/
on Saturday; **~ ahora** (*al despedirse*) see you
in a minute; **~ pronto** see you soon
hay *vb* V **haber**
Haya ['aja] *nf*: **la ~** The Hague
haya *etc* ['aja] *vb* V **haber** ⊳ *nf* beech tree
haz [aθ] *vb* V **hacer** ⊳ *nm* (*de luz*) beam
hazaña [a'θaɲa] *nf* feat, exploit
hazmerreír [aθmerre'ir] *nm inv* laughing
stock
he *vb* V **haber**
hebilla [e'βiʎa] *nf* buckle, clasp
hebra ['eβra] *nf* thread; (*Bot: fibra*) fibre,
grain
hebreo, -a [e'βreo, a] *adj*, *nm/f* Hebrew
⊳ *nm* (*Ling*) Hebrew
hechizar [etʃi'θar] *vt* to cast a spell on,
bewitch
hechizo [e'tʃiθo] *nm* witchcraft, magic;
(*acto de magía*) spell, charm
hecho, -a ['etʃo, a] *pp de* **hacer** ⊳ *adj*
(*carne*) done; (*Costura*) ready-to-wear ⊳ *nm*
deed, act; (*dato*) fact; (*cuestión*) matter;
(*suceso*) event ⊳ *excl* agreed!, done!; **de ~** in
fact, as a matter of fact; **el ~ es que** ... the
fact is that ...; **¡bien ~!** well done!
hechura [e'tʃura] *nf* (*forma*) form, shape;
(*de persona*) build
hectárea [ek'tarea] *nf* hectare
helada [e'laða] *nf* frost
heladera [ela'ðera] (LAM) *nf* (*refrigerador*)
refrigerator
helado, -a [e'laðo, a] *adj* frozen; (*glacial*)
icy; (*fig*) chilly, cold ⊳ *nm* ice cream
helar [e'lar] *vt* to freeze, ice (up); (*dejar
atónito*) to amaze; (*desalentar*) to discourage
⊳ *vi* to freeze; **helarse** *vr* to freeze
helecho [e'letʃo] *nm* fern
hélice ['eliθe] *nf* (*Tec*) propeller
helicóptero [eli'koptero] *nm* helicopter
hembra ['embra] *nf* (*Bot, Zool*) female;
(*mujer*) woman; (*Tec*) nut
hemorragia [emo'rraxja] *nf*
haemorrhage
hemorroides [emo'rroiðes] *nfpl*
haemorrhoids, piles
hemos *vb* V **haber**
heno ['eno] *nm* hay
heredar [ere'ðar] *vt* to inherit; **heredero,
-a** *nm/f* heir(ess)
hereje [e'rexe] *nmf* heretic
herencia [e'renθja] *nf* inheritance
herida [e'riða] *nf* wound, injury; V tb
herido
herido, -a [e'riðo, a] *adj* injured,
wounded ⊳ *nm/f* casualty
herir [e'rir] *vt* to wound, injure; (*fig*) to
offend
hermanastro, -a [erma'nastro, a] *nm/f*
stepbrother/sister
hermandad [erman'dað] *nf* brotherhood
hermano, -a [er'mano, a] *nm/f* brother/
sister; **hermano(-a) gemelo(-a)**, twin
brother/sister; **hermano(-a) político(-a)**,
brother-in-law/sister-in-law
hermético, -a [er'metiko, a] *adj*
hermetic; (*fig*) watertight
hermoso, -a [er'moso, a] *adj* beautiful,
lovely; (*estupendo*) splendid; (*guapo*)
handsome; **hermosura** *nf* beauty
hernia ['ernja] *nf* hernia; **hernia discal**
slipped disc
héroe ['eroe] *nm* hero
heroína [ero'ina] *nf* (*mujer*) heroine;
(*droga*) heroin
herradura [erra'ðura] *nf* horseshoe
herramienta [erra'mjenta] *nf* tool
herrero ['errero] *nm* blacksmith
hervidero [erβi'ðero] *nm* (*fig*) swarm; (*Pol
etc*) hotbed
hervir [er'βir] *vi* to boil; (*burbujear*) to
bubble; **~ a fuego lento** to simmer; **hervor**
nm boiling; (*fig*) ardour, fervour
heterosexual [eterosek'swal] *adj*
heterosexual
hice *etc vb* V **hacer**
hidratante [iðra'tante] *adj*: **crema ~**
moisturizing cream, moisturizer; **hidratar**
vt (*piel*) to moisturize; **hidrato** *nm* hydrate;

hidratos de carbono carbohydrates
hidráulico, -a [i'ðrauliko, a] *adj*
hydraulic
hidro... [iðro] *prefijo* hydro..., water-...;
hidroeléctrico, -a *adj* hydroelectric;
hidrógeno *nm* hydrogen
hiedra ['jeðra] *nf* ivy
hiel [jel] *nf* gall, bile; (*fig*) bitterness
hiela *etc vb* V **helar**
hielo ['jelo] *nm* (*gen*) ice; (*escarcha*) frost;
(*fig*) coldness, reserve
hiena ['jena] *nf* hyena
hierba ['jerβa] *nf* (*pasto*) grass; (*Culin,
Med: planta*) herb; **mala ~** weed; (*fig*) evil
influence; **hierbabuena** *nf* mint
hierro ['jerro] *nm* (*metal*) iron; (*objeto*) iron
object
hígado ['iɣaðo] *nm* liver
higiene [i'xjene] *nf* hygiene; **higiénico, -a**
adj hygienic
higo ['iɣo] *nm* fig; **higo seco** dried fig;
higuera *nf* fig tree
hijastro, -a [i'xastro, a] *nm/f* stepson/
daughter
hijo, -a ['ixo, a] *nm/f* son/daughter, child;
hijos *nmpl* children, sons and daughters;
hijo adoptivo adopted child; **hijo de papá/
mamá** daddy's/mummy's boy; **hijo de puta**
(*fam!*) bastard (!), son of a bitch (!); **hijo/a
político/a** son-/daughter-in-law
hilera [i'lera] *nf* row, file
hilo ['ilo] *nm* thread; (*Bot*) fibre; (*metal*)
wire; (*de agua*) trickle, thin stream
hilvanar [ilβa'nar] *vt* (*Costura*) to tack
(*BRIT*), baste (*US*); (*fig*) to do hurriedly
himno ['imno] *nm* hymn; **himno nacional**
national anthem
hincapié [inka'pje] *nm*: **hacer ~ en** to
emphasize
hincar [in'kar] *vt* to drive (in), thrust (in)
hincha ['intʃa] (*fam*) *nmf* fan
hinchado, -a [in'tʃaðo, a] *adj* (*gen*)
swollen; (*persona*) pompous
hinchar [in'tʃar] *vt* (*gen*) to swell; (*inflar*)
to blow up, inflate; (*fig*) to exaggerate;
hincharse *vr* (*inflarse*) to swell up; (*fam: de
comer*) to stuff o.s.; **hinchazón** *nf* (*Med*)
swelling; (*altivez*) arrogance
hinojo [i'noxo] *nm* fennel
hipermercado [ipermer'kaðo] *nm*
hypermarket, superstore
hípico, -a ['ipiko, a] *adj* horse *cpd*
hipnotismo [ipno'tismo] *nm* hypnotism;
hipnotizar *vt* to hypnotize
hipo ['ipo] *nm* hiccups *pl*
hipocresía [ipokre'sia] *nf* hypocrisy;
hipócrita *adj* hypocritical ⊳ *nmf* hypocrite
hipódromo [i'poðromo] *nm* racetrack

hipopótamo [ipo'potamo] *nm*
hippopotamus
hipoteca [ipo'teka] *nf* mortgage
hipótesis [i'potesis] *nf inv* hypothesis
hispánico, -a [is'paniko, a] *adj* Hispanic
hispano, -a [is'pano, a] *adj* Hispanic,
Spanish, Hispano- ⊳ *nm/f* Spaniard;
Hispanoamérica *nf* Latin America;
hispanoamericano, -a *adj, nm/f* Latin
American
histeria [is'terja] *nf* hysteria
historia [is'torja] *nf* history; (*cuento*) story,
tale; **historias** *nfpl* (*chismes*) gossip *sg*;
dejarse de ~s to come to the point; **pasar
a la ~** to go down in history; **historiador, a**
nm/f historian; **historial** *nm* (*profesional*)
curriculum vitae, C.V.; (*Med*) case history;
histórico, -a *adj* historical; (*memorable*)
historic
historieta [isto'rjeta] *nf* tale, anecdote;
(*dibujos*) comic strip
hito ['ito] *nm* (*fig*) landmark
hizo *vb* V **hacer**
hocico [o'θiko] *nm* snout
hockey ['xokei] *nm* hockey; **hockey sobre
hielo/patines** ice/roller hockey
hogar [o'ɣar] *nm* fireplace, hearth; (*casa*)
home; (*vida familiar*) home life; **hogareño, -a**
adj home *cpd*; (*persona*) home-loving
hoguera [o'ɣera] *nf* (*gen*) bonfire
hoja ['oxa] *nf* (*gen*) leaf; (*de flor*) petal; (*de
papel*) sheet; (*página*) page; **hoja de afeitar**
(*LAM*) razor blade; **hoja electrónica** *o* **de
cálculo** spreadsheet; **hoja informativa**
leaflet, handout
hojalata [oxa'lata] *nf* tin(plate)
hojaldre [o'xaldre] *nm* (*Culin*) puff pastry
hojear [oxe'ar] *vt* to leaf through, turn
the pages of
hojuela [o'xwela] (*MÉX*) *nf* flake
hola ['ola] *excl* hello!
holá [o'la] (*RPL*) *excl* hello!
Holanda [o'landa] *nf* Holland;
holandés, -esa *adj* Dutch ⊳ *nm/f*
Dutchman(-woman) ⊳ *nm* (*Ling*) Dutch
holgado, -a [ol'ɣaðo, a] *adj* (*ropa*) loose,
baggy; (*rico*) comfortable
holgar [ol'ɣar] *vi* (*descansar*) to rest;
(*sobrar*) to be superfluous
holgazán, -ana [olɣa'θan, ana] *adj* idle,
lazy ⊳ *nm/f* loafer
hollín [o'ʎin] *nm* soot
hombre ['ombre] *nm* (*gen*) man; (*raza
humana*): **el ~** man(kind) ⊳ *excl*: **¡sí ~!**
(*claro*) of course!; (*para énfasis*) man, old
boy; **hombre de negocios** businessman;
hombre de pro honest man; **hombre-rana**
frogman

hombrera [om'brera] nf shoulder strap

hombro ['ombro] nm shoulder

homenaje [ome'naxe] nm (gen) homage; (tributo) tribute

homicida [omi'θiða] adj homicidal ▷ nmf murderer; **homicidio** nm murder, homicide

homologar [omolo'ðar] vt (Com: productos, tamaños) to standardize

homólogo, -a [o'moloxo, a] nm/f: **su** etc ~ his etc counterpart o opposite number

homosexual [omosek'swal] adj, nmf homosexual

honda ['onda] (cs) nf catapult

hondo, -a ['ondo, a] adj deep; **lo ~** the depth(s) pl, the bottom; **hondonada** nf hollow, depression; (cañón) ravine

Honduras [on'duras] nf Honduras

hondureño, -a [ondu'reno, a] adj, nm/f Honduran

honestidad [onesti'ðað] nf purity, chastity; (decencia) decency; **honesto, -a** adj chaste; decent; honest; (justo) just

hongo ['ongo] nm (Bot: gen) fungus; (: comestible) mushroom; (: venenoso) toadstool

honor [o'nor] nm (gen) honour; **en ~ a la verdad** to be fair; **honorable** adj honourable

honorario, -a [ono'rarjo, a] adj honorary; **honorarios** nmpl fees

honra ['onra] nf (gen) honour; (renombre) good name; **honradez** nf honesty; (de persona) integrity; **honrado, -a** adj honest, upright; **honrar** [on'rar] vt to honour

hora ['ora] nf (una hora) hour; (tiempo) time; **¿qué ~ es?** what time is it?; **¿a qué ~?** at what time?; **media ~** half an hour; **a la ~ de recreo** at playtime; **a primera ~** first thing (in the morning); **a última ~** at the last moment; **a altas ~s** in the small hours; **¡a buena ~!** about time too!; **pedir ~** to make an appointment; **dar la ~** to strike the hour; **horas de oficina/trabajo** office/working hours; **horas de visita** visiting times; **horas extras** o **extraordinarias** overtime sg; **horas pico** (LAM) rush o peak hours; **horas punta** (ESP) rush hours

horario, -a [o'rarjo, a] adj hourly, hour cpd ▷ nm timetable; **horario comercial** business hours pl

horca ['orka] nf gallows sg

horcajadas [orka'xaðas]: **a ~** adv astride

horchata [or'tʃata] nf cold drink made from tiger nuts and water, tiger nut milk

horizontal [oriθon'tal] adj horizontal

horizonte [ori'θonte] nm horizon

horma ['orma] nf mould

hormiga [or'miɣa] nf ant; **hormigas** nfpl (Med) pins and needles

hormigón [ormi'ɣon] nm concrete; **hormigón armado/pretensado** reinforced/prestressed concrete; **hormigonera** nf cement mixer

hormigueo [ormi'ɣeo] nm (comezón) itch

hormona [or'mona] nf hormone

hornillo [or'niʎo] nm (cocina) portable stove; **hornillo de gas** gas ring

horno ['orno] nm (Culin) oven; (Tec) furnace; **alto ~** blast furnace

horóscopo [o'roskopo] nm horoscope

horquilla [or'kiʎa] nf hairpin; (Agr) pitchfork

horrendo, -a [o'rrendo, a] adj horrendous, frightful

horrible [o'rriβle] adj horrible, dreadful

horripilante [orripi'lante] adj hair-raising, horrifying

horror [o'rror] nm horror, dread; (atrocidad) atrocity; **¡qué ~!** (fam) how awful!; **horrorizar** vt to horrify, frighten; **horrorizarse** vr to be horrified; **horroroso, -a** adj horrifying, ghastly

hortaliza [orta'liθa] nf vegetable

hortelano, -a [orte'lano, a] nm/f (market) gardener

hortera [or'tera] (fam) adj tacky

hospedar [ospe'ðar] vt to put up; **hospedarse** vr to stay, lodge

hospital [ospi'tal] nm hospital

hospitalario, -a [ospita'larjo, a] adj (acogedor) hospitable; **hospitalidad** nf hospitality

hostal [os'tal] nm small hotel

hostelería [ostele'ria] nf hotel business o trade

hostia ['ostja] nf (Rel) host, consecrated wafer; (fam!: golpe) whack, punch ▷ excl (fam!): **¡~(s)!** damn!

hostil [os'til] adj hostile

hotdog [ot'dog] (LAM) nm hot dog

hotel [o'tel] nm hotel; **hotelero, -a** adj hotel cpd ▷ nm/f hotelier

● **HOTEL**

● In Spain you can choose from
● the following categories of
● accommodation, in descending order of
● quality and price: **hotel** (from 5 stars to
● 1), **hostal**, **pensión**, **casa de huéspedes**,
● **fonda**. The State also runs luxury hotels
● called **paradores**, which are usually
● sited in places of particular historical
● interest and are often historic buildings
● themselves.

hoy [oi] *adv* (*este día*) today; (*la actualidad*)
now(adays) ▷*nm* present time; **~ (en) día**
now(adays)

hoyo ['ojo] *nm* hole, pit

hoz [oθ] *nf* sickle

hube *etc vb* V **haber**

hucha ['utʃa] *nf* money box

hueco, -a ['weko, a] *adj* (*vacío*) hollow,
empty; (*resonante*) booming ▷*nm* hollow,
cavity

huelga *etc* ['welɣa] *vb* V **holgar** ▷*nf*
strike; **declararse en ~** to go on strike,
come out on strike; **huelga de hambre**
hunger strike; **huelga general** general
strike

huelguista [wel'ɣista] *nmf* striker

huella ['weʎa] *nf* (*pisada*) tread; (*marca
del paso*) footprint, footstep; (: *de animal,
máquina*) track; **huella dactilar** fingerprint

huelo *etc vb* V **oler**

huérfano, -a ['werfano, a] *adj*
orphan(ed) ▷*nm/f* orphan

huerta ['werta] *nf* market garden; (*en
Murcia y Valencia*) irrigated region

huerto ['werto] *nm* kitchen garden; (*de
árboles frutales*) orchard

hueso ['weso] *nm* (*Anat*) bone; (*de fruta*)
stone

huésped ['wespeð] *nmf* guest

hueva ['weβa] *nf* roe

huevera [we'βera] *nf* eggcup

huevo ['weβo] *nm* egg; **huevo a la copa**
(CS) soft-boiled egg; **huevo duro/escalfado**
hard-boiled/poached egg; **huevo
estrellado** (LAM) fried egg; **huevo frito** (ESP)
fried egg; **huevo pasado por agua** soft-
boiled egg; **huevos revueltos** scrambled
eggs; **huevo tibio** (MÉX) soft-boiled egg

huida [u'iða] *nf* escape, flight

huir [u'ir] *vi* (*escapar*) to flee, escape; (*evitar*)
to avoid

hule ['ule] *nm* oilskin; (MÉX: *goma*) rubber

hulera [u'lera] (MÉX) *nf* catapult

humanidad [umani'ðað] *nf* (*género
humano*) man(kind); (*cualidad*) humanity

humanitario, -a [umani'tarjo, a] *adj*
humanitarian

humano, -a [u'mano, a] *adj* (*gen*) human;
(*humanitario*) humane ▷*nm* human; **ser ~**
human being

humareda [uma'reða] *nf* cloud of smoke

humedad [ume'ðað] *nf* (*de clima*)
humidity; (*de pared etc*) dampness; **a prueba
de ~** damp-proof; **humedecer** *vt* to
moisten, wet; **humedecerse** *vr* to get wet

húmedo, -a ['umeðo, a] *adj* (*mojado*)
damp, wet; (*tiempo etc*) humid

humilde [u'milde] *adj* humble, modest

humillación [umiʎa'θjon] *nf*
humiliation; **humillante** *adj* humiliating

humillar [umi'ʎar] *vt* to humiliate

humo ['umo] *nm* (*de fuego*) smoke; (*gas
nocivo*) fumes *pl*; (*vapor*) steam, vapour;
humos *nmpl* (*fig*) conceit *sg*

humor [u'mor] *nm* (*disposición*) mood,
temper; (*lo que divierte*) humour; **de buen/
mal ~** in a good/bad mood; **humorista**
nmf comic; **humorístico, -a** *adj* funny,
humorous

hundimiento [undi'mjento] *nm* (*gen*)
sinking; (*colapso*) collapse

hundir [un'dir] *vt* to sink; (*edificio, plan*) to
ruin, destroy; **hundirse** *vr* to sink, collapse

húngaro, -a ['ungaro, a] *adj, nm/f*
Hungarian

Hungría [un'gria] *nf* Hungary

huracán [ura'kan] *nm* hurricane

huraño, -a [u'raɲo, a] *adj* (*antisocial*)
unsociable

hurgar [ur'ɣar] *vt* to poke, jab; (*remover*) to
stir (up); **hurgarse** *vr*: **~se (las narices)** to
pick one's nose

hurón, -ona [u'ron, ona] *nm* (*Zool*) ferret

hurtadillas [urta'ðiʎas]: **a ~** *adv* stealthily,
on the sly

hurtar [ur'tar] *vt* to steal; **hurto** *nm*
theft, stealing

husmear [usme'ar] *vt* (*oler*) to sniff out,
scent; (*fam*) to pry into

huyo *etc vb* V **huir**

iba etc vb V **ir**

ibérico, -a [i'βeriko, a] adj Iberian

iberoamericano, -a [iβeroameri'kano, a] adj, nm/f Latin American

Ibiza [i'βiθa] nf Ibiza

iceberg [iθe'βer] nm iceberg

icono [i'kono] nm ikon, icon

ida ['iða] nf going, departure; **~ y vuelta** round trip, return

idea [i'ðea] nf idea; **no tengo la menor ~** I haven't a clue

ideal [iðe'al] adj, nm ideal; **idealista** nmf idealist; **idealizar** vt to idealize

ídem ['iðem] pron ditto

idéntico, -a [i'ðentiko, a] adj identical

identidad [iðenti'ðað] nf identity

identificación [iðentifika'θjon] nf identification

identificar [iðentifi'kar] vt to identify; **identificarse** vr: **~se con** to identify with

ideología [iðeolo'xia] nf ideology

idilio [i'ðiljo] nm love-affair

idioma [i'ðjoma] nm (gen) language

▌ No confundir **idioma** con la palabra inglesa idiom.

idiota [i'ðjota] adj idiotic ▷nmf idiot

ídolo ['iðolo] nm (tb fig) idol

idóneo, -a [i'ðoneo, a] adj suitable

iglesia [i'ɣlesja] nf church

ignorante [iɣno'rante] adj ignorant, uninformed ▷nmf ignoramus

ignorar [iɣno'rar] vt not to know, be ignorant of; (no hacer caso a) to ignore

igual [i'ɣwal] adj (gen) equal; (similar) like, similar; (mismo) (the) same; (constante) constant; (temperatura) even ▷nmf equal; **~ que** like, the same as; **me da o es ~** I don't care; **son ~es** they're the same; **al ~ que** (prep, conj) like, just like

igualar [iɣwa'lar] vt (gen) to equalize, make equal; (allanar, nivelar) to level (off),

even (out); **igualarse** vr (platos de balanza) to balance out

igualdad [iɣwal'dað] nf equality; (similaridad) sameness; (uniformidad) uniformity

igualmente [iɣwal'mente] adv equally; (también) also, likewise ▷excl the same to you!

ilegal [ile'ɣal] adj illegal

ilegítimo, -a [ile'xitimo, a] adj illegitimate

ileso, -a [i'leso, a] adj unhurt

ilimitado, -a [ilimi'taðo, a] adj unlimited

iluminación [ilumina'θjon] nf illumination; (alumbrado) lighting

iluminar [ilumi'nar] vt to illuminate, light (up); (fig) to enlighten

ilusión [ilu'sjon] nf illusion; (quimera) delusion; (esperanza) hope; **hacerse ilusiones** to build up one's hopes; **ilusionado, -a** adj excited; **ilusionar** vi: **le ilusiona ir de vacaciones** he's looking forward to going on holiday; **ilusionarse** vr: **ilusionarse (con)** to get excited (about)

iluso, -a [i'luso, a] adj easily deceived ▷nm/f dreamer

ilustración [ilustra'θjon] nf illustration; (saber) learning, erudition; **la I~** the Enlightenment; **ilustrado, -a** adj illustrated; learned

ilustrar [ilus'trar] vt to illustrate; (instruir) to instruct; (explicar) to explain, make clear

ilustre [i'lustre] adj famous, illustrious

imagen [i'maxen] nf (gen) image; (dibujo) picture

imaginación [imaxina'θjon] nf imagination

imaginar [imaxi'nar] vt (gen) to imagine; (idear) to think up; (suponer) to suppose; **imaginarse** vr to imagine; **imaginario, -a** adj imaginary; **imaginativo, -a** adj imaginative

imán [i'man] nm magnet

imbécil [im'beθil] nmf imbecile, idiot

imitación [imita'θjon] nf imitation; **de ~** imitation cpd

imitar [imi'tar] vt to imitate; (parodiar, remedar) to mimic, ape

impaciente [impa'θjente] adj impatient; (nervioso) anxious

impacto [im'pakto] nm impact

impar [im'par] adj odd

imparcial [impar'θjal] adj impartial, fair

impecable [impe'kaβle] adj impeccable

impedimento [impeði'mento] nm impediment, obstacle

impedir [impe'ðir] vt (obstruir) to impede, obstruct; (estorbar) to prevent; **~ a algn**

hacer *o* **que algn haga algo** to prevent sb (from) doing sth, stop sb doing sth

imperativo, -a [impera'tiβo, a] *adj* (*urgente, Ling*) imperative

imperdible [imper'ðiβle] *nm* safety pin

imperdonable [imperðo'naβle] *adj* unforgivable, inexcusable

imperfecto, -a [imper'fekto, a] *adj* imperfect

imperio [im'perjo] *nm* empire; (*autoridad*) rule, authority; (*fig*) pride, haughtiness

impermeable [imperme'aβle] *adj* waterproof ▷ *nm* raincoat, mac (*BRIT*)

impersonal [imperso'nal] *adj* impersonal

impertinente [imperti'nente] *adj* impertinent

ímpetu ['impetu] *nm* (*impulso*) impetus, impulse; (*impetuosidad*) impetuosity; (*violencia*) violence

implantar [implan'tar] *vt* to introduce

implemento [imple'mento] (*LAM*) *nm* tool, implement

implicar [impli'kar] *vt* to involve; (*entrañar*) to imply

implícito, -a [im'pliθito, a] *adj* (*tácito*) implicit; (*sobreentendido*) implied

imponente [impo'nente] *adj* (*impresionante*) impressive, imposing; (*solemne*) grand

imponer [impo'ner] *vt* (*gen*) to impose; (*exigir*) to exact; **imponerse** *vr* to assert o.s.; (*prevalecer*) to prevail; **imponible** *adj* (*Com*) taxable

impopular [impopu'lar] *adj* unpopular

importación [importa'θjon] *nf* (*acto*) importing; (*mercancías*) imports *pl*

importancia [impor'tanθja] *nf* importance; (*valor*) value, significance; (*extensión*) size, magnitude; **no tiene ~** it's nothing; **importante** *adj* important; valuable, significant

importar [impor'tar] *vt* (*del extranjero*) to import; (*costar*) to amount to ▷ *vi* to be important, matter; **me importa un rábano** I couldn't care less; **no importa** it doesn't matter; **¿le importa que fume?** do you mind if I smoke?

importe [im'porte] *nm* (*total*) amount; (*valor*) value

imposible [impo'siβle] *adj* (*gen*) impossible; (*insoportable*) unbearable, intolerable

imposición [imposi'θjon] *nf* imposition; (*Com: impuesto*) tax; (: *inversión*) deposit

impostor, a [impos'tor, a] *nm/f* impostor

impotencia [impo'tenθja] *nf* impotence; **impotente** *adj* impotent

impreciso, -a [impre'θiso, a] *adj* imprecise, vague

impregnar [impreɣ'nar] *vt* to impregnate; **impregnarse** *vr* to become impregnated

imprenta [im'prenta] *nf* (*acto*) printing; (*aparato*) press; (*casa*) printer's; (*letra*) print

imprescindible [impresθin'diβle] *adj* essential, vital

impresión [impre'sjon] *nf* (*gen*) impression; (*Imprenta*) printing; (*edición*) edition; (*Foto*) print; (*marca*) imprint; **impresión digital** fingerprint

impresionante [impresjo'nante] *adj* impressive; (*tremendo*) tremendous; (*maravilloso*) great, marvellous

impresionar [impresjo'nar] *vt* (*conmover*) to move; (*afectar*) to impress, strike; (*película fotográfica*) to expose; **impresionarse** *vr* to be impressed; (*conmoverse*) to be moved

impreso, -a [im'preso, a] *pp de* **imprimir** ▷ *adj* printed; **impresos** *nmpl* printed matter; **impresora** *nf* printer

imprevisto, -a [impre'βisto, a] *adj* (*gen*) unforeseen; (*inesperado*) unexpected

imprimir [impri'mir] *vt* to imprint, impress, stamp; (*textos*) to print; (*Inform*) to output, print out

improbable [impro'βaβle] *adj* improbable; (*inverosímil*) unlikely

impropio, -a [im'propjo, a] *adj* improper

improvisado, -a [improβi'saðo, a] *adj* improvised

improvisar [improβi'sar] *vt* to improvise

improviso, -a [impro'βiso, a] *adj*: **de ~** unexpectedly, suddenly

imprudencia [impru'ðenθja] *nf* imprudence; (*indiscreción*) indiscretion; (*descuido*) carelessness; **imprudente** *adj* unwise, imprudent; (*indiscreto*) indiscreet

impuesto, -a [im'pwesto, a] *adj* imposed ▷ *nm* tax; **impuesto al valor agregado** *o* **añadido** (*LAM*) value added tax (*BRIT*) ≈ sales tax (*US*); **impuesto sobre el valor añadido** (*ESP*) value added tax (*BRIT*) ≈ sales tax (*US*)

impulsar [impul'sar] *vt* to drive; (*promover*) to promote, stimulate

impulsivo, -a [impul'siβo, a] *adj* impulsive; **impulso** *nm* impulse; (*fuerza, empuje*) thrust, drive; (*fig: sentimiento*) urge, impulse

impureza [impu'reθa] *nf* impurity; **impuro, -a** *adj* impure

inaccesible [inakθe'siβle] *adj* inaccessible

inaceptable [inaθep'taβle] *adj* unacceptable

inactivo, -a [inak'tiβo, a] *adj* inactive

inadecuado, -a [inaðe'kwaðo, a] *adj*

(*insuficiente*) inadequate; (*inapto*) unsuitable

inadvertido, -a [inaðβer'tiðo, a] *adj* (*no visto*) unnoticed

inaguantable [inaɣwan'taβle] *adj* unbearable

inanimado, -a [inani'maðo, a] *adj* inanimate

inaudito, -a [inau'ðito, a] *adj* unheard-of

inauguración [inauɣura'θjon] *nf* inauguration; opening

inaugurar [inauɣu'rar] *vt* to inaugurate; (*exposición*) to open

inca ['inka] *nmf* Inca

incalculable [inkalku'laβle] *adj* incalculable

incandescente [inkandes'θente] *adj* incandescent

incansable [inkan'saβle] *adj* tireless, untiring

incapacidad [inkapaθi'ðað] *nf* incapacity; (*incompetencia*) incompetence; **incapacidad física/mental** physical/mental disability

incapacitar [inkapaθi'tar] *vt* (*inhabilitar*) to incapacitate, render unfit; (*descalificar*) to disqualify

incapaz [inka'paθ] *adj* incapable

incautarse [inkau'tarse] *vr*: **~ de** to seize, confiscate

incauto, -a [in'kauto, a] *adj* (*imprudente*) incautious, unwary

incendiar [inθen'djar] *vt* to set fire to; (*fig*) to inflame; **incendiarse** *vr* to catch fire; **incendiario, -a** *adj* incendiary

incendio [in'θendjo] *nm* fire

incentivo [inθen'tiβo] *nm* incentive

incertidumbre [inθerti'ðumbre] *nf* (*inseguridad*) uncertainty; (*duda*) doubt

incesante [inθe'sante] *adj* incessant

incesto [in'θesto] *nm* incest

incidencia [inθi'ðenθja] *nf* (*Mat*) incidence

incidente [inθi'ðente] *nm* incident

incidir [inθi'ðir] *vi* (*influir*) to influence; (*afectar*) to affect

incienso [in'θjenso] *nm* incense

incierto, -a [in'θjerto, a] *adj* uncertain

incineración [inθinera'θjon] *nf* incineration; (*de cadáveres*) cremation

incinerar [inθine'rar] *vt* to burn; (*cadáveres*) to cremate

incisión [inθi'sjon] *nf* incision

incisivo, -a [inθi'siβo, a] *adj* sharp, cutting; (*fig*) incisive

incitar [inθi'tar] *vt* to incite, rouse

inclemencia [inkle'menθja] *nf* (*severidad*) harshness, severity; (*del tiempo*) inclemency

inclinación [inklina'θjon] *nf* (*gen*)

inclination; (*de tierras*) slope, incline; (*de cabeza*) nod, bow; (*fig*) leaning, bent

inclinar [inkli'nar] *vt* to incline; (*cabeza*) to nod, bow ▷ *vi* to lean, slope; **inclinarse** *vr* to bow; (*encorvarse*) to stoop; **~se a** (*parecerse a*) to take after, resemble; **~se ante** to bow down to; **me inclino a pensar que ...** I'm inclined to think that ...

incluir [inklu'ir] *vt* to include; (*incorporar*) to incorporate; (*meter*) to enclose

inclusive [inklu'siβe] *adv* inclusive ▷ *prep* including

incluso [in'kluso] *adv* even

incógnita [in'koɣnita] *nf* (*Mat*) unknown quantity

incógnito [in'koɣnito] *nm*: **de ~** incognito

incoherente [inkoe'rente] *adj* incoherent

incoloro, -a [inko'loro, a] *adj* colourless

incomodar [inkomo'ðar] *vt* to inconvenience; (*molestar*) to bother, trouble; (*fastidiar*) to annoy

incomodidad [inkomoði'ðað] *nf* inconvenience; (*fastidio, enojo*) annoyance; (*de vivienda*) discomfort

incómodo, -a [in'komoðo, a] *adj* (*inconfortable*) uncomfortable; (*molesto*) annoying; (*inconveniente*) inconvenient

incomparable [inkompa'raβle] *adj* incomparable

incompatible [inkompa'tiβle] *adj* incompatible

incompetente [inkompe'tente] *adj* incompetent

incompleto, -a [inkom'pleto, a] *adj* incomplete, unfinished

incomprensible [inkompren'siβle] *adj* incomprehensible

incomunicado, -a [inkomuni'kaðo, a] *adj* (*aislado*) cut off, isolated; (*confinado*) in solitary confinement

incondicional [inkondiθjo'nal] *adj* unconditional; (*apoyo*) wholehearted; (*partidario*) staunch

inconfundible [inkonfun'diβle] *adj* unmistakable

incongruente [inkon'grwente] *adj* incongruous

inconsciente [inkons'θjente] *adj* unconscious; thoughtless

inconsecuente [inkonse'kwente] *adj* inconsistent

inconstante [inkons'tante] *adj* inconstant

incontable [inkon'taβle] *adj* countless, innumerable

inconveniencia [inkombe'njenθja] *nf* unsuitability, inappropriateness;

(*descortesía*) impoliteness; **inconveniente** *adj* unsuitable; impolite ▷ *nm* obstacle; (*desventaja*) disadvantage; **el inconveniente es que ...** the trouble is that ...

incordiar [inkor'ðjar] (*fam*) *vt* to bug, annoy

incorporar [inkorpo'rar] *vt* to incorporate; **incorporarse** *vr* to sit up; **~se a** to join

incorrecto, -a [inko'rrekto, a] *adj* (*gen*) incorrect, wrong; (*comportamiento*) bad-mannered

incorregible [inkorre'xiβle] *adj* incorrigible

incrédulo, -a [in'kreðulo, a] *adj* incredulous, unbelieving; sceptical

increíble [inkre'iβle] *adj* incredible

incremento [inkre'mento] *nm* increment; (*aumento*) rise, increase

increpar [inkre'par] *vt* to reprimand

incruento, -a [in'krwento, a] *adj* bloodless

incrustar [inkrus'tar] *vt* to incrust; (*piedras: en joya*) to inlay

incubar [inku'βar] *vt* to incubate

inculcar [inkul'kar] *vt* to inculcate

inculto, -a [in'kulto, a] *adj* (*persona*) uneducated; (*grosero*) uncouth ▷ *nm/f* ignoramus

incumplimiento [inkumpli'mjento] *nm* non-fulfilment; **incumplimiento de contrato** breach of contract

incurrir [inku'rrir] *vi:* **~ en** to incur; (*crimen*) to commit

indagar [inda'ɣar] *vt* to investigate; to search; (*averiguar*) to ascertain

indecente [inde'θente] *adj* indecent, improper; (*lascivo*) obscene

indeciso, -a [inde'θiso, a] *adj* (*por decidir*) undecided; (*vacilante*) hesitant

indefenso, -a [inde'fenso, a] *adj* defenceless

indefinido, -a [indefi'niðo, a] *adj* indefinite; (*vago*) vague, undefined

indemne [in'demne] *adj* (*objeto*) undamaged; (*persona*) unharmed, unhurt

indemnizar [indemni'θar] *vt* to indemnify; (*compensar*) to compensate

independencia [indepen'denθja] *nf* independence

independiente [indepen'djente] *adj* (*libre*) independent; (*autónomo*) self-sufficient

indeterminado, -a [indetermi'naðo, a] *adj* indefinite; (*desconocido*) indeterminate

India ['indja] *nf:* **la ~** India

indicación [indika'θjon] *nf* indication;

(*señal*) sign; (*sugerencia*) suggestion, hint

indicado, -a [indi'kaðo, a] *adj* (*momento, método*) right; (*tratamiento*) appropriate; (*solución*) likely

indicador [indika'ðor] *nm* indicator; (*Tec*) gauge, meter

indicar [indi'kar] *vt* (*mostrar*) to indicate, show; (*termómetro etc*) to read, register; (*señalar*) to point to

índice ['indiθe] *nm* index; (*catálogo*) catalogue; (*Anat*) index finger, forefinger; **índice de materias** table of contents

indicio [in'diθjo] *nm* indication, sign; (*en pesquisa etc*) clue

indiferencia [indife'renθja] *nf* indifference; (*apatía*) apathy; **indiferente** *adj* indifferent

indígena [in'dixena] *adj* indigenous, native ▷ *nmf* native

indigestión [indixes'tjon] *nf* indigestion

indigesto, -a [indi'xesto, a] *adj* (*alimento*) indigestible; (*fig*) turgid

indignación [indixna'θjon] *nf* indignation

indignar [indix'nar] *vt* to anger, make indignant; **indignarse** *vr:* **~se por** to get indignant about

indigno, -a [in'dixno, a] *adj* (*despreciable*) low, contemptible; (*inmerecido*) unworthy

indio, -a ['indjo, a] *adj, nm/f* Indian

indirecta [indi'rekta] *nf* insinuation, innuendo; (*sugerencia*) hint

indirecto, -a [indi'rekto, a] *adj* indirect

indiscreción [indiskre'θjon] *nf* (*imprudencia*) indiscretion; (*irreflexión*) tactlessness; (*acto*) gaffe, faux pas

indiscreto, -a [indis'kreto, a] *adj* indiscreet

indiscutible [indisku'tiβle] *adj* indisputable, unquestionable

indispensable [indispen'saβle] *adj* indispensable, essential

indispuesto, -a [indis'pwesto, a] *adj* (*enfermo*) unwell, indisposed

indistinto, -a [indis'tinto, a] *adj* indistinct; (*vago*) vague

individual [indiβi'ðwal] *adj* individual; (*habitación*) single ▷ *nm* (*Deporte*) singles *sg*

individuo, -a [indi'βiðwo, a] *adj, nm* individual

índole ['indole] *nf* (*naturaleza*) nature; (*clase*) sort, kind

inducir [indu'θir] *vt* to induce; (*inferir*) to infer; (*persuadir*) to persuade

indudable [indu'ðaβle] *adj* undoubted; (*incuestionable*) unquestionable

indultar [indul'tar] *vt* (*perdonar*) to pardon, reprieve; (*librar de pago*) to exempt;

indulto *nm* pardon; exemption
industria [in'dustrja] *nf* industry;
(*habilidad*) skill; **industrial** *adj* industrial
▷ *nm* industrialist
inédito, -a [in'eðito, a] *adj* (*texto*)
unpublished; (*nuevo*) new
ineficaz [inefi'kaθ] *adj* (*inútil*) ineffective;
(*ineficiente*) inefficient
ineludible [inelu'ðiβle] *adj* inescapable,
unavoidable
ineptitud [inepti'tuð] *nf* ineptitude,
incompetence; **inepto, -a** *adj* inept,
incompetent
inequívoco, -a [ine'kiβoko, a] *adj*
unequivocal; (*inconfundible*) unmistakable
inercia [in'erθja] *nf* inertia; (*pasividad*)
passivity
inerte [in'erte] *adj* inert; (*inmóvil*)
motionless
inesperado, -a [inespe'raðo, a] *adj*
unexpected, unforeseen
inestable [ines'taβle] *adj* unstable
inevitable [ineβi'taβle] *adj* inevitable
inexacto, -a [inek'sakto, a] *adj*
inaccurate; (*falso*) untrue
inexperto, -a [inek'sperto, a] *adj*
(*novato*) inexperienced
infalible [infa'liβle] *adj* infallible; (*plan*)
foolproof
infame [in'fame] *adj* infamous; (*horrible*)
dreadful; **infamia** *nf* infamy; (*deshonra*)
disgrace
infancia [in'fanθja] *nf* infancy, childhood
infantería [infante'ria] *nf* infantry
infantil [infan'til] *adj* (*pueril, aniñado*)
infantile; (*cándido*) childlike; (*literatura, ropa
etc*) children's
infarto [in'farto] *nm* (*tb:* ~ **de miocardio**)
heart attack
infatigable [infati'xaβle] *adj* tireless,
untiring
infección [infek'θjon] *nf* infection;
infeccioso, -a *adj* infectious
infectar [infek'tar] *vt* to infect;
infectarse *vr* to become infected
infeliz [infe'liθ] *adj* unhappy, wretched
▷ *nmf* wretch
inferior [infe'rjor] *adj* inferior; (*situación*)
lower ▷ *nmf* inferior, subordinate
inferir [infe'rir] *vt* (*deducir*) to infer,
deduce; (*causar*) to cause
infidelidad [infiðeli'ðað] *nf* (*gen*)
infidelity, unfaithfulness
infiel [in'fjel] *adj* unfaithful, disloyal;
(*erróneo*) inaccurate ▷ *nmf* infidel,
unbeliever
infierno [in'fjerno] *nm* hell
infiltrarse [infil'trarse] *vr:* ~ **en** to

infiltrate in(to); (*persona*) to work one's
way in(to)
ínfimo, -a ['infimo, a] *adj* (*más bajo*)
lowest; (*despreciable*) vile, mean
infinidad [infini'ðað] *nf* infinity;
(*abundancia*) great quantity
infinito, -a [infi'nito, a] *adj, nm* infinite
inflación [infla'θjon] *nf* (*hinchazón*)
swelling; (*monetaria*) inflation; (*fig*) conceit
inflamable [infl'maβle] *adj* flammable
inflamar [infla'mar] *vt* (*Med: fig*) to
inflame; **inflamarse** *vr* to catch fire; to
become inflamed
inflar [in'flar] *vt* (*hinchar*) to inflate, blow
up; (*fig*) to exaggerate; **inflarse** *vr* to swell
(up); (*fig*) to get conceited
inflexible [inflek'siβle] *adj* inflexible; (*fig*)
unbending
influencia [influ'enθja] *nf* influence
influir [influ'ir] *vt* to influence
influjo [in'fluxo] *nm* influence
influya *etc vb* V **influir**
influyente [influ'jente] *adj* influential
información [informa'θjon] *nf*
information; (*noticias*) news *sg*; (*Jur*) inquiry;
I~ (*oficina*) Information Office; (*mostrador*)
Information Desk; (*Tel*) Directory Enquiries
informal [infor'mal] *adj* (*gen*) informal
informar [infor'mar] *vt* (*gen*) to inform;
(*revelar*) to reveal, make known ▷ *vi* (*Jur*) to
plead; (*denunciar*) to inform; (*dar cuenta de*)
to report on; **informarse** *vr* to find out; ~ **se
de** to inquire into
informática [infor'matika] *nf* computer
science, information technology
informe [in'forme] *adj* shapeless ▷ *nm*
report
infracción [infrak'θjon] *nf* infraction,
infringement
infravalorar [infrabalo'rar] *vt* to
undervalue, underestimate
infringir [infrin'xir] *vt* to infringe,
contravene
infundado, -a [infun'daðo, a] *adj*
groundless, unfounded
infundir [infun'dir] *vt* to infuse, instil
infusión [infu'sjon] *nf* infusion; **infusión
de manzanilla** camomile tea
ingeniería [inxenje'ria] *nf* engineering;
ingeniería genética genetic engineering;
ingeniero, -a *nm/f* engineer; **ingeniero
civil** *o* **de caminos** civil engineer
ingenio [in'xenjo] *nm* (*talento*) talent;
(*agudeza*) wit; (*habilidad*) ingenuity,
inventiveness; **ingenio azucarero** (*LAM*)
sugar refinery; **ingenioso, -a** [inxe'njoso,
a] *adj* ingenious, clever; (*divertido*) witty;
ingenuo, -a *adj* ingenuous

ingerir [inxe'rir] vt to ingest; (*tragar*) to swallow; (*consumir*) to consume

Inglaterra [ingla'terra] nf England

ingle ['ingle] nf groin

inglés, -esa [in'gles, esa] adj English ▷ nm/f Englishman(-woman) ▷ nm (*Ling*) English

ingrato, -a [in'grato, a] adj (*gen*) ungrateful

ingrediente [ingre'ðjente] nm ingredient

ingresar [ingre'sar] vt (*dinero*) to deposit ▷ vi to come in; **~ en el hospital** to go into hospital

ingreso [in'greso] nm (*entrada*) entry; (*en hospital etc*) admission; **ingresos** nmpl (*dinero*) income sg; (*Com*) takings pl

inhabitable [inaβi'taβle] adj uninhabitable

inhalar [ina'lar] vt to inhale

inhibir [ini'βir] vt to inhibit

inhóspito, -a [i'nospito, a] adj (*región, paisaje*) inhospitable

inhumano, -a [inu'mano, a] adj inhuman

inicial [ini'θjal] adj, nf initial

iniciar [ini'θjar] vt (*persona*) to initiate; (*empezar*) to begin, commence; (*conversación*) to start up

iniciativa [iniθja'tiβa] nf initiative; **iniciativa privada** private enterprise

ininterrumpido, -a [ininterrum'piðo, a] adj uninterrupted

injertar [inxer'tar] vt to graft; **injerto** nm graft

injuria [in'xurja] nf (*agravio, ofensa*) offence; (*insulto*) insult

▌No confundir **injuria** con la palabra inglesa *injury*.

injusticia [inxus'tiθja] nf injustice

injusto, -a [in'xusto, a] adj unjust, unfair

inmadurez [inmaðu're θ] nf immaturity

inmediaciones [inmeðja'θjones] nfpl neighbourhood sg, environs

inmediato, -a [inme'ðjato, a] adj immediate; (*contiguo*) adjoining; (*rápido*) prompt; (*próximo*) neighbouring, next; **de ~** immediately

inmejorable [inmexo'raβle] adj unsurpassable; (*precio*) unbeatable

inmenso, -a [in'menso, a] adj immense, huge

inmigración [inmiɣra'θjon] nf immigration

inmobiliaria [inmoβi'ljarja] nf estate agency

inmolar [inmo'lar] vt to immolate, sacrifice

inmoral [inmo'ral] adj immoral

inmortal [inmor'tal] adj immortal; **inmortalizar** vt to immortalize

inmóvil [in'moβil] adj immobile

inmueble [in'mweβle] adj: **bienes ~s** real estate, landed property ▷ nm property

inmundo, -a [in'mundo, a] adj filthy

inmune [in'mune] adj: **~ (a)** (*Med*) immune (to)

inmunidad [inmuni'ðað] nf immunity

inmutarse [inmu'tarse] vr to turn pale; **no se inmutó** he didn't turn a hair

innato, -a [in'nato, a] adj innate

innecesario, -a [inneθe'sarjo, a] adj unnecessary

innovación [innoβa'θjon] nf innovation

innovar [inno'βar] vt to introduce

inocencia [ino'θenθja] nf innocence

inocentada [inoθen'taða] nf practical joke

inocente [ino'θente] adj (*ingenuo*) naive, innocent; (*inculpable*) innocent; (*sin malicia*) harmless ▷ nmf simpleton; **el día de los (Santos) I~s** ≈ April Fools' Day

> ● **DÍA DE LOS (SANTOS)**
> ● **INOCENTES**
> ●
> ● The 28th December, el **día de los**
> ● **(Santos) Inocentes**, is when the
> ● Church commemorates the story of
> ● Herod's slaughter of the innocent
> ● children of Judaea. On this day
> ● Spaniards play **inocentadas** (practical
> ● jokes) on each other, much like our April
> ● Fool's Day pranks.

inodoro [ino'ðoro] nm toilet, lavatory (BRIT)

inofensivo, -a [inofen'siβo, a] adj inoffensive, harmless

inolvidable [inolβi'ðaβle] adj unforgettable

inoportuno, -a [inopor'tuno, a] adj untimely; (*molesto*) inconvenient

inoxidable [inoksi'ðaβle] adj: **acero ~** stainless steel

inquietar [inkje'tar] vt to worry, trouble; **inquietarse** vr to worry, get upset; **inquieto, -a** adj anxious, worried; **inquietud** nf anxiety, worry

inquilino, -a [inki'lino, a] nm/f tenant

insaciable [insa'θjaβle] adj insatiable

inscribir [inskri'βir] vt to inscribe; **~ a algn en** (*lista*) to put sb on; (*censo*) to register sb on

inscripción [inskrip'θjon] nf inscription; (*Escol etc*) enrolment; (*en censo*) registration

insecticida [insekti'θiða] nm insecticide

insecto [in'sekto] nm insect
inseguridad [inseɣuri'ðað] nf insecurity;
inseguridad ciudadana lack of safety in
the streets
inseguro, -a [inse'ɣuro, a] adj insecure;
(inconstante) unsteady; (incierto) uncertain
insensato, -a [insen'sato, a] adj foolish,
stupid
insensible [insen'siβle] adj (gen)
insensitive; (movimiento) imperceptible; (sin
sentido) numb
insertar [inser'tar] vt to insert
inservible [inser'βiβle] adj useless
insignia [in'siɣnja] nf (señal distintiva)
badge; (estandarte) flag
insignificante [insiɣnifi'kante] adj
insignificant
insinuar [insi'nwar] vt to insinuate,
imply
insípido, -a [in'sipiðo, a] adj insipid
insistir [insis'tir] vi to insist; **~ en algo** to
insist on sth; (enfatizar) to stress sth
insolación [insola'θjon] nf (Med)
sunstroke
insolente [inso'lente] adj insolent
insólito, -a [in'solito, a] adj unusual
insoluble [inso'luβle] adj insoluble
insomnio [in'somnjo] nm insomnia
insonorizado, -a [insonori'θaðo, a] adj
(cuarto etc) soundproof
insoportable [insopor'taβle] adj
unbearable
inspección [inspek'θjon] nf inspection,
check; **inspeccionar** vt (examinar) to
inspect, examine; (controlar) to check
inspector, a [inspek'tor, a] nm/f
inspector
inspiración [inspira'θjon] nf inspiration
inspirar [inspi'rar] vt to inspire; (Med) to
inhale; **inspirarse** vr: **~se en** to be inspired
by
instalación [instala'θjon] nf (equipo)
fittings pl, equipment; **instalación
eléctrica** wiring
instalar [insta'lar] vt (establecer) to instal;
(erguir) to set up, erect; **instalarse** vr to
establish o.s.; (en una vivienda) to move into
instancia [ins'tanθja] nf (Jur) petition;
(ruego) request; **en última ~** as a last resort
instantáneo, -a [instan'taneo, a] adj
instantaneous; **café ~** instant coffee
instante [ins'tante] nm instant, moment;
al ~ right now
instar [ins'tar] vt to press, urge
instaurar [instau'rar] vt (costumbre)
to establish; (normas, sistema) to bring in,
introduce; (gobierno) to instal
instigar [insti'ɣar] vt to instigate

instinto [ins'tinto] nm instinct; **por ~**
instinctively
institución [institu'θjon] nf institution,
establishment
instituir [institu'ir] vt to establish;
(fundar) to found; **instituto** nm (gen)
institute; (ESP Escol) ≈ comprehensive (BRIT)
o high (US) school
institutriz [institu'triθ] nf governess
instrucción [instruk'θjon] nf instruction
instruir [instru'ir] vt (gen) to instruct;
(enseñar) to teach, educate
instrumento [instru'mento] nm (gen)
instrument; (herramienta) tool, implement
insubordinarse [insuβorði'narse] vr to
rebel
insuficiente [insufi'θjente] adj
(gen) insufficient; (Escol: calificación)
unsatisfactory
insular [insu'lar] adj insular
insultar [insul'tar] vt to insult; **insulto**
nm insult
insuperable [insupe'raβle] adj
(excelente) unsurpassable; (problema etc)
insurmountable
insurrección [insurrek'θjon] nf
insurrection, rebellion
intachable [inta'tʃaβle] adj
irreproachable
intacto, -a [in'takto, a] adj intact
integral [inte'ɣral] adj integral; (completo)
complete; **pan ~** wholemeal (BRIT) o
wholewheat (US) bread
integrar [inte'ɣrar] vt to make up,
compose; (Mat: fig) to integrate
integridad [inteɣri'ðað] nf wholeness;
(carácter) integrity; **íntegro, -a** adj whole,
entire; (honrado) honest
intelectual [intelek'twal] adj, nmf
intellectual
inteligencia [inteli'xenθja] nf
intelligence; (ingenio) ability; **inteligente**
adj intelligent
intemperie [intem'perje] nf: **a la ~** out in
the open, exposed to the elements
intención [inten'θjon] nf (gen) intention,
purpose; **con segundas intenciones**
maliciously; **con ~** deliberately
intencionado, -a [intenθjo'naðo, a] adj
deliberate; **mal ~** ill-disposed, hostile
intensidad [intensi'ðað] nf (gen)
intensity; (Elec, Tec) strength; **llover con ~**
to rain hard
intenso, -a [in'tenso, a] adj intense;
(sentimiento) profound, deep
intentar [inten'tar] vt (tratar) to try,
attempt; **intento** nm attempt
interactivo, -a [interak'tiβo, a] adj

(*Inform*) interactive
intercalar [interka'lar] *vt* to insert
intercambio [inter'kambjo] *nm*
exchange, swap
interceder [interθe'ðer] *vi* to intercede
interceptar [interθep'tar] *vt* to intercept
interés [inte'res] *nm* (*gen*) interest; (*parte*)
share, part; (*pey*) self-interest; **intereses
creados** vested interests
interesado, -a [intere'saðo, a] *adj*
interested; (*prejuiciado*) prejudiced; (*pey*)
mercenary, self-seeking
interesante [intere'sante] *adj*
interesting
interesar [intere'sar] *vt, vi* to interest, be
of interest to; **interesarse** *vr*: **~se en** *o* **por**
to take an interest in
interferir [interfe'rir] *vt* to interfere with;
(*Tel*) to jam ▷ *vi* to interfere
interfón [inter'fon] (*MÉX*) *nm* entry
phone
interino, -a [inte'rino, a] *adj* temporary
▷ *nm/f* temporary holder of a post; (*Med*)
locum; (*Escol*) supply teacher
interior [inte'rjor] *adj* inner, inside;
(*Com*) domestic, internal ▷ *nm* interior,
inside; (*fig*) soul, mind; **Ministerio del I~**
≈ Home Office (*BRIT*), ≈ Department of the
Interior (*us*); **interiorista** (*ESP*) *nmf* interior
designer
interjección [interxek'θjon] *nf*
interjection
interlocutor, a [interloku'tor, a] *nm/f*
speaker
intermedio, -a [inter'meðjo, a] *adj*
intermediate ▷ *nm* interval
interminable [intermi'naβle] *adj*
endless
intermitente [intermi'tente] *adj*
intermittent ▷ *nm* (*Auto*) indicator
internacional [internaθjo'nal] *adj*
international
internado [inter'naðo] *nm* boarding
school
internar [inter'nar] *vt* to intern; (*en
un manicomio*) to commit; **internarse** *vr*
(*penetrar*) to penetrate
internauta [inter'nauta] *nmf* web surfer,
Internet user
Internet, internet [inter'net] *nm o f*
Internet
interno, -a [in'terno, a] *adj* internal,
interior; (*Pol etc*) domestic ▷ *nm/f* (*alumno*)
boarder
interponer [interpo'ner] *vt* to interpose,
put in; **interponerse** *vr* to intervene
interpretación [interpreta'θjon] *nf*
interpretation

interpretar [interpre'tar] *vt* to interpret;
(*Teatro, Mús*) to perform, play; **intérprete**
nmf (*Ling*) interpreter, translator; (*Mús,
Teatro*) performer, artist(e)
interrogación [interroxa'θjon] *nf*
interrogation; (*Ling*: *tb*: **signo de ~**)
question mark
interrogar [interro'xar] *vt* to interrogate,
question
interrumpir [interrum'pir] *vt* to
interrupt
interrupción [interrup'θjon] *nf*
interruption
interruptor [interrup'tor] *nm* (*Elec*)
switch
intersección [intersek'θjon] *nf*
intersection
interurbano, -a [interur'βano, a]
adj: **llamada interurbana** long-distance
call
intervalo [inter'βalo] *nm* interval;
(*descanso*) break
intervenir [interβe'nir] *vt* (*controlar*) to
control, supervise; (*Med*) to operate on ▷ *vi*
(*participar*) to take part, participate; (*mediar*)
to intervene
interventor, a [interβen'tor, a] *nm/f*
inspector; (*Com*) auditor
intestino [intes'tino] *nm* (*Med*) intestine
intimar [inti'mar] *vi* to become friendly
intimidad [intimi'ðað] *nf* intimacy;
(*familiaridad*) familiarity; (*vida privada*)
private life; (*Jur*) privacy
íntimo, -a ['intimo, a] *adj* intimate
intolerable [intole'raβle] *adj* intolerable,
unbearable
intoxicación [intoksika'θjon] *nf*
poisoning; **intoxicación alimenticia** food
poisoning
intranet [intra'net] *nf* intranet
intranquilo, -a [intran'kilo, a] *adj*
worried
intransitable [intransi'taβle] *adj*
impassable
intrépido, -a [in'trepiðo, a] *adj* intrepid
intriga [in'trixa] *nf* intrigue; (*plan*) plot;
intrigar *vt, vi* to intrigue
intrínseco, -a [in'trinseko, a] *adj*
intrinsic
introducción [introðuk'θjon] *nf*
introduction
introducir [introðu'θir] *vt* (*gen*) to
introduce; (*moneda etc*) to insert; (*Inform*) to
input, enter
intromisión [intromi'sjon] *nf*
interference, meddling
introvertido, -a [introβer'tiðo, a] *adj*,
nm/f introvert

intruso, -a [in'truso, a] *adj* intrusive
▷ *nm/f* intruder
intuición [intwi'θjon] *nf* intuition
inundación [inunda'θjon] *nf* flood(ing);
inundar *vt* to flood; (*fig*) to swamp,
inundate
inusitado, -a [inusi'taðo, a] *adj* unusual,
rare
inútil [in'util] *adj* useless; (*esfuerzo*) vain,
fruitless
inutilizar [inutili'θar] *vt* to make o render
useless
invadir [imba'ðir] *vt* to invade
inválido, -a [im'baliðo, a] *adj* invalid
▷ *nm/f* invalid
invasión [imba'sjon] *nf* invasion
invasor, a [imba'sor, a] *adj* invading
▷ *nm/f* invader
invención [imben'θjon] *nf* invention
inventar [imben'tar] *vt* to invent
inventario [imben'tarjo] *nm* inventory
invento [im'bento] *nm* invention
inventor, a [imben'tor, a] *nm/f* inventor
invernadero [imberna'ðero] *nm*
greenhouse
inverosímil [imbero'simil] *adj*
implausible
inversión [imber'sjon] *nf* (*Com*)
investment
inverso, -a [im'berso, a] *adj* inverse,
opposite; **en el orden ~** in reverse order; **a la
inversa** inversely, the other way round
inversor, a [imber'sor, a] *nm/f* (*Com*)
investor
invertir [imber'tir] *vt* (*Com*) to invest;
(*volcar*) to turn upside down; (*tiempo etc*)
to spend
investigación [imbestiɣa'θjon]
nf investigation; (*Escol*) research;
investigación y desarrollo research and
development
investigar [imbesti'ɣar] *vt* to investigate;
(*Escol*) to do research into
invierno [im'bjerno] *nm* winter
invisible [imbi'siβle] *adj* invisible
invitado, -a [imbi'taðo, a] *nm/f* guest
invitar [imbi'tar] *vt* to invite; (*incitar*) to
entice; (*pagar*) to buy, pay for
invocar [imbo'kar] *vt* to invoke, call on
involucrar [imbolu'krar] *vt*: **~ en** to
involve in; **involucrarse** *vr* (*persona*): **~se
en** to get mixed up in
involuntario, -a [imbolun'tarjo, a]
adj (*movimiento, gesto*) involuntary; (*error*)
unintentional
inyección [injek'θjon] *nf* injection
inyectar [injek'tar] *vt* to inject
iPod® ['ipoð] (*pl* **~s**) *nm* iPod®

○ **PALABRA CLAVE**

ir [ir] *vi* **1** to go; (*a pie*) to walk; (*viajar*) to
travel; **ir caminando** to walk; **fui en tren** I
went o travelled by train; **¡(ahora) voy!** (I'm
just) coming!
2: **ir (a) por**: **ir (a) por el médico** to fetch
the doctor
3 (*progresar: persona, cosa*) to go; **el trabajo
va muy bien** work is going very well; **¿cómo
te va?** how are things going?; **me va muy
bien** I'm getting on very well; **le fue fatal** it
went awfully badly for him
4 (*funcionar*): **el coche no va muy bien** the
car isn't running very well
5: **te va estupendamente ese color** that
colour suits you fantastically well
6 (*locuciones*): **¿vino? - ¡que va!** did he come?
– of course not!; **vamos, no llores** come on,
don't cry; **¡vaya coche!** what a car!, that's
some car!
7: **no vaya a ser: tienes que correr, no
vaya a ser que pierdas el tren** you'll have
to run so as not to miss the train
8 (+ *pp*): **iba vestido muy bien** he was very
well dressed
9: **ni me** *etc* **va ni me** *etc* **viene** I *etc* don't
care
▷ *vb aux* **1** **ir a: voy/iba a hacerlo hoy** I am/
was going to do it today
2 (+ *gerundio*): **iba anocheciendo** it was
getting dark; **todo se me iba aclarando**
everything was gradually becoming clearer
to me
3 (+ *pp* = *pasivo*): **van vendidos 300
ejemplares** 300 copies have been sold so far
irse *vr* **1**: **¿por dónde se va al zoológico?**
which is the way to the zoo?
2 (*marcharse*) to leave; **ya se habrán ido** they
must already have left o gone

ira ['ira] *nf* anger, rage
Irak [i'rak] *nm* = **Iraq**
Irán [i'ran] *nm* Iran; **iraní** *adj, nmf* Iranian
Iraq [i'rak] *nm* Iraq; **iraquí** *adj, nmf* Iraqi
iris ['iris] *nm inv* (*tb*: **arco ~**) rainbow;
(*Anat*) iris
Irlanda [ir'landa] *nf* Ireland; **irlandés,
-esa** *adj* Irish ▷ *nm/f* Irishman(-woman);
los irlandeses the Irish
ironía [iro'nia] *nf* irony; **irónico, -a** *adj*
ironic(al)
IRPF *nm abr* (= *Impuesto sobre la Renta de las
Personas Físicas*) (personal) income tax
irreal [irre'al] *adj* unreal
irregular [irreɣu'lar] *adj* (*gen*) irregular;
(*situación*) abnormal
irremediable [irreme'ðjaβle] *adj*

irremediable; (vicio) incurable
irreparable [irrepa'raβle] adj (daños)
irreparable; (pérdida) irrecoverable
irrespetuoso, -a [irrespe'twoso, a] adj
disrespectful
irresponsable [irrespon'saβle] adj
irresponsible
irreversible [irreβer'sible] adj irreversible
irrigar [irri'ɣar] vt to irrigate
irrisorio, -a [irri'sorjo, a] adj derisory,
ridiculous
irritar [irri'tar] vt to irritate, annoy
irrupción [irrup'θjon] nf irruption;
(invasión) invasion
isla ['isla] nf island
Islam [is'lam] nm Islam; **las enseñanzas
del ~** the teachings of Islam; **islámico, -a**
adj Islamic
islandés, -esa [islan'des, esa] adj
Icelandic ▷ nm/f Icelander
Islandia [is'landja] nf Iceland
isleño, -a [is'leɲo, a] adj island cpd ▷ nm/f
islander
Israel [isra'el] nm Israel; **israelí** adj, nmf
Israeli
istmo ['istmo] nm isthmus
Italia [i'talja] nf Italy; **italiano, -a** adj,
nm/f Italian
itinerario [itine'rarjo] nm itinerary, route
ITV (ESP) nf abr (= inspección técnica de
vehículos) roadworthiness test, ≈ MOT (BRIT)
IVA ['iβa] nm abr (= impuesto sobre el valor
añadido) VAT
izar [i'θar] vt to hoist
izdo, -a abr (= izquierdo, a) l
izquierda [iθ'kjerda] nf left; (Pol) left
(wing); **a la ~** (estar) on the left; (torcer etc)
(to the) left
izquierdo, -a [iθ'kjerðo, a] adj left

J

jabalí [xaβa'li] nm wild boar
jabalina [xaβa'lina] nf javelin
jabón [xa'βon] nm soap
jaca ['xaka] nf pony
jacal [xa'kal] (MÉX) nm shack
jacinto [xa'θinto] nm hyacinth
jactarse [xak'tarse] vr to boast, brag
jadear [xaðe'ar] vi to pant, gasp for breath
jaguar [xa'ɣwar] nm jaguar
jaiba ['xaiβa] (LAM) nf crab
jalar [xa'lar] (LAM) vt to pull
jalea [xa'lea] nf jelly
jaleo [xa'leo] nm racket, uproar; **armar un
~** to kick up a racket
jalón [xa'lon] (LAM) nm tug
jamás [xa'mas] adv never
jamón [xa'mon] nm ham; **jamón dulce**
o **de York** cooked ham; **jamón serrano**
cured ham
Japón [xa'pon] nm Japan; **japonés, -esa**
adj, nm/f Japanese ▷ nm (Ling) Japanese
jaque ['xake] nm (Ajedrez) check; **jaque
mate** checkmate
jaqueca [xa'keka] nf (very bad) headache,
migraine
jarabe [xa'raβe] nm syrup
jardín [xar'ðin] nm garden; **jardín infantil**
o **de infancia** nursery (school); **jardinería**
nf gardening; **jardinero, -a** nm/f gardener
jarra ['xarra] nf jar; (jarro) jug
jarro ['xarro] nm jug
jarrón [xa'rron] nm vase
jaula ['xaula] nf cage
jauría [xau'ria] nf pack of hounds
jazmín [xaθ'min] nm jasmine
J.C. abr (= Jesucristo) J.C.
jeans [jins, dʒins] (LAM) nmpl jeans,
denims; **unos ~** a pair of jeans
jefatura [xefa'tura] nf (tb: ~ **de policía**)
police headquarters sg
jefe, -a ['xefe, a] nm/f (gen) chief, head;

(*patrón*) boss; **jefe de cocina** chef; **jefe de estación** stationmaster; **jefe de Estado** head of state; **jefe de estudios** (*Escol*) director of studies; **jefe de gobierno** head of government

jengibre [xen'xiβre] *nm* ginger

jeque ['xeke] *nm* sheik

jerárquico, -a [xe'rarkiko, a] *adj* hierarchic(al)

jerez [xe'reθ] *nm* sherry

jerga ['xerɣa] *nf* jargon

jeringa [xe'ringa] *nf* syringe; (*LAM: molestia*) annoyance, bother; **jeringuilla** *nf* syringe

jeroglífico [xero'ɣlifiko] *nm* hieroglyphic

jersey [xer'sei] (*pl* **~s**) *nm* jersey, pullover, jumper

Jerusalén [xerusa'len] *n* Jerusalem

Jesucristo [xesu'kristo] *nm* Jesus Christ

jesuita [xe'swita] *adj, nm* Jesuit

Jesús [xe'sus] *nm* Jesus; **¡~!** good heavens!; (*al estornudar*) bless you!

jinete [xi'nete] *nmf* horseman(-woman), rider

jipijapa [xipi'xapa] (*LAM*) *nm* straw hat

jirafa [xi'rafa] *nf* giraffe

jirón [xi'ron] *nm* rag, shred

jitomate [xito'mate] (*MÉX*) *nm* tomato

joder [xo'ðer] (*fam!*) *vt, vi* to fuck (*!*)

jogging ['joɣin] (*RPL*) *nm* tracksuit (*BRIT*), sweat suit (*US*)

jornada [xor'naða] *nf* (*viaje de un día*) day's journey; (*camino o viaje entero*) journey; (*día de trabajo*) working day

jornal [xor'nal] *nm* (day's) wage; **jornalero** *nm* (day) labourer

joroba [xo'roβa] *nf* hump, hunched back; **jorobado, -a** *adj* hunchbacked ▷ *nm/f* hunchback

jota ['xota] *nf* (the letter) J; (*danza*) Aragonese dance; **no saber ni ~** to have no idea

joven ['xoβen] (*pl* **jóvenes**) *adj* young ▷ *nm* young man, youth ▷ *nf* young woman, girl

joya ['xoja] *nf* jewel, gem; (*fig: persona*) gem; **joyas de fantasía** costume *o* imitation jewellery; **joyería** *nf* (*joyas*) jewellery; (*tienda*) jeweller's (shop); **joyero** *nm* (*persona*) jeweller; (*caja*) jewel case

juanete [xwa'nete] *nm* (*del pie*) bunion

jubilación [xuβila'θjon] *nf* (*retiro*) retirement

jubilado, -a [xuβi'laðo, a] *adj* retired ▷ *nm/f* pensioner (*BRIT*), senior citizen

jubilar [xuβi'lar] *vt* to pension off, retire; (*fam*) to discard; **jubilarse** *vr* to retire

júbilo ['xuβilo] *nm* joy, rejoicing; **jubiloso,**

-a *adj* jubilant

judía [xu'ðia] (*ESP*) *nf* (*Culin*) bean; **judía blanca/verde** haricot/French bean; V tb **judío**

judicial [xuði'θjal] *adj* judicial

judío, -a [xu'ðio, a] *adj* Jewish ▷ *nm/f* Jew(ess)

judo ['juðo] *nm* judo

juego etc ['xweɣo] vb V **jugar** ▷ *nm* (*gen*) play; (*pasatiempo, partido*) game; (*en casino*) gambling; (*conjunto*) set; **fuera de ~** (*Deporte: persona*) offside; (*: pelota*) out of play; **juego de palabras** pun, play on words; **Juegos Olímpicos** Olympic Games

juerga ['xwerɣa] (*ESP: fam*) *nf* binge; (*fiesta*) party; **ir de ~** to go out on a binge

jueves ['xweβes] *nm inv* Thursday

juez [xweθ] *nmf* judge; **juez de instrucción** examining magistrate; **juez de línea** linesman; **juez de salida** starter

jugada [xu'ɣaða] *nf* play; **buena ~** good move *o* shot *o* stroke etc

jugador, a [xuɣa'ðor, a] *nm/f* player; (*en casino*) gambler

jugar [xu'ɣar] *vt, vi* to play; (*en casino*) to gamble; (*apostar*) to bet; **~ al fútbol** to play football

juglar [xu'ɣlar] *nm* minstrel

jugo ['xuɣo] *nm* (*Bot*) juice; (*fig*) essence, substance; **jugo de naranja** (*LAM*) orange juice; **jugoso, -a** *adj* juicy; (*fig*) substantial, important

juguete [xu'ɣete] *nm* toy; **juguetear** *vi* to play; **juguetería** *nf* toyshop

juguetón, -ona [xuɣe'ton, ona] *adj* playful

juicio ['xwiθjo] *nm* judgement; (*razón*) sanity, reason; (*opinión*) opinion

julio ['xuljo] *nm* July

jumper ['dʒumper] (*LAM*) *nm* pinafore dress (*BRIT*), jumper (*US*)

junco ['xunko] *nm* rush, reed

jungla ['xungla] *nf* jungle

junio ['xunjo] *nm* June

junta ['xunta] *nf* (*asamblea*) meeting, assembly; (*comité, consejo*) council, committee; (*Com, Finanzas*) board; (*Tec*) joint; **junta directiva** board of directors

juntar [xun'tar] *vt* to join, unite; (*maquinaria*) to assemble, put together; (*dinero*) to collect; **juntarse** *vr* to join, meet; (*reunirse: personas*) to meet, assemble; (*arrimarse*) to approach, draw closer; **~se con algn** to join sb

junto, -a ['xunto, a] *adj* joined; (*unido*) united; (*anexo*) near, close; (*contiguo, próximo*) next, adjacent ▷ *adv*: **todo ~** all at once; **~s** together; **~ a** near (to), next to; **~**

con (together) with

jurado [xu'raðo] nm (Jur: individuo) juror; (: grupo) jury; (de concurso: grupo) panel (of judges); (: individuo) member of a panel

juramento [xura'mento] nm oath; (maldición) oath, curse; **prestar ~** to take the oath; **tomar ~ a** to swear in, administer the oath to

jurar [xu'rar] vt, vi to swear; **~ en falso** to commit perjury; **tenérsela jurada a algn** to have it in for sb

jurídico, -a [xu'riðiko, a] adj legal

jurisdicción [xurisðik'θjon] nf (poder, autoridad) jurisdiction; (territorio) district

justamente [xusta'mente] adv justly, fairly; (precisamente) just, exactly

justicia [xus'tiθja] nf justice; (equidad) fairness, justice

justificación [xustifika'θjon] nf justification; **justificar** vt to justify

justo, -a ['xusto, a] adj (equitativo) just, fair, right; (preciso) exact, correct; (ajustado) tight ▷ adv (precisamente) exactly, precisely; (LAM: apenas a tiempo) just in time

juvenil [xuβe'nil] adj youthful

juventud [xuβen'tuð] nf (adolescencia) youth; (jóvenes) young people pl

juzgado [xuθ'ɣaðo] nm tribunal; (Jur) court

juzgar [xuθ'ɣar] vt to judge; **a ~ por ...** to judge by ..., judging by ...

kárate ['karate] nm karate

kg abr (= kilogramo) kg

kilo ['kilo] nm kilo; **kilogramo** nm kilogramme; **kilometraje** nm distance in kilometres ≈ mileage; **kilómetro** nm kilometre; **kilovatio** nm kilowatt

kiosco ['kjosko] nm = **quiosco**

kleenex® [kli'neks] nm paper handkerchief, tissue

Kosovo [ko'soβo] nm Kosovo

km abr (= kilómetro) km

kv abr (= kilovatio) kw

l *abr* (= *litro*) l

la [la] *art def* the ▷ *pron* her; (*Ud.*) you; (*cosa*) it ▷ *nm* (*Mús*) la; **~ del sombrero rojo** the girl in the red hat; *V tb* **el**

laberinto [laβe'rinto] *nm* labyrinth

labio ['laβjo] *nm* lip

labor [la'βor] *nf* labour; (*Agr*) farm work; (*tarea*) job, task; (*Costura*) needlework; **labores domésticas** *o* **del hogar** household chores; **laborable** *adj* (*Agr*) workable; **día laborable** working day; **laboral** *adj* (*accidente*) at work; (*jornada*) working

laboratorio [laβora'torjo] *nm* laboratory

laborista [laβo'rista] *adj*: **Partido L~** Labour Party

labrador, a [laβra'ðor, a] *adj* farming *cpd* ▷ *nm/f* farmer

labranza [la'βranθa] *nf* (*Agr*) cultivation

labrar [la'βrar] *vt* (*gen*) to work; (*madera etc*) to carve; (*fig*) to cause, bring about

laca ['laka] *nf* lacquer

lacio, -a ['laθjo, a] *adj* (*pelo*) straight

lacón [la'kon] *nm* shoulder of pork

lactancia [lak'tanθja] *nf* lactation

lácteo, -a ['lakteo, a] *adj*: **productos ~s** dairy products

ladear [laðe'ar] *vt* to tip, tilt ▷ *vi* to tilt; **ladearse** *vr* to lean

ladera [la'ðera] *nf* slope

lado ['laðo] *nm* (*gen*) side; (*fig*) protection; (*Mil*) flank; **al ~ de** beside; **poner de ~** to put on its side; **poner a un ~** to put aside; **por todos ~s** on all sides, all round (BRIT)

ladrar [la'ðrar] *vi* to bark; **ladrido** *nm* bark, barking

ladrillo [la'ðriʎo] *nm* (*gen*) brick; (*azulejo*) tile

ladrón, -ona [la'ðron, ona] *nm/f* thief

lagartija [laɣar'tixa] *nf* (*Zool*) (small) lizard

lagarto [la'ɣarto] *nm* (*Zool*) lizard

lago ['laɣo] *nm* lake

lágrima ['laɣrima] *nf* tear

laguna [la'ɣuna] *nf* (*lago*) lagoon; (*hueco*) gap

lamentable [lamen'taβle] *adj* lamentable, regrettable; (*miserable*) pitiful

lamentar [lamen'tar] *vt* (*sentir*) to regret; (*deplorar*) to lament; **lamentarse** *vr* to lament; **lo lamento mucho** I'm very sorry

lamer [la'mer] *vt* to lick

lámina ['lamina] *nf* (*plancha delgada*) sheet; (*para estampar, estampa*) plate

lámpara ['lampara] *nf* lamp; **lámpara de alcohol/gas** spirit/gas lamp; **lámpara de pie** standard lamp

lana ['lana] *nf* wool

lancha ['lantʃa] *nf* launch; **lancha motora** motorboat, speedboat

langosta [lan'gosta] *nf* (*crustáceo*) lobster; (: *de río*) crayfish; **langostino** *nm* Dublin Bay prawn

lanza ['lanθa] *nf* (*arma*) lance, spear

lanzamiento [lanθa'mjento] *nm* (*gen*) throwing; (*Náut, Com*) launch, launching; **lanzamiento de peso** putting the shot

lanzar [lan'θar] *vt* (*gen*) to throw; (*Deporte: pelota*) to bowl; (*Náut, Com*) to launch; (*Jur*) to evict; **lanzarse** *vr* to throw o.s.

lapa ['lapa] *nf* limpet

lapicero [lapi'θero] (CAM) *nm* (*bolígrafo*) ballpoint pen, Biro®

lápida ['lapiða] *nf* stone; **lápida mortuoria** headstone

lápiz ['lapiθ] *nm* pencil; **lápiz de color** coloured pencil; **lápiz de labios** lipstick; **lápiz de ojos** eyebrow pencil

largar [lar'xar] *vt* (*soltar*) to release; (*aflojar*) to loosen; (*lanzar*) to launch; (*fam*) to let fly; (*velas*) to unfurl; (LAM: *lanzar*) to throw; **largarse** *vr* (*fam*) to beat it; **~se a** (CS: *empezar*) to start to

largo, -a ['larxo, a] *adj* (*longitud*) long; (*tiempo*) lengthy; (*fig*) generous ▷ *nm* length; (*Mús*) largo; **dos años ~s** two long years; **tiene 9 metros de ~** it is 9 metres long; **a la larga** in the long run; **a lo ~ de** along; (*tiempo*) all through, throughout

> No confundir **largo** con la palabra inglesa *large*.

largometraje *nm* feature film

laringe [la'rinxe] *nf* larynx; **laringitis** *nf* laryngitis

las [las] *art def* the ▷ *pron* them; **~ que cantan** the ones *o* women *o* girls who sing; *V tb* **el**

lasaña [la'saɲa] *nf* lasagne, lasagna

láser ['laser] *nm* laser

lástima ['lastima] nf (pena) pity; **dar ~** to be pitiful; **es una ~ que ...** it's a pity that ...; **¡qué ~!** what a pity!; **está hecha una ~** she looks pitiful

lastimar [lasti'mar] vt (herir) to wound; (ofender) to offend; **lastimarse** vr to hurt o.s.

lata ['lata] nf (metal) tin; (caja) tin (BRIT), can; (fam) nuisance; **en ~** tinned (BRIT), canned; **dar la ~** to be a nuisance

latente [la'tente] adj latent

lateral [late'ral] adj side cpd, lateral ▷ nm (Teatro) wings

latido [la'tiðo] nm (de corazón) beat

latifundio [lati'fundjo] nm large estate

latigazo [lati'γaθo] nm (golpe) lash; (sonido) crack

látigo ['latiγo] nm whip

latín [la'tin] nm Latin

latino, -a [la'tino, a] adj Latin; **latinoamericano, -a** adj, nm/f Latin-American

latir [la'tir] vi (corazón, pulso) to beat

latitud [lati'tuð] nf (Geo) latitude

latón [la'ton] nm brass

laurel [lau'rel] nm (Bot) laurel; (Culin) bay

lava ['laβa] nf lava

lavabo [la'βaβo] nm (pila) washbasin; (tb: **~s**) toilet

lavado [la'βaðo] nm washing; (de ropa) laundry; (Arte) wash; **lavado de cerebro** brainwashing; **lavado en seco** dry-cleaning

lavadora [laβa'ðora] nf washing machine

lavanda [la'βanda] nf lavender

lavandería [laβande'ria] nf laundry; (automática) launderette

lavaplatos [laβa'platos] nm inv dishwasher

lavar [la'βar] vt to wash; (borrar) to wipe away; **lavarse** vr to wash o.s.; **~se las manos** to wash one's hands; **~se los dientes** to brush one's teeth; **~ y marcar** (pelo) to shampoo and set; **~ en seco** to dry-clean; **~ los platos** to wash the dishes

lavarropas [laβa'rropas] (RPL) nm inv washing machine

lavavajillas [laβaβa'xiλas] nm inv dishwasher

laxante [lak'sante] nm laxative

lazarillo [laθa'riλo] nm (tb: **perro ~**) guide dog

lazo ['laθo] nm knot; (lazada) bow; (para animales) lasso; (trampa) snare; (vínculo) tie

le [le] pron (directo) him (o her); (: usted) you; (indirecto) to him (o her o it); (: usted) to you

leal [le'al] adj loyal; **lealtad** nf loyalty

lección [lek'θjon] nf lesson

leche ['letʃe] nf milk; **tiene mala ~** (fam!) he's a swine (!); **leche condensada** condensed milk; **leche desnatada** skimmed milk

lecho ['letʃo] nm (cama: de río) bed; (Geo) layer

lechón [le'tʃon] nm sucking (BRIT) o suckling (US) pig

lechoso, -a [le'tʃoso, a] adj milky

lechuga [le'tʃuγa] nf lettuce

lechuza [le'tʃuθa] nf owl

lector, a [lek'tor, a] nm/f reader ▷ nm: **~ de discos compactos** CD player

lectura [lek'tura] nf reading

leer [le'er] vt to read

legado [le'γaðo] nm (don) bequest; (herencia) legacy; (enviado) legate

legajo [le'γaxo] nm file

legal [le'γal] adj (gen) legal; (persona) trustworthy; **legalizar** [leγali'θar] vt to legalize; (documento) to authenticate

legaña [le'γaɲa] nf sleep (in eyes)

legión [le'xjon] nf legion; **legionario, -a** adj legionary ▷ nm legionnaire

legislación [lexisla'θjon] nf legislation

legislar [lexis'lar] vi to legislate

legislatura [lexisla'tura] nf (Pol) period of office

legítimo, -a [le'xitimo, a] adj (genuino) authentic; (legal) legitimate

legua ['leγwa] nf league

legumbres [le'γumbres] nfpl pulses

leído, -a [le'iðo, a] adj well-read

lejanía [lexa'nia] nf distance; **lejano, -a** adj far-off; (en el tiempo) distant; (fig) remote

lejía [le'xia] nf bleach

lejos ['lexos] adv far, far away; **a lo ~** in the distance; **de o desde ~** from afar; **~ de** far from

lema ['lema] nm motto; (Pol) slogan

lencería [lenθe'ria] nf linen, drapery

lengua ['lengwa] nf tongue; (Ling) language; **morderse la ~** to hold one's tongue

lenguado [len'gwaðo] nm sole

lenguaje [len'gwaxe] nm language; **lenguaje de programación** program(m)ing language

lengüeta [len'gweta] nf (Anat) epiglottis; (zapatos) tongue; (Mús) reed

lente ['lente] nf lens; (lupa) magnifying glass; **lentes** nfpl lenses ▷ nmpl (LAM: gafas) glasses; **lentes bifocales/de sol** (LAM) bifocals/sunglasses; **lentes de contacto** contact lenses

lenteja [len'texa] nf lentil; **lentejuela** nf sequin

lentilla [len'tiλa] nf contact lens

lentitud [lenti'tuð] nf slowness; **con ~**

slowly

lento, -a ['lento, a] *adj* slow

leña ['leɲa] *nf* firewood; **leñador, a** *nm/f* woodcutter

leño ['leɲo] *nm* (*trozo de árbol*) log; (*madero*) timber; (*fig*) blockhead

Leo ['leo] *nm* Leo

león [le'on] *nm* lion; **león marino** sea lion

leopardo [leo'parðo] *nm* leopard

leotardos [leo'tarðos] *nmpl* tights

lepra ['lepra] *nf* leprosy; **leproso, -a** *nm/f* leper

les [les] *pron* (*directo*) them; (: *ustedes*) you; (*indirecto*) to them; (: *ustedes*) to you

lesbiana [les'βjana] *adj, nf* lesbian

lesión [le'sjon] *nf* wound, lesion; (*Deporte*) injury; **lesionado, -a** *adj* injured ▷ *nm/f* injured person

letal [le'tal] *adj* lethal

letanía [leta'nia] *nf* litany

letra ['letra] *nf* letter; (*escritura*) handwriting; (*Mús*) lyrics *pl*; **letra de cambio** bill of exchange; **letra de imprenta** print; **letrado, -a** *adj* learned ▷ *nm/f* lawyer; **letrero** *nm* (*cartel*) sign; (*etiqueta*) label

letrina [le'trina] *nf* latrine

leucemia [leu'θemja] *nf* leukaemia

levadura [leβa'ðura] *nf* (*para el pan*) yeast; (*de cerveza*) brewer's yeast

levantar [leβan'tar] *vt* (*gen*) to raise; (*del suelo*) to pick up; (*hacia arriba*) to lift (up); (*plan*) to make, draw up; (*mesa*) to clear; (*campamento*) to strike; (*fig*) to cheer up, hearten; **levantarse** *vr* to get up; (*enderezarse*) to straighten up; (*rebelarse*) to rebel; **~ el ánimo** to cheer up

levante [le'βante] *nm* east coast; **el L~** *region of Spain extending from Castellón to Murcia*

levar [le'βar] *vt* to weigh

leve ['leβe] *adj* light; (*fig*) trivial

levita [le'βita] *nf* frock coat

léxico ['leksiko] *nm* (*vocabulario*) vocabulary

ley [lei] *nf* (*gen*) law; (*metal*) standard

leyenda [le'jenda] *nf* legend

leyó *etc vb* V **leer**

liar [li'ar] *vt* to tie (up); (*unir*) to bind; (*envolver*) to wrap (up); (*enredar*) to confuse; (*cigarrillo*) to roll; **liarse** *vr* (*fam*) to get involved; **~se a palos** to get involved in a fight

Líbano ['liβano] *nm*: **el ~** the Lebanon

libélula [li'βelula] *nf* dragonfly

liberación [liβera'θjon] *nf* liberation; (*de la cárcel*) release

liberal [liβe'ral] *adj, nmf* liberal

liberar [liβe'rar] *vt* to liberate

libertad [liβer'taθ] *nf* liberty, freedom; **libertad bajo fianza** bail; **libertad bajo palabra** parole; **libertad condicional** probation; **libertad de culto/de prensa/de comercio** freedom of worship/of the press/of trade

libertar [liβer'tar] *vt* (*preso*) to set free; (*de una obligación*) to release; (*eximir*) to exempt

libertino, -a [liβer'tino, a] *adj* permissive ▷ *nm/f* permissive person

libra ['liβra] *nf* pound; **L~** (*Astrología*) Libra; **libra esterlina** pound sterling

libramiento [liβra'mjento] (*Méx*) *nm* ring road (*Brit*), beltway (*Us*)

librar [li'βrar] *vt* (*de peligro*) to save; (*batalla*) to wage, fight; (*de impuestos*) to exempt; (*cheque*) to make out; (*Jur*) to exempt; **librarse** *vr*: **~se de** to escape from, free o.s. from

libre ['liβre] *adj* free; (*lugar*) unoccupied; (*asiento*) vacant; (*de deudas*) free of debts; **~ de impuestos** free of tax; **tiro ~** free kick; **los 100 metros ~s** the 100 metres free-style (race); **al aire ~** in the open air

librería [liβre'ria] *nf* (*tienda*) bookshop

▌No confundir **librería** con la palabra inglesa *library*.

librero, -a *nm/f* bookseller

libreta [li'βreta] *nf* notebook

libro ['liβro] *nm* book; **libro de bolsillo** paperback; **libro de texto** textbook; **libro electrónico** e-book

Lic. *abr* = **licenciado, a**

licencia [li'θenθja] *nf* (*gen*) licence; (*permiso*) permission; **licencia de caza** game licence; **licencia por enfermedad** (*Méx, Rpl*) sick leave; **licenciado, -a** *adj* licensed ▷ *nm/f* graduate; **licenciar** *vt* (*empleado*) to dismiss; (*permitir*) to permit, allow; (*soldado*) to discharge; (*estudiante*) to confer a degree upon; **licenciarse** *vr*: **licenciarse en Derecho** to graduate in law

lícito, -a ['liθito, a] *adj* (*legal*) lawful; (*justo*) fair, just; (*permisible*) permissible

licor [li'kor] *nm* spirits *pl* (*Brit*), liquor (*Us*); (*de frutas etc*) liqueur

licuadora [likwa'ðora] *nf* blender

líder ['liðer] *nmf* leader; **liderato** *nm* leadership; **liderazgo** *nm* leadership

lidia ['liðja] *nf* bullfighting; (*una lidia*) bullfight; **toros de ~** fighting bulls; **lidiar** *vt, vi* to fight

liebre ['ljeβre] *nf* hare

lienzo ['ljenθo] *nm* linen; (*Arte*) canvas; (*Arq*) wall

liga ['liɣa] *nf* (*de medias*) garter, suspender; (*Lam: goma*) rubber band; (*confederación*)

league
ligadura [liɣa'ðura] *nf* bond, tie; (*Med, Mús*) ligature
ligamento [liɣa'mento] *nm* ligament
ligar [li'ɣar] *vt* (*atar*) to tie; (*unir*) to join; (*Med*) to bind up; (*Mús*) to slur ▷ *vi* to mix, blend; (*fam*) **(él) liga mucho** he pulls a lot of women; **ligarse** *vr* to commit o.s.
ligero, -a [li'ɣero, a] *adj* (*de peso*) light; (*tela*) thin; (*rápido*) swift, quick; (*ágil*) agile, nimble; (*de importancia*) slight; (*de carácter*) flippant, superficial ▷ *adv*: **a la ligera** superficially
liguero [li'ɣero] *nm* suspender (*BRIT*) o garter (*US*) belt
lija ['lixa] *nf* (*Zool*) dogfish; (*tb*: **papel de ~**) sandpaper
lila ['lila] *nf* lilac
lima ['lima] *nf* file; (*Bot*) lime; **lima de uñas** nailfile; **limar** *vt* to file
limitación [limita'θjon] *nf* limitation, limit
limitar [limi'tar] *vt* to limit; (*reducir*) to reduce, cut down ▷ *vi*: **~ con** to border on; **limitarse** *vr*: **~se a** to limit o.s. to
límite ['limite] *nm* (*gen*) limit; (*fin*) end; (*frontera*) border; **límite de velocidad** speed limit
limítrofe [li'mitrofe] *adj* neighbouring
limón [li'mon] *nm* lemon ▷ *adj*: **amarillo ~** lemon-yellow; **limonada** *nf* lemonade
limosna [li'mosna] *nf* alms *pl*; **vivir de ~** to live on charity
limpiador [limpja'ðor] (*MÉX*) *nm* = **limpiaparabrisas**
limpiaparabrisas [limpjapara'βrisas] *nm inv* windscreen (*BRIT*) o windshield (*US*) wiper
limpiar [lim'pjar] *vt* to clean; (*con trapo*) to wipe; (*quitar*) to wipe away; (*zapatos*) to shine, polish; (*fig*) to clean up
limpieza [lim'pjeθa] *nf* (*estado*) cleanliness; (*acto*) cleaning; (: *de las calles*) cleansing; (: *de zapatos*) polishing; (*habilidad*) skill; (*fig: Policía*) clean-up; (*pureza*) purity; (*Mil*): **operación de ~** mopping-up operation; **limpieza en seco** dry cleaning
limpio, -a ['limpjo, a] *adj* clean; (*moralmente*) pure; (*Com*) clear, net; (*fam*) honest ▷ *adv*: **jugar ~** to play fair; **pasar a** (*ESP*) o **en** (*LAM*) **~** to make a clean copy of
lince ['linθe] *nm* lynx
linchar [lin'tʃar] *vt* to lynch
lindar [lin'dar] *vi* to adjoin; **~ con** to border on
lindo, -a ['lindo, a] *adj* pretty, lovely ▷ *adv*: **nos divertimos de lo ~** we had a marvellous time; **canta muy ~** (*LAM*) he

sings beautifully
línea ['linea] *nf* (*gen*) line; **en ~** (*Inform*) on line; **línea aérea** airline; **línea de meta** goal line; (*en carrera*) finishing line; **línea discontinua** (*Auto*) broken line; **línea recta** straight line
lingote [lin'gote] *nm* ingot
lingüista [lin'gwista] *nmf* linguist; **lingüística** *nf* linguistics *sg*
lino ['lino] *nm* linen; (*Bot*) flax
linterna [lin'terna] *nf* torch (*BRIT*), flashlight (*US*)
lío ['lio] *nm* bundle; (*fam*) fuss; (*desorden*) muddle, mess; **armar un ~** to make a fuss
liquen ['liken] *nm* lichen
liquidación [likiða'θjon] *nf* liquidation; **venta de ~** clearance sale
liquidar [liki'ðar] *vt* (*mercancías*) to liquidate; (*deudas*) to pay off; (*empresa*) to wind up
líquido, -a ['likiðo, a] *adj* liquid; (*ganancia*) net ▷ *nm* liquid; **líquido imponible** net taxable income
lira ['lira] *nf* (*Mús*) lyre; (*moneda*) lira
lírico, -a ['liriko, a] *adj* lyrical
lirio ['lirjo] *nm* (*Bot*) iris
lirón [li'ron] *nm* (*Zool*) dormouse; (*fig*) sleepyhead
Lisboa [lis'βoa] *n* Lisbon
lisiar [li'sjar] *vt* to maim
liso, -a ['liso, a] *adj* (*terreno*) flat; (*cabello*) straight; (*superficie*) even; (*tela*) plain
lista ['lista] *nf* list; (*de alumnos*) school register; (*de libros*) catalogue; (*de platos*) menu; (*de precios*) price list; **pasar ~** to call the roll; **tela de ~s** striped material; **lista de espera** waiting list; **lista de precios** price list; **listín** *nm* (*tb*: **listín telefónico** o **de teléfonos**) telephone directory
listo, -a ['listo, a] *adj* (*perspicaz*) smart, clever; (*preparado*) ready
listón [lis'ton] *nm* (*de madera, metal*) strip
litera [li'tera] *nf* (*en barco, tren*) berth; (*en dormitorio*) bunk, bunk bed
literal [lite'ral] *adj* literal
literario, -a [lite'rarjo, a] *adj* literary
literato, -a [lite'rato, a] *adj* literary ▷ *nm/f* writer
literatura [litera'tura] *nf* literature
litigio [li'tixjo] *nm* (*Jur*) lawsuit; (*fig*): **en ~ con** in dispute with
litografía [litoɣra'fia] *nf* lithography; (*una litografía*) lithograph
litoral [lito'ral] *adj* coastal ▷ *nm* coast, seaboard
litro ['litro] *nm* litre
lívido, -a ['liβiðo, a] *adj* livid
llaga ['ʎaɣa] *nf* wound

llama ['ʎama] nf flame; (Zool) llama
llamada [ʎa'maða] nf call; **llamada a cobro revertido** reverse-charge (BRIT) o collect (US) call; **llamada al orden** call to order; **llamada de atención** warning; **llamada local** (LAM) local call; **llamada metropolitana** (ESP) local call; **llamada por cobrar** (MÉX) reverse-charge (BRIT) o collect (US) call
llamamiento [ʎama'mjento] nm call
llamar [ʎa'mar] vt to call; (atención) to attract ▷ vi (por teléfono) to telephone; (a la puerta) to knock (o ring); (por señas) to beckon; (Mil) to call up; **llamarse** vr to be called, be named; **¿cómo se llama (usted)?** what's your name?
llamativo, -a [ʎama'tiβo, a] adj showy; (color) loud
llano, -a ['ʎano, a] adj (superficie) flat; (persona) straightforward; (estilo) clear ▷ nm plain, flat ground
llanta ['ʎanta] nf (ESP) (wheel) rim; **llanta (de goma)** (LAM: neumático) tyre; (: cámara) inner (tube); **llanta de repuesto** (LAM) spare tyre
llanto ['ʎanto] nm weeping
llanura [ʎa'nura] nf plain
llave ['ʎaβe] nf key; (del agua) tap; (Mecánica) spanner; (de la luz) switch; (Mús) key; **echar la ~ a** to lock up; **llave de contacto** (ESP Auto) ignition key; **llave de encendido** (LAM Auto) ignition key; **llave de paso** stopcock; **llave inglesa** monkey wrench; **llave maestra** master key; **llavero** nm keyring
llegada [ʎe'ɣaða] nf arrival
llegar [ʎe'ɣar] vi to arrive; (alcanzar) to reach; (bastar) to be enough; **llegarse** vr: **~se a** to approach; **~ a** to manage to, succeed in; **~ a saber** to find out; **~ a ser** to become; **~ a las manos de** to come into the hands of
llenar [ʎe'nar] vt to fill; (espacio) to cover; (formulario) to fill in o up; (fig) to heap
lleno, -a ['ʎeno, a] adj full, filled; (repleto) full up ▷ nm (Teatro) full house; **dar de ~ contra un muro** to hit a wall head-on
llevadero, -a [ʎeβa'ðero, a] adj bearable, tolerable
llevar [ʎe'βar] vt to take; (ropa) to wear; (cargar) to carry; (quitar) to take away; (en coche) to drive; (transportar) to transport; (traer: dinero) to carry; (conducir) to lead; (Mat) to carry ▷ vi (suj: camino etc): **~ a** to lead to; **llevarse** vr to carry off, take away; **llevamos dos días aquí** we have been here for two days; **él me lleva 2 años** he's 2 years older than me; **~ los libros** (Com) to keep the

books; **~se bien** to get on well (together)
llorar [ʎo'rar] vt, vi to cry, weep; **~ de risa** to cry with laughter
llorón, -ona [ʎo'ron, ona] adj tearful ▷ nm/f cry-baby
lloroso, -a [ʎo'roso, a] adj (gen) weeping, tearful; (triste) sad, sorrowful
llover [ʎo'βer] vi to rain
llovizna [ʎo'βiθna] nf drizzle; **lloviznar** vi to drizzle
llueve etc vb V **llover**
lluvia ['ʎuβja] nf rain; **lluvia radioactiva** (radioactive) fallout; **lluvioso, -a** adj rainy
lo [lo] art def: **~ bel~** the beautiful, what is beautiful, that which is beautiful ▷ pron (persona) him; (cosa) it; **~ que sea** whatever; V tb **el**
loable [lo'aβle] adj praiseworthy
lobo ['loβo] nm wolf; **lobo de mar** (fig) sea dog
lóbulo ['loβulo] nm lobe
local [lo'kal] adj local ▷ nm place, site; (oficinas) premises pl; **localidad** nf (barrio) locality; (lugar) location; (Teatro) seat, ticket; **localizar** vt (ubicar) to locate, find; (restringir) to localize; (situar) to place
loción [lo'θjon] nf lotion
loco, -a ['loko, a] adj mad ▷ nm/f lunatic, mad person; **estar ~ con** o **por algo/por algn** to be mad about sth/sb
locomotora [lokomo'tora] nf engine, locomotive
locuaz [lo'kwaθ] adj loquacious
locución [loku'θjon] nf expression
locura [lo'kura] nf madness; (acto) crazy act
locutor, a [loku'tor, a] nm/f (Radio) announcer; (comentarista) commentator; (TV) newsreader
locutorio [loku'torjo] nm (en telefónica) telephone booth
lodo ['loðo] nm mud
lógica ['loxika] nf logic
lógico, -a ['loxiko, a] adj logical
login ['loxin] nm login
logística [lo'xistika] nf logistics sg
logotipo [loðo'tipo] nm logo
logrado, -a [lo'ðraðo, a] adj (interpretación, reproducción) polished, excellent
lograr [lo'ɣrar] vt to achieve; (obtener) to get, obtain; **~ hacer** to manage to do; **~ que algn venga** to manage to get sb to come
logro ['loɣro] nm achievement, success
lóker ['loker] (LAM) nm locker
loma ['loma] nf hillock (BRIT), small hill
lombriz [lom'briθ] nf worm
lomo ['lomo] nm (de animal) back; (Culin: de

cerdo) pork loin; (: *de vaca*) rib steak; (*de libro*)
spine

lona ['lona] *nf* canvas

loncha ['lontʃa] *nf* = **lonja**

lonchería [lontʃe'ria] (*LAM*) *nf* snack bar,
diner (*us*)

Londres ['londres] *n* London

longaniza [longa'niθa] *nf* pork sausage

longitud [lonxi'tuð] *nf* length; (*Geo*)
longitude; **tener 3 metros de ~** to be 3
metres long; **longitud de onda** wavelength

lonja ['lonxa] *nf* slice; (*de tocino*) rasher;
lonja de pescado fish market

loro ['loro] *nm* parrot

los [los] *art def* the ▷ *pron* them; (*ustedes*)
you; **mis libros y ~ tuyos** my books and
yours; V tb **el**

losa ['losa] *nf* stone

lote ['lote] *nm* portion; (*Com*) lot

lotería [lote'ria] *nf* lottery; (*juego*) lotto

● **LOTERÍA**
●
● Millions of pounds are spent on lotteries
● each year in Spain, two of which are
● state-run: the **Lotería Primitiva** and
● the **Lotería Nacional**, with money
● raised going directly to the government.
● One of the most famous lotteries is run
● by the wealthy and influential society
● for the blind, "la ONCE".

loza ['loθa] *nf* crockery

lubina [lu'βina] *nf* sea bass

lubricante [luβri'kante] *nm* lubricant

lubricar [luβri'kar] *vt* to lubricate

lucha ['lutʃa] *nf* fight, struggle; **lucha de
clases** class struggle; **lucha libre** wrestling;
luchar *vi* to fight

lúcido, -a ['luθiðo, a] *adj* (*persona*) lucid;
(*mente*) logical; (*idea*) crystal-clear

luciérnaga [lu'θjernaxa] *nf* glow-worm

lucir [lu'θir] *vt* to illuminate, light (up);
(*ostentar*) to show off ▷ *vi* (*brillar*) to shine;
lucirse *vr* (*irónico*) to make a fool of o.s.

lucro ['lukro] *nm* profit, gain

lúdico, -a ['luðiko, a] *adj* (*aspecto,
actividad*) play *cpd*

luego ['lweɣo] *adv* (*después*) next; (*más
tarde*) later, afterwards

lugar [lu'ɣar] *nm* place; (*sitio*) spot; **en
primer ~** in the first place, firstly; **en ~ de**
instead of; **hacer ~** to make room; **fuera de
~** out of place; **sin ~ a dudas** without doubt,
undoubtedly; **dar ~ a** to give rise to; **tener ~**
to take place; **yo en su ~** if I were him; **lugar
común** commonplace

lúgubre ['luɣuβre] *adj* mournful

lujo ['luxo] *nm* luxury; (*fig*) profusion,
abundance; **de ~** luxury *cpd*, de luxe; **lujoso,
-a** *adj* luxurious

lujuria [lu'xurja] *nf* lust

lumbre ['lumbre] *nf* fire; (*para cigarrillo*)
light

luminoso, -a [lumi'noso, a] *adj*
luminous, shining

luna ['luna] *nf* moon; (*de un espejo*) glass;
(*de gafas*) lens; (*fig*) crescent; **estar en la ~**
to have one's head in the clouds; **luna de
miel** honeymoon; **luna llena/nueva** full/
new moon

lunar [lu'nar] *adj* lunar ▷ *nm* (*Anat*) mole;
tela de ~es spotted material

lunes ['lunes] *nm inv* Monday

lupa ['lupa] *nf* magnifying glass

lustre ['lustre] *nm* polish; (*fig*) lustre; **dar
~ a** to polish

luto ['luto] *nm* mourning; **llevar el** o
vestirse de ~ to be in mourning

Luxemburgo [luksem'burxo] *nm*
Luxembourg

luz [luθ] (*pl* **luces**) *nf* light; **dar a ~ un niño**
to give birth to a child; **sacar a la ~** to bring
to light; **dar** o **encender** (*ESP*) o **prender**
(*LAM*)**/apagar la ~** to switch the light on/
off; **tener pocas luces** to be dim o stupid;
traje de luces bullfighter's costume; **luces
de tráfico** traffic lights; **luz de freno** brake
light; **luz roja/verde** red/green light

I

m *abr* (= *metro*) m; (= *minuto*) m

macana [ma'kana] (MÉX) *nf* truncheon (BRIT), billy club (US)

macarrones [maka'rrones] *nmpl* macaroni *sg*

macedonia [maθe'ðonja] *nf* (*tb*: **~ de frutas**) fruit salad

maceta [ma'θeta] *nf* (*de flores*) pot of flowers; (*para plantas*) flowerpot

machacar [matʃa'kar] *vt* to crush, pound ▷ *vi* (*insistir*) to go on, keep on

machete [ma'tʃete] *nm* machete, (large) knife

machetear [matʃete'ar] (MÉX) *vt* to swot (BRIT), grind away (US)

machismo [ma'tʃismo] *nm* male chauvinism; **machista** *adj, nm* sexist

macho ['matʃo] *adj* male; (*fig*) virile ▷ *nm* male; (*fig*) he-man

macizo, -a [ma'θiθo, a] *adj* (*grande*) massive; (*fuerte, sólido*) solid ▷ *nm* mass, chunk

madeja [ma'ðexa] *nf* (*de lana*) skein, hank; (*de pelo*) mass, mop

madera [ma'ðera] *nf* wood; (*fig*) nature, character; **una ~** a piece of wood

madrastra [ma'ðrastra] *nf* stepmother

madre ['maðre] *adj* mother *cpd* ▷ *nf* mother; (*de vino etc*) dregs *pl*; **madre política/soltera** mother-in-law/unmarried mother

Madrid [ma'ðrið] *n* Madrid

madriguera [maðri'ɣera] *nf* burrow

madrileño, -a [maðri'leɲo, a] *adj* of o from Madrid ▷ *nm/f* native of Madrid

madrina [ma'ðrina] *nf* godmother; (*Arq*) prop, shore; (*Tec*) brace; (*de boda*) bridesmaid

madrugada [maðru'ɣaða] *nf* early morning; (*alba*) dawn, daybreak

madrugador, a [maðruɣa'ðor, a] *adj* early-rising

madrugar [maðru'ɣar] *vi* to get up early; (*fig*) to get ahead

madurar [maðu'rar] *vt, vi* (*fruta*) to ripen; (*fig*) to mature; **madurez** *nf* ripeness; maturity; **maduro, -a** *adj* ripe; mature

maestra *nf* V **maestro**

maestría [maes'tria] *nf* mastery; (*habilidad*) skill, expertise

maestro, -a [ma'estro, a] *adj* masterly; (*principal*) main ▷ *nm/f* master/mistress; (*profesor*) teacher ▷ *nm* (*autoridad*) authority; (*Mús*) maestro; (*experto*) master; **maestro albañil** master mason

magdalena [maɣða'lena] *nf* fairy cake

magia ['maxja] *nf* magic; **mágico, -a** *adj* magic(al) ▷ *nm/f* magician

magisterio [maxis'terjo] *nm* (*enseñanza*) teaching; (*profesión*) teaching profession; (*maestros*) teachers *pl*

magistrado [maxis'traðo] *nm* magistrate

magistral [maxis'tral] *adj* magisterial; (*fig*) masterly

magnate [maɣ'nate] *nm* magnate, tycoon

magnético, -a [maɣ'netiko, a] *adj* magnetic

magnetofón [maɣneto'fon] *nm* tape recorder

magnetófono [maɣne'tofono] *nm* = **magnetofón**

magnífico, -a [maɣ'nifiko, a] *adj* splendid, magnificent

magnitud [maɣni'tuð] *nf* magnitude

mago, -a ['maxo, a] *nm/f* magician; **los Reyes M~s** the Three Wise Men

magro, -a ['maɣro, a] *adj* (*carne*) lean

mahonesa [mao'nesa] *nf* mayonnaise

maître ['metre] *nm* head waiter

maíz [ma'iθ] *nm* maize (BRIT), corn (US); sweet corn

majestad [maxes'tað] *nf* majesty

majo, -a ['maxo, a] *adj* nice; (*guapo*) attractive, good-looking; (*elegante*) smart

mal [mal] *adv* badly; (*equivocadamente*) wrongly ▷ *adj* = **malo** ▷ *nm* evil; (*desgracia*) misfortune; (*daño*) harm, damage; (*Med*) illness; **~ que bien** rightly or wrongly; **ir de ~ en peor** to get worse and worse

malabarista [malaβa'rista] *nmf* juggler

malaria [ma'larja] *nf* malaria

malcriado, -a [mal'krjaðo, a] *adj* spoiled

maldad [mal'dað] *nf* evil, wickedness

maldecir [malde'θir] *vt* to curse

maldición [maldi'θjon] *nf* curse

maldito, -a [mal'dito, a] *adj* (*condenado*) damned; (*perverso*) wicked; **¡~ sea!** damn it!

malecón [male'kon] (LAM) *nm* sea front,

promenade

maleducado, -a [maleðu'kaðo, a] *adj*
bad-mannered, rude

malentendido [malenten'diðo] *nm*
misunderstanding

malestar [males'tar] *nm* (*gen*) discomfort;
(*fig: inquietud*) uneasiness; (*Pol*) unrest

maleta [ma'leta] *nf* case, suitcase; (*Auto*)
boot (BRIT), trunk (US); **hacer las ~s** to pack;
maletero *nm* (*Auto*) boot (BRIT), trunk (US);
maletín *nm* small case, bag

maleza [ma'leθa] *nf* (*malas hierbas*) weeds
pl; (*arbustos*) thicket

malgastar [malɣas'tar] *vt* (*tiempo, dinero*)
to waste; (*salud*) to ruin

malhechor, a [male'tʃor, a] *nm/f*
delinquent

malhumorado, -a [malumo'raðo, a] *adj*
bad-tempered

malicia [ma'liθja] *nf* (*maldad*)
wickedness; (*astucia*) slyness, guile; (*mala
intención*) malice, spite; (*carácter travieso*)
mischievousness

maligno, -a [ma'liɣno, a] *adj* evil;
(*malévolo*) malicious; (*Med*) malignant

malla ['maʎa] *nf* mesh; (*de baño*) swimsuit;
(*de ballet, gimnasia*) leotard; **mallas** *nfpl*
tights; **malla de alambre** wire mesh

Mallorca [ma'ʎorka] *nf* Majorca

malo, -a ['malo, a] *adj* bad, false ▷ *nm/f*
villain; **estar ~** to be ill

malograr [malo'ɣrar] *vt* to spoil; (*plan*) to
upset; (*ocasión*) to waste

malparado, -a [malpa'raðo, a] *adj*: **salir
~** to come off badly

malpensado, -a [malpen'saðo, a] *adj*
nasty

malteada [malte'aða] (LAM) *nf* milkshake

maltratar [maltra'tar] *vt* to ill-treat,
mistreat

malvado, -a [mal'βaðo, a] *adj* evil,
villainous

Malvinas [mal'βinas] *nfpl* (*tb:* **Islas ~**)
Falklands, Falkland Islands

mama ['mama] *nf* (*de animal*) teat; (*de
mujer*) breast

mamá [ma'ma] (*pl* **~s**) (*fam*) *nf* mum,
mummy

mamar [ma'mar] *vt, vi* to suck

mamarracho [mama'rratʃo] *nm* sight,
mess

mameluco [mameluko] (RPL) *nm*
dungarees *pl* (BRIT), overalls *pl* (US)

mamífero [ma'mifero] *nm* mammal

mampara [mam'para] *nf* (*entre
habitaciones*) partition; (*biombo*) screen

mampostería [mamposte'ria] *nf*
masonry

manada [ma'naða] *nf* (*Zool*) herd; (: *de
leones*) pride; (: *de lobos*) pack

manantial [manan'tjal] *nm* spring

mancha ['mantʃa] *nf* stain, mark; (*Zool*)
patch; **manchar** *vt* (*gen*) to stain, mark;
(*ensuciar*) to soil, dirty

manchego, -a [man'tʃeɣo, a] *adj* of o
from La Mancha

manco, -a ['manko, a] *adj* (*de un brazo*)
one-armed; (*de una mano*) one-handed; (*fig*)
defective, faulty

mancuernas [man'kwernas] (MÉX) *nfpl*
cufflinks

mandado [man'daðo] (LAM) *nm* errand

mandamiento [manda'mjento]
nm (*orden*) order, command; (*Rel*)
commandment

mandar [man'dar] *vt* (*ordenar*) to order;
(*dirigir*) to lead, command; (*enviar*) to send;
(*pedir*) to order, ask for ▷ *vi* to be in charge;
(*pey*) to be bossy; **¿mande?** (MÉX: *¿cómo dice?*)
pardon?, excuse me?; **~ hacer un traje** to
have a suit made

mandarina [manda'rina] (ESP) *nf*
tangerine, mandarin (orange)

mandato [man'dato] *nm* (*orden*) order;
(*Pol: período*) term of office; (: *territorio*)
mandate

mandíbula [man'diβula] *nf* jaw

mandil [man'dil] *nm* apron

mando ['mando] *nm* (*Mil*) command; (*de
país*) rule; (*el primer lugar*) lead; (*Pol*) term
of office; (*Tec*) control; **~ a la izquierda**
left-hand drive; **mando a distancia** remote
control

mandón, -ona [man'don, ona] *adj*
bossy, domineering

manejar [mane'xar] *vt* to manage;
(*máquina*) to work, operate; (*caballo etc*) to
handle; (*casa*) to run, manage; (LAM: *coche*)
to drive; **manejarse** *vr* (*comportarse*) to act,
behave; (*arreglárselas*) to manage; **manejo**
nm (*de bicicleta*) handling; (*de negocio*)
management, running; (LAM *Auto*) driving;
(*facilidad de trato*) ease, confidence; **manejos**
nmpl (*intrigas*) intrigues

manera [ma'nera] *nf* way, manner,
fashion; **maneras** *nfpl* (*modales*) manners;
su ~ de ser the way he is; (*aire*) his manner;
de ninguna ~ no way, by no means; **de
otra ~** otherwise; **de todas ~s** at any rate;
no hay ~ de persuadirle there's no way of
convincing him

manga ['manga] *nf* (*de camisa*) sleeve; (*de
riego*) hose

mango ['mango] *nm* handle; (*Bot*) mango

manguera [man'gera] *nf* hose

maní [ma'ni] (LAM) *nm* peanut

manía [ma'nia] *nf* (*Med*) mania; (*fig: moda*) rage, craze; (*disgusto*) dislike; (*malicia*) spite; **coger ~ a algn** to take a dislike to sb; **tener ~ a algn** to dislike sb; **maníaco, -a** *adj* maniac(al) ▷ *nm/f* maniac

maniático, -a [ma'njatiko, a] *adj* maniac(al) ▷ *nm/f* maniac

manicomio [mani'komjo] *nm* mental hospital (*BRIT*), insane asylum (*US*)

manifestación [manifesta'θjon] *nf* (*declaración*) statement, declaration; (*de emoción*) show, display; (*Pol: desfile*) demonstration; (: *concentración*) mass meeting

manifestar [manifes'tar] *vt* to show, manifest; (*declarar*) to state, declare; **manifiesto, -a** *adj* clear, manifest ▷ *nm* manifesto

manillar [mani'ʎar] *nm* handlebars *pl*

maniobra [ma'njoβra] *nf* manoeuvre; **maniobras** *nfpl* (*Mil*) manoeuvres; **maniobrar** *vt* to manoeuvre

manipulación [manipula'θjon] *nf* manipulation

manipular [manipu'lar] *vt* to manipulate; (*manejar*) to handle

maniquí [mani'ki] *nm* dummy ▷ *nmf* model

manivela [mani'βela] *nf* crank

manjar [man'xar] *nm* (tasty) dish

mano ['mano] *nf* hand; (*Zool*) foot, paw; (*de pintura*) coat; (*serie*) lot, series; **a ~** by hand; **a ~ derecha/izquierda** on the right(-hand side)/left(-hand side); **de primera ~** (at) first hand; **de segunda ~** (at) second hand; **robo a ~ armada** armed robbery; **estrechar la ~ a algn** to shake sb's hand; **mano de obra** labour, manpower; **manos libres** *adj inv* (*teléfono, dispositivo*) hands-free ▷ *nm inv* hands-free kit

manojo [ma'noxo] *nm* handful, bunch; (*de llaves*) bunch

manopla [ma'nopla] *nf* mitten

manosear [manose'ar] *vt* (*tocar*) to handle, touch; (*desordenar*) to mess up, rumple; (*insistir en*) to overwork; (*LAM: acariciar*) to caress, fondle

manotazo [mano'taθo] *nm* slap, smack

mansalva [man'salβa]: **a ~** *adv* indiscriminately

mansión [man'sjon] *nf* mansion

manso, -a ['manso, a] *adj* gentle, mild; (*animal*) tame

manta ['manta] (*ESP*) *nf* blanket

manteca [man'teka] *nf* fat; (*cs: mantequilla*) butter; **manteca de cerdo** lard

mantecado [mante'kaðo] (*ESP*) *nm* Christmas sweet made from flour, almonds and lard

mantel [man'tel] *nm* tablecloth

mantendré *etc vb* V **mantener**

mantener [mante'ner] *vt* to support, maintain; (*alimentar*) to sustain; (*conservar*) to keep; (*Tec*) to maintain, service; **mantenerse** *vr* (*seguir de pie*) to be still standing; (*no ceder*) to hold one's ground; (*subsistir*) to sustain o.s., keep going; **mantenimiento** *nm* maintenance; sustenance; (*sustento*) support

mantequilla [mante'kiʎa] *nf* butter

mantilla [man'tiʎa] *nf* mantilla; **mantillas** *nfpl* (*de bebé*) baby clothes

manto ['manto] *nm* (*capa*) cloak; (*de ceremonia*) robe, gown

mantuve *etc vb* V **mantener**

manual [ma'nwal] *adj* manual ▷ *nm* manual, handbook

manuscrito, -a [manus'krito, a] *adj* handwritten ▷ *nm* manuscript

manutención [manuten'θjon] *nf* maintenance; (*sustento*) support

manzana [man'θana] *nf* apple; (*Arq*) block (of houses)

manzanilla [manθa'niʎa] *nf* (*planta*) camomile; (*infusión*) camomile tea

manzano [man'θano] *nm* apple tree

maña ['maɲa] *nf* (*gen*) skill, dexterity; (*pey*) guile; (*destreza*) trick, knack

mañana [ma'ɲana] *adv* tomorrow ▷ *nm* future ▷ *nf* morning; **de o por la ~** in the morning; **¡hasta ~!** see you tomorrow!; **~ por la ~** tomorrow morning

mapa ['mapa] *nm* map

maple ['maple] (*LAM*) *nm* maple

maqueta [ma'keta] *nf* (scale) model

maquiladora [makila'ðora] (*MÉX*) *nf* (*Com*) bonded assembly plant

maquillaje [maki'ʎaxe] *nm* make-up; (*acto*) making up

maquillar [maki'ʎar] *vt* to make up; **maquillarse** *vr* to put on (some) make-up

máquina ['makina] *nf* machine; (*de tren*) locomotive, engine; (*Foto*) camera; (*fig*) machinery; **escrito a ~** typewritten; **máquina de coser** sewing machine; **máquina de escribir** typewriter; **máquina fotográfica** camera

maquinaria [maki'narja] *nf* (*máquinas*) machinery; (*mecanismo*) mechanism, works *pl*

maquinilla [maki'niʎa] (*ESP*) *nf* (tb: **~ de afeitar**) razor

maquinista [maki'nista] *nmf* (*de tren*) engine driver; (*Tec*) operator; (*Náut*) engineer

mar [mar] nm of sea; **~ adentro** out at sea; **en alta ~** on the high seas; **la ~ de** (fam) lots of; **el Mar Negro/Báltico** the Black/ Baltic Sea

maraña [ma'raɲa] nf (maleza) thicket; (confusión) tangle

maravilla [mara'βiʎa] nf marvel, wonder; (Bot) marigold; **maravillar** vt to astonish, amaze; **maravillarse** vr to be astonished, be amazed; **maravilloso, -a** adj wonderful, marvellous

marca ['marka] nf (gen) mark; (sello) stamp; (Com) make, brand; **de ~** excellent, outstanding; **marca de fábrica** trademark; **marca registrada** registered trademark

marcado, -a [mar'kaðo, a] adj marked, strong

marcador [marka'ðor] nm (Deporte) scoreboard; (: persona) scorer

marcapasos [marka'pasos] nm inv pacemaker

marcar [mar'kar] vt (gen) to mark; (número de teléfono) to dial; (gol) to score; (números) to record, keep a tally of; (pelo) to set ▷ vi (Deporte) to score; (Tel) to dial

marcha ['martʃa] nf march; (Tec) running, working; (Auto) gear; (velocidad) speed; (fig) progress; (dirección) course; **poner en ~** to put into gear; (fig) to set in motion, get going; **dar ~ atrás** to reverse, put into reverse; **estar en ~** to be under way, be in motion

marchar [mar'tʃar] vi (ir) to go; (funcionar) to work, go; **marcharse** vr to go (away), leave

marchitar [martʃi'tar] vt to wither, dry up; **marchitarse** vr (Bot) to wither; (fig) to fade away; **marchito, -a** adj withered, faded; (fig) in decline

marciano, -a [mar'θjano, a] adj, nm/f Martian

marco ['marko] nm frame; (moneda) mark; (fig) framework

marea [ma'rea] nf tide; **marea negra** oil slick

marear [mare'ar] vt (fig) to annoy, upset; (Med): **~ a algn** to make sb feel sick; **marearse** vr (tener náuseas) to feel sick; (desvanecerse) to feel faint; (aturdirse) to feel dizzy; (fam: emborracharse) to get tipsy

maremoto [mare'moto] nm tidal wave

mareo [ma'reo] nm (náusea) sick feeling; (en viaje) travel sickness; (aturdimiento) dizziness; (fam: lata) nuisance

marfil [mar'fil] nm ivory

margarina [marɣa'rina] nf margarine

margarita [marɣa'rita] nf (Bot) daisy; (Tip) daisywheel

margen ['marxen] nm (borde) edge, border; (fig) margin, space ▷ nf (de río etc) bank; **dar ~ para** to give an opportunity for; **mantenerse al ~** to keep out (of things)

marginar [marxi'nar] vt (socialmente) to marginalize, ostracize

mariachi [ma'rjatʃi] nm (persona) mariachi musician; (grupo) mariachi band

⬤ **MARIACHI**
⬤
⬤ Mariachi music is the musical style
⬤ most characteristic of Mexico. From the
⬤ state of Jalisco in the 19th century, this
⬤ music spread rapidly throughout the
⬤ country, until each region had its own
⬤ particular style of the Mariachi "sound".
⬤ A Mariachi band can be made up of
⬤ several singers, up to eight violins, two
⬤ trumpets, guitars, a "vihuela" (an old
⬤ form of guitar), and a harp. The dance
⬤ associated with this music is called the
⬤ "zapateado".

marica [ma'rika] (fam) nm sissy

maricón [mari'kon] (fam) nm queer

marido [ma'riðo] nm husband

marihuana [mari'wana] nf marijuana, cannabis

marina [ma'rina] nf navy; **marina mercante** merchant navy

marinero, -a [mari'nero, a] adj sea cpd ▷ nm sailor, seaman

marino, -a [ma'rino, a] adj sea cpd, marine ▷ nm sailor

marioneta [marjo'neta] nf puppet

mariposa [mari'posa] nf butterfly

mariquita [mari'kita] nf ladybird (BRIT), ladybug (US)

marisco [ma'risko] (ESP) nm shellfish inv, seafood; **mariscos** (LAM) nmpl = **marisco**

marítimo, -a [ma'ritimo, a] adj sea cpd, maritime

mármol ['marmol] nm marble

marqués, -esa [mar'kes, esa] nm/f marquis/marchioness

marrón [ma'rron] adj brown

marroquí [marro'ki] adj, nmf Moroccan ▷ nm Morocco (leather)

Marruecos [ma'rrwekos] nm Morocco

martes ['martes] nm inv Tuesday; **~ y trece** ≈ Friday 13th

⬤ **MARTES Y TRECE**
⬤
⬤ According to Spanish superstition
⬤ Tuesday is an unlucky day, even more so
⬤ if it falls on the 13th of the month.

martillo [mar'tiʎo] *nm* hammer
mártir ['martir] *nmf* martyr; **martirio** *nm*
martyrdom; *(fig)* torture, torment
marxismo [mark'sismo] *nm* Marxism
marzo ['marθo] *nm* March

○ **PALABRA CLAVE**

más [mas] *adj, adv* **1: más (que** *o* **de)**
(compar) more (than), ...+er (than);
más grande/inteligente bigger/more
intelligent; **trabaja más (que yo)** he works
more (than me); *V tb* **cada**
2 *(superl)*: **el más** the most, ...+est; **el más**
grande/inteligente (de) the biggest/most
intelligent (in)
3 *(negativo)*: **no tengo más dinero** I haven't
got any more money; **no viene más por**
aquí he doesn't come round here any more
4 *(adicional)*: **no le veo más solución que**
... I see no other solution than to ...; **¿quién**
más? anybody else?
5 (+ *adj: valor intensivo*): **¡qué perro más**
sucio! what a filthy dog!; **¡es más tonto!**
he's so stupid!
6 *(locuciones)*: **más o menos** more or less;
los más most people; **es más** furthermore;
más bien rather; **¡qué más da!** what does it
matter!; *V tb* **no**
7: **por más: por más que te esfuerces** no
matter how hard you try; **por más que**
quisiera ... much as I should like to ...
8: **de más: veo que aquí estoy de más** I can
see I'm not needed here; **tenemos uno de**
más we've got one extra ▷ *prep*: **2 más 2 son**
4 2 and 0 plus 2 are 4
▷ *nm inv*: **este trabajo tiene sus más y sus**
menos this job's got its good points and its
bad points

mas [mas] *conj* but
masa ['masa] *nf (mezcla)* dough; *(volumen)*
volume, mass; *(Física)* mass; **en ~** en masse;
las ~s *(Pol)* the masses
masacre [ma'sakre] *nf* massacre
masaje [ma'saxe] *nm* massage
máscara ['maskara] *nf* mask; **máscara**
antigás/de oxígeno gas/oxygen mask;
mascarilla *nf (de belleza, Med)* mask
masculino, -a [masku'lino, a] *adj*
masculine; *(Bio)* male
masía [ma'sia] *nf* farmhouse
masivo, -a [ma'siβo, a] *adj* mass *cpd*
masoquista [maso'kista] *nmf* masochist
máster ['master] *(ESP) nm* master
masticar [masti'kar] *vt* to chew
mástil ['mastil] *nm (de navío)* mast; *(de*
guitarra) neck

mastín [mas'tin] *nm* mastiff
masturbarse [mastur'βarse] *vr* to
masturbaṭe
mata ['mata] *nf (arbusto)* bush, shrub; *(de*
hierba) tuft
matadero [mata'ðero] *nm*
slaughterhouse, abattoir
matamoscas [mata'moskas] *nm inv*
(pala) fly swat
matanza [ma'tanθa] *nf* slaughter
matar [ma'tar] *vt, vi* to kill; **matarse**
vr (suicidarse) to kill o.s., commit suicide;
(morir) to be *o* get killed; **~ el hambre** to
stave off hunger
matasellos [mata'seʎos] *nm inv*
postmark
mate ['mate] *adj* matt ▷ *nm (en ajedrez)*
(check)mate; *(LAM: hierba)* maté; *(: vasija)*
gourd
matemáticas [mate'matikas] *nfpl*
mathematics; **matemático, -a** *adj*
mathematical ▷ *nm/f* mathematician
materia [ma'terja] *nf (gen)* matter;
(Tec) material; *(Escol)* subject; **en ~ de**
on the subject of; **materia prima** raw
material; **material** *adj* material ▷ *nm*
material; *(Tec)* equipment; **materialista**
adj materialist(ic); **materialmente** *adv*
materially; *(fig)* absolutely
maternal [mater'nal] *adj* motherly,
maternal
maternidad [materni'ðað] *nf*
motherhood, maternity; **materno, -a** *adj*
maternal; *(lengua)* mother *cpd*
matinal [mati'nal] *adj* morning *cpd*
matiz [ma'tiθ] *nm* shade; **matizar** *vt*
(variar) to vary; *(Arte)* to blend; **matizar de**
to tinge with
matón [ma'ton] *nm* bully
matorral [mato'rral] *nm* thicket
matrícula [ma'trikula] *nf (registro)*
register; *(Auto)* registration number; *(: placa)*
number plate; **matrícula de honor** *(Univ)*
top marks in a subject at university with the
right to free registration the following year;
matricular *vt* to register, enrol
matrimonio [matri'monjo] *nm (pareja)*
(married) couple; *(unión)* marriage
matriz [ma'triθ] *nf (Anat)* womb; *(Tec)*
mould
matrona [ma'trona] *nf (persona de edad)*
matron; *(comadrona)* midwife
matufia [ma'tufja] *(RPL: fam) nf* put-up
job
maullar [mau'ʎar] *vi* to mew, miaow
maxilar [maksi'lar] *nm* jaw(bone)
máxima ['maksima] *nf* maxim
máximo, -a ['maksimo, a] *adj*

maximum; (*más alto*) highest; (*más grande*) greatest ▷ *nm* maximum; **como ~** at most
mayo ['majo] *nm* May
mayonesa [majo'nesa] *nf* mayonnaise
mayor [ma'jor] *adj* main, chief; (*adulto*) adult; (*de edad avanzada*) elderly; (*Mús*) major; (*compar: de tamaño*) bigger; (: *de edad*) older; (*superl: de tamaño*) biggest; (: *de edad*) oldest ▷ *nm* (*adulto*) adult; **mayores** *nmpl* (*antepasados*) ancestors; **al por ~** wholesale; **mayor de edad** adult
mayoral [majo'ral] *nm* foreman
mayordomo [major'ðomo] *nm* butler
mayoría [majo'ria] *nf* majority, greater part
mayorista [majo'rista] *nmf* wholesaler
mayoritario, -a [majori'tarjo, a] *adj* majority *cpd*
mayúscula [ma'juskula] *nf* capital letter
mazapán [maθa'pan] *nm* marzipan
mazo ['maθo] *nm* (*martillo*) mallet; (*de flores*) bunch; (*Deporte*) bat
me [me] *pron* (*directo*) me; (*indirecto*) (to) me; (*reflexivo*) (to) myself; **¡dá~lo!** give it to me!
mear [me'ar] (*fam*) *vi* to pee, piss (!)
mecánica [me'kanika] *nf* (*Escol*) mechanics *sg*; (*mecanismo*) mechanism; *V tb* **mecánico**
mecánico, -a [me'kaniko, a] *adj* mechanical ▷ *nm/f* mechanic
mecanismo [meka'nismo] *nm* mechanism; (*marcha*) gear
mecanografía [mekanoɤra'fia] *nf* typewriting; **mecanógrafo, -a** *nm/f* typist
mecate [me'kate] (*MÉX, CAM*) *nm* rope
mecedora [meθe'ðora] *nf* rocking chair
mecer [me'θer] *vt* (*cuna*) to rock; **mecerse** *vr* to rock; (*rama*) to sway
mecha ['metʃa] *nf* (*de vela*) wick; (*de bomba*) fuse
mechero [me'tʃero] *nm* (cigarette) lighter
mechón [me'tʃon] *nm* (*gen*) tuft; (*de pelo*) lock
medalla [me'ðaʎa] *nf* medal
media ['meðja] *nf* stocking; (*LAM: calcetín*) sock; (*promedio*) average
mediado, -a [me'ðjaðo, a] *adj* half-full; (*trabajo*) half-completed; **a ~s de** in the middle of, halfway through
mediano, -a [me'ðjano, a] *adj* (*regular*) medium, average; (*mediocre*) mediocre
medianoche [meðja'notʃe] *nf* midnight
mediante [me'ðjante] *adv* by (means of), through
mediar [me'ðjar] *vi* (*interceder*) to mediate, intervene
medicamento [meðika'mento] *nm* medicine, drug

medicina [meði'θina] *nf* medicine
médico, -a ['meðiko, a] *adj* medical ▷ *nm/f* doctor
medida [me'ðiða] *nf* measure; (*medición*) measurement; (*prudencia*) moderation, prudence; **en cierta/gran ~** up to a point/ to a great extent; **un traje a la ~** a made-to-measure suit; **~ de cuello** collar size; **a ~ de** in proportion to; (*de acuerdo con*) in keeping with; **a ~ que** (*conforme*) as; **medidor** (*LAM*) *nm* meter
medio, -a ['meðjo, a] *adj* half (a); (*punto*) mid, middle; (*promedio*) average ▷ *adv* half ▷ *nm* (*centro*) middle, centre; (*promedio*) average; (*método*) means, way; (*ambiente*) environment; **medios** *nmpl* means, resources; **~ litro** half a litre; **las tres y media** half past three; **a ~ terminar** half finished; **pagar a medias** to share the cost; **medio ambiente** environment; **medio de transporte** means of transport; **Medio Oriente** Middle East; **medios de comunicación** media; **medioambiental** *adj* (*política, efectos*) environmental
mediocre [me'ðjokre] *adj* mediocre
mediodía [meðjo'ðia] *nm* midday, noon
medir [me'ðir] *vt, vi* (*gen*) to measure
meditar [meði'tar] *vt* to ponder, think over, meditate on; (*planear*) to think out
mediterráneo, -a [meðite'rraneo, a] *adj* Mediterranean ▷ *nm*: **el M~** the Mediterranean
médula ['meðula] *nf* (*Anat*) marrow; **médula espinal** spinal cord
medusa [me'ðusa] (*ESP*) *nf* jellyfish
megáfono [me'ɤafono] *nm* megaphone
megapíxel [meɤa'piksel] (*pl* **megapixels** *or* **~es**) *nm* megapixel
mejilla [me'xiʎa] *nf* cheek
mejillón [mexi'ʎon] *nm* mussel
mejor [me'xor] *adj, adv* (*compar*) better; (*superl*) best; **a lo ~** probably; (*quizá*) maybe; **~ dicho** rather; **tanto ~** so much the better
mejora [me'xora] *nf* improvement; **mejorar** *vt* to improve, make better ▷ *vi* to improve, get better; **mejorarse** *vr* to improve, get better
melancólico, -a [melan'koliko, a] *adj* (*triste*) sad, melancholy; (*soñador*) dreamy
melena [me'lena] *nf* (*de persona*) long hair; (*Zool*) mane
mellizo, -a [me'ʎiθo, a] *adj, nm/f* twin
melocotón [meloko'ton] (*ESP*) *nm* peach
melodía [melo'ðia] *nf* melody, tune
melodrama [melo'ðrama] *nm* melodrama; **melodramático, -a** *adj* melodramatic

m

melón [me'lon] *nm* melon

membrete [mem'brete] *nm* letterhead

membrillo [mem'briʎo] *nm* quince;
(carne de) ~ quince jelly

memoria [me'morja] *nf* (*gen*) memory;
memorias *nfpl* (*de autor*) memoirs;
memorizar *vt* to memorize

menaje [me'naxe] *nm* (*tb*: **artículos de ~**)
household items

mencionar [menθjo'nar] *vt* to mention

mendigo, -a [men'diɣo, a] *nm/f* beggar

menear [mene'ar] *vt* to move; **menearse**
vr to shake; (*balancearse*) to sway; (*moverse*)
to move; (*fig*) to get a move on

menestra [me'nestra] *nf* (*tb*: **~ de
verduras**) vegetable stew

menopausia [meno'pausja] *nf*
menopause

menor [me'nor] *adj* (*más pequeño: compar*)
smaller; (: *superl*) smallest; (*más
joven: compar*) younger; (: *superl*) youngest;
(*Mús*) minor ▷ *nmf* (*joven*) young person,
juvenile; **no tengo la ~ idea** I haven't the
faintest idea; **al por ~** retail; **menor de edad**
person under age

Menorca [me'norka] *nf* Minorca

○ **PALABRA CLAVE**

menos [menos] *adj* **1**: **menos (que** *o* **de)**
(*compar: cantidad*) less (than); (: *número*)
fewer (than); **con menos entusiasmo**
with less enthusiasm; **menos gente** fewer
people; V *tb* **cada**

2 (*superl*): **es el que menos culpa tiene** he is
the least to blame

▷ *adv* **1** (*compar*): **menos (que** *o* **de)** less
(than); **me gusta menos que el otro** I like it
less than the other one

2 (*superl*): **es el menos listo (de su clase)**
he's the least bright in his class; **de todas
ellas es la que menos me agrada** out of all
of them she's the one I like least

3 (*locuciones*): **no quiero verle y menos
visitarle** I don't want to see him, let alone
visit him; **tenemos siete de menos** we're
seven short; **(por) lo menos** at (the very)
least; **¡menos mal!** thank goodness!

▷ *prep* except; (*cifras*) minus; **todos menos
él** everyone except (for) him; **5 menos 2** 5
minus 2

▷ *conj*: **a menos que: a menos que venga
mañana** unless he comes tomorrow

menospreciar [menospre'θjar] *vt* to
underrate, undervalue; (*despreciar*) to scorn,
despise

mensaje [men'saxe] *nm* message; **enviar**
un ~ a algn (*por móvil*) to text sb, send sb
a text message; **mensaje de texto** text
message; **mensajero, -a** *nm/f* messenger

menso, -a ['menso, a] (*MÉX: fam*) *adj*
stupid

menstruación [menstrua'θjon] *nf*
menstruation

mensual [men'swal] *adj* monthly; **100
euros ~es** 100 euros a month; **mensualidad**
nf (*salario*) monthly salary; (*Com*) monthly
payment, monthly instalment

menta ['menta] *nf* mint

mental [men'tal] *adj* mental; **mentalidad**
nf mentality; **mentalizar** *vt* (*sensibilizar*) to
make aware; (*convencer*) to convince; (*padres*)
to prepare (mentally); **mentalizarse**
vr (*concienciarse*) to become aware;
mentalizarse (de) to get used to the idea
(of); **mentalizarse de que ...** (*convencerse*)
to get it into one's head that ...

mente ['mente] *nf* mind

mentir [men'tir] *vi* to lie

mentira [men'tira] *nf* (*una mentira*) lie;
(*acto*) lying; (*invención*) fiction; **parece
mentira que ...** it seems incredible that
..., I can't believe that ...; **mentiroso, -a**
[menti'roso, a] *adj* lying ▷ *nm/f* liar

menú [me'nu] (*pl* **~s**) *nm* menu; **menú del
día** set menu; **menú turístico** tourist menu

menudencias [menu'ðenθjas] (*LAM*)
nfpl giblets

menudo, -a [me'nuðo, a] *adj* (*pequeño*)
small, tiny; (*sin importancia*) petty,
insignificant; **¡~ negocio!** (*fam*) some deal!;
a ~ often, frequently

meñique [me'ɲike] *nm* little finger

mercadillo [merka'ðiʎo] (*ESP*) *nm* flea
market

mercado [mer'kaðo] *nm* market;
mercado de pulgas (*LAM*) flea market

mercancía [merkan'θia] *nf* commodity;
mercancías *nfpl* goods, merchandise *sg*

mercenario, -a [merθe'narjo, a] *adj, nm*
mercenary

mercería [merθe'ria] *nf* haberdashery
(*BRIT*), notions *pl* (*US*); (*tienda*) haberdasher's
(*BRIT*), notions store (*US*)

mercurio [mer'kurjo] *nm* mercury

merecer [mere'θer] *vt* to deserve, merit
▷ *vi* to be deserving, be worthy; **merece
la pena** it's worthwhile; **merecido, -a** *adj*
(well) deserved; **llevar su merecido** to get
one's deserts

merendar [meren'dar] *vt* to have for
tea ▷ *vi* to have tea; (*en el campo*) to have a
picnic; **merendero** *nm* open-air cafe

merengue [me'renge] *nm* meringue

meridiano [meri'ðjano] *nm* (*Geo*)

meridian
merienda [me'rjenda] nf (light) tea,
afternoon snack; (de campo) picnic
mérito ['merito] nm merit; (valor) worth,
value
merluza [mer'luθa] nf hake
mermelada [merme'laða] nf jam
mero, -a ['mero, a] adj mere; (MÉX,
CAM: fam) very
merodear [meroðe'ar] vi: ~ **por** to prowl
about
mes [mes] nm month
mesa ['mesa] nf table; (de trabajo) desk;
(Geo) plateau; **poner/quitar la ~** to lay/clear
the table; **mesa electoral** officials in charge
of a polling station; **mesa redonda** (reunión)
round table; **mesero, -a** (LAM) nm/f waiter/
waitress
meseta [me'seta] nf (Geo) plateau,
tableland
mesilla [me'siʎa] nf (tb: ~ **de noche**)
bedside table
mesón [me'son] nm inn
mestizo, -a [mes'tiθo, a] adj half-caste,
of mixed race ▷ nm/f half-caste
meta ['meta] nf goal; (de carrera) finish
metabolismo [metaβo'lismo] nm
metabolism
metáfora [me'tafora] nf metaphor
metal [me'tal] nm (materia) metal; (Mús)
brass; **metálico, -a** adj metallic; (de metal)
metal ▷ nm (dinero contante) cash
meteorología [meteorolo'xia] nf
meteorology
meter [me'ter] vt (colocar) to put, place;
(introducir) to put in, insert; (involucrar) to
involve; (causar) to make, cause; **meterse**
vr: ~**se en** to go into, enter; (fig) to interfere
in, meddle in; ~**se a** to start; ~**se a escritor**
to become a writer; ~**se con uno** to provoke
sb, pick a quarrel with sb
meticuloso, -a [metiku'loso, a] adj
meticulous, thorough
metódico, -a [me'toðiko, a] adj
methodical
método ['metoðo] nm method
metralleta [metra'ʎeta] nf sub-machine-
gun
métrico, -a ['metriko, a] adj metric
metro ['metro] nm metre; (tren)
underground (BRIT), subway (US)
metrosexual [metrosek'swal] adj, nm
metrosexual
mexicano, -a [mexi'kano, a] adj, nm/f
Mexican
México ['mexiko] nm Mexico; **Ciudad de
~** Mexico City
mezcla ['meθkla] nf mixture; **mezcladora**

(MÉX) nf (tb: **mezcladora de cemento**)
cement mixer; **mezclar** vt to mix (up);
mezclarse vr to mix, mingle; **mezclarse
en** to get mixed up in, get involved in
mezquino, -a [meθ'kino, a] adj mean
mezquita [meθ'kita] nf mosque
mg. abr (= miligramo) mg
mi [mi] adj pos my ▷ nm (Mús) E
mí [mi] pron me; myself
mía pron V **mío**
michelín [mitʃe'lin] (fam) nm (de grasa)
spare tyre
microbio [mi'kroβjo] nm microbe
micrófono [mi'krofono] nm microphone
microondas [mikro'ondas] nm inv
(tb: **horno ~**) microwave (oven)
microscopio [mikro'skopjo] nm
microscope
miedo ['mjeðo] nm fear; (nerviosismo)
apprehension, nervousness; **tener ~** to be
afraid; **de ~** wonderful, marvellous; **hace un
frío de ~** (fam) it's terribly cold; **miedoso, -a**
adj fearful, timid
miel [mjel] nf honey
miembro ['mjembro] nm limb; (socio)
member; **miembro viril** penis
mientras ['mjentras] conj while;
(duración) as long as ▷ adv meanwhile; ~
tanto meanwhile
miércoles ['mjerkoles] nm inv Wednesday
mierda ['mjerða] (fam!) nf shit (!)
miga ['miɣa] nf crumb; (fig: meollo)
essence; **hacer buenas ~s** (fam) to get on
well
mil [mil] num thousand; **dos ~ libras** two
thousand pounds
milagro [mi'laɣro] nm miracle;
milagroso, -a adj miraculous
milésima [mi'lesima] nf (de segundo)
thousandth
mili ['mili] (ESP: fam) nf: **hacer la ~** to do
one's military service
milímetro [mi'limetro] nm millimetre
militante [mili'tante] adj militant
militar [mili'tar] adj military ▷ nmf
soldier ▷ vi (Mil) to serve; (en un partido) to
be a member
milla ['miʎa] nf mile
millar [mi'ʎar] nm thousand
millón [mi'ʎon] num million; **millonario,
-a** nm/f millionaire
milusos [mi'lusos] (MÉX) nm inv odd-job
man
mimar [mi'mar] vt to spoil, pamper
mimbre ['mimbre] nm wicker
mímica ['mimika] nf (para comunicarse)
sign language; (imitación) mimicry
mimo ['mimo] nm (caricia) caress; (de niño)

spoiling; (*Teatro*) mime; (: *actor*) mime artist
mina ['mina] *nf* mine
mineral [mine'ral] *adj* mineral ▷ *nm*
(*Geo*) mineral; (*mena*) ore
minero, -a [mi'nero, a] *adj* mining *cpd*
▷ *nm/f* miner
miniatura [minja'tura] *adj inv, nf*
miniature
minidisco [mini'disko] *nm* MiniDisc®
minifalda [mini'falda] *nf* miniskirt
mínimo, -a ['minimo, a] *adj, nm*
minimum
minino, -a [mi'nino, a] (*fam*) *nm/f* puss,
pussy
ministerio [minis'terjo] *nm* Ministry;
**Ministerio de Hacienda/de Asuntos
Exteriores** Treasury (*BRIT*), Treasury
Department (*us*)/Foreign Office (*BRIT*),
State Department (*us*)
ministro, -a [mi'nistro, a] *nm/f* minister
minoría [mino'ria] *nf* minority
minúscula [mi'nuskula] *nf* small letter
minúsculo, -a [mi'nuskulo, a] *adj* tiny,
minute
minusválido, -a [minus'βaliðo, a]
adj (physically) handicapped ▷ *nm/f*
(physically) handicapped person
minuta [mi'nuta] *nf* (*de comida*) menu
minutero [minu'tero] *nm* minute hand
minuto [mi'nuto] *nm* minute
mío, -a ['mio, a] *pron*: **el ~/la mía** mine; **un
amigo ~** a friend of mine; **lo ~** what is mine
miope [mi'ope] *adj* short-sighted
mira ['mira] *nf* (*de arma*) sight(s) (*pl*); (*fig*)
aim, intention
mirada [mi'raða] *nf* look, glance;
(*expresión*) look, expression; **clavar la ~ en** to
stare at; **echar una ~ a** to glance at
mirado, -a [mi'raðo, a] *adj* (*sensato*)
sensible; (*considerado*) considerate; **bien/
mal ~** (*estimado*) well/not well thought of;
bien ~ ... all things considered ...
mirador [mira'ðor] *nm* viewpoint,
vantage point
mirar [mi'rar] *vt* to look at; (*observar*) to
watch; (*considerar*) to consider, think over;
(*vigilar, cuidar*) to watch, look after ▷ *vi* to
look; (*Arq*) to face; **mirarse** *vr* (*dos personas*)
to look at each other; **~ bien/mal** to think
highly of/have a poor opinion of; **~se al
espejo** to look at o.s. in the mirror
mirilla [mi'riʎa] *nf* spyhole, peephole
mirlo ['mirlo] *nm* blackbird
misa ['misa] *nf* mass
miserable [mise'raβle] *adj* (*avaro*)
mean, stingy; (*nimio*) miserable, paltry;
(*lugar*) squalid; (*fam*) vile, despicable ▷ *nmf*
(*malvado*) rogue

miseria [mi'serja] *nf* (*pobreza*) poverty;
(*tacañería*) meanness, stinginess;
(*condiciones*) squalor; **una ~** a pittance
misericordia [miseri'korðja] *nf*
(*compasión*) compassion, pity; (*piedad*) mercy
misil [mi'sil] *nm* missile
misión [mi'sjon] *nf* mission; **misionero,
-a** *nm/f* missionary
mismo, -a ['mismo, a] *adj* (*semejante*)
same; (*después de pron*) -self; (*para énfasis*)
very ▷ *adv*: **aquí/hoy ~** right here/this very
day; **ahora ~** right now ▷ *conj*: **lo ~ que** just
like o as; **el ~ traje** the same suit; **en ese ~
momento** at that very moment; **vino el ~
ministro** the minister himself came; **yo ~
lo vi** I saw it myself; **lo ~** the same (thing);
da lo ~ it's all the same; **quedamos en las
mismas** we're no further forward; **por lo ~**
for the same reason
misterio [mis'terjo] *nm* mystery;
misterioso, -a *adj* mysterious
mitad [mi'tað] *nf* (*medio*) half; (*centro*)
middle; **a ~ de precio** (at) half-price; **en o a ~
del camino** halfway along the road; **cortar
por la ~** to cut through the middle
mitin ['mitin] (*pl* **mítines**) *nm* meeting
mito ['mito] *nm* myth
mixto, -a ['miksto, a] *adj* mixed
ml. *abr* (= *mililitro*) ml
mm. *abr* (= *milímetro*) mm
mobiliario [moβi'ljarjo] *nm* furniture
mochila [mo'tʃila] *nf* rucksack (*BRIT*),
back-pack
moco ['moko] *nm* mucus; **mocos** *nmpl*
(*fam*) snot; **limpiarse los ~s de la nariz** (*fam*)
to wipe one's nose
moda ['moða] *nf* fashion; (*estilo*) style; **a la
o de ~** in fashion, fashionable; **pasado de ~**
out of fashion
modales [mo'ðales] *nmpl* manners
modelar [moðe'lar] *vt* to model
modelo [mo'ðelo] *adj inv, nmf* model
módem ['moðem] *nm* (*Inform*) modem
moderado, -a [moðe'raðo, a] *adj*
moderate
moderar [moðe'rar] *vt* to moderate;
(*violencia*) to restrain, control; (*velocidad*)
to reduce; **moderarse** *vr* to restrain o.s.,
control o.s.
modernizar [moðerni'θar] *vt* to
modernize
moderno, -a [mo'ðerno, a] *adj* modern;
(*actual*) present-day
modestia [mo'ðestja] *nf* modesty;
modesto, -a *adj* modest
modificar [moðifi'kar] *vt* to modify
modisto, -a [mo'ðisto, a] *nm/f* (*diseñador*)
couturier, designer; (*que confecciona*)

dressmaker

modo ['moðo] nm way, manner; (Mús) mode; **modos** nmpl manners; **de ningún ~** in no way; **de todos ~s** at any rate; **modo de empleo** directions pl (for use)

mofarse [mo'farse] vr: **~ de** to mock, scoff at

mofle ['mofle] (MÉX, CAM) nm silencer (BRIT), muffler (US)

mogollón [moɣo'ʎon] (ESP: fam) adv a hell of a lot

moho ['moo] nm mould, mildew; (en metal) rust

mojar [mo'xar] vt to wet; (humedecer) to damp(en), moisten; (calar) to soak; **mojarse** vr to get wet

molcajete [molka'xete] (MÉX) nm mortar

molde ['molde] nm mould; (Costura) pattern; (fig) model; **moldeado** nm soft perm; **moldear** vt to mould

mole ['mole] nf mass, bulk; (edificio) pile

moler [mo'ler] vt to grind, crush

molestar [moles'tar] vt to bother; (fastidiar) to annoy; (incomodar) to inconvenience, put out ▷ vi to be a nuisance; **molestarse** vr to bother; (incomodarse) to go to trouble; (ofenderse) to take offence; **¿(no) te molesta si …?** do you mind if …?

▌ No confundir **molestar** con la palabra inglesa molest.

molestia [mo'lestja] nf bother, trouble; (incomodidad) inconvenience; (Med) discomfort; **es una ~** it's a nuisance; **molesto, -a** adj (que fastidia) annoying; (incómodo) inconvenient; (inquieto) uncomfortable, ill at ease; (enfadado) annoyed

molido, -a [mo'liðo, a] adj: **estar ~** (fig) to be exhausted o dead beat

molinillo [moli'niʎo] nm hand mill; **molinillo de café** coffee grinder

molino [mo'lino] nm (edificio) mill; (máquina) grinder

momentáneo, -a [momen'taneo, a] adj momentary

momento [mo'mento] nm moment; **de ~** at o for the moment

momia ['momja] nf mummy

monarca [mo'narka] nmf monarch, ruler; **monarquía** nf monarchy

monasterio [monas'terjo] nm monastery

mondar [mon'dar] vt to peel; **mondarse** vr (ESP): **~se de risa** (fam) to split one's sides laughing

mondongo [mon'dongo] (LAM) nm tripe

moneda [mo'neða] nf (tipo de dinero) currency, money; (pieza) coin; **una ~ de 2**

euros a 2 euro piece; **monedero** nm purse

monitor, a [moni'tor, a] nm/f instructor, coach ▷ nm (TV) set; (Inform) monitor

monja ['monxa] nf nun

monje ['monxe] nm monk

mono, -a ['mono, a] adj (bonito) lovely, pretty; (gracioso) nice, charming ▷ nm/f monkey, ape ▷ nm dungarees pl; (overoles) overalls pl

monopatín [monopa'tin] nm skateboard

monopolio [mono'poljo] nm monopoly; **monopolizar** vt to monopolize

monótono, -a [mo'notono, a] adj monotonous

monstruo ['monstrwo] nm monster ▷ adj inv fantastic; **monstruoso, -a** adj monstrous

montaje [mon'taxe] nm assembly; (Teatro) décor; (Cine) montage

montaña [mon'taɲa] nf (monte) mountain; (sierra) mountains pl, mountainous area; **montaña rusa** roller coaster; **montañero, -a** nm/f mountaineer; **montañismo** nm mountaineering

montar [mon'tar] vt (subir a) to mount, get on; (Tec) to assemble, put together; (negocio) to set up; (arma) to cock; (colocar) to lift on to; (Culin) to beat ▷ vi to mount, get on; (sobresalir) to overlap; **~ en bicicleta** to ride a bicycle; **~ en cólera** to get angry; **~ a caballo** to ride, go horseriding

monte ['monte] nm (montaña) mountain; (bosque) woodland; (área sin cultivar) wild area, wild country; **monte de piedad** pawnshop

montón [mon'ton] nm heap, pile; (fig): **un ~ de** heaps o lots of

monumento [monu'mento] nm monument

moño ['moɲo] nm bun

moqueta [mo'keta] nf fitted carpet

mora ['mora] nf blackberry; V tb **moro**

morado, -a [mo'raðo, a] adj purple, violet ▷ nm bruise

moral [mo'ral] adj moral ▷ nf (ética) ethics pl; (moralidad) morals pl, morality; (ánimo) morale

moraleja [mora'lexa] nf moral

morboso, -a [mor'βoso, a] adj morbid

morcilla [mor'θiʎa] nf blood sausage ≈ black pudding (BRIT)

mordaza [mor'ðaθa] nf (para la boca) gag; (Tec) clamp

morder [mor'ðer] vt to bite; (fig: consumir) to eat away, eat into; **mordisco** nm bite

moreno, -a [mo'reno, a] adj (color) (dark) brown; (de tez) dark; (de pelo moreno) dark-haired; (*negro*) black

morfina [mor'fina] *nf* morphine

moribundo, -a [mori'βundo, a] *adj* dying

morir [mo'rir] *vi* to die; (*fuego*) to die down; (*luz*) to go out; **morirse** *vr* to die; (*fig*) to be dying; **murió en un accidente** he was killed in an accident; **~se por algo** to be dying for sth

moro, -a ['moro, a] *adj* Moorish ▷ *nm/f* Moor

moroso, -a [mo'roso, a] *nm/f* bad debtor, defaulter

morraña [mo'rraɲa] (*MÉX*) *nf* (*cambio*) small o loose change

morro ['morro] *nm* (*Zool*) snout, nose; (*Auto, Aviac*) nose

morsa ['morsa] *nf* walrus

mortadela [morta'ðela] *nf* mortadella

mortal [mor'tal] *adj* mortal; (*golpe*) deadly; **mortalidad** *nf* mortality

mortero [mor'tero] *nm* mortar

mosca ['moska] *nf* fly

Moscú [mos'ku] *n* Moscow

mosquearse [moske'arse] (*fam*) *vr* (*enojarse*) to get cross; (*ofenderse*) to take offence

mosquitero [moski'tero] *nm* mosquito net

mosquito [mos'kito] *nm* mosquito

mostaza [mos'taθa] *nf* mustard

mosto ['mosto] *nm* (unfermented) grape juice

mostrador [mostra'ðor] *nm* (*de tienda*) counter; (*de café*) bar

mostrar [mos'trar] *vt* to show; (*exhibir*) to display, exhibit; (*explicar*) to explain; **mostrarse** *vr*: **~se amable** to be kind; to prove to be kind; **no se muestra muy inteligente** he doesn't seem (to be) very intelligent

mota ['mota] *nf* speck, tiny piece; (*en diseño*) dot

mote ['mote] *nm* nickname

motín [mo'tin] *nm* (*del pueblo*) revolt, rising; (*del ejército*) mutiny

motivar [moti'βar] *vt* (*causar*) to cause, motivate; (*explicar*) to explain, justify; **motivo** *nm* motive, reason

moto ['moto] (*fam*) *nf* = **motocicleta**

motocicleta [motoθi'kleta] *nf* motorbike (*BRIT*), motorcycle

motoneta [moto'neta] (*CS*) *nf* scooter

motor [mo'tor] *nm* motor, engine; **motor a chorro** o **de reacción/de explosión** jet engine/internal combustion engine

motora [mo'tora] *nf* motorboat

movedizo, -a *adj* V **arena**

mover [mo'βer] *vt* to move; (*cabeza*) to shake; (*accionar*) to drive; (*fig*) to cause, provoke; **moverse** *vr* to move; (*fig*) to get a move on

móvil ['moβil] *adj* mobile; (*pieza de máquina*) moving; (*mueble*) movable ▷ *nm* (*motivo*) motive; (*teléfono*) mobile

movimiento [moβi'mjento] *nm* movement; (*Tec*) motion; (*actividad*) activity

mozo, -a ['moθo, a] *adj* (*joven*) young ▷ *nm/f* youth, young man/girl; (*cs: mesero*) waiter/waitress

MP3 *nm* MP3; **reproductor (de) ~** MP3 player

mucama [mu'kama] (*RPL*) *nf* maid

muchacho, -a [mu'tʃatʃo, a] *nm/f* (*niño*) boy/girl; (*criado*) servant; (*criada*) maid

muchedumbre [mutʃe'ðumbre] *nf* crowd

○ **PALABRA CLAVE**

mucho, -a ['mutʃo, a] *adj* **1** (*cantidad*) a lot of, much; (*número*) lots of, a lot of, many; **mucho dinero** a lot of money; **hace mucho calor** it's very hot; **muchas amigas** lots o a lot of friends

2 (*sg: grande*): **ésta es mucha casa para él** this house is much too big for him

▷ *pron*: **tengo mucho que hacer** I've got a lot to do; **muchos dicen que ...** a lot of people say that ...; V *tb* **tener**

▷ *adv* **1 me gusta mucho** I like it a lot; **lo siento mucho** I'm very sorry; **come mucho** he eats a lot; **¿te vas a quedar mucho?** are you going to be staying long?

2 (*respuesta*) very; **¿estás cansado? – ¡mucho!** are you tired? – very!

3 (*locuciones*): **como mucho** at (the) most; **con mucho: el mejor con mucho** by far the best; **ni mucho menos: no es rico ni mucho menos** he's far from being rich

4: **por mucho que: por mucho que le creas** no matter how o however much you believe her

muda ['muða] *nf* change of clothes

mudanza [mu'ðanθa] *nf* (*de casa*) move

mudar [mu'ðar] *vt* to change; (*Zool*) to shed ▷ *vi* to change; **mudarse** *vr* (*ropa*) to change; **~se de casa** to move house

mudo, -a ['muðo, a] *adj* dumb; (*callado, Cine*) silent

mueble ['mweβle] *nm* piece of furniture; **muebles** *nmpl* furniture *sg*

mueca ['mweka] *nf* face, grimace; **hacer ~s a** to make faces at

muela ['mwela] *nf* back tooth; **muela del**

juicio wisdom tooth
muelle ['mweʎe] *nm* spring; (*Náut*) wharf; (*malecón*) pier
muero *etc vb* V **morir**
muerte ['mwerte] *nf* death; (*homicidio*) murder; **dar ~ a** to kill
muerto, -a ['mwerto, a] *pp de* **morir**
▷ *adj* dead ▷ *nm/f* dead man/woman; (*difunto*) deceased; (*cadáver*) corpse; **estar ~ de cansancio** to be dead tired; **Día de los Muertos** (*MÉX*) All Souls' Day

● **DÍA DE LOS MUERTOS**
●
●
● All Souls' Day (or "Day of the Dead")
● in Mexico coincides with All Saints'
● Day, which is celebrated in the
● Catholic countries of Latin America on
● November 1st and 2nd. All Souls' Day
● is actually a celebration which begins
● in the evening of October 31st and
● continues until November 2nd. It is a
● combination of the Catholic tradition
● of honouring the Christian saints and
● martyrs, and the ancient Mexican or
● Aztec traditions, in which death was
● not something sinister. For this reason
● all the dead are honoured by bringing
● offerings of food, flowers and candles to
● the cemetery.

muestra ['mwestra] *nf* (*señal*) indication, sign; (*demostración*) demonstration; (*prueba*) proof; (*estadística*) sample; (*modelo*) model, pattern; (*testimonio*) token
muestro *etc vb* V **mostrar**
muevo *etc vb* V **mover**
mugir [mu'xir] *vi* (*vaca*) to moo
mugre ['muxre] *nf* dirt, filth
mujer [mu'xer] *nf* woman; (*esposa*) wife; **mujeriego** *nm* womanizer
mula ['mula] *nf* mule
muleta [mu'leta] *nf* (*para andar*) crutch; (*Taur*) stick with red cape attached
multa ['multa] *nf* fine; **poner una ~ a** to fine; **multar** *vt* to fine
multicines [multi'θines] *nmpl* multiscreen cinema *sg*
multinacional [multinaθjo'nal] *nf* multinational
múltiple ['multiple] *adj* multiple; (*pl*) many, numerous
multiplicar [multipli'kar] *vt* (*Mat*) to multiply; (*fig*) to increase; **multiplicarse** *vr* (*Bio*) to multiply; (*fig*) to be everywhere at once
multitud [multi'tuð] *nf* (*muchedumbre*) crowd; **~ de** lots of

mundial [mun'djal] *adj* world-wide, universal; (*guerra, récord*) world *cpd*
mundo ['mundo] *nm* world; **todo el ~** everybody; **tener ~** to be experienced, know one's way around
munición [muni'θjon] *nf* ammunition
municipal [muniθi'pal] *adj* municipal, local
municipio [muni'θipjo] *nm* (*ayuntamiento*) town council, corporation; (*territorio administrativo*) town, municipality
muñeca [mu'ɲeka] *nf* (*Anat*) wrist; (*juguete*) doll
muñeco [mu'ɲeko] *nm* (*figura*) figure; (*marioneta*) puppet; (*fig*) puppet, pawn
mural [mu'ral] *adj* mural, wall *cpd* ▷ *nm* mural
muralla [mu'raʎa] *nf* (*city*) wall(s) (*pl*)
murciélago [mur'θjelaxo] *nm* bat
murmullo [mur'muʎo] *nm* murmur(ing); (*cuchicheo*) whispering
murmurar [murmu'rar] *vi* to murmur, whisper; (*cotillear*) to gossip
muro ['muro] *nm* wall
muscular [musku'lar] *adj* muscular
músculo ['muskulo] *nm* muscle
museo [mu'seo] *nm* museum; **museo de arte** art gallery
musgo ['musxo] *nm* moss
música ['musika] *nf* music; V tb **músico**
músico, -a ['musiko, a] *adj* musical ▷ *nm/f* musician
muslo ['muslo] *nm* thigh
musulmán, -ana [musul'man, ana] *nm/f* Moslem
mutación [muta'θjon] *nf* (*Bio*) mutation; (*cambio*) (sudden) change
mutilar [muti'lar] *vt* to mutilate; (*a una persona*) to maim
mutuo, -a ['mutwo, a] *adj* mutual
muy [mwi] *adv* very; (*demasiado*) too; **M~ Señor mío** Dear Sir; **~ de noche** very late at night; **eso es ~ de él** that's just like him

m

n

N abr (= norte) N

nabo ['naβo] nm turnip

nacer [na'θer] vi to be born; (de huevo) to hatch; (vegetal) to sprout; (río) to rise; **nací en Barcelona** I was born in Barcelona; **nacido, -a** adj born; **recién nacido** newborn; **nacimiento** nm birth; (de Navidad) Nativity; (de río) source

nación [na'θjon] nf nation; **nacional** adj national; **nacionalismo** nm nationalism

nada ['naða] pron nothing ▷ adv not at all, in no way; **no decir ~** to say nothing, not to say anything; **~ más** nothing else; **de ~** don't mention it

nadador, a [naða'ðor, a] nm/f swimmer

nadar [na'ðar] vi to swim

nadie ['naðje] pron nobody, no-one; **~ habló** nobody spoke; **no había ~** there was nobody there, there wasn't anybody there

nado ['naðo] **a nado**: adv: **pasar a ~** to swim across

nafta ['nafta] (RPL) nf petrol (BRIT), gas (US)

naipe ['naipe] nm (playing) card; **naipes** nmpl cards

nalgas ['nalɣas] nfpl buttocks

nalguear [nalɣe'ar] (MÉX, CAM) vt to spank

nana ['nana] (ESP) nf lullaby

naranja [na'ranxa] adj inv, nf orange; **media ~** (fam) better half; **naranjada** nf orangeade; **naranjo** nm orange tree

narciso [nar'θiso] nm narcissus

narcótico, -a [nar'kotiko, a] adj, nm narcotic; **narcotizar** vt to drug; **narcotráfico** nm drug trafficking o running

nariz [na'riθ] nf nose; **nariz chata/ respingona** snub/turned-up nose

narración [narra'θjon] nf narration

narrar [na'rrar] vt to narrate, recount; **narrativa** nf narrative

nata ['nata] nf cream; **nata montada** whipped cream

natación [nata'θjon] nf swimming

natal [na'tal] adj: **ciudad ~** home town; **natalidad** nf birth rate

natillas [na'tiʎas] nfpl custard sg

nativo, -a [na'tiβo, a] adj, nm/f native

natural [natu'ral] adj natural; (fruta etc) fresh ▷ nmf native ▷ nm (disposición) nature

naturaleza [natura'leθa] nf nature; (género) nature, kind; **naturaleza muerta** still life

naturalmente [natural'mente] adv (de modo natural) in a natural way; **¡~!** of course!

naufragar [naufra'ɣar] vi to sink; **naufragio** nm shipwreck

nauseabundo, -a [nausea'βundo, a] adj nauseating, sickening

náuseas ['nauseas] nfpl nausea sg; **me da ~** it makes me feel sick

náutico, -a ['nautiko, a] adj nautical

navaja [na'βaxa] nf knife; (de barbero, peluquero) razor

naval [na'βal] adj naval

Navarra [na'βarra] n Navarre

nave ['naβe] nf (barco) ship, vessel; (Arq) nave; **nave espacial** spaceship; **nave industrial** factory premises pl

navegador [naβeɣa'ðor] nm (Inform) browser

navegante [naβe'ɣante] nmf navigator

navegar [naβe'ɣar] vi (barco) to sail; (avión) to fly; **~ por Internet** to surf the Net

Navidad [naβi'ðað] nf Christmas; **Navidades** nfpl Christmas time; **¡Feliz ~!** Merry Christmas!; **navideño, -a** adj Christmas cpd

nazca etc vb V **nacer**

nazi ['naθi] adj, nmf Nazi

NE abr (= nor(d)este) NE

neblina [ne'βlina] nf mist

necesario, -a [neθe'sarjo, a] adj necessary

neceser [neθe'ser] nm toilet bag; (bolsa grande) holdall

necesidad [neθesi'ðað] nf need; (lo inevitable) necessity; (miseria) poverty; **en caso de ~** in case of need o emergency; **hacer sus ~es** to relieve o.s.

necesitado, -a [neθesi'taðo, a] adj needy, poor; **~ de** in need of

necesitar [neθesi'tar] vt to need, require

necio, -a ['neθjo, a] adj foolish

nectarina [nekta'rina] nf nectarine

nefasto, -a [ne'fasto, a] adj ill-fated, unlucky

negación [neɣa'θjon] nf negation;

(*rechazo*) refusal, denial

negar [ne'ɣar] *vt* (*renegar, rechazar*) to refuse; (*prohibir*) to refuse, deny; (*desmentir*) to deny; **negarse** *vr*: ~**se a** to refuse to

negativa [neɣa'tiβa] *nf* negative; (*rechazo*) refusal, denial

negativo, -a [neɣa'tiβo, a] *adj, nm* negative

negociante [neɣo'θjante] *nmf* businessman/woman

negociar [neɣo'θjar] *vt, vi* to negotiate; ~ **en** to deal *o* trade in

negocio [ne'ɣoθjo] *nm* (*Com*) business; (*asunto*) affair, business; (*operación comercial*) deal, transaction; (*lugar*) place of business; **los ~s** business *sg*; **hacer ~** to do business

negra ['neɣra] *nf* (*Mús*) crotchet; V *tb* **negro**

negro, -a ['neɣro, a] *adj* black; (*suerte*) awful ▷ *nm* black ▷ *nm/f* black man/ woman

nene, -a ['nene, a] *nm/f* baby, small child

neón [ne'on] *nm*: **luces/lámpara de ~** neon lights/lamp

neoyorquino, -a [neojor'kino, a] *adj* (of) New York

nervio ['nerβjo] *nm* nerve; **nerviosismo** *nm* nervousness, nerves *pl*; **nervioso, -a** *adj* nervous

neto, -a ['neto, a] *adj* net

neumático, -a [neu'matiko, a] *adj* pneumatic ▷ *nm* (*ESP*) tyre (*BRIT*), tire (*US*); **neumático de recambio** spare tyre

neurólogo, -a [neu'roloɣo, a] *nm/f* neurologist

neurona [neu'rona] *nf* nerve cell

neutral [neu'tral] *adj* neutral; **neutralizar** *vt* to neutralize; (*contrarrestar*) to counteract

neutro, -a ['neutro, a] *adj* (*Bio, Ling*) neuter

neutrón [neu'tron] *nm* neutron

nevada [ne'βaða] *nf* snowstorm; (*caída de nieve*) snowfall

nevar [ne'βar] *vi* to snow

nevera [ne'βera] (*ESP*) *nf* refrigerator (*BRIT*), icebox (*US*)

nevería [neβe'ria] (*MÉX*) *nf* ice-cream parlour

nexo ['nekso] *nm* link, connection

ni [ni] *conj* nor, neither; (*tb*: ~ **siquiera**) not ... even; ~ **aunque** even if; ~ **blanco** ~ **negro** neither white nor black

Nicaragua [nika'raɣwa] *nf* Nicaragua; **nicaragüense** *adj, nmf* Nicaraguan

nicho ['nitʃo] *nm* niche

nicotina [niko'tina] *nf* nicotine

nido ['niðo] *nm* nest

niebla ['njeβla] *nf* fog; (*neblina*) mist

niego *etc vb* V **negar**

nieto, -a ['njeto, a] *nm/f* grandson/ daughter; **nietos** *nmpl* grandchildren

nieve *etc* ['njeβe] *vb* V **nevar** ▷ *nf* snow; (*MÉX: helado*) ice cream

NIF *nm abr* (= *Número de Identificación Fiscal*) *personal identification number used for financial and tax purposes*

ninfa ['ninfa] *nf* nymph

ningún *adj* V **ninguno**

ninguno, -a [nin'guno, a] (*adj* **ningún**) no ▷ *pron* (*nadie*) nobody; (*ni uno*) none, not one; (*ni uno ni otro*) neither; **de ninguna manera** by no means, not at all

niña ['niɲa] *nf* (*Anat*) pupil; V *tb* **niño**

niñera [ni'ɲera] *nf* nursemaid, nanny

niñez [ni'ɲeθ] *nf* childhood; (*infancia*) infancy

niño, -a ['niɲo, a] *adj* (*joven*) young; (*inmaduro*) immature ▷ *nm/f* child, boy/girl

nipón, -ona [ni'pon, ona] *adj, nm/f* Japanese

níquel ['nikel] *nm* nickel

níspero ['nispero] *nm* medlar

nítido, -a ['nitiðo, a] *adj* clear; sharp

nitrato [ni'trato] *nm* nitrate

nitrógeno [ni'troxeno] *nm* nitrogen

nivel [ni'βel] *nm* (*Geo*) level; (*norma*) level, standard; (*altura*) height; **nivel de aceite** oil level; **nivel de aire** spirit level; **nivel de vida** standard of living; **nivelar** *vt* to level out; (*fig*) to even up; (*Com*) to balance

no [no] *adv* no; not; (*con verbo*) not ▷ *excl* no!; ~ **tengo nada** I don't have anything, I have nothing; ~ **es el mío** it's not mine; **ahora ~** not now; **¿~ lo sabes?** don't you know?; ~ **mucho** not much; ~ **bien termine, lo entregaré** as soon as I finish, I'll hand it over; ~ **más: ayer ~ más** just yesterday; **¡pase ~ más!** come in!; **¡a que ~ lo sabes!** I bet you don't know!; **¡cómo ~!** of course!; **la ~ intervención** non-intervention

noble ['noβle] *adj, nmf* noble; **nobleza** *nf* nobility

noche ['notʃe] *nf* night, night-time; (*la tarde*) evening; **de ~, por la ~** at night; **es de ~** it's dark; **Noche de San Juan** *see below*

● **NOCHE DE SAN JUAN**

● The **Noche de San Juan** on the 24th June
● is a **fiesta** coinciding with the summer
● solstice and which has taken the
● place of other ancient pagan festivals.
● Traditionally fire plays a major part in
● these festivities with celebrations and
● dancing taking place around bonfires
● in towns and villages across the country.

nochebuena [notʃe'βwena] nf Christmas Eve

nochevieja [notʃe'βjexa] nf New Year's Eve

nocivo, -a [no'θiβo, a] adj harmful

noctámbulo, -a [nok'tambulo, a] nm/f sleepwalker

nocturno, -a [nok'turno, a] adj (de la noche) nocturnal, night cpd; (de la tarde) evening cpd ▷ nm nocturne

nogal [no'ɣal] nm walnut tree

nómada ['nomaða] adj nomadic ▷ nmf nomad

nombrar [nom'brar] vt (designar) to name; (mencionar) to mention; (dar puesto a) to appoint

nombre ['nombre] nm name; (sustantivo) noun; **~ y apellidos** name in full; **poner ~ a** to call, name; **nombre común/propio** common/proper noun; **nombre de pila/de soltera** Christian/maiden name

nómina ['nomina] nf (lista) payroll; (hoja) payslip

nominal [nomi'nal] adj nominal

nominar [nomi'nar] vt to nominate

nominativo, -a [nomina'tiβo, a] adj (Com): **cheque ~ a X** cheque made out to X

nordeste [nor'ðeste] adj north-east, north-eastern, north-easterly ▷ nm north-east

nórdico, -a ['norðiko, a] adj Nordic

noreste [no'reste] adj, nm = **nordeste**

noria ['norja] nf (Agr) waterwheel; (de carnaval) big (BRIT) o Ferris (US) wheel

norma ['norma] nf rule (of thumb)

normal [nor'mal] adj (corriente) normal; (habitual) usual, natural; **normalizarse** vr to return to normal; **normalmente** adv normally

normativa [norma'tiβa] nf (set of) rules pl, regulations pl

noroeste [noro'este] adj north-west, north-western, north-westerly ▷ nm north-west

norte ['norte] adj north, northern, northerly ▷ nm north; (fig) guide

norteamericano, -a [norteameri'kano, a] adj, nm/f (North) American

Noruega [no'rweɣa] nf Norway

noruego, -a [no'rweɣo, a] adj, nm/f Norwegian

nos [nos] pron (directo) us; (indirecto) us; to us; for us; from us; (reflexivo) (to) ourselves; (recíproco) (to) each other; **~ levantamos a las 7** we get up at 7

nosotros, -as [no'sotros, as] pron (sujeto) we; (después de prep) us

nostalgia [nos'talxja] nf nostalgia

nota ['nota] nf note; (Escol) mark

notable [no'taβle] adj notable; (Escol) outstanding

notar [no'tar] vt to notice, note; **notarse** vr to be obvious; **se nota que ...** one observes that ...

notario [no'tarjo] nm notary

noticia [no'tiθja] nf (información) piece of news; **las ~s** the news sg; **tener ~s de algn** to hear from sb

▌ No confundir **noticia** con la palabra inglesa notice.

noticiero [noti'θjero] (LAM) nm news bulletin

notificar [notifi'kar] vt to notify, inform

notorio, -a [no'torjo, a] adj (público) well-known; (evidente) obvious

novato, -a [no'βato, a] adj inexperienced ▷ nm/f beginner, novice

novecientos, -as [noβe'θjentos, as] num nine hundred

novedad [noβe'ðað] nf (calidad de nuevo) newness; (noticia) piece of news; (cambio) change, (new) development

novel [no'βel] adj new; (inexperto) inexperienced ▷ nmf beginner

novela [no'βela] nf novel

noveno, -a [no'βeno, a] adj ninth

noventa [no'βenta] num ninety

novia nf V **novio**

novicio, -a [no'βiθjo, a] nm/f novice

noviembre [no'βjembre] nm November

novillada [noβi'ʎaða] nf (Taur) bullfight with young bulls; **novillero** nm novice bullfighter; **novillo** nm young bull, bullock; **hacer novillos** (fam) to play truant

novio, -a [no'βjo, a] nm/f boyfriend/girlfriend; (prometido) fiancé/fiancée; (recién casado) bridegroom/bride; **los ~s** the newly-weds

nube ['nuβe] nf cloud

nublado, -a [nu'βlaðo, a] adj cloudy; **nublarse** vr to grow dark

nubosidad [nuβosi'ðað] nf cloudiness;

había mucha ~ it was very cloudy
nuca ['nuka] *nf* nape of the neck
nuclear [nukle'ar] *adj* nuclear
núcleo ['nukleo] *nm* (*centro*) core; (*Física*) nucleus; **núcleo urbano** city centre
nudillo [nu'ðiʎo] *nm* knuckle
nudista [nu'ðista] *adj* nudist
nudo ['nuðo] *nm* knot; (*de carreteras*) junction
nuera ['nwera] *nf* daughter-in-law
nuestro, -a ['nwestro, a] *adj pos* our ▷ *pron* ours; **~ padre** our father; **un amigo ~** a friend of ours; **es el ~** it's ours
Nueva York [-jɔrk] *n* New York
Nueva Zelanda [-θe'landa] *nf* New Zealand
nueve ['nweβe] *num* nine
nuevo, -a ['nweβo, a] *adj* (*gen*) new; **de ~** again
nuez [nweθ] *nf* walnut; (*Anat*) Adam's apple; **nuez moscada** nutmeg
nulo, -a ['nulo, a] *adj* (*inepto, torpe*) useless; (*inválido*) (null and) void; (*Deporte*) drawn, tied
núm. *abr* (= *número*) no.
numerar [nume'rar] *vt* to number
número ['numero] *nm* (*gen*) number; (*tamaño: de zapato*) size; (*ejemplar: de diario*) number, issue; **sin ~** numberless, unnumbered; **número atrasado** back number; **número de matrícula/teléfono** registration/telephone number; **número impar/par** odd/even number; **número romano** Roman numeral
numeroso, -a [nume'roso, a] *adj* numerous
nunca ['nunka] *adv* (*jamás*) never; **~ lo pensé** I never thought it; **no viene ~** he never comes; **~ más** never again; **más que ~** more than ever
nupcias ['nupθjas] *nfpl* wedding *sg*, nuptials
nutria ['nutrja] *nf* otter
nutrición [nutri'θjon] *nf* nutrition
nutrir [nu'trir] *vt* (*alimentar*) to nourish; (*dar de comer*) to feed; (*fig*) to strengthen; **nutritivo, -a** *adj* nourishing, nutritious
nylon [ni'lon] *nm* nylon

ñango, -a ['ɲango, a] (*MÉX*) *adj* puny
ñapa ['ɲapa] (*LAM*) *nf* extra
ñata ['ɲata] (*LAM: fam*) *nf* nose; V tb **ñato**
ñato, -a ['ɲato, a] (*LAM*) *adj* snub-nosed
ñoñería [ɲoɲe'ria] *nf* insipidness
ñoño, -a ['ɲoɲo, a] *adj* (*fam: tonto*) silly, stupid; (*soso*) insipid; (*persona*) spineless; (*ESP: película, novela*) sentimental

ñ

O

O *abr* (= *oeste*) W

o [o] *conj* or

oasis [o'asis] *nm inv* oasis

obcecarse [oβθe'karse] *vr* to get o become stubborn

obedecer [oβeðe'θer] *vt* to obey; **obediente** *adj* obedient

obertura [oβer'tura] *nf* overture

obeso, -a [o'βeso, a] *adj* obese

obispo [o'βispo] *nm* bishop

obituario [oβɪ'twarjo] (*LAM*) *nm* obituary

objetar [oβxe'tar] *vt*, *vi* to object

objetivo, -a [oβxe'tiβo, a] *adj*, *nm* objective

objeto [oβ'xeto] *nm* (*cosa*) object; (*fin*) aim

objetor, a [oβxe'tor, a] *nm/f* objector

obligación [oβliɣa'θjon] *nf* obligation; (*Com*) bond

obligar [oβli'ɣar] *vt* to force; **obligarse** *vr* to bind o.s.; **obligatorio, -a** *adj* compulsory, obligatory

oboe [o'βoe] *nm* oboe

obra ['oβra] *nf* work; (*Arq*) construction, building; (*Teatro*) play; **por ~ de** thanks to · (the efforts of); **obra maestra** masterpiece; **obras públicas** public works; **obrar** *vt* to work; (*tener efecto*) to have an effect on ▷ *vi* to act, behave; (*tener efecto*) to have an effect; **la carta obra en su poder** the letter is in his/her possession

obrero, -a [o'βrero, a] *adj* (*clase*) working; (*movimiento*) labour *cpd* ▷ *nm/f* (*gen*) worker; (*sin oficio*) labourer

obsceno, -a [oβs'θeno, a] *adj* obscene

obscu... = **oscu...**

obsequiar [oβse'kjar] *vt* (*ofrecer*) to present with; (*agasajar*) to make a fuss of, lavish attention on; **obsequio** *nm* (*regalo*) gift; (*cortesía*) courtesy, attention

observación [oβserβa'θjon] *nf* observation; (*reflexión*) remark

observador, a [oβserβa'ðor, a] *nm/f* observer

observar [oβser'βar] *vt* to observe; (*anotar*) to notice; **observarse** *vr* to keep to, observe

obsesión [oβse'sjon] *nf* obsession; **obsesivo, -a** *adj* obsessive

obstáculo [oβs'takulo] *nm* obstacle; (*impedimento*) hindrance, drawback

obstante [oβs'tante]: **no ~** *adv* nevertheless

obstinado, -a [oβsti'naðo, a] *adj* obstinate, stubborn

obstinarse [oβsti'narse] *vr* to be obstinate; **~ en** to persist in

obstruir [oβstru'ir] *vt* to obstruct

obtener [oβte'ner] *vt* (*gen*) to obtain; (*premio*) to win

obturador [oβtura'ðor] *nm* (*Foto*) shutter

obvio, -a ['oββjo, a] *adj* obvious

oca ['oka] *nf* (*animal*) goose; (*juego*) ≈ snakes and ladders

ocasión [oka'sjon] *nf* (*oportunidad*) opportunity, chance; (*momento*) occasion, time; (*causa*) cause; **de ~** secondhand; **ocasionar** *vt* to cause

ocaso [o'kaso] *nm* (*fig*) decline

occidente [okθi'ðente] *nm* west

OCDE *nf abr* (= *Organización de Cooperación y Desarrollo Económico*) OECD

océano [o'θeano] *nm* ocean; **Océano Índico** Indian Ocean

ochenta [o'tʃenta] *num* eighty

ocho ['otʃo] *num* eight; **dentro de ~ días** within a week

ocio ['oθjo] *nm* (*tiempo*) leisure; (*pey*) idleness

octavilla [okta'viʎa] *nf* leaflet, pamphlet

octavo, -a [ok'taβo, a] *adj* eighth

octubre [ok'tuβre] *nm* October

oculista [oku'lista] *nmf* oculist

ocultar [okul'tar] *vt* (*esconder*) to hide; (*callar*) to conceal; **oculto, -a** *adj* hidden; (*fig*) secret

ocupación [okupa'θjon] *nf* occupation

ocupado, -a [oku'paðo, a] *adj* (*persona*) busy; (*plaza*) occupied, taken; (*teléfono*) engaged; **ocupar** *vt* (*gen*) to occupy; **ocuparse** *vr*: **ocuparse de** o **en** (*gen*) to concern o.s. with; (*cuidar*) to look after

ocurrencia [oku'rrenθja] *nf* (*idea*) bright idea

ocurrir [oku'rrir] *vi* to happen; **ocurrirse** *vr*: **se me ocurrió que ...** it occurred to me that ...

odiar [o'ðjar] *vt* to hate; **odio** *nm* hate, hatred; **odioso, -a** *adj* (*gen*) hateful; (*malo*) nasty

odontólogo, -a [oðon'toloxo, a] *nm/f* dentist, dental surgeon

oeste [o'este] *nm* west; **una película del ~** a western

ofender [ofen'der] *vt* (*agraviar*) to offend; (*insultar*) to insult; **ofenderse** *vr* to take offence; **ofensa** *nf* offence; **ofensiva** *nf* offensive; **ofensivo, -a** *adj* offensive

oferta [o'ferta] *nf* offer; (*propuesta*) proposal; **la ~ y la demanda** supply and demand; **artículos en ~** goods on offer

oficial [ofi'θjal] *adj* official ▷ *nm* (*Mil*) officer

oficina [ofi'θina] *nf* office; **oficina de correos** post office; **oficina de información** information bureau; **oficina de turismo** tourist office; **oficinista** *nmf* clerk

oficio [o'fiθjo] *nm* (*profesión*) profession; (*puesto*) post; (*Rel*) service; **ser del ~** to be an old hand; **tener mucho ~** to have a lot of experience; **oficio de difuntos** funeral service

ofimática [ofi'matika] *nf* office automation

ofrecer [ofre'θer] *vt* (*dar*) to offer; (*proponer*) to propose; **ofrecerse** *vr* (*persona*) to offer o.s., volunteer; (*situación*) to present itself; **¿qué se le ofrece?, ¿se le ofrece algo?** what can I do for you?, can I get you anything?

ofrecimiento [ofreθi'mjento] *nm* offer

oftalmólogo, -a [oftal'moloxo, a] *nm/f* ophthalmologist

oída [o'iða] *nf*: **de ~s** by hearsay

oído [o'iðo] *nm* (*Anat*) ear; (*sentido*) hearing

oigo *etc vb* ∨ **oír**

oír [o'ir] *vt* (*gen*) to hear; (*atender a*) to listen to; **¡oiga!** listen!; **~ misa** to attend mass

OIT *nf abr* (= *Organización Internacional del Trabajo*) ILO

ojal [o'xal] *nm* buttonhole

ojalá [oxa'la] *excl* if only (it were so)!, some hope! ▷ *conj* if only ...!, would that ...!; **~ (que) venga hoy** I hope he comes today

ojeada [oxe'aða] *nf* glance

ojera [o'xera] *nf*: **tener ~s** to have bags under one's eyes

ojo ['oxo] *nm* eye; (*de puente*) span; (*de cerradura*) keyhole ▷ *excl* careful!; **tener ~ para** to have an eye for; **ojo de buey** porthole

okey ['okei] (*LAM*) *excl* O.K.

okupa [o'kupa] (*ESP: fam*) *nmf* squatter

ola ['ola] *nf* wave

olé [o'le] *excl* bravo!, olé!

oleada [ole'aða] *nf* big wave, swell; (*fig*) wave

oleaje [ole'axe] *nm* swell

óleo ['oleo] *nm* oil; **oleoducto** *nm* (oil) pipeline

oler [o'ler] *vt* (*gen*) to smell; (*inquirir*) to pry into; (*fig: sospechar*) to sniff out ▷ *vi* to smell; **~ a** to smell of

olfatear [olfate'ar] *vt* to smell; (*inquirir*) to pry into; **olfato** *nm* sense of smell

olimpiada [olim'piaða] *nf*: **las O~s** the Olympics; **olímpico, -a** [o'limpiko, a] *adj* Olympic

oliva [o'liβa] *nf* (*aceituna*) olive; **aceite de ~** olive oil; **olivo** *nm* olive tree

olla ['oʎa] *nf* pan; (*comida*) stew; **olla exprés** *o* **a presión** (*ESP*) pressure cooker; **olla podrida** *type of Spanish stew*

olmo ['olmo] *nm* elm (tree)

olor [o'lor] *nm* smell; **oloroso, -a** *adj* scented

olvidar [olβi'ðar] *vt* to forget; (*omitir*) to omit; **olvidarse** *vr* (*fig*) to forget o.s.; **se me olvidó** I forgot

olvido [ol'βiðo] *nm* oblivion; (*despiste*) forgetfulness

ombligo [om'blixo] *nm* navel

omelette [ome'lete] (*LAM*) *nf* omelet(te)

omisión [omi'sjon] *nf* (*abstención*) omission; (*descuido*) neglect

omiso, -a [o'miso, a] *adj*: **hacer caso ~ de** to ignore, pass over

omitir [omi'tir] *vt* to omit

omnipotente [omnipo'tente] *adj* omnipotent

omóplato [o'moplato] *nm* shoulder blade

OMS *nf abr* (= *Organización Mundial de la Salud*) WHO

once ['onθe] *num* eleven; **onces** (*CS*) *nfpl* tea break *sg*

onda ['onda] *nf* wave; **onda corta/larga/media** short/long/medium wave; **ondear** *vt, vi* to wave; (*tener ondas*) to be wavy; (*agua*) to ripple

ondulación [ondula'θjon] *nf* undulation; **ondulado, -a** *adj* wavy

ONG *nf abr* (= *organización no gubernamental*) NGO

ONU ['onu] *nf abr* (= *Organización de las Naciones Unidas*) UNO

opaco, -a [o'pako, a] *adj* opaque

opción [op'θjon] *nf* (*gen*) option; (*derecho*) right, option

OPEP ['opep] *nf abr* (= *Organización de Países Exportadores de Petróleo*) OPEC

ópera ['opera] *nf* opera; **ópera bufa** *o* **cómica** comic opera

operación [opera'θjon] *nf* (*gen*) operation; (*Com*) transaction, deal

operador, a [opera'ðor, a] *nm/f* operator; (*Cine: de proyección*) projectionist; (*: de rodaje*) cameraman

operar [ope'rar] *vt* (*producir*) to produce, bring about; (*Med*) to operate on ▷ *vi* (*Com*) to operate, deal; **operarse** *vr* to occur; (*Med*) to have an operation

opereta [ope'reta] *nf* operetta

opinar [opi'nar] *vt* to think ▷ *vi* to give one's opinion; **opinión** *nf* (*creencia*) belief; (*criterio*) opinion

opio ['opjo] *nm* opium

oponer [opo'ner] *vt* (*resistencia*) to put up, offer; **oponerse** *vr* (*objetar*) to object; (*estar frente a frente*) to be opposed; (*dos personas*) to oppose each other; **~ A a B** to set A against B; **me opongo a pensar que ...** I refuse to believe o think that ...

oportunidad [oportuni'ðað] *nf* (*ocasión*) opportunity; (*posibilidad*) chance

oportuno, -a [opor'tuno, a] *adj* (*en su tiempo*) opportune, timely; (*respuesta*) suitable; **en el momento ~** at the right moment

oposición [oposi'θjon] *nf* opposition; **oposiciones** *nfpl* (*Escol*) public examinations

opositor, a [oposi'tor, a] *nm/f* (*adversario*) opponent; (*candidato*): **~ (a)** candidate (for)

opresión [opre'sjon] *nf* oppression; **opresor, a** *nm/f* oppressor

oprimir [opri'mir] *vt* to squeeze; (*fig*) to oppress

optar [op'tar] *vi* (*elegir*) to choose; **~ por** to opt for; **optativo, -a** *adj* optional

óptico, -a ['optiko, a] *adj* optic(al) ▷ *nm/f* optician; **óptica** *nf* optician's (shop); **desde esta óptica** from this point of view

optimismo [opti'mismo] *nm* optimism; **optimista** *nmf* optimist

opuesto, -a [o'pwesto, a] *adj* (*contrario*) opposite; (*antagónico*) opposing

oración [ora'θjon] *nf* (*Rel*) prayer; (*Ling*) sentence

orador, a [ora'ðor, a] *nm/f* (*conferenciante*) speaker, orator

oral [o'ral] *adj* oral

orangután [orangu'tan] *nm* orangutan

orar [o'rar] *vi* to pray

oratoria [ora'torja] *nf* oratory

órbita ['orβita] *nf* orbit

orden ['orðen] *nm* (*gen*) order ▷ *nf* (*gen*) order; (*Inform*) command; **en ~ de prioridad** in order of priority; **orden del día** agenda

ordenado, -a [orðe'naðo, a] *adj* (*metódico*) methodical; (*arreglado*) orderly

ordenador [orðena'ðor] *nm* computer; **ordenador central** mainframe computer

ordenar [orðe'nar] *vt* (*mandar*) to order; (*poner orden*) to put in order, arrange;

ordenarse *vr* (*Rel*) to be ordained

ordeñar [orðe'ɲar] *vt* to milk

ordinario, -a [orði'narjo, a] *adj* (*común*) ordinary, usual; (*vulgar*) vulgar, common

orégano [o'reɣano] *nm* oregano

oreja [o'rexa] *nf* ear; (*Mecánica*) lug, flange

orfanato [orfa'nato] *nm* orphanage

orfebrería [orfeβre'ria] *nf* gold/silver work

orgánico, -a [or'ɣaniko, a] *adj* organic

organismo [orɣa'nismo] *nm* (*Bio*) organism; (*Pol*) organization

organización [orɣaniθa'θjon] *nf* organization; **organizar** *vt* to organize

órgano ['orɣano] *nm* organ

orgasmo [or'ɣasmo] *nm* orgasm

orgía [or'xia] *nf* orgy

orgullo [or'ɣuʎo] *nm* pride; **orgulloso, -a** *adj* (*gen*) proud; (*altanero*) haughty

orientación [orjenta'θjon] *nf* (*posición*) position; (*dirección*) direction

oriental [orjen'tal] *adj* eastern; (*del Extremo Oriente*) oriental

orientar [orjen'tar] *vt* (*situar*) to orientate; (*señalar*) to point; (*dirigir*) to direct; (*guiar*) to guide; **orientarse** *vr* to get one's bearings

oriente [o'rjente] *nm* east; **el O~ Medio** the Middle East; **el Próximo/Extremo O~** the Near/Far East

origen [o'rixen] *nm* origin

original [orixi'nal] *adj* (*nuevo*) original; (*extraño*) odd, strange; **originalidad** *nf* originality

originar [orixi'nar] *vt* to start, cause; **originarse** *vr* to originate; **originario, -a** *adj* original; **originario de** native of

orilla [o'riʎa] *nf* (*borde*) border; (*de río*) bank; (*de bosque, tela*) edge; (*de mar*) shore

orina [o'rina] *nf* urine; **orinal** *nm* (*chamber*) pot; **orinar** *vi* to urinate; **orinarse** *vr* to wet o.s.

oro ['oro] *nm* gold; **oros** *nmpl* (*Naipes*) hearts

orquesta [or'kesta] *nf* orchestra; **orquesta sinfónica** symphony orchestra

orquídea [or'kiðea] *nf* orchid

ortiga [or'tiɣa] *nf* nettle

ortodoxo, -a [orto'ðokso, a] *adj* orthodox

ortografía [ortoɣra'fia] *nf* spelling

ortopedia [orto'peðja] *nf* orthopaedics *sg*; **ortopédico, -a** *adj* orthopaedic

oruga [o'ruɣa] *nf* caterpillar

orzuelo [or'θwelo] *nm* stye

os [os] *pron* (*gen*) you; (*a vosotros*) to you

osa ['osa] *nf* (she-)bear; **Osa Mayor/Menor** Great/Little Bear

osadía [osa'ðia] nf daring
osar [o'sar] vi to dare
oscilación [osθila'θjon] nf (movimiento) oscillation; (fluctuación) fluctuation
oscilar [osθi'lar] vi to oscillate; to fluctuate
oscurecer [oskure'θer] vt to darken ▷ vi to grow dark; **oscurecerse** vr to grow o get dark
oscuridad [oskuri'ðað] nf obscurity; (tinieblas) darkness
oscuro, -a [os'kuro, a] adj dark; (fig) obscure; **a oscuras** in the dark
óseo, -a ['oseo, a] adj bone cpd
oso ['oso] nm bear; **oso de peluche** teddy bear; **oso hormiguero** anteater
ostentar [osten'tar] vt (gen) to show; (pey) to flaunt, show off; (poseer) to have, possess
ostión [os'tjon] (MÉX) nm = **ostra**
ostra ['ostra] nf oyster
OTAN ['otan] nf abr (= Organización del Tratado del Atlántico Norte) NATO
otitis [o'titis] nf earache
otoñal [oto'ɲal] adj autumnal
otoño [o'toɲo] nm autumn
otorgar [otor'ɣar] vt (conceder) to concede; (dar) to grant
otorrino, -a [oto'rrino, a], **otorrinolaringólogo, -a** [otorrinolarin'goloɣo, a] nm/f ear, nose and throat specialist

○ PALABRA CLAVE

otro, -a ['otro, a] adj **1** (distinto: sg) another; (: pl) other; **con otros amigos** with other o different friends
2 (adicional): **tráigame otro café (más), por favor** can I have another coffee please; **otros diez días más** another ten days
▷ pron **1** **el otro** the other one; **(los) otros** (the) others; **de otro** somebody else's; **que lo haga otro** let somebody else do it
2 (recíproco): **se odian (la) una a (la) otra** they hate one another o each other
3: **otro tanto: comer otro tanto** to eat the same o as much again; **recibió una decena de telegramas y otras tantas llamadas** he got about ten telegrams and as many calls

ovación [oβa'θjon] nf ovation
oval [o'βal] adj oval; **ovalado, -a** adj oval; **óvalo** nm oval
ovario [o'βarjo] nm ovary
oveja [o'βexa] nf sheep
overol [oβe'rol] (LAM) nm overalls pl
ovillo [o'βiʎo] nm (de lana) ball of wool
OVNI ['oβni] nm abr (= objeto volante no identificado) UFO
ovulación [oβula'θjon] nf ovulation; **óvulo** nm ovum
oxidación [oksiða'θjon] nf rusting
oxidar [oksi'ðar] vt to rust; **oxidarse** vr to go rusty
óxido ['oksiðo] nm oxide
oxigenado, -a [oksixe'naðo, a] adj (Quím) oxygenated; (pelo) bleached
oxígeno [ok'sixeno] nm oxygen
oyente [o'jente] nmf listener
oyes etc vb V **oír**
ozono [o'θono] nm ozone

P

pabellón [paβe'ʎon] nm bell tent; (Arq) pavilion; (de hospital etc) block, section; (bandera) flag

pacer [pa'θer] vi to graze

paciencia [pa'θjenθja] nf patience

paciente [pa'θjente] adj, nmf patient

pacificación [paθifika'θjon] nf pacification

pacífico, -a [pa'θifiko, a] adj (persona) peaceable; (existencia) peaceful; **el (Océano) P~** the Pacific (Ocean)

pacifista [paθi'fista] nmf pacifist

pacotilla [pako'tiʎa] nf: **de ~** (actor, escritor) third-rate

pactar [pak'tar] vt to agree to o on ▷ vi to come to an agreement

pacto ['pakto] nm (tratado) pact; (acuerdo) agreement

padecer [paðe'θer] vt (sufrir) to suffer; (soportar) to endure, put up with; **padecimiento** nm suffering

padrastro [pa'ðrastro] nm stepfather

padre ['paðre] nm father ▷ adj (fam): **un éxito ~** a tremendous success; **padres** nmpl parents; **padre político** father-in-law

padrino [pa'ðrino] nm (Rel) godfather; (tb: **~ de boda**) best man; (fig) sponsor, patron; **padrinos** nmpl godparents

padrón [pa'ðron] nm (censo) census, roll

padrote [pa'ðrote] (MÉX: fam) nm pimp

paella [pa'eʎa] nf paella, dish of rice with meat, shellfish etc

paga ['paɣa] nf (pago) payment; (sueldo) pay, wages pl

pagano, -a [pa'ɣano, a] adj, nm/f pagan, heathen

pagar [pa'ɣar] vt to pay; (las compras, crimen) to pay for; (fig: favor) to repay ▷ vi to pay; **~ al contado/a plazos** to pay (in) cash/in instalments

pagaré [paɣa're] nm I.O.U.

página ['paxina] nf page; **página de inicio** (Inform) home page; **página web** (Inform) web page

pago ['paɣo] nm (dinero) payment; **en ~ de** in return for; **pago anticipado/a cuenta/contra reembolso/en especie** advance payment/payment on account/cash on delivery/payment in kind

pág(s). abr (= página(s)) p(p).

pague etc vb V **pagar**

país [pa'is] nm (gen) country; (región) land; **los P~es Bajos** the Low Countries; **el P~ Vasco** the Basque Country

paisaje [pai'saxe] nm landscape, scenery

paisano, -a [pai'sano, a] adj of the same country ▷ nm/f (compatriota) fellow countryman/woman; **vestir de ~** (soldado) to be in civvies; (guardia) to be in plain clothes

paja ['paxa] nf straw; (fig) rubbish (BRIT), trash (US)

pajarita [paxa'rita] nf (corbata) bow tie

pájaro ['paxaro] nm bird; **pájaro carpintero** woodpecker

pajita [pa'xita] nf (drinking) straw

pala ['pala] nf spade, shovel; (raqueta etc) bat; (: de tenis) racquet; (Culin) slice; **pala mecánica** power shovel

palabra [pa'laβra] nf word; (facultad) (power of) speech; (derecho de hablar) right to speak; **tomar la ~** (en mitin) to take the floor

palabrota [pala'brota] nf swearword

palacio [pa'laθjo] nm palace; (mansión) mansion, large house; **palacio de justicia** courthouse; **palacio municipal** town o city hall

paladar [pala'ðar] nm palate; **paladear** vt to taste

palanca [pa'lanka] nf lever; (fig) pull, influence

palangana [palan'gana] nf washbasin

palco ['palko] nm box

Palestina [pales'tina] nf Palestine; **palestino, -a** nm/f Palestinian

paleta [pa'leta] nf (de pintor) palette; (de albañil) trowel; (de ping-pong) bat; (MÉX, CAM: helado) ice lolly (BRIT), Popsicle® (US)

palidecer [paliðe'θer] vi to turn pale; **palidez** nf paleness; **pálido, -a** adj pale

palillo [pa'liʎo] nm (mondadientes) toothpick; (para comer) chopstick

palito [pa'lito] (RPL) nm (helado) ice lolly (BRIT), Popsicle® (US)

paliza [pa'liθa] nf beating, thrashing

palma ['palma] nf (Anat) palm; (árbol) palm tree; **batir o dar ~s** to clap, applaud; **palmada** nf slap; **palmadas** nfpl clapping *sg*, applause *sg*

palmar [pal'mar] *(fam)* *vi* *(tb:* **~la)** to die, kick the bucket

palmear [palme'ar] *vi* to clap

palmera [pal'mera] *nf* *(Bot)* palm tree

palmo ['palmo] *nm* *(medida)* span; *(fig)* small amount; **~ a ~** inch by inch

palo ['palo] *nm* stick; *(poste)* post; *(de tienda de campaña)* pole; *(mango)* handle, shaft; *(golpe)* blow, hit; *(de golf)* club; *(de béisbol)* bat; *(Náut)* mast; *(Naipes)* suit

paloma [pa'loma] *nf* dove, pigeon

palomitas [palo'mitas] *nfpl* popcorn *sg*

palpar [pal'par] *vt* to touch, feel

palpitar [palpi'tar] *vi* to palpitate; *(latir)* to beat

palta ['palta] *(cs)* *nf* avocado

paludismo [palu'ðismo] *nm* malaria

pamela [pa'mela] *nf* picture hat, sun hat

pampa ['pampa] *nf* pampas, prairie

pan [pan] *nm* bread; *(una barra)* loaf; **pan integral** wholemeal *(BRIT)* o wholewheat *(US)* bread; **pan rallado** breadcrumbs *pl*; **pan tostado** *(MÉX: tostada)* toast

pana ['pana] *nf* corduroy

panadería [panaðe'ria] *nf* baker's (shop); **panadero, -a** *nm/f* baker

Panamá [pana'ma] *nm* Panama; **panameño, -a** *adj* Panamanian

pancarta [pan'karta] *nf* placard, banner

panceta [pan'θeta] *(ESP, RPL)* *nf* bacon

pancho ['pantʃo] *(RPL)* *nm* hot dog

pancito [pan'θito] *nm* (bread) roll

panda ['panda] *nm* *(Zool)* panda

pandereta [pande'reta] *nf* tambourine

pandilla [pan'diʎa] *nf* set, group; *(de criminales)* gang; *(pey: camarilla)* clique

panecillo [pane'θiʎo] *(ESP)* *nm* (bread) roll

panel [pa'nel] *nm* panel; **panel solar** solar panel

panfleto [pan'fleto] *nm* pamphlet

pánico ['paniko] *nm* panic

panorama [pano'rama] *nm* panorama; *(vista)* view

panqueque [pan'keke] *(LAM)* *nm* pancake

pantalla [pan'taʎa] *nf* *(de cine)* screen; *(de lámpara)* lampshade

pantalón [panta'lon] *nm* trousers; **pantalones** *nmpl* trousers; **pantalones cortes** shorts

pantano [pan'tano] *nm* *(ciénaga)* marsh, swamp; *(depósito: de agua)* reservoir; *(fig)* jam, difficulty

panteón [pante'on] *nm* *(monumento)* pantheon

pantera [pan'tera] *nf* panther

pantimedias [panti'meðjas] *(MÉX)* *nfpl*

= **pantis**

pantis ['pantis] *nmpl* tights *(BRIT)*, pantyhose *(US)*

pantomima [panto'mima] *nf* pantomime

pantorrilla [panto'rriʎa] *nf* calf (of the leg)

pants [pants] *(MÉX)* *nmpl* tracksuit *(BRIT)*, sweat suit *(US)*

pantufla [pan'tufla] *nf* slipper

panty(s) ['panti(s)] *nm(pl)* tights *(BRIT)*, pantyhose *(US)*

panza ['panθa] *nf* belly, paunch

pañal [pa'ɲal] *nm* nappy *(BRIT)*, diaper *(US)*; **pañales** *nmpl* *(fig)* early stages, infancy *sg*

paño ['paɲo] *nm* *(tela)* cloth; *(pedazo de tela)* (piece of) cloth; *(trapo)* duster, rag; **paños menores** underclothes

pañuelo [pa'ɲwelo] *nm* handkerchief, hanky; *(fam: para la cabeza)* (head)scarf

papa ['papa] *nm:* **el P~** the Pope ▷ *nf* *(LAM: patata)* potato; **papas fritas** *(LAM)* French fries, chips *(BRIT)*; *(de bolsa)* crisps *(BRIT)*, potato chips *(US)*

papá [pa'pa] *(fam)* *nm* dad(dy), pa *(US)*

papada [pa'paða] *nf* double chin

papagayo [papa'ɣajo] *nm* parrot

papalote [papa'lote] *(MÉX, CAM)* *nm* kite

papanatas [papa'natas] *(fam)* *nm inv* simpleton

papaya [pa'paja] *nf* papaya

papear [pape'ar] *(fam)* *vt, vi* to scoff

papel [pa'pel] *nm* paper; *(hoja de papel)* sheet of paper; *(Teatro: fig)* role; **papel de aluminio** aluminium *(BRIT)* o aluminum *(US)* foil; **papel de arroz/envolver/fumar** rice/wrapping/cigarette paper; **papel de estaño** o **plata** tinfoil; **papel de lija** sandpaper; **papel higiénico** toilet paper; **papel moneda** paper money; **papel secante** blotting paper

papeleo [pape'leo] *nm* red tape

papelera [pape'lera] *nf* wastepaper basket; *(en la calle)* litter bin; **papelera (de reciclaje)** *(Inform)* wastebasket

papelería [papele'ria] *nf* stationer's (shop)

papeleta [pape'leta] *(ESP)* *nf* *(Pol)* ballot paper

paperas [pa'peras] *nfpl* mumps *sg*

papilla [pa'piʎa] *nf* *(de bebé)* baby food

paquete [pa'kete] *nm* *(de cigarrillos etc)* packet; *(Correos etc)* parcel

par [par] *adj* *(igual)* like, equal; *(Mat)* even ▷ *nm* equal; *(de guantes)* pair; *(de veces)* couple; *(Pol)* peer; *(Golf, Com)* par; **abrir de ~ en ~** to open wide

para ['para] *prep* for; **no es ~ comer** it's not for eating; **decir ~ sí** to say to o.s.; **¿~ qué lo quieres?** what do you want it for?; **se casaron ~ separarse otra vez** they married only to separate again; **lo tendré ~ mañana** I'll have it (for) tomorrow; **ir ~ casa** to go home, head for home; **~ profesor es muy estúpido** he's very stupid for a teacher; **¿quién es usted ~ gritar así?** who are you to shout like that?; **tengo bastante ~ vivir** I have enough to live on; *V tb* **con**

parabién [para'βjen] *nm* congratulations *pl*

parábola [pa'raβola] *nf* parable; (*Mat*) parabola; **parabólica** *nf* (*tb*: **antena parabólica**) satellite dish

parabrisas [para'βrisas] *nm inv* windscreen (*BRIT*), windshield (*US*)

paracaídas [paraka'iðas] *nm inv* parachute; **paracaidista** *nmf* parachutist; (*Mil*) paratrooper

parachoques [para'tʃokes] *nm inv* (*Auto*) bumper; (*Mecánica etc*) shock absorber

parada [pa'raða] *nf* stop; (*acto*) stopping; (*de industria*) shutdown, stoppage; (*lugar*) stopping place; **parada de autobús** bus stop; **parada de taxis** taxi stand *o* rank (*BRIT*)

paradero [para'ðero] *nm* stopping-place; (*situación*) whereabouts

parado, -a [pa'raðo, a] *adj* (*persona*) motionless, standing still; (*fábrica*) closed, at a standstill; (*coche*) stopped; (*LAM: de pie*) standing (up); (*ESP: sin empleo*) unemployed, idle

paradoja [para'ðoxa] *nf* paradox

parador [para'ðor] *nm* parador, state-run hotel

paragolpes [para'golpes] (*RPL*) *nm inv* (*Auto*) bumper, fender (*US*)

paraguas [pa'raɣwas] *nm inv* umbrella

Paraguay [para'ɣwai] *nm* Paraguay; **paraguayo, -a** *adj, nm/f* Paraguayan

paraíso [para'iso] *nm* paradise, heaven

paraje [pa'ɾaxe] *nm* place, spot

paralelo, -a [para'lelo, a] *adj* parallel

parálisis [pa'ralisis] *nf inv* paralysis; **paralítico, -a** *adj, nm/f* paralytic

paralizar [parali'θar] *vt* to paralyse; **paralizarse** *vr* to become paralysed; (*fig*) to come to a standstill

páramo ['paramo] *nm* bleak plateau

paranoico, -a [para'noiko, a] *nm/f* paranoiac

parapente [para'pente] *nm* (*deporte*) paragliding; (*aparato*) paraglider

parapléjico, -a [para'plexiko, a] *adj, nm/f* paraplegic

parar [pa'rar] *vt* to stop; (*golpe*) to ward off ▷ *vi* to stop; **pararse** *vr* to stop; (*LAM: ponerse de pie*) to stand up; **ha parado de llover** it has stopped raining; **van a ir a ~ a comisaría** they're going to end up in the police station; **~se en** to pay attention to

pararrayos [para'rrajos] *nm inv* lightning conductor

parásito, -a [pa'rasito, a] *nm/f* parasite

parcela [par'θela] *nf* plot, piece of ground

parche ['partʃe] *nm* (*gen*) patch

parchís [par'tʃis] *nm* ludo

parcial [par'θjal] *adj* (*pago*) part-; (*eclipse*) partial; (*Jur*) prejudiced, biased; (*Pol*) partisan

parecer [pare'θer] *nm* (*opinión*) opinion, view; (*aspecto*) looks *pl* ▷ *vi* (*tener apariencia*) to seem, look; (*asemejarse*) to look *o* seem like; (*aparecer, llegar*) to appear; **parecerse** *vr* to look alike, resemble each other; **al ~** apparently; **según parece** evidently, apparently; **~se a** to look like, resemble; **me parece que** I think (that), it seems to me that

parecido, -a [pare'θiðo, a] *adj* similar ▷ *nm* similarity, likeness, resemblance; **bien ~** good-looking, nice-looking

pared [pa'reð] *nf* wall

pareja [pa'rexa] *nf* (*par*) pair; (*dos personas*) couple; (*otro: de un par*) other one (of a pair); (*persona*) partner

parentesco [paren'tesko] *nm* relationship

paréntesis [pa'rentesis] *nm inv* parenthesis; (*en escrito*) bracket

parezco *etc vb* *V* **parecer**

pariente [pa'rjente] *nmf* relative, relation

▎No confundir **pariente** con la palabra inglesa *parent*.

parir [pa'rir] *vt* to give birth to ▷ *vi* (*mujer*) to give birth, have a baby

París [pa'ris] *n* Paris

parka ['parka] (*LAM*) *nf* anorak

parking ['parkin] *nm* car park (*BRIT*), parking lot (*US*)

parlamentar [parlamen'tar] *vi* to parley

parlamentario, -a [parlamen'tarjo, a] *adj* parliamentary ▷ *nm/f* member of parliament

parlamento [parla'mento] *nm* parliament

parlanchín, -ina [parlan'tʃin, ina] *adj* indiscreet ▷ *nm/f* chatterbox

parlar [par'lar] *vi* to chatter (away)

paro ['paro] *nm* (*huelga*) stoppage (of work), strike; (*ESP: desempleo*) unemployment; (: *subsidio*) unemployment benefit; **estar en ~** (*ESP*) to be unemployed;

paro cardíaco cardiac arrest
parodia [pa'roðja] nf parody; **parodiar**
vt to parody
parpadear [parpaðe'ar] vi (ojos) to blink;
(luz) to flicker
párpado ['parpaðo] nm eyelid
parque ['parke] nm (lugar verde) park;
(MÉX: munición) ammunition; **parque
de atracciones** fairground; **parque de
bomberos** (ESP) fire station; **parque
infantil/temático/zoológico** playground/
theme park/zoo
parqué [par'ke] nm parquet (flooring)
parquímetro [par'kimetro] nm parking
meter
parra ['parra] nf (grape)vine
párrafo ['parrafo] nm paragraph; **echar
un ~** (fam) to have a chat
parranda [pa'rranda] (fam) nf spree,
binge
parrilla [pa'rriʎa] nf (Culin) grill; (de coche)
grille; **(carne a la) ~** barbecue; **parrillada**
nf barbecue
párroco ['parroko] nm parish priest
parroquia [pa'rrokja] nf parish; (iglesia)
parish church; (Com) clientele, customers pl;
parroquiano, -a nm/f parishioner; (Com)
client, customer
parte ['parte] nm message; (informe)
report ▷ nf part; (lado, cara) side; (de reparto)
share; (Jur) party; **en alguna ~ de Europa**
somewhere in Europe; **en o por todas ~s**
everywhere; **en gran ~** to a large extent; **la
mayor ~ de los españoles** most Spaniards;
de un tiempo a esta ~ for some time past;
de ~ de algn on sb's behalf; **¿de ~ de quién?**
(Tel) who is speaking?; **por ~ de** on the part
of; **yo por mi ~** I for my part; **por otra ~** on
the other hand; **dar ~** to inform; **tomar ~** to
take part; **parte meteorológico** weather
forecast o report
participación [partiθipa'θjon] nf (acto)
participation, taking part; (parte, Com)
share; (de lotería) shared prize; (aviso) notice,
notification
participante [partiθi'pante] nmf
participant
participar [partiθi'par] vt to notify,
inform ▷ vi to take part, participate
partícipe [par'tiθipe] nmf participant
particular [partiku'lar] adj (especial)
particular, special; (individual, personal)
private, personal ▷ nm (punto, asunto)
particular, point; (individuo) individual;
tiene coche ~ he has a car of his own
partida [par'tiða] nf (salida) departure;
(Com) entry, item; (juego) game; (grupo de
personas) band, group; **mala ~** dirty trick;

**partida de nacimiento/matrimonio/
defunción** (ESP) birth/marriage/death
certificate
partidario, -a [parti'ðarjo, a] adj
partisan ▷ nm/f supporter, follower
partido [par'tiðo] nm (Pol) party; (Deporte)
game, match; **sacar ~ de** to profit o benefit
from; **tomar ~** to take sides
partir [par'tir] vt (dividir) to split, divide;
(compartir, distribuir) to share (out),
distribute; (romper) to break open, split
open; (rebanada) to cut (off) ▷ vi (ponerse en
camino) to set off o out; (comenzar) to start
(off o out); **partirse** vr to crack o split o
break (in two etc); **a ~ de** (starting) from
partitura [parti'tura] nf (Mús) score
parto ['parto] nm birth; (fig) product,
creation; **estar de ~** to be in labour
parvulario [parβu'larjo] (ESP) nm
nursery school, kindergarten
pasa ['pasa] nf raisin; **pasa de Corinto**
currant
pasacintas [pasa'θintas] (LAM) nm
cassette player
pasada [pa'saða] nf passing, passage;
de ~ in passing, incidentally; **una mala ~** a
dirty trick
pasadizo [pasa'ðiθo] nm (pasillo) passage,
corridor; (callejuela) alley
pasado, -a [pa'saðo, a] adj past;
(malo: comida, fruta) bad; (muy cocido)
overdone; (anticuado) out of date ▷ nm past;
~ mañana the day after tomorrow; **el mes
~** last month
pasador [pasa'ðor] nm (cerrojo) bolt; (de
pelo) hair slide; (horquilla) grip
pasaje [pa'saxe] nm passage; (pago de
viaje) fare; (los pasajeros) passengers pl;
(pasillo) passageway
pasajero, -a [pasa'xero, a] adj passing;
(situación, estado) temporary; (amor,
enfermedad) brief ▷ nm/f passenger
pasamontañas [pasamon'taɲas] nm inv
balaclava helmet
pasaporte [pasa'porte] nm passport
pasar [pa'sar] vt to pass; (tiempo) to spend;
(desgracias) to suffer, endure; (noticia) to
give, pass on; (río) to cross; (barrera) to
pass through; (falta) to overlook, tolerate;
(contrincante) to surpass, do better than;
(coche) to overtake; (Cine) to show;
(enfermedad) to give, infect with ▷ vi (gen)
to pass; (terminarse) to be over; (ocurrir) to
happen; **pasarse** vr (flores) to fade; (comida)
to go bad o off; (fig) to overdo it, go too far;
~ de to go beyond, exceed; **~ por** (LAM) to
fetch; **~lo bien/mal** to have a good/bad
time; **¡pase!** come in!; **hacer ~** to show in;

lo que pasa es que ... the thing is ...; **~se al enemigo** to go over to the enemy; **se me pasó** I forgot; **no se le pasa nada** he misses nothing; **pase lo que pase** come what may; **¿qué pasa?** what's going on?, what's up?; **¿qué te pasa?** what's wrong?

pasarela [pasa'rela] *nf* footbridge; (*en barco*) gangway

pasatiempo [pasa'tjempo] *nm* pastime, hobby

Pascua ['paskwa] *nf* (*en Semana Santa*) Easter; **Pascuas** *nfpl* Christmas (time); **¡felices ~s!** Merry Christmas!

pase ['pase] *nm* pass; (*Cine*) performance, showing

pasear [pase'ar] *vt* to take for a walk; (*exhibir*) to parade, show off ▷ *vi* to walk, go for a walk; **pasearse** *vr* to walk, go for a walk; **~ en coche** to go for a drive; **paseo** *nm* (*avenida*) avenue; (*distancia corta*) walk, stroll; **dar un** o **ir de paseo** to go for a walk; **paseo marítimo** (*ESP*) promenade

pasillo [pa'siʎo] *nm* passage, corridor

pasión [pa'sjon] *nf* passion

pasivo, -a [pa'siβo, a] *adj* passive; (*inactivo*) inactive ▷ *nm* (*Com*) liabilities *pl*, debts *pl*

pasmoso, -a [pas'moso, a] *adj* amazing, astonishing

paso, -a ['paso, a] *adj* dried ▷ *nm* step; (*modo de andar*) walk; (*huella*) footprint; (*rapidez*) speed, pace, rate; (*camino accesible*) way through, passage; (*cruce*) crossing; (*pasaje*) passing, passage; (*Geo*) pass; (*estrecho*) strait; **a ese ~** (*fig*) at that rate; **salir al ~ de** o **a** to waylay; **estar de ~** to be passing through; **prohibido el ~** no entry; **ceda el ~** give way; **paso a nivel** (*Ferro*) level-crossing; **paso (de) cebra** (*ESP*) zebra crossing; **paso de peatones** pedestrian crossing; **paso elevado** flyover

pasota [pa'sota] (*ESP: fam*) *adj, nmf* ≈ dropout; **ser un ~** to be a bit of a dropout; (*ser indiferente*) not to care about anything

pasta ['pasta] *nf* paste; (*Culin: masa*) dough; (: *de bizcochos etc*) pastry; (*fam*) dough; **pastas** *nfpl* (*bizcochos*) pastries, small cakes; (*fideos, espaguetis etc*) pasta; **pasta dentífrica** o **de dientes** toothpaste

pastar [pas'tar] *vt, vi* to graze

pastel [pas'tel] *nm* (*dulce*) cake; (*Arte*) pastel; **pastel de carne** meat pie; **pastelería** *nf* cake shop

pastilla [pas'tiʎa] *nf* (*de jabón, chocolate*) bar; (*píldora*) tablet, pill

pasto ['pasto] *nm* (*hierba*) grass; (*lugar*) pasture, field; **pastor, a** [pas'tor, a] *nm/f* shepherd/ess ▷ *nm* (*Rel*) clergyman, pastor;

pastor alemán Alsatian

pata ['pata] *nf* (*pierna*) leg; (*pie*) foot; (*de muebles*) leg; **~s arriba** upside down; **metedura de ~** (*fam*) gaffe; **meter la ~** (*fam*) to put one's foot in it; **tener buena/mala ~** to be lucky/unlucky; **pata de cabra** (*Tec*) crowbar; **patada** *nf* kick; (*en el suelo*) stamp

patata [pa'tata] *nf* potato; **patatas fritas** chips, French fries; (*de bolsa*) crisps

paté [pa'te] *nm* pâté

patente [pa'tente] *adj* obvious, evident; (*Com*) patent ▷ *nf* patent

paternal [pater'nal] *adj* fatherly, paternal; **paterno, -a** *adj* paternal

patético, -a [pa'tetiko, a] *adj* pathetic, moving

patilla [pa'tiʎa] *nf* (*de gafas*) side(piece); **patillas** *nfpl* sideburns

patín [pa'tin] *nm* skate; (*de trineo*) runner; **patín de ruedas** roller skate; **patinaje** *nm* skating; **patinar** *vi* to skate; (*resbalarse*) to skid, slip; (*fam*) to slip up, blunder

patineta [pati'neta] *nf* (*MÉX: patinete*) scooter; (*cs: monopatín*) skateboard

patinete [pati'nete] *nm* scooter

patio ['patjo] *nm* (*de casa*) patio, courtyard; **patio de recreo** playground

pato ['pato] *nm* duck; **pagar el ~** (*fam*) to take the blame, carry the can

patoso, -a [pa'toso, a] (*fam*) *adj* clumsy

patotero [pato'tero] (*cs*) *nm* hooligan, lout

patraña [pa'traɲa] *nf* story, fib

patria ['patrja] *nf* native land, mother country

patrimonio [patri'monjo] *nm* inheritance; (*fig*) heritage

patriota [pa'trjota] *nmf* patriot

patrocinar [patroθi'nar] *vt* to sponsor

patrón, -ona [pa'tron, ona] *nm/f* (*jefe*) boss, chief, master(mistress); (*propietario*) landlord/lady; (*Rel*) patron saint ▷ *nm* (*Tec, Costura*) pattern

patronato [patro'nato] *nm* sponsorship; (*acto*) patronage; (*fundación benéfica*) trust, foundation

patrulla [pa'truʎa] *nf* patrol

pausa ['pausa] *nf* pause, break

pauta ['pauta] *nf* line, guide line

pava ['paβa] (*RPL*) *nf* kettle

pavimento [paβi'mento] *nm* (*de losa*) pavement, paving

pavo ['paβo] *nm* turkey; **pavo real** peacock

payaso, -a [pa'jaso, a] *nm/f* clown

payo, -a ['pajo, a] *nm/f* non-gipsy

paz [paθ] *nf* peace; (*tranquilidad*) peacefulness, tranquillity; **hacer las paces** to make peace; (*fig*) to make up; **¡déjame en**

~! leave me alone!

PC *nm* PC, personal computer

P.D. *abr* (= *posdata*) P.S., p.s.

peaje [pe'axe] *nm* toll

peatón [pea'ton] *nm* pedestrian; **peatonal** *adj* pedestrian

peca ['peka] *nf* freckle

pecado [pe'kaðo] *nm* sin; **pecador, a** *adj* sinful ▷ *nm/f* sinner

pecaminoso, -a [pekami'noso, a] *adj* sinful

pecar [pe'kar] *vi* (*Rel*) to sin; **peca de generoso** he is generous to a fault

pecera [pe'θera] *nf* fish tank; (*redonda*) goldfish bowl

pecho ['petʃo] *nm* (*Anat*) chest; (*de mujer*) breast; **dar el ~ a** to breast-feed; **tomar algo a ~** to take sth to heart

pechuga [pe'tʃuxa] *nf* breast

peculiar [peku'ljar] *adj* special, peculiar; (*característico*) typical, characteristic

pedal [pe'ðal] *nm* pedal; **pedalear** *vi* to pedal

pedante [pe'ðante] *adj* pedantic ▷ *nmf* pedant

pedazo [pe'ðaθo] *nm* piece, bit; **hacerse ~s** to smash, shatter

pediatra [pe'ðjatra] *nmf* paediatrician

pedido [pe'ðiðo] *nm* (*Com*) order; (*petición*) request

pedir [pe'ðir] *vt* to ask for, request; (*comida, Com: mandar*) to order; (*necesitar*) to need, demand, require ▷ *vi* to ask; **me pidió que cerrara la puerta** he asked me to shut the door; **¿cuánto piden por el coche?** how much are they asking for the car?

pedo ['peðo] (*fam!*) *nm* fart

pega ['pexa] *nf* snag; **poner ~s (a)** to complain (about)

pegadizo, -a [pexa'ðiθo, a] *adj* (*Mús*) catchy

pegajoso, -a [pexa'xoso, a] *adj* sticky, adhesive

pegamento [pexa'mento] *nm* gum, glue

pegar [pe'xar] *vt* (*papel, sellos*) to stick (on); (*cartel*) to stick up; (*coser*) to sew (on); (*unir: partes*) to join, fix together; (*Comput*) to paste; (*Med*) to give, infect with; (*dar: golpe*) to give, deal ▷ *vi* (*adherirse*) to stick, adhere; (*ir juntos: colores*) to match, go together; (*golpear*) to hit; (*quemar: el sol*) to strike hot, burn; **pegarse** *vr* (*gen*) to stick; (*dos personas*) to hit each other, fight; (*fam*): **~ un grito** to let out a yell; **~ un salto** to jump (with fright); **~ en** to touch; **~se un tiro** to shoot o.s.

pegatina [pexa'tina] *nf* sticker

pegote [pe'xote] (*fam*) *nm* eyesore, sight

peinado [pei'naðo] *nm* hairstyle

peinar [pei'nar] *vt* to comb; (*hacer estilo*) to style; **peinarse** *vr* to comb one's hair

peine ['peine] *nm* comb; **peineta** *nf* ornamental comb

p.ej. *abr* (= *por ejemplo*) e.g.

Pekín [pe'kin] *n* Pekin(g)

pelado, -a [pe'laðo, a] *adj* (*fruta, patata etc*) peeled; (*cabeza*) shorn; (*campo, fig*) bare; (*fam: sin dinero*) broke

pelar [pe'lar] *vt* (*fruta, patatas etc*) to peel; (*cortar el pelo a*) to cut the hair of; (*quitar la piel: animal*) to skin; **pelarse** *vr* (*la piel*) to peel off; **voy a ~me** I'm going to get my hair cut

peldaño [pel'daɲo] *nm* step

pelea [pe'lea] *nf* (*lucha*) fight; (*discusión*) quarrel, row; **peleado, -a** [pele'aðo, a] *adj*: **estar peleado (con algn)** to have fallen out (with sb); **pelear** [pele'ar] *vi* to fight; **pelearse** *vr* to fight; (*reñirse*) to fall out, quarrel

pelela [pe'lela] (*cs*) *nf* potty

peletería [pelete'ria] *nf* furrier's, fur shop

pelícano [pe'likano] *nm* pelican

película [pe'likula] *nf* film; (*cobertura ligera*) thin covering; (*Foto: rollo*) roll o reel of film; **película de dibujos (animados)/del oeste** cartoon/western

peligro [pe'lixro] *nm* danger; (*riesgo*) risk; **correr el ~ de** to run the risk of; **peligroso, -a** *adj* dangerous; risky

pelirrojo, -a [peli'rroxo, a] *adj* red-haired, red-headed ▷ *nm/f* redhead

pellejo [pe'ʎexo] *nm* (*de animal*) skin, hide

pellizcar [peʎiθ'kar] *vt* to pinch, nip

pelma ['pelma] (*ESP: fam*) *nmf* pain (in the neck)

pelmazo [pel'maθo] (*fam*) *nm* = **pelma**

pelo ['pelo] *nm* (*cabellos*) hair; (*de barba, bigote*) whisker; (*de animal: pellejo*) hair, fur, coat; **venir al ~** to be exactly what one needs; **un hombre de ~ en pecho** a brave man; **por los ~s** by the skin of one's teeth; **no tener ~s en la lengua** to be outspoken, not to mince one's words; **con ~s y señales** in minute detail; **tomar el ~ a algn** to pull sb's leg

pelota [pe'lota] *nf* ball; **en ~** stark naked; **hacer la ~ (a algn)** (*ESP: fam*) to creep (to sb); **pelota vasca** pelota

pelotón [pelo'ton] *nm* (*Mil*) squad, detachment

peluca [pe'luka] *nf* wig

peluche [pe'lutʃe] *nm*: **oso/muñeco de ~** teddy bear/soft toy

peludo, -a [pe'luðo, a] *adj* hairy, shaggy

peluquería [peluke'ria] *nf* hairdresser's;

peluquero, -a *nm/f* hairdresser
pelusa [pe'lusa] *nf* (*Bot*) down; (*en tela*) fluff
pena ['pena] *nf* (*congoja*) grief, sadness; (*remordimiento*) regret; (*dificultad*) trouble; (*dolor*) pain; (*Jur*) sentence; **merecer** *o* **valer la ~** to be worthwhile; **a duras ~s** with great difficulty; **¡qué ~!** what a shame!; **pena capital** capital punishment; **pena de muerte** death penalty
penal [pe'nal] *adj* penal ▷ *nm* (*cárcel*) prison
penalidad [penali'ðað] *nf* (*problema, dificultad*) trouble, hardship; (*Jur*) penalty, punishment; **penalidades** *nfpl* trouble *sg*, hardship *sg*
penalti [pe'nalti] *nm* = **penalty**
penalty [pe'nalti] (*pl* **~s** *o* **penalties**) *nm* penalty (kick)
pendiente [pen'djente] *adj* pending, unsettled ▷ *nm* earring ▷ *nf* hill, slope
pene ['pene] *nm* penis
penetrante [pene'trante] *adj* (*herida*) deep; (*persona, arma*) sharp; (*sonido*) penetrating, piercing; (*mirada*) searching; (*viento, ironía*) biting
penetrar [pene'trar] *vt* to penetrate, pierce; (*entender*) to grasp ▷ *vi* to penetrate, go in; (*entrar*) to enter, go in; (*líquido*) to soak in; (*fig*) to pierce
penicilina [peniθi'lina] *nf* penicillin
península [pe'ninsula] *nf* peninsula; **peninsular** *adj* peninsular
penique [pe'nike] *nm* penny
penitencia [peni'tenθja] *nf* penance
penoso, -a [pe'noso, a] *adj* (*lamentable*) distressing; (*difícil*) arduous, difficult
pensador, a [pensa'ðor, a] *nm/f* thinker
pensamiento [pensa'mjento] *nm* thought; (*mente*) mind; (*idea*) idea
pensar [pen'sar] *vt* to think; (*considerar*) to think over, think out; (*proponerse*) to intend, plan; (*imaginarse*) to think up, invent ▷ *vi* to think; **~ en** to aim at, aspire to; **pensativo, -a** *adj* thoughtful, pensive
pensión [pen'sjon] *nf* (*casa*) boarding *o* guest house; (*dinero*) pension; (*cama y comida*) board and lodging; **media ~** half-board; **pensión completa** full board; **pensionista** *nmf* (*jubilado*) (old-age) pensioner; (*huésped*) lodger
penúltimo, -a [pe'nultimo, a] *adj* penultimate, last but one
penumbra [pe'numbra] *nf* half-light
peña ['peɲa] *nf* (*roca*) rock; (*cuesta*) cliff, crag; (*grupo*) group, circle; (*LAM: club*) folk club
peñasco [pe'ɲasko] *nm* large rock, boulder

peñón [pe'ɲon] *nm* wall of rock; **el P~** the Rock (of Gibraltar)
peón [pe'on] *nm* labourer; (*LAM Agr*) farm labourer, farmhand; (*Ajedrez*) pawn
peonza [pe'onθa] *nf* spinning top
peor [pe'or] *adj* (*comparativo*) worse; (*superlativo*) worst ▷ *adv* worse; worst; **de mal en ~** from bad to worse
pepinillo [pepi'niʎo] *nm* gherkin
pepino [pe'pino] *nm* cucumber; **(no) me importa un ~** I don't care one bit
pepita [pe'pita] *nf* (*Bot*) pip; (*Minería*) nugget
pepito [pe'pito] (*ESP*) *nm* (*tb*: **~ de ternera**) steak sandwich
pequeño, -a [pe'keɲo, a] *adj* small, little
pera ['pera] *nf* pear; **peral** *nm* pear tree
percance [per'kanθe] *nm* setback, misfortune
percatarse [perka'tarse] *vr*: **~ de** to notice, take note of
percebe [per'θeβe] *nm* barnacle
percepción [perθep'θjon] *nf* (*vista*) perception; (*idea*) notion, idea
percha ['pertʃa] *nf* (coat) hanger; (*ganchos*) coat hooks *pl*; (*de ave*) perch
percibir [perθi'βir] *vt* to perceive, notice; (*Com*) to earn, get
percusión [perku'sjon] *nf* percussion
perdedor, a [perðe'ðor, a] *adj* losing ▷ *nm/f* loser
perder [per'ðer] *vt* to lose; (*tiempo, palabras*) to waste; (*oportunidad*) to lose, miss; (*tren*) to miss ▷ *vi* to lose; **perderse** *vr* (*extraviarse*) to get lost; (*desaparecer*) to disappear, be lost to view; (*arruinarse*) to be ruined; **echar a ~** (*comida*) to spoil, ruin; (*oportunidad*) to waste
pérdida ['perðiða] *nf* loss; (*de tiempo*) waste; **pérdidas** *nfpl* (*Com*) losses
perdido, -a [per'ðiðo, a] *adj* lost
perdiz [per'ðiθ] *nf* partridge
perdón [per'ðon] *nm* (*disculpa*) pardon, forgiveness; (*clemencia*) mercy; **¡~!** sorry!, I beg your pardon!; **perdonar** *vt* to pardon, forgive; (*la vida*) to spare; (*excusar*) to exempt, excuse; **¡perdone (usted)!** sorry!, I beg your pardon!
perecedero, -a [pereθe'ðero, a] *adj* perishable
perecer [pere'θer] *vi* to perish, die
peregrinación [pereɣrina'θjon] *nf* (*Rel*) pilgrimage
peregrino, -a [pere'ɣrino, a] *adj* (*idea*) strange, absurd ▷ *nm/f* pilgrim
perejil [pere'xil] *nm* parsley
perenne [pe'renne] *adj* everlasting, perennial

pereza [pe'reθa] nf laziness, idleness;
  perezoso, -a adj lazy, idle
perfección [perfek'θjon] nf perfection;
  perfeccionar vt to perfect; (mejorar) to
  improve; (acabar) to complete, finish
perfecto, -a [per'fekto, a] adj perfect;
  (total) complete
perfil [per'fil] nm profile; (contorno)
  silhouette, outline; (Arq) (cross) section;
  perfiles nmpl features
perforación [perfora'θjon] nf
  perforation; (con taladro) drilling;
  perforadora nf punch
perforar [perfo'rar] vt to perforate;
  (agujero) to drill, bore; (papel) to punch a hole
  in ⊳ vi to drill, bore
perfume [per'fume] nm perfume, scent
periferia [peri'ferja] nf periphery; (de
  ciudad) outskirts pl
periférico [peri'feriko] (LAM) nm ring road
  (BRIT), beltway (US)
perilla [pe'riʎa] nf (barba) goatee; (LAM: de
  puerta) doorknob, door handle
perímetro [pe'rimetro] nm perimeter
periódico, -a [pe'rjoðiko, a] adj
  periodic(al) ⊳ nm newspaper
periodismo [perjo'ðismo] nm
  journalism; **periodista** nmf journalist
periodo [pe'rjoðo] nm period
período [pe'rioðo] nm = periodo
periquito [peri'kito] nm budgerigar,
  budgie
perito, -a [pe'rito, a] adj (experto) expert;
  (diestro) skilled, skilful ⊳ nm/f expert;
  skilled worker; (técnico) technician
perjudicar [perxuði'kar] vt (gen) to
  damage, harm; **perjudicial** adj damaging,
  harmful; (en detrimento) detrimental;
  perjuicio nm damage, harm
perjurar [perxu'rar] vi to commit perjury
perla ['perla] nf pearl; **me viene de ~s** it
  suits me fine
permanecer [permane'θer] vi (quedarse)
  to stay, remain; (seguir) to continue to be
permanente [perma'nente] adj
  permanent, constant ⊳ nf perm
permiso [per'miso] nm permission;
  (licencia) permit, licence; **con ~** excuse me;
  estar de ~ (Mil) to be on leave; **permiso de
  conducir** driving licence (BRIT), driver's
  license (US); **permiso por enfermedad**
  (LAM) sick leave
permitir [permi'tir] vt to permit, allow
pernera [per'nera] nf trouser leg
pero ['pero] conj but; (aún) yet ⊳ nm
  (defecto) flaw, defect; (reparo) objection
perpendicular [perpendiku'lar] adj
  perpendicular

perpetuo, -a [per'petwo, a] adj perpetual
perplejo, -a [per'plexo, a] adj perplexed,
  bewildered
perra ['perra] nf (Zool) bitch; **estar sin una
  ~** (ESP: fam) to be flat broke
perrera [pe'rrera] nf kennel
perrito [pe'rrito] nm (tb: ~ caliente) hot
  dog
perro ['perro] nm dog
persa ['persa] adj, nmf Persian
persecución [perseku'θjon] nf pursuit,
  chase; (Rel, Pol) persecution
perseguir [perse'ɣir] vt to pursue, hunt;
  (cortejar) to chase after; (molestar) to pester,
  annoy; (Rel, Pol) to persecute
persiana [per'sjana] nf (Venetian) blind
persistente [persis'tente] adj persistent
persistir [persis'tir] vi to persist
persona [per'sona] nf person; **persona
  mayor** elderly person
personaje [perso'naxe] nm important
  person, celebrity; (Teatro etc) character
personal [perso'nal] adj (particular)
  personal; (para una persona) single, for
  one person ⊳ nm personnel, staff;
  personalidad nf personality
personarse [perso'narse] vr to appear
  in person
personificar [personifi'kar] vt to
  personify
perspectiva [perspek'tiβa] nf
  perspective; (vista, panorama) view,
  panorama; (posibilidad futura) outlook,
  prospect
persuadir [perswa'ðir] vt (gen) to
  persuade; (convencer) to convince;
  persuadirse vr to become convinced;
  persuasión nf persuasion
pertenecer [pertene'θer] vi to
  belong; (fig) to concern; **perteneciente**
  adj: **perteneciente a** belonging to;
  pertenencia nf ownership; **pertenencias**
  nfpl (bienes) possessions, property sg
pertenezca etc vb V **pertenecer**
pértiga ['pertiɣa] nf: **salto de ~** pole vault
pertinente [perti'nente] adj relevant,
  pertinent; (apropiado) appropriate; **~ a**
  concerning, relevant to
perturbación [perturβa'θjon] nf (Pol)
  disturbance; (Med) upset, disturbance
Perú [pe'ru] nm Peru; **peruano, -a** adj,
  nm/f Peruvian
perversión [perβer'sjon] nf perversion;
  perverso, -a adj perverse; (depravado)
  depraved
pervertido, -a [perβer'tiðo, a] adj
  perverted ⊳ nm/f pervert
pervertir [perβer'tir] vt to pervert,

P

corrupt

pesa ['pesa] nf weight; (Deporte) shot

pesadez [pesa'ðeθ] nf (peso) heaviness; (lentitud) slowness; (aburrimiento) tediousness

pesadilla [pesa'ðiʎa] nf nightmare, bad dream

pesado, -a [pe'saðo, a] adj heavy; (lento) slow; (difícil, duro) tough, hard; (aburrido) boring, tedious; (tiempo) sultry

pésame ['pesame] nm expression of condolence, message of sympathy; **dar el ~** to express one's condolences

pesar [pe'sar] vt to weigh ▷ vi to weigh; (ser pesado) to weigh a lot, be heavy; (fig: opinión) to carry weight; **no pesa mucho** it's not very heavy ▷ nm (arrepentimiento) regret; (pena) grief, sorrow; **a ~ de** o **pese a (que)** in spite of, despite

pesca ['peska] nf (acto) fishing; (lo pescado) catch; **ir de ~** to go fishing

pescadería [peskaðe'ria] nf fish shop, fishmonger's (BRIT)

pescadilla [peska'ðiʎa] nf whiting

pescado [pes'kaðo] nm fish

pescador, a [peska'ðor, a] nm/f fisherman/woman

pescar [pes'kar] vt (tomar) to catch; (intentar tomar) to fish for; (conseguir: trabajo) to manage to get ▷ vi to fish, go fishing

pesebre [pe'seβre] nm manger

peseta [pe'seta] nf (Hist) peseta

pesimista [pesi'mista] adj pessimistic ▷ nmf pessimist

pésimo, -a ['pesimo, a] adj awful, dreadful

peso ['peso] nm weight; (balanza) scales pl; (moneda) peso; **vender al ~** to sell by weight; **peso bruto/neto** gross/net weight; **peso pesado/pluma** heavyweight/featherweight

pesquero, -a [pes'kero, a] adj fishing cpd

pestaña [pes'taɲa] nf (Anat) eyelash; (borde) rim

peste ['peste] nf plague; (mal olor) stink, stench

pesticida [pesti'θiða] nm pesticide

pestillo [pes'tiʎo] nm (cerrojo) bolt; (picaporte) door handle

petaca [pe'taka] nf (de cigarros) cigarette case; (de pipa) tobacco pouch; (MÉX: maleta) suitcase

pétalo ['petalo] nm petal

petardo [pe'tarðo] nm firework, firecracker

petición [peti'θjon] nf (pedido) request, plea; (memorial) petition; (Jur) plea

peto ['peto] (ESP) nm dungarees pl,

overalls pl (US)

petróleo [pe'troleo] nm oil, petroleum; **petrolero, -a** adj petroleum cpd ▷ nm (oil) tanker

peyorativo, -a [pejora'tiβo, a] adj pejorative

pez [peθ] nm fish; **pez espada** swordfish

pezón [pe'θon] nm teat, nipple

pezuña [pe'θuɲa] nf hoof

pianista [pja'nista] nmf pianist

piano ['pjano] nm piano

piar [pjar] vi to cheep

pibe, -a ['piβe, a] (RPL) nm/f boy/girl

picadero [pika'ðero] nm riding school

picadillo [pika'ðiʎo] nm mince, minced meat

picado, -a [pi'kaðo, a] adj pricked, punctured; (Culin) minced, chopped; (mar) choppy; (diente) bad; (tabaco) cut; (enfadado) cross

picador [pika'ðor] nm (Taur) picador; (minero) faceworker

picadura [pika'ðura] nf (pinchazo) puncture; (de abeja) sting; (de mosquito) bite; (tabaco picado) cut tobacco

picante [pi'kante] adj hot; (comentario) racy, spicy

picaporte [pika'porte] nm (manija) doorhandle; (pestillo) latch

picar [pi'kar] vt (agujerear, perforar) to prick, puncture; (abeja) to sting; (mosquito, serpiente) to bite; (Culin) to mince, chop; (incitar) to incite, goad; (dañar, irritar) to annoy, bother; (quemar: lengua) to burn, sting ▷ vi (pez) to bite, take the bait; (sol) to burn, scorch; (abeja, Med) to sting; (mosquito) to bite; **picarse** vr (agriarse) to turn sour, go off; (ofenderse) to take offence

picardía [pikar'ðia] nf villainy; (astucia) slyness, craftiness; (una picardía) dirty trick; (palabra) rude/bad word o expression

pícaro, -a ['pikaro, a] adj (malicioso) villainous; (travieso) mischievous ▷ nm (astuto) crafty sort; (sinvergüenza) rascal, scoundrel

pichi ['pitʃi] (ESP) nm pinafore dress (BRIT), jumper (US)

pichón [pi'tʃon] nm young pigeon

pico ['piko] nm (de ave) beak; (punta) sharp point; (Tec) pick, pickaxe; (Geo) peak, summit; **y ~** and a bit; **las seis y ~** six and a bit

picor [pi'kor] nm itch

picoso, -a [pi'koso, a] (MÉX) adj (comida) hot

picudo, -a [pi'kuðo, a] adj pointed, with a point

pidió etc vb V **pedir**

pido etc vb V **pedir**

pie [pje] (pl **~s**) nm foot; (fig: motivo) motive, basis; (: fundamento) foothold; **ir a ~** to go on foot, walk; **estar de ~** to be standing (up); **ponerse de ~** to stand up; **de ~s a cabeza** from top to bottom; **al ~ de la letra** (citar) literally, verbatim; (copiar) exactly, word for word; **en ~ de guerra** on a war footing; **dar ~ a** to give cause for; **hacer ~** (en el agua) to touch (the) bottom

piedad [pje'ðað] nf (lástima) pity, compassion; (clemencia) mercy; (devoción) piety, devotion

piedra ['pjeðra] nf stone; (roca) rock; (de mechero) flint; (Meteorología) hailstone; **piedra preciosa** precious stone

piel [pjel] nf (Anat) skin; (Zool) skin, hide, fur; (cuero) leather; (Bot) skin, peel

pienso etc vb V **pensar**

pierdo etc vb V **perder**

pierna ['pjerna] nf leg

pieza ['pjeθa] nf piece; (habitación) room; **pieza de recambio** o **repuesto** spare (part)

pigmeo, -a [pix'meo, a] adj, nm/f pigmy

pijama [pi'xama] nm pyjamas pl (BRIT), pajamas pl (US)

pila ['pila] nf (Elec) battery; (montón) heap, pile; (lavabo) sink

píldora ['pildora] nf pill; **la ~ (anticonceptiva)** the (contraceptive) pill

pileta [pi'leta] (RPL) nf (fregadero) (kitchen) sink; (piscina) swimming pool

pillar [pi'ʎar] vt (saquear) to pillage, plunder; (fam: coger) to catch; (: agarrar) to grasp, seize; (: entender) to grasp, catch on to; **pillarse** vr: **~se un dedo con la puerta** to catch one's finger in the door

pillo, -a ['piʎo, a] adj villainous; (astuto) sly, crafty ▷ nm/f rascal, rogue, scoundrel

piloto [pi'loto] nm pilot; (de aparato) (pilot) light; (Auto: luz) tail o rear light; (: conductor) driver; **piloto automático** automatic pilot

pimentón [pimen'ton] nm paprika

pimienta [pi'mjenta] nf pepper

pimiento [pi'mjento] nm pepper, pimiento

pin [pin] (pl **~s**) nm badge

pinacoteca [pinako'teka] nf art gallery

pinar [pi'nar] nm pine forest (BRIT), pine grove (US)

pincel [pin'θel] nm paintbrush

pinchadiscos [pintʃa'ðiskos] (ESP) nmf inv disc-jockey, DJ

pinchar [pin'tʃar] vt (perforar) to prick, pierce; (neumático) to puncture; (fig) to prod; (Inform) to click

pinchazo [pin'tʃaθo] nm (perforación) prick; (de neumático) puncture; (fig) prod

pincho ['pintʃo] nm savoury (snack); **pincho de tortilla** small slice of omelette; **pincho moruno** shish kebab

ping-pong ['pin'pon] nm table tennis

pingüino [pin'gwino] nm penguin

pino ['pino] nm pine (tree)

pinta ['pinta] nf spot; (de líquidos) spot, drop; (aspecto) appearance, look(s) (pl); **pintado, -a** adj spotted; (de colores) colourful; **pintadas** nfpl graffiti sg

pintalabios [pinta'laβjos] (ESP) nm inv lipstick

pintar [pin'tar] vt to paint ▷ vi to paint; (fam) to count, be important; **pintarse** vr to put on make-up

pintor, a [pin'tor, a] nm/f painter

pintoresco, -a [pinto'resko, a] adj picturesque

pintura [pin'tura] nf painting; **pintura al óleo** oil painting

pinza ['pinθa] nf (Zool) claw; (para colgar ropa) clothes peg; (Tec) pincers pl; **pinzas** nfpl (para depilar etc) tweezers pl

piña ['pina] nf (de pino) pine cone; (fruta) pineapple; (fig) group

piñata [pi'nata] nf container hung up at parties to be beaten with sticks until sweets or presents fall out

PIÑATA

Piñata is a very popular party game in Mexico. The **piñata** itself is a hollow figure made of papier maché, or, traditionally, from adobe, in the shape of an object, a star, a person or an animal. It is filled with either sweets and toys, or fruit and yam beans. The game consists of hanging the **piñata** from the ceiling, and beating it with a stick, blindfolded, until it breaks and the presents fall out.

piñón [pi'non] nm (fruto) pine nut; (Tec) pinion

pío, -a ['pio, a] adj (devoto) pious, devout; (misericordioso) merciful

piojo ['pjoxo] nm louse

pipa ['pipa] nf pipe; **pipas** nfpl (Bot) (edible) sunflower seeds

pipí [pi'pi] (fam) nm: **hacer ~** to have a wee(-wee) (BRIT), have to go (wee-wee) (US)

pique ['pike] nm (resentimiento) pique, resentment; (rivalidad) rivalry, competition; **irse a ~** to sink; (esperanza, familia) to be ruined

piqueta [pi'keta] nf pick(axe)

piquete [pi'kete] nm (Mil) squad, party;

(*de obreros*) picket; (*MÉX: de insecto*) bite;
piquetear (*LAM*) *vt* to picket
pirado, -a [pi'raðo, a] (*fam*) *adj* round the
bend ▷ *nm/f* nutter
piragua [pi'raɣwa] *nf* canoe; **piragüismo**
nm canoeing
pirámide [pi'ramiðe] *nf* pyramid
pirata [pi'rata] *adj*, *nmf* pirate; **pirata
informático** hacker
Pirineo(s) [piri'neo(s)] *nm(pl)* Pyrenees *pl*
pirómano, -a [pi'romano, a] *nm/f* (*Med,
Jur*) arsonist
piropo [pi'ropo] *nm* compliment, (piece
of) flattery
pirueta [pi'rweta] *nf* pirouette
piruleta [piru'leta] (*ESP*) *nf* lollipop
pis [pis] (*fam*) *nm* pee, piss; **hacer ~** to have
a pee; (*para niños*) to wee-wee
pisada [pi'saða] *nf* (*paso*) footstep; (*huella*)
footprint
pisar [pi'sar] *vt* (*caminar sobre*) to walk on,
tread on; (*apretar con el pie*) to press; (*fig*)
to trample on, walk all over ▷ *vi* to tread,
step, walk
piscina [pis'θina] *nf* swimming pool
Piscis [ˈpisθis] *nm* Pisces
piso [ˈpiso] *nm* (*suelo, planta*) floor;
(*ESP: apartamento*) flat (*BRIT*), apartment;
primer ~ (*ESP*) first floor; (*LAM: planta baja*)
ground floor
pisotear [pisote'ar] *vt* to trample (on *o*
underfoot)
pista [ˈpista] *nf* track, trail; (*indicio*) clue;
pista de aterrizaje runway; **pista de baile**
dance floor; **pista de hielo** ice rink; **pista de
tenis** (*ESP*) tennis court
pistola [pis'tola] *nf* pistol; (*Tec*) spray-gun
pistón [pis'ton] *nm* (*Tec*) piston; (*Mús*) key
pitar [pi'tar] *vt* (*silbato*) to blow; (*rechiflar*)
to whistle at, boo ▷ *vi* to whistle; (*Auto*)
to sound *o* toot one's horn; (*LAM: fumar*) to
smoke
pitillo [pi'tiʎo] *nm* cigarette
pito [ˈpito] *nm* whistle; (*de coche*) horn
pitón [pi'ton] *nm* (*Zool*) python
pitonisa [pito'nisa] *nf* fortune-teller
pitorreo [pito'rreo] *nm* joke; **estar de ~**
to be joking
píxel [ˈpiksel] (*pl* **pixels** *or* **~es**) *nm* pixel
piyama [pi'jama] (*LAM*) *nm* pyjamas *pl*
(*BRIT*), pajamas *pl* (*US*)
pizarra [pi'θarra] *nf* (*piedra*) slate;
(*ESP: encerado*) blackboard; **pizarra
blanca** whiteboard; **pizarra interactiva**
interactive whiteboard
pizarrón [piθa'rron] (*LAM*) *nm* blackboard
pizca [ˈpiθka] *nf* pinch, spot; (*fig*) spot,
speck; **ni ~** not a bit

placa [ˈplaka] *nf* plate; (*distintivo*) badge,
insignia; **placa de matrícula** (*LAM*) number
plate
placard [pla'kar] (*RPL*) *nm* cupboard
placer [pla'θer] *nm* pleasure ▷ *vt* to please
plaga [ˈplaɣa] *nf* pest; (*Med*) plague;
(*abundancia*) abundance
plagio [ˈplaxjo] *nm* plagiarism
plan [plan] *nm* (*esquema, proyecto*) plan;
(*idea, intento*) idea, intention; **tener ~** (*fam*)
to have a date; **tener un ~** (*fam*) to have an
affair; **en ~ económico** (*fam*) on the cheap;
vamos en ~ de turismo we're going as
tourists; **si te pones en ese ~ ...** if that's
your attitude ...
plana [ˈplana] *nf* sheet (of paper), page;
(*Tec*) trowel; **en primera ~** on the front page
plancha [ˈplantʃa] *nf* (*para planchar*) iron;
(*rótulo*) plate, sheet; (*Náut*) gangway; **a la ~**
(*Culin*) grilled; **planchar** *vt* to iron ▷ *vi* to
do the ironing
planear [plane'ar] *vt* to plan ▷ *vi* to glide
planeta [pla'neta] *nm* planet
plano, -a [ˈplano, a] *adj* flat, level, even
▷ *nm* (*Mat, Tec*) plane; (*Foto*) shot; (*Arq*) plan;
(*Geo*) map; (*de ciudad*) map, street plan;
primer ~ close-up
planta [ˈplanta] *nf* (*Bot, Tec*) plant;
(*Anat*) sole of the foot, foot; (*piso*) floor;
(*LAM: personal*) staff; **planta baja** ground
floor
plantar [plan'tar] *vt* (*Bot*) to plant;
(*levantar*) to erect, set up; **plantarse** *vr* to
stand firm; **~ a algn en la calle** to throw sb
out; **dejar plantado a algn** (*fam*) to stand
sb up
plantear [plante'ar] *vt* (*problema*) to pose;
(*dificultad*) to raise
plantilla [plan'tiʎa] *nf* (*de zapato*) insole;
(*ESP: personal*) personnel; **ser de ~** (*ESP*) to be
on the staff
plantón [plan'ton] *nm* (*Mil*) guard, sentry;
(*fam*) long wait; **dar (un) ~ a algn** to stand
sb up
plasta [ˈplasta] (*ESP: fam*) *adj inv* boring
▷ *nmf* bore
plástico, -a [ˈplastiko, a] *adj* plastic ▷ *nm*
plastic
Plastilina® [plasti'lina] *nf* Plasticine®
plata [ˈplata] *nf* (*metal*) silver; (*cosas hechas
de plata*) silverware; (*cs: dinero*) cash, dough
plataforma [plata'forma] *nf* platform;
plataforma de lanzamiento/perforación
launch(ing) pad/drilling rig
plátano [ˈplatano] *nm* (*fruta*) banana;
(*árbol*) plane tree; banana tree
platea [pla'tea] *nf* (*Teatro*) pit
plática [ˈplatika] *nf* talk, chat; **platicar** *vi*

to talk, chat

platillo [pla'tiʎo] nm saucer; **platillos** nmpl (Mús) cymbals; **platillo volante** flying saucer

platino [pla'tino] nm platinum; **platinos** nmpl (Auto) contact points

plato ['plato] nm plate, dish; (parte de comida) course; (comida) dish; **primer ~** first course; **plato combinado** set main course (served on one plate); **plato fuerte** main course

playa ['plaja] nf beach; (costa) seaside; **playa de estacionamiento** (cs) car park (BRIT), parking lot (US)

playera [pla'jera] nf (MÉX: camiseta) T-shirt; **playeras** nfpl (zapatos) canvas shoes

plaza ['plaθa] nf square; (mercado) market (place); (sitio) room, space; (de vehículo) seat, place; (colocación) post, job; **plaza de toros** bullring

plazo ['plaθo] nm (lapso de tiempo) time, period; (fecha de vencimiento) expiry date; (pago parcial) instalment; **a corto/largo ~** short-/long-term; **comprar algo a ~s** to buy sth on hire purchase (BRIT) o on time (US)

plazoleta [plaθo'leta] nf small square

plebeyo, -a [ple'βejo, a] adj plebeian; (pey) coarse, common

plegable [ple'ɣaβle] adj collapsible; (silla) folding

pleito ['pleito] nm (Jur) lawsuit, case; (fig) dispute, feud

plenitud [pleni'tuð] nf plenitude, fullness; (abundancia) abundance

pleno, -a ['pleno, a] adj full; (completo) complete ▷ nm plenum; **en ~ día** in broad daylight; **en ~ verano** at the height of summer; **en plena cara** full in the face

pliego etc ['pljeɣo] vb V **plegar** ▷ nm (hoja) sheet (of paper); (carta) sealed letter/document; **pliego de condiciones** details pl, specifications pl

pliegue etc ['pljeɣe] vb V **plegar** ▷ nm fold, crease; (de vestido) pleat

plomería [plome'ria] (LAM) nf plumbing; **plomero** (LAM) nm plumber

plomo ['plomo] nm (metal) lead; (Elec) fuse; **sin ~** unleaded

pluma ['pluma] nf feather; (para escribir): **~ (estilográfica)** ink pen; **~ fuente** (LAM) fountain pen

plumero [plu'mero] nm (para el polvo) feather duster

plumón [plu'mon] nm (de ave) down

plural [plu'ral] adj plural

pluriempleo [pluriem'pleo] nm having more than one job

plus [plus] nm bonus

población [poβla'θjon] nf population; (pueblo, ciudad) town, city

poblado, -a [po'βlaðo, a] adj inhabited ▷ nm (aldea) village; (pueblo) (small) town; **densamente ~** densely populated

poblador, a [poβla'ðor, a] nm/f settler, colonist

pobre ['poβre] adj poor ▷ nmf poor person; **pobreza** nf poverty

pocilga [po'θilɣa] nf pigsty

○ PALABRA CLAVE

poco, -a ['poko, a] adj 1 (sg) little, not much; **poco tiempo** little o not much time; **de poco interés** of little interest, not very interesting; **poca cosa** not much
2 (pl) few, not many; **unos pocos** a few, some; **pocos niños comen lo que les conviene** few children eat what they should ▷ adv 1 little, not much; **cuesta poco** it doesn't cost much
2 (+ adj: negativo, antónimo): **poco amable/inteligente** not very nice/intelligent
3: **por poco me caigo** I almost fell
4: **a poco: a poco de haberse casado** shortly after getting married
5: **poco a poco** little by little ▷ nm a little, a bit; **un poco triste/de dinero** a little sad/money

podar [po'ðar] vt to prune

○ PALABRA CLAVE

poder [po'ðer] vi 1 (tener capacidad) can, be able to; **no puedo hacerlo** I can't do it, I'm unable to do it
2 (tener permiso) can, may, be allowed to; **¿se puede?** may I (o we)?; **puedes irte ahora** you may go now; **no se puede fumar en este hospital** smoking is not allowed in this hospital
3 (tener posibilidad) may, might, could; **puede llegar mañana** he may o might arrive tomorrow; **pudiste haberte hecho daño** you might o could have hurt yourself; **¡podías habérmelo dicho antes!** you might have told me before!
4: **puede ser** perhaps; **puede ser que lo sepa Tomás** Tomás may o might know
5: **¡no puedo más!** I've had enough!; **es tonto a más no poder** he's as stupid as they come
6: **poder con: no puedo con este crío** this kid's too much for me

P

▷ *nm* power; **detentar** o **ocupar** o **estar en el poder** to be in power; **poder adquisitivo/ejecutivo/legislativo** purchasing/executive/legislative power; **poder judicial** judiciary

poderoso, -a [poðe'roso, a] *adj* (*político, país*) powerful
podio ['poðjo] *nm* (*Deporte*) podium
podium ['poðjum] = **podio**
podrido, -a [po'ðriðo, a] *adj* rotten, bad; (*fig*) rotten, corrupt
podrir [po'ðrir] = **pudrir**
poema [po'ema] *nm* poem
poesía [poe'sia] *nf* poetry
poeta [po'eta] *nmf* poet; **poético, -a** *adj* poetic(al)
poetisa [poe'tisa] *nf* (woman) poet
póker ['poker] *nm* poker
polaco, -a [po'lako, a] *adj* Polish ▷ *nm/f* Pole
polar [po'lar] *adj* polar
polea [po'lea] *nf* pulley
polémica [po'lemika] *nf* polemics *sg*; (*una polémica*) controversy, polemic
polen ['polen] *nm* pollen
policía [poli'θia] *nmf* policeman/woman ▷ *nf* police; **policíaco, -a** *adj* police *cpd*; **novela policíaca** detective story; **policial** *adj* police *cpd*
polideportivo [poliðepor'tiβo] *nm* sports centre o complex
polígono [po'liɣono] *nm* (*Mat*) polygon; **polígono industrial** (*ESP*) industrial estate
polilla [po'liʎa] *nf* moth
polio ['poljo] *nf* polio
política [po'litika] *nf* politics *sg*; (*económica, agraria etc*) policy; V *tb* **político**
político, -a [po'litiko, a] *adj* political; (*discreto*) tactful; (*de familia*) ...-in-law ▷ *nm/f* politician; **padre ~** father-in-law
póliza ['poliθa] *nf* certificate, voucher; (*impuesto*) tax stamp; **póliza de seguro(s)** insurance policy
polizón [poli'θon] *nm* stowaway
pollera [po'ʎera] (*cs*) *nf* skirt
pollo ['poʎo] *nm* chicken
polo ['polo] *nm* (*Geo, Elec*) pole; (*helado*) ice lolly (*BRIT*), Popsicle® (*US*); (*Deporte*) polo; (*suéter*) polo-neck; **polo Norte/Sur** North/South Pole
Polonia [po'lonja] *nf* Poland
poltrona [pol'trona] *nf* easy chair
polución [polu'θjon] *nf* pollution
polvera [pol'βera] *nf* powder compact
polvo ['polβo] *nm* dust; (*Quím, Culin, Med*) powder; **polvos** *nmpl* (*maquillaje*) powder *sg*; **en ~** powdered; **quitar el ~** to dust; **estar**

hecho ~ (*fam*) to be worn out o exhausted; **polvos de talco** talcum powder *sg*
pólvora ['polβora] *nf* gunpowder
polvoriento, -a [polβo'rjento, a] *adj* (*superficie*) dusty; (*sustancia*) powdery
pomada [po'maða] *nf* cream, ointment
pomelo [po'melo] *nm* grapefruit
pómez ['pomeθ] *nf*: **piedra ~** pumice stone
pomo ['pomo] *nm* doorknob
pompa ['pompa] *nf* (*burbuja*) bubble; (*bomba*) pump; (*esplendor*) pomp, splendour
pómulo ['pomulo] *nm* cheekbone
pon [pon] *vb* V **poner**
ponchadura [pontʃa'dura] (*MÉX*) *nf* puncture (*BRIT*), flat (*US*); **ponchar** (*MÉX*) *vt* (*llanta*) to puncture
ponche ['pontʃe] *nm* punch
poncho ['pontʃo] *nm* poncho
pondré *etc vb* V **poner**

○ **PALABRA CLAVE**

poner [po'ner] *vt* **1** (*colocar*) to put; (*telegrama*) to send; (*obra de teatro*) to put on; (*película*) to show; **ponlo más fuerte** turn it up; **¿qué ponen en el Excelsior?** what's on at the Excelsior?
2 (*tienda*) to open; (*instalar: gas etc*) to put in; (*radio, TV*) to switch o turn on
3 (*suponer*): **pongamos que ...** let's suppose that ...
4 (*contribuir*): **el gobierno ha puesto otro millón** the government has contributed another million
5 (*Tel*): **póngame con el Sr. López** can you put me through to Mr. López?
6: **poner de: le han puesto de director general** they've appointed him general manager
7 (+ *adj*) to make; **me estás poniendo nerviosa** you're making me nervous
8 (*dar nombre*): **al hijo le pusieron Diego** they called their son Diego
▷ *vi* (*gallina*) to lay
ponerse *vr* **1** (*colocarse*): **se puso a mi lado** he came and stood beside me; **tú ponte en esa silla** you go and sit on that chair
2 (*vestido, cosméticos*) to put on; **¿por qué no te pones el vestido nuevo?** why don't you put on o wear your new dress?
3 (+ *adj*) to turn; to get, become; **se puso muy serio** he got very serious; **después de lavarla la tela se puso azul** after washing it the material turned blue
4: **ponerse a: se puso a llorar** he started to cry; **tienes que ponerte a estudiar** you must get down to studying

pongo etc vb V **poner**

poniente [po'njente] nm (occidente) west; (viento) west wind

pontífice [pon'tifiθe] nm pope, pontiff

popa ['popa] nf stern

popote [po'pote] (MÉX) nm straw

popular [popu'lar] adj popular; (cultura) of the people, folk cpd; **popularidad** nf popularity

○ **PALABRA CLAVE**

por [por] prep **1** (objetivo) for; **luchar por la patria** to fight for one's country

2 (+ infin) **por no llegar tarde** so as not to arrive late; **por citar unos ejemplos** to give a few examples

3 (causa) out of, because of; **por escasez de fondos** through o for lack of funds

4 (tiempo) **por la mañana/noche** in the morning/at night; **se queda por una semana** she's staying (for) a week

5 (lugar) **pasar por Madrid** to pass through Madrid; **ir a Guayaquil por Quito** to go to Guayaquil via Quito; **caminar por la calle** to walk along the street; V tb **todo**

6 (cambio, precio): **te doy uno nuevo por el que tienes** I'll give you a new one (in return) for the one you've got

7 (valor distributivo): **6 euros por hora/cabeza** 6 euros an o per hour/a o per head

8 (modo, medio) by; **por correo/avión** by post/air; **entrar por la entrada principal** to go in through the main entrance

9: **10 por 10 son 100** 10 times 10 is 100

10 (en lugar de): **vino él por su jefe** he came instead of his boss

11: **por mí que revienten** as far as I'm concerned they can drop dead

12: **¿por qué?** why?; **¿por qué no?** why not?

porcelana [porθe'lana] nf porcelain; (china) china

porcentaje [porθen'taxe] nm percentage

porción [por'θjon] nf (parte) portion, share; (cantidad) quantity, amount

porfiar [por'fjar] vi to persist, insist; (disputar) to argue stubbornly

pormenor [porme'nor] nm detail, particular

pornografía [pornoɣra'fia] nf pornography

poro ['poro] nm pore

pororó [poro'ro] (RPL) nm popcorn

poroso, -a [po'roso, a] adj porous

poroto [po'roto] (CS) nm bean

porque ['porke] conj (a causa de) because; (ya que) since; (con el fin de) so that, in order

that

porqué [por'ke] nm reason, cause

porquería [porke'ria] nf (suciedad) filth, dirt; (acción) dirty trick; (objeto) small thing, trifle; (fig) rubbish

porra ['porra] (ESP) nf (arma) stick, club

porrazo [po'rraθo] nm blow, bump

porro ['porro] (fam) nm (droga) joint (fam)

porrón [po'rron] nm glass wine jar with a long spout

portaaviones [porta'(a)βjones] nm inv aircraft carrier

portada [por'taða] nf (de revista) cover

portador, a [porta'ðor, a] nm/f carrier, bearer; (Com) bearer, payee

portaequipajes [portaeki'paxes] nm inv (Auto: maletero) boot; (: baca) luggage rack

portafolio [porta'foljo] (LAM) nm briefcase

portal [por'tal] nm (entrada) vestibule, hall; (portada) porch, doorway; (puerta de entrada) main door; (Internet) portal; **portales** nmpl (LAM) arcade sg

portamaletas [portama'letas] nm inv (Auto: maletero) boot; (: baca) roof rack

portarse [por'tarse] vr to behave, conduct o.s.

portátil [por'tatil] adj portable

portavoz [porta'βoθ] nmf spokesman/woman

portazo [por'taθo] nm: **dar un ~** to slam the door

porte ['porte] nm (Com) transport; (precio) transport charges pl

portentoso, -a [porten'toso, a] adj marvellous, extraordinary

porteño, -a [por'teɲo, a] adj of o from Buenos Aires

portería [porte'ria] nf (oficina) porter's office; (Deporte) goal

portero, -a [por'tero, a] nm/f porter; (conserje) caretaker; (ujier) doorman; (Deporte) goalkeeper; **portero automático** (ESP) entry phone

pórtico ['portiko] nm (patio) portico, porch; (fig) gateway; (arcada) arcade

portorriqueño, -a [portorri'keɲo, a] adj Puerto Rican

Portugal [portu'ɣal] nm Portugal; **portugués, -esa** adj, nm/f Portuguese ▷ nm (Ling) Portuguese

porvenir [porβe'nir] nm future

pos [pos] prep: **en ~ de** after, in pursuit of

posaderas [posa'ðeras] nfpl backside sg, buttocks

posar [po'sar] vt (en el suelo) to lay down, put down; (la mano) to place, put gently ▷ vi (modelo) to sit, pose; **posarse** vr to settle;

(*pájaro*) to perch; (*avión*) to land, come down

posavasos [posa'basos] *nm inv* coaster; (*para cerveza*) beermat

posdata [pos'ðata] *nf* postscript

pose ['pose] *nf* pose

poseedor, a [posee'ðor, a] *nm/f* owner, possessor; (*de récord, puesto*) holder

poseer [pose'er] *vt* to possess, own; (*ventaja*) to enjoy; (*récord, puesto*) to hold

posesivo, -a [pose'siβo, a] *adj* possessive

posibilidad [posiβili'ðað] *nf* possibility; (*oportunidad*) chance; **posibilitar** *vt* to make possible; (*hacer realizable*) to make feasible

posible [po'siβle] *adj* possible; (*realizable*) feasible; **de ser ~** if possible; **en lo ~** as far as possible

posición [posi'θjon] *nf* position; (*rango social*) status

positivo, -a [posi'tiβo, a] *adj* positive

poso ['poso] *nm* sediment; (*heces*) dregs *pl*

posponer [pospo'ner] *vt* (*relegar*) to put behind/below; (*aplazar*) to postpone

posta ['posta] *nf*: **a ~** deliberately, on purpose

postal [pos'tal] *adj* postal ▷ *nf* postcard

poste ['poste] *nm* (*de telégrafos etc*) post, pole; (*columna*) pillar

póster ['poster] (*pl* **~es, ~s**) *nm* poster

posterior [poste'rjor] *adj* back, rear; (*siguiente*) following, subsequent; (*más tarde*) later

postgrado [post'graðo] *nm* = **posgrado**

postizo, -a [pos'tiθo, a] *adj* false, artificial ▷ *nm* hairpiece

postre ['postre] *nm* sweet, dessert

póstumo, -a ['postumo, a] *adj* posthumous

postura [pos'tura] *nf* (*del cuerpo*) posture, position; (*fig*) attitude, position

potable [po'taβle] *adj* drinkable; **agua ~** drinking water

potaje [po'taxe] *nm* thick vegetable soup

potencia [po'tenθja] *nf* power; **potencial** [poten'θjal] *adj, nm* potential

potente [po'tente] *adj* powerful

potro, -a ['potro, a] *nm/f* (*Zool*) colt/filly ▷ *nm* (*de gimnasia*) vaulting horse

pozo ['poθo] *nm* well; (*de río*) deep pool; (*de mina*) shaft

PP (*ESP*) *nm abr* = **Partido Popular**

práctica ['praktika] *nf* practice; (*método*) method; (*arte, capacidad*) skill; **en la ~** in practice

practicable [prakti'kaβle] *adj* practicable; (*camino*) passable

practicante [prakti'kante] *nmf* (*Med: ayudante de doctor*) medical assistant;

(: *enfermero*) nurse; (*quien practica algo*) practitioner ▷ *adj* practising

practicar [prakti'kar] *vt* to practise; (*Deporte*) to play; (*realizar*) to carry out, perform

práctico, -a ['praktiko, a] *adj* practical; (*instruído: persona*) skilled, expert

practique *etc vb* V **practicar**

pradera [pra'ðera] *nf* meadow; (*us etc*) prairie

prado ['praðo] *nm* (*campo*) meadow, field; (*pastizal*) pasture

Praga ['praɣa] *n* Prague

pragmático, -a [praɣ'matiko, a] *adj* pragmatic

precario, -a [pre'karjo, a] *adj* precarious

precaución [prekau'θjon] *nf* (*medida preventiva*) preventive measure, precaution; (*prudencia*) caution, wariness

precedente [preθe'ðente] *adj* preceding; (*anterior*) former ▷ *nm* precedent

preceder [preθe'ðer] *vt, vi* to precede, go before, come before

precepto [pre'θepto] *nm* precept

precinto [pre'θinto] *nm* (*tb:* **~ de garantía**) seal

precio ['preθjo] *nm* price; (*costo*) cost; (*valor*) value, worth; (*de viaje*) fare; **precio al contado/de coste/de oportunidad** cash/cost/bargain price; **precio al por menor** retail price; **precio de ocasión** bargain price; **precio de venta al público** retail price; **precio tope** top price

preciosidad [preθjosi'ðað] *nf* (*valor*) (high) value, (great) worth; (*encanto*) charm; (*cosa bonita*) beautiful thing; **es una ~** it's lovely, it's really beautiful

precioso, -a [pre'θjoso, a] *adj* precious; (*de mucho valor*) valuable; (*fam*) lovely, beautiful

precipicio [preθi'piθjo] *nm* cliff, precipice; (*fig*) abyss

precipitación [preθipita'θjon] *nf* haste; (*lluvia*) rainfall

precipitado, -a [preθipi'taðo, a] *adj* (*conducta*) hasty, rash; (*salida*) hasty, sudden

precipitar [preθipi'tar] *vt* (*arrojar*) to hurl down, throw; (*apresurar*) to hasten; (*acelerar*) to speed up, accelerate; **precipitarse** *vr* to throw o.s.; (*apresurarse*) to rush; (*actuar sin pensar*) to act rashly

precisamente [preθisa'mente] *adv* precisely; (*exactamente*) precisely, exactly

precisar [preθi'sar] *vt* (*necesitar*) to need, require; (*fijar*) to determine exactly, fix; (*especificar*) to specify

precisión [preθi'sjon] *nf* (*exactitud*) precision

preciso, -a [pre'θiso, a] *adj* (*exacto*)
precise; (*necesario*) necessary, essential

preconcebido, -a [prekonθe'βiðo, a] *adj*
preconceived

precoz [pre'koθ] *adj* (*persona*) precocious;
(*calvicie etc*) premature

predecir [preðe'θir] *vt* to predict, forecast

predestinado, -a [preðesti'naðo, a] *adj*
predestined

predicar [preði'kar] *vt, vi* to preach

predicción [preðik'θjon] *nf* prediction

predilecto, -a [preði'lekto, a] *adj*
favourite

predisposición [preðisposi'θjon] *nf*
inclination; prejudice, bias

predominar [preðomi'nar] *vt* to
dominate ▷ *vi* to predominate; (*prevalecer*)
to prevail; **predominio** *nm* predominance;
prevalence

preescolar [pre(e)sko'lar] *adj* preschool

prefabricado, -a [prefaβri'kaðo, a] *adj*
prefabricated

prefacio [pre'faθjo] *nm* preface

preferencia [prefe'renθja] *nf* preference;
de ~ preferably, for preference

preferible [prefe'riβle] *adj* preferable

preferir [prefe'rir] *vt* to prefer

prefiero *etc vb* V **preferir**

prefijo [pre'fixo] *nm* (*Tel*) (dialling) code

pregunta [pre'ɣunta] *nf* question;
hacer una ~ to ask a question; **preguntas
frecuentes** FAQs, frequently asked
questions

preguntar [preɣun'tar] *vt* to ask;
(*cuestionar*) to question ▷ *vi* to ask;
preguntarse *vr* to wonder; **preguntar
por algn** to ask for sb; **preguntón, -ona**
[preɣun'ton, ona] *adj* inquisitive

prehistórico, -a [preis'toriko, a] *adj*
prehistoric

prejuicio [pre'xwiθjo] *nm* (*acto*)
prejudgement; (*idea preconcebida*)
preconception; (*parcialidad*) prejudice, bias

preludio [pre'luðjo] *nm* prelude

prematuro, -a [prema'turo, a] *adj*
premature

premeditar [premeði'tar] *vt* to
premeditate

premiar [pre'mjar] *vt* to reward; (*en un
concurso*) to give a prize to

premio ['premjo] *nm* reward; prize; (*Com*)
premium

prenatal [prena'tal] *adj* antenatal,
prenatal

prenda ['prenda] *nf* (*ropa*) garment, article
of clothing; (*garantía*) pledge; **prendas** *nfpl*
(*talentos*) talents, gifts

prender [pren'der] *vt* (*captar*) to catch,

capture; (*detener*) to arrest; (*Costura*) to
pin, attach; (*sujetar*) to fasten ▷ *vi* to
catch; (*arraigar*) to take root; **prenderse** *vr*
(*encenderse*) to catch fire

prendido, -a [pren'diðo, a] (*LAM*) *adj* (*luz
etc*) on

prensa ['prensa] *nf* press; **la ~** the press

preñado, -a [pre'ɲaðo, a] *adj* pregnant; **~
de** pregnant with, full of

preocupación [preokupa'θjon] *nf* worry,
concern; (*ansiedad*) anxiety

preocupado, -a [preoku'paðo, a] *adj*
worried, concerned; (*ansioso*) anxious

preocupar [preoku'par] *vt* to worry;
preocuparse *vr* to worry; **~se de algo**
(*hacerse cargo*) to take care of sth

preparación [prepara'θjon] *nf*
(*acto*) preparation; (*estado*) readiness;
(*entrenamiento*) training

preparado, -a [prepa'raðo, a] *adj*
(*dispuesto*) prepared; (*Culin*) ready (to serve)
▷ *nm* preparation

preparar [prepa'rar] *vt* (*disponer*)
to prepare, get ready; (*Tec: tratar*) to
prepare, process; (*entrenar*) to teach, train;
prepararse *vr*: **~se a** *o* **para** to prepare to
o for, get ready to *o* for; **preparativo, -a** *adj*
preparatory, preliminary; **preparativos**
nmpl preparations; **preparatoria** (*MÉX*)
nf sixth-form college (*BRIT*), senior high
school (*US*)

presa ['presa] *nf* (*cosa apresada*) catch;
(*víctima*) victim; (*de animal*) prey; (*de agua*)
dam

presagiar [presa'xjar] *vt* to presage,
forebode; **presagio** *nm* omen

prescindir [presθin'dir] *vi*: **~ de** (*privarse
de*) to do *o* go without; (*descartar*) to
dispense with

prescribir [preskri'βir] *vt* to prescribe

presencia [pre'senθja] *nf* presence;
presenciar *vt* to be present at; (*asistir a*) to
attend; (*ver*) to see, witness

presentación [presenta'θjon] *nf*
presentation; (*introducción*) introduction

presentador, a [presenta'ðor, a] *nm/f*
presenter, compère

presentar [presen'tar] *vt* to present;
(*ofrecer*) to offer; (*mostrar*) to show, display;
(*a una persona*) to introduce; **presentarse**
vr (*llegar inesperadamente*) to appear, turn
up; (*ofrecerse: como candidato*) to run, stand;
(*aparecer*) to show, appear; (*solicitar empleo*)
to apply

presente [pre'sente] *adj* present ▷ *nm*
present; **hacer ~** to state, declare; **tener ~** to
remember, bear in mind

presentimiento [presenti'mjento] *nm*

premonition, presentiment
presentir [presen'tir] *vt* to have a premonition of
preservación [preserβa'θjon] *nf* protection, preservation
preservar [preser'βar] *vt* to protect, preserve; **preservativo** *nm* sheath, condom
presidencia [presi'ðenθja] *nf* presidency; (*de comité*) chairmanship
presidente [presi'ðente] *nmf* president; (*de comité*) chairman/woman
presidir [presi'ðir] *vt* (*dirigir*) to preside at, preside over; (: *comité*) to take the chair at; (*dominar*) to dominate, rule ▷ *vi* to preside; to take the chair
presión [pre'sjon] *nf* pressure; **presión atmosférica** atmospheric *o* air pressure; **presionar** *vt* to press; (*fig*) to press, put pressure on ▷ *vi*: **presionar para** to press for
preso, -a ['preso, a] *nm/f* prisoner; **tomar** *o* **llevar ~ a algn** to arrest sb, take sb prisoner
prestación [presta'θjon] *nf* service; (*subsidio*) benefit; **prestaciones** *nfpl* (*Tec, Auto*) performance features
prestado, -a [pres'taðo, a] *adj* on loan; **pedir ~** to borrow
prestamista [presta'mista] *nmf* moneylender
préstamo ['prestamo] *nm* loan; **préstamo hipotecario** mortgage
prestar [pres'tar] *vt* to lend, loan; (*atención*) to pay; (*ayuda*) to give
prestigio [pres'tixjo] *nm* prestige; **prestigioso, -a** *adj* (*honorable*) prestigious; (*famoso, renombrado*) renowned, famous
presumido, -a [presu'miðo, a] *adj* (*persona*) vain
presumir [presu'mir] *vt* to presume ▷ *vi* (*tener aires*) to be conceited; **presunto, -a** *adj* (*supuesto*) supposed, presumed; (*así llamado*) so-called; **presuntuoso, -a** *adj* conceited, presumptuous
presupuesto [presu'pwesto] *pp de* **presuponer** ▷ *nm* (*Finanzas*) budget; (*estimación: de costo*) estimate
pretencioso, -a [preten'θjoso, a] *adj* pretentious
pretender [preten'der] *vt* (*intentar*) to try to, seek to; (*reivindicar*) to claim; (*buscar*) to seek, try for; (*cortejar*) to woo, court; **~ que** to expect that

▎No confundir **pretender** con la palabra inglesa *pretend*.

pretendiente *nmf* (*amante*) suitor; (*al trono*) pretender; **pretensión** *nf* (*aspiración*) aspiration; (*reivindicación*) claim; (*orgullo*)

pretension
pretexto [pre'teksto] *nm* pretext; (*excusa*) excuse
prevención [preβen'θjon] *nf* prevention; (*precaución*) precaution
prevenido, -a [preβe'niðo, a] *adj* prepared, ready; (*cauteloso*) cautious
prevenir [preβe'nir] *vt* (*impedir*) to prevent; (*predisponer*) to prejudice, bias; (*avisar*) to warn; (*preparar*) to prepare, get ready; **prevenirse** *vr* to get ready, prepare; **~se contra** to take precautions against; **preventivo, -a** *adj* preventive, precautionary
prever [pre'βer] *vt* to foresee
previo, -a ['preβjo, a] *adj* (*anterior*) previous; (*preliminar*) preliminary ▷ *prep*: **~ acuerdo de los otros** subject to the agreement of the others
previsión [preβi'sjon] *nf* (*perspicacia*) foresight; (*predicción*) forecast; **previsto, -a** *adj* anticipated, forecast
prima ['prima] *nf* (*Com*) bonus; (*de seguro*) premium; *V tb* **primo**
primario, -a [pri'marjo, a] *adj* primary
primavera [prima'βera] *nf* spring(-time)
primera [pri'mera] *nf* (*Auto*) first gear; (*Ferro: tb*: **~ clase**) first class; **de ~** (*fam*) first-class, first-rate
primero, -a [pri'mero, a] (*adj* **primer**) first; (*principal*) prime *adv* first; (*más bien*) sooner, rather; **primera plana** front page
primitivo, -a [primi'tiβo, a] *adj* primitive; (*original*) original
primo, -a ['primo, a] *adj* prime ▷ *nm/f* cousin; (*fam*) fool, idiot; **materias primas** raw materials; **primo hermano** first cousin
primogénito, -a [primo'xenito, a] *adj* first-born
primoroso, -a [primo'roso, a] *adj* exquisite, delicate
princesa [prin'θesa] *nf* princess
principal [prinθi'pal] *adj* principal, main ▷ *nm* (*jefe*) chief, principal
príncipe ['prinθipe] *nm* prince
principiante [prinθi'pjante] *nmf* beginner
principio [prin'θipjo] *nm* (*comienzo*) beginning, start; (*origen*) origin; (*primera etapa*) rudiment, basic idea; (*moral*) principle; **desde el ~** from the first; **en un ~** at first; **a ~s de** at the beginning of
pringue ['pringe] *nm* (*grasa*) grease, fat, dripping
prioridad [priori'ðað] *nf* priority
prisa ['prisa] *nf* (*apresuramiento*) hurry, haste; (*rapidez*) speed; (*urgencia*) (sense of) urgency; **a** *o* **de ~** quickly; **correr ~** to be

urgent; **darse ~** to hurry up; **tener ~** to be
in a hurry
prisión [pri'sjon] nf (cárcel) prison; (período
de cárcel) imprisonment; **prisionero, -a**
nm/f prisoner
prismáticos [pris'matikos] nmpl
binoculars
privado, -a [pri'βaðo, a] adj private
privar [pri'βar] vt to deprive; **privativo, -a**
adj exclusive
privilegiar [priβile'xjar] vt to grant a
privilege to; (favorecer) to favour
privilegio [priβi'lexjo] nm privilege;
(concesión) concession
pro [pro] nm of profit, advantage
▷ prep: **asociación ~ ciegos** association
for the blind ▷ prefijo: **~ americano** pro-
American; **en ~ de** on behalf of, for; **los ~s y
los contras** the pros and cons
proa ['proa] nf bow, prow; **de ~** bow cpd,
fore
probabilidad [proβaβili'ðað] nf
probability, likelihood; (oportunidad,
posibilidad) chance, prospect; **probable** adj
probable, likely
probador [proβa'ðor] nm (en tienda)
fitting room
probar [pro'βar] vt (demostrar) to prove;
(someter a prueba) to test, try out; (ropa) to try
on; (comida) to taste ▷ vi to try; **~se un traje**
to try on a suit
probeta [pro'βeta] nf test tube
problema [pro'βlema] nm problem
procedente [proθe'ðente] adj (razonable)
reasonable; (conforme a derecho) proper,
fitting; **~ de** coming from, originating in
proceder [proθe'ðer] vi (avanzar) to
proceed; (actuar) to act; (ser correcto) to
be right (and proper), be fitting ▷ nm
(comportamiento) behaviour, conduct; **~ de**
to come from, originate in; **procedimiento**
nm procedure; (proceso) process; (método)
means pl, method
procesador [proθesa'ðor] nm processor;
procesador de textos word processor
procesar [proθe'sar] vt to try, put on trial
procesión [proθe'sjon] nf procession
proceso [pro'θeso] nm process; (Jur) trial
proclamar [prokla'mar] vt to proclaim
procrear [prokre'ar] vt, vi to procreate
procurador, a [prokura'ðor, a] nm/f
attorney
procurar [proku'rar] vt (intentar) to
try, endeavour; (conseguir) to get, obtain;
(asegurar) to secure; (producir) to produce
prodigio [pro'ðixjo] nm prodigy; (milagro)
wonder, marvel; **prodigioso, -a** adj
prodigious, marvellous

pródigo, -a ['proðixo, a] adj: **hijo ~**
prodigal son
producción [proðuk'θjon] nf (gen)
production; (producto) output; **producción
en serie** mass production
producir [proðu'θir] vt to produce;
(causar) to cause, bring about; **producirse**
vr (cambio) to come about; (accidente) to
take place; (problema etc) to arise; (hacerse) to
be produced, be made; (estallar) to break out
productividad [proðuktiβi'ðað]
nf productivity; **productivo, -a** adj
productive; (provechoso) profitable
producto [pro'ðukto] nm product
productor, a [proðuk'tor, a] adj
productive, producing ▷ nm/f producer
proeza [pro'eθa] nf exploit, feat
profano, -a [pro'fano, a] adj profane
▷ nm/f layman/woman
profecía [profe'θia] nf prophecy
profesión [profe'sjon] nf profession; (en
formulario) occupation; **profesional** adj
professional
profesor, a [profe'sor, a] nm/f teacher;
profesorado nm teaching profession
profeta [pro'feta] nmf prophet
prófugo, -a ['profuxo, a] nm/f fugitive;
(Mil: desertor) deserter
profundidad [profundi'ðað] nf depth;
profundizar vi: **profundizar en** to go
deeply into; **profundo, -a** adj deep;
(misterio, pensador) profound
progenitor [proxeni'tor] nm ancestor;
progenitores nmpl (padres) parents
programa [pro'ɣrama] nm programme
(BRIT), program (US); **programa de estudios**
curriculum, syllabus; **programación** nf
programming; **programador, a** nm/f
programmer; **programar** vt to program
progresar [proɣre'sar] vi to progress,
make progress; **progresista** adj,
nmf progressive; **progresivo, -a** adj
progressive; (gradual) gradual; (continuo)
continuous; **progreso** nm progress
prohibición [proiβi'θjon] nf prohibition,
ban
prohibir [proi'βir] vt to prohibit, ban,
forbid; **prohibido o se prohibe fumar** no
smoking; **"prohibido el paso"** "no entry"
prójimo, -a ['proximo, a] nm/f fellow
man; (vecino) neighbour
prólogo ['proloɣo] nm prologue
prolongar [prolon'xar] vt to extend;
(reunión etc) to prolong; (calle, tubo) to extend
promedio [pro'meðjo] nm average; (de
distancia) middle, mid-point
promesa [pro'mesa] nf promise
prometer [prome'ter] vt to promise ▷ vi

P

prominente | 166

to show promise; **prometerse** vr (novios) to get engaged; **prometido, -a** adj promised; engaged ▷ nm/f fiancé/fiancée
prominente [promi'nente] adj prominent
promoción [promo'θjon] nf promotion
promotor [promo'tor] nm promoter; (instigador) instigator
promover [promo'βer] vt to promote; (causar) to cause; (instigar) to instigate, stir up
promulgar [promul'ɣar] vt to promulgate; (anunciar) to proclaim
pronombre [pro'nombre] nm pronoun
pronosticar [pronosti'kar] vt to predict, foretell, forecast; **pronóstico** nm prediction, forecast; **pronóstico del tiempo** weather forecast
pronto, -a ['pronto, a] adj (rápido) prompt, quick; (preparado) ready ▷ adv quickly, promptly; (en seguida) at once, right away; (dentro de poco) soon; (temprano) early ▷ nm: **tiene unos ~s muy malos** he gets ratty all of a sudden (inf); **de ~** suddenly; **por lo ~** meanwhile, for the present
pronunciación [pronunθja'θjon] nf pronunciation
pronunciar [pronun'θjar] vt to pronounce; (discurso) to make, deliver; **pronunciarse** vr to revolt, rebel; (declararse) to declare o.s.
propagación [propaɣa'θjon] nf propagation
propaganda [propa'ɣanda] nf (Pol) propaganda; (Com) advertising
propenso, -a [pro'penso, a] adj inclined to; **ser ~ a** to be inclined to, have a tendency to
propicio, -a [pro'piθjo, a] adj favourable, propitious
propiedad [propje'ðað] nf property; (posesión) possession, ownership; **propiedad particular** private property
propietario, -a [propje'tarjo, a] nm/f owner, proprietor
propina [pro'pina] nf tip
propio, -a ['propjo, a] adj own, of one's own; (característico) characteristic, typical; (debido) proper; (mismo) selfsame, very; **el ~ ministro** the minister himself; **¿tienes casa propia?** have you a house of your own?
proponer [propo'ner] vt to propose, put forward; (problema) to pose; **proponerse** vr to propose, intend
proporción [propor'θjon] nf proportion; (Mat) ratio; **proporciones** nfpl (dimensiones) dimensions; (fig) size sg; **proporcionado, -a** adj proportionate; (regular) medium,

middling; (justo) just right; **proporcionar** vt (dar) to give, supply, provide
proposición [proposi'θjon] nf proposition; (propuesta) proposal
propósito [pro'posito] nm purpose; (intento) aim, intention ▷ adv: **a ~** by the way, incidentally; (a posta) on purpose, deliberately; **a ~ de** about, with regard to
propuesta [pro'pwesta] vb V **proponer** ▷ nf proposal
propulsar [propul'sar] vt to drive, propel; (fig) to promote, encourage; **propulsión** nf propulsion; **propulsión a chorro** o **por reacción** jet propulsion
prórroga ['prorroɣa] nf extension; (Jur) stay; (Com) deferment; (Deporte) extra time; **prorrogar** vt (período) to extend; (decisión) to defer, postpone
prosa ['prosa] nf prose
proseguir [prose'ɣir] vt to continue, carry on ▷ vi to continue, go on
prospecto [pros'pekto] nm prospectus
prosperar [prospe'rar] vi to prosper, thrive, flourish; **prosperidad** nf prosperity; (éxito) success; **próspero, -a** adj prosperous, flourishing; (que tiene éxito) successful
prostíbulo [pros'tiβulo] nm brothel (BRIT), house of prostitution (US)
prostitución [prostitu'θjon] nf prostitution
prostituir [prosti'twir] vt to prostitute; **prostituirse** vr to prostitute o.s., become a prostitute
prostituta [prosti'tuta] nf prostitute
protagonista [protaɣo'nista] nmf protagonist
protección [protek'θjon] nf protection
protector, a [protek'tor, a] adj protective, protecting ▷ nm/f protector
proteger [prote'xer] vt to protect; **protegido, -a** nm/f protégé/protégée
proteína [prote'ina] nf protein
protesta [pro'testa] nf protest; (declaración) protestation
protestante [protes'tante] adj Protestant
protestar [protes'tar] vt to protest, declare ▷ vi to protest
protocolo [proto'kolo] nm protocol
prototipo [proto'tipo] nm prototype
provecho [pro'βetʃo] nm advantage, benefit; (Finanzas) profit; **¡buen ~!** bon appétit!; **en ~ de** to the benefit of; **sacar ~ de** to benefit from, profit by
provenir [proβe'nir] vi: **~ de** to come o stem from
proverbio [pro'βerβjo] nm proverb

providencia [proβi'ðenθja] *nf* providence
provincia [pro'βinθja] *nf* province
provisión [proβi'sjon] *nf* provision;
(*abastecimiento*) provision, supply; (*medida*)
measure, step
provisional [proβisjo'nal] *adj* provisional
provocar [proβo'kar] *vt* (*alentar*) to tempt, invite; (*causar*) to bring
about, lead to; (*promover*) to promote;
(*estimular*) to rouse, stimulate; **¿te provoca
un café?** (*CAM*) would you like a coffee?;
provocativo, -a *adj* provocative
proxeneta [prokse'neta] *nm* pimp
próximamente [proksima'mente] *adv*
shortly, soon
proximidad [proksimi'ðað] *nf* closeness,
proximity; **próximo, -a** *adj* near, close;
(*vecino*) neighbouring; (*siguiente*) next
proyectar [projek'tar] *vt* (*objeto*) to hurl,
throw; (*luz*) to cast, shed; (*Cine*) to screen,
show; (*planear*) to plan
proyectil [projek'til] *nm* projectile,
missile
proyecto [pro'jekto] *nm* plan; (*estimación
de costo*) detailed estimate
proyector [projek'tor] *nm* (*Cine*) projector
prudencia [pru'ðenθja] *nf* (*sabiduría*)
wisdom; (*cuidado*) care; **prudente** *adj*
sensible, wise; (*conductor*) careful
prueba *etc* ['prweβa] *vb* V **probar** ▷ *nf*
proof; (*ensayo*) test, trial; (*degustación*)
tasting, sampling; (*de ropa*) fitting; **a ~ on
trial; a ~ de** proof against; **a ~ de agua/
fuego** waterproof/fireproof; **someter a ~** to
put to the test
psico... [siko] *prefijo* psycho...;
psicología *nf* psychology; **psicológico,
-a** *adj* psychological; **psicólogo, -a** *nm/f*
psychologist; **psicópata** *nmf* psychopath;
psicosis *nf inv* psychosis
psiquiatra [si'kjatra] *nmf* psychiatrist;
psiquiátrico, -a *adj* psychiatric
PSOE [pe'soe] (*ESP*) *nm abr* = **Partido
Socialista Obrero Español**
púa ['pua] *nf* (*Bot, Zool*) prickle, spine; (*para
guitarra*) plectrum (*BRIT*), pick (*US*); **alambre
de ~** barbed wire
pubertad [puβer'tað] *nf* puberty
publicación [puβlika'θjon] *nf*
publication
publicar [puβli'kar] *vt* (*editar*) to publish;
(*hacer público*) to publicize; (*divulgar*) to make
public, divulge
publicidad [puβliði'ðað] *nf* publicity;
(*Com: propaganda*) advertising; **publicitario,
-a** *adj* publicity *cpd*; advertising *cpd*
público, -a ['puβliko, a] *adj* public ▷ *nm*
public; (*Teatro etc*) audience

puchero [pu'tʃero] *nm* (*Culin: guiso*) stew;
(: *olla*) cooking pot; **hacer ~s** to pout
pucho ['putʃo] (*cs: fam*) *nm* cigarette,
fag (*BRIT*)
pude *etc vb* V **poder**
pudiente [pu'ðjente] *adj* (*rico*) wealthy,
well-to-do
pudiera *etc vb* V **poder**
pudor [pu'ðor] *nm* modesty
pudrir [pu'ðrir] *vt* to rot; **pudrirse** *vr* to
rot, decay
pueblo ['pweβlo] *nm* people; (*nación*)
nation; (*aldea*) village
puedo *etc vb* V **poder**
puente ['pwente] *nm* bridge; **hacer ~**
(*fam*) to take extra days off work between 2
public holidays; to take a long weekend;
puente aéreo shuttle service; **puente
colgante** suspension bridge; **puente
levadizo** drawbridge

HACER PUENTE

When a public holiday in Spain falls on
a Tuesday or Thursday it is common
practice for employers to make the
Monday or Friday a holiday as well and
to give everyone a four-day weekend.
This is known as **hacer puente**. When
a named public holiday such as the **Día
de la Constitución** falls on a Tuesday
or Thursday, people refer to the whole
holiday period as e.g. the **puente de la
Constitución**.

puerco, -a ['pwerko, a] *nm/f* pig/
sow ▷ *adj* (*sucio*) dirty, filthy; (*obsceno*)
disgusting; **puerco espín** porcupine
pueril [pwe'ril] *adj* childish
puerro ['pwerro] *nm* leek
puerta ['pwerta] *nf* door; (*de jardín*) gate;
(*portal*) doorway; (*fig*) gateway; (*portería*)
goal; **a la ~** at the door; **a ~ cerrada** behind
closed doors; **puerta giratoria** revolving
door
puerto ['pwerto] *nm* port; (*paso*) pass; (*fig*)
haven, refuge
Puerto Rico [pwerto'riko] *nm* Puerto
Rico; **puertorriqueño, -a** *adj, nm/f* Puerto
Rican
pues [pwes] *adv* (*entonces*) then; (*bueno*)
well, well then; (*así que*) so ▷ *conj* (*ya que*)
since; **¡~ sí!** yes!, certainly!
puesta ['pwesta] *nf* (*apuesta*) bet, stake;
puesta al día updating; **puesta a punto**
fine tuning; **puesta de sol** sunset; **puesta
en marcha** starting
puesto, -a ['pwesto, a] *pp de* **poner**

▷ adj: **tener algo ~** to have sth on, be wearing sth ▷ nm (lugar, posición) place; (trabajo) post, job; (Com) stall ▷ conj: **~ que** since, as

púgil ['puxil] nm boxer

pulga ['pulɣa] nf flea

pulgada [pul'ɣaða] nf inch

pulgar [pul'ɣar] nm thumb

pulir [pu'lir] vt to polish; (alisar) to smooth; (fig) to polish up, touch up

pulmón [pul'mon] nm lung; **pulmonía** nf pneumonia

pulpa ['pulpa] nf pulp; (de fruta) flesh, soft part

pulpería [pulpe'ria] (LAM) nf (tienda) small grocery store

púlpito ['pulpito] nm pulpit

pulpo ['pulpo] nm octopus

pulque ['pulke] nm pulque

● **PULQUE**
●
● **Pulque** is a thick, white, alcoholic
● drink which is very popular in Mexico.
● In ancient times it was considered
● sacred by the Aztecs. It is produced by
● fermenting the juice of the **maguey**,
● a Mexican cactus similar to the agave.
● It can be drunk by itself or mixed with
● fruit or vegetable juice.

pulsación [pulsa'θjon] nf beat; **pulsaciones** pulse rate

pulsar [pul'sar] vt (tecla) to touch, tap; (Mús) to play; (botón) to press, push ▷ vi to pulsate; (latir) to beat, throb

pulsera [pul'sera] nf bracelet

pulso ['pulso] nm (Anat) pulse; (fuerza) strength; (firmeza) steadiness, steady hand

pulverizador [pulβeriθa'ðor] nm spray, spray gun

pulverizar [pulβeri'θar] vt to pulverize; (líquido) to spray

puna ['puna] (CAM) nf mountain sickness

punta ['punta] nf point, tip; (extremo) end; (fig) touch, trace; **horas ~** peak o rush hours; **sacar ~ a** to sharpen

puntada [pun'taða] nf (Costura) stitch

puntal [pun'tal] nm prop, support

puntapié [punta'pje] nm kick

puntería [punte'ria] nf (de arma) aim, aiming; (destreza) marksmanship

puntero, -a [pun'tero, a] adj leading ▷ nm (palo) pointer

puntiagudo, -a [puntja'ɣuðo, a] adj sharp, pointed

puntilla [pun'tiʎa] nf (encaje) lace edging o trim; **(andar) de ~s** (to walk) on tiptoe

punto ['punto] nm (gen) point; (señal diminuta) spot, dot; (Costura, Med) stitch; (lugar) spot, place; (momento) point, moment; **a ~** ready; **estar a ~ de** to be on the point of o about to; **en ~** on the dot; **hasta cierto ~** to some extent; **hacer ~** (ESP: tejer) to knit; **dos ~s** (Ling) colon; **punto de interrogación** question mark; **punto de vista** point of view, viewpoint; **punto final** full stop (BRIT), period (US); **punto muerto** dead center; (Auto) neutral (gear); **punto y aparte** (en dictado) full stop, new paragraph; **punto y coma** semicolon

puntocom [punto'kom] adj inv, nf inv dotcom

puntuación [puntwa'θjon] nf punctuation; (puntos: en examen) mark(s) (pl); (Deporte) score

puntual [pun'twal] adj (a tiempo) punctual; (exacto) exact, accurate; **puntualidad** nf punctuality; exactness, accuracy

puntuar [pun'twar] vi (Deporte) to score, count

punzante [pun'θante] adj (dolor) shooting, sharp; (herramienta) sharp

puñado [pu'ɲaðo] nm handful

puñal [pu'ɲal] nm dagger; **puñalada** nf stab

puñetazo [puɲe'taθo] nm punch

puño ['puɲo] nm (Anat) fist; (cantidad) fistful, handful; (Costura) cuff; (de herramienta) handle

pupila [pu'pila] nf pupil

pupitre [pu'pitre] nm desk

puré [pu're] nm purée; (sopa) (thick) soup; **puré de papas** (LAM) mashed potatoes; **puré de patatas** (ESP) mashed potatoes

purga ['purɣa] nf purge; **purgante** adj, nm purgative

purgatorio [purɣa'torjo] nm purgatory

purificar [purifi'kar] vt to purify; (refinar) to refine

puritano, -a [puri'tano, a] adj (actitud) puritanical; (iglesia, tradición) puritan ▷ nm/f puritan

puro, -a ['puro, a] adj pure; (verdad) simple, plain ▷ nm cigar

púrpura ['purpura] nf purple

pus [pus] nm pus

puse etc vb V **poder**

pusiera etc vb V **poder**

puta ['puta] (fam!) nf whore, prostitute

putrefacción [putrefak'θjon] nf rotting, putrefaction

PVP nm abr (= precio de venta al público) RRP

pyme, PYME ['pime] nf abr (= Pequeña y Mediana Empresa) SME

q

fraction

quebrantar [keβran'tar] vt (infringir) to violate, transgress

quebrar [ke'βrar] vt to break, smash ▷ vi to go bankrupt

quedar [ke'ðar] vi to stay, remain; (encontrarse: sitio) to be; (haber aún) to remain, be left; **quedarse** vr to remain, stay (behind); **~se (con) algo** to keep sth; **~ en** (acordar) to agree on/to; **~ en nada** to come to nothing; **~ por hacer** to be still to be done; **~ ciego/mudo** to be left blind/ dumb; **no te queda bien ese vestido** that dress doesn't suit you; **eso queda muy lejos** that's a long way (away); **quedamos a las seis** we agreed to meet at six

quedo, -a ['keðo, a] adj still ▷ adv softly, gently

quehacer [kea'θer] nm task, job; **quehaceres (domésticos)** nmpl household chores

queja ['kexa] nf complaint; **quejarse** vr (enfermo) to moan, groan; (protestar) to complain; **quejarse de que** to complain that; **quejido** nm moan

quemado, -a [ke'maðo, a] adj burnt

quemadura [kema'ðura] nf burn, scald

quemar [ke'mar] vt to burn; (fig: malgastar) to burn up, squander ▷ vi to be burning hot; **quemarse** vr (consumirse) to burn (up); (del sol) to get sunburnt

quemarropa [kema'rropa]: **a ~** adv point-blank

quepo etc vb V **caber**

querella [ke'reʎa] nf (Jur) charge; (disputa) dispute

que [ke] conj **1** (con oración subordinada: muchas veces no se traduce) that; **dijo que vendría** he said (that) he would come; **espero que lo encuentres** I hope (that) you find it; V tb **el**

2 (en oración independiente): **¡que entre!** send him in; **¡que aproveche!** enjoy your meal!; **¡que se mejore tu padre!** I hope your father gets better

3 (enfático): **¿me quieres? – ¡que sí!** do you love me? – of course!

4 (consecutivo: muchas veces no se traduce) that; **es tan grande que no lo puedo levantar** it's so big (that) I can't lift it

5 (comparaciones) than; **yo que tú/él** if I were you/him; V tb **más, menos, mismo**

6 (valor disyuntivo): **que le guste o no** whether he likes it or not; **que venga o que no venga** whether he comes or not

7 (porque): **no puedo, que tengo que quedarme en casa** I can't, I've got to stay in ▷ pron **1** (cosa) that, which; (+ prep) which; **el sombrero que te compraste** the hat (that o which) you bought; **la cama en que dormí** the bed (that o which) I slept in

2 (persona: suj) that, who; (: objeto) that, whom; **el amigo que me acompañó al museo** the friend that o who went to the museum with me; **la chica que invité** the girl (that o whom) I invited

qué [ke] adj what?, which? ▷ pron what?; **¡~ divertido!** how funny!; **¿~ edad tienes?** how old are you?; **¿de ~ me hablas?** what are you saying to me?; **¿~ tal?** how are you?, how are things?; **¿~ hay (de nuevo)?** what's new?

quebrado, -a [ke'βraðo, a] adj (roto) broken ▷ nm/f bankrupt ▷ nm (Mat)

querer [ke'rer] vt **1** (desear) to want; **quiero más dinero** I want more money; **quisiera o querría un té** I'd like a tea; **sin querer** unintentionally; **quiero ayudar/que vayas** I want to help/you to go

2 (preguntas: para pedir algo): **¿quiere abrir la ventana?** could you open the window?; **¿quieres echarme una mano?** can you give me a hand?

3 (amar) to love; (tener cariño a) to be fond of; **te quiero** I love you; **quiere mucho a sus hijos** he's very fond of his children

4 **le pedí que me dejara ir pero no quiso** I asked him to let me go but he refused

querido, -a [ke'riðo, a] adj dear ▷ nm/f darling; (amante) lover

queso ['keso] nm cheese; **queso crema** (LAM) cream cheese; **queso de untar** (ESP) cream cheese; **queso manchego** *sheep's milk cheese made in La Mancha*

quicio ['kiθjo] *nm* hinge; **sacar a algn de ~** to get on sb's nerves

quiebra ['kjeβra] *nf* break, split; (*Com*) bankruptcy; (*Econ*) slump

quiebro ['kjeβro] *nm* (*del cuerpo*) swerve

quien [kjen] *pron* who; **hay ~ piensa que** there are those who think that; **no hay ~ lo haga** no-one will do it

quién [kjen] *pron* who, whom; **¿~ es?** who's there?

quienquiera [kjen'kjera] (*pl* **quienesquiera**) *pron* whoever

quiero *etc vb* V **querer**

quieto, -a ['kjeto, a] *adj* still; (*carácter*) placid

▍ No confundir **quieto** con la palabra inglesa *quiet*.

quietud *nf* stillness

químico, -a ['kimiko, a] *adj* chemical ▷ *nm/f* chemist ▷ *nf* chemistry

quincalla [kin'kaʎa] *nf* hardware, ironmongery (BRIT)

quince ['kinθe] *num* fifteen; **~ días** a fortnight; **quinceañero, -a** *nm/f* teenager; **quincena** *nf* fortnight; (*pago*) fortnightly pay; **quincenal** *adj* fortnightly

quiniela [ki'njela] *nf* football pools *pl*; **quinielas** *nfpl* (*impreso*) pools coupon *sg*

quinientos, -as [ki'njentos, as] *adj, num* five hundred

quinto, -a ['kinto, a] *adj* fifth ▷ *nf* country house; (*Mil*) call-up, draft

quiosco ['kjosko] *nm* (*de música*) bandstand; (*de periódicos*) news stand

quirófano [ki'rofano] *nm* operating theatre

quirúrgico, -a [ki'rurxiko, a] *adj* surgical

quise *etc vb* V **querer**

quisiera *etc vb* V **querer**

quisquilloso, -a [kiski'ʎoso, a] *adj* (*susceptible*) touchy; (*meticuloso*) pernickety

quiste ['kiste] *nm* cyst

quitaesmalte [kitaes'malte] *nm* nail-polish remover

quitamanchas [kita'mantʃas] *nm inv* stain remover

quitanieves [kita'njeβes] *nm inv* snowplough (BRIT), snowplow (US)

quitar [ki'tar] *vt* to remove, take away; (*ropa*) to take off; (*dolor*) to relieve; **¡quita de ahí!** get away!; **quitarse** *vr* to withdraw; (*ropa*) to take off; **se quitó el sombrero** he took off his hat

Quito ['kito] *n* Quito

quizá(s) [ki'θa(s)] *adv* perhaps, maybe

rábano ['raβano] *nm* radish; **me importa un ~** I don't give a damn

rabia ['raβja] *nf* (*Med*) rabies *sg*; (*ira*) fury, rage; **rabiar** *vi* to have rabies; to rage, be furious; **rabiar por algo** to long for sth

rabieta [ra'βjeta] *nf* tantrum, fit of temper

rabino [ra'βino] *nm* rabbi

rabioso, -a [ra'βjoso, a] *adj* rabid; (*fig*) furious

rabo ['raβo] *nm* tail

racha ['ratʃa] *nf* gust of wind; **buena/mala ~** spell of good/bad luck

racial [ra'θjal] *adj* racial, race *cpd*

racimo [ra'θimo] *nm* bunch

ración [ra'θjon] *nf* portion; **raciones** *nfpl* rations

racional [raθjo'nal] *adj* (*razonable*) reasonable; (*lógico*) rational

racionar [raθjo'nar] *vt* to ration (out)

racismo [ra'θismo] *nm* racism; **racista** *adj, nm* racist

radar [ra'ðar] *nm* radar

radiador [raðja'ðor] *nm* radiator

radiante [ra'ðjante] *adj* radiant

radical [raði'kal] *adj, nmf* radical

radicar [raði'kar] *vi*: **~ en** (*dificultad, problema*) to lie in; (*solución*) to consist in

radio ['raðjo] *nf* radio; (*aparato*) radio (set) ▷ *nm* (*Mat*) radius; (*Quím*) radium; **radioactividad** *nf* radioactivity; **radioactivo, -a** *adj* radioactive; **radiografía** *nf* X-ray; **radioterapia** *nf* radiotherapy; **radioyente** *nmf* listener

ráfaga ['rafaxa] *nf* gust; (*de luz*) flash; (*de tiros*) burst

raíz [ra'iθ] *nf* root; **a ~ de** as a result of; **raíz cuadrada** square root

raja ['raxa] *nf* (*de melón etc*) slice; (*grieta*) crack; **rajar** *vt* to split; (*fam*) to slash; **rajarse** *vr* to split, crack; **rajarse de** to back out of

rajatabla [raxa'taβla]: **a ~** adv
(estrictamente) strictly, to the letter
rallador [raʎa'ðor] nm grater
rallar [ra'ʎar] vt to grate
rama ['rama] nf branch; **ramaje** nm
branches pl, foliage; **ramal** nm (de cuerda)
strand; (Ferro) branch line (BRIT); (Auto)
branch (road) (BRIT)
rambla ['rambla] nf (avenida) avenue
ramo ['ramo] nm branch; (sección)
department, section
rampa ['rampa] nf ramp; **rampa de
acceso** entrance ramp
rana ['rana] nf frog; **salto de ~** leapfrog
ranchero [ran'tʃero] (MÉX) nm (hacendado)
rancher; smallholder
rancho ['rantʃo] nm (grande) ranch;
(pequeño) small farm
rancio, -a ['ranθjo, a] adj (comestibles)
rancid; (vino) aged, mellow; (fig) ancient
rango ['rango] nm rank, standing
ranura [ra'nura] nf groove; (de teléfono
etc) slot
rapar [ra'par] vt to shave; (los cabellos)
to crop
rapaz [ra'paθ] (nf ~a) nmf young boy/girl
▷ adj (Zool) predatory
rape ['rape] nm (pez) monkfish; **al ~**
cropped
rapé [ra'pe] nm snuff
rapidez [rapi'ðeθ] nf speed, rapidity;
rápido, -a adj fast, quick ▷ adv quickly
▷ nm (Ferro) express; **rápidos** nmpl rapids
rapiña [ra'piɲa] nm robbery; **ave de ~**
bird of prey
raptar [rap'tar] vt to kidnap; **rapto** nm
kidnapping; (impulso) sudden impulse;
(éxtasis) ecstasy, rapture
raqueta [ra'keta] nf racquet
raquítico, -a [ra'kitiko, a] adj stunted;
(fig) poor, inadequate
rareza [ra'reθa] nf rarity; (fig) eccentricity
raro, -a ['raro, a] adj (poco común)
rare; (extraño) odd, strange; (excepcional)
remarkable
ras [ras] nm: **a ~ de** level with; **a ~ de tierra**
at ground level
rasar [ra'sar] vt (igualar) to level
rascacielos [raska'θjelos] nm inv
skyscraper
rascar [ras'kar] vt (con las uñas etc) to
scratch; (raspar) to scrape; **rascarse** vr to
scratch (o.s.)
rasgar [ras'xar] vt to tear, rip (up)
rasgo ['rasxo] nm (con pluma) stroke;
rasgos nmpl (facciones) features,
characteristics; **a grandes ~s** in outline,
broadly

rasguño [ras'xuɲo] nm scratch
raso, -a ['raso, a] adj (liso) flat, level; (a baja
altura) very low ▷ nm satin; **cielo ~** clear sky
raspadura [raspa'ðura] nf (acto) scrape,
scraping; (marca) scratch; **raspaduras** nfpl
(de papel etc) scrapings
raspar [ras'par] vt to scrape; (arañar) to
scratch; (limar) to file
rastra ['rastra] nf (Agr) rake; **a ~s** by
dragging; (fig) unwillingly
rastrear [rastre'ar] vt (seguir) to track
rastrero, -a [ras'trero, a] adj (Bot, Zool)
creeping; (fig) despicable, mean
rastrillo [ras'triʎo] nm rake
rastro ['rastro] nm (Agr) rake; (pista) track,
trail; (vestigio) trace; **el R~** (ESP) the Madrid
fleamarket
rasurado [rasu'raðo] (MÉX) nm shaving;
rasuradora [rasura'ðora] (MÉX) nf electric
shaver; **rasurar** [rasu'rar] (MÉX) vt to
shave; **rasurarse** vr to shave
rata ['rata] nf rat
ratear [rate'ar] vt (robar) to steal
ratero, -a [ra'tero, a] adj light-fingered
▷ nm/f (carterista) pickpocket; (ladrón) petty
thief
rato ['rato] nm while, short time; **a ~s** from
time to time; **hay para ~** there's still a long
way to go; **al poco ~** soon afterwards; **pasar
el ~** to kill time; **pasar un buen/mal ~** to
have a good/rough time; **en mis ~s libres** in
my spare time
ratón [ra'ton] nm mouse; **ratonera** nf
mousetrap
raudal [rau'ðal] nm torrent; **a ~es** in
abundance
raya ['raja] nf line; (marca) scratch; (en tela)
stripe; (de pelo) parting; (límite) boundary;
(pez) ray; (puntuación) dash; **a ~s** striped;
pasarse de la ~ to go too far; **tener a ~** to
keep in check; **rayar** vt to line; to scratch;
(subrayar) to underline ▷ vi: **rayar en o con**
to border on
rayo ['rajo] nm (del sol) ray, beam; (de luz)
shaft; (en una tormenta) (flash of) lightning;
rayos X X-rays
raza ['raθa] nf race; **raza humana** human
race
razón [ra'θon] nf reason; (justicia) right,
justice; (razonamiento) reasoning; (motivo)
reason, motive; (Mat) ratio; **a ~ de 10
cada día** at the rate of 10 a day; **en ~ de**
with regard to; **dar ~ a algn** to agree that
sb is right; **tener ~** to be right; **razón de
ser** raison d'être; **razón directa/inversa**
direct/inverse proportion; **razonable**
adj reasonable; (justo, moderado) fair;
razonamiento nm (juicio) judg(e)ment;

(*argumento*) reasoning; **razonar** *vt, vi* to reason, argue

re [re] *nm* (*Mús*) D

reacción [reak'θjon] *nf* reaction; **avión a ~** jet plane; **reacción en cadena** chain reaction; **reaccionar** *vi* to react

reacio, -a [re'aθjo, a] *adj* stubborn

reactivar [reakti'βar] *vt* to revitalize

reactor [reak'tor] *nm* reactor

real [re'al] *adj* real; (*del rey, fig*) royal

realidad [reali'ðað] *nf* reality, fact; (*verdad*) truth

realista [rea'lista] *nmf* realist

realización [realiθa'θjon] *nf* fulfilment

realizador, a [realiθa'ðor, a] *nm/f* film-maker

realizar [reali'θar] *vt* (*objetivo*) to achieve; (*plan*) to carry out; (*viaje*) to make, undertake; **realizarse** *vr* to come about, come true

realmente [real'mente] *adv* really, actually

realzar [real'θar] *vt* to enhance; (*acentuar*) to highlight

reanimar [reani'mar] *vt* to revive; (*alentar*) to encourage; **reanimarse** *vr* to revive

reanudar [reanu'ðar] *vt* (*renovar*) to renew; (*historia, viaje*) to resume

reaparición [reapari'θjon] *nf* reappearance

rearme [re'arme] *nm* rearmament

rebaja [re'βaxa] *nf* (*Com*) reduction; (: *descuento*) discount; **rebajas** *nfpl* (*Com*) sale; **rebajar** *vt* (*bajar*) to lower; (*reducir*) to reduce; (*disminuir*) to lessen; (*humillar*) to humble

rebanada [reβa'naða] *nf* slice

rebañar [reβa'ɲar] *vt* (*comida*) to scrape up; (*plato*) to scrape clean

rebaño [re'βaɲo] *nm* herd; (*de ovejas*) flock

rebatir [reβa'tir] *vt* to refute

rebeca [re'βeka] *nf* cardigan

rebelarse [reβe'larse] *vr* to rebel, revolt

rebelde [re'βelde] *adj* rebellious; (*niño*) unruly ▷ *nmf* rebel; **rebeldía** *nf* rebelliousness; (*desobediencia*) disobedience

rebelión [reβe'ljon] *nf* rebellion

reblandecer [reβlande'θer] *vt* to soften

rebobinar [reβoβi'nar] *vt* (*cinta, película de video*) to rewind

rebosante [reβo'sante] *adj* overflowing

rebosar [reβo'sar] *vi* (*líquido, recipiente*) to overflow; (*abundar*) to abound, be plentiful

rebotar [reβo'tar] *vt* to bounce; (*rechazar*) to repel ▷ *vi* (*pelota*) to bounce; (*bala*) to ricochet; **rebote** *nm* rebound; **de rebote** on the rebound

rebozado, -a [reβo'θaðo, a] *adj* fried in batter o breadcrumbs

rebozar [reβo'θar] *vt* to wrap up; (*Culin*) to fry in batter o breadcrumbs

rebuscado, -a [reβus'kaðo, a] *adj* (*amanerado*) affected; (*palabra*) recherché; (*idea*) far-fetched

rebuscar [reβus'kar] *vi*: **~ (en/por)** to search carefully (in/for)

recado [re'kaðo] *nm* (*mensaje*) message; (*encargo*) errand; **tomar un ~** (*Tel*) to take a message

recaer [reka'er] *vi* to relapse; **~ en** to fall to o on; (*criminal etc*) to fall back into, relapse into; **recaída** *nf* relapse

recalcar [rekal'kar] *vt* (*fig*) to stress, emphasize

recalentar [rekalen'tar] *vt* (*volver a calentar*) to reheat; (*calentar demasiado*) to overheat

recámara [re'kamara] (*MÉX*) *nf* bedroom

recambio [re'kambjo] *nm* spare; (*de pluma*) refill

recapacitar [rekapaθi'tar] *vi* to reflect

recargado, -a [rekar'ɣaðo, a] *adj* overloaded

recargar [rekar'ɣar] *vt* to overload; (*batería*) to recharge; **~ el saldo de** (*Tel*) to top up; **recargo** *nm* surcharge; (*aumento*) increase

recatado, -a [reka'taðo, a] *adj* (*modesto*) modest, demure; (*prudente*) cautious

recaudación [rekauða'θjon] *nf* (*acción*) collection; (*cantidad*) takings pl; (*en deporte*) gate; **recaudador, a** *nm/f* tax collector

recelar [reθe'lar] *vt*: **~ que** (*sospechar*) to suspect that ...; (*temer*) to fear that ... ▷ *vi*: **~ de** to distrust; **recelo** *nm* distrust, suspicion

recepción [reθep'θjon] *nf* reception; **recepcionista** *nmf* receptionist

receptor, a [reθep'tor, a] *nm/f* recipient ▷ *nm* (*Tel*) receiver

recesión [reθe'sjon] *nf* (*Com*) recession

receta [re'θeta] *nf* (*Culin*) recipe; (*Med*) prescription

No confundir **receta** con la palabra inglesa *receipt*.

rechazar [retʃa'θar] *vt* to reject; (*oferta*) to turn down; (*ataque*) to repel

rechazo [re'tʃaθo] *nm* rejection

rechinar [retʃi'nar] *vi* to creak; (*dientes*) to grind

rechistar [retʃis'tar] *vi*: **sin ~** without a murmur

rechoncho, -a [re'tʃontʃo, a] (*fam*) *adj* thickset (*BRIT*), heavy-set (*US*)

rechupete [retʃu'pete]: **de ~** *adj* (*comida*)

delicious, scrumptious

recibidor [reθiβi'ðor] *nm* entrance hall

recibimiento [reθiβi'mjento] *nm* reception, welcome

recibir [reθi'βir] *vt* to receive; *(dar la bienvenida)* to welcome ▷ *vi* to entertain; **recibo** *nm* receipt

reciclable [reθi'klaβle] *adj* recyclable

reciclar [reθi'klar] *vt* to recycle

recién [re'θjen] *adv* recently, newly; **los ~ casados** the newly-weds; **el ~ llegado** the newcomer; **el ~ nacido** the newborn child

reciente [re'θjente] *adj* recent; *(fresco)* fresh

recinto [re'θinto] *nm* enclosure; *(área)* area, place

recio, -a ['reθjo, a] *adj* strong, tough; *(voz)* loud ▷ *adv* hard, loud(ly)

recipiente [reθi'pjente] *nm* receptacle

recíproco, -a [re'θiproco, a] *adj* reciprocal

recital [reθi'tal] *nm* (*Mús*) recital; (*Literatura*) reading

recitar [reθi'tar] *vt* to recite

reclamación [reklama'θjon] *nf* claim, demand; *(queja)* complaint

reclamar [rekla'mar] *vt* to claim, demand ▷ *vi*: **~ contra** to complain about; **reclamo** *nm* (*anuncio*) advertisement; (*tentación*) attraction

reclinar [rekli'nar] *vt* to recline, lean; **reclinarse** *vr* to lean back

reclusión [reklu'sjon] *nf* (*prisión*) prison; *(refugio)* seclusion

recluta [re'kluta] *nmf* recruit ▷ *nf* recruitment; **reclutar** *vt* (*datos*) to collect; (*dinero*) to collect up; **reclutamiento** *nm* recruitment

recobrar [reko'βrar] *vt* (*salud*) to recover; *(rescatar)* to get back; **recobrarse** *vr* to recover

recodo [re'koðo] *nm* (*de río, camino*) bend

recogedor [rekoxe'ðor] *nm* dustpan

recoger [reko'xer] *vt* to collect; (*Agr*) to harvest; (*levantar*) to pick up; (*juntar*) to gather; (*pasar a buscar*) to come for, get; (*dar asilo*) to give shelter to; (*faldas*) to gather up; (*pelo*) to put up; **recogerse** *vr* (*retirarse*) to retire; **recogido, -a** *adj* (*lugar*) quiet, secluded; (*pequeño*) small ▷ *nf* (*Correos*) collection; (*Agr*) harvest

recolección [rekolek'θjon] *nf* (*Agr*) harvesting; (*colecta*) collection

recomendación [rekomenda'θjon] *nf* (*sugerencia*) suggestion, recommendation; (*referencia*) reference

recomendar [rekomen'dar] *vt* to suggest, recommend; (*confiar*) to entrust

recompensa [rekom'pensa] *nf* reward, recompense; **recompensar** *vt* to reward, recompense

reconciliación [rekonθilja'θjon] *nf* reconciliation

reconciliar [rekonθi'ljar] *vt* to reconcile; **reconciliarse** *vr* to become reconciled

recóndito, -a [re'kondito, a] *adj* (*lugar*) hidden, secret

reconocer [rekono'θer] *vt* to recognize; (*registrar*) to search; (*Med*) to examine; **reconocido, -a** *adj* recognized; (*agradecido*) grateful; **reconocimiento** *nm* recognition; search; examination; gratitude; (*confesión*) admission

reconquista [rekon'kista] *nf* reconquest; **la R~** the Reconquest (of Spain)

reconstituyente [rekonstitu'jente] *nm* tonic

reconstruir [rekonstru'ir] *vt* to reconstruct

reconversión [rekonβer'sjon] *nf* (*reestructuración*) restructuring; **reconversión industrial** industrial rationalization

recopilación [rekopila'θjon] *nf* (*resumen*) summary; (*compilación*) compilation; **recopilar** *vt* to compile

récord ['rekorð] (*pl* **~s**) *adj inv, nm* record

recordar [rekor'ðar] *vt* (*acordarse de*) to remember; (*acordar a otro*) to remind ▷ *vi* to remember

▎ No confundir **recordar** con la palabra inglesa *record*.

recorrer [reko'rrer] *vt* (*país*) to cross, travel through; (*distancia*) to cover; (*registrar*) to search; (*repasar*) to look over; **recorrido** *nm* run, journey; **tren de largo recorrido** main-line train

recortar [rekor'tar] *vt* to cut out; **recorte** *nm* (*acción, de prensa*) cutting; (*de telas, chapas*) trimming; **recorte presupuestario** budget cut

recostar [rekos'tar] *vt* to lean; **recostarse** *vr* to lie down

recoveco [reko'βeko] *nm* (*de camino, río etc*) bend; (*en casa*) cubby hole

recreación [rekrea'θjon] *nf* recreation

recrear [rekre'ar] *vt* (*entretener*) to entertain; (*volver a crear*) to recreate; **recreativo, -a** *adj* recreational; **recreo** *nm* recreation; (*Escol*) break, playtime

recriminar [rekrimi'nar] *vt* to reproach ▷ *vi* to recriminate; **recriminarse** *vr* to reproach each other

recrudecer [rekruðe'θer] *vt, vi* to worsen; **recrudecerse** *vr* to worsen

recta ['rekta] *nf* straight line

rectángulo, -a [rek'taŋgulo, a] *adj* rectangular ▷ *nm* rectangle
rectificar [rektifi'kar] *vt* to rectify; (*volverse recto*) to straighten ▷ *vi* to correct o.s.
rectitud [rekti'tuð] *nf* straightness
recto, -a ['rekto, a] *adj* straight; (*persona*) honest, upright; **siga todo ~** go straight on ▷ *nm* rectum
rector, a [rek'tor, a] *adj* governing
recuadro [re'kwaðro] *nm* box; (*Tip*) inset
recubrir [reku'βrir] *vt*: **~ (con)** (*pintura, crema*) to cover (with)
recuento [re'kwento] *nm* inventory; **hacer el ~ de** to count *o* reckon up
recuerdo [re'kwerðo] *nm* souvenir; **recuerdos** *nmpl* (*memorias*) memories; **¡~s a tu madre!** give my regards to your mother!
recular [reku'lar] *vi* to back down
recuperación [rekupera'θjon] *nf* recovery
recuperar [rekupe'rar] *vt* to recover; (*tiempo*) to make up; **recuperarse** *vr* to recuperate
recurrir [reku'rrir] *vi* (*Jur*) to appeal; **~ a** to resort to; (*persona*) to turn to; **recurso** *nm* resort; (*medios*) means *pl*, resources *pl*; (*Jur*) appeal
red [reð] *nf* net, mesh; (*Ferro etc*) network; (*trampa*) trap; **la R~** (*Internet*) the Net
redacción [reðak'θjon] *nf* (*acción*) editing; (*personal*) editorial staff; (*Escol*) essay, composition
redactar [reðak'tar] *vt* to draw up, draft; (*periódico*) to edit
redactor, a [reðak'tor, a] *nm/f* editor
redada [re'ðaða] *nf* (*de policía*) raid, round-up
rededor [reðe'ðor] *nm*: **al** *o* **en ~** around, round about
redoblar [reðo'βlar] *vt* to redouble ▷ *vi* (*tambor*) to roll
redonda [re'ðonda] *nf*: **a la ~** around, round about
redondear [reðonde'ar] *vt* to round, round off
redondel [reðon'del] *nm* (*círculo*) circle; (*Taur*) bullring, arena
redondo, -a [re'ðondo, a] *adj* (*circular*) round; (*completo*) complete
reducción [reðuk'θjon] *nf* reduction
reducido, -a [reðu'θiðo, a] *adj* reduced; (*limitado*) limited; (*pequeño*) small
reducir [reðu'θir] *vt* to reduce; to limit; **reducirse** *vr* to diminish
redundancia [reðun'danθja] *nf* redundancy

reembolsar [re(e)mbol'sar] *vt* (*persona*) to reimburse; (*dinero*) to repay, pay back; (*depósito*) to refund; **reembolso** *nm* reimbursement; refund
reemplazar [re(e)mpla'θar] *vt* to replace; **reemplazo** *nm* replacement; **de reemplazo** (*Mil*) reserve
reencuentro [re(e)n'kwentro] *nm* reunion
reescribible [reeskri'βiβle] *adj* rewritable
refacción [refak'θjon] (*MÉX*) *nf* spare (part)
referencia [refe'renθja] *nf* reference; **con ~ a** with reference to
referéndum [refe'rendum] (*pl* **~s**) *nm* referendum
referente [refe'rente] *adj*: **~ a** concerning, relating to
réferi ['referi] (*LAM*) *nmf* referee
referir [refe'rir] *vt* (*contar*) to tell, recount; (*relacionar*) to refer, relate; **referirse** *vr*: **~se a** to refer to
refilón [refi'lon]: **de ~** *adv* obliquely
refinado, -a [refi'naðo, a] *adj* refined
refinar [refi'nar] *vt* to refine; **refinería** *nf* refinery
reflejar [refle'xar] *vt* to reflect; **reflejo, -a** *adj* reflected; (*movimiento*) reflex ▷ *nm* reflection; (*Anat*) reflex
reflexión [reflek'sjon] *nf* reflection; **reflexionar** *vt* to reflect on ▷ *vi* to reflect; (*detenerse*) to pause (to think)
reflexivo, -a [reflek'siβo, a] *adj* thoughtful; (*Ling*) reflexive
reforma [re'forma] *nf* reform; (*Arq etc*) repair; **reforma agraria** agrarian reform
reformar [refor'mar] *vt* to reform; (*modificar*) to change, alter; (*Arq*) to repair; **reformarse** *vr* to mend one's ways
reformatorio [reforma'torjo] *nm* reformatory
reforzar [refor'θar] *vt* to strengthen; (*Arq*) to reinforce; (*fig*) to encourage
refractario, -a [refrak'tarjo, a] *adj* (*Tec*) heat-resistant
refrán [re'fran] *nm* proverb, saying
refregar [refre'xar] *vt* to scrub
refrescante [refres'kante] *adj* refreshing, cooling
refrescar [refres'kar] *vt* to refresh ▷ *vi* to cool down; **refrescarse** *vr* to get cooler; (*tomar aire fresco*) to go out for a breath of fresh air; (*beber*) to have a drink
refresco [re'fresko] *nm* soft drink, cool drink; **"~s"** "refreshments"
refriega [re'frjexa] *nf* scuffle, brawl
refrigeración [refrixera'θjon] *nf* refrigeration; (*de sala*) air-conditioning

refrigerador [refrixera'ðor] *nm* refrigerator (BRIT), icebox (US)

refrigerar [refrixe'rar] *vt* to refrigerate; (*sala*) to air-condition

refuerzo [re'fwerθo] *nm* reinforcement; (*Tec*) support

refugiado, -a [refu'xjaðo, a] *nm/f* refugee

refugiarse [refu'xjarse] *vr* to take refuge, shelter

refugio [re'fuxjo] *nm* refuge; (*protección*) shelter

refunfuñar [refunfu'ɲar] *vi* to grunt, growl; (*quejarse*) to grumble

regadera [reɣa'ðera] *nf* watering can

regadío [reɣa'ðio] *nm* irrigated land

regalado, -a [reɣa'laðo, a] *adj* comfortable, luxurious; (*gratis*) free, for nothing

regalar [reɣa'lar] *vt* (*dar*) to give (as a present); (*entregar*) to give away; (*mimar*) to pamper, make a fuss of

regaliz [reɣa'liθ] *nm* liquorice

regalo [re'ɣalo] *nm* (*obsequio*) gift, present; (*gusto*) pleasure

regañadientes [reɣaɲa'ðjentes]: **a ~** *adv* reluctantly

regañar [reɣa'ɲar] *vt* to scold ▷ *vi* to grumble; **regañón, -ona** *adj* nagging

regar [re'ɣar] *vt* to water, irrigate; (*fig*) to scatter, sprinkle

regatear [reɣate'ar] *vt* (*Com*) to bargain over; (*escatimar*) to be mean with ▷ *vi* to bargain, haggle; (*Deporte*) to dribble; **regateo** *nm* bargaining; dribbling; (*del cuerpo*) swerve, dodge

regazo [re'ɣaθo] *nm* lap

regenerar [rexene'rar] *vt* to regenerate

régimen ['reximen] (*pl* **regímenes**) *nm* regime; (*Med*) diet

regimiento [rexi'mjento] *nm* regiment

regio, -a ['rexjo, a] *adj* royal, regal; (*fig: suntuoso*) splendid; (*cs: fam*) great, terrific

región [re'xjon] *nf* region

regir [re'xir] *vt* to govern, rule; (*dirigir*) to manage, run ▷ *vi* to apply, be in force

registrar [rexis'trar] *vt* (*buscar*) to search; (: *en cajón*) to look through; (*inspeccionar*) to inspect; (*anotar*) to register, record; (*Inform*) to log; **registrarse** *vr* to register; (*ocurrir*) to happen

registro [re'xistro] *nm* (*acto*) registration; (*Mús, libro*) register; (*inspección*) inspection, search; **registro civil** registry office

regla ['reɣla] *nf* (*ley*) rule, regulation; (*de medir*) ruler, rule; (*Med: período*) period; **en ~** in order

reglamentación [reɣlamenta'θjon] *nf* (*acto*) regulation; (*lista*) rules *pl*

reglamentar [reɣlamen'tar] *vt* to regulate; **reglamentario, -a** *adj* statutory; **reglamento** *nm* rules *pl*, regulations *pl*

regocijarse [reɣoθi'xarse] *vr* (*alegrarse*) to rejoice; **regocijo** *nm* joy, happiness

regrabadora [reɣraβa'ðora] *nf* rewriter; **regrabadora de DVD** DVD rewriter

regresar [reɣre'sar] *vi* to come back, go back, return; **regreso** *nm* return

reguero [re'ɣero] *nm* (*de sangre etc*) trickle; (*de humo*) trail

regulador [reɣula'ðor] *nm* regulator; (*de radio etc*) knob, control

regular [reɣu'lar] *adj* regular; (*normal*) normal, usual; (*común*) ordinary; (*organizado*) regular, orderly; (*mediano*) average; (*fam*) not bad, so-so ▷ *adv* so-so, alright ▷ *vt* (*controlar*) to control, regulate; (*Tec*) to adjust; **por lo ~** as a rule; **regularidad** *nf* regularity; **regularizar** *vt* to regularize

rehabilitación [reaβilita'θjon] *nf* rehabilitation; (*Arq*) restoration

rehabilitar [reaβili'tar] *vt* to rehabilitate; (*Arq*) to restore; (*reintegrar*) to reinstate

rehacer [rea'θer] *vt* (*reparar*) to mend, repair; (*volver a hacer*) to redo, repeat; **rehacerse** *vr* (*Med*) to recover

rehén [re'en] *nm* hostage

rehuir [reu'ir] *vt* to avoid, shun

rehusar [reu'sar] *vt, vi* to refuse

reina ['reina] *nf* queen; **reinado** *nm* reign

reinar [rei'nar] *vi* to reign

reincidir [reinθi'ðir] *vi* to relapse

reincorporarse [reinkorpo'rarse] *vr*: **~ a** to rejoin

reino ['reino] *nm* kingdom; **reino animal/ vegetal** animal/plant kingdom; **el Reino Unido** the United Kingdom

reintegrar [reinte'ɣrar] *vt* (*reconstituir*) to reconstruct; (*persona*) to reinstate; (*dinero*) to refund, pay back; **reintegrarse** *vr*: **~se a** to return to

reír [re'ir] *vi* to laugh; **reírse** *vr* to laugh; **~se de** to laugh at

reiterar [reite'rar] *vt* to reiterate

reivindicación [reiβindika'θjon] *nf* (*demanda*) claim, demand; (*justificación*) vindication

reivindicar [reiβindi'kar] *vt* to claim

reja ['rexa] *nf* (*de ventana*) grille, bars *pl*; (*en la calle*) grating

rejilla [re'xiʎa] *nf* grating, grille; (*muebles*) wickerwork; (*de ventilación*) vent; (*de coche etc*) luggage rack

rejoneador [rexonea'ðor] *nm* mounted bullfighter

rejuvenecer [rexuβene'θer] *vt, vi* to rejuvenate

relación [rela'θjon] *nf* relation, relationship; (*Mat*) ratio; (*narración*) report; **con ~ a, en ~ con** in relation to; **relaciones públicas** public relations; **relacionar** *vt* to relate, connect; **relacionarse** *vr* to be connected, be linked

relajación [relaxa'θjon] *nf* relaxation

relajar [rela'xar] *vt* to relax; **relajarse** *vr* to relax

relamerse [rela'merse] *vr* to lick one's lips

relámpago [re'lampaɣo] *nm* flash of lightning; **visita ~** lightning visit

relatar [rela'tar] *vt* to tell, relate

relativo, -a [rela'tiβo, a] *adj* relative; **en lo ~ a** concerning

relato [re'lato] *nm* (*narración*) story, tale

relegar [rele'xar] *vt* to relegate

relevante [rele'βante] *adj* eminent, outstanding

relevar [rele'βar] *vt* (*sustituir*) to relieve; **relevarse** *vr* to relay; **~ a algn de un cargo** to relieve sb of his post

relevo [re'leβo] *nm* relief; **carrera de ~s** relay race

relieve [re'ljeβe] *nm* (*Arte, Tec*) relief; (*fig*) prominence, importance; **bajo ~** bas-relief

religión [reli'xjon] *nf* religion; **religioso, -a** *adj* religious ▷ *nm/f* monk/nun

relinchar [relin'tʃar] *vi* to neigh

reliquia [re'likja] *nf* relic; **reliquia de familia** heirloom

rellano [re'ʎano] *nm* (*Arq*) landing

rellenar [reʎe'nar] *vt* (*llenar*) to fill up; (*Culin*) to stuff; (*Costura*) to pad; **relleno, -a** *adj* full up; stuffed ▷ *nm* stuffing; (*de tapicería*) padding

reloj [re'lo(x)] *nm* clock; **poner el ~ (en hora)** to set one's watch (*o* the clock); **reloj (de pulsera)** wristwatch; **reloj despertador** alarm (clock); **reloj digital** digital watch; **relojero, -a** *nm/f* clockmaker; watchmaker

reluciente [relu'θjente] *adj* brilliant, shining

relucir [relu'θir] *vi* to shine; (*fig*) to excel

remachar [rema'tʃar] *vt* to rivet; (*fig*) to hammer home, drive home; **remache** *nm* rivet

remangar [reman'gar] *vt* to roll up

remanso [re'manso] *nm* pool

remar [re'mar] *vi* to row

rematado, -a [rema'taðo, a] *adj* complete, utter

rematar [rema'tar] *vt* to finish off; (*Com*) to sell off cheap ▷ *vi* to end, finish off; (*Deporte*) to shoot

remate [re'mate] *nm* end, finish; (*punta*) tip; (*Deporte*) shot; (*Arq*) top; **de** *o* **para ~** to crown it all (*BRIT*), to top it off

remedar [reme'ðar] *vt* to imitate

remediar [reme'ðjar] *vt* to remedy; (*subsanar*) to make good, repair; (*evitar*) to avoid

remedio [re'meðjo] *nm* remedy; (*alivio*) relief, help; (*Jur*) recourse, remedy; **poner ~ a** to correct, stop; **no tener más ~** to have no alternative; **¡qué ~!** there's no choice!; **sin ~** hopeless

remendar [remen'dar] *vt* to repair; (*con parche*) to patch

remiendo [re'mjendo] *nm* mend; (*con parche*) patch; (*cosido*) darn

remilgado, -a [remil'ɣaðo, a] *adj* prim; (*afectado*) affected

remiso, -a [re'miso, a] *adj* slack, slow

remite [re'mite] *nm* (*en sobre*) name and address of sender

remitir [remi'tir] *vt* to remit, send ▷ *vi* to slacken; (*en carta*): **remite: X** sender: X; **remitente** *nmf* sender

remo ['remo] *nm* (*de barco*) oar; (*Deporte*) rowing

remojar [remo'xar] *vt* to steep, soak; (*galleta etc*) to dip, dunk

remojo [re'moxo] *nm*: **dejar la ropa en ~** to leave clothes to soak

remolacha [remo'latʃa] *nf* beet, beetroot

remolcador [remolka'ðor] *nm* (*Náut*) tug; (*Auto*) breakdown lorry

remolcar [remol'kar] *vt* to tow

remolino [remo'lino] *nm* eddy; (*de agua*) whirlpool; (*de viento*) whirlwind; (*de gente*) crowd

remolque [re'molke] *nm* tow, towing; (*cuerda*) towrope; **llevar a ~** to tow

remontar [remon'tar] *vt* to mend; **remontarse** *vr* to soar; **~se a** (*Com*) to amount to; **~ el vuelo** to soar

remorder [remor'ðer] *vt* to distress, disturb; **~le la conciencia a algn** to have a guilty conscience; **remordimiento** *nm* remorse

remoto, -a [re'moto, a] *adj* remote

remover [remo'βer] *vt* to stir; (*tierra*) to turn over; (*objetos*) to move round

remuneración [remunera'θjon] *nf* remuneration

remunerar [remune'rar] *vt* to remunerate; (*premiar*) to reward

renacer [rena'θer] *vi* to be reborn; (*fig*) to revive; **renacimiento** *nm* rebirth; **el Renacimiento** the Renaissance

renacuajo [rena'kwaxo] *nm* (*Zool*) tadpole

renal [re'nal] *adj* renal, kidney *cpd*

rencilla [ren'θiʎa] *nf* quarrel

rencor [ren'kor] *nm* rancour, bitterness; **rencoroso, -a** *adj* spiteful

rendición [rendi'θjon] *nf* surrender

rendido, -a [ren'diðo, a] *adj* (*sumiso*) submissive; (*cansado*) worn-out, exhausted

rendija [ren'dixa] *nf* (*hendedura*) crack, cleft

rendimiento [rendi'mjento] *nm* (*producción*) output; (*Tec, Com*) efficiency

rendir [ren'dir] *vt* (*vencer*) to defeat; (*producir*) to produce; (*dar beneficio*) to yield; (*agotar*) to exhaust ▷ *vi* to pay; **rendirse** *vr* (*someterse*) to surrender; (*cansarse*) to wear o.s. out; **~ homenaje** *o* **culto a** to pay homage to

renegar [rene'xar] *vi* (*renunciar*) to renounce; (*blasfemar*) to blaspheme; (*quejarse*) to complain

RENFE ['renfe] *nf abr* (= *Red Nacional de los Ferrocarriles Españoles*)

renglón [ren'glon] *nm* (*línea*) line; (*Com*) item, article; **a ~ seguido** immediately after

renombre [re'nombre] *nm* renown

renovación [renoβa'θjon] *nf* (*de contrato*) renewal; (*Arq*) renovation

renovar [reno'βar] *vt* to renew; (*Arq*) to renovate

renta ['renta] *nf* (*ingresos*) income; (*beneficio*) profit; (*alquiler*) rent; **renta vitalicia** annuity; **rentable** *adj* profitable

renuncia [re'nunθja] *nf* resignation; **renunciar** [renun'θjar] *vt* to renounce; (*tabaco, alcohol etc*): **renunciar a** to give up; (*oferta, oportunidad*) to turn down; (*puesto*) to resign ▷ *vi* to resign

reñido, -a [re'niðo, a] *adj* (*batalla*) bitter, hard-fought; **estar ~ con algn** to be on bad terms with sb

reñir [re'nir] *vt* (*regañar*) to scold ▷ *vi* (*estar peleado*) to quarrel, fall out; (*combatir*) to fight

reo ['reo] *nmf* culprit, offender; (*acusado*) accused, defendant

reojo [re'oxo]: **de ~** *adv* out of the corner of one's eye

reparación [repara'θjon] *nf* (*acto*) mending, repairing; (*Tec*) repair; (*fig*) amends *pl*, reparation

reparar [repa'rar] *vt* to repair; (*fig*) to make amends for; (*observar*) to observe ▷ *vi*: **~ en** (*darse cuenta de*) to notice; (*prestar atención a*) to pay attention to

reparo [re'paro] *nm* (*advertencia*) observation; (*duda*) doubt; (*dificultad*) difficulty; **poner ~s (a)** to raise objections (to)

repartidor, a [reparti'ðor, a] *nm/f* distributor

repartir [repar'tir] *vt* to distribute, share out; (*Correos*) to deliver; **reparto** *nm* distribution; delivery; (*Teatro, Cine*) cast; (*CAM: urbanización*) housing estate (*BRIT*), real estate development (*US*)

repasar [repa'sar] *vt* (*Escol*) to revise; (*Mecánica*) to check, overhaul; (*Costura*) to mend; **repaso** *nm* revision; overhaul, checkup; mending

repecho [re'petʃo] *nm* steep incline

repelente [repe'lente] *adj* repellent, repulsive

repeler [repe'ler] *vt* to repel

repente [re'pente] *nm*: **de ~** suddenly

repentino, -a [repen'tino, a] *adj* sudden

repercusión [reperku'sjon] *nf* repercussion

repercutir [reperku'tir] *vi* (*objeto*) to rebound; (*sonido*) to echo; **~ en** (*fig*) to have repercussions on

repertorio [reper'torjo] *nm* list; (*Teatro*) repertoire

repetición [repeti'θjon] *nf* repetition

repetir [repe'tir] *vt* to repeat; (*plato*) to have a second helping of ▷ *vi* to repeat; (*sabor*) to come back; **repetirse** *vr* (*volver sobre un tema*) to repeat o.s.

repetitivo, -a [repeti'tiβo, a] *adj* repetitive, repetitious

repique [re'pike] *nm* pealing, ringing; **repiqueteo** *nm* pealing; (*de tambor*) drumming

repisa [re'pisa] *nf* ledge, shelf; (*de ventana*) windowsill; **la ~ de la chimenea** the mantelpiece

repito *etc vb* V **repetir**

replantearse [replante'arse] *vr*: **~ un problema** to reconsider a problem

repleto, -a [re'pleto, a] *adj* replete, full up

réplica ['replika] *nf* answer; (*Arte*) replica

replicar [repli'kar] *vi* to answer; (*objetar*) to argue, answer back

repliegue [re'pljexe] *nm* (*Mil*) withdrawal

repoblación [repoβla'θjon] *nf* repopulation; (*de río*) restocking; **repoblación forestal** reafforestation

repoblar [repo'βlar] *vt* to repopulate; (*con árboles*) to reafforest

repollito [repo'ʎito] (*cs*) *nm*: **~s de Bruselas** (Brussels) sprouts

repollo [re'poʎo] *nm* cabbage

reponer [repo'ner] *vt* to replace, put back; (*Teatro*) to revive; **reponerse** *vr* to recover; **~ que ...** to reply that ...

reportaje [repor'taxe] *nm* report, article

reportero, -a [repor'tero, a] *nm/f*

reporter

reposacabezas [reposaka'βeθas] *nm inv* headrest

reposar [repo'sar] *vi* to rest, repose

reposera [repo'sera] (*RPL*) *nf* deck chair

reposición [reposi'θjon] *nf* replacement; (*Cine*) remake

reposo [re'poso] *nm* rest

repostar [repos'tar] *vt* to replenish; (*Auto*) to fill up (with petrol (*BRIT*) o gasoline (*US*))

repostería [reposte'ria] *nf* confectioner's (shop)

represa [re'presa] *nf* dam; (*lago artificial*) lake, pool

represalia [repre'salja] *nf* reprisal

representación [representa'θjon] *nf* representation; (*Teatro*) performance; **representante** *nmf* representative; performer

representar [represen'tar] *vt* to represent; (*Teatro*) to perform; (*edad*) to look; **representarse** *vr* to imagine; **representativo, -a** *adj* representative

represión [repre'sjon] *nf* repression

reprimenda [repri'menda] *nf* reprimand, rebuke

reprimir [repri'mir] *vt* to repress

reprobar [repro'βar] *vt* to censure, reprove

reprochar [repro'tʃar] *vt* to reproach; **reproche** *nm* reproach

reproducción [reproðuk'θjon] *nf* reproduction

reproducir [reproðu'θir] *vt* to reproduce; **reproducirse** *vr* to breed; (*situación*) to recur

reproductor, a [reproðuk'tor, a] *adj* reproductive ▷ *nm* player; **reproductor de CD** CD player

reptil [rep'til] *nm* reptile

república [re'puβlika] *nf* republic; **República Dominicana** Dominican Republic; **republicano, -a** *adj, nm* republican

repudiar [repu'ðjar] *vt* to repudiate; (*fe*) to renounce

repuesto [re'pwesto] *nm* (*pieza de recambio*) spare (part); (*abastecimiento*) supply; **rueda de ~** spare wheel

repugnancia [repuɣ'nanθja] *nf* repugnance; **repugnante** *adj* repugnant, repulsive

repugnar [repuɣ'nar] *vt* to disgust

repulsa [re'pulsa] *nf* rebuff

repulsión [repul'sjon] *nf* repulsion, aversion; **repulsivo, -a** *adj* repulsive

reputación [reputa'θjon] *nf* reputation

requerir [reke'rir] *vt* (*pedir*) to ask, request; (*exigir*) to require; (*llamar*) to send for, summon

requesón [reke'son] *nm* cottage cheese

requete... [re'kete] *prefijo* extremely

réquiem ['rekjem] (*pl* **-s**) *nm* requiem

requisito [reki'sito] *nm* requirement, requisite

res [res] *nf* beast, animal

resaca [re'saka] *nf* (*de mar*) undertow, undercurrent; (*fam*) hangover

resaltar [resal'tar] *vi* to project, stick out; (*fig*) to stand out

resarcir [resar'θir] *vt* to compensate; **resarcirse** *vr* to make up for

resbaladero [resβala'ðero] (*MÉX*) *nm* slide

resbaladizo, -a [resβala'ðiθo, a] *adj* slippery

resbalar [resβa'lar] *vi* to slip, slide; (*fig*) to slip (up); **resbalarse** *vr* to slip, slide; to slip (up); **resbalón** *nm* (*acción*) slip

rescatar [reska'tar] *vt* (*salvar*) to save, rescue; (*objeto*) to get back, recover; (*cautivos*) to ransom

rescate [res'kate] *nm* rescue; (*de objeto*) recovery; **pagar un ~** to pay a ransom

rescindir [resθin'dir] *vt* to rescind

rescisión [resθi'sjon] *nf* cancellation

resecar [rese'kar] *vt* to dry thoroughly; (*Med*) to cut out, remove; **resecarse** *vr* to dry up

reseco, -a [re'seko, a] *adj* very dry; (*fig*) skinny

resentido, -a [resen'tiðo, a] *adj* resentful

resentimiento [resenti'mjento] *nm* resentment, bitterness

resentirse [resen'tirse] *vr* (*debilitarse: persona*) to suffer; **~ de** (*consecuencias*) to feel the effects of; **~ de (**o **por) algo** to resent sth, be bitter about sth

reseña [re'seɲa] *nf* (*cuenta*) account; (*informe*) report; (*Literatura*) review

reseñar [rese'ɲar] *vt* to describe, (*Literatura*) to review

reserva [re'serβa] *nf* reserve; (*reservación*) reservation

reservado, -a [reser'βaðo, a] *adj* reserved; (*retraído*) cold, distant ▷ *nm* private room

reservar [reser'βar] *vt* (*guardar*) to keep; (*habitación, entrada*) to reserve; **reservarse** *vr* to save o.s.; (*callar*) to keep to o.s.

resfriado [resfri'aðo] *nm* cold; **resfriarse** *vr* to cool; (*Med*) to catch a cold

resguardar [resxwar'ðar] *vt* to protect, shield; **resguardarse** *vr*: **~se de** to guard against; **resguardo** *nm* defence; (*vale*) voucher; (*recibo*) receipt, slip

residencia [resi'ðenθja] *nf* residence;
residencia de ancianos residential
home, old people's home; **residencia
universitaria** hall of residence; **residencial**
nf (*urbanización*) housing estate
residente [resi'ðente] *adj, nmf* resident
residir [resi'ðir] *vi* to reside, live; **~ en** to
reside in, lie in
residuo [re'siðwo] *nm* residue
resignación [resiɣna'θjon] *nf*
resignation; **resignarse** *vr*: **resignarse a** *o*
con to resign o.s. to, be resigned to
resina [re'sina] *nf* resin
resistencia [resis'tenθja] *nf* (*dureza*)
endurance, strength; (*oposición, Elec*)
resistance; **resistente** *adj* strong, hardy;
resistant
resistir [resis'tir] *vt* (*soportar*) to bear;
(*oponerse a*) to resist, oppose; (*aguantar*)
to put up with ▷ *vi* to resist; (*aguantar*) to
last, endure; **resistirse** *vr*: **~se a** to refuse
to, resist
resoluto, -a [reso'luto, a] *adj* resolute
resolver [resol'βer] *vt* to resolve;
(*solucionar*) to solve, resolve; (*decidir*) to
decide, settle; **resolverse** *vr* to make up
one's mind
resonar [reso'nar] *vi* to ring, echo
resoplar [reso'plar] *vi* to snort; **resoplido**
nm heavy breathing
resorte [re'sorte] *nm* spring; (*fig*) lever
resortera [resor'tera] (*MÉX*) *nf* catapult
respaldar [respal'dar] *vt* to back (up),
support; **respaldarse** *vr* to lean back;
~se con *o* **en** (*fig*) to take one's stand on;
respaldo *nm* (*de sillón*) back; (*fig*) support,
backing
respectivo, -a [respek'tiβo, a] *adj*
respective; **en lo ~ a** with regard to
respecto [res'pekto] *nm*: **al ~** on this
matter; **con ~ a, ~ de** with regard to, in
relation to
respetable [respe'taβle] *adj* respectable
respetar [respe'tar] *vt* to respect; **respeto**
nm respect; (*acatamiento*) deference;
respetos *nmpl* respects; **respetuoso, -a**
adj respectful
respingo [res'pingo] *nm* start, jump
respiración [respira'θjon] *nf* breathing;
(*Med*) respiration; (*ventilación*) ventilation;
respiración asistida artificial respiration
(*by machine*)
respirar [respi'rar] *vi* to breathe;
respiratorio, -a *adj* respiratory; **respiro**
nm breathing; (*fig: descanso*) respite
resplandecer [resplande'θer] *vi* to shine;
resplandeciente *adj* resplendent, shining;
resplandor *nm* brilliance, brightness; (*de*

luz, fuego) blaze
responder [respon'der] *vt* to answer ▷ *vi*
to answer; (*fig*) to respond; (*pey*) to answer
back; **~ de** *o* **por** to answer for; **respondón,
-ona** *adj* cheeky
responsabilidad [responsaβili'ðað] *nf*
responsibility
responsabilizarse [responsaβili'θarse]
vr to make o.s. responsible, take charge
responsable [respon'saβle] *adj*
responsible
respuesta [res'pwesta] *nf* answer, reply
resquebrajar [reskeβra'xar] *vt* to crack,
split; **resquebrajarse** *vr* to crack, split
resquicio [res'kiθjo] *nm* chink; (*hendedura*)
crack
resta ['resta] *nf* (*Mat*) remainder
restablecer [restaβle'θer] *vt* to re-
establish, restore; **restablecerse** *vr* to
recover
restante [res'tante] *adj* remaining; **lo ~**
the remainder
restar [res'tar] *vt* (*Mat*) to subtract; (*fig*) to
take away ▷ *vi* to remain, be left
restauración [restaura'θjon] *nf*
restoration
restaurante [restau'rante] *nm*
restaurant
restaurar [restau'rar] *vt* to restore
restituir [restitu'ir] *vt* (*devolver*) to return,
give back; (*rehabilitar*) to restore
resto ['resto] *nm* (*residuo*) rest, remainder;
(*apuesta*) stake; **restos** *nmpl* remains
restorán [resto'ran] *nm* (*Lam*) restaurant
restregar [restre'xar] *vt* to scrub, rub
restricción [restrik'θjon] *nf* restriction
restringir [restrin'xir] *vt* to restrict, limit
resucitar [resuθi'tar] *vt, vi* to resuscitate,
revive
resuelto, -a [re'swelto, a] *pp de* **resolver**
▷ *adj* resolute, determined
resultado [resul'taðo] *nm* result;
(*conclusión*) outcome; **resultante** *adj*
resulting, resultant
resultar [resul'tar] *vi* (*ser*) to be; (*llegar a
ser*) to turn out to be; (*salir bien*) to turn out
well; (*Com*) to amount to; **~ de** to stem from;
me resulta difícil hacerlo it's difficult for
me to do it
resumen [re'sumen] (*pl* **resúmenes**) *nm*
summary, résumé; **en ~** in short
resumir [resu'mir] *vt* to sum up; (*cortar*)
to abridge, cut down; (*condensar*) to
summarize

   No confundir **resumir** con la palabra
inglesa *resume*.

resurgir [resur'xir] *vi* (*reaparecer*) to
reappear

resurrección [resurre(k)'θjon] *nf* resurrection

retablo [re'taβlo] *nm* altarpiece

retaguardia [reta'ɣwarðja] *nf* rearguard

retahíla [reta'ila] *nf* series, string

retal [re'tal] *nm* remnant

retar [re'tar] *vt* to challenge; (*desafiar*) to defy, dare

retazo [re'taθo] *nm* snippet (BRIT), fragment

retención [reten'θjon] *nf* (*tráfico*) hold-up; **retención fiscal** deduction for tax purposes

retener [rete'ner] *vt* (*intereses*) to withhold

reticente [reti'θente] *adj* (*tono*) insinuating; (*postura*) reluctant; **ser ~ a hacer algo** to be reluctant *o* unwilling to do sth

retina [re'tina] *nf* retina

retintín [retin'tin] *nm* jangle, jingle

retirada [reti'raða] *nf* (*Mil, refugio*) retreat; (*de dinero*) withdrawal; (*de embajador*) recall; **retirado, -a** *adj* (*lugar*) remote; (*vida*) quiet; (*jubilado*) retired

retirar [reti'rar] *vt* to withdraw; (*quitar*) to remove; (*jubilar*) to retire, pension off; **retirarse** *vr* to retreat, withdraw; to retire; (*acostarse*) to retire, go to bed; **retiro** *nm* retreat; retirement; (*pago*) pension

reto ['reto] *nm* dare, challenge

retocar [reto'kar] *vt* (*fotografía*) to touch up, retouch

retoño [re'toɲo] *nm* sprout, shoot; (*fig*) offspring, child

retoque [re'toke] *nm* retouching

retorcer [retor'θer] *vt* to twist; (*manos, lavado*) to wring; **retorcerse** *vr* to become twisted; (*mover el cuerpo*) to writhe

retorcido, -a [retor'θiðo, a] *adj* (*persona*) devious

retorcijón [retorθi'jon] (LAM) *nm* (tb: **~ de tripas**) stomach cramp

retórica [re'torika] *nf* rhetoric; (*pey*) affectedness

retorno [re'torno] *nm* return

retortijón [retorti'xon] (ESP) *nm* (tb: **~ de tripas**) stomach cramp

retozar [reto'θar] *vi* (*juguetear*) to frolic, romp; (*saltar*) to gambol

retracción [retrak'θjon] *nf* retraction

retraerse [retra'erse] *vr* to retreat, withdraw; **retraído, -a** *adj* shy, retiring; **retraimiento** *nm* retirement; (*timidez*) shyness

retransmisión [retransmi'sjon] *nf* repeat (broadcast)

retransmitir [retransmi'tir] *vt* (*mensaje*) to relay; (*TV etc*) to repeat, retransmit; (: *en vivo*) to broadcast live

retrasado, -a [retra'saðo, a] *adj* late; (*Med*) mentally retarded; (*país etc*) backward, underdeveloped

retrasar [retra'sar] *vt* (*demorar*) to postpone, put off; (*retardar*) to slow down ▷ *vi* (*atrasarse*) to be late; (*reloj*) to be slow; (*producción*) to fall (off); (*quedarse atrás*) to lag behind; **retrasarse** *vr* to be late; to be slow; to fall (off); to lag behind

retraso [re'traso] *nm* (*demora*) delay; (*lentitud*) slowness; (*tardanza*) lateness; (*atraso*) backwardness; **retrasos** *nmpl* (*Finanzas*) arrears; **llegar con ~** to arrive late; **retraso mental** mental deficiency

retratar [retra'tar] *vt* (*Arte*) to paint the portrait of; (*fotografiar*) to photograph; (*fig*) to depict, describe; **retrato** *nm* portrait; (*fig*) likeness; **retrato-robot** (ESP) *nm* Identikit®

retrete [re'trete] *nm* toilet

retribuir [retri'βwir] *vt* (*recompensar*) to reward; (*pagar*) to pay

retro... ['retro] *prefijo* retro...

retroceder [retroθe'ðer] *vi* (*echarse atrás*) to move back(wards); (*fig*) to back down

retroceso [retro'θeso] *nm* backward movement; (*Med*) relapse; (*fig*) backing down

retrospectivo, -a [retrospek'tiβo, a] *adj* retrospective

retrovisor [retroβi'sor] *nm* (tb: **espejo ~**) rear-view mirror

retumbar [retum'bar] *vi* to echo, resound

reúma [re'uma], **reuma** ['reuma] *nm* rheumatism

reunión [reu'njon] *nf* (*asamblea*) meeting; (*fiesta*) party

reunir [reu'nir] *vt* (*juntar*) to reunite, join (together); (*recoger*) to gather (together); (*personas*) to get together; (*cualidades*) to combine; **reunirse** *vr* (*personas: en asamblea*) to meet, gather

revalidar [reβali'ðar] *vt* (*ratificar*) to confirm, ratify

revalorizar [reβalori'θar] *vt* to revalue, reassess

revancha [re'βantʃa] *nf* revenge

revelación [reβela'θjon] *nf* revelation

revelado [reβe'laðo] *nm* developing

revelar [reβe'lar] *vt* to reveal; (*Foto*) to develop

reventa [re'βenta] *nf* (*de entradas: para concierto*) touting

reventar [reβen'tar] *vt* to burst, explode

reventón [reβen'ton] *nm* (*Auto*) blow-out (BRIT), flat (US)

reverencia [reβe'renθja] *nf* reverence; **reverenciar** *vt* to revere

reverendo, -a [reβe'rendo, a] *adj* reverend

reverente [reβe'rente] *adj* reverent

reversa [re'βersa] (*MÉX*, *CAM*) *nf* reverse (gear)

reversible [reβer'siβle] *adj* (*prenda*) reversible

reverso [re'βerso] *nm* back, other side; (*de moneda*) reverse

revertir [reβer'tir] *vi* to revert

revés [re'βes] *nm* back, wrong side; (*fig*) reverse, setback; (*Deporte*) backhand; **al ~** the wrong way round; (*de arriba abajo*) upside down; (*ropa*) inside out; **volver algo del ~** to turn sth round; (*ropa*) to turn sth inside out

revisar [reβi'sar] *vt* (*examinar*) to check; (*texto etc*) to revise; **revisión** *nf* revision; **revisión salarial** wage review

revisor, a [reβi'sor, a] *nm/f* inspector; (*Ferro*) ticket collector

revista [re'βista] *nf* magazine, review; (*Teatro*) revue; (*inspección*) inspection; **pasar ~ a** to review, inspect; **revista del corazón** *magazine featuring celebrity gossip and real-life romance stories*

revivir [reβi'βir] *vi* to revive

revolcarse [reβol'karse] *vr* to roll about

revoltijo [reβol'tixo] *nm* mess, jumble

revoltoso, -a [reβol'toso, a] *adj* (*travieso*) naughty, unruly

revolución [reβolu'θjon] *nf* revolution; **revolucionario, -a** *adj*, *nm/f* revolutionary

revolver [reβol'βer] *vt* (*desordenar*) to disturb, mess up; (*mover*) to move about ▷ *vi*: **~ en** to go through, rummage (about) in; **revolverse** *vr* (*volver contra*) to turn on o against

revólver [re'βolβer] *nm* revolver

revuelo [re'βwelo] *nm* fluttering; (*fig*) commotion

revuelta [re'βwelta] *nf* (*motín*) revolt; (*agitación*) commotion

revuelto, -a [re'βwelto, a] *pp de* **revolver** ▷ *adj* (*mezclado*) mixed-up, in disorder

rey [rei] *nm* king; **Día de R~es** Twelfth Night; **los R~es Magos** the Three Wise Men, the Magi

the town by land or sea to the delight of the children.

reyerta [re'jerta] *nf* quarrel, brawl

rezagado, -a [reθa'ɣaðo, a] *nm/f* straggler

rezar [re'θar] *vi* to pray; **~ con** (*fam*) to concern, have to do with; **rezo** *nm* prayer

rezumar [reθu'mar] *vt* to ooze

ría ['ria] *nf* estuary

riada [ri'aða] *nf* flood

ribera [ri'βera] *nf* (*de río*) bank; (: *área*) riverside

ribete [ri'βete] *nm* (*de vestido*) border; (*fig*) addition

ricino [ri'θino] *nm*: **aceite de ~** castor oil

rico, -a ['riko, a] *adj* rich; (*adinerado*) wealthy, rich; (*lujoso*) luxurious; (*comida*) delicious; (*niño*) lovely, cute ▷ *nm/f* rich person

ridiculez [riðiku'leθ] *nf* absurdity

ridiculizar [riðikuli'θar] *vt* to ridicule

ridículo, -a [ri'ðikulo, a] *adj* ridiculous; **hacer el ~** to make a fool of o.s.; **poner a algn en ~** to make a fool of sb

riego ['rjeɣo] *nm* (*aspersión*) watering; (*irrigación*) irrigation; **riego sanguíneo** blood flow o circulation

riel [rjel] *nm* rail

rienda ['rjenda] *nf* rein; **dar ~ suelta a** to give free rein to

riesgo ['rjesɣo] *nm* risk; **correr el ~ de** to run the risk of

rifa ['rifa] *nf* (*lotería*) raffle; **rifar** *vt* to raffle

rifle ['rifle] *nm* rifle

rigidez [rixi'ðeθ] *nf* rigidity, stiffness; (*fig*) strictness; **rígido, -a** *adj* rigid, stiff; strict, inflexible

rigor [ri'ɣor] *nm* strictness, rigour; (*inclemencia*) harshness; **de ~** de rigueur, essential; **riguroso, -a** *adj* rigorous; harsh; (*severo*) severe

rimar [ri'mar] *vi* to rhyme

rimbombante [rimbom'bante] *adj* pompous

rímel ['rimel] *nm* mascara

rímmel ['rimel] *nm* =**rímel**

rin [rin] (*MÉX*) *nm* (wheel) rim

rincón [rin'kon] *nm* corner (inside)

rinoceronte [rinoθe'ronte] *nm* rhinoceros

riña ['riɲa] *nf* (*disputa*) argument; (*pelea*) brawl

riñón [ri'ɲon] *nm* kidney

río *etc* ['rio] *vb* V **reír** ▷ *nm* river; (*fig*) torrent, stream; **río abajo/arriba** downstream/upstream; **Río de la Plata** River Plate

r

rioja [ri'oxa] *nm* (*vino*) rioja (wine)

rioplatense [riopla'tense] *adj* of o from the River Plate region

riqueza [ri'keθa] *nf* wealth, riches *pl*; (*cualidad*) richness

risa ['risa] *nf* laughter; (*una risa*) laugh; **¡qué ~!** what a laugh!

risco ['risko] *nm* crag, cliff

ristra ['ristra] *nf* string

risueño, -a [ri'sweɲo, a] *adj* (*sonriente*) smiling; (*contento*) cheerful

ritmo ['ritmo] *nm* rhythm; **a ~ lento** slowly; **trabajar a ~ lento** to go slow; **ritmo cardíaco** heart rate

rito ['rito] *nm* rite

ritual [ri'twal] *adj, nm* ritual

rival [ri'βal] *adj, nmf* rival; **rivalidad** *nf* rivalry; **rivalizar** *vi*: **rivalizar con** to rival, vie with

rizado, -a [ri'θaðo, a] *adj* curly ▷ *nm* curls *pl*

rizar [ri'θar] *vt* to curl; **rizarse** *vr* (*pelo*) to curl; (*agua*) to ripple; **rizo** *nm* curl; ripple

RNE *nf abr* = **Radio Nacional de España**

robar [ro'βar] *vt* to rob; (*objeto*) to steal; (*casa etc*) to break into; (*Naipes*) to draw

roble ['roβle] *nm* oak; **robledal** *nm* oakwood

robo ['roβo] *nm* robbery, theft

robot [ro'βot] *nm* robot; **robot (de cocina)** (*ESP*) food processor

robustecer [roβuste'θer] *vt* to strengthen

robusto, -a [ro'βusto, a] *adj* robust, strong

roca ['roka] *nf* rock

roce ['roθe] *nm* (*caricia*) brush; (*Tec*) friction; (*en la piel*) graze; **tener ~ con** to be in close contact with

rociar [ro'θjar] *vt* to spray

rocín [ro'θin] *nm* nag, hack

rocío [ro'θio] *nm* dew

rocola [ro'kola] (*LAM*) *nf* jukebox

rocoso, -a [ro'koso, a] *adj* rocky

rodaballo [roða'baʎo] *nm* turbot

rodaja [ro'ðaxa] *nf* slice

rodaje [ro'ðaxe] *nm* (*Cine*) shooting, filming; (*Auto*): **en ~** running in

rodar [ro'ðar] *vt* (*vehículo*) to wheel (along); (*escalera*) to roll down; (*viajar por*) to travel (over) ▷ *vi* to roll; (*coche*) to go, run; (*Cine*) to shoot, film

rodear [roðe'ar] *vt* to surround ▷ *vi* to go round; **rodearse** *vr*: **~se de amigos** to surround o.s. with friends

rodeo [ro'ðeo] *nm* (*ruta indirecta*) detour; (*evasión*) evasion; (*Deporte*) rodeo; **hablar sin ~s** to come to the point, speak plainly

rodilla [ro'ðiʎa] *nf* knee; **de ~s** kneeling;

ponerse de ~s to kneel (down)

rodillo [ro'ðiʎo] *nm* roller; (*Culin*) rolling-pin

roedor, a [roe'ðor, a] *adj* gnawing ▷ *nm* rodent

roer [ro'er] *vt* (*masticar*) to gnaw; (*corroer, fig*) to corrode

rogar [ro'ɣar] *vt, vi* (*pedir*) to ask for; (*suplicar*) to beg, plead; **se ruega no fumar** please do not smoke

rojizo, -a [ro'xiθo, a] *adj* reddish

rojo, -a ['roxo, a] *adj, nm* red; **al ~ vivo** red-hot

rol [rol] *nm* list, roll; (*papel*) role

rollito [ro'ʎito] *nm* (*tb*: **~ de primavera**) spring roll

rollizo, -a [ro'ʎiθo, a] *adj* (*objeto*) cylindrical; (*persona*) plump

rollo ['roʎo] *nm* roll; (*de cuerda*) coil; (*madera*) log; (*ESP*: *fam*) bore; **¡qué ~!** (*ESP*: *fam*) what a carry-on!

Roma ['roma] *n* Rome

romance [ro'manθe] *nm* (*amoroso*) romance; (*Literatura*) ballad

romano, -a [ro'mano, a] *adj, nm/f* Roman; **a la romana** in batter

romanticismo [romanti'θismo] *nm* romanticism

romántico, -a [ro'mantiko, a] *adj* romantic

rombo ['rombo] *nm* (*Geom*) rhombus

romería [rome'ria] *nf* (*Rel*) pilgrimage; (*excursión*) trip, outing

● **ROMERÍA**
●
● Originally a pilgrimage to a shrine or
● church to express devotion to the Virgin
● Mary or a local Saint, the **romería** has
● also become a rural festival which
● accompanies the pilgrimage. People
● come from all over to attend, bringing
● their own food and drink, and spend the
● day in celebration.

romero, -a [ro'mero, a] *nm/f* pilgrim ▷ *nm* rosemary

romo, -a ['romo, a] *adj* blunt; (*fig*) dull

rompecabezas [rompeka'βeθas] *nm inv* riddle, puzzle; (*juego*) jigsaw (puzzle)

rompehuelgas [rompe'welɣas] (*LAM*) *nm inv* strikebreaker, scab

rompeolas [rompe'olas] *nm inv* breakwater

romper [rom'per] *vt* to break; (*hacer pedazos*) to smash; (*papel, tela etc*) to tear, rip ▷ *vi* (*olas*) to break; (*sol, diente*) to break through; **romperse** *vr* to break; **~ un**

contrato to break a contract; **~ a** (*empezar a*) to start (suddenly) to; **~ a llorar** to burst into tears; **~ con algn** to fall out with sb
ron [ron] *nm* rum
roncar [ron'kar] *vi* to snore
ronco, -a ['ronko, a] *adj* (*afónico*) hoarse; (*áspero*) raucous
ronda ['ronda] *nf* (*gen*) round; (*patrulla*) patrol; **rondar** *vt* to patrol ▷ *vi* to patrol; (*fig*) to prowl round
ronquido [ron'kiðo] *nm* snore, snoring
ronronear [ronrone'ar] *vi* to purr
roña ['rona] *nf* (*Veterinaria*) mange; (*mugre*) dirt, grime; (*óxido*) rust
roñoso, -a [ro'noso, a] *adj* (*mugriento*) filthy; (*tacaño*) mean
ropa ['ropa] *nf* clothes *pl*, clothing; **ropa blanca** linen; **ropa de cama** bed linen; **ropa de color** coloureds *pl*; **ropa interior** underwear; **ropa sucia** dirty washing; **ropaje** *nm* gown, robes *pl*
ropero [ro'pero] *nm* linen cupboard; (*guardarropa*) wardrobe
rosa ['rosa] *adj* pink ▷ *nf* rose
rosado, -a [ro'saðo, a] *adj* pink ▷ *nm* rosé
rosal [ro'sal] *nm* rosebush
rosario [ro'sarjo] *nm* (*Rel*) rosary; **rezar el ~** to say the rosary
rosca ['roska] *nf* (*de tornillo*) thread; (*de humo*) coil, spiral; (*pan, postre*) ring-shaped roll/pastry
rosetón [rose'ton] *nm* rosette; (*Arq*) rose window
rosquilla [ros'kiʎa] *nf* doughnut-shaped fritter
rostro ['rostro] *nm* (*cara*) face
rotativo, -a [rota'tiβo, a] *adj* rotary
roto, -a ['roto, a] *pp de* **romper** ▷ *adj* broken
rotonda [ro'tonda] *nf* roundabout
rótula ['rotula] *nf* kneecap; (*Tec*) ball-and-socket joint
rotulador [rotula'ðor] *nm* felt-tip pen
rótulo ['rotulo] *nm* heading, title; label; (*letrero*) sign
rotundamente [rotunda'mente] *adv* (*negar*) flatly; (*responder, afirmar*) emphatically; **rotundo, -a** *adj* round; (*enfático*) emphatic
rotura [ro'tura] *nf* (*acto*) breaking; (*Med*) fracture
rozadura [roθa'ðura] *nf* abrasion, graze
rozar [ro'θar] *vt* (*frotar*) to rub; (*arañar*) to scratch; (*tocar ligeramente*) to shave, touch lightly; **~se** *vr* to rub (together); **~se con** (*fam*) to rub shoulders with
rte. *abr* (= *remite, remitente*) sender
RTVE *nf abr* = **Radiotelevisión Española**

rubí [ru'βi] *nm* ruby; (*de reloj*) jewel
rubio, -a ['ruβjo, a] *adj* fair-haired, blond(e) ▷ *nm/f* blond/blonde; **tabaco ~** Virginia tobacco
rubor [ru'βor] *nm* (*sonrojo*) blush; (*timidez*) bashfulness; **ruborizarse** *vr* to blush
rúbrica ['ruβrika] *nf* (*de la firma*) flourish; **rubricar** *vt* (*firmar*) to sign with a flourish; (*concluir*) to sign and seal
rudimentario, -a [ruðimen'tarjo, a] *adj* rudimentary
rudo, -a ['ruðo, a] *adj* (*sin pulir*) unpolished; (*grosero*) coarse; (*violento*) violent; (*sencillo*) simple
rueda ['rweða] *nf* wheel; (*círculo*) ring, circle; (*rodaja*) slice, round; **rueda de auxilio** (*RPL*) spare tyre; **rueda delantera/trasera/ de repuesto** front/back/spare wheel; **rueda de prensa** press conference; **rueda gigante** (*LAM*) big (*BRIT*) o Ferris (*US*) wheel
ruedo ['rweðo] *nm* (*círculo*) circle; (*Taur*) arena, bullring
ruego *etc* ['rweɣo] *vb* V **rogar** ▷ *nm* request
rugby ['ruɣβi] *nm* rugby
rugido [ru'xiðo] *nm* roar
rugir [ru'xir] *vi* to roar
rugoso, -a [ru'ɣoso, a] *adj* (*arrugado*) wrinkled; (*áspero*) rough; (*desigual*) ridged
ruido ['rwiðo] *nm* noise; (*sonido*) sound; (*alboroto*) racket, row; (*escándalo*) commotion, rumpus; **ruidoso, -a** *adj* noisy, loud; (*fig*) sensational
ruin [rwin] *adj* contemptible, mean
ruina ['rwina] *nf* ruin; (*colapso*) collapse; (*de persona*) ruin, downfall
ruinoso, -a [rwi'noso, a] *adj* ruinous; (*destartalado*) dilapidated, tumbledown; (*Com*) disastrous
ruiseñor [rwise'nor] *nm* nightingale
rulero [ru'lero] (*RPL*) *nm* roller
ruleta [ru'leta] *nf* roulette
rulo ['rulo] *nm* (*para el pelo*) curler
Rumanía [ruma'nia] *nf* Rumania
rumba ['rumba] *nf* rumba
rumbo ['rumbo] *nm* (*ruta*) route, direction; (*ángulo de dirección*) course, bearing; (*fig*) course of events; **ir con ~ a** to be heading for
rumiante [ru'mjante] *nm* ruminant
rumiar [ru'mjar] *vt* to chew; (*fig*) to chew over ▷ *vi* to chew the cud
rumor [ru'mor] *nm* (*ruido sordo*) low sound; (*murmuración*) murmur, buzz; **rumorearse** *vr*: **se rumorea que ...** it is rumoured that ...
rupestre [ru'pestre] *adj* rock *cpd*
ruptura [rup'tura] *nf* rupture
rural [ru'ral] *adj* rural

Rusia ['rusja] *nf* Russia; **ruso, -a** *adj, nm/f*
Russian
rústico, -a ['rustiko, a] *adj* rustic;
(*ordinario*) coarse, uncouth ▷ *nm/f* yokel
ruta ['ruta] *nf* route
rutina [ru'tina] *nf* routine

S

S *abr* (= *santo, a*) St; (= *sur*) S
s. *abr* (= *siglo*) C.; (= *siguiente*) foll
S.A. *abr* (= *Sociedad Anónima*) Ltd. (BRIT),
Inc. (US)
sábado ['saβaðo] *nm* Saturday
sábana ['saβana] *nf* sheet
sabañón [saβa'ɲon] *nm* chilblain
saber [sa'βer] *vt* to know; (*llegar a conocer*)
to find out, learn; (*tener capacidad de*) to
know how to ▷ *vi*: ~ **a** to taste of, taste like
▷ *nm* knowledge, learning; **a** ~ namely;
¿sabes conducir/nadar? can you drive/
swim?; **¿sabes francés?** do you speak
French?; ~ **de memoria** to know by heart;
hacer ~ **algo a algn** to inform sb of sth, let
sb know sth
sabiduría [saβiðu'ria] *nf* (*conocimientos*)
wisdom; (*instrucción*) learning
sabiendas [sa'βjendas]: **a** ~ *adv* knowingly
sabio, -a ['saβjo,a] *adj* (*docto*) learned;
(*prudente*) wise, sensible
sabor [sa'βor] *nm* taste, flavour; **saborear**
vt to taste, savour; (*fig*) to relish
sabotaje [saβo'taxe] *nm* sabotage
sabré *etc vb* V **saber**
sabroso, -a [sa'βroso, a] *adj* tasty;
(*fig: fam*) racy, salty
sacacorchos [saka'kortʃos] *nm inv*
corkscrew
sacapuntas [saka'puntas] *nm inv* pencil
sharpener
sacar [sa'kar] *vt* to take out; (*fig: extraer*)
to get (out); (*quitar*) to remove, get out;
(*hacer salir*) to bring out; (*conclusión*) to draw;
(*novela etc*) to publish, bring out; (*ropa*) to
take off; (*obra*) to make; (*premio*) to receive;
(*entradas*) to get; (*Tenis*) to serve; ~ **adelante**
(*niño*) to bring up; (*negocio*) to carry on, go on
with; ~ **a algn a bailar** to get sb up to dance;
~ **una foto** to take a photo; ~ **la lengua** to
stick out one's tongue; ~ **buenas/malas**

notas to get good/bad marks

sacarina [saka'rina] *nf* saccharin(e)

sacerdote [saθer'ðote] *nm* priest

saciar [sa'θjar] *vt* (*hambre, sed*) to satisfy; **saciarse** *vr* (*de comida*) to get full up

saco ['sako] *nm* bag; (*grande*) sack; (*su contenido*) bagful; (LAM: *chaqueta*) jacket; **saco de dormir** sleeping bag

sacramento [sakra'mento] *nm* sacrament

sacrificar [sakrifi'kar] *vt* to sacrifice; **sacrificio** *nm* sacrifice

sacristía [sakris'tia] *nf* sacristy

sacudida [saku'ðiða] *nf* (*agitación*) shake, shaking; (*sacudimiento*) jolt, bump; **sacudida eléctrica** electric shock

sacudir [saku'ðir] *vt* to shake; (*golpear*) to hit

Sagitario [saxi'tarjo] *nm* Sagittarius

sagrado, -a [sa'ɣraðo, a] *adj* sacred, holy

Sáhara ['saara] *nm*: **el ~** the Sahara (desert)

sal [sal] *vb* V **salir** ▷ *nf* salt; **sales de baño** bath salts

sala ['sala] *nf* room; (*tb*: **~ de estar**) living room; (*Teatro*) house, auditorium; (*de hospital*) ward; **sala de espera** waiting room; **sala de estar** living room; **sala de fiestas** dance hall

salado, -a [sa'laðo, a] *adj* salty; (*fig*) witty, amusing; **agua salada** salt water

salar [sa'lar] *vt* to salt, add salt to

salario [sa'larjo] *nm* wage, pay

salchicha [sal'tʃitʃa] *nf* (pork) sausage; **salchichón** *nm* (salami-type) sausage

saldo ['saldo] *nm* (*pago*) settlement; (*de una cuenta*) balance; (*lo restante*) remnant(s) (*pl*), remainder; (*de móvil*) credit; **saldos** *nmpl* (*en tienda*) sale

saldré *etc vb* V **salir**

salero [sa'lero] *nm* salt cellar

salgo *etc vb* V **salir**

salida [sa'liða] *nf* (*puerta etc*) exit, way out; (*acto*) leaving, going out; (*de tren, Aviac*) departure; (*Tec*) output, production; (*fig*) way out; (*Com*) opening; (*Geo, válvula*) outlet; (*de gas*) leak; **calle sin ~** cul-de-sac; **salida de baño** (RPL) bathrobe; **salida de emergencia/incendios** emergency exit/fire escape

○ **PALABRA CLAVE**

salir [sa'lir] *vi* **1** (*partir: tb*: **salir de**) to leave; **Juan ha salido** Juan is out; **salió de la cocina** he came out of the kitchen

2 (*aparecer*) to appear; (*disco, libro*) to come out; **anoche salió en la tele** she appeared o was on TV last night; **salió en todos los periódicos** it was in all the papers

3 (*resultar*): **la muchacha nos salió muy trabajadora** the girl turned out to be a very hard worker; **la comida te ha salido exquisita** the food was delicious; **sale muy caro** it's very expensive

4: **salirle a uno algo: la entrevista que hice me salió bien/mal** the interview I did went o turned out well/badly

5: **salir adelante: no sé cómo haré para salir adelante** I don't know how I'll get by

salirse *vr* (*líquido*) to spill; (*animal*) to escape

saliva [sa'liβa] *nf* saliva

salmo ['salmo] *nm* psalm

salmón [sal'mon] *nm* salmon

salmonete [salmo'nete] *nm* red mullet

salón [sa'lon] *nm* (*de casa*) living room, lounge; (*muebles*) lounge suite; **salón de baile** dance hall; **salón de belleza** beauty parlour

salpicadera [salpika'ðera] (MÉX) *nf* mudguard (BRIT), fender (US)

salpicadero [salpika'ðero] *nm* (*Auto*) dashboard

salpicar [salpi'kar] *vt* (*rociar*) to sprinkle, spatter; (*esparcir*) to scatter

salpicón [salpi'kon] *nm* (*tb*: **~ de marisco**) seafood salad

salsa ['salsa] *nf* sauce; (*con carne asada*) gravy; (*fig*) spice

saltamontes [salta'montes] *nm inv* grasshopper

saltar [sal'tar] *vt* to jump (over), leap (over); (*dejar de lado*) to skip, miss out ▷ *vi* to jump, leap; (*pelota*) to bounce; (*al aire*) to fly up; (*quebrarse*) to break; (*al agua*) to dive; (*fig*) to explode, blow up

salto ['salto] *nm* jump, leap; (*al agua*) dive; **salto de agua** waterfall; **salto de altura/longitud** high/long jump

salud [sa'luð] *nf* health; **¡(a su) ~!** cheers!, good health!; **saludable** *adj* (*de buena salud*) healthy; (*provechoso*) good, beneficial

saludar [salu'ðar] *vt* to greet; (*Mil*) to salute; **saludo** *nm* greeting; **"saludos"** (*en carta*) "best wishes", "regards"

salvación [salβa'θjon] *nf* salvation; (*rescate*) rescue

salvado [sal'βaðo] *nm* bran

salvaje [sal'βaxe] *adj* wild; (*tribu*) savage

salvamanteles [salβaman'teles] *nm inv* table mat

salvamento [salβa'mento] *nm* rescue

salvapantallas [salβapan'taʎas] *nm inv* screen saver

salvar [sal'βar] *vt* (*rescatar*) to save, rescue; (*resolver*) to overcome, resolve; (*cubrir* *distancias*) to cover, travel; (*hacer excepción*) to except, exclude; (*barco*) to salvage

salvavidas [salβa'βiðas] *adj inv*: **bote/chaleco ~** lifeboat/life jacket

salvo, -a ['salβo, a] *adj* safe ▷ *adv* except (for), save; **a ~** out of danger; **~ que** unless

san [san] *adj* saint; **S~ Juan** St John

sanar [sa'nar] *vt* (*herida*) to heal; (*persona*) to cure ▷ *vi* (*persona*) to get well, recover; (*herida*) to heal

sanatorio [sana'torjo] *nm* sanatorium

sanción [san'θjon] *nf* sanction

sancochado, -a [sanko'tʃado, a] (*MÉX*) *adj* (*Culin*) underdone, rare

sandalia [san'dalja] *nf* sandal

sandía [san'dia] *nf* watermelon

sandwich ['sandwitʃ] (*pl* **~s, ~es**) *nm* sandwich

sanfermines [sanfer'mines] *nmpl* *festivities in celebration of San Fermín (Pamplona)*

SANFERMINES

The **Sanfermines** is a week-long festival in Pamplona made famous by Ernest Hemingway. From the 7th July, the feast of "San Fermín", crowds of mainly young people take to the streets drinking, singing and dancing. Early in the morning bulls are released along the narrow streets leading to the bullring, and young men risk serious injury to show their bravery by running out in front of them, a custom which is also typical of many Spanish villages.

sangrar [san'grar] *vt, vi* to bleed; **sangre** *nf* blood

sangría [san'gria] *nf* sangria, *sweetened drink of red wine with fruit*

sangriento, -a [san'grjento, a] *adj* bloody

sanguíneo, -a [san'gineo, a] *adj* blood *cpd*

sanidad [sani'ðað] *nf* (*tb*: **~ pública**) public health

San Isidro [sani'sidro] *nm* patron saint of Madrid

SAN ISIDRO

San Isidro is the patron saint of Madrid, and gives his name to the week-long festivities which take place around the 15th May. Originally an 18th-century trade fair, the **San Isidro** celebrations

now include music, dance, a famous **romería**, theatre and bullfighting.

sanitario, -a [sani'tarjo, a] *adj* health *cpd*; **sanitarios** *nmpl* toilets (*BRIT*), washroom (*US*)

sano, -a ['sano, a] *adj* healthy; (*sin daños*) sound; (*comida*) wholesome; (*entero*) whole, intact; **~ y salvo** safe and sound

No confundir **sano** con la palabra inglesa *sane*.

Santiago [san'tjaɣo] *nm*: **~ (de Chile)** Santiago

santiamén [santja'men] *nm*: **en un ~** in no time at all

santidad [santi'ðað] *nf* holiness, sanctity

santiguarse [santi'ɣwarse] *vr* to make the sign of the cross

santo, -a ['santo, a] *adj* holy; (*fig*) wonderful, miraculous ▷ *nm/f* saint ▷ *nm* saint's day; **~ y seña** password

santuario [san'twarjo] *nm* sanctuary, shrine

sapo ['sapo] *nm* toad

saque ['sake] *nm* (*Tenis*) service, serve; (*Fútbol*) throw-in; **saque de esquina** corner (kick)

saquear [sake'ar] *vt* (*Mil*) to sack; (*robar*) to loot, plunder; (*fig*) to ransack

sarampión [saram'pjon] *nm* measles *sg*

sarcástico, -a [sar'kastiko, a] *adj* sarcastic

sardina [sar'ðina] *nf* sardine

sargento [sar'xento] *nm* sergeant

sarmiento [sar'mjento] *nm* (*Bot*) vine shoot

sarna ['sarna] *nf* itch; (*Med*) scabies

sarpullido [sarpu'ʎiðo] *nm* (*Med*) rash

sarro ['sarro] *nm* (*en dientes*) tartar, plaque

sartén [sar'ten] *nf* frying pan

sastre ['sastre] *nm* tailor; **sastrería** *nf* (*arte*) tailoring; (*tienda*) tailor's (shop)

Satanás [sata'nas] *nm* Satan

satélite [sa'telite] *nm* satellite

sátira ['satira] *nf* satire

satisfacción [satisfak'θjon] *nf* satisfaction

satisfacer [satisfa'θer] *vt* to satisfy; (*gastos*) to meet; (*pérdida*) to make good; **satisfacerse** *vr* to satisfy o.s., be satisfied; (*vengarse*) to take revenge; **satisfecho, -a** *adj* satisfied; (*contento*) content(ed), happy; (*tb*: **satisfecho de sí mismo**) self-satisfied, smug

saturar [satu'rar] *vt* to saturate; **saturarse** *vr* (*mercado, aeropuerto*) to reach saturation point

sauce ['sauθe] *nm* willow; **sauce llorón**

weeping willow
sauna ['sauna] nf sauna
savia ['saβja] nf sap
saxofón [sakso'fon] nm saxophone
sazonar [saθo'nar] vt to ripen; (Culin) to flavour, season
scooter [e'skuter] (ESP) nf scooter
Scotch® [skotʃ] (LAM) nm Sellotape® (BRIT), Scotch tape® (US)
SE abr (= sudeste) SE

○ **PALABRA CLAVE**

se [se] pron **1** (reflexivo: sg: m) himself; (: f) herself; (: pl) themselves; (: cosa) itself; (: de Vd) yourself; (: de Vds) yourselves; **se está preparando** she's preparing herself **2** (con complemento indirecto) to him; to her; to them; to it; to you; **a usted se lo dije ayer** I told you yesterday; **se compró un sombrero** he bought himself a hat; **se rompió la pierna** he broke his leg **3** (uso recíproco) each other, one another; **se miraron (el uno al otro)** they looked at each other o one another **4** (en oraciones pasivas): **se han vendido muchos libros** a lot of books have been sold **5** (impers): **se dice que ...** people say that ..., it is said that ...; **allí se come muy bien** the food there is very good, you can eat very well there

sé etc [se] vb V **saber; ser**
sea etc vb V **ser**
sebo ['seβo] nm fat, grease
secador [seka'ðor] nm: **~ de pelo** hairdryer
secadora [seka'ðora] nf tumble dryer
secar [se'kar] vt to dry; **secarse** vr to dry (off); (río, planta) to dry up
sección [sek'θjon] nf section
seco, -a ['seko, a] adj dry; (carácter) cold; (respuesta) sharp, curt; **parar en ~** to stop dead; **decir algo a secas** to say sth curtly
secretaría [sekreta'ria] nf secretariat
secretario, -a [sekre'tarjo, a] nm/f secretary
secreto, -a [se'kreto, a] adj secret; (persona) secretive ▷ nm secret; (calidad) secrecy
secta ['sekta] nf sect
sector [sek'tor] nm sector
secuela [se'kwela] nf consequence
secuencia [se'kwenθja] nf sequence
secuestrar [sekwes'trar] vt to kidnap; (bienes) to seize, confiscate; **secuestro** nm kidnapping; seizure, confiscation
secundario, -a [sekun'darjo, a] adj secondary

sed [seð] nf thirst; **tener ~** to be thirsty
seda ['seða] nf silk
sedal [se'ðal] nm fishing line
sedán [se'ðan] (LAM) nm saloon (BRIT), sedan (US)
sedante [se'ðante] nm sedative
sede ['seðe] nf (de gobierno) seat; (de compañía) headquarters pl; **Santa S~** Holy See
sedentario, -a [seðen'tario, a] adj sedentary
sediento, -a [se'ðjento, a] adj thirsty
sedimento [seði'mento] nm sediment
seducción [seðuk'θjon] nf seduction
seducir [seðu'θir] vt to seduce; (cautivar) to charm, fascinate; (atraer) to attract; **seductor, a** adj seductive; charming, fascinating; attractive ▷ nm/f seducer
segar [se'ɣar] vt (mies) to reap, cut; (hierba) to mow, cut
seglar [se'ɣlar] adj secular, lay
seguida [se'ɣiða] nf: **en ~** at once, right away
seguido, -a [se'ɣiðo, a] adj (continuo) continuous, unbroken; (recto) straight ▷ adv (directo) straight (on); (después) after; (LAM: a menudo) often; **~s** consecutive, successive; **5 días ~s** 5 days running, 5 days in a row
seguir [se'ɣir] vt to follow; (venir después) to follow on, come after; (proseguir) to continue; (perseguir) to chase, pursue ▷ vi (gen) to follow; (continuar) to continue, carry o go on; **seguirse** vr to follow; **sigo sin comprender** I still don't understand; **sigue lloviendo** it's still raining
según [se'ɣun] prep according to ▷ adv: **¿irás? - ~** are you going? – it all depends ▷ conj as; **~ caminamos** while we walk
segundo, -a [se'ɣundo, a] adj second ▷ nm second ▷ nf second meaning; **de segunda mano** second-hand; **segunda (clase)** second class; **segunda (marcha)** (Auto) second (gear)
seguramente [seɣura'mente] adv surely; (con certeza) for sure, with certainty
seguridad [seɣuri'ðað] nf safety; (del estado, de casa etc) security; (certidumbre) certainty; (confianza) confidence; (estabilidad) stability; **seguridad social** social security
seguro, -a [se'ɣuro, a] adj (cierto) sure, certain; (fiel) trustworthy; (libre de peligro) safe; (bien defendido, firme) secure ▷ adv for sure, certainly ▷ nm (Com) insurance; **seguro contra terceros/a todo riesgo** third party/comprehensive insurance;

seguros sociales social security *sg*
seis [seis] *num* six
seísmo [se'ismo] *nm* tremor, earthquake
selección [selek'θjon] *nf* selection;
 seleccionar *vt* to pick, choose, select
selectividad [selektiβi'ðað] (ESP) *nf*
 university entrance examination
selecto, -a [se'lekto, a] *adj* select, choice;
 (*escogido*) selected
sellar [se'ʎar] *vt* (*documento oficial*) to seal;
 (*pasaporte, visado*) to stamp
sello ['seʎo] *nm* stamp; (*precinto*) seal
selva ['selβa] *nf* (*bosque*) forest, woods *pl*;
 (*jungla*) jungle
semáforo [se'maforo] *nm* (*Auto*) traffic
 lights *pl*; (*Ferro*) signal
semana [se'mana] *nf* week; **entre ~**
 during the week; **Semana Santa** Holy
 Week; **semanal** *adj* weekly; **semanario** *nm*
 weekly magazine

● **SEMANA SANTA**
●
● In Spain celebrations for **Semana Santa**
● (Holy Week) are often spectacular.
● "Viernes Santo", "Sábado Santo" and
● "Domingo de Resurrección" (Good
● Friday, Holy Saturday, Easter Sunday)
● are all national public holidays,
● with additional days being given as
● local holidays. There are fabulous
● **procesiones** all over the country, with
● members of "cofradías" (brotherhoods)
● dressing in hooded robes and parading
● their "pasos" (religious floats and
● sculptures) through the streets. Seville
● has the most famous Holy Week
● processions.

sembrar [sem'brar] *vt* to sow; (*objetos*)
 to sprinkle, scatter about; (*noticias etc*) to
 spread
semejante [seme'xante] *adj* (*parecido*)
 similar ▷ *nm* fellow man, fellow creature;
 ~s alike, similar, **nunca hizo cosa ~** he
 never did any such thing; **semejanza** *nf*
 similarity, resemblance
semejar [seme'xar] *vi* to seem like,
 resemble; **semejarse** *vr* to look alike, be
 similar
semen ['semen] *nm* semen
semestral [semes'tral] *adj* half-yearly,
 bi-annual
semicírculo [semi'θirkulo] *nm* semicircle
semidesnatado, -a [semiðesna'taðo, a]
 adj semi-skimmed
semifinal [semifi'nal] *nf* semifinal
semilla [se'miʎa] *nf* seed

seminario [semi'narjo] *nm* (*Rel*)
 seminary; (*Escol*) seminar
sémola ['semola] *nf* semolina
senado [se'naðo] *nm* senate; **senador, a**
 nm/f senator
sencillez [senθi'ʎeθ] *nf* simplicity; (*de
 persona*) naturalness; **sencillo, -a** *adj*
 simple; natural, unaffected
senda ['senda] *nf* path, track
senderismo [sende'rismo] *nm* hiking
sendero [sen'dero] *nm* path, track
sendos, -as ['sendos, as] *adj pl*: **les dio ~
 golpes** he hit both of them
senil [se'nil] *adj* senile
seno ['seno] *nm* (*Anat*) bosom, bust; (*fig*)
 bosom; **~s** breasts
sensación [sensa'θjon] *nf* sensation;
 (*sentido*) sense; (*sentimiento*) feeling;
 sensacional *adj* sensational
sensato, -a [sen'sato, a] *adj* sensible
sensible [sen'sible] *adj* sensitive;
 (*apreciable*) perceptible, appreciable;
 (*pérdida*) considerable

▎No confundir **sensible** con la palabra
 inglesa *sensible*.

sensiblero, -a [sensi'βlero, a] *adj* sentimental
sensitivo, -a [sensi'tiβo, a] *adj* sense *cpd*
sensorial [senso'rjal] *adj* sensory
sensual [sen'swal] *adj* sensual
sentada [sen'taða] *nf* sitting; (*protesta*)
 sit-in
sentado, -a [sen'taðo, a] *adj*: **estar ~** to
 sit, be sitting (down); **dar por ~** to take for
 granted, assume
sentar [sen'tar] *vt* to sit, seat; (*fig*) to
 establish ▷ *vi* (*vestido*) to suit; (*alimento*): **~
 bien/mal a** to agree/disagree with;
 sentarse *vr* (*persona*) to sit, sit down; (*los
 depósitos*) to settle
sentencia [sen'tenθja] *nf* (*máxima*)
 maxim, saying; (*Jur*) sentence; **sentenciar**
 vt to sentence
sentido, -a [sen'tiðo, a] *adj* (*pérdida*)
 regrettable; (*carácter*) sensitive ▷ *nm* sense;
 (*sentimiento*) feeling; (*significado*) sense,
 meaning; (*dirección*) direction; **mi más ~
 pésame** my deepest sympathy; **tener ~**
 to make sense; **sentido común** common
 sense; **sentido del humor** sense of humour;
 sentido único one-way (street)
sentimental [sentimen'tal] *adj*
 sentimental; **vida ~** love life
sentimiento [senti'mjento] *nm* feeling
sentir [sen'tir] *vt* to feel; (*percibir*) to
 perceive, sense; (*lamentar*) to regret, be
 sorry for ▷ *vi* (*tener la sensación*) to feel;
 (*lamentarse*) to feel sorry ▷ *nm* opinion,
 judgement; **~se bien/mal** to feel well/ill; **lo**

siento I'm sorry

seña ['seɲa] nf sign; (Mil) password; **señas** nfpl (dirección) address sg; **señas personales** personal description sg

señal [se'ɲal] nf sign; (síntoma) symptom; (Ferro, Tel) signal; (marca) mark; (Com) deposit; **en ~ de** as a token o sign of; **señalar** vt to mark; (indicar) to point out, indicate

señor [se'ɲor] nm (hombre) man; (caballero) gentleman; (dueño) owner, master; (trato: antes de nombre propio) Mr; (: hablando directamente) sir; **muy ~ mío** Dear Sir; **el ~ alcalde/presidente** the mayor/president

señora [se'ɲora] nf (dama) lady; (trato: antes de nombre propio) Mrs; (: hablando directamente) madam; (esposa) wife; **Nuestra S~** Our Lady

señorita [seɲo'rita] nf (con nombre y/o apellido) Miss; (mujer joven) young lady

señorito [seɲo'rito] nm young gentleman; (pey) rich kid

sepa etc vb V **saber**

separación [separa'θjon] nf separation; (división) division; (hueco) gap

separar [sepa'rar] vt to separate; (dividir) to divide; **separarse** vr (parte) to come away; (partes) to come apart; (persona) to leave, go away; (matrimonio) to separate; **separatismo** nm separatism

sepia ['sepja] nf cuttlefish

septentrional [septentrjo'nal] adj northern

septiembre [sep'tjembre] nm September

séptimo, -a ['septimo, a] adj, nm seventh

sepulcral [sepul'kral] adj (fig: silencio, atmósfera) deadly; **sepulcro** nm tomb, grave

sepultar [sepul'tar] vt to bury; **sepultura** nf (acto) burial; (tumba) grave, tomb

sequía [se'kia] nf drought

séquito ['sekito] nm (de rey etc) retinue; (seguidores) followers pl

○ **PALABRA CLAVE**

ser [ser] vi **1** (descripción) to be; **es médica/ muy alta** she's a doctor/very tall; **la familia es de Cuzco** his (o her etc) family is from Cuzco; **soy Ana** (Tel) Ana speaking o here

2 (propiedad): **es de Joaquín** it's Joaquín's, it belongs to Joaquín

3 (horas, fechas, números): **es la una** it's one o'clock; **son las seis y media** it's half-past six; **es el 1 de junio** it's the first of June; **somos/son seis** there are six of us/them

4 (en oraciones pasivas): **ha sido descubierto ya** it's already been discovered

5: **es de esperar que ...** it is to be hoped o I etc hope that ...

6 (locuciones con sub): **o sea** that is to say; **sea él sea su hermana** either him or his sister

7: **a no ser por él ...** but for him ...

8: **a no ser que: a no ser que tenga uno ya** unless he's got one already ▷ nm being; **ser humano** human being

sereno, -a [se'reno, a] adj (persona) calm, unruffled; (el tiempo) fine, settled; (ambiente) calm, peaceful ▷ nm night watchman

serial [ser'jal] nm serial

serie ['serje] nf series; (cadena) sequence, succession; **fuera de ~** out of order; (fig) special, out of the ordinary; **fabricación en ~** mass production

seriedad [serje'ðað] nf seriousness; (formalidad) reliability; **serio, -a** adj serious; reliable, dependable; grave, serious; **en serio** adv seriously

serigrafía [seriɣra'fia] nf silk-screen printing

sermón [ser'mon] nm (Rel) sermon

seropositivo, -a [seroposi'tiβo] adj HIV positive

serpentear [serpente'ar] vi to wriggle; (camino, río) to wind, snake

serpentina [serpen'tina] nf streamer

serpiente [ser'pjente] nf snake; **serpiente de cascabel** rattlesnake

serranía [serra'nia] nf mountainous area

serrar [se'rrar] vt = **aserrar**

serrín [se'rrin] nm sawdust

serrucho [se'rrutʃo] nm saw

service ['serβis] (RPL) nm (Auto) service

servicio [ser'βiθjo] nm service; (LAM Auto) service; **servicios** nmpl (ESP) toilet(s); **servicio incluido** service charge included; **servicio militar** military service

servidumbre [serβi'ðumbre] nf (sujeción) servitude; (criados) servants pl, staff

servil [ser'βil] adj servile

servilleta [serβi'ʎeta] nf serviette, napkin

servir [ser'βir] vt to serve ▷ vi to serve; (tener utilidad) to be of use, be useful; **servirse** vr to serve o help o.s.; **~se de algo** to make use of sth, use sth; **sírvase pasar** please come in

sesenta [se'senta] num sixty

sesión [se'sjon] nf (Pol) session, sitting; (Cine) showing

seso ['seso] nm brain; **sesudo, -a** adj sensible, wise

seta ['seta] nf mushroom; **seta venenosa** toadstool

setecientos, -as [sete'θjentos, as] adj, num seven hundred

setenta [se'tenta] num seventy

seto ['seto] nm hedge

severo, -a [se'βero, a] *adj* severe
Sevilla [se'βiʎa] *n* Seville; **sevillano, -a** *adj*
of o from Seville ▷ *nm/f* native o inhabitant
of Seville
sexo ['sekso] *nm* sex
sexto, -a ['seksto, a] *adj, nm* sixth
sexual [sek'swal] *adj* sexual; **vida ~** sex life
si [si] *conj* if ▷ *nm* (*Mús*) B; **me pregunto ~**
... I wonder if o whether ...
sí [si] *adv* yes ▷ *nm* consent ▷ *pron* (*uso
impersonal*) oneself; (*sg: m*) himself; (: *f*)
herself; (: *de cosa*) itself; (*de usted*) yourself;
(*pl*) themselves; (*de ustedes*) yourselves;
(*recíproco*) each other; **él no quiere pero yo
~** he doesn't want to but I do; **ella ~ vendrá**
she will certainly come, she is sure to come;
claro que ~ of course; **creo que ~** I think so
siamés, -esa [sja'mes, esa] *adj, nm/f*
Siamese
SIDA ['siða] *nm abr* (= *Síndrome de
Inmunodeficiencia Adquirida*) AIDS
siderúrgico, -a [siðe'rurxico, a] *adj* iron
and steel *cpd*
sidra ['siðra] *nf* cider
siembra ['sjembra] *nf* sowing
siempre ['sjempre] *adv* always; (*todo
el tiempo*) all the time; **~ que** (*cada vez*)
whenever; (*dado que*) provided that; **como ~**
as usual; **para ~** for ever
sien [sjen] *nf* temple
siento *etc* ['sjento] *vb* V **sentar; sentir**
sierra ['sjerra] *nf* (*Tec*) saw; (*cadena de
montañas*) mountain range
siervo, -a ['sjerβo, a] *nm/f* slave
siesta ['sjesta] *nf* siesta, nap; **echar la ~** to
have an afternoon nap o a siesta
siete ['sjete] *num* seven
sifón [si'fon] *nm* syphon
sigla ['siɣla] *nf* abbreviation; acronym
siglo ['siɣlo] *nm* century; (*fig*) age
significado [siɣnifi'kaðo] *nm* (*de palabra
etc*) meaning
significar [siɣnifi'kar] *vt* to mean,
signify; (*notificar*) to make known, express
signo ['siɣno] *nm* sign; **signo de
admiración** o **exclamación** exclamation
mark; **signo de interrogación** question
mark
sigo *etc vb* V **seguir**
siguiente [si'ɣjente] *adj* next, following
siguió *etc vb* V **seguir**
sílaba ['silaβa] *nf* syllable
silbar [sil'βar] *vt, vi* to whistle; **silbato** *nm*
whistle; **silbido** *nm* whistle, whistling
silenciador [silenθja'ðor] *nm* silencer
silenciar [silen'θjar] *vt* (*persona*) to
silence; (*escándalo*) to hush up; **silencio** *nm*
silence, quiet; **silencioso, -a** *adj* silent,

quiet
silla ['siʎa] *nf* (*asiento*) chair; (*tb: ~ de
montar*) saddle; **silla de ruedas** wheelchair
sillón [si'ʎon] *nm* armchair, easy chair
silueta [si'lweta] *nf* silhouette; (*de edificio*)
outline; (*figura*) figure
silvestre [sil'βestre] *adj* wild
simbólico, -a [sim'boliko, a] *adj*
symbolic(al)
simbolizar [simboli'θar] *vt* to symbolize
símbolo ['simbolo] *nm* symbol
similar [simi'lar] *adj* similar
simio ['simjo] *nm* ape
simpatía [simpa'tia] *nf* liking; (*afecto*)
affection; (*amabilidad*) kindness; **simpático,
-a** *adj* nice, pleasant; kind
▌No confundir **simpático** con la palabra
inglesa *sympathetic*.
simpatizante [simpati'θante] *nmf*
sympathizer
simpatizar [simpati'θar] *vi*: **~ con** to get
on well with
simple ['simple] *adj* simple; (*elemental*)
simple, easy; (*mero*) mere; (*puro*) pure, sheer
▷ *nmf* simpleton; **simpleza** *nf* simpleness;
(*necedad*) silly thing; **simplificar** *vt* to
simplify
simposio [sim'posjo] *nm* symposium
simular [simu'lar] *vt* to simulate
simultáneo, -a [simul'taneo, a] *adj*
simultaneous
sin [sin] *prep* without; **la ropa está ~ lavar**
the clothes are unwashed; **~ que** without; **~
embargo** however, still
sinagoga [sina'ɣoɣa] *nf* synagogue
sinceridad [sinθeri'ðað] *nf* sincerity;
sincero, -a *adj* sincere
sincronizar [sinkroni'θar] *vt* to
synchronize
sindical [sindi'kal] *adj* union *cpd*, trade-
union *cpd*; **sindicalista** *adj, nmf* trade
unionist
sindicato [sindi'kato] *nm* (*de trabajadores*)
trade(s) union; (*de negociantes*) syndicate
síndrome ['sindrome] *nm* (*Med*)
syndrome; **síndrome de abstinencia**
(*Med*) withdrawal symptoms; **síndrome
de la clase turista** (*Med*) economy-class
syndrome
sinfín [sin'fin] *nm*: **un ~ de** a great many,
no end of
sinfonía [sinfo'nia] *nf* symphony
singular [singu'lar] *adj* singular; (*fig*)
outstanding, exceptional; (*raro*) peculiar,
odd
siniestro, -a [si'njestro, a] *adj* sinister
▷ *nm* (*accidente*) accident
sinnúmero [sin'numero] *nm* = **sinfín**

sino ['sino] *nm* fate, destiny ▷ *conj* (*pero*) but; (*salvo*) except, save

sinónimo, -a [si'nonimo, a] *adj* synonymous ▷ *nm* synonym

síntesis ['sintesis] *nf* synthesis; **sintético, -a** *adj* synthetic

sintió *vb* V **sentir**

síntoma ['sintoma] *nm* symptom

sintonía [sinto'nia] *nf* (*Radio, Mús: de programa*) tuning; **sintonizar** *vt* (*Radio: emisora*) to tune (in)

sinvergüenza [simber'ɣwenθa] *nmf* rogue, scoundrel; **¡es un ~!** he's got a nerve!

siquiera [si'kjera] *conj* even if, even though ▷ *adv* at least; **ni ~** not even

Siria ['sirja] *nf* Syria

sirviente, -a [sir'βjente, a] *nm/f* servant

sirvo *etc vb* V **servir**

sistema [sis'tema] *nm* system; (*método*) method; **sistema educativo** education system; **sistemático, -a** *adj* systematic

sitiar [si'tjar] *vt* to besiege, lay siege to

sitio ['sitjo] *nm* (*lugar*) place; (*espacio*) room, space; (*Mil*) siege; **sitio de taxis** (*MÉX: parada*) taxi stand *o* rank (*BRIT*); **sitio web** (*Inform*) website

situación [sitwa'θjon] *nf* situation, position; (*estatus*) position, standing

situado, -a [situ'aðo] *adj* situated, placed

situar [si'twar] *vt* to place, put; (*edificio*) to locate, situate

slip [slip] *nm* pants *pl*, briefs *pl*

smoking ['smokin, es'mokin] (*pl* **~s**) *nm* dinner jacket (*BRIT*), tuxedo (*US*)

▌No confundir **smoking** con la palabra inglesa *smoking*.

SMS *nm* (*mensaje*) text message, SMS message

snob [es'nob] = **esnob**

SO *abr* (= *suroeste*) SW

sobaco [so'βako] *nm* armpit

sobar [so'βar] *vt* (*ropa*) to rumple; (*comida*) to play around with

soberanía [soβera'nia] *nf* sovereignty;

soberano, -a *adj* sovereign; (*fig*) supreme ▷ *nm/f* sovereign

soberbia [so'βerβja] *nf* pride; haughtiness, arrogance; magnificence

soberbio, -a [so'βerβjo, a] *adj* (*orgulloso*) proud; (*altivo*) arrogant; (*estupendo*) magnificent, superb

sobornar [soβor'nar] *vt* to bribe; **soborno** *nm* bribe

sobra ['soβra] *nf* excess, surplus; **sobras** *nfpl* left-overs, scraps; **de ~** surplus, extra; **tengo de ~** I've more than enough; **sobrado, -a** *adj* (*más que suficiente*) more than enough; (*superfluo*) excessive; **sobrante** *adj* remaining, extra ▷ *nm* surplus, remainder

sobrar [so'βrar] *vt* to exceed, surpass ▷ *vi* (*tener de más*) to be more than enough; (*quedar*) to remain, be left (over)

sobrasada [soβra'saða] *nf* pork sausage spread

sobre ['soβre] *prep* (*gen*) on; (*encima*) on (top of); (*por encima de, arriba de*) over, above; (*más que*) more than; (*además*) in addition to, besides; (*alrededor de*) about ▷ *nm* envelope; **~ todo** above all

sobrecama [soβre'kama] *nf* bedspread

sobrecargar [soβrekar'ɣar] *vt* (*camión*) to overload; (*Com*) to surcharge

sobredosis [soβre'ðosis] *nf inv* overdose

sobreentender [soβre(e)nten'der] *vt* to deduce, infer; **sobreentenderse** *vr*: **se sobreentiende que ...** it is implied that ...

sobrehumano, -a [soβreu'mano, a] *adj* superhuman

sobrellevar [soβreʎe'βar] *vt* to bear, endure

sobremesa [soβre'mesa] *nf*: **durante la ~** after dinner

sobrenatural [soβrenatu'ral] *adj* supernatural

sobrenombre [soβre'nombre] *nm* nickname

sobrepasar [soβrepa'sar] *vt* to exceed, surpass

sobreponerse [soβrepo'nerse] *vr*: **~ a** to overcome

sobresaliente [soβresa'ljente] *adj* outstanding, excellent

sobresalir [soβresa'lir] *vi* to project, jut out; (*fig*) to stand out, excel

sobresaltar [soβresal'tar] *vt* (*asustar*) to scare, frighten; (*sobrecoger*) to startle; **sobresalto** *nm* (*movimiento*) start; (*susto*) scare; (*turbación*) sudden shock

sobretodo [soβre'toðo] *nm* overcoat

sobrevenir [soβreβe'nir] *vi* (*ocurrir*) to happen (unexpectedly); (*resultar*) to follow, ensue

sobrevivir [soβreβi'βir] vi to survive

sobrevolar [soβreβo'lar] vt to fly over

sobriedad [soβrje'ðað] nf sobriety, soberness; (moderación) moderation, restraint

sobrino, -a [so'βrino, a] nm/f nephew/ niece

sobrio, -a ['soβrjo, a] adj sober; (moderado) moderate, restrained

socarrón, -ona [soka'rron, ona] adj (sarcástico) sarcastic, ironic(al)

socavón [soka'βon] nm (hoyo) hole

sociable [so'θjaβle] adj (persona) sociable, friendly; (animal) social

social [so'θjal] adj social; (Com) company cpd

socialdemócrata [soθjalde'mokrata] nmf social democrat

socialista [soθja'lista] adj, nm socialist

socializar [soθjali'θar] vt to socialize

sociedad [soθje'ðað] nf society; (Com) company; **sociedad anónima** limited company; **sociedad de consumo** consumer society

socio, -a ['soθjo, a] nm/f (miembro) member; (Com) partner

sociología [soθjolo'xia] nf sociology; **sociólogo, -a** nm/f sociologist

socorrer [soko'rrer] vt to help; **socorrista** nmf first aider; (en piscina, playa) lifeguard; **socorro** nm (ayuda) help, aid; (Mil) relief; **¡socorro!** help!

soda ['soða] nf (sosa) soda; (bebida) soda (water)

sofá [so'fa] (pl **~s**) nm sofa, settee; **sofá-cama** nm studio couch; sofa bed

sofocar [sofo'kar] vt to suffocate; (apagar) to smother, put out; **sofocarse** vr to suffocate; (fig) to blush, feel embarrassed; **sofoco** nm suffocation; embarrassment

sofreír [sofre'ir] vt (Culin) to fry lightly

soga ['soxa] nf rope

sois etc vb V **ser**

soja ['soxa] nf soya

sol [sol] nm sun; (luz) sunshine, sunlight; (Mús) G; **hace ~** it's sunny

solamente [sola'mente] adv only, just

solapa [so'lapa] nf (de chaqueta) lapel; (de libro) jacket

solapado, -a [sola'paðo, a] adj (intenciónes) underhand; (gestos, movimiento) sly

solar [so'lar] adj solar, sun cpd

soldado [sol'daðo] nm soldier; **soldado raso** private

soldador [solda'ðor] nm soldering iron; (persona) welder

soldar [sol'dar] vt to solder, weld

soleado, -a [sole'aðo, a] adj sunny

soledad [sole'ðað] nf solitude; (estado infeliz) loneliness

solemne [so'lemne] adj solemn

soler [so'ler] vi to be in the habit of, be accustomed to; **suele salir a las ocho** she usually goes out at eight o'clock

solfeo [sol'feo] nm solfa

solicitar [soliθi'tar] vt (permiso) to ask for, seek; (puesto) to apply for; (votos) to canvass for; (atención) to attract

solícito, -a [so'liθito, a] adj (diligente) diligent; (cuidadoso) careful; **solicitud** nf (calidad) great care; (petición) request; (a un puesto) application

solidaridad [soliðari'ðað] nf solidarity; **solidario, -a** adj (participación) joint, common; (compromiso) mutually binding

sólido, -a ['soliðo, a] adj solid

soliloquio [soli'lokjo] nm soliloquy

solista [so'lista] nmf soloist

solitario, -a [soli'tarjo, a] adj (persona) lonely, solitary; (lugar) lonely, desolate ▷ nm/f (recluso) recluse; (en la sociedad) loner ▷ nm solitaire

sollozar [soλo'θar] vi to sob; **sollozo** nm sob

solo, -a ['solo, a] adj (único) single, sole; (sin compañía) alone; (solitario) lonely; **hay una sola dificultad** there is just one difficulty; **a solas** alone, by oneself

sólo ['solo] adv only, just

solomillo [solo'miλo] nm sirloin

soltar [sol'tar] vt (dejar ir) to let go of; (desprender) to unfasten, loosen; (librar) to release, set free; (risa etc) to let out

soltero, -a [sol'tero, a] adj single, unmarried ▷ nm/f bachelor/single woman; **solterón, -ona** nm/f old bachelor/spinster

soltura [sol'tura] nf looseness, slackness; (de los miembros) agility, ease of movement; (en el hablar) fluency, ease

soluble [so'luβle] adj (Quím) soluble; (problema) solvable; **~ en agua** soluble in water

solución [solu'θjon] nf solution; **solucionar** vt (problema) to solve; (asunto) to settle, resolve

solventar [solβen'tar] vt (pagar) to settle, pay; (resolver) to resolve; **solvente** adj (Econ: empresa, persona) solvent

sombra ['sombra] nf shadow; (como protección) shade; **sombras** nfpl (oscuridad) darkness sg, shadows; **tener buena/mala ~** to be lucky/unlucky

sombrero [som'brero] nm hat

sombrilla [som'briλa] nf parasol,

sunshade

sombrío, -a [som'brio, a] *adj (oscuro)* dark; *(triste)* sombre, sad; *(persona)* gloomy

someter [some'ter] *vt (país)* to conquer; *(persona)* to subject to one's will; *(informe)* to present, submit; **someterse** *vr* to give in, yield, submit; **~ a** to subject to

somier [so'mjer] *(pl* **~s)** *n* spring mattress

somnífero [som'nifero] *nm* sleeping pill

somos *vb* V **ser**

son [son] *vb* V **ser** ▷ *nm* sound

sonaja [so'naxa] *(MÉX) nf* = **sonajero**

sonajero [sona'xero] *nm* (baby's) rattle

sonambulismo [sonambu'lismo] *nm* sleepwalking; **sonámbulo, -a** *nm/f* sleepwalker

sonar [so'nar] *vt* to ring ▷ *vi* to sound; *(hacer ruido)* to make a noise; *(pronunciarse)* to be sounded, be pronounced; *(ser conocido)* to sound familiar; *(campana)* to ring; *(reloj)* to strike, chime; **sonarse** *vr:* **~se (las narices)** to blow one's nose; **me suena ese nombre** that name rings a bell

sonda ['sonda] *nf (Náut)* sounding; *(Tec)* bore, drill; *(Med)* probe

sondear [sonde'ar] *vt* to sound; to bore (into), drill; to probe, sound; *(fig)* to sound out; **sondeo** *nm* sounding; boring, drilling; *(fig)* poll, enquiry

sonido [so'niðo] *nm* sound

sonoro, -a [so'noro, a] *adj* sonorous; *(resonante)* loud, resonant

sonreír [sonre'ir] *vi* to smile; **sonreírse** *vr* to smile; **sonriente** *adj* smiling; **sonrisa** *nf* smile

sonrojarse [sonro'xarse] *vr* to blush, go red; **sonrojo** *nm* blush

soñador, a [soɲa'ðor, a] *nm/f* dreamer

soñar [so'ɲar] *vt, vi* to dream; **~ con** to dream about o of

soñoliento, -a [soɲo'ljento, a] *adj* sleepy, drowsy

sopa ['sopa] *nf* soup

soplar [so'plar] *vt (polvo)* to blow away, blow off; *(inflar)* to blow up; *(vela)* to blow out ▷ *vi* to blow; **soplo** *nm* blow, puff; *(de viento)* puff, gust

soplón, -ona [so'plon, ona] *(fam) nm/f (niño)* telltale; *(de policía)* grass *(fam)*

soporífero [sopo'rifero] *nm* sleeping pill

soportable [sopor'taβle] *adj* bearable

soportar [sopor'tar] *vt* to bear, carry; *(fig)* to bear, put up with

▌No confundir **soportar** con la palabra inglesa *support*.

soporte *nm* support; *(fig)* pillar, support

soprano [so'prano] *nf* soprano

sorber [sor'βer] *vt (chupar)* to sip; *(absorber)* to soak up, absorb

sorbete [sor'βete] *nm* iced fruit drink

sorbo ['sorβo] *nm (trago: grande)* gulp, swallow; *(: pequeño)* sip

sordera [sor'ðera] *nf* deafness

sórdido, -a ['sorðiðo, a] *adj* dirty, squalid

sordo, -a ['sorðo, a] *adj (persona)* deaf ▷ *nm/f* deaf person; **sordomudo, -a** *adj* deaf and dumb

sorna ['sorna] *nf* sarcastic tone

soroche [so'rotʃe] *(CAM) nm* mountain sickness

sorprendente [sorpren'dente] *adj* surprising

sorprender [sorpren'der] *vt* to surprise; **sorpresa** *nf* surprise

sortear [sorte'ar] *vt* to draw lots for; *(rifar)* to raffle; *(dificultad)* to avoid; **sorteo** *nm (en lotería)* draw; *(rifa)* raffle

sortija [sor'tixa] *nf* ring; *(rizo)* ringlet, curl

sosegado, -a [sose'ɣaðo, a] *adj* quiet, calm

sosiego [so'sjeɣo] *nm* quiet(ness), calm(ness)

soso, -a ['soso, a] *adj (Culin)* tasteless; *(aburrido)* dull, uninteresting

sospecha [sos'petʃa] *nf* suspicion; **sospechar** *vt* to suspect; **sospechoso, -a** *adj* suspicious; *(testimonio, opinión)* suspect ▷ *nm/f* suspect

sostén [sos'ten] *nm (apoyo)* support; *(sujetador)* bra; *(alimentación)* sustenance, food

sostener [soste'ner] *vt* to support; *(mantener)* to keep up, maintain; *(alimentar)* to sustain, keep going; **sostenerse** *vr* to support o.s.; *(seguir)* to continue, remain; **sostenido, -a** *adj* continuous, sustained; *(prolongado)* prolonged

sotana [so'tana] *nf (Rel)* cassock

sótano ['sotano] *nm* basement

soy [soi] *vb* V **ser**

soya ['soja] *(LAM) nf* soya *(BRIT)*, soy *(US)*

Sr. *abr* (= *Señor*) Mr

Sra. *abr* (= *Señora*) Mrs

Sres. *abr* (= *Señores*) Messrs

Srta. *abr* (= *Señorita*) Miss

Sta. *abr* (= *Santa*) St

Sto. *abr* (= *Santo*) St

su [su] *pron (de él)* his; *(de ella)* her; *(de una cosa)* its; *(de ellos, ellas)* their; *(de usted, ustedes)* your

suave ['swaβe] *adj* gentle; *(superficie)* smooth; *(trabajo)* easy; *(música, voz)* soft, sweet; **suavidad** *nf* gentleness; smoothness; softness, sweetness; **suavizante** *nm (de ropa)* softener; *(del pelo)* conditioner; **suavizar** *vt* to soften; *(quitar* *la aspereza*) to smooth (out)

subasta [suˈβasta] *nf* auction; **subastar** *vt* to auction (off)

subcampeón, -ona [suβkampeˈon, ona] *nm/f* runner-up

subconsciente [suβkonsˈθjente] *adj, nm* subconscious

subdesarrollado, -a [suβðesarroˈʎaðo, a] *adj* underdeveloped

subdesarrollo [suβðesaˈrroʎo] *nm* underdevelopment

subdirector, a [suβðirekˈtor, a] *nm/f* assistant director

súbdito, -a [ˈsuβðito, a] *nm/f* subject

subestimar [suβestiˈmar] *vt* to underestimate, underrate

subida [suˈβiða] *nf* (*de montaña etc*) ascent, climb; (*de precio*) rise, increase; (*pendiente*) slope, hill

subir [suˈβir] *vt* (*objeto*) to raise, lift up; (*cuesta, calle*) to go up; (*colina, montaña*) to climb; (*precio*) to raise, put up ▷ *vi* to go up, come up; (*a un coche*) to get in; (*a un autobús, tren o avión*) to get on, board; (*precio*) to rise, go up; (*río, marea*) to rise; **subirse** *vr* to get up, climb

súbito, -a [ˈsuβito, a] *adj* (*repentino*) sudden; (*imprevisto*) unexpected

subjetivo, -a [suβxeˈtiβo, a] *adj* subjective

sublevar [suβleˈβar] *vt* to rouse to revolt; **sublevarse** *vr* to revolt, rise

sublime [suˈβlime] *adj* sublime

submarinismo [suβmariˈnismo] *nm* scuba diving

submarino, -a [suβmaˈrino, a] *adj* underwater ▷ *nm* submarine

subnormal [suβnorˈmal] *adj* subnormal ▷ *nmf* subnormal person

subordinado, -a [suβorðiˈnaðo, a] *adj, nm/f* subordinate

subrayar [suβraˈjar] *vt* to underline

subsanar [suβsaˈnar] *vt* to rectify

subsidio [suβˈsiðjo] *nm* (*ayuda*) aid, financial help; (*subvención*) subsidy, grant; (*de enfermedad, paro etc*) benefit, allowance

subsistencia [suβsisˈtenθja] *nf* subsistence

subsistir [suβsisˈtir] *vi* to subsist; (*sobrevivir*) to survive, endure

subte [ˈsuβte] (*RPL*) *nm* underground (*BRIT*), subway (*US*)

subterráneo, -a [suβteˈrraneo, a] *adj* underground, subterranean ▷ *nm* underpass, underground passage

subtítulo [suβˈtitulo] *nm* (*Cine*) subtitle

suburbio [suˈβurβjo] *nm* (*barrio*) slum quarter

subvención [suββenˈθjon] *nf* (*Econ*) subsidy, grant; **subvencionar** *vt* to subsidize

sucedáneo, -a [suθeˈðaneo, a] *adj* substitute ▷ *nm* substitute (food)

suceder [suθeˈðer] *vt, vi* to happen; (*seguir*) to succeed, follow; **lo que sucede es que ...** the fact is that ...; **sucesión** *nf* succession; (*serie*) sequence, series

sucesivamente [suθesiβaˈmente] *adv*: **y así ~** and so on

sucesivo, -a [suθeˈsiβo, a] *adj* successive, following; **en lo ~** in future, from now on

suceso [suˈθeso] *nm* (*hecho*) event, happening; (*incidente*) incident

▌No confundir **suceso** con la palabra inglesa *success*.

suciedad [suθjeˈðað] *nf* (*estado*) dirtiness; (*mugre*) dirt, filth

sucio, -a [ˈsuθjo, a] *adj* dirty

suculento, -a [sukuˈlento, a] *adj* succulent

sucumbir [sukumˈbir] *vi* to succumb

sucursal [sukurˈsal] *nf* branch (office)

sudadera [suðaˈðera] *nf* sweatshirt

Sudáfrica [suðˈafrika] *nf* South Africa

Sudamérica [suðaˈmerika] *nf* South America; **sudamericano, -a** *adj, nm/f* South American

sudar [suˈðar] *vt, vi* to sweat

sudeste [suˈðeste] *nm* south-east

sudoeste [suðoˈeste] *nm* south-west

sudor [suˈðor] *nm* sweat; **sudoroso, -a** *adj* sweaty, sweating

Suecia [ˈsweθja] *nf* Sweden; **sueco, -a** *adj* Swedish ▷ *nm/f* Swede

suegro, -a [ˈswexro, a] *nm/f* father-/mother-in-law

suela [ˈswela] *nf* sole

sueldo [ˈsweldo] *nm* pay, wage(s) (*pl*)

suele *etc vb* V **soler**

suelo [ˈswelo] *nm* (*tierra*) ground; (*de casa*) floor

suelto, -a [ˈswelto, a] *adj* loose; (*libre*) free; (*separado*) detached; (*ágil*) quick, agile ▷ *nm* (*loose*) change, small change

sueñito [sweˈɲito] (*LAM*) *nm* nap

sueño *etc* [ˈsweɲo] *vb* V **soñar** ▷ *nm* sleep; (*somnolencia*) sleepiness, drowsiness; (*lo soñado, fig*) dream; **tener ~** to be sleepy

suero [ˈswero] *nm* (*Med*) serum; (*de leche*) whey

suerte [ˈswerte] *nf* (*fortuna*) luck; (*azar*) chance; (*destino*) fate, destiny; (*especie*) sort, kind; **tener ~** to be lucky

suéter [ˈsweter] *nm* sweater

suficiente [sufiˈθjente] *adj* enough, sufficient ▷ *nm* (*Escol*) pass

sufragio [su'fraxjo] *nm* (*voto*) vote; (*derecho de voto*) suffrage

sufrido, -a [su'friðo, a] *adj* (*persona*) tough; (*paciente*) long-suffering, patient

sufrimiento [sufri'mjento] *nm* (*dolor*) suffering

sufrir [su'frir] *vt* (*padecer*) to suffer; (*soportar*) to bear, put up with; (*apoyar*) to hold up, support ▷ *vi* to suffer

sugerencia [suxe'renθja] *nf* suggestion

sugerir [suxe'rir] *vt* to suggest; (*sutilmente*) to hint

sugestión [suxes'tjon] *nf* suggestion; (*sutil*) hint; **sugestionar** *vt* to influence

sugestivo, -a [suxes'tiβo, a] *adj* stimulating; (*fascinante*) fascinating

suicida [sui'θiða] *adj* suicidal ▷ *nmf* suicidal person; (*muerto*) suicide, person who has committed suicide; **suicidarse** *vr* to commit suicide, kill o.s.; **suicidio** *nm* suicide

Suiza ['swiθa] *nf* Switzerland; **suizo, -a** *adj, nm/f* Swiss

sujeción [suxe'θjon] *nf* subjection

sujetador [suxeta'ðor] *nm* (*sostén*) bra

sujetar [suxe'tar] *vt* (*fijar*) to fasten; (*detener*) to hold down; **sujetarse** *vr* to subject o.s.; **sujeto, -a** *adj* fastened, secure ▷ *nm* subject; (*individuo*) individual; **sujeto a** subject to

suma ['suma] *nf* (*cantidad*) total, sum; (*de dinero*) sum; (*acto*) adding (up), addition; **en ~** in short

sumamente [suma'mente] *adv* extremely, exceedingly

sumar [su'mar] *vt* to add (up) ▷ *vi* to add up

sumergir [sumer'xir] *vt* to submerge; (*hundir*) to sink

suministrar [suminis'trar] *vt* to supply, provide; **suministro** *nm* supply; (*acto*) supplying, providing

sumir [su'mir] *vt* to sink, submerge; (*fig*) to plunge

sumiso, -a [su'miso, a] *adj* submissive, docile

sumo, -a ['sumo, a] *adj* great, extreme; (*autoridad*) highest, supreme

suntuoso, -a [sun'twoso, a] *adj* sumptuous, magnificent

supe *etc vb* V **saber**

super... [super] *prefijo* super..., over...

superbueno, -a [super'bweno, a] *adj* great, fantastic

súper ['super] *nf* (*gasolina*) four-star (petrol)

superar [supe'rar] *vt* (*sobreponerse a*) to overcome; (*rebasar*) to surpass, do better

than; (*pasar*) to go beyond; **superarse** *vr* to excel o.s.

superficial [superfi'θjal] *adj* superficial; (*medida*) surface *cpd*, of the surface

superficie [super'fiθje] *nf* surface; (*área*) area

superfluo, -a [su'perflwo, a] *adj* superfluous

superior [supe'rjor] *adj* (*piso, clase*) upper; (*temperatura, número, nivel*) higher; (*mejor: calidad, producto*) superior, better ▷ *nmf* superior; **superioridad** *nf* superiority

supermercado [supermer'kaðo] *nm* supermarket

superponer [superpo'ner] *vt* to superimpose

superstición [supersti'θjon] *nf* superstition; **supersticioso, -a** *adj* superstitious

supervisar [superβi'sar] *vt* to supervise

supervivencia [superβi'βenθja] *nf* survival

superviviente [superβi'βjente] *adj* surviving

supiera *etc vb* V **saber**

suplantar [suplan'tar] *vt* to supplant

suplemento [suple'mento] *nm* supplement

suplente [su'plente] *adj, nm* substitute

supletorio, -a [suple'torjo, a] *adj* supplementary ▷ *nm* supplement; **teléfono ~** extension

súplica ['suplika] *nf* request; (*Jur*) petition

suplicar [supli'kar] *vt* (*cosa*) to beg (for), plead for; (*persona*) to beg, plead with

suplicio [su'pliθjo] *nm* torture

suplir [su'plir] *vt* (*compensar*) to make good, make up for; (*reemplazar*) to replace, substitute ▷ *vi*: **~ a** to take the place of, substitute for

supo *etc vb* V **saber**

suponer [supo'ner] *vt* to suppose; **suposición** *nf* supposition

suprimir [supri'mir] *vt* to suppress; (*derecho, costumbre*) to abolish; (*palabra etc*) to delete; (*restricción*) to cancel, lift

supuesto, -a [su'pwesto, a] *pp de* **suponer** ▷ *adj* (*hipotético*) supposed ▷ *nm* assumption, hypothesis; **~ que** since; **por ~** of course

sur [sur] *nm* south

surcar [sur'kar] *vt* to plough; **surco** *nm* (*en metal, disco*) groove; (*Agr*) furrow

surgir [sur'xir] *vi* to arise, emerge; (*dificultad*) to come up, crop up

suroeste [suro'este] *nm* south-west

surtido, -a [sur'tiðo, a] *adj* mixed,

assorted ▷ *nm* (*selección*) selection, assortment; (*abastecimiento*) supply, stock; **surtidor** *nm* (*tb*: **surtidor de gasolina**) petrol pump (BRIT), gas pump (US)

surtir [sur'tir] *vt* to supply, provide ▷ *vi* to spout, spurt

susceptible [susθep'tiβle] *adj* susceptible; (*sensible*) sensitive; **~ de** capable of

suscitar [susθi'tar] *vt* to cause, provoke; (*interés, sospechas*) to arouse

suscribir [suskri'βir] *vt* (*firmar*) to sign; (*respaldar*) to subscribe to, endorse; **suscribirse** *vr* to subscribe; **suscripción** *nf* subscription

susodicho, -a [suso'ðitʃo, a] *adj* above-mentioned

suspender [suspen'der] *vt* (*objeto*) to hang (up), suspend; (*trabajo*) to stop, suspend; (*Escol*) to fail; (*interrumpir*) to adjourn; (*atrasar*) to postpone

suspense [sus'pense] (*ESP*) *nm* suspense; **película/novela de ~** thriller

suspensión [suspen'sjon] *nf* suspension; (*fig*) stoppage, suspension

suspenso, -a [sus'penso, a] *adj* hanging, suspended; (*ESP Escol*) failed ▷ *nm* (*ESP Escol*) fail; **película** *o* **novela de ~** (*LAM*) thriller; **quedar** *o* **estar en ~** to be pending

suspicaz [suspi'kaθ] *adj* suspicious, distrustful

suspirar [suspi'rar] *vi* to sigh; **suspiro** *nm* sigh

sustancia [sus'tanθja] *nf* substance

sustento [sus'tento] *nm* support; (*alimento*) sustenance, food

sustituir [sustitu'ir] *vt* to substitute, replace; **sustituto, -a** *nm/f* substitute, replacement

susto ['susto] *nm* fright, scare

sustraer [sustra'er] *vt* to remove, take away; (*Mat*) to subtract

susurrar [susu'rrar] *vi* to whisper; **susurro** *nm* whisper

sutil [su'til] *adj* (*aroma, diferencia*) subtle; (*tenue*) thin; (*inteligencia, persona*) sharp

suyo, -a ['sujo, a] (*con artículo o después del verbo* **ser**) *adj* (*de él*) his; (*de ella*) hers; (*de ellos, ellas*) theirs; (*de Ud, Uds*) yours; **un amigo ~** a friend of his (*o* hers *o* theirs *o* yours)

Tabacalera [taβaka'lera] *nf* Spanish state tobacco monopoly

tabaco [ta'βako] *nm* tobacco; (*ESP: fam*) cigarettes *pl*

tabaquería [tabake'ria] (*LAM*) *nf* tobacconist's (shop) (BRIT), smoke shop (US); **tabaquero, -a** (*LAM*) *nm/f* tobacconist

taberna [ta'βerna] *nf* bar, pub (BRIT)

tabique [ta'βike] *nm* partition (wall)

tabla ['taβla] *nf* (*de madera*) plank; (*estante*) shelf; (*de vestido*) pleat; (*Arte*) panel; **tablas** *nfpl*: **estar** *o* **quedar en ~s** to draw; **tablado** *nm* (*plataforma*) platform; (*Teatro*) stage

tablao [ta'βlao] *nm* (*tb*: **~ flamenco**) flamenco show

tablero [ta'βlero] *nm* (*de madera*) plank, board; (*de ajedrez, damas*) board; **tablero de mandos** (*LAM Auto*) dashboard

tableta [ta'βleta] *nf* (*Med*) tablet; (*de chocolate*) bar

tablón [ta'βlon] *nm* (*de suelo*) plank; (*de techo*) beam; **tablón de anuncios** notice (BRIT) *o* bulletin (US) board

tabú [ta'βu] *nm* taboo

taburete [taβu'rete] *nm* stool

tacaño, -a [ta'kaɲo, a] *adj* mean

tacha ['tatʃa] *nf* flaw; (*Tec*) stud; **tachar** *vt* (*borrar*) to cross out; **tachar de** to accuse of

tacho ['tatʃo] (*CS*) *nm* (*balde*) bucket; **tacho de la basura** rubbish bin (BRIT), trash can (US)

taco ['tako] *nm* (*Billar*) cue; (*de billetes*) book; (*CS: de zapato*) heel; (*tarugo*) peg; (*palabrota*) swear word

tacón [ta'kon] *nm* heel; **de ~ alto** high-heeled

táctica ['taktika] *nf* tactics *pl*

táctico, -a ['taktiko, a] *adj* tactical

tacto ['takto] *nm* touch; (*fig*) tact

tajada [ta'xaða] *nf* slice

tajante [ta'xante] *adj* sharp

tajo ['taxo] nm (corte) cut; (Geo) cleft

tal [tal] adj such ▷ pron (persona) someone,
such a one; (cosa) something, such a thing
▷ adv: **~ como** (igual) just as ▷ conj: **con ~
de que** provided that; **~ cual** (como es) just
as it is; **~ vez** perhaps; **~ como** such as; **~
para cual** (dos iguales) two of a kind; **¿qué
~?** how are things?; **¿qué ~ te gusta?** how
do you like it?

taladrar [tala'ðrar] vt to drill; **taladro**
nm drill

talante [ta'lante] nm (humor) mood;
(voluntad) will, willingness

talar [ta'lar] vt to fell, cut down; (devastar)
to devastate

talco ['talko] nm (polvos) talcum powder

talento [ta'lento] nm talent; (capacidad)
ability

TALGO ['talxo] (ESP) nm abr (= tren
articulado ligero Goicoechea-Oriol) ≈ HST (BRIT)

talismán [talis'man] nm talisman

talla ['taʎa] nf (estatura, fig, Med) height,
stature; (palo) measuring rod; (Arte) carving;
(medida) size

tallar [ta'ʎar] vt (madera) to carve; (metal
etc) to engrave; (medir) to measure

tallarines [taʎa'rines] nmpl noodles

talle ['taʎe] nm (Anat) waist; (fig)
appearance

taller [ta'ʎer] nm (Tec) workshop; (de
artista) studio

tallo ['taʎo] nm (de planta) stem; (de hierba)
blade; (brote) shoot

talón [ta'lon] nm (Anat) heel; (Com)
counterfoil; (cheque) cheque (BRIT), check
(US)

talonario [talo'narjo] nm (de cheques)
chequebook (BRIT), checkbook (US); (de
recibos) receipt book

tamaño, -a [ta'maɲo, a] adj (tan grande)
such a big; (tan pequeño) such a small ▷ nm
size; **de ~ natural** full-size

tamarindo [tama'rindo] nm tamarind

tambalearse [tambale'arse] vr (persona)
to stagger; (vehículo) to sway

también [tam'bjen] adv (igualmente) also,
too, as well; (además) besides

tambor [tam'bor] nm drum; (Anat)
eardrum; **tambor del freno** brake drum

tamizar [tami'θar] vt to sieve

tampoco [tam'poko] adv nor, neither; **yo
~ lo compré** I didn't buy it either

tampón [tam'pon] nm tampon

tan [tan] adv so; **~ es así que ...** so much
so that ...

tanda ['tanda] nf (gen) series; (turno) shift

tangente [tan'xente] nf tangent

tangerina [tanxe'rina] (LAM) nf
tangerine

tangible [tan'xiβle] adj tangible

tanque ['tanke] nm (cisterna, Mil) tank;
(Auto) tanker

tantear [tante'ar] vt (calcular) to reckon
(up); (medir) to take the measure of; (probar)
to test, try out; (tomar la medida: persona) to
take the measurements of; (situación) to
weigh up; (persona: opinión) to sound out
▷ vi (Deporte) to score; **tanteo** nm (cálculo)
(rough) calculation; (prueba) test, trial;
(Deporte) scoring

tanto, -a ['tanto, a] adj (cantidad) so
much, as much ▷ adv (cantidad) so much,
as much; (tiempo) so long, as long ▷ conj: **en
~ que** while ▷ nm (suma) certain amount;
(proporción) so much; (punto) point; (gol)
goal; **un ~ perezoso** somewhat lazy
▷ pron: **cada uno paga ~** each one pays so
much; **~s** so many, as many; **20 y ~s** 20-odd;
hasta ~ (que) until such time as; **~ tú como
yo** both you and I; **~ como eso** as much as
that; **~ más ... cuanto que** all the more ...
because; **~ mejor/peor** so much the better/
the worse; **~ si viene como si va** whether
he comes or whether he goes; **~ es así que**
so much so that; **por (lo) ~** therefore; **entre
~** meanwhile; **estar al ~** to be up to date;
me he vuelto ronco de o con ~ hablar I
have become hoarse with so much talking;
a ~s de agosto on such and such a day in
August

tapa ['tapa] nf (de caja, olla) lid; (de botella)
top; (de libro) cover; (comida) snack

tapadera [tapa'ðera] nf lid, cover

tapar [ta'par] vt (cubrir) to cover; (envolver)
to wrap o cover up; (la vista) to obstruct;
(persona, falta) to conceal; (MÉX, CAM: diente)
to fill; **taparse** vr to wrap o.s. up

taparrabo [tapa'rraβo] nm loincloth

tapete [ta'pete] nm table cover

tapia ['tapja] nf (garden) wall

tapicería [tapiθe'ria] nf tapestry; (para
muebles) upholstery; (tienda) upholsterer's
(shop)

tapiz [ta'piθ] nm (alfombra) carpet; (tela
tejida) tapestry; **tapizar** vt (muebles) to
upholster

tapón [ta'pon] nm (de botella) top; (de
lavabo) plug; **tapón de rosca** screw-top

taquigrafía [takixra'fia] nf shorthand;
taquígrafo, -a nm/f shorthand writer,
stenographer

taquilla [ta'kiʎa] nf (donde se compra)
booking office; (suma recogida) takings pl

tarántula [ta'rantula] nf tarantula

tararear [tarare'ar] vi to hum

tardar [tar'ðar] vi (tomar tiempo) to take a

long time; (*llegar tarde*) to be late; (*demorar*) to delay; **¿tarda mucho el tren?** does the train take (very) long?; **a más ~** at the latest; **no tardes en venir** come soon

tarde ['tarðe] *adv* late ▷ *nf* (*de día*) afternoon; (*al anochecer*) evening; **de ~ en ~** from time to time; **¡buenas ~s!** good afternoon!; **a o por la ~** in the afternoon; in the evening

tardío, -a [tar'ðio, a] *adj* (*retrasado*) late; (*lento*) slow (to arrive)

tarea [ta'rea] *nf* task; (*faena*) chore; (*Escol*) homework

tarifa [ta'rifa] *nf* (*lista de precios*) price list; (*precio*) tariff

tarima [ta'rima] *nf* (*plataforma*) platform

tarjeta [tar'xeta] *nf* card; **tarjeta de crédito/de Navidad/postal/telefónica** credit card/Christmas card/postcard/phonecard; **tarjeta de embarque** boarding pass; **tarjeta de memoria** memory card; **tarjeta prepago** top-up card; **tarjeta SIM** SIM card

tarro ['tarro] *nm* jar, pot

tarta ['tarta] *nf* (*pastel*) cake; (*de base dura*) tart

tartamudear [tartamuðe'ar] *vi* to stammer; **tartamudo, -a** *adj* stammering ▷ *nm/f* stammerer

tártaro, -a ['tartaro, a] *adj*: **salsa tártara** tartar(e) sauce

tasa ['tasa] *nf* (*precio*) (fixed) price, rate; (*valoración*) valuation; (*medida, norma*) measure, standard; **tasa de cambio/interés** exchange/interest rate; **tasas de aeropuerto** airport tax; **tasas universitarias** university fees

tasar [ta'sar] *vt* (*arreglar el precio*) to fix a price for; (*valorar*) to value, assess

tasca ['taska] (*fam*) *nf* pub

tatarabuelo, -a [tatara'βwelo, a] *nm/f* great-great-grandfather/mother

tatuaje [ta'twaxe] *nm* (*dibujo*) tattoo; (*acto*) tattooing

tatuar [ta'twar] *vt* to tattoo

taurino, -a [tau'rino, a] *adj* bullfighting *cpd*

Tauro ['tauro] *nm* Taurus

tauromaquia [tauro'makja] *nf* tauromachy, (art of) bullfighting

taxi ['taksi] *nm* taxi; **taxista** [tak'sista] *nmf* taxi driver

taza ['taθa] *nf* cup; (*de retrete*) bowl; **~ para café** coffee cup; **taza de café** cup of coffee; **tazón** *nm* (*taza grande*) mug, large cup; (*de fuente*) basin

te [te] *pron* (*complemento de objeto*) you; (*complemento indirecto*) (to) you; (*reflexivo*) (to) yourself; **¿~ duele mucho el brazo?** does your arm hurt a lot?; **~ equivocas** you're wrong; **¡cálma~!** calm down!

té [te] *nm* tea

teatral [tea'tral] *adj* theatre *cpd*; (*fig*) theatrical

teatro [te'atro] *nm* theatre; (*Literatura*) plays *pl*, drama

tebeo [te'βeo] *nm* comic

techo ['tetʃo] *nm* (*externo*) roof; (*interno*) ceiling; **techo corredizo** sunroof

tecla ['tekla] *nf* key; **teclado** *nm* keyboard; **teclear** *vi* (*Mús*) to strum; (*con los dedos*) to tap ▷ *vt* (*Inform*) to key in

técnica ['teknika] *nf* technique; (*tecnología*) technology; *V tb* **técnico**

técnico, -a ['tekniko, a] *adj* technical ▷ *nm/f* technician; (*experto*) expert

tecnología [teknolo'xia] *nf* technology; **tecnológico, -a** *adj* technological

tecolote [teko'lote] *nm* (*MÉX*) owl

tedioso, -a [te'ðjoso, a] *adj* boring, tedious

teja ['texa] *nf* tile; (*Bot*) lime (tree); **tejado** *nm* (tiled) roof

tejemaneje [texema'nexe] *nm* (*lío*) fuss; (*intriga*) intrigue

tejer [te'xer] *vt* to weave; (*hacer punto*) to knit; (*fig*) to fabricate; **tejido** *nm* (*tela*) material, fabric; (*telaraña*) web; (*Anat*) tissue

tel [tel] *abr*. (= *teléfono*) tel

tela ['tela] *nf* (*tejido*) material; (*telaraña*) web; (*en líquido*) skin; **telar** *nm* (*máquina*) loom

telaraña [tela'raɲa] *nf* cobweb

tele ['tele] (*fam*) *nf* telly (*BRIT*), tube (*US*)

tele... ['tele] *prefijo* tele...; **telebasura** *nf* trash TV; **telecomunicación** *nf* telecommunication; **telediario** *nm* television news; **teledirigido, -a** *adj* remote-controlled

teleférico [tele'feriko] *nm* (*de esquí*) ski-lift

telefonear [telefone'ar] *vi* to telephone

telefónico, -a [tele'foniko, a] *adj* telephone *cpd*

telefonillo [telefo'niʎo] *nm* (*de puerta*) intercom

telefonista [telefo'nista] *nmf* telephonist

teléfono [te'lefono] *nm* (tele)phone; **estar hablando al ~** to be on the phone; **llamar a algn por ~** to ring sb (up) o phone sb (up); **teléfono celular** (*LAM*) mobile phone; **teléfono con cámara** camera phone; **teléfono inalámbrico** cordless phone; **teléfono móvil** (*ESP*) mobile phone

telégrafo [te'lexrafo] *nm* telegraph

telegrama [tele'xrama] *nm* telegram

tele: telenovela nf soap (opera);
teleobjetivo nm telephoto lens; **telepatía**
nf telepathy; **telepático, -a** adj telepathic;
telerrealidad nf reality TV; **telescopio**
nm telescope; **telesilla** nm chairlift;
telespectador, a nm/f viewer; **telesquí**
nm ski-lift; **teletarjeta** nf phonecard;
teletipo nm teletype; **teletrabajador,
a** nm/f teleworker; **teletrabajo** nm
teleworking; **televentas** nfpl telesales
televidente [teleβi'ðente] nmf viewer
televisar [teleβi'sar] vt to televise
televisión [teleβi'sjon] nf television;
televisión digital digital television
televisor [teleβi'sor] nm television set
télex ['teleks] nm inv telex
telón [te'lon] nm curtain; **telón de acero**
(Pol) iron curtain; **telón de fondo** backcloth,
background
tema ['tema] nm (asunto) subject, topic;
(Mús) theme; **temático, -a** adj thematic
temblar [tem'blar] vi to shake, tremble;
(por frío) to shiver; **temblor** nm trembling;
(de tierra) earthquake; **tembloroso, -a** adj
trembling
temer [te'mer] vt to fear ▷ vi to be afraid;
temo que llegue tarde I am afraid he may
be late
temible [te'miβle] adj fearsome
temor [te'mor] nm (miedo) fear; (duda)
suspicion
témpano ['tempano] nm (tb: ~ de hielo)
ice-floe
temperamento [tempera'mento] nm
temperament
temperatura [tempera'tura] nf
temperature
tempestad [tempes'tað] nf storm
templado, -a [tem'plaðo, a] adj
(moderado) moderate; (frugal) frugal; (agua)
lukewarm; (clima) mild; (Mús) well-tuned;
templanza nf moderation; mildness
templar [tem'plar] vt (moderar) to
moderate; (furia) to restrain; (calor) to
reduce; (afinar) to tune (up); (acero) to
temper; (tuerca) to tighten up; **temple**
nm (ajuste) tempering; (afinación) tuning;
(pintura) tempera
templo ['templo] nm (iglesia) church;
(pagano etc) temple
temporada [tempo'raða] nf time, period;
(estación) season
temporal [tempo'ral] adj (no permanente)
temporary ▷ nm storm
temprano, -a [tem'prano, a] adj early;
(demasiado pronto) too soon, too early
ten vb V **tener**
tenaces [te'naθes] adj pl V **tenaz**

tenaz [te'naθ] adj (material) tough;
(persona) tenacious; (creencia, resistencia)
stubborn
tenaza(s) [te'naθa(s)] nf(pl) (Med) forceps;
(Tec) pliers; (Zool) pincers
tendedero [tende'ðero] nm (para ropa)
drying place; (cuerda) clothes line
tendencia [ten'denθja] nf tendency;
tener ~ a to tend to, have a tendency to
tender [ten'der] vt (extender) to spread out;
(colgar) to hang out; (vía férrea, cable) to lay;
(estirar) to stretch ▷ vi: **~ a** to tend to, have
a tendency towards; **tenderse** vr to lie
down; **~ la cama/mesa** (LAM) to make the
bed/lay (BRIT) o set (US) the table
tenderete [tende'rete] nm (puesto) stall;
(exposición) display of goods
tendero, -a [ten'dero, a] nm/f
shopkeeper
tendón [ten'don] nm tendon
tendré etc vb V **tener**
tenebroso, -a [tene'βroso, a] adj (oscuro)
dark; (fig) gloomy
tenedor [tene'ðor] nm (Culin) fork
tenencia [te'nenθja] nf (de casa) tenancy;
(de oficio) tenure; (de propiedad) possession

○ **PALABRA CLAVE**

tener [te'ner] vt **1** (poseer, gen) to have; (en
la mano) to hold; **¿tienes un boli?** have you
got a pen?; **va a tener un niño** she's going
to have a baby; **¡ten (o tenga)!, ¡aquí tienes
(o tiene)!** here you are!
2 (edad, medidas) to be; **tiene 7 años** she's 7
(years old); **tiene 15 cm de largo** it's 15 cm
long; V **calor; hambre etc**
3 (considerar): **lo tengo por brillante** I
consider him to be brilliant; **tener en
mucho a algn** to think very highly of sb
4 (+ pp: = pretérito): **tengo terminada ya la
mitad del trabajo** I've done half the work
already
5: tener que hacer algo to have to do sth;
tengo que acabar este trabajo hoy I have
to finish this job today
6: ¿qué tienes, estás enfermo? what's the
matter with you, are you ill?
tenerse vr **1: tenerse en pie** to stand up
2: tenerse por to think o.s.

tengo etc vb V **tener**
tenia ['tenja] nf tapeworm
teniente [te'njente] nm (rango)
lieutenant; (ayudante) deputy
tenis ['tenis] nm tennis; **tenis de mesa**
table tennis; **tenista** nmf tennis player
tenor [te'nor] nm (sentido) meaning; (Mús)

tenor; **a ~ de** on the lines of

tensar [ten'sar] *vt* to tighten; (*arco*) to draw

tensión [ten'sjon] *nf* tension; (*Tec*) stress; **tener la ~ alta** to have high blood pressure; **tensión arterial** blood pressure

tenso, -a ['tenso, a] *adj* tense

tentación [tenta'θjon] *nf* temptation

tentáculo [ten'takulo] *nm* tentacle

tentador, a [tenta'ðor, a] *adj* tempting

tentar [ten'tar] *vt* (*seducir*) to tempt; (*atraer*) to attract

tentempié [tentem'pje] *nm* snack

tenue ['tenwe] *adj* (*delgado*) thin, slender; (*neblina*) light; (*lazo, vínculo*) slight

teñir [te'ɲir] *vt* to dye; (*fig*) to tinge; **teñirse** *vr* to dye; **~se el pelo** to dye one's hair

teología [teolo'xia] *nf* theology

teoría [teo'ria] *nf* theory; **en ~** in theory; **teórico, -a** *adj* theoretic(al) ▷ *nm/f* theoretician, theorist; **teorizar** *vi* to theorize

terapéutico, -a [tera'peutiko, a] *adj* therapeutic

terapia [te'rapja] *nf* therapy

tercer *adj* V **tercero**

tercermundista [terθermun'dista] *adj* Third World *cpd*

tercero, -a [ter'θero, a] (*delante de nmsg*: **tercer**) *adj* third ▷ *nm* (*Jur*) third party

terceto [ter'θeto] *nm* trio

terciar [ter'θjar] *vi* (*participar*) to take part; (*hacer de árbitro*) to mediate; **terciario, -a** *adj* tertiary

tercio ['terθjo] *nm* third

terciopelo [terθjo'pelo] *nm* velvet

terco, -a ['terko, a] *adj* obstinate

tergal® [ter'xal] *nm* type of polyester

tergiversar [terxiβer'sar] *vt* to distort

termal [ter'mal] *adj* thermal

termas ['termas] *nfpl* hot springs

térmico, -a ['termiko, a] *adj* thermal

terminal [termi'nal] *adj, nm, nf* terminal

terminante [termi'nante] *adj* (*final*) final, definitive; (*tajante*) categorical; **terminantemente** *adv*: **terminantemente prohibido** strictly forbidden

terminar [termi'nar] *vt* (*completar*) to complete, finish; (*concluir*) to end ▷ *vi* (*llegar a su fin*) to end; (*parar*) to stop; (*acabar*) to finish; **terminarse** *vr* to come to an end; **~ por hacer algo** to end up (by) doing sth

término ['termino] *nm* end, conclusion; (*parada*) terminus; (*límite*) boundary; **en último ~** (*a fin de cuentas*) in the last analysis; (*como último recurso*) as a last resort; **término medio** average; (*fig*) middle way

termómetro [ter'mometro] *nm* thermometer

termo(s)® ['termo(s)] *nm* Thermos®

termostato [termo'stato] *nm* thermostat

ternero, -a [ter'nero, a] *nm/f* (*animal*) calf ▷ *nf* (*carne*) veal

ternura [ter'nura] *nf* (*trato*) tenderness; (*palabra*) endearment; (*cariño*) fondness

terrado [te'rraðo] *nm* terrace

terraplén [terra'plen] *nm* embankment

terrateniente [terrate'njente] *nmf* landowner

terraza [te'rraθa] *nf* (*balcón*) balcony; (*tejado*) (flat) roof; (*Agr*) terrace

terremoto [terre'moto] *nm* earthquake

terrenal [terre'nal] *adj* earthly

terreno [te'rreno] *nm* (*tierra*) land; (*parcela*) plot; (*suelo*) soil; (*fig*) field; **un ~** a piece of land

terrestre [te'rrestre] *adj* terrestrial; (*ruta*) land *cpd*

terrible [te'rriβle] *adj* terrible, awful

territorio [terri'torjo] *nm* territory

terrón [te'rron] *nm* (*de azúcar*) lump; (*de tierra*) clod, lump

terror [te'rror] *nm* terror; **terrorífico, -a** *adj* terrifying; **terrorista** *adj, nmf* terrorist; **terrorista suicida** suicide bomber

terso, -a ['terso, a] *adj* (*liso*) smooth; (*pulido*) polished

tertulia [ter'tulja] *nf* (*reunión informal*) social gathering; (*grupo*) group, circle

tesis ['tesis] *nf inv* thesis

tesón [te'son] *nm* (*firmeza*) firmness; (*tenacidad*) tenacity

tesorero, -a [teso'rero, a] *nm/f* treasurer

tesoro [te'soro] *nm* treasure; (*Com, Pol*) treasury

testamento [testa'mento] *nm* will

testarudo, -a [testa'ruðo, a] *adj* stubborn

testículo [tes'tikulo] *nm* testicle

testificar [testifi'kar] *vt* to testify; (*fig*) to attest ▷ *vi* to give evidence

testigo [tes'tixo] *nmf* witness; **testigo de cargo/descargo** witness for the prosecution/defence; **testigo ocular** eye witness

testimonio [testi'monjo] *nm* testimony

teta ['teta] *nf* (*de biberón*) teat; (*Anat: fam*) breast

tétanos ['tetanos] *nm* tetanus

tetera [te'tera] *nf* teapot

tétrico, -a ['tetriko, a] *adj* gloomy, dismal

textil [teks'til] *adj* textile

texto ['teksto] *nm* text; **textual** *adj* textual

textura [teks'tura] nf (de tejido) texture
tez [teθ] nf (cutis) complexion
ti [ti] pron you; (reflexivo) yourself
tía ['tia] nf (pariente) aunt; (fam) chick, bird
tibio, -a ['tiβjo, a] adj lukewarm
tiburón [tiβu'ron] nm shark
tic [tik] nm (ruido) click; (de reloj) tick;
(Med): **~ nervioso** nervous tic
tictac [tik'tak] nm (de reloj) tick tock
tiempo ['tjempo] nm time; (época, período)
age, period; (Meteorología) weather; (Ling)
tense; (Deporte) half; **a ~** in time; **a un o al
mismo ~** at the same time; **al poco ~** very
soon (after); **se quedó poco ~** he didn't
stay very long; **hace poco ~** not long ago;
mucho ~ a long time; **de ~ en ~** from time to
time; **hace buen/mal ~** the weather is fine/
bad; **estar a ~** to be in time; **hace ~** some
time ago; **hacer ~** to while away the time;
motor de 2 ~s two-stroke engine; **primer
~** first half
tienda ['tjenda] nf shop, store; **tienda
de abarrotes** (MÉX, CAM) grocer's (BRIT),
grocery store (US); **tienda de alimentación
o comestibles** grocer's (BRIT), grocery store
(US); **tienda de campaña** tent
tienes etc vb V tener
tienta etc ['tjenta] vb V tentar ▷nf: **andar
a ~s** to grope one's way along
tiento etc ['tjento] vb V tentar ▷nm
(tacto) touch; (precaución) wariness
tierno, -a ['tjerno, a] adj (blando) tender;
(fresco) fresh; (amable) sweet
tierra ['tjerra] nf earth; (suelo) soil; (mundo)
earth, world; (país) country, land; **~ adentro**
inland
tieso, -a ['tjeso, a] adj (rígido) rigid; (duro)
stiff; (fam: orgulloso) conceited
tiesto ['tjesto] nm flowerpot
tifón [ti'fon] nm typhoon
tifus ['tifus] nm typhus
tigre ['tixre] nm tiger
tijera [ti'xera] nf scissors pl; (Zool) claw;
tijeras nfpl scissors; (para plantas) shears
tila ['tila] nf lime blossom tea
tildar [til'dar] vt: **~ de** to brand as
tilde ['tilde] nf (Tip) tilde
tilín [ti'lin] nm tinkle
timar [ti'mar] vt (estafar) to swindle
timbal [tim'bal] nm small drum
timbre ['timbre] nm (sello) stamp;
(campanilla) bell; (tono) timbre; (Com) stamp
duty
timidez [timi'ðeθ] nf shyness; **tímido,
-a** adj shy
timo ['timo] nm swindle
timón [ti'mon] nm helm, rudder; **timonel**
nm helmsman

tímpano ['timpano] nm (Anat) eardrum;
(Mús) small drum
tina ['tina] nf tub; (baño) bath(tub); **tinaja**
nf large jar
tinieblas [ti'njeβlas] nfpl darkness sg;
(sombras) shadows
tino ['tino] nm (habilidad) skill; (juicio)
insight
tinta ['tinta] nf ink; (Tec) dye; (Arte) colour
tinte ['tinte] nm dye
tintero [tin'tero] nm inkwell
tinto ['tinto] nm red wine
tintorería [tintore'ria] nf dry cleaner's
tío ['tio] nm (pariente) uncle; (fam: individuo)
bloke (BRIT), guy
tiovivo [tio'βiβo] nm merry-go-round
típico, -a ['tipiko, a] adj typical
tipo ['tipo] nm (clase) type, kind; (hombre)
fellow; (Anat: de hombre) build; (: de mujer)
figure; (Imprenta) type; **tipo bancario/de
descuento/de interés/de cambio** bank/
discount/interest/exchange rate
tipografía [tipoxra'fia] nf printing cpd
tíquet ['tiket] (pl **~s**) nm ticket; (en tienda)
cash slip
tiquismiquis [tikis'mikis] nm inv fussy
person ▷nmpl (querellas) squabbling sg;
(escrúpulos) silly scruples
tira ['tira] nf strip; (fig) abundance; **tira y
afloja** give and take
tirabuzón [tiraβu'θon] nm (rizo) curl
tirachinas [tira'tʃinas] nm inv catapult
tirada [ti'raða] nf (acto) cast, throw; (serie)
series; (Tip) printing, edition; **de una ~** at
one go
tirado, -a [ti'raðo, a] adj (barato) dirt-
cheap; (fam: fácil) very easy
tirador [tira'ðor] nm (mango) handle
tirano, -a [ti'rano, a] adj tyrannical
▷nm/f tyrant
tirante [ti'rante] adj (cuerda etc) tight,
taut; (relaciones) strained ▷nm (Arq) brace;
(Tec) stay; **tirantes** nmpl (de pantalón)
braces (BRIT), suspenders (US); **tirantez** nf
tightness; (fig) tension
tirar [ti'rar] vt to throw; (dejar caer) to
drop; (volcar) to upset; (derribar) to knock
down o over; (desechar) to throw out o away;
(dinero) to squander; (imprimir) to print ▷vi
(disparar) to shoot; (de la puerta etc) to pull;
(fam: andar) to go; (tender a, buscar realizar)
to tend to; (Deporte) to shoot; **tirarse** vr to
throw o.s.; **~ abajo** to bring down, destroy;
tira más a su padre he takes more after his
father; **ir tirando** to manage
tirita [ti'rita] nf (sticking) plaster (BRIT),
Bandaid® (US)
tiritar [tiri'tar] vi to shiver

tiro ['tiro] nm (lanzamiento) throw; (disparo) shot; (Deporte) shot; (Golf, Tenis) drive; (alcance) range; **caballo de ~** cart-horse; **tiro al blanco** target practice

tirón [ti'ron] nm (sacudida) pull, tug; **de un ~** in one go, all at once

tiroteo [tiro'teo] nm exchange of shots, shooting

tisis ['tisis] nf inv consumption, tuberculosis

títere ['titere] nm puppet

titubear [tituβe'ar] vi to stagger; to stammer; (fig) to hesitate; **titubeo** nm staggering; stammering; hesitation

titulado, -a [titu'laðo, a] adj (libro) entitled; (persona) titled

titular [titu'lar] adj titular ▷ nmf holder ▷ nm headline ▷ vt to title; **titularse** vr to be entitled; **título** nm title; (de diario) headline; (certificado) professional qualification; (universitario) (university) degree; **a título de** in the capacity of

tiza ['tiθa] nf chalk

toalla [to'aʎa] nf towel

tobillo [to'βiʎo] nm ankle

tobogán [toβo'ɣan] nm (montaña rusa) roller-coaster; (de niños) chute, slide

tocadiscos [toka'ðiskos] nm inv record player

tocado, -a [to'kaðo, a] adj (fam) touched ▷ nm headdress

tocador [toka'ðor] nm (mueble) dressing table; (cuarto) boudoir; (fam) ladies' toilet (BRIT) o room (US)

tocar [to'kar] vt to touch; (Mús) to play; (referirse a) to allude to; (timbre) to ring ▷ vi (a la puerta) to knock (on o at the door); (ser de turno) to fall to, be the turn of; (ser hora) to be due; **tocarse** vr (cubrirse la cabeza) to cover one's head; (tener contacto) to touch (each other); **por lo que a mí me toca** as far as I am concerned; **te toca a ti** it's your turn

tocayo, -a [to'kajo, a] nm/f namesake

tocino [to'θino] nm bacon

todavía [toða'βia] adv (aun) even; (aún) still, yet; **~ más** yet more; **~ no** not yet

todo, -a ['toðo, a] adj **1** (con artículo sg) all; **toda la carne** all the meat; **toda la noche** all night, the whole night; **todo el libro** the whole book; **toda una botella** a whole bottle; **todo lo contrario** quite the opposite; **está toda sucia** she's all dirty; **por todo el país** throughout the whole country
2 (con artículo pl) all; every; **todos los libros**

all the books; **todas las noches** every night; **todos los que quieran salir** all those who want to leave
▷ pron **1** everything, all; **todos** everyone, everybody; **lo sabemos todo** we know everything; **todos querían más tiempo** everybody o everyone wanted more time; **nos marchamos todos** all of us left
2: **con todo: con todo él me sigue gustando** even so I still like him
▷ adv all; **vaya todo seguido** keep straight on o ahead
▷ nm: **como un todo** as a whole; **del todo: no me agrada del todo** I don't entirely like it

todopoderoso, -a [toðopoðe'roso, a] adj all powerful; (Rel) almighty

todoterreno [toðote'rreno] sm inv four-wheel drive, SUV (ESP US)

toga ['toɣa] nf toga; (Escol) gown

Tokio ['tokjo] n Tokyo

toldo ['toldo] nm (para el sol) sunshade (BRIT), parasol; (tienda) marquee

tolerancia [tole'ranθja] nf tolerance; **tolerante** adj (sociedad) liberal; (persona) open-minded

tolerar [tole'rar] vt to tolerate; (resistir) to endure

toma ['toma] nf (acto) taking; (Med) dose; **toma de corriente** socket; **toma de tierra** earth (wire); **tomacorriente** (LAM) nm socket

tomar [to'mar] vt to take; (aspecto) to take on; (beber) to drink ▷ vi to take; (LAM: beber) to drink; **tomarse** vr to take; **~se por** to consider o.s. to be; **~ a bien/mal** to take well/badly; **~ en serio** to take seriously; **~ el pelo a algn** to pull sb's leg; **~la con algn** to pick a quarrel with sb; **¡tome!** here you are!; **~ el sol** to sunbathe

tomate [to'mate] nm tomato

tomillo [to'miʎo] nm thyme

tomo ['tomo] nm (libro) volume

ton [ton] abr = **tonelada** ▷ nm: **sin ~ ni son** without rhyme or reason

tonalidad [tonali'ðað] nf tone

tonel [to'nel] nm barrel

tonelada [tone'laða] nf ton; **tonelaje** nm tonnage

tónica ['tonika] nf (Mús) tonic; (fig) keynote

tónico, -a ['toniko, a] adj tonic ▷ nm (Med) tonic

tono ['tono] nm tone; **fuera de ~** inappropriate

tontería [tonte'ria] nf (estupidez) foolishness; (cosa) stupid thing; (acto) foolish act; **tonterías** nfpl (disparates) rubbish sg, nonsense sg

tonto, -a ['tonto, a] adj stupid, silly ▷ nm/f fool

topar [to'par] vi: **~ contra** o **en** to run into; **~ con** to run up against

tope ['tope] adj maximum ▷ nm (fin) end; (límite) limit; (Ferro) buffer; (Auto) bumper; **al ~** end to end

tópico, -a ['topiko, a] adj topical ▷ nm platitude

topo ['topo] nm (Zool) mole; (fig) blunderer

toque etc ['toke] vb V **tocar** ▷ nm touch; (Mús) beat; (de campana) peal; **dar un ~ a** to warn; **toque de queda** curfew

toqué etc vb V **tocar**

toquetear [tokete'ar] vt to finger

toquilla [to'kiʎa] nf (pañuelo) headscarf; (chal) shawl

tórax ['toraks] nm thorax

torbellino [torbe'ʎino] nm whirlwind; (fig) whirl

torcedura [torθe'ðura] nf twist; (Med) sprain

torcer [tor'θer] vt to twist; (la esquina) to turn; (Med) to sprain ▷ vi (desviar) to turn off; **torcerse** vr (ladearse) to bend; (desviarse) to go astray; (fracasar) to go wrong; **torcido, -a** adj twisted; (fig) crooked ▷ nm curl

tordo, -a ['torðo, a] adj dappled ▷ nm thrush

torear [tore'ar] vt (fig: evadir) to avoid; (jugar con) to tease ▷ vi to fight bulls; **toreo** nm bullfighting; **torero, -a** nm/f bullfighter

tormenta [tor'menta] nf storm; (fig: confusión) turmoil

tormento [tor'mento] nm torture; (fig) anguish

tornar [tor'nar] vt (devolver) to return, give back; (transformar) to transform ▷ vi to go back

tornasolado, -a [tornaso'laðo, a] adj (brillante) iridescent; (reluciente) shimmering

torneo [tor'neo] nm tournament

tornillo [tor'niʎo] nm screw

torniquete [torni'kete] nm (Med) tourniquet

torno ['torno] nm (Tec) winch; (tambor) drum; **en ~ (a)** round, about

toro ['toro] nm bull; (fam) he-man; **los ~s** bullfighting

toronja [to'ronxa] nf grapefruit

torpe ['torpe] adj (poco hábil) clumsy, awkward; (necio) dim; (lento) slow

torpedo [tor'peðo] nm torpedo

torpeza [tor'peθa] nf (falta de agilidad) clumsiness; (lentitud) slowness; (error) mistake

torre ['torre] nf tower; (de petróleo) derrick

torrefacto, -a [torre'fakto, a] adj roasted

torrente [to'rrente] nm torrent

torrija [to'rrixa] nf French toast

torsión [tor'sjon] nf twisting

torso ['torso] nm torso

torta ['torta] nf cake; (fam) slap

tortícolis [tor'tikolis] nm inv stiff neck

tortilla [tor'tiʎa] nf omelette; (LAM: de maíz) maize pancake; **tortilla de papas** (LAM) potato omelette; **tortilla de patatas** (ESP) potato omelette; **tortilla francesa** (ESP) plain omelette

tórtola ['tortola] nf turtledove

tortuga [tor'tuxa] nf tortoise

tortuoso, -a [tor'twoso, a] adj winding

tortura [tor'tura] nf torture; **torturar** vt to torture

tos [tos] nf cough; **tos ferina** whooping cough

toser [to'ser] vi to cough

tostada [tos'taða] nf piece of toast; **tostado, -a** adj toasted; (por el sol) dark brown; (piel) tanned

tostador [tosta'ðor] (ESP) nm toaster; **tostadora** (LAM) nf = **tostador**

tostar [tos'tar] vt to toast; (café) to roast; (persona) to tan; **tostarse** vr to get brown

total [to'tal] adj total ▷ adv in short; (al fin y al cabo) when all is said and done ▷ nm total; **en ~** in all; **~ que ...** to cut (BRIT) o make (US) a long story short ...

totalidad [totali'ðað] nf whole

totalitario, -a [totali'tarjo, a] adj totalitarian

tóxico, -a ['toksiko, a] adj toxic ▷ nm poison; **toxicómano, -a** nm/f drug addict

toxina [to'ksina] nf toxin

tozudo, -a [to'θuðo, a] adj obstinate

trabajador, a [traβaxa'ðor, a] adj hard-working ▷ nm/f worker; **trabajador autónomo** o **por cuenta propia** self-employed person

trabajar [traβa'xar] vt to work; (Agr) to till; (empeñarse en) to work at; (convencer) to persuade ▷ vi to work; (esforzarse) to strive; **trabajo** nm work; (tarea) task; (Pol) labour; (fig) effort; **tomarse el trabajo de** to take the trouble to; **trabajo a destajo** piecework; **trabajo en equipo** teamwork; **trabajo por turnos** shift work; **trabajos forzados** hard labour sg

trabalenguas [traβa'lengwas] nm inv tongue twister

tracción [trak'θjon] nf traction; **tracción delantera/trasera** front-wheel/rear-wheel drive

tractor [trak'tor] *nm* tractor
tradición [traði'θjon] *nf* tradition;
 tradicional *adj* traditional
traducción [traðuk'θjon] *nf* translation
traducir [traðu'θir] *vt* to translate;
 traductor, a *nm/f* translator
traer [tra'er] *vt* to bring; (*llevar*) to carry;
 (*llevar puesto*) to wear; (*incluir*) to carry;
 (*causar*) to cause; **traerse** *vr*: **~se algo** to
 be up to sth
traficar [trafi'kar] *vi* to trade
tráfico ['trafiko] *nm* (*Com*) trade; (*Auto*)
 traffic
tragaluz [traɣa'luθ] *nm* skylight
tragamonedas [traɣamo'neðas] (*LAM*) *nf
 inv* slot machine
tragaperras [traɣa'perras] (*ESP*) *nf inv*
 slot machine
tragar [tra'ɣar] *vt* to swallow; (*devorar*) to
 devour, bolt down; **tragarse** *vr* to swallow
tragedia [tra'xeðja] *nf* tragedy; **trágico,
 -a** *adj* tragic
trago ['traɣo] *nm* (*líquido*) drink; (*bocado*)
 gulp; (*fam: de bebida*) swig; (*desgracia*) blow;
 echar un ~ to have a drink
traición [trai'θjon] *nf* treachery; (*Jur*)
 treason; (*una traición*) act of treachery;
 traicionar *vt* to betray
traidor, a [trai'ðor, a] *adj* treacherous
 ▷ *nm/f* traitor
traigo *etc vb* V **traer**
traje ['traxe] *vb* V **traer** ▷ *nm* (*de hombre*)
 suit; (*de mujer*) dress; (*vestido típico*) costume;
 traje de baño/chaqueta swimsuit/suit;
 traje de etiqueta dress suit; **traje de luces**
 bullfighter's costume
trajera *etc vb* V **traer**
trajín [tra'xin] *nm* (*fam: movimiento*) bustle;
 trajinar *vi* (*moverse*) to bustle about
trama ['trama] *nf* (*intriga*) plot; (*de tejido*)
 weft (*BRIT*), woof (*US*); **tramar** *vt* to plot;
 (*Tec*) to weave
tramitar [trami'tar] *vt* (*asunto*) to
 transact; (*negociar*) to negotiate
trámite ['tramite] *nm* (*paso*) step; (*Jur*)
 transaction; **trámites** *nmpl* (*burocracia*)
 procedure *sg*; (*Jur*) proceedings
tramo ['tramo] *nm* (*de tierra*) plot; (*de
 escalera*) flight; (*de vía*) section
trampa ['trampa] *nf* trap; (*en el suelo*)
 trapdoor; (*truco*) trick; (*engaño*) fiddle;
 trampear *vt, vi* to cheat
trampolín [trampo'lin] *nm* (*de piscina etc*)
 diving board
tramposo, -a [tram'poso, a] *adj* crooked,
 cheating ▷ *nm/f* crook, cheat
tranca ['tranka] *nf* (*palo*) stick; (*de puerta,
 ventana*) bar; **trancar** *vt* to bar

trance ['tranθe] *nm* (*momento difícil*)
 difficult moment *o* juncture; (*estado
 hipnotizado*) trance
tranquilidad [trankili'ðað] *nf* (*calma*)
 calmness, stillness; (*paz*) peacefulness
tranquilizar [trankili'θar] *vt* (*calmar*)
 to calm (down); (*asegurar*) to reassure;
 tranquilizarse *vr* to calm down;
 tranquilo, -a *adj* (*calmado*) calm; (*apacible*)
 peaceful; (*mar*) calm; (*mente*) untroubled
transacción [transak'θjon] *nf*
 transaction
transbordador [transβorða'ðor] *nm*
 ferry
transbordo [trans'βorðo] *nm* transfer;
 hacer ~ to change (trains *etc*)
transcurrir [transku'rrir] *vi* (*tiempo*) to
 pass; (*hecho*) to take place
transcurso [trans'kurso] *nm*: **~ del
 tiempo** lapse (of time)
transeúnte [transe'unte] *nmf* passer-by
transferencia [transfe'renθja] *nf*
 transference; (*Com*) transfer
transferir [transfe'rir] *vt* to transfer
transformador [transforma'ðor] *nm*
 (*Elec*) transformer
transformar [transfor'mar] *vt* to
 transform; (*convertir*) to convert
transfusión [transfu'sjon] *nf* transfusion
transgénico, -a [trans'xeniko, a] *adj*
 genetically modified, GM
transición [transi'θjon] *nf* transition
transigir [transi'xir] *vi* to compromise,
 make concessions
transitar [transi'tar] *vi* to go (from place
 to place); **tránsito** *nm* transit; (*Auto*)
 traffic; **transitorio, -a** *adj* transitory
transmisión [transmi'sjon] *nf* (*Tec*)
 transmission; (*transferencia*) transfer;
 transmisión exterior/en directo outside/
 live broadcast
transmitir [transmi'tir] *vt* to transmit;
 (*Radio, TV*) to broadcast
transparencia [transpa'renθja] *nf*
 transparency; (*claridad*) clearness, clarity;
 (*foto*) slide
transparentar [transparen'tar] *vt* to
 reveal ▷ *vi* to be transparent; **transparente**
 adj transparent; (*claro*) clear
transpirar [transpi'rar] *vi* to perspire
transportar [transpor'tar] *vt* to
 transport; (*llevar*) to carry; **transporte** *nm*
 transport; (*Com*) haulage
transversal [transβer'sal] *adj* transverse,
 cross
tranvía [tram'bia] *nm* tram
trapeador [trapea'ðor] (*LAM*) *nm* mop;
 trapear (*LAM*) *vt* to mop

trapecio [tra'peθjo] nm trapeze;
 trapecista nmf trapeze artist
trapero, -a [tra'pero, a] nm/f ragman
trapicheo [trapi'tʃeo] (fam) nm scheme,
 fiddle
trapo ['trapo] nm (tela) rag; (de cocina) cloth
tráquea ['trakea] nf windpipe
traqueteo [trake'teo] nm rattling
tras [tras] prep (detrás) behind; (después)
 after
trasatlántico [trasat'lantiko] nm (barco)
 (cabin) cruiser
trascendencia [trasθen'denθja] nf
 (importancia) importance; (Filosofía)
 transcendence
trascendental [trasθenden'tal] adj
 important; (Filosofía) transcendental
trasero, -a [tra'sero, a] adj back, rear
 ▷ nm (Anat) bottom
trasfondo [tras'fondo] nm background
trasgredir [trasɣre'ðir] vt to contravene
trashumante [trasu'mante] adj
 (animales) migrating
trasladar [trasla'ðar] vt to move;
 (persona) to transfer; (postergar) to postpone;
 (copiar) to copy; **trasladarse** vr (mudarse) to
 move; **traslado** nm move; (mudanza) move,
 removal
traslucir [traslu'θir] vt to show
trasluz [tras'luθ] nm reflected light; **al ~**
 against o up to the light
trasnochador, a [trasnotʃa'ðor, a] nm/f
 night owl
trasnochar [trasno'tʃar] vi (acostarse
 tarde) to stay up late
traspapelar [traspape'lar] vt (documento,
 carta) to mislay, misplace
traspasar [traspa'sar] vt (suj: bala etc)
 to pierce, go through; (propiedad) to sell,
 transfer; (calle) to cross over; (límites) to go
 beyond; (ley) to break; **traspaso** nm (venta)
 transfer, sale
traspatio [tras'patjo] (LAM) nm backyard
traspié [tras'pje] nm (tropezón) trip; (error)
 blunder
trasplantar [trasplan'tar] vt to
 transplant
traste ['traste] nm (Mús) fret; **dar al ~ con**
 algo to ruin sth
trastero [tras'tero] nm storage room
trastienda [tras'tjenda] nf back of shop
trasto ['trasto] (pey) nm (cosa) piece of
 junk; (persona) dead loss
trastornado, -a [trastor'naðo, a] adj
 (loco) mad, crazy
trastornar [trastor'nar] vt (fig: planes) to
 disrupt; (: nervios) to shatter; (: persona) to
 drive crazy; **trastornarse** vr (volverse loco)

to go mad o crazy; **trastorno** nm (acto)
 overturning; (confusión) confusion
tratable [tra'taβle] adj friendly
tratado [tra'taðo] nm (Pol) treaty; (Com)
 agreement
tratamiento [trata'mjento] nm
 treatment; **tratamiento de textos** (Inform)
 word processing cpd
tratar [tra'tar] vt (ocuparse de) to treat;
 (manejar, Tec) to handle; (Med) to treat;
 (dirigirse a: persona) to address ▷ vi: **~**
 de (hablar sobre) to deal with, be about;
 (intentar) to try to; **tratarse** vr to treat each
 other; **~ con** (Com) to trade in; (negociar) to
 negotiate with; (tener contactos) to have
 dealings with; **¿de qué se trata?** what's it
 about?; **trato** nm dealings pl; (relaciónes)
 relationship; (comportamiento) manner;
 (Com) agreement
trauma ['trauma] nm trauma
través [tra'βes] nm (fig) reverse; **al ~**
 across, crossways; **a ~ de** across; (sobre)
 over; (por) through
travesaño [traβe'saɲo] nm (Arq)
 crossbeam; (Deporte) crossbar
travesía [traβe'sia] nf (calle) cross-street;
 (Náut) crossing
travesura [traβe'sura] nf (broma) prank;
 (ingenio) wit
travieso, -a [tra'βjeso, a] adj (niño)
 naughty
trayecto [tra'jekto] nm (ruta) road, way;
 (viaje) journey; (tramo) stretch; **trayectoria**
 nf trajectory; (fig) path
traza ['traθa] nf (aspecto) looks pl; (señal)
 sign; **trazado, -a** adj: **bien trazado** shapely,
 well-formed ▷ nm (Arq) plan, design; (fig)
 outline
trazar [tra'θar] vt (Arq) to plan; (Arte) to
 sketch; (fig) to trace; (plan) to draw up; **trazo**
 nm (línea) line; (bosquejo) sketch
trébol ['treβol] nm (Bot) clover
trece ['treθe] num thirteen
trecho ['tretʃo] nm (distancia) distance;
 (tiempo) while
tregua ['treɣwa] nf (Mil) truce; (fig) respite
treinta ['treinta] num thirty
tremendo, -a [tre'mendo, a] adj (terrible)
 terrible; (imponente: cosa) imposing;
 (fam: fabuloso) tremendous
tren [tren] nm train; **tren de aterrizaje**
 undercarriage; **tren de cercanías** suburban
 train
trenca ['trenka] nf duffel coat
trenza ['trenθa] nf (de pelo) plait (BRIT),
 braid (US)
trepadora [trepa'ðora] nf (Bot) climber
trepar [tre'par] vt, vi to climb

tres [tɾes] *num* three
tresillo [tɾe'siʎo] *nm* three-piece suite; (*Mús*) triplet
treta ['tɾeta] *nf* trick
triángulo ['tɾjangulo] *nm* triangle
tribu ['tɾiβu] *nf* tribe
tribuna [tɾi'βuna] *nf* (*plataforma*) platform; (*Deporte*) (grand)stand
tribunal [tɾiβu'nal] *nm* (*Jur*) court; (*comisión, fig*) tribunal; ~ **popular** jury
tributo [tɾi'βuto] *nm* (*Com*) tax
trigal [tɾi'ɣal] *nm* wheat field
trigo ['tɾiɣo] *nm* wheat
trigueño, -a [tɾi'ɣeɲo, a] *adj* (*pelo*) corn-coloured
trillar [tɾi'ʎaɾ] *vt* (*Agr*) to thresh
trimestral [tɾimes'tɾal] *adj* quarterly; (*Escol*) termly
trimestre [tɾi'mestɾe] *nm* (*Escol*) term
trinar [tɾi'naɾ] *vi* (*pájaros*) to sing; (*rabiar*) to fume, be angry
trinchar [tɾin'tʃaɾ] *vt* to carve
trinchera [tɾin'tʃeɾa] *nf* (*fosa*) trench
trineo [tɾi'neo] *nm* sledge
trinidad [tɾini'ðað] *nf* trio; (*Rel*): **la T~** the Trinity
tripa ['tɾipa] *nf* (*Anat*) intestine; (*fam*: *tb*: ~**s**) insides *pl*
triple ['tɾiple] *adj* triple
triplicado, -a [tɾipli'kaðo, a] *adj*: **por ~** in triplicate
tripulación [tɾipula'θjon] *nf* crew
tripulante [tɾipu'lante] *nmf* crewman/woman
tripular [tɾipu'laɾ] *vt* (*barco*) to man; (*Auto*) to drive
triquiñuela [tɾiki'ɲwela] *nf* trick
tris [tɾis] *nm inv* crack
triste ['tɾiste] *adj* sad; (*lamentable*) sorry, miserable; **tristeza** *nf* (*aflicción*) sadness; (*melancolía*) melancholy
triturar [tɾitu'raɾ] *vt* (*moler*) to grind; (*mascar*) to chew
triunfar [tɾjun'faɾ] *vi* (*tener éxito*) to triumph; (*ganar*) to win; **triunfo** *nm* triumph
trivial [tɾi'βjal] *adj* trivial
triza ['tɾiθa] *nf*: **hacer ~s** to smash to bits; (*papel*) to tear to shreds
trocear [tɾoθe'aɾ] *vt* (*carne, manzana*) to cut up, cut into pieces
trocha ['tɾotʃa] *nf* short cut
trofeo [tɾo'feo] *nm* (*premio*) trophy; (*éxito*) success
tromba ['tɾomba] *nf* downpour
trombón [tɾom'bon] *nm* trombone
trombosis [tɾom'bosis] *nf inv* thrombosis
trompa ['tɾompa] *nf* horn; (*trompo*) humming top; (*hocico*) snout; (*fam*): **cogerse una ~** to get tight
trompazo [tɾom'paθo] *nm* bump, bang
trompeta [tɾom'peta] *nf* trumpet; (*clarín*) bugle
trompicón [tɾompi'kon]: **a trompicones** *adv* in fits and starts
trompo ['tɾompo] *nm* spinning top
trompón [tɾom'pon] *nm* bump
tronar [tɾo'naɾ] *vt* (*MÉX, CAM*: *fusilar*) to shoot; (*MÉX*: *examen*) to flunk ▷ *vi* to thunder; (*fig*) to rage
tronchar [tɾon'tʃaɾ] *vt* (*árbol*) to chop down; (*fig*: *vida*) to cut short; (*: esperanza*) to shatter; (*persona*) to tire out; **troncharse** *vr* to fall down
tronco ['tɾonko] *nm* (*de árbol, Anat*) trunk
trono ['tɾono] *nm* throne
tropa ['tɾopa] *nf* (*Mil*) troop; (*soldados*) soldiers *pl*
tropezar [tɾope'θaɾ] *vi* to trip, stumble; (*errar*) to slip up; ~ **con** to run into; (*topar con*) to bump into; **tropezón** *nm* trip; (*fig*) blunder
tropical [tɾopi'kal] *adj* tropical
trópico ['tɾopiko] *nm* tropic
tropiezo [tɾo'pjeθo] *vb* V **tropezar** ▷ *nm* (*error*) slip, blunder; (*desgracia*) misfortune; (*obstáculo*) snag
trotamundos [tɾota'mundos] *nm inv* globetrotter
trotar [tɾo'taɾ] *vi* to trot; **trote** *nm* trot; (*fam*) travelling; **de mucho trote** hard-wearing
trozar [tɾo'θaɾ] (*LAM*) *vt* to cut up, cut into pieces
trozo ['tɾoθo] *nm* bit, piece
trucha ['tɾutʃa] *nf* trout
truco ['tɾuko] *nm* (*habilidad*) knack; (*engaño*) trick
trueno ['tɾweno] *nm* thunder; (*estampido*) bang
trueque *etc* ['tɾweke] *vb* V **trocar** ▷ *nm* exchange; (*Com*) barter
trufa ['tɾufa] *nf* (*Bot*) truffle
truhán, -ana [tɾu'an, ana] *nm/f* rogue
truncar [tɾun'kaɾ] *vt* (*cortar*) to truncate; (*fig*: *la vida etc*) to cut short; (*: el desarrollo*) to stunt
tu [tu] *adj* your
tú [tu] *pron* you
tubérculo [tu'βeɾkulo] *nm* (*Bot*) tuber
tuberculosis [tuβeɾku'losis] *nf inv* tuberculosis
tubería [tuβe'ria] *nf* pipes *pl*; (*conducto*) pipeline
tubo ['tuβo] *nm* tube, pipe; **tubo de ensayo** test tube; **tubo de escape** exhaust

(pipe)

tuerca ['twerka] nf nut

tuerto, -a ['twerto, a] adj blind in one eye
▷ nm/f one-eyed person

tuerza etc vb V **torcer**

tuétano ['twetano] nm marrow; (Bot) pith

tufo ['tufo] nm (hedor) stench

tul [tul] nm tulle

tulipán [tuli'pan] nm tulip

tullido, -a [tu'ʎiðo, a] adj crippled

tumba ['tumba] nf (sepultura) tomb

tumbar [tum'bar] vt to knock down;
tumbarse vr (echarse) to lie down;
(extenderse) to stretch out

tumbo ['tumbo] nm: **dar ~s** to stagger

tumbona [tum'bona] nf (butaca) easy
chair; (de playa) deckchair (BRIT), beach
chair (US)

tumor [tu'mor] nm tumour

tumulto [tu'multo] nm turmoil

tuna ['tuna] nf (Mús) student music group;
V tb **tuno**

tunante [tu'nante] nmf rascal

tunear [tune'ar] vt (Auto) to style, mod
(inf)

túnel ['tunel] nm tunnel

tuning ['tunin] nm (Auto) car styling,
modding (inf)

tuno, -a ['tuno, a] nm/f (fam) rogue ▷ nm
member of student music group

tupido, -a [tu'piðo, a] adj (denso) dense;
(tela) close-woven

turbante [tur'βante] nm turban

turbar [tur'βar] vt (molestar) to disturb;
(incomodar) to upset

turbina [tur'βina] nf turbine

turbio, -a ['turβjo, a] adj cloudy; (tema
etc) confused

turbulencia [turβu'lenθja] nf
turbulence; (fig) restlessness; **turbulento,
-a** adj turbulent; (fig: intranquilo) restless;
(: ruidoso) noisy

turco, -a ['turko, a] adj Turkish ▷ nm/f

Turk

turismo [tu'rismo] nm tourism; (coche)
car; **turista** nmf tourist; **turístico, -a** adj
tourist cpd

turnar [tur'nar] vi to take (it in) turns;
turnarse vr to take (it in) turns; **turno** nm
(de trabajo) shift; (en juegos etc) turn

turquesa [tur'kesa] nf turquoise

Turquía [tur'kia] nf Turkey

turrón [tu'rron] nm (dulce) nougat

tutear [tute'ar] vt to address as familiar
"tú"; **tutearse** vr to be on familiar terms

tutela [tu'tela] nf (legal) guardianship;
tutelar adj tutelary ▷ vt to protect

tutor, a [tu'tor, a] nm/f (legal) guardian;
(Escol) tutor

tuve etc vb V **tener**

tuviera etc vb V **tener**

tuyo, -a ['tujo, a] adj yours, of yours
▷ pron yours; **un amigo ~** a friend of yours;
los ~s (fam) your relations o family

TV nf abr (= televisión) TV

TVE nf abr = **Televisión Española**

t

u [u] *conj* or

ubicar [uβi'kar] *vt* to place, situate; (*LAM: encontrar*) to find; **ubicarse** *vr* (*LAM: encontrarse*) to lie, be located

ubre ['uβre] *nf* udder

UCI *nf abr* (= *Unidad de Cuidados Intensivos*) ICU

Ud(s) *abr* = **usted(es)**

UE *nf abr* (= *Unión Europea*) EU

ufanarse [ufa'narse] *vr* to boast; **ufano, -a** *adj* (*arrogante*) arrogant; (*presumido*) conceited

UGT (*ESP*) *nf abr* = **Unión General de Trabajadores**

úlcera ['ulθera] *nf* ulcer

ulterior [ulte'rjor] *adj* (*más allá*) farther, further; (*subsecuente, siguiente*) subsequent

últimamente ['ultimamente] *adv* (*recientemente*) lately, recently

ultimar [ulti'mar] *vt* to finish; (*finalizar*) to finalize; (*LAM: matar*) to kill

ultimátum [ulti'matum] (*pl* **-s**) *nm* ultimatum

último, -a ['ultimo, a] *adj* last; (*más reciente*) latest, most recent; (*más bajo*) bottom; (*más alto*) top; **en las últimas** on one's last legs; **por ~** finally

ultra ['ultra] *adj* ultra ▷ *nmf* extreme right-winger

ultraje [ul'traxe] *nm* outrage; insult

ultramar [ultra'mar] *nm*: **de** *o* **en ~** abroad, overseas

ultramarinos [ultrama'rinos] *nmpl* groceries; **tienda de ~** grocer's (shop)

ultranza [ul'tranθa]: **a ~** *adv* (*a todo trance*) at all costs; (*completo*) outright

umbral [um'bral] *nm* (*gen*) threshold

un, una [un, 'una] *art indef* a; (*antes de vocal*) an; **una mujer/naranja** a woman/ an orange

▷ *adj*: **unos** (*o* **unas**): **hay unos regalos para ti** there are some presents for you; **hay unas cervezas en la nevera** there are some beers in the fridge

unánime [u'nanime] *adj* unanimous; **unanimidad** *nf* unanimity

undécimo, -a [un'deθimo, a] *adj* eleventh

ungir [un'xir] *vt* to anoint

ungüento [un'gwento] *nm* ointment

único, -a ['uniko, a] *adj* only, sole; (*sin par*) unique

unidad [uni'ðað] *nf* unity; (*Com, Tec etc*) unit

unido, -a [u'niðo, a] *adj* joined, linked; (*fig*) united

unificar [unifi'kar] *vt* to unite, unify

uniformar [unifor'mar] *vt* to make uniform, level up; (*persona*) to put into uniform

uniforme [uni'forme] *adj* uniform, equal; (*superficie*) even ▷ *nm* uniform

unilateral [unilate'ral] *adj* unilateral

unión [u'njon] *nf* union; (*acto*) uniting, joining; (*unidad*) unity; (*Tec*) joint; **Unión Europea** European Union

unir [u'nir] *vt* (*juntar*) to join, unite; (*atar*) to tie, fasten; (*combinar*) to combine; **unirse** *vr* to join together, unite; (*empresas*) to merge

unísono [u'nisono] *nm*: **al ~** in unison

universal [uniβer'sal] *adj* universal; (*mundial*) world *cpd*

universidad [uniβersi'ðað] *nf* university

universitario, -a [uniβersi'tarjo, a] *adj* university *cpd* ▷ *nm/f* (*profesor*) lecturer; (*estudiante*) (university) student; (*graduado*) graduate

universo [uni'βerso] *nm* universe

uno, -a ['uno, a] *adj* one; **unos pocos** a few; **unos cien** about a hundred ▷ *pron*

1 one; **quiero sólo uno** I only want one; **uno de ellos** one of them

2 (*alguien*) somebody, someone; **conozco a uno que se te parece** I know somebody *o* someone who looks like you; **uno mismo** oneself; **unos querían quedarse** some (people) wanted to stay

3 (**los**) **unos ...** (**los**) **otros ...** some ... others

▷ *nf* one; **es la una** it's one o'clock

▷ *nm* (*number*) one

untar [un'tar] *vt* (*mantequilla*) to spread; (*engrasar*) to grease, oil

uña ['uɲa] *nf* (Anat) nail; (*garra*) claw; (*casco*) hoof; (*arrancaclavos*) claw

uranio [u'ranjo] *nm* uranium

urbanización [urβaniθa'θjon] *nf* (*barrio*, *colonia*) housing estate

urbanizar [urβani'θar] *vt* (*zona*) to develop, urbanize

urbano, -a [ur'βano, a] *adj* (*de ciudad*) urban; (*cortés*) courteous, polite

urbe ['urβe] *nf* large city

urdir [ur'ðir] *vt* to warp; (*complot*) to plot, contrive

urgencia [ur'xenθja] *nf* urgency; (*prisa*) haste, rush; (*emergencia*) emergency; **servicios de ~** emergency services; **"U~s"** "Casualty"; **urgente** *adj* urgent

urgir [ur'xir] *vi* to be urgent; **me urge** I'm in a hurry for it

urinario, -a [uri'narjo, a] *adj* urinary ▷ *nm* urinal

urna ['urna] *nf* urn; (*Pol*) ballot box

urraca [u'rraka] *nf* magpie

URSS [urs] *nf* (Hist): **la URSS** the USSR

Uruguay [uru'ɣwai] *nm* (tb: **el ~**) Uruguay; **uruguayo, -a** *adj, nm/f* Uruguayan

usado, -a [u'saðo, a] *adj* used; (*de segunda mano*) secondhand

usar [u'sar] *vt* to use; (*ropa*) to wear; (*tener costumbre*) to be in the habit of; **usarse** *vr* to be used; **uso** *nm* use; wear; (*costumbre*) usage, custom; (*moda*) fashion; **al uso** in keeping with custom; **al uso de** in the style of; **de uso externo** (Med) for external use

usted [us'teð] *pron* (sg) you *sg*; (pl): **~es** you *pl*

usual [u'swal] *adj* usual

usuario, -a [usu'arjo, a] *nm/f* user

usurpar [usur'par] *vt* to usurp

utensilio [uten'siljo] *nm* tool; (Culin) utensil

útero ['utero] *nm* uterus, womb

útil ['util] *adj* useful ▷ *nm* tool; **utilidad** *nf* usefulness; (Com) profit; **utilizar** *vt* to use, utilize

uva ['uβa] *nf* grape

LAS UVAS

In Spain **Las uvas** play a big part on New Year's Eve (**Nochevieja**), when on the stroke of midnight people gather at home, in restaurants or in the **plaza mayor** and eat a grape for each stroke of the clock of the **Puerta del Sol** in Madrid. It is said to bring luck for the following year.

---

v *abr* (= *voltio*) v

va *vb* V **ir**

vaca ['baka] *nf* (*animal*) cow; **carne de ~** beef

vacaciones [baka'θjones] *nfpl* holidays

vacante [ba'kante] *adj* vacant, empty ▷ *nf* vacancy

vaciar [ba'θjar] *vt* to empty out; (*ahuecar*) to hollow out; (*moldear*) to cast; **vaciarse** *vr* to empty

vacilar [baθi'lar] *vi* to be unsteady; (*al hablar*) to falter; (*dudar*) to hesitate, waver; (*memoria*) to fail

vacío, -a [ba'θio, a] *adj* empty; (*puesto*) vacant; (*desocupado*) idle; (*vano*) vain ▷ *nm* emptiness; (*Física*) vacuum; (*un vacío*) (empty) space

vacuna [ba'kuna] *nf* vaccine; **vacunar** *vt* to vaccinate

vacuno, -a [ba'kuno, a] *adj* cow *cpd*; **ganado ~** cattle

vadear [baðe'ar] *vt* (*río*) to ford; **vado** *nm* ford

vagabundo, -a [baɣa'βundo, a] *adj* wandering ▷ *nm* tramp

vagancia [ba'ɣanθja] *nf* (*pereza*) idleness, laziness

vagar [ba'ɣar] *vi* to wander; (*no hacer nada*) to idle

vagina [ba'xina] *nf* vagina

vago, -a ['baɣo, a] *adj* vague; (*perezoso*) lazy ▷ *nm/f* (*vagabundo*) tramp; (*flojo*) lazybones *sg*, idler

vagón [ba'ɣon] *nm* (Ferro: *de pasajeros*) carriage; (: *de mercancías*) wagon

vaho ['bao] *nm* (*vapor*) vapour, steam; (*respiración*) breath

vaina ['baina] *nf* sheath

vainilla [bai'niʎa] *nf* vanilla

vais *vb* V **ir**

vaivén [bai'βen] *nm* to-and-fro

movement; (de tránsito) coming and going;
vaivenes nmpl (fig) ups and downs
vajilla [ba'xiʎa] nf crockery, dishes pl;
(juego) service, set
valdré etc vb V **valer**
vale ['bale] nm voucher; (recibo) receipt;
(pagaré) IOU
valedero, -a [bale'ðero, a] adj valid
valenciano, -a [balen'θjano, a] adj
Valencian
valentía [balen'tia] nf courage, bravery
valer [ba'ler] vt to be worth; (Mat) to
equal; (costar) to cost ▷ vi (ser útil) to be
useful; (ser válido) to be valid; **valerse** vr
to take care of oneself; **~se de** to make
use of, take advantage of; **~ la pena** to be
worthwhile; **¿vale?** (ESP) OK?; **más vale que
nos vayamos** we'd better go; **¡eso a mí no
me vale!** (MÉX: fam: no importar) I couldn't
care less about that
valeroso, -a [bale'roso, a] adj brave,
valiant
valgo etc vb V **valer**
valía [ba'lia] nf worth, value
validar [bali'ðar] vt to validate; **validez** nf
validity; **válido, -a** adj valid
valiente [ba'ljente] adj brave, valiant
▷ nm hero
valija [ba'lixa] (cs) nf (suit)case
valioso, -a [ba'ljoso, a] adj valuable
valla ['baʎa] nf fence; (Deporte) hurdle;
valla publicitaria hoarding; **vallar** vt to
fence in
valle ['baʎe] nm valley
valor [ba'lor] nm value, worth; (precio)
price; (valentía) valour, courage; (importancia)
importance; **valores** nmpl (Com) securities;
valorar vt to value
vals [bals] nm inv waltz
válvula ['balβula] nf valve
vamos vb V **ir**
vampiro, -resa [bam'piro, 'resa] nm/f
vampire
van vb V **ir**
vanguardia [ban'gwardja] nf vanguard;
(Arte etc) avant-garde
vanidad [bani'ðað] nf vanity; **vanidoso,
-a** adj vain, conceited
vano, -a ['bano, a] adj vain
vapor [ba'por] nm vapour; (vaho) steam;
al ~ (Culin) steamed; **vapor de agua** water
vapour; **vaporizador** nm atomizer;
vaporizar vt to vaporize; **vaporoso, -a** adj
vaporous
vaquero, -a [ba'kero, a] adj cattle cpd
▷ nm cowboy; **vaqueros** nmpl (pantalones)
jeans
vaquilla [ba'kiʎa] nf (Zool) heifer

vara ['bara] nf stick; (Tec) rod
variable [ba'rjaβle] adj, nf variable
variación [baria'θjon] nf variation
variar [ba'rjar] vt to vary; (modificar) to
modify; (cambiar de posición) to switch
around ▷ vi to vary
varicela [bari'θela] nf chickenpox
varices [ba'riθes] nfpl varicose veins
variedad [barje'ðað] nf variety
varilla [ba'riʎa] nf stick; (Bot) twig; (Tec)
rod; (de rueda) spoke
vario, -a ['barjo, a] adj varied; **~s** various,
several
varita [ba'rita] nf (tb: ~ **mágica**) magic
wand
varón [ba'ron] nm male, man; **varonil** adj
manly, virile
Varsovia [bar'soβja] n Warsaw
vas vb V **ir**
vasco, -a ['basko, a] adj, nm/f Basque;
vascongado, -a [baskon'gaðo, a] adj
Basque; **las Vascongadas** the Basque
Country
vaselina [base'lina] nf Vaseline®
vasija [ba'sixa] nf container, vessel
vaso ['baso] nm glass, tumbler; (Anat)
vessel

⏐ No confundir **vaso** con la palabra inglesa
vase.

vástago ['bastaɣo] nm (Bot) shoot; (Tec)
rod; (fig) offspring
vasto, -a ['basto, a] adj vast, huge
Vaticano [bati'kano] nm: **el ~** the Vatican
vatio ['batjo] nm (Elec) watt
vaya etc vb V **ir**
Vd(s) abr = **usted(es)**
ve [be] vb V **ir; ver**
vecindad [beθin'dað] nf neighbourhood;
(habitantes) residents pl
vecindario [beθin'darjo] nm
neighbourhood; residents pl
vecino, -a [be'θino, a] adj neighbouring
▷ nm/f neighbour; (residente) resident
veda ['beða] nf prohibition; **vedar**
[be'ðar] vt (prohibir) to ban, prohibit;
(impedir) to stop, prevent
vegetación [bexeta'θjon] nf vegetation
vegetal [bexe'tal] adj, nm vegetable
vegetariano, -a [bexeta'rjano, a] adj,
nm/f vegetarian
vehículo [be'ikulo] nm vehicle; (Med)
carrier
veía etc vb V **ver**
veinte ['beinte] num twenty
vejar [be'xar] vt (irritar) to annoy, vex;
(humillar) to humiliate
vejez [be'xeθ] nf old age
vejiga [be'xiɣa] nf (Anat) bladder

vela ['bela] nf (de cera) candle; (Náut) sail; (insomnio) sleeplessness; (vigilia) vigil; (Mil) sentry duty; **estar a dos ~s** (fam: sin dinero) to be skint

velado, -a [be'laðo, a] adj veiled; (sonido) muffled; (Foto) blurred ▷ nf soirée

velar [be'lar] vt (vigilar) to keep watch over ▷ vi to stay awake; **~ por** to watch over, look after

velatorio [bela'torjo] nm (funeral) wake

velero [be'lero] nm (Náut) sailing ship; (Aviac) glider

veleta [be'leta] nf weather vane

veliz [be'lis] (MÉX) nm (suit)case

vello ['beʎo] nm down, fuzz

velo ['belo] nm veil

velocidad [beloθi'ðað] nf speed; (Tec, Auto) gear

velocímetro [belo'θimetro] nm speedometer

velorio [be'lorjo] (LAM) nm (funeral) wake

veloz [be'loθ] adj fast

ven vb V **venir**

vena ['bena] nf vein

venado [be'naðo] nm deer

vencedor, a [benθe'ðor, a] adj victorious ▷ nm/f victor, winner

vencer [ben'θer] vt (dominar) to defeat, beat; (derrotar) to vanquish; (superar, controlar) to overcome, master ▷ vi (triunfar) to win (through), triumph; (plazo) to expire; **vencido, -a** adj (derrotado) defeated, beaten; (Com) due ▷ adv: **pagar vencido** to pay in arrears

venda ['benda] nf bandage; **vendaje** nm bandage, dressing; **vendar** vt to bandage; **vendar los ojos** to blindfold

vendaval [benda'βal] nm (viento) gale

vendedor, a [bende'ðor, a] nm/f seller

vender [ben'der] vt to sell; **venderse** vr (estar a la venta) to be on sale; **~ al contado/al por mayor/al por menor** to sell for cash/wholesale/retail; **"se vende"** "for sale"

vendimia [ben'dimja] nf grape harvest

vendré etc vb V **venir**

veneno [be'neno] nm poison; (de serpiente) venom; **venenoso, -a** adj poisonous; venomous

venerable [bene'raβle] adj venerable; **venerar** vt (respetar) to revere; (adorar) to worship

venéreo, -a [be'nereo, a] adj: **enfermedad venérea** venereal disease

venezolano, -a [beneθo'lano, a] adj Venezuelan

Venezuela [bene'θwela] nf Venezuela

venganza [ben'ganθa] nf vengeance, revenge; **vengar** vt to avenge; **vengarse**

vr to take revenge; **vengativo, -a** adj (persona) vindictive

vengo etc vb V **venir**

venia ['benja] nf (perdón) pardon; (permiso) consent

venial [be'njal] adj venial

venida [be'niða] nf (llegada) arrival; (regreso) return

venidero, -a [beni'ðero, a] adj coming, future

venir [be'nir] vi to come; (llegar) to arrive; (ocurrir) to happen; (fig): **~ de** to stem from; **~ bien/mal** to be suitable/unsuitable; **el año que viene** next year; **~se abajo** to collapse

venta ['benta] nf (Com) sale; **"en ~"** "for sale"; **estar a la o en ~** to be (up) for sale o on the market; **venta a domicilio** door-to-door selling; **venta a plazos** hire purchase; **venta al contado/al por mayor/al por menor** cash sale/wholesale/retail

ventaja [ben'taxa] nf advantage; **ventajoso, -a** adj advantageous

ventana [ben'tana] nf window; **ventanilla** nf (de taquilla) window (of booking office etc)

ventilación [bentila'θjon] nf ventilation; (corriente) draught

ventilador [bentila'ðor] nm fan

ventilar [benti'lar] vt to ventilate; (para secar) to put out to dry; (asunto) to air, discuss

ventisca [ben'tiska] nf blizzard

ventrílocuo, -a [ben'trilokwo, a] nm/f ventriloquist

ventura [ben'tura] nf (felicidad) happiness; (buena suerte) luck; (destino) fortune; **a la (buena) ~** at random; **venturoso, -a** adj happy; (afortunado) lucky, fortunate

veo etc vb V **ver**

ver [ber] vt to see; (mirar) to look at, watch; (entender) to understand; (investigar) to look into ▷ vi to see; to understand; **verse** vr (encontrarse) to meet; (dejarse ver) to be seen; (hallarse: en un apuro) to find o.s., be; **(vamos) a ~** let's see; **no tener nada que ~ con** to have nothing to do with; **a mi modo de ~** as I see it; **ya ~emos** we'll see

vera ['bera] nf edge, verge; (de río) bank

veranear [berane'ar] vi to spend the summer; **veraneo** nm summer holiday; **veraniego, -a** adj summer cpd

verano [be'rano] nm summer

veras ['beras] nfpl truth sg; **de ~** really, truly

verbal [ber'βal] adj verbal

verbena [ber'βena] nf (baile) open-air dance

V

verbo ['berβo] *nm* verb

verdad [ber'ðað] *nf* truth; (*fiabilidad*) reliability; **de ~** real, proper; **a decir ~** to tell the truth; **verdadero, -a** *adj* (*veraz*) true, truthful; (*fiable*) reliable; (*fig*) real

verde ['berðe] *adj* green; (*chiste*) blue, dirty ▷ *nm* green; **viejo ~** dirty old man; **verdear** *vi* to turn green; **verdor** *nm* greenness

verdugo [ber'ðuxo] *nm* executioner

verdulero, -a [berðu'lero, a] *nm/f* greengrocer

verduras [ber'ðuras] *nfpl* (*Culin*) greens

vereda [be'reða] *nf* path; (*cs: acera*) pavement (*BRIT*), sidewalk (*US*)

veredicto [bere'ðikto] *nm* verdict

vergonzoso, -a [berɣon'θoso, a] *adj* shameful; (*tímido*) timid, bashful

vergüenza [ber'ɣwenθa] *nf* shame, sense of shame; (*timidez*) bashfulness; (*pudor*) modesty; **me da ~** I'm ashamed

verídico, -a [be'riðiko, a] *adj* true, truthful

verificar [berifi'kar] *vt* to check; (*corroborar*) to verify; (*llevar a cabo*) to carry out; **verificarse** *vr* (*predicción*) to prove to be true

verja ['berxa] *nf* (*cancela*) iron gate; (*valla*) iron railings *pl*; (*de ventana*) grille

vermut [ber'mut] (*pl ~s*) *nm* vermouth

verosímil [bero'simil] *adj* likely, probable; (*relato*) credible

verruga [be'rruxa] *nf* wart

versátil [ber'satil] *adj* versatile

versión [ber'sjon] *nf* version

verso ['berso] *nm* verse; **un ~ a** line of poetry

vértebra ['berteβra] *nf* vertebra

verter [ber'ter] *vt* (*líquido: adrede*) to empty, pour (out); (*: sin querer*) to spill; (*basura*) to dump ▷ *vi* to flow

vertical [berti'kal] *adj* vertical

vértice ['bertiθe] *nm* vertex, apex

vertidos [ber'tiðos] *nmpl* waste *sg*

vertiente [ber'tjente] *nf* slope; (*fig*) aspect

vértigo ['bertixo] *nm* vertigo; (*mareo*) dizziness

vesícula [be'sikula] *nf* blister

vespino® [bes'pino] *nm o nf* moped

vestíbulo [bes'tiβulo] *nm* hall; (*de teatro*) foyer

vestido [bes'tiðo] *nm* (*ropa*) clothes *pl*, clothing; (*de mujer*) dress, frock ▷ *pp de* **vestir**; **~ de azul/marinero** dressed in blue/as a sailor

vestidor [besti'ðor] (*MÉX*) *nm* (*Deporte*) changing (*BRIT*) o locker (*US*) room

vestimenta [besti'menta] *nf* clothing

vestir [bes'tir] *vt* (*poner: ropa*) to put on; (*llevar: ropa*) to wear; (*proveer de ropa a*) to clothe; (*sastre*) to make clothes for ▷ *vi* to dress; (*verse bien*) to look good; **vestirse** *vr* to get dressed, dress o.s.

vestuario [bes'twarjo] *nm* clothes *pl*, wardrobe; (*Teatro: cuarto*) dressing room; (*Deporte*) changing (*BRIT*) o locker (*US*) room

vetar [be'tar] *vt* to veto

veterano, -a [bete'rano, a] *adj, nm* veteran

veterinaria [beteri'narja] *nf* veterinary science; *V tb* **veterinario**

veterinario, -a [beteri'narjo, a] *nm/f* vet(erinary surgeon)

veto ['beto] *nm* veto

vez [beθ] *nf* time; (*turno*) turn; **a la ~ que** at the same time as; **a su ~** in its turn; **otra ~** again; **una ~** once; **de una ~** in one go; **de una ~ para siempre** once and for all; **en ~ de** instead of; **a o algunas veces** sometimes; **una y otra ~** repeatedly; **de ~ en cuando** from time to time; **7 veces 9** 7 times 9; **hacer las veces de** to stand in for; **tal ~** perhaps

vía ['bia] *nf* track, route; (*Ferro*) line; (*fig*) way; (*Anat*) passage, tube ▷ *prep* via, by way of; **por ~ judicial** by legal means; **en ~s de** in the process of; **vía aérea** airway; **Vía Láctea** Milky Way; **vía pública** public road o thoroughfare

viable ['bjaβle] *adj* (*solución, plan, alternativa*) feasible

viaducto [bja'ðukto] *nm* viaduct

viajante [bja'xante] *nm* commercial traveller

viajar [bja'xar] *vi* to travel; **viaje** *nm* journey; (*gira*) tour; (*Náut*) voyage; **estar de viaje** to be on a trip; **viaje de ida y vuelta** round trip; **viaje de novios** honeymoon; **viajero, -a** *adj* travelling; (*Zool*) migratory ▷ *nm/f* (*quien viaja*) traveller; (*pasajero*) passenger

víbora ['biβora] *nf* (*Zool*) viper; (*: MÉX: venenoso*) poisonous snake

vibración [biβra'θjon] *nf* vibration

vibrar [bi'βrar] *vt, vi* to vibrate

vicepresidente [biθepresi'ðente] *nmf* vice-president

viceversa [biθe'βersa] *adv* vice versa

vicio ['biθjo] *nm* vice; (*mala costumbre*) bad habit; **vicioso, -a** *adj* (*muy malo*) vicious; (*corrompido*) depraved ▷ *nm/f* depraved person

víctima ['biktima] *nf* victim

victoria [bik'torja] *nf* victory; **victorioso, -a** *adj* victorious

vid [bið] *nf* vine

vida ['biða] *nf* (*gen*) life; (*duración*) lifetime;

de por ~ for life; **en la** o **mi ~** never; **estar con ~** to be still alive; **ganarse la ~** to earn one's living

vídeo ['biðeo] nm video ▷ adj inv: **película de ~** video film; **videocámara** nf camcorder; **videocasete** nm video cassette, videotape; **videoclub** nm video club; **videojuego** nm video game; **videollamada** nf video call; **videoteléfono** nf videophone

vidrio ['biðrjo] nm glass

vieira ['bjeira] nf scallop

viejo, -a ['bjexo, a] adj old ▷ nm/f old man/woman; **hacerse ~** to get old

Viena ['bjena] n Vienna

vienes etc vb V **venir**

vienés, -esa [bje'nes, esa] adj Viennese

viento ['bjento] nm wind; **hacer ~** to be windy

vientre ['bjentre] nm belly; (matriz) womb

viernes ['bjernes] nm inv Friday; **Viernes Santo** Good Friday

Vietnam [bjet'nam] nm Vietnam; **vietnamita** adj Vietnamese

viga ['biɣa] nf beam, rafter; (de metal) girder

vigencia [bi'xenθja] nf validity; **estar en ~** to be in force; **vigente** adj valid, in force; (imperante) prevailing

vigésimo, -a [bi'xesimo, a] adj twentieth

vigía [bi'xia] nm look-out

vigilancia [bixi'lanθja] nf: **tener a algn bajo ~** to keep watch on sb

vigilar [bixi'lar] vt to watch over ▷ vi (gen) to be vigilant; (hacer guardia) to keep watch; **~ por** to take care of

vigilia [vi'xilja] nf wakefulness, being awake; (Rel) fast

vigor [bi'ɣor] nm vigour, vitality; **en ~** in force; **entrar/poner en ~** to come/put into effect; **vigoroso, -a** adj vigorous

VIH nm abr (= virus de la inmunodeficiencia humana) HIV; **VIH negativo/positivo** HIV-negative/-positive

vil [bil] adj vile, low

villa ['biʎa] nf (casa) villa; (pueblo) small town; (municipalidad) municipality

villancico [biʎan'θiko] nm (Christmas) carol

vilo ['bilo]: **en ~** adv in the air, suspended; (fig) on tenterhooks, in suspense

vinagre [bi'naɣre] nm vinegar

vinagreta [bina'ɣreta] nf vinaigrette, French dressing

vinculación [binkula'θjon] nf (lazo) link, bond; (acción) linking

vincular [binku'lar] vt to link, bind;

vínculo nm link, bond

vine etc vb V **venir**

vinicultura [binikul'tura] nf wine growing

viniera etc vb V **venir**

vino ['bino] vb V **venir** ▷ nm wine; **vino blanco/tinto** white/red wine

viña ['bina] nf vineyard; **viñedo** nm vineyard

viola ['bjola] nf viola

violación [bjola'θjon] nf violation; (sexual) rape

violar [bjo'lar] vt to violate; (sexualmente) to rape

violencia [bjo'lenθja] nf violence, force; (incomodidad) embarrassment; (acto injusto) unjust act; **violentar** vt to force; (casa) to break into; (agredir) to assault; (violar) to violate; **violento, -a** adj violent; (furioso) furious; (situación) embarrassing; (acto) forced, unnatural

violeta [bjo'leta] nf violet

violín [bjo'lin] nm violin

violón [bjo'lon] nm double bass

virar [bi'rar] vt to change direction

virgen ['birxen] adj, nf virgin

Virgo ['birɣo] nm Virgo

viril [bi'ril] adj virile; **virilidad** nf virility

virtud [bir'tuð] nf virtue; **en ~ de** by virtue of; **virtuoso, -a** adj virtuous ▷ nm/f virtuoso

viruela [bi'rwela] nf smallpox

virulento, -a [biru'lento, a] adj virulent

virus ['birus] nm inv virus

visa ['bisa] (LAM) nf = **visado**

visado [bi'saðo] (ESP) nm visa

víscera ['bisθera] nf (Anat, Zool) gut, bowel; **vísceras** nfpl entrails

visceral [bisθe'ral] adj (odio) intense; **reacción ~** gut reaction

visera [bi'sera] nf visor

visibilidad [bisiβili'ðað] nf visibility; **visible** adj visible; (fig) obvious

visillos [bi'siʎos] nmpl lace curtains

visión [bi'sjon] nf (Anat) vision, (eye)sight; (fantasía) vision, fantasy

visita [bi'sita] nf call, visit; (persona) visitor; **hacer una ~** to pay a visit; **visitar** [bisi'tar] vt to visit, call on

visón [bi'son] nm mink

visor [bi'sor] nm (Foto) viewfinder

víspera ['bispera] nf: **la ~ de ...** the day before ...

vista ['bista] nf sight, vision; (capacidad de ver) (eye)sight; (mirada) look(s) (pl); **a primera ~** at first glance; **hacer la ~ gorda** to turn a blind eye; **volver la ~** to look back; **está a la ~ que** it's obvious that; **en ~ de** in view of; **en ~ de que** in view of the fact that; **¡hasta la ~!** so long!, see you!; **con ~s a** with a view to; **vistazo** *nm* glance; **dar** *o* **echar un vistazo a** to glance at

visto, -a ['bisto, a] *pp de* **ver** ▷ *vb V tb* **vestir** ▷ *adj* seen; (*considerado*) considered ▷ *nm*: **~ bueno** approval; **por lo ~** apparently; **está ~ que** it's clear that; **está bien/mal ~** it's acceptable/unacceptable; **~ que** since, considering that

vistoso, -a [bis'toso, a] *adj* colourful

visual [bi'swal] *adj* visual

vital [bi'tal] *adj* life *cpd*, living *cpd*; (*fig*) vital; (*persona*) lively, vivacious; **vitalicio, -a** *adj* for life; **vitalidad** *nf* (*de persona, negocio*) energy; (*de ciudad*) liveliness

vitamina [bita'mina] *nf* vitamin

vitorear [bitore'ar] *vt* to cheer, acclaim

vitrina [bi'trina] *nf* showcase; (*LAM: escaparate*) shop window

viudo, -a ['bjuðo, a] *nm/f* widower/widow

viva ['biβa] *excl* hurrah!; **¡~ el rey!** long live the king!

vivaracho, -a [biβa'ratʃo, a] *adj* jaunty, lively; (*ojos*) bright, twinkling

vivaz [bi'βaθ] *adj* lively

víveres ['biβeres] *nmpl* provisions

vivero [bi'βero] *nm* (*para plantas*) nursery; (*para peces*) fish farm; (*fig*) hotbed

viveza [bi'βeθa] *nf* liveliness; (*agudeza: mental*) sharpness

vivienda [bi'βjenda] *nf* housing; (*una vivienda*) house; (*piso*) flat (BRIT), apartment (US)

viviente [bi'βjente] *adj* living

vivir [bi'βir] *vt, vi* to live ▷ *nm* life, living

vivo, -a ['biβo, a] *adj* living, alive; (*fig: descripción*) vivid; (*persona: astuto*) smart, clever; **en ~** (*transmisión etc*) live

vocablo [bo'kaβlo] *nm* (*palabra*) word; (*término*) term

vocabulario [bokaβu'larjo] *nm* vocabulary

vocación [boka'θjon] *nf* vocation; **vocacional** (LAM) *nf* ≈ technical college

vocal [bo'kal] *adj* vocal ▷ *nf* vowel; **vocalizar** *vt* to vocalize

vocero [bo'θero] (LAM) *nmf* spokesman/woman

voces ['boθes] *pl de* **voz**

vodka ['boðka] *nm o f* vodka

vol *abr* = **volumen**

volado [bo'laðo] (MÉX) *adv* in a rush, hastily

volador, a [bola'ðor, a] *adj* flying

volandas [bo'landas]: **en ~** *adv* in the air

volante [bo'lante] *adj* flying ▷ *nm* (*de*

coche) steering wheel; (*de reloj*) balance

volar [bo'lar] *vt* (*edificio*) to blow up ▷ *vi* to fly

volátil [bo'latil] *adj* volatile

volcán [bol'kan] *nm* volcano; **volcánico, -a** *adj* volcanic

volcar [bol'kar] *vt* to upset, overturn; (*tumbar, derribar*) to knock over; (*vaciar*) to empty out ▷ *vi* to overturn; **volcarse** *vr* to tip over

voleibol [bolei'βol] *nm* volleyball

volqué *etc vb V* **volcar**

voltaje [bol'taxe] *nm* voltage

voltear [bolte'ar] *vt* to turn over; (*volcar*) to turn upside down

voltereta [bolte'reta] *nf* somersault

voltio ['boltjo] *nm* volt

voluble [bo'luβle] *adj* fickle

volumen [bo'lumen] (*pl* **volúmenes**) *nm* volume; **voluminoso, -a** *adj* voluminous; (*enorme*) massive

voluntad [bolun'tað] *nf* will; (*resolución*) willpower; (*deseo*) desire, wish

voluntario, -a [bolun'tarjo, a] *adj* voluntary ▷ *nm/f* volunteer

volver [bol'βer] *vt* (*gen*) to turn; (*dar vuelta a*) to turn (over); (*voltear*) to turn round, turn upside down; (*poner al revés*) to turn inside out; (*devolver*) to return ▷ *vi* to return, go back, come back; **volverse** *vr* to turn round; **~ la espalda** to turn one's back; **~ triste** *etc* **a algn** to make sb sad *etc*; **~ a hacer** to do again; **~ en sí** to come to; **~se insoportable/muy caro** to get *o* become unbearable/very expensive; **~se loco** to go mad

vomitar [bomi'tar] *vt, vi* to vomit; **vómito** *nm* vomit

voraz [bo'raθ] *adj* voracious

vos [bos] (LAM) *pron* you

vosotros, -as [bo'sotros, as] (ESP) *pron* you; (*reflexivo*): **entre/para ~** among/for yourselves

votación [bota'θjon] *nf* (*acto*) voting; (*voto*) vote

votar [bo'tar] *vi* to vote; **voto** *nm* vote; (*promesa*) vow; **votos** *nmpl* (good) wishes

voy *vb V* **ir**

voz [boθ] *nf* voice; (*grito*) shout; (*rumor*) rumour; (*Ling*) word; **dar voces** to shout, yell; **de viva ~** verbally; **en ~ alta** aloud; **en ~ baja** in a low voice, in a whisper; **voz de mando** command

vuelco ['bwelko] *vb V* **volcar** ▷ *nm* spill, overturning

vuelo ['bwelo] *vb V* **volar** ▷ *nm* flight; (*encaje*) lace, frill; **coger al ~** to catch in flight; **vuelo chárter/regular** charter/

scheduled flight; **vuelo libre** (*Deporte*) hang-gliding

vuelque *etc vb* V **volcar**

vuelta ['bwelta] *nf* (*gen*) turn; (*curva*) bend, curve; (*regreso*) return; (*revolución*) revolution; (*de circuito*) lap; (*de papel, tela*) reverse; (*cambio*) change; **a la ~** on one's return; **a la ~ (de la esquina)** round the corner; **a ~ de correo** by return of post; **dar ~s** (*cabeza*) to spin; **dar(se) la ~** (*volverse*) to turn round; **dar ~s a una idea** to turn over an idea (in one's head); **estar de ~** to be back; **dar una ~** to go for a walk; (*en coche*) to go for a drive; **vuelta ciclista** (*Deporte*) (cycle) tour

vuelto ['bwelto] *pp de* **volver**

vuelvo *etc vb* V **volver**

vuestro, -a ['bwestro, a] *adj pos* your; **un amigo ~** a friend of yours ▷ *pron:* **el ~/la vuestra, los ~s/las vuestras** yours

vulgar [bul'ɣar] *adj* (*ordinario*) vulgar; (*común*) common; **vulgaridad** *nf* commonness; (*acto*) vulgarity; (*expresión*) coarse expression

vulnerable [bulne'raβle] *adj* vulnerable

vulnerar [bulne'rar] *vt* (*ley, acuerdo*) to violate, breach; (*derechos, intimidad*) to violate; (*reputación*) to damage

walkie-talkie [walki-'talki] (*pl* ~**s**) *nm* walkie-talkie

Walkman® ['walkman] *nm* Walkman®

wáter ['bater] *nm* (*taza*) toilet; (*LAM: lugar*) toilet (*BRIT*), rest room (*US*)

web [web] *nm o f* (*página*) website; (*red*) (World Wide) Web; **webcam** *nf* webcam; **webmaster** *nmf* webmaster; **website** *nm* website

western ['western] (*pl* ~**s**) *nm* western

whisky ['wiski] *nm* whisky, whiskey

windsurf ['winsurf] *nm* windsurfing; **hacer ~** to go windsurfing

X y

xenofobia [kseno'foβja] *nf* xenophobia
xilófono [ksi'lofono] *nm* xylophone
xocoyote, -a [ksoko'yote, a] (*MÉX*) *nm/f*
   baby of the family, youngest child

y [i] *conj* and
ya [ja] *adv* (*gen*) already; (*ahora*) now; (*en
   seguida*) at once; (*pronto*) soon ▷ *excl* all
   right! ▷ *conj* (*ahora que*) now that; **~ lo sé**
   I know; **~ que ...** since; **¡~ está bien!** that's
   (quite) enough!; **¡~ voy!** coming!
yacaré [jaka're] (*CS*) *nm* cayman
yacer [ja'θer] *vi* to lie
yacimiento [jaθi'mjento] *nm* (*de mineral*)
   deposit; (*arqueológico*) site
yanqui ['janki] *adj, nmf* Yankee
yate ['jate] *nm* yacht
yazco *etc vb* V **yacer**
yedra ['jeðra] *nf* ivy
yegua ['jeɣwa] *nf* mare
yema ['jema] *nf* (*del huevo*) yolk; (*Bot*) leaf
   bud; (*fig*) best part; **yema del dedo** fingertip
yerno ['jerno] *nm* son-in-law
yeso ['jeso] *nm* plaster
yo [jo] *pron* I; **soy ~** it's me
yodo ['joðo] *nm* iodine
yoga ['joɣa] *nm* yoga
yogur(t) [jo'ɣur(t)] *nm* yoghurt
yuca ['juka] *nf* (*alimento*) cassava, manioc
   root
Yugoslavia [juɣos'laβja] *nf* (*Hist*)
   Yugoslavia
yugular [juɣu'lar] *adj* jugular
yunque ['junke] *nm* anvil
yuyo ['jujo] (*RPL*) *nm* (*mala hierba*) weed

Z

zafar [θa'far] vt (*soltar*) to untie; (*superficie*) to clear; **zafarse** vr (*escaparse*) to escape; (*Tec*) to slip off

zafiro [θa'firo] nm sapphire

zaga ['θaɣa] nf: **a la ~** behind

zaguán [θa'ɣwan] nm hallway

zalamero, -a [θala'mero, a] adj flattering; (*cobista*) suave

zamarra [θa'marra] nf (*chaqueta*) sheepskin jacket

zambullirse [θambu'ʎirse] vr to dive

zampar [θam'par] vt to gobble down

zanahoria [θana'orja] nf carrot

zancadilla [θanka'ðiʎa] nf trip

zanco ['θanko] nm stilt

zanja ['θanxa] nf ditch; **zanjar** vt (*resolver*) to resolve

zapata [θa'pata] nf (*Mecánica*) shoe

zapatería [θapate'ria] nf (*oficio*) shoemaking; (*tienda*) shoe shop; (*fábrica*) shoe factory; **zapatero, -a** nm/f shoemaker

zapatilla [θapa'tiʎa] nf slipper; **zapatilla de deporte** training shoe

zapato [θa'pato] nm shoe

zapping ['θapin] nm channel-hopping; **hacer ~** to channel-hop

zar [θar] nm tsar, czar

zarandear [θarande'ar] (*fam*) vt to shake vigorously

zarpa ['θarpa] nf (*garra*) claw

zarpar [θar'par] vi to weigh anchor

zarza ['θarθa] nf (*Bot*) bramble; **zarzamora** nf blackberry

zarzuela [θar'θwela] nf Spanish light opera

zigzag [θiɣ'θaɣ] nm zigzag

zinc [θink] nm zinc

zíper ['θiper] (*MÉX, CAM*) nm zip (fastener) (*BRIT*), zipper (*US*)

zócalo ['θokalo] nm (*Arq*) plinth, base; (*de pared*) skirting board (*BRIT*), baseboard (*US*); (*MÉX: plaza*) main o public square

zoclo ['θoklo] (*MÉX*) nm skirting board (*BRIT*), baseboard (*US*)

zodíaco [θo'ðiako] nm zodiac

zona ['θona] nf zone; **zona fronteriza** border area; **zona roja** (*LAM*) red-light district

zonzo, -a (*LAM: fam*) ['θonθo, a] adj silly ▷ nm/f fool

zoo ['θoo] nm zoo

zoología [θoolo'xia] nf zoology; **zoológico, -a** adj zoological ▷ nm (*tb*: **parque zoológico**) zoo; **zoólogo, -a** nm/f zoologist

zoom [θum] nm zoom lens

zopilote [θopi'lote] (*MÉX, CAM*) nm buzzard

zoquete [θo'kete] nm (*fam*) blockhead

zorro, -a ['θorro, a] adj crafty ▷ nm/f fox/ vixen

zozobrar [θoθo'βrar] vi (*hundirse*) to capsize; (*fig*) to fail

zueco ['θweko] nm clog

zumbar [θum'bar] vt (*golpear*) to hit ▷ vi to buzz; **zumbido** nm buzzing

zumo ['θumo] nm juice

zurcir [θur'θir] vt (*coser*) to darn

zurdo, -a ['θurðo, a] adj left-handed

zurrar [θu'rrar] (*fam*) vt to wallop

a

A [eɪ] n (Mus) la m

a [ə] (before vowel or silent h: an) indef art **1** un(a); **a book** un libro; **an apple** una manzana; **she's a doctor** (ella) es médica **2** (instead of the number "one") un(a); **a year ago** hace un año; **a hundred/thousand** etc **pounds** cien/mil etc libras **3** (in expressing ratios, prices etc): **3 a day/week** 3 al día/a la semana; **10 km an hour** 10 km por hora; **£5 a person** £5 por persona; **30p a kilo** 30p el kilo

A2 (BRIT: Scol) n segunda parte de los "A levels"
A.A. n abbr (BRIT: = Automobile Association) ≈ RACE m (SP); (= Alcoholics Anonymous) Alcohólicos Anónimos
A.A.A. (US) n abbr (= American Automobile Association) ≈ RACE m (SP)
aback [ə'bæk] adv: **to be taken ~** quedar desconcertado
abandon [ə'bændən] vt abandonar; (give up) renunciar a
abattoir ['æbətwɑ:*] (BRIT) n matadero
abbey ['æbɪ] n abadía
abbreviation [ə'bri:vɪ'eɪʃən] n (short form) abreviatura
abdomen ['æbdəmən] n abdomen m
abduct [æb'dʌkt] vt raptar, secuestrar
abide [ə'baɪd] vt: **I can't ~ it/him** no lo/le puedo ver; **abide by** vt fus atenerse a
ability [ə'bɪlɪtɪ] n habilidad f, capacidad f; (talent) talento
able ['eɪbl] adj capaz; (skilled) hábil; **to be ~ to do sth** poder hacer algo
abnormal [æb'nɔ:məl] adj anormal
aboard [ə'bɔ:d] adv a bordo ▷ prep a bordo de
abolish [ə'bɔlɪʃ] vt suprimir, abolir

abolition [æbəu'lɪʃən] n supresión f, abolición f
abort [ə'bɔ:t] vt, vi abortar; **abortion** [ə'bɔ:ʃən] n aborto; **to have an abortion** abortar, hacerse abortar

about [ə'baut] adv **1** (approximately) más o menos, aproximadamente; **about a hundred/thousand** etc unos(unas) cien/mil etc; **it takes about 10 hours** se tarda unas or más o menos 10 horas; **at about 2 o'clock** sobre las dos; **I've just about finished** casi he terminado
2 (referring to place) por todas partes; **to leave things lying about** dejar las cosas (tiradas) por ahí; **to run about** correr por todas partes; **to walk about** pasearse, ir y venir
3: **to be about to do sth** estar a punto de hacer algo
▷ prep **1** (relating to) de, sobre, acerca de; **a book about London** un libro sobre or acerca de Londres; **what is it about?** ¿de qué se trata?; **we talked about it** hablamos de eso or ello; **what** or **how about doing this?** ¿qué tal si hacemos esto?
2 (referring to place) por; **to walk about the town** caminar por la ciudad

above [ə'bʌv] adv encima, por encima, arriba ▷ prep encima de; (greater than: in number) más de; (: in rank) superior a; **mentioned ~** susodicho; **~ all** sobre todo
abroad [ə'brɔ:d] adv (to be) en el extranjero; (to go) al extranjero
abrupt [ə'brʌpt] adj (sudden) brusco; (curt) áspero
abscess ['æbsɪs] n absceso
absence ['æbsəns] n ausencia
absent ['æbsənt] adj ausente; **absent-minded** adj distraído
absolute ['æbsəlu:t] adj absoluto; **absolutely** [-'lu:tlɪ] adv (totally) totalmente; (certainly!) ¡por supuesto (que sí)!
absorb [əb'zɔ:b] vt absorber; **to be ~ed in a book** estar absorto en un libro; **absorbent cotton** (US) n algodón m hidrófilo; **absorbing** adj absorbente
abstain [əb'steɪn] vi: **to ~ (from)** abstenerse (de)
abstract ['æbstrækt] adj abstracto
absurd [əb'sə:d] adj absurdo
abundance [ə'bʌndəns] n abundancia
abundant [ə'bʌndənt] adj abundante
abuse [n ə'bju:s, vb ə'bju:z] n (insults)

insultos *mpl*, injurias *fpl*; (*ill-treatment*) malos tratos *mpl*; (*misuse*) abuso ▷ *vt* insultar; maltratar; abusar de; **abusive** *adj* ofensivo

abysmal [ə'bɪzməl] *adj* pésimo; (*failure*) garrafal; (*ignorance*) supino

academic [ækə'dɛmɪk] *adj* académico, universitario; (*pej: issue*) puramente teórico ▷ *n* estudioso/a, profesor(a) *m/f* universitario/a; **academic year** *n* (*Univ*) año *m* académico; (*Scol*) año *m* escolar

academy [ə'kædəmɪ] *n* (*learned body*) academia; (*school*) instituto, colegio; **~ of music** conservatorio

accelerate [æk'sɛləreɪt] *vt, vi* acelerar; **acceleration** [æksɛlə'reɪʃən] *n* aceleración *f*; **accelerator** (*BRIT*) *n* acelerador *m*

accent ['æksɛnt] *n* acento; (*fig*) énfasis *m*

accept [ək'sɛpt] *vt* aceptar; (*responsibility, blame*) admitir; **acceptable** *adj* aceptable; **acceptance** *n* aceptación *f*

access ['æksɛs] *n* acceso; **to have ~ to** tener libre acceso a; **accessible** [-'sɛsəbl] *adj* (*place, person*) accesible; (*knowledge etc*) asequible

accessory [æk'sɛsərɪ] *n* accesorio; (*Law*): **~ to** cómplice de

accident ['æksɪdənt] *n* accidente *m*; (*chance event*) casualidad *f*; **by ~** (*unintentionally*) sin querer; (*by chance*) por casualidad; **accidental** [-'dɛntl] *adj* accidental, fortuito; **accidentally** [-'dɛntəlɪ] *adv* sin querer; por casualidad; **Accident and Emergency Department** *n* (*BRIT*) Urgencias *fpl*; **accident insurance** *n* seguro contra accidentes

acclaim [ə'kleɪm] *vt* aclamar, aplaudir ▷ *n* aclamación *f*, aplausos *mpl*

accommodate [ə'kɔmədeɪt] *vt* (*person*) alojar, hospedar; (*: car, hotel etc*) tener cabida para; (*oblige, help*) complacer

accommodation [əkɔmə'deɪʃən] (*us* **accommodations**) *n* alojamiento

accompaniment [ə'kʌmpənɪmənt] *n* acompañamiento

accompany [ə'kʌmpənɪ] *vt* acompañar

accomplice [ə'kʌmplɪs] *n* cómplice *mf*

accomplish [ə'kʌmplɪʃ] *vt* (*finish*) concluir; (*achieve*) lograr; **accomplishment** *n* (*skill: gen pl*) talento; (*completion*) realización *f*

accord [ə'kɔːd] *n* acuerdo ▷ *vt* conceder; **of his own ~** espontáneamente; **accordance** *n*: **in accordance with** de acuerdo con; **according ▷ according to** *prep* según; (*in accordance with*) conforme a; **accordingly** *adv* (*appropriately*) de acuerdo con esto; (*as a result*) en consecuencia

account [ə'kaunt] *n* (*Comm*) cuenta; (*report*) informe *m*; **accounts** *npl* (*Comm*) cuentas *fpl*; **of no ~** de ninguna importancia; **on ~** a cuenta; **on no ~** bajo ningún concepto; **on ~ of** a causa de, por motivo de; **to take into ~, take ~ of** tener en cuenta; **account for** *vt fus* (*explain*) explicar; (*represent*) representar; **accountable** *adj*: **accountable (to)** responsable (ante); **accountant** *n* contable *mf*, contador(a) *m/f*; **account number** *n* (*at bank etc*) número de cuenta

accumulate [ə'kjuːmjuleɪt] *vt* acumular ▷ *vi* acumularse

accuracy ['ækjurəsɪ] *n* (*of total*) exactitud *f*; (*of description etc*) precisión *f*

accurate ['ækjurɪt] *adj* (*total*) exacto; (*description*) preciso; (*person*) cuidadoso; (*device*) de precisión; **accurately** *adv* con precisión

accusation [ækju'zeɪʃən] *n* acusación *f*

accuse [ə'kjuːz] *vt*: **to ~ sb (of sth)** acusar a algn (de algo); **accused** *n* (*Law*) acusado/a

accustomed [ə'kʌstəmd] *adj*: **~ to** acostumbrado a

ace [eɪs] *n* as *m*

ache [eɪk] *n* dolor *m* ▷ *vi* doler; **my head ~s** me duele la cabeza

achieve [ə'tʃiːv] *vt* (*aim, result*) alcanzar; (*success*) lograr, conseguir; **achievement** *n* (*completion*) realización *f*; (*success*) éxito

acid ['æsɪd] *adj* ácido; (*taste*) agrio ▷ *n* (*Chem, inf: LSD*) ácido

acknowledge [ək'nɔlɪdʒ] *vt* (*letter: also:* **~ receipt of**) acusar recibo de; (*fact, situation, person*) reconocer; **acknowledgement** *n* acuse *m* de recibo

acne ['æknɪ] *n* acné *m*

acorn ['eɪkɔːn] *n* bellota

acoustic [ə'kuːstɪk] *adj* acústico

acquaintance [ə'kweɪntəns] *n* (*person*) conocido/a; (*with person, subject*) conocimiento

acquire [ə'kwaɪə*] *vt* adquirir; **acquisition** [ækwɪ'zɪʃən] *n* adquisición *f*

acquit [ə'kwɪt] *vt* absolver, exculpar; **to ~ o.s. well** salir con éxito

acre ['eɪkə*] *n* acre *m*

acronym ['ækrənɪm] *n* siglas *fpl*

across [ə'krɔs] *prep* (*on the other side of*) al otro lado de, del otro lado de; (*crosswise*) a través de ▷ *adv* de un lado a otro, de una parte a otra; a través, al través; (*measurement*): **the road is 10m ~** la carretera tiene 10m de ancho; **to run/swim ~** atravesar corriendo/nadando; **~ from** enfrente de

acrylic [ə'krɪlɪk] *adj* acrílico ▷ *n* acrílica

act [ækt] n acto, acción f; (of play) acto; (in music hall etc) número; (Law) decreto, ley f ▷ vi (behave) comportarse; (have effect: drug, chemical) hacer efecto; (Theatre) actuar; (pretend) fingir; (take action) obrar ▷ vt (part) hacer el papel de; **in the ~ of: to catch sb in the ~ of …** pillar a algn en el momento en que …; **to ~ as** actuar or hacer de; **act up** (inf) vi (person) portarse mal; **acting** adj suplente ▷ n (activity) actuación f; (profession) profesión f de actor

action ['ækʃən] n acción f, acto; (Mil) acción f, batalla; (Law) proceso, demanda; **out of ~** (person) fuera de combate; (thing) estropeado; **to take ~** tomar medidas; **action replay** n (TV) repetición f

activate ['æktɪveɪt] vt activar

active ['æktɪv] adj activo, enérgico; (volcano) en actividad; **actively** adv (participate) activamente; (discourage, dislike) enérgicamente

activist ['æktɪvɪst] n activista m/f

activity [-'tɪvɪtɪ] n actividad f; **activity holiday** n vacaciones con actividades organizadas

actor ['æktə*] n actor m, actriz f

actress ['aektrɪs] n actriz f

actual ['æktjuəl] adj verdadero, real; (emphatic use) propiamente dicho

> Be careful not to translate **actual** by the Spanish word actual.

actually ['æktjuəlɪ] adv realmente, en realidad; (even) incluso

> Be careful not to translate **actually** by the Spanish word actualmente.

acupuncture ['ækjupʌŋktʃə*] n acupuntura

acute [ə'kju:t] adj agudo

ad [æd] n abbr = **advertisement**

A.D. adv abbr (= anno Domini) DC

adamant ['ædəmənt] adj firme, inflexible

adapt [ə'dæpt] vt adaptar ▷ vi: **to ~ (to)** adaptarse a, ajustarse (a); **adapter** (us **adaptor**) n (Elec) adaptador m; (for several plugs) ladrón m

add [æd] vt añadir, agregar; **add up** vt (figures) sumar ▷ vi (fig): **it doesn't add up** no tiene sentido; **add up to** vt fus (Math) sumar, ascender a; (fig: mean) querer decir, venir a ser

addict ['ædɪkt] n adicto/a; (enthusiast) entusiasta m/f; **addicted** [ə'dɪktɪd] adj: **to be addicted to** ser adicto a, ser fanático de; **addiction** [ə'dɪkʃən] n (to drugs etc) adicción f; **addictive** [ə'dɪktɪv] adj que causa adicción

addition [ə'dɪʃən] n (adding up) adición f; (thing added) añadidura, añadido; **in ~**

además, por añadidura; **in ~ to** además de; **additional** adj adicional

additive ['ædɪtɪv] n aditivo

address [ə'drɛs] n dirección f, señas fpl; (speech) discurso ▷ vt (letter) dirigir; (speak to) dirigirse a, dirigir la palabra a; (problem) tratar; **address book** n agenda (de direcciones)

adequate ['ædɪkwɪt] adj (satisfactory) adecuado; (enough) suficiente

adhere [əd'hɪə*] vi: **to ~ to** (stick to) pegarse a; (fig: abide by) observar; (: belief etc) ser partidario de

adhesive [əd'hi:zɪv] n adhesivo; **adhesive tape** n (BRIT) cinta adhesiva; (US Med) esparadrapo

adjacent [ə'dʒeɪsənt] adj: **~ to** contiguo a, inmediato a

adjective ['ædʒɛktɪv] n adjetivo

adjoining [ə'dʒɔɪnɪŋ] adj contiguo, vecino

adjourn [ə'dʒə:n] vt aplazar ▷ vi suspenderse

adjust [ə'dʒʌst] vt (change) modificar; (clothing) arreglar; (machine) ajustar ▷ vi: **to ~ (to)** adaptarse (a); **adjustable** adj ajustable; **adjustment** n adaptación f; (to machine, prices) ajuste m

administer [əd'mɪnɪstə*] vt administrar; **administration** [-'treɪʃən] n (management) administración f; (government) gobierno; **administrative** [-trətɪv] adj administrativo

administrator [əd'mɪnɪstreɪtə*] n administrador(a) m/f

admiral ['ædmərəl] n almirante m

admiration [ædmə'reɪʃən] n admiración f

admire [əd'maɪə*] vt admirar; **admirer** (fan) admirador(a) m/f

admission [əd'mɪʃən] n (to university, club) ingreso; (entry fee) entrada; (confession) confesión f

admit [əd'mɪt] vt (confess) confesar; (permit to enter) dejar entrar, dar entrada a; (to club, organization) admitir; (accept: defeat) reconocer; **to be ~ted to hospital** ingresar en el hospital; **admit to** vt fus confesarse culpable de; **admittance** n entrada; **admittedly** adv es cierto or verdad que

adolescent [ædəu'lɛsnt] adj, n adolescente mf

adopt [ə'dɔpt] vt adoptar; **adopted** adj adoptivo; **adoption** [ə'dɔpʃən] n adopción f

adore [ə'dɔ:*] vt adorar

adorn [ə'dɔ:n] vt adornar

Adriatic [eɪdrɪ'ætɪk] n: **the ~ (Sea)** el (Mar) Adriático

adrift [ə'drɪft] *adv* a la deriva
adult ['ædʌlt] *n* adulto/a ▷ *adj* (grown-up)
adulto; (for adults) para adultos; **adult
education** *n* educación *f* para adultos
adultery [ə'dʌltərɪ] *n* adulterio
advance [əd'vɑːns] *n* (progress) adelanto,
progreso; (money) anticipo, préstamo;
(Mil) avance *m* ▷ *adj*: **~ booking** venta
anticipada; **~ notice, ~ warning** previo
aviso ▷ *vt* (money) anticipar; (theory, idea)
proponer (para la discusión) ▷ *vi* avanzar,
adelantarse; **to take ~ of** (person) aprovecharse
de; (opportunity) aprovechar
advance [əd'vɑːntɪdʒ] *n* (also Tennis)
ventaja; **to take ~ of** (person) aprovecharse
de; (opportunity) aprovechar
advent ['ædvənt] *n* advenimiento; **A~**
Adviento
adventure [əd'ventʃə*] *n* aventura;
adventurous [-tʃərəs] *adj* atrevido;
aventurero
adverb ['ædvɜːb] *n* adverbio
adversary ['ædvəsərɪ] *n* adversario,
contrario
adverse ['ædvɜːs] *adj* adverso, contrario
advert ['ædvɜːt] (BRIT) *n abbr* =
advertisement
advertise ['ædvətaɪz] *vi* (in newspaper etc)
anunciar, hacer publicidad; **to ~ for** (staff,
accommodation etc) buscar por medio de
anuncios ▷ *vt* anunciar; **advertisement**
[əd'vɜːtɪsmənt] *n* (Comm) anuncio;
advertiser *n* anunciante *mf*; **advertising**
n publicidad *f*, anuncios *mpl*; (industry)
industria publicitaria
advice [əd'vaɪs] *n* consejo, consejos *mpl*;
(notification) aviso; **a piece of ~** un consejo;
to take legal ~ consultar con un abogado
advisable [əd'vaɪzəbl] *adj* aconsejable,
conveniente
advise [əd'vaɪz] *vt* aconsejar; (inform): **to
~ sb of sth** informar a algn de algo; **to ~
sb against sth/doing sth** desaconsejar
algo a algn/aconsejar a algn que no haga
algo; **adviser, advisor** *n* consejero/a;
(consultant) asesor(a) *m/f*; **advisory** *adj*
consultivo
advocate [vb 'ædvəkeɪt, n -kɪt] *vt* abogar
por ▷ *n* (lawyer) abogado/a; (supporter): **~ of**
defensor *m/f* de
Aegean [iː'dʒiːən] *n*: **the ~ (Sea)** el (Mar)
Egeo
aerial ['ɛərɪəl] *n* antena ▷ *adj* aéreo
aerobics [ɛə'rəubɪks] *n* aerobic *m*
aeroplane ['ɛərəpleɪn] (BRIT) *n* avión *m*
aerosol ['ɛərəsɔl] *n* aerosol *m*

affair [ə'fɛə*] *n* asunto; (also: **love ~**)
aventura (amorosa)
affect [ə'fɛkt] *vt* (influence) afectar,
influir en; (afflict, concern) afectar; (move)
conmover; **affected** *adj* afectado;
affection *n* afecto, cariño; **affectionate**
adj afectuoso, cariñoso
afflict [ə'flɪkt] *vt* afligir
affluent ['æfluənt] *adj* (wealthy)
acomodado; **the ~ society** la sociedad
opulenta
afford [ə'fɔːd] *vt* (provide) proporcionar;
can we ~ (to buy) it? ¿tenemos bastante
dinero para comprarlo?; **affordable** *adj*
asequible
Afghanistan [æf'gænɪstæn] *n*
Afganistán *m*
afraid [ə'freɪd] *adj*: **to be ~ of** (person) tener
miedo a; (thing) tener miedo de; **to be ~ to**
tener miedo de, temer; **I am ~ that** me temo
que; **I am ~ not/so** lo siento, pero no/es así
Africa ['æfrɪkə] *n* África; **African** *adj, n*
africano/a *m/f*; **African-American** *adj, n*
afroamericano/a
after ['ɑːftə*] *prep* (time) después de; (place,
order) detrás de, tras ▷ *adv* después ▷ *conj*
después (de) que; **what/who are you ~?**
¿qué/a quién busca usted?; **~ having done/
he left** después de haber hecho/después
de que se marchó; **to name sb ~ sb** llamar
a algn por algn; **it's twenty ~ eight** (US)
son las ocho y veinte; **to ask ~ sb** preguntar
por algn; **~ all** después de todo, al fin y al
cabo; **~ you!** ¡pase usted!; **after-effects** *npl*
consecuencias *fpl*, efectos *mpl*; **aftermath**
n consecuencias *fpl*, resultados *mpl*;
afternoon *n* tarde *f*; **after-shave (lotion)**
n aftershave *m*; **aftersun (lotion/cream)**
n loción *f*/crema para después del sol,
aftersun *m*; **afterwards** (US **afterward**) *adv*
después, más tarde
again [ə'gɛn] *adv* otra vez, de nuevo; **to
do sth ~** volver a hacer algo; **~ and ~** una y
otra vez
against [ə'gɛnst] *prep* (in opposition to)
en contra de; (leaning on, touching) contra,
junto a
age [eɪdʒ] *n* edad *f*; (period) época ▷ *vi*
envejecer(se) ▷ *vt* envejecer; **she is 20
years of ~** tiene 20 años; **to come of ~** llegar
a la mayoría de edad; **it's been ~s since I
saw you** hace siglos que no te veo; **~d 10** de
10 años de edad; **age group** *n*: **to be in the
same age group** tener la misma edad; **age
limit** *n* edad *f* mínima (or máxima)
agency ['eɪdʒənsɪ] *n* agencia
agenda [ə'dʒɛndə] *n* orden *m* del día
⬛ Be careful not to translate **agenda** by the

■ Spanish word *agenda*.

agent ['eɪdʒənt] *n* agente *mf*; (*Comm: holding concession*) representante *mf*, delegado/a; (*Chem, fig*) agente *m*

aggravate ['ægrəveɪt] *vt* (*situation*) agravar; (*person*) irritar

aggression [ə'greʃən] *n* agresión *f*

aggressive [ə'grɛsɪv] *adj* (*belligerent*) agresivo; (*assertive*) enérgico

agile ['ædʒaɪl] *adj* ágil

agitated ['ædʒɪteɪtɪd] *adj* agitado

AGM *n abbr* (= *annual general meeting*) asamblea anual

ago [ə'gəu] *adv*: **2 days ~** hace 2 días; **not long ~** hace poco; **how long ~?** ¿hace cuánto tiempo?

agony ['ægənɪ] *n* (*pain*) dolor *m* agudo; (*distress*) angustia; **to be in ~** retorcerse de dolor

agree [ə'griː] *vt* (*price, date*) acordar, quedar en ▷ *vi* (*have same opinion*): **to ~ (with/that)** estar de acuerdo (con/que); (*correspond*) coincidir, concordar; (*consent*) acceder; **to ~ with** (*person*) estar de acuerdo con, ponerse de acuerdo con; (: *food*) sentar bien a; (*Ling*) concordar con; **to ~ to sth/ to do sth** consentir en algo/aceptar hacer algo; **to ~ that** (*admit*) estar de acuerdo en que; **agreeable** *adj* (*sensation*) agradable; (*person*) simpático; (*willing*) de acuerdo, conforme; **agreed** *adj* (*time, place*) convenido; **agreement** *n* acuerdo; (*contract*) contrato; **in agreement** de acuerdo, conforme

agricultural [ægrɪ'kʌltʃərəl] *adj* agrícola

agriculture ['ægrɪkʌltʃə*] *n* agricultura

ahead [ə'hɛd] *adv* (*in front*) delante; (*into the future*): **she had no time to think ~** no tenía tiempo de hacer planes para el futuro; **~ of** delante de; (*in advance of*) antes de; **~ of time** antes de la hora; **go right** *or* **straight ~** (*direction*) siga adelante; (*permission*) hazlo (*or* hágalo)

aid [eɪd] *n* ayuda, auxilio; (*device*) aparato ▷ *vt* ayudar, auxiliar; **in ~ of** a beneficio de

aide [eɪd] *n* (*person, also Mil*) ayudante *mf*

AIDS [eɪdz] *n abbr* (= *acquired immune deficiency syndrome*) SIDA *m*

ailing ['eɪlɪŋ] *adj* (*person, economy*) enfermizo

ailment ['eɪlmənt] *n* enfermedad *f*, achaque *m*

aim [eɪm] *vt* (*gun, camera*) apuntar; (*missile, remark*) dirigir; (*blow*) asestar ▷ *vi* (*also*: **take ~**) apuntar ▷ *n* (*in shooting: skill*) puntería; (*objective*) propósito, meta; **to ~ at** (*with weapon*) apuntar a; (*objective*) aspirar a, pretender; **to ~ to do** tener la intención

de hacer

ain't [eɪnt] (*inf*) = **am not; aren't; isn't**

air [ɛə*] *n* aire *m*; (*appearance*) aspecto ▷ *vt* (*room*) ventilar; (*clothes, ideas*) airear ▷ *cpd* aéreo; **to throw sth into the ~** (*ball etc*) lanzar algo al aire; **by ~** (*travel*) en avión; **to be on the ~** (*Radio, TV*) estar en antena; **airbag** *n* airbag *m inv*; **airbed** (*BRIT*) *n* colchón *m* neumático; **airborne** *adj* (*in the air*) en el aire; **as soon as the plane was airborne** tan pronto como el avión estuvo en el aire; **air-conditioned** *adj* climatizado; **air conditioning** *n* aire acondicionado; **aircraft** *n inv* avión *m*; **airfield** *n* campo de aviación; **Air Force** *n* fuerzas *fpl* aéreas, aviación *f*; **air hostess** (*BRIT*) *n* azafata; **airing cupboard** *n* (*BRIT*) armario *m* para oreo; **airlift** *n* puente *m* aéreo; **airline** *n* línea aérea; **airliner** *n* avión *m* de pasajeros; **airmail** *n*: **by airmail** por avión; **airplane** (*US*) *n* avión *m*; **airport** *n* aeropuerto; **air raid** *n* ataque *m* aéreo; **airsick** *adj*: **to be airsick** marearse (en avión); **airspace** *n* espacio aéreo; **airstrip** *n* pista de aterrizaje; **air terminal** *n* terminal *f*; **airtight** *adj* hermético; **air-traffic controller** *n* controlador(a) *m/f* aéreo/a; **airy** *adj* (*room*) bien ventilado; (*fig: manner*) desenfadado

aisle [aɪl] *n* (*of church*) nave *f*; (*of theatre, supermarket*) pasillo; **aisle seat** *n* (*on plane*) asiento de pasillo

ajar [ə'dʒɑː*] *adj* entreabierto

à la carte [ælæ'kɑːt] *adv* a la carta

alarm [ə'lɑːm] *n* (*in shop, bank*) alarma; (*anxiety*) inquietud *f* ▷ *vt* asustar, inquietar; **alarm call** *n* (*in hotel etc*) alarma; **alarm clock** *n* despertador *m*; **alarmed** *adj* (*person*) alarmado, asustado; (*house, car etc*) con alarma; **alarming** *adj* alarmante

Albania [æl'beɪnɪə] *n* Albania

albeit [ɔːl'biːɪt] *conj* aunque

album ['ælbəm] *n* álbum *m*; (*L.P.*) elepé *m*

alcohol ['ælkəhɔl] *n* alcohol *m*; **alcohol-free** *adj* sin alcohol; **alcoholic** [-'hɔlɪk] *adj*, *n* alcohólico/a *m/f*

alcove ['ælkəuv] *n* nicho, hueco

ale [eɪl] *n* cerveza

alert [ə'lɜːt] *adj* (*attentive*) atento; (*to danger, opportunity*) alerta ▷ *n* alerta *m*, alarma ▷ *vt* poner sobre aviso; **to be on the ~** (*also Mil*) estar alerta *or* sobre aviso

algebra ['ældʒɪbrə] *n* álgebra

Algeria [æl'dʒɪərɪə] *n* Argelia

alias ['eɪlɪəs] *adv* alias, conocido por ▷ *n* (*of criminal*) apodo; (*of writer*) seudónimo

alibi ['ælɪbaɪ] *n* coartada

alien ['eɪlɪən] *n* (*foreigner*) extranjero/a;

(*extraterrestrial*) extraterrestre *mf* ▷ *adj*: **~ to** ajeno a; **alienate** *vt* enajenar, alejar

alight [ə'laɪt] *adj* ardiendo; (*eyes*) brillante ▷ *vi* (*person*) apearse, bajar; (*bird*) posarse

align [ə'laɪn] *vt* alinear

alike [ə'laɪk] *adj* semejantes, iguales ▷ *adv* igualmente, del mismo modo; **to look ~** parecerse

alive [ə'laɪv] *adj* vivo; (*lively*) alegre

○ **KEYWORD**

all [ɔːl] *adj* (*sg*) todo/a; (*pl*) todos/as; **all day** todo el día; **all night** toda la noche; **all men** todos los hombres; **all five came** vinieron los cinco; **all the books** todos los libros; **all his life** toda su vida
▷ *pron* **1** todo; **I ate it all, I ate all of it** me lo comí todo; **all of us went** fuimos todos; **all the boys went** fueron todos los chicos; **is that all?** ¿eso es todo?, ¿algo más?; (*in shop*) ¿algo más?, ¿alguna cosa más?
2 (*in phrases*): **above all** sobre todo; por encima de todo; **after all** después de todo; **at all: not at all** (*in answer to question*) en absoluto; (*in answer to thanks*) ¡de nada!, ¡no hay de qué!; **I'm not at all tired** no estoy nada cansado/a; **anything at all will do** cualquier cosa viene bien; **all in all** a fin de cuentas
▷ *adv*: **all alone** completamente solo/a; **it's not as hard as all that** no es tan difícil como lo pintas; **all the more/the better** tanto más/mejor; **all but** casi; **the score is 2 all** están empatados a 2

Allah ['ælə] *n* Alá *m*

allegation [ælɪ'geɪʃən] *n* alegato

alleged [ə'lɛdʒd] *adj* supuesto, presunto; **allegedly** *adv* supuestamente, según se afirma

allegiance [ə'liːdʒəns] *n* lealtad *f*

allergic [ə'lɜːdʒɪk] *adj*: **~ to** alérgico a

allergy ['ælədʒɪ] *n* alergia

alleviate [ə'liːvɪeɪt] *vt* aliviar

alley ['ælɪ] *n* callejuela

alliance [ə'laɪəns] *n* alianza

allied ['ælaɪd] *adj* aliado

alligator ['ælɪgeɪtə*] *n* (*Zool*) caimán *m*

all-in (*BRIT*) ['ɔːlɪn] *adj, adv* (*charge*) todo incluido

allocate ['æləkeɪt] *vt* (*money etc*) asignar

allot [ə'lɒt] *vt* asignar

all-out [ɔːl'aut] *adj* (*effort etc*) supremo

allow [ə'lau] *vt* permitir, dejar; (*a claim*) admitir; (*sum, time etc*) dar, conceder; (*concede*): **to ~ that** reconocer que; **to ~ sb to do** permitir a algn hacer; **he is ~ed to**

... se le permite ...; **allow for** *vt fus* tener en cuenta; **allowance** *n* subvención *f*; (*welfare payment*) subsidio, pensión *f*; (*pocket money*) dinero de bolsillo; (*tax allowance*) desgravación *f*; **to make allowances for** (*person*) disculpar a; (*thing*) tener en cuenta

all right *adv* bien; (*as answer*) ¡conforme!, ¡está bien!

ally ['ælaɪ] *n* aliado/a ▷ *vt*: **to ~ o.s. with** aliarse con

almighty [ɔːl'maɪtɪ] *adj* todopoderoso; (*row etc*) imponente

almond ['ɑːmənd] *n* almendra

almost ['ɔːlməust] *adv* casi

alone [ə'ləun] *adj, adv* solo; **to leave sb ~** dejar a algn en paz; **to leave sth ~** no tocar algo, dejar algo sin tocar; **let ~ ...** y mucho menos ...

along [ə'lɒŋ] *prep* a lo largo de, por ▷ *adv*: **is he coming ~ with us?** ¿viene con nosotros?; **he was limping ~** iba cojeando; **~ with** junto con; **all ~** (*all the time*) desde el principio; **alongside** *prep* al lado de ▷ *adv* al lado

aloof [ə'luːf] *adj* reservado ▷ *adv*: **to stand ~** mantenerse apartado

aloud [ə'laud] *adv* en voz alta

alphabet ['ælfəbɛt] *n* alfabeto

Alps [ælps] *npl*: **the ~** los Alpes

already [ɔːl'rɛdɪ] *adv* ya

alright ['ɔːl'raɪt] (*BRIT*) *adv* = **all right**

also ['ɔːlsəu] *adv* también, además

altar ['ɔːltə*] *n* altar *m*

alter ['ɔːltə*] *vt* cambiar, modificar ▷ *vi* cambiar; **alteration** [ɔːltə'reɪʃən] *n* cambio; (*to clothes*) arreglo; (*to building*) arreglos *mpl*

alternate [*adj* ɔl'tɜːnɪt, *vb* 'ɔːltəneɪt] *adj* (*actions etc*) alternativo; (*events*) alterno; (*US*) = **alternative** ▷ *vi*: **to ~ (with)** alternar (con); **on ~ days** un día sí y otro no

alternative [ɔl'tɜːnətɪv] *adj* alternativo ▷ *n* alternativa; **~ medicine** medicina alternativa; **alternatively** *adv*: **alternatively one could ...** por otra parte se podría ...

although [ɔːl'ðəu] *conj* aunque

altitude ['æltɪtjuːd] *n* altura

altogether [ɔːltə'gɛðə*] *adv* completamente, del todo; (*on the whole*) en total, en conjunto

aluminium [ælju'mɪnɪəm] (*BRIT*), **aluminum** [ə'luːmɪnəm] (*US*) *n* aluminio

always ['ɔːlweɪz] *adv* siempre

Alzheimer's (disease) ['æltshaɪməz-] *n* enfermedad *f* de Alzheimer

am [æm] *vb see* **be**

amalgamate [ə'mælgəmeɪt] *vi*

amalgamarse ▷ vt amalgamar, unir
amass [əˈmæs] vt amontonar, acumular
amateur [ˈæmətəʳ] n aficionado/a,
amateur mf
amaze [əˈmeɪz] vt asombrar, pasmar; **to
be ~d (at)** quedar pasmado (de); **amazed**
adj asombrado; **amazement** n asombro,
sorpresa; **amazing** adj extraordinario;
(fantastic) increíble
Amazon [ˈæməzən] n (Geo) Amazonas m
ambassador [æmˈbæsədəʳ] n
embajador(a) m/f
amber [ˈæmbəʳ] n ámbar m; **at ~** (BRIT Aut)
en el amarillo
ambiguous [æmˈbɪgjuəs] adj ambiguo
ambition [æmˈbɪʃən] n ambición f;
ambitious [-ʃəs] adj ambicioso
ambulance [ˈæmbjuləns] n ambulancia
ambush [ˈæmbuʃ] n emboscada ▷ vt
tender una emboscada a
amen [ɑːˈmɛn] excl amén
amend [əˈmɛnd] vt enmendar; **to make
~s** dar cumplida satisfacción; **amendment**
n enmienda
amenities [əˈmiːnɪtɪz] npl comodidades
fpl
America [əˈmɛrɪkə] n (USA) Estados mpl
Unidos; **American** adj, n norteamericano/a;
estadounidense mf; **American football** n
(BRIT) fútbol m americano
amicable [ˈæmɪkəbl] adj amistoso,
amigable
amid(st) [əˈmɪd(st)] prep entre, en medio
de
ammunition [æmjuˈnɪʃən] n municiones
fpl
amnesty [ˈæmnɪstɪ] n amnistía
among(st) [əˈmʌŋ(st)] prep entre, en
medio de
amount [əˈmaunt] n (gen) cantidad f; (of
bill etc) suma, importe m ▷ vi: **to ~ to** sumar;
(be same as) equivaler a, significar
amp(ère) [ˈæmp(ɛəʳ)] n amperio
ample [ˈæmpl] adj (large) grande;
(abundant) abundante; (enough) bastante,
suficiente
amplifier [ˈæmplɪfaɪəʳ] n amplificador m
amputate [ˈæmpjuteɪt] vt amputar
Amtrak [ˈæmtræk] (US) n empresa nacional
de ferrocarriles de los EEUU
amuse [əˈmjuːz] vt divertir; (distract)
distraer, entretener; **amusement** n
diversión f; (pastime) pasatiempo; (laughter)
risa; **amusement arcade** n salón m de
juegos; **amusement park** n parque m de
atracciones
amusing [əˈmjuːzɪŋ] adj divertido
an [æn] indef art see **a**

anaemia [əˈniːmɪə] (US **anemia**) n
anemia
anaemic [əˈniːmɪk] (US **anemic**) adj
anémico; (fig) soso, insípido
anaesthetic [ænɪsˈθɛtɪk] (US **anesthetic**)
n anestesia
analog(ue) [ˈænələg] adj (computer,
watch) analógico
analogy [əˈnælədʒɪ] n analogía
analyse [ˈænəlaɪz] (US **analyze**) vt
analizar; **analysis** [əˈnæləsɪs] (pl **analyses**)
n análisis m inv; **analyst** [-lɪst] n (political
analyst, psychoanalyst) analista mf
analyze [ˈænəlaɪz] (US) vt = **analyse**
anarchy [ˈænəkɪ] n anarquía, desorden m
anatomy [əˈnætəmɪ] n anatomía
ancestor [ˈænsɪstəʳ] n antepasado
anchor [ˈæŋkəʳ] n ancla, áncora ▷ vi
(also: **to drop ~**) anclar ▷ vt anclar; **to
weigh ~** levar anclas
anchovy [ˈæntʃəvɪ] n anchoa
ancient [ˈeɪnʃənt] adj antiguo
and [ænd] conj y; (before i-, hi- + consonant)
e; **men ~ women** hombres y mujeres;
father ~ son padre e hijo; **trees ~ grass**
árboles y hierba; **~ so on** etcétera, y así
sucesivamente; **try ~ come** procura venir;
he talked ~ talked habló sin parar; **better ~
better** cada vez mejor
Andes [ˈændiːz] npl: **the ~** los Andes
Andorra [ænˈdɔːrə] n Andorra
anemia etc [əˈniːmɪə] (US) = **anaemia** etc
anesthetic [ænɪsˈθɛtɪk] (US) =
anaesthetic
angel [ˈeɪndʒəl] n ángel m
anger [ˈæŋgəʳ] n cólera
angina [ænˈdʒaɪnə] n angina (del pecho)
angle [ˈæŋgl] n ángulo; **from their ~** desde
su punto de vista
angler [ˈæŋgləʳ] n pescador(a) m/f (de
caña)
Anglican [ˈæŋglɪkən] adj, n anglicano/a
m/f
angling [ˈæŋglɪŋ] n pesca con caña
angrily [ˈæŋgrɪlɪ] adv coléricamente,
airadamente
angry [ˈæŋgrɪ] adj enfadado, airado;
(wound) inflamado; **to be ~ with sb/at sth**
estar enfadado con algn/por algo; **to get ~**
enfadarse, enojarse
anguish [ˈæŋgwɪʃ] n (physical) tormentos
mpl; (mental) angustia
animal [ˈænɪməl] n animal m; (pej: person)
bestia ▷ adj animal
animated [-meɪtɪd] adj animado
animation [ænɪˈmeɪʃən] n animación f
aniseed [ˈænɪsiːd] n anís m
ankle [ˈæŋkl] n tobillo

annex [n 'æneks, vb æ'neks] n (BRIT: also:
~e: building) edificio anexo ▷ vt (territory)
anexionar
anniversary [ænɪ'vəːsərɪ] n aniversario
announce [ə'nauns] vt anunciar;
announcement n anuncio; (official)
declaración f; **announcer** n (Radio)
locutor(a) m/f; (TV) presentador(a) m/f
annoy [ə'nɔɪ] vt molestar, fastidiar; **don't
get ~ed!** ¡no se enfade!; **annoying** adj
molesto, fastidioso; (person) pesado
annual ['ænjuəl] adj anual ▷ n (Bot)
anual m; (book) anuario; **annually** adv
anualmente, cada año
annum ['ænəm] n see **per**
anonymous [ə'nɔnɪməs] adj anónimo
anorak ['ænəræk] n anorak m
anorexia [ænə'reksɪə] n (Med: also: ~
nervosa) anorexia
anorexic [ænə'reksɪk] adj, n anoréxico/a
m/f
another [ə'nʌðə*] adj (one more, a different
one) otro ▷ pron otro; see **one**
answer ['ɑːnsə*] n contestación f,
respuesta; (to problem) solución f ▷ vi
contestar, responder ▷ vt (reply to)
contestar a, responder a; (problem) resolver;
(prayer) escuchar; **in ~ to your letter**
contestando or en contestación a su
carta; **to ~ the phone** contestar or coger el
teléfono; **to ~ the bell** or **the door** acudir
a la puerta; **answer back** vi replicar, ser
respondón/ona; **answerphone** n (esp BRIT)
contestador m (automático)
ant [ænt] n hormiga
Antarctic [ænt'ɑːktɪk] n: **the ~** el
Antártico
antelope ['æntɪləup] n antílope m
antenatal ['æntɪ'neɪtl] adj antenatal,
prenatal
antenna [æn'tɛnə, pl -niː] (pl **antennae**)
n antena
anthem ['ænθəm] n: **national ~** himno
nacional
anthology [æn'θɔlədʒɪ] n antología
anthrax ['ænθræks] n ántrax m
anthropology [ænθrə'pɔlədʒɪ] n
antropología
anti [æntɪ] prefix anti; **antibiotic**
[-baɪ'ɔtɪk] n antibiótico; **antibody**
['æntɪbɔdɪ] n anticuerpo
anticipate [æn'tɪsɪpeɪt] vt prever;
(expect) esperar, contar con; (look forward to)
esperar con ilusión; (do first) anticiparse a,
adelantarse a; **anticipation** [-'peɪʃən] n
(expectation) previsión f; (eagerness) ilusión f,
expectación f
anticlimax [æntɪ'klaɪmæks] n

decepción f
anticlockwise [æntɪ'klɔkwaɪz] (BRIT)
adv en dirección contraria a la de las agujas
del reloj
antics ['æntɪks] npl gracias fpl
anti: antidote ['æntɪdəut] n antídoto;
antifreeze ['æntɪfriːz] n anticongelante
m; **antihistamine** [-'hɪstəmiːn] n
antihistamínico; **antiperspirant**
['æntɪpəːspɪrənt] n antitranspirante m
antique [æn'tiːk] n antigüedad f ▷ adj
antiguo; **antique shop** n tienda de
antigüedades
antiseptic [æntɪ'septɪk] adj, n
antiséptico
antisocial [æntɪ'səuʃəl] adj antisocial
antivirus [æntɪ'vaɪərəs] adj (program,
software) antivirus inv
antlers ['æntləz] npl cuernas fpl,
cornamenta sg
anxiety [æŋ'zaɪətɪ] n inquietud f; (Med)
ansiedad f; **~ to do** deseo de hacer
anxious ['æŋkʃəs] adj inquieto,
preocupado; (worrying) preocupante;
(keen): **to be ~ to do** tener muchas ganas
de hacer

○ **KEYWORD**

any ['enɪ] adj 1 (in questions etc) algún/
alguna; **have you any butter/children?**
¿tienes mantequilla/hijos?; **if there are
any tickets left** si quedan billetes, si queda
algún billete
2 (with negative): **I haven't any money/
books** no tengo dinero/libros
3 (no matter which) cualquier; **any excuse
will do** valdrá or servirá cualquier excusa;
choose any book you like escoge el libro
que quieras
4 (in phrases): **in any case** de todas formas,
en cualquier caso; **any day now** cualquier
día (de estos); **at any moment** en cualquier
momento, de un momento a otro; **at any
rate** en todo caso; **any time: come (at)
any time** ven cuando quieras; **he might
come (at) any time** podría llegar de un
momento a otro
▷ pron 1 (in questions etc): **have you got
any?** ¿tienes alguno(s)/a(s)?; **can any of
you sing?** ¿sabe cantar alguno de vosotros/
ustedes?
2 (with negative): **I haven't any (of them)** no
tengo ninguno
3 (no matter which one(s)): **take any of those
books (you like)** toma el libro que quieras
de ésos
▷ adv 1 (in questions etc): **do you want any**

more soup/sandwiches? ¿quieres más sopa/bocadillos?; **are you feeling any better?** ¿te sientes algo mejor? **2** (with negative): **I can't hear him any more** ya no le oigo; **don't wait any longer** no esperes más

any: anybody pron cualquiera; (in interrogative sentences) alguien; (in negative sentences): **I don't see anybody** no veo a nadie; **if anybody should phone ...** si llama alguien ...; **anyhow** adv (at any rate) de todos modos, de todas formas; (haphazard): **do it anyhow you like** hazlo como quieras; **she leaves things just anyhow** deja las cosas como quiera or de cualquier modo; **I shall go anyhow** de todos modos iré; **anyone** pron **=anybody**; **anything** pron (in questions etc) algo, alguna cosa; (with negative) nada; **can you see anything?** ¿ves algo?; **if anything happens to me ...** si algo me ocurre ...; (no matter what): **you can say anything you like** puedes decir lo que quieras; **anything will do** vale todo or cualquier cosa; **he'll eat anything** come de todo or lo que sea; **anytime** adv (at any moment) en cualquier momento, de un momento a otro; (whenever) no importa cuándo, cuando quiera; **anyway** adv (at any rate) de todos modos, de todas formas; **I shall go anyway** iré de todos modos; (besides): **anyway, I couldn't come even if I wanted to** además, no podría venir aunque quisiera; **why are you phoning, anyway?** ¿entonces, por qué llamas?, ¿por qué llamas, pues?; **anywhere** adv (in questions etc): **can you see him anywhere?** ¿le ves por algún lado?; **are you going anywhere?** ¿vas a algún sitio?; (with negative): **I can't see him anywhere** no le veo por ninguna parte; **anywhere in the world** (no matter where) en cualquier parte (del mundo); **put the books down anywhere** deja los libros donde quieras

apart [əˈpɑːt] adv (aside) aparte; (situation): **~ (from)** separado (de); (movement): **to pull ~** separar; **10 miles ~** separados por 10 millas; **to take ~** desmontar; **~ from** prep aparte de

apartment [əˈpɑːtmənt] n (us) piso (SP), departamento (LAM), apartamento; (room) cuarto; **apartment building** (us) n edificio de apartamentos

apathy [ˈæpəθɪ] n apatía, indiferencia

ape [eɪp] n mono ▷ vt imitar, remedar

aperitif [əˈpɛrɪtɪf] n aperitivo

aperture [ˈæpətʃjuə*] n rendija,

resquicio; (Phot) abertura

APEX [ˈeɪpɛks] n abbr (=Advanced Purchase Excursion Fare) tarifa f APEX

apologize [əˈpɒlədʒaɪz] vi: **to ~ (for sth to sb)** disculparse (con algn de algo)

apology [əˈpɒlədʒɪ] n disculpa, excusa

> Be careful not to translate **apology** by the Spanish word apología.

apostrophe [əˈpɒstrəfɪ] n apóstrofo

appal [əˈpɔːl] (us **appall**) vt horrorizar, espantar; **appalling** adj espantoso; (awful) pésimo

apparatus [æpəˈreɪtəs] n (equipment) equipo; (organization) aparato; (in gymnasium) aparatos mpl

apparent [əˈpærənt] adj aparente; (obvious) evidente; **apparently** adv por lo visto, al parecer

appeal [əˈpiːl] vi (Law) apelar ▷ n (Law) apelación f; (request) llamamiento; (plea) petición f; (charm) atractivo; **to ~ for** reclamar; **to ~ to** (be attractive to) atraer; **it doesn't ~ to me** no me atrae, no me llama la atención; **appealing** adj (attractive) atractivo

appear [əˈpɪə*] vi aparecer, presentarse; (Law) comparecer; (publication) salir (a luz), publicarse; (seem) parecer; **to ~ on TV/in "Hamlet"** salir por la tele/hacer un papel en "Hamlet"; **it would ~ that** parecería que; **appearance** n aparición f; (look) apariencia, aspecto

appendices [əˈpɛndɪsiːz] npl of **appendix**

appendicitis [əpɛndɪˈsaɪtɪs] n apendicitis f

appendix [əˈpɛndɪks] (pl **appendices**) n apéndice m

appetite [ˈæpɪtaɪt] n apetito; (fig) deseo, anhelo

appetizer [ˈæpɪtaɪzə*] n (drink) aperitivo; (food) tapas fpl (SP)

applaud [əˈplɔːd] vt, vi aplaudir

applause [əˈplɔːz] n aplausos mpl

apple [ˈæpl] n manzana; **apple pie** n pastel m de manzana, pay m de manzana (LAM)

appliance [əˈplaɪəns] n aparato

applicable [əˈplɪkəbl] adj (relevant): **to be ~ (to)** referirse (a)

applicant [ˈæplɪkənt] n candidato/a; solicitante mf

application [æplɪˈkeɪʃən] n aplicación f; (for a job etc) solicitud f, petición f; **application form** n solicitud f

apply [əˈplaɪ] vt (paint etc) poner; (law etc: put into practice) poner en vigor ▷ vi: **to ~ to** (ask) dirigirse a; (be applicable) ser aplicable a; **to ~ for** (permit, grant, job)

solicitar; **to ~ o.s. to** aplicarse a, dedicarse a
appoint [ə'pɔɪnt] vt (to post) nombrar a
> ▌ Be careful not to translate **appoint** by the
> Spanish word apuntar.

appointment n (with client) cita; (act)
nombramiento; (post) puesto; (at hairdresser
etc): **to have an appointment** tener hora;
to make an appointment (with sb) citarse
(con algn)
appraisal [ə'preɪzl] n valoración f
appreciate [ə'pri:ʃɪeɪt] vt apreciar,
tener en mucho; (be grateful for) agradecer;
(be aware) comprender ▷ vi (Comm)
aumentar(se) en valor; **appreciation**
[-'eɪʃən] n apreciación f; (gratitude)
reconocimiento, agradecimiento; (Comm)
aumento en valor
apprehension [æprɪ'hɛnʃən] n (fear)
aprensión f
apprehensive [æprɪ'hɛnsɪv] adj
aprensivo
apprentice [ə'prɛntɪs] n aprendiz(a) m/f
approach [ə'prəʊtʃ] vi acercarse
▷ vt acercarse a; (ask, apply to) dirigirse
a; (situation, problem) abordar ▷ n
acercamiento; (access) acceso; (to problem,
situation): **~ (to)** actitud f (ante)
appropriate [adj ə'prəʊprɪɪt,
vb ə'prəʊprɪeɪt] adj apropiado,
conveniente ▷ vt (take) apropiarse de
approval [ə'pru:vəl] n aprobación f, visto
bueno; (permission) consentimiento; **on ~**
(Comm) a prueba
approve [ə'pru:v] vt aprobar; **approve of**
vt fus (thing) aprobar; (person): **they don't
approve of her** (ella) no les parece bien
approximate [ə'prɒksɪmɪt] adj
aproximado; **approximately** adv
aproximadamente, más o menos
Apr. abbr (=April) abr
apricot ['eɪprɪkɒt] n albaricoque m,
chabacano (MEX), damasco (RPL)
April ['eɪprəl] n abril m; **April Fools' Day** n
el primero de abril, ≈ día m de los Inocentes
(28 December)
apron ['eɪprən] n delantal m
apt [æpt] adj acertado, apropiado;
(likely): **~ to do** propenso a hacer
aquarium [ə'kwɛərɪəm] n acuario
Aquarius [ə'kwɛərɪəs] n Acuario
Arab ['ærəb] adj, n árabe mf
Arabia [ə'reɪbɪə] n Arabia; **Arabian**
adj árabe; **Arabic** ['ærəbɪk] adj árabe;
(numerals) arábigo ▷ n árabe m
arbitrary ['ɑ:bɪtrərɪ] adj arbitrario
arbitration [ɑ:bɪ'treɪʃən] n arbitraje m
arc [ɑ:k] n arco
arcade [ɑ:'keɪd] n (round a square)

soportales mpl; (shopping mall) galería
comercial
arch [ɑ:tʃ] n arco; (of foot) arco del pie ▷ vt
arquear
archaeology [ɑ:kɪ'ɔlədʒɪ] (US **archeology**)
n arqueología
archbishop [ɑ:tʃ'bɪʃəp] n arzobispo
archeology [ɑ:kɪ'ɔlədʒɪ] (US) =
archaeology
architect ['ɑ:kɪtɛkt] n arquitecto/a;
architectural [ɑ:kɪ'tɛktʃərəl] adj
arquitectónico; **architecture** n
arquitectura
archive ['ɑ:kaɪv] n (often pl: also Comput)
archivo
Arctic ['ɑ:ktɪk] adj ártico ▷ n: **the ~** el
Ártico
are [ɑ:*] vb see **be**
area ['ɛərɪə] n área, región f; (part of
place) zona; (Math etc) área, superficie f; (in
room: e.g. dining area) parte f; (of knowledge,
experience) campo; **area code** (US) n (Tel)
prefijo
arena [ə'ri:nə] n estadio; (of circus) pista
aren't [ɑ:nt] = **are not**
Argentina [ɑ:dʒən'ti:nə] n Argentina;
Argentinian [-'tɪnɪən] adj, n argentino/a
m/f
arguably ['ɑ:gjuəblɪ] adv posiblemente
argue ['ɑ:gju:] vi (quarrel) discutir,
pelearse; (reason) razonar, argumentar; **to ~
that** sostener que
argument ['ɑ:gjumənt] n discusión f,
pelea; (reasons) argumento
Aries ['ɛərɪz] n Aries m
arise [ə'raɪz] (pt **arose**, pp **arisen**) vi surgir,
presentarse
arithmetic [ə'rɪθmətɪk] n aritmética
arm [ɑ:m] n brazo ▷ vt armar; **arms**
npl armas fpl; **~ in ~** cogidos del brazo;
armchair ['ɑ:mtʃɛə*] n sillón m, butaca
armed [ɑ:md] adj armado; **armed
robbery** n robo a mano armada
armour ['ɑ:mə*] (US **armor**) n armadura;
(Mil: tanks) blindaje m
armpit ['ɑ:mpɪt] n sobaco, axila
armrest ['ɑ:mrɛst] n apoyabrazos m inv
army ['ɑ:mɪ] n ejército; (fig) multitud f
A road n (BRIT) ≈ carretera f nacional
aroma [ə'rəʊmə] n aroma m, fragancia;
aromatherapy n aromaterapia
arose [ə'rəʊz] pt of **arise**
around [ə'raʊnd] adv alrededor; (in the
area): **there is no one else ~** no hay nadie
más por aquí ▷ prep alrededor de
arouse [ə'raʊz] vt despertar; (anger)
provocar
arrange [ə'reɪndʒ] vt arreglar, ordenar;

(*organize*) organizar; **to ~ to do sth** quedar en hacer algo; **arrangement** n arreglo; (*agreement*) acuerdo; **arrangements** npl (*preparations*) preparativos mpl

array [ə'reɪ] n: **~ of** (*things*) serie f de; (*people*) conjunto de

arrears [ə'rɪəz] npl atrasos mpl; **to be in ~ with one's rent** estar retrasado en el pago del alquiler

arrest [ə'rɛst] vt detener; (*sb's attention*) llamar ▷ n detención f; **under ~** detenido

arrival [ə'raɪvəl] n llegada; **new ~** recién llegado/a; (*baby*) recién nacido

arrive [ə'raɪv] vi llegar; (*baby*) nacer; **arrive at** vt fus (*decision, solution*) llegar a

arrogance ['ærəgəns] n arrogancia, prepotencia (LAM)

arrogant ['ærəgənt] adj arrogante

arrow ['ærəʊ] n flecha

arse [ɑːs] (BRIT: inf!) n culo, trasero

arson ['ɑːsn] n incendio premeditado

art [ɑːt] n arte m; (*skill*) destreza; **art college** n escuela f de Bellas Artes

artery ['ɑːtərɪ] n arteria

art gallery n pinacoteca; (*saleroom*) galería de arte

arthritis [ɑː'θraɪtɪs] n artritis f

artichoke ['ɑːtɪtʃəʊk] n alcachofa; **Jerusalem ~** aguaturma

article ['ɑːtɪkl] n artículo

articulate [adj ɑː'tɪkjulɪt, vb ɑː'tɪkjuleɪt] adj claro, bien expresado ▷ vt expresar

artificial [ɑːtɪ'fɪʃəl] adj artificial; (*affected*) afectado

artist ['ɑːtɪst] n artista mf; (Mus) intérprete mf; **artistic** [ɑː'tɪstɪk] adj artístico

art school n escuela de bellas artes

○ **KEYWORD**

as [æz] conj **1** (*referring to time*) cuando, mientras; a medida que; **as the years went by** con el paso de los años; **he came in as I was leaving** entró cuando me marchaba; **as from tomorrow** desde or a partir de mañana

2 (*in comparisons*): **as big as** tan grande como; **twice as big as** el doble de grande que; **as much money/many books as** tanto dinero/tantos libros como; **as soon as** en cuanto

3 (*since, because*) como, ya que; **he left early as he had to be home by 10** se fue temprano ya que tenía que estar en casa a las 10

4 (*referring to manner, way*): **do as you wish** haz lo que quieras; **as she said** como dijo;

he gave it to me as a present me lo dio de regalo

5 (*in the capacity of*): **he works as a barman** trabaja de barman; **as chairman of the company, he ...** como presidente de la compañía ...

6 (*concerning*): **as for** or **to that** por or en lo que respecta a eso

7: **as if** or **though** como si; **he looked as if he was ill** parecía como si estuviera enfermo, tenía aspecto de enfermo; *see also* **long; such; well**

a.s.a.p. abbr (= *as soon as possible*) cuanto antes

asbestos [æz'bɛstəs] n asbesto, amianto

ascent [ə'sɛnt] n subida; (*slope*) cuesta, pendiente f

ash [æʃ] n ceniza; (*tree*) fresno

ashamed [ə'ʃeɪmd] adj avergonzado, apenado (LAM); **to be ~ of** avergonzarse de

ashore [ə'ʃɔː*] adv en tierra; (*swim etc*) a tierra

ashtray ['æʃtreɪ] n cenicero

Ash Wednesday n miércoles m de Ceniza

Asia ['eɪʃə] n Asia; **Asian** adj, n asiático/a m/f

aside [ə'saɪd] adv a un lado ▷ n aparte m

ask [ɑːsk] vt (*question*) preguntar; (*invite*) invitar; **to ~ sb sth/to do sth** preguntar algo a algn/pedir a algn que haga algo; **to ~ sb about sth** preguntar algo a algn; **to ~ (sb) a question** hacer una pregunta (a algn); **to ~ sb out to dinner** invitar a cenar a algn; **ask for** vt fus pedir; (*trouble*) buscar

asleep [ə'sliːp] adj dormido; **to fall ~** dormirse, quedarse dormido

asparagus [əs'pærəgəs] n (*plant*) espárrago; (*food*) espárragos mpl

aspect ['æspɛkt] n aspecto, apariencia; (*direction in which a building etc faces*) orientación f

aspirations [æspə'reɪʃənz] npl aspiraciones fpl; (*ambition*) ambición f

aspire [əs'paɪə*] vi: **to ~ to** aspirar a, ambicionar

aspirin ['æsprɪn] n aspirina

ass [æs] n asno, burro; (inf: idiot) imbécil mf; (US: inf!) culo, trasero

assassin [ə'sæsɪn] n asesino/a; **assassinate** vt asesinar

assault [ə'sɔːlt] n asalto; (Law) agresión f ▷ vt asaltar, atacar; (*sexually*) violar

assemble [ə'sɛmbl] vt reunir, juntar; (Tech) montar ▷ vi reunirse, juntarse

assembly [ə'sɛmblɪ] n reunión f, asamblea; (*parliament*) parlamento; (*construction*) montaje m

assert [ə'sə:t] vt afirmar; (authority) hacer valer; **assertion** [-ʃən] n afirmación f

assess [ə'ses] vt valorar, calcular; (tax, damages) fijar; (for tax) gravar; **assessment** n valoración f; (for tax) gravamen m

asset ['æset] n ventaja; **assets** npl (Comm) activo; (property, funds) fondos mpl

assign [ə'saɪn] vt: **to ~ (to)** (date) fijar (para); (task) asignar (a); (resources) destinar (a); **assignment** n tarea

assist [ə'sɪst] vt ayudar; **assistance** n ayuda, auxilio; **assistant** n ayudante mf; (BRIT: also: **shop assistant**) dependiente/a m/f

associate [adj, n ə'səʊʃiɪt, vb ə'səʊʃieɪt] adj asociado ▷ n (at work) colega mf ▷ vt asociar; (ideas) relacionar ▷ vi: **to ~ with sb** tratar con algn

association [əsəʊsɪ'eɪʃən] n asociación f

assorted [ə'sɔ:tɪd] adj surtido, variado

assortment [ə'sɔ:tmənt] n (of shapes, colours) surtido; (of books) colección f; (of people) mezcla

assume [ə'sju:m] vt suponer; (responsibilities) asumir; (attitude) adoptar, tomar

assumption [ə'sʌmpʃən] n suposición f, presunción f; (of power etc) toma

assurance [ə'ʃʊərəns] n garantía, promesa; (confidence) confianza, aplomo; (insurance) seguro

assure [ə'ʃʊə*] vt asegurar

asterisk ['æstərɪsk] n asterisco

asthma ['æsmə] n asma

astonish [ə'stɒnɪʃ] vt asombrar, pasmar; **astonished** adj estupefacto, pasmado; **to be astonished (at)** asombrarse (de); **astonishing** adj asombroso, pasmoso; **I find it astonishing that …** me asombra or pasma que …; **astonishment** n asombro, sorpresa

astound [ə'staʊnd] vt asombrar, pasmar

astray [ə'streɪ] adv: **to go ~** extraviarse; **to lead ~** (morally) llevar por mal camino

astrology [æs'trɒlədʒɪ] n astrología

astronaut ['æstrənɔ:t] n astronauta mf

astronomer [əs'trɒnəmə*] n astrónomo/a

astronomical [æstrə'nɒmɪkəl] adj astronómico

astronomy [æs'trɒnəmɪ] n astronomía

astute [əs'tju:t] adj astuto

asylum [ə'saɪləm] n (refuge) asilo; (mental hospital) manicomio

○ **KEYWORD**

at [æt] prep **1** (referring to position) en; (direction) a; **at the top** en lo alto; **at home/school** en casa/la escuela; **to look at sth/sb** mirar algo/a algn

2 (referring to time): **at 4 o'clock** a las 4; **at night** por la noche; **at Christmas** en Navidad; **at times** a veces

3 (referring to rates, speed etc): **at £1 a kilo** a una libra el kilo; **two at a time** de dos en dos; **at 50 km/h** a 50 km/h

4 (referring to manner): **at a stroke** de un golpe; **at peace** en paz

5 (referring to activity): **to be at work** estar trabajando; (in the office etc) estar en el trabajo; **to play at cowboys** jugar a los vaqueros; **to be good at sth** ser bueno en algo

6 (referring to cause): **shocked/surprised/annoyed at sth** asombrado/sorprendido/fastidiado por algo; **I went at his suggestion** fui a instancias suyas

7 (symbol) arroba

ate [eɪt] pt of **eat**

atheist ['eɪθɪɪst] n ateo/a

Athens ['æθɪnz] n Atenas

athlete ['æθli:t] n atleta mf

athletic [æθ'lɛtɪk] adj atlético; **athletics** n atletismo

Atlantic [ət'læntɪk] adj atlántico ▷ n: **the ~ (Ocean)** el (Océano) Atlántico

atlas ['ætləs] n atlas m inv

A.T.M. n abbr (= automated telling machine) cajero automático

atmosphere ['ætməsfɪə*] n atmósfera; (of place) ambiente m

atom ['ætəm] n átomo; **atomic** [ə'tɒmɪk] adj atómico; **atom(ic) bomb** n bomba atómica

A to Z® n (map) callejero

atrocity [ə'trɒsɪtɪ] n atrocidad f

attach [ə'tætʃ] vt (fasten) atar; (join) unir, sujetar; (document, letter) adjuntar; (importance etc) dar, conceder; **to be ~ed to sb/sth** (to like) tener cariño a algn/algo; **attachment** n (tool) accesorio; (Comput) archivo, documento adjunto; (love): **attachment (to)** apego (a)

attack [ə'tæk] vt (Mil) atacar; (criminal) agredir, asaltar; (criticize) criticar; (task) emprender ▷ n ataque m, asalto; (on sb's life) atentado; (fig: criticism) crítica; (of illness) ataque m; **heart ~** infarto (de miocardio); **attacker** n agresor(a) m/f, asaltante mf

attain [ə'teɪn] vt (also: **~ to**) alcanzar; (achieve) lograr, conseguir

attempt [ə'tempt] n tentativa, intento; (attack) atentado ▷ vt intentar

attend [ə'tend] vt asistir a; (patient)

atender; **attend to** *vt fus* ocuparse de; (*customer, patient*) atender a; **attendance** *n* asistencia, presencia; (*people present*) concurrencia; **attendant** *n* ayudante *mf*; (*in garage etc*) encargado/a ▷ *adj* (*dangers*) concomitante

attention [ə'tɛnʃən] *n* atención *f*; (*care*) atenciones *fpl* ▷ *excl* (*Mil*) ¡firme(s)!; **for the ~ of...** (*Admin*) atención...

attic ['ætɪk] *n* desván *m*

attitude ['ætɪtjuːd] *n* actitud *f*; (*disposition*) disposición *f*

attorney [ə'təːnɪ] *n* (*lawyer*) abogado/a; **Attorney General** *n* (*BRIT*) ≈ Presidente *m* del Consejo del Poder Judicial (*SP*); (*US*) ≈ ministro de Justicia

attract [ə'trækt] *vt* atraer; (*sb's attention*) llamar; **attraction** [ə'trækʃən] *n* encanto; (*gen pl: amusements*) diversiones *fpl*; (*Physics*) atracción *f*; (*fig: towards sb, sth*) atractivo; **attractive** *adj* guapo; (*interesting*) atrayente

attribute [*n* 'ætrɪbjuːt, *vb* ə'trɪbjuːt] *n* atributo ▷ *vt*: **to ~ sth to** atribuir algo a

aubergine ['əubəʒiːn] (*BRIT*) *n* berenjena; (*colour*) morado

auburn ['ɔːbən] *adj* color castaño rojizo

auction ['ɔːkʃən] *n* (*also*: **sale by ~**) subasta ▷ *vt* subastar

audible ['ɔːdɪbl] *adj* audible, que se puede oír

audience ['ɔːdɪəns] *n* público; (*Radio*) radioescuchas *mpl*; (*TV*) telespectadores *mpl*; (*interview*) audiencia

audit ['ɔːdɪt] *vt* revisar, intervenir

audition [ɔː'dɪʃən] *n* audición *f*

auditor ['ɔːdɪtə*] *n* interventor(a) *m/f*, censor(a) *m/f* de cuentas

auditorium [ɔːdɪ'tɔːrɪəm] *n* auditorio

Aug. *abbr* (= *August*) ag

August ['ɔːgəst] *n* agosto

aunt [ɑːnt] *n* tía; **auntie** *n diminutive of* **aunt**; **aunty** *n diminutive of* **aunt**

au pair ['əu'pɛə*] *n* (*also*: **~ girl**) (chica) au pair *f*

aura ['ɔːrə] *n* aura; (*atmosphere*) ambiente *m*

austerity [ɔ'stɛrɪtɪ] *n* austeridad *f*

Australia [ɔs'treɪlɪə] *n* Australia; **Australian** *adj, n* australiano/a *m/f*

Austria ['ɔstrɪə] *n* Austria; **Austrian** *adj, n* austríaco/a *m/f*

authentic [ɔː'θɛntɪk] *adj* auténtico

author ['ɔːθə*] *n* autor(a) *m/f*

authority [ɔː'θɔrɪtɪ] *n* autoridad *f*; (*official permission*) autorización *f*; **the authorities** *npl* las autoridades

authorize ['ɔːθəraɪz] *vt* autorizar

auto ['ɔːtəu] (*US*) *n* coche *m* (*SP*), carro (*LAM*), automóvil *m*

auto: autobiography [ɔːtəbaɪ'ɔgrəfɪ] *n* autobiografía; **autograph** ['ɔːtəgrɑːf] *n* autógrafo ▷ *vt* (*photo etc*) dedicar; (*programme*) firmar; **automatic** [ɔːtə'mætɪk] *adj* automático ▷ *n* (*gun*) pistola automática; (*car*) coche *m* automático; **automatically** *adv* automáticamente; **automobile** ['ɔːtəməbiːl] (*US*) *n* coche *m* (*SP*), carro (*LAM*), automóvil *m*; **autonomous** [ɔː'tɔnəməs] *adj* autónomo; **autonomy** [ɔː'tɔnəmɪ] *n* autonomía

autumn ['ɔːtəm] *n* otoño

auxiliary [ɔːg'zɪlɪərɪ] *adj, n* auxiliar *mf*

avail [ə'veɪl] *vt*: **to ~ o.s. of** aprovechar(se) de ▷ *n*: **to no ~** en vano, sin resultado

availability [əveɪlə'bɪlɪtɪ] *n* disponibilidad *f*

available [ə'veɪləbl] *adj* disponible; (*unoccupied*) libre; (*person: unattached*) soltero y sin compromiso

avalanche ['ævəlɑːnʃ] *n* alud *m*, avalancha

Ave. *abbr* = **avenue**

avenue ['ævənjuː] *n* avenida; (*fig*) camino

average ['ævərɪdʒ] *n* promedio, término medio ▷ *adj* medio, de término medio; (*ordinary*) regular, corriente ▷ *vt* sacar un promedio de; **on ~** por regla general

avert [ə'vəːt] *vt* prevenir; (*blow*) desviar; (*one's eyes*) apartar

avid ['ævɪd] *adj* ávido

avocado [ævə'kɑːdəu] *n* (*also BRIT*: **~ pear**) aguacate *m*, palta (*SC*)

avoid [ə'vɔɪd] *vt* evitar, eludir

await [ə'weɪt] *vt* esperar, aguardar

awake [ə'weɪk] (*pt* awoke, *pp* awoken *or* awaked) *adj* despierto ▷ *vt* despertar ▷ *vi* despertarse; **to be ~** estar despierto

award [ə'wɔːd] *n* premio; (*Law: damages*) indemnización *f* ▷ *vt* otorgar, conceder; (*Law: damages*) adjudicar

aware [ə'wɛə*] *adj*: **~ (of)** consciente (de); **to become ~ of/that** (*realize*) darse cuenta de/de que; (*learn*) enterarse de/de que; **awareness** *n* conciencia; (*knowledge*) conocimiento

away [ə'weɪ] *adv* fuera; (*movement*): **she went ~** se marchó; **far ~** lejos; **two kilometres ~** a dos kilómetros de distancia; **two hours ~ by car** a dos horas en coche; **the holiday was two weeks ~** faltaban dos semanas para las vacaciones; **he's ~ for a week** estará ausente una semana; **to take ~ (from)** quitar (a); (*subtract*) substraer (de); **to work/pedal ~** seguir

trabajando/pedaleando; **to fade ~** (*colour*)
desvanecerse; (*sound*) apagarse
awe [ɔ:] *n* admiración *f* respetuosa;
 awesome ['ɔ:səm] (*US*) *adj* (*excellent*)
 formidable
awful ['ɔ:fəl] *adj* horroroso; (*quantity*): **an
 ~ lot (of)** cantidad (de); **awfully** *adv* (*very*)
 terriblemente
awkward ['ɔ:kwəd] *adj* desmañado,
 torpe; (*shape*) incómodo; (*embarrassing*)
 delicado, difícil
awoke [ə'wəuk] *pt of* **awake**
awoken [ə'wəukən] *pp of* **awake**
axe [æks] (*US* **ax**) *n* hacha ▷ *vt* (*project*)
 cortar; (*jobs*) reducir
axle ['æksl] *n* eje *m*, árbol *m*
ay(e) [aɪ] *excl* sí
azalea [ə'zeɪlɪə] *n* azalea

B [bi:] *n* (*Mus*) si *m*
B.A. *abbr* = **Bachelor of Arts**
baby ['beɪbɪ] *n* bebé *mf*; (*US: inf: darling*)
 mi amor; **baby carriage** (*US*) *n* cochecito;
 baby-sit *vi* hacer de canguro; **baby-sitter**
 n canguro/a; **baby wipe** *n* toallita húmeda
 (*para bebés*)
bachelor ['bætʃələ*] *n* soltero; **B~ of Arts/
 Science** licenciado/a en Filosofía y Letras/
 Ciencias
back [bæk] *n* (*of person*) espalda; (*of
 animal*) lomo; (*of hand*) dorso; (*as opposed
 to front*) parte *f* de atrás; (*of chair*) respaldo;
 (*of page*) reverso; (*of book*) final *m*; (*Football*)
 defensa *m*; (*of crowd*): **the ones at the ~**
 los del fondo ▷ *vt* (*candidate: also: ~ up*)
 respaldar, apoyar; (*horse: at races*) apostar
 a; (*car*) dar marcha atrás a *or* con ▷ *vi* (*car
 etc*) ir (*or* salir *or* entrar) marcha atrás
 ▷ *adj* (*payment, rent*) atrasado; (*seats,
 wheels*) de atrás ▷ *adv* (*not forward*) (*hacia*)
 atrás; (*returned*): **he's ~** está de vuelta,
 ha vuelto; **he ran ~** volvió corriendo;
 (*restitution*): **throw the ball ~** devuelve la
 pelota; **can I have it ~?** ¿me lo devuelve?;
 (*again*): **he called ~** llamó de nuevo; **back
 down** *vi* echarse atrás; **back out** *vi* (*of
 promise*) volverse atrás; **back up** *vt* (*person*)
 apoyar, respaldar; (*theory*) defender;
 (*Comput*) hacer una copia preventiva
 or de reserva; **backache** *n* dolor *m* de
 espalda; **backbencher** (*BRIT*) *n* miembro del
 parlamento sin cargo relevante; **backbone** *n*
 columna vertebral; **back door** *n* puerta
 f trasera; **backfire** *vi* (*Aut*) petardear;
 (*plans*) fallar, salir mal; **backgammon** *n*
 backgammon *m*; **background** *n* fondo; (*of
 events*) antecedentes *mpl*; (*basic knowledge*)
 bases *fpl*; (*experience*) conocimientos *mpl*,
 educación *f*; **family background** origen *m*,
 antecedentes *mpl*; **backing** *n* (*fig*) apoyo,

respaldo; **backlog** n: **backlog of work** trabajo atrasado; **backpack** n mochila; **backpacker** n mochilero/a; **backslash** n pleca, barra inversa; **backstage** adv entre bastidores; **backstroke** n espalda; **backup** adj suplementario; (Comput) de reserva ▷ n (support) apoyo; (also: **backup file**) copia preventiva or de reserva; **backward** adj (person, country) atrasado; **backwards** adv hacia atrás; (read a list) al revés; (fall) de espaldas; **backyard** n traspatio

bacon ['beɪkən] n tocino, beicon m

bacteria [bæk'tɪərɪə] npl bacterias fpl

bad [bæd] adj malo; (mistake, accident) grave; (food) podrido, pasado; **his ~ leg** su pierna lisiada; **to go ~** (food) pasarse

badge [bædʒ] n insignia; (policeman's) chapa, placa

badger ['bædʒə*] n tejón m

badly ['bædlɪ] adv mal; **to reflect ~ on sb** influir negativamente en la reputación de algn; **~ wounded** gravemente herido; **he needs it ~** le hace gran falta; **to be ~ off (for money)** andar mal de dinero

bad-mannered ['bæd'mænəd] adj mal educado

badminton ['bædmɪntən] n bádminton m

bad-tempered ['bæd'tempəd] adj de mal genio or carácter; (temporarily) de mal humor

bag [bæg] n bolsa; (handbag) bolso; (satchel) mochila; (case) maleta; **~s of** (inf) un montón de; **baggage** n equipaje m; **baggage allowance** n límite m de equipaje; **baggage reclaim** n recogida de equipajes; **baggy** adj amplio; **bagpipes** npl gaita

bail [beɪl] n fianza ▷ vt (prisoner: gen: grant bail to) poner en libertad bajo fianza; (boat: also: **~ out**) achicar; **on ~** (prisoner) bajo fianza; **to ~ sb out** obtener la libertad de algn bajo fianza

bait [beɪt] n cebo ▷ vt poner cebo en; (tease) tomar el pelo a

bake [beɪk] vt cocer (al horno) ▷ vi cocerse; **baked beans** npl judías fpl en salsa de tomate; **baked potato** n patata al horno; **baker** n panadero; **bakery** n panadería; (for cakes) pastelería; **baking** n (act) amasar m; (batch) hornada; **baking powder** n levadura (en polvo)

balance ['bæləns] n equilibrio; (Comm: sum) balance m; (remainder) resto; (scales) balanza ▷ vt equilibrar; (budget) nivelar; (account) saldar; (make equal) equilibrar; **~ of trade/payments** balanza de comercio/pagos; **balanced** adj (personality, diet) equilibrado; (report) objetivo; **balance sheet** n balance m

balcony ['bælkənɪ] n (open) balcón m; (closed) galería; (in theatre) anfiteatro

bald [bɔːld] adj calvo; (tyre) liso

Balearics [bælɪ'ærɪks] npl: **the ~** las Baleares

ball [bɔːl] n pelota; (football) balón m; (of wool, string) ovillo; (dance) baile m; **to play ~** (fig) cooperar

ballerina [bælə'riːnə] n bailarina

ballet ['bæleɪ] n ballet m; **ballet dancer** n bailarín/ina m/f

balloon [bə'luːn] n globo

ballot ['bælət] n votación f

ballpoint (pen) ['bɔːlpɔɪnt-] n bolígrafo

ballroom ['bɔːlrum] n salón m de baile

Baltic ['bɔːltɪk] n: **the ~ (Sea)** el (Mar) Báltico

bamboo [bæm'buː] n bambú m

ban [bæn] n prohibición f, proscripción f ▷ vt prohibir, proscribir

banana [bə'nɑːnə] n plátano, banana (LAM), banano (CAM)

band [bænd] n grupo; (strip) faja, tira; (stripe) lista; (Mus: jazz) orquesta; (: rock) grupo; (Mil) banda

bandage ['bændɪdʒ] n venda, vendaje m ▷ vt vendar

Band-Aid® ['bændeɪd] (US) n tirita

bandit ['bændɪt] n bandido

bang [bæŋ] n (of gun, exhaust) estallido, detonación f; (of door) portazo; (blow) golpe m ▷ vt (door) cerrar de golpe; (one's head) golpear ▷ vi estallar; (door) cerrar de golpe

Bangladesh [bɑːŋglə'deʃ] n Bangladesh m

bangle ['bæŋgl] n brazalete m, ajorca

bangs [bæŋz] (US) npl flequillo

banish ['bænɪʃ] vt desterrar

banister(s) ['bænɪstə(z)] n(pl) barandilla, pasamanos m inv

banjo ['bændʒəu] (pl **~es** or **~s**) n banjo

bank [bæŋk] n (Comm) banco; (of river, lake) ribera, orilla; (of earth) terraplén m ▷ vi (Aviat) ladearse; **bank on** vt fus contar con; **bank account** n cuenta de banco; **bank balance** n saldo; **bank card** n tarjeta bancaria; **bank charges** npl comisión fsg; **banker** n banquero; **bank holiday** n (BRIT) día m festivo or de fiesta; **banking** n banca; **bank manager** n director(a) m/f (de sucursal) de banco; **banknote** n billete m de banco

● **BANK HOLIDAY**

El término **bank holiday** se aplica en el Reino Unido a todo día festivo oficial en el que cierran bancos y comercios.

bankrupt | 234

- Los más importantes son en Navidad,
- Semana Santa, finales de mayo y
- finales de agosto y, al contrario que
- en los países de tradición católica, no
- coinciden necesariamente con una
- celebración religiosa.

bankrupt ['bæŋkrʌpt] *adj* quebrado, insolvente; **to go ~** hacer bancarrota; **to be ~** estar en quiebra; **bankruptcy** *n* quiebra
bank statement *n* balance *m* or detalle *m* de cuenta
banner ['bænə*] *n* pancarta
bannister(s) ['bænɪstə(z)] *n(pl)* = **banister(s)**
banquet ['bæŋkwɪt] *n* banquete *m*
baptism ['bæptɪzəm] *n* bautismo; (*act*) bautizo
baptize [bæp'taɪz] *vt* bautizar
bar [bɑ:*] *n* (*pub*) bar *m*; (*counter*) mostrador *m*; (*rod*) barra; (*of window, cage*) reja; (*of soap*) pastilla; (*of chocolate*) tableta; (*fig: hindrance*) obstáculo; (*prohibition*) proscripción *f*; (*Mus*) barra ▷ *vt* (*road*) obstruir; (*person*) excluir; (*activity*) prohibir; **the B~** (*Law*) la abogacía; **behind ~s** entre rejas; **~ none** sin excepción
barbaric [bɑ:'bærɪk] *adj* bárbaro
barbecue ['bɑ:bɪkju:] *n* barbacoa
barbed wire ['bɑ:bd-] *n* alambre *m* de púas
barber ['bɑ:bə*] *n* peluquero, barbero; **barber's (shop)** (*US* **barber (shop)**) *n* peluquería
bar code *n* código de barras
bare [bɛə*] *adj* desnudo; (*trees*) sin hojas; (*necessities etc*) básico ▷ *vt* desnudar; (*teeth*) enseñar; **barefoot** *adj, adv* descalzo; **barely** *adv* apenas
bargain ['bɑ:gɪn] *n* pacto, negocio; (*good buy*) ganga ▷ *vi* negociar; (*haggle*) regatear; **into the ~** además, por añadidura; **bargain for** *vt fus*: **he got more than he bargained for** le resultó peor de lo que esperaba
barge [bɑ:dʒ] *n* barcaza; **barge in** *vi* irrumpir; (*interrupt: conversation*) interrumpir
bark [bɑ:k] *n* (*of tree*) corteza; (*of dog*) ladrido ▷ *vi* ladrar
barley ['bɑ:lɪ] *n* cebada
barmaid ['bɑ:meɪd] *n* camarera
barman ['bɑ:mən] (*irreg*) *n* camarero, barman *m*
barn [bɑ:n] *n* granero
barometer [bə'rɔmɪtə*] *n* barómetro
baron ['bærən] *n* barón *m*; (*press baron etc*) magnate *m*; **baroness** *n* baronesa
barracks ['bærəks] *npl* cuartel *m*
barrage ['bærɑ:ʒ] *n* (*Mil*) descarga,

bombardeo; (*dam*) presa; (*of criticism*) lluvia, aluvión *m*
barrel ['bærəl] *n* barril *m*; (*of gun*) cañón *m*
barren ['bærən] *adj* estéril
barrette [bə'ret] (*US*) *n* pasador *m* (*LAM, SP*), broche *m* (*MEX*)
barricade [bærɪ'keɪd] *n* barricada
barrier ['bærɪə*] *n* barrera
barring ['bɑ:rɪŋ] *prep* excepto, salvo
barrister ['bærɪstə*] (*BRIT*) *n* abogado/a
barrow ['bærəu] *n* (*cart*) carretilla (de mano)
bartender ['bɑ:tendə*] (*US*) *n* camarero, barman *m*
base [beɪs] *n* base *f* ▷ *vt*: **to ~ sth on** basar *or* fundar algo en ▷ *adj* bajo, infame
baseball ['beɪsbɔ:l] *n* béisbol *m*; **baseball cap** *n* gorra *f* de béisbol
basement ['beɪsmənt] *n* sótano
bases¹ ['beɪsi:z] *npl of* **basis**
bases² ['beɪsɪz] *npl of* **base**
bash [bæʃ] (*inf*) *vt* golpear
basic ['beɪsɪk] *adj* básico; **basically** *adv* fundamentalmente, en el fondo; (*simply*) sencillamente; **basics** *npl*: **the basics** los fundamentos
basil ['bæzl] *n* albahaca
basin ['beɪsn] *n* cuenco, tazón *m*; (*Geo*) cuenca; (*also*: **wash~**) lavabo
basis ['beɪsɪs] (*pl* **bases**) *n* base *f*; **on a part-time/trial ~** a tiempo parcial/a prueba
basket ['bɑ:skɪt] *n* cesta, cesto; canasta; **basketball** *n* baloncesto
bass [beɪs] *n* (*Mus: instrument*) bajo; (*double bass*) contrabajo; (*singer*) bajo
bastard ['bɑ:stəd] *n* bastardo; (*inf!*) hijo de puta (!)
bat [bæt] *n* (*Zool*) murciélago; (*for ball games*) palo; (*BRIT: for table tennis*) pala ▷ *vt*: **he didn't ~ an eyelid** ni pestañeó
batch [bætʃ] *n* (*of bread*) hornada; (*of letters etc*) lote *m*
bath [bɑ:θ, *pl* bɑ:ðz] *n* (*action*) baño; (*bathtub*) bañera (*SP*), tina (*LAM*), bañadera (*RPL*) ▷ *vt* bañar; **to have a ~** bañarse, tomar un baño; *see also* **baths**
bathe [beɪð] *vi* bañarse ▷ *vt* (*wound*) lavar
bathing ['beɪðɪŋ] *n* el bañarse; **bathing costume** (*US* **bathing suit**) *n* traje *m* de baño
bath: bathrobe *n* (*man's*) batín *m*; (*woman's*) bata; **bathroom** *n* (cuarto de) baño; **baths** [bɑ:ðz] *npl* (*also*: **swimming baths**) piscina; **bath towel** *n* toalla de baño; **bathtub** *n* bañera
baton ['bætən] *n* (*Mus*) batuta; (*Athletics*) testigo; (*weapon*) porra

batter ['bætə*] vt maltratar; (rain etc) azotar ▷ n masa (para rebozar); **battered** adj (hat, pan) estropeado

battery ['bætərɪ] n (Aut) batería; (of torch) pila; **battery farming** n cría intensiva

battle ['bætl] n batalla; (fig) lucha ▷ vi luchar; **battlefield** n campo m de batalla

bay [beɪ] n (Geo) bahía; **B~ of Biscay** ≈ mar Cantábrico; **to hold sb at ~** mantener a algn a raya

bazaar [bə'zɑ:*] n bazar m; (fete) venta con fines benéficos

B. & B. n abbr = **bed and breakfast**; (place) pensión f; (terms) cama y desayuno

BBC n abbr (= British Broadcasting Corporation) cadena de radio y televisión estatal británica

B.C. adv abbr (= before Christ) a. de C.

○ **KEYWORD**

be [bi:] (pt **was**, **were**, pp **been**) aux vb
1 (with present participle: forming continuous tenses): **what are you doing?** ¿qué estás haciendo?, ¿qué haces?; **they're coming tomorrow** vienen mañana; **I've been waiting for you for hours** llevo horas esperándote
2 (with pp: forming passives) ser (but often replaced by active or reflexive constructions); **to be murdered** ser asesinado; **the box had been opened** habían abierto la caja; **the thief was nowhere to be seen** no se veía al ladrón por ninguna parte
3 (in tag questions): **it was fun, wasn't it?** fue divertido, ¿no? or ¿verdad?; **he's good-looking, isn't he?** es guapo, ¿no te parece?; **she's back again, is she?** entonces, ¿ha vuelto?
4 (+to +infin): **the house is to be sold** (necessity) hay que vender la casa; (future) van a vender la casa; **he's not to open it** no tiene que abrirlo ▷ vb +complement
1 (with n or num complement, but see also 3, 4, 5 and impers vb below) ser; **he's a doctor** es médico; **2 and 2 are 4** 2 y 2 son 4
2 (with adj complement: expressing permanent or inherent quality) ser; (: expressing state seen as temporary or reversible) estar; **I'm English** soy inglés/esa; **she's tall/pretty** es alta/bonita; **he's young** es joven; **be careful/good/quiet** ten cuidado/pórtate bien/cállate; **I'm tired** estoy cansado/a; **it's dirty** está sucio/a
3 (of health) estar; **how are you?** ¿cómo estás?; **he's very ill** está muy enfermo; **I'm better now** ya estoy mejor
4 (of age) tener; **how old are you?** ¿cuántos años tienes?; **I'm sixteen (years old)** tengo dieciséis años
5 (cost) costar; ser; **how much was the meal?** ¿cuánto fue or costó la comida?; **that'll be £5.75, please** son £5.75, por favor; **this shirt is £17** esta camisa cuesta £17 ▷ vi 1 (exist, occur etc) existir, haber; **the best singer that ever was** el mejor cantante que existió jamás; **is there a God?** ¿hay un Dios?, ¿existe Dios?; **be that as it may** sea como sea; **so be it** así sea
2 (referring to place) estar; **I won't be here tomorrow** no estaré aquí mañana
3 (referring to movement): **where have you been?** ¿dónde has estado? ▷ impers vb 1 (referring to time): **it's 5 o'clock** son las 5; **it's the 28th of April** estamos a 28 de abril
2 (referring to distance): **it's 10 km to the village** el pueblo está a 10 km
3 (referring to the weather): **it's too hot/cold** hace demasiado calor/frío; **it's windy today** hace viento hoy
4 (emphatic): **it's me** soy yo; **it was Maria who paid the bill** fue María la que pagó la cuenta

beach [bi:tʃ] n playa ▷ vt varar

beacon ['bi:kən] n (lighthouse) faro; (marker) guía

bead [bi:d] n cuenta; (of sweat etc) gota; **beads** npl (necklace) collar m

beak [bi:k] n pico

beam [bi:m] n (Arch) viga, travesaño; (of light) rayo, haz m de luz ▷ vi brillar; (smile) sonreír

bean [bi:n] n judía; **runner/broad ~** habichuela/haba; **coffee ~** grano de café; **beansprouts** npl brotes mpl de soja

bear [bɛə*] (pt **bore**, pp **borne**) n oso ▷ vt (weight etc) llevar; (cost) pagar; (responsibility) tener; (endure) soportar, aguantar; (children) parir, tener; (fruit) dar ▷ vi: **to ~ right/left** torcer a la derecha/izquierda

beard [bɪəd] n barba

bearer ['bɛərə*] n portador(a) m/f

bearing ['bɛərɪŋ] n porte m, comportamiento; (connection) relación f

beast [bi:st] n bestia; (inf) bruto, salvaje m

beat [bi:t] (pt **~**, pp **beaten**) n (of heart) latido; (Mus) ritmo, compás m; (of policeman) ronda ▷ vt pegar, golpear; (eggs) batir; (defeat: opponent) vencer, derrotar; (: record) sobrepasar ▷ vi latir; (drum) redoblar; (rain, wind) azotar; **off the ~en track** aislado; **to ~ it** (inf) largarse; **beat up** vt (attack) dar una paliza a; **beating** n paliza

beautiful ['bju:tɪful] adj precioso,

hermoso, bello; **beautifully** adv maravillosamente

beauty ['bjuːtɪ] n belleza; **beauty parlour** (US **beauty parlor**) n salón m de belleza; **beauty salon** n salón m de belleza; **beauty spot** n (Tourism) lugar m pintoresco

beaver ['biːvə*] n castor m

became [bɪ'keɪm] pt of **become**

because [bɪ'kɔz] conj porque; **~ of** debido a, a causa de

beckon ['bɛkən] vt (also: **~ to**) llamar con señas

become [bɪ'kʌm] (pt **became**, pp **~**) vt (suit) favorecer, sentar bien a ▷ vi (+ n) hacerse, llegar a ser; (+ adj) ponerse, volverse; **to ~ fat** engordar

bed [bɛd] n cama; (of flowers) macizo; (of coal, clay) capa; (of river) lecho; (of sea) fondo; **to go to ~** acostarse; **bed and breakfast** n (place) pensión f; (terms) cama y desayuno; **bedclothes** npl ropa de cama; **bedding** n ropa de cama; **bed linen** n (BRIT) ropa f de cama

⬤ **BED AND BREAKFAST**
⬤
⬤ Se llama **bed and breakfast** a una forma
⬤ de alojamiento, en el campo o la ciudad,
⬤ que ofrece cama y desayuno a precios
⬤ inferiores a los de un hotel. El servicio
⬤ se suele anunciar con carteles en los
⬤ que a menudo se usa únicamente la
⬤ abreviatura **B.& B.**

bed: bedroom n dormitorio; **bedside** n: **at the bedside of** a la cabecera de; **bedside lamp** n lámpara de noche; **bedside table** n mesilla de noche; **bedsit(ter)** (BRIT) n cuarto de alquiler; **bedspread** n cubrecama m, colcha; **bedtime** n hora de acostarse

bee [biː] n abeja

beech [biːtʃ] n haya

beef [biːf] n carne f de vaca; **roast ~** rosbif m; **beefburger** n hamburguesa; **Beefeater** n alabardero de la Torre de Londres

been [biːn] pp of **be**

beer [bɪə*] n cerveza; **beer garden** n (BRIT) terraza f de verano, jardín m (de un bar)

beet [biːt] (US) n (also: **red ~**) remolacha

beetle ['biːtl] n escarabajo

beetroot ['biːtruːt] (BRIT) n remolacha

before [bɪ'fɔː*] prep (of time) antes de; (of space) delante de ▷ conj antes (de) que ▷ adv antes, anteriormente; delante, adelante; **~ going** antes de marcharse; **~ she goes** antes de que se vaya; **the week ~** la semana anterior; **I've never seen it ~** no lo he visto nunca; **beforehand** adv de antemano, con anticipación

beg [bɛg] vi pedir limosna ▷ vt pedir, rogar; (entreat) suplicar; **to ~ sb to do sth** rogar a algn que haga algo; see also **pardon**

began [bɪ'gæn] pt of **begin**

beggar ['bɛgə*] n mendigo/a

begin [bɪ'gɪn] (pt **began**, pp **begun**) vt, vi empezar, comenzar; **to ~ doing** or **to do sth** empezar a hacer algo; **beginner** n principiante mf; **beginning** n principio, comienzo

begun [bɪ'gʌn] pp of **begin**

behalf [bɪ'hɑːf] n: **on ~ of** en nombre de, por; (for benefit of) en beneficio de; **on my/ his ~** por mí/él

behave [bɪ'heɪv] vi (person) portarse, comportarse; (well: also: **~ o.s.**) portarse bien; **behaviour** (US **behavior**) n comportamiento, conducta

behind [bɪ'haɪnd] prep detrás de; (supporting): **to be ~ sb** apoyar a algn ▷ adv detrás, por detrás, atrás ▷ n trasero; **to be ~ (schedule)** ir retrasado; **~ the scenes** (fig) entre bastidores

beige [beɪʒ] adj color beige

Beijing ['beɪ'dʒɪŋ] n Pekín m

being ['biːɪŋ] n ser m; (existence): **in ~** existente; **to come into ~** aparecer

belated [bɪ'leɪtɪd] adj atrasado, tardío

belch [bɛltʃ] vi eructar ▷ vt (gen: belch out: smoke etc) arrojar

Belgian ['bɛldʒən] adj, n belga mf

Belgium ['bɛldʒəm] n Bélgica

belief [bɪ'liːf] n opinión f; (faith) fe f

believe [bɪ'liːv] vt, vi creer; **to ~ in** creer en; **believer** n partidario/a; (Rel) creyente mf, fiel mf

bell [bɛl] n campana; (small) campanilla; (on door) timbre m

bellboy ['bɛlbɔɪ] (BRIT) n botones m inv

bellhop ['bɛlhɔp] (US) n = **bellboy**

bellow ['bɛləʊ] vi bramar; (person) rugir

bell pepper n (esp US) pimiento, pimentón m (LAM)

belly ['bɛlɪ] n barriga, panza; **belly button** (inf) n ombligo

belong [bɪ'lɔŋ] vi: **to ~ to** pertenecer a; (club etc) ser socio de; **this book ~s here** este libro va aquí; **belongings** npl pertenencias fpl

beloved [bɪ'lʌvɪd] adj querido/a

below [bɪ'ləʊ] prep bajo, debajo de; (less than) inferior a ▷ adv abajo, (por) debajo; **see ~** véase más abajo

belt [bɛlt] n cinturón m; (Tech) correa, cinta ▷ vt (thrash) pegar con correa; **beltway** (US)

n (*Aut*) carretera de circunvalación
bemused [bɪ'mjuːzd] *adj* perplejo
bench [bɛntʃ] *n* banco; (*BRIT Pol*): **the Government/Opposition ~es** (los asientos de) los miembros del Gobierno/ de la Oposición; **the B~** (*Law*: *judges*) magistratura
bend [bɛnd] (*pt, pp* **bent**) *vt* doblar ▷ *vi* inclinarse ▷ *n* (*BRIT*: *in road, river*) curva; (*in pipe*) codo; **bend down** *vi* inclinarse, doblarse; **bend over** *vi* inclinarse
beneath [bɪ'niːθ] *prep* bajo, debajo de; (*unworthy*) indigno de ▷ *adv* abajo, (por) debajo
beneficial [bɛnɪ'fɪʃəl] *adj* beneficioso
benefit ['bɛnɪfɪt] *n* beneficio; (*allowance of money*) subsidio ▷ *vt* beneficiar ▷ *vi*: **he'll ~ from it** le sacará provecho
benign [bɪ'naɪn] *adj* benigno; (*smile*) afable
bent [bɛnt] *pt, pp of* **bend** ▷ *n* inclinación *f* ▷ *adj*: **to be ~ on** estar empeñado en
bereaved [bɪ'riːvd] *npl*: **the ~** los íntimos de una persona afligidos por su muerte
beret ['bɛreɪ] *n* boina
Berlin [bəː'lɪn] *n* Berlín
Bermuda [bəː'mjuːdə] *n* las Bermudas
berry ['bɛrɪ] *n* baya
berth [bəːθ] *n* (*bed*) litera; (*cabin*) camarote *m*; (*for ship*) amarradero ▷ *vi* atracar, amarrar
beside [bɪ'saɪd] *prep* junto a, al lado de; **to be ~ o.s. with anger** estar fuera de sí; **that's ~ the point** eso no tiene nada que ver; **besides** *adv* además ▷ *prep* además de
best [bɛst] *adj* (el/la) mejor ▷ *adv* (lo) mejor; **the ~ part of** (*quantity*) la mayor parte de; **at ~** en el mejor de los casos; **to make the ~ of sth** sacar el mejor partido de algo; **to do one's ~** hacer todo lo posible; **to the ~ of my knowledge** que yo sepa; **to the ~ of my ability** como mejor puedo; **best-before date** *n* fecha de consumo preferente; **best man** (*irreg*) *n* padrino de boda; **bestseller** *n* éxito de librería, bestseller *m*
bet [bɛt] (*pt, pp* **~** *or* **~ted**) *n* apuesta ▷ *vt*: **to ~ money on** apostar dinero por ▷ *vi* apostar; **to ~ sb sth** apostar algo a algn
betray [bɪ'treɪ] *vt* traicionar; (*trust*) faltar a
better ['bɛtə*] *adj, adv* mejor ▷ *vt* superar ▷ *n*: **to get the ~ of sb** quedar por encima de algn; **you had ~ do it** más vale que lo hagas; **he thought ~ of it** cambió de parecer; **to get ~** (*Med*) mejorar(se)
betting ['bɛtɪŋ] *n* juego, el apostar; **betting shop** (*BRIT*) *n* agencia de apuestas
between [bɪ'twiːn] *prep* entre ▷ *adv*

(*time*) mientras tanto; (*place*) en medio
beverage ['bɛvərɪdʒ] *n* bebida
beware [bɪ'wɛə*] *vi*: **to ~ (of)** tener cuidado (con); **"~ of the dog"** "perro peligroso"
bewildered [bɪ'wɪldəd] *adj* aturdido, perplejo
beyond [bɪ'jɔnd] *prep* más allá de; (*past: understanding*) fuera de; (*after: date*) después de, más allá de; (*above*) superior a ▷ *adv* (*in space*) más allá; (*in time*) posteriormente; **~ doubt** fuera de toda duda; **~ repair** irreparable
bias ['baɪəs] *n* (*prejudice*) prejuicio, pasión *f*; (*preference*) predisposición *f*; **bias(s)ed** *adj* parcial
bib [bɪb] *n* babero
Bible ['baɪbl] *n* Biblia
bicarbonate of soda [baɪ'kɑːbənɪt-] *n* bicarbonato sódico
biceps ['baɪsɛps] *n* bíceps *m*
bicycle ['baɪsɪkl] *n* bicicleta; **bicycle pump** *n* bomba de bicicleta
bid [bɪd] (*pt* **bade** *or* **~**, *pp* **bidden** *or* **~**) *n* oferta, postura; (*in tender*) licitación *f*; (*attempt*) tentativa, conato ▷ *vi* hacer una oferta ▷ *vt* (*offer*) ofrecer; **to ~ sb good day** dar a algn los buenos días; **bidder** *n*: **the highest bidder** el mejor postor
bidet ['biːdeɪ] *n* bidet *m*
big [bɪg] *adj* grande; (*brother, sister*) mayor; **bigheaded** *adj* engreído; **big toe** *n* dedo gordo (del pie)
bike [baɪk] *n* bici *f*; **bike lane** *n* carril-bici *m*
bikini [bɪ'kiːnɪ] *n* bikini *m*
bilateral [baɪ'lætərl] *adj* (*agreement*) bilateral
bilingual [baɪ'lɪŋgwəl] *adj* bilingüe
bill [bɪl] *n* cuenta; (*invoice*) factura; (*Pol*) proyecto de ley; (*US*: *banknote*) billete *m*; (*of bird*) pico; (*of show*) programa *m*; **"post no ~s"** "prohibido fijar carteles"; **to fit** *or* **fill the ~** (*fig*) cumplir con los requisitos; **billboard** (*US*) *n* cartelera; **billfold** ['bɪlfəuld] (*US*) *n* cartera
billiards ['bɪljədz] *n* billar *m*
billion ['bɪljən] *n* (*BRIT*) billón *m* (*millón de millones*); (*US*) mil millones *mpl*
bin [bɪn] *n* (*for rubbish*) cubo *or* bote *m* (*MEX*) *or* tacho (*SC*) de la basura; (*container*) recipiente *m*
bind [baɪnd] (*pt, pp* **bound**) *vt* atar; (*book*) encuadernar; (*oblige*) obligar ▷ *n* (*inf: nuisance*) lata
binge [bɪndʒ] (*inf*) *n*: **to go on a ~** ir de juerga
bingo ['bɪŋgəu] *n* bingo *m*

binoculars [bɪˈnɔkjuləz] npl prismáticos mpl

bio... [baɪəˈ] prefix: **biochemistry** n bioquímica; **biodegradable** [baɪə udrɪˈgreɪdəbl] adj biodegradable; **biography** [baɪˈɔɡrəfɪ] n biografía; **biological** adj biológico; **biology** [baɪˈɔlədʒɪ] n biología; **biometric** [baɪəˈmɛtrɪk] adj biométrico

birch [bəːtʃ] n (tree) abedul m

bird [bəːd] n ave f, pájaro; (BRIT: inf: girl) chica, **bird flu** n gripe f aviar; **bird of prey** n ave f de presa; **birdwatching** n: **he likes to go birdwatching on Sundays** los domingos le gusta ir a ver pájaros

Biro® [ˈbaɪrəu] n boli

birth [bəːθ] n nacimiento; **to give ~ to** parir, dar a luz; **birth certificate** n partida de nacimiento; **birth control** n (policy) control m de natalidad; (methods) métodos mpl anticonceptivos; **birthday** n cumpleaños m inv ▷ cpd (cake, card etc) de cumpleaños; **birthmark** n antojo, marca de nacimiento; **birthplace** n lugar m de nacimiento

biscuit [ˈbɪskɪt] (BRIT) n galleta

bishop [ˈbɪʃəp] n obispo; (Chess) alfil m

bistro [ˈbiːstrəu] n café-bar m

bit [bɪt] pt of **bite** ▷ n trozo, pedazo, pedacito; (Comput) bit m, bitio; (for horse) freno, bocado; **a ~ of** un poco de; **a ~ mad** un poco loco; **~ by ~** poco a poco

bitch [bɪtʃ] n perra; (inf!: woman) zorra (!)

bite [baɪt] (pt **bit**, pp **bitten**) vt, vi morder; (insect etc) picar ▷ n (insect bite) picadura; (mouthful) bocado; **to ~ one's nails** comerse las uñas; **let's have a ~ (to eat)** (inf) vamos a comer algo

bitten [ˈbɪtn] pp of **bite**

bitter [ˈbɪtə*] adj amargo; (wind) cortante, penetrante; (battle) encarnizado ▷ n (BRIT: beer) cerveza típica británica a base de lúpulos

bizarre [bɪˈzɑː*] adj raro, extraño

black [blæk] adj negro; (tea, coffee) solo ▷ n color m negro; (person): **B~** negro/a ▷ vt (BRIT Industry) boicotear; **to give sb a ~ eye** ponerle a algn el ojo morado; **~ and blue** (bruised) amoratado; **to be in the ~** (bank account) estar en números negros; **black out** vi (faint) desmayarse; **blackberry** n zarzamora; **blackbird** n mirlo; **blackboard** n pizarra; **black coffee** n café m solo; **blackcurrant** n grosella negra; **black ice** n hielo invisible en la carretera; **blackmail** n chantaje m ▷ vt chantajear; **black market** n mercado negro; **blackout** n (Mil) oscurecimiento; (power cut) apagón

m; (TV, Radio) interrupción f de programas; (fainting) desvanecimiento; **black pepper** n pimienta f negra; **black pudding** n morcilla; **Black Sea** n: **the Black Sea** el Mar Negro

bladder [ˈblædə*] n vejiga

blade [bleɪd] n hoja; (of propeller) paleta; **a ~ of grass** una brizna de hierba

blame [bleɪm] n culpa ▷ vt: **to ~ sb for sth** echar a algn la culpa de algo; **to be to ~ (for)** tener la culpa (de)

bland [blænd] adj (music, taste) soso

blank [blæŋk] adj en blanco; (look) sin expresión ▷ n (of memory): **my mind is a ~** no puedo recordar nada; (on form) blanco, espacio en blanco; (cartridge) cartucho sin bala or de fogueo

blanket [ˈblæŋkɪt] n manta (SP), cobija (LAM); (of snow) capa; (of fog) manto

blast [blɑːst] n (of wind) ráfaga, soplo; (of explosive) explosión f ▷ vt (blow up) volar

blatant [ˈbleɪtənt] adj descarado

blaze [bleɪz] n (fire) fuego; (fig: of colour) despliegue m; (: of glory) esplendor m ▷ vi arder en llamas; (fig) brillar ▷ vt: **to ~ a trail** (fig) abrir (un) camino; **in a ~ of publicity** con gran publicidad

blazer [ˈbleɪzə*] n chaqueta de uniforme de colegial o de socio de club

bleach [bliːtʃ] n (also: **household ~**) lejía ▷ vt blanquear; **bleachers** (US) npl (Sport) gradas fpl al sol

bleak [bliːk] adj (countryside) desierto; (prospect) poco prometedor(a); (weather) crudo; (smile) triste

bled [bled] pt, pp of **bleed**

bleed [bliːd] (pt, pp **bled**) vt, vi sangrar; **my nose is ~ing** me está sangrando la nariz

blemish [ˈblɛmɪʃ] n marca, mancha; (on reputation) tacha

blend [blɛnd] n mezcla ▷ vt mezclar; (colours etc) combinar, mezclar ▷ vi (colours etc: also: **~ in**) combinarse, mezclarse; **blender** n (Culin) batidora

bless [blɛs] (pt, pp **~ed** or **blest**) vt bendecir; **~ you!** (after sneeze) ¡Jesús!; **blessing** n (approval) aprobación f; (godsend) don m del cielo, bendición f; (advantage) beneficio, ventaja

blew [bluː] pt of **blow**

blight [blaɪt] vt (hopes etc) frustrar, arruinar

blind [blaɪnd] adj ciego; (fig): **~ (to)** ciego (a) ▷ n (for window) persiana ▷ vt cegar; (dazzle) deslumbrar; (deceive): **to ~ sb to ...** cegar a algn a ...; **the blind** npl los ciegos; **blind alley** n callejón m sin salida; **blindfold** n venda ▷ adv con los ojos

vendados ▷ vt vendar los ojos a
blink [blɪŋk] vi parpadear, pestañear;
(light) oscilar
bliss [blɪs] n felicidad f
blister ['blɪstə*] n ampolla ▷ vi (paint)
ampollarse
blizzard ['blɪzəd] n ventisca
bloated ['bləʊtɪd] adj hinchado;
(person: full) ahíto
blob [blɔb] n (drop) gota; (indistinct object)
bulto
block [blɔk] n bloque m; (in pipes)
obstáculo; (of buildings) manzana (SP),
cuadra (LAM) ▷ vt obstruir, cerrar; (progress)
estorbar; **~ of flats** (BRIT) bloque m de pisos;
mental ~ bloqueo mental; **block up** vt
tapar, obstruir; (pipe) atascar; **blockade**
[-'keɪd] n bloqueo ▷ vt bloquear; **blockage**
n estorbo, obstrucción f; **blockbuster** n
(book) bestseller m; (film) éxito de público;
block capitals npl mayúsculas fpl; **block
letters** npl mayúsculas fpl
blog [blɔg] n blog m
bloke [bləʊk] (BRIT: inf) n tipo, tío
blond(e) [blɔnd] adj, n rubio/a m/f
blood [blʌd] n sangre f; **blood donor**
n donante mf de sangre; **blood group**
n grupo sanguíneo; **blood poisoning**
n envenenamiento de la sangre; **blood
pressure** n presión f sanguínea;
bloodshed n derramamiento de sangre;
bloodshot adj inyectado en sangre;
bloodstream n corriente f sanguínea;
blood test n análisis m inv de sangre;
blood transfusion n transfusión f de
sangre; **blood type** n grupo sanguíneo;
blood vessel n vaso sanguíneo; **bloody**
adj sangriento; (nose etc) lleno de sangre;
(BRIT: infl): **this bloody ...** este condenado o
puñetero ... (!) ▷ adv: **bloody strong/good**
(BRIT: infl) terriblemente fuerte/bueno
bloom [bluːm] n flor f ▷ vi florecer
blossom ['blɔsəm] n flor f ▷ vi florecer
blot [blɔt] n borrón m; (fig) mancha ▷ vt
(stain) manchar
blouse [blauz] n blusa
blow [bləʊ] (pt **blew**, pp **blown**) n golpe
m; (with sword) espadazo ▷ vi soplar; (dust,
sand etc) volar; (fuse) fundirse ▷ vt (wind)
llevarse; (fuse) quemar; (instrument) tocar;
to ~ one's nose sonarse; **blow away** vt
llevarse, arrancar; **blow out** vi apagarse;
blow up vi estallar ▷ vt volar; (tyre) inflar;
(Phot) ampliar; **blow-dry** n moldeado (con
secador)
blown [bləʊn] pp of blow
blue [bluː] adj azul; (depressed) deprimido;
~ film/joke película/chiste m verde;

out of the ~ (fig) de repente; **bluebell** n
campanilla, campánula azul; **blueberry**
n arándano; **blue cheese** n queso azul;
blues npl: **the blues** (Mus) el blues; **to have
the blues** estar triste; **bluetit** n herrerillo
m (común)
bluff [blʌf] vi tirarse un farol, farolear ▷ n
farol m; **to call sb's ~** coger a algn la palabra
blunder ['blʌndə*] n patinazo, metedura
de pata ▷ vi cometer un error, meter la pata
blunt [blʌnt] adj (pencil) despuntado;
(knife) desafilado, romo; (person) franco,
directo
blur [blə:*] n (shape): **to become a ~**
hacerse borroso ▷ vt (vision) enturbiar;
(distinction) borrar; **blurred** adj borroso
blush [blʌʃ] vi ruborizarse, ponerse
colorado ▷ n rubor m; **blusher** n colorete
m
board [bɔːd] n (cardboard) cartón m;
(wooden) tabla, tablero; (on wall) tablón
m; (for chess etc) tablero; (committee)
junta, consejo; (in firm) mesa or junta
directiva; (Naut, Aviat): **on ~** a bordo ▷ vt
(ship) embarcarse en; (train) subir a; **full
~** (BRIT) pensión completa; **half ~** (BRIT)
media pensión; **to go by the ~** (fig) ser
abandonado or olvidado; **board game** n
juego de tablero; **boarding card** (BRIT) n
tarjeta de embarque; **boarding pass** (US)
n = **boarding card**; **boarding school** n
internado; **board room** n sala de juntas
boast [bəʊst] vi: **to ~ (about or of)** alardear
(de)
boat [bəʊt] n barco, buque m; (small)
barca, bote m
bob [bɔb] vi (also: **~ up and down**)
menearse, balancearse
bobby pin ['bɔbɪ-] (US) n horquilla
body ['bɔdɪ] n cuerpo; (corpse) cadáver m;
(of car) caja, carrocería; (fig: group) grupo;
(: organization) organismo; **body-building**
n culturismo; **bodyguard** n guardaespaldas
m inv; **bodywork** n carrocería
bog [bɔg] n pantano, ciénaga ▷ vt: **to get
~ged down** (fig) empantanarse, atascarse
bogus ['bəʊgəs] adj falso, fraudulento
boil [bɔɪl] vt (water) hervir; (eggs) pasar
por agua, cocer ▷ vi hervir; (fig: with anger)
estar furioso; (: with heat) asfixiarse ▷ n
(Med) furúnculo, divieso; **to come to the
~, to come to a ~** (US) comenzar a hervir;
to ~ down to (fig) reducirse a; **boil over** vi
salirse, rebosar; (anger etc) llegar al colmo;
boiled egg n (soft) huevo tibio (MEX) or
pasado por agua or a la copa (SC); (hard)
huevo duro; **boiled potatoes** npl patatas
fpl (SP) or papas fpl (LAM) cocidas; **boiler** n

caldera; **boiling** ['bɔɪlɪŋ] *adj*: **I'm boiling (hot)** (*inf*) estoy asado; **boiling point** *n* punto de ebullición

bold [bəuld] *adj* valiente, audaz; (*pej*) descarado; (*colour*) llamativo

Bolivia [bə'lɪvɪə] *n* Bolivia; **Bolivian** *adj, n* boliviano/a *m/f*

bollard ['bɔləd] (*BRIT*) *n* (*Aut*) poste *m*

bolt [bəult] *n* (*lock*) cerrojo; (*with nut*) perno, tornillo ▷ *adv*: **~ upright** rígido, erguido ▷ *vt* (*door*) echar el cerrojo a; (*also*: **~ together**) sujetar con tornillos; (*food*) engullir ▷ *vi* fugarse; (*horse*) desbocarse

bomb [bɔm] *n* bomba ▷ *vt* bombardear; **bombard** [bɔm'bɑːd] *vt* bombardear; (*fig*) asediar; **bomber** *n* (*Aviat*) bombardero; **bomb scare** *n* amenaza de bomba

bond [bɔnd] *n* (*promise*) fianza; (*Finance*) bono; (*link*) vínculo, lazo; (*Comm*): **in ~** en depósito bajo fianza; **bonds** *npl* (*chains*) cadenas *fpl*

bone [bəun] *n* hueso; (*of fish*) espina ▷ *vt* deshuesar; quitar las espinas a

bonfire ['bɔnfaɪə*] *n* hoguera, fogata

bonnet ['bɔnɪt] *n* gorra; (*BRIT: of car*) capó *m*

bonus ['bəunəs] *n* (*payment*) paga extraordinaria, plus *m*; (*fig*) bendición *f*

boo [buː] *excl* ¡uh! ▷ *vt* abuchear, rechiflar

book [buk] *n* libro; (*of tickets*) taco; (*of stamps etc*) librito ▷ *vt* (*ticket*) sacar; (*seat, room*) reservar; **books** *npl* (*Comm*) cuentas *fpl*, contabilidad *f*; **book in** *vi* (*at hotel*) registrarse; **book up** *vt*: **to be booked up** (*hotel*) estar completo; **bookcase** *n* librería, estante *m* para libros; **booking** *n* reserva; **booking office** *n* (*BRIT Rail*) despacho de billetes (*SP*) *or* boletos (*LAM*); (*Theatre*) taquilla (*SP*), boletería (*LAM*); **book-keeping** *n* contabilidad *f*; **booklet** *n* folleto; **bookmaker** *n* corredor *m* de apuestas; **bookmark** *n* (*also Comput*) marcador; **bookseller** *n* librero; **bookshelf** *n* estante *m* (para libros); **bookshop, book store** *n* librería

boom [buːm] *n* (*noise*) trueno, estampido; (*in prices etc*) alza rápida; (*Econ, in population*) boom *m* ▷ *vi* (*cannon*) hacer gran estruendo, retumbar; (*Econ*) estar en alza

boost [buːst] *n* estímulo, empuje *m* ▷ *vt* estimular, empujar

boot [buːt] *n* bota; (*BRIT: of car*) maleta, maletero ▷ *vt* (*Comput*) arrancar; **to ~** (*in addition*) además, por añadidura

booth [buːð] *n* (*telephone booth, voting booth*) cabina

booze [buːz] (*inf*) *n* bebida

border ['bɔːdə*] *n* borde *m*, margen *m*; (*of a country*) frontera; (*for flowers*) arriate *m* ▷ *vt* (*road*) bordear; (*another country: also*: **~ on**) lindar con; **borderline** *n*: **on the borderline** en el límite

bore [bɔː*] *pt of* **bear** ▷ *vt* (*hole*) hacer un agujero en; (*well*) perforar; (*person*) aburrir ▷ *n* (*person*) pelmazo, pesado; (*of gun*) calibre *m*; **bored** *adj* aburrido; **he's bored to tears** *or* **to death** *or* **stiff** está aburrido como una ostra, está muerto de aburrimiento; **boredom** *n* aburrimiento

boring ['bɔːrɪŋ] *adj* aburrido

born [bɔːn] *adj*: **to be ~** nacer; **I was ~ in 1960** nací en 1960

borne [bɔːn] *pp of* **bear**

borough ['bʌrə] *n* municipio

borrow ['bɔrəu] *vt*: **to ~ sth (from sb)** tomar algo prestado (a algn)

Bosnia(-Herzegovina) ['bɔːsnɪə(hɜːzə'gəuvɪːnə)] *n* Bosnia(-Herzegovina); **Bosnian** ['bɔznɪən] *adj, n* bosnio/a

bosom ['buzəm] *n* pecho

boss [bɔs] *n* jefe *m* ▷ *vt* (*also*: **~ about** *or* **around**) mangonear; **bossy** *adj* mandón/ona

both [bəuθ] *adj, pron* ambos/as, los dos (las dos); **~ of us went, we ~ went** fuimos los dos, ambos fuimos ▷ *adv*: **~ A and B** tanto A como B

bother ['bɔðə*] *vt* (*worry*) preocupar; (*disturb*) molestar, fastidiar ▷ *vi* (*also*: **~ o.s.**) molestarse ▷ *n* (*trouble*) dificultad *f*; (*nuisance*) molestia, lata; **to ~ doing** tomarse la molestia de hacer

bottle ['bɔtl] *n* botella; (*small*) frasco; (*baby's*) biberón *m* ▷ *vt* embotellar; **bottle bank** *n* contenedor *m* de vidrio; **bottle-opener** *n* abrebotellas *m inv*

bottom ['bɔtəm] *n* (*of box, sea*) fondo; (*buttocks*) trasero, culo; (*of page*) pie *m*; (*of list*) final *m*; (*of class*) último/a ▷ *adj* (*lowest*) más bajo; (*last*) último

bought [bɔːt] *pt, pp of* **buy**

boulder ['bəuldə*] *n* canto rodado

bounce [bauns] *vi* (*ball*) (re)botar; (*cheque*) ser rechazado ▷ *vt* hacer (re)botar ▷ *n* (*rebound*) (re)bote *m*; **bouncer** (*inf*) *n* gorila *m* (*que echa a los alborotadores de un bar, club etc*)

bound [baund] *pt, pp of* **bind** ▷ *n* (*leap*) salto; (*gen pl: limit*) límite *m* ▷ *vi* (*leap*) saltar ▷ *vt* (*border*) rodear ▷ *adj*: **~ by** rodeado de; **to be ~ to do sth** (*obliged*) tener el deber de hacer algo; **he's ~ to come** es seguro que vendrá; **out of ~s** prohibido el paso; **~ for** con destino a

boundary ['baundrɪ] *n* límite *m*

bouquet ['bukeɪ] *n* (*of flowers*) ramo
bourbon ['buəbən] (*US*) *n* (*also*: ~
whiskey) whisky *m* americano, bourbon *m*
bout [baut] *n* (*of malaria etc*) ataque *m*; (*of
activity*) período; (*Boxing etc*) combate *m*,
encuentro
boutique [buːˈtiːk] *n* boutique *f*, tienda
de ropa
bow¹ [bəu] *n* (*knot*) lazo; (*weapon*, *Mus*) arco
bow² [bau] *n* (*of the head*) reverencia;
(*Naut*: *also*: ~s) proa ▷ *vi* inclinarse, hacer
una reverencia
bowels [bauəlz] *npl* intestinos *mpl*,
vientre *m*; (*fig*) entrañas *fpl*
bowl [bəul] *n* tazón *m*, cuenco; (*ball*) bola
▷ *vi* (*Cricket*) arrojar la pelota; *see also* **bowls**;
bowler *n* (*Cricket*) lanzador *m* (de la pelota);
(*BRIT*: *also*: **bowler hat**) hongo, bombín *m*;
bowling *n* (*game*) bochas *fpl*, bolos *mpl*;
bowling alley *n* bolera; **bowling green**
n pista para bochas; **bowls** *n* juego de las
bochas, bolos *mpl*
bow tie ['bəu-] *n* corbata de lazo, pajarita
box [bɔks] *n* (*also*: **cardboard** ~) caja,
cajón *m*; (*Theatre*) palco ▷ *vt* encajonar ▷ *vi*
(*Sport*) boxear; **boxer** *n* ['bɔksə*] (*person*)
boxeador *m*; **boxer shorts** ['bɔksəfɔːts]
pl n bóxers; **a pair of boxer shorts** unos
bóxers; **boxing** ['bɔksɪŋ] *n* (*Sport*) boxeo;
Boxing Day (*BRIT*) *n* día en que se dan los
aguinaldos, 26 de diciembre; **boxing gloves**
npl guantes *mpl* de boxeo; **boxing ring** *n*
ring *m*, cuadrilátero; **box office** *n* taquilla
(*SP*), boletería (*LAM*)
boy [bɔɪ] *n* (*young*) niño; (*older*) muchacho,
chico; (*son*) hijo; **boy band** *n* boy band *m*
(*grupo musical de chicos*)
boycott ['bɔɪkɔt] *n* boicot *m* ▷ *vt*
boicotear
boyfriend ['bɔɪfrɛnd] *n* novio
bra [brɑː] *n* sostén *m*, sujetador *m*
brace [breɪs] *n* (*BRIT*: *also*: ~s: *on teeth*)
corrector *m*, aparato; (*tool*) berbiquí *m* ▷ *vt*
(*knees*, *shoulders*) tensionar; **braces** *npl*
(*BRIT*) tirantes *mpl*; **to ~ o.s.** (*fig*) prepararse
bracelet ['breɪslɪt] *n* pulsera, brazalete *m*
bracket ['brækɪt] *n* (*Tech*) soporte *m*,
puntal *m*; (*group*) clase *f*, categoría; (*also*:
brace ~) soporte *m*, abrazadera; (*also*: **round**
~) paréntesis *m inv*; (*also*: **square** ~) corchete
m ▷ *vt* (*word etc*) poner entre paréntesis
brag [bræg] *vi* jactarse
braid [breɪd] *n* (*trimming*) galón *m*; (*of hair*)
trenza
brain [breɪn] *n* cerebro; **brains** *npl* sesos
mpl; **she's got ~s** es muy lista
braise [breɪz] *vt* cocer a fuego lento
brake [breɪk] *n* (*on vehicle*) freno ▷ *vi*

frenar; **brake light** *n* luz *f* de frenado
bran [bræn] *n* salvado
branch [brɑːntʃ] *n* rama; (*Comm*) sucursal
f; **branch off** *vi*: **a small road branches off
to the right** hay una carretera pequeña que
sale hacia la derecha; **branch out** *vi* (*fig*)
extenderse
brand [brænd] *n* marca; (*fig*: *type*) tipo ▷ *vt*
(*cattle*) marcar con hierro candente; **brand
name** *n* marca; **brand-new** *adj* flamante,
completamente nuevo
brandy ['brændɪ] *n* coñac *m*
brash [bræʃ] *adj* (*forward*) descarado
brass [brɑːs] *n* latón *m*; **the** ~ (*Mus*) los
cobres; **brass band** *n* banda de metal
brat [bræt] (*pej*) *n* mocoso/a
brave [breɪv] *adj* valiente, valeroso ▷ *vt*
(*face up to*) desafiar; **bravery** *n* valor *m*,
valentía
brawl [brɔːl] *n* pelea, reyerta
Brazil [brəˈzɪl] *n* (el) Brasil; **Brazilian** *adj*, *n*
brasileño/a *m/f*
breach [briːtʃ] *vt* abrir brecha en ▷ *n* (*gap*)
brecha; (*breaking*): ~ **of contract** infracción
f de contrato; ~ **of the peace** perturbación *f*
del órden público
bread [brɛd] *n* pan *m*; **breadbin** *n* panera;
breadbox (*US*) *n* panera; **breadcrumbs** *npl*
migajas *fpl*; (*Culin*) pan rallado
breadth [brɛtθ] *n* anchura; (*fig*) amplitud *f*
break [breɪk] (*pt* **broke**, *pp* **broken**) *vt*
romper; (*promise*) faltar a; (*law*) violar,
infringir; (*record*) batir ▷ *vi* romperse,
quebrarse; (*storm*) estallar; (*weather*)
cambiar; (*dawn*) despuntar; (*news etc*) darse
a conocer ▷ *n* (*gap*) abertura; (*fracture*)
fractura; (*time*) intervalo; (: *at school*)
(período de) recreo; (*chance*) oportunidad *f*;
to ~ the news to sb comunicar la noticia a
algn; **break down** *vt* (*figures*, *data*) analizar,
descomponer ▷ *vi* (*machine*) estropearse;
(*Aut*) averiarse; (*person*) romper a llorar;
(*talks*) fracasar; **break in** *vt* (*horse etc*)
domar ▷ *vi* (*burglar*) forzar una entrada;
(*interrupt*) interrumpir; **break into** *vt
fus* (*house*) forzar; **break off** *vi* (*speaker*)
pararse, detenerse; (*branch*) partir; **break
out** *vi* estallar; (*prisoner*) escaparse; **to
break out in spots** salirle a algn granos;
break up *vi* (*ship*) hacerse pedazos; (*crowd*,
meeting) disolverse; (*marriage*) deshacerse;
(*Scol*) terminar (el curso); (*line*) cortarse ▷ *vt*
(*rocks etc*) partir; (*journey*) partir; (*fight etc*)
acabar con; **the line's** *or* **you're breaking
up** se corta; **breakdown** *n* (*Aut*) avería; (*in
communications*) interrupción *f*; (*Med*: *also*:
nervous breakdown) colapso, crisis *f*
nerviosa; (*of marriage*, *talks*) fracaso; (*of*

statistics) análisis *m inv*; **breakdown truck, breakdown van** *n* (camión *m*) grúa
breakfast ['brɛkfəst] *n* desayuno
break: break-in *n* robo con allanamiento de morada; **breakthrough** *n* (*also fig*) avance *m*
breast [brɛst] *n* (*of woman*) pecho, seno; (*chest*) pecho; (*of bird*) pechuga; **breast-feed** (*pt, pp* **breast-fed**) *vt, vi* amamantar, criar a los pechos; **breast-stroke** *n* braza (de pecho)
breath [brɛθ] *n* aliento, respiración *f*; **to take a deep ~** respirar hondo; **out of ~** sin aliento, sofocado
Breathalyser® ['brɛθəlaɪzə*] (*BRIT*) *n* alcoholímetro
breathe [bri:ð] *vt, vi* respirar; **breathe in** *vt, vi* aspirar; **breathe out** *vt, vi* espirar; **breathing** *n* respiración *f*
breath: breathless *adj* sin aliento, jadeante; **breathtaking** *adj* imponente, pasmoso; **breath test** *n* prueba de la alcoholemia
bred [brɛd] *pt, pp of* **breed**
breed [bri:d] (*pt, pp* **bred**) *vt* criar ▷ *vi* reproducirse, procrear ▷ *n* (*Zool*) raza, casta; (*type*) tipo
breeze [bri:z] *n* brisa
breezy ['bri:zɪ] *adj* de mucho viento, ventoso; (*person*) despreocupado
brew [bru:] *vt* (*tea*) hacer; (*beer*) elaborar ▷ *vi* (*fig: trouble*) prepararse; (*storm*) amenazar; **brewery** *n* fábrica de cerveza, cervecería
bribe [braɪb] *n* soborno ▷ *vt* sobornar, cohechar; **bribery** *n* soborno, cohecho
bric-a-brac ['brɪkəbræk] *n inv* baratijas *fpl*
brick [brɪk] *n* ladrillo; **bricklayer** *n* albañil *m*
bride [braɪd] *n* novia; **bridegroom** *n* novio; **bridesmaid** *n* dama de honor
bridge [brɪdʒ] *n* puente *m*; (*Naut*) puente *m* de mando; (*of nose*) caballete *m*; (*Cards*) bridge *m* ▷ *vt* (*fig*): **to ~ a gap** llenar un vacío
bridle ['braɪdl] *n* brida, freno
brief [bri:f] *adj* breve, corto ▷ *n* (*Law*) escrito; (*task*) cometido, encargo ▷ *vt* informar; **briefs** *npl* (*for men*) calzoncillos *mpl*; (*for women*) bragas *fpl*; **briefcase** *n* cartera (*SP*), portafolio (*LAM*); **briefing** *n* (*Press*) informe *m*; **briefly** *adv* (*glance*) fugazmente; (*say*) en pocas palabras
brigadier [brɪgə'dɪə*] *n* general *m* de brigada
bright [braɪt] *adj* brillante; (*room*) luminoso; (*day*) de sol; (*person: clever*) listo,

inteligente; (: *lively*) alegre; (*colour*) vivo; (*future*) prometedor(a)
brilliant ['brɪljənt] *adj* brillante; (*inf*) fenomenal
brim [brɪm] *n* borde *m*; (*of hat*) ala
brine [braɪn] *n* (*Culin*) salmuera
bring [brɪŋ] (*pt, pp* **brought**) *vt* (*thing, person: with you*) traer; (: *to sb*) llevar, conducir; (*trouble, satisfaction*) causar; **bring about** *vt* ocasionar, producir; **bring back** *vt* volver a traer; (*return*) devolver; **bring down** *vt* (*government, plane*) derribar; (*price*) rebajar; **bring in** *vt* (*harvest*) recoger; (*person*) hacer entrar *or* pasar; (*object*) traer; (*Pol: bill, law*) presentar; (*produce: income*) producir, rendir; **bring on** *vt* (*illness, attack*) producir, causar; (*player, substitute*) sacar (de la reserva), hacer salir; **bring out** *vt* sacar; (*book etc*) publicar; (*meaning*) subrayar; **bring up** *vt* subir; (*person*) educar, criar; (*question*) sacar a colación; (*food: vomit*) devolver, vomitar
brink [brɪŋk] *n* borde *m*
brisk [brɪsk] *adj* (*abrupt: tone*) brusco; (*person*) enérgico, vigoroso; (*pace*) rápido; (*trade*) activo
bristle ['brɪsl] *n* cerda ▷ *vi*: **to ~ in anger** temblar de rabia
Brit [brɪt] *n abbr* (*inf: = British person*) británico/a
Britain ['brɪtən] *n* (*also*: **Great ~**) Gran Bretaña
British ['brɪtɪʃ] *adj* británico ▷ *npl*: **the ~** los británicos; **British Isles** *npl*: **the British Isles** las Islas Británicas
Briton ['brɪtən] *n* británico/a
brittle ['brɪtl] *adj* quebradizo, frágil
broad [brɔːd] *adj* ancho; (*range*) amplio; (*smile*) abierto; (*general: outlines etc*) general; (*accent*) cerrado; **in ~ daylight** en pleno día; **broadband** *n* banda ancha; **broad bean** *n* haba; **broadcast** (*pt, pp* **~**) *n* emisión *f* ▷ *vt* (*Radio*) emitir; (*TV*) transmitir ▷ *vi* emitir; transmitir; **broaden** *vt* ampliar ▷ *vi* ensancharse; **to broaden one's mind** hacer más tolerante a algn; **broadly** *adv* en general; **broad-minded** *adj* tolerante, liberal
broccoli ['brɔkəlɪ] *n* brécol *m*
brochure ['brəuʃjuə*] *n* folleto
broil [brɔɪl] *vt* (*Culin*) asar a la parrilla
broiler ['brɔɪlə*] *n* (*grill*) parrilla
broke [brəuk] *pt of* **break** ▷ *adj* (*inf*) pelado, sin blanca
broken ['brəukən] *pp of* **break** ▷ *adj* roto; (*machine: also*: **~ down**) averiado; **~ leg** pierna rota; **in ~ English** en un inglés imperfecto

broker ['brəukə*] n agente mf, bolsista mf; (insurance broker) agente de seguros

bronchitis [brɔŋ'kaɪtɪs] n bronquitis f

bronze [brɔnz] n bronce m

brooch [brəutʃ] n prendedor m, broche m

brood [bru:d] n camada, cría ▷ vi (person) dejarse obsesionar

broom [brum] n escoba; (Bot) retama

Bros. abbr (= Brothers) Hnos

broth [brɔθ] n caldo

brothel ['brɔθl] n burdel m

brother ['brʌðə*] n hermano; **brother-in-law** n cuñado

brought [brɔ:t] pt, pp of **bring**

brow [brau] n (forehead) frente m; (eyebrow) ceja; (of hill) cumbre f

brown [braun] adj (colour) marrón; (hair) castaño; (tanned) bronceado, moreno ▷ n (colour) color m marrón or pardo ▷ vt (Culin) dorar; **brown bread** n pan integral

Brownie ['braunɪ] n niña exploradora

brown rice n arroz m integral

brown sugar n azúcar m terciado

browse [brauz] vi (through book) hojear; (in shop) mirar; **browser** n (Comput) navegador m

bruise [bru:z] n cardenal m (SP), moretón m ▷ vt magullar

brunette [bru:'nɛt] n morena

brush [brʌʃ] n cepillo; (for painting, shaving etc) brocha; (artist's) pincel m; (with police etc) roce m ▷ vt (sweep) barrer; (groom) cepillar; (also: ~ **against**) rozar al pasar

Brussels ['brʌslz] n Bruselas

Brussels sprout n col f de Bruselas

brutal ['bru:tl] adj brutal

B.Sc. abbr (= Bachelor of Science) licenciado en Ciencias

BSE n abbr (= bovine spongiform encephalopathy) encefalopatía espongiforme bovina

bubble ['bʌbl] n burbuja ▷ vi burbujear, borbotar; **bubble bath** n espuma para el baño; **bubble gum** n chicle m de globo; **bubblejet printer** ['bʌbldʒɛt-] n impresora de inyección por burbujas

buck [bʌk] n (rabbit) conejo macho; (deer) gamo; (us: inf) dólar m ▷ vi corcovear; **to pass the ~ (to sb)** echar (a algn) el muerto

bucket ['bʌkɪt] n cubo, balde m

buckle ['bʌkl] n hebilla ▷ vt abrochar con hebilla ▷ vi combarse

bud [bʌd] n (of plant) brote m, yema; (of flower) capullo ▷ vi brotar, echar brotes

Buddhism ['budɪzm] n Budismo

Buddhist ['budɪst] adj, n budista m/f

buddy ['bʌdɪ] n (us) compañero, compinche m

budge [bʌdʒ] vt mover; (fig) hacer ceder ▷ vi moverse, ceder

budgerigar ['bʌdʒərɪgɑ:*] n periquito

budget ['bʌdʒɪt] n presupuesto ▷ vi: **to ~ for sth** presupuestar algo

budgie ['bʌdʒɪ] n = **budgerigar**

buff [bʌf] adj (colour) color de ante ▷ n (inf: enthusiast) entusiasta mf

buffalo ['bʌfələu] (pl ~ or ~**es**) n (BRIT) búfalo; (us: bison) bisonte m

buffer ['bʌfə*] n (Comput) memoria intermedia; (Rail) tope m

buffet[1] ['bʌfɪt] vt golpear

buffet[2] ['bufeɪ] n (BRIT: in station) bar m, cafetería; (food) buffet m; **buffet car** (BRIT) n (Rail) coche-comedor m

bug [bʌg] n (esp us: insect) bicho, sabandija; (Comput) error m; (germ) microbio, bacilo; (spy device) micrófono oculto ▷ vt (inf: annoy) fastidiar; (room) poner micrófono oculto en

buggy ['bʌgɪ] n cochecito de niño

build [bɪld] (pt, pp **built**) n (of person) tipo ▷ vt construir, edificar; **build up** vt (morale, forces, production) acrecentar; (stocks) acumular; **builder** n (contractor) contratista mf; **building** n construcción f; (structure) edificio; **building site** n obra; **building society** (BRIT) n sociedad f inmobiliaria

built [bɪlt] pt, pp of **build**; **built-in** adj (cupboard) empotrado; (device) interior, incorporado; **built-up** adj (area) urbanizado

bulb [bʌlb] n (Bot) bulbo; (Elec) bombilla, foco (MEX), bujía (CAM), bombita (RPL)

Bulgaria [bʌl'gɛərɪə] n Bulgaria; **Bulgarian** adj, n búlgaro/a m/f

bulge [bʌldʒ] n bulto, protuberancia ▷ vi bombearse, pandearse; (pocket etc): **to ~ (with)** rebosar (de)

bulimia [bə'lɪmɪə] n bulimia

bulimic [bju:'lɪmɪk] adj, n bulímico/a m/f

bulk [bʌlk] n masa, mole f; **in ~** (Comm) a granel; **the ~ of** la mayor parte de; **bulky** adj voluminoso, abultado

bull [bul] n toro; (male elephant, whale) macho

bulldozer ['buldəuzə*] n bulldozer m

bullet ['bulɪt] n bala

bulletin ['bulɪtɪn] n anuncio, parte m; (journal) boletín m; **bulletin board** n (us) tablón m de anuncios; (Comput) tablero de noticias

bullfight ['bulfaɪt] n corrida de toros; **bullfighter** n torero; **bullfighting** n los toros, el toreo

bully ['bulɪ] n valentón m, matón m ▷ vt

intimidar, tiranizar

bum [bʌm] *n* (*inf: backside*) culo; (*esp us: tramp*) vagabundo

bumblebee ['bʌmblbiː] *n* abejorro

bump [bʌmp] *n* (*blow*) tope *m*, choque *m*; (*jolt*) sacudida; (*on road etc*) bache *m*; (*on head etc*) chichón *m* ▷ *vt* (*strike*) chocar contra; **bump into** *vt fus* chocar contra, tropezar con; (*person*) topar con; **bumper** *n* (*Aut*) parachoques *m inv* ▷ *adj*: **bumper crop** or **harvest** cosecha abundante; **bumpy** *adj* (*road*) lleno de baches

bun [bʌn] *n* (*BRIT: cake*) pastel *m*; (*us: bread*) bollo; (*of hair*) moño

bunch [bʌntʃ] *n* (*of flowers*) ramo; (*of keys*) manojo; (*of bananas*) piña; (*of people*) grupo; **bunches** *npl* (*in hair*) coletas *fpl*

bundle ['bʌndl] *n* bulto, fardo; (*of sticks*) haz *m*; (*of papers*) legajo ▷ *vt* (*also:* **~ up**) atar, envolver; **to ~ sth/sb into** meter algo/a algn precipitadamente en

bungalow ['bʌŋgələu] *n* bungalow *m*, chalé *m*

bungee jumping ['bʌndʒiː'dʒʌmpɪŋ] *n* puenting *m*, banyi *m*

bunion ['bʌnjən] *n* juanete *m*

bunk [bʌŋk] *n* litera; **bunk beds** *npl* literas *fpl*

bunker ['bʌŋkə*] *n* (*coal store*) carbonera; (*Mil*) refugio; (*Golf*) bunker *m*

bunny ['bʌnɪ] *n* (*inf: also:* **~ rabbit**) conejito

buoy [bɔɪ] *n* boya; **buoyant** *adj* (*ship*) capaz de flotar; (*economy*) boyante; (*person*) optimista

burden ['bəːdn] *n* carga ▷ *vt* cargar

bureau [bjuə'rəu] (*pl* **~x**) *n* (*BRIT: writing desk*) escritorio, buró *m*; (*us: chest of drawers*) cómoda; (*office*) oficina, agencia

bureaucracy [bjuə'rɔkrəsɪ] *n* burocracia

bureaucrat ['bjuərəkræt] *n* burócrata *m/f*

bureau de change [-də'ʃɑ̃ʒ] (*pl* **bureaux de change**) *n* caja *f* de cambio

bureaux ['bjuərəuz] *npl of* **bureau**

burger ['bəːgə*] *n* hamburguesa

burglar ['bəːglə*] *n* ladrón/ona *m/f*; **burglar alarm** *n* alarma *f* antirrobo; **burglary** *n* robo con allanamiento, robo de una casa

burial ['bɛrɪəl] *n* entierro

burn [bəːn] (*pt, pp* **~ed** *or* **~t**) *vt* quemar; (*house*) incendiar ▷ *vi* quemarse, arder; incendiarse; (*sting*) escocer ▷ *n* quemadura; **burn down** *vt* incendiar; **burn out** *vt* (*writer etc*): **to burn o.s. out** agotarse; **burning** *adj* (*building etc*) en llamas; (*hot: sand etc*) abrasador(a); (*ambition*) ardiente

Burns' Night [bəːnz-] *n ver abajo*

burnt [bəːnt] *pt, pp of* **burn**

burp [bəːp] (*inf*) *n* eructo ▷ *vi* eructar

burrow ['bʌrəu] *n* madriguera ▷ *vi* hacer una madriguera; (*rummage*) hurgar

burst [bəːst] (*pt, pp* **~**) *vt* reventar; (*river: banks etc*) romper ▷ *vi* reventarse; (*tyre*) pincharse ▷ *n* (*of gunfire*) ráfaga; (*also:* **~ pipe**) reventón *m*; **a ~ of energy/speed/ enthusiasm** una explosión de energía/ un ímpetu de velocidad/un arranque de entusiasmo; **to ~ into flames** estallar en llamas; **to ~ into tears** deshacerse en lágrimas; **to ~ out laughing** soltar la carcajada; **to ~ open** abrirse de golpe; **to be ~ing with** (*container*) estar lleno a rebosar de; (*: person*) reventar por or de; **burst into** *vt fus* (*room etc*) irrumpir en

bury ['bɛrɪ] *vt* enterrar; (*body*) enterrar, sepultar

bus [bʌs] (*pl* **~es**) *n* autobús *m*

bush [buʃ] *n* arbusto; (*scrub land*) monte *m*; **to beat about the ~** andar(se) con rodeos

business ['bɪznɪs] *n* (*matter*) asunto; (*trading*) comercio, negocios *mpl*; (*firm*) empresa, casa; (*occupation*) oficio; **to be away on ~** estar en viaje de negocios; **it's my ~ to ...** me toca *or* corresponde ...; **it's none of my ~** yo no tengo nada que ver; **he means ~** habla en serio; **business class** *n* (*Aer*) clase *f* preferente; **businesslike** *adj* eficiente; **businessman** (*irreg*) *n* hombre *m* de negocios; **business trip** *n* viaje *m* de negocios; **businesswoman** (*irreg*) *n* mujer *f* de negocios

busker ['bʌskə*] (*BRIT*) *n* músico/a ambulante

bus: bus pass *n* bonobús; **bus shelter** *n* parada cubierta; **bus station** *n* estación *f* de autobuses; **bus stop** *n* parada de autobús

bust [bʌst] *n* (*Anat*) pecho; (*sculpture*) busto

▷ *adj* (*inf: broken*) roto, estropeado; **to go ~** quebrar

bustling [ˈbʌslɪŋ] *adj* (*town*) animado, bullicioso

busy [ˈbɪzɪ] *adj* ocupado, atareado; (*shop, street*) concurrido, animado; (*Tel: line*) comunicando ▷ *vt*: **to ~ o.s. with** ocuparse en; **busy signal** (*us*) *n* (*Tel*) señal *f* de comunicando

○ **KEYWORD**

but [bʌt] *conj* **1** pero; **he's not very bright, but he's hard-working** no es muy inteligente, pero es trabajador

2 (*in direct contradiction*) sino; **he's not English but French** no es inglés sino francés; **he didn't sing but he shouted** no cantó sino que gritó

3 (*showing disagreement, surprise etc*): **but that's far too expensive!** ¡pero eso es carísimo!; **but it does work!** ¡(pero) sí que funciona!

▷ *prep* (*apart from, except*) menos, salvo; **we've had nothing but trouble** no hemos tenido más que problemas; **no-one but him can do it** nadie más que él puede hacerlo; **who but a lunatic would do such a thing** ¡sólo un loco haría una cosa así!; **but for you/your help** si no fuera por ti/tu ayuda; **anything but that** cualquier cosa menos eso

▷ *adv* (*just, only*) **she's but a child** no es más que una niña; **had I but known** si lo hubiera sabido; **I can but try** al menos lo puedo intentar; **it's all but finished** está casi acabado

butcher [ˈbutʃə*] *n* carnicero ▷ *vt* hacer una carnicería con; (*cattle etc*) matar; **butcher's (shop)** *n* carnicería

butler [ˈbʌtlə*] *n* mayordomo

butt [bʌt] *n* (*barrel*) tonel *m*; (*of gun*) culata; (*of cigarette*) colilla; (*BRIT: fig: target*) blanco ▷ *vt* dar cabezadas contra, top(et)ar

butter [ˈbʌtə*] *n* mantequilla ▷ *vt* untar con mantequilla; **buttercup** *n* botón *m* de oro

butterfly [ˈbʌtəflaɪ] *n* mariposa; (*Swimming: also: ~ stroke*) braza de mariposa

buttocks [ˈbʌtəks] *npl* nalgas *fpl*

button [ˈbʌtn] *n* botón *m*; (*us*) placa, chapa ▷ *vt* (*also: ~ up*) abotonar, abrochar ▷ *vi* abrocharse

buy [baɪ] (*pt, pp* **bought**) *vt* comprar ▷ *n* compra; **to ~ sb sth/sth from sb** comprarle algo a algn; **to ~ sb a drink** invitar a algn a tomar algo; **buy out** *vt* (*partner*) comprar

la parte de; **buy up** *vt* (*property*) acaparar; (*stock*) comprar todas las existencias de; **buyer** *n* comprador(a) *m/f*

buzz [bʌz] *n* zumbido; (*inf: phone call*) llamada (por teléfono) ▷ *vi* zumbar; **buzzer** *n* timbre *m*

○ **KEYWORD**

by [baɪ] *prep* **1** (*referring to cause, agent*) por; de; **killed by lightning** muerto por un relámpago; **a painting by Picasso** un cuadro de Picasso

2 (*referring to method, manner, means*): **by bus/car/train** en autobús/coche/tren; **to pay by cheque** pagar con un cheque; **by moonlight/candlelight** a la luz de la luna/una vela; **by saving hard he ...** ahorrando ...

3 (*via, through*) por; **we came by Dover** vinimos por Dover

4 (*close to, past*): **the house by the river** la casa junto al río; **she rushed by me** pasó a mi lado como una exhalación; **I go by the post office every day** paso por delante de Correos todos los días

5 (*time: not later than*) para; (: *during*): **by daylight** de día; **by 4 o'clock** para las cuatro; **by this time tomorrow** mañana a estas horas; **by the time I got here it was too late** cuando llegué ya era demasiado tarde

6 (*amount*): **by the metre/kilo** por metro/kilo; **paid by the hour** pagado por hora

7 (*Math, measure*): **to divide/multiply by 3** dividir/multiplicar por 3; **a room 3 metres by 4** una habitación de 3 metros por 4; **it's broader by a metre** es un metro más ancho

8 (*according to*) según, de acuerdo con; **it's 3 o'clock by my watch** según mi reloj, son las tres; **it's all right by me** por mí, está bien

9: **(all) by oneself** *etc* todo solo; **he did it (all) by himself** lo hizo él solo; **he was standing (all) by himself in a corner** estaba de pie solo en un rincón

10: **by the way** a propósito, por cierto; **this wasn't my idea, by the way** pues, no fue idea mía

▷ *adv* **1** *see* **go**; **pass** *etc*

2: **by and by** finalmente; **they'll come back by and by** acabarán volviendo; **by and large** en líneas generales, en general

bye(-bye) [ˈbaɪ(ˈbaɪ)] *excl* adiós, hasta luego

by-election (*BRIT*) *n* elección *f* parcial

bypass [ˈbaɪpɑːs] *n* carretera de circunvalación; (*Med*) (*operación f de*) by-pass *f* ▷ *vt* evitar

byte [baɪt] *n* (*Comput*) byte *m*, octeto

C

C [si:] n (Mus) do m
cab [kæb] n taxi m; (of truck) cabina
cabaret ['kæbəreɪ] n cabaret m
cabbage ['kæbɪdʒ] n col f, berza
cabin ['kæbɪn] n cabaña; (on ship) camarote m; (on plane) cabina; **cabin crew** n tripulación f de cabina
cabinet ['kæbɪnɪt] n (Pol) consejo de ministros; (furniture) armario; (also: **display ~**) vitrina; **cabinet minister** n ministro/a (del gabinete)
cable ['keɪbl] n cable m ⊳ vt cablegrafiar; **cable car** n teleférico; **cable television** n televisión f por cable
cactus ['kæktəs] (pl **cacti**) n cacto
café ['kæfeɪ] n café m
cafeteria [kæfɪ'tɪərɪə] n cafetería
caffein(e) ['kæfi:n] n cafeína
cage [keɪdʒ] n jaula
cagoule [kə'gu:l] n chubasquero
cake [keɪk] n (Culin: large) tarta; (: small) pastel m; (of soap) pastilla
calcium ['kælsɪəm] n calcio
calculate ['kælkjuleɪt] vt calcular; **calculation** [-'leɪʃən] n cálculo, cómputo; **calculator** n calculadora
calendar ['kæləndə*] n calendario
calf [kɑːf] (pl **calves**) n (of cow) ternero, becerro; (of other animals) cría; (also: **~skin**) piel f de becerro; (Anat) pantorrilla
calibre ['kælɪbə*] (us **caliber**) n calibre m
call [kɔːl] vt llamar; (meeting) convocar ⊳ vi (shout) llamar; (Tel) llamar (por teléfono); (visit: also: **~ in, ~ round**) hacer una visita ⊳ n llamada; (of bird) canto; **to be ~ed** llamarse; **on ~** (on duty) de guardia; **call back** vi (return) volver; (Tel) volver a llamar; **call for** vt fus (demand) pedir, exigir; (fetch) pasar a recoger; **call in** vt (doctor, expert, police) llamar; **call off** vt (cancel: meeting, race) cancelar; (: deal) anular; (: strike)

desconvocar; **call on** vt fus (visit) visitar; (turn to) acudir a; **call out** vi gritar; **call up** vt (Mil) llamar al servicio militar; (Tel) llamar; **callbox** (BRIT) n cabina telefónica; **call centre** (us **call center**) n centro de atención al cliente; **caller** n visita; (Tel) usuario/a
callous ['kæləs] adj insensible, cruel
calm [kɑːm] adj tranquilo; (sea) liso, en calma ⊳ n calma, tranquilidad f ⊳ vt calmar, tranquilizar; **calm down** vi calmarse, tranquilizarse ⊳ vt calmar, tranquilizar; **calmly** ['kɑːmlɪ] adv tranquilamente, con calma
Calor gas® ['kælə*-] n butano
calorie ['kælərɪ] n caloría
calves [kɑːvz] npl of **calf**
camcorder ['kæmkɔːdə*] n videocámara
came [keɪm] pt of **come**
camel ['kæməl] n camello
camera ['kæmərə] n máquina fotográfica; (Cinema, TV) cámara; **in ~** (Law) a puerta cerrada; **cameraman** (irreg) n cámara m; **camera phone** n teléfono con cámara
camouflage ['kæməflɑːʒ] n camuflaje m ⊳ vt camuflar
camp [kæmp] n campamento, camping m; (Mil) campamento; (for prisoners) campo; (fig: faction) bando ⊳ vi acampar ⊳ adj afectado, afeminado
campaign [kæm'peɪn] n (Mil, Pol etc) campaña ⊳ vi hacer campaña; **campaigner** n: **campaigner for** defensor(a) m/f de
camp: campbed (BRIT) n cama de campaña; **camper** n campista mf; (vehicle) caravana; **campground** (us) n camping m, campamento; **camping** n camping m; **to go camping** hacer camping; **campsite** n camping m
campus ['kæmpəs] n ciudad f universitaria
can[1] [kæn] n (of oil, water) bidón m; (tin) lata, bote m ⊳ vt enlatar

○ KEYWORD

can[2] [kæn] (negative **cannot, can't**, conditional and pt **could**) aux vb **1** (be able to) poder; **you can do it if you try** puedes hacerlo si lo intentas; **I can't see you** no te veo

2 (know how to) saber; **I can swim/play tennis/drive** sé nadar/jugar al tenis/conducir; **can you speak French?** ¿hablas or sabes hablar francés?

3 (may) poder; **can I use your phone?** ¿me dejas or puedo usar tu teléfono?

4 (expressing disbelief, puzzlement etc): **it can't**

be true! ¡no puede ser (verdad)!; **what CAN he want?** ¿qué querrá?

5 (*expressing possibility, suggestion etc*): **he could be in the library** podría estar en la biblioteca; **she could have been delayed** pudo haberse retrasado

Canada ['kænədə] *n* (el) Canadá; **Canadian** [kə'neɪdɪən] *adj, n* canadiense *mf*

canal [kə'næl] *n* canal *m*

canary [kə'nɛərɪ] *n* canario

Canary Islands [kə'nɛərɪ'aɪləndz] *npl*: **the ~** las (Islas) Canarias

cancel ['kænsəl] *vt* cancelar; (*train*) suprimir; (*cross out*) tachar, borrar; **cancellation** [-'leɪʃən] *n* cancelación *f*; supresión *f*

Cancer ['kænsə*] *n* (*Astrology*) Cáncer *m*

cancer ['kænsə*] *n* cáncer *m*

candidate ['kændɪdeɪt] *n* candidato/a

candle ['kændl] *n* vela; (*in church*) cirio; **candlestick** *n* (*single*) candelero; (*low*) palmatoria; (*bigger, ornate*) candelabro

candy ['kændɪ] *n* azúcar *m* cande; (*us*) caramelo; **candy bar** (*us*) *n* barrita (*dulce*); **candyfloss** (*BRIT*) *n* algodón *m* (azucarado)

cane [keɪn] *n* (*Bot*) caña; (*stick*) vara, palmeta; (*for furniture*) mimbre *f* ▷ *vt* (*BRIT: Scol*) castigar (con vara)

canister ['kænɪstə*] *n* bote *m*, lata; (*of gas*) bombona

cannabis ['kænəbɪs] *n* marijuana

canned [kænd] *adj* en lata, de lata

cannon ['kænən] (*pl ~ or ~s*) *n* cañón *m*

cannot ['kænɔt] = **can not**

canoe [kə'nuː] *n* canoa; (*Sport*) piragua; **canoeing** *n* piragüismo

canon ['kænən] *n* (*clergyman*) canónigo; (*standard*) canon *m*

can-opener ['kænəupnə*] *n* abrelatas *m inv*

can't [kɑːnt] = **can not**

canteen [kæn'tiːn] *n* (*eating place*) cantina; (*BRIT: of cutlery*) juego

canter ['kæntə*] *vi* ir a medio galope

canvas ['kænvəs] *n* (*material*) lona; (*painting*) lienzo; (*Naut*) velas *fpl*

canvass ['kænvəs] *vi* (*Pol*): **to ~ for** solicitar votos por ▷ *vt* (*Comm*) sondear

canyon ['kænjən] *n* cañón *m*

cap [kæp] *n* (*hat*) gorra; (*of pen*) capuchón *m*; (*of bottle*) tapa, tapón *m*; (*contraceptive*) diafragma *m*; (*for toy gun*) cápsula ▷ *vt* (*outdo*) superar; (*limit*) recortar

capability [keɪpə'bɪlɪtɪ] *n* capacidad *f*

capable ['keɪpəbl] *adj* capaz

capacity [kə'pæsɪtɪ] *n* capacidad *f*; (*position*) calidad *f*

cape [keɪp] *n* capa; (*Geo*) cabo

caper ['keɪpə*] *n* (*Culin: gen pl*) alcaparra; (*prank*) broma

capital ['kæpɪtl] *n* (*also: ~ city*) capital *f*; (*money*) capital *m*; (*also: ~ letter*) mayúscula; **capitalism** *n* capitalismo; **capitalist** *adj, n* capitalista *mf*; **capital punishment** *n* pena de muerte

Capitol ['kæpɪtl] *n ver abajo*

● **CAPITOL**
●
● El Capitolio (**Capitol**) es el edificio del
● Congreso (**Congress**) de los Estados
● Unidos, situado en la ciudad de
● Washington. Por extensión, también
● se suele llamar así al edificio en el que
● tienen lugar las sesiones parlamentarias
● de la cámara de representantes de
● muchos de los estados.

Capricorn ['kæprɪkɔːn] *n* Capricornio

capsize [kæp'saɪz] *vt* volcar, hacer zozobrar ▷ *vi* volcarse, zozobrar

capsule ['kæpsjuːl] *n* cápsula

captain ['kæptɪn] *n* capitán *m*

caption ['kæpʃən] *n* (*heading*) título; (*to picture*) leyenda

captivity [kæp'tɪvɪtɪ] *n* cautiverio

capture ['kæptʃə*] *vt* prender, apresar; (*animal, Comput*) capturar; (*place*) tomar; (*attention*) captar, llamar ▷ *n* apresamiento; captura; toma; (*data capture*) formulación *f* de datos

car [kɑː*] *n* coche *m*, carro (*LAM*), automóvil *m*; (*US Rail*) vagón *m*

carafe [kə'ræf] *n* jarra

caramel ['kærəməl] *n* caramelo

carat ['kærət] *n* quilate *m*

caravan ['kærəvæn] *n* (*BRIT*) caravana, ruló *f*; (*in desert*) caravana; **caravan site** (*BRIT*) *n* camping *m* para caravanas

carbohydrate [kɑːbəu'haɪdreɪt] *n* hidrato de carbono; (*food*) fécula

carbon ['kɑːbən] *n* carbono; **carbon dioxide** *n* dióxido de carbono, anhídrido carbónico; **carbon monoxide** *n* monóxido de carbono

car boot sale *n* mercadillo organizado en un aparcamiento, en el que se exponen las mercancías en el maletero del coche

carburettor [kɑːbju'retə*] (*US* **carburetor**) *n* carburador *m*

card [kɑːd] *n* (*material*) cartulina; (*index card etc*) ficha; (*playing card*) carta, naipe *m*; (*visiting card, greetings card etc*) tarjeta; **cardboard** *n* cartón *m*; **card game** *n*

juego de naipes or cartas
cardigan ['kɑːdɪgən] n rebeca
cardinal ['kɑːdɪnl] adj cardinal;
(importance, principal) esencial ▷ n cardenal
m
cardphone ['kɑːdfəun] n cabina que
funciona con tarjetas telefónicas
care [kɛə*] n cuidado; (worry) inquietud
f; (charge) cargo, custodia ▷ vi: **to ~ about**
(person, animal) tener cariño a; (thing, idea)
preocuparse por; **~ of** en casa de, al cuidado
de; **in sb's ~** a cargo de algn; **to take ~ to**
cuidarse de, tener cuidado de; **to take ~ of**
cuidar; (problem etc) ocuparse de; **I don't
~** no me importa; **I couldn't ~ less** eso me
trae sin cuidado; **care for** vt fus cuidar a;
(like) querer
career [kə'rɪə*] n profesión f; (in work,
school) carrera ▷ vi (also: **~ along**) correr a
toda velocidad
care: carefree adj despreocupado; **careful**
adj cuidadoso; (cautious) cauteloso; **(be)
careful!** ¡tenga cuidado!; **carefully** adv con
cuidado, cuidadosamente; con cautela;
caregiver (us) n (professional) enfermero/a
m/f; (unpaid) persona que cuida a un pariente o
vecino; **careless** adj descuidado; (heedless)
poco atento; **carelessness** n descuido,
falta de atención; **carer** ['kɛərə*] n
(professional) enfermero/a m/f; (unpaid)
persona que cuida a un pariente o vecino;
caretaker n portero/a, conserje mf
car-ferry ['kɑːfɛrɪ] n transbordador m
para coches
cargo ['kɑːgəu] (pl **~es**) n cargamento,
carga
car hire n alquiler m de automóviles
Caribbean [kærɪ'biːən] n: **the ~ (Sea)** el
(Mar) Caribe
caring ['kɛərɪŋ] adj humanitario;
(behaviour) afectuoso
carnation [kɑː'neɪʃən] n clavel m
carnival ['kɑːnɪvəl] n carnaval m;
(us: funfair) parque m de atracciones
carol ['kærəl] n: **(Christmas) ~** villancico
carousel [kærə'sɛl] (us) n tiovivo,
caballitos mpl
car park (BRIT) n aparcamiento, parking m
carpenter ['kɑːpɪntə*] n carpintero/a
carpet ['kɑːpɪt] n alfombra; (fitted)
moqueta ▷ vt alfombrar
car rental (us) n alquiler m de coches
carriage ['kærɪdʒ] n (BRIT Rail) vagón m;
(horse-drawn) coche m; (of goods) transporte
m; (: cost) porte m, flete m; **carriageway**
(BRIT) n (part of road) calzada
carrier ['kærɪə*] n (transport company)
transportista, empresa de transportes;

(Med) portador(a) m/f; **carrier bag** (BRIT) n
bolsa de papel or plástico
carrot ['kærət] n zanahoria
carry ['kærɪ] vt (person) llevar; (transport)
transportar; (involve: responsibilities etc)
entrañar, implicar; (Med) ser portador de
▷ vi (sound) oírse; **to get carried away**
(fig) entusiasmarse; **carry on** vi (continue)
seguir (adelante), continuar ▷ vt proseguir,
continuar; **carry out** vt (orders) cumplir;
(investigation) llevar a cabo, realizar
cart [kɑːt] n carro, carreta ▷ vt
(inf: transport) acarrear
carton ['kɑːtən] n (box) caja (de cartón); (of
milk etc) bote m; (of yogurt) tarrina
cartoon [kɑː'tuːn] n (Press) caricatura;
(comic strip) tira cómica; (film) dibujos mpl
animados
cartridge ['kɑːtrɪdʒ] n cartucho; (of pen)
recambio
carve [kɑːv] vt (meat) trinchar; (wood,
stone) cincelar, esculpir; (initials etc) grabar;
carving n (object) escultura; (design) talla;
(art) tallado
car wash n lavado de coches
case [keɪs] n (container) caja; (Med) caso;
(for jewels etc) estuche m; (Law) causa,
proceso; (BRIT: also: **suit~**) maleta; **in ~ of**
en caso de; **in any ~** en todo caso; **just in ~**
por si acaso
cash [kæʃ] n dinero en efectivo, dinero
contante ▷ vt cobrar, hacer efectivo; **to
pay (in) ~** pagar al contado; **~ on delivery**
cóbrese al entregar; **cashback** n (discount)
devolución f; (at supermarket etc) retirada de
dinero en efectivo de un establecimiento donde se
ha pagado con tarjeta; también dinero retirado;
cash card n tarjeta f dinero; **cash desk**
(BRIT) n caja; **cash dispenser** n cajero
automático
cashew [kæ'ʃuː] n (also: **~ nut**) anacardo
cashier [kæ'ʃɪə*] n cajero/a
cashmere ['kæʃmɪə*] n cachemira
cash point n cajero automático
cash register n caja
casino [kə'siːnəu] n casino
casket ['kɑːskɪt] n cofre m, estuche m;
(us: coffin) ataúd m
casserole ['kæsərəul] n (food, pot) cazuela
cassette [kæ'sɛt] n casete f; **cassette
player, cassette recorder** n casete m
cast [kɑːst] (pt, pp **~**) vt (throw) echar,
arrojar, lanzar; (glance, eyes) dirigir;
(Theatre): **to ~ sb as Othello** dar a algn el
papel de Otelo ▷ vi (Fishing) lanzar ▷ n
(Theatre) reparto; (also: **plaster ~**) vaciado;
to ~ one's vote votar; **to ~ doubt on**
suscitar dudas acerca de; **cast off** vi (Naut)

desamarrar; (*Knitting*) cerrar (los puntos)

castanets [kæstə'nɛts] *npl* castañuelas *fpl*

caster sugar ['kɑːstə*-] (*BRIT*) *n* azúcar *m* extrafino

Castile [kæs'tiːl] *n* Castilla; **Castilian** *adj*, *n* castellano/a *m/f*

cast-iron ['kɑːstaɪən] *adj* (*lit*) (hecho) de hierro fundido; (*fig: case*) irrebatible

castle ['kɑːsl] *n* castillo; (*Chess*) torre *f*

casual ['kæʒjul] *adj* fortuito; (*irregular: work etc*) eventual, temporero; (*unconcerned*) despreocupado; (*clothes*) informal

▌ Be careful not to translate **casual** by the Spanish word *casual*.

casualty ['kæʒjultɪ] *n* víctima, herido/a; (*dead*) muerto/a; (*Med: department*) urgencias *fpl*

cat [kæt] *n* gato; (*big cat*) felino

Catalan ['kætəlæn] *adj*, *n* catalán/ana *m/f*

catalogue ['kætəlɒg] (*US* **catalog**) *n* catálogo ▷ *vt* catalogar

Catalonia [kætə'ləunɪə] *n* Cataluña

catalytic converter [kætə'lɪtɪkkən'vɜːtə*] *n* catalizador *m*

cataract ['kætərækt] *n* (*Med*) cataratas *fpl*

catarrh [kə'tɑː*] *n* catarro

catastrophe [kə'tæstrəfɪ] *n* catástrofe *f*

catch [kætʃ] (*pt, pp* **caught**) *vt* coger (*SP*), agarrar (*LAM*); (*arrest*) detener; (*grasp*) asir; (*breath*) contener; (*surprise: person*) sorprender; (*attract: attention*) captar; (*hear*) oír; (*Med*) contagiarse de, coger; (*also:* **~ up**) alcanzar ▷ *vi* (*fire*) encenderse; (*in branches etc*) enredarse ▷ *n* (*fish etc*) pesca; (*act of catching*) cogida; (*hidden problem*) dificultad *f*; (*game*) pilla-pilla; (*of lock*) pestillo, cerradura; **to ~ fire** encenderse; **to ~ sight of** divisar; **catch up** *vi* (*fig*) ponerse al día; **catching** ['kætʃɪŋ] *adj* (*Med*) contagioso

category ['kætɪgərɪ] *n* categoría, clase *f*

cater ['keɪtə*] *vi*: **to ~ for** (*BRIT*) abastecer a; (*needs*) atender a; (*Comm: parties etc*) proveer comida a

caterpillar ['kætəpɪlə*] *n* oruga, gusano

cathedral [kə'θiːdrəl] *n* catedral *f*

Catholic ['kæθəlɪk] *adj*, *n* (*Rel*) católico/a *m/f*

Catseye® ['kætsaɪ] (*BRIT*) *n* (*Aut*) catafoto

cattle ['kætl] *npl* ganado

catwalk ['kætwɔːk] *n* pasarela

caught [kɔːt] *pt, pp of* **catch**

cauliflower ['kɒlɪflauə*] *n* coliflor *f*

cause [kɔːz] *n* causa, motivo, razón *f*; (*principle: also Pol*) causa ▷ *vt* causar

caution ['kɔːʃən] *n* cautela, prudencia; (*warning*) advertencia, amonestación *f*

▷ *vt* amonestar; **cautious** *adj* cauteloso, prudente, precavido

cave [keɪv] *n* cueva, caverna; **cave in** *vi* (*roof etc*) derrumbarse, hundirse

caviar(e) ['kævɪɑː*] *n* caviar *m*

cavity ['kævɪtɪ] *n* hueco, cavidad *f*

cc *abbr* (= *cubic centimetres*) c.c.; (= *carbon copy*) copia hecha con papel del carbón

CCTV *n abbr* (= *closed-circuit television*) circuito cerrado de televisión

CD *n abbr* (= *compact disc*) CD *m*; (*player*) (reproductor *m* de) CD; **CD player** *n* reproductor *m* de CD; **CD-ROM** [siːdiː'rɔm] *n abbr* CD-ROM *m*; **CD writer** *n* grabadora de CD

cease [siːs] *vt, vi* cesar; **ceasefire** *n* alto *m* el fuego

cedar ['siːdə*] *n* cedro

ceilidh ['keɪlɪ] *n* baile con música y danzas tradicionales escocesas o irlandesas

ceiling ['siːlɪŋ] *n* techo; (*fig*) límite *m*

celebrate ['sɛlɪbreɪt] *vt* celebrar ▷ *vi* divertirse; **celebration** [-'breɪʃən] *n* fiesta, celebración *f*

celebrity [sɪ'lɛbrɪtɪ] *n* celebridad *f*

celery ['sɛlərɪ] *n* apio

cell [sɛl] *n* celda; (*Biol*) célula; (*Elec*) elemento

cellar ['sɛlə*] *n* sótano; (*for wine*) bodega

cello ['tʃɛləu] *n* violoncelo

Cellophane® ['sɛləfeɪn] *n* celofán *m*

cellphone ['sɛlfəʊn] *n* teléfono celular

Celsius ['sɛlsɪəs] *adj* centígrado

Celtic ['kɛltɪk] *adj* celta

cement [sə'mɛnt] *n* cemento

cemetery ['sɛmɪtrɪ] *n* cementerio

censor ['sɛnsə*] *n* censor *m* ▷ *vt* (*cut*) censurar; **censorship** *n* censura

census ['sɛnsəs] *n* censo

cent [sɛnt] *n* (*unit of dollar*) centavo, céntimo; (*unit of euro*) céntimo; *see also* **per**

centenary [sɛn'tiːnərɪ] *n* centenario

centennial [sɛn'tɛnɪəl] (*US*) *n* centenario

center ['sɛntə*] (*US*) = **centre**

centi... [sɛntɪ] *prefix*: **centigrade** *adj* centígrado; **centimetre** (*US* **centimeter**) *n* centímetro; **centipede** ['sɛntɪpiːd] *n* ciempiés *m inv*

central ['sɛntrəl] *adj* central; (*house etc*) céntrico; **Central America** *n* Centroamérica; **central heating** *n* calefacción *f* central; **central reservation** *n* (*BRIT Aut*) mediana

centre ['sɛntə*] (*US* **center**) *n* centro; (*fig*) núcleo ▷ *vt* centrar; **centre-forward** *n* (*Sport*) delantero centro; **centre-half** *n* (*Sport*) medio centro

century ['sɛntjurɪ] *n* siglo; **20th ~** siglo

veinte

CEO *n abbr* = **chief executive officer**

ceramic [sɪ'ræmɪk] *adj* cerámico

cereal ['si:rɪəl] *n* cereal *m*

ceremony ['sɛrɪmənɪ] *n* ceremonia; **to stand on ~** hacer ceremonias, estar de cumplido

certain ['sɜ:tən] *adj* seguro; (*person*): **a ~ Mr Smith** un tal Sr. Smith; (*particular, some*) cierto; **for ~** a ciencia cierta; **certainly** *adv* (*undoubtedly*) ciertamente; (*of course*) desde luego, por supuesto; **certainty** *n* certeza, certidumbre *f*, seguridad *f*; (*inevitability*) certeza

certificate [sə'tɪfɪkɪt] *n* certificado

certify ['sɜ:tɪfaɪ] *vt* certificar; (*award diploma to*) conceder un diploma a; (*declare insane*) declarar loco

cf. *abbr* (= *compare*) cfr

CFC *n abbr* (= *chlorofluorocarbon*) CFC *m*

chain [tʃeɪn] *n* cadena; (*of mountains*) cordillera; (*of events*) sucesión *f* ▷ *vt* (*also: ~ up*) encadenar; **chain-smoke** *vi* fumar un cigarrillo tras otro

chair [tʃɛə*] *n* silla; (*armchair*) sillón *m*, butaca; (*of university*) cátedra; (*of meeting etc*) presidencia ▷ *vt* (*meeting*) presidir; **chairlift** *n* telesilla; **chairman** (*irreg*) *n* presidente *m*; **chairperson** *n* presidente/a *m/f*; **chairwoman** (*irreg*) *n* presidenta

chalet ['ʃæleɪ] *n* chalet *m* (de madera)

chalk [tʃɔ:k] *n* (*Geo*) creta; (*for writing*) tiza, gis *m* (MEX); **chalkboard** (US) *n* pizarrón (LAM), pizarra (SP)

challenge ['tʃælɪndʒ] *n* desafío, reto ▷ *vt* desafiar, retar; (*statement, right*) poner en duda; **to ~ sb to do sth** retar a algn a que haga algo; **challenging** *adj* exigente; (*tone*) de desafío

chamber ['tʃeɪmbə*] *n* cámara, sala; (*Pol*) cámara; (BRIT Law: *gen pl*) despacho; **~ of commerce** cámara de comercio; **chambermaid** *n* camarera

champagne [ʃæm'peɪn] *n* champaña *m*, champán *m*

champion ['tʃæmpɪən] *n* campeón/ona *m/f*; (*of cause*) defensor(a) *m/f*; **championship** *n* campeonato

chance [tʃɑ:ns] *n* (*opportunity*) ocasión *f*, oportunidad *f*; (*likelihood*) posibilidad *f*; (*risk*) riesgo ▷ *vt* arriesgar, probar ▷ *adj* fortuito, casual; **to ~ it** arriesgarse, intentarlo; **to take a ~** arriesgarse; **by ~** por casualidad

chancellor ['tʃɑ:nsələ*] *n* canciller *m*; **Chancellor of the Exchequer** (BRIT) *n* Ministro de Hacienda

chandelier [ʃændə'lɪə*] *n* araña (de luces)

change [tʃeɪndʒ] *vt* cambiar; (*replace*) cambiar, reemplazar; (*gear, clothes, job*) cambiar de; (*transform*) transformar ▷ *vi* cambiar(se); (*change trains*) hacer transbordo; (*traffic lights*) cambiar de color; (*be transformed*): **to ~ into** transformarse en ▷ *n* cambio; (*alteration*) modificación *f*; (*transformation*) transformación *f*; (*of clothes*) muda; (*coins*) suelto, sencillo; (*money returned*) vuelta; **to ~ gear** (*Aut*) cambiar de marcha; **to ~ one's mind** cambiar de opinión o idea; **for a ~** para variar; **change over** *vi* (*from sth to sth*) cambiar; (*players etc*) cambiar(se) ▷ *vt* cambiar; **changeable** *adj* (*weather*) cambiable; **change machine** *n* máquina de cambio; **changing room** (BRIT) *n* vestuario

channel ['tʃænl] *n* (*TV*) canal *m*; (*of river*) cauce *m*; (*groove*) conducto; (*fig: medium*) medio ▷ *vt* (*river etc*) encauzar; **the (English) C~** el Canal (de la Mancha); **the C~ Islands** las Islas Normandas; **Channel Tunnel** *n*: **the Channel Tunnel** el túnel del Canal de la Mancha, el Eurotúnel

chant [tʃɑ:nt] *n* (*of crowd*) gritos *mpl*; (*Rel*) canto ▷ *vt* (*slogan, word*) repetir a gritos

chaos ['keɪɔs] *n* caos *m*

chaotic [keɪ'ɔtɪk] *adj* caótico

chap [tʃæp] (BRIT: *inf*) *n* (*man*) tío, tipo

chapel ['tʃæpəl] *n* capilla

chapped [tʃæpt] *adj* agrietado

chapter ['tʃæptə*] *n* capítulo

character ['kærɪktə*] *n* carácter *m*, naturaleza, índole *f*; (*moral strength, personality*) carácter; (*in novel, film*) personaje *m*; **characteristic** [-'rɪstɪk] *adj* característico ▷ *n* característica; **characterize** ['kærɪktəraɪz] *vt* caracterizar

charcoal ['tʃɑ:kəul] *n* carbón *m* vegetal; (*Art*) carboncillo

charge [tʃɑ:dʒ] *n* (*Law*) cargo, acusación *f*; (*cost*) precio, coste *m*; (*responsibility*) cargo ▷ *vt* (*Law*): **to ~ (with)** acusar (de); (*battery*) cargar; (*price*) pedir; (*customer*) cobrar ▷ *vi* precipitarse; (*Mil*) cargar, atacar; **charge card** *n* tarjeta de cuenta; **charger** *n* (*also*: **battery charger**) cargador *m* (de baterías)

charismatic [kærɪz'mætɪk] *adj* carismático

charity ['tʃærɪtɪ] *n* caridad *f*; (*organization*) sociedad *f* benéfica; (*money, gifts*) limosnas *fpl*; **charity shop** *n* (BRIT) *tienda de artículos de segunda mano que dedica su recaudación a causas benéficas*

charm [tʃɑ:m] *n* encanto, atractivo; (*talisman*) hechizo; (*on bracelet*) dije *m* ▷ *vt* encantar; **charming** *adj* encantador(a)

chart [tʃɑːt] n (diagram) cuadro; (graph) gráfica; (map) carta de navegación ▷ vt (course) trazar; (progress) seguir; **charts** npl (Top 40): **the ~s** ≈ los 40 principales (SP)

charter ['tʃɑːtə*] vt (plane) alquilar; (ship) fletar ▷ n (document) carta; (of university, company) estatutos mpl; **chartered accountant** (BRIT) n contable m/f diplomado/a; **charter flight** n vuelo chárter

chase [tʃeɪs] vt (pursue) perseguir; (also: **~ away**) ahuyentar ▷ n persecución f

chat [tʃæt] vi (also: **have a ~**) charlar; (on Internet) chatear ▷ n charla; **chat up** vt (inf: girl) ligar con, enrollarse con; **chat room** n (Internet) chat m, canal m de charla; **chat show** (BRIT) n programa m de entrevistas

chatter ['tʃætə*] vi (person) charlar; (teeth) castañetear ▷ n (of birds) parloteo; (of people) charla, cháchara

chauffeur ['ʃəufə*] n chófer m

chauvinist ['ʃəuvɪnɪst] n (male chauvinist) machista m; (nationalist) chovinista mf

cheap [tʃiːp] adj barato; (joke) de mal gusto; (poor quality) de mala calidad ▷ adv barato; **cheap day return** n billete de ida y vuelta el mismo día; **cheaply** adv barato, a bajo precio

cheat [tʃiːt] vi hacer trampa ▷ vt: **to ~ sb (out of sth)** estafar (algo) a algn ▷ n (person) tramposo/a; **cheat on** vt fus engañar

Chechnya [tʃɪtʃ'njɑː] n Chechenia

check [tʃɛk] vt (examine) controlar; (facts) comprobar; (halt) parar, detener; (restrain) refrenar, restringir ▷ n (inspection) control m, inspección f; (curb) freno; (US: bill) nota, cuenta; (US) = **cheque**; (pattern: gen pl) cuadro; **check in** vi (at hotel) firmar el registro; (at airport) facturar el equipaje ▷ vt (luggage) facturar; **check off** vt (esp US: check) comprobar; (cross off) tachar; **check out** vi (of hotel) marcharse; **check up** vi: **to check up on sth** comprobar algo; **to check up on sb** investigar a algn; **checkbook** (US) = **chequebook**; **checked** adj a cuadros; **checkers** (US) n juego de damas; **check-in** (also: **check-in desk**: at airport) mostrador m de facturación; **checking account** (US) n cuenta corriente; **checklist** n lista (de control); **checkmate** n jaque m mate; **checkout** n caja; **checkpoint** n (punto de) control m; **checkroom** (US) n consigna; **checkup** n (Med) reconocimiento general

cheddar ['tʃedə*] n (also: **~ cheese**) queso m cheddar

cheek [tʃiːk] n mejilla; (impudence) descaro; **what a ~!** ¡qué cara!; **cheekbone** n pómulo; **cheeky** adj fresco, descarado

cheer [tʃɪə*] vt vitorear, aplaudir; (gladden) alegrar, animar ▷ vi dar vivas ▷ n viva m; **cheer up** vi animarse ▷ vt alegrar, animar; **cheerful** adj alegre

cheerio [tʃɪərɪ'əu] (BRIT) excl ¡hasta luego!

cheerleader ['tʃɪəliːdə*] n animador(a) m/f

cheese [tʃiːz] n queso; **cheeseburger** n hamburguesa con queso; **cheesecake** n pastel m de queso

chef [ʃef] n jefe/a m/f de cocina

chemical ['kemɪkəl] adj químico ▷ n producto químico

chemist ['kemɪst] n (BRIT: pharmacist) farmacéutico/a; (scientist) químico/a; **chemistry** n química; **chemist's (shop)** (BRIT) n farmacia

cheque [tʃek] (US **check**) n cheque m; **chequebook** n talonario de cheques (SP), chequera (LAM); **cheque card** n tarjeta de cheque

cherry ['tʃerɪ] n cereza; (also: **~ tree**) cerezo

chess [tʃes] n ajedrez m

chest [tʃest] n (Anat) pecho; (box) cofre m, cajón m

chestnut ['tʃesnʌt] n castaña; (also: **~ tree**) castaño

chest of drawers n cómoda

chew [tʃuː] vt mascar, masticar; **chewing gum** n chicle m

chic [ʃiːk] adj elegante

chick [tʃɪk] n pollito, polluelo; (inf: girl) chica

chicken ['tʃɪkɪn] n gallina, pollo; (food) pollo; (inf: coward) gallina mf; **chicken out** (inf) vi rajarse; **chickenpox** n varicela

chickpea ['tʃɪkpiː] n garbanzo

chief [tʃiːf] n jefe/a m/f ▷ adj principal; **chief executive (officer)** n director(a) m/f general; **chiefly** adv principalmente

child [tʃaɪld] (pl **~ren**) n niño/a; (offspring) hijo/a; **child abuse** n (with violence) malos tratos mpl a niños; (sexual) abuso m sexual de niños; **child benefit** n (BRIT) subsidio por cada hijo pequeño; **childbirth** n parto; **childcare** n cuidado de los niños; **childhood** n niñez f, infancia; **childish** adj pueril, aniñado; **child minder** (BRIT) n madre f de día; **children** ['tʃɪldrən] npl of **child**

Chile ['tʃɪlɪ] n Chile m; **Chilean** adj, n chileno/a m/f

chill [tʃɪl] n frío; (Med) resfriado ▷ vt enfriar; (Culin) congelar; **chill out** vi (esp US: inf) tranquilizarse

chil(l)i ['tʃɪlɪ] (BRIT) n chile m, ají m (SC)

chilly ['tʃɪlɪ] adj frío

chimney ['tʃɪmnɪ] n chimenea
chimpanzee [tʃɪmpæn'ziː] n chimpancé m
chin [tʃɪn] n mentón m, barbilla
China ['tʃaɪnə] n China
china ['tʃaɪnə] n porcelana; (crockery) loza
Chinese [tʃaɪ'niːz] adj chino ▷ n inv chino/a m/f; (Ling) chino
chip [tʃɪp] n (gen pl: Culin: BRIT) patata (SP) or papa (LAM) frita; (: US: also: **potato ~**) patata or papa frita; (of wood) astilla; (of glass, stone) lasca; (at poker) ficha; (Comput) chip m ▷ vt (cup, plate) desconchar;
chip shop pescadería (donde se vende principalmente pescado rebozado y patatas fritas)
chiropodist [kɪ'rɒpədɪst] (BRIT) n pedicuro/a, callista m/f
chisel ['tʃɪzl] n (for wood) escoplo; (for stone) cincel m
chives [tʃaɪvz] npl cebollinos mpl
chlorine ['klɔːriːn] n cloro
choc-ice ['tʃɒkaɪs] n (BRIT) helado m cubierto de chocolate
chocolate ['tʃɒklɪt] n chocolate m; (sweet) bombón m
choice [tʃɔɪs] n elección f, selección f; (option) opción f; (preference) preferencia ▷ adj escogido
choir ['kwaɪə*] n coro
choke [tʃəuk] vi ahogarse; (on food) atragantarse ▷ vt estrangular, ahogar; (block): **to be ~d with** estar atascado de ▷ n (Aut) estárter m
cholesterol [kə'lɛstərʊl] n colesterol m
choose [tʃuːz] (pt **chose**, pp **chosen**) vt escoger, elegir; (team) seleccionar; **to ~ to do sth** optar por hacer algo
chop [tʃɒp] vt (wood) cortar, tajar; (Culin: also: **~ up**) picar ▷ n (Culin) chuleta; **chop down** vt (tree) talar; **chop off** vt cortar (de un tajo); **chopsticks** ['tʃɒpstɪks] npl palillos mpl
chord [kɔːd] n (Mus) acorde m
chore [tʃɔː*] n faena, tarea; (routine task) trabajo rutinario
chorus ['kɔːrəs] n coro; (repeated part of song) estribillo
chose [tʃəuz] pt of **choose**
chosen [tʃəuzn] pp of **choose**
Christ [kraɪst] n Cristo
christen ['krɪsn] vt bautizar; **christening** n bautizo
Christian ['krɪstɪən] adj, n cristiano/a m/f; **Christianity** [-'ænɪtɪ] n cristianismo; **Christian name** n nombre m de pila
Christmas ['krɪsməs] n Navidad f; **Merry ~!** ¡Felices Pascuas!; **Christmas**

card n crismas m inv, tarjeta de Navidad; **Christmas carol** n villancico m; **Christmas Day** n día m de Navidad; **Christmas Eve** n Nochebuena; **Christmas pudding** n (esp BRIT) pudin m de Navidad; **Christmas tree** n árbol m de Navidad
chrome [krəum] n cromo
chronic ['krɒnɪk] adj crónico
chrysanthemum [krɪ'sænθəməm] n crisantemo
chubby ['tʃʌbɪ] adj regordete
chuck [tʃʌk] (inf) vt lanzar, arrojar; (BRIT: also: **~ up**) abandonar; **chuck out** vt (person) echar (fuera); (rubbish etc) tirar
chuckle ['tʃʌkl] vi reírse entre dientes
chum [tʃʌm] n compañero/a
chunk [tʃʌŋk] n pedazo, trozo
church [tʃəːtʃ] n iglesia; **churchyard** n cementerio
churn [tʃəːn] n (for butter) mantequera; (for milk) lechera
chute [ʃuːt] n (also: **rubbish ~**) vertedero; (for coal etc) rampa de caída
chutney ['tʃʌtnɪ] n condimento a base de frutas de la India
CIA (US) n abbr (= Central Intelligence Agency) CIA f
CID (BRIT) n abbr (= Criminal Investigation Department) ≈ B.I.C. f (SP)
cider ['saɪdə*] n sidra
cigar [sɪ'gɑː*] n puro
cigarette [sɪgə'rɛt] n cigarrillo; **cigarette lighter** n mechero
cinema ['sɪnəmə] n cine m
cinnamon ['sɪnəmən] n canela
circle ['səːkl] n círculo; (in theatre) anfiteatro ▷ vi dar vueltas ▷ vt (surround) rodear, cercar; (move round) dar la vuelta a
circuit ['səːkɪt] n circuito; (tour) gira; (track) pista; (lap) vuelta
circular ['səːkjulə*] adj circular ▷ n circular f
circulate ['səːkjuleɪt] vi circular; (person: at party etc) hablar con los invitados ▷ vt poner en circulación; **circulation** [-'leɪʃən] n circulación f; (of newspaper) tirada
circumstances ['səːkəmstənsɪz] npl circunstancias fpl; (financial condition) situación f económica
circus ['səːkəs] n circo
cite [saɪt] vt citar
citizen ['sɪtɪzn] n (Pol) ciudadano/a; (of city) vecino/a, habitante m/f; **citizenship** n ciudadanía; (BRIT: Scol) civismo
citrus fruits ['sɪtrəs-] npl agrios mpl
city ['sɪtɪ] n ciudad f; **the C~** centro financiero de Londres; **city centre** (BRIT)

n centro de la ciudad; **city technology college** *n* centro de formación profesional (*centro de enseñanza secundaria que da especial importancia a la ciencia y tecnología.*)

civic ['sɪvɪk] *adj* cívico; (*authorities*) municipal

civil ['sɪvɪl] *adj* civil; (*polite*) atento, cortés; **civilian** [sɪ'vɪlɪən] *adj* civil (*no militar*) ▷ *n* civil *mf*, paisano/a

civilization [sɪvɪlaɪ'zeɪʃən] *n* civilización *f*

civilized ['sɪvɪlaɪzd] *adj* civilizado

civil: civil law *n* derecho civil; **civil rights** *npl* derechos *mpl* civiles; **civil servant** *n* funcionario/a del Estado; **Civil Service** *n* administración *f* pública; **civil war** *n* guerra civil

CJD *n abbr* (= *Creutzfeldt-Jakob disease*) enfermedad de Creutzfeldt-Jakob

claim [kleɪm] *vt* exigir, reclamar; (*rights etc*) reivindicar; (*assert*) pretender ▷ *vi* (*for insurance*) reclamar ▷ *n* reclamación *f*; pretensión *f*; **claim form** *n* solicitud *f*

clam [klæm] *n* almeja

clamp [klæmp] *n* abrazadera, grapa ▷ *vt* (*two things together*) cerrar fuertemente; (*one thing on another*) afianzar (con abrazadera); (*Aut: wheel*) poner el cepo a

clan [klæn] *n* clan *m*

clap [klæp] *vi* aplaudir

claret ['klærət] *n* burdeos *m inv*

clarify ['klærɪfaɪ] *vt* aclarar

clarinet [klærɪ'nɛt] *n* clarinete *m*

clarity ['klærɪtɪ] *n* claridad *f*

clash [klæʃ] *n* enfrentamiento; choque *m*; desacuerdo; estruendo ▷ *vi* (*fight*) enfrentarse; (*beliefs*) chocar; (*disagree*) estar en desacuerdo; (*colours*) desentonar; (*two events*) coincidir

clasp [klɑːsp] *n* (*hold*) apretón *m*; (*of necklace, bag*) cierre *m* ▷ *vt* apretar; abrazar

class [klɑːs] *n* clase *f* ▷ *vt* clasificar

classic ['klæsɪk] *adj*, *n* clásico; **classical** *adj* clásico

classification [klæsɪfɪ'keɪʃən] *n* clasificación *f*

classify ['klæsɪfaɪ] *vt* clasificar

classmate ['klɑːsmeɪt] *n* compañero/a de clase

classroom ['klɑːsrum] *n* aula; **classroom assistant** *n* profesor(a) *m/f* de apoyo

classy ['klɑːsɪ] *adj* (*inf*) elegante, con estilo

clatter ['klætə*] *n* estrépito ▷ *vi* hacer ruido *or* estrépito

clause [klɔːz] *n* cláusula; (*Ling*) oración *f*

claustrophobic [klɔːstrə'fəʊbɪk] *adj* claustrofóbico; **I feel ~** me entra claustrofobia

claw [klɔː] *n* (*of cat*) uña; (*of bird of prey*)

garra; (*of lobster*) pinza

clay [kleɪ] *n* arcilla

clean [kliːn] *adj* limpio; (*record, reputation*) bueno, intachable; (*joke*) decente ▷ *vt* limpiar; (*hands etc*) lavar; **clean up** *vt* limpiar, asear; **cleaner** *n* (*person*) asistenta; (*substance*) producto para la limpieza; **cleaner's** *n* tintorería; **cleaning** *n* limpieza

cleanser ['klɛnzə*] *n* (*for face*) crema limpiadora

clear [klɪə*] *adj* claro; (*road, way*) libre; (*conscience*) limpio, tranquilo; (*skin*) terso; (*sky*) despejado ▷ *vt* (*space*) despejar, limpiar; (*Law: suspect*) absolver; (*obstacle*) salvar, saltar por encima de; (*cheque*) aceptar ▷ *vi* (*fog etc*) despejarse ▷ *adv*: **~ of** a distancia de; **to ~ the table** recoger *or* levantar la mesa; **clear away** *vt* (*things, clothes etc*) quitar (de en medio); (*dishes*) retirar; **clear up** *vt* limpiar; (*mystery*) aclarar, resolver; **clearance** *n* (*removal*) despeje *m*; (*permission*) acreditación *f*; **clear-cut** *adj* bien definido, nítido; **clearing** *n* (*in wood*) claro; **clearly** *adv* claramente; (*evidently*) sin duda; **clearway** (*BRIT*) *n* carretera donde no se puede parar

clench [klɛntʃ] *vt* apretar, cerrar

clergy ['klɜːdʒɪ] *n* clero

clerk [klɑːk, (*US*) klɜːrk] *n* (*BRIT*) oficinista *mf*; (*US*) dependiente/a *m/f*

clever ['klɛvə*] *adj* (*intelligent*) inteligente, listo; (*skilful*) hábil; (*device, arrangement*) ingenioso

cliché ['kliːʃeɪ] *n* cliché *m*, frase *f* hecha

click [klɪk] *vt* (*tongue*) chasquear; (*heels*) taconear ▷ *vi* (*Comput*) hacer clic; **to ~ on an icon** hacer clic en un icono

client ['klaɪənt] *n* cliente *m/f*

cliff [klɪf] *n* acantilado

climate ['klaɪmɪt] *n* clima *m*; **climate change** *n* cambio climático

climax ['klaɪmæks] *n* (*of battle, career*) apogeo; (*of film, book*) punto culminante; (*sexual*) orgasmo

climb [klaɪm] *vi* subir; (*plant*) trepar; (*move with effort*): **to ~ over a wall/into a car** trepar a una tapia/subir a un coche ▷ *vt* (*stairs*) subir; (*tree*) trepar a; (*mountain*) escalar ▷ *n* subida; **climb down** *vi* (*fig*) volverse atrás; **climber** *n* alpinista *mf* (*SP, MEX*), andinista *mf* (*LAM*); **climbing** *n* alpinismo (*SP, MEX*), andinismo (*LAM*)

clinch [klɪntʃ] *vt* (*deal*) cerrar; (*argument*) remachar

cling [klɪŋ] (*pt, pp* **clung**) *vi*: **to ~ to** agarrarse a; (*clothes*) pegarse a

Clingfilm® ['klɪŋfɪlm] *n* plástico

adherente

clinic ['klınık] n clínica

clip [klıp] n (for hair) horquilla; (also:
paper ~) sujetapapeles m inv, clip m; (TV,
Cinema) fragmento ▷ vt (cut) cortar; (also:
~ together) unir; **clipping** n (newspaper)
recorte m

cloak [kləuk] n capa, manto ▷ vt (fig)
encubrir, disimular; **cloakroom** n
guardarropa; (BRIT: WC) lavabo (SP), aseos
mpl (SP), baño (LAM)

clock [klɔk] n reloj m; **clock in** or **on** vi
(with card) fichar, picar; (start work) entrar
a trabajar; **clock off** or **out** vi (with card)
fichar or picar la salida; (leave work) salir del
trabajar; **clockwise** adv en el sentido de las
agujas del reloj; **clockwork** n aparato de
relojería ▷ adj (toy) de cuerda

clog [klɔg] n zueco, chanclo ▷ vt atascar
▷ vi (also: **~ up**) atascarse

clone [kləun] n clon m ▷ vt clonar

close¹ [kləus] adj (near): **~ (to)** cerca
(de); (friend) íntimo; (connection) estrecho;
(examination) detallado, minucioso;
(weather) bochornoso ▷ adv cerca; **~ by, ~
at hand** muy cerca; **to have a ~ shave** (fig)
escaparse por un pelo

close² [kləuz] vt (shut) cerrar; (end)
concluir, terminar ▷ vi (shop etc) cerrarse;
(end) concluirse, terminarse ▷ n (end) fin
m, final m, conclusión f; **close down** vi
cerrarse definitivamente; **closed** adj (shop
etc) cerrado

closely ['kləuslı] adv (study) con detalle;
(watch) de cerca; (resemble) estrechamente

closet ['klɔzıt] n armario

close-up ['kləusʌp] n primer plano

closing time n hora de cierre

closure ['kləuʒə*] n cierre m

clot [klɔt] n (gen) coágulo; (inf: idiot)
imbécil m/f ▷ vi (blood) coagularse

cloth [klɔθ] n (material) tela, paño; (rag)
trapo

clothes [kləuðz] npl ropa; **clothes line** n
cuerda (para tender la ropa); **clothes peg**
(US **clothes pin**) n pinza

clothing ['kləuðıŋ] n = **clothes**

cloud [klaud] n nube f; **cloud over** vi (also
fig) nublarse; **cloudy** adj nublado, nubloso;
(liquid) turbio

clove [kləuv] n clavo; **~ of garlic** diente
m de ajo

clown [klaun] n payaso ▷ vi (also: **~
about, ~ around**) hacer el payaso

club [klʌb] n (society) club m; (weapon)
porra, cachiporra; (also: **golf ~**) palo ▷ vt
aporrear ▷ vi: **to ~ together** (for gift)
comprar entre todos; **clubs** npl (Cards)

tréboles mpl; **club class** n (Aviat) clase f
preferente

clue [klu:] n pista; (in crosswords)
indicación f; **I haven't a ~** no tengo ni idea

clump [klʌmp] n (of trees) grupo

clumsy ['klʌmzı] adj (person) torpe,
desmañado; (tool) difícil de manejar;
(movement) desgarbado

clung [klʌŋ] pt, pp of **cling**

cluster ['klʌstə*] n grupo ▷ vi agruparse,
apiñarse

clutch [klʌtʃ] n (Aut) embrague m;
(grasp): **~es** garras fpl ▷ vt asir; agarrar

cm abbr (= centimetre) cm

Co. abbr = **county; company**

c/o abbr (= care of) c/a, a/c

coach [kəutʃ] n autocar m (SP), coche m
de línea; (horse-drawn) coche m; (of train)
vagón m, coche m; (Sport) entrenador(a) m/f,
instructor(a) m/f; (tutor) profesor(a) m/f
particular ▷ vt (Sport) entrenar; (student)
preparar, enseñar; **coach station** n (BRIT)
estación f de autobuses etc; **coach trip** n
excursión f en autocar

coal [kəul] n carbón m

coalition [kəuə'lıʃən] n coalición f

coarse [kɔːs] adj basto, burdo; (vulgar)
grosero, ordinario

coast [kəust] n costa, litoral m ▷ vi (Aut)
ir en punto muerto; **coastal** adj costero,
costanero; **coastguard** n guardacostas m
inv; **coastline** n litoral m

coat [kəut] n abrigo; (of animal) pelaje
m, lana; (of paint) mano f, capa ▷ vt cubrir,
revestir; **coat hanger** n percha (SP),
gancho (LAM); **coating** n capa, baño

coax [kəuks] vt engatusar

cob [kɔb] n see **corn**

cobbled ['kɔbld] adj: **~ street** calle f
empedrada, calle f adoquinada

cobweb ['kɔbwɛb] n telaraña

cocaine [kə'keın] n cocaína

cock [kɔk] n (rooster) gallo; (male bird)
macho ▷ vt (gun) amartillar; **cockerel** n
gallito

cockney ['kɔknı] n habitante de ciertos
barrios de Londres

cockpit ['kɔkpıt] n cabina

cockroach ['kɔkrəutʃ] n cucaracha

cocktail ['kɔkteıl] n coctel m, cóctel m

cocoa ['kəukəu] n cacao; (drink) chocolate
m

coconut ['kəukənʌt] n coco

cod [kɔd] n bacalao

C.O.D. abbr (= cash on delivery) C.A.E.

code [kəud] n código; (cipher) clave f;
(dialling code) prefijo; (post code) código
postal

coeducational [kəʊɛdjuˈkeɪʃənl] *adj* mixto

coffee [ˈkɒfɪ] *n* café *m*; **coffee bar** (BRIT) *n* cafetería; **coffee bean** *n* grano de café; **coffee break** *n* descanso (para tomar café); **coffee maker** *n* máquina de hacer café, cafetera; **coffeepot** *n* cafetera; **coffee shop** *n* café *m*; **coffee table** *n* mesita (para servir el café)

coffin [ˈkɒfɪn] *n* ataúd *m*

cog [kɒg] *n* (*wheel*) rueda dentada; (*tooth*) diente *m*

cognac [ˈkɒnjæk] *n* coñac *m*

coherent [kəʊˈhɪərənt] *adj* coherente

coil [kɔɪl] *n* rollo; (*Elec*) bobina, carrete *m*; (*contraceptive*) espiral *f* ▷ *vt* enrollar

coin [kɔɪn] *n* moneda ▷ *vt* (*word*) inventar, idear

coincide [kəʊɪnˈsaɪd] *vi* coincidir; (*agree*) estar de acuerdo; **coincidence** [kəʊˈɪnsɪdəns] *n* casualidad *f*

Coke® [kəʊk] *n* Coca-Cola®

coke [kəʊk] *n* (*coal*) coque *m*

colander [ˈkɒləndə*] *n* colador *m*, escurridor *m*

cold [kəʊld] *adj* frío ▷ *n* frío; (*Med*) resfriado; **it's ~** hace frío; **to be ~** (*person*) tener frío; **to catch (a) ~** resfriarse; **in ~ blood** a sangre fría; **cold sore** *n* herpes *mpl or fpl*

coleslaw [ˈkəʊlslɔː] *n* especie de ensalada de col

colic [ˈkɒlɪk] *n* cólico

collaborate [kəˈlæbəreɪt] *vi* colaborar

collapse [kəˈlæps] *vi* hundirse, derrumbarse; (*Med*) sufrir un colapso ▷ *n* hundimiento, derrumbamiento; (*Med*) colapso

collar [ˈkɒlə*] *n* (*of coat, shirt*) cuello; (*of dog etc*) collar; **collarbone** *n* clavícula

colleague [ˈkɒliːg] *n* colega *mf*; (*at work*) compañero/a

collect [kəˈlɛkt] *vt* (*litter, mail etc*) recoger; (*as a hobby*) coleccionar; (BRIT: *call and pick up*) recoger; (*debts, subscriptions etc*) recaudar ▷ *vi* reunirse; (*dust*) acumularse; **to call ~** (US Tel) llamar a cobro revertido; **collection** [kəˈlɛkʃən] *n* colección *f*; (*of mail, for charity*) recogida; **collective** [kəˈlɛktɪv] *adj* colectivo; **collector** *n* coleccionista *mf*

college [ˈkɒlɪdʒ] *n* colegio mayor; (*of agriculture, technology*) escuela universitaria

collide [kəˈlaɪd] *vi* chocar

collision [kəˈlɪʒən] *n* choque *m*

cologne [kəˈləʊn] *n* (*also:* **eau de ~**) (agua de) colonia

Colombia [kəˈlɒmbɪə] *n* Colombia; **Colombian** *adj, n* colombiano/a

colon [ˈkəʊlən] *n* (*sign*) dos puntos; (*Med*) colon *m*

colonel [ˈkɜːnl] *n* coronel *m*

colonial [kəˈləʊnɪəl] *adj* colonial

colony [ˈkɒlənɪ] *n* colonia

colour *etc* [ˈkʌlə*] (US **color** *etc*) *n* color *m* ▷ *vt* color(e)ar; (*dye*) teñir; (*fig: account*) adornar; (: *judgement*) distorsionar ▷ *vi* (*blush*) sonrojarse; **colour in** *vt* colorear; **colour-blind** *adj* daltónico; **coloured** *adj* de color; (*photo*) en color; **colour film** *n* película en color; **colourful** *adj* lleno de color; (*story*) fantástico; (*person*) excéntrico; **colouring** *n* (*complexion*) tez *f*; (*in food*) colorante *m*; **colour television** *n* televisión *f* en color

column [ˈkɒləm] *n* columna

coma [ˈkəʊmə] *n* coma *m*

comb [kəʊm] *n* peine *m*; (*ornamental*) peineta ▷ *vt* (*hair*) peinar; (*area*) registrar a fondo

combat [ˈkɒmbæt] *n* combate *m* ▷ *vt* combatir

combination [kɒmbɪˈneɪʃən] *n* combinación *f*

combine [*vb* kəmˈbaɪn, *n* ˈkɒmbaɪn] *vt* combinar; (*qualities*) reunir ▷ *vi* combinarse ▷ *n* (*Econ*) cartel *m*

○ **KEYWORD**

come [kʌm] (*pt* **came**, *pp* **come**) *vi*
1 (*movement towards*) venir; **to come running** venir corriendo
2 (*arrive*) llegar; **he's come here to work** ha venido aquí para trabajar; **to come home** volver a casa
3 (*reach*): **to come to** llegar a; **the bill came to £40** la cuenta ascendía a cuarenta libras
4 (*occur*): **an idea came to me** se me ocurrió una idea
5 (*be, become*): **to come loose/undone** *etc* aflojarse/desabrocharse/desatarse *etc*; **I've come to like him** por fin ha llegado a gustarme

come across *vt fus* (*person*) topar con; (*thing*) dar con

come along *vi* (BRIT: *progress*) ir

come back *vi* (*return*) volver

come down *vi* (*price*) bajar; (*tree, building*) ser derribado

come from *vt fus* (*place, source*) ser de

come in *vi* (*visitor*) entrar; (*train, report*) llegar; (*fashion*) ponerse de moda; (*on deal etc*) entrar

come off *vi* (*button*) soltarse, desprenderse; (*attempt*) salir bien

come on *vi* (*pupil*) progresar; (*work, project*)

desarrollarse; (*lights*) encenderse; (*electricity*) volver; **come on!** ¡vamos!

come out *vi* (*fact*) salir a la luz; (*book, sun*) salir; (*stain*) quitarse

come round *vi* (*after faint, operation*) volver en sí

come to *vi* (*wake*) volver en sí

come up *vi* (*sun*) salir; (*problem*) surgir; (*event*) aproximarse; (*in conversation*) mencionarse

come up with *vt fus* (*idea*) sugerir; (*money*) conseguir

comeback ['kʌmbæk] *n*: **to make a ~** (*Theatre*) volver a las tablas

comedian [kə'miːdɪən] *n* humorista *mf*

comedy ['kɔmɪdɪ] *n* comedia; (*humour*) comicidad *f*

comet ['kɔmɪt] *n* cometa *m*

comfort ['kʌmfət] *n* bienestar *m*; (*relief*) alivio ▷ *vt* consolar; **comfortable** *adj* cómodo; (*financially*) acomodado; (*easy*) fácil; **comfort station** (*us*) *n* servicios *mpl*

comic ['kɔmɪk] *adj* (*also*: **~al**) cómico ▷ *n* (*comedian*) cómico; (*BRIT: for children*) tebeo; (*BRIT: for adults*) comic *m*; **comic book** (*us*) *n* libro *m* de cómics; **comic strip** *n* tira cómica

comma ['kɔmə] *n* coma

command [kə'mɑːnd] *n* orden *f*, mandato; (*Mil: authority*) mando; (*mastery*) dominio ▷ *vt* (*troops*) mandar; (*give orders to*): **to ~ sb to do** mandar *or* ordenar a algn hacer; **commander** *n* (*Mil*) comandante *mf*, jefe/a *m/f*

commemorate [kə'mɛməreɪt] *vt* conmemorar

commence [kə'mɛns] *vt, vi* comenzar, empezar; **commencement** (*us*) *n* (*Univ*) (*ceremonia de*) graduación *f*

commend [kə'mɛnd] *vt* elogiar, alabar; (*recommend*) recomendar

comment ['kɔmɛnt] *n* comentario ▷ *vi*: **to ~ on** hacer comentarios sobre; **"no ~"** (*written*) "sin comentarios"; (*spoken*) "no tengo nada que decir"; **commentary** ['kɔməntərɪ] *n* comentario; **commentator** ['kɔmənteɪtə*] *n* comentarista *mf*

commerce ['kɔmɜːs] *n* comercio

commercial [kə'mɜːʃəl] *adj* comercial ▷ *n* (*TV, Radio*) anuncio; **commercial break** *n* intermedio para publicidad

commission [kə'mɪʃən] *n* (*committee, fee*) comisión *f* ▷ *vt* (*work of art*) encargar; **out of ~** fuera de servicio; **commissioner** *n* (*Police*) comisario de policía

commit [kə'mɪt] *vt* (*act*) cometer; (*resources*) dedicar; (*to sb's care*) entregar;

to ~ o.s. (to do) comprometerse (a hacer); **to ~ suicide** suicidarse; **commitment** *n* compromiso; (*to ideology etc*) entrega

committee [kə'mɪtɪ] *n* comité *m*

commodity [kə'mɔdɪtɪ] *n* mercancía

common ['kɔmən] *adj* común; (*pej*) ordinario ▷ *n* campo común; **commonly** *adv* comúnmente; **commonplace** *adj* de lo más común; **Commons** (*BRIT*) *npl* (*Pol*): **the Commons** (la Cámara de) los Comunes; **common sense** *n* sentido común; **Commonwealth** *n*: **the Commonwealth** la Commonwealth

communal ['kɔmjuːnl] *adj* (*property*) comunal; (*kitchen*) común

commune [*n* 'kɔmjuːn, *vb* kə'mjuːn] *n* (*group*) comuna ▷ *vi*: **to ~ with** comulgar *or* conversar con

communicate [kə'mjuːnɪkeɪt] *vt* comunicar ▷ *vi*: **to ~ (with)** comunicarse (con); (*in writing*) estar en contacto (con)

communication [kəmjuːnɪ'keɪʃən] *n* comunicación *f*

communion [kə'mjuːnɪən] *n* (*also*: **Holy ~**) comunión *f*

communism ['kɔmjunɪzəm] *n* comunismo; **communist** *adj, n* comunista *mf*

community [kə'mjuːnɪtɪ] *n* comunidad *f*; (*large group*) colectividad *f*; **community centre** (*us* **community center**) *n* centro social; **community service** *n* trabajo *m* comunitario (*prestado en lugar de cumplir una pena de prisión*)

commute [kə'mjuːt] *vi* viajar a diario de la casa al trabajo ▷ *vt* conmutar; **commuter** *n* persona que viaja a diario de la casa al trabajo

compact [*adj* kəm'pækt, *n* 'kɔmpækt] *adj* compacto ▷ *n* (*also*: **powder ~**) polvera; **compact disc** *n* compact disc *m*; **compact disc player** *n* reproductor *m* de disco compacto, compact disc *m*

companion [kəm'pænɪən] *n* compañero/a

company ['kʌmpənɪ] *n* compañía; (*Comm*) sociedad *f*, compañía; **to keep sb ~** acompañar a algn; **company car** *n* coche *m* de la empresa; **company director** *n* director(a) *m/f* de empresa

comparable ['kɔmpərəbl] *adj* comparable

comparative [kəm'pærətɪv] *adj* relativo; (*study*) comparativo; **comparatively** *adv* (*relatively*) relativamente

compare [kəm'pɛə*] *vt*: **to ~ sth/sb with** *or* **to** comparar algo/a algn con ▷ *vi*: **to ~ (with)** compararse (con); **comparison** [-'pærɪsn] *n* comparación *f*

compartment [kəm'pɑːtmənt] n
(also: Rail) compartim(i)ento
compass ['kʌmpəs] n brújula;
compasses npl (Math) compás m
compassion [kəm'pæʃən] n compasión f
compatible [kəm'pætɪbl] adj compatible
compel [kəm'pɛl] vt obligar; **compelling**
adj (fig: argument) convincente
compensate ['kɒmpənseɪt] vt
compensar ▷ vi: **to ~ for** compensar;
compensation [-'seɪʃən] n (for loss)
indemnización f
compete [kəm'piːt] vi (take part) tomar
parte, concurrir; (vie with): **to ~ with**
competir con, hacer competencia a
competent ['kɒmpɪtənt] adj
competente, capaz
competition [kɒmpɪ'tɪʃən] n (contest)
concurso; (rivalry) competencia
competitive [kəm'pɛtɪtɪv] adj (Econ,
Sport) competitivo
competitor [kəm'pɛtɪtə*] n (rival)
competidor(a) m/f; (participant) concursante
mf
complacent [kəm'pleɪsənt] adj
autocomplaciente
complain [kəm'pleɪn] vi quejarse; (Comm)
reclamar; **complaint** n queja; reclamación
f; (Med) enfermedad f
complement [n 'kɒmplɪmənt, vb
'kɒmplɪment] n complemento; (esp
of ship's crew) dotación f ▷ vt (enhance)
complementar; **complementary**
[kɒmplɪ'mɛntərɪ] adj complementario
complete [kəm'pliːt] adj (full) completo;
(finished) acabado ▷ vt (fulfil) completar;
(finish) acabar; (a form) llenar; **completely**
adv completamente; **completion**
[-'pliːʃən] n terminación f; (of contract)
realización f
complex ['kɒmplɛks] adj, n complejo
complexion [kəm'plɛkʃən] n (of face) tez
f, cutis m
compliance [kəm'plaɪəns] n (submission)
sumisión f; (agreement) conformidad f; **in ~
with** de acuerdo con
complicate ['kɒmplɪkeɪt] vt complicar;
complicated adj complicado;
complication [-'keɪʃən] n complicación f
compliment ['kɒmplɪmənt] n (formal)
cumplido ▷ vt felicitar; **complimentary**
[-'mɛntərɪ] adj lisonjero; (free) de favor
comply [kəm'plaɪ] vi: **to ~ with** cumplir
con
component [kəm'pəunənt] adj
componente ▷ n (Tech) pieza
compose [kəm'pəuz] vt: **to be ~d of**
componerse de; (music etc) componer;

to ~ o.s. tranquilizarse; **composer** n
(Mus) compositor(a) m/f; **composition**
[kɒmpə'zɪʃən] n composición f
composure [kəm'pəuʒə*] n serenidad
f, calma
compound ['kɒmpaund] n (Chem)
compuesto; (Ling) palabra compuesta;
(enclosure) recinto ▷ adj compuesto;
(fracture) complicado
comprehension [-'hɛnʃən] n
comprensión f
comprehensive [kɒmprɪ'hɛnsɪv] adj
exhaustivo; (Insurance) contra todo riesgo;
comprehensive (school) n centro estatal de
enseñanza secundaria ≈ Instituto Nacional de
Bachillerato (SP)
compress [vb kəm'prɛs, n 'kɒmprɛs] vt
comprimir; (information) condensar ▷ n
(Med) compresa
comprise [kəm'praɪz] vt (also: **be ~d
of**) comprender, constar de; (constitute)
constituir
compromise ['kɒmprəmaɪz] n
(agreement) arreglo ▷ vt comprometer ▷ vi
transigir
compulsive [kəm'pʌlsɪv] adj compulsivo;
(viewing, reading) obligado
compulsory [kəm'pʌlsərɪ] adj
obligatorio
computer [kəm'pjuːtə*] n ordenador m,
computador m, computadora; **computer
game** n juego para ordenador; **computer-
generated** adj realizado por ordenador,
creado por ordenador; **computerize** vt
(data) computerizar; (system) informatizar;
we're computerized now ya nos hemos
informatizado; **computer programmer**
n programador(a) m/f; **computer
programming** n programación f;
computer science n informática;
computer studies npl informática fsg,
computación fsg (LAM); **computing** [kəm-
'pjuːtɪŋ] n (activity, science) informática
con [kɒn] vt (deceive) engañar; (cheat)
estafar ▷ n estafa
conceal [kən'siːl] vt ocultar
concede [kən'siːd] vt (point, argument)
reconocer; (territory) ceder; **to ~ (defeat)**
darse por vencido; **to ~ that** admitir que
conceited [kən'siːtɪd] adj presumido
conceive [kən'siːv] vt, vi concebir
concentrate ['kɒnsəntreɪt] vi
concentrarse ▷ vt concentrar
concentration [kɒnsən'treɪʃən] n
concentración f
concept ['kɒnsɛpt] n concepto
concern [kən'sɜːn] n (matter) asunto;
(Comm) empresa; (anxiety) preocupación

f ▷vt (worry) preocupar; (involve) afectar; (relate to) tener que ver con; **to be ~ed (about)** interesarse (por), preocuparse (por); **concerning** prep sobre, acerca de

concert ['kɔnsət] n concierto; **concert hall** n sala de conciertos

concerto [kən'tʃəːtəu] n concierto

concession [kən'sɛʃən] n concesión f; **tax ~** privilegio fiscal

concise [kən'saɪs] adj conciso

conclude [kən'kluːd] vt concluir; (treaty etc) firmar; (agreement) llegar a; (decide) llegar a la conclusión de; **conclusion** [-'kluːʒən] n conclusión f; firma

concrete ['kɔnkriːt] n hormigón m ▷adj de hormigón; (fig) concreto

concussion [kən'kʌʃən] n conmoción f cerebral

condemn [kən'dɛm] vt condenar; (building) declarar en ruina

condensation [kɔndɛn'seɪʃən] n condensación f

condense [kən'dɛns] vi condensarse ▷vt condensar, abreviar

condition [kən'dɪʃən] n condición f, estado; (requirement) condición f ▷vt condicionar; **on ~ that** a condición (de) que; **conditional** [kən'dɪʃənl] adj condicional; **conditioner** n suavizante

condo ['kɔndəu] (us) n (inf) = **condominium**

condom ['kɔndəm] n condón m

condominium [kɔndə'mɪnɪəm] (us) n (building) bloque m de pisos or apartamentos (propiedad de quienes lo habitan), condominio (LAM); (apartment) piso or apartamento (en propiedad), condominio (LAM)

condone [kən'dəun] vt condonar

conduct [n 'kɔndʌkt, vb kən'dʌkt] n conducta, comportamiento ▷vt (lead) conducir; (manage) llevar a cabo, dirigir; (Mus) dirigir; **to ~ o.s.** comportarse; **conducted tour** (BRIT) n visita acompañada; **conductor** n (of orchestra) director m; (us: on train) revisor(a) m/f; (on bus) cobrador m; (Elec) conductor m

cone [kəun] n cono; (pine cone) piña; (on road) pivote m; (for ice-cream) cucurucho

confectionery [kən'fɛkʃənrɪ] n dulces mpl

confer [kən'fəː*] vt: **to ~ sth on** otorgar algo a ▷vi conferenciar

conference ['kɔnfərns] n (meeting) reunión f; (convention) congreso

confess [kən'fɛs] vt confesar ▷vi admitir; **confession** [-'fɛʃən] n confesión f

confide [kən'faɪd] vi: **to ~ in** confiar en

confidence ['kɔnfɪdns] n (also: self-~)

confianza; (secret) confidencia; **in ~** (speak, write) en confianza; **confident** adj seguro de sí mismo; (certain) seguro; **confidential** [kɔnfɪ'dɛnʃəl] adj confidencial

confine [kən'faɪn] vt (limit) limitar; (shut up) encerrar; **confined** adj (space) reducido

confirm [kən'fəːm] vt confirmar; **confirmation** [kɔnfə'meɪʃən] n confirmación f

confiscate ['kɔnfɪskeɪt] vt confiscar

conflict [n 'kɔnflɪkt, vb kən'flɪkt] n conflicto ▷vi (opinions) chocar

conform [kən'fɔːm] vi conformarse; **to ~ to** ajustarse a

confront [kən'frʌnt] vt (problems) hacer frente a; (enemy, danger) enfrentarse con; **confrontation** [kɔnfrən'teɪʃən] n enfrentamiento

confuse [kən'fjuːz] vt (perplex) aturdir, desconcertar; (mix up) confundir; (complicate) complicar; **confused** adj confuso; (person) perplejo; **confusing** adj confuso; **confusion** [-'fjuːʒən] n confusión f

congestion [kən'dʒɛstʃən] n congestión f

congratulate [kən'grætjuleɪt] vt: **to ~ sb (on)** felicitar a algn (por); **congratulations** [-'leɪʒənz] npl felicitaciones fpl; **congratulations!** ¡enhorabuena!

congregation [-'geɪʃən] n (of a church) feligreses mpl

congress ['kɔŋgrɛs] n congreso; (us): **C~** Congreso; **congressman** (irreg: us) n miembro del Congreso; **congresswoman** (irreg: us) n diputada, miembro f del Congreso

conifer ['kɔnɪfə*] n conífera

conjugate ['kɔndʒugeɪt] vt conjugar

conjugation [kɔndʒə'geɪʃən] n conjugación f

conjunction [kən'dʒʌŋkʃən] n conjunción f; **in ~ with** junto con

conjure ['kʌndʒə*] vi hacer juegos de manos

connect [kə'nɛkt]. vt juntar, unir; (Elec) conectar; (Tel: subscriber) poner; (: caller) poner al habla; (fig) relacionar, asociar ▷vi: **to ~ with** (train) enlazar con; **to be ~ed with** (associated) estar relacionado con; **connecting flight** n vuelo m de enlace; **connection** [-ʃən] n juntura, unión f; (Elec) conexión f; (Rail) enlace m; (Tel) comunicación f; (fig) relación f

conquer ['kɔŋkə*] vt (territory) conquistar; (enemy, feelings) vencer

conquest ['kɔŋkwɛst] n conquista

cons [kɔnz] npl see **convenience; pro; mod**

conscience ['kɔnʃəns] n conciencia
conscientious [kɔnʃɪˈɛnʃəs] adj concienzudo; (objection) de conciencia
conscious ['kɔnʃəs] adj (deliberate) deliberado; (awake, aware) consciente; **consciousness** n conciencia; (Med) conocimiento
consecutive [kənˈsɛkjutɪv] adj consecutivo; **on 3 ~ occasions** en 3 ocasiones consecutivas
consensus [kənˈsɛnsəs] n consenso
consent [kənˈsɛnt] n consentimiento ▷ vi: **to ~ (to)** consentir (en)
consequence ['kɔnsɪkwəns] n consecuencia; (significance) importancia
consequently ['kɔnsɪkwəntlɪ] adv por consiguiente
conservation [kɔnsəˈveɪʃən] n conservación f
conservative [kənˈsə:vətɪv] adj conservador(a); (estimate etc) cauteloso; **Conservative** (BRIT) adj, n (Pol) conservador(a) m/f
conservatory [kənˈsə:vətrɪ] n invernadero; (Mus) conservatorio
consider [kənˈsɪdə*] vt considerar; (take into account) tener en cuenta; (study) estudiar, examinar; **to ~ doing sth** pensar en (la posibilidad de) hacer algo; **considerable** adj considerable; **considerably** adv notablemente; **considerate** adj considerado; **consideration** [-ˈreɪʃən] n consideración f; (factor) factor m; **to give sth further consideration** estudiar algo más a fondo; **considering** prep teniendo en cuenta
consignment [kənˈsaɪnmənt] n envío
consist [kənˈsɪst] vi: **to ~ of** consistir en
consistency [kənˈsɪstənsɪ] n (of argument etc) coherencia; consecuencia; (thickness) consistencia
consistent [kənˈsɪstənt] adj (person) consecuente; (argument etc) coherente
consolation [kɔnsəˈleɪʃən] n consuelo
console¹ [kənˈsəul] vt consolar
console² ['kɔnsəul] n consola
consonant ['kɔnsənənt] n consonante f
conspicuous [kənˈspɪkjuəs] adj (visible) visible
conspiracy [kənˈspɪrəsɪ] n conjura, complot m
constable ['kʌnstəbl] (BRIT) n policía mf; **chief ~** ≈ jefe m de policía
constant ['kɔnstənt] adj constante; **constantly** adv constantemente
constipated ['kɔnstɪpeɪtəd] adj estreñido
▌Be careful not to translate **constipated**

▌by the Spanish word constipado.
constipation [kɔnstɪˈpeɪʃən] n estreñimiento
constituency [kənˈstɪtjuənsɪ] n (Pol: area) distrito electoral; (: electors) electorado
constitute ['kɔnstɪtjuːt] vt constituir
constitution [kɔnstɪˈtjuːʃən] n constitución f
constraint [kənˈstreɪnt] n obligación f; (limit) restricción f
construct [kənˈstrʌkt] vt construir; **construction** [-ʃən] n construcción f; **constructive** adj constructivo
consul ['kɔnsl] n cónsul mf; **consulate** ['kɔnsjulɪt] n consulado
consult [kənˈsʌlt] vt consultar; **consultant** n (BRIT Med) especialista mf; (other specialist) asesor(a) m/f; **consultation** [kɔnsəlˈteɪʃən] n consulta; **consulting room** (BRIT) n consultorio
consume [kənˈsjuːm] vt (eat) comerse; (drink) beberse; (fire etc, Comm) consumir; **consumer** n consumidor(a) m/f
consumption [kənˈsʌmpʃən] n consumo
cont. abbr (= continued) sigue
contact ['kɔntækt] n contacto; (person) contacto; (: pej) enchufe m ▷ vt ponerse en contacto con; **contact lenses** npl lentes fpl de contacto
contagious [kənˈteɪdʒəs] adj contagioso
contain [kənˈteɪn] vt contener; **to ~ o.s.** contenerse; **container** n recipiente m; (for shipping etc) contenedor m
contaminate [kənˈtæmɪneɪt] vt contaminar
cont'd abbr (= continued) sigue
contemplate ['kɔntəmpleɪt] vt contemplar; (reflect upon) considerar
contemporary [kənˈtɛmpərərɪ] adj, n contemporáneo/a m/f
contempt [kənˈtɛmpt] n desprecio; **~ of court** (Law) desacato (a los tribunales)
contend [kənˈtɛnd] vt (argue) afirmar ▷ vi: **to ~ with/for** luchar contra/por
content [adj, vb kənˈtɛnt, n 'kɔntɛnt] adj (happy) contento; (satisfied) satisfecho ▷ vt contentar; satisfacer ▷ n contenido; **contents** npl contenido; **(table of) ~s** índice m de materias; **contented** adj contento; satisfecho
contest [n 'kɔntɛst, vb kənˈtɛst] n lucha; (competition) concurso ▷ vt (dispute) impugnar; (Pol) presentarse como candidato/a en
▌Be careful not to translate **contest** by the Spanish word contestar.
contestant [kənˈtɛstənt] n concursante

mf; (in fight) contendiente *mf*

context ['kɔntɛkst] *n* contexto

continent ['kɔntɪnənt] *n* continente *m*; **the C~** (BRIT) el continente europeo; **continental** [-'nɛntl] *adj* continental; **continental breakfast** *n* desayuno estilo europeo; **continental quilt** (BRIT) *n* edredón *m*

continual [kən'tɪnjuəl] *adj* continuo; **continually** *adv* constantemente

continue [kən'tɪnjuː] *vi, vt* seguir, continuar

continuity [kɔntɪ'njuɪtɪ] *n (also Cine)* continuidad *f*

continuous [kən'tɪnjuəs] *adj* continuo; **continuous assessment** *n* (BRIT) evaluación *f* continua; **continuously** *adv* continuamente

contour ['kɔntuə*] *n* contorno; *(also: ~ line)* curva de nivel

contraception [kɔntrə'sɛpʃən] *n* contracepción *f*

contraceptive [kɔntrə'sɛptɪv] *adj, n* anticonceptivo

contract [*n* 'kɔntrækt, *vb* kən'trækt] *n* contrato ⊳ *vi (Comm)*: **to ~ to do sth** comprometerse por contrato a hacer algo; *(become smaller)* contraerse, encogerse ⊳ *vt* contraer; **contractor** *n* contratista *mf*

contradict [kɔntrə'dɪkt] *vt* contradecir; **contradiction** [-ʃən] *n* contradicción *f*

contrary[1] ['kɔntrərɪ] *adj* contrario ⊳ *n* lo contrario; **on the ~** al contrario; **unless you hear to the ~** a no ser que le digan lo contrario

contrary[2] [kən'trɛərɪ] *adj (perverse)* terco

contrast [*n* 'kɔntrɑːst, *vt* kən'trɑːst] *n* contraste *m* ⊳ *vt* comparar; **in ~ to** en contraste con

contribute [kən'trɪbjuːt] *vi* contribuir ⊳ *vt*: **to ~ £10/an article to** contribuir con 10 libras/un artículo a; **to ~ to** *(charity)* donar a; *(newspaper)* escribir para; *(discussion)* intervenir en; **contribution** [kɔntrɪ'bjuː-ʃən] *n (donation)* donativo; (BRIT: *for social security)* cotización *f; (to debate)* intervención *f; (to journal)* colaboración *f*; **contributor** *n* contribuyente *mf*; *(to newspaper)* colaborador(a) *m/f*

control [kən'trəul] *vt* controlar; *(process etc)* dirigir; *(machinery)* manejar; *(temper)* dominar; *(disease)* contener ⊳ *n* control *m*; **controls** *npl (of vehicle)* instrumentos *mpl* de mando; *(of radio)* controles *mpl*; *(governmental)* medidas *fpl* de control; **under ~** bajo control; **to be in ~ of** tener el mando de; **the car went out of ~** se perdió el control del coche; **control tower** *n (Aviat)*

torre *f* de control

controversial [kɔntrə'vəːʃl] *adj* polémico

controversy ['kɔntrəvəːsɪ] *n* polémica

convenience [kən'viːnɪəns] *n (easiness)* comodidad *f; (suitability)* idoneidad *f; (advantage)* ventaja; **at your ~** cuando le sea conveniente; **all modern ~s, all mod cons** (BRIT) todo confort

convenient [kən'viːnɪənt] *adj (useful)* útil; *(place, time)* conveniente

convent ['kɔnvənt] *n* convento

convention [kən'vɛnʃən] *n* convención *f; (meeting)* asamblea; *(agreement)* convenio; **conventional** *adj* convencional

conversation [kɔnvə'seɪʃən] *n* conversación *f*

conversely [-'vəːslɪ] *adv* a la inversa

conversion [kən'vəːʃən] *n* conversión *f*

convert [*vb* kən'vəːt, *n* 'kɔnvəːt] *vt (Rel, Comm)* convertir; *(alter)*: **to ~ sth into/to** transformar algo en/convertir algo a ⊳ *n* converso/a; **convertible** *adj* convertible ⊳ *n* descapotable *m*

convey [kən'veɪ] *vt* llevar; *(thanks)* comunicar; *(idea)* expresar; **conveyor belt** *n* cinta transportadora

convict [*vb* kən'vɪkt, *n* 'kɔnvɪkt] *vt (find guilty)* declarar culpable a ⊳ *n* presidiario/a; **conviction** [-ʃən] *n* condena; *(belief, certainty)* convicción *f*

convince [kən'vɪns] *vt* convencer; **convinced** *adj*: **convinced of/that** convencido de/de que; **convincing** *adj* convincente

convoy ['kɔnvɔɪ] *n* convoy *m*

cook [kuk] *vt (stew etc)* guisar; *(meal)* preparar ⊳ *vi* cocer; *(person)* cocinar ⊳ *n* cocinero/a; **cook book** *n* libro de cocina; **cooker** *n* cocina; **cookery** *n* cocina; **cookery book** (BRIT) *n* = **cook book**; **cookie** (US) *n* galleta; **cooking** *n* cocina

cool [kuːl] *adj* fresco; *(not afraid)* tranquilo; *(unfriendly)* frío ⊳ *vt* enfriar ⊳ *vi* enfriarse; **cool down** *vi* enfriarse; *(fig: person, situation)* calmarse; **cool off** *vi (become calmer)* calmarse, apaciguarse; *(lose enthusiasm)* perder (el) interés, enfriarse

cop [kɔp] *(inf) n* poli *mf* (SP), tira *mf* (MEX)

cope [kəup] *vi*: **to ~ with** *(problem)* hacer frente a

copper ['kɔpə*] *n (metal)* cobre *m; (BRIT: inf)* poli *mf*, tira *mf* (MEX)

copy ['kɔpɪ] *n* copia; *(of book etc)* ejemplar *m* ⊳ *vt* copiar; **copyright** *n* derechos *mpl* de autor

coral ['kɔrəl] *n* coral *m*

cord [kɔːd] *n* cuerda; *(Elec)* cable *m; (fabric)* pana; **cords** *npl (trousers)* pantalones *mpl* de

pana; **cordless** *adj* sin hilos
corduroy ['kɔːdərɔɪ] *n* pana
core [kɔː*] *n* centro, núcleo; (*of fruit*)
corazón *m*; (*of problem*) meollo ▷ *vt* quitar
el corazón de
coriander [kɔrɪ'ændə*] *n* culantro
cork [kɔːk] *n* corcho; (*tree*) alcornoque *m*;
corkscrew *n* sacacorchos *m inv*
corn [kɔːn] *n* (*BRIT: cereal crop*) trigo;
(*US: maize*) maíz *m*; (*on foot*) callo; ~ **on the**
cob (*Culin*) mazorca, elote *m* (*MEX*), choclo
(*SC*)
corned beef ['kɔːnd-] *n* carne *f* acecinada
(en lata)
corner ['kɔːnə*] *n* (*outside*) esquina; (*inside*)
rincón *m*; (*in road*) curva; (*Football*) córner
m; (*Boxing*) esquina ▷ *vt* (*trap*) arrinconar;
(*Comm*) acaparar ▷ *vi* (*in car*) tomar las
curvas; **corner shop** (*BRIT*) tienda de la
esquina
cornflakes ['kɔːnfleɪks] *npl* copos *mpl* de
maíz, cornflakes *mpl*
cornflour ['kɔːnflauə*] (*BRIT*) *n* harina
de maíz
cornstarch ['kɔːnstɑːtʃ] (*US*) *n* = **cornflour**
Cornwall ['kɔːnwəl] *n* Cornualles *m*
coronary ['kɔrənərɪ] *n* (*also:* ~
thrombosis) infarto
coronation [kɔrə'neɪʃən] *n* coronación *f*
coroner ['kɔrənə*] *n* juez *mf* de
instrucción
corporal ['kɔːpərl] *n* cabo ▷ *adj:* ~
punishment castigo corporal
corporate ['kɔːpərɪt] *adj* (*action,
ownership*) colectivo; (*finance, image*)
corporativo
corporation [kɔːpə'reɪʃən] *n* (*of town*)
ayuntamiento; (*Comm*) corporación *f*
corps [kɔː*, *pl* kɔːz] *n inv* cuerpo;
diplomatic ~ cuerpo diplomático; **press** ~
gabinete *m* de prensa
corpse [kɔːps] *n* cadáver *m*
correct [kə'rɛkt] *adj* justo, exacto;
(*proper*) correcto ▷ *vt* corregir; (*exam*)
corregir, calificar; **correction** [-ʃən] *n* (*act*)
corrección *f*; (*instance*) rectificación *f*
correspond [kɔrɪs'pɔnd] *vi* (*write*): **to**
~ **(with)** escribirse (con); (*be equivalent
to*): **to** ~ **(to)** corresponder (a); (*be in
accordance*): **to** ~ **(with)** corresponder (con);
correspondence *n* correspondencia;
correspondent *n* corresponsal *mf*;
corresponding *adj* correspondiente
corridor ['kɔrɪdɔː*] *n* pasillo
corrode [kə'rəud] *vt* corroer ▷ *vi*
corroerse
corrupt [kə'rʌpt] *adj* (*person*) corrupto;
(*Comput*) corrompido ▷ *vt* corromper;

(*Comput*) degradar; **corruption** *n*
corrupción *f*; (*of data*) alteración *f*
Corsica ['kɔːsɪkə] *n* Córcega
cosmetic [kɔz'mɛtɪk] *adj, n* cosmético;
cosmetic surgery *n* cirugía *f* estética
cosmopolitan [kɔzmə'pɔlɪtn] *adj*
cosmopolita
cost [kɔst] (*pt, pp* ~) *n* (*price*) precio ▷ *vi*
costar, valer ▷ *vt* preparar el presupuesto
de; **how much does it** ~**?** ¿cuánto cuesta?;
to ~ **sb time/effort** costarle a algn tiempo/
esfuerzo; **it** ~ **him his life** le costó la vida;
at all ~**s** cueste lo que cueste; **costs** *npl*
(*Comm*) costes *mpl*; (*Law*) costas *fpl*
co-star ['kəustɑː*] *n* coprotagonista *mf*
Costa Rica ['kɔstə'riːkə] *n* Costa Rica;
Costa Rican *adj, n* costarriqueño/a
costly ['kɔstlɪ] *adj* costoso
cost of living *n* costo or coste *m* (*Sp*) de
la vida
costume ['kɔstjuːm] *n* traje *m*; (*BRIT: also:*
swimming ~) traje de baño
cosy ['kəuzɪ] (*US* **cozy**) *adj* (*person*)
cómodo; (*room*) acogedor(a)
cot [kɔt] *n* (*BRIT: child's*) cuna; (*US: campbed*)
cama de campaña
cottage ['kɔtɪdʒ] *n* casita de campo;
(*rustic*) barraca; **cottage cheese** *n*
requesón *m*
cotton ['kɔtn] *n* algodón *m*; (*thread*) hilo;
cotton on *vi* (*inf*): **to cotton on (to sth)**
caer en la cuenta (de algo); **cotton bud** *n*
(*BRIT*) bastoncillo *m* de algodón; **cotton
candy** (*US*) *n* algodón *m* (azucarado);
cotton wool (*BRIT*) *n* algodón *m* (hidrófilo)
couch [kautʃ] *n* sofá *m*; (*doctor's etc*) diván
m
cough [kɔf] *vi* toser ▷ *n* tos *f*; **cough
mixture** *n* jarabe *m* para la tos
could [kud] *pt of* **can²**; **couldn't** = **could
not**
council ['kaunsl] *n* consejo; **city** *or* **town**
~ consejo municipal; **council estate** (*BRIT*)
n urbanización de viviendas municipales de
alquiler; **council house** (*BRIT*) *n* vivienda
municipal de alquiler; **councillor** (*US*
councilor) *n* concejal(a) *m/f*; **council tax** *n*
(*BRIT*) contribución *f* municipal (*dependiente
del valor de la vivienda*)
counsel ['kaunsl] *n* (*advice*) consejo;
(*lawyer*) abogado/a ▷ *vt* aconsejar;
counselling (*US* **counseling**) *n* (*Psych*)
asistencia *f* psicológica; **counsellor** (*US*
counselor) *n* consejero/a, abogado/a
count [kaunt] *vt* contar; (*include*) incluir
▷ *vi* contar ▷ *n* cuenta; (*of votes*) escrutinio;
(*level*) nivel *m*; (*nobleman*) conde *m*; **count in**
(*inf*) *vt:* **to count sb in on sth** contar con

algn para algo; **count on** vt fus contar con;
countdown n cuenta atrás

counter ['kauntə*] n (in shop) mostrador
m; (in games) ficha ▷ vt contrarrestar
▷ adv: **to run ~ to** ser contrario a, ir en
contra de; **counter clockwise** (US) adv en
sentido contrario al de las agujas del reloj

counterfeit ['kauntəfɪt] n falsificación
f, simulación f ▷ vt falsificar ▷ adj falso,
falsificado

counterpart ['kauntəpɑːt] n
homólogo/a

countess ['kauntɪs] n condesa

countless ['kauntlɪs] adj innumerable

country ['kʌntrɪ] n país m; (native land)
patria; (as opposed to town) campo; (region)
región f, tierra; **country and western
(music)** n música country; **country house**
n casa de campo; **countryside** n campo

county ['kauntɪ] n condado

coup [kuː] (pl ~s) n (also: ~ d'état) golpe m
(de estado); (achievement) éxito

couple ['kʌpl] n (of things) par m; (of people)
pareja; (married couple) matrimonio; **a ~ of**
un par de

coupon ['kuːpɔn] n cupón m; (voucher)
valé m

courage ['kʌrɪdʒ] n valor m, valentía;
courageous [kə'reɪdʒəs] adj valiente

courgette [kuə'ʒet] (BRIT) n calabacín m,
calabacita (MEX)

courier ['kurɪə*] n mensajero/a; (for
tourists) guía mf (de turismo)

course [kɔːs] n (direction) dirección f;
(of river, Scol) curso; (process) transcurso;
(Med): ~ **of treatment** tratamiento; (of ship)
rumbo; (part of meal) plato; (Golf) campo; **of
~** desde luego, naturalmente; **of ~!** ¡claro!

court [kɔːt] n (royal) corte f; (Law) tribunal
m, juzgado; (Tennis etc) pista, cancha ▷ vt
(woman) cortejar a; **to take to ~** demandar

courtesy ['kɜːtəsɪ] n cortesía; **(by) ~ of**
por cortesía de; **courtesy bus, courtesy
coach** n autobús m gratuito

court: court-house ['kɔːthaus] (US) n
palacio de justicia; **courtroom** ['kɔːtrum]
n sala de justicia; **courtyard** ['kɔːtjɑːd]
n patio

cousin ['kʌzn] n primo/a; **first ~** primo/a
carnal, primo/a hermano/a

cover ['kʌvə*] vt cubrir; (feelings, mistake)
ocultar; (with lid) tapar; (book etc) forrar;
(distance) recorrer; (include) abarcar;
(protect: also: Insurance) cubrir; (Press)
investigar; (discuss) tratar ▷ n cubierta; (lid)
tapa; (for chair etc) funda; (envelope) sobre
m; (for book) forro; (of magazine) portada;
(shelter) abrigo; (Insurance) cobertura; (of

spy) cobertura; **covers** npl (on bed) sábanas;
mantas; **to take ~** (shelter) protegerse,
resguardarse; **under ~** (indoors) bajo techo;
under ~ of darkness al amparo de la
oscuridad; **under separate ~** (Comm) por
separado; **cover up** vi: **to cover up for sb**
encubrir a algn; **coverage** n (TV, Press)
cobertura; **cover charge** n precio del
cubierto; **cover-up** n encubrimiento

cow [kau] n vaca; (inf!: woman) bruja ▷ vt
intimidar

coward ['kauəd] n cobarde mf; **cowardly**
adj cobarde

cowboy ['kaubɔɪ] n vaquero

cozy ['kəuzɪ] (US) adj = **cosy**

crab [kræb] n cangrejo

crack [kræk] n grieta; (noise) crujido; (drug)
crack m ▷ vt agrietar, romper; (nut) cascar;
(solve: problem) resolver; (: code) descifrar;
(whip etc) chasquear; (knuckles) crujir; (joke)
contar ▷ adj (expert) de primera; **crack
down on** vt fus adoptar fuertes medidas
contra; **cracked** adj (cup, window) rajado;
(wall) resquebrajado; **cracker** n (biscuit)
cráquer m; (Christmas cracker) petardo
sorpresa

crackle ['krækl] vi crepitar

cradle ['kreɪdl] n cuna

craft [krɑːft] n (skill) arte m; (trade) oficio;
(cunning) astucia; (boat: pl inv) barco;
(plane: pl inv) avión m; **craftsman** (irreg)
n artesano; **craftsmanship** n (quality)
destreza

cram [kræm] vt (fill): **to ~ sth with** llenar
algo (a reventar) de; (put): **to ~ sth into**
meter algo a la fuerza en ▷ vi (for exams)
empollar

cramp [kræmp] n (Med) calambre m;
cramped adj apretado, estrecho

cranberry ['krænbərɪ] n arándano agrio

crane [kreɪn] n (Tech) grúa; (bird) grulla

crap [kræp] n (inf!) mierda (!)

crash [kræʃ] n (noise) estrépito; (of cars
etc) choque m; (of plane) accidente m de
aviación; (Comm) quiebra ▷ vt (car, plane)
estrellar ▷ vi (car, plane) estrellarse; (two
cars) chocar; (Comm) quebrar; **crash course**
n curso acelerado; **crash helmet** n casco
(protector)

crate [kreɪt] n cajón m de embalaje; (for
bottles) caja

crave [kreɪv] vt, vi: **to ~ (for)** ansiar,
anhelar

crawl [krɔːl] vi (drag o.s.) arrastrarse; (child)
andar a gatas, gatear; (vehicle) avanzar
(lentamente) ▷ n (Swimming) crol m

crayfish ['kreɪfɪʃ] n inv (freshwater)
cangrejo de río; (saltwater) cigala

crayon ['kreɪən] n lápiz m de color
craze [kreɪz] n (fashion) moda
crazy ['kreɪzɪ] adj (person) loco; (idea)
disparatado; (inf: keen): **~ about sb/sth** loco
por algn/algo
creak [kriːk] vi (floorboard) crujir; (hinge etc)
chirriar, rechinar
cream [kriːm] n (of milk) nata, crema;
(lotion) crema; (fig) flor f y nata ▷ adj (colour)
color crema; **cream cheese** n queso
blanco; **creamy** adj cremoso; (colour) color
crema
crease [kriːs] n (fold) pliegue m; (in trousers)
raya; (wrinkle) arruga ▷ vt (wrinkle) arrugar
▷ vi (wrinkle up) arrugarse
create [kriː'eɪt] vt crear; **creation** [-ʃən] n
creación f; **creative** adj creativo; **creator** n
creador(a) m/f
creature ['kriːtʃə*] n (animal) animal m,
bicho; (person) criatura
crèche [krɛʃ] n guardería (infantil)
credentials [krɪ'dɛnʃlz] npl (references)
referencias fpl; (identity papers) documentos
mpl de identidad
credibility [krɛdɪ'bɪlɪtɪ] n credibilidad f
credible ['krɛdɪbl] adj creíble; (trustworthy)
digno de confianza
credit ['krɛdɪt] n crédito; (merit) honor m,
mérito ▷ vt (Comm) abonar; (believe: also:
give ~ to) creer, prestar fe a ▷ adj crediticio;
credits npl (Cinema) fichas fpl técnicas; **to
be in ~** (person) tener saldo a favor; **to ~ sb
with** (fig) reconocer a algn el mérito de;
credit card n tarjeta de crédito
creek [kriːk] n cala, ensenada; (US)
riachuelo
creep [kriːp] (pt, pp **crept**) vi arrastrarse
cremate [krɪ'meɪt] vt incinerar
crematorium [krɛmə'tɔːrɪəm] (pl
crematoria) n crematorio
crept [krɛpt] pt, pp of **creep**
crescent ['krɛsnt] n media luna; (street)
calle f (en forma de semicírculo)
cress [krɛs] n berro
crest [krɛst] n (of bird) cresta; (of hill) cima,
cumbre f; (of coat of arms) blasón m
crew [kruː] n (of ship etc) tripulación f;
(TV, Cinema) equipo; **crew-neck** n cuello
a la caja
crib [krɪb] n cuna ▷ vt (inf) plagiar
cricket ['krɪkɪt] n (insect) grillo; (game)
críquet m; **cricketer** n jugador(a) m/f de
críquet
crime [kraɪm] n (no pl: illegal activities)
crimen m; (illegal action) delito; **criminal**
['krɪmɪnl] n criminal mf, delincuente mf
▷ adj criminal; (illegal) delictivo; (law) penal
crimson ['krɪmzn] adj carmesí

cringe [krɪndʒ] vi agacharse, encogerse
cripple ['krɪpl] n lisiado/a, cojo/a ▷ vt
lisiar, mutilar
crisis ['kraɪsɪs] (pl **crises**) n crisis f inv
crisp [krɪsp] adj fresco; (vegetables etc)
crujiente; (manner) seco; **crispy** adj
crujiente
criterion [kraɪ'tɪərɪən] (pl **criteria**) n
criterio
critic ['krɪtɪk] n crítico/a; **critical** adj
crítico; (illness) grave; **criticism** ['krɪtɪsɪzm]
n crítica; **criticize** ['krɪtɪsaɪz] vt criticar
Croat ['krəuæt] adj, n = **Croatian**
Croatia [krəu'eɪʃə] n Croacia; **Croatian**
adj, n croata m/f ▷ n (Ling) croata m
crockery ['krɔkərɪ] n loza, vajilla
crocodile ['krɔkədaɪl] n cocodrilo
crocus ['krəukəs] n croco, crocus m
croissant ['krwasŋ] n croissant m,
medialuna (esp LAM)
crook [kruk] n ladrón/ona m/f; (of
shepherd) cayado; **crooked** ['krukɪd] adj
torcido; (dishonest) nada honrado
crop [krɔp] n (produce) cultivo; (amount
produced) cosecha; (riding crop) látigo de
montar ▷ vt cortar, recortar; **crop up** vi
surgir, presentarse
cross [krɔs] n cruz f; (hybrid) cruce m ▷ vt
(street etc) cruzar, atravesar ▷ adj de mal
humor, enojado; **cross off** vt tachar;
cross out vt tachar; **cross over** vi cruzar;
cross-Channel ferry ['krɔs'tʃænl-] n
transbordador m que cruza el Canal de la
Mancha; **crosscountry (race)** n carrera
a campo traviesa, cross m; **crossing** n
(sea passage) travesía; (also: **pedestrian
crossing**) paso para peatones; **crossing
guard** (US) n persona encargada de ayudar a
los niños a cruzar la calle; **crossroads** n cruce
m, encrucijada; **crosswalk** (US) n paso de
peatones; **crossword** n crucigrama m
crotch [krɔtʃ] n (Anat, of garment)
entrepierna
crouch [krautʃ] vi agacharse, acurrucarse
crouton ['kruːtɔn] n cubito de pan frito
crow [krəu] n (bird) cuervo; (of cock) canto,
cacareo ▷ vi (cock) cantar
crowd [kraud] n muchedumbre f,
multitud f ▷ vt (fill) llenar ▷ vi (gather): **to
~ round** reunirse en torno a; (cram): **to
~ in** entrar en tropel; **crowded** adj (full)
atestado; (densely populated) superpoblado
crown [kraun] n corona; (of head)
coronilla; (for tooth) funda; (of hill) cumbre
f ▷ vt coronar; (fig) completar, rematar;
crown jewels npl joyas fpl reales
crucial ['kruːʃl] adj decisivo
crucifix ['kruːsɪfɪks] n crucifijo

crude [kru:d] *adj* (*materials*) bruto;
(*fig: basic*) tosco; (: *vulgar*) ordinario; **crude
(oil)** *n* (petróleo) crudo
cruel ['kruəl] *adj* cruel; **cruelty** *n* crueldad
f
cruise [kru:z] *n* crucero ▷ *vi* (*ship*) hacer
un crucero; (*car*) ir a velocidad de crucero
crumb [krʌm] *n* miga, migaja
crumble ['krʌmbl] *vt* desmenuzar ▷ *vi*
(*building, also fig*) desmoronarse
crumpet ['krʌmpɪt] *n* ≈ bollo para tostar
crumple ['krʌmpl] *vt* (*paper*) estrujar;
(*material*) arrugar
crunch [krʌntʃ] *vt* (*with teeth*) mascar;
(*underfoot*) hacer crujir ▷ *n* (*fig*) hora
or momento de la verdad; **crunchy** *adj*
crujiente
crush [krʌʃ] *n* (*crowd*) aglomeración *f*;
(*infatuation*): **to have a ~ on sb** estar loco
por algn; (*drink*): **lemon ~** limonada ▷ *vt*
aplastar; (*paper*) estrujar; (*cloth*) arrugar;
(*fruit*) exprimir; (*opposition*) aplastar; (*hopes*)
destruir
crust [krʌst] *n* corteza; (*of snow, ice*)
costra; **crusty** *adj* (*bread*) crujiente; (*person*)
de mal carácter
crutch [krʌtʃ] *n* muleta
cry [kraɪ] *vi* llorar ▷ *n* (*shriek*) chillido;
(*shout*) grito; **cry out** *vi* (*call out, shout*)
lanzar un grito, echar un grito ▷ *vt* gritar
crystal ['krɪstl] *n* cristal *m*
cub [kʌb] *n* cachorro; (*also*: **~ scout**) niño
explorador
Cuba ['kju:bə] *n* Cuba; **Cuban** *adj, n*
cubano/a *m/f*
cube [kju:b] *n* cubo ▷ *vt* (*Math*) cubicar
cubicle ['kju:bɪkl] *n* (*at pool*) caseta; (*for
bed*) cubículo
cuckoo ['kuku:] *n* cuco
cucumber ['kju:kʌmbə*] *n* pepino
cuddle ['kʌdl] *vt* abrazar ▷ *vi* abrazarse
cue [kju:] *n* (*snooker cue*) taco; (*Theatre etc*)
señal *f*
cuff [kʌf] *n* (*of sleeve*) puño; (*us: of trousers*)
vuelta; (*blow*) bofetada ▷ **off the ~** *adv* de
improviso; **cufflinks** *npl* gemelos *mpl*
cuisine [kwɪ'zi:n] *n* cocina
cul-de-sac ['kʌldəsæk] *n* callejón *m* sin
salida
cull [kʌl] *vt* (*idea*) sacar ▷ *n* (*of animals*)
matanza selectiva
culminate ['kʌlmɪneɪt] *vi*: **to ~ in**
terminar en
culprit ['kʌlprɪt] *n* culpable *mf*
cult [kʌlt] *n* culto
cultivate ['kʌltɪveɪt] *vt* cultivar
cultural ['kʌltʃərəl] *adj* cultural
culture ['kʌltʃə*] *n* (*also fig*) cultura; (*Biol*)

cultivo
cumin ['kʌmɪn] *n* (*spice*) comino
cunning ['kʌnɪŋ] *n* astucia ▷ *adj* astuto
cup [kʌp] *n* taza; (*as prize*) copa
cupboard ['kʌbəd] *n* armario; (*in kitchen*)
alacena
cup final *n* (*Football*) final *f* de copa
curator [kjuə'reɪtə*] *n* director(a) *m/f*
curb [kə:b] *vt* refrenar; (*person*) reprimir
▷ *n* freno; (*us*) bordillo
curdle ['kə:dl] *vi* cuajarse
cure [kjuə*] *vt* curar ▷ *n* cura, curación *f*;
(*fig: solution*) remedio
curfew ['kə:fju:] *n* toque *m* de queda
curiosity [kjuərɪ'ɔsɪtɪ] *n* curiosidad *f*
curious ['kjuərɪəs] *adj* curioso;
(*person: interested*): **to be ~** sentir curiosidad
curl [kə:l] *n* rizo ▷ *vt* (*hair*) rizar ▷ *vi*
rizarse; **curl up** *vi* (*person*) hacerse un ovillo;
curler *n* rulo; **curly** *adj* rizado
currant ['kʌrnt] *n* pasa (de Corinto);
(*blackcurrant, redcurrant*) grosella
currency ['kʌrnsɪ] *n* moneda; **to gain ~**
(*fig*) difundirse
current ['kʌrnt] *n* corriente *f* ▷ *adj*
(*accepted*) corriente; (*present*) actual; **current
account** (BRIT) *n* cuenta corriente; **current
affairs** *npl* noticias *fpl* de actualidad;
currently *adv* actualmente
curriculum [kə'rɪkjuləm] (*pl* **~s**
or **curricula**) *n* plan *m* de estudios;
curriculum vitae *n* currículum *m*
curry ['kʌrɪ] *n* curry *m* ▷ *vt*: **to ~ favour
with** buscar favores con; **curry powder** *n*
curry *m* en polvo
curse [kə:s] *vi* soltar tacos ▷ *vt* maldecir
▷ *n* maldición *f*; (*swearword*) palabrota, taco
cursor ['kə:sə*] *n* (*Comput*) cursor *m*
curt [kə:t] *adj* corto, seco
curtain ['kə:tn] *n* cortina; (*Theatre*) telón *m*
curve [kə:v] *n* curva ▷ *vi* (*road*) hacer una
curva; (*line etc*) curvarse; **curved** *adj* curvo
cushion ['kuʃən] *n* cojín *m*; (*of air*) colchón
m ▷ *vt* (*shock*) amortiguar
custard ['kʌstəd] *n* natillas *fpl*
custody ['kʌstədɪ] *n* custodia; **to take
into ~** detener
custom ['kʌstəm] *n* costumbre *f*; (*Comm*)
clientela
customer ['kʌstəmə*] *n* cliente *m/f*
customized ['kʌstəmaɪzd] *adj* (*car etc*)
hecho a encargo
customs ['kʌstəmz] *npl* aduana; **customs
officer** *n* aduanero/a
cut [kʌt] (*pt, pp* **~**) *vt* cortar; (*price*) rebajar;
(*text, programme*) acortar; (*reduce*) reducir
▷ *vi* cortar ▷ *n* (*of garment*) corte *m*; (*in skin*)
cortadura; (*in salary etc*) rebaja; (*in spending*)

reducción f, recorte m; (*slice of meat*) tajada;
to ~ a tooth echar un diente; **to ~ and
paste** (*Comput*) cortar y pegar; **cut back**
vt (*plants*) podar; (*production, expenditure*)
reducir; **cut down** vt (*tree*) derribar; (*reduce*)
reducir; **cut off** vt cortar; (*person, place*)
aislar; (*Tel*) desconectar; **cut out** vt (*shape*)
recortar; (*stop: activity etc*) dejar; (*remove*)
quitar; **cut up** vt cortar (en pedazos);
cutback n reducción f
cute [kju:t] adj mono
cutlery ['kʌtlərɪ] n cubiertos mpl
cutlet ['kʌtlɪt] n chuleta; (*nut etc cutlet*)
plato vegetariano hecho con nueces y verdura en
forma de chuleta
cut-price ['kʌt'praɪs] (BRIT) adj a precio
reducido
cut-rate ['kʌt'reɪt] (US) adj = **cut-price**
cutting ['kʌtɪŋ] adj (*remark*) mordaz ⊳ n
(BRIT: *from newspaper*) recorte m; (*from plant*)
esqueje m
CV n abbr = **curriculum vitae**
cwt abbr = **hundredweight(s)**
cybercafé ['saɪbəkæfeɪ] n cibercafé m
cyberspace ['saɪbəspeɪs] n ciberespacio
cycle ['saɪkl] n ciclo; (*bicycle*) bicicleta ⊳ vi
ir en bicicleta; **cycle hire** n alquiler m de
bicicletas; **cycle lane** n carril-bici m; **cycle
path** n carril-bici m; **cycling** n ciclismo;
cyclist n ciclista mf
cyclone ['saɪkləun] n ciclón m
cylinder ['sɪlɪndə*] n cilindro; (*of gas*)
bombona
cymbal ['sɪmbl] n címbalo, platillo
cynical ['sɪnɪkl] adj cínico
Cypriot ['sɪprɪət] adj, n chipriota m/f
Cyprus ['saɪprəs] n Chipre f
cyst [sɪst] n quiste m; **cystitis** [-'taɪtɪs]
n cistitis f
czar [zɑ:*] n zar m
Czech [tʃɛk] adj, n checo/a m/f; **Czech
Republic** n: **the Czech Republic** la
República Checa

d

D [di:] n (*Mus*) re m
dab [dæb] vt (*eyes, wound*) tocar
(ligeramente); (*paint, cream*) poner un
poco de
dad [dæd] n = **daddy**
daddy ['dædɪ] n papá m
daffodil ['dæfədɪl] n narciso
daft [dɑ:ft] adj tonto
dagger ['dægə*] n puñal m, daga
daily ['deɪlɪ] adj diario, cotidiano ⊳ adv
todos los días, cada día
dairy ['dɛərɪ] n (*shop*) lechería; (*on farm*)
vaquería; **dairy produce** n productos mpl
lácteos
daisy ['deɪzɪ] n margarita
dam [dæm] n presa ⊳ vt construir una
presa sobre, represar
damage ['dæmɪdʒ] n lesión f; daño; (*dents
etc*) desperfectos mpl; (*fig*) perjuicio ⊳ vt
dañar, perjudicar; (*spoil, break*) estropear;
damages npl (*Law*) daños mpl y perjuicios
damn [dæm] vt condenar; (*curse*) maldecir
⊳ n (*inf*): **I don't give a ~** me importa un
pito ⊳ adj (*inf: also: ~ed*) maldito; **~ (it)!**
¡maldito sea!
damp [dæmp] adj húmedo, mojado ⊳ n
humedad f ⊳ vt (*also: ~en: cloth, rag*) mojar;
(: *enthusiasm*) enfriar
dance [dɑ:ns] n baile m ⊳ vi bailar;
dance floor n pista f de baile; **dancer** n
bailador(a) m/f; (*professional*) bailarín/ina
m/f; **dancing** n baile m
dandelion ['dændɪlaɪən] n diente m de
león
dandruff ['dændrəf] n caspa
Dane [deɪn] n danés/esa m/f
danger ['deɪndʒə*] n peligro; (*risk*) riesgo;
~! (*on sign*) ¡peligro de muerte!; **to be in ~ of**
correr riesgo de; **dangerous** adj peligroso
dangle ['dæŋgl] vt colgar ⊳ vi pender,
colgar

Danish ['deɪnɪʃ] *adj* danés/esa ▷ *n* (*Ling*) danés *m*

dare [dɛə*] *vt*: **to ~ sb to do** desafiar a algn a hacer ▷ *vi*: **to ~ (to) do sth** atreverse a hacer algo; **I ~ say** (*I suppose*) puede ser (que); **daring** *adj* atrevido, osado ▷ *n* atrevimiento, osadía

dark [dɑːk] *adj* oscuro; (*hair, complexion*) moreno ▷ *n*: **in the ~** a oscuras; **to be in the ~ about** (*fig*) no saber nada de; **after ~** después del anochecer; **darken** *vt* (*colour*) hacer más oscuro ▷ *vi* oscurecerse; **darkness** *n* oscuridad *f*; **darkroom** *n* cuarto oscuro

darling ['dɑːlɪŋ] *adj, n* querido/a *m/f*

dart [dɑːt] *n* dardo; (*in sewing*) sisa ▷ *vi* precipitarse; **dartboard** *n* diana; **darts** *n* (*game*) dardos *mpl*

dash [dæʃ] *n* (*small quantity: of liquid*) gota, chorrito; (*sign*) raya ▷ *vt* (*throw*) tirar; (*hopes*) defraudar ▷ *vi* precipitarse, ir de prisa

dashboard ['dæʃbɔːd] *n* (*Aut*) salpicadero

data ['deɪtə] *npl* datos *mpl*; **database** *n* base *f* de datos; **data processing** *n* proceso de datos

date [deɪt] *n* (*day*) fecha; (*with friend*) cita; (*fruit*) dátil *m* ▷ *vt* fechar; (*person*) salir con; **~ of birth** fecha de nacimiento; **to ~** *adv* hasta la fecha; **dated** *adj* anticuado

daughter ['dɔːtə*] *n* hija; **daughter-in-law** *n* nuera, hija política

daunting ['dɔːntɪŋ] *adj* desalentador(a)

dawn [dɔːn] *n* alba, amanecer *m*; (*fig*) nacimiento ▷ *vi* (*day*) amanecer; (*fig*): **it ~ed on him that ...** cayó en la cuenta de que ...

day [deɪ] *n* día *m*; (*working day*) jornada; (*heyday*) tiempos *mpl*, días *mpl*; **the ~ before/after** el día anterior/siguiente; **the ~ after tomorrow** pasado mañana; **the ~ before yesterday** anteayer; **the following ~** el día siguiente; **by ~** de día; **day-care centre** ['deɪkɛə-] *n* centro de día; (*for children*) guardería infantil; **daydream** *vi* soñar despierto; **daylight** *n* luz *f* (del día); **day return** (*BRIT*) *n* billete *m* de ida y vuelta (en un día); **daytime** *n* día *m*; **day-to-day** *adj* cotidiano; **day trip** *n* excursión *f* (de un día)

dazed [deɪzd] *adj* aturdido

dazzle ['dæzl] *vt* deslumbrar; **dazzling** *adj* (*light, smile*) deslumbrante; (*colour*) fuerte

DC *abbr* (= *direct current*) corriente *f* continua

dead [dɛd] *adj* muerto; (*limb*) dormido; (*telephone*) cortado; (*battery*) agotado ▷ *adv* (*completely*) totalmente; (*exactly*) exactamente; **to shoot sb ~** matar a algn a tiros; **~ tired** muerto (de cansancio); **to stop ~** parar en seco; **dead end** *n* callejón *m* sin salida; **deadline** *n* fecha (*or* hora) tope; **deadly** *adj* mortal, fatal; **Dead Sea** *n*: **the Dead Sea** el Mar Muerto

deaf [dɛf] *adj* sordo; **deafen** *vt* ensordecer; **deafening** *adj* ensordecedor/a

deal [diːl] (*pt, pp* **~t**) *n* (*agreement*) pacto, convenio; (*business deal*) trato ▷ *vt* dar; (*card*) repartir; **a great ~ (of)** bastante, mucho; **deal with** *vt fus* (*people*) tratar con; (*problem*) ocuparse de; (*subject*) tratar de; **dealer** *n* comerciante *m/f*; (*Cards*) mano *f*; **dealings** *npl* (*Comm*) transacciones *fpl*; (*relations*) relaciones *fpl*

dealt [dɛlt] *pt, pp of* **deal**

dean [diːn] *n* (*Rel*) deán *m*; (*Scol*: *BRIT*) decano; (: *US*) decano; rector *m*

dear [dɪə*] *adj* querido; (*expensive*) caro ▷ *n*: **my ~** mi querido/a ▷ *excl*: **~ me!** ¡Dios mío!; **D~ Sir/Madam** (*in letter*) Muy Señor Mío, Estimado Señor/Estimada Señora; **D~ Mr/Mrs X** Estimado/a Señor(a) X; **dearly** *adv* (*love*) mucho; (*pay*) caro

death [dɛθ] *n* muerte *f*; **death penalty** *n* pena de muerte; **death sentence** *n* condena a muerte

debate [dɪ'beɪt] *n* debate *m* ▷ *vt* discutir

debit ['dɛbɪt] *n* debe *m* ▷ *vt*: **to ~ a sum to sb** *or* **to sb's account** cargar una suma en cuenta a algn; **debit card** *n* tarjeta *f* de débito

debris ['dɛbriː] *n* escombros *mpl*

debt [dɛt] *n* deuda; **to be in ~** tener deudas

debut ['deɪbjuː] *n* presentación *f*

Dec. *abbr* (= *December*) dic

decade ['dɛkeɪd] *n* decenio, década

decaffeinated [dɪ'kæfɪneɪtɪd] *adj* descafeinado

decay [dɪ'keɪ] *n* (*of building*) desmoronamiento; (*of tooth*) caries *f inv* ▷ *vi* (*rot*) pudrirse

deceased [dɪ'siːst] *n*: **the ~** el(la) difunto/a

deceit [dɪ'siːt] *n* engaño; **deceive** [dɪ'siːv] *vt* engañar

December [dɪ'sɛmbə*] *n* diciembre *m*

decency ['diːsənsɪ] *n* decencia

decent ['diːsənt] *adj* (*proper*) decente; (*person: kind*) amable, bueno

deception [dɪ'sɛpʃən] *n* engaño

deceptive [dɪ'sɛptɪv] *adj* engañoso

■ Be careful not to translate **deception** by the Spanish word *decepción*.

decide [dɪ'saɪd] *vt* (*person*) decidir; (*question, argument*) resolver ▷ *vi* decidir; **to ~ to do/that** decidir hacer/que; **to ~ on sth** decidirse por algo

decimal ['dɛsɪməl] *adj* decimal ▷ *n* decimal *m*

decision [dɪˈsɪʒən] n decisión f
decisive [dɪˈsaɪsɪv] adj decisivo; (person) decidido
deck [dɛk] n (Naut) cubierta; (of bus) piso; (record deck) platina; (of cards) baraja; **deckchair** n tumbona
declaration [dɛkləˈreɪʃən] n declaración f
declare [dɪˈklɛə*] vt declarar
decline [dɪˈklaɪn] n disminución f, descenso ▷ vt rehusar ▷ vi (person, business) decaer; (strength) disminuir
decorate [ˈdɛkəreɪt] vt (adorn): **to ~ (with)** adornar (de), decorar (de); (paint) pintar; (paper) empapelar; **decoration** [-ˈreɪʃən] n adorno; (act) decoración f; (medal) condecoración f; **decorator** n (workman) pintor m (decorador)
decrease [n ˈdiːkriːs, vb diːˈkriːs] n: **~ (in)** disminución f (de) ▷ vt disminuir, reducir ▷ vi reducirse
decree [dɪˈkriː] n decreto
dedicate [ˈdɛdɪkeɪt] vt dedicar; **dedicated** adj dedicado; (Comput) especializado; **dedicated word processor** procesador m de textos especializado o dedicado; **dedication** [-ˈkeɪʃən] n (devotion) dedicación f; (in book) dedicatoria
deduce [dɪˈdjuːs] vt deducir
deduct [dɪˈdʌkt] vt restar; descontar; **deduction** [dɪˈdʌkʃən] n (amount deducted) descuento; (conclusion) deducción f, conclusión f
deed [diːd] n hecho, acto; (feat) hazaña; (Law) escritura
deem [diːm] vt (formal) juzgar, considerar
deep [diːp] adj profundo; (expressing measurements) de profundidad; (voice) bajo; (breath) profundo; (colour) intenso ▷ adv: **the spectators stood 20 ~** los espectadores se formaron de 20 en fondo; **to be 4 metres ~** tener 4 metros de profundidad; **deep-fry** vt freír en aceite abundante; **deeply** adv (breathe) a pleno pulmón; (interested, moved, grateful) profundamente, hondamente
deer [dɪə*] n inv ciervo
default [dɪˈfɔːlt] n: **by ~ (win)** por incomparecencia ▷ adj (Comput) por defecto
defeat [dɪˈfiːt] n derrota ▷ vt derrotar, vencer
defect [n ˈdiːfɛkt, vb dɪˈfɛkt] n defecto ▷ vi: **to ~ to the enemy** pasarse al enemigo; **defective** [dɪˈfɛktɪv] adj defectuoso
defence [dɪˈfɛns] (us **defense**) n defensa
defend [dɪˈfɛnd] vt defender; **defendant** n acusado/a; (in civil case) demandado/a; **defender** n defensor(a) m/f; (Sport) defensa mf

defense [dɪˈfɛns] (us) = **defence**
defensive [dɪˈfɛnsɪv] adj defensivo ▷ n: **on the ~** a la defensiva
defer [dɪˈfə:*] vt aplazar
defiance [dɪˈfaɪəns] n desafío; **in ~ of** en contra de; **defiant** [dɪˈfaɪənt] adj (challenging) desafiante, retador(a)
deficiency [dɪˈfɪʃənsɪ] n (lack) falta; (defect) defecto; **deficient** [dɪˈfɪʃənt] adj deficiente
deficit [ˈdɛfɪsɪt] n déficit m
define [dɪˈfaɪn] vt (word etc) definir; (limits etc) determinar
definite [ˈdɛfɪnɪt] adj (fixed) determinado; (obvious) claro; (certain) indudable; **he was ~ about it** no dejó lugar a dudas (sobre ello); **definitely** adv desde luego, por supuesto
definition [dɛfɪˈnɪʃən] n definición f; (clearness) nitidez f
deflate [diːˈfleɪt] vt desinflar
deflect [dɪˈflɛkt] vt desviar
defraud [dɪˈfrɔːd] vt: **to ~ sb of sth** estafar algo a algn
defrost [diːˈfrɒst] vt descongelar
defuse [diːˈfjuːz] vt desactivar; (situation) calmar
defy [dɪˈfaɪ] vt (resist) oponerse a; (challenge) desafiar; (fig): **it defies description** resulta imposible describirlo
degree [dɪˈgriː] n grado; (Scol) título; **to have a ~ in maths** tener una licenciatura en matemáticas; **by ~s** (gradually) poco a poco, por etapas; **to some ~** hasta cierto punto
dehydrated [diːhaɪˈdreɪtɪd] adj deshidratado; (milk) en polvo
de-icer [diːˈaɪsə*] n descongelador m
delay [dɪˈleɪ] vt demorar, aplazar; (person) entretener; (train) retrasar ▷ vi tardar ▷ n demora, retraso; **to be ~ed** retrasarse; **without ~** en seguida, sin tardar
delegate [n ˈdɛlɪgɪt, vb ˈdɛlɪgeɪt] n delegado/a ▷ vt (person) delegar en; (task) delegar
delete [dɪˈliːt] vt suprimir, tachar
deli [ˈdɛlɪ] n = **delicatessen**
deliberate [adj dɪˈlɪbərɪt, vb dɪˈlɪbəreɪt] adj (intentional) intencionado; (slow) pausado, lento ▷ vi deliberar; **deliberately** adv (on purpose) a propósito
delicacy [ˈdɛlɪkəsɪ] n delicadeza; (choice food) manjar m
delicate [ˈdɛlɪkɪt] adj delicado; (fragile) frágil
delicatessen [dɛlɪkəˈtɛsn] n ultramarinos mpl finos
delicious [dɪˈlɪʃəs] adj delicioso
delight [dɪˈlaɪt] n (feeling) placer m, deleite m; (person, experience etc) encanto,

delicia ▷ *vt* encantar, deleitar; **to take ~ in**
deleitarse en; **delighted** *adj*: **delighted (at**
or **with/to do)** encantado (con/de hacer);
delightful *adj* encantador(a), delicioso
delinquent [dɪˈlɪŋkwənt] *adj*, *n*
delincuente *mf*
deliver [dɪˈlɪvə*] *vt* (*distribute*) repartir;
(*hand over*) entregar; (*message*) comunicar;
(*speech*) pronunciar; (*Med*) asistir al parto
de; **delivery** *n* reparto; entrega; (*of*
speaker) modo de expresarse; (*Med*) parto,
alumbramiento; **to take delivery of** recibir
delusion [dɪˈluːʒən] *n* ilusión *f*, engaño
de luxe [dəˈlʌks] *adj* de lujo
delve [dɛlv] *vi*: **to ~ into** hurgar en
demand [dɪˈmɑːnd] *vt* (*gen*) exigir; (*rights*)
reclamar ▷ *n* exigencia; (*claim*) reclamación
f; (*Econ*) demanda; **to be in ~** ser muy
solicitado; **on ~** a solicitud; **demanding** *adj*
(*boss*) exigente; (*work*) absorbente
demise [dɪˈmaɪz] *n* (*death*) fallecimiento
demo [ˈdɛməu] (*inf*) *n abbr* (= *demonstration*)
manifestación *f*
democracy [dɪˈmɔkrəsɪ] *n* democracia;
democrat [ˈdɛməkræt] *n* demócrata
mf; **democratic** [dɛməˈkrætɪk] *adj*
democrático; (*US*) demócrata
demolish [dɪˈmɔlɪʃ] *vt* derribar, demoler;
(*fig*: *argument*) destruir
demolition [dɛməˈlɪʃən] *n* derribo,
demolición *f*
demon [ˈdiːmən] *n* (*evil spirit*) demonio
demonstrate [ˈdɛmənstreɪt] *vt*
demostrar; (*skill, appliance*) mostrar ▷ *vi*
manifestarse;
[-ˈstreɪʃən] *n* (*Pol*) manifestación *f*; (*proof,*
exhibition) demostración *f*; **demonstrator**
n (*Pol*) manifestante *mf*; (*Comm*)
demostrador(a) *m/f*; vendedor(a) *m/f*
demote [dɪˈməut] *vt* degradar
den [dɛn] *n* (*of animal*) guarida; (*room*)
habitación *f*
denial [dɪˈnaɪəl] *n* (*refusal*) negativa; (*of*
report etc) negación *f*
denim [ˈdɛnɪm] *n* tela vaquera; **denims**
npl vaqueros *mpl*
Denmark [ˈdɛnmɑːk] *n* Dinamarca
denomination [dɪnɔmɪˈneɪʃən] *n* valor
m; (*Rel*) confesión *f*
denounce [dɪˈnauns] *vt* denunciar
dense [dɛns] *adj* (*crowd*) denso; (*thick*)
espeso; (: *foliage etc*) tupido; (*inf*: *stupid*)
torpe
density [ˈdɛnsɪtɪ] *n* densidad *f* ▷ **single/**
double-~ disk *n* (*Comput*) disco de densidad
sencilla/de doble densidad
dent [dɛnt] *n* abolladura ▷ *vt* (*also*: **make**
a ~ in) abollar

dental [ˈdɛntl] *adj* dental; **dental floss**
[-flɔs] *n* seda dental; **dental surgery** *n*
clínica *f* dental, consultorio *m* dental
dentist [ˈdɛntɪst] *n* dentista *mf*
dentures [ˈdɛntʃəz] *npl* dentadura
(postiza)
deny [dɪˈnaɪ] *vt* negar; (*charge*) rechazar
deodorant [diːˈəudərənt] *n* desodorante
m
depart [dɪˈpɑːt] *vi* irse, marcharse; (*train*)
salir; **to ~ from** (*fig*: *differ from*) apartarse de
department [dɪˈpɑːtmənt] *n* (*Comm*)
sección *f*; (*Scol*) departamento; (*Pol*)
ministerio; **department store** *n* gran
almacén *m*
departure [dɪˈpɑːtʃə*] *n* partida, ida; (*of*
train) salida; (*of employee*) marcha; **a new ~**
un nuevo rumbo; **departure lounge** *n* (*at*
airport) sala de embarque
depend [dɪˈpɛnd] *vi*: **to ~ on** depender de;
(*rely on*) contar con; **it ~s** depende, según;
~ing on the result según el resultado;
dependant *n* dependiente *mf*; **dependent**
adj: **to be dependent on** depender de ▷ *n* =
dependant
depict [dɪˈpɪkt] *vt* (*in picture*) pintar;
(*describe*) representar
deport [dɪˈpɔt] *vt* deportar
deposit [dɪˈpɔzɪt] *n* depósito; (*Chem*)
sedimento; (*of ore, oil*) yacimiento ▷ *vt*
(*gen*) depositar; **deposit account** (*BRIT*) *n*
cuenta de ahorros
depot [ˈdɛpəu] *n* (*storehouse*) depósito; (*for*
vehicles) parque *m*; (*US*) estación *f*
depreciate [dɪˈpriːʃɪeɪt] *vi* depreciarse,
perder valor
depress [dɪˈprɛs] *vt* deprimir; (*wages*
etc) hacer bajar; (*press down*) apretar;
depressed *adj* deprimido; **depressing**
adj deprimente; **depression** [dɪˈprɛʃən] *n*
depresión *f*
deprive [dɪˈpraɪv] *vt*: **to ~ sb of** privar a
algn de; **deprived** *adj* necesitado
dept. *abbr* (= *department*) dto
depth [dɛpθ] *n* profundidad *f*; (*of cupboard*)
fondo; **to be in the ~s of despair** sentir la
mayor desesperación; **to be out of one's**
~ (*in water*) no hacer pie; (*fig*) sentirse
totalmente perdido
deputy [ˈdɛpjutɪ] *adj*: **~ head**
subdirector(a) *m/f* ▷ *n* sustituto/a,
suplente *mf*; (*US Pol*) diputado/a; (*US*: *also*: **~**
sheriff) agente *m* del sheriff
derail [dɪˈreɪl] *vt*: **to be ~ed** descarrilarse
derelict [ˈdɛrɪlɪkt] *adj* abandonado
derive [dɪˈraɪv] *vt* (*benefit etc*) obtener
▷ *vi*: **to ~ from** derivarse de
descend [dɪˈsɛnd] *vt*, *vi* descender, bajar;

to ~ from descender de; **to ~ to** rebajarse a;
descendant *n* descendiente *mf*

descent [dɪˈsɛnt] *n* descenso; (*origin*)
descendencia

describe [dɪsˈkraɪb] *vt* describir;
description [-ˈkrɪpʃən] *n* descripción *f*;
(*sort*) clase *f*, género

desert [*n* ˈdɛzət, *vb* dɪˈzəːt] *n* desierto ▷ *vt*
abandonar ▷ *vi* (*Mil*) desertar; **deserted**
[dɪˈzəːtɪd] *adj* desierto

deserve [dɪˈzəːv] *vt* merecer, ser digno de

design [dɪˈzaɪn] *n* (*sketch*) bosquejo;
(*layout, shape*) diseño; (*pattern*) dibujo;
(*intention*) intención *f* ▷ *vt* diseñar; **design
and technology** (*BRIT: Scol*) *n* ≈ dibujo y
tecnología

designate [*vb* ˈdɛzɪgneɪt, *adj* ˈdɛzɪgnɪt] *vt*
(*appoint*) nombrar; (*destine*) designar ▷ *adj*
designado

designer [dɪˈzaɪnə*] *n* diseñador(a) *m/f*;
(*fashion designer*) modisto/a, diseñador(a)
m/f de moda

desirable [dɪˈzaɪərəbl] *adj* (*proper*)
deseable; (*attractive*) atractivo

desire [dɪˈzaɪə*] *n* deseo ▷ *vt* desear

desk [dɛsk] *n* (*in office*) escritorio; (*for pupil*)
pupitre *m*; (*in hotel, at airport*) recepción
f; (*BRIT: in shop, restaurant*) caja; **desk-top
publishing** [ˈdɛsktɔp-] *n* autoedición *f*

despair [dɪsˈpɛə*] *n* desesperación *f*
▷ *vi*: **to ~ of** perder la esperanza de

despatch [dɪsˈpætʃ] *n, vt* = **dispatch**

desperate [ˈdɛspərɪt] *adj* desesperado;
(*fugitive*) peligroso; **to be ~ for sth/to
do** necesitar urgentemente algo/hacer;
desperately *adv* desesperadamente; (*very*)
terriblemente, gravemente

desperation [dɛspəˈreɪʃən]
n desesperación *f*; **in (sheer) ~**
(absolutamente) desesperado

despise [dɪsˈpaɪz] *vt* despreciar

despite [dɪsˈpaɪt] *prep* a pesar de, pese a

dessert [dɪˈzəːt] *n* postre *m*;
dessertspoon *n* cuchara (de postre)

destination [dɛstɪˈneɪʃən] *n* destino

destined [ˈdɛstɪnd] *adj*: **~ for London** con
destino a Londres

destiny [ˈdɛstɪnɪ] *n* destino

destroy [dɪsˈtrɔɪ] *vt* destruir; (*animal*)
sacrificar

destruction [dɪsˈtrʌkʃən] *n* destrucción *f*

destructive [dɪsˈtrʌktɪv] *adj* destructivo,
destructor(a)

detach [dɪˈtætʃ] *vt* separar; (*unstick*)
despegar; **detached** *adj* (*attitude*) objetivo,
imparcial; **detached house** *n* ≈ chalé *m*,
≈ chalet *m*

detail [ˈdiːteɪl] *n* detalle *m*; (*no pl*; (: *in*

picture etc) detalles *mpl*; (*trifle*) pequeñez
f ▷ *vt* detallar; (*Mil*) destacar; **in ~**
detalladamente; **detailed** *adj* detallado

detain [dɪˈteɪn] *vt* retener; (*in captivity*)
detener

detect [dɪˈtɛkt] *vt* descubrir; (*Med, Police*)
identificar; (*Mil, Radar, Tech*) detectar;
detection [dɪˈtɛkʃən] *n* descubrimiento;
identificación *f*; **detective** *n* detective *mf*;
detective story *n* novela policíaca

detention [dɪˈtɛnʃən] *n* detención *f*,
arresto; (*Scol*) castigo

deter [dɪˈtəː*] *vt* (*dissuade*) disuadir

detergent [dɪˈtəːdʒənt] *n* detergente *m*

deteriorate [dɪˈtɪərɪəreɪt] *vi* deteriorarse

determination [dɪtəːmɪˈneɪʃən] *n*
resolución *f*

determine [dɪˈtəːmɪn] *vt* determinar;
determined *adj* (*person*) resuelto, decidido;
determined to do resuelto a hacer

deterrent [dɪˈtɛrənt] *n* (*Mil*) fuerza de
disuasión

detest [dɪˈtɛst] *vt* aborrecer

detour [ˈdiːtuə*] *n* (*gen, US Aut*) desviación
f

detract [dɪˈtrækt] *vt*: **to ~ from** quitar
mérito a, desvirtuar

detrimental [dɛtrɪˈmɛntl] *adj*: **~ (to)**
perjudicial (a)

devastating [ˈdɛvəsteɪtɪŋ] *adj*
devastador(a); (*fig*) arrollador(a)

develop [dɪˈvɛləp] *vt* desarrollar; (*Phot*)
revelar; (*disease*) coger; (*habit*) adquirir;
(*fault*) empezar a tener ▷ *vi* desarrollarse;
(*advance*) progresar; (*facts, symptoms*)
aparecer; **developing country** *n* país *m*
en (vías de) desarrollo; **development** *n*
desarrollo; (*advance*) progreso; (*of affair, case*)
desenvolvimiento; (*of land*) urbanización *f*

device [dɪˈvaɪs] *n* (*apparatus*) aparato,
mecanismo

devil [ˈdɛvl] *n* diablo, demonio

devious [ˈdiːvɪəs] *adj* taimado

devise [dɪˈvaɪz] *vt* idear, inventar

devote [dɪˈvəut] *vt*: **to ~ sth to** dedicar
algo a; **devoted** *adj* (*loyal*) leal, fiel; **to be
devoted to sb** querer con devoción a algn;
the book is devoted to politics el libro
trata de la política; **devotion** *n* dedicación
f; (*Rel*) devoción *f*

devour [dɪˈvauə*] *vt* devorar

devout [dɪˈvaut] *adj* devoto

dew [djuː] *n* rocío

diabetes [daɪəˈbiːtiːz] *n* diabetes *f*

diabetic [daɪəˈbɛtɪk] *adj, n* diabético/a
m/f

diagnose [ˈdaɪəgnəuz] *vt* diagnosticar

diagnosis [daɪəgˈnəusɪs] (*pl* **-ses**) *n*

diagnóstico

diagonal [daɪ'ægənl] *adj, n* diagonal *f*

diagram ['daɪəgræm] *n* diagrama *m*, esquema *m*

dial ['daɪəl] *n* esfera (SP), cara (LAM); (*on radio etc*) dial *m*; (*of phone*) disco ▷ *vt* (*number*) marcar

dialect ['daɪəlɛkt] *n* dialecto

dialling code ['daɪəlɪŋ-] *n* prefijo

dialling tone (US **dial tone**) *n* (BRIT) señal *f* or tono de marcar

dialogue ['daɪəlɔg] (US **dialog**) *n* diálogo

diameter [daɪ'æmɪtə*] *n* diámetro

diamond ['daɪəmənd] *n* diamante *m*; (*shape*) rombo; **diamonds** *npl* (*Cards*) diamantes *mpl*

diaper ['daɪəpə*] (US) *n* pañal *m*

diarrhoea [daɪə'riːə] (US **diarrhea**) *n* diarrea

diary ['daɪərɪ] *n* (*daily account*) diario; (*book*) agenda

dice [daɪs] *n inv* dados *mpl* ▷ *vt* (*Culin*) cortar en cuadritos

dictate [dɪk'teɪt] *vt* dictar; (*conditions*) imponer; **dictation** [-'teɪʃən] *n* dictado; (*giving of orders*) órdenes *fpl*

dictator [dɪk'teɪtə*] *n* dictador *m*

dictionary ['dɪkʃənrɪ] *n* diccionario

did [dɪd] *pt of* **do**

didn't ['dɪdənt] = **did not**

die [daɪ] *vi* morir; (*fig: fade*) desvanecerse, desaparecer; **to be dying for sth/to do sth** morirse por algo/de ganas de hacer algo; **die down** *vi* apagarse; (*wind*) amainar; **die out** *vi* desaparecer

diesel ['diːzəl] *n* vehículo con motor Diesel

diet ['daɪət] *n* dieta; (*restricted food*) régimen *m* ▷ *vi* (*also*: **be on a ~**) estar a dieta, hacer régimen

differ ['dɪfə*] *vi*: **to ~ (from)** (*be different*) ser distinto (a), diferenciarse (de); (*disagree*) discrepar (de); **difference** *n* diferencia; (*disagreement*) desacuerdo; **different** *adj* diferente, distinto; **differentiate** [-'rɛnʃɪeɪt] *vi*: **to differentiate (between)** distinguir (entre); **differently** *adv* de otro modo, en forma distinta

difficult ['dɪfɪkəlt] *adj* difícil; **difficulty** *n* dificultad *f*

dig [dɪg] (*pt, pp* **dug**) *vt* (*hole, ground*) cavar ▷ *n* (*prod*) empujón *m*; (*archaeological*) excavación *f*; (*remark*) indirecta; **to ~ one's nails into** clavar las uñas en; **dig up** *vt* (*information*) desenterrar; (*plant*) desarraigar

digest [*vb* daɪ'dʒɛst, *n* 'daɪdʒɛst] *vt* (*food*) digerir; (*facts*) asimilar ▷ *n* resumen *m*; **digestion** [dɪ'dʒɛstʃən] *n* digestión *f*

digit ['dɪdʒɪt] *n* (*number*) dígito; (*finger*)

dedo; **digital** *adj* digital; **digital camera** *n* cámara digital; **digital TV** *n* televisión *f* digital

dignified ['dɪgnɪfaɪd] *adj* grave, solemne

dignity ['dɪgnɪtɪ] *n* dignidad *f*

digs [dɪgz] (BRIT: *inf*) *npl* pensión *f*, alojamiento

dilemma [daɪ'lɛmə] *n* dilema *m*

dill [dɪl] *n* eneldo

dilute [daɪ'luːt] *vt* diluir

dim [dɪm] *adj* (*light*) débil; (*outline*) indistinto; (*room*) oscuro; (*inf: stupid*) lerdo ▷ *vt* (*light*) bajar

dime [daɪm] (US) *n* moneda de diez centavos

dimension [dɪ'mɛnʃən] *n* dimensión *f*

diminish [dɪ'mɪnɪʃ] *vt, vi* disminuir

din [dɪn] *n* estruendo, estrépito

dine [daɪn] *vi* cenar; **diner** *n* (*person*) comensal *mf*

dinghy ['dɪŋgɪ] *n* bote *m*; (*also*: **rubber ~**) lancha (neumática)

dingy ['dɪndʒɪ] *adj* (*room*) sombrío; (*colour*) sucio

dining car ['daɪnɪŋ-] (BRIT) *n* (*Rail*) coche-comedor *m*

dining room ['daɪnɪŋ-] *n* comedor *m*

dining table *n* mesa *f* de comedor

dinner ['dɪnə*] *n* (*evening meal*) cena; (*lunch*) comida; (*public*) cena, banquete *m*; **dinner jacket** *n* smoking *m*; **dinner party** *n* cena; **dinner time** *n* (*evening*) hora de cenar; (*midday*) hora de comer

dinosaur ['daɪnəsɔː*] *n* dinosaurio

dip [dɪp] *n* (*slope*) pendiente *m*; (*in sea*) baño; (*Culin*) salsa ▷ *vt* (*in water*) mojar; (*ladle etc*) meter; (BRIT Aut): **to ~ one's lights** poner luces de cruce ▷ *vi* (*road etc*) descender, bajar

diploma [dɪ'pləumə] *n* diploma *m*

diplomacy [dɪ'pləuməsɪ] *n* diplomacia

diplomat ['dɪpləmæt] *n* diplomático/a; **diplomatic** [dɪplə'mætɪk] *adj* diplomático

dipstick ['dɪpstɪk] (BRIT) *n* (*Aut*) varilla de nivel (del aceite)

dire [daɪə*] *adj* calamitoso

direct [daɪ'rɛkt] *adj* directo; (*challenge*) claro; (*person*) franco ▷ *vt* dirigir; (*order*): **to ~ sb to do sth** mandar a algn hacer algo ▷ *adv* derecho; **can you ~ me to ...?** ¿puede indicarme dónde está ...?; **direct debit** (BRIT) *n* domiciliación *f* bancaria de recibos

direction [dɪ'rɛkʃən] *n* dirección *f*; **sense of ~** sentido de la dirección; **directions** *npl* (*instructions*) instrucciones *fpl*; **~s for use** modo de empleo

directly [dɪ'rɛktlɪ] *adv* (*in straight line*) directamente; (*at once*) en seguida

director [dɪ'rɛktə*] *n* director(a) *m/f*

directory [dɪ'rɛktərɪ] n (Tel) guía (telefónica); (Comput) directorio; **directory enquiries** (US **directory assistance**) n (servicio de) información f

dirt [də:t] n suciedad f; (earth) tierra; **dirty** adj sucio; (joke) verde, colorado (MEX) ▷ vt ensuciar; (stain) manchar

disability [dɪsə'bɪlɪtɪ] n incapacidad f

disabled [dɪs'eɪbld] adj: **to be physically ~** ser minusválido/a; **to be mentally ~** ser deficiente mental

disadvantage [dɪsəd'vɑːntɪdʒ] n desventaja, inconveniente m

disagree [dɪsə'griː] vi (differ) discrepar; **to ~ (with)** no estar de acuerdo (con); **disagreeable** adj desagradable; (person) antipático; **disagreement** n desacuerdo

disappear [dɪsə'pɪə*] vi desaparecer; **disappearance** n desaparición f

disappoint [dɪsə'pɔɪnt] vt decepcionar, defraudar; **disappointed** adj decepcionado; **disappointing** adj decepcionante; **disappointment** n decepción f

disapproval [dɪsə'pruːvəl] n desaprobación f

disapprove [dɪsə'pruːv] vi: **to ~ of** ver mal

disarm [dɪs'ɑːm] vt desarmar; **disarmament** [dɪs'ɑːməmənt] n desarme m

disaster [dɪ'zɑːstə*] n desastre m

disastrous [dɪ'zɑːstrəs] adj desastroso

disbelief [dɪsbə'liːf] n incredulidad f

disc [dɪsk] n disco; (Comput) = **disk**

discard [dɪs'kɑːd] vt (old things) tirar; (fig) descartar

discharge [vb dɪs'tʃɑːdʒ, n 'dɪstʃɑːdʒ] vt (task, duty) cumplir; (waste) verter; (patient) dar de alta; (employee) despedir; (soldier) licenciar; (defendant) poner en libertad ▷ n (Elec) descarga; (Med) supuración f; (dismissal) despedida; (of duty) desempeño; (of debt) pago, descargo

discipline ['dɪsɪplɪn] n disciplina ▷ vt disciplinar; (punish) castigar

disc jockey n pinchadiscos mf inv

disclose [dɪs'kləuz] vt revelar

disco ['dɪskəu] n abbr discoteca

discoloured [dɪs'kʌləd] (US **discolored**) adj descolorido

discomfort [dɪs'kʌmfət] n incomodidad f; (unease) inquietud f; (physical) malestar m

disconnect [dɪskə'nɛkt] vt separar; (Elec etc) desconectar

discontent [dɪskən'tɛnt] n descontento

discontinue [dɪskən'tɪnjuː] vt interrumpir; (payments) suspender; **"~d"** (Comm) "ya no se fabrica"

discount [n 'dɪskaunt, vb dɪs'kaunt] n descuento ▷ vt descontar

discourage [dɪs'kʌrɪdʒ] vt desalentar; (advise against): **to ~ sb from doing** disuadir a algn de hacer

discover [dɪs'kʌvə*] vt descubrir; (error) darse cuenta de; **discovery** n descubrimiento

discredit [dɪs'krɛdɪt] vt desacreditar

discreet [dɪ'skriːt] adj (tactful) discreto; (careful) prudente

discrepancy [dɪ'skrɛpənsɪ] n diferencia

discretion [dɪ'skrɛʃən] n (tact) discreción f; **at the ~ of** a criterio de

discriminate [dɪ'skrɪmɪneɪt] vi: **to ~ between** distinguir entre; **to ~ against** discriminar contra; **discrimination** ['neɪʃən] n (discernment) perspicacia; (bias) discriminación f

discuss [dɪ'skʌs] vt discutir; (a theme) tratar; **discussion** [dɪ'skʌʃən] n discusión f

disease [dɪ'ziːz] n enfermedad f

disembark [dɪsɪm'bɑːk] vt, vi desembarcar

disgrace [dɪs'greɪs] n ignominia; (shame) vergüenza, escándalo ▷ vt deshonrar; **disgraceful** adj vergonzoso

disgruntled [dɪs'grʌntld] adj disgustado, descontento

disguise [dɪs'gaɪz] n disfraz m ▷ vt disfrazar; **in ~** disfrazado

disgust [dɪs'gʌst] n repugnancia ▷ vt repugnar, dar asco a

 ▌Be careful not to translate **disgust** by the Spanish word disgustar.

disgusted [dɪs'gʌstɪd] adj indignado
 ▌Be careful not to translate **disgusted** by the Spanish word disgustado.

disgusting [dɪs'gʌstɪŋ] adj repugnante, asqueroso; (behaviour etc) vergonzoso

dish [dɪʃ] n (gen) plato; **to do** or **wash the ~es** fregar los platos; **dishcloth** n estropajo

dishonest [dɪs'ɔnɪst] adj (person) poco honrado, tramposo; (means) fraudulento

dishtowel ['dɪʃtauəl] (US) n estropajo

dishwasher ['dɪʃwɔʃə*] n lavaplatos m inv

disillusion [dɪsɪ'luːʒən] vt desilusionar

disinfectant [dɪsɪn'fɛktənt] n desinfectante m

disintegrate [dɪs'ɪntɪgreɪt] vi disgregarse, desintegrarse

disk [dɪsk] n (esp US) = **disc**; (Comput) disco, disquete m; **single-/double-sided ~** disco de una cara/dos caras; **disk drive** n disc drive m; **diskette** n = **disk**

dislike [dɪs'laɪk] n antipatía, aversión f ▷ vt tener antipatía a

dislocate ['dɪsləkeɪt] vt dislocar

disloyal [dɪs'lɔɪəl] adj desleal

dismal ['dɪzml] adj (gloomy) deprimente, triste; (very bad) malísimo, fatal

dismantle [dɪs'mæntl] vt desmontar, desarmar

dismay [dɪs'meɪ] n consternación f ▷ vt consternar

dismiss [dɪs'mɪs] vt (worker) despedir; (pupils) dejar marchar; (soldiers) dar permiso para irse; (idea, Law) rechazar; (possibility) descartar; **dismissal** n despido

disobedient [dɪsə'biːdɪənt] adj desobediente

disobey [dɪsə'beɪ] vt desobedecer

disorder [dɪs'ɔːdə*] n desorden m; (rioting) disturbios mpl; (Med) trastorno

disorganized [dɪs'ɔːgənaɪzd] adj desorganizado

disown [dɪs'əun] vt (action) renegar de; (person) negar cualquier tipo de relación con

dispatch [dɪs'pætʃ] vt enviar ▷ n (sending) envío; (Press) informe m; (Mil) parte m

dispel [dɪs'pɛl] vt disipar

dispense [dɪs'pɛns] vt (medicines) preparar; **dispense with** vt fus prescindir de; **dispenser** n (container) distribuidor m automático

disperse [dɪs'pə:s] vt dispersar ▷ vi dispersarse

display [dɪs'pleɪ] n (in shop window) escaparate m; (exhibition) exposición f; (Comput) visualización f; (of feeling) manifestación f ▷ vt exponer; manifestar; (ostentatiously) lucir

displease [dɪs'pliːz] vt (offend) ofender; (annoy) fastidiar

disposable [dɪs'pəuzəbl] adj desechable; (income) disponible

disposal [dɪs'pəuzl] n (of rubbish) destrucción f; **at one's ~** a su disposición

dispose [dɪs'pəuz] vi: **to ~ of** (unwanted goods) deshacerse de; (problem etc) resolver; **disposition** [dɪspə'zɪʃən] n (nature) temperamento; (inclination) propensión f

disproportionate [dɪsprə'pɔːʃənət] adj desproporcionado

dispute [dɪs'pjuːt] n disputa; (also: **industrial ~**) conflicto (laboral) ▷ vt (argue) disputar, discutir; (question) cuestionar

disqualify [dɪs'kwɔlɪfaɪ] vt (Sport) desclasificar; **to ~ sb for sth/from doing sth** incapacitar a algn para algo/hacer algo

disregard [dɪsrɪ'gɑːd] vt (ignore) no hacer caso de

disrupt [dɪs'rʌpt] vt (plans) desbaratar, trastornar; (conversation) interrumpir; **disruption** [dɪs'rʌpʃən] n trastorno, desbaratamiento; interrupción f

dissatisfaction [dɪssætɪs'fækʃən] n disgusto, descontento

dissatisfied [dɪs'sætɪsfaɪd] adj insatisfecho

dissect [dɪ'sɛkt] vt disecar

dissent [dɪ'sɛnt] n disensión f

dissertation [dɪsə'teɪʃən] n tesina

dissolve [dɪ'zɔlv] vt disolver ▷ vi disolverse; **to ~ in(to) tears** deshacerse en lágrimas

distance ['dɪstəns] n distancia; **in the ~** a lo lejos

distant ['dɪstənt] adj lejano; (manner) reservado, frío

distil [dɪs'tɪl] (us **distill**) vt destilar; **distillery** n destilería

distinct [dɪs'tɪŋkt] adj (different) distinto; (clear) claro; (unmistakeable) inequívoco; **as ~ from** a diferencia de; **distinction** [dɪs'tɪŋkʃən] n distinción f; (honour) honor m; (in exam) sobresaliente m; **distinctive** adj distintivo

distinguish [dɪs'tɪŋgwɪʃ] vt distinguir; **to ~ o.s.** destacarse; **distinguished** adj (eminent) distinguido

distort [dɪs'tɔːt] vt distorsionar; (shape, image) deformar

distract [dɪs'trækt] vt distraer; **distracted** adj distraído; **distraction** [dɪs'trækʃən] n distracción f; (confusion) aturdimiento

distraught [dɪs'trɔːt] adj loco de inquietud

distress [dɪs'trɛs] n (anguish) angustia, aflicción f ▷ vt afligir; **distressing** adj angustioso; doloroso

distribute [dɪs'trɪbjuːt] vt distribuir; (share out) repartir; **distribution** [-'bjuːʃən] n distribución f, reparto; **distributor** n (Aut) distribuidor m; (Comm) distribuidora

district ['dɪstrɪkt] n (of country) zona, región f; (of town) barrio; (Admin) distrito; **district attorney** (us) n fiscal mf

distrust [dɪs'trʌst] n desconfianza ▷ vt desconfiar de

disturb [dɪs'tə:b] vt (person: bother, interrupt) molestar; (: upset) perturbar, inquietar; (disorganize) alterar; **disturbance** n (upheaval) perturbación f; (political etc: gen pl) disturbio; (of mind) trastorno; **disturbed** adj (worried, upset) preocupado, angustiado; **emotionally disturbed** trastornado; (childhood) inseguro; **disturbing** adj inquietante, perturbador(a)

ditch [dɪtʃ] n zanja; (irrigation ditch) acequia ▷ vt (inf: partner) deshacerse de; (: plan, car etc) abandonar

ditto ['dɪtəu] adv ídem, lo mismo

dive [daɪv] n (from board) salto; (underwater) buceo; (of submarine) sumersión f ▷ vi (swimmer: into water) saltar; (: under water) zambullirse, bucear; (fish, submarine) sumergirse; (bird) lanzarse en picado; **to ~ into** (bag etc) meter la mano en; (place) meterse de prisa en; **diver** n (underwater) buzo

diverse [daɪˈvəːs] adj diversos/as, varios/as

diversion [daɪˈvəːʃən] n (BRIT Aut) desviación f; (distraction, Mil) diversión f; (of funds) distracción f

diversity [daɪˈvəːsɪtɪ] n diversidad f

divert [daɪˈvəːt] vt (turn aside) desviar

divide [dɪˈvaɪd] vt dividir; (separate) separar ▷ vi dividirse; (road) bifurcarse; **divided highway** (US) n carretera de doble calzada

divine [dɪˈvaɪn] adj (also fig) divino

diving [ˈdaɪvɪŋ] n (Sport) salto; (underwater) buceo; **diving board** n trampolín m

division [dɪˈvɪʒən] n división f; (sharing out) reparto; (disagreement) diferencias fpl; (Comm) sección f

divorce [dɪˈvɔːs] n divorcio ▷ vt divorciarse de; **divorced** adj divorciado; **divorcee** [-ˈsiː] n divorciado/a

D.I.Y. (BRIT) adj, n abbr = **do-it-yourself**

dizzy [ˈdɪzɪ] adj (spell) de mareo; **to feel ~** marearse

DJ n abbr = **disc jockey**

DNA n abbr (= deoxyribonucleic acid) ADN m

○ **KEYWORD**

do [duː] (pt **did**, pp **done**) n (inf: party etc): **we're having a little do on Saturday** damos una fiestecita el sábado; **it was rather a grand do** fue un acontecimiento a lo grande
▷ aux vb **1** (in negative constructions: not translated): **I don't understand** no entiendo
2 (to form questions: not translated): **didn't you know?** ¿no lo sabías?; **what do you think?** ¿qué opinas?
3 (for emphasis, in polite expressions): **people do make mistakes sometimes** sí que se cometen errores a veces; **she does seem rather late** a mí también me parece que se ha retrasado; **do sit down/help yourself** siéntate/sírvete por favor; **do take care!** ¡ten cuidado(, te pido)!
4 (used to avoid repeating vb): **she sings better than I do** canta mejor que yo; **do you agree? - yes, I do/no, I don't** ¿estás de acuerdo? - sí (lo estoy)/no (lo estoy); **she lives in Glasgow - so do I** vive en Glasgow

- yo también; **he didn't like it and neither did we** no le gustó y a nosotros tampoco; **who made this mess? - I did** ¿quién hizo esta chapuza? - yo; **he asked me to help him and I did** me pidió que le ayudara y lo hice
5 (in question tags): **you like him, don't you?** te gusta, ¿verdad? or ¿no?; **I don't know him, do I?** creo que no le conozco
▷ vt **1** (gen, carry out, perform etc): **what are you doing tonight?** ¿qué haces esta noche?; **what can I do for you?** ¿en qué puedo servirle?; **to do the washing-up/cooking** fregar los platos/cocinar; **to do one's teeth/hair/nails** lavarse los dientes/arreglarse el pelo/arreglarse las uñas
2 (Aut etc): **the car was doing 100** el coche iba a 100; **we've done 200 km already** ya hemos hecho 200 km; **he can do 100 in that car** puede ir a 100 en ese coche
▷ vi **1** (act, behave) hacer; **do as I do** haz como yo
2 (get on, fare): **he's doing well/badly at school** va bien/mal en la escuela; **the firm is doing well** la empresa anda or va bien; **how do you do?** mucho gusto; (less formal) ¿qué tal?
3 (suit): **will it do?** ¿sirve?, ¿está or va bien?
4 (be sufficient) bastar; **will £10 do?** ¿será bastante con £10?; **that'll do** así está bien; **that'll do!** (in annoyance) ¡ya está bien!, ¡basta ya!; **to make do (with)** arreglárselas (con)

do up vt (laces) atar; (zip, dress, shirt) abrochar; (renovate: room, house) renovar

do with vt fus (need): **I could do with a drink/some help** no me vendría mal un trago/un poco de ayuda; (be connected) tener que ver con; **what has it got to do with you?** ¿qué tiene que ver contigo?

do without vi pasar sin; **if you're late for tea then you'll do without** si llegas tarde tendrás que quedarte sin cenar
▷ vt fus pasar sin; **I can do without a car** puedo pasar sin coche

dock [dɔk] n (Naut) muelle m; (Law) banquillo (de los acusados) ▷ vi (enter dock) atracar (la) muelle; (Space) acoplarse; **docks** npl (Naut) muelles mpl, puerto sg

doctor [ˈdɔktə*] n médico/a; (Ph.D. etc) doctor(a) m/f ▷ vt (drink etc) adulterar; **Doctor of Philosophy** n Doctor en Filosofía y Letras

document [ˈdɔkjumənt] n documento; **documentary** [-ˈmɛntərɪ] adj documental ▷ n documental m; **documentation** [-mɛnˈteɪʃən] n documentación f

dodge [dɔdʒ] n (fig) truco ▷ vt evadir; (blow) esquivar

dodgy ['dɔdʒɪ] adj (inf: uncertain) dudoso; (suspicious) sospechoso; (risky) arriesgado

does [dʌz] vb see **do**

doesn't ['dʌznt] = **does not**

dog [dɔg] n perro ▷ vt seguir los pasos de; (bad luck) perseguir; **doggy bag** ['dɔgɪ-] n bolsa para llevarse las sobras de la comida

do-it-yourself ['duːɪtjɔːˈsɛlf] n bricolaje m

dole [dəul] (BRIT) n (payment) subsidio de paro; **on the ~** parado

doll [dɔl] n muñeca; (US: inf: woman) muñeca, gachí f

dollar ['dɔlə*] n dólar m

dolphin ['dɔlfɪn] n delfín m

dome [dəum] n (Arch) cúpula

domestic [dəˈmɛstɪk] adj (animal, duty) doméstico; (flight, policy) nacional; **domestic appliance** n aparato m doméstico, aparato m de uso doméstico

dominant ['dɔmɪnənt] adj dominante

dominate ['dɔmɪneɪt] vt dominar

domino ['dɔmɪnəu] (pl **-es**) n ficha de dominó; **dominoes** n (game) dominó

donate [dəˈneɪt] vt donar; **donation** [dəˈneɪʃən] n donativo

done [dʌn] pp of **do**

donkey ['dɔŋkɪ] n burro

donor ['dəunə*] n donante mf; **donor card** n carnet m de donante

don't [dəunt] = **do not**

donut ['dəunʌt] (US) n = **doughnut**

doodle ['duːdl] vi hacer dibujitos or garabatos

doom [duːm] n (fate) suerte f ▷ vt: **to be ~ed to failure** estar condenado al fracaso

door [dɔː*] n puerta; **doorbell** n timbre m; **door handle** n tirador m; (of car) manija; **doorknob** n pomo m de la puerta, manilla f (LAM); **doorstep** n peldaño; **doorway** n entrada, puerta

dope [dəup] n (inf: illegal drug) droga; (: person) imbécil mf ▷ vt (horse etc) drogar

dormitory ['dɔːmɪtrɪ] n (BRIT) dormitorio; (US) colegio mayor

DOS n abbr (= disk operating system) DOS m

dosage ['dəusɪdʒ] n dosis f inv

dose [dəus] n dosis f inv

dot [dɔt] n punto ▷ vi: **~ted with** salpicado de; **on the ~** en punto; **dotcom** [dɔtˈkɔm] n puntocom f inv; **dotted line** ['dɔtɪd-] n: **to sign on the dotted line** firmar

double ['dʌbl] adj doble ▷ adv (twice): **to cost ~** costar el doble ▷ n doble m ▷ vt doblar ▷ vi doblarse; **on the ~**, **at the ~** (BRIT) corriendo; **double back** vi (person)

volver sobre sus pasos; **double bass** n contrabajo; **double bed** n cama de matrimonio; **double-check** vt volver a revisar ▷ vi: **I'll double-check** voy a revisarlo otra vez; **double-click** vi (Comput) hacer doble clic; **double-cross** vt (trick) engañar; (betray) traicionar; **doubledecker** n autobús m de dos pisos; **double glazing** (BRIT) n doble acristalamiento; **double room** n habitación f doble; **doubles** n (Tennis) juego de dobles; **double yellow lines** npl (BRIT: Aut) línea doble amarilla de prohibido aparcar, ≈ línea fsg amarilla continua

doubt [daut] n duda ▷ vt dudar; (suspect) dudar de; **to ~ that** dudar que; **doubtful** adj dudoso; (person): **to be doubtful about sth** tener dudas sobre algo; **doubtless** adv sin duda

dough [dəu] n masa, pasta; **doughnut** (US **donut**) n ≈ rosquilla

dove [dʌv] n paloma

down [daun] n (feathers) plumón m, flojel m ▷ adv (downwards) abajo, hacia abajo; (on the ground) por or en tierra ▷ prep abajo ▷ vt (inf: drink) beberse; **~ with X!** ¡abajo X!; **down-and-out** n vagabundo/a; **downfall** n caída, ruina; **downhill** adv: **to go downhill** (also fig) ir cuesta abajo

Downing Street ['daunɪŋ-] n (BRIT) Downing Street f

down: download vt (Comput) bajar; **downright** adj (nonsense, lie) manifiesto; (refusal) terminante

Down's syndrome ['daunz-] n síndrome m de Down

down: downstairs adv (below) (en el piso de) abajo; (downwards) escaleras abajo; **down-to-earth** adj práctico; **downtown** adv en el centro de la ciudad; **down under** adv en Australia (or Nueva Zelanda); **downward** [-wəd] adj, adv hacia abajo; **downwards** [-wədz] adv hacia abajo

doz. abbr = **dozen**

doze [dəuz] vi dormitar

dozen ['dʌzn] n docena; **a ~ books** una docena de libros; **~s of** cantidad de

Dr. abbr = **doctor**; **drive**

drab [dræb] adj gris, monótono

draft [drɑːft] n (first copy) borrador m; (Pol: of bill) anteproyecto; (US: call-up) quinta ▷ vt (plan) preparar; (write roughly) hacer un borrador de; see also **draught**

drag [dræg] vt arrastrar; (river) dragar, rastrear ▷ vi (time) pasar despacio; (play, film etc) hacerse pesado ▷ n (inf) lata; (women's clothing): **in ~** vestido de travesti; **to ~ and drop** (Comput) arrastrar y soltar

dragon ['drægən] n dragón m
dragonfly ['drægənflaɪ] n libélula
drain [dreɪn] n desaguadero; (in street) sumidero; (source of loss): **to be a ~ on** consumir, agotar ▷ vt (land, marshes) desaguar; (reservoir) desecar; (vegetables) escurrir ▷ vi escurrirse; **drainage** n (act) desagüe m; (Med, Agr) drenaje m; (sewage) alcantarillado; **drainpipe** n tubo de desagüe
drama ['drɑːmə] n (art) teatro; (play) drama m; (excitement) emoción f; **dramatic** [drə'mætɪk] adj dramático; (sudden, marked) espectacular
drank [dræŋk] pt of **drink**
drape [dreɪp] vt (cloth) colocar; (flag) colgar; **drapes** npl (us) cortinas fpl
drastic ['dræstɪk] adj (measure) severo; (change) radical, drástico
draught [drɑːft] (us **draft**) n (of air) corriente f de aire; (Naut) calado; **on ~** (beer) de barril; **draught beer** n cerveza de barril; **draughts** (BRIT) n (game) juego de damas
draw [drɔː] (pt **drew**, pp **drawn**) vt (picture) dibujar; (cart) tirar de; (curtain) correr; (take out) sacar; (attract) atraer; (money) retirar; (wages) cobrar ▷ vi (Sport) empatar ▷ n (Sport) empate m; (lottery) sorteo; **draw out** vi (lengthen) alargarse ▷ vt sacar; **draw up** vi (stop) pararse ▷ vt (chair) acercar; (document) redactar; **drawback** n inconveniente m, desventaja
drawer [drɔː*] n cajón m
drawing ['drɔːɪŋ] n dibujo; **drawing pin** (BRIT) n chincheta; **drawing room** n salón m
drawn [drɔːn] pp of **draw**
dread [drɛd] n pavor m, terror m ▷ vt temer, tener miedo or pavor a; **dreadful** adj horroroso
dream [driːm] (pt, pp **~ed** or **~t**) n sueño ▷ vt, vi soñar; **dreamer** n soñador(a) m/f
dreamt [drɛmt] pt, pp of **dream**
dreary ['drɪərɪ] adj monótono
drench [drɛntʃ] vt empapar
dress [drɛs] n vestido; (clothing) ropa ▷ vt vestir; (wound) vendar ▷ vi vestirse; **to get ~ed** vestirse; **dress up** vi vestirse de etiqueta; (in fancy dress) disfrazarse; **dress circle** (BRIT) n principal m; **dresser** n (furniture) aparador m; (: us) cómoda (con espejo); **dressing** n (Med) vendaje m; (Culin) aliño; **dressing gown** (BRIT) n bata; **dressing room** n (Theatre) camarín m; (Sport) vestuario; **dressing table** n tocador m; **dressmaker** n modista, costurera
drew [druː] pt of **draw**
dribble ['drɪbl] vi (baby) babear ▷ vt (ball) regatear
dried [draɪd] adj (fruit) seco; (milk) en polvo
drier ['draɪə*] n = **dryer**
drift [drɪft] n (of current etc) flujo; (of snow) ventisquero; (meaning) significado ▷ vi (boat) ir a la deriva; (sand, snow) amontonarse
drill [drɪl] n (drill bit) broca; (tool for DIY etc) taladro; (of dentist) fresa; (for mining etc) perforadora, barrena; (Mil) instrucción f ▷ vt perforar, taladrar; (troops) enseñar la instrucción a ▷ vi (for oil) perforar
drink [drɪŋk] (pt **drank**, pp **drunk**) n bebida; (sip) trago ▷ vt, vi beber; **to have a ~** tomar algo; tomar una copa or un trago; **a ~ of water** un trago de agua; **drink-driving** n: **to be charged with drink-driving** ser acusado de conducir borracho or en estado de embriaguez; **drinker** n bebedor(a) m/f; **drinking water** n agua potable
drip [drɪp] n (act) goteo; (one drip) gota; (Med) gota a gota m ▷ vi gotear
drive [draɪv] (pt **drove**, pp **driven**) n (journey) viaje m (en coche); (also: **~way**) entrada; (energy) energía, vigor m; (Comput: also: **disk ~**) drive m ▷ vt (car) conducir (SP), manejar (LAM); (nail) clavar; (push) empujar; (Tech: motor) impulsar ▷ vi (Aut: at controls) conducir; (: travel) pasearse en coche; **left-/right-hand ~** conducción f por la izquierda/derecha; **to ~ sb mad** volverle loco a algn; **drive out** vt (force out) expulsar, echar; **drive-in** adj (esp us): **drive-in cinema** autocine m
driven ['drɪvn] pp of **drive**
driver ['draɪvə*] n conductor(a) m/f (SP), chofer mf (LAM); (of taxi, bus) chófer mf (SP), chofer mf (LAM); **driver's license** (us) n carnet m de conducir
driveway ['draɪvweɪ] n entrada
driving ['draɪvɪŋ] n el conducir (SP), el manejar (LAM); **driving instructor** n profesor(a) m/f de autoescuela (SP), instructor(a) m/f de manejo (LAM); **driving lesson** n clase f de conducir (SP) or manejar (LAM); **driving licence** (BRIT) n licencia de manejo (LAM), carnet m de conducir (SP); **driving test** n examen m de conducir (SP) or manejar (LAM)
drizzle ['drɪzl] n llovizna
droop [druːp] vi (flower) marchitarse; (shoulders) encorvarse; (head) inclinarse
drop [drɔp] n (of water) gota; (lessening) baja; (fall) caída ▷ vt dejar caer; (voice, eyes, price) bajar; (passenger) dejar; (omit) omitir ▷ vi (object) caer; (wind) amainar; **drop in** vi (inf: visit): **to drop in (on)** pasar por casa (de); **drop off** vi (sleep) dormirse ▷ vt

(*passenger*) dejar; **drop out** *vi* (*withdraw*) retirarse

drought [draut] *n* sequía

drove [drəuv] *pt of* **drive**

drown [draun] *vt* ahogar ▷ *vi* ahogarse

drowsy ['drauzı] *adj* soñoliento; **to be ~** tener sueño

drug [drʌg] *n* medicamento; (*narcotic*) droga ▷ *vt* drogar; **to be on ~s** drogarse; **drug addict** *n* drogadicto/a; **drug dealer** *n* traficante *mf* de drogas; **druggist** (*us*) *n* farmacéutico; **drugstore** (*us*) *n* farmacia

drum [drʌm] *n* tambor *m*; (*for oil, petrol*) bidón *m*; **drums** *npl* batería; **drummer** *n* tambor *m*

drunk [drʌŋk] *pp of* **drink** ▷ *adj* borracho ▷ *n* (*also*: **~ard**) borracho/a; **drunken** *adj* borracho; (*laughter, party*) de borrachos

dry [draı] *adj* seco; (*day*) sin lluvia; (*climate*) árido, seco ▷ *vt* secar; (*tears*) enjugarse ▷ *vi* secarse; **dry off** *vi* secarse ▷ *vt* secar; **dry up** *vi* (*river*) secarse; **dry-cleaner's** *n* tintorería; **dry-cleaning** *n* lavado en seco; **dryer** *n* (*for hair*) secador *m*; (*us: for clothes*) secadora

DSS *n abbr* = **Department of Social Security**

D & T (*BRIT: Scol*) *n abbr* (= *design and technology*) ≈ dibujo y tecnología

DTP *n abbr* (= *desk-top publishing*) autoedición *f*

dual ['djuəl] *adj* doble; **dual carriageway** (*BRIT*) *n* carretera de doble calzada

dubious ['dju:bıəs] *adj* indeciso; (*reputation, company*) sospechoso

duck [dʌk] *n* pato ▷ *vi* agacharse

due [dju:] *adj* (*owed*): **he is ~ £10** se le deben 10 libras; (*expected: event*): **the meeting is ~ on Wednesday** la reunión tendrá lugar el miércoles; (: *arrival*): **the train is ~ at 8am** el tren tiene su llegada para las 8; (*proper*) debido ▷ *n*: **to give sb his** (*or* **her**) **~** ser justo con algn ▷ *adv*: **~ north** derecho al norte

duel ['djuəl] *n* duelo

duet [dju:'ɛt] *n* dúo

dug [dʌg] *pt, pp of* **dig**

duke [dju:k] *n* duque *m*

dull [dʌl] *adj* (*light*) débil; (*stupid*) torpe; (*boring*) pesado; (*sound, pain*) sordo; (*weather, day*) gris ▷ *vt* (*pain, grief*) aliviar; (*mind, senses*) entorpecer

dumb [dʌm] *adj* mudo; (*pej: stupid*) estúpido

dummy ['dʌmı] *n* (*tailor's dummy*) maniquí *m*; (*mock-up*) maqueta; (*BRIT: for baby*) chupete *m* ▷ *adj* falso, postizo

dump [dʌmp] *n* (*also*: **rubbish ~**) basurero, vertedero; (*inf: place*) cuchitril *m* ▷ *vt* (*put down*) dejar; (*get rid of*) deshacerse de; (*Comput: data*) transferir

dumpling ['dʌmplıŋ] *n* bola de masa hervida

dune [dju:n] *n* duna

dungarees [dʌŋgə'ri:z] *npl* mono

dungeon ['dʌndʒən] *n* calabozo

duplex ['dju:plɛks] *n* dúplex *m*

duplicate [*n* 'dju:plıkət, *vb* 'dju:plıkeıt] *n* duplicado ▷ *vt* duplicar; (*photocopy*) fotocopiar; (*repeat*) repetir; **in ~** por duplicado

durable ['djuərəbl] *adj* duradero

duration [djuə'reıʃən] *n* duración *f*

during ['djuərıŋ] *prep* durante

dusk [dʌsk] *n* crepúsculo, anochecer *m*

dust [dʌst] *n* polvo ▷ *vt* quitar el polvo a, desempolvar; (*cake etc*): **to ~ with** espolvorear de; **dustbin** (*BRIT*) *n* cubo or bote *m* (*MEX*) or tacho (*SC*) de la basura; **duster** *n* paño, trapo; **dustman** (*BRIT: irreg*) *n* basurero; **dustpan** *n* cogedor *m*; **dusty** *adj* polvoriento

Dutch [dʌtʃ] *adj* holandés/esa ▷ *n* (*Ling*) holandés *m*; **the Dutch** *npl* los holandeses; **to go ~** (*inf*) pagar cada uno lo suyo; **Dutchman** (*irreg*) *n* holandés *m*; **Dutchwoman** (*irreg*) *n* holandésa

duty ['dju:tı] *n* deber *m*; (*tax*) derechos *mpl* de aduana; **on ~** de servicio; (*at night etc*) de guardia; **off ~** libre (de servicio); **duty-free** *adj* libre de impuestos

duvet ['du:veı] (*BRIT*) *n* edredón *m*

DVD *n abbr* (= *digital versatile or video disc*) DVD *m*; **DVD player** *n* lector *m* de DVD; **DVD writer** *n* grabadora de DVD

dwarf [dwɔ:f] (*pl* **dwarves**) *n* enano/a ▷ *vt* empequeñecer

dwell [dwɛl] (*pt, pp* **dwelt**) *vi* morar; **dwell on** *vt fus* explayarse en

dwelt [dwɛlt] *pt, pp of* **dwell**

dwindle ['dwındl] *vi* disminuir

dye [daı] *n* tinte *m* ▷ *vt* teñir

dying ['daııŋ] *adj* moribundo

dynamic [daı'næmık] *adj* dinámico

dynamite ['daınəmaıt] *n* dinamita

dyslexia [dıs'lɛksıə] *n* dislexia

dyslexic [dıs'lɛksık] *adj, n* disléxico/a *m/f*

e

E [i:] n (Mus) mi m

E111 n abbr (= form E111) impreso E111

each [i:tʃ] adj cada inv ▷ pron cada uno; **~ other** el uno al otro; **they hate ~ other** se odian (entre ellos or mutuamente); **they have 2 books ~** tienen 2 libros por persona

eager ['i:gə*] adj (keen) entusiasmado; **to be ~ to do sth** tener muchas ganas de hacer algo, impacientarse por hacer algo; **to be ~ for** tener muchas ganas de

eagle ['i:gl] n águila

ear [ɪə*] n oreja; oído; (of corn) espiga; **earache** n dolor m de oídos; **eardrum** n tímpano

earl [ə:l] n conde m

earlier ['ə:lɪə*] adj anterior ▷ adv antes

early ['ə:lɪ] adv temprano; (before time) con tiempo, con anticipación ▷ adj temprano; (settlers etc) primitivo; (death, departure) prematuro; (reply) pronto; **to have an ~ night** acostarse temprano; **in the ~** or **~ in the spring/19th century** a principios de primavera/del siglo diecinueve; **early retirement** n jubilación f anticipada

earmark ['ɪəmɑ:k] vt: **to ~ (for)** reservar (para), destinar (a)

earn [ə:n] vt (salary) percibir; (interest) devengar; (praise) merecerse

earnest ['ə:nɪst] adj (wish) fervoroso; (person) serio, formal; **in ~** en serio

earnings ['ə:nɪŋz] npl (personal) sueldo, ingresos mpl; (company) ganancias fpl

ear: earphones npl auriculares mpl; **earplugs** npl tapones mpl para los oídos; **earring** n pendiente m, arete m

earth [ə:θ] n tierra; (BRIT Elec) cable m de toma de tierra ▷ vt (BRIT Elec) conectar a tierra; **earthquake** n terremoto

ease [i:z] n facilidad f; (comfort) comodidad f ▷ vt (lessen: problem) mitigar; (: pain) aliviar; (: tension) reducir; **to ~ sth in/out** meter/sacar algo con cuidado; **at ~!** (Mil) ¡descansen!

easily ['i:zɪlɪ] adv fácilmente

east [i:st] n este m ▷ adj del este, oriental; (wind) este ▷ adv al este, hacia el este; **the E~** el Oriente; (Pol) los países del Este; **eastbound** adj en dirección este

Easter ['i:stə*] n Pascua (de Resurrección); **Easter egg** n huevo de Pascua

eastern ['i:stən] adj del este, oriental; (oriental) oriental

Easter Sunday n Domingo de Resurrección

easy ['i:zɪ] adj fácil; (simple) sencillo; (comfortable) holgado, cómodo; (relaxed) tranquilo ▷ adv: **to take it** or **things ~** (not worry) tomarlo con calma; (rest) descansar; **easy-going** adj acomodadizo

eat [i:t] (pt **ate**, pp **eaten**) vt comer; **eat out** vi comer fuera

eavesdrop ['i:vzdrɔp] vi: **to ~ (on)** escuchar a escondidas

e-book ['i:buk] n libro electrónico

e-business ['i:bɪznɪs] n (company) negocio electrónico; (commerce) comercio electrónico

EC n abbr (= European Community) CE f

eccentric [ɪk'sɛntrɪk] adj, n excéntrico/a m/f

echo ['ɛkəu] (pl **~es**) n eco ▷ vt (sound) repetir ▷ vi resonar, hacer eco

eclipse [ɪ'klɪps] n eclipse m

eco-friendly ['i:kəufrɛndlɪ] adj ecológico

ecological [i:kə'lɔdʒɪkl] adj ecológico

ecology [ɪ'kɔlədʒɪ] n ecología

e-commerce n abbr comercio electrónico

economic [i:kə'nɔmɪk] adj económico; (business etc) rentable; **economical** adj económico; **economics** n (Scol) economía ▷ npl (of project etc) rentabilidad f

economist [ɪ'kɔnəmɪst] n economista m/f

economize [ɪ'kɔnəmaɪz] vi economizar, ahorrar

economy [ɪ'kɔnəmɪ] n economía; **economy class** n (Aviat) clase f económica; **economy class syndrome** n síndrome m de la clase turista

ecstasy ['ɛkstəsɪ] n éxtasis m inv; (drug) éxtasis m inv; **ecstatic** [ɛks'tætɪk] adj extático

eczema ['ɛksɪmə] n eczema m

edge [ɛdʒ] n (of knife) filo; (of object) borde m; (of lake) orilla ▷ vt (Sewing) ribetear; **on ~** (fig) = **edgy**; **to ~ away from** alejarse poco a poco de

edgy ['ɛdʒɪ] adj nervioso, inquieto

edible ['ɛdɪbl] adj comestible

Edinburgh ['ɛdɪnbərə] n Edimburgo
edit ['ɛdɪt] vt (be editor of) dirigir; (text, report) corregir, preparar; **edition** [ɪ'dɪʃən] n edición f; **editor** n (of newspaper) director(a) m/f; (of column): **foreign/political editor** encargado de la sección de extranjero/política; (of book) redactor(a) m/f; **editorial** [-'tɔ:rɪəl] adj editorial ▷ n editorial m
educate ['ɛdjukeɪt] vt (gen) educar; (instruct) instruir; **educated** ['ɛdjukeɪtɪd] adj culto
education [ɛdju'keɪʃən] n educación f; (schooling) enseñanza; (Scol) pedagogía; **educational** adj (policy etc) educacional; (experience) docente; (toy) educativo
eel [i:l] n anguila
eerie ['ɪərɪ] adj misterioso
effect [ɪ'fɛkt] n efecto ▷ vt efectuar, llevar a cabo; **to take ~** (law) entrar en vigor or vigencia; (drug) surtir efecto; **in ~** en realidad; **effects** npl (property) efectos mpl.
effective adj eficaz; (actual) verdadero; **effectively** adv eficazmente; (in reality) efectivamente
efficiency [ɪ'fɪʃənsɪ] n eficiencia; rendimiento
efficient [ɪ'fɪʃənt] adj eficiente; (machine) de buen rendimiento; **efficiently** adv eficientemente, de manera eficiente
effort ['ɛfət] n esfuerzo; **effortless** adj sin ningún esfuerzo; (style) natural
e.g. adv abbr (= exempli gratia) p. ej.
egg [ɛg] n huevo; **hard-boiled/soft-boiled ~** huevo duro/pasado por agua; **eggcup** n huevera; **eggplant** (esp us) n berenjena; **eggshell** n cáscara de huevo; **egg white** n clara de huevo; **egg yolk** n yema de huevo
ego ['i:gəu] n ego
Egypt ['i:dʒɪpt] n Egipto; **Egyptian** [ɪ'dʒɪpʃən] adj, n egipcio/a m/f
eight [eɪt] num ocho; **eighteen** num diez y ocho, dieciocho; **eighteenth** adj decimoctavo; **the eighteenth floor** la planta dieciocho; **the eighteenth of August** el dieciocho de agosto; **eighth** num octavo; **eightieth** ['eɪtɪɪθ] adj octogésimo
eighty ['eɪtɪ] num ochenta
Eire ['ɛərə] n Eire m
either ['aɪðə*] adj cualquiera de los dos; (both, each) cada ▷ pron: **~ (of them)** cualquiera (de los dos) ▷ adv tampoco ▷ conj: **~ yes or no** o sí o no; **on ~ side** en ambos lados; **I don't like ~** no me gusta ninguno/a de los(las) dos; **no, I don't ~** no, yo tampoco
eject [ɪ'dʒɛkt] vt echar, expulsar; (tenant) desahuciar
elaborate [adj ɪ'læbərɪt, vb ɪ'læbəreɪt] adj

(complex) complejo ▷ vt (expand) ampliar; (refine) refinar ▷ vi explicar con más detalles
elastic [ɪ'læstɪk] n elástico ▷ adj elástico; (fig) flexible; **elastic band** (BRIT) n gomita
elbow ['ɛlbəu] n codo
elder ['ɛldə*] adj mayor ▷ n (tree) saúco; (person) mayor; **elderly** adj de edad, mayor ▷ npl: **the elderly** los mayores
eldest ['ɛldɪst] adj, n el/la mayor
elect [ɪ'lɛkt] vt elegir ▷ adj: **the president ~** el presidente electo; **to ~ to do** optar por hacer; **election** n elección f; **electoral** adj electoral; **electorate** n electorado
electric [ɪ'lɛktrɪk] adj eléctrico; **electrical** adj eléctrico; **electric blanket** n manta eléctrica; **electric fire** n estufa eléctrica; **electrician** [ɪlɛk'trɪʃən] n electricista mf; **electricity** [ɪlɛk'trɪsɪtɪ] n electricidad f; **electric shock** n electrochoque m; **electrify** [ɪ'lɛktrɪfaɪ] vt (Rail) electrificar; (fig: audience) electrizar
electronic [ɪlɛk'trɔnɪk] adj electrónico; **electronic mail** n correo electrónico; **electronics** n electrónica
elegance ['ɛlɪgəns] n elegancia
elegant ['ɛlɪgənt] adj elegante
element ['ɛlɪmənt] n elemento; (of kettle etc) resistencia
elementary [ɛlɪ'mɛntərɪ] adj elemental; (primitive) rudimentario; **elementary school** (us) n escuela de enseñanza primaria
elephant ['ɛlɪfənt] n elefante m
elevate ['ɛlɪveɪt] vt (gen) elevar; (in rank) ascender
elevator ['ɛlɪveɪtə*] (us) n ascensor m; (in warehouse etc) montacargas m inv
eleven [ɪ'lɛvn] num once; **eleventh** num undécimo
eligible ['ɛlɪdʒəbl] adj: **an ~ young man/woman** un buen partido; **to be ~ for sth** llenar los requisitos para algo
eliminate [ɪ'lɪmɪneɪt] vt (suspect, possibility) descartar
elm [ɛlm] n olmo
eloquent ['ɛləkwənt] adj elocuente
else [ɛls] adv: **something ~** otra cosa; **somewhere ~** en otra parte; **everywhere ~** en todas partes menos aquí; **where ~?** ¿dónde más?, ¿en qué otra parte?; **there was little ~ to do** apenas quedaba otra cosa que hacer; **nobody ~ spoke** no habló nadie más; **elsewhere** adv (be) en otra parte; (go) a otra parte
elusive [ɪ'lu:sɪv] adj esquivo; (quality) difícil de encontrar
e-mail ['i:meɪl] n abbr (= electronic mail) correo electrónico, e-mail m; **e-mail**

address n dirección f electrónica, email m

embankment [ɪm'bæŋkmənt] n
terraplén m

embargo [ɪm'bɑ:gəʊ] (pl **~es**) n (Comm,
Naut) embargo; (prohibition) prohibición f; **to
put an ~ on sth** poner un embargo en algo

embark [ɪm'bɑ:k] vi embarcarse ▷ vt
embarcar; **to ~ on** (journey) emprender;
(course of action) lanzarse a

embarrass [ɪm'bærəs] vt avergonzar;
(government etc) dejar en mal lugar;
embarrassed adj (laugh, silence)
embarazoso

▌ Be careful not to translate **embarrassed**
by the Spanish word embarazada.

embarrassing adj (situation) violento;
(question) embarazoso; **embarrassment**
n (shame) vergüenza; (problem): **to be an
embarrassment for sb** poner en un aprieto
a algn

embassy ['embəsɪ] n embajada

embrace [ɪm'breɪs] vt abrazar, dar un
abrazo a; (include) abarcar ▷ vi abrazarse
▷ n abrazo

embroider [ɪm'brɔɪdə*] vt bordar;
embroidery n bordado

embryo ['embrɪəʊ] n embrión m

emerald ['emərəld] n esmeralda

emerge [ɪ'mɜ:dʒ] vi salir; (arise) surgir

emergency [ɪ'mɜ:dʒənsɪ] n crisis f inv;
in an ~ en caso de urgencia; **state of ~**
estado de emergencia; **emergency brake**
(us) n freno de mano; **emergency exit** n
salida de emergencia; **emergency landing**
n aterrizaje m forzoso; **emergency room**
(us: Med) n sala f de urgencias; **emergency
services** npl (fire, police, ambulance)
servicios mpl de urgencia or emergencia

emigrate ['emɪgreɪt] vi emigrar;
emigration [emɪ'greɪʃən] n emigración f

eminent ['emɪnənt] adj eminente

emissions [ɪ'mɪʃənz] npl emisión f

emit [ɪ'mɪt] vt emitir; (smoke) arrojar;
(smell) despedir; (sound) producir

emotion [ɪ'məʊʃən] n emoción f;
emotional adj (needs) emocional; (person)
sentimental; (scene) conmovedor(a),
emocionante; (speech) emocionado

emperor ['empərə*] n emperador m

emphasis ['emfəsɪs] (pl **-ses**) n énfasis
m inv

emphasize ['emfəsaɪz] vt (word, point)
subrayar, recalcar; (feature) hacer resaltar

empire ['empaɪə*] n imperio

employ [ɪm'plɔɪ] vt emplear; **employee**
[-'i:] n empleado/a; **employer** n patrón/
ona m/f; empresario; **employment** n
(work) trabajo; **employment agency** n
agencia de colocaciones

empower [ɪm'paʊə*] vt: **to ~ sb to do sth**
autorizar a algn para hacer algo

empress ['emprɪs] n emperatriz f

emptiness ['emptɪnɪs] n vacío m; (of life etc)
vaciedad f

empty ['emptɪ] adj vacío; (place) desierto;
(house) desocupado; (threat) vano ▷ vt
vaciar; (place) dejar vacío ▷ vi vaciarse;
(house etc) quedar desocupado; **empty-
handed** adj con las manos vacías

EMU n abbr (= European Monetary Union)
UME f

emulsion [ɪ'mʌlʃən] n emulsión f; (also: ~
paint) pintura emulsión

enable [ɪ'neɪbl] vt: **to ~ sb to do sth**
permitir a algn hacer algo

enamel [ɪ'næməl] n esmalte m; (also: ~
paint) pintura esmaltada

enchanting [ɪn'tʃɑ:ntɪŋ] adj
encantador(a)

encl. abbr (= enclosed) adj

enclose [ɪn'kləʊz] vt (land) cercar; (letter
etc) adjuntar; **please find ~d** le mandamos
adjunto

enclosure [ɪn'kləʊʒə*] n cercado, recinto

encore [ɔŋ'kɔ:*] excl ¡otra!, ¡bis! ▷ n bis m

encounter [ɪn'kaʊntə*] n encuentro
▷ vt encontrar, encontrarse con; (difficulty)
tropezar con

encourage [ɪn'kʌrɪdʒ] vt alentar, animar;
(activity) fomentar; (growth) estimular;
encouragement n estímulo; (of industry)
fomento

encouraging [ɪn'kʌrɪdʒɪŋ] adj
alentador(a)

encyclop(a)edia [ensaɪkləʊ'pi:dɪə] n
enciclopedia

end [end] n fin m; (of table) extremo; (of
street) final m; (Sport) lado ▷ vt terminar,
acabar; (also: **bring to an ~, put an ~ to**)
acabar con ▷ vi terminar, acabar; **in the
~** al fin; **on ~** (object) de punta, de cabeza;
to stand on ~ (hair) erizarse; **for hours on
~** hora tras hora; **end up** vi: **to end up in**
terminar en; (place) ir a parar en

endanger [ɪn'deɪndʒə*] vt poner en
peligro; **an ~ed species** una especie en
peligro de extinción

endearing [ɪn'dɪərɪŋ] adj simpático,
atractivo

endeavour [ɪn'devə*] (us **endeavor**) n
esfuerzo; (attempt) tentativa ▷ vi: **to ~ to do**
esforzarse por hacer; (try) procurar hacer

ending ['endɪŋ] n (of book) desenlace m;
(Ling) terminación f

endless ['endlɪs] adj interminable,
inacabable

endorse [ɪn'dɔːs] vt (cheque) endosar; (approve) aprobar; **endorsement** n (on driving licence) nota de inhabilitación

endurance [ɪn'djuərəns] n resistencia

endure [ɪn'djuə*] vt (bear) aguantar, soportar ▷ vi (last) durar

enemy ['ɛnəmɪ] adj, n enemigo/a m/f

energetic [ɛnə'dʒɛtɪk] adj enérgico

energy ['ɛnədʒɪ] n energía

enforce [ɪn'fɔːs] vt (Law) hacer cumplir

engaged [ɪn'geɪdʒd] adj (BRIT: busy, in use) ocupado; (betrothed) prometido; **to get ~** prometerse; **engaged tone** (BRIT) n (Tel) señal f de comunicando

engagement [ɪn'geɪdʒmənt] n (appointment) compromiso, cita; (booking) contratación f; (to marry) compromiso; (period) noviazgo; **engagement ring** n anillo de prometida

engaging [ɪn'geɪdʒɪŋ] adj atractivo

engine ['ɛndʒɪn] n (Aut) motor m; (Rail) locomotora

engineer [ɛndʒɪ'nɪə*] n ingeniero; (BRIT: for repairs) mecánico; (on ship, US Rail) maquinista m; **engineering** n ingeniería

England ['ɪŋɡlənd] n Inglaterra

English ['ɪŋɡlɪʃ] adj inglés/esa ▷ n (Ling) inglés m; **the English** npl los ingleses mpl; **English Channel** n: **the English Channel** (el Canal de) la Mancha; **Englishman** (irreg) n inglés m; **Englishwoman** (irreg) n inglésa

engrave [ɪn'greɪv] vt grabar

engraving [ɪn'greɪvɪŋ] n grabado

enhance [ɪn'hɑːns] vt (gen) aumentar; (beauty) realzar

enjoy [ɪn'dʒɔɪ] vt (health, fortune) disfrutar de, gozar de; (like) gustarle a algn; **to ~ o.s.** divertirse; **enjoyable** adj agradable; (amusing) divertido; **enjoyment** n (joy) placer m; (activity) diversión f

enlarge [ɪn'lɑːdʒ] vt aumentar; (broaden) extender; (Phot) ampliar ▷ vi: **to ~ on** (subject) tratar con más detalles; **enlargement** n (Phot) ampliación f

enlist [ɪn'lɪst] vt alistar; (support) conseguir ▷ vi alistarse

enormous [ɪ'nɔːməs] adj enorme

enough [ɪ'nʌf] adj: **~ time/books** bastante tiempo/bastantes libros ▷ pron bastante(s) ▷ adv: **big ~** bastante grande; **he has not worked ~** no ha trabajado bastante; **have you got ~?** ¿tiene usted bastante(s)?; **~ to eat** (lo) suficiente or (lo) bastante para comer; **~!** ¡basta ya!; **that's ~, thanks** con eso basta, gracias; **I've had ~ of him** estoy harto de él; **… which, funnily** or **oddly ~ …** … lo que, por extraño que parezca …

enquire [ɪn'kwaɪə*] vt, vi = **inquire**

enquiry [ɪn'kwaɪərɪ] n (official investigation) investigación

enrage [ɪn'reɪdʒ] vt enfurecer

enrich [ɪn'rɪtʃ] vt enriquecer

enrol [ɪn'rəul] (US **enroll**) vt (members) inscribir; (Scol) matricular ▷ vi inscribirse; matricularse; **enrolment** (US **enrollment**) n inscripción f; matriculación f

en route [ɔn'ruːt] adv durante el viaje

en suite [ɔn'swiːt] adj: **with ~ bathroom** con baño

ensure [ɪn'ʃuə*] vt asegurar

entail [ɪn'teɪl] vt suponer

enter ['ɛntə*] vt (room) entrar en; (club) hacerse socio de; (army) alistarse en; (sb for a competition) inscribir; (write down) anotar, apuntar; (Comput) meter ▷ vi entrar

enterprise ['ɛntəpraɪz] n empresa; (spirit) iniciativa; **free ~** la libre empresa; **private ~** la iniciativa privada; **enterprising** adj emprendedor(a)

entertain [ɛntə'teɪn] vt (amuse) divertir; (invite: guest) invitar (a casa); (idea) abrigar; **entertainer** n artista mf; **entertaining** adj divertido, entretenido; **entertainment** n (amusement) diversión f; (show) espectáculo

enthusiasm [ɪn'θuːzɪæzəm] n entusiasmo

enthusiast [ɪn'θuːzɪæst] n entusiasta mf; **enthusiastic** [-'æstɪk] adj entusiasta; **to be enthusiastic about** entusiasmarse por

entire [ɪn'taɪə*] adj entero; **entirely** adv totalmente

entitle [ɪn'taɪtl] vt: **to ~ sb to sth** dar a algn derecho a algo; **entitled** adj (book) titulado; **to be entitled to do** tener derecho a hacer

entrance [n 'ɛntrəns, vb ɪn'trɑːns] n entrada ▷ vt encantar, hechizar; **to gain ~ to** (university etc) ingresar en; **entrance examination** n examen m de ingreso; **entrance fee** n cuota; **entrance ramp** (US) n (Aut) rampa de acceso

entrant ['ɛntrənt] n (in race, competition) participante mf; (in examination) candidato/a

entrepreneur [ɔntrəprə'nəː] n empresario

entrust [ɪn'trʌst] vt: **to ~ sth to sb** confiar algo a algn

entry ['ɛntrɪ] n entrada; (in competition) participación f; (in register) apunte m; (in account) partida; (in reference book) artículo; **"no ~"** "prohibido el paso"; (Aut) "dirección prohibida"; **entry phone** n portero automático

envelope ['ɛnvələup] n sobre m

envious ['ɛnvɪəs] adj envidioso; (look) de

envidia

environment [ɪnˈvaɪərnmənt] n
(*surroundings*) entorno; (*natural world*):
the ~ el medio ambiente; **environmental**
[-ˈmɛntl] adj ambiental; medioambiental;
environmentally [-ˈmɛntəlɪ]
adv: **environmentally sound/friendly**
ecológico

envisage [ɪnˈvɪzɪdʒ] vt prever

envoy [ˈɛnvɔɪ] n enviado

envy [ˈɛnvɪ] n envidia ▷vt tener envidia a;
to ~ sb sth envidiar algo a algn

epic [ˈɛpɪk] n épica ▷adj épico

epidemic [ɛpɪˈdɛmɪk] n epidemia

epilepsy [ˈɛpɪlɛpsɪ] n epilepsia

epileptic [ɛpɪˈlɛptɪk] adj, n epiléptico/a
m/f; **epileptic fit** [ɛpɪˈlɛptɪk-] n ataque m
de epilepsia, acceso m epiléptico

episode [ˈɛpɪsəud] n episodio

equal [ˈiːkwl] adj igual; (*treatment*)
equitativo ▷n igual m f ▷vt ser igual a;
(*fig*) igualar; **to be ~ to** (*task*) estar a la altura
de; **equality** [iːˈkwɔlɪtɪ] n igualdad f;
equalize vi (*Sport*) empatar; **equally** adv
igualmente; (*share etc*) a partes iguales

equation [ɪˈkweɪʒən] n (*Math*) ecuación f

equator [ɪˈkweɪtə*] n ecuador m

equip [ɪˈkwɪp] vt equipar; (*person*) proveer;
to be well ~ped estar bien equipado;
equipment n equipo; (*tools*) avíos mpl

equivalent [ɪˈkwɪvələnt] adj: **~ (to)**
equivalente (a) ▷n equivalente m

ER abbr (BRIT: = *Elizabeth Regina*) la reina
Isabel; (US: *Med*) = **emergency room**

era [ˈɪərə] n era, época

erase [ɪˈreɪz] vt borrar; **eraser** n goma
de borrar

erect [ɪˈrɛkt] adj erguido ▷vt erigir,
levantar; (*assemble*) montar; **erection** [-ʃən]
n construcción f; (*assembly*) montaje m;
(*Physiol*) erección f

ERM n abbr (= *Exchange Rate Mechanism*) tipo
de cambio europeo

erode [ɪˈrəud] vt (*Geo*) erosionar; (*metal*)
corroer, desgastar; (*fig*) desgastar

erosion [ɪˈrəuʒən] n erosión f; desgaste m

erotic [ɪˈrɔtɪk] adj erótico

errand [ˈɛrnd] n recado (SP), mandado
(LAM)

erratic [ɪˈrætɪk] adj desigual, poco
uniforme

error [ˈɛrə*] n error m, equivocación f

erupt [ɪˈrʌpt] vi entrar en erupción; (*fig*)
estallar; **eruption** [ɪˈrʌpʃən] n erupción f;
(*of war*) estallido

escalate [ˈɛskəleɪt] vi extenderse,
intensificarse

escalator [ˈɛskəleɪtə*] n escalera móvil

escape [ɪˈskeɪp] n fuga ▷vi escaparse;
(*flee*) huir, evadirse; (*leak*) fugarse
▷vt (*responsibility etc*) evitar, eludir;
(*consequences*) escapar a; (*elude*): **his name**
~s me no me sale su nombre; **to ~ from**
(*place*) escaparse de; (*person*) escaparse a

escort [n ˈɛskɔːt, vb ɪˈskɔːt] n
acompañante mf; (*Mil*) escolta mf ▷vt
acompañar

especially [ɪˈspɛʃlɪ] adv (*above all*)
sobre todo; (*particularly*) en particular,
especialmente

espionage [ˈɛspɪənɑːʒ] n espionaje m

essay [ˈɛseɪ] n (*Literature*) ensayo;
(*Scol: short*) redacción f; (: *long*) trabajo

essence [ˈɛsns] n esencia

essential [ɪˈsɛnʃl] adj (*necessary*)
imprescindible; (*basic*) esencial; **essentially**
adv esencialmente; **essentials** npl lo
imprescindible, lo esencial

establish [ɪˈstæblɪʃ] vt establecer;
(*prove*) demostrar; (*relations*) entablar;
(*reputation*) ganarse; **establishment** n
establecimiento; **the Establishment** la
clase dirigente

estate [ɪˈsteɪt] n (*land*) finca, hacienda;
(*inheritance*) herencia; (BRIT: *also*: **housing**
~) urbanización f; **estate agent** (BRIT) n
agente mf inmobiliario/a; **estate car** (BRIT)
n furgoneta

estimate [n ˈɛstɪmət, vb ˈɛstɪmeɪt] n
estimación f, apreciación f; (*assessment*)
tasa, cálculo; (*Comm*) presupuesto ▷vt
estimar, tasar; calcular

etc abbr (= *et cetera*) etc

eternal [ɪˈtəːnl] adj eterno

eternity [ɪˈtəːnɪtɪ] n eternidad f

ethical [ˈɛθɪkl] adj ético; **ethics** [ˈɛθɪks] n
ética ▷npl moralidad f

Ethiopia [iːˈθɪˈəupɪə] n Etiopía

ethnic [ˈɛθnɪk] adj étnico; **ethnic**
minority n minoría étnica

e-ticket [ˈiːtɪkɪt] n billete m electrónico
(SP), boleto electrónico (LAM)

etiquette [ˈɛtɪkɛt] n etiqueta

EU n abbr (= *European Union*) UE f

euro n euro

Europe [ˈjuərəp] n Europa; **European**
[-ˈpiːən] adj, n europeo/a m/f; **European**
Community n Comunidad f Europea;
European Union n Unión f Europea

Eurostar® [ˈjuərəustɑː*] n Eurostar® m

evacuate [ɪˈvækjueɪt] vt (*people*) evacuar;
(*place*) desocupar

evade [ɪˈveɪd] vt evadir, eludir

evaluate [ɪˈvæljueɪt] vt evaluar; (*value*)
tasar; (*evidence*) interpretar

evaporate [ɪˈvæpəreɪt] vi evaporarse; (*fig*)

desvanecerse

eve [iːv] n: **on the ~ of** en vísperas de

even ['iːvn] adj (level) llano; (smooth) liso; (speed, temperature) uniforme; (number) par ▷ adv hasta, incluso; (introducing a comparison) aún, todavía; **~ if, ~ though** aunque +subjun; **~ more** aun más; **~ so** aun así; **not ~** ni siquiera; **~ he was there** hasta él estuvo allí; **~ on Sundays** incluso los domingos; **to get ~ with sb** ajustar cuentas con algn

evening ['iːvnɪŋ] n tarde f; (late) noche f; **in the ~** por la tarde; **evening class** n clase f nocturna; **evening dress** n (no pl: formal clothes) traje m de etiqueta; (woman's) traje m de noche

event [ɪ'vɛnt] n suceso, acontecimiento; (Sport) prueba; **in the ~ of** en caso de; **eventful** adj (life) activo; (day) ajetreado

eventual [ɪ'vɛntʃuəl] adj final

⬛ Be careful not to translate **eventual** by the Spanish word eventual.

eventually adv (finally) finalmente; (in time) con el tiempo

ever ['ɛvə*] adv (at any time) nunca, jamás; (at all times) siempre; (in question): **why ~ not?** ¿y por qué no?; **the best ~** lo nunca visto; **have you ~ seen it?** ¿lo ha visto usted alguna vez?; **better than ~** mejor que nunca; **~ since** adv desde entonces ▷ conj después de que; **evergreen** n árbol m de hoja perenne

○ **KEYWORD**

every ['ɛvrɪ] adj **1** (each) cada; **every one of them** (persons) todos ellos/as; (objects) cada uno de ellos/as; **every shop in the town was closed** todas las tiendas de la ciudad estaban cerradas **2** (all possible) todo/a; **I gave you every assistance** te di toda la ayuda posible; **I have every confidence in him** tiene toda mi confianza; **we wish you every success** te deseamos toda suerte de éxitos **3** (showing recurrence) todo/a; **every day/week** todos los días/todas las semanas; **every other car had been broken into** habían forzado uno de cada dos coches; **she visits me every other/third day** me visita cada dos/tres días; **every now and then** de vez en cuando

every: everybody pron = **everyone**; **everyday** adj (daily) cotidiano, de todos los días; (usual) acostumbrado; **everyone** pron todos/as, todo el mundo; **everything** pron todo; **this shop sells everything** esta tienda vende de todo; **everywhere** adv: **I've been looking for you everywhere** te he estado buscando por todas partes; **everywhere you go you meet ...** en todas partes encuentras ...

evict [ɪ'vɪkt] vt desahuciar

evidence ['ɛvɪdəns] n (proof) prueba; (of witness) testimonio; (sign) indicios mpl; **to give ~** prestar declaración, dar testimonio

evident ['ɛvɪdənt] adj evidente, manifiesto; **evidently** adv por lo visto

evil ['iːvl] adj malo; (influence) funesto ▷ n mal m

evoke [ɪ'vəuk] vt evocar

evolution [iːvə'luːʃən] n evolución f

evolve [ɪ'vɔlv] vt desarrollar ▷ vi evolucionar, desarrollarse

ewe [juː] n oveja

ex [ɛks] (inf) n: **my ~** mi ex

ex- [ɛks] prefix ex

exact [ɪg'zækt] adj exacto; (person) meticuloso ▷ vt: **to ~ sth (from)** exigir algo (de); **exactly** adv exactamente; (indicating agreement) exacto

exaggerate [ɪg'zædʒəreɪt] vt, vi exagerar; **exaggeration** [-'reɪʃən] n exageración f

exam [ɪg'zæm] n abbr (Scol) = **examination**

examination [ɪgzæmɪ'neɪʃən] n examen m; (Med) reconocimiento

examine [ɪg'zæmɪn] vt examinar; (inspect) inspeccionar, escudriñar; (Med) reconocer; **examiner** n examinador(a) m/f

example [ɪg'zɑːmpl] n ejemplo; **for ~** por ejemplo

exasperated [ɪg'zɑːspəreɪtɪd] adj exasperado

excavate ['ɛkskəveɪt] vt excavar

exceed [ɪk'siːd] vt (amount) exceder; (number) pasar de; (speed limit) sobrepasar; (powers) excederse en; (hopes) superar; **exceedingly** adv sumamente, sobremanera

excel [ɪk'sɛl] vi sobresalir; **to ~ o.s** lucirse

excellence ['ɛksələns] n excelencia

excellent ['ɛksələnt] adj excelente

except [ɪk'sɛpt] prep (also: **~ for, ~ing**) excepto, salvo ▷ vt exceptuar, excluir; **~ if/when** excepto si/cuando; **~ that** salvo que; **exception** [ɪk'sɛpʃən] n excepción f; **to take exception to** ofenderse por; **exceptional** [ɪk'sɛpʃənl] adj excepcional; **exceptionally** [ɪk'sɛpʃənəlɪ] adv excepcionalmente, extraordinariamente

excerpt ['ɛksəːpt] n extracto

excess [ɪk'sɛs] n exceso; **excess baggage** n exceso de equipaje; **excessive** adj excesivo

exchange [ɪks'tʃeɪndʒ] n intercambio; (conversation) diálogo; (also: **telephone ~**)

central f (telefónica) ▷ vt: **to ~ (for)** cambiar (por); **exchange rate** n tipo de cambio

excite [ɪk'saɪt] vt (stimulate) estimular; (arouse) excitar; **excited** adj: **to get excited** emocionarse; **excitement** n (agitation) excitación f; (exhilaration) emoción f; **exciting** adj emocionante

exclaim [ɪk'skleɪm] vi exclamar; **exclamation** [ɛksklə'meɪʃən] n exclamación f; **exclamation mark** n punto de admiración; **exclamation point** (US) = **exclamation mark**

exclude [ɪk'sklu:d] vt excluir; exceptuar **excluding** [ɪks'klu:dɪŋ] prep: **~ VAT** IVA no incluido

exclusion [ɪk'sklu:ʒən] n exclusión f; **to the ~ of** con exclusión de

exclusive [ɪk'sklu:sɪv] adj exclusivo; (club, district) selecto; **~ of tax** excluyendo impuestos; **exclusively** adv únicamente

excruciating [ɪk'skru:ʃɪeɪtɪŋ] adj (pain) agudísimo, atroz; (noise, embarrassment) horrible

excursion [ɪk'skə:ʃən] n (tourist excursion) excursión f

excuse [n ɪk'skju:s, vb ɪk'skju:z] n disculpa, excusa; (pretext) pretexto ▷ vt (justify) justificar; (forgive) disculpar, perdonar; **to ~ sb from doing sth** dispensar a algn de hacer algo; **~ me!** (attracting attention) ¡por favor!; (apologizing) ¡perdón!; **if you will ~ me** con su permiso

ex-directory ['ɛksdɪ'rɛktərɪ] (BRIT) adj que no consta en la guía

execute ['ɛksɪkju:t] vt (plan) realizar; (order) cumplir; (person) ajusticiar, ejecutar; **execution** [-'kju:ʃən] n realización f; cumplimiento; ejecución f

executive [ɪg'zɛkjutɪv] n (person, committee) ejecutivo; (Pol: committee) poder m ejecutivo ▷ adj ejecutivo

exempt [ɪg'zɛmpt] adj: **~ from** exento de ▷ vt: **to ~ sb from** eximir a algn de

exercise ['ɛksəsaɪz] n ejercicio ▷ vt (patience) usar de; (right) valerse de; (dog) llevar de paseo; (mind) preocupar ▷ vi (also: **to take ~**) hacer ejercicio(s); **exercise book** n cuaderno

exert [ɪg'zə:t] vt ejercer; **to ~ o.s.** esforzarse; **exertion** [-ʃən] n esfuerzo

exhale [ɛks'heɪl] vt despedir ▷ vi exhalar

exhaust [ɪg'zɔ:st] n (Aut: also: **~ pipe**) escape m; (: fumes) gases mpl de escape ▷ vt agotar; **exhausted** adj agotado; **exhaustion** [ɪg'zɔ:stʃən] n agotamiento; **nervous exhaustion** postración f nerviosa

exhibit [ɪg'zɪbɪt] n (Art) obra expuesta; (Law) objeto expuesto ▷ vt (show: emotions)

manifestar; (: courage, skill) demostrar; (paintings) exponer; **exhibition** [ɛksɪ'bɪʃən] n exposición f; (of talent etc) demostración f

exhilarating [ɪg'zɪləreɪtɪŋ] adj estimulante, tónico

exile ['ɛksaɪl] n exilio; (person) exiliado/a ▷ vt desterrar, exiliar

exist [ɪg'zɪst] vi existir; (live) vivir; **existence** n existencia; **existing** adj existente, actual

exit ['ɛksɪt] n salida ▷ vi (Theatre) hacer mutis; (Comput) salir (del sistema)

▌ Be careful not to translate **exit** by the Spanish word éxito.

exit ramp (US) n (Aut) vía de acceso

exotic [ɪg'zɒtɪk] adj exótico

expand [ɪk'spænd] vt ampliar; (number) aumentar ▷ vi (population) aumentar; (trade etc) expandirse; (gas, metal) dilatarse

expansion [ɪk'spænʃən] n (of population) aumento; (of trade) expansión f

expect [ɪk'spɛkt] vt esperar; (require) contar con; (suppose) suponer ▷ vi: **to be ~ing** (pregnant woman) estar embarazada; **expectation** [ɛkspɛk'teɪʃən] n (hope) esperanza; (belief) expectativa

expedition [ɛkspə'dɪʃən] n expedición f

expel [ɪk'spɛl] vt arrojar; (from place) expulsar

expenditure [ɪks'pɛndɪtʃə*] n gastos mpl, desembolso; consumo

expense [ɪk'spɛns] n gasto, gastos mpl; (high cost) costa; **expenses** npl (Comm) gastos mpl; **at the ~ of** a costa de; **expense account** n cuenta de gastos

expensive [ɪk'spɛnsɪv] adj caro, costoso

experience [ɪk'spɪərɪəns] n experiencia ▷ vt experimentar; (suffer) sufrir; **experienced** adj experimentado

experiment [ɪk'spɛrɪmənt] n experimento ▷ vi hacer experimentos; **experimental** [-'mɛntl] adj experimental; **the process is still at the experimental stage** el proceso está todavía en prueba

expert ['ɛkspə:t] adj experto, perito ▷ n experto/a, perito/a; (specialist) especialista mf; **expertise** [-'ti:z] n pericia

expire [ɪk'spaɪə*] vi caducar, vencer; **expiry** n vencimiento; **expiry date** n (of medicine, food item) fecha de caducidad

explain [ɪk'spleɪn] vt explicar; **explanation** [ɛksplə'neɪʃən] n explicación f

explicit [ɪk'splɪsɪt] adj explícito

explode [ɪk'spləud] vi estallar, explotar; (population) crecer rápidamente; (with anger) reventar

exploit [n 'ɛksplɔɪt, vb ɪk'splɔɪt] n hazaña

▷ *vt* explotar; **exploitation** [-'teɪʃən] *n* explotación *f*
explore [ɪk'splɔ:*] *vt* explorar; (*fig*) examinar; investigar; **explorer** *n* explorador(a) *m/f*
explosion [ɪk'spləuʒən] *n* explosión *f*; **explosive** [ɪks'pləusɪv] *adj, n* explosivo
export [*vb* ɛk'spɔ:t, *n, cpd* 'ɛkspɔ:t] *vt* exportar ▷ *n* (*process*) exportación *f*; (*product*) producto de exportación ▷ *cpd* de exportación; **exporter** *n* exportador *m*
expose [ɪk'spəuz] *vt* exponer; (*unmask*) desenmascarar; **exposed** *adj.* expuesto
exposure [ɪk'spəuʒə*] *n* exposición *f*; (*publicity*) publicidad *f*; (*Phot: speed*) velocidad *f* de obturación; (: *shot*) fotografía; **to die from ~** (*Med*) morir de frío
express [ɪk'sprɛs] *adj* (*definite*) expreso, explícito; (*BRIT: letter etc*) urgente ▷ *vt* expresar; **expression** [ɪk'sprɛʃən] *n* expresión *f*; (*of actor etc*) sentimiento; **expressway** (*US*) *n* (*urban motorway*) autopista
exquisite [ɛk'skwɪzɪt] *adj* exquisito
extend [ɪk'stɛnd] *vt* (*visit, street*) prolongar; (*building*) ampliar; (*invitation*) ofrecer ▷ *vi* (*land*) extenderse; (*period of time*) prolongarse
extension [ɪk'stɛnʃən] *n* extensión *f*; (*building*) ampliación *f*; (*of time*) prolongación *f*; (*Tel: in private house*) línea derivada; (: *in office*) extensión *f*; **extension lead** *n* alargador *m*, alargadera
extensive [ɪk'stɛnsɪv] *adj* extenso; (*damage*) importante; (*knowledge*) amplio
extent [ɪk'stɛnt] *n* (*breadth*) extensión *f*; (*scope*) alcance *m*; **to some ~** hasta cierto punto; **to the ~ of ...** hasta el punto de ...; **to such an ~ that ...** hasta tal punto que ...; **to what ~?** ¿hasta qué punto?
exterior [ɛk'stɪərɪə*] *adj* exterior, externo ▷ *n* exterior *m*
external [ɛk'stə:nl] *adj* externo
extinct [ɪk'stɪŋkt] *adj* (*volcano*) extinguido; (*race*) extinto; **extinction** *n* extinción *f*
extinguish [ɪk'stɪŋgwɪʃ] *vt* extinguir, apagar
extra ['ɛkstrə] *adj* adicional ▷ *adv* (*in addition*) de más ▷ *n* (*luxury, addition*) extra *m*; (*Cinema, Theatre*) extra *mf*, comparsa *mf*
extract [*vb* ɪk'strækt, *n* 'ɛkstrækt] *vt* sacar; (*tooth*) extraer; (*money, promise*) obtener ▷ *n* extracto
extradite ['ɛkstrədaɪt] *vt* extraditar
extraordinary [ɪk'strɔ:dnrɪ] *adj* extraordinario; (*odd*) raro
extravagance [ɪk'strævəgəns] *n* derroche *m*, despilfarro; (*thing bought*) extravagancia
extravagant [ɪk'strævəgənt] *adj* (*lavish: person*) pródigo; (: *gift*) (demasiado) caro; (*wasteful*) despilfarrador(a)
extreme [ɪk'stri:m] *adj* extremo, extremado ▷ *n* extremo; **extremely** *adv* sumamente, extremadamente
extremist [ɪk'stri:mɪst] *adj, n* extremista *m/f*
extrovert ['ɛkstrəvə:t] *n* extrovertido/a
eye [aɪ] *n* ojo ▷ *vt* mirar de soslayo, ojear; **to keep an ~ on** vigilar; **eyeball** *n* globo ocular; **eyebrow** *n* ceja; **eyedrops** *npl* gotas *fpl* para los ojos, colino; **eyelash** *n* pestaña; **eyelid** *n* párpado; **eyeliner** *n* delineador *m* (de ojos); **eyeshadow** *n* sombreador *m* de ojos; **eyesight** *n* vista; **eye witness** *n* testigo *mf* presencial

f

F [ɛf] n (Mus) fa m

fabric ['fæbrɪk] n tejido, tela

⏐ Be careful not to translate **fabric** by the Spanish word *fábrica*.

fabulous ['fæbjʊləs] adj fabuloso

face [feɪs] n (Anat) cara, rostro; (of clock) esfera (SP), cara (LAM); (of mountain) cara, ladera; (of building) fachada ▷ vt (direction) estar de cara a; (situation) hacer frente a; (facts) aceptar; **~ down** (person, card) boca abajo; **to lose ~** desprestigiarse; **to make** or **pull a ~** hacer muecas; **in the ~ of** (difficulties etc) ante; **on the ~ of it** a primera vista; **~ to ~** cara a cara; **face up to** vt fus hacer frente a, arrostrar; **face cloth** n (BRIT) manopla; **face pack** n (BRIT) mascarilla

facial ['feɪʃəl] adj de la cara ▷ n (also: **beauty ~**) tratamiento facial, limpieza

facilitate [fə'sɪlɪteɪt] vt facilitar

facilities [fə'sɪlɪtɪz] npl (buildings) instalaciones fpl; (equipment) servicios mpl; **credit ~** facilidades fpl de crédito

fact [fækt] n hecho; **in ~** en realidad

faction ['fækʃən] n facción f

factor ['fæktə*] n factor m

factory ['fæktərɪ] n fábrica

factual ['fæktjʊəl] adj basado en los hechos

faculty ['fækəltɪ] n facultad f; (US: teaching staff) personal m docente

fad [fæd] n novedad f, moda

fade [feɪd] vi desteñirse; (sound, smile) desvanecerse; (light) apagarse; (flower) marchitarse; (hope, memory) perderse; **fade away** vi (sound) apagarse

fag [fæg] (BRIT: inf) n (cigarette) pitillo (SP), cigarro

Fahrenheit ['fɑːrənhaɪt] n Fahrenheit m

fail [feɪl] vt (candidate, test) suspender (SP), reprobar (LAM); (memory etc) fallar a ▷ vi suspender (SP), reprobar (LAM); (be unsuccessful) fracasar; (strength, brakes) fallar; (light) acabarse; **to ~ to do sth** (neglect) dejar de hacer algo; (be unable) no poder hacer algo; **without ~** sin falta; **failing** n falta, defecto ▷ prep a falta de; **failure** ['feɪljə*] n fracaso; (person) fracasado/a; (mechanical etc) fallo

faint [feɪnt] adj débil; (recollection) vago; (mark) apenas visible ▷ n desmayo ▷ vi desmayarse; **to feel ~** estar mareado, marearse; **faintest** adj: **I haven't the faintest idea** no tengo la más remota idea; **faintly** adv débilmente; (vaguely) vagamente

fair [fɛə*] adj justo; (hair, person) rubio; (weather) bueno; (good enough) regular; (considerable) considerable ▷ adv (play) limpio ▷ n feria; (BRIT: funfair) parque m de atracciones; **fairground** n recinto ferial; **fair-haired** adj (person) rubio; **fairly** adv (justly) con justicia; (quite) bastante; **fair trade** n comercio justo; **fairway** n (Golf) calle f

fairy ['fɛərɪ] n hada; **fairy tale** n cuento de hadas

faith [feɪθ] n fe f; (trust) confianza; (sect) religión f; **faithful** adj (loyal: troops etc) leal; (spouse) fiel; (account) exacto; **faithfully** adv fielmente; **yours faithfully** (BRIT: in letters) le saluda atentamente

fake [feɪk] n (painting etc) falsificación f; (person) impostor(a) m/f ▷ adj falso ▷ vt fingir; (painting etc) falsificar

falcon ['fɔːlkən] n halcón m

fall [fɔːl] (pt fell, pp fallen) n caída; (in price etc) descenso; (US) otoño ▷ vi caer(se); (price) bajar, descender; **falls** npl (waterfall) cascada, salto de agua; **to ~ flat** (on one's face) caerse (boca abajo); (plan) fracasar; (joke, story) no hacer gracia; **fall apart** vi deshacerse; **fall down** vi (person) caerse; (building, hopes) derrumbarse; **fall for** vt fus (trick) dejarse engañar por; (person) enamorarse de; **fall off** vi caerse; (diminish) disminuir; **fall out** vi (friends etc) reñir; (hair, teeth) caerse; **fall over** vi caer(se); **fall through** vi (plan, project) fracasar

fallen ['fɔːlən] pp of **fall**

fallout ['fɔːlaʊt] n lluvia radioactiva

false [fɔːls] adj falso; **under ~ pretences** con engaños; **false alarm** n falsa alarma; **false teeth** (BRIT) npl dentadura postiza

fame [feɪm] n fama

familiar [fə'mɪlɪə*] adj conocido, familiar; (tone) de confianza; **to be ~ with** (subject) conocer (bien); **familiarize** [fə'mɪlɪəraɪz] vt: **to familiarize o.s. with** familiarizarse con

family ['fæmɪlɪ] n familia; **family doctor** n médico/a de cabecera; **family planning** n planificación f familiar

famine ['fæmɪn] n hambre f, hambruna

famous ['feɪməs] adj famoso, célebre

fan [fæn] n abanico; (Elec) ventilador m; (of pop star) fan mf; (Sport) hincha mf ▷ vt abanicar; (fire, quarrel) atizar

fanatic [fə'nætɪk] n fanático/a

fan belt n correa del ventilador

fan club n club m de fans

fancy ['fænsɪ] n (whim) capricho, antojo; (imagination) imaginación f ▷ adj (luxury) lujoso, de lujo ▷ vt (feel like, want) tener ganas de; (imagine) imaginarse; (think) creer; **to take a ~ to sb** tomar cariño a algn; **he fancies her** (inf) le gusta (ella) mucho; **fancy dress** n disfraz m

fan heater n calefactor m de aire

fantasize ['fæntəsaɪz] vi fantasear, hacerse ilusiones

fantastic [fæn'tæstɪk] adj (enormous) enorme; (strange, wonderful) fantástico

fantasy ['fæntəzɪ] n (dream) sueño; (unreality) fantasía

fanzine ['fænziːn] n fanzine m

FAQs abbr (= frequently asked questions) preguntas frecuentes

far [fɑː*] adj (distant) lejano ▷ adv lejos; (much, greatly) mucho; **~ away, ~ off** (a lo) lejos; **~ better** mucho mejor; **~ from** lejos de; **by ~** con mucho; **go as ~ as the farm** vaya hasta la granja; **as ~ as I know** que yo sepa; **how ~?** ¿hasta dónde?; (fig) ¿hasta qué punto?

farce [fɑːs] n farsa

fare [fɛə*] n (on trains, buses) precio (del billete); (in taxi: cost) tarifa; (food) comida; **half ~** medio pasaje m; **full ~** pasaje completo

Far East n: **the ~** el Extremo Oriente

farewell [fɛə'wɛl] excl, n adiós m

farm [fɑːm] n cortijo (SP), hacienda (LAM), rancho (MEX), estancia (RPL) ▷ vt cultivar; **farmer** n granjero, hacendado (LAM), ranchero (MEX), estanciero (RPL); **farmhouse** n granja, casa del hacendado (LAM), rancho (MEX), casco de la estancia (RPL); **farming** n agricultura; (of crops) cultivo; (of animals) cría; **farmyard** n corral m

far-reaching [fɑː'riːtʃɪŋ] adj (reform, effect) de gran alcance

fart [fɑːt] (inf!) vi tirarse un pedo (!)

farther ['fɑːðə*] adv más lejos, más allá ▷ adj más lejano

farthest ['fɑːðɪst] superlative of **far**

fascinate ['fæsɪneɪt] vt fascinar;

fascinated adj fascinado

fascinating ['fæsɪneɪtɪŋ] adj fascinante

fascination [-'neɪʃən] n fascinación f

fascist ['fæʃɪst] adj, n fascista m/f

fashion ['fæʃən] n moda; (fashion industry) industria de la moda; (manner) manera ▷ vt formar; **in ~** a la moda; **out of ~** pasado de moda; **fashionable** adj de moda; **fashion show** n desfile m de modelos

fast [fɑːst] adj rápido; (dye, colour) resistente; (clock): **to be ~** estar adelantado ▷ adv rápidamente, de prisa; (stuck, held) firmemente ▷ n ayuno ▷ vi ayunar; **~ asleep** profundamente dormido

fasten ['fɑːsn] vt atar, sujetar; (coat, belt) abrochar ▷ vi atarse; abrocharse

fast food n comida rápida, platos mpl preparados

fat [fæt] adj gordo; (book) grueso; (profit) grande, pingüe ▷ n grasa; (on person) carnes fpl; (lard) manteca

fatal ['feɪtl] adj (mistake) fatal; (injury) mortal; **fatality** [fə'tælɪtɪ] n (road death etc) víctima; **fatally** adv fatalmente; mortalmente

fate [feɪt] n destino; (of person) suerte f

father ['fɑːðə*] n padre m; **Father Christmas** n Papá m Noel; **father-in-law** n suegro

fatigue [fə'tiːg] n fatiga, cansancio

fattening ['fætnɪŋ] adj (food) que hace engordar

fatty ['fætɪ] adj (food) graso ▷ n (inf) gordito/a, gordinflón/ona m/f

faucet ['fɔːsɪt] (US) n grifo (SP), llave f, canilla (RPL)

fault [fɔːlt] n (blame) culpa; (defect: in person, machine) defecto; (Geo) falla ▷ vt criticar; **it's my ~** es culpa mía; **to find ~ with** criticar, poner peros a; **at ~** culpable; **faulty** adj defectuoso

fauna ['fɔːnə] n fauna

favour etc ['feɪvə*] (US **favor** etc) n favor m; (approval) aprobación f ▷ vt (proposition) estar a favor de, aprobar; (assist) ser propicio a; **to do sb a ~** hacer un favor a algn; **to find ~ with sb** caer en gracia a algn; **in ~ of** a favor de; **favourable** adj favorable; **favourite** ['feɪvrɪt] adj, n favorito, preferido

fawn [fɔːn] n cervato ▷ adj (also: **~-coloured**) color de cervato, leonado ▷ vi: **to ~ (up)on** adular

fax [fæks] n (document) fax m; (machine) telefax m ▷ vt mandar por telefax

FBI (US) n abbr (= Federal Bureau of Investigation) ≈ BIC f (SP)

fear [fɪə*] n miedo, temor m ▷ vt tener

miedo de, temer; **for ~ of** por si; **fearful**
adj temeroso, miedoso; *(awful)* terrible;
fearless *adj* audaz
feasible ['fi:zəbl] *adj* factible
feast [fi:st] *n* banquete *m*; *(Rel: also:* **~ day)**
fiesta ▷ *vi* festejar
feat [fi:t] *n* hazaña
feather ['fɛðə*] *n* pluma
feature ['fi:tʃə*] *n* característica; *(article)*
artículo de fondo ▷ *vt (film)* presentar
▷ *vi:* **to ~ in** tener un papel destacado en;
features *npl (of face)* facciones *fpl;* **feature
film** *n* largometraje *m*
Feb. *abbr* (= *February)* feb
February ['fɛbruərɪ] *n* febrero
fed [fɛd] *pt, pp of* **feed**
federal ['fɛdərəl] *adj* federal
federation [fɛdə'reɪʃən] *n* federación *f*
fed up [fɛd'ʌp] *adj:* **to be ~ (with)** estar
harto (de)
fee [fi:] *n* pago; *(professional)* derechos *mpl,*
honorarios *mpl; (of club)* cuota; **school ~s**
matrícula
feeble ['fi:bl] *adj* débil; *(joke)* flojo
feed [fi:d] *(pt, pp* **fed)** *n* comida; *(of
animal)* pienso; *(on printer)* dispositivo
de alimentación ▷ *vt* alimentar;
(BRIT: baby: breastfeed) dar el pecho a; *(animal)*
dar de comer a; *(data, information):* **to ~
into** meter en; **feedback** *n* reacción *f,*
feedback *m*
feel [fi:l] *(pt, pp* **felt)** *n (sensation)* sensación
f; (sense of touch) tacto; *(impression):* **to have
the ~ of** parecerse a ▷ *vt* tocar; *(pain etc)*
sentir; *(think, believe)* creer; **to ~ hungry/
cold** tener hambre/frío; **to ~ lonely/
better** sentirse solo/mejor; **I don't ~ well**
no me siento bien; **it ~s soft** es suave al
tacto; **to ~ like** *(want)* tener ganas de;
feeling *n (physical)* sensación *f; (foreboding)*
presentimiento; *(emotion)* sentimiento
feet [fi:t] *npl of* **foot**
fell [fɛl] *pt of* **fall** ▷ *vt (tree)* talar
fellow ['fɛləu] *n* tipo, tío *(SP); (comrade)*
compañero; *(of learned society)* socio/a;
fellow citizen *n* conciudadano/a; **fellow
countryman** *(irreg)* *n* compatriota
m; **fellow men** *npl* semejantes *mpl;*
fellowship *n* compañerismo; *(grant)* beca
felony ['fɛlənɪ] *n* crimen *m*
felt [fɛlt] *pt, pp of* **feel** ▷ *n* fieltro; **felt-tip**
n (also: **felt-tip pen)** rotulador *m*
female ['fi:meɪl] *n (pej: woman)* mujer *f,*
tía; *(Zool)* hembra ▷ *adj* femenino; hembra
feminine ['fɛmɪnɪn] *adj* femenino
feminist ['fɛmɪnɪst] *n* feminista
fence [fɛns] *n* valla, cerca ▷ *vt (also:* **~ in)**
cercar ▷ *vi (Sport)* hacer esgrima; **fencing**

n esgrima
fend [fɛnd] *vi:* **to ~ for o.s.** valerse por
sí mismo; **fend off** *vt (attack)* rechazar;
(questions) evadir
fender ['fɛndə*] *(US)* *n* guardafuego; *(Aut)*
parachoques *m inv*
fennel ['fɛnl] *n* hinojo
ferment *[vb* fə'mɛnt, *n* 'fə:mɛnt] *vi*
fermentar ▷ *n (fig)* agitación *f*
fern [fə:n] *n* helecho
ferocious [fə'rəuʃəs] *adj* feroz
ferret ['fɛrɪt] *n* hurón *m*
ferry ['fɛrɪ] *n (small)* barca (de pasaje),
balsa; *(large: also:* **~boat)** transbordador *m,*
ferry *m* ▷ *vt* transportar
fertile ['fə:taɪl] *adj* fértil; *(Biol)* fecundo;
fertilize ['fə:tɪlaɪz] *vt (Biol)* fecundar; *(Agr)*
abonar; **fertilizer** *n* abono
festival ['fɛstɪvəl] *n (Rel)* fiesta; *(Art, Mus)*
festival *m*
festive ['fɛstɪv] *adj* festivo; **the ~ season**
(BRIT: *Christmas)* las Navidades
fetch [fɛtʃ] *vt* ir a buscar; *(sell for)* venderse
por
fête [feɪt] *n* fiesta
fetus ['fi:təs] *(US)* *n* = **foetus**
feud [fju:d] *n (hostility)* enemistad *f;*
(quarrel) disputa
fever ['fi:və*] *n* fiebre *f;* **feverish** *adj* febril
few [fju:] *adj (not many)* pocos ▷ *pron*
pocos; algunos; **a ~** *adj* unos pocos,
algunos; **fewer** *adj* menos; **fewest** *adj*
los(las) menos
fiancé [fɪ'ɑ̃:ŋseɪ] *n* novio, prometido;
fiancée *n* novia, prometida
fiasco [fɪ'æskəu] *n* fiasco
fib [fɪb] *n* mentirilla
fibre ['faɪbə*] *(US* **fiber)** *n* fibra; **fibreglass**
(US **Fiberglass®)** *n* fibra de vidrio
fickle ['fɪkl] *adj* inconstante
fiction ['fɪkʃən] *n* ficción *f;* **fictional** *adj*
novelesco
fiddle ['fɪdl] *n (Mus)* violín *m; (cheating)*
trampa ▷ *vt (BRIT: accounts)* falsificar; **fiddle
with** *vt fus* juguetear con
fidelity [fɪ'dɛlɪtɪ] *n* fidelidad *f*
field [fi:ld] *n* campo; *(fig)* campo, esfera;
(Sport) campo *(SP),* cancha *(LAM);* **field
marshal** *n* mariscal *m*
fierce [fɪəs] *adj* feroz; *(wind, heat)* fuerte;
(fighting, enemy) encarnizado
fifteen [fɪf'ti:n] *num* quince; **fifteenth** *adj*
decimoquinto; **the fifteenth floor** la planta
quince; **the fifteenth of August** el quince
de agosto
fifth [fɪfθ] *num* quinto
fiftieth ['fɪftɪɪθ] *adj* quincuagésimo
fifty ['fɪftɪ] *num* cincuenta; **fifty-fifty** *adj*

fig | 288

(*deal, split*) a medias ▷ *adv* a medias, mitad
por mitad
fig [fɪg] n higo
fight [faɪt] (*pt, pp* **fought**) n (*gen*)
pelea; (*Mil*) combate m; (*struggle*) lucha
▷ *vt* luchar contra; (*cancer, alcoholism*)
combatir; (*election*) intentar ganar; (*emotion*)
resistir ▷ *vi* pelear, luchar; **fight back**
vi defenderse; (*after illness*) recuperarse
▷ *vt* (*tears*) contener; **fight off** *vt* (*attack,
attacker*) rechazar; (*disease, sleep, urge*) luchar
contra; **fighting** n combate m, pelea
figure ['fɪgə*] n (*Drawing, Geom*) figura,
dibujo; (*number, cipher*) cifra; (*body, outline*)
tipo; (*personality*) figura ▷ *vt* (*esp us*)
imaginar ▷ *vi* (*appear*) figurar; **figure out** *vt*
(*work out*) resolver
file [faɪl] n (*tool*) lima; (*dossier*) expediente
m; (*folder*) carpeta; (*Comput*) fichero; (*row*)
fila ▷ *vt* limar; (*Law: claim*) presentar;
(*store*) archivar; **filing cabinet** n fichero,
archivador m
Filipino [fɪlɪ'piːnəu] *adj* filipino ▷ n
(*person*) filipino/a m/f; (*Ling*) tagalo
fill [fɪl] *vt* (*space*): **to ~ (with)** llenar (de);
(*vacancy, need*) cubrir ▷ n: **to eat one's ~**
llenarse; **fill in** *vt* rellenar; **fill out** *vt* (*form,
receipt*) rellenar; **fill up** *vt* llenar (hasta el
borde) ▷ *vi* (*Aut*) poner gasolina
fillet ['fɪlɪt] n filete m; **fillet steak** n filete
m de ternera
filling ['fɪlɪŋ] n (*Culin*) relleno; (*for tooth*)
empaste m; **filling station** n estación f de
servicio
film [fɪlm] n película ▷ *vt* (*scene*) filmar
▷ *vi* rodar (una película); **film star** n astro,
estrella de cine
filter ['fɪltə*] n filtro ▷ *vt* filtrar; **filter lane**
(*BRIT*) n carril m de selección
filth [fɪlθ] n suciedad f; **filthy** *adj* sucio;
(*language*) obsceno
fin [fɪn] n (*gen*) aleta
final ['faɪnl] *adj* (*last*) final, último;
(*definitive*) definitivo, terminante ▷ n (*BRIT
Sport*) final f; **finals** npl (*Scol*) examen m final;
(*us Sport*) final f
finale [fɪ'nɑːlɪ] n final m
final: finalist n (*Sport*) finalista mf; **finalize**
vt concluir, completar; **finally** *adv* (*lastly*)
por último, finalmente; (*eventually*) por fin
finance [faɪ'næns] n (*money*) fondos mpl
▷ *vt* financiar; **finances** npl finanzas fpl;
(*personal finances*) situación f económica;
financial [-'nænʃəl] *adj* financiero;
financial year n ejercicio (financiero)
find [faɪnd] (*pt, pp* **found**) *vt* encontrar,
hallar; (*come upon*) descubrir ▷ n hallazgo;
descubrimiento; **to ~ sb guilty** (*Law*)

declarar culpable a algn; **find out** *vt*
averiguar; (*truth, secret*) descubrir; **to find
out about** (*subject*) informarse sobre; (*by
chance*) enterarse de; **findings** npl (*Law*)
veredicto, fallo; (*of report*) recomendaciones
fpl
fine [faɪn] *adj* excelente; (*thin*) fino ▷ *adv*
(*well*) bien ▷ n (*Law*) multa ▷ *vt* (*Law*)
multar; **to be ~** (*person*) estar bien; (*weather*)
hacer buen tiempo; **fine arts** npl bellas
artes fpl
finger ['fɪŋgə*] n dedo ▷ *vt* (*touch*)
manosear; **little/index ~** (dedo) meñique
m/índice m; **fingernail** n uña; **fingerprint**
n huella dactilar; **fingertip** n yema del
dedo
finish ['fɪnɪʃ] n (*end*) fin m; (*Sport*) meta;
(*polish etc*) acabado ▷ *vt*, vi terminar;
to ~ doing sth acabar de hacer algo; **to ~
third** llegar el tercero; **finish off** *vt* acabar,
terminar; (*kill*) acabar con; **finish up** *vt*
acabar, terminar ▷ *vi* ir a parar, terminar
Finland ['fɪnlənd] n Finlandia
Finn [fɪn] n finlandés/esa m/f; **Finnish** *adj*
finlandés/esa ▷ n (*Ling*) finlandés m
fir [fəː*] n abeto
fire ['faɪə*] n fuego; (*in hearth*) lumbre
f; (*accidental*) incendio; (*heater*) estufa
▷ *vt* (*gun*) disparar; (*interest*) despertar;
(*inf: dismiss*) despedir ▷ *vi* (*shoot*) disparar;
on ~ ardiendo, en llamas; **fire alarm** n
alarma de incendios; **firearm** n arma de
fuego; **fire brigade** (us **fire department**) n
(cuerpo de) bomberos mpl; **fire engine** (BRIT)
n coche m de bomberos; **fire escape** n
escalera de incendios; **fire exit** n salida de
incendios; **fire extinguisher** n extintor m
(de incendios); **fireman** (*irreg*) n bombero;
fireplace n chimenea; **fire station** n
parque m de bomberos; **firetruck** (us) n =
fire engine; **firewall** n (*Internet*) firewall m;
firewood n leña; **fireworks** npl fuegos mpl
artificiales
firm [fəːm] *adj* firme; (*look, voice*)
resuelto ▷ n firma, empresa; **firmly** *adv*
firmemente; resueltamente
first [fəːst] *adj* primero ▷ *adv* (*before others*)
primero; (*when listing reasons etc*) en primer
lugar, primeramente ▷ n (*person: in race*)
primero/a; (*Aut*) primera; (*BRIT Scol*) título
de licenciado con calificación de sobresaliente;
at ~ al principio; **~ of all** ante todo; **first
aid** n primera ayuda, primeros auxilios
mpl; **first-aid kit** n botiquín m; **first-class**
adj (*excellent*) de primera (categoría); (*ticket
etc*) de primera clase; **first-hand** *adj* de
primera mano; **first lady** n (*esp us*) primera
dama; **firstly** *adv* en primer lugar; **first**

name n nombre m (de pila); **first-rate** adj estupendo

fiscal ['fɪskəl] adj fiscal; **fiscal year** n año fiscal, ejercicio

fish [fɪʃ] n inv pez m; (food) pescado ▷ vt, vi pescar; **to go ~ing** ir de pesca; **~ and chips** pescado frito con patatas fritas; **fisherman** (irreg) n pescador m; **fish fingers** (BRIT) npl croquetas fpl de pescado; **fishing** n pesca; **fishing boat** n barca de pesca; **fishing line** n sedal m; **fishmonger** n (BRIT) pescadero/a; **fishmonger's (shop)** (BRIT) n pescadería; **fish sticks** (US) npl = **fish fingers**; **fishy** (inf) adj sospechoso

fist [fɪst] n puño

fit [fɪt] adj (healthy) en (buena) forma; (proper) adecuado, apropiado ▷ vt (clothes) estar or sentar bien a; (instal) poner; (equip) proveer, dotar; (facts) cuadrar or corresponder con ▷ vi (clothes) sentar bien; (in space, gap) caber; (facts) coincidir ▷ n (Med) ataque m; **~ to** (ready) a punto de; **~ for** apropiado para; **a ~ of anger/pride** un arranque de cólera/orgullo; **this dress is a good ~** este vestido me sienta bien; **by ~s and starts** a rachas; **fit in** vi (fig: person) llevarse bien (con todos); **fitness** n (Med) salud f; **fitted** adj (jacket, shirt) entallado; (sheet) de cuatro picos; **fitted carpet** n moqueta; **fitted kitchen** n cocina amueblada; **fitting** adj apropiado ▷ n (of dress) prueba; (of piece of equipment) instalación f; **fitting room** n probador m; **fittings** npl instalaciones fpl

five [faɪv] num cinco; **fiver** (inf) n (BRIT) billete m de cinco libras; (US) billete m de cinco dólares

fix [fɪks] vt (secure) fijar, asegurar; (mend) arreglar; (prepare) preparar ▷ n: **to be in a ~** estar en un aprieto; **fix up** vt (meeting) arreglar; **to fix sb up with sth** proveer a algn de algo; **fixed** adj (prices etc) fijo; **fixture** n (Sport) encuentro

fizzy ['fɪzɪ] adj (drink) gaseoso

flag [flæg] n bandera; (stone) losa ▷ vi decaer ▷ vt: **to ~ sb down** hacer señas a algn para que se pare; **flagpole** n asta de bandera

flair [flɛə*] n aptitud f especial

flak [flæk] n (Mil) fuego antiaéreo; (inf: criticism) lluvia de críticas

flake [fleɪk] n (of rust, paint) escama; (of snow, soap powder) copo ▷ vi (also: **~ off**) desconcharse

flamboyant [flæm'bɔɪənt] adj (dress) vistoso; (person) extravagante

flame [fleɪm] n llama

flamingo [flə'mɪŋɡəu] n flamenco

flammable ['flæməbl] adj inflamable

flan [flæn] (BRIT) n tarta

| Be careful not to translate **flan** by the Spanish word *flan*.

flank [flæŋk] n (of animal) ijar m; (of army) flanco ▷ vt flanquear

flannel ['flænl] n (BRIT: also: **face ~**) manopla; (fabric) franela

flap [flæp] n (of pocket, envelope) solapa ▷ vt (wings, arms) agitar ▷ vi (sail, flag) ondear

flare [flɛə*] n llamarada; (Mil) bengala; (in skirt etc) vuelo; **flares** npl (trousers) pantalones mpl de campana; **flare up** vi encenderse; (fig: person) encolerizarse; (: revolt) estallar

flash [flæʃ] n relámpago; (also: **news ~**) noticias fpl de última hora; (Phot) flash m ▷ vt (light, headlights) lanzar un destello con; (news, message) transmitir; (smile) lanzar ▷ vi brillar; (hazard light etc) lanzar destellos; **in a ~** en un instante; **he ~ed by** or **past** pasó como un rayo; **flashback** n (Cinema) flashback m; **flashbulb** n bombilla fusible; **flashlight** n linterna

flask [flɑːsk] n frasco; (also: **vacuum ~**) termo

flat [flæt] adj llano; (smooth) liso; (tyre) desinflado; (battery) descargado; (beer) muerto; (refusal etc) rotundo; (Mus) desafinado; (rate) fijo ▷ n (BRIT: apartment) piso (SP), departamento (LAM), apartamento; (Aut) pinchazo; (Mus) bemol m; **to work ~ out** trabajar a toda mecha; **flatten** vt (also: **flatten out**) allanar; (smooth out) alisar; (building, plants) arrasar

flatter ['flætə*] vt adular, halagar; **flattering** adj halagüeño; (dress) que favorece

flaunt [flɔːnt] vt ostentar, lucir

flavour etc ['fleɪvə*] (US **flavor** etc) n sabor m, gusto ▷ vt sazonar, condimentar; **strawberry-flavoured** con sabor a fresa; **flavouring** n (in product) aromatizante m

flaw [flɔː] n defecto; **flawless** adj impecable

flea [fliː] n pulga; **flea market** n rastro, mercadillo

flee [fliː] (pt, pp **fled**) vt huir de ▷ vi huir, fugarse

fleece [fliːs] n vellón m; (wool) lana; (top) forro polar ▷ vt (inf) desplumar

fleet [fliːt] n flota; (of lorries etc) escuadra

fleeting ['fliːtɪŋ] adj fugaz

Flemish ['flemɪʃ] adj flamenco

flesh [fleʃ] n carne f; (skin) piel f; (of fruit) pulpa

flew [fluː] pt of **fly**

flex [flɛks] n cordón m ▷ vt (muscles)

tensar; **flexibility** n flexibilidad f; **flexible** adj flexible; **flexitime** (us **flextime**) n horario flexible

flick [flɪk] n capirotazo; chasquido ▷ vt (with hand) dar un capirotazo a; (whip etc) chasquear; (switch) accionar; **flick through** vt fus hojear

flicker ['flɪkə*] vi (light) parpadear; (flame) vacilar

flies [flaɪz] npl of **fly**

flight [flaɪt] n vuelo; (escape) huida, fuga; (also: **~ of steps**) tramo (de escaleras); **flight attendant** n auxiliar mf de vuelo

flimsy ['flɪmzɪ] adj (thin) muy ligero; (building) endeble; (excuse) flojo

flinch [flɪntʃ] vi encogerse; **to ~ from** retroceder ante

fling [flɪŋ] (pt, pp **flung**) vt arrojar

flint [flɪnt] n pedernal m; (in lighter) piedra

flip [flɪp] vt dar la vuelta a; (switch: turn on) encender; (turn) apagar; (coin) echar a cara o cruz

flip-flops ['flɪpflɔps] npl (esp BRIT) chancletas fpl

flipper ['flɪpə*] n aleta

flirt [flə:t] vi coquetear, flirtear ▷ n coqueta

float [fləut] n flotador m; (in procession) carroza; (money) reserva ▷ vi flotar; (swimmer) hacer la plancha

flock [flɔk] n (of sheep) rebaño; (of birds) bandada ▷ vi: **to ~ to** acudir en tropel a

flood [flʌd] n inundación f; (of letters, imports etc) avalancha ▷ vt inundar ▷ vi (place) inundarse; (people): **to ~ into** inundar; **flooding** n inundaciones fpl; **floodlight** n foco

floor [flɔ:*] n suelo; (storey) piso; (of sea) fondo ▷ vt (question) dejar sin respuesta; (: blow) derribar; **ground ~, first ~** (us) planta baja; **first ~, second ~** (us) primer piso; **floorboard** n tabla; **flooring** n suelo; (material) solería; **floor show** n cabaret m

flop [flɔp] n fracaso ▷ vi (fail) fracasar; (fall) derrumbarse; **floppy** adj flojo ▷ n (Comput: also: **floppy disk**) floppy m

flora ['flɔ:rə] n flora

floral ['flɔ:rl] adj (pattern) floreado

florist ['flɔrɪst] n florista mf; **florist's (shop)** n floristería

flotation [fləu'teɪʃən] n (of shares) emisión f; (of company) lanzamiento

flour ['flauə*] n harina

flourish ['flʌrɪʃ] vi florecer ▷ n ademán m, movimiento (ostentoso)

flow [fləu] n (movement) flujo; (of traffic) circulación f; (tide) corriente f ▷ vi (river, blood) fluir; (traffic) circular

flower ['flauə*] n flor f ▷ vi florecer; **flower bed** n macizo; **flowerpot** n tiesto

flown [fləun] pp of **fly**

fl. oz. abbr (= fluid ounce)

flu [flu:] n: **to have ~** tener la gripe

fluctuate ['flʌktjueɪt] vi fluctuar

fluent ['flu:ənt] adj (linguist) que habla perfectamente; (speech) elocuente; **he speaks ~ French, he's ~ in French** domina el francés

fluff [flʌf] n pelusa; **fluffy** adj de pelo suave

fluid ['flu:ɪd] adj (movement) fluido, líquido; (situation) inestable ▷ n fluido, líquido; **fluid ounce** n onza f líquida

fluke [flu:k] (inf) n chiripa

flung [flʌŋ] pt, pp of **fling**

fluorescent [fluə'resnt] adj fluorescente

fluoride ['fluəraɪd] n fluoruro

flurry ['flʌrɪ] n (of snow) temporal m; **~ of activity** frenesí m de actividad

flush [flʌʃ] n rubor m; (fig: of youth etc) resplandor m ▷ vt limpiar con agua ▷ vi ruborizarse ▷ adj: **~ with** a ras de; **to ~ the toilet** hacer funcionar la cisterna

flute [flu:t] n flauta

flutter ['flʌtə*] n (of wings) revoloteo, aleteo; (fig): **a ~ of panic/excitement** una oleada de pánico/excitación ▷ vi revolotear

fly [flaɪ] (pt **flew**, pp **flown**) n mosca; (on trousers: also: **flies**) bragueta ▷ vt (plane) pilot(e)ar; (cargo) transportar (en avión); (distances) recorrer (en avión) ▷ vi volar; (passengers) ir en avión; (escape) evadirse; (flag) ondear; **fly away, fly off** vi emprender el vuelo; **fly-drive** n: **fly-drive holiday** vacaciones que incluyen vuelo y alquiler de coche; **flying** n (activity) (el) volar; (action) vuelo ▷ adj: **flying visit** visita relámpago; **with flying colours** con lucimiento; **flying saucer** n platillo volante; **flyover** (BRIT) n paso a desnivel or superior

FM abbr (Radio) (= frequency modulation) FM

foal [fəul] n potro

foam [fəum] n espuma ▷ vi hacer espuma

focus ['fəukəs] (pl **~es**) n foco; (centre) centro ▷ vt (field glasses etc) enfocar ▷ vi: **to ~ (on)** enfocar (a); (issue etc) centrarse en; **in/out of ~** enfocado/desenfocado

foetus ['fi:təs] (us **fetus**) n feto

fog [fɔg] n niebla; **foggy** adj: **it's foggy** hay niebla, está brumoso; **fog lamp** (us **fog light**) n (Aut) faro de niebla

foil [fɔil] vt frustrar ▷ n hoja; (kitchen foil) papel m (de) aluminio; (complement) complemento; (Fencing) florete m

fold [fəuld] n (bend, crease) pliegue m; (Agr)

redil m ▷vt doblar; (arms) cruzar; **fold up**
vi plegarse, doblarse; (business) quebrar
▷vt (map etc) plegar; **folder** n (for papers)
carpeta; (Comput) directorio; **folding** adj
(chair, bed) plegable
foliage ['fəulɪɪdʒ] n follaje m
folk [fəuk] npl gente f ▷adj popular,
folklórico; **folks** npl (family) familia sg,
parientes mpl; **folklore** ['fəuklɔː*] n
folklore m; **folk music** n música folk; **folk
song** n canción f popular
follow ['fɔləu] vt seguir ▷vi seguir;
(result) resultar; **to ~ suit** hacer lo mismo;
follow up vt (letter, offer) responder a; (case)
investigar; **follower** n (of person, belief)
partidario/a; **following** adj siguiente
▷n afición f, partidarios mpl; **follow-up** n
continuación f
fond [fɔnd] adj (memory, smile etc) cariñoso;
(hopes) ilusorio; **to be ~ of** tener cariño a;
(pastime, food) ser aficionado a
food [fuːd] n comida; **food mixer** n
batidora; **food poisoning** n intoxicación
f alimenticia; **food processor** n robot m
de cocina; **food stamp** (US) n vale m para
comida
fool [fuːl] n tonto/a; (Culin) puré m de
frutas con nata ▷vt engañar ▷vi (gen)
bromear; **fool about, fool around** vi
hacer el tonto; **foolish** adj tonto; (careless)
imprudente; **foolproof** adj (plan etc)
infalible
foot [fut] (pl **feet**) n pie m; (measure) pie m
(=304 mm); (of animal) pata ▷vt (bill) pagar;
on ~ a pie; **footage** n (Cinema) imágenes
fpl; **foot-and-mouth (disease)**
[futənd'mauθ-] n fiebre f aftosa; **football**
n balón m; (game: BRIT) fútbol m; (: US) fútbol
m americano; **footballer** n (BRIT) = **football
player**; **football match** n partido de
fútbol; **football player** n (BRIT) futbolista
mf; (US) jugador m de fútbol americano;
footbridge n puente m para peatones;
foothills npl estribaciones fpl; **foothold**
n pie m firme; **footing** n (fig) posición f; **to
lose one's footing** perder el pie; **footnote**
n nota (al pie de la página); **footpath**
n sendero; **footprint** n huella, pisada;
footstep n paso; **footwear** n calzado

○ KEYWORD

for [fɔː] prep **1** (indicating destination,
intention) para; **the train for London** el
tren con destino a or de Londres; **he left for
Rome** marchó para Roma; **he went for the
paper** fue por el periódico; **is this for me?**
¿es esto para mí?; **it's time for lunch** es la

hora de comer
2 (indicating purpose) para; **what('s it) for?**
¿para qué (es)?; **to pray for peace** rezar
por la paz
3 (on behalf of, representing): **the MP for Hove**
el diputado por Hove; **he works for the
government/a local firm** trabaja para el
gobierno/en una empresa local; **I'll ask him
for you** se
lo pediré por ti; **G for George** G de Gerona
4 (because of) por esta razón; **for fear of
being criticized** por temor a ser criticado
5 (with regard to) para; **it's cold for July** hace
frío para julio; **he has a gift for languages**
tiene don de lenguas
6 (in exchange for) por; **I sold it for £5** lo vendí
por £5; **to pay 50 pence for a ticket** pagar
50 peniques por un billete
7 (in favour of): **are you for or against us?**
¿estás con nosotros o contra nosotros?; **I'm
all for it** estoy totalmente a favor; **vote for
X** vote (a) X
8 (referring to distance): **there are roadworks
for 5 km** hay obras en 5 km; **we walked for
miles** caminamos kilómetros y kilómetros
9 (referring to time): **he was away for two
years** estuvo fuera (durante) dos años; **it
hasn't rained for 3 weeks** no ha llovido
durante or en 3 semanas; **I have known her
for years** la conozco desde hace años; **can
you do it for tomorrow?** ¿lo podrás hacer
para mañana?
10 (with infinitive clauses): **it is not for me to
decide** la decisión no es cosa mía; **it would
be best for you to leave** sería mejor que
te fueras; **there is still time for you to do
it** todavía te queda tiempo para hacerlo;
for this to be possible ... para que esto sea
posible ...
11 (in spite of) a pesar de; **for all his
complaints** a pesar de sus quejas ▷conj
(since, as: rather formal) puesto que

forbid [fə'bɪd] (pt **forbad(e)**, pp **forbidden**)
vt prohibir; **to ~ sb to do sth** prohibir a algn
hacer algo; **forbidden** pt of **forbid** ▷adj
(food, area) prohibido; (word, subject) tabú
force [fɔːs] n fuerza ▷vt forzar; (push)
meter a la fuerza; **to ~ o.s. to do** hacer un
esfuerzo por hacer; **forced** adj forzado;
forceful adj enérgico
ford [fɔːd] n vado
fore [fɔː*] n: **to come to the ~** empezar
a destacar; **forearm** n antebrazo;
forecast (pt, pp **forecast**) n pronóstico
▷vt pronosticar; **forecourt** n patio;
forefinger n (dedo) índice m; **forefront**
n: **in the forefront of** en la vanguardia de;

foreground n primer plano; **forehead** ['fɔrɪd] n frente f

foreign ['fɔrɪn] adj extranjero; (trade) exterior; (object) extraño; **foreign currency** n divisas fpl; **foreigner** n extranjero/a; **foreign exchange** n divisas fpl; **Foreign Office** (BRIT) n Ministerio de Asuntos Exteriores; **Foreign Secretary** (BRIT) n Ministro de Asuntos Exteriores

fore: foreman (irreg) n capataz m; (in construction) maestro de obras; **foremost** adj principal ▷ adv: **first and foremost** ante todo; **forename** n nombre m (de pila)

forensic [fə'rɛnsɪk] adj forense

foresee [fɔː'siː] (pt **foresaw**, pp **foreseen**) vt prever; **foreseeable** adj previsible

forest ['fɔrɪst] n bosque m; **forestry** n silvicultura

forever [fə'rɛvə*] adv para siempre; (endlessly) constantemente

foreword ['fɔːwəːd] n prefacio

forfeit ['fɔːfɪt] vt perder

forgave [fə'geɪv] pt of **forgive**

forge [fɔːdʒ] n herrería ▷ vt (signature, money) falsificar; (metal) forjar; **forger** n falsificador(a) m/f; **forgery** n falsificación f

forget [fə'gɛt] (pt **forgot**, pp **forgotten**) vt olvidar ▷ vi olvidarse; **forgetful** adj despistado

forgive [fə'gɪv] (pt **forgave**, pp **forgiven**) vt perdonar; **to ~ sb for sth** perdonar algo a algn

forgot [fə'gɒt] pt of **forget**

forgotten [fə'gɒtn] pp of **forget**

fork [fɔːk] n (for eating) tenedor m; (for gardening) horca; (of roads) bifurcación f ▷ vi (road) bifurcarse

forlorn [fə'lɔːn] adj (person) triste, melancólico; (place) abandonado; (attempt, hope) desesperado

form [fɔːm] n forma; (BRIT Scol) clase f; (document) formulario ▷ vt formar; (idea) concebir; (habit) adquirir; **in top ~** en plena forma; **to ~ a queue** hacer cola

formal ['fɔːməl] adj (offer, receipt) por escrito; (person etc) correcto; (occasion, dinner) de etiqueta; (dress) correcto; (garden) (de estilo) clásico; **formality** [-'mælɪtɪ] n (procedure) trámite m; corrección f; etiqueta

format ['fɔːmæt] n formato ▷ vt (Comput) formatear

formation [fɔː'meɪʃən] n formación f

former ['fɔːmə*] adj anterior; (earlier) antiguo; (ex) ex; **the ~ ... the latter ...** aquél ... éste ...; **formerly** adv antes

formidable ['fɔːmɪdəbl] adj formidable

formula ['fɔːmjulə] n fórmula

fort [fɔːt] n fuerte m

forthcoming [fɔːθ'kʌmɪŋ] adj próximo, venidero; (help, information) disponible; (character) comunicativo

fortieth ['fɔːtɪɪθ] adj cuadragésimo

fortify ['fɔːtɪfaɪ] vt (city) fortificar; (person) fortalecer

fortnight ['fɔːtnaɪt] (BRIT) n quince días mpl; quincena; **fortnightly** adj de cada quince días, quincenal ▷ adv cada quince días, quincenalmente

fortress ['fɔːtrɪs] n fortaleza

fortunate ['fɔːtʃənɪt] adj afortunado; **it is ~ that ...** (es una) suerte que ...; **fortunately** adv afortunadamente

fortune ['fɔːtʃən] n suerte f; (wealth) fortuna; **fortune-teller** n adivino/a

forty ['fɔːtɪ] num cuarenta

forum ['fɔːrəm] n foro

forward ['fɔːwəd] adj (movement, position) avanzado; (front) delantero; (in time) adelantado; (not shy) atrevido ▷ n (Sport) delantero ▷ vt (letter) remitir; (career) promocionar; **to move ~** avanzar; **forwarding address** n destinatario; **forward(s)** adv (hacia) adelante; **forward slash** n barra diagonal

fossil ['fɒsl] n fósil m

foster ['fɒstə*] vt (child) acoger en una familia; fomentar; **foster child** n hijo/a adoptivo/a; **foster mother** n madre f adoptiva

fought [fɔːt] pt, pp of **fight**

foul [faul] adj sucio, puerco; (weather, smell etc) asqueroso; (language) grosero; (temper) malísimo ▷ n (Sport) falta ▷ vt (dirty) ensuciar; **foul play** n (Law) muerte f violenta

found [faund] pt, pp of **find** ▷ vt fundar; **foundation** [-'deɪʃən] n (act) fundación f; (basis) base f; (also: **foundation cream**) crema base; **foundations** npl (of building) cimientos mpl

founder ['faundə*] n fundador(a) m/f ▷ vi hundirse

fountain ['fauntɪn] n fuente f; **fountain pen** n (pluma) estilográfica (SP), pluma-fuente f (LAM)

four [fɔː*] num cuatro; **on all ~s** a gatas; **four-letter word** n taco; **four-poster** n (also: **four-poster bed**) cama de columnas; **fourteen** num catorce; **fourteenth** adj decimocuarto; **fourth** num cuarto; **four-wheel drive** n tracción f a las cuatro ruedas

fowl [faul] n ave f (de corral)

fox [fɒks] n zorro ▷ vt confundir

foyer ['fɔɪeɪ] n vestíbulo

fraction ['frækʃən] n fracción f

fracture ['fræktʃə*] n fractura

fragile ['frædʒaɪl] *adj* frágil
fragment ['frægmənt] *n* fragmento
fragrance ['freɪgrəns] *n* fragancia
frail [freɪl] *adj* frágil; *(person)* débil
frame [freɪm] *n (Tech)* armazón *m*; *(of person)* cuerpo; *(of picture, door etc)* marco; *(of spectacles: also:* **~s**) montura ▷ *vt* enmarcar;
  framework *n* marco
France [frɑːns] *n* Francia
franchise ['fræntʃaɪz] *n (Pol)* derecho de votar, sufragio; *(Comm)* licencia, concesión *f*
frank [fræŋk] *adj* franco ▷ *vt* franquear; **frankly** *adv* francamente
frantic ['fræntɪk] *adj (distraught)* desesperado; *(hectic)* frenético
fraud [frɔːd] *n* fraude *m*; *(person)* impostor(a) *m/f*
fraught [frɔːt] *adj:* **~ with** lleno de
fray [freɪ] *vi* deshilacharse
freak [friːk] *n (person)* fenómeno; *(event)* suceso anormal
freckle ['frɛkl] *n* peca
free [friː] *adj* libre; *(gratis)* gratuito ▷ *vt (prisoner etc)* poner en libertad; *(jammed object)* soltar; **~ (of charge), for ~** gratis; **freedom** *n* libertad *f*; **Freefone®** *n* número gratuito; **free gift** *n* prima; **free kick** *n* tiro libre; **freelance** *adj* independiente ▷ *adv* por cuenta propia; **freely** *adv* libremente; *(liberally)* generosamente; **Freepost®** *n* porte *m* pagado; **free-range** *adj (hen, eggs)* de granja; **freeway** *(US) n* autopista; **free will** *n* libre albedrío; **of one's own free will** por su propia voluntad
freeze [friːz] *(pt* froze, *pp* frozen) *vi (weather)* helar; *(liquid, pipe, person)* helarse, congelarse ▷ *vt* helar; *(food, prices, salaries)* congelar ▷ *n* helada; *(on arms, wages)* congelación *f*; **freezer** *n* congelador *m*, freezer *m (SC)*
freezing ['friːzɪŋ] *adj* helado; **three degrees below ~** tres grados bajo cero; **freezing point** *n* punto de congelación
freight [freɪt] *n (goods)* carga; *(money charged)* flete *m*; **freight train** *(US) n* tren *m* de mercancías
French [frɛntʃ] *adj* francés/esa ▷ *n (Ling)* francés *m*; **the French** *npl* los franceses; **French bean** *n* judía verde; **French bread** *n* pan *m* francés; **French dressing** *n (Culin)* vinagreta; **French fried potatoes, French fries** *(US) npl* patatas *fpl (SP)* or papas *fpl (LAM)* fritas; **Frenchman** *(irreg) n* francés *m*; **Frenchwoman** *(irreg) n* francesa; **French stick** *n* barra de pan; **French window** *n* puerta de cristal
frenzy ['frɛnzɪ] *n* frenesí *m*

frequency ['friːkwənsɪ] *n* frecuencia
frequent [*adj* 'friːkwənt, *vb* frɪ'kwɛnt] *adj* frecuente ▷ *vt* frecuentar; **frequently** [-əntlɪ] *adv* frecuentemente, a menudo
fresh [frɛʃ] *adj* fresco; *(bread)* tierno; *(new)* nuevo; **freshen** *vi (wind, air)* soplar más recio; **freshen up** *vi (person)* arreglarse, lavarse; **fresher** *(BRIT: inf) n (Univ)* estudiante *mf* de primer año; **freshly** *adv (made, painted etc)* recién; **freshman** *(US: irreg) n* = **fresher**; **freshwater** *adj (fish)* de agua dulce
fret [frɛt] *vi* inquietarse
Fri *abbr (=* Friday*)* vier
friction ['frɪkʃən] *n* fricción *f*
Friday ['fraɪdɪ] *n* viernes *m inv*
fridge [frɪdʒ] *(BRIT) n* frigorífico *(SP)*, nevera *(SP)*, refrigerador *m (LAM)*, heladera *(RPL)*
fried [fraɪd] *adj* frito
friend [frɛnd] *n* amigo/a; **friendly** *adj* simpático; *(government)* amigo; *(place)* acogedor(a); *(match)* amistoso; **friendship** *n* amistad *f*
fries [fraɪz] *(esp US) npl* = **French fried potatoes**
frigate ['frɪgɪt] *n* fragata
fright [fraɪt] *n (terror)* terror *m*; *(scare)* susto; **to take ~** asustarse; **frighten** *vt* asustar; **frightened** *adj* asustado; **frightening** *adj* espantoso; **frightful** *adj* espantoso, horrible
frill [frɪl] *n* volante *m*
fringe [frɪndʒ] *n (BRIT: of hair)* flequillo; *(on lampshade etc)* flecos *mpl*; *(of forest etc)* borde *m*, margen *m*
Frisbee® ['frɪzbɪ] *n* frisbee® *m*
fritter ['frɪtə*] *n* buñuelo
frivolous ['frɪvələs] *adj* frívolo
fro [frəu] *see* **to**
frock [frɔk] *n* vestido
frog [frɔg] *n* rana; **frogman** *(irreg) n* hombre-rana *m*

○ **KEYWORD**

from [frɔm] *prep* **1** *(indicating starting place)* de, desde; **where do you come from?** ¿de dónde eres?; **from London to Glasgow** de Londres a Glasgow; **to escape from sth/sb** escaparse de algo/algn
2 *(indicating origin etc)* de; **a letter/ telephone call from my sister** una carta/ llamada de mi hermana; **tell him from me that ...** dígale de mi parte que ...
3 *(indicating time)* **from one o'clock to** or **until** or **till two** de(sde) la una a or hasta las dos; **from January (on)** a partir de enero

4 (*indicating distance*) de; **the hotel is 1 km from the beach** el hotel está a 1 km de la playa

5 (*indicating price, number etc*) de; **prices range from £10 to £50** los precios van desde £10 a or hasta £50; **the interest rate was increased from 9% to 10%** el tipo de interés fue incrementado de un 9% a un 10%

6 (*indicating difference*) de; **he can't tell red from green** no sabe distinguir el rojo del verde; **to be different from sb/sth** ser diferente a algn/algo

7 (*because of, on the basis of*): **from what he says** por lo que dice; **weak from hunger** debilitado por el hambre

front [frʌnt] *n* (*foremost part*) parte *f* delantera; (*of house*) fachada; (*of dress*) delantero; (*promenade: also:* **sea ~**) paseo marítimo; (*Mil, Pol, Meteorology*) frente *m*; (*fig: appearances*) apariencias *fpl* ▷ *adj* (*wheel, leg*) delantero; (*row, line*) primero; **in ~ (of)** delante (de); **front door** *n* puerta principal; **frontier** ['frʌntɪə*] *n* frontera; **front page** *n* primera plana; **front-wheel drive** *n* tracción *f* delantera

frost [frɒst] *n* helada; (*also:* **hoar~**) escarcha; **frostbite** *n* congelación *f*; **frosting** *n* (*esp us: icing*) glaseado; **frosty** *adj* (*weather*) de helada; (*welcome etc*) glacial

froth [frɒθ] *n* espuma

frown [fraun] *vi* fruncir el ceño

froze [frəuz] *pt of* **freeze**

frozen ['frəuzn] *pp of* **freeze**

fruit [fruːt] *n inv* fruta; fruto; (*fig*) fruto; resultados *mpl*; **fruit juice** *n* zumo (*sp*) or jugo (*LAM*) de fruta; **fruit machine** (*BRIT*) *n* máquina *f* tragaperras; **fruit salad** *n* macedonia (*sp*) or ensalada (*LAM*) de frutas

frustrate [frʌs'treɪt] *vt* frustrar; **frustrated** *adj* frustrado

fry [fraɪ] (*pt, pp* **fried**) *vt* freír; **small ~** gente *f* menuda; **frying pan** *n* sartén *f*

ft. *abbr* = **foot; feet**

fudge [fʌdʒ] *n* (*Culin*) caramelo blando

fuel [fjuəl] *n* (*for heating*) combustible *m*; (*coal*) carbón *m*; (*wood*) leña; (*for engine*) carburante *m*; **fuel tank** *n* depósito (de combustible)

fulfil [ful'fɪl] *vt* (*function*) cumplir con; (*condition*) satisfacer; (*wish, desire*) realizar

full [ful] *adj* lleno; (*fig*) pleno; (*complete*) completo; (*maximum*) máximo; (*information*) detallado; (*price*) íntegro; (*skirt*) amplio ▷ *adv*: **to know ~ well that** saber perfectamente que; **I'm ~ (up)** no puedo más; **~ employment** pleno empleo; **a ~ two hours** dos horas completas; **at ~ speed** a

máxima velocidad; **in ~** (*reproduce, quote*) íntegramente; **full-length** *adj* (*novel etc*) entero; (*coat*) largo; (*portrait*) de cuerpo entero; **full moon** *n* luna llena; **full-scale** *adj* (*attack, war*) en gran escala; (*model*) de tamaño natural; **full stop** *n* punto; **full-time** *adj* (*work*) de tiempo completo ▷ *adv*: **to work full-time** trabajar a tiempo completo; **fully** *adv* completamente; (*at least*) por lo menos

fumble ['fʌmbl] *vi*: **to ~ with** manejar torpemente

fume [fjuːm] *vi* (*rage*) estar furioso; **fumes** *npl* humo, gases *mpl*

fun [fʌn] *n* (*amusement*) diversión *f*; **to have ~** divertirse; **for ~** en broma; **to make ~ of** burlarse de

function ['fʌŋkʃən] *n* función *f* ▷ *vi* funcionar

fund [fʌnd] *n* fondo; (*reserve*) reserva; **funds** *npl* (*money*) fondos *mpl*

fundamental [fʌndə'mentl] *adj* fundamental

funeral ['fjuːnərəl] *n* (*burial*) entierro; (*ceremony*) funerales *mpl*; **funeral director** *n* director(a) *m/f* de pompas fúnebres; **funeral parlour** (*BRIT*) *n* funeraria

funfair ['fʌnfɛə*] (*BRIT*) *n* parque *m* de atracciones

fungus ['fʌŋgəs] (*pl* **fungi**) *n* hongo; (*mould*) moho

funnel ['fʌnl] *n* embudo; (*of ship*) chimenea

funny ['fʌnɪ] *adj* gracioso, divertido; (*strange*) curioso, raro

fur [fəː*] *n* piel *f*; (*BRIT: in kettle etc*) sarro; **fur coat** *n* abrigo de pieles

furious ['fjuərɪəs] *adj* furioso; (*effort*) violento

furnish ['fəːnɪʃ] *vt* amueblar; (*supply*) suministrar; (*information*) facilitar; **furnishings** *npl* muebles *mpl*

furniture ['fəːnɪtʃə*] *n* muebles *mpl*; **piece of ~** mueble *m*

furry ['fəːrɪ] *adj* peludo

further ['fəːðə*] *adj* (*new*) nuevo, adicional ▷ *adv* más lejos; (*more*) más; (*moreover*) además ▷ *vt* promover, adelantar; **further education** *n* educación *f* superior; **furthermore** *adv* además

furthest ['fəːðɪst] *superlative of* **far**

fury ['fjuərɪ] *n* furia

fuse [fjuːz] (*us* **fuze**) *n* fusible *m*; (*for bomb etc*) mecha ▷ *vt* (*metal*) fundir; (*fig*) fusionar ▷ *vi* fundirse; fusionarse; (*BRIT Elec*): **to ~ the lights** fundir los plomos; **fuse box** *n* caja de fusibles

fusion ['fjuːʒən] *n* fusión *f*

fuss [fʌs] *n* (*excitement*) conmoción *f*; (*trouble*) alboroto; **to make a ~** armar un lío *or* jaleo; **to make a ~ of sb** mimar a algn; **fussy** *adj* (*person*) exigente; (*too ornate*) recargado

future ['fju:tʃə*] *adj* futuro; (*coming*) venidero ▷ *n* futuro; (*prospects*) porvenir *m*; **in ~** de ahora en adelante; **futures** *npl* (*Comm*) operaciones *fpl* a término, futuros *mpl*

fuze [fju:z] (*US*) = **fuse**

fuzzy ['fʌzɪ] *adj* (*Phot*) borroso; (*hair*) muy rizado

G [dʒi:] *n* (*Mus*) sol *m*

g. *abbr* (= *gram(s)*) gr.

gadget ['gædʒɪt] *n* aparato

Gaelic ['geɪlɪk] *adj, n* (*Ling*) gaélico

gag [gæg] *n* (*on mouth*) mordaza; (*joke*) chiste *m* ▷ *vt* amordazar

gain [geɪn] *n*: **~ (in)** aumento (de); (*profit*) ganancia ▷ *vt* ganar ▷ *vi* (*watch*) adelantarse; **to ~ from/by sth** sacar provecho de algo; **to ~ on sb** ganar terreno a algn; **to ~ 3 lbs (in weight)** engordar 3 libras

gal. *abbr* = **gallon**

gala ['gɑːlə] *n* fiesta

galaxy ['gæləksɪ] *n* galaxia

gale [geɪl] *n* (*wind*) vendaval *m*

gall bladder ['gɔːl-] *n* vesícula biliar

gallery ['gælərɪ] *n* (*also*: **art ~**: *public*) pinacoteca; (: *private*) galería de arte; (*for spectators*) tribuna

gallon ['gæln] *n* galón *m* (BRIT = 4,546 *litros*, US = 3,785 *litros*)

gallop ['gæləp] *n* galope *m* ▷ *vi* galopar

gallstone ['gɔːlstəun] *n* cálculo biliario

gamble ['gæmbl] *n* (*risk*) riesgo ▷ *vt* jugar, apostar ▷ *vi* (*take a risk*) jugárselas; (*bet*) apostar; **to ~ on** apostar a; (*success etc*) contar con; **gambler** *n* jugador(a) *m/f*; **gambling** *n* juego

game [geɪm] *n* juego; (*match*) partido; (*of cards*) partida; (*Hunting*) caza ▷ *adj* (*willing*): **to be ~ for anything** atreverse a todo; **big ~** caza mayor (*contest*) juegos; (BRIT: *Scol*) deportes *mpl*; **games console** [geɪmz-] *n* consola de juegos; **game show** *n* programa *m* concurso *m*, concurso

gammon ['gæmən] *n* (*bacon*) tocino ahumado; (*ham*) jamón *m* ahumado

gang [gæŋ] *n* (*of criminals*) pandilla; (*of friends etc*) grupo; (*of workmen*) brigada

gangster ['gæŋstə*] *n* gángster *m*

gap [gæp] *n* vacío (SP), hueco (LAM);

(*in trees, traffic*) claro; (*in time*) intervalo;
(*difference*): **~ (between)** diferencia (entre)
gape [geɪp] *vi* mirar boquiabierto; (*shirt
etc*) abrirse (completamente)
gap year *n* año sabático (antes de
empezar a estudiar en la universidad)
garage ['gærɑːʒ] *n* garaje *m*; (*for repairs*)
taller *m*; **garage sale** *n* venta de objetos
usados (*en el jardín de una casa particular*)
garbage ['gɑːbɪdʒ] (*US*) *n* basura;
(*inf: nonsense*) tonterías *fpl*; **garbage
can** *n* cubo or bote *m* (*MEX*) or tacho (*SC*)
de la basura; **garbage collector** (*US*) *n*
basurero/a
garden ['gɑːdn] *n* jardín *m*; **gardens**
npl (*park*) parque *m*; **garden centre**
(*BRIT*) *n* centro de jardinería; **gardener** *n*
jardinero/a; **gardening** *n* jardinería
garlic ['gɑːlɪk] *n* ajo
garment ['gɑːmənt] *n* prenda (de vestir)
garnish ['gɑːnɪʃ] *vt* (*Culin*) aderezar
garrison ['gærɪsn] *n* guarnición *f*
gas [gæs] *n* gas *m*; (*fuel*) combustible *m*;
(*US: gasoline*) gasolina ▷ *vt* asfixiar con gas;
gas cooker (*BRIT*) *n* cocina de gas; **gas
cylinder** *n* bombona de gas; **gas fire** *n*
estufa de gas
gasket ['gæskɪt] *n* (*Aut*) junta de culata
gasoline ['gæsəliːn] (*US*) *n* gasolina
gasp [gɑːsp] *n* boqueada; (*of shock etc*)
grito sofocado ▷ *vi* (*pant*) jadear
gas: **gas pedal** *n* (*esp US*) acelerador *m*; **gas
station** (*US*) *n* gasolinera; **gas tank** (*US*) *n*
(*Aut*) depósito (de gasolina)
gate [geɪt] *n* puerta; (*iron gate*) verja
gateau ['gætəu] (*pl* **~x**) *n* tarta
gatecrash ['geɪtkræʃ] (*BRIT*) *vt* colarse en
gateway ['geɪtweɪ] *n* puerta
gather ['gæðə*] *vt* (*flowers, fruit*) coger (*SP*),
recoger; (*assemble*) reunir; (*pick up*) recoger;
(*Sewing*) fruncir; (*understand*) entender
▷ *vi* (*assemble*) reunirse; **to ~ speed**
ganar velocidad; **gathering** *n* reunión *f*,
asamblea
gauge [geɪdʒ] *n* (*instrument*) indicador *m*
▷ *vt* medir; (*fig*) juzgar
gave [geɪv] *pt of* **give**
gay [geɪ] *adj* (*homosexual*) gay; (*joyful*)
alegre; (*colour*) vivo
gaze [geɪz] *n* mirada fija ▷ *vi*: **to ~ at sth**
mirar algo fijamente
GB *abbr* = **Great Britain**
GCSE (*BRIT*) *n abbr* (= *General Certificate of
Secondary Education*) examen de reválida que se
hace a los 16 años
gear [gɪə*] *n* equipo, herramientas
fpl; (*Tech*) engranaje *m*; (*Aut*) velocidad *f*,
marcha ▷ *vt* (*fig: adapt*): **to ~ sth to** adaptar

or ajustar algo a; **top** *or* **high** (*US*)**/low ~**
cuarta/primera velocidad; **in ~** en marcha;
gear up *vi* prepararse; **gear box** *n* caja de
cambios; **gear lever** *n* palanca de cambio;
gear shift (*US*) *n* = **gear lever**; **gear stick** *n*
(*BRIT*) palanca de cambios
geese [giːs] *npl of* **goose**
gel [dʒɛl] *n* gel *m*
gem [dʒɛm] *n* piedra preciosa
Gemini ['dʒɛmɪnaɪ] *n* Géminis *m*, Gemelos
mpl
gender ['dʒɛndə*] *n* género
gene [dʒiːn] *n* gen(e)*m*
general ['dʒɛnərl] *n* general *m* ▷ *adj*
general; **in ~** en general; **general
anaesthetic** (*US* **general anesthetic**) *n*
anestesia general; **general election** *n*
elecciones *fpl* generales; **generalize** *vi*
generalizar; **generally** *adv* generalmente,
en general; **general practitioner** *n* médico
general; **general store** *n* tienda (*que vende
de todo*) (*LAM, SP*), almacén *m* (*SC, SP*)
generate ['dʒɛnəreɪt] *vt* (*Elec*) generar;
(*jobs, profits*) producir
generation [dʒɛnə'reɪʃən] *n* generación *f*
generator ['dʒɛnəreɪtə*] *n* generador *m*
generosity [dʒɛnə'rɔsɪtɪ] *n* generosidad *f*
generous ['dʒɛnərəs] *adj* generoso
genetic [dʒɪ'nɛtɪk] *adj*: **~ engineering**
ingeniería genética; **~ fingerprinting**
identificación *f* genética; **genetically
modified** *adj* transgénico; **genetics** *n*
genética
genitals ['dʒɛnɪtlz] *npl* (órganos *mpl*)
genitales *mpl*
genius ['dʒiːnɪəs] *n* genio
genome ['giːnəum] *n* genoma *m*
gent [dʒɛnt] *n abbr* (*BRIT inf*) = **gentleman**
gentle ['dʒɛntl] *adj* apacible, dulce;
(*animal*) manso; (*breeze, curve etc*) suave

 ┃ Be careful not to translate **gentle** by the
 ┃ Spanish word *gentil*.

gentleman ['dʒɛntlmən] (*irreg*) *n* señor
m; (*well-bred man*) caballero
gently ['dʒɛntlɪ] *adv* dulcemente;
suavemente
gents [dʒɛnts] *n* aseos *mpl* (de caballeros)
genuine ['dʒɛnjuɪn] *adj* auténtico;
(*person*) sincero; **genuinely** *adv*
sinceramente
geographic(al) [dʒɪə'græfɪk(l)] *adj*
geográfico
geography [dʒɪ'ɔgrəfɪ] *n* geografía
geology [dʒɪ'ɔlədʒɪ] *n* geología
geometry [dʒɪ'ɔmətrɪ] *n* geometría
geranium [dʒɪ'reɪnjəm] *n* geranio
geriatric [dʒɛrɪ'ætrɪk] *adj, n* geriátrico/a
m/f

germ [dʒə:m] n (microbe) microbio,
bacteria; (seed, fig) germen m
German ['dʒə:mən] adj alemán/ana ⊳ n
alemán/ana m/f; (Ling) alemán m; **German
measles** n rubéola
Germany ['dʒə:mənɪ] n Alemania
gesture ['dʒɛstjə*] n gesto; (symbol)
muestra

○ KEYWORD

get [gɛt] (pt, pp **got**, pp **gotten** (US)) vi
1 (become, be) ponerse, volverse; **to get old/
tired** envejecer/cansarse; **to get drunk**
emborracharse; **to get dirty** ensuciarse;
to get married casarse; **when do I get
paid?** ¿cuándo me pagan or se me paga?; **it's
getting late** se está haciendo tarde
2 (go): **to get to/from** llegar a/de; **to get
home** llegar a casa
3 (begin) empezar a; **to get to know sb**
(llegar a) conocer a algn; **I'm getting to like
him** me está empezando a gustar; **let's get
going** or **started** ¡vamos (a empezar)!
4 (modal aux vb): **you've got to do it** tienes
que hacerlo
⊳ vt **1: to get sth done** (finish) terminar
algo; (have done) mandar hacer algo; **to get
one's hair cut** cortarse el pelo; **to get the
car going** or **to go** arrancar el coche; **to get
sb to do sth** conseguir or hacer que algn
haga algo; **to get sth/sb ready** preparar
algo/a algn
2 (obtain: money, permission, results)
conseguir; (find: job, flat) encontrar;
(fetch: person, doctor) buscar; (object) ir a
buscar, traer; **to get sth for sb** conseguir
algo para algn; **get me Mr Jones, please**
(Tel) póngame (SP) or comuníqueme (LAM)
con el Sr. Jones, por favor; **can I get you a
drink?** ¿quieres algo de beber?
3 (receive: present, letter) recibir;
(acquire: reputation) alcanzar; (: prize) ganar;
what did you get for your birthday?
¿qué te regalaron por tu cumpleaños?;
how much did you get for the painting?
¿cuánto sacaste por el cuadro?
4 (catch) coger (SP), agarrar (LAM); (hit: target
etc) dar en; **to get sb by the arm/throat**
coger or agarrar a algn por el brazo/cuello;
get him! ¡cógelo! (SP), ¡atrápalo! (LAM); **the
bullet got him in the leg** la bala le dio en
la pierna
5 (take, move) llevar; **to get sth to sb** hacer
llegar algo a algn; **do you think we'll get it
through the door?** ¿crees que lo podremos
meter por la puerta?
6 (catch, take: plane, bus etc) coger (SP),

tomar (LAM); **where do I get the train for
Birmingham?** ¿dónde se coge or se toma el
tren para Birmingham?
7 (understand) entender; (hear) oír; **I've got
it!** ¡ya lo tengo!, ¡eureka!; **I don't get your
meaning** no te entiendo; **I'm sorry, I didn't
get your name** lo siento, no cogí tu nombre
8 (have, possess): **to have got** tener
get away vi marcharse; (escape) escaparse
get away with vt fus hacer impunemente
get back vi (return) volver ⊳ vt recobrar
get in vi entrar; (train) llegar; (arrive home)
volver a casa, regresar
get into vt fus entrar en; (vehicle) subir a; **to
get into a rage** enfadarse
get off vi (from train etc) bajar;
(depart: person, car) marcharse ⊳ vt (remove)
quitar ⊳ vt fus (train, bus) bajar de
get on vi (at exam etc): **how are you
getting on?** ¿cómo te va?; (agree): **to get on
(with)** llevarse bien (con) ⊳ vt fus subir a
get out vi salir; (of vehicle) bajar ⊳ vt sacar
get out of vt fus salir de; (duty etc)
escaparse de
get over vt fus (illness) recobrarse de
get through vi (Tel) (lograr) comunicarse
get up vi (rise) levantarse ⊳ vt fus subir

getaway ['gɛtəweɪ] n fuga
Ghana ['gɑ:nə] n Ghana
ghastly ['gɑ:stlɪ] adj horrible
ghetto ['gɛtəʊ] n gueto
ghost [gəʊst] n fantasma m
giant ['dʒaɪənt] n gigante mf ⊳ adj
gigantesco, gigante
gift [gɪft] n regalo; (ability) talento; **gifted**
adj dotado; **gift shop** (US **gift store**) n
tienda de regalos; **gift token, gift voucher**
n vale m canjeable por un regalo
gig [gɪg] n (inf: concert) actuación f
gigabyte ['dʒɪgəbaɪt] n gigabyte m
gigantic [dʒaɪ'gæntɪk] adj gigantesco
giggle ['gɪgl] vi reírse tontamente
gills [gɪlz] npl (of fish) branquias fpl, agallas
fpl
gilt [gɪlt] adj, n dorado
gimmick ['gɪmɪk] n truco
gin [dʒɪn] n ginebra
ginger ['dʒɪndʒə*] n jengibre m
gipsy ['dʒɪpsɪ] n = **gypsy**
giraffe [dʒɪ'rɑ:f] n jirafa
girl [gə:l] n (small) niña; (young woman)
chica, joven f, muchacha; (daughter) hija;
an English ~ una (chica) inglesa; **girl band**
n girl band m (grupo musical de chicas);
girlfriend n (of girl) amiga; (of boy) novia;
Girl Scout (US) n = **Girl Guide**
gist [dʒɪst] n lo esencial

give [gɪv] (*pt* **gave**, *pp* **given**) *vt* dar; (*deliver*) entregar; (*as gift*) regalar ▷*vi* (*break*) romperse; (*stretch: fabric*) dar de sí; **to ~ sb sth**, **~ sth to sb** dar algo a algn; **give away** *vt* (*give free*) regalar; (*betray*) traicionar; (*disclose*) revelar; **give back** *vt* devolver; **give in** *vi* ceder ▷*vt* entregar; **give out** *vt* distribuir; **give up** *vi* rendirse, darse por vencido ▷*vt* renunciar a; **to give up smoking** dejar de fumar; **to give o.s. up** entregarse

given ['gɪvn] *pp of* **give** ▷*adj* (*fixed: time, amount*) determinado ▷*conj*: **~ (that) ...** dado (que) ...; **~ the circumstances ...** dadas las circunstancias ...

glacier ['glæsɪə*] *n* glaciar *m*

glad [glæd] *adj* contento; **gladly** ['-lɪ] *adv* con mucho gusto

glamour ['glæmər] (*US* **glamor**) *n* encanto, atractivo; **glamorous** *adj* encantador(a), atractivo

glance [glɑːns] *n* ojeada, mirada ▷*vi*: **to ~ at** echar una ojeada a

gland [glænd] *n* glándula

glare [glɛə*] *n* (*of anger*) mirada feroz; (*of light*) deslumbramiento, brillo; **to be in the ~ of publicity** ser el foco de la atención pública ▷*vi* deslumbrar; **to ~ at** mirar con odio a; **glaring** *adj* (*mistake*) manifiesto

glass [glɑːs] *n* vidrio, cristal *m*; (*for drinking*) vaso; (: *with stem*) copa; **glasses** *npl* (*spectacles*) gafas *fpl*

glaze [gleɪz] *vt* (*window*) poner cristales a; (*pottery*) vidriar ▷*n* vidriado

gleam [gliːm] *vi* brillar

glen [glɛn] *n* cañada

glide [glaɪd] *vi* deslizarse; (*Aviat: birds*) planear; **glider** *n* (*Aviat*) planeador *m*

glimmer ['glɪmə*] *n* luz *f* tenue; (*of interest*) muestra; (*of hope*) rayo

glimpse [glɪmps] *n* vislumbre *m* ▷*vt* vislumbrar, entrever

glint [glɪnt] *vi* centellear

glisten ['glɪsn] *vi* relucir, brillar

glitter ['glɪtə*] *vi* relucir, brillar

global ['gləubl] *adj* mundial; **globalization** *n* globalización *f*; **global warming** *n* (re)calentamiento global *or* de la tierra

globe [gləub] *n* globo; (*model*) globo terráqueo

gloom [gluːm] *n* oscuridad *f*; (*sadness*) tristeza; **gloomy** *adj* (*dark*) oscuro; (*sad*) triste; (*pessimistic*) pesimista

glorious ['glɔːrɪəs] *adj* glorioso; (*weather etc*) magnífico

glory ['glɔːrɪ] *n* gloria

gloss [glɔs] *n* (*shine*) brillo; (*paint*) pintura de aceite

glossary ['glɔsərɪ] *n* glosario

glossy ['glɔsɪ] *adj* lustroso; (*magazine*) de lujo

glove [glʌv] *n* guante *m*; **glove compartment** *n* (*Aut*) guantera

glow [gləu] *vi* brillar

glucose ['gluːkəus] *n* glucosa

glue [gluː] *n* goma (de pegar), cemento ▷*vt* pegar

GM *adj abbr* (= *genetically modified*) transgénico

gm *abbr* (= *gram*) g

GMO *n abbr* (= *genetically modified organism*) organismo transgénico

GMT *abbr* (= *Greenwich Mean Time*) GMT

gnaw [nɔː] *vt* roer

go [gəu] (*pt* **went**, *pp* **gone**, *pl* **~es**) *vi* ir; (*travel*) viajar; (*depart*) irse, marcharse; (*work*) funcionar, marchar; (*be sold*) venderse; (*time*) pasar; (*fit, suit*): **to ~ with** hacer juego con; (*become*) ponerse; (*break etc*) estropearse, romperse ▷*n*: **to have a ~ (at)** probar suerte (con); **to be on the ~** no parar; **whose ~ is it?** ¿a quién le toca?; **he's ~ing to do it** va a hacerlo; **to ~ for a walk** ir de paseo; **to ~ dancing** ir a bailar; **how did it ~?** ¿qué tal salió *or* resultó?, ¿cómo ha ido?; **to ~ round the back** pasar por detrás; **go ahead** *vi* seguir adelante; **go away** *vi* irse, marcharse; **go back** *vi* volver; **go by** *vi* (*time*) pasar ▷*vt fus* guiarse por; **go down** *vi* bajar; (*ship*) hundirse; (*sun*) ponerse ▷*vt fus* bajar; **go for** *vt fus* (*fetch*) ir por; (*like*) gustar; (*attack*) atacar; **go in** *vi* entrar; **go into** *vt fus* entrar en; (*investigate*) investigar; (*embark on*) dedicarse a; **go off** *vi* irse, marcharse; (*food*) pasarse; (*explode*) estallar; (*event*) realizarse ▷*vt fus* dejar de gustar; **I'm going off him/the idea** ya no me gusta tanto él/la idea; **go on** *vi* (*continue*) seguir, continuar; (*happen*) pasar, ocurrir; **to go on doing sth** seguir haciendo algo; **go out** *vi* salir; (*fire, light*) apagarse; **go over** *vi* (*ship*) zozobrar ▷*vt fus* (*check*) revisar; **go past** *vi*, *vt fus* pasar; **go round** *vi* (*circulate: news, rumour*) correr; (*suffice*) alcanzar, bastar; (*revolve*) girar, dar vueltas; (*visit*): **to go round (to sb's)** pasar a ver (a algn); **to go round (by)** (*make a detour*) dar la vuelta (por); **go through** *vt fus* (*town etc*) atravesar; **go up** *vi*, *vt fus* subir; **go with** *vt fus* (*accompany*) ir con, acompañar a; **go without** *vt fus* pasarse sin

go-ahead ['gəuəhɛd] *adj* (*person*) dinámico; (*firm*) innovador(a) ▷*n* luz *f* verde

goal [gəul] *n* meta; (*score*) gol *m*;

goalkeeper n portero; **goal-post** n poste m (de la portería)

goat [gəut] n cabra

gobble ['gɔbl] vt (also: ~ **down**, ~ **up**) tragarse, engullir

God [gɔd] n Dios m; **godchild** n ahijado/a; **goddaughter** n ahijada; **goddess** n diosa; **godfather** n padrino; **godmother** n madrina; **godson** n ahijado

goggles ['gɔglz] npl gafas fpl

going ['gəuɪŋ] n (conditions) estado del terreno ▷ adj: **the ~ rate** la tarifa corriente or en vigor

gold [gəuld] n oro ▷ adj de oro; **golden** adj (made of gold) de oro; (gold in colour) dorado; **goldfish** n pez m de colores; **goldmine** n (also fig) mina de oro; **gold-plated** adj chapado en oro

golf [gɔlf] n golf m; **golf ball** n (for game) pelota de golf; (on typewriter) esfera; **golf club** n club m de golf; (stick) palo (de golf); **golf course** n campo de golf; **golfer** n golfista mf

gone [gɔn] pp of **go**

gong [gɔŋ] n gong m

good [gud] adj bueno; (pleasant) agradable; (kind) bueno, amable; (well-behaved) educado ▷ n bien m, provecho; **goods** npl (Comm) mercancías fpl; **~!** ¡qué bien!; **to be ~ at** tener aptitud para; **to be ~ for** servir para; **it's ~ for you** te hace bien; **would you be ~ enough to ...?** ¿podría hacerme el favor de ...?, ¿sería tan amable de ...?; **a ~ deal (of)** mucho; **a ~ many** muchos; **to make ~** reparar; **it's no ~ complaining** no vale la pena (de) quejarse; **for ~** para siempre, definitivamente; **~ morning/afternoon!** ¡buenos días/buenas tardes!; **~ evening!** ¡buenas noches!; **~ night!** ¡buenas noches!

goodbye [gud'baɪ] excl ¡adiós!; **to say ~ (to)** (person) despedirse (de)

good: Good Friday n Viernes m Santo; **good-looking** adj guapo; **good-natured** adj amable, simpático; **goodness** n (of person) bondad f; **for goodness sake!** ¡por Dios!; **goodness gracious!** ¡Dios mío!; **goods train** (BRIT) n tren m de mercancías; **goodwill** n buena voluntad f

Google® ['gu:gəl] n Google® m ▷ vi hacer búsquedas en Internet ▷ vt buscar información en Internet sobre

goose [gu:s] (pl **geese**) n ganso, oca

gooseberry ['guzbərɪ] n grosella espinosa; **to play ~** hacer de carabina

goose bumps, goose pimples npl carne f de gallina

gorge [gɔ:dʒ] n barranco ▷ vr: **to ~ o.s. (on)** atracarse (de)

gorgeous ['gɔ:dʒəs] adj (thing) precioso; (weather) espléndido; (person) guapísimo

gorilla [gə'rɪlə] n gorila m

gosh [gɔʃ] (inf) excl ¡cielos!

gospel ['gɔspl] n evangelio

gossip ['gɔsɪp] n (scandal) cotilleo, chismes mpl; (chat) charla; (scandalmonger) cotilla m/f, chismoso/a ▷ vi cotillear; **gossip column** n ecos mpl de sociedad

got [gɔt] pt, pp of **get**

gotten (US) ['gɔtn] pp of **get**

gourmet ['guəmeɪ] n gastrónomo/a m/f

govern ['gʌvən] vt gobernar; (influence) dominar; **government** n gobierno; **governor** n gobernador(a) m/f; (of school etc) miembro del consejo; (of jail) director(a) m/f

gown [gaun] n traje m; (of teacher, BRIT: of judge) toga

G.P. n abbr = **general practitioner**

grab [græb] vt coger (SP), agarrar (LAM), arrebatar ▷ vi: **to ~ at** intentar agarrar

grace [greɪs] n gracia ▷ vt honrar; (adorn) adornar; **5 days' ~** un plazo de 5 días; **graceful** adj grácil, ágil; (style, shape) elegante, gracioso; **gracious** ['greɪʃəs] adj amable

grade [greɪd] n (quality) clase f, calidad f; (in hierarchy) grado; (Scol: mark) nota; (US: school class) curso ▷ vt clasificar; **grade crossing** (US) n paso a nivel; **grade school** (US) n escuela primaria

gradient ['greɪdɪənt] n pendiente f

gradual ['grædjuəl] adj paulatino; **gradually** adv paulatinamente

graduate [n 'grædjuɪt, vb 'grædjueɪt] n (US: of high school) graduado/a; (of university) licenciado/a ▷ vi graduarse; licenciarse; **graduation** [-'eɪʃən] n (ceremony) entrega del título

graffiti [grə'fi:tɪ] n pintadas fpl

graft [gra:ft] n (Agr, Med) injerto; (BRIT: inf) trabajo duro; (bribery) corrupción f ▷ vt injertar

grain [greɪn] n (single particle) grano; (corn) granos mpl, cereales mpl; (of wood) fibra

gram [græm] n gramo

grammar ['græmə*] n gramática; **grammar school** (BRIT) n ≈ instituto de segunda enseñanza, liceo (SP)

gramme [græm] n = **gram**

gran [græn] (inf) n (BRIT) abuelita

grand [grænd] adj magnífico, imponente; (wonderful) estupendo; (gesture etc) grandioso; **grandad** n = **granddad**; **grandchild** (pl **grandchildren**) n nieto/a m/f; **granddad** (inf) n yayo, abuelito;

granddaughter *n* nieta; **grandfather** *n*
abuelo; **grandma** (*inf*) *n* yaya, abuelita;
grandmother *n* abuela; **grandpa** (*inf*) *n* =
granddad; **grandparents** *npl* abuelos *mpl*;
grand piano *n* piano de cola; **Grand Prix**
['grã:'pri:] *n* (*Aut*) gran premio, Grand Prix
m; **grandson** *n* nieto
granite ['grænɪt] *n* granito
granny ['grænɪ] (*inf*) *n* abuelita, yaya
grant [grɑːnt] *vt* (*concede*) conceder;
(*admit*) reconocer ▷ *n* (*Scol*) beca; (*Admin*)
subvención *f*; **to take sth/sb for ~ed** dar
algo por sentado/no hacer ningún caso
a algn
grape [greɪp] *n* uva
grapefruit ['greɪpfruːt] *n* pomelo (*SP*, *SC*),
toronja (*LAM*)
graph [grɑːf] *n* gráfica; **graphic** ['græfɪk]
adj gráfico; **graphics** *n* artes *fpl* gráficas
▷ *npl* (*drawings*) dibujos *mpl*
grasp [grɑːsp] *vt* agarrar, asir; (*understand*)
comprender ▷ *n* (*grip*) asimiento;
(*understanding*) comprensión *f*
grass [grɑːs] *n* hierba; (*lawn*) césped *m*;
grasshopper *n* saltamontes *m inv*
grate [greɪt] *n* parrilla de chimenea
▷ *vi*: **to ~ (on)** chirriar (sobre) ▷ *vt* (*Culin*)
rallar
grateful ['greɪtful] *adj* agradecido
grater ['greɪtə*] *n* rallador *m*
gratitude ['grætɪtjuːd] *n* agradecimiento
grave [greɪv] *n* tumba ▷ *adj* serio, grave
gravel ['grævl] *n* grava
gravestone ['greɪvstəun] *n* lápida
graveyard ['greɪvjɑːd] *n* cementerio
gravity ['grævɪtɪ] *n* gravedad *f*
gravy ['greɪvɪ] *n* salsa de carne
gray [greɪ] *adj* = **grey**
graze [greɪz] *vi* pacer ▷ *vt* (*touch lightly*)
rozar; (*scrape*) raspar ▷ *n* (*Med*) abrasión *f*
grease [griːs] *n* (*fat*) grasa; (*lubricant*)
lubricante *m* ▷ *vt* engrasar; lubrificar;
greasy *adj* grasiento
great [greɪt] *adj* grande; (*inf*) magnífico,
estupendo; **Great Britain** *n* Gran Bretaña;
great-grandfather *n* bisabuelo; **great-grandmother** *n* bisabuela; **greatly** *adv*
muy; (*with verb*) mucho
Greece [griːs] *n* Grecia
greed [griːd] *n* (*also*: **~iness**) codicia,
avaricia; (*for food*) gula; (*for power etc*) avidez
f; **greedy** *adj* avaro; (*for food*) glotón/ona
Greek [griːk] *adj* griego ▷ *n* griego/a;
(*Ling*) griego
green [griːn] *adj* (*also Pol*) verde;
(*inexperienced*) novato ▷ *n* verde *m*; (*stretch
of grass*) césped *m*; (*Golf*) green; *m* **greens**
npl (*vegetables*) verduras *fpl*; **green card**

n (*Aut*) carta verde; (*US*: *work permit*)
*permiso de trabajo para los extranjeros en
EE. UU.*; **greengage** *n* (ciruela) claudia;
greengrocer (*BRIT*) *n* verdulero/a;
greenhouse *n* invernadero; **greenhouse
effect** *n* efecto invernadero
Greenland ['griːnlənd] *n* Groenlandia
green salad *n* ensalada *f* (*de lechuga,
pepino, pimiento verde, etc*)
greet [griːt] *vt* (*welcome*) dar la bienvenida
a; (*receive*: *news*) recibir; **greeting** *n*
(*welcome*) bienvenida; **greeting(s) card** *n*
tarjeta de felicitación
grew [gruː] *pt of* **grow**
grey [greɪ] (*US* **gray**) *adj* gris; (*weather*)
sombrío; **grey-haired** *adj* canoso;
greyhound *n* galgo
grid [grɪd] *n* reja; (*Elec*) red *f*; **gridlock** *n*
(*traffic jam*) retención *f*
grief [griːf] *n* dolor *m*, pena
grievance ['griːvəns] *n* motivo de queja,
agravio
grieve [griːv] *vi* afligirse, acongojarse ▷ *vt*
dar pena a; **to ~ for** llorar por
grill [grɪl] *n* (*on cooker*) parrilla; (*also*: **mixed
~**) parrillada ▷ *vt* (*BRIT*) asar a la parrilla;
(*inf*: *question*) interrogar
grille [grɪl] *n* reja; (*Aut*) rejilla
grim [grɪm] *adj* (*place*) sombrío; (*situation*)
triste; (*person*) ceñudo
grime [graɪm] *n* mugre *f*, suciedad *f*
grin [grɪn] *n* sonrisa abierta ▷ *vi* sonreír
abiertamente
grind [graɪnd] (*pt*, *pp* **ground**) *vt* (*coffee,
pepper etc*) moler; (*US*: *meat*) picar; (*make
sharp*) afilar ▷ *n* (*work*) rutina
grip [grɪp] *n* (*hold*) asimiento; (*control*)
control *m*, dominio; (*of tyre etc*): **to have a
good/bad ~** agarrarse bien/mal; (*handle*)
asidero; (*holdall*) maletín *m* ▷ *vt* agarrar;
(*viewer, reader*) fascinar; **to get to ~s with**
enfrentarse con; **gripping** *adj* absorbente
grit [grɪt] *n* gravilla; (*courage*) valor *m* ▷ *vt*
(*road*) poner gravilla en; **to ~ one's teeth**
apretar los dientes
grits [grɪts] (*US*) *npl* maíz *msg* a medio
moler
groan [grəun] *n* gemido; quejido ▷ *vi*
gemir; quejarse
grocer ['grəusə*] *n* tendero (de
ultramarinos (*SP*)); **groceries** *npl*
comestibles *mpl*; **grocer's (shop)** *n* tienda
de comestibles *or* (*MEX*, *CAM*) abarrotes,
almacén (*SC*); **grocery** *n* (*shop*) tienda de
ultramarinos
groin [grɔɪn] *n* ingle *f*
groom [gruːm] *n* mozo/a de cuadra;
(*also*: **bride~**) novio ▷ *vt* (*horse*) almohazar;

(*fig*): **to ~ sb for** preparar a algn para; **well-~ed** de buena presencia

groove [gru:v] *n* ranura, surco

grope [grəup] *vi*: **to ~ for** buscar a tientas

gross [grəus] *adj* (*neglect, injustice*) grave; (*vulgar: behaviour*) grosero; (: *appearance*) de mal gusto; (*Comm*) bruto; **grossly** *adv* (*greatly*) enormemente

grotesque [grə'tɛsk] *adj* grotesco

ground [graund] *pt, pp of* **grind** ▷ *n* suelo, tierra; (*Sport*) campo, terreno; (*reason: gen pl*) causa, razón *f*; (*us: also*: **~ wire**) tierra ▷ *vt* (*plane*) mantener en tierra; (*us Elec*) conectar con tierra; **grounds** *npl* (*of coffee etc*) poso; (*gardens etc*) jardines *mpl*, parque *m*; **on the ~** en el suelo; **to the ~** al suelo; **to gain/lose ~** ganar/perder terreno; **ground floor** *n* (*BRIT*) planta baja; **groundsheet** (*BRIT*) *n* tela impermeable; suelo; **groundwork** *n* preparación *f*

group [gru:p] *n* grupo; (*musical*) conjunto ▷ *vt* (*also*: **~ together**) agrupar ▷ *vi* (*also*: **~ together**) agruparse

grouse [graus] *n inv* (*bird*) urogallo ▷ *vi* (*complain*) quejarse

grovel ['grɔvl] *vi* (*fig*): **to ~ before** humillarse ante

grow [grəu] (*pt* **grew**, *pp* **grown**) *vi* crecer; (*increase*) aumentar; (*expand*) desarrollarse; (*become*) volverse; **to ~ rich/weak** enriquecerse/debilitarse ▷ *vt* cultivar; (*hair, beard*) dejar crecer; **grow on** *vt fus*: **that painting is growing on me** ese cuadro me gusta cada vez más; **grow up** *vi* crecer, hacerse hombre/mujer

growl [graul] *vi* gruñir

grown [grəun] *pp of* **grow**; **grown-up** *n* adulto/a, mayor *mf*

growth [grəuθ] *n* crecimiento, desarrollo; (*what has grown*) brote *m*; (*Med*) tumor *m*

grub [grʌb] *n* larva, gusano; (*inf: food*) comida

grubby ['grʌbɪ] *adj* sucio, mugriento

grudge [grʌdʒ] *n* (*motivo de*) rencor *m* ▷ *vt*: **to ~ sb sth** dar algo a algn de mala gana; **to bear sb a ~** guardar rencor a algn

gruelling ['gruəlɪŋ] (*us* **grueling**) *adj* penoso, duro

gruesome ['gru:səm] *adj* horrible

grumble ['grʌmbl] *vi* refunfuñar, quejarse

grumpy ['grʌmpɪ] *adj* gruñón/ona

grunt [grʌnt] *vi* gruñir

guarantee [gærən'ti:] *n* garantía ▷ *vt* garantizar

guard [gɑ:d] *n* (*squad*) guardia; (*one man*) guardia *mf*; (*BRIT Rail*) jefe *m* de tren; (*on machine*) dispositivo de seguridad; (*also*: **fire~**) rejilla de protección ▷ *vt* guardar;

(*prisoner*) vigilar; **to be on one's ~** estar alerta; **guardian** *n* guardián/ana *m/f*; (*of minor*) tutor(a) *m/f*

guerrilla [gə'rɪlə] *n* guerrillero/a

guess [gɛs] *vi* adivinar; (*us*) suponer ▷ *vt* adivinar; suponer ▷ *n* suposición *f*, conjetura; **to take** *or* **have a ~** tratar de adivinar

guest [gɛst] *n* invitado/a; (*in hotel*) huésped *mf*; **guest house** *n* casa de huéspedes, pensión *f*; **guest room** *n* cuarto de huéspedes

guidance ['gaɪdəns] *n* (*advice*) consejos *mpl*

guide [gaɪd] *n* (*person*) guía *mf*; (*book, fig*) guía; (*also*: **Girl ~**) guía ▷ *vt* (*round museum etc*) guiar; (*lead*) conducir; (*direct*) orientar; **guidebook** *n* guía; **guide dog** *n* perro *m* guía; **guided tour** *n* visita *f* con guía; **guidelines** *npl* (*advice*) directrices *fpl*

guild [gɪld] *n* gremio

guilt [gɪlt] *n* culpabilidad *f*; **guilty** *adj* culpable

guinea pig ['gɪnɪ-] *n* cobaya; (*fig*) conejillo de Indias

guitar [gɪ'tɑ:*] *n* guitarra; **guitarist** *n* guitarrista *m/f*

gulf [gʌlf] *n* golfo; (*abyss*) abismo

gull [gʌl] *n* gaviota

gulp [gʌlp] *vi* tragar saliva ▷ *vt* (*also*: **~ down**) tragarse

gum [gʌm] *n* (*Anat*) encía; (*glue*) goma, cemento; (*sweet*) caramelo de goma; (*also*: **chewing-~**) chicle *m* ▷ *vt* pegar con goma

gun [gʌn] *n* (*small*) pistola, revólver *m*; (*shotgun*) escopeta; (*rifle*) fusil *m*; (*cannon*) cañón *m*; **gunfire** *n* disparos *mpl*; **gunman** (*irreg*) *n* pistolero; **gunpoint** *n*: **at gunpoint** a mano armada; **gunpowder** *n* pólvora; **gunshot** *n* escopetazo

gush [gʌʃ] *vi* salir a raudales; (*person*) deshacerse en efusiones

gust [gʌst] *n* (*of wind*) ráfaga

gut [gʌt] *n* intestino; **guts** *npl* (*Anat*) tripas *fpl*; (*courage*) valor *m*

gutter ['gʌtə*] *n* (*of roof*) canalón *m*; (*in street*) cuneta

guy [gaɪ] *n* (*also*: **~rope**) cuerda; (*inf: man*) tío (*sp*), tipo; (*figure*) monigote *m*

Guy Fawkes' Night [gaɪ'fɔ:ks-] *n ver abajo*

GUY FAWKES' NIGHT

La noche del cinco de noviembre, **Guy Fawkes' Night**, se celebra en el Reino Unido el fracaso de la conspiración de la pólvora ("Gunpowder Plot"), un intento

fallido de volar el parlamento de Jaime
I en 1605. Esa noche se lanzan fuegos
artificiales y se hacen hogueras en las
que se queman unos muñecos de trapo
que representan a **Guy Fawkes**, uno
de los cabecillas de la revuelta. Días
antes, los niños tienen por costumbre
pedir a los transeúntes "a penny for the
guy", dinero que emplean en comprar
cohetes y petardos.

gym [dʒɪm] n gimnasio; **gymnasium** n
gimnasio mf; **gymnast** n gimnasta mf;
gymnastics n gimnasia; **gym shoes** npl
zapatillas fpl (de deporte)
gynaecologist [gaɪnɪ'kɔlədʒɪst] (US
gynecologist) n ginecólogo/a
gypsy ['dʒɪpsɪ] n gitano/a

haberdashery [hæbə'dæʃərɪ] (BRIT) n
mercería
habit ['hæbɪt] n hábito, costumbre f; (drug
habit) adicción f; (costume) hábito
habitat ['hæbɪtæt] n hábitat m
hack [hæk] vt (cut) cortar; (slice) tajar ▷ n
(pej: writer) escritor(a) m/f a sueldo; **hacker**
n (Comput) pirata mf informático/a
had [hæd] pt, pp of **have**
haddock ['hædək] (pl ~ or ~s) n especie de
merluza
hadn't ['hædnt] = **had not**
haemorrhage ['hɛmərɪdʒ] (US
hemorrhage) n hemorragia
haemorrhoids ['hɛmərɔɪdz] (US
hemorrhoids) npl hemorroides fpl
haggle ['hægl] vi regatear
Hague [heɪg] n: The ~ La Haya
hail [heɪl] n granizo; (fig) lluvia ▷ vt
saludar; (taxi) llamar a; (acclaim) aclamar
▷ vi granizar; **hailstone** n (piedra de)
granizo
hair [hɛə*] n pelo, cabellos mpl; (one hair)
pelo, cabello; (on legs etc) vello; **to do one's
~** arreglarse el pelo; **to have grey ~** tener
canas fpl; **hairband** n cinta; **hairbrush** n
cepillo (para el pelo); **haircut** n corte m (de
pelo); **hairdo** n peinado; **hairdresser** n
peluquero/a; **hairdresser's** n peluquería;
hair dryer n secador m de pelo; **hair gel**
n fijador; **hair spray** n laca; **hairstyle**
n peinado; **hairy** adj peludo; velludo;
(inf: frightening) espeluznante
hake [heɪk] (pl ~ or ~s) n merluza
half [hɑːf] (pl **halves**) n mitad f; (of beer)
≈ caña (SP), media pinta; (Rail, Bus) billete
m de niño ▷ adj medio ▷ adv medio, a
medias; **two and a ~** dos y media; **~ a dozen**
media docena; **~ a pound** media libra; **to
cut sth in ~** cortar algo por la mitad; **half
board** n (BRIT: in hotel) media pensión; **half-**

brother n hermanastro; **half day** n medio día m, media jornada; **half fare** n medio pasaje m; **half-hearted** adj indiferente, poco entusiasta; **half-hour** n media hora; **half-price** adj, adv a mitad de precio; **half term** (BRIT) n (Scol) vacaciones de mediados del trimestre; **half-time** n descanso; **halfway** adv a medio camino; **halfway through** a mitad de

hall [hɔːl] n (for concerts) sala; (entrance way) hall m; vestíbulo

hallmark ['hɔːlmɑːk] n sello

hallo [hə'ləʊ] excl = **hello**

hall of residence (BRIT) n residencia

Hallowe'en [hæləʊ'iːn] n víspera de Todos los Santos

⬤ **HALLOWE'EN**
⬤
⬤ La tradición anglosajona dice que en
⬤ la noche del 31 de octubre, **Hallowe'en**,
⬤ víspera de Todos los Santos, es posible
⬤ ver a brujas y fantasmas. En este día los
⬤ niños se disfrazan y van de puerta en
⬤ puerta llevando un farol hecho con una
⬤ calabaza en forma de cabeza humana.
⬤ Cuando se les abre la puerta gritan "trick
⬤ or treat", amenazando con gastar una
⬤ broma a quien no les dé golosinas o algo
⬤ de calderilla.

hallucination [həluːsɪ'neɪʃən] n alucinación f

hallway ['hɔːlweɪ] n vestíbulo

halo ['heɪləʊ] n (of saint) halo, aureola

halt [hɔːlt] n (stop) alto, parada ▷ vt parar; interrumpir ▷ vi pararse

halve [hɑːv] vt partir por la mitad

halves [hɑːvz] npl of **half**

ham [hæm] n jamón m (cocido)

hamburger ['hæmbəːgə*] n hamburguesa

hamlet ['hæmlɪt] n aldea

hammer ['hæmə*] n martillo ▷ vt (nail) clavar; (force): **to ~ an idea into sb/a message home** meter una idea en la cabeza a algn/machacar una idea ▷ vi dar golpes

hammock ['hæmək] n hamaca

hamper ['hæmpə*] vt estorbar ▷ n cesto

hamster ['hæmstə*] n hámster m

hamstring ['hæmstrɪŋ] n (Anat) tendón m de la corva

hand [hænd] n mano f; (of clock) aguja; (writing) letra; (worker) obrero ▷ vt dar, pasar; **to give** or **lend sb a ~** echar una mano a algn, ayudar a algn; **at ~** a mano; **in ~** (time) libre; (job etc) entre manos; **on ~** (person, services) a mano, al alcance; **to ~** (information

etc) a mano; **on the one ~ ..., on the other ~ ...** por una parte ... por otra (parte) ...; **hand down** vt pasar, bajar; (tradition) transmitir; (heirloom) dejar en herencia; (us: sentence, verdict) imponer; **hand in** vt entregar; **hand out** vt distribuir; **hand over** vt (deliver) entregar; **handbag** n bolso (SP), cartera (LAM), bolsa (MEX); **hand baggage** n = **hand luggage**; **handbook** n manual m; **handbrake** n freno de mano; **handcuffs** npl esposas fpl; **handful** n puñado

handicap ['hændɪkæp] n minusvalía; (disadvantage) desventaja; (Sport) handicap m ▷ vt estorbar; **to be mentally ~ped** ser mentalmente m/f discapacitado; **to be physically ~ped** ser minusválido/a

handkerchief ['hæŋkətʃɪf] n pañuelo

handle ['hændl] n (of door etc) tirador m; (of cup etc) asa; (of knife etc) mango; (for winding) manivela ▷ vt (touch) tocar; (deal with) encargarse de; (treat: people) manejar; **"~ with care"** "(manéjese) con cuidado"; **to fly off the ~** perder los estribos; **handlebar(s)** n(pl) manillar m

hand: hand luggage n equipaje m de mano; **handmade** adj hecho a mano; **handout** n (money etc) limosna; (leaflet) folleto; **hands-free** adj (phone) manos libres inv; **hands-free kit** n manos libres m inv

handsome ['hænsəm] adj guapo; (building) bello; (fig: profit) considerable

handwriting ['hændraɪtɪŋ] n letra

handy ['hændɪ] adj (close at hand) a la mano; (tool etc) práctico; (skilful) hábil, diestro

hang [hæŋ] (pt, pp **hung**) vt colgar; (criminal: pt, pp hanged) ahorcar ▷ vi (painting, coat etc) colgar; (hair, drapery) caer; **to get the ~ of sth** (inf) lograr dominar algo; **hang about** or **around** vi haraganear; **hang down** vi colgar, pender; **hang on** vi (wait) esperar; **hang out** vt (washing) tender, colgar ▷ vi (inf: live) vivir; (spend time) pasar el rato; **to hang out of sth** colgar fuera de algo; **hang round** vi = **hang around**; **hang up** vi (Tel) colgar ▷ vt colgar

hanger ['hæŋə*] n percha

hang-gliding ['-glaɪdɪŋ] n vuelo libre

hangover ['hæŋəʊvə*] n (after drinking) resaca

hankie, hanky ['hæŋkɪ] n abbr = **handkerchief**

happen ['hæpən] vi suceder, ocurrir; (chance): **he ~ed to hear/see** dió la casualidad de que oyó/vió; **as it ~s** da la casualidad de que

happily ['hæpɪlɪ] adv (luckily)

h

afortunadamente; (*cheerfully*) alegremente
happiness ['hæpɪnɪs] *n* felicidad *f*;
(*cheerfulness*) alegría
happy ['hæpɪ] *adj* feliz; (*cheerful*) alegre; **to
be ~ (with)** estar contento (con); **to be ~ to
do** estar encantado de hacer; **~ birthday!**
¡feliz cumpleaños!
harass ['hærəs] *vt* acosar, hostigar;
harassment *n* persecución *f*
harbour ['hɑːbə*] (*us* **harbor**) *n* puerto
▷ *vt* (*fugitive*) dar abrigo a; (*hope etc*) abrigar
hard [hɑːd] *adj* duro; (*difficult*) difícil; (*work*)
arduo; (*person*) severo; (*fact*) innegable ▷ *adv*
(*work*) mucho, duro; (*think*) profundamente;
to look ~ at clavar los ojos en; **to try ~**
esforzarse; **no ~ feelings!** ¡sin rencor(es)!;
to be ~ of hearing ser duro de oído; **to
be ~ done by** ser tratado injustamente;
hardback *n* libro en cartoné; **hardboard**
n aglomerado *m* (*de madera*); **hard disk** *n*
(*Comput*) disco duro or rígido; **harden** *vt*
endurecer; (*fig*) curtir ▷ *vi* endurecerse;
curtirse
hardly ['hɑːdlɪ] *adv* apenas; **~ ever** casi
nunca
hard: hardship *n* privación *f*; **hard
shoulder** (*BRIT*) *n* (*Aut*) arcén *m*; **hard-up**
(*inf*) *adj* sin un duro (*SP*), pelado, sin un
centavo (*MEX*), pato (*SC*); **hardware** *n*
ferretería; (*Comput*) hardware *m*; (*Mil*)
armamento; **hardware shop** (*us* **hardware
store**) ferretería; **hard-working** *adj*
trabajador(a)
hardy ['hɑːdɪ] *adj* fuerte; (*plant*) resistente
hare [hɛə*] *n* liebre *f*
harm [hɑːm] *n* daño, mal *m* ▷ *vt* (*person*)
hacer daño a; (*health, interests*) perjudicar;
(*thing*) dañar; **out of ~'s way** a salvo;
harmful *adj* dañino; **harmless** *adj* (*person*)
inofensivo; (*joke etc*) inocente
harmony ['hɑːmənɪ] *n* armonía
harness ['hɑːnɪs] *n* arreos *mpl*; (*for child*)
arnés *m*; (*safety harness*) arneses *mpl* ▷ *vt*
(*horse*) enjaezar; (*resources*) aprovechar
harp [hɑːp] *n* arpa ▷ *vi*: **to ~ on (about)**
machacar (con)
harsh [hɑːʃ] *adj* (*cruel*) duro, cruel;
(*severe*) severo; (*sound*) áspero; (*light*)
deslumbrador(a)
harvest ['hɑːvɪst] *n* (*harvest time*) siega;
(*of cereals etc*) cosecha; (*of grapes*) vendimia
▷ *vt* cosechar
has [hæz] *vb see* **have**
hasn't ['hæznt] = **has not**
hassle ['hæsl] (*inf*) *n* lata
haste [heɪst] *n* prisa; **hasten** ['heɪsn]
vt acelerar ▷ *vi* darse prisa; **hastily** *adv*
de prisa; precipitadamente; **hasty** *adj*

apresurado; (*rash*) precipitado
hat [hæt] *n* sombrero
hatch [hætʃ] *n* (*Naut: also:* **~way**) escotilla;
(*also:* **service ~**) ventanilla ▷ *vi* (*bird*) salir
del cascarón ▷ *vt* incubar; (*plot*) tramar; **5
eggs have ~ed** han salido 5 pollos
hatchback ['hætʃbæk] *n* (*Aut*) tres *or*
cinco puertas *m*
hate [heɪt] *vt* odiar, aborrecer ▷ *n* odio;
hatred ['heɪtrɪd] *n* odio
haul [hɔːl] *vt* tirar ▷ *n* (*of fish*) redada; (*of
stolen goods etc*) botín *m*
haunt [hɔːnt] *vt* (*ghost*) aparecerse en;
(*obsess*) obsesionar ▷ *n* guarida; **haunted**
adj (*castle etc*) embrujado; (*look*) de angustia

○ **KEYWORD**

have [hæv] (*pt, pp* **had**) *aux vb* **1** (*gen*)
haber; **to have arrived/eaten** haber
llegado/comido; **having finished** *or* **when
he had finished, he left** cuando hubo
acabado, se fue
2 (*in tag questions*): **you've done it, haven't
you?** lo has hecho, ¿verdad? *or* ¿no?
3 (*in short answers and questions*): **I haven't**
no; **so I have** pues, es verdad; **we haven't
paid - yes we have!** no hemos pagado –
¡sí que hemos pagado!; **I've been there
before, have you?** he estado allí antes,
¿y tú?
▷ *modal aux vb* (*be obliged*): **to have (got) to
do sth** tener que hacer algo; **you haven't to
tell her** no hay que *or* no debes decírselo
▷ *vt* **1** (*possess*): **he has (got) blue eyes/
dark hair** tiene los ojos azules/el pelo negro
2 (*referring to meals etc*): **to have breakfast/
lunch/dinner** desayunar/comer/cenar;
to have a drink/a cigarette tomar algo/
fumar un cigarrillo
3 (*receive*) recibir; (*obtain*) obtener; **may
I have your address?** ¿puedes darme tu
dirección?; **you can have it for £5** te lo
puedes quedar por £5; **I must have it by
tomorrow** lo necesito para mañana; **to
have a baby** tener un niño *or* bebé
4 (*maintain, allow*): **I won't have it/this
nonsense!** ¡no lo permitiré!/¡no permitiré
estas tonterías!; **we can't have that** no
podemos permitir eso
5 to have sth done hacer *or* mandar hacer
algo; **to have one's hair cut** cortarse el
pelo; **to have sb do sth** hacer que algn
haga algo
6 (*experience, suffer*): **to have a cold/flu**
tener un resfriado/la gripe; **she had her
bag stolen/her arm broken** le robaron
el bolso/se rompió un brazo; **to have an**

operation operarse
7 (+ *noun*): **to have a swim/walk/bath/
rest** nadar/dar un paseo/darse un baño/
descansar; **let's have a look** vamos a ver;
to have a meeting/party celebrar una
reunión/una fiesta; **let me have a try**
déjame intentarlo

haven ['heɪvn] *n* puerto; (*fig*) refugio
haven't ['hævnt] = **have not**
havoc ['hævək] *n* estragos *mpl*
Hawaii [hə'waɪiː] *n* (Islas *fpl*) Hawai *fpl*
hawk [hɔːk] *n* halcón *m*
hawthorn ['hɔːθɔːn] *n* espino
hay [heɪ] *n* heno; **hay fever** *n* fiebre *f* del
heno; **haystack** *n* almiar *m*
hazard ['hæzəd] *n* peligro ▷ *vt* aventurar;
hazardous *adj* peligroso; **hazard warning
lights** *npl* (*Aut*) señales *fpl* de emergencia
haze [heɪz] *n* neblina
hazel ['heɪzl] *n* (*tree*) avellano ▷ *adj* (*eyes*)
color *m* de avellano; **hazelnut** *n* avellana
hazy ['heɪzɪ] *adj* brumoso; (*idea*) vago
he [hiː] *pron* él; **~ who ...** él que ..., quien ...
head [hɛd] *n* cabeza; (*leader*) jefe/a *m/f*; (*of
school*) director(a) *m/f* ▷ *vt* (*list*) encabezar;
(*group*) capitanear; (*company*) dirigir; **~s
(or tails)** cara (o cruz); **~ first** de cabeza;
~ over heels (*in love*) perdidamente; **to ~
the ball** cabecear (la pelota); **head for** *vt
fus* dirigirse a; (*disaster*) ir camino de; **head
off** *vt* (*threat, danger*) evitar; **headache**
n dolor *m* de cabeza; **heading** *n* título;
headlamp (*BRIT*) *n* = **headlight**; **headlight**
n faro; **headline** *n* titular *m*; **head office** *n*
oficina central, central *f*; **headphones** *npl*
auriculares *mpl*; **headquarters** *npl* sede *f*
central; (*Mil*) cuartel *m* general; **headroom**
n (*in car*) altura interior; (*under bridge*)
(límite *m* de) altura; **headscarf** *n* pañuelo;
headset *n* cascos *mpl*; **headteacher** *n*
director(directora); **head waiter** *n* maître
m
heal [hiːl] *vt* curar ▷ *vi* cicatrizarse
health [hɛlθ] *n* salud *f*; **health care** *n*
asistencia sanitaria; **health centre** (*BRIT*) *n*
ambulatorio, centro médico; **health food**
n alimentos *mpl* orgánicos; **Health Service**
(*BRIT*) *n* el servicio de salud pública, ≈ el
Insalud (*SP*); **healthy** *adj* sano, saludable
heap [hiːp] *n* montón *m* ▷ *vt*: **to ~ (up)**
amontonar; **to ~ sth with** llenar algo hasta
arriba de; **~s of** un montón de
hear [hɪə*] (*pt, pp* **~d**) *vt* (*also Law*) oír;
(*news*) saber ▷ *vi* oír; **to ~ about** oír hablar
de; **to ~ from sb** tener noticias de algn
heard [hɜːd] *pt, pp of* **hear**
hearing [hɪərɪŋ] *n* (*sense*) oído; (*Law*) vista;

hearing aid *n* audífono
hearse [hɜːs] *n* coche *m* fúnebre
heart [hɑːt] *n* corazón *m*; (*fig*) valor
m; (*of lettuce*) cogollo; **hearts** *npl*
(*Cards*) corazones *mpl*; **to lose/take ~**
descorazonarse/cobrar ánimo; **at ~** en
el fondo; **by ~** (*learn, know*) de memoria;
heart attack *n* infarto (de miocardio);
heartbeat *n* latido (del corazón);
heartbroken *adj*: **she was heartbroken
about it** esto le partió el corazón;
heartburn *n* acedía; **heart disease** *n*
enfermedad *f* cardíaca
hearth [hɑːθ] *n* (*fireplace*) chimenea
heartless ['hɑːtlɪs] *adj* despiadado
hearty ['hɑːtɪ] *adj* (*person*) campechano;
(*laugh*) sano; (*dislike, support*) absoluto
heat [hiːt] *n* calor *m*; (*Sport: also*:
qualifying ~) prueba eliminatoria ▷ *vt*
calentar; **heat up** *vi* calentarse ▷ *vt*
calentar; **heated** *adj* caliente; (*fig*)
acalorado; **heater** *n* estufa; (*in car*)
calefacción *f*
heather ['hɛðə*] *n* brezo
heating ['hiːtɪŋ] *n* calefacción *f*
heatwave ['hiːtweɪv] *n* ola de calor
heaven ['hɛvn] *n* cielo; (*fig*) una maravilla;
heavenly *adj* celestial; (*fig*) maravilloso
heavily ['hɛvɪlɪ] *adv* pesadamente;
(*drink, smoke*) con exceso; (*sleep, sigh*)
profundamente; (*depend*) mucho
heavy ['hɛvɪ] *adj* pesado; (*work, blow*)
duro; (*sea, rain, meal*) fuerte; (*drinker, smoker*)
grande; (*responsibility*) grave; (*schedule*)
ocupado; (*weather*) bochornoso
Hebrew ['hiːbruː] *adj, n* (*Ling*) hebreo
hectare ['hɛktɑː*] *n* (*BRIT*) hectárea
hectic ['hɛktɪk] *adj* agitado
he'd [hiːd] = **he would**; **he had**
hedge [hɛdʒ] *n* seto ▷ *vi* contestar con
evasivas; **to ~ one's bets** (*fig*) cubrirse
hedgehog ['hɛdʒhɔg] *n* erizo
heed [hiːd] *vt* (*also*: **take ~**: *pay attention to*)
hacer caso de
heel [hiːl] *n* talón *m*; (*of shoe*) tacón *m* ▷ *vt*
(*shoe*) poner tacón a
hefty ['hɛftɪ] *adj* (*person*) fornido; (*parcel,
profit*) gordo
height [haɪt] *n* (*of person*) estatura; (*of
building*) altura; (*high ground*) cerro; (*altitude*)
altitud *f*; (*fig: of season*): **at the ~ of summer**
en los días más calurosos del verano; (: *of
power etc*) cúspide *f*; (: *of stupidity etc*) colmo;
heighten *vt* elevar; (*fig*) aumentar
heir [ɛə*] *n* heredero; **heiress** *n* heredera
held [hɛld] *pt, pp of* **hold**
helicopter ['hɛlɪkɔptə*] *n* helicóptero
hell [hɛl] *n* infierno; **~!** (*inf*) ¡demonios!

he'll [hi:l] = **he will; he shall**
hello [hə'ləʊ] excl ¡hola!; (to attract
attention) ¡oiga!; (surprise) ¡caramba!
helmet ['hɛlmɪt] n casco
help [hɛlp] n ayuda; (cleaner etc) criada,
asistenta ▷ vt ayudar; ~! ¡socorro!; ~
yourself sírvete; **he can't ~ it** no es culpa
suya; **help out** vi ayudar, echar una mano
▷ vt: **to help sb out** ayudar a algn, echar una
mano a algn; **helper** n ayudante mf; **helpful**
adj útil; (person) servicial; (advice) útil;
helping n ración f; **helpless** adj (incapable)
incapaz; (defenceless) indefenso; **helpline** n
teléfono de asistencia al público
hem [hɛm] n dobladillo ▷ vt poner or
coser el dobladillo de
hemisphere ['hɛmɪsfɪə*] n hemisferio
hemorrhage ['hɛmərɪdʒ] (US) n =
haemorrhage
hemorrhoids ['hɛmərɔɪdz] (US) npl =
haemorrhoids
hen [hɛn] n gallina; (female bird) hembra
hence [hɛns] adv (therefore) por lo tanto; **2
years ~** de aquí a 2 años
hen night, hen party n (inf) despedida
de soltera
hepatitis [hɛpə'taɪtɪs] n hepatitis f
her [hə:*] pron (direct) la; (indirect) le;
(stressed, after prep) ella ▷ adj su; see also
me; my
herb [hə:b] n hierba; **herbal** adj de
hierbas; **herbal tea** n infusión f de hierbas
herd [hə:d] n rebaño
here [hɪə*] adv aquí; (at this point) en este
punto; ~! (present) ¡presente!; ~ **is/are** aquí
está/están; ~ **she is** aquí está
hereditary [hɪ'rɛdɪtrɪ] adj hereditario
heritage ['hɛrɪtɪdʒ] n patrimonio
hernia ['hə:nɪə] n hernia
hero ['hɪərəʊ] (pl ~es) n héroe m; (in book,
film) protagonista m; **heroic** [hɪ'rəʊɪk] adj
heroico
heroin ['hɛrəʊɪn] n heroína
heroine ['hɛrəʊɪn] n heroína; (in book,
film) protagonista
heron ['hɛrən] n garza
herring ['hɛrɪŋ] n arenque m
hers [hə:z] pron (el) suyo/(la) suya etc; see
also **mine¹**
herself [hə:'sɛlf] pron (reflexive) se;
(emphatic) ella misma; (after prep) sí (misma);
see also **oneself**
he's [hi:z] = **he is; he has**
hesitant ['hɛzɪtənt] adj vacilante
hesitate ['hɛzɪteɪt] vi vacilar; (in
speech) titubear; (be unwilling) resistirse
a; **hesitation** ['-teɪʃən] n indecisión f;
titubeo; dudas fpl

heterosexual [hɛtərəʊ'sɛksjuəl] adj
heterosexual
hexagon ['hɛksəgən] n hexágono
hey [heɪ] excl ¡oye!, ¡oiga!
heyday ['heɪdeɪ] n: **the ~ of** el apogeo de
HGV n abbr (= heavy goods vehicle) vehículo
pesado
hi [haɪ] excl ¡hola!; (to attract attention)
¡oiga!
hibernate ['haɪbəneɪt] vi invernar
hiccough ['hɪkʌp] = **hiccup**
hiccup ['hɪkʌp] vi hipar
hid [hɪd] pt of **hide**
hidden ['hɪdn] pp of **hide** ▷ adj: ~ **agenda**
plan m encubierto
hide [haɪd] (pt **hid**, pp **hidden**) n (skin) piel
f ▷ vt esconder, ocultar ▷ vi: **to ~ (from sb)**
esconderse or ocultarse (de algn)
hideous ['hɪdɪəs] adj horrible
hiding ['haɪdɪŋ] n (beating) paliza; **to be in
~** (concealed) estar escondido
hi-fi ['haɪfaɪ] n estéreo, hifi m ▷ adj de alta
fidelidad
high [haɪ] adj alto; (speed, number) grande;
(price) elevado; (wind) fuerte; (voice) agudo
▷ adv alto, a gran altura; **it is 20 m ~** tiene
20 m de altura; ~ **in the air** en las alturas;
highchair n silla alta; **high-class** adj
(hotel) de lujo; (person) distinguido, de
categoría; (food) de alta categoría; **higher
education** n educación f or enseñanza
superior; **high heels** npl (heels) tacones
mpl altos; (shoes) zapatos mpl de tacón; **high
jump** n (Sport) salto de altura; **highlands**
['haɪləndz] npl tierras fpl altas; **the
Highlands** (in Scotland) las Tierras Altas de
Escocia; **highlight** n (fig: of event) punto
culminante ▷ vt subrayar; **highlights**
npl (in hair) reflejos mpl; **highlighter** n
rotulador; **highly** adv (paid) muy bien;
(critical, confidential) sumamente; (a lot): **to
speak/think highly of** hablar muy bien
de/tener en mucho a; **highness** n altura;
Her/His Highness Su Alteza; **high-rise** n
(also: **high-rise block, high-rise building**)
torre f de pisos; **high school** n ≈ Instituto
Nacional de Bachillerato (SP); **high season**
(BRIT) n temporada alta; **high street**
(BRIT) n calle f mayor; **high-tech** (inf) adj
al-tec (inf), de alta tecnología; **highway**
n carretera; (US) carretera nacional;
autopista; **Highway Code** (BRIT) n código
de la circulación
hijack ['haɪdʒæk] vt secuestrar; **hijacker**
n secuestrador(a) m/f
hike [haɪk] vi (go walking) ir de excursión (a
pie) ▷ n caminata; **hiker** n excursionista
mf; **hiking** n senderismo

hilarious [hɪˈlɛərɪəs] *adj* divertidísimo
hill [hɪl] *n* colina; *(high)* montaña; *(slope)* cuesta; **hillside** *n* ladera; **hill walking** *n* senderismo (de montaña); **hilly** *adj* montañoso
him [hɪm] *pron (direct)* le, lo; *(indirect)* le; *(stressed, after prep)* él; *see also* **me**; **himself** *pron (reflexive)* se; *(emphatic)* él mismo; *(after prep)* sí (mismo); *see also* **oneself**
hind [haɪnd] *adj* posterior
hinder [ˈhɪndə*] *vt* estorbar, impedir
hindsight [ˈhaɪndsaɪt] *n*: **with ~** en retrospectiva
Hindu [ˈhɪnduː] *n* hindú *mf*; **Hinduism** *n (Rel)* hinduismo
hinge [hɪndʒ] *n* bisagra, gozne *m* ⊳ *vi (fig)*: **to ~ on** depender de
hint [hɪnt] *n* indirecta; *(advice)* consejo; *(sign)* dejo ⊳ *vt*: **to ~ that** insinuar que ⊳ *vi*: **to ~ at** hacer alusión a
hip [hɪp] *n* cadera
hippie [ˈhɪpɪ] *n* hippie *m/f*, jipi *m/f*
hippo [ˈhɪpəʊ] *(pl* **~s)** *n* hipopótamo
hippopotamus [hɪpəˈpɔtəməs] *(pl* **~es** *or* **hippopotami)** *n* hipopótamo
hippy [ˈhɪpɪ] *n* = **hippie**
hire [ˈhaɪə*] *vt (BRIT: car, equipment)* alquilar; *(worker)* contratar ⊳ *n* alquiler *m*; **for ~** se alquila; *(taxi)* libre; **hire(d) car** *(BRIT)* *n* coche *m* de alquiler; **hire purchase** *(BRIT)* *n* compra a plazos
his [hɪz] *pron (el)* suyo((la) suya) *etc* ⊳ *adj* su; *see also* **mine¹; my**
Hispanic [hɪsˈpænɪk] *adj* hispánico
hiss [hɪs] *vi* silbar
historian [hɪˈstɔːrɪən] *n* historiador(a) *m/f*
historic(al) [hɪˈstɔrɪk(l)] *adj* histórico
history [ˈhɪstərɪ] *n* historia
hit [hɪt] *(pt, pp* **~)** *vt (strike)* golpear, pegar; *(reach: target)* alcanzar; *(collide with: car)* chocar contra; *(fig: affect)* afectar ⊳ *n* golpe *m*; *(success)* éxito; *(on website)* visita; *(in web search)* correspondencia; **to ~ it off with sb** llevarse bien con algn; **hit back** *vi* defenderse; *(fig)* devolver golpe por golpe
hitch [hɪtʃ] *vt (fasten)* atar, amarrar; *(also: ~ up)* remangar ⊳ *n (difficulty)* dificultad *f*; **to ~ a lift** hacer autostop
hitch-hike [ˈhɪtʃhaɪk] *vi* hacer autostop; **hitch-hiker** *n* autostopista *m/f*; **hitch-hiking** *n* autostop *m*
hi-tech [haɪˈtɛk] *adj* de alta tecnología
hitman [ˈhɪtmæn] *(irreg)* *n* asesino a sueldo
HIV *n abbr (= human immunodeficiency virus)* VIH *m*; **~-negative/positive** VIH negativo/positivo

hive [haɪv] *n* colmena
hoard [hɔːd] *n (treasure)* tesoro; *(stockpile)* provisión *f* ⊳ *vt* acumular; *(goods in short supply)* acaparar
hoarse [hɔːs] *adj* ronco
hoax [həʊks] *n* trampa
hob [hɔb] *n* quemador *m*
hobble [ˈhɔbl] *vi* cojear
hobby [ˈhɔbɪ] *n* pasatiempo, afición *f*
hobo [ˈhəʊbəʊ] *(US)* *n* vagabundo
hockey [ˈhɔkɪ] *n* hockey *m*; **hockey stick** *n* palo *m* de hockey
hog [hɔg] *n* cerdo, puerco ⊳ *vt (fig)* acaparar; **to go the whole ~** poner toda la carne en el asador
Hogmanay [hɔgməˈneɪ] *n ver abajo*

hoist [hɔɪst] *n (crane)* grúa ⊳ *vt* levantar, alzar; *(flag, sail)* izar
hold [həʊld] *(pt, pp* **held)** *vt* sostener; *(contain)* contener; *(have: power, qualification)* tener; *(keep back)* retener; *(believe)* sostener; *(consider)* considerar; *(keep in position)*: **to ~ one's head up** mantener la cabeza alta; *(meeting)* celebrar ⊳ *vi (withstand pressure)* resistir; *(be valid)* valer ⊳ *n (grasp)* asimiento; *(fig)* dominio; **~ the line!** *(Tel)* ¡no cuelgue!; **to ~ one's own** *(fig)* defenderse; **to catch** *or* **get (a) ~ of** agarrarse *or* asirse de; **hold back** *vt* retener; *(secret)* ocultar; **hold on** *vi* agarrarse bien; *(wait)* esperar; **hold on!** *(Tel)* ¡(espere) un momento!; **hold out** *vt* ofrecer ⊳ *vi (resist)* resistir; **hold up** *vt (raise)* levantar; *(support)* apoyar; *(delay)* retrasar; *(rob)* asaltar; **holdall** *(BRIT)* *n* bolsa; **holder** *n (container)* receptáculo; *(of ticket, record)* poseedor(a) *m/f*; *(of office, title etc)* titular *mf*
hole [həʊl] *n* agujero
holiday [ˈhɔlədɪ] *n* vacaciones *fpl*; *(public holiday)* (día *m* de) fiesta, día *m* feriado; **on ~** de vacaciones; **holiday camp** *n (BRIT: also:* **holiday centre)** centro de vacaciones; **holiday job** *n (BRIT)* trabajillo extra para las

vacaciones; **holiday-maker** (BRIT) n turista mf; **holiday resort** n centro turístico

Holland ['hɔlənd] n Holanda

hollow ['hɔləu] adj hueco; (claim) vacío; (eyes) hundido; (sound) sordo ▷ n hueco; (in ground) hoyo ▷ vt: **to ~ out** excavar

holly ['hɔlɪ] n acebo

Hollywood ['hɔlɪwud] n Hollywood m

holocaust ['hɔləkɔːst] n holocausto

holy ['həulɪ] adj santo, sagrado; (water) bendito

home [həum] n casa; (country) patria; (institution) asilo ▷ cpd (domestic) casero, de casa; (Econ, Pol) nacional ▷ adv (direction) a casa; (right in: nail etc) a fondo; **at ~** en casa; (in country) en el país; (fig) como pez en el agua; **to go/come ~** ir/volver a casa; **make yourself at ~** ¡estás en tu casa!; **home address** n domicilio; **homeland** n tierra natal; **homeless** adj sin hogar, sin casa; **homely** adj (simple) sencillo; **home-made** adj casero; **home match** n partido en casa; **Home Office** (BRIT) n Ministerio del Interior; **home owner** n propietario/a m/f de una casa; **home page** n página de inicio; **Home Secretary** (BRIT) n Ministro del Interior; **homesick** adj: **to be homesick** tener morriña, sentir nostalgia; **home town** n ciudad f natal; **homework** n deberes mpl

homicide ['hɔmɪsaɪd] (US) n homicidio

homoeopathic [həumɪɔ'pəθɪk] (US **homeopathic**) adj homeopático

homoeopathy [həumɪ'ɔpəθɪ] (US **homeopathy**) n homeopatía

homosexual [hɔməu'sɛksjuəl] adj, n homosexual mf

honest ['ɔnɪst] adj honrado; (sincere) franco, sincero; **honestly** adv honradamente; francamente; **honesty** n honradez f

honey ['hʌnɪ] n miel f; **honeymoon** n luna de miel; **honeysuckle** n madreselva

Hong Kong ['hɔŋ'kɔŋ] n Hong-Kong m

honorary ['ɔnərərɪ] adj (member, president) de honor; (title) honorífico; **~ degree** doctorado honoris causa

honour ['ɔnə*] (US **honor**) vt honrar; (commitment, promise) cumplir con ▷ n honor m, honra; **to graduate with ~s** ≈ licenciarse con matrícula (de honor); **honourable** (US **honorable**) adj honorable; **honours degree** n (Scol) título de licenciado con calificación alta

hood [hud] n capucha; (BRIT Aut) capota; (US Aut) capó m; (of cooker) campana de humos; **hoodie** n (top) jersey m con capucha

hoof [huːf] (pl **hooves**) n pezuña

hook [huk] n gancho; (on dress) corchete m, broche m; (for fishing) anzuelo ▷ vt enganchar; (fish) pescar

hooligan ['huːlɪgən] n gamberro

hoop [huːp] n aro

hooray [huː'reɪ] excl = **hurray**

hoot [huːt] (BRIT) vi (Aut) tocar el pito, pitar; (siren) (hacer) sonar; (owl) ulular

Hoover® ['huːvə*] (BRIT) n aspiradora ▷ vt: **to hoover** pasar la aspiradora por

hooves [huːvz] npl of **hoof**

hop [hɔp] vi saltar, brincar; (on one foot) saltar con un pie

hope [həup] vt, vi esperar ▷ n esperanza; **I ~ so/not** espero que sí/no; **hopeful** adj (person) optimista; (situation) prometedor(a); **hopefully** adv con esperanza; (one hopes): **hopefully he will recover** esperamos que se recupere; **hopeless** adj desesperado; (person): **to be hopeless** ser un desastre

hops [hɔps] npl lúpulo

horizon [hə'raɪzn] n horizonte m; **horizontal** [hɔrɪ'zɔntl] adj horizontal

hormone ['hɔːməun] n hormona

horn [hɔːn] n cuerno; (Mus: also: **French ~**) trompa; (Aut) pito, claxon m

horoscope ['hɔrəskəup] n horóscopo

horrendous [hɔ'rɛndəs] adj horrendo

horrible ['hɔrɪbl] adj horrible

horrid ['hɔrɪd] adj horrible, horroroso

horrific [hɔ'rɪfɪk] adj (accident) horroroso; (film) horripilante

horrifying ['hɔrɪfaɪɪŋ] adj horroroso

horror ['hɔrə*] n horror m; **horror film** n película de horror

hors d'œuvre [ɔː'dəːvrə] n entremeses mpl

horse [hɔːs] n caballo; **horseback** n: **on horseback** a caballo; **horse chestnut** n (tree) castaño de Indias; (nut) castaña de Indias; **horsepower** n caballo (de fuerza); **horse-racing** n carreras fpl de caballos; **horseradish** n rábano picante; **horse riding** n (BRIT) equitación f

hose [həuz] n manguera; **hosepipe** n manguera

hospital ['hɔspɪtl] n hospital m

hospitality [hɔspɪ'tælɪtɪ] n hospitalidad f

host [həust] n anfitrión m; (TV, Radio) presentador m; (Rel) hostia; (large number): **a ~ of** multitud de

hostage ['hɔstɪdʒ] n rehén m

hostel ['hɔstl] n hostal m; **(youth) ~** albergue m juvenil

hostess ['həustɪs] n anfitriona; (BRIT: air hostess) azafata; (TV, Radio) presentadora

hostile ['hɔstaɪl] *adj* hostil
hostility [hɔ'stɪlɪtɪ] *n* hostilidad *f*
hot [hɔt] *adj* caliente; (*weather*) caluroso, de calor; (*as opposed to warm*) muy caliente; (*spicy*) picante; **to be ~** (*person*) tener calor; (*object*) estar caliente; (*weather*) hacer calor; **hot dog** *n* perro caliente
hotel [həʊ'tel] *n* hotel *m*
hot-water bottle [hɔt'wɔːtə*-] *n* bolsa de agua caliente
hound [haʊnd] *vt* acosar ▷ *n* perro (de caza)
hour ['aʊə*] *n* hora; **hourly** *adj* (de) cada hora
house [*n* haus, *pl* 'hauzɪz, *vb* hauz] *n* (*gen, firm*) casa; (*Pol*) cámara; (*Theatre*) sala ▷ *vt* (*person*) alojar; (*collection*) albergar; **on the ~** (*fig*) la casa invita; **household** *n* familia; (*home*) casa; **householder** *n* propietario/a; (*head of house*) cabeza de familia; **housekeeper** *n* ama de llaves; **housekeeping** *n* (*work*) trabajos *mpl* domésticos; **housewife** (*irreg*) *n* ama de casa; **house wine** *n* vino *m* de la casa; **housework** *n* faenas *fpl* (de la casa)
housing ['haʊzɪŋ] *n* (*act*) alojamiento; (*houses*) viviendas *fpl*; **housing development, housing estate** (*BRIT*) *n* urbanización *f*
hover ['hɔvə*] *vi* flotar (en el aire); **hovercraft** *n* aerodeslizador *m*
how [hau] *adv* (*in what way*) cómo; **~ are you?** ¿cómo estás?; **~ much milk/many people?** ¿cuánta leche/gente?; **~ much does it cost?** ¿cuánto cuesta?; **~ long have you been here?** ¿cuánto hace que estás aquí?; **~ old are you?** ¿cuántos años tienes?; **~ tall is he?** ¿cómo es de alto?; **~ is school?** ¿cómo (te) va (en) la escuela?; **~ was the film?** ¿qué tal la película?; **~ lovely/awful!** ¡qué bonito/horror!
however [hau'evə*] *adv*: **~ I do it** lo haga como lo haga; **~ cold it is** por mucho frío que haga; **~ fast he runs** por muy rápido que corra; **~ did you do it?** ¿cómo lo hiciste? ▷ *conj* sin embargo, no obstante
howl [haul] *n* aullido ▷ *vi* aullar; (*person*) dar alaridos; (*wind*) ulular
H.P. *n abbr* = **hire purchase**
h.p. *abbr* = **horsepower**
HQ *n abbr* = **headquarters**
hr(s) *abbr* (= *hour(s)*) h
HTML *n abbr* (= *hypertext markup language*) lenguaje *m* de hipertexto
hubcap ['hʌbkæp] *n* tapacubos *m inv*
huddle ['hʌdl] *vi*: **to ~ together** acurrucarse
huff [hʌf] *n*: **in a ~** enojado

hug [hʌg] *vt* abrazar; (*thing*) apretar con los brazos
huge [hjuːdʒ] *adj* enorme
hull [hʌl] *n* (*of ship*) casco
hum [hʌm] *vt* tararear, canturrear ▷ *vi* tararear, canturrear; (*insect*) zumbar
human ['hjuːmən] *adj, n* humano
humane [hjuː'meɪn] *adj* humano, humanitario
humanitarian [hjuːmænɪ'tɛərɪən] *adj* humanitario
humanity [hjuː'mænɪtɪ] *n* humanidad *f*
human rights *npl* derechos *mpl* humanos
humble ['hʌmbl] *adj* humilde
humid ['hjuːmɪd] *adj* húmedo; **humidity** [-'mɪdɪtɪ] *n* humedad *f*
humiliate [hjuː'mɪlɪeɪt] *vt* humillar
humiliating [hjuː'mɪlɪeɪtɪŋ] *adj* humillante, vergonzoso
humiliation [hjuːmɪlɪ'eɪʃən] *n* humillación *f*
hummus ['huməs] *n* paté de garbanzos
humorous ['hjuːmərəs] *adj* gracioso, divertido
humour ['hjuːmə*] (*US* **humor**) *n* humorismo, sentido del humor; (*mood*) humor *m* ▷ *vt* (*person*) complacer
hump [hʌmp] *n* (*in ground*) montículo; (*camel's*) giba
hunch [hʌntʃ] *n* (*premonition*) presentimiento
hundred ['hʌndrəd] *num* ciento; (*before n*) cien; **~s of** centenares de; **hundredth** [-ɪdθ] *adj* centésimo
hung [hʌŋ] *pt, pp of* **hang**
Hungarian [hʌŋ'gɛərɪən] *adj, n* húngaro/a *m/f*
Hungary ['hʌŋgərɪ] *n* Hungría
hunger ['hʌŋgə*] *n* hambre *f* ▷ *vi*: **to ~ for** (*fig*) tener hambre de, anhelar
hungry ['hʌŋgrɪ] *adj*: **~ (for)** hambriento (de); **to be ~** tener hambre
hunt [hʌnt] *vt* (*seek*) buscar; (*Sport*) cazar ▷ *vi* (*search*): **to ~ (for)** buscar; (*Sport*) cazar ▷ *n* búsqueda; caza, cacería; **hunter** *n* cazador(a) *m/f*; **hunting** *n* caza
hurdle ['həːdl] *n* (*Sport*) valla; (*fig*) obstáculo
hurl [həːl] *vt* lanzar, arrojar
hurrah [hu'rɑː] *excl* = **hurray**
hurray [hu'reɪ] *excl* ¡viva!
hurricane ['hʌrɪkən] *n* huracán *m*
hurry ['hʌrɪ] *n* prisa ▷ *vt* (*also*: **~ up**: *person*) dar prisa a; (: *work*) apresurar, hacer de prisa; **to be in a ~** tener prisa; **hurry up** *vi* darse prisa, apurarse (*LAM*)
hurt [həːt] (*pt, pp* **~**) *vt* hacer daño a ▷ *vi* doler ▷ *adj* lastimado

h

husband ['hʌzbənd] n marido
hush [hʌʃ] n silencio ⊳vt hacer callar; ~!
¡chitón!, ¡cállate!
husky ['hʌskɪ] adj ronco ⊳n perro
esquimal
hut [hʌt] n cabaña; (shed) cobertizo
hyacinth ['haɪəsɪnθ] n jacinto
hydrangea [haɪ'dreɪnʒə] n hortensia
hydrofoil ['haɪdrəfɔɪl] n aerodeslizador m
hydrogen ['haɪdrədʒən] n hidrógeno
hygiene ['haɪdʒiːn] n higiene f; **hygienic**
[-'dʒiːnɪk] adj higiénico
hymn [hɪm] n himno
hype [haɪp] (inf) n bombardeo publicitario
hyphen ['haɪfn] n guión m
hypnotize ['hɪpnətaɪz] vt hipnotizar
hypocrite ['hɪpəkrɪt] n hipócrita mf
hypocritical [hɪpə'krɪtɪkl] adj hipócrita
hypothesis [haɪ'pɔθɪsɪs] (pl **hypotheses**)
n hipótesis f inv
hysterical [hɪ'stɛrɪkl] adj histérico;
(funny) para morirse de risa
hysterics [hɪ'stɛrɪks] npl histeria; **to be in**
~ (fig) morirse de risa

◆

I [aɪ] pron yo
ice [aɪs] n hielo; (ice cream) helado ⊳vt
(cake) alcorzar ⊳vi (also: ~ over, ~ up)
helarse; **iceberg** n iceberg m; **ice cream**
n helado; **ice cube** n cubito de hielo; **ice
hockey** n hockey m sobre hielo
Iceland ['aɪslənd] n Islandia; **Icelander**
n islandés/esa m/f; **Icelandic** [aɪs'lændɪk]
adj islandés/esa ⊳n (Ling) islandés m
ice: ice lolly (BRIT) n polo; **ice rink** n pista
de hielo; **ice skating** n patinaje m sobre
hielo
icing ['aɪsɪŋ] n (Culin) alcorza; **icing sugar**
(BRIT) n azúcar m glas(eado)
icon ['aɪkɔn] n icono
ICT (BRIT: Scol) n abbr (= information and
communications technology) informática
icy ['aɪsɪ] adj helado
I'd [aɪd] = **I would; I had**
ID card n (identity card) DNI m
idea [aɪ'dɪə] n idea
ideal [aɪ'dɪəl] n ideal m ⊳adj ideal; **ideally**
[-dɪəlɪ] adv idealmente; **they're ideally
suited** hacen una pareja ideal
identical [aɪ'dɛntɪkl] adj idéntico
identification [aɪdɛntɪfɪ'keɪʃən] n
identificación f; **(means of)** ~ documentos
mpl personales
identify [aɪ'dɛntɪfaɪ] vt identificar
identity [aɪ'dɛntɪtɪ] n identidad f;
identity card n carnet m de identidad;
identity theft n robo de identidad
ideology [aɪdɪ'ɔlədʒɪ] n ideología
idiom ['ɪdɪəm] n modismo; (style of
speaking) lenguaje m

▌Be careful not to translate **idiom** by the
Spanish word idioma.

idiot ['ɪdɪət] n idiota mf
idle ['aɪdl] adj (inactive) ocioso; (lazy)
holgazán/ana; (unemployed) parado,
desocupado; (machinery etc) parado; (talk etc)

frívolo ▷ *vi* (*machine*) marchar en vacío

idol ['aɪdl] *n* ídolo

idyllic [ɪ'dɪlɪk] *adj* idílico

i.e. *abbr* (= *that is*) esto es

if [ɪf] *conj* si; **~ necessary** si fuera
necesario, si hiciese falta; **~ I were you** yo
en tu lugar; **~ so/not** de ser así/si no; **~ only
I could!** ¡ojalá pudiera!; *see also* **as; even**

ignite [ɪg'naɪt] *vt* (*set fire to*) encender ▷ *vi*
encenderse

ignition [ɪg'nɪʃən] *n* (*Aut: process*) ignición
f; (*: mechanism*) encendido; **to switch on/off
the ~** arrancar/apagar el motor

ignorance ['ɪgnərəns] *n* ignorancia

ignorant ['ɪgnərənt] *adj* ignorante; **to be
~ of** ignorar

ignore [ɪg'nɔ:*] *vt* (*person, advice*) no hacer
caso de; (*fact*) pasar por alto

I'll [aɪl] = **I will; I shall**

ill [ɪl] *adj* enfermo, malo ▷ *n* mal *m* ▷ *adv*
mal; **to be taken ~** ponerse enfermo

illegal [ɪ'li:gl] *adj* ilegal

illegible [ɪ'lɛdʒɪbl] *adj* ilegible

illegitimate [ɪlɪ'dʒɪtɪmət] *adj* ilegítimo

ill health *n* mala salud *f*; **to be in ~** estar
mal de salud

illiterate [ɪ'lɪtərət] *adj* analfabeto

illness ['ɪlnɪs] *n* enfermedad *f*

illuminate [ɪ'lu:mɪneɪt] *vt* (*room, street*)
iluminar, alumbrar

illusion [ɪ'lu:ʒən] *n* ilusión *f*; (*trick*) truco

illustrate ['ɪləstreɪt] *vt* ilustrar

illustration [ɪlə'streɪʃən] *n* (*act of
illustrating*) ilustración *f*; (*example*) ejemplo,
ilustración *f*; (*in book*) lámina

I'm [aɪm] = **I am**

image ['ɪmɪdʒ] *n* imagen *f*

imaginary [ɪ'mædʒɪnərɪ] *adj* imaginario

imagination [ɪmædʒɪ'neɪʃən] *n*
imaginación *f*; (*inventiveness*) inventiva

imaginative [ɪ'mædʒɪnətɪv] *adj*
imaginativo

imagine [ɪ'mædʒɪn] *vt* imaginarse

imbalance [ɪm'bæləns] *n* desequilibrio

imitate ['ɪmɪteɪt] *vt* imitar; **imitation**
[ɪmɪ'teɪʃən] *n* imitación *f*; (*copy*) copia

immaculate [ɪ'mækjulət] *adj*
inmaculado

immature [ɪmə'tjuə*] *adj* (*person*)
inmaduro

immediate [ɪ'mi:dɪət] *adj* inmediato;
(*pressing*) urgente, apremiante;
(*nearest: family*) próximo; (*: neighbourhood*)
inmediato; **immediately** *adv* (*at once*)
en seguida; (*directly*) inmediatamente;
immediately next to muy junto a

immense [ɪ'mɛns] *adj* inmenso, enorme;
(*importance*) enorme; **immensely** *adv*

enormemente

immerse [ɪ'mə:s] *vt* (*submerge*) sumergir;
to be ~d in (*fig*) estar absorto en

immigrant ['ɪmɪgrənt] *n* inmigrante *mf*;
immigration [ɪmɪ'greɪʃən] *n* inmigración
f

imminent ['ɪmɪnənt] *adj* inminente

immoral [ɪ'mɔrl] *adj* inmoral

immortal [ɪ'mɔ:tl] *adj* inmortal

immune [ɪ'mju:n] *adj*; **~ (to)** inmune (a);
immune system *n* sistema *m* inmunitario

immunize ['ɪmjunaɪz] *vt* inmunizar

impact ['ɪmpækt] *n* impacto

impair [ɪm'pɛə*] *vt* perjudicar

impartial [ɪm'pɑ:ʃl] *adj* imparcial

impatience [ɪm'peɪʃəns] *n* impaciencia

impatient [ɪm'peɪʃənt] *adj* impaciente;
to get *or* **grow ~** impacientarse

impeccable [ɪm'pɛkəbl] *adj* impecable

impending [ɪm'pɛndɪŋ] *adj* inminente

imperative [ɪm'pɛrətɪv] *adj* (*tone*)
imperioso; (*need*) imprescindible

imperfect [ɪm'pə:fɪkt] *adj* (*goods etc*)
defectuoso ▷ *n* (*Ling: also:* **~ tense**)
imperfecto

imperial [ɪm'pɪərɪəl] *adj* imperial

impersonal [ɪm'pə:sənl] *adj* impersonal

impersonate [ɪm'pə:səneɪt] *vt* hacerse
pasar por; (*Theatre*) imitar

impetus ['ɪmpətəs] *n* ímpetu *m*; (*fig*)
impulso

implant [ɪm'plɑ:nt] *vt* (*Med*) injertar,
implantar; (*fig: idea, principle*) inculcar

implement [*n* 'ɪmplɪmənt, *vb* 'ɪmplɪmɛnt]
n herramienta; (*for cooking*) utensilio ▷ *vt*
(*regulation*) hacer efectivo; (*plan*) realizar

implicate ['ɪmplɪkeɪt] *vt* (*compromise*)
comprometer; **to ~ sb in sth** comprometer
a algn en algo

implication [ɪmplɪ'keɪʃən] *n*
consecuencia; **by ~** indirectamente

implicit [ɪm'plɪsɪt] *adj* implícito; (*belief,
trust*) absoluto

imply [ɪm'plaɪ] *vt* (*involve*) suponer; (*hint*)
dar a entender que

impolite [ɪmpə'laɪt] *adj* mal educado

import [*vb* ɪm'pɔ:t, *n* 'ɪmpɔ:t] *vt* importar
▷ *n* (*Comm*) importación *f*; (*: article*)
producto importado; (*meaning*) significado,
sentido

importance [ɪm'pɔ:təns] *n* importancia

important [ɪm'pɔ:tənt] *adj* importante;
it's not ~ no importa, no tiene importancia

importer [ɪm'pɔ:tə*] *n* importador(a) *m/f*

impose [ɪm'pəuz] *vt* imponer ▷ *vi*: **to
~ on sb** abusar de algn; **imposing** *adj*
imponente, impresionante

impossible [ɪm'pɔsɪbl] *adj* imposible;

(person) insoportable

impotent ['ɪmpətənt] adj impotente
impoverished [ɪm'pɔvərɪʃt] adj
necesitado
impractical [ɪm'præktɪkl] adj (person,
plan) poco práctico
impress [ɪm'prɛs] vt impresionar; (mark)
estampar; **to ~ sth on sb** hacer entender
algo a algn
impression [ɪm'prɛʃən] n impresión f;
(imitation) imitación f; **to be under the ~
that** tener la impresión de que
impressive [ɪm'prɛsɪv] adj
impresionante
imprison [ɪm'prɪzn] vt encarcelar;
imprisonment n encarcelamiento; (term of
imprisonment) cárcel f
improbable [ɪm'prɔbəbl] adj improbable,
inverosímil
improper [ɪm'prɔpə*] adj
(unsuitable: conduct etc) incorrecto;
(: activities) deshonesto
improve [ɪm'pru:v] vt mejorar; (foreign
language) perfeccionar ▷ vi mejorarse;
improvement n mejoramiento;
perfección f; progreso
improvise ['ɪmprəvaɪz] vt, vi improvisar
impulse ['ɪmpʌls] n impulso; **to act on ~**
obrar sin reflexión; **impulsive** [ɪm'pʌlsɪv]
adj irreflexivo

○ **KEYWORD**

in [ɪn] prep 1 (indicating place, position, with
place names) en; **in the house/garden** en
(la) casa/el jardín; **in here/there** aquí/
ahí or allí dentro; **in London/England** en
Londres/Inglaterra
2 (indicating time) en; **in spring** en (la)
primavera; **in the afternoon** por la tarde;
at 4 o'clock in the afternoon a las 4 de la
tarde; **I did it in 3 hours/days** lo hice en 3
horas/días; **I'll see you in 2 weeks** or **in 2
weeks' time** te veré dentro de 2 semanas
3 (indicating manner etc) en; **in a loud/soft
voice** en voz alta/baja; **in pencil/ink** a
lápiz/bolígrafo; **the boy in the blue shirt** el
chico de la camisa azul
4 (indicating circumstances): **in the sun/
shade/rain** al sol/a la sombra/bajo la
lluvia; **a change in policy** un cambio de
política
5 (indicating mood, state): **in tears** en
lágrimas, llorando; **in anger/despair**
enfadado/desesperado; **to live in luxury**
vivir lujosamente
6 (with ratios, numbers): **1 in 10 households,
1 household in 10** una de cada 10 familias;

20 pence in the pound 20 peniques por
libra; **they lined up in twos** se alinearon de
dos en dos
7 (referring to people, works) en; entre;
the disease is common in children la
enfermedad es común entre los niños; **in
(the works of) Dickens** en (las obras de)
Dickens
8 (indicating profession etc): **to be in teaching**
estar en la enseñanza
9 (after superlative) de; **the best pupil in the
class** el(la) mejor alumno/a de la clase
10 (with present participle): **in saying this** al
decir esto
▷ adv: **to be in** (person: at home) estar en
casa; (at work) estar; (train, ship, plane) haber
llegado; (in fashion) estar de moda; **she'll be
in later today** llegará más tarde hoy; **to ask
sb in** hacer pasar a algn; **to run/limp** etc **in**
entrar corriendo/cojeando etc
▷ n: **the ins and outs** (of proposal, situation
etc) los detalles

inability [ɪnə'bɪlɪtɪ] n: **~ (to do)**
incapacidad f (de hacer)
inaccurate [ɪn'ækjurət] adj inexacto,
incorrecto
inadequate [ɪn'ædɪkwət] adj (income,
reply etc) insuficiente; (person) incapaz
inadvertently [ɪnəd'və:tntlɪ] adv por
descuido
inappropriate [ɪnə'prəuprɪət] adj
inadecuado; (improper) poco oportuno
inaugurate [ɪ'nɔ:gjureɪt] vt inaugurar;
(president, official) investir
Inc. (us) abbr (= incorporated) S.A.
incapable [ɪn'keɪpəbl] adj incapaz
incense [n 'ɪnsɛns, vb ɪn'sɛns] n incienso
▷ vt (anger) indignar, encolerizar
incentive [ɪn'sɛntɪv] n incentivo,
estímulo
inch [ɪntʃ] n pulgada; **to be within an ~ of**
estar a dos dedos de; **he didn't give an ~** no
dio concesión alguna
incidence ['ɪnsɪdns] n (of crime, disease)
incidencia
incident ['ɪnsɪdnt] n incidente m
incidentally [ɪnsɪ'dɛntəlɪ] adv (by the
way) a propósito
inclination [ɪnklɪ'neɪʃən] n (tendency)
tendencia, inclinación f; (desire) deseo;
(disposition) propensión f
incline [n 'ɪnklaɪn, vb ɪn'klaɪn] n
pendiente m, cuesta ▷ vt (head) poner de
lado ▷ vi inclinarse; **to be ~d to** (tend) tener
tendencia a hacer algo
include [ɪn'klu:d] vt (incorporate) incluir;
(in letter) adjuntar; **including** prep incluso,

inclusive

inclusion [ɪn'kluːʒən] n inclusión f

inclusive [ɪn'kluːsɪv] adj inclusivo; **~ of tax** incluidos los impuestos

income ['ɪŋkʌm] n (earned) ingresos mpl; (from property etc) renta; (from investment etc) rédito; **income support** n (BRIT) ≈ ayuda familiar; **income tax** n impuesto sobre la renta

incoming ['ɪnkʌmɪŋ] adj (flight, government etc) entrante

incompatible [ɪnkəm'pætɪbl] adj incompatible

incompetence [ɪn'kɔmpɪtəns] n incompetencia

incompetent [ɪn'kɔmpɪtənt] adj incompetente

incomplete [ɪnkəm'pliːt] adj (partial: achievement etc) incompleto; (unfinished: painting etc) inacabado

inconsistent [ɪnkən'sɪstənt] adj inconsecuente; (contradictory) incongruente; **~ with** (que) no concuerda con

inconvenience [ɪnkən'viːnjəns] n inconvenientes mpl; (trouble) molestia, incomodidad f ▷ vt incomodar

inconvenient [ɪnkən'viːnjənt] adj incómodo, poco práctico; (time, place, visitor) inoportuno

incorporate [ɪn'kɔːpəreɪt] vt incorporar; (contain) comprender; (add) agregar

incorrect [ɪnkə'rɛkt] adj incorrecto

increase [n 'ɪnkriːs, vb ɪn'kriːs] n aumento ▷ vi aumentar; (grow) crecer; (price) subir ▷ vt aumentar; (price) subir; **increasingly** adv cada vez más, más y más

incredible [ɪn'krɛdɪbl] adj increíble; **incredibly** adv increíblemente

incur [ɪn'kəː*] vt (expenditure) incurrir; (loss) sufrir; (anger, disapproval) provocar

indecent [ɪn'diːsnt] adj indecente

indeed [ɪn'diːd] adv efectivamente, en realidad; (in fact) en efecto; (furthermore) es más; **yes ~!** ¡claro que sí!

indefinitely [ɪn'dɛfɪnɪtlɪ] adv (wait) indefinidamente

independence [ɪndɪ'pɛndns] n independencia; **Independence Day** (US) n Día m de la Independencia

independent [ɪndɪ'pɛndənt] adj independiente; **independent school** n (BRIT) escuela f privada, colegio m privado

index ['ɪndɛks] (pl **~es**) n (in book) índice m; (: in library etc) catálogo; (pl **indices**: ratio, sign) exponente m

India ['ɪndɪə] n la India; **Indian** adj, n indio/a; **Red Indian** piel roja mf

indicate ['ɪndɪkeɪt] vt indicar; **indication** [-'keɪʃən] n indicio, señal f; **indicative** [ɪn'dɪkətɪv] adj: **to be indicative of** indicar; **indicator** n indicador m; (Aut) intermitente m

indices ['ɪndɪsiːz] npl of **index**

indict [ɪn'daɪt] vt acusar; **indictment** n acusación f

indifference [ɪn'dɪfrəns] n indiferencia

indifferent [ɪn'dɪfrənt] adj indiferente; (mediocre) regular

indigenous [ɪn'dɪdʒɪnəs] adj indígena

indigestion [ɪndɪ'dʒɛstʃən] n indigestión f

indignant [ɪn'dɪgnənt] adj: **to be ~ at sth/ with sb** indignarse por algo/con algn

indirect [ɪndɪ'rɛkt] adj indirecto

indispensable [ɪndɪ'spɛnsəbl] adj indispensable, imprescindible

individual [ɪndɪ'vɪdjuəl] n individuo ▷ adj individual; (personal) personal; (particular) particular; **individually** adv (singly) individualmente

Indonesia [ɪndə'niːzɪə] n Indonesia

indoor ['ɪndɔː*] adj (swimming pool) cubierto; (plant) de interior; (sport) bajo cubierta; **indoors** [ɪn'dɔːz] adv dentro

induce [ɪn'djuːs] vt inducir, persuadir; (bring about) producir; (labour) provocar

indulge [ɪn'dʌldʒ] vt (whim) satisfacer; (person) complacer; (child) mimar ▷ vi: **to ~ in** darse el gusto de; **indulgent** adj indulgente

industrial [ɪn'dʌstrɪəl] adj industrial; **industrial estate** (BRIT) n polígono (SP) or zona (LAM) industrial; **industrialist** n industrial mf; **industrial park** (US) n = **industrial estate**

industry ['ɪndəstrɪ] n industria; (diligence) aplicación f

inefficient [ɪnɪ'fɪʃənt] adj ineficaz, ineficiente

inequality [ɪnɪ'kwɔlɪtɪ] n desigualdad f

inevitable [ɪn'ɛvɪtəbl] adj inevitable; **inevitably** adv inevitablemente

inexpensive [ɪnɪk'spɛnsɪv] *adj*
económico
inexperienced [ɪnɪk'spɪərɪənst] *adj*
inexperto
inexplicable [ɪnɪk'splɪkəbl] *adj*
inexplicable
infamous ['ɪnfəməs] *adj* infame
infant ['ɪnfənt] *n* niño/a; (*baby*) niño/a
pequeño/a, bebé *mf*; (*pej*) aniñado
infantry ['ɪnfəntrɪ] *n* infantería
infant school (*BRIT*) *n* parvulario
infect [ɪn'fɛkt] *vt* (*wound*) infectar; (*food*)
contaminar; (*person, animal*) contagiar;
infection [ɪn'fɛkʃən] *n* infección *f*; (*fig*)
contagio; **infectious** [ɪn'fɛkʃəs] *adj* (*also
fig*) contagioso
infer [ɪn'fə:*] *vt* deducir, inferir
inferior [ɪn'fɪərɪə*] *adj, n* inferior *mf*
infertile [ɪn'fə:taɪl] *adj* estéril; (*person*)
infecundo
infertility [ɪnfə:'tɪlɪtɪ] *n* esterilidad *f*;
infecundidad *f*
infested [ɪn'fɛstɪd] *adj*: **~ with** plagado de
infinite ['ɪnfɪnɪt] *adj* infinito; **infinitely**
adv infinitamente
infirmary [ɪn'fə:mərɪ] *n* hospital *m*
inflamed [ɪn'fleɪmd] *adj*: **to become ~**
inflamarse
inflammation [ɪnflə'meɪʃən] *n*
inflamación *f*
inflatable [ɪn'fleɪtəbl] *adj* (*ball, boat*)
inflable
inflate [ɪn'fleɪt] *vt* (*tyre, price etc*) inflar;
(*fig*) hinchar; **inflation** [ɪn'fleɪʃən] *n* (*Econ*)
inflación *f*
inflexible [ɪn'flɛksəbl] *adj* (*rule*) rígido;
(*person*) inflexible
inflict [ɪn'flɪkt] *vt*: **to ~ sth on sb** infligir
algo en algn
influence ['ɪnfluəns] *n* influencia
▷ *vt* influir en, influenciar; **under the
~ of alcohol** en estado de embriaguez;
influential [-'ɛnʃl] *adj* influyente
influx ['ɪnflʌks] *n* afluencia
info (*inf*) ['ɪnfəu] *n* = **information**
inform [ɪn'fɔ:m] *vt*: **to ~ sb of sth** informar
a algn sobre *or* de algo ▷ *vi*: **to ~ on sb**
delatar a algn
informal [ɪn'fɔ:məl] *adj* (*manner, tone*)
familiar; (*dress, interview, occasion*) informal;
(*visit, meeting*) extraoficial
information [ɪnfə'meɪʃən] *n* información
f; (*knowledge*) conocimientos *mpl*; **a piece
of ~** un dato; **information office** *n*
información *f*; **information technology** *n*
informática
informative [ɪn'fɔ:mətɪv] *adj*
informativo

infra-red [ɪnfrə'rɛd] *adj* infrarrojo
infrastructure ['ɪnfrəstrʌktʃə*] *n* (*of
system etc*) infraestructura
infrequent [ɪn'fri:kwənt] *adj* infrecuente
infuriate [ɪn'fjuərɪeɪt] *vt*: **to become ~d**
ponerse furioso
infuriating [ɪn'fjuərɪeɪtɪŋ] *adj* (*habit,
noise*) enloquecedor(a)
ingenious [ɪn'dʒi:njəs] *adj* ingenioso
ingredient [ɪn'gri:dɪənt] *n* ingrediente *m*
inhabit [ɪn'hæbɪt] *vt* vivir en; **inhabitant**
n habitante *mf*
inhale [ɪn'heɪl] *vt* inhalar ▷ *vi* (*breathe
in*) aspirar; (*in smoking*) tragar; **inhaler** *n*
inhalador *m*
inherent [ɪn'hɪərənt] *adj*: **~ in** *or* **to**
inherente a
inherit [ɪn'hɛrɪt] *vt* heredar; **inheritance**
n herencia; (*fig*) patrimonio
inhibit [ɪn'hɪbɪt] *vt* inhibir, impedir;
inhibition [-'bɪʃən] *n* cohibición *f*
initial [ɪ'nɪʃl] *adj* primero ▷ *n* inicial *f*
▷ *vt* firmar con las iniciales; **initials** *npl* (*as
signature*) iniciales *fpl*; (*abbreviation*) siglas
fpl; **initially** *adv* al principio
initiate [ɪ'nɪʃɪeɪt] *vt* iniciar; **to ~
proceedings against sb** (*Law*) entablar
proceso contra algn
initiative [ɪ'nɪʃətɪv] *n* iniciativa
inject [ɪn'dʒɛkt] *vt* inyectar; **to ~ sb
with sth** inyectar algo a algn; **injection**
[ɪn'dʒɛkʃən] *n* inyección *f*
injure ['ɪndʒə*] *vt* (*hurt*) herir, lastimar;
(*fig: reputation etc*) perjudicar; **injured** *adj*
(*person, arm*) herido, lastimado; **injury** *n*
herida, lesión *f*; (*wrong*) perjuicio, daño
▎ Be careful not to translate **injury** by the
▎ Spanish word *injuria*.
injustice [ɪn'dʒʌstɪs] *n* injusticia
ink [ɪŋk] *n* tinta; **ink-jet printer**
['ɪŋkdʒɛt-] *n* impresora de chorro de tinta
inland [*adj* 'ɪnlənd, *adv* ɪn'lænd] *adj*
(*waterway, port etc*) interior ▷ *adv* tierra
adentro; **Inland Revenue** (*BRIT*) *n*
departamento de impuestos ≈ Hacienda
(*SP*)
in-laws ['ɪnlɔ:z] *npl* suegros *mpl*
inmate ['ɪnmeɪt] *n* (*in prison*) preso/a,
presidiario/a; (*in asylum*) internado/a
inn [ɪn] *n* posada, mesón *m*
inner ['ɪnə*] *adj* (*courtyard, calm*) interior;
(*feelings*) íntimo; **inner-city** *adj* (*schools,
problems*) de las zonas céntricas pobres, de
los barrios céntricos pobres
inning ['ɪnɪŋ] *n* (*US: Baseball*) inning *m*,
entrada; **~s** (*Cricket*) entrada, turno
innocence ['ɪnəsns] *n* inocencia
innocent ['ɪnəsnt] *adj* inocente

innovation [ɪnəʊ'veɪʃən] *n* novedad *f*
innovative ['ɪnəʊveɪtɪv] *adj* innovador
in-patient ['ɪnpeɪʃənt] *n* paciente *m/f*
interno/a
input ['ɪnput] *n* entrada; (*of resources*)
inversión *f*; (*Comput*) entrada de datos
inquest ['ɪnkwest] *n* (*coroner's*) encuesta
judicial
inquire [ɪn'kwaɪə*] *vi* preguntar ▷ *vt*: **to**
~ whether preguntar si; **to ~ about** (*person*)
preguntar por; (*fact*) informarse de; **inquiry**
n pregunta; (*investigation*) investigación *f*,
pesquisa; **"Inquiries"** "Información"
ins. *abbr* =**inches**
insane [ɪn'seɪn] *adj* loco; (*Med*) demente
insanity [ɪn'sænɪtɪ] *n* demencia, locura
insect ['ɪnsekt] *n* insecto; **insect**
repellent *n* loción *f* contra insectos
insecure [ɪnsɪ'kjuə*] *adj* inseguro
insecurity [ɪnsɪ'kjuərɪtɪ] *n* inseguridad *f*
insensitive [ɪn'sensɪtɪv] *adj* insensible
insert [*vb* ɪn'səːt, *n* 'ɪnsəːt] *vt* (*into sth*)
introducir ▷ *n* encarte *m*
inside ['ɪn'saɪd] *n* interior *m* ▷ *adj* interior,
interno ▷ *adv* (*be*) (por) dentro; (*go*) hacia
dentro ▷ *prep* dentro de; (*of time*): **~ 10**
minutes en menos de 10 minutos; **inside**
lane *n* (*Aut: in Britain*) carril *m* izquierdo;
(: *in US, Europe etc*) carril *m* derecho; **inside**
out *adv* (*turn*) al revés; (*know*) a fondo
insight ['ɪnsaɪt] *n* perspicacia
insignificant [ɪnsɪg'nɪfɪknt] *adj*
insignificante
insincere [ɪnsɪn'sɪə*] *adj* poco sincero
insist [ɪn'sɪst] *vi* insistir; **to ~ on** insistir
en; **to ~ that** insistir en que; (*claim*) exigir
que; **insistent** *adj* insistente; (*noise, action*)
persistente
insomnia [ɪn'sɔmnɪə] *n* insomnio
inspect [ɪn'spekt] *vt* inspeccionar,
examinar; (*troops*) pasar revista a;
inspection [ɪn'spekʃən] *n* inspección *f*,
examen *m*; (*of troops*) revista; **inspector**
n inspector(a) *m/f*; (BRIT: *on buses, trains*)
revisor(a) *m/f*
inspiration [ɪnspə'reɪʃən] *n* inspiración
f; **inspire** [ɪn'spaɪə*] *vt* inspirar; **inspiring**
adj inspirador(a)
instability [ɪnstə'bɪlɪtɪ] *n* inestabilidad *f*
install [ɪn'stɔːl] (US **instal**) *vt* instalar;
(*official*) nombrar; **installation** [ɪnstə'leɪʃən]
n instalación *f*
instalment [ɪn'stɔːlmənt] (US
installment) *n* plazo; (*of story*) entrega;
(*of TV serial etc*) capítulo; **in ~s** (*pay, receive*)
a plazos
instance ['ɪnstəns] *n* ejemplo, caso; **for ~**
por ejemplo; **in the first ~** en primer lugar

instant ['ɪnstənt] *n* instante *m*, momento
▷ *adj* inmediato; (*coffee etc*) instantáneo;
instantly *adv* en seguida; **instant**
messaging *n* mensajería instantánea
instead [ɪn'sted] *adv* en cambio; **~ of** en
lugar de, en vez de
instinct ['ɪnstɪŋkt] *n* instinto; **instinctive**
adj instintivo
institute ['ɪnstɪtjuːt] *n* instituto;
(*professional body*) colegio ▷ *vt* (*begin*)
iniciar, empezar; (*proceedings*) entablar;
(*system, rule*) establecer
institution [ɪnstɪ'tjuːʃən] *n* institución
f; (*Med: home*) asilo; (: *asylum*) manicomio;
(*of system etc*) establecimiento; (*of custom*)
iniciación *f*
instruct [ɪn'strʌkt] *vt*: **to ~ sb in sth**
instruir a algn en *or* sobre algo; **to ~ sb to**
do sth dar instrucciones a algn de hacer
algo; **instruction** [ɪn'strʌkʃən] *n* (*teaching*)
instrucción *f*; **instructions** *npl* (*orders*)
órdenes *fpl*; **instructions (for use)** modo de
empleo; **instructor** *n* instructor(a) *m/f*
instrument ['ɪnstrəmənt] *n*
instrumento; **instrumental** [-'mentl] *adj*
(*Mus*) instrumental; **to be instrumental in**
ser (el) artífice de
insufficient [ɪnsə'fɪʃənt] *adj* insuficiente
insulate ['ɪnsjuleɪt] *vt* aislar; **insulation**
[-'leɪʃən] *n* aislamiento
insulin ['ɪnsjulɪn] *n* insulina
insult [*n* 'ɪnsʌlt, *vb* ɪn'sʌlt] *n* insulto ▷ *vt*
insultar; **insulting** *adj* insultante
insurance [ɪn'ʃuərəns] *n* seguro; **fire/**
life ~ seguro contra incendios/sobre la
vida; **insurance company** *n* compañía *f*
de seguros; **insurance policy** *n* póliza (de
seguros)
insure [ɪn'ʃuə*] *vt* asegurar
intact [ɪn'tækt] *adj* íntegro; (*unharmed*)
intacto
intake ['ɪnteɪk] *n* (*of food*) ingestión *f*; (*of*
air) consumo; (BRIT *Scol*): **an ~ of 200 a year**
200 matriculados al año
integral ['ɪntɪgrəl] *adj* (*whole*) íntegro;
(*part*) integrante
integrate ['ɪntɪgreɪt] *vt* integrar ▷ *vi*
integrarse
integrity [ɪn'tegrɪtɪ] *n* honradez *f*,
rectitud *f*
intellect ['ɪntəlekt] *n* intelecto;
intellectual [-'lektjuəl] *adj, n* intelectual
mf
intelligence [ɪn'telɪdʒəns] *n* inteligencia
intelligent [ɪn'telɪdʒənt] *adj* inteligente
intend [ɪn'tend] *vt* (*gift etc*): **to ~ sth**
for destinar algo a; **to ~ to do sth** tener
intención de *or* pensar hacer algo

intense [ɪnˈtɛns] *adj* intenso
intensify [ɪnˈtɛnsɪfaɪ] *vt* intensificar; (*increase*) aumentar
intensity [ɪnˈtɛnsɪtɪ] *n* (*gen*) intensidad *f*
intensive [ɪnˈtɛnsɪv] *adj* intensivo; **intensive care** *n*: **to be in intensive care** estar bajo cuidados intensivos; **intensive care unit** *n* unidad *f* de vigilancia intensiva
intent [ɪnˈtɛnt] *n* propósito; (*Law*) premeditación *f* ▷ *adj* (*absorbed*) absorto; (*attentive*) atento; **to all ~s and purposes** prácticamente; **to be ~ on doing sth** estar resuelto a hacer algo
intention [ɪnˈtɛnʃən] *n* intención *f*, propósito; **intentional** *adj* deliberado
interact [ɪntərˈækt] *vi* influirse mutuamente; **interaction** [ɪntərˈækʃən] *n* interacción *f*, acción *f* recíproca; **interactive** *adj* (*Comput*) interactivo
intercept [ɪntəˈsɛpt] *vt* interceptar; (*stop*) detener
interchange [ˈɪntətʃeɪndʒ] *n* intercambio; (*on motorway*) intersección *f*
intercourse [ˈɪntəkɔːs] *n* (*sexual*) relaciones *fpl* sexuales
interest [ˈɪntrɪst] *n* (*also Comm*) interés *m* ▷ *vt* interesar; **interested** *adj* interesado; **to be interested in** interesarse por; **interesting** *adj* interesante; **interest rate** *n* tipo *or* tasa de interés
interface [ˈɪntəfeɪs] *n* (*Comput*) junción *f*
interfere [ɪntəˈfɪə*] *vi*: **to ~ in** entrometerse en; **to ~ with** (*hinder*) estorbar; (*damage*) estropear
interference [ɪntəˈfɪərəns] *n* intromisión *f*; (*Radio, TV*) interferencia
interim [ˈɪntərɪm] *n*: **in the ~** en el ínterin ▷ *adj* provisional
interior [ɪnˈtɪərɪə*] *n* interior *m* ▷ *adj* interior; **interior design** *n* interiorismo, decoración *f* de interiores
intermediate [ɪntəˈmiːdɪət] *adj* intermedio
intermission [ɪntəˈmɪʃən] *n* intermisión *f*; (*Theatre*) descanso
intern [*vb* ɪnˈtəːn, *n* ˈɪntəːn] (*us*) *vt* internar ▷ *n* interno/a
internal [ɪnˈtəːnl] *adj* (*layout, pipes, security*) interior; (*injury, structure, memo*) internal; **Internal Revenue Service** (*us*) *n* departamento de impuestos, ≈ Hacienda (*sp*)
international [ɪntəˈnæʃənl] *adj* internacional ▷ *n* (*BRIT: match*) partido internacional
Internet [ˈɪntənɛt] *n*: **the ~** Internet *m or f*; **Internet café** *n* cibercafé *m*; **Internet Service Provider** *n* proveedor *m* de (acceso

a) Internet; **Internet user** *n* internauta *mf*
interpret [ɪnˈtəːprɪt] *vt* interpretar; (*translate*) traducir; (*understand*) entender ▷ *vi* hacer de intérprete; **interpretation** [ɪntəːprɪˈteɪʃən] *n* interpretación *f*; traducción *f*; **interpreter** *n* intérprete *mf*
interrogate [ɪnˈtɛrəugeɪt] *vt* interrogar; **interrogation** [-ˈgeɪʃən] *n* interrogatorio
interrogative [ɪntəˈrɔgətɪv] *adj* interrogativo
interrupt [ɪntəˈrʌpt] *vt, vi* interrumpir; **interruption** [-ˈrʌpʃən] *n* interrupción *f*
intersection [ɪntəˈsɛkʃən] *n* (*of roads*) cruce *m*
interstate [ˈɪntəsteɪt] (*us*) *n* carretera interestatal
interval [ˈɪntəvl] *n* intervalo; (*BRIT Theatre, Sport*) descanso; (*Scol*) recreo; **at ~s** a ratos, de vez en cuando
intervene [ɪntəˈviːn] *vi* intervenir; (*event*) interponerse; (*time*) transcurrir
interview [ˈɪntəvjuː] *n* entrevista ▷ *vt* entrevistarse con; **interviewer** *n* entrevistador(a) *m/f*
intimate [*adj* ˈɪntɪmət, *vb* ˈɪntɪmeɪt] *adj* íntimo; (*friendship*) estrecho; (*knowledge*) profundo ▷ *vt* dar a entender
intimidate [ɪnˈtɪmɪdeɪt] *vt* intimidar, amedrentar
intimidating [ɪnˈtɪmɪdeɪtɪŋ] *adj* amedrentador, intimidante
into [ˈɪntuː] *prep* en; (*towards*) a; (*inside*) hacia el interior de; **~ 3 pieces/French** en 3 pedazos/al francés
intolerant [ɪnˈtɔlərənt] *adj*: **~ (of)** intolerante (con *or* para)
intranet [ˈɪntrənɛt] *n* intranet *f*
intransitive [ɪnˈtrænsɪtɪv] *adj* intransitivo
intricate [ˈɪntrɪkət] *adj* (*design, pattern*) intrincado
intrigue [ɪnˈtriːg] *n* intriga ▷ *vt* fascinar; **intriguing** *adj* fascinante
introduce [ɪntrəˈdjuːs] *vt* introducir, meter; (*speaker, TV show etc*) presentar; **to ~ sb (to sb)** presentar a algn (a algn); **to ~ sb to** (*pastime, technique*) introducir a algn a; **introduction** [-ˈdʌkʃən] *n* introducción *f*; (*of person*) presentación *f*; **introductory** [-ˈdʌktərɪ] *adj* introductorio; (*lesson, offer*) de introducción
intrude [ɪnˈtruːd] *vi* (*person*) entrometerse; **to ~ on** estorbar; **intruder** *n* intruso/a
intuition [ɪntjuːˈɪʃən] *n* intuición *f*
inundate [ˈɪnʌndeɪt] *vt*: **to ~ with** inundar de
invade [ɪnˈveɪd] *vt* invadir

invalid [n 'ɪnvəlɪd, adj ɪn'vælɪd] n (Med) minusválido/a ▷ adj (not valid) inválido, nulo

invaluable [ɪn'væljuəbl] adj inestimable

invariably [ɪn'vɛərɪəblɪ] adv sin excepción, siempre; **she is ~ late** siempre llega tarde

invasion [ɪn'veɪʒən] n invasión f

invent [ɪn'vɛnt] vt inventar; **invention** [ɪn'vɛnʃən] n invento; (lie) ficción f, mentira; **inventor** n inventor(a) m/f

inventory ['ɪnvəntrɪ] n inventario

inverted commas [ɪn'vəːtɪd-] (BRIT) npl comillas fpl

invest [ɪn'vɛst] vt invertir ▷ vi: **to ~ in** (company etc) invertir dinero en; (fig: sth useful) comprar

investigate [ɪn'vɛstɪgeɪt] vt investigar; **investigation** [-'geɪʃən] n investigación f, pesquisa

investigator [ɪn'vɛstɪgeɪtə*] n investigador(a) m/f; **private ~** investigador(a) m/f privado/a

investment [ɪn'vɛstmənt] n inversión f

investor [ɪn'vɛstə*] n inversionista mf

invisible [ɪn'vɪzɪbl] adj invisible

invitation [ɪnvɪ'teɪʃən] n invitación f

invite [ɪn'vaɪt] vt invitar; (opinions etc) solicitar, pedir; **inviting** adj atractivo; (food) apetitoso

invoice ['ɪnvɔɪs] n factura ▷ vt facturar

involve [ɪn'vɔlv] vt suponer, implicar; tener que ver con; (concern, affect) corresponder; **to ~ sb (in sth)** comprometer a algn (con algo); **involved** adj complicado; **to be involved in** (take part) tomar parte en; (be engrossed) estar muy metido en; **involvement** n participación f; dedicación f

inward ['ɪnwəd] adj (movement) interior, interno; (thought, feeling) íntimo; **inward(s)** adv hacia dentro

iPod ® ['aɪpɒd] n iPod ® m

IQ n abbr (= intelligence quotient) cociente m intelectual

IRA n abbr (= Irish Republican Army) IRA m

Iran [ɪ'rɑːn] n Irán m; **Iranian** [ɪ'reɪnɪən] adj, n iraní mf

Iraq [ɪ'rɑːk] n Iraq; **Iraqi** adj, n iraquí mf

Ireland ['aɪələnd] n Irlanda

iris ['aɪrɪs] (pl **-es**) n (Anat) iris m; (Bot) lirio

Irish ['aɪrɪʃ] adj irlandés/esa ▷ npl: **the ~** los irlandeses; **Irishman** (irreg) n irlandés m; **Irishwoman** (irreg) n irlandésa

iron ['aɪən] n hierro; (for clothes) plancha ▷ cpd de hierro ▷ vt (clothes) planchar

ironic(al) [aɪ'rɒnɪk(l)] adj irónico; **ironically** adv irónicamente

ironing ['aɪənɪŋ] n (activity) planchado; (clothes: ironed) ropa planchada; (: to be ironed) ropa por planchar; **ironing board** n tabla de planchar

irony ['aɪrənɪ] n ironía

irrational [ɪ'ræʃənl] adj irracional

irregular [ɪ'rɛgjulə*] adj irregular; (surface) desigual; (action, event) anómalo; (behaviour) poco ortodoxo

irrelevant [ɪ'rɛləvənt] adj fuera de lugar, inoportuno

irresistible [ɪrɪ'zɪstɪbl] adj irresistible

irresponsible [ɪrɪ'spɒnsɪbl] adj (act) irresponsable; (person) poco serio

irrigation [ɪrɪ'geɪʃən] n riego

irritable ['ɪrɪtəbl] adj (person) de mal humor

irritate ['ɪrɪteɪt] vt fastidiar; (Med) picar; **irritating** adj fastidioso; **irritation** [-'teɪʃən] n fastidio; enfado; picazón f

IRS (US) n abbr = **Internal Revenue Service**

is [ɪz] vb see **be**

ISDN n abbr (= Integrated Services Digital Network) RDSI f

Islam ['ɪzlɑːm] n Islam m; **Islamic** [ɪz'læmɪk] adj islámico

island ['aɪlənd] n isla; **islander** n isleño/a

isle [aɪl] n isla

isn't ['ɪznt] = **is not**

isolated ['aɪsəleɪtɪd] adj aislado

isolation [aɪsə'leɪʃən] n aislamiento

ISP n abbr = **Internet Service Provider**

Israel ['ɪzreɪl] n Israel m; **Israeli** [ɪz'reɪlɪ] adj, n israelí mf

issue ['ɪsjuː] n (problem, subject) cuestión f; (outcome) resultado; (of banknotes etc) emisión f; (of newspaper etc) edición f ▷ vt (rations, equipment) distribuir, repartir; (orders) dar; (certificate, passport) expedir; (decree) promulgar; (magazine) publicar; (cheques) extender; (banknotes, stamps) emitir; **at ~** en cuestión; **to take ~ with sb (over)** estar en desacuerdo con algn (sobre); **to make an ~ of sth** hacer una cuestión de algo

IT n abbr = **information technology**

○ **KEYWORD**

it [ɪt] pron **1** (specific subject: not generally translated) él (ella); (: direct object) lo, la; (: indirect object) le; (after prep) él (ella); (abstract concept) ello; **it's on the table** está en la mesa; **I can't find it** no lo (or la) encuentro; **give it to me** dámelo (or dámela); **I spoke to him about it** le hablé del asunto; **what did you learn from it?** ¿qué aprendiste de él (or ella)?; **did you go**

to it? (party, concert etc) ¿fuiste?
2 (impersonal): it's raining llueve, está
lloviendo; it's 6 o'clock/the 10th of
August son las 6/es el 10 de agosto; how far
is it? – it's 10 miles/2 hours on the train ¿a
qué distancia está? – a 10 millas/2 horas en
tren; who is it? – it's me ¿quién es? – soy yo

Italian [ɪˈtæljən] adj italiano ▷ n
italiano/a; (Ling) italiano
italics [ɪˈtælɪks] npl cursiva
Italy [ˈɪtəlɪ] n Italia
itch [ɪtʃ] n picazón f ▷ vi (part of body)
picar; **to ~ to do sth** rabiar por hacer algo;
itchy adj: **my hand is itchy** me pica la
mano
it'd [ˈɪtd] = **it would; it had**
item [ˈaɪtəm] n artículo; (on agenda)
asunto (a tratar); (also: **news ~**) noticia
itinerary [aɪˈtɪnərərɪ] n itinerario
it'll [ˈɪtl] = **it will; it shall**
its [ɪts] adj su; sus pl
it's [ɪts] = **it is; it has**
itself [ɪtˈsɛlf] pron (reflexive) sí mismo/a;
(emphatic) él mismo(ella misma)
ITV n abbr (BRIT: = Independent Television)
cadena de televisión comercial independiente
del Estado
I've [aɪv] = **I have**
ivory [ˈaɪvərɪ] n marfil m
ivy [ˈaɪvɪ] n (Bot) hiedra

jab [dʒæb] vt: **to ~ sth into sth** clavar algo
en algo ▷ n (inf: Med) pinchazo
jack [dʒæk] n (Aut) gato; (Cards) sota
jacket [ˈdʒækɪt] n chaqueta, americana
(SP), saco (LAM); (of book) sobrecubierta;
jacket potato n patata asada (con piel)
jackpot [ˈdʒækpɒt] n premio gordo
Jacuzzi® [dʒəˈkuːzɪ] n jacuzzi® m
jagged [ˈdʒægɪd] adj dentado
jail [dʒeɪl] n cárcel f ▷ vt encarcelar; **jail
sentence** n pena f de cárcel
jam [dʒæm] n mermelada; (also: **traffic ~**)
embotellamiento; (inf: difficulty) apuro ▷ vt
(passage etc) obstruir; (mechanism, drawer etc)
atascar; (Radio) interferir ▷ vi atascarse,
trabarse; **to ~ sth into sth** meter algo a la
fuerza en algo
Jamaica [dʒəˈmeɪkə] n Jamaica
jammed [dʒæmd] adj atascado
Jan abbr (= January) ene
janitor [ˈdʒænɪtə*] n (caretaker) portero,
conserje m
January [ˈdʒænjuərɪ] n enero
Japan [dʒəˈpæn] n (el) Japón; **Japanese**
[dʒæpəˈniːz] adj japonés/esa ▷ n inv
japonés/esa m/f; (Ling) japonés m
jar [dʒɑː*] n tarro, bote m ▷ vi (sound)
chirriar; (colours) desentonar
jargon [ˈdʒɑːgən] n jerga
javelin [ˈdʒævlɪn] n jabalina
jaw [dʒɔː] n mandíbula
jazz [dʒæz] n jazz m
jealous [ˈdʒɛləs] adj celoso; (envious)
envidioso; **jealousy** n celos mpl; envidia
jeans [dʒiːnz] npl vaqueros mpl, tejanos mpl
Jello® [ˈdʒɛləʊ] (us) n gelatina
jelly [ˈdʒɛlɪ] n (jam) jalea; (dessert etc)
gelatina; **jellyfish** n inv medusa, aguaviva
(RPL)
jeopardize [ˈdʒɛpədaɪz] vt arriesgar,
poner en peligro

jerk [dʒəːk] n (jolt) sacudida; (wrench) tirón m; (inf) imbécil mf ▷ vt tirar bruscamente de ▷ vi (vehicle) traquetear

Jersey ['dʒəːzɪ] n Jersey m

jersey ['dʒəːzɪ] n jersey m; (fabric) (tejido de) punto

Jesus ['dʒiːzəs] n Jesús m

jet [dʒɛt] n (of gas, liquid) chorro; (Aviat) avión m a reacción; **jet lag** n desorientación f después de un largo vuelo; **jet-ski** vi practicar el motociclismo acuático

jetty ['dʒɛtɪ] n muelle m, embarcadero

Jew [dʒuː] n judío/a

jewel ['dʒuːəl] n joya; (in watch) rubí m; **jeweller** (US **jeweler**) n joyero/a; **jeweller's (shop)** (US **jewelry store**) n joyería; **jewellery** (US **jewelry**) n joyas fpl, alhajas fpl

Jewish ['dʒuːɪʃ] adj judío

jigsaw ['dʒɪgsɔː] n (also: ~ **puzzle**) rompecabezas m inv, puzle m

job [dʒɔb] n (task) tarea; (post) empleo; **it's not my ~** no me incumbe a mí; **it's a good ~ that ...** menos mal que ...; **just the ~!** ¡estupendo!; **job centre** (BRIT) n oficina estatal de colocaciones; **jobless** adj sin trabajo

jockey ['dʒɔkɪ] n jockey mf ▷ vi: **to ~ for position** maniobrar para conseguir una posición

jog [dʒɔg] vt empujar (ligeramente) ▷ vi (run) hacer footing; **to ~ sb's memory** refrescar la memoria a algn; **jogging** n footing m

join [dʒɔɪn] vt (things) juntar, unir; (club) hacerse socio de; (Pol: party) afiliarse a; (queue) ponerse en; (meet: people) reunirse con ▷ vi (roads) juntarse; (rivers) confluir ▷ n juntura; **join in** vi tomar parte, participar ▷ vt fus tomar parte or participar en; **join up** vi reunirse; (Mil) alistarse

joiner ['dʒɔɪnə*] (BRIT) n carpintero/a

joint [dʒɔɪnt] n (Tech) junta, unión f; (Anat) articulación f; (BRIT Culin) pieza de carne (para asar); (inf: place) tugurio; (: of cannabis) porro ▷ adj (common) común; (combined) combinado; **joint account** n (with bank etc) cuenta común; **jointly** adv (gen) en común; (together) conjuntamente

joke [dʒəuk] n chiste m; (also: **practical ~**) broma ▷ vi bromear; **to play a ~ on** gastar una broma a; **joker** n (Cards) comodín m

jolly ['dʒɔlɪ] adj (merry) alegre; (enjoyable) divertido ▷ adv (BRIT: inf) muy, terriblemente

jolt [dʒəult] n (jerk) sacudida; (shock) susto ▷ vt (physically) sacudir; (emotionally) asustar

Jordan ['dʒɔːdən] n (country) Jordania; (river) Jordán m

journal ['dʒəːnl] n (magazine) revista; (diary) periódico, diario; **journalism** n periodismo; **journalist** n periodista mf, reportero/a

journey ['dʒəːnɪ] n viaje m; (distance covered) trayecto

joy [dʒɔɪ] n alegría; **joyrider** n gamberro que roba un coche para dar una vuelta y luego abandonarlo; **joy stick** n (Aviat) palanca de mando; (Comput) palanca de control

Jr abbr = **junior**

judge [dʒʌdʒ] n juez mf; (fig: expert) perito ▷ vt juzgar; (consider) considerar

judo ['dʒuːdəu] n judo

jug [dʒʌg] n jarra

juggle ['dʒʌgl] vi hacer juegos malabares; **juggler** n malabarista mf

juice [dʒuːs] n zumo (SP), jugo (LAM); **juicy** adj jugoso

Jul abbr (= July) jul

July [dʒuːˈlaɪ] n julio

jumble ['dʒʌmbl] n revoltijo ▷ vt (also: ~ up) revolver; **jumble sale** (BRIT) n venta de objetos usados con fines benéficos

JUMBLE SALE

Los **jumble sales** son unos mercadillos que se organizan con fines benéficos en los locales de un colegio, iglesia u otro centro público. En ellos puede comprarse todo tipo de artículos baratos de segunda mano, sobre todo ropa, juguetes, libros, vajillas o muebles.

jumbo ['dʒʌmbəu] n (also: ~ **jet**) jumbo

jump [dʒʌmp] vi saltar, dar saltos; (with fear etc) pegar un bote; (increase) aumentar ▷ vt saltar ▷ n salto; aumento; **to ~ the queue** (BRIT) colarse

jumper ['dʒʌmpə*] n (BRIT: pullover) suéter m, jersey m; (US: dress) mandil m

jumper cables (US) npl = **jump leads**

jump leads (BRIT) npl cables mpl puente de batería

Jun. abbr = **junior**

junction ['dʒʌŋkʃən] n (BRIT: of roads) cruce m; (Rail) empalme m

June [dʒuːn] n junio

jungle ['dʒʌŋgl] n selva, jungla

junior ['dʒuːnɪə*] adj (in age) menor, más joven; (brother/sister etc): **seven years her ~** siete años menor que ella; (position) subalterno ▷ n menor mf, joven mf; **junior high school** (US) n centro de educación secundaria; *see also* **high school**; **junior school** (*BRIT*) *n* escuela primaria

junk [dʒʌŋk] *n* (*cheap goods*) baratijas *fpl*; (*rubbish*) basura; **junk food** *n* alimentos preparados y envasados de escaso valor nutritivo

junkie ['dʒʌŋkɪ] (*inf*) *n* drogadicto/a, yonqui *mf*

junk mail *n* propaganda de buzón

Jupiter ['dʒuːpɪtə*] *n* (*Mythology, Astrology*) Júpiter *m*

jurisdiction [dʒuərɪs'dɪkʃən] *n* jurisdicción *f*; **it falls** *or* **comes within/ outside our ~** es/no es de nuestra competencia

jury ['dʒuərɪ] *n* jurado

just [dʒʌst] *adj* justo ▷ *adv* (*exactly*) exactamente; (*only*) sólo, solamente; **he's ~ done it/left** acaba de hacerlo/irse; **~ right** perfecto; **~ two o'clock** las dos en punto; **she's ~ as clever as you** (ella) es tan lista como tú; **~ as well that ...** menos mal que ...; **~ as he was leaving** en el momento en que se marchaba; **~ before/enough** justo antes/lo suficiente; **~ here** aquí mismo; **he ~ missed** ha fallado por poco; **~ listen to this** escucha esto un momento

justice ['dʒʌstɪs] *n* justicia; (*us: judge*) juez *mf*; **to do ~ to** (*fig*) hacer justicia a

justification [dʒʌstɪfɪ'keɪʃən] *n* justificación *f*

justify ['dʒʌstɪfaɪ] *vt* justificar; (*text*) alinear

jut [dʒʌt] *vi* (*also: ~ out*) sobresalir

juvenile ['dʒuːvənaɪl] *adj* (*court*) de menores; (*humour, mentality*) infantil ▷ *n* menor *m* de edad

K *abbr* (= *one thousand*) mil; (= *kilobyte*) kilobyte *m*, kiloocteto

kangaroo [kæŋgə'ruː] *n* canguro

karaoke [kɑːrə'əukɪ] *n* karaoke

karate [kə'rɑːtɪ] *n* karate *m*

kebab [kə'bæb] *n* pincho moruno

keel [kiːl] *n* quilla; **on an even ~** (*fig*) en equilibrio

keen [kiːn] *adj* (*interest, desire*) grande, vivo; (*eye, intelligence*) agudo; (*competition*) reñido; (*edge*) afilado; (*eager*) entusiasta; **to be ~ to do** *or* **on doing sth** tener muchas ganas de hacer algo; **to be ~ on sth/sb** interesarse por algo/algn

keep [kiːp] (*pt, pp* **kept**) *vt* (*preserve, store*) guardar; (*hold back*) quedarse con; (*maintain*) mantener; (*detain*) detener; (*shop*) ser propietario de; (*feed: family etc*) mantener; (*promise*) cumplir; (*chickens, bees etc*) criar; (*accounts*) llevar; (*diary*) escribir; (*prevent*): **to ~ sb from doing sth** impedir a algn hacer algo ▷ *vi* (*food*) conservarse; (*remain*) seguir, continuar ▷ *n* (*of castle*) torreón *m*; (*food etc*) comida, subsistencia; (*inf*): **for ~s** para siempre; **to ~ doing sth** seguir haciendo algo; **to ~ sb happy** tener a algn contento; **to ~ a place tidy** mantener un lugar limpio; **to ~ sth to o.s.** guardar algo para sí mismo; **to ~ sth (back) from sb** ocultar algo a algn; **to ~ time** (*clock*) mantener la hora exacta; **keep away** *vt*: **to keep sth/sb away from sb** mantener algo/a algn apartado de algn ▷ *vi*: **to keep away (from)** mantenerse apartado (de); **keep back** *vt* (*crowd, tears*) contener; (*money*) quedarse con; (*conceal: information*): **to keep sth back from sb** ocultar algo a algn ▷ *vi* hacerse a un lado; **keep off** *vt* (*dog, person*) mantener a distancia ▷ *vi*: **if the rain keeps off** so no lleuve; **keep your hands off!** ¡no toques!; **"keep off the grass"** "prohibido pisar el césped"; **keep on** vi: **to keep on doing** seguir or continuar haciendo; **to keep on (about sth)** no parar de hablar (de algo); **keep out** vi (*stay out*) permanecer fuera; **"keep out"** prohibida la entrada"; **keep up** vt mantener, conservar ▷ vi no retrasarse; **to keep up with** (*pace*) ir al paso de; (*level*) mantenerse a la altura de; **keeper** n guardián/ana m/f; **keeping** n (*care*) cuidado; **in keeping with** de acuerdo con

kennel ['kɛnl] n perrera; **kennels** npl residencia canina

Kenya ['kɛnjə] n Kenia

kept [kɛpt] pt, pp of **keep**

kerb [kəːb] (*BRIT*) n bordillo

kerosene ['kɛrəsiːn] n keroseno

ketchup ['kɛtʃəp] n salsa de tomate, catsup m

kettle ['kɛtl] n hervidor m de agua

key [kiː] n llave f; (*Mus*) tono; (*of piano, typewriter*) tecla ▷ adj (*issue etc*) clave inv ▷ vt (*also:* **~ in**) teclear; **keyboard** n teclado; **keyhole** n ojo (de la cerradura); **keyring** n llavero

kg abbr (= kilogram) kg

khaki ['kɑːkɪ] n caqui

kick [kɪk] vt dar una patada or un puntapié a; (*inf: habit*) quitarse de ▷ vi (*horse*) dar coces ▷ n patada; puntapié m; (*of animal*) coz f; (*thrill*): **he does it for ~s** lo hace por pura diversión; **kick off** vi (*Sport*) hacer el saque inicial; **kick-off** n saque inicial; **the kick-off is at 10 o'clock** el partido empieza a las diez

kid [kɪd] n (*inf: child*) chiquillo/a; (*animal*) cabrito; (*leather*) cabritilla ▷ vi (*inf*) bromear

kidnap ['kɪdnæp] vt secuestrar; **kidnapping** n secuestro

kidney ['kɪdnɪ] n riñón m; **kidney bean** n judía, alubia

kill [kɪl] vt matar; (*murder*) asesinar ▷ n matanza; **to ~ time** matar el tiempo; **killer** n asesino/a; **killing** n (*one*) asesinato; (*several*) matanza; **to make a killing** (*fig*) hacer su agosto

kiln [kɪln] n horno

kilo ['kiːləu] n kilo; **kilobyte** n (*Comput*) kilobyte m, kilocteto; **kilogram(me)** n kilo, kilogramo; **kilometre** ['kɪləmiːtə*] (*US* **kilometer**) n kilómetro; **kilowatt** n kilovatio

kilt [kɪlt] n falda escocesa

kin [kɪn] n see **next-of-kin**

kind [kaɪnd] adj amable, atento ▷ n clase f, especie f; (*species*) género; **in ~** (*Comm*) en especie; **a ~ of** una especie de; **to be two of a ~** ser tal para cual

kindergarten ['kɪndəgɑːtn] n jardín m de la infancia

kindly ['kaɪndlɪ] adj bondadoso; cariñoso ▷ adv bondadosamente, amablemente; **will you ~ ...** sea usted tan amable de ...

kindness ['kaɪndnɪs] n (*quality*) bondad f, amabilidad f; (*act*) favor m

king [kɪŋ] n rey m; **kingdom** n reino; **kingfisher** n martín m pescador; **king-size(d) bed** n cama de matrimonio extragrande

kiosk ['kiːɔsk] n quiosco; (*BRIT Tel*) cabina

kipper ['kɪpə*] n arenque m ahumado

kiss [kɪs] n beso ▷ vt besar; **to ~ (each other)** besarse; **kiss of life** n respiración f boca a boca

kit [kɪt] n (*equipment*) equipo; (*tools etc*) (caja de) herramientas fpl; (*assembly kit*) juego de armar

kitchen ['kɪtʃɪn] n cocina

kite [kaɪt] n (*toy*) cometa

kitten ['kɪtn] n gatito/a

kiwi ['kiːwiː-] n (*also:* **~ fruit**) kiwi m

km abbr (= kilometre) km

km/h abbr (= kilometres per hour) km/h

knack [næk] n: **to have the ~ of doing sth** tener el don de hacer algo

knee [niː] n rodilla; **kneecap** n rótula

kneel [niːl] (*pt, pp* **knelt**) vi (*also:* **~ down**) arrodillarse

knelt [nɛlt] pt, pp of **kneel**

knew [njuː] pt of **know**

knickers ['nɪkəz] (*BRIT*) npl bragas fpl

knife [naɪf] (*pl* **knives**) n cuchillo ▷ vt acuchillar

knight [naɪt] n caballero; (*Chess*) caballo

knit [nɪt] vt tejer, tricotar ▷ vi hacer punto, tricotar; (*bones*) soldarse; **to ~ one's brows** fruncir el ceño; **knitting** n labor f de punto; **knitting needle** n aguja de hacer punto; **knitwear** n prendas fpl de punto

knives [naɪvz] npl of **knife**

knob [nɔb] n (*of door*) tirador m; (*of stick*) puño; (*on radio, TV*) botón m

knock [nɔk] vt (*strike*) golpear; (*bump into*) chocar contra; (*inf*) criticar ▷ vi (*at door etc*): **to ~ at/on** llamar a ▷ n golpe m; (*on door*) llamada; **knock down** vt atropellar; **knock off** (*inf*) vi (*finish*) salir del trabajo ▷ vt (*from price*) descontar; (*inf: steal*) birlar; **knock out** vt dejar sin sentido; (*Boxing*) poner fuera de combate, dejar K.O.; (*in competition*) eliminar; **knock over** vt (*object*) tirar; (*person*) atropellar; **knockout** n (*Boxing*) K.O. m, knockout m ▷ cpd (*competition etc*) eliminatorio

knot [nɔt] n nudo ▷ vt anudar

know [nəu] (*pt* **knew**, *pp* **known**) vt (*facts*) saber; (*be acquainted with*) conocer;

(*recognize*) reconocer, conocer; **to ~ how to swim** saber nadar; **to ~ about** *or* **of sb/sth** saber de algn/algo; **know-all** *n* sabelotodo *mf*; **know-how** *n* conocimientos *mpl*; **knowing** *adj* (*look*) de complicidad; **knowingly** *adv* (*purposely*) adrede; (*smile, look*) con complicidad; **know-it-all** (*us*) *n* = **know-all**

knowledge ['nɔlɪdʒ] *n* conocimiento; (*learning*) saber *m*, conocimientos *mpl*; **knowledgeable** *adj* entendido

known [nəʊn] *pp of* **know** ▷ *adj* (*thief, facts*) conocido; (*expert*) reconocido

knuckle ['nʌkl] *n* nudillo

koala [kəʊ'ɑːlə] *n* (*also:* **~ bear**) koala *m*

Koran [kɔ'rɑːn] *n* Corán *m*

Korea [kə'rɪə] *n* Corea; **Korean** *adj*, *n* coreano/a *m/f*

kosher ['kəʊʃə*] *adj* autorizado por la ley judía

Kosovar ['kɔsəvɑ*], **Kosovan** ['kɔːsəvən] *adj* kosovar

Kosovo ['kɔsəvəʊ] *n* Kosovo

Kremlin ['kremlɪn] *n*: **the ~** el Kremlin

Kuwait [ku'weɪt] *n* Kuwait *m*

L (*BRIT*) *abbr* = **learner driver**

l. *abbr* (= *litre*) l

lab [læb] *n abbr* = **laboratory**

label ['leɪbl] *n* etiqueta ▷ *vt* poner etiqueta a

labor *etc* ['leɪbə*] (*us*) = **labour** *etc*

laboratory [lə'bɔrətərɪ] *n* laboratorio

Labor Day (*us*) *n* día *m* de los trabajadores (*primer lunes de septiembre*)

labor union (*us*) *n* sindicato

labour ['leɪbə*] (*us* **labor**) *n* (*hard work*) trabajo; (*labour force*) mano *f* de obra; (*Med*): **to be in ~** estar de parto ▷ *vi*: **to ~ (at sth)** trabajar (en algo) ▷ *vt*: **to ~ a point** insistir en un punto; **L~, the L~ party** (*BRIT*) el partido laborista, los laboristas *mpl*; **labourer** *n* peón *m*; **farm labourer** peón *m*; (*day labourer*) jornalero

lace [leɪs] *n* encaje *m*; (*of shoe etc*) cordón *m* ▷ *vt* (*shoes: also:* **~ up**) atarse (los zapatos)

lack [læk] *n* (*absence*) falta ▷ *vt* faltarle a algn, carecer de; **through** *or* **for ~ of** por falta de; **to be ~ing** faltar, no haber; **to be ~ing in sth** faltarle a algn algo

lacquer ['lækə*] *n* laca

lacy ['leɪsɪ] *adj* (*of lace*) de encaje; (*like lace*) como de encaje

lad [læd] *n* muchacho, chico

ladder ['lædə*] *n* escalera (de mano); (*BRIT: in tights*) carrera

ladle ['leɪdl] *n* cucharón *m*

lady ['leɪdɪ] *n* señora; (*dignified, graceful*) dama; **"ladies and gentlemen ..."** "señoras y caballeros ..."; **young ~** señorita; **the ladies' (room)** los servicios de señoras; **ladybird** (*us* **ladybug**) *n* mariquita

lag [læg] *n* retraso ▷ *vi* (*also:* **~ behind**) retrasarse, quedarse atrás ▷ *vt* (*pipes*) revestir

lager ['lɑːgə*] *n* cerveza (rubia)

lagoon [lə'guːn] *n* laguna

laid [leɪd] *pt, pp of* **lay**; **laid back** (*inf*) *adj* relajado
lain [leɪn] *pp of* **lie**
lake [leɪk] *n* lago
lamb [læm] *n* cordero; (*meat*) (carne f de) cordero
lame [leɪm] *adj* cojo; (*excuse*) poco convincente
lament [lə'mɛnt] *n* quejo ▷ *vt* lamentarse de
lamp [læmp] *n* lámpara; **lamppost** (*BRIT*) *n* (poste m de) farol m; **lampshade** *n* pantalla
land [lænd] *n* tierra; (*country*) país m; (*piece of land*) terreno; (*estate*) tierras fpl, finca ▷ *vi* (*from ship*) desembarcar; (*Aviat*) aterrizar; (*fig: fall*) caer, terminar ▷ *vt* (*passengers, goods*) desembarcar; **to ~ sb with sth** (*inf*) hacer cargar a algn con algo; **landing** *n* aterrizaje m; (*of staircase*) rellano; **landing card** *n* tarjeta de desembarque; **landlady** *n* (*of rented house, pub etc*) dueña; **landlord** *n* propietario; (*of pub etc*) patrón m; **landmark** *n* lugar m conocido; **to be a landmark** (*fig*) marcar un hito histórico; **landowner** *n* terrateniente mf; **landscape** *n* paisaje m; **landslide** *n* (*Geo*) corrimiento de tierras; (*fig: Pol*) victoria arrolladora
lane [leɪn] *n* (*in country*) camino; (*Aut*) carril m; (*in race*) calle f
language ['læŋgwɪdʒ] *n* lenguaje m; (*national tongue*) idioma m, lengua; **bad ~** palabrotas fpl; **language laboratory** *n* laboratorio de idiomas; **language school** *n* academia de idiomas
lantern ['læntn] *n* linterna, farol m
lap [læp] *n* (*of track*) vuelta; (*of body*) regazo ▷ *vt* (*also: ~ up*) beber a lengüetadas ▷ *vi* (*waves*) chapotear; **to sit on sb's ~** sentarse en las rodillas de algn
lapel [lə'pɛl] *n* solapa
lapse [læps] *n* fallo; (*moral*) desliz m; (*of time*) intervalo ▷ *vi* (*expire*) caducar; (*time*) pasar, transcurrir; **to ~ into bad habits** caer en malos hábitos
laptop (computer) ['læptɔp-] *n* (ordenador m) portátil m
lard [lɑːd] *n* manteca (de cerdo)
larder ['lɑːdə*] *n* despensa
large [lɑːdʒ] *adj* grande; **at ~** (*free*) en libertad; (*generally*) en general

▎Be careful not to translate **large** by the Spanish word *largo*.

largely *adv* (*mostly*) en su mayor parte; (*introducing reason*) en gran parte; **large-scale** *adj* (*map*) en gran escala; (*fig*) importante
lark [lɑːk] *n* (*bird*) alondra; (*joke*) broma

laryngitis [lærɪn'dʒaɪtɪs] *n* laringitis f
lasagne [lə'zænjə] *n* lasaña
laser ['leɪzə*] *n* láser m; **laser printer** *n* impresora (por) láser
lash [læʃ] *n* latigazo; (*also: eye~*) pestaña ▷ *vt* azotar; (*tie*): **to ~ together** atar a/atar; **lash out** *vi*: **to lash out (at sb)** (*hit*) arremeter (contra algn); **to lash out against sb** lanzar invectivas contra algn
lass [læs] (*BRIT*) *n* chica
last [lɑːst] *adj* último; (*end: of series etc*) final ▷ *adv* (*most recently*) la última vez; (*finally*) por último ▷ *vi* durar; (*continue*) continuar, seguir; **~ night** anoche; **~ week** la semana pasada; **at ~** por fin; **~ but one** penúltimo; **lastly** *adv* por último, finalmente; **last-minute** *adj* de última hora
latch [lætʃ] *n* pestillo; **latch onto** *vt fus* (*person, group*) pegarse a; (*idea*) agarrarse a
late [leɪt] *adj* (*far on: in time, process etc*) al final de; (*not on time*) tarde, atrasado; (*dead*) fallecido ▷ *adv* tarde; (*behind time, schedule*) con retraso; **of ~** últimamente; **~ at night** a última hora de la noche; **in ~ May** hacia fines de mayo; **the ~ Mr X** el difunto Sr X; **latecomer** *n* recién llegado/a; **lately** *adv* últimamente; **later** *adj* (*date etc*) posterior; (*version etc*) más reciente ▷ *adv* más tarde, después; **latest** ['leɪtɪst] *adj* último; **at the latest** a más tardar
lather ['lɑːðə*] *n* espuma (de jabón) ▷ *vt* enjabonar
Latin ['lætɪn] *n* latín m ▷ *adj* latino; **Latin America** *n* América latina; **Latin American** *adj, n* latinoamericano/a m/f
latitude ['lætɪtjuːd] *n* latitud f; (*fig*) libertad f
latter ['lætə*] *adj* último; (*of two*) segundo ▷ *n*: **the ~** el último, éste
laugh [lɑːf] *n* risa ▷ *vi* reír(se); **(to do sth) for a ~** (hacer algo) en broma; **laugh at** *vt fus* reírse de; **laughter** *n* risa
launch [lɔːntʃ] *n* lanzamiento; (*boat*) lancha ▷ *vt* (*ship*) botar; (*rocket etc*) lanzar; (*fig*) comenzar; **launch into** *vt fus* lanzarse a
launder ['lɔːndə*] *vt* lavar
Launderette® [lɔːn'drɛt] (*BRIT*) *n* lavandería (automática)
Laundromat® ['lɔːndrəmæt] (*US*) *n* = **Launderette**
laundry ['lɔːndrɪ] *n* (*dirty*) ropa sucia; (*clean*) colada; (*room*) lavadero
lava ['lɑːvə] *n* lava
lavatory ['lævətərɪ] *n* wáter m
lavender ['lævəndə*] *n* lavanda
lavish ['lævɪʃ] *adj* (*amount*) abundante;

(person): ~ **with** pródigo en ▷ *vt*: **to ~ sth on sb** colmar a algn de algo

law [lɔ:] *n* ley *f*; *(Scol)* derecho; *(a rule)* regla; *(professions connected with law)* jurisprudencia; **lawful** *adj* legítimo, lícito; **lawless** *adj* *(action)* criminal

lawn [lɔ:n] *n* césped *m*; **lawnmower** *n* cortacésped *m*

lawsuit ['lɔ:su:t] *n* pleito

lawyer ['lɔ:jə*] *n* abogado/a; *(for sales, wills etc)* notario/a

lax [læks] *adj* laxo

laxative ['læksətɪv] *n* laxante *m*

lay [leɪ] *(pt, pp* **laid**) *pt of* **lie** ▷ *adj* laico; *(not expert)* lego ▷ *vt* *(place)* colocar; *(eggs, table)* poner; *(cable)* tender; *(carpet)* extender; **lay down** *vt* *(pen etc)* dejar; *(rules etc)* establecer; **to lay down the law** *(pej)* imponer las normas; **lay off** *vt* *(workers)* despedir; **lay on** *vt* *(meal, facilities)* proveer; **lay out** *vt* *(spread out)* disponer, exponer; **lay-by** *n* *(BRIT Aut)* área de aparcamiento

layer ['leɪə*] *n* capa

layman ['leɪmən] *(irreg)* *n* lego

layout ['leɪaut] *n* *(design)* plan *m*, trazado; *(Press)* composición *f*

lazy ['leɪzɪ] *adj* perezoso, vago; *(movement)* lento

lb. *abbr* = **pound** *(weight)*

lead¹ [li:d] *(pt, pp* **led**) *n* *(front position)* delantera; *(clue)* pista; *(Elec)* cable *m*; *(for dog)* correa; *(Theatre)* papel *m* principal ▷ *vt* *(walk etc in front)* ir a la cabeza de; *(guide)*: **to ~ sb somewhere** conducir a algn a algún sitio; *(be leader)* dirigir; *(start, guide: activity)* protagonizar ▷ *vi* *(road, pipe etc)* conducir a; *(Sport)* ir primero; **to be in the ~** *(Sport)* llevar la delantera; *(fig)* ir a la cabeza; **to ~ the way** llevar la delantera; **lead up to** *vt fus* *(events)* conducir a; *(in conversation)* preparar el terreno para

lead² [lɛd] *n* *(metal)* plomo; *(in pencil)* mina

leader ['li:də*] *n* jefe/a *m/f*, líder *mf*; *(Sport)* líder *mf*; **leadership** *n* dirección *f*; *(position)* mando; *(quality)* iniciativa

lead-free ['lɛdfri:] *adj* sin plomo

leading ['li:dɪŋ] *adj* *(main)* principal; *(first)* primero; *(front)* delantero

lead singer [li:d-] *n* cantante *mf*

leaf [li:f] *(pl* **leaves**) *n* hoja ▷ *vi*: **to ~ through** hojear; **to turn over a new ~** reformarse

leaflet ['li:flɪt] *n* folleto

league [li:g] *n* sociedad *f*; *(Football)* liga; **to be in ~ with** haberse confabulado con

leak [li:k] *n* *(of liquid, gas)* escape *m*, fuga; *(in pipe)* agujero; *(in roof)* gotera; *(in security)* filtración *f* ▷ *vi* *(shoes, ship)* hacer agua;

(pipe) tener *(un)* escape; *(roof)* gotear; *(liquid, gas)* escaparse, fugarse; *(fig)* divulgarse ▷ *vt* *(fig)* filtrar

lean [li:n] *(pt, pp* **~ed** *or* **~t**) *adj* *(thin)* flaco; *(meat)* magro ▷ *vt*: **to ~ sth on sth** apoyar algo en algo ▷ *vi* *(slope)* inclinarse; **to ~ against** apoyarse contra; **to ~ on** apoyarse en; **lean forward** *vi* inclinarse hacia adelante; **lean over** *vi* inclinarse; **leaning** *n*: **leaning (towards)** inclinación *f* *(hacia)*

leant [lɛnt] *pt, pp of* **lean**

leap [li:p] *(pt, pp* **~ed** *or* **~t**) *n* salto ▷ *vi* saltar

leapt [lɛpt] *pt, pp of* **leap**

leap year *n* año bisiesto

learn [lə:n] *(pt, pp* **~ed** *or* **~t**) *vt* aprender ▷ *vi* aprender; **to ~ about sth** enterarse de algo; **to ~ to do sth** aprender a hacer algo; **learner** *n* *(BRIT: also:* **learner driver**) principiante *mf*; **learning** *n* el saber *m*, conocimientos *mpl*

learnt [lə:nt] *pp of* **learn**

lease [li:s] *n* arriendo ▷ *vt* arrendar

leash [li:ʃ] *n* correa

least [li:st] *adj*: **the ~** *(slightest)* el menor, el más pequeño; *(smallest amount of)* mínimo ▷ *adv* *(+ vb)* menos; *(+ adj)*: **the ~ expensive** el *(la)* menos costoso/a; **the ~ possible effort** el menor esfuerzo posible; **at ~** por lo menos, al menos; **you could at ~ have written** por lo menos podías haber escrito; **not in the ~** en absoluto

leather ['lɛðə*] *n* cuero

leave [li:v] *(pt, pp* **left**) *vt* dejar; *(go away from)* abandonar; *(place etc: permanently)* salir de ▷ *vi* irse; *(train etc)* salir ▷ *n* permiso; **to ~ sth to sb** *(money etc)* legar algo a algn; *(responsibility etc)* encargar a algn de algo; **to be left** quedar, sobrar; **there's some milk left over** sobra *or* queda algo de leche; **on ~** de permiso; **leave behind** *vt* *(on purpose)* dejar; *(accidentally)* dejarse; **leave out** *vt* omitir

leaves [li:vz] *npl of* **leaf**

Lebanon ['lɛbənən] *n*: **the ~** el Líbano

lecture ['lɛktʃə*] *n* conferencia; *(Scol)* clase *f* ▷ *vi* dar una clase ▷ *vt* *(scold)*: **to ~ sb on** *or* **about sth** echar una reprimenda a algn por algo; **to give a ~ on** dar una conferencia sobre; **lecture hall** *n* sala de conferencias; *(Univ)* aula; **lecturer** *n* conferenciante *mf*; *(BRIT: at university)* profesor(a) *m/f*; **lecture theatre** *n* = **lecture hall**

led [lɛd] *pt, pp of* **lead¹**

ledge [lɛdʒ] *n* repisa; *(of window)* alféizar *m*; *(of mountain)* saliente *m*

leek [li:k] *n* puerro

left [lɛft] *pt, pp of* **leave** ▷ *adj* izquierdo;

(*remaining*): **there are two ~** quedan dos ▷ *n* izquierda ▷ *adv* a la izquierda; **on** *or* **to the ~** a la izquierda; **the L~** (*Pol*) la izquierda; **left-hand** *adj*: **the left-hand side** la izquierda; **left-hand drive** *adj*: **a left-hand drive car** un coche con el volante a la izquierda; **left-handed** *adj* zurdo; **left-luggage locker** *n* (*BRIT*) consigna *f* automática; **left-luggage (office)** (*BRIT*) *n* consigna; **left-overs** *npl* sobras *fpl*; **left-wing** *adj* (*Pol*) de izquierdas, izquierdista

leg [lɛg] *n* pierna; (*of animal, chair*) pata; (*trouser leg*) pernera; (*Culin: of lamb*) pierna; (: *of chicken*) pata; (*of journey*) etapa

legacy ['lɛgəsɪ] *n* herencia

legal ['liːgl] *adj* (*permitted by law*) lícito; (*of law*) legal; **legal holiday** (*US*) *n* fiesta oficial; **legalize** *vt* legalizar; **legally** *adv* legalmente

legend ['lɛdʒənd] *n* (*also fig: person*) leyenda; **legendary** [-ərɪ] *adj* legendario

leggings ['lɛgɪŋz] *npl* mallas *fpl*, leggins *mpl*

legible ['lɛdʒəbl] *adj* legible

legislation [lɛdʒɪs'leɪʃən] *n* legislación *f*

legislative ['lɛdʒɪslətɪv] *adj* legislativo

legitimate [lɪ'dʒɪtɪmət] *adj* legítimo

leisure ['lɛʒə*] *n* ocio, tiempo libre; **at ~** con tranquilidad; **leisure centre** (*BRIT*) *n* centro de recreo; **leisurely** *adj* sin prisa; lento

lemon ['lɛmən] *n* limón *m*; **lemonade** *n* (*fizzy*) gaseosa; **lemon tea** *n* té *m* con limón

lend [lɛnd] (*pt, pp* **lent**) *vt*: **to ~ sth to sb** prestar algo a algn

length [lɛŋθ] *n* (*size*) largo, longitud *f*; (*distance*): **the ~ of** todo lo largo de; (*of swimming pool, cloth*) largo; (*of wood, string*) trozo; (*amount of time*) duración *f*; **at ~** (*at last*) por fin, finalmente; (*lengthily*) largamente; **lengthen** *vt* alargar ▷ *vi* alargarse; **lengthways** *adv* a lo largo; **lengthy** *adj* largo, extenso

lens [lɛnz] *n* (*of spectacles*) lente *f*; (*of camera*) objetivo

Lent [lɛnt] *n* Cuaresma

lent [lɛnt] *pt, pp of* **lend**

lentil ['lɛntl] *n* lenteja

Leo ['liːəu] *n* Leo

leopard ['lɛpəd] *n* leopardo

leotard ['liːətɑːd] *n* mallas *fpl*

leprosy ['lɛprəsɪ] *n* lepra

lesbian ['lɛzbɪən] *n* lesbiana

less [lɛs] *adj* (*in size, degree etc*) menor; (*in quality*) menos ▷ *pron, adv* menos ▷ *prep*: **~ tax/10% discount** menos impuestos/el 10 por ciento de descuento; **~ than half** menos de la mitad; **~ than ever** menos que nunca; **~ and ~** cada vez menos; **the ~ he works ...** cuanto menos trabaja ...; **lessen** *vi* disminuir, reducirse ▷ *vt* disminuir, reducir; **lesser** ['lɛsə*] *adj* menor; **to a lesser extent** en menor grado

lesson ['lɛsn] *n* clase *f*; (*warning*) lección *f*

let [lɛt] (*pt, pp* **~**) *vt* (*allow*) dejar, permitir; (*BRIT: lease*) alquilar; **to ~ sb do sth** dejar que algn haga algo; **to ~ sb know sth** comunicar algo a algn; **~'s go** ¡vamos!; **~ him come** que venga; "**to ~**" "se alquila"; **let down** *vt* (*tyre*) desinflar; (*disappoint*) defraudar; **let in** *vt* dejar entrar; (*visitor etc*) hacer pasar; **let off** *vt* (*culprit*) dejar escapar; (*gun*) disparar; (*bomb*) accionar; (*firework*) hacer estallar; **let out** *vt* dejar salir; (*sound*) soltar

lethal ['liːθl] *adj* (*weapon*) mortífero; (*poison, wound*) mortal

letter ['lɛtə*] *n* (*of alphabet*) letra; (*correspondence*) carta; **letterbox** (*BRIT*) *n* buzón *m*

lettuce ['lɛtɪs] *n* lechuga

leukaemia [luː'kiːmɪə] (*US* **leukemia**) *n* leucemia

level ['lɛvl] *adj* (*flat*) llano ▷ *adv*: **to draw ~ with** llegar a la altura de ▷ *n* nivel *m*; (*height*) altura ▷ *vt* nivelar; allanar; (*destroy: building*) derribar; (: *forest*) arrasar; **to be ~ with** estar a nivel de; **A ~s** (*BRIT*) ≈ exámenes *mpl* de bachillerato superior, B.U.P.; **AS ~** (*BRIT*) asignatura aprobada entre los "GCSEs" y los "A levels"; **on the ~** (*fig: honest*) serio; **level crossing** (*BRIT*) *n* paso a nivel

lever ['liːvə*] *n* (*also fig*) palanca ▷ *vt*: **to ~ up** levantar con palanca; **leverage** *n* (*using bar etc*) apalancamiento; (*fig: influence*) influencia

levy ['lɛvɪ] *n* impuesto ▷ *vt* exigir, recaudar

liability [laɪə'bɪlɪtɪ] *n* (*pej: person, thing*) estorbo, lastre *m*; (*Jur: responsibility*) responsabilidad *f*

liable ['laɪəbl] *adj* (*subject*): **~ to** sujeto a; (*responsible*): **~ for** responsable de; (*likely*): **~ to do** propenso a hacer

liaise [lɪ'eɪz] *vi*: **to ~ with** enlazar con

liar ['laɪə*] *n* mentiroso/a

liberal ['lɪbərəl] *adj* liberal; (*offer, amount etc*) generoso; **Liberal Democrat** *n* (*BRIT*) demócrata *m/f* liberal

liberate ['lɪbəreɪt] *vt* (*people: from poverty etc*) librar; (*prisoner*) libertar; (*country*) liberar

liberation [lɪbə'reɪʃən] *n* liberación *f*

liberty ['lɪbətɪ] *n* libertad *f*; **to be at ~** (*criminal*) estar en libertad; **to be at ~ to do** estar libre para hacer; **to take the ~ of doing sth** tomarse la libertad de hacer algo

Libra ['liːbrə] *n* Libra

librarian [laɪˈbrɛərɪən] n bibliotecario/a
library ['laɪbrərɪ] n biblioteca

Be careful not to translate **library** by the Spanish word *librería*.

Libya ['lɪbɪə] n Libia
lice [laɪs] npl of **louse**
licence ['laɪsəns] (us **license**) n licencia; (*permit*) permiso; (*also*: **driving ~**) carnet m de conducir (sp), licencia de manejo (LAM)
license ['laɪsəns] n (us) = **licence** ▷ vt autorizar, dar permiso a; **licensed** adj (*for alcohol*) autorizado para vender bebidas alcohólicas; (*car*) matriculado; **license plate** (us) n placa (de matrícula); **licensing hours** (BRIT) npl horas durante las cuales se permite la venta y consumo de alcohol (en un bar etc)
lick [lɪk] vt lamer; (*inf: defeat*) dar una paliza a; **to ~ one's lips** relamerse
lid [lɪd] n (*of box, case*) tapa; (*of pan*) tapadera
lie [laɪ] (*pt* **lay**, *pp* **lain**) vi (*rest*) estar echado, estar acostado; (*of object: be situated*) estar, encontrarse; (*tell lies: pt, pp* **lied**) mentir ▷ n mentira; **to ~ low** (*fig*) mantenerse a escondidas; **lie about** or **around** vi (*things*) estar tirado; (BRIT: *people*) estar tumbado; **lie down** vi echarse, tumbarse
Liechtenstein ['lɪktənstaɪn] n Liechtenstein m
lie-in ['laɪɪn] (BRIT) n: **to have a ~** quedarse en la cama
lieutenant [lɛfˈtɛnənt, us luːˈtɛnənt] n (*Mil*) teniente mf
life [laɪf] (*pl* **lives**) n vida; **to come to ~** animarse; **life assurance** (BRIT) n seguro de vida; **lifeboat** n lancha de socorro; **lifeguard** n vigilante mf, socorrista mf; **life insurance** n = **life assurance**; **life jacket** n chaleco salvavidas; **lifelike** adj (*model etc*) que parece vivo; (*realistic*) realista; **life preserver** (us) n cinturón m/chaleco salvavidas; **life sentence** n cadena perpetua; **lifestyle** n estilo de vida; **lifetime** n (*of person*) vida; (*of thing*) período de vida
lift [lɪft] vt levantar; (*end: ban, rule*) levantar, suprimir ▷ vi (*fog*) disiparse ▷ n (BRIT: *machine*) ascensor m; **to give sb a ~** (BRIT) llevar a algn en el coche; **lift up** vt levantar; **lift-off** n despegue m
light [laɪt] (*pt, pp* **~ed** or **lit**) n luz f; (*lamp*) luz f, lámpara; (*Aut*) faro; (*for cigarette etc*): **have you got a ~?** ¿tienes fuego? ▷ vt (*candle, cigarette, fire*) encender (sp), prender (LAM); (*room*) alumbrar ▷ adj (*colour*) claro; (*not heavy, also fig*) ligero; (*room*) con mucha

luz; (*gentle, graceful*) ágil; **lights** npl (*traffic lights*) semáforos mpl; **to come to ~** salir a luz; **in the ~ of** (*new evidence etc*) a la luz de; **light up** vi (*smoke*) encender un cigarrillo; (*face*) iluminarse ▷ vt (*illuminate*) iluminar, alumbrar; (*set fire to*) encender; **light bulb** n bombilla (sp), foco (MEX), bujía (CAM), bombita (RPL); **lighten** vt (*make less heavy*) aligerar; **lighter** n (*also*: **cigarette lighter**) encendedor m, mechero; **light-hearted** adj (*person*) alegre; (*remark etc*) divertido; **lighthouse** n faro; **lighting** n (*system*) alumbrado; **lightly** adv ligeramente; (*not seriously*) con poca seriedad; **to get off lightly** ser castigado con poca severidad
lightning ['laɪtnɪŋ] n relámpago, rayo
lightweight ['laɪtweɪt] adj (*suit*) ligero ▷ n (*Boxing*) peso ligero
like [laɪk] vt gustarle a algn ▷ prep como ▷ adj parecido, semejante ▷ n: **and the ~** y otros por el estilo; **his ~s and dislikes** sus gustos y aversiones; **I would ~, I'd ~** me gustaría; (*for purchase*) quisiera; **would you ~ a coffee?** ¿te apetece un café?; **I ~ swimming** me gusta nadar; **she ~s apples** le gustan las manzanas; **to be** or **look ~ sb/ sth** parecerse a algn/algo; **what does it look/taste/sound ~?** ¿cómo es/a qué sabe/ cómo suena?; **that's just ~ him** es muy de él, es característico de él; **do it ~ this** hazlo así; **it is nothing ~ ...** no tiene parecido alguno con ...; **likeable** adj simpático, agradable
likelihood ['laɪklɪhud] n probabilidad f
likely ['laɪklɪ] adj probable; **he's ~ to leave** es probable que se vaya; **not ~!** ¡ni hablar!
likewise ['laɪkwaɪz] adv igualmente; **to do ~** hacer lo mismo
liking ['laɪkɪŋ] n: **~ (for)** (*person*) cariño (a); (*thing*) afición (a); **to be to sb's ~** ser del gusto de algn
lilac ['laɪlək] n (*tree*) lilo; (*flower*) lila
Lilo® ['laɪləu] n colchoneta inflable
lily ['lɪlɪ] n lirio, azucena; **~ of the valley** lirio de los valles
limb [lɪm] n miembro
limbo ['lɪmbəu] n: **to be in ~** (*fig*) quedar a la expectativa
lime [laɪm] n (*tree*) limero; (*fruit*) lima; (*Geo*) cal f
limelight ['laɪmlaɪt] n: **to be in the ~** (*fig*) ser el centro de atención
limestone ['laɪmstəun] n piedra caliza
limit ['lɪmɪt] n límite m ▷ vt limitar; **limited** adj limitado; **to be limited to** limitarse a
limousine ['lɪməziːn] n limusina
limp [lɪmp] n: **to have a ~** tener cojera ▷ vi

cojear ▷ *adj* flojo; (*material*) fláccido

line [laɪn] *n* línea; (*rope*) cuerda; (*for fishing*) sedal *m*; (*wire*) hilo; (*row, series*) fila, hilera; (*of writing*) renglón *m*, línea; (*of song*) verso; (*on face*) arruga; (*Rail*) vía ▷ *vt* (*road etc*) llenar; (*Sewing*) forrar; **to ~ the streets** llenar las aceras; **in ~ with** alineado con; (*according to*) de acuerdo con; **line up** *vi* hacer cola ▷ *vt* alinear; (*prepare*) preparar; organizar

linear ['lɪnɪə*] *adj* lineal

linen ['lɪnɪn] *n* ropa blanca; (*cloth*) lino

liner ['laɪnə*] *n* vapor *m* de línea, transatlántico; (*for bin*) bolsa (de basura)

line-up ['laɪnʌp] *n* (*us: queue*) cola; (*Sport*) alineación *f*

linger ['lɪŋgə*] *vi* retrasarse, tardar en marcharse; (*smell, tradition*) persistir

lingerie ['lænʒəriː] *n* lencería

linguist ['lɪŋgwɪst] *n* lingüista *mf*; **linguistic** *adj* lingüístico

lining ['laɪnɪŋ] *n* forro; (*Anat*) (membrana) mucosa

link [lɪŋk] *n* (*of a chain*) eslabón *m*; (*relationship*) relación *f*, vínculo; (*Internet*) link *m*, enlace *m* ▷ *vt* vincular, unir; (*associate*): **to ~ with** *or* **to** relacionar con; **links** *npl* (*Golf*) campo de golf; **link up** *vt* acoplar ▷ *vi* unirse

lion ['laɪən] *n* león *m*; **lioness** *n* leona

lip [lɪp] *n* labio; **lipread** *vi* leer los labios; **lip salve** *n* crema protectora para labios; **lipstick** *n* lápiz *m* de labios, carmín *m*

liqueur [lɪ'kjuə*] *n* licor *m*

liquid ['lɪkwɪd] *adj, n* líquido; **liquidizer** [-aɪzə*] *n* licuadora

liquor ['lɪkə*] *n* licor *m*, bebidas *fpl* alcohólicas; **liquor store** (*us*) *n* bodega, tienda de vinos y bebidas alcohólicas

Lisbon ['lɪzbən] *n* Lisboa

lisp [lɪsp] *n* ceceo ▷ *vi* cecear

list [lɪst] *n* lista ▷ *vt* (*mention*) enumerar; (*put on a list*) poner en una lista

listen ['lɪsn] *vi* escuchar, oír; **to ~ to sb/sth** escuchar a algn/algo; **listener** *n* oyente *mf*; (*Radio*) radioyente *mf*

lit [lɪt] *pt, pp of* **light**

liter ['liːtə*] (*us*) *n* = **litre**

literacy ['lɪtərəsɪ] *n* capacidad *f* de leer y escribir

literal ['lɪtərl] *adj* literal; **literally** *adv* literalmente

literary ['lɪtərərɪ] *adj* literario

literate ['lɪtərət] *adj* que sabe leer y escribir; (*educated*) culto

literature ['lɪtərɪtʃə*] *n* literatura; (*brochures etc*) folletos *mpl*

litre ['liːtə*] (*us* **liter**) *n* litro

litter ['lɪtə*] *n* (*rubbish*) basura; (*young animals*) camada, cría; **litter bin** (*BRIT*) *n* papelera; **littered** *adj*: **littered with** (*scattered*) lleno de

little ['lɪtl] *adj* (*small*) pequeño; (*not much*) poco ▷ *adv* poco; **a ~** un poco (de); **~ house/bird** casita/pajarito; **a ~ bit** un poquito; **~ by ~** poco a poco; **little finger** *n* dedo meñique

live¹ [laɪv] *adj* (*animal*) vivo; (*wire*) conectado; (*broadcast*) en directo; (*shell*) cargado

live² [lɪv] *vi* vivir; **live together** *vi* vivir juntos; **live up to** *vt fus* (*fulfil*) cumplir con

livelihood ['laɪvlɪhud] *n* sustento

lively ['laɪvlɪ] *adj* vivo; (*interesting: place, book etc*) animado

liven up ['laɪvn-] *vt* animar ▷ *vi* animarse

liver ['lɪvə*] *n* hígado

lives [laɪvz] *npl of* **life**

livestock ['laɪvstɔk] *n* ganado

living ['lɪvɪŋ] *adj* (*alive*) vivo ▷ *n*: **to earn** *or* **make a ~** ganarse la vida; **living room** *n* sala (de estar)

lizard ['lɪzəd] *n* lagarto; (*small*) lagartija

load [ləud] *n* carga; (*weight*) peso ▷ *vt* (*Comput*) cargar; (*also*: ~ **up**): **to ~ (with)** cargar (con *or* de); **a ~ of rubbish** (*inf*) tonterías *fpl*; **a ~ of, ~s of** (*fig*) (gran) cantidad de, montones de; **loaded** *adj* (*vehicle*): **to be loaded with** estar cargado de

loaf [ləuf] (*pl* **loaves**) *n* (barra de) pan *m*

loan [ləun] *n* préstamo ▷ *vt* prestar; **on ~** prestado

loathe [ləuð] *vt* aborrecer; (*person*) odiar

loaves [ləuvz] *npl of* **loaf**

lobby ['lɔbɪ] *n* vestíbulo, sala de espera; (*Pol: pressure group*) grupo de presión ▷ *vt* presionar

lobster ['lɔbstə*] *n* langosta

local ['ləukl] *adj* local ▷ *n* (*pub*) bar *m*; **the locals** *npl* los vecinos, los del lugar; **local anaesthetic** *n* (*Med*) anestesia local; **local authority** *n* municipio, ayuntamiento (*SP*); **local government** *n* gobierno municipal; **locally** [-kəlɪ] *adv* en la vecindad; por aquí

locate [ləu'keɪt] *vt* (*find*) localizar; (*situate*): **to be ~d in** estar situado en

location [ləu'keɪʃən] *n* situación *f*; **on ~** (*Cinema*) en exteriores

loch [lɔx] *n* lago

lock [lɔk] *n* (*of door, box*) cerradura; (*of canal*) esclusa; (*of hair*) mechón *m* ▷ *vt* (*with key*) cerrar (con llave) ▷ *vi* (*door etc*) cerrarse (con llave); (*wheels*) trabarse; **lock in** *vt* encerrar; **lock out** *vt* (*person*) cerrar la puerta a; **lock up** *vt* (*criminal*) meter en la cárcel; (*mental patient*) encerrar; (*house*) cerrar (con llave) ▷ *vi* echar la llave

locker ['lɔkə*] *n* casillero; **locker-room** (US) *n* (*Sport*) vestuario

locksmith ['lɔksmɪθ] *n* cerrajero/a

locomotive [ləukə'məutɪv] *n* locomotora

lodge [lɔdʒ] *n* casita (del guarda) ▷ *vi* (*person*): **to ~ (with)** alojarse (en casa de); (*bullet, bone*) incrustarse ▷ *vt* presentar; **lodger** *n* huésped *mf*

lodging ['lɔdʒɪŋ] *n* alojamiento, hospedaje *m*

loft [lɔft] *n* desván *m*

log [lɔg] *n* (*of wood*) leño, tronco; (*written account*) diario ▷ *vt* anotar; **log in, log on** *vi* (*Comput*) entrar en el sistema; **log off, log out** *vi* (*Comput*) salir del sistema

logic ['lɔdʒɪk] *n* lógica; **logical** *adj* lógico

logo ['ləugəu] *n* logotipo

lollipop ['lɔlɪpɔp] *n* pirulí *m*; **lollipop man/lady** (BRIT: *irreg*) *n* persona encargada de ayudar a los niños a cruzar la calle

lolly ['lɔlɪ] *n* (*inf: ice cream*) polo; (: *lollipop*) piruleta; (: *money*) guita

London ['lʌndən] *n* Londres; **Londoner** *n* londinense *mf*

lone [ləun] *adj* solitario

loneliness ['ləunlɪnɪs] *n* soledad *f*; aislamiento

lonely ['ləunlɪ] *adj* (*situation*) solitario; (*person*) solo; (*place*) aislado

long [lɔŋ] *adj* largo ▷ *adv* mucho tiempo, largamente ▷ *vi*: **to ~ for sth** anhelar algo; **so** *or* **as ~ as** mientras, con tal que; **don't be ~!** ¡no tardes!, ¡vuelve pronto!; **how ~ is the street?** ¿cuánto tiene la calle de largo?; **how ~ is the lesson?** ¿cuánto dura la clase?; **6 metres ~** que mide 6 metros, de 6 metros de largo; **6 months ~** que dura 6 meses, de 6 meses de duración; **all night ~** toda la noche; **he no ~er comes** ya no viene; **I can't stand it any ~er** ya no lo aguanto más; **~ before** mucho antes; **before ~** (+ *future*) dentro de poco; (+ *past*) poco tiempo después; **at ~ last** al fin, por fin; **long-distance** *adj* (*race*) de larga distancia; (*call*) interurbano; **long-haul** *adj* (*flight*) de larga distancia; **longing** *n* anhelo, ansia; (*nostalgia*) nostalgia ▷ *adj* anhelante

longitude ['lɔŋgɪtjuːd] *n* longitud *f*

long: long jump *n* salto de longitud; **long-life** *adj* (*batteries*) de larga duración; (*milk*) uperizado; **long-sighted** (BRIT) *adj* présbita; **long-standing** *adj* de mucho tiempo; **long-term** *adj* a largo plazo

loo [luː] (BRIT: *inf*) *n* wáter *m*

look [luk] *vi* mirar; (*seem*) parecer; (*building etc*): **to ~ south/on to the sea** dar al sur/al mar ▷ *n* (*gen*): **to have a ~** mirar; (*glance*)

mirada; (*appearance*) aire *m*, aspecto; **looks** *npl* (*good looks*) belleza; **~ (here)!** (*expressing annoyance etc*) ¡oye!; **~!** (*expressing surprise*) ¡mira!; **look after** *vt fus* (*care for*) cuidar a; (*deal with*) encargarse de; **look around** *vi* echar una mirada alrededor; **look at** *vt fus* mirar; (*read quickly*) echar un vistazo a; **look back** *vi* mirar hacia atrás; **look down on** *vt fus* (*fig*) despreciar, mirar con desprecio; **look for** *vt fus* buscar; **look forward to** *vt fus* esperar con ilusión; (*in letters*): **we look forward to hearing from you** quedamos a la espera de sus gratas noticias; **look into** *vt* investigar; **look out** *vi* (*beware*): **to look out (for)** tener cuidado (de); **look out for** *vt fus* (*seek*) buscar; (*await*) esperar; **look round** *vi* volver la cabeza; **look through** *vt fus* (*examine*) examinar; **look up** *vi* mirar hacia arriba; (*improve*) mejorar ▷ *vt* (*word*) buscar; **look up to** *vt fus* admirar; **lookout** *n* (*tower etc*) puesto de observación; (*person*) vigía *mf*; **to be on the lookout for sth** estar al acecho de algo

loom [luːm] *vi*: **~ (up)** (*threaten*) surgir, amenazar; (*event: approach*) aproximarse

loony ['luːnɪ] (*inf*) *n, adj* loco/a *m/f*

loop [luːp] *n* lazo ▷ *vt*: **to ~ sth round sth** pasar algo alrededor de algo; **loophole** *n* escapatoria

loose [luːs] *adj* suelto; (*clothes*) ancho; (*morals, discipline*) relajado; **to be on the ~** estar en libertad; **to be at a ~ end** *or* **at ~ ends** (US) no saber qué hacer; **loosely** *adv* libremente, aproximadamente; **loosen** *vt* aflojar

loot [luːt] *n* botín *m* ▷ *vt* saquear

lop-sided ['lɔp'saɪdɪd] *adj* torcido

lord [lɔːd] *n* señor *m*; **L~ Smith** Lord Smith; **the L~** el Señor; **my ~** (*to bishop*) Ilustrísima; (*to noble etc*) Señor; **good L~!** ¡Dios mío!; **Lords** *npl* (BRIT: *Pol*): **the (House of) Lords** la Cámara de los Lores

lorry ['lɔrɪ] (BRIT) *n* camión *m*; **lorry driver** (BRIT) *n* camionero/a

lose [luːz] (*pt, pp* lost) *vt* perder ▷ *vi* perder, ser vencido; **to ~ (time)** (*clock*) atrasarse; **lose out** *vi* salir perdiendo; **loser** *n* perdedor(a) *m/f*

loss [lɔs] *n* pérdida; **heavy ~es** (*Mil*) grandes pérdidas; **to be at a ~** no saber qué hacer; **to make a ~** sufrir pérdidas

lost [lɔst] *pt, pp* *of* lose ▷ *adj* perdido; **lost property** (US **lost and found**) *n* objetos *mpl* perdidos

lot [lɔt] *n* (*group: of things*) grupo; (*at auctions*) lote *m*; **the ~** el todo, todos; **a ~** (*large number: of books etc*) muchos; (*a great deal*) mucho, bastante; **a ~ of, ~s**

of mucho(s) (*pl*); **I read a ~** leo bastante; **to draw ~s (for sth)** echar suertes (para decidir algo)

lotion ['ləʊʃən] *n* loción *f*

lottery ['lɔtərɪ] *n* lotería

loud [laʊd] *adj* (*voice, sound*) fuerte; (*laugh, shout*) estrepitoso; (*condemnation etc*) enérgico; (*gaudy*) chillón/ona ▷ *adv* (*speak etc*) fuerte; **out ~** en voz alta; **loudly** *adv* (*noisily*) fuerte; (*aloud*) en voz alta; **loudspeaker** *n* altavoz *m*

lounge [laʊndʒ] *n* salón *m*, sala (de estar); (*at airport etc*) sala; (*BRIT: also:* **~-bar**) salón-bar *m* ▷ *vi* (*also:* **~ about** *or* **around**) reposar, holgazanear

louse [laʊs] (*pl* **lice**) *n* piojo

lousy ['laʊzɪ] (*inf*) *adj* (*bad quality*) malísimo, asqueroso; (*ill*) fatal

love [lʌv] *n* (*romantic, sexual*) amor *m*; (*kind, caring*) cariño ▷ *vt* amar, querer; (*thing, activity*) encantarle a algn; **"~ from Anne"** (*on letter*) "un abrazo (de) Anne"; **to ~ to do** encantarle a algn hacer; **to be/fall in ~ with** estar enamorado/enamorarse de; **to make ~** hacer el amor; **for the ~ of** por amor de; **"15 ~"** (*Tennis*) "15 a cero"; **I ~ you** te quiero; **I ~ paella** me encanta la paella; **love affair** *n* aventura sentimental; **love life** *n* vida sentimental

lovely ['lʌvlɪ] *adj* (*delightful*) encantador(a); (*beautiful*) precioso

lover ['lʌvə*] *n* amante *mf*; (*person in love*) enamorado; (*amateur*): **a ~ of** un(a) aficionado/a *or* un(a) amante de

loving ['lʌvɪŋ] *adj* amoroso, cariñoso; (*action*) tierno

low [ləʊ] *adj, adv* bajo ▷ *n* (*Meteorology*) área de baja presión; **to be ~ on** (*supplies etc*) andar mal de; **to feel ~** sentirse deprimido; **to turn (down) ~** bajar; **low-alcohol** *adj* de bajo contenido en alcohol; **low-calorie** *adj* bajo en calorías

lower ['ləʊə*] *adj* más bajo; (*less important*) menos importante ▷ *vt* bajar; (*reduce*) reducir ▷ *vr*: **to ~ o.s. to** (*fig*) rebajarse a

low-fat *adj* (*milk, yoghurt*) desnatado; (*diet*) bajo en calorías

loyal ['lɔɪəl] *adj* leal; **loyalty** *n* lealtad *f*; **loyalty card** *n* tarjeta cliente

L.P. *n abbr* (= *long-playing record*) elepé *m*

L-plates ['ɛl-] (*BRIT*) *npl* placas *fpl* de aprendiz de conductor

L-PLATES

En el Reino Unido las personas que están aprendiendo a conducir deben llevar en la parte delantera y trasera de su vehículo unas placas blancas con una L en rojo conocidas como **L-Plates** (de **learner**). No es necesario que asistan a clases teóricas sino que, desde el principio, se le sentrega un carnet de conducir provisional ("provisional driving licence") para que realicen sus prácticas, aunque no pueden circular por las autopistas y deben ir siempre acompañadas por un conductor con carnet definitivo ("full driving licence").

Lt *abbr* (= *lieutenant*) Tte.

Ltd *abbr* (= *limited company*) S.A.

luck [lʌk] *n* suerte *f*; **bad ~** mala suerte; **good ~!** ¡que tengas suerte!, ¡suerte!; **bad** *or* **hard** *or* **tough ~!** ¡qué pena!; **luckily** *adv* afortunadamente; **lucky** *adj* afortunado; (*at cards etc*) con suerte; (*object*) que trae suerte

lucrative ['lu:krətɪv] *adj* lucrativo

ludicrous ['lu:dɪkrəs] *adj* absurdo

luggage ['lʌgɪdʒ] *n* equipaje *m*; **luggage rack** *n* (*on car*) baca, portaequipajes *m inv*

lukewarm ['lu:kwɔ:m] *adj* tibio

lull [lʌl] *n* tregua ▷ *vt*: **to ~ sb to sleep** arrullar a algn; **to ~ sb into a false sense of security** dar a algn una falsa sensación de seguridad

lullaby ['lʌləbaɪ] *n* nana

lumber ['lʌmbə*] *n* (*junk*) trastos *mpl* viejos; (*wood*) maderos *mpl*

luminous ['lu:mɪnəs] *adj* luminoso

lump [lʌmp] *n* terrón *m*; (*fragment*) trozo; (*swelling*) bulto ▷ *vt* (*also:* **~ together**) juntar; **lump sum** *n* suma global; **lumpy** *adj* (*sauce*) lleno de grumos; (*mattress*) lleno de bultos

lunatic ['lu:nətɪk] *adj* loco

lunch [lʌntʃ] *n* almuerzo, comida ▷ *vi* almorzar; **lunch break, lunch hour** *n* hora del almuerzo; **lunch time** *n* hora de comer

lung [lʌŋ] *n* pulmón *m*

lure [luə*] *n* (*attraction*) atracción *f* ▷ *vt* tentar

lurk [lə:k] *vi* (*person, animal*) estar al acecho; (*fig*) acechar

lush [lʌʃ] *adj* exuberante

lust [lʌst] *n* lujuria; (*greed*) codicia

Luxembourg ['lʌksəmbə:g] *n* Luxemburgo

luxurious [lʌg'zjuərɪəs] *adj* lujoso

luxury ['lʌkʃərɪ] *n* lujo ▷ *cpd* de lujo

Lycra® ['laɪkrə] *n* licra®

lying ['laɪɪŋ] *n* mentiras *fpl* ▷ *adj* mentiroso

lyrics ['lɪrɪks] *npl* (*of song*) letra

m. *abbr* = **metre; mile; million**

M.A. *abbr* = **Master of Arts**

ma (*inf*) [mɑ:] *n* mamá

mac [mæk] (BRIT) *n* impermeable *m*

macaroni [mækə'rəunɪ] *n* macarrones *mpl*

Macedonia [mæsɪ'dəunɪə] *n* Macedonia; **Macedonian** [-'dəunɪən] *adj* macedonio ▷ *n* macedonio/a; (*Ling*) macedonio

machine [mə'ʃi:n] *n* máquina ▷ *vt* (*dress etc*) coser a máquina; (*Tech*) hacer a máquina; **machine gun** *n* ametralladora; **machinery** *n* maquinaria; (*fig*) mecanismo; **machine washable** *adj* lavable a máquina

macho ['mætʃəu] *adj* machista

mackerel ['mækrl] *n inv* caballa

mackintosh ['mækɪntɔʃ] (BRIT) *n* impermeable *m*

mad [mæd] *adj* loco; (*idea*) disparatado; (*angry*) furioso; (*keen*): **to be ~ about sth** volverle loco a algn algo

Madagascar [mædə'gæskə*] *n* Madagascar *m*

madam ['mædəm] *n* señora

mad cow disease *n* encefalopatía espongiforme bovina

made [meɪd] *pt, pp of* **make; made-to-measure** (BRIT) *adj* hecho a la medida; **made-up** ['meɪdʌp] *adj* (*story*) ficticio

madly ['mædlɪ] *adv* locamente

madman ['mædmən] (*irreg*) *n* loco

madness ['mædnɪs] *n* locura

Madrid [mə'drɪd] *n* Madrid

Mafia ['mæfɪə] *n* Mafia

mag [mæg] *n abbr* (BRIT *inf*) = **magazine**

magazine [mægə'zi:n] *n* revista; (*Radio, TV*) programa *m* magazine

maggot ['mægət] *n* gusano

magic ['mædʒɪk] *n* magia ▷ *adj* mágico; **magical** *adj* mágico; **magician**

[mə'dʒɪʃən] *n* mago/a; (*conjurer*) prestidigitador(a) *m/f*

magistrate ['mædʒɪstreɪt] *n* juez *mf* (municipal)

magnet ['mægnɪt] *n* imán *m*; **magnetic** [-'nɛtɪk] *adj* magnético; (*personality*) atrayente

magnificent [mæg'nɪfɪsənt] *adj* magnífico

magnify ['mægnɪfaɪ] *vt* (*object*) ampliar; (*sound*) aumentar; **magnifying glass** *n* lupa

magpie ['mægpaɪ] *n* urraca

mahogany [mə'hɔgənɪ] *n* caoba

maid [meɪd] *n* criada; **old ~** (*pej*) solterona

maiden name *n* nombre *m* de soltera

mail [meɪl] *n* correo; (*letters*) cartas *fpl* ▷ *vt* echar al correo; **mailbox** (US) *n* buzón *m*; **mailing list** *n* lista de direcciones; **mailman** (US: *irreg*) *n* cartero; **mail-order** *n* pedido postal

main [meɪn] *adj* principal, mayor ▷ *n* (*pipe*) cañería maestra; (US) red *f* eléctrica ▷ **the ~s** *npl* (BRIT *Elec*) la red eléctrica; **in the ~** en general; **main course** *n* (*Culin*) plato principal; **mainland** *n* tierra firme; **mainly** *adv* principalmente; **main road** *n* carretera; **mainstream** *n* corriente *f* principal; **main street** *n* calle *f* mayor

maintain [meɪn'teɪn] *vt* mantener; **maintenance** ['meɪntənəns] *n* mantenimiento; (*Law*) manutención *f*

maisonette [meɪzə'nɛt] *n* dúplex *m*

maize [meɪz] (BRIT) *n* maíz *m*, choclo (SC)

majesty ['mædʒɪstɪ] *n* majestad *f*; (*title*): **Your M~** Su Majestad

major ['meɪdʒə*] *n* (*Mil*) comandante *mf* ▷ *adj* principal; (*Mus*) mayor

Majorca [mə'jɔ:kə] *n* Mallorca

majority [mə'dʒɔrɪtɪ] *n* mayoría

make [meɪk] (*pt, pp* **made**) *vt* hacer; (*manufacture*) fabricar; (*mistake*) cometer; (*speech*) pronunciar; (*cause to be*): **to ~ sb sad** poner triste a algn; (*force*): **to ~ sb do sth** obligar a algn a hacer algo; (*earn*) ganar; (*equal*): **2 and 2 ~ 4** 2 y 2 son 4 ▷ *n* marca; **to ~ the bed** hacer la cama; **to ~ a fool of sb** poner a algn en ridículo; **to ~ a profit/loss** obtener ganancias/sufrir pérdidas; **to ~ it** (*arrive*) llegar; (*achieve sth*) tener éxito; **what time do you ~ it?** ¿qué hora tienes?; **to ~ do with** contentarse con; **make off** *vi* largarse; **make out** *vt* (*decipher*) descifrar; (*understand*) entender; (*see*) distinguir; (*cheque*) extender; **make up** *vt* (*invent*) inventar; (*prepare*) hacer; (*constitute*) constituir ▷ *vi* reconciliarse; (*with cosmetics*) maquillarse; **make up for** *vt*

fus compensar; **makeover** ['meɪkəuvə*]
n (*by beautician*) sesión *f* de maquillaje y
peluquería; (*change of image*) lavado de cara;
maker *n* fabricante *mf*; (*of film, programme*)
autor(a) *m/f*; **makeshift** *adj* improvisado;
make-up *n* maquillaje *m*
making ['meɪkɪŋ] *n* (*fig*): **in the ~** en vías
de formación; **to have the ~s of** (*person*)
tener madera de
malaria [mə'lɛərɪə] *n* malaria
Malaysia [mə'leɪzɪə] *n* Malasia, Malaysia
male [meɪl] *n* (*Biol*) macho ▷ *adj* (*sex,
attitude*) masculino; (*child etc*) varón
malicious [mə'lɪʃəs] *adj* malicioso;
rencoroso
malignant [mə'lɪgnənt] *adj* (*Med*)
maligno
mall [mɔ:l] (*US*) *n* (*also*: **shopping ~**) centro
comercial
mallet ['mælɪt] *n* mazo
malnutrition [mælnju:'trɪʃən] *n*
desnutrición *f*
malpractice [mæl'præktɪs] *n*
negligencia profesional
malt [mɔ:lt] *n* malta; (*whisky*) whisky *m*
de malta
Malta ['mɔ:ltə] *n* Malta; **Maltese** [-'ti:z]
adj, n inv maltés/esa *m/f*
mammal ['mæml] *n* mamífero
mammoth ['mæməθ] *n* mamut *m* ▷ *adj*
gigantesco
man [mæn] (*pl* **men**) *n* hombre *m*;
(*mankind*) el hombre ▷ *vt* (*Naut*) tripular;
(*Mil*) guarnecer; (*operate: machine*) manejar;
an old ~ un viejo; **~ and wife** marido y
mujer
manage ['mænɪdʒ] *vi* arreglárselas,
ir tirando ▷ *vt* (*be in charge of*) dirigir;
(*control: person*) manejar; (: *ship*)
gobernar; **manageable** *adj* manejable;
management *n* dirección *f*; **manager** *n*
director(a) *m/f*; (*of pop star*) mánager *mf*;
(*Sport*) entrenador(a) *m/f*; **manageress**
n directora; entrenadora; **managerial**
[-ə'dʒɪərɪəl] *adj* directivo; **managing
director** *n* director(a) *m/f* general
mandarin ['mændərɪn] *n* (*also*: **~ orange**)
mandarina; (*person*) mandarín *n*
mandate ['mændeɪt] *n* mandato
mandatory ['mændətərɪ] *adj* obligatorio
mane [meɪn] *n* (*of horse*) crin *f*; (*of lion*)
melena
maneuver [mə'nu:və*] (*US*) = **manoeuvre**
mangetout [mɔnʒ'tu:] *n* tirabeque *m*
mango ['mæŋgəu] (*pl* **~es**) *n* mango
man: manhole *n* agujero de acceso;
manhood *n* edad *f* viril; (*state*) virilidad *f*
mania ['meɪnɪə] *n* manía; **maniac**

['meɪnɪæk] *n* maníaco/a; (*fig*) maniático
manic ['mænɪk] *adj* frenético
manicure ['mænɪkjuə*] *n* manicura
manifest ['mænɪfɛst] *vt* manifestar,
mostrar ▷ *adj* manifiesto
manifesto [mænɪ'fɛstəu] *n* manifiesto
manipulate [mə'nɪpjuleɪt] *vt* manipular
man: mankind [mæn'kaɪnd] *n*
humanidad *f*, género humano; **manly** *adj*
varonil; **man-made** *adj* artificial
manner ['mænə*] *n* manera, modo;
(*behaviour*) conducta, manera de ser;
(*type*): **all ~ of things** toda clase de cosas;
manners *npl* (*behaviour*) modales *mpl*; **bad
~s** mala educación
manoeuvre [mə'nu:və*] (*US* **maneuver**)
vt, vi maniobrar ▷ *n* maniobra
manpower ['mænpauə*] *n* mano *f* de
obra
mansion ['mænʃən] *n* palacio, casa
grande
manslaughter ['mænslɔ:tə*] *n*
homicidio no premeditado
mantelpiece ['mæntlpi:s] *n* repisa,
chimenea
manual ['mænjuəl] *adj* manual ▷ *n*
manual *m*
manufacture [mænju'fæktʃə*] *vt*
fabricar ▷ *n* fabricación *f*; **manufacturer** *n*
fabricante *mf*
manure [mə'njuə*] *n* estiércol *m*
manuscript ['mænjuskrɪpt] *n*
manuscrito
many ['mɛnɪ] *adj, pron* muchos/as; **a
great ~** muchísimos, un buen número de; **~
a time** muchas veces
map [mæp] *n* mapa *m* ▷ **to ~ out** *vt*
proyectar
maple ['meɪpl] *n* arce *m*, maple *m* (*LAM*)
Mar *abbr* (= *March*) mar
mar [mɑ:*] *vt* estropear
marathon ['mærəθən] *n* maratón *m*
marble ['mɑ:bl] *n* mármol *m*; (*toy*) canica
March [mɑ:tʃ] *n* marzo
march [mɑ:tʃ] *vi* (*Mil*) marchar;
(*demonstrators*) manifestarse ▷ *n* marcha;
(*demonstration*) manifestación *f*
mare [mɛə*] *n* yegua
margarine [mɑ:dʒə'ri:n] *n* margarina
margin ['mɑ:dʒɪn] *n* margen *m*;
(*Comm: profit margin*) margen *m* de
beneficios; **marginal** *adj* marginal;
marginally *adv* ligeramente
marigold ['mærɪgəuld] *n* caléndula
marijuana [mærɪ'wɑ:nə] *n* marijuana
marina [mə'ri:nə] *n* puerto deportivo
marinade [mærɪ'neɪd] *n* adobo
marinate ['mærɪneɪt] *vt* marinar

marine [mə'riːn] *adj* marino ▷ *n* soldado de marina

marital ['mærɪtl] *adj* matrimonial; **marital status** *n* estado *m* civil

maritime ['mærɪtaɪm] *adj* marítimo

marjoram ['mɑːdʒərəm] *n* mejorana

mark [mɑːk] *n* marca, señal *f*; (*in snow, mud etc*) huella; (*stain*) mancha; (BRIT Scol) nota ▷ *vt* marcar; manchar; (*damage: furniture*) rayar; (*indicate: place etc*) señalar; (BRIT Scol) calificar, corregir; **to ~ time** marcar el paso; (*fig*) marcar(se) un ritmo; **marked** *adj* (*obvious*) marcado, acusado; **marker** *n* (*sign*) marcador *m*; (*bookmark*) señal *f* (de libro)

market ['mɑːkɪt] *n* mercado ▷ *vt* (Comm) comercializar; **marketing** *n* márketing *m*; **marketplace** *n* mercado; **market research** *n* análisis *m inv* de mercados

marmalade ['mɑːməleɪd] *n* mermelada de naranja

maroon [mə'ruːn] *vt*: **to be ~ed** quedar aislado; (*fig*) quedar abandonado ▷ *n* (*colour*) granate *m*

marquee [mɑːˈkiː] *n* entoldado

marriage ['mærɪdʒ] *n* (*relationship, institution*) matrimonio; (*wedding*) boda; (*act*) casamiento; **marriage certificate** *n* partida de casamiento

married ['mærɪd] *adj* casado; (*life, love*) conyugal

marrow ['mærəu] *n* médula; (*vegetable*) calabacín *m*

marry ['mærɪ] *vt* casarse con; (*father, priest etc*) casar ▷ *vi* (*also*: **get married**) casarse

Mars [mɑːz] *n* Marte *m*

marsh [mɑːʃ] *n* pantano; (*salt marsh*) marisma

marshal ['mɑːʃl] *n* (Mil) mariscal *m*; (*at sports meeting etc*) oficial *m*; (US: *of police, fire department*) jefe/a *m/f* ▷ *vt* (*thoughts etc*) ordenar; (*soldiers*) formar

martyr ['mɑːtə*] *n* mártir *mf*

marvel ['mɑːvl] *n* maravilla, prodigio ▷ *vi*: **to ~ (at)** maravillarse (de); **marvellous** (US **marvelous**) *adj* maravilloso

Marxism ['mɑːksɪzəm] *n* marxismo

Marxist ['mɑːksɪst] *adj, n* marxista *mf*

marzipan ['mɑːzɪpæn] *n* mazapán *m*

mascara [mæs'kɑːrə] *n* rímel *m*

mascot ['mæskət] *n* mascota

masculine ['mæskjulɪn] *adj* masculino

mash [mæʃ] *vt* machacar; **mashed potato(es)** *n(pl)* puré *m* de patatas (SP) or papas (LAM)

mask [mɑːsk] *n* máscara ▷ *vt* (*cover*): **to ~ one's face** ocultarse la cara; (*hide: feelings*) esconder

mason ['meɪsn] *n* (*also*: **stone~**) albañil *m*; (*also*: **free~**) masón *m*; **masonry** *n* (*in building*) mampostería

mass [mæs] *n* (*people*) muchedumbre *f*; (*of air, liquid etc*) masa; (*of detail, hair etc*) gran cantidad *f*; (Rel) misa ▷ *cpd* masivo ▷ *vi* reunirse; concentrarse; **the masses** *npl* las masas; **~es of** (*inf*) montones de

massacre ['mæsəkə*] *n* masacre *f*

massage ['mæsɑːʒ] *n* masaje *m* ▷ *vt* dar masaje en

massive ['mæsɪv] *adj* enorme; (*support, changes*) masivo

mass media *npl* medios *mpl* de comunicación

mass-produce ['mæsprə'djuːs] *vt* fabricar en serie

mast [mɑːst] *n* (Naut) mástil *m*; (Radio etc) torre *f*

master ['mɑːstə*] *n* (*of servant*) amo; (*of situation*) dueño, maestro; (*in primary school*) maestro; (*in secondary school*) profesor *m*; (*title for boys*): **M~ X** Señorito X ▷ *vt* dominar; **mastermind** *n* inteligencia superior ▷ *vt* dirigir, planear; **Master of Arts/Science** *n* licenciatura superior en Letras/Ciencias; **masterpiece** *n* obra maestra

masturbate ['mæstəbeɪt] *vi* masturbarse

mat [mæt] *n* estera; (*also*: **door~**) felpudo; (*also*: **table ~**) salvamanteles *m inv*, posavasos *m inv* ▷ *adj* = **matt**

match [mætʃ] *n* cerilla, fósforo; (*game*) partido; (*equal*) igual *m/f* ▷ *vt* (*go well with*) hacer juego con; (*equal*) igualar; (*correspond to*) corresponderse con; (*pair: also*: **~ up**) casar con ▷ *vi* hacer juego; **to be a good ~** hacer juego; **matchbox** *n* caja de cerillas; **matching** *adj* que hace juego

mate [meɪt] *n* (*workmate*) colega *mf*; (*inf: friend*) amigo/a; (*animal*) macho/ hembra; (*in merchant navy*) segundo de a bordo ▷ *vi* acoplarse, aparearse ▷ *vt* aparear

material [mə'tɪərɪəl] *n* (*substance*) materia; (*information*) material *m*; (*cloth*) tela, tejido ▷ *adj* material; (*important*) esencial; **materials** *npl* materiales *mpl*

materialize [mə'tɪərɪəlaɪz] *vi* materializarse

maternal [mə'təːnl] *adj* maternal

maternity [mə'təːnɪtɪ] *n* maternidad *f*; **maternity hospital** *n* hospital *m* de maternidad; **maternity leave** *n* baja por maternidad

math [mæθ] (US) *n* = **mathematics**

mathematical [mæθə'mætɪkl] *adj* matemático

mathematician [mæθəmə'tɪʃən] n matemático/a

mathematics [mæθə'mætɪks] n matemáticas fpl

maths [mæθs] (BRIT) n = **mathematics**

matinée ['mætɪneɪ] n sesión f de tarde

matron ['meɪtrən] n enfermera f jefe; (in school) ama de llaves

matt [mæt] adj mate

matter ['mætə*] n cuestión f, asunto; (Physics) sustancia, materia; (reading matter) material m; (Med: pus) pus m ▷ vi importar; **matters** npl (affairs) asuntos mpl, temas mpl; **it doesn't ~** no importa; **what's the ~?** ¿qué pasa?; **no ~ what** pase lo que pase; **as a ~ of course** por rutina; **as a ~ of fact** de hecho

mattress ['mætrɪs] n colchón m

mature [mə'tjuə*] adj maduro ▷ vi madurar; **mature student** n estudiante de más de 21 años; **maturity** n madurez f

maul [mɔːl] vt magullar

mauve [məuv] adj de color malva (SP) or guinda (LAM)

max abbr = **maximum**

maximize ['mæksɪmaɪz] vt (profits etc) llevar al máximo; (chances) maximizar

maximum ['mæksɪməm] (pl **maxima**) adj máximo ▷ n máximo

May [meɪ] n mayo

may [meɪ] (conditional **might**) vi (indicating possibility): **he ~ come** puede que venga; (be allowed to): **~ I smoke?** ¿puedo fumar?; (wishes): **~ God bless you!** ¡que Dios le bendiga!; **you ~ as well go** bien puedes irte

maybe ['meɪbiː] adv quizá(s)

May Day n el primero de Mayo

mayhem ['meɪhɛm] n caos m total

mayonnaise [meɪə'neɪz] n mayonesa

mayor [mɛə*] n alcalde m; **mayoress** n alcaldesa

maze [meɪz] n laberinto

MD n abbr = **managing director**

me [miː] pron (direct) me; (stressed, after pron) mí; **can you hear ~?** ¿me oyes?; **he heard ME** ¡me oyó a mí!; **it's ~** soy yo; **give them to ~** dámelos/las; **with/without ~** conmigo/sin mí

meadow ['mɛdəu] n prado, pradera

meagre ['miːgə*] (US **meager**) adj escaso, pobre

meal [miːl] n comida; (flour) harina; **mealtime** n hora de comer

mean [miːn] (pt, pp **~t**) adj (with money) tacaño; (unkind) mezquino, malo; (shabby) humilde; (average) medio ▷ vt (signify) querer decir, significar; (refer to) referirse a; (intend): **to ~ to do sth** pensar or pretender hacer algo ▷ n medio, término medio; **means** npl (way) medio, manera; (money) recursos mpl, medios mpl; **by ~s of** mediante, por medio de; **by all ~s!** ¡naturalmente!, ¡claro que sí!; **do you ~ it?** ¿lo dices en serio?; **what do you ~?** ¿qué quiere decir?; **to be ~t for sb/sth** ser para algn/algo

meaning ['miːnɪŋ] n significado, sentido; (purpose) sentido, propósito; **meaningful** adj significativo; **meaningless** adj sin sentido

meant [mɛnt] pt, pp of **mean**

meantime ['miːntaɪm] adv (also: **in the ~**) mientras tanto

meanwhile ['miːnwaɪl] adv = **meantime**

measles ['miːzlz] n sarampión m

measure ['mɛʒə*] vt, vi medir ▷ n medida; (ruler) regla; **measurement** ['mɛʒəmənt] n (measure) medida; (act) medición f; **to take sb's measurements** tomar las medidas a algn

meat [miːt] n carne f; **cold ~** fiambre m; **meatball** n albóndiga

Mecca ['mɛkə] n La Meca

mechanic [mɪ'kænɪk] n mecánico/a; **mechanical** adj mecánico

mechanism ['mɛkənɪzəm] n mecanismo

medal ['mɛdl] n medalla; **medallist** (US **medalist**) n (Sport) medallista mf

meddle ['mɛdl] vi: **to ~ in** entrometerse en; **to ~ with sth** manosear algo

media ['miːdɪə] npl medios mpl de comunicación ▷ npl of **medium**

mediaeval [mɛdɪ'iːvl] adj = **medieval**

mediate ['miːdɪeɪt] vi mediar

medical ['mɛdɪkl] adj médico ▷ n reconocimiento médico; **medical certificate** n certificado m médico

medicated ['mɛdɪkeɪtɪd] adj medicinal

medication [mɛdɪ'keɪʃən] n medicación f

medicine ['mɛdsɪn] n medicina; (drug) medicamento

medieval [mɛdɪ'iːvl] adj medieval

mediocre [miːdɪ'əukə*] adj mediocre

meditate ['mɛdɪteɪt] vi meditar

meditation [mɛdɪ'teɪʃən] n meditación f

Mediterranean [mɛdɪtə'reɪnɪən] adj mediterráneo; **the ~ (Sea)** el (Mar) Mediterráneo

medium ['miːdɪəm] (pl **media**) adj mediano, regular ▷ n (means) medio; (pl **mediums**: person) médium mf; **medium-sized** adj de tamaño mediano; (clothes) de (la) talla mediana; **medium wave** n onda media

meek [miːk] adj manso, sumiso

meet [miːt] (pt, pp **met**) vt encontrar;

m

(*accidentally*) encontrarse con, tropezar con; (*by arrangement*) reunirse con; (*for the first time*) conocer; (*go and fetch*) ir a buscar; (*opponent*) enfrentarse con; (*obligations*) cumplir; (*encounter: problem*) hacer frente a; (*need*) satisfacer ▷ *vi* encontrarse; (*in session*) reunirse; (*join: objects*) unirse; (*for the first time*) conocerse; **meet up** *vi*: **to meet up with sb** reunirse con algn; **meet with** *vt fus* (*difficulty*) tropezar con; **to meet with success** tener éxito; **meeting** *n* encuentro; (*arranged*) cita, compromiso; (*business meeting*) reunión *f*; (*Pol*) mítin *m*; **meeting place** *n* lugar *m* de reunión *or* encuentro

megabyte ['mɛɡəbaɪt] *n* (*Comput*) megabyte *m*, megaocteto

megaphone ['mɛɡəfəʊn] *n* megáfono

megapixel ['mɛɡəpɪksl] *n* megapíxel *m*

melancholy ['mɛlənkəlɪ] *n* melancolía ▷ *adj* melancólico

melody ['mɛlədɪ] *n* melodía

melon ['mɛlən] *n* melón *m*

melt [mɛlt] *vi* (*metal*) fundirse; (*snow*) derretirse ▷ *vt* fundir

member ['mɛmbə*] *n* (*gen, Anat*) miembro; (*of club*) socio/a; **Member of Congress** (*us*) *n* miembro *mf* del Congreso; **Member of Parliament** *n* (*BRIT*) diputado/a *m/f*, parlamentario/a *m/f*; **Member of the European Parliament** *n* diputado/a *m/f* del Parlamento Europeo, eurodiputado/a *m/f*; **Member of the Scottish Parliament** (*BRIT*) diputado/a del Parlamento escocés; **membership** *n* (*members*) número de miembros; (*state*) filiación *f*; **membership card** *n* carnet *m* de socio

memento [mə'mɛntəʊ] *n* recuerdo

memo ['mɛməʊ] *n* apunte *m*, nota

memorable ['mɛmərəbl] *adj* memorable

memorandum [mɛmə'rændəm] (*pl* **memoranda**) *n* apunte *m*, nota; (*official note*) acta

memorial [mɪ'mɔ:rɪəl] *n* monumento conmemorativo ▷ *adj* conmemorativo

memorize ['mɛməraɪz] *vt* aprender de memoria

memory ['mɛmərɪ] *n* (*also: Comput*) memoria; (*instance*) recuerdo; (*of dead person*): **in ~ of** a la memoria de; **memory card** *n* (*for digital camera*) tarjeta de memoria

men [mɛn] *npl of* **man**

menace ['mɛnəs] *n* amenaza ▷ *vt* amenazar

mend [mɛnd] *vt* reparar, arreglar; (*darn*) zurcir ▷ *vi* reponerse ▷ *n* arreglo, reparación *f* zurcido ▷ *n*: **to be on the ~** ir mejorando; **to ~ one's ways** enmendarse

meningitis [mɛnɪn'dʒaɪtɪs] *n* meningitis *f*

menopause ['mɛnəupɔ:z] *n* menopausia

men's room (*us*) *n*: **the ~** el servicio de caballeros

menstruation [mɛnstru'eɪʃən] *n* menstruación *f*

menswear ['mɛnzwɛə*] *n* confección *f* de caballero

mental ['mɛntl] *adj* mental; **mental hospital** *n* (*hospital m*) psiquiátrico;

mentality [mɛn'tælɪtɪ] *n* mentalidad *f*;

mentally *adv*: **to be mentally ill** tener una enfermedad mental

menthol ['mɛnθɒl] *n* mentol *m*

mention ['mɛnʃən] *n* mención *f* ▷ *vt* mencionar; (*speak*) hablar de; **don't ~ it!** ¡de nada!

menu ['mɛnju:] *n* (*set menu*) menú *m*; (*printed*) carta; (*Comput*) menú *m*

MEP *n abbr* = **Member of the European Parliament**

mercenary ['mə:sɪnərɪ] *adj, n* mercenario/a

merchandise ['mə:tʃəndaɪz] *n* mercancías *fpl*

merchant ['mə:tʃənt] *n* comerciante *mf*; **merchant navy** (*us*)**, merchant marine** *n* marina mercante

merciless ['mə:sɪlɪs] *adj* despiadado

mercury ['mə:kjurɪ] *n* mercurio

mercy ['mə:sɪ] *n* compasión *f*; (*Rel*) misericordia; **at the ~ of** a la merced de

mere [mɪə*] *adj* simple, mero; **merely** *adv* simplemente, sólo

merge [mə:dʒ] *vt* (*join*) unir ▷ *vi* unirse; (*Comm*) fusionarse; (*colours etc*) fundirse; **merger** *n* (*Comm*) fusión *f*

meringue [mə'ræŋ] *n* merengue *m*

merit ['mɛrɪt] *n* mérito ▷ *vt* merecer

mermaid ['mə:meɪd] *n* sirena

merry ['mɛrɪ] *adj* alegre; **M~ Christmas!** ¡Felices Pascuas!; **merry-go-round** *n* tiovivo

mesh [mɛʃ] *n* malla

mess [mɛs] *n* (*muddle: of situation*) confusión *f*; (*: of room*) revoltijo; (*dirt*) porquería; (*Mil*) comedor *m*; **mess about** *or* **around** (*inf*) *vi* perder el tiempo; (*pass the time*) entretenerse; **mess up** *vt* (*spoil*) estropear; (*dirty*) ensuciar; **mess with** (*inf*) *vt fus* (*challenge, confront*) meterse con (*inf*); (*interfere with*) interferir con

message ['mɛsɪdʒ] *n* recado, mensaje *m*

messenger ['mɛsɪndʒə*] *n* mensajero/a

Messrs *abbr* (*on letters*) (= *Messieurs*) Sres

messy ['mɛsɪ] *adj* (*dirty*) sucio; (*untidy*) desordenado

met [mɛt] *pt, pp of* **meet**

metabolism [mɛ'tæbəlɪzəm] *n* metabolismo

metal ['mɛtl] *n* metal *m*; **metallic** [-'tælɪk] *adj* metálico

metaphor ['mɛtəfə*] *n* metáfora

meteor ['mi:tɪə*] *n* meteoro; **meteorite** [-aɪt] *n* meteorito

meteorology [mi:tɪɔ'rɔlədʒɪ] *n* meteorología

meter ['mi:tə*] *n* (*instrument*) contador *m*; (*US*: *unit*) = **metre** ▷ *vt* (*US Post*) franquear

method ['mɛθəd] *n* método; **methodical** [mɪ'θɔdɪkl] *adj* metódico

meths [mɛθs] *n* (*BRIT*) alcohol *m* metilado *or* desnaturalizado

meticulous [mɛ'tɪkjuləs] *adj* meticuloso

metre ['mi:tə*] (*US* **meter**) *n* metro

metric ['mɛtrɪk] *adj* métrico

metro ['mɛtrəu] *n* metro

metropolitan [mɛtrə'pɔlɪtən] *adj* metropolitano; **the M~ Police** (*BRIT*) la policía londinense

Mexican ['mɛksɪkən] *adj, n* mexicano/a , mejicano/a

Mexico ['mɛksɪkəu] *n* México, Méjico (*SP*)

mg *abbr* (= *milligram*) mg

mice [maɪs] *npl of* **mouse**

micro... [maɪkrəu] *prefix* micro...; **microchip** *n* microplaqueta; **microphone** *n* micrófono; **microscope** *n* microscopio; **microwave** *n* (*also*: **microwave oven**) horno microondas

mid [mɪd] *adj*: **in ~ May** a mediados de mayo; **in ~ afternoon** a media tarde; **in ~ air** en el aire; **midday** *n* mediodía *m*

middle ['mɪdl] *n* centro; (*half-way point*) medio; (*waist*) cintura ▷ *adj* de en medio; (*course, way*) intermedio; **in the ~ of the night** en plena noche; **middle-aged** *adj* de mediana edad; **Middle Ages** *npl*: **the Middle Ages** la Edad Media; **middle-class** *adj* de clase media; **the middle class(es)** la clase media; **Middle East** *n* Oriente *m* Medio; **middle name** *n* segundo nombre; **middle school** *n* (*US*) colegio para niños de doce a catorce años; (*BRIT*) colegio para niños de ocho o nueve a doce o trece años

midge [mɪdʒ] *n* mosquito

midget ['mɪdʒɪt] *n* enano/a

midnight ['mɪdnaɪt] *n* medianoche *f*

midst [mɪdst] *n*: **in the ~ of** (*crowd*) en medio de; (*situation, action*) en mitad de

midsummer [mɪd'sʌmə*] *n*: **in ~** en pleno verano

midway [mɪd'weɪ] *adj, adv*: **~ (between)** a medio camino (entre); **~ through** a la mitad (de)

midweek [mɪd'wi:k] *adv* entre semana

midwife ['mɪdwaɪf] (*irreg*) *n* comadrona, partera

midwinter [mɪd'wɪntə*] *n*: **in ~** en pleno invierno

might [maɪt] *vb see* **may** ▷ *n* fuerza, poder *m*; **mighty** *adj* fuerte, poderoso

migraine ['mi:greɪn] *n* jaqueca

migrant ['maɪgrənt] *n, adj* (*bird*) migratorio; (*worker*) emigrante

migrate [maɪ'greɪt] *vi* emigrar

migration [maɪ'greɪʃən] *n* emigración *f*

mike [maɪk] *n abbr* (= *microphone*) micro

mild [maɪld] *adj* (*person*) apacible; (*climate*) templado; (*slight*) ligero; (*taste*) suave; (*illness*) leve; **mildly** ['-lɪ] *adv* ligeramente; suavemente; **to put it mildly** para no decir más

mile [maɪl] *n* milla; **mileage** *n* número de millas ≈ kilometraje *m*; **mileometer** [maɪ'lɔmɪtə] *n* ≈ cuentakilómetros *m inv*; **milestone** *n* mojón *m*

military ['mɪlɪtərɪ] *adj* militar

militia [mɪ'lɪʃə] *n* milicia

milk [mɪlk] *n* leche *f* ▷ *vt* (*cow*) ordeñar; (*fig*) chupar; **milk chocolate** *n* chocolate *m* con leche; **milkman** (*irreg*) *n* lechero; **milky** *adj* lechoso

mill [mɪl] *n* (*windmill etc*) molino; (*coffee mill*) molinillo; (*factory*) fábrica ▷ *vt* moler ▷ *vi* (*also*: **~ about**) arremolinarse

millennium [mɪ'lɛnɪəm] (*pl* **~s** *or* **millennia**) *n* milenio, milenario

milli... ['mɪlɪ] *prefix*: **milligram(me)** *n* miligramo; **millilitre** (*US* **milliliter**) ['mɪlɪli:tə*] *n* mililitro; **millimetre** (*US* **millimeter**) *n* milímetro

million ['mɪljən] *n* millón *m*; **a ~ times** un millón de veces; **millionaire** [-jə'nɛə*] *n* millonario/a; **millionth** [-θ] *adj* millonésimo

milometer [maɪ'lɔmɪtə*] (*BRIT*) *n* = **mileometer**

mime [maɪm] *n* mímica; (*actor*) mimo/a ▷ *vt* remedar ▷ *vi* actuar de mimo

mimic ['mɪmɪk] *n* imitador(a) *m/f* ▷ *adj* mímico ▷ *vt* remedar, imitar

min. *abbr* = **minimum**; **minute(s)**

mince [mɪns] *vt* picar ▷ *n* (*BRIT Culin*) carne *f* picada; **mincemeat** *n* conserva de fruta picada; (*US*: *meat*) carne *f* picada; **mince pie** *n* empanadilla rellena de fruta picada

mind [maɪnd] *n* mente *f*; (*intellect*) intelecto; (*contrasted with matter*) espíritu *m* ▷ *vt* (*attend to, look after*) ocuparse de, cuidar; (*be careful*) tener cuidado con; (*object to*): **I don't ~ the noise** no me molesta el ruido; **it is on my ~** me preocupa; **to bear**

sth in ~ tomar or tener algo en cuenta; **to make up one's** ~ decidirse; **I don't** ~ me es igual; **~ you ...** te advierto que ...; **never ~!** ¡es igual!, ¡no importa!; (don't worry) ¡no te preocupes!; **"~ the step"** "cuidado con el escalón"; **mindless** adj (crime) sin motivo; (work) de autómata

mine¹ [maɪn] pron el mío/la mía etc; **a friend of** ~ un(a) amigo/a mío/mía ▷ adj: **this book is** ~ este libro es mío

mine² [maɪn] n mina ▷ vt (coal) extraer; (bomb: beach etc) minar; **minefield** n campo de minas; **miner** n minero/a

mineral ['mɪnərəl] adj mineral ▷ n mineral m; **mineral water** n agua mineral

mingle ['mɪŋɡl] vi: **to** ~ **with** mezclarse con

miniature ['mɪnətʃə*] adj (en) miniatura ▷ n miniatura

minibar ['mɪnɪbɑ:*] n minibar m

minibus ['mɪnɪbʌs] n microbús m

minicab ['mɪnɪkæb] n taxi m (que sólo puede pedirse por teléfono)

minimal ['mɪnɪml] adj mínimo

minimize ['mɪnɪmaɪz] vt minimizar; (play down) empequeñecer

minimum ['mɪnɪməm] (pl **minima**) n, adj mínimo

mining ['maɪnɪŋ] n explotación f minera

miniskirt ['mɪnɪskə:t] n minifalda

minister ['mɪnɪstə*] n (BRIT Pol) ministro/a (SP), secretario/a (LAM); (Rel) pastor m ▷ vi: **to** ~ **to** atender a

ministry ['mɪnɪstrɪ] n (BRIT Pol) ministerio, secretaría (MEX); (Rel) sacerdocio

minor ['maɪnə*] adj (repairs, injuries) leve; (poet, planet) menor; (Mus) menor ▷ n (Law) menor m de edad

Minorca [mɪ'nɔ:kə] n Menorca

minority [maɪ'nɔrɪtɪ] n minoría

mint [mɪnt] n (plant) menta, hierbabuena; (sweet) caramelo de menta ▷ vt (coins) acuñar; **the (Royal) M~, the (US) M~** la Casa de la Moneda; **in** ~ **condition** en perfecto estado

minus ['maɪnəs] n (also: ~ **sign**) signo de menos ▷ prep menos; **12** ~ **6 equals 6** 12 menos 6 son 6; **~ 24°C** menos 24 grados

minute¹ ['mɪnɪt] n minuto; (fig) momento; **minutes** npl (of meeting) actas fpl; **at the last** ~ a última hora

minute² [maɪ'nju:t] adj diminuto; (search) minucioso

miracle ['mɪrəkl] n milagro

miraculous [mɪ'rækjuləs] adj milagroso

mirage ['mɪrɑ:ʒ] n espejismo

mirror ['mɪrə*] n espejo; (in car) retrovisor m

misbehave [mɪsbɪ'heɪv] vi portarse mal

misc. abbr = **miscellaneous**

miscarriage ['mɪskærɪdʒ] n (Med) aborto; ~ **of justice** error m judicial

miscellaneous [mɪsɪ'leɪnɪəs] adj varios/as, diversos/as

mischief ['mɪstʃɪf] n travesuras fpl, diabluras fpl; (maliciousness) malicia; **mischievous** [-ʃɪvəs] adj travieso

misconception [mɪskən'sɛpʃən] n idea equivocada; equivocación f

misconduct [mɪs'kɔndʌkt] n mala conducta; **professional** ~ falta profesional

miser ['maɪzə*] n avaro/a

miserable ['mɪzərəbl] adj (unhappy) triste, desgraciado; (unpleasant, contemptible) miserable

misery ['mɪzərɪ] n tristeza; (wretchedness) miseria, desdicha

misfortune [mɪs'fɔ:tʃən] n desgracia

misgiving [mɪs'ɡɪvɪŋ] n (apprehension) presentimiento; **to have ~s about sth** tener dudas acerca de algo

misguided [mɪs'ɡaɪdɪd] adj equivocado

mishap ['mɪshæp] n desgracia, contratiempo

misinterpret [mɪsɪn'tə:prɪt] vt interpretar mal

misjudge [mɪs'dʒʌdʒ] vt juzgar mal

mislay [mɪs'leɪ] vt extraviar, perder

mislead [mɪs'li:d] vt llevar a conclusiones erróneas; **misleading** adj engañoso

misplace [mɪs'pleɪs] vt extraviar

misprint ['mɪsprɪnt] n errata, error m de imprenta

misrepresent [mɪsrɛprɪ'zɛnt] vt falsificar

Miss [mɪs] n Señorita

miss [mɪs] vt (train etc) perder; (fail to hit: target) errar; (regret the absence of): **I** ~ **him** (yo) le echo de menos or a faltar; (fail to see): **you can't** ~ **it** no tiene pérdida ▷ vi fallar ▷ n (shot) tiro fallido or perdido; **miss out** (BRIT) vt omitir; **miss out on** vt fus (fun, party, opportunity) perderse

missile ['mɪsaɪl] n (Aviat) mísil m; (object thrown) proyectil m

missing ['mɪsɪŋ] adj (pupil) ausente; (thing) perdido; (Mil): ~ **in action** desaparecido en combate

mission ['mɪʃən] n misión f; (official representation) delegación f; **missionary** n misionero/a

misspell [mɪs'spɛl] (pt, pp **misspelt** (BRIT) or **~ed**) vt escribir mal

mist [mɪst] n (light) neblina; (heavy) niebla; (at sea) bruma ▷ vi (eyes: also: ~ **over**, ~ **up**) llenarse de lágrimas; (BRIT: windows: also: ~

over, ~ up) empañarse

mistake [mɪs'teɪk] (vt: irreg) n error m
▷ vt entender mal; **by ~** por equivocación;
to make a ~ equivocarse; **to ~ A for B**
confundir A con B; **mistaken** pp of **mistake**
▷ adj equivocado; **to be mistaken**
equivocarse, engañarse

mister ['mɪstə*] (inf) n señor m; see **Mr**

mistletoe ['mɪsltəʊ] n muérdago

mistook [mɪs'tʊk] pt of **mistake**

mistress ['mɪstrɪs] n (lover) amante
f; (of house) señora (de la casa); (BRIT: in
primary school) maestra; (in secondary school)
profesora; (of situation) dueña

mistrust [mɪs'trʌst] vt desconfiar de

misty ['mɪstɪ] adj (day) de niebla; (glasses
etc) empañado

misunderstand [mɪsʌndə'stænd] (irreg)
vt, vi entender mal; **misunderstanding** n
malentendido

misunderstood [mɪsʌndə'stud] pt,
pp of **misunderstand** ▷ adj (person)
incomprendido

misuse [n mɪs'juːs, vb mɪs'juːz] n mal uso;
(of power) abuso; (of funds) malversación f
▷ vt abusar de; malversar

mitt(en) ['mɪt(n)] n manopla

mix [mɪks] vt mezclar; (combine) unir ▷ vi
mezclarse; (people) llevarse bien ▷ n mezcla;
mix up vt mezclar; (confuse) confundir;
mixed adj mixto; (feelings etc) encontrado;
mixed grill n (BRIT) parrillada mixta;
mixed salad n ensalada mixta; **mixed-up**
adj (confused) confuso, revuelto; **mixer** n
(for food) licuadora; (for drinks) coctelera;
(person): **he's a good mixer** tiene don de
gentes; **mixture** n mezcla; (also: **cough
mixture**) jarabe m; **mix-up** n confusión f

ml abbr (= millilitre(s)) ml

mm abbr (= millimetre) mm

moan [məʊn] n gemido ▷ vi gemir;
(inf: complain): **to ~ (about)** quejarse (de)

moat [məʊt] n foso

mob [mɔb] n multitud f ▷ vt acosar

mobile ['məʊbaɪl] adj móvil ▷ n móvil m;
mobile home n caravana; **mobile phone** n
teléfono móvil

mobility [məʊ'bɪlɪtɪ] n movilidad f

mobilize ['məʊbɪlaɪz] vt movilizar

mock [mɔk] vt (ridicule) ridiculizar; (laugh
at) burlarse de ▷ adj fingido; **~ exam**
examen preparatorio antes de los exámenes
oficiales° (BRIT: Scol: inf) exámenes mpl de
prueba; **mockery** n burla

mod cons ['mɔd'kɔnz] npl abbr (= modern
conveniences) see **convenience**

mode [məʊd] n modo

model ['mɔdl] n modelo; (fashion model,

artist's model) modelo mf ▷ adj modelo ▷ vt
(with clay etc) modelar; (copy): **to ~ o.s. on**
tomar como modelo a ▷ vi ser modelo; **to ~
clothes** pasar modelos, ser modelo

modem ['məʊdəm] n modem m

moderate [adj 'mɔdərət, vb 'mɔdəreɪt]
adj moderado/a ▷ vi moderarse, calmarse
▷ vt moderar

moderation [mɔdə'reɪʃən] n moderación
f; **in ~** con moderación

modern ['mɔdən] adj moderno;
modernize vt modernizar; **modern
languages** npl lenguas fpl modernas

modest ['mɔdɪst] adj modesto; (small)
módico; **modesty** n modestia

modification [mɔdɪfɪ'keɪʃən] n
modificación f

modify ['mɔdɪfaɪ] vt modificar

module ['mɔdjuːl] n (unit, component,
Space) módulo

mohair ['məʊhɛə*] n mohair m

Mohammed [mə'hæmɛd] n Mahoma m

moist [mɔɪst] adj húmedo; **moisture**
['mɔɪstʃə*] n humedad f; **moisturizer**
['mɔɪstʃəraɪzə*] n crema hidratante

mold etc [məʊld] (US) = **mould** etc

mole [məʊl] n (animal, spy) topo; (spot)
lunar m

molecule ['mɔlɪkjuːl] n molécula

molest [məʊ'lɛst] vt importunar; (assault
sexually) abusar sexualmente de

┃ Be careful not to translate **molest** by the
┃ Spanish word molestar.

molten ['məʊltən] adj fundido; (lava)
líquido

mom [mɔm] (US) n = **mum**

moment ['məʊmənt] n momento; **at the
~** de momento, por ahora; **momentarily**
adv momentáneamente; (US: very soon)
de un momento a otro; **momentary** adj
momentáneo; **momentous** [-'mɛntəs] adj
trascendental, importante

momentum [məʊ'mɛntəm] n momento;
(fig) ímpetu m; **to gather ~** cobrar
velocidad; (fig) ganar fuerza

mommy ['mɔmɪ] (US) n = **mummy**

Mon abbr (= Monday) lun

Monaco ['mɔnəkəʊ] n Mónaco

monarch ['mɔnək] n monarca mf;
monarchy n monarquía

monastery ['mɔnəstərɪ] n monasterio

Monday ['mʌndɪ] n lunes m inv

monetary ['mʌnɪtərɪ] adj monetario

money ['mʌnɪ] n dinero; (currency)
moneda; **to make ~** ganar dinero; **money
belt** n riñonera; **money order** n giro

mongrel ['mʌŋgrəl] n (dog) perro mestizo

monitor ['mɔnɪtə*] n (Scol) monitor m;

(also: **television ~**) receptor *m* de control; (of computer) monitor *m* ▷ *vt* controlar

monk [mʌŋk] *n* monje *m*

monkey ['mʌŋkɪ] *n* mono

monologue ['mɒnəlɒg] *n* monólogo

monopoly [mə'nɒpəlɪ] *n* monopolio

monosodium glutamate [mɒnə'səʊdɪəm'glu:təmeɪt] *n* glutamato monosódico

monotonous [mə'nɒtənəs] *adj* monótono

monsoon [mɒn'su:n] *n* monzón *m*

monster ['mɒnstə*] *n* monstruo

month [mʌnθ] *n* mes *m*; **monthly** *adj* mensual ▷ *adv* mensualmente

monument ['mɒnjumənt] *n* monumento

mood [mu:d] *n* humor *m*; (of crowd, group) clima *m*; **to be in a good/bad ~** estar de buen/mal humor; **moody** *adj* (changeable) de humor variable; (sullen) malhumorado

moon [mu:n] *n* luna; **moonlight** *n* luz *f* de la luna

moor [muə*] *n* páramo ▷ *vt* (ship) amarrar ▷ *vi* echar las amarras

moose [mu:s] *n inv* alce *m*

mop [mɒp] *n* fregona; (of hair) greña, melena ▷ *vt* fregar; **mop up** *vt* limpiar

mope [məup] *vi* estar *or* andar deprimido

moped ['məupɛd] *n* ciclomotor *m*

moral ['mɒrl] *adj* moral ▷ *n* moraleja; **morals** *npl* moralidad *f*, moral *f*

morale [mɒ'rɑ:l] *n* moral *f*

morality [mə'rælɪtɪ] *n* moralidad *f*

morbid ['mɔ:bɪd] *adj* (interest) morboso; (Med) mórbido

○ **KEYWORD**

more [mɔ:*] *adj* **1** (greater in number etc) más; **more people/work than before** más gente/trabajo que antes

2 (additional) más; **do you want (some) more tea?** ¿quieres más té?; **is there any more wine?** ¿queda vino?; **it'll take a few more weeks** tardará unas semanas más; **it's 2 kms more to the house** faltan 2 kms para la casa; **more time/letters than we expected** más tiempo del que/más cartas de las que esperábamos

▷ *pron* (greater amount, additional amount) más; **more than 10** más de 10; **it cost more than the other one/than we expected** costó más que el otro/más de lo que esperábamos; **is there any more?** ¿hay más?; **many/much more** muchos(as)/mucho(a) más

▷ *adv* más; **more dangerous/easily (than)** más peligroso/fácilmente (que); **more and more expensive** cada vez más caro; **more or less** más o menos; **more than ever** más que nunca

moreover [mɔ:'rəuvə*] *adv* además, por otra parte

morgue [mɔ:g] *n* depósito de cadáveres

morning ['mɔ:nɪŋ] *n* mañana; (early morning) madrugada ▷ *cpd* matutino, de la mañana; **in the ~** por la mañana; **7 o'clock in the ~** las 7 de la mañana; **morning sickness** *n* náuseas *fpl* matutinas

Moroccan [mə'rɔkən] *adj, n* marroquí *m/f*

Morocco [mə'rɔkəu] *n* Marruecos *m*

moron ['mɔ:rɒn] (inf) *n* imbécil *mf*

morphine ['mɔ:fi:n] *n* morfina

Morse [mɔ:s] *n* (also: **~ code**) (código) Morse

mortal ['mɔ:tl] *adj, n* mortal *m*

mortar ['mɔ:tə*] *n* argamasa

mortgage ['mɔ:gɪdʒ] *n* hipoteca ▷ *vt* hipotecar

mortician [mɔ:'tɪʃən] (US) *n* director/a *m/f* de pompas fúnebres

mortified ['mɔ:tɪfaɪd] *adj*: **I was ~** me dio muchísima vergüenza

mortuary ['mɔ:tjuərɪ] *n* depósito de cadáveres

mosaic [məu'zeɪɪk] *n* mosaico

Moslem ['mɒzləm] *adj, n* = **Muslim**

mosque [mɒsk] *n* mezquita

mosquito [mɒs'ki:təu] (pl **~es**) *n* mosquito (SP), zancudo (LAM)

moss [mɒs] *n* musgo

most [məust] *adj* la mayor parte de, la mayoría de ▷ *pron* la mayor parte, la mayoría ▷ *adv* el más; (very) muy; **the ~** (also: + adj) el más; **~ of them** la mayor parte de ellos; **I saw the ~** yo vi el que más; **at the (very) ~** a lo sumo, todo lo más; **to make the ~ of** aprovechar (al máximo); **a ~ interesting book** un libro interesantísimo; **mostly** *adv* en su mayor parte, principalmente

MOT (BRIT) *n abbr* = **Ministry of Transport**; **the ~ (test)** inspección (anual) obligatoria de coches y camiones

motel [məu'tɛl] *n* motel *m*

moth [mɒθ] *n* mariposa nocturna; (clothes moth) polilla

mother ['mʌðə*] *n* madre *f* ▷ *adj* materno ▷ *vt* (care for) cuidar (como una madre); **motherhood** *n* maternidad *f*; **mother-in-law** *n* suegra; **mother-of-pearl** *n* nácar *m*; **Mother's Day** *n* Día *m* de la Madre; **mother-to-be** *n* futura madre *f*; **mother tongue** *n* lengua materna

motif [məu'ti:f] n motivo

motion ['məuʃən] n movimiento; (gesture) ademán m, señal f; (at meeting) moción f ▷ vt, vi: **to ~ (to) sb to do sth** hacer señas a algn para que haga algo; **motionless** adj inmóvil; **motion picture** n película

motivate ['məutıveıt] vt motivar

motivation [məutı'veıʃən] n motivación f

motive ['məutıv] n motivo

motor ['məutə*] n motor m; (BRIT: inf: vehicle) coche m (SP), carro (LAM), automóvil m ▷ adj motor (f: motora or motriz); **motorbike** n moto f; **motorboat** n lancha motora; **motorcar** (BRIT) n coche m, carro, automóvil m; **motorcycle** n motocicleta; **motorcyclist** n motociclista mf; **motoring** (BRIT) n automovilismo; **motorist** n conductor(a) m/f, automovilista mf; **motor racing** (BRIT) n carreras fpl de coches, automovilismo; **motorway** (BRIT) n autopista

motto ['mɔtəu] (pl **~es**) n lema m; (watchword) consigna

mould [məuld] (US **mold**) n molde m; (mildew) moho ▷ vt moldear; (fig) formar; **mouldy** adj enmohecido

mound [maund] n montón m, montículo

mount [maunt] n monte m ▷ vt montar, subir a; (jewel) engarzar; (picture) enmarcar; (exhibition etc) organizar ▷ vi (increase) aumentar; **mount up** vi aumentar

mountain ['mauntın] n montaña ▷ cpd de montaña; **mountain bike** n bicicleta de montaña; **mountaineer** n alpinista mf (SP, MEX), andinista mf (LAM); **mountaineering** n alpinismo (SP, MEX), andinismo (LAM); **mountainous** adj montañoso; **mountain range** n sierra

mourn [mɔ:n] vt llorar, lamentar ▷ vi: **to ~ for** llorar la muerte de; **mourner** n doliente mf; dolorido/a; **mourning** n luto; **in mourning** de luto

mouse [maus] (pl **mice**) n (Zool, Comput) ratón m; **mouse mat** n (Comput) alfombrilla

moussaka [mu'sɑ:kə] n musaca

mousse [mu:s] n (Culin) crema batida; (for hair) espuma (moldeadora)

moustache [məs'tɑ:ʃ] (US **mustache**) n bigote m

mouth [mauθ, pl mauðz] n boca; (of river) desembocadura; **mouthful** n bocado; **mouth organ** n armónica; **mouthpiece** n (of musical instrument) boquilla; (spokesman) portavoz mf; **mouthwash** n enjuague m

move [mu:v] n (movement) movimiento; (in game) jugada; (: turn to play) turno; (change: of house) mudanza; (: of job) cambio de trabajo ▷ vt mover; (emotionally) conmover; (Pol: resolution etc) proponer ▷ vi moverse; (traffic) circular; (also: **~ house**) trasladarse, mudarse; **to ~ sb to do sth** mover a algn a hacer algo; **to get a ~ on** darse prisa; **move back** vi retroceder; **move in** vi (to a house) instalarse; (police, soldiers) intervenir; **move off** vi ponerse en camino; **move on** vi ponerse en camino; **move out** vi (of house) mudarse; **move over** vi apartarse, hacer sitio; **move up** vi (employee) ser ascendido; **movement** n movimiento

movie ['mu:vı] n película; **to go to the ~s** ir al cine; **movie theater** (US) n cine m

moving ['mu:vıŋ] adj (emotional) conmovedor(a); (that moves) móvil

mow [məu] (pt **~ed**, pp mowed or **mown**) vt (grass, corn) cortar, segar; **mower** n (also: **lawnmower**) cortacéspedes m inv

Mozambique [məuzæm'bi:k] n Mozambique m

MP n abbr = **Member of Parliament**

MP3 n MP3; **MP3 player** n reproductor m (de) MP3

mpg n abbr = **miles per gallon**

m.p.h. abbr = **miles per hour** (60 m.p.h. = 96 k.p.h.)

Mr ['mıstə*] (US **Mr.**) n: **~ Smith** (el) Sr. Smith

Mrs ['mısız] (US **Mrs.**) n: **~ Smith** (la) Sra. Smith

Ms [mız] (US **Ms.**) n = **Miss** or **Mrs**; **~ Smith** (la) Sr(t)a. Smith

MSP n abbr = **Member of the Scottish Parliament**

Mt abbr (Geo) (= **mount**) m

much [mʌtʃ] adj mucho ▷ adv mucho; (before pp) muy ▷ n or pron mucho; **how ~ is it?** ¿cuánto es?, ¿cuánto cuesta?; **too ~** demasiado; **it's not ~** no es mucho; **as ~ as** tanto como; **however ~ he tries** por mucho que se esfuerce

muck [mʌk] n suciedad f; **muck up** (inf) vt arruinar, estropear; **mucky** adj (dirty) sucio

mucus ['mju:kəs] n mucosidad f, moco

mud [mʌd] n barro, lodo

muddle ['mʌdl] n desorden m, confusión f; (mix-up) embrollo, lío ▷ vt (also: **~ up**) embrollar, confundir

muddy ['mʌdı] adj fangoso, cubierto de lodo

mudguard ['mʌdgɑ:d] n guardabarros m inv

muesli ['mju:zlı] n muesli m

muffin ['mʌfın] n panecillo dulce

muffled ['mʌfld] adj (noise etc) amortiguado, apagado

muffler (US) ['mʌflə*] n (Aut) silenciador m

mug [mʌg] n taza grande (sin platillo); (for beer) jarra; (inf: face) jeta ▷ vt (assault) asaltar; **mugger** ['mʌgə*] n atracador(a) m/f; **mugging** n asalto

muggy ['mʌgɪ] adj bochornoso

mule [mju:l] n mula

multicoloured ['mʌltɪkʌləd] (US), **multicolored** adj multicolor

multimedia ['mʌltɪ'mi:dɪə] adj multimedia

multinational [mʌltɪ'næʃənl] n multinacional f ▷ adj multinacional

multiple ['mʌltɪpl] adj múltiple ▷ n múltiplo; **multiple choice (test)** n examen m de tipo test; **multiple sclerosis** n esclerosis f múltiple

multiplex cinema ['mʌltɪplɛks-] n multicines mpl

multiplication [mʌltɪplɪ'keɪʃən] n multiplicación f

multiply ['mʌltɪplaɪ] vt multiplicar ▷ vi multiplicarse

multistorey [mʌltɪ'stɔ:rɪ] (BRIT) adj de muchos pisos

mum [mʌm] (BRIT: inf) n mamá ▷ adj: **to keep ~** mantener la boca cerrada

mumble ['mʌmbl] vt, vi hablar entre dientes, refunfuñar

mummy ['mʌmɪ] n (BRIT: mother) mamá; (embalmed) momia

mumps [mʌmps] n paperas fpl

munch [mʌntʃ] vt, vi mascar

municipal [mju:'nɪsɪpl] adj municipal

mural ['mjuərl] n (pintura) mural m

murder ['mə:də*] n asesinato; (in law) homicidio ▷ vt asesinar, matar; **murderer** n asesino

murky ['mə:kɪ] adj (water) turbio; (street, night) lóbrego

murmur ['mə:mə*] n murmullo ▷ vt, vi murmurar

muscle ['mʌsl] n músculo; (fig: strength) garra, fuerza; **muscular** ['mʌskjulə*] adj muscular; (person) musculoso

museum [mju:'zɪəm] n museo

mushroom ['mʌʃrum] n seta, hongo; (Culin) champiñón m ▷ vi crecer de la noche a la mañana

music ['mju:zɪk] n música; **musical** adj musical; (sound) melodioso; (person) con talento musical ▷ n (show) comedia musical; **musical instrument** n instrumento musical; **musician** [-'zɪʃən] n músico/a

Muslim ['mʌzlɪm] adj, n musulmán/ana m/f

muslin ['mʌzlɪn] n muselina

mussel ['mʌsl] n mejillón m

must [mʌst] aux vb (obligation): **I ~ do it** debo hacerlo, tengo que hacerlo; (probability): **he ~ be there by now** ya debe (de) estar allí ▷ n: **it's a ~** es imprescindible

mustache ['mʌstæʃ] (US) n = **moustache**

mustard ['mʌstəd] n mostaza

mustn't ['mʌsnt] = **must not**

mute [mju:t] adj, n mudo/a m/f

mutilate ['mju:tɪleɪt] vt mutilar

mutiny ['mju:tɪnɪ] n motín m ▷ vi amotinarse

mutter ['mʌtə*] vt, vi murmurar

mutton ['mʌtn] n carne f de cordero

mutual ['mju:tʃuəl] adj mutuo; (interest) común

muzzle ['mʌzl] n hocico; (for dog) bozal m; (of gun) boca ▷ vt (dog) poner un bozal a

my [maɪ] adj mi(s); **~ house/brother/sisters** mi casa/mi hermano/mis hermanas; **I've washed ~ hair/cut ~ finger** me he lavado el pelo/cortado un dedo; **is this ~ pen or yours?** ¿es este bolígrafo mío o tuyo?

myself [maɪ'sɛlf] pron (reflexive) me; (emphatic) yo mismo; (after prep) mí (mismo); see also **oneself**

mysterious [mɪs'tɪərɪəs] adj misterioso

mystery ['mɪstərɪ] n misterio

mystical ['mɪstɪkl] adj místico

mystify ['mɪstɪfaɪ] vt (perplex) dejar perplejo

myth [mɪθ] n mito; **mythology** [mɪ'θɒlədʒɪ] n mitología

n

n/a *abbr* (= *not applicable*) no interesa
nag [næg] *vt* (*scold*) regañar
nail [neɪl] *n* (*human*) uña; (*metal*) clavo ▷ *vt* clavar; **to ~ sth to sth** clavar algo en algo; **to ~ sb down to doing sth** comprometer a algn a que haga algo; **nailbrush** *n* cepillo para las uñas; **nailfile** *n* lima para las uñas; **nail polish** *n* esmalte *m or* laca para las uñas; **nail polish remover** *n* quitaesmalte *m*; **nail scissors** *npl* tijeras *fpl* para las uñas; **nail varnish** (*BRIT*) *n* =**nail polish**
naïve [naɪˈiːv] *adj* ingenuo
naked [ˈneɪkɪd] *adj* (*nude*) desnudo; (*flame*) expuesto al aire
name [neɪm] *n* nombre *m*; (*surname*) apellido; (*reputation*) fama, renombre *m* ▷ *vt* (*child*) poner nombre a; (*criminal*) identificar; (*price, date etc*) fijar; **what's your ~?** ¿cómo se llama?; **by ~** de nombre; **in the ~ of** en nombre de; **to give one's ~ and address** dar sus señas; **namely** *adv* a saber
nanny [ˈnænɪ] *n* niñera
nap [næp] *n* (*sleep*) sueñecito, siesta
napkin [ˈnæpkɪn] *n* (*also*: **table ~**) servilleta
nappy [ˈnæpɪ] (*BRIT*) *n* pañal *m*
narcotics *npl* (*illegal drugs*) estupefacientes *mpl*, narcóticos *mpl*
narrative [ˈnærətɪv] *n* narrativa ▷ *adj* narrativo
narrator [nəˈreɪtə*] *n* narrador(a) *m/f*
narrow [ˈnærəu] *adj* estrecho, angosto; (*fig: majority etc*) corto; (: *ideas etc*) estrecho ▷ *vi* (*road*) estrecharse; (*diminish*) reducirse; **to have a ~ escape** escaparse por los pelos; **narrow down** *vt* (*search, investigation, possibilities*) restringir, limitar; (*list*) reducir; **narrowly** *adv* (*miss*) por poco; **narrow-minded** *adj* de miras estrechas
nasal [ˈneɪzl] *adj* nasal
nasty [ˈnɑːstɪ] *adj* (*remark*) feo; (*person*)

antipático; (*revolting: taste, smell*) asqueroso; (*wound, disease etc*) peligroso, grave
nation [ˈneɪʃən] *n* nación *f*
national [ˈnæʃənl] *adj, n* nacional *m/f*; **national anthem** *n* himno nacional; **national dress** *n* vestido nacional; **National Health Service** (*BRIT*) *n* servicio nacional de salud pública ≈ Insalud *m* (*SP*); **National Insurance** (*BRIT*) *n* seguro social nacional; **nationalist** *adj, n* nacionalista *mf*; **nationality** [-ˈnælɪtɪ] *n* nacionalidad *f*; **nationalize** *vt* nacionalizar; **national park** (*BRIT*) *n* parque *m* nacional; **National Trust** *n* (*BRIT*) *organización encargada de preservar el patrimonio histórico británico*
nationwide [ˈneɪʃənwaɪd] *adj* en escala *or* a nivel nacional
native [ˈneɪtɪv] *n* (*local inhabitant*) natural *mf*, nacional *mf* ▷ *adj* (*indigenous*) indígena; (*country*) natal; (*innate*) natural, innato; **a ~ of Russia** un(a) natural *mf* de Rusia; **Native American** *adj, n* americano/a indígena, amerindio/a; **native speaker** *n* hablante *mf* nativo/a
NATO [ˈneɪtəu] *n abbr* (= *North Atlantic Treaty Organization*) OTAN *f*
natural [ˈnætʃrəl] *adj* natural; **natural gas** *n* gas *m* natural; **natural history** *n* historia natural; **naturally** *adv* (*speak etc*) naturalmente; (*of course*) desde luego, por supuesto; **natural resources** *npl* recursos *mpl* naturales
nature [ˈneɪtʃə*] *n* (*also*: **N~**) naturaleza; (*group, sort*) género, clase *f*; (*character*) carácter *m*, genio; **by ~** por *or* de naturaleza; **nature reserve** *n* reserva natural
naughty [ˈnɔːtɪ] *adj* (*child*) travieso
nausea [ˈnɔːsɪə] *n* náuseas *fpl*
naval [ˈneɪvl] *adj* naval, de marina
navel [ˈneɪvl] *n* ombligo
navigate [ˈnævɪgeɪt] *vt* gobernar ▷ *vi* navegar; (*Aut*) ir de copiloto; **navigation** [-ˈgeɪʃən] *n* (*action*) navegación *f*; (*science*) náutica
navy [ˈneɪvɪ] *n* marina de guerra; (*ships*) armada, flota
Nazi [ˈnɑːtsɪ] *n* nazi *mf*
NB *abbr* (= *nota bene*) nótese
near [nɪə*] *adj* (*place, relation*) cercano; (*time*) próximo ▷ *adv* cerca ▷ *prep* (*also*: **~ to**: *space*) cerca de, junto a; (: *time*) cerca de ▷ *vt* acercarse a, aproximarse a; **nearby** [nɪəˈbaɪ] *adj* cercano, próximo ▷ *adv* cerca; **nearly** *adv* casi, por poco; **I nearly fell** por poco me caigo; **near-sighted** *adj* miope, corto de vista
neat [niːt] *adj* (*place*) ordenado, bien cuidado; (*person*) pulcro; (*plan*) ingenioso;

(spirits) solo; **neatly** adv (tidily) con esmero; (skilfully) ingeniosamente

necessarily ['nɛsɪsrɪlɪ] adv necesariamente

necessary ['nɛsɪsrɪ] adj necesario, preciso

necessity [nɪ'sɛsɪtɪ] n necesidad f

neck [nɛk] n (of person, garment, bottle) cuello; (of animal) pescuezo ▷ vi (inf) besuquearse; ~ **and** ~ parejos; **necklace** ['nɛklɪs] n collar m; **necktie** ['nɛktaɪ] n corbata

nectarine ['nɛktərɪn] n nectarina

need [niːd] n (lack) escasez f, falta; (necessity) necesidad f ▷ vt (require) necesitar; **I** ~ **to do it** tengo que or debo hacerlo; **you don't** ~ **to go** no hace falta que (te) vayas

needle ['niːdl] n aguja ▷ vt (fig: inf) picar, fastidiar

needless ['niːdlɪs] adj innecesario; ~ **to say** huelga decir que

needlework ['niːdlwəːk] n (activity) costura, labor f de aguja

needn't ['niːdnt] = **need not**

needy ['niːdɪ] adj necesitado

negative ['nɛgətɪv] n (Phot) negativo; (Ling) negación f ▷ adj negativo

neglect [nɪ'glɛkt] vt (one's duty) faltar a, no cumplir con; (child) descuidar, desatender ▷ n (of house, garden etc) abandono; (of child) desatención f; (of duty) incumplimiento

negotiate [nɪ'gəuʃɪeɪt] vt (treaty, loan) negociar; (obstacle) franquear; (bend in road) tomar ▷ vi: **to** ~ **(with)** negociar (con)

negotiations [nɪgəuʃɪ'eɪʃənz] pl n negociaciones

negotiator [nɪ'gəuʃɪeɪtə*] n negociador(a) m/f

neighbour ['neɪbə*] (US **neighbor** etc) n vecino/a; **neighbourhood** n (place) vecindad f, barrio; (people) vecindario; **neighbouring** adj vecino

neither ['naɪðə*] adj ni ▷ conj: **I didn't move and** ~ **did John** no me he movido, ni Juan tampoco ▷ pron ninguno ▷ adv: ~ **good nor bad** ni bueno ni malo; ~ **is true** ninguno/a de los(las) dos es cierto/a

neon ['niːɔn] n neón m

Nepal [nɪ'pɔːl] n Nepal m

nephew ['nɛvjuː] n sobrino

nerve [nəːv] n (Anat) nervio; (courage) valor m; (impudence) descaro, frescura (nervousness) nerviosismo msg, nervios mpl; **a fit of** ~**s** un ataque de nervios

nervous ['nəːvəs] adj (anxious, Anat) nervioso; (timid) tímido, miedoso; **nervous breakdown** n crisis f nerviosa

nest [nɛst] n (of bird) nido; (wasps' nest) avispero ▷ vi anidar

net [nɛt] n (gen) red f; (fabric) tul m ▷ adj (Comm) neto, líquido ▷ vt coger (SP) or agarrar (LAM) con red; (Sport) marcar; **netball** n básquet m

Netherlands ['nɛðələndz] npl: **the** ~ los Países Bajos

nett [nɛt] adj = **net**

nettle ['nɛtl] n ortiga

network ['nɛtwəːk] n red f

neurotic [njuə'rɔtɪk] adj neurótico/a

neuter ['njuːtə*] adj (Ling) neutro ▷ vt castrar, capar

neutral ['njuːtrəl] adj (person) neutral; (colour etc, Elec) neutro ▷ n (Aut) punto muerto

never ['nɛvə*] adv nunca, jamás; **I** ~ **went** no fui nunca; ~ **in my life** jamás en la vida; see also **mind**; **never-ending** adj interminable, sin fin; **nevertheless** [nɛvəðə'lɛs] adv sin embargo, no obstante

new [njuː] adj nuevo; (brand new) a estrenar; (recent) reciente; **New Age** n Nueva Era; **newborn** adj recién nacido; **newcomer** ['njuːkʌmə*] n recién venido/a or llegado/a; **newly** adv nuevamente, recién

news [njuːz] n noticias fpl; **a piece of** ~ una noticia; **the** ~ (Radio, TV) las noticias fpl; **news agency** n agencia de noticias; **newsagent** (BRIT) n vendedor(a) m/f de periódicos; **newscaster** n presentador(a) m/f, locutor(a) m/f; **news dealer** (US) n = **newsagent**; **newsletter** n hoja informativa, boletín m; **newspaper** n periódico, diario; **newsreader** n = **newscaster**

newt [njuːt] n tritón m

New Year n Año Nuevo; **New Year's Day** n Día m de Año Nuevo; **New Year's Eve** n Nochevieja

New Zealand [njuː'ziːlənd] n Nueva Zelanda; **New Zealander** n neozelandés/esa m/f

next [nɛkst] adj (house, room) vecino; (bus stop, meeting) próximo; (following: page etc) siguiente ▷ adv después; **the** ~ **day** el día siguiente; ~ **time** la próxima vez; ~ **year** el año próximo or que viene; ~ **to** junto a, al lado de; ~ **to nothing** casi nada; ~ **please!** ¡el siguiente!; **next door** adv en la casa de al lado ▷ adj vecino, de al lado; **next-of-kin** n pariente m más cercano

NHS n abbr = **National Health Service**

nibble ['nɪbl] vt mordisquear, mordiscar

nice [naɪs] adj (likeable) simpático; (kind) amable; (pleasant) agradable;

(*attractive*) bonito, lindo (*LAM*); **nicely** *adv* amablemente; bien

niche [niːʃ] *n* (*Arch*) nicho, hornacina

nick [nɪk] *n* (*wound*) rasguño; (*cut, indentation*) mella, muesca ▷ *vt* (*inf*) birlar, robar; **in the ~ of time** justo a tiempo

nickel ['nɪkl] *n* níquel *m*; (*US*) moneda de 5 centavos

nickname ['nɪkneɪm] *n* apodo, mote *m* ▷ *vt* apodar

nicotine ['nɪkətiːn] *n* nicotina

niece [niːs] *n* sobrina

night [naɪt] *n* noche *f*; (*evening*) tarde *f*; **the ~ before last** anteanoche; **at ~, by ~** de noche, por la noche; **night club** *n* cabaret *m*; **nightdress** (*BRIT*) *n* camisón *m*; **nightie** ['naɪtɪ] *n* = **nightdress**; **nightlife** *n* vida nocturna; **nightly** *adj* de todas las noches ▷ *adv* todas las noches, cada noche; **nightmare** *n* pesadilla; **night school** *n* clase(s) *f(pl)* nocturna(s); **night shift** *n* turno nocturno *or* de noche; **night-time** *n* noche *f*

nil [nɪl] (*BRIT*) *n* (*Sport*) cero, nada

nine [naɪn] *num* nueve; **nineteen** *num* diecinueve, diez y nueve; **nineteenth** [naɪn'tiːnθ] *adj* decimonoveno, decimonono; **ninetieth** ['naɪntɪɪθ] *adj* nonagésimo; **ninety** *num* noventa

ninth [naɪnθ] *adj* noveno

nip [nɪp] *vt* (*pinch*) pellizcar; (*bite*) morder

nipple ['nɪpl] *n* (*Anat*) pezón *m*

nitrogen ['naɪtrədʒən] *n* nitrógeno

○ **KEYWORD**

no [nəu] (*pl* **noes**) *adv* (*opposite of "yes"*) no; **are you coming? – no (I'm not)** ¿vienes? – no; **would you like some more? – no thank you** ¿quieres más? – no gracias ▷ *adj* (*not any*): **I have no money/time/books** no tengo dinero/tiempo/libros; **no other man would have done it** ningún otro lo hubiera hecho; **"no entry"** "prohibido el paso"; **"no smoking"** "prohibido fumar" ▷ *n* no *m*

nobility [nəu'bɪlɪtɪ] *n* nobleza

noble ['nəubl] *adj* noble

nobody ['nəubədɪ] *pron* nadie

nod [nɔd] *vi* saludar con la cabeza; (*in agreement*) decir que sí con la cabeza; (*doze*) dar cabezadas ▷ *vt*: **to ~ one's head** inclinar la cabeza ▷ *n* inclinación *f* de cabeza; **nod off** *vi* dar cabezadas

noise [nɔɪz] *n* ruido; (*din*) escándalo, estrépito; **noisy** *adj* ruidoso; (*child*) escandaloso

nominal ['nɔmɪnl] *adj* nominal

nominate ['nɔmɪneɪt] *vt* (*propose*) proponer; (*appoint*) nombrar; **nomination** [nɔmɪ'neɪʃən] *n* propuesta; nombramiento; **nominee** [-'niː] *n* candidato/a

none [nʌn] *pron* ninguno/a ▷ *adv* de ninguna manera; **~ of you** ninguno de vosotros; **I've ~ left** no me queda ninguno/a; **he's ~ the worse for it** no le ha hecho ningún mal

nonetheless [nʌnðə'lɛs] *adv* sin embargo, no obstante

non-fiction [nɔn'fɪkʃən] *n* literatura no novelesca

nonsense ['nɔnsəns] *n* tonterías *fpl*, disparates *fpl*; **~!** ¡qué tonterías!

non: non-smoker *n* no fumador(a) *m/f*; **non-smoking** *adj* (de) no fumador; **non-stick** *adj* (*pan, surface*) antiadherente

noodles ['nuːdlz] *npl* tallarines *mpl*

noon [nuːn] *n* mediodía *m*

no-one ['nəuwʌn] *pron* = **nobody**

nor [nɔː*] *conj* = **neither** ▷ *adv* *see* **neither**

norm [nɔːm] *n* norma

normal ['nɔːml] *adj* normal; **normally** *adv* normalmente

north [nɔːθ] *n* norte *m* ▷ *adj* del norte, norteño ▷ *adv* al *or* hacia el norte; **North America** *n* América del Norte; **North American** *adj, n* norteamericano/a *m/f*; **northbound** ['nɔːθbaund] *adj* (*traffic*) que se dirige al norte; (*carriageway*) de dirección norte; **north-east** *n* nor(d)este *m*; **northeastern** *adj* nor(d)este, del nor(d)este; **northern** ['nɔːðən] *adj* norteño, del norte; **Northern Ireland** *n* Irlanda del Norte; **North Korea** *n* Corea del Norte; **North Pole** *n* Polo Norte; **North Sea** *n* Mar *m* del Norte; **north-west** *n* nor(d)oeste *m*; **northwestern** ['nɔːθ'westən] *adj* noroeste, del noroeste

Norway ['nɔːweɪ] *n* Noruega; **Norwegian** [-'wiːdʒən] *adj* noruego/a ▷ *n* noruego/a; (*Ling*) noruego

nose [nəuz] *n* (*Anat*) nariz *f*; (*Zool*) hocico; (*sense of smell*) olfato ▷ *vi*: **to ~ about** curiosear; **nosebleed** *n* hemorragia nasal; **nosey** (*inf*) *adj* curioso, fisgón/ona

nostalgia [nɔs'tældʒɪə] *n* nostalgia

nostalgic [nɔs'tældʒɪk] *adj* nostálgico

nostril ['nɔstrɪl] *n* ventana de la nariz

nosy ['nəuzɪ] (*inf*) *adj* = **nosey**

not [nɔt] *adv* no; **~ that** ... no es que ...; **it's too late, isn't it?** es demasiado tarde, ¿verdad *or* no?; **~ yet/now** todavía/ahora no; **why ~?** ¿por qué no?; *see also* **all; only**

notable ['nəʊtəbl] *adj* notable; **notably**
adv especialmente
notch [nɒtʃ] *n* muesca, corte *m*
note [nəʊt] *n* (*Mus, record, letter*) nota;
(*banknote*) billete *m*; (*tone*) tono ▷ *vt*
(*observe*) notar, observar; (*write down*)
apuntar, anotar; **notebook** *n* libreta,
cuaderno; **noted** ['nəʊtɪd] *adj* célebre,
conocido; **notepad** *n* bloc *m*; **notepaper** *n*
papel *m* para cartas
nothing ['nʌθɪŋ] *n* nada; (*zero*) cero; **he
does ~** no hace nada; **~ new** nada nuevo; **~
much** no mucho; **for ~** (*free*) gratis, sin pago;
(*in vain*) en balde
notice ['nəʊtɪs] *n* (*announcement*) anuncio;
(*warning*) aviso; (*dismissal*) despido;
(*resignation*) dimisión *f*; (*period of time*) plazo
▷ *vt* (*observe*) notar, observar; **to bring sth
to sb's ~** (*attention*) llamar la atención de
algn sobre algo; **to take ~ of** tomar nota
de, prestar atención a; **at short ~** con poca
anticipación; **until further ~** hasta nuevo
aviso; **to hand in one's ~** dimitir

▌ Be careful not to translate **notice** by the
Spanish word *noticia*.

noticeable *adj* evidente, obvio
notify ['nəʊtɪfaɪ] *vt*: **to ~ sb (of sth)**
comunicar (algo) a algn
notion ['nəʊʃən] *n* idea; (*opinion*) opinión
f; **notions** *npl* (*us*) mercería
notorious [nəʊ'tɔːrɪəs] *adj* notorio
notwithstanding [nɒtwɪθ'stændɪŋ] *adv*
no obstante, sin embargo; **~ this** a pesar
de esto
nought [nɔːt] *n* cero
noun [naʊn] *n* nombre *m*, sustantivo
nourish ['nʌrɪʃ] *vt* nutrir; (*fig*) alimentar;
nourishment *n* alimento, sustento
Nov. *abbr* (= *November*) nov
novel ['nɒvl] *n* novela ▷ *adj* (*new*) nuevo,
original; (*unexpected*) insólito; **novelist** *n*
novelista *mf*; **novelty** *n* novedad *f*
November [nəʊ'vembə*] *n* noviembre *m*
novice ['nɒvɪs] *n* (*Rel*) novicio/a
now [naʊ] *adv* (*at the present time*) ahora;
(*these days*) actualmente, hoy día ▷ *conj*: **~
(that)** ya que, ahora que; **right ~** ahora
mismo; **by ~** ya; **just ~** ahora mismo; **~
and then, ~ and again** de vez en cuando;
from ~ on de ahora en adelante; **nowadays**
['naʊədeɪz] *adv* hoy (en) día, actualmente
nowhere ['nəʊwɛə*] *adv* (*direction*) a
ninguna parte; (*location*) en ninguna parte
nozzle ['nɒzl] *n* boquilla
nr *abbr* (*BRIT*) = **near**
nuclear ['njuːklɪə*] *adj* nuclear
nucleus ['njuːklɪəs] (*pl* **nuclei**) *n* núcleo
nude [njuːd] *adj, n* desnudo/a *m/f*; **in the
~** desnudo
nudge [nʌdʒ] *vt* dar un codazo a
nudist ['njuːdɪst] *n* nudista *mf*
nudity ['njuːdɪtɪ] *n* desnudez *f*
nuisance ['njuːsns] *n* molestia, fastidio;
(*person*) pesado, latoso; **what a ~!** ¡qué lata!
numb [nʌm] *adj*: **~ with cold/fear**
entumecido por el frío/paralizado de miedo
number ['nʌmbə*] *n* número; (*quantity*)
cantidad *f* ▷ *vt* (*pages etc*) numerar, poner
número a; (*amount to*) sumar, ascender a; **to
be ~ed among** figurar entre; **a ~ of** varios,
algunos; **they were ten in ~** eran diez;
number plate (*BRIT*) *n* matrícula, placa;
Number Ten *n* (*BRIT*: 10 *Downing Street*)
residencia del primer ministro
numerical [njuː'merɪkl] *adj* numérico
numerous ['njuːmərəs] *adj* numeroso
nun [nʌn] *n* monja, religiosa
nurse [nɜːs] *n* enfermero/a; (*also*: **~maid**)
niñera ▷ *vt* (*patient*) cuidar, atender
nursery ['nɜːsərɪ] *n* (*institution*) guardería
infantil; (*room*) cuarto de los niños; (*for
plants*) criadero, semillero; **nursery
rhyme** *n* canción *f* infantil; **nursery
school** *n* parvulario, escuela de párvulos;
nursery slope (*BRIT*) *n* (*Ski*) cuesta para
principiantes
nursing ['nɜːsɪŋ] *n* (*profession*) profesión
f de enfermera; (*care*) asistencia, cuidado;
nursing home *n* clínica de reposo
nurture ['nɜːtʃə*] *vt* (*child, plant*)
alimentar, nutrir
nut [nʌt] *n* (*Tech*) tuerca; (*Bot*) nuez *f*
nutmeg ['nʌtmeg] *n* nuez *f* moscada
nutrient ['njuːtrɪənt] *adj* nutritivo ▷ *n*
elemento nutritivo
nutrition [njuː'trɪʃən] *n* nutrición *f*,
alimentación *f*
nutritious [njuː'trɪʃəs] *adj* nutritivo,
alimenticio
nuts [nʌts] (*inf*) *adj* loco
NVQ *n abbr* (*BRIT*) = **National Vocational
Qualification**
nylon ['naɪlɒn] *n* nilón *m* ▷ *adj* de nilón

oath [əuθ] *n* juramento; (*swear word*) palabrota; **on** (*BRIT*) *or* **under ~** bajo juramento

oak [əuk] *n* roble *m* ▷ *adj* de roble

O.A.P. (*BRIT*) *n, abbr* = **old-age pensioner**

oar [ɔ:*] *n* remo

oasis [əu'eisis] (*pl* **oases**) *n* oasis *m inv*

oath [əuθ] *n* juramento; (*swear word*) palabrota; **on** (*BRIT*) *or* **under ~** bajo juramento

oatmeal ['əutmi:l] *n* harina de avena

oats [əuts] *npl* avena

obedience [ə'bi:diəns] *n* obediencia

obedient [ə'bi:diənt] *adj* obediente

obese [əu'bi:s] *adj* obeso

obesity [əu'bi:siti] *n* obesidad *f*

obey [ə'bei] *vt* obedecer; (*instructions, regulations*) cumplir

obituary [ə'bitjuəri] *n* necrología

object [*n* 'ɔbdʒikt, *vb* əb'dʒɛkt] *n* objeto; (*purpose*) objeto, propósito; (*Ling*) complemento ▷ *vi*: **to ~ to** estar en contra de; (*proposal*) oponerse a; **to ~ that** objetar que; **expense is no ~** no importa cuánto cuesta; **I ~!** ¡yo protesto!; **objection** [əb'dʒɛkʃən] *n* protesta; **I have no objection to …** no tengo inconveniente en que …; **objective** *adj*, *n* objetivo

obligation [ɔbli'geiʃən] *n* obligación *f*; (*debt*) deber *m*; **without ~** sin compromiso

obligatory [ə'bligətəri] *adj* obligatorio

oblige [ə'blaidʒ] *vt* (*do a favour for*) complacer, hacer un favor a; **to ~ sb to do sth** forzar *or* obligar a algn a hacer algo; **to be ~d to sb for sth** estarle agradecido a algn por algo

oblique [ə'bli:k] *adj* oblicuo; (*allusion*) indirecto

obliterate [ə'blitəreit] *vt* borrar

oblivious [ə'bliviəs] *adj*: **~ of** inconsciente de

oblong ['ɔblɔŋ] *adj* rectangular ▷ *n* rectángulo

obnoxious [əb'nɔkʃəs] *adj* odioso, detestable; (*smell*) nauseabundo

oboe ['əubəu] *n* oboe *m*

obscene [əb'si:n] *adj* obsceno

obscure [əb'skjuə*] *adj* oscuro ▷ *vt* oscurecer; (*hide: sun*) esconder

observant [əb'zə:vnt] *adj* observador(a)

observation [ɔbzə'veiʃən] *n* observación *f*; (*Med*) examen *m*

observatory [əb'zə:vətri] *n* observatorio

observe [əb'zə:v] *vt* observar; (*rule*) cumplir; **observer** *n* observador(a) *m/f*

obsess [əb'sɛs] *vt* obsesionar; **obsession** [əb'sɛʃən] *n* obsesión *f*; **obsessive** *adj* obsesivo; obsesionante

obsolete ['ɔbsəli:t] *adj*: **to be ~** estar en desuso

obstacle ['ɔbstəkl] *n* obstáculo; (*nuisance*) estorbo

obstinate ['ɔbstinit] *adj* terco, porfiado; (*determined*) obstinado

obstruct [əb'strʌkt] *vt* obstruir; (*hinder*) estorbar, obstaculizar; **obstruction** [əb'strʌkʃən] *n* (*action*) obstrucción *f*; (*object*) estorbo, obstáculo

obtain [əb'tein] *vt* obtener; (*achieve*) conseguir

obvious ['ɔbviəs] *adj* obvio, evidente; **obviously** *adv* evidentemente, naturalmente; **obviously not** por supuesto que no

occasion [ə'keiʒən] *n* oportunidad *f*, ocasión *f*; (*event*) acontecimiento; **occasional** *adj* poco frecuente, ocasional; **occasionally** *adv* de vez en cuando

occult [ɔ'kʌlt] *adj* (*gen*) oculto

occupant ['ɔkjupənt] *n* (*of house*) inquilino/a; (*of car*) ocupante *mf*

occupation [ɔkju'peiʃən] *n* ocupación *f*; (*job*) trabajo; (*pastime*) ocupaciones *fpl*

occupy ['ɔkjupai] *vt* (*seat, post, time*) ocupar; (*house*) habitar; **to ~ o.s. in doing** pasar el tiempo haciendo

occur [ə'kə:*] *vi* pasar, suceder; **to ~ to sb** ocurrírsele a algn; **occurrence** [ə'kʌrəns] *n* acontecimiento; (*existence*) existencia

ocean ['əuʃən] *n* océano

o'clock [ə'klɔk] *adv*: **it is 5 ~** son las 5

Oct. *abbr* (= *October*) oct

October [ɔk'təubə*] *n* octubre *m*

octopus ['ɔktəpəs] *n* pulpo

odd [ɔd] *adj* extraño, raro; (*number*) impar; (*sock, shoe etc*) suelto; **60-~** 60 y pico; **at ~ times** de vez en cuando; **to be the ~ one out** estar de más; **oddly** *adv* curiosamente, extrañamente; *see also* **enough**; **odds** *npl*

(*in betting*) puntos *mpl* de ventaja; **it makes no odds** da lo mismo; **at odds** reñidos/as; **odds and ends** minucias *fpl*
odometer [ɔˈdɒmɪtə*] (*us*) *n* cuentakilómetros *m inv*
odour [ˈəʊdə*] (*us* **odor**) *n* olor *m*; (*unpleasant*) hedor *m*

○ **KEYWORD**

of [ɔv, əv] *prep* **1** (*gen*) de; **a friend of ours** un amigo nuestro; **a boy of 10** un chico de 10 años; **that was kind of you** eso fue muy amable por or de tu parte
2 (*expressing quantity, amount, dates etc*) de; **a kilo of flour** un kilo de harina; **there were three of them** había tres; **three of us went** tres de nosotros fuimos; **the 5th of July** el 5 de julio
3 (*from, out of*) de; **made of wood** (hecho) de madera

off [ɔf] *adj, adv* (*engine*) desconectado; (*light*) apagado; (*tap*) cerrado; (*BRIT: food: bad*) pasado, malo; (: *milk*) cortado; (*cancelled*) cancelado ▷ *prep* de; **to be ~** (*to leave*) irse, marcharse; **to be ~ sick** estar enfermo or de baja; **a day ~** un día libre or sin trabajar; **to have an ~ day** tener un día malo; **he had his coat ~** se había quitado el abrigo; **10% ~** (*Comm*) (con el) 10% de descuento; **5 km ~ (the road)** a 5 km (de la carretera); **~ the coast** frente a la costa; **I'm ~ meat** (*no longer eat/like it*) paso de la carne; **on the ~ chance** por si acaso; **~ and on** de vez en cuando
offence [əˈfɛns] (*us* **offense**) *n* (*crime*) delito; **to take ~ at** ofenderse por
offend [əˈfɛnd] *vt* (*person*) ofender; **offender** *n* delincuente *mf*
offense [əˈfɛns] (*us*) *n* = **offence**
offensive [əˈfɛnsɪv] *adj* ofensivo; (*smell etc*) repugnante ▷ *n* (*Mil*) ofensiva
offer [ˈɔfə*] *n* oferta, ofrecimiento; (*proposal*) propuesta ▷ *vt* ofrecer; (*opportunity*) facilitar; **"on ~"** (*Comm*) "en oferta"
offhand [ɔfˈhænd] *adj* informal ▷ *adv* de improviso
office [ˈɔfɪs] *n* (*place*) oficina; (*room*) despacho; (*position*) carga, oficio; **doctor's ~** (*us*) consultorio; **to take ~** entrar en funciones; **office block** (*us*), **office building** *n* bloque *m* de oficinas; **office hours** *npl* horas *fpl* de oficina; (*us Med*) horas *fpl* de consulta
officer [ˈɔfɪsə*] *n* (*Mil etc*) oficial *mf*; (*also*: **police ~**) agente *mf* de policía; (*of*

organization) director(a) *m/f*
office worker *n* oficinista *mf*
official [əˈfɪʃl] *adj* oficial, autorizado ▷ *n* funcionario/a, oficial *mf*
off: **off-licence** (*BRIT*) *n* (*shop*) bodega *tienda de vinos y bebidas alcohólicas*; **off-line** *adj, adv* (*Comput*) fuera de línea; **off-peak** *adj* (*electricity*) de banda económica; (*ticket*) *billete de precio reducido por viajar fuera de las horas punta*; **off-putting** (*BRIT*) *adj* (*person*) asqueroso; (*remark*) desalentador(a); **off-season** *adj, adv* fuera de temporada

◉ **OFF-LICENCE**
◉
◉ En el Reino Unido la venta de bebidas
◉ alcohólicas está estrictamente regulada
◉ y se necesita una licencia especial, con
◉ la que cuentan los bares, restaurantes
◉ y los establecimientos de **off-licence**,
◉ los únicos lugares en donde se pueden
◉ adquirir bebidas alcohólicas para su
◉ consumo fuera del local, de donde viene
◉ su nombre. También venden bebidas
◉ no alcohólicas, tabaco, chocolatinas,
◉ patatas fritas, etc. y a menudo forman
◉ parte de una cadena nacional.

offset [ˈɔfsɛt] *vt* contrarrestar, compensar
offshore [ɔfˈʃɔː*] *adj* (*breeze, island*) costera; (*fishing*) de bajura
offside [ˈɔfsaɪd] *adj* (*Sport*) fuera de juego; (*Aut: in UK*) del lado derecho; (: *in US, Europe etc*) del lado izquierdo
offspring [ˈɔfsprɪŋ] *n inv* descendencia
often [ˈɔfn] *adv* a menudo, con frecuencia; **how ~ do you go?** ¿cada cuánto vas?
oh [əʊ] *excl* ¡ah!
oil [ɔɪl] *n* aceite *m*; (*petroleum*) petróleo; (*for heating*) aceite *m* combustible ▷ *vt* engrasar; **oil filter** *n* (*Aut*) filtro de aceite; **oil painting** *n* pintura al óleo; **oil refinery** *n* refinería de petróleo; **oil rig** *n* torre *f* de perforación; **oil slick** *n* marea negra; **oil tanker** *n* petrolero; (*truck*) camión *m* cisterna; **oil well** *n* pozo (de petróleo); **oily** *adj* aceitoso; (*food*) grasiento
ointment [ˈɔɪntmənt] *n* ungüento
O.K., okay [ˈəʊˈkeɪ] *excl* ¡O.K.!, ¡está bien!, ¡vale! (*SP*) ▷ *adj* bien ▷ *vt* dar el visto bueno a
old [əʊld] *adj* viejo; (*former*) antiguo; **how ~ are you?** ¿cuántos años tienes?, ¿qué edad tienes?; **he's 10 years ~** tiene 10 años; **~er brother** hermano mayor; **old age** *n* vejez *f*; **old-age pension** *n* (*BRIT*) jubilación *f*, pensión *f*; **old-age pensioner** (*BRIT*) *n* jubilado/a; **old-fashioned** *adj* anticuado,

pasado de moda; **old people's home** n (esp BRIT) residencia f de ancianos

olive ['ɔlɪv] n (fruit) aceituna; (tree) olivo ▷ adj (also: **~-green**) verde oliva; **olive oil** n aceite m de oliva

Olympic [əu'lɪmpɪk] adj olímpico; **the ~ Games, the ~s** las Olimpiadas

omelet(te) ['ɔmlɪt] n tortilla francesa (SP), omelette f (LAM)

omen ['əumən] n presagio

ominous ['ɔmɪnəs] adj de mal agüero, amenazador(a)

omit [əu'mɪt] vt omitir

○ KEYWORD

on [ɔn] prep 1 (indicating position) en; sobre; **on the wall** en la pared; **it's on the table** está sobre or en la mesa; **on the left** a la izquierda

2 (indicating means, method, condition etc): **on foot** a pie; **on the train/plane** (go) en tren/ avión; (be) en el tren/el avión; **on the radio/ television/telephone** por or en la radio/ televisión/al teléfono; **to be on drugs** drogarse; (Med) estar a tratamiento; **to be on holiday/business** estar de vacaciones/ en viaje de negocios

3 (referring to time): **on Friday** el viernes; **on Fridays** los viernes; **on June 20th** el 20 de junio; **a week on Friday** del viernes en una semana; **on arrival** al llegar; **on seeing this** al ver esto

4 (about, concerning) sobre, acerca de; **a book on physics** un libro de or sobre física ▷ adv 1 (referring to dress): **to have one's coat on** tener or llevar el abrigo puesto; **she put her gloves on** se puso los guantes

2 (referring to covering): **"screw the lid on tightly"** "cerrar bien la tapa"

3 (further, continuously): **to walk** etc **on** seguir caminando etc

▷ adj 1 (functioning, in operation: machine, radio, TV, light) encendido/a (SP), prendido/a (LAM); (: tap) abierto/a; (: brakes) echado/a, puesto/a; **is the meeting still on?** (in progress) ¿todavía continúa la reunión?; (not cancelled) ¿va a haber reunión al fin?; **there's a good film on at the cinema** ponen una buena película en el cine

2 **that's not on!** (inf: not possible) ¡eso ni hablar!; (: not acceptable) ¡eso no se hace!

once [wʌns] adv una vez; (formerly) antiguamente ▷ conj una vez que; **~ he had left/it was done** una vez que se había marchado/se hizo; **at ~** en seguida, inmediatamente; (simultaneously) a la vez;

~ a week una vez por semana; **~ more** otra vez; **~ and for all** de una vez por todas; **~ upon a time** érase una vez

oncoming ['ɔnkʌmɪŋ] adj (traffic) que viene de frente

○ KEYWORD

one [wʌn] num un(o)/una; **one hundred and fifty** ciento cincuenta; **one by one** uno a uno

▷ adj 1 (sole) único; **the one book which** el único libro que; **the one man who** el único que

2 (same) mismo/a; **they came in the one car** vinieron en un solo coche

▷ pron 1 **this one** éste(ésta); **that one** ése(ésa); (more remote) aquél(aquella); **I've already got (a red) one** ya tengo uno/a rojo/a; **one by one** uno/a por uno/a

2 **one another** os (SP), se (+ el uno al otro, unos a otros etc); **do you two ever see one another?** ¿vosotros dos os veis alguna vez? (SP), ¿se ven ustedes dos alguna vez?; **the boys didn't dare look at one another** los chicos no se atrevieron a mirarse (el uno al otro); **they all kissed one another** se besaron unos a otros

3 (impers): **one never knows** nunca se sabe; **to cut one's finger** cortarse el dedo; **one needs to eat** hay que comer

one-off (BRIT: inf) n (event) acontecimiento único

oneself [wʌn'sɛlf] pron (reflexive) se; (after prep) sí; (emphatic) uno/a mismo/a; **to hurt ~** hacerse daño; **to keep sth for ~** guardarse algo; **to talk to ~** hablar solo

one: one-shot [wʌn'ʃɔt] (US) n = **one-off**; **one-sided** adj (argument) parcial; **one-to-one** adj (relationship) de dos; **one-way** adj (street) de sentido único

ongoing ['ɔngəuɪŋ] adj continuo

onion ['ʌnjən] n cebolla

on-line ['ɔnlaɪn] adj, adv (Comput) en línea

onlooker ['ɔnlukə*] n espectador(a) m/f

only ['əunlɪ] adv solamente, sólo ▷ adj único, solo ▷ conj solamente que, pero; **an ~ child** un hijo único; **not ~ ... but also ...** no sólo ... sino también ...

on-screen [ɔn'skriːn] adj (Comput etc) en pantalla; (romance, kiss) cinematográfico

onset ['ɔnsɛt] n comienzo

onto ['ɔntu] prep = **on to**

onward(s) ['ɔnwəd(z)] adv (move) (hacia) adelante; **from that time ~** desde entonces en adelante

oops [ups] excl (also: **~-a-daisy!**) ¡huy!

ooze [uːz] *vi* rezumar

opaque [əuˈpeɪk] *adj* opaco

open [ˈəupn] *adj* abierto; (*car*) descubierto; (*road, view*) despejado; (*meeting*) público; (*admiration*) manifiesto ▷ *vt* abrir ▷ *vi* abrirse; (*book etc: commence*) comenzar; **in the ~ (air)** al aire libre; **open up** *vt* abrir; (*blocked road*) despejar ▷ *vi* abrirse, empezar; **open-air** *adj* al aire libre; **opening** *n* abertura; (*start*) comienzo; (*opportunity*) oportunidad *f*; **opening hours** *npl* horario de apertura; **open learning** *n* enseñanza flexible a tiempo parcial; **openly** *adv* abiertamente; **open-minded** *adj* imparcial; **open-necked** *adj* (*shirt*) desabrochado; sin corbata; **open-plan** *adj*: **open-plan office** gran oficina sin particiones; **Open University** *n* (BRIT) ≈ Universidad *f* Nacional de Enseñanza a Distancia, UNED *f*

● OPEN UNIVERSITY
●
● La **Open University**, fundada en
● 1969, está especializada en impartir
● cursos a distancia que no exigen una
● dedicación exclusiva. Cuenta con sus
● propios materiales de apoyo, entre
● ellos programas de radio y televisión
● emitidos por la **BBC** y para conseguir los
● créditos de la licenciatura es necesaria
● la presentación de unos trabajos y la
● asistencia a los cursos de verano.

opera [ˈɔpərə] *n* ópera; **opera house** *n* teatro de la ópera; **opera singer** *n* cantante *m/f* de ópera

operate [ˈɔpəreɪt] *vt* (*machine*) hacer funcionar; (*company*) dirigir ▷ *vi* funcionar; **to ~ on sb** (Med) operar a algn

operating room [ˈɔpəreɪtɪŋ-] (US) *n* quirófano, sala de operaciones

operating theatre (BRIT) *n* sala de operaciones

operation [ɔpəˈreɪʃən] *n* operación *f*; (*of machine*) funcionamiento; **to be in ~** estar funcionando *or* en funcionamiento; **to have an ~** (Med) ser operado; **operational** *adj* operacional, en buen estado

operative [ˈɔpərətɪv] *adj* en vigor

operator [ˈɔpəreɪtə*] *n* (*of machine*) maquinista *mf*, operario/a; (Tel) operador(a) *m/f*, telefonista *mf*

opinion [əˈpɪnɪən] *n* opinión *f*; **in my ~** en mi opinión, a mi juicio; **opinion poll** *n* encuesta, sondeo

opponent [əˈpəunənt] *n* adversario/a, contrincante *mf*

opportunity [ɔpəˈtjuːnɪtɪ] *n* oportunidad *f*; **to take the ~ of doing** aprovechar la ocasión para hacer

oppose [əˈpəuz] *vt* oponerse a; **to be ~d to sth** oponerse a algo; **as ~d to** a diferencia de

opposite [ˈɔpəzɪt] *adj* opuesto, contrario a; (*house etc*) de enfrente ▷ *adv* en frente ▷ *prep* en frente de, frente a ▷ *n* lo contrario

opposition [ɔpəˈzɪʃən] *n* oposición *f*

oppress [əˈpres] *vt* oprimir

opt [ɔpt] *vi*: **to ~ for** optar por; **to ~ to do** optar por hacer; **opt out** *vi*: **to opt out of** optar por no hacer

optician [ɔpˈtɪʃən] *n* óptico *m/f*

optimism [ˈɔptɪmɪzəm] *n* optimismo

optimist [ˈɔptɪmɪst] *n* optimista *mf*; **optimistic** [-ˈmɪstɪk] *adj* optimista

optimum [ˈɔptɪməm] *adj* óptimo

option [ˈɔpʃən] *n* opción *f*; **optional** *adj* facultativo, discrecional

or [ɔː*] *conj* o; (*before o, ho*) u; (*with negative*): **he hasn't seen ~ heard anything** no ha visto ni oído nada; **~ else** si no

oral [ˈɔːrəl] *adj* oral ▷ *n* examen *m* oral

orange [ˈɔrɪndʒ] *n* (*fruit*) naranja ▷ *adj* color naranja; **orange juice** *n* jugo *m* de naranja, zumo *m* de naranja (SP); **orange squash** *n* naranjada

orbit [ˈɔːbɪt] *n* órbita ▷ *vt*, *vi* orbitar

orchard [ˈɔːtʃəd] *n* huerto

orchestra [ˈɔːkɪstrə] *n* orquesta; (US: *seating*) platea

orchid [ˈɔːkɪd] *n* orquídea

ordeal [ɔːˈdiːl] *n* experiencia horrorosa

order [ˈɔːdə*] *n* orden *m*; (*command*) orden *f*; (*good order*) buen estado; (Comm) pedido ▷ *vt* (*also*: **put in ~**) arreglar, poner en orden; (Comm) pedir; (*command*) mandar, ordenar; **in ~** en orden; (*of document*) en regla; **in (working) ~** en funcionamiento; **in ~ to do/that** para hacer/que; **on ~** (Comm) pedido; **to be out of ~** estar desordenado; (*not working*) no funcionar; **to ~ sb to do sth** mandar a algn hacer algo; **order form** *n* hoja de pedido; **orderly** *n* (Mil) ordenanza *m*; (Med) enfermero/a (auxiliar) ▷ *adj* ordenado

ordinary [ˈɔːdnrɪ] *adj* corriente, normal; (*pej*) común y corriente; **out of the ~** fuera de lo común

ore [ɔː*] *n* mineral *m*

oregano [ɔrɪˈgɑːnəu] *n* orégano

organ [ˈɔːgən] *n* órgano; **organic** [ɔːˈgænɪk] *adj* orgánico; **organism** *n* organismo

organization [ɔːgənaɪˈzeɪʃən] *n* organización *f*

organize [ˈɔːgənaɪz] *vt* organizar;

organized ['ɔ:gənaizd] *adj* organizado;
organizer *n* organizador(a) *m/f*
orgasm ['ɔ:gæzəm] *n* orgasmo
orgy ['ɔ:dʒɪ] *n* orgía
oriental [ɔ:rɪ'entl] *adj* oriental
orientation [ɔ:rɪen'teɪʃən] *n* orientación *f*
origin ['ɔrɪdʒɪn] *n* origen *m*
original [ə'rɪdʒɪnl] *adj* original; (*first*)
primero; (*earlier*) primitivo ▷ *n* original *m*;
originally *adv* al principio
originate [ə'rɪdʒɪneɪt] *vi*: **to ~ from, to ~
in** surgir de, tener su origen en
Orkneys ['ɔ:knɪz] *npl*: **the ~** (*also*: **the
Orkney Islands**) las Orcadas
ornament ['ɔ:nəmənt] *n* adorno; (*trinket*)
chuchería; **ornamental** [-'mɛntl] *adj*
decorativo, de adorno
ornate [ɔ:'neɪt] *adj* muy ornado, vistoso
orphan ['ɔ:fn] *n* huérfano/a
orthodox ['ɔ:θədɔks] *adj* ortodoxo
orthopaedic [ɔ:θə'pi:dɪk] (*us* **orthopedic**)
adj ortopédico
osteopath ['ɔstɪəpæθ] *n* osteópata *mf*
ostrich ['ɔstrɪtʃ] *n* avestruz *m*
other ['ʌðə*] *adj* otro ▷ *pron*: **the ~ (one)**
el(la) otro/a ▷ *adv*: **~ than** aparte de;
otherwise *adv* de otra manera ▷ *conj* (*if
not*) si no
otter ['ɔtə*] *n* nutria
ouch [autʃ] *excl* ¡ay!
ought [ɔ:t] (*pt* **~**) *aux vb*: **I ~ to do it** debería
hacerlo; **this ~ to have been corrected**
esto debiera haberse corregido; **he ~ to win**
(*probability*) debe *or* debiera ganar
ounce [auns] *n* onza (*28.35g*)
our ['auə*] *adj* nuestro; *see also* **my**; **ours**
pron (el) nuestro/(la) nuestra *etc*; *see also*
mine¹; **ourselves** *pron pl* (*reflexive, after
prep*) nosotros; (*emphatic*) nosotros mismos,
see also **oneself**
oust [aust] *vt* desalojar
out [aut] *adv* fuera, afuera; (*not at home*)
fuera (de casa); (*light, fire*) apagado; **~ there**
allí (fuera); **he's ~** (*absent*) no está, ha salido;
to be ~ in one's calculations equivocarse
(en sus cálculos); **to run ~** salir corriendo;
~ loud en alta voz; **~ of** (*outside*) fuera
de; (*because of: anger etc*) por; **~ of petrol**
sin gasolina; **"~ of order"** "no funciona";
outback *n* interior *m*; **outbound** *adj*
(*flight*) de salida; (*flight: not return*) de ida;
outbreak *n* (*of war*) comienzo; (*of disease*)
epidemia; (*of violence etc*) ola; **outburst** *n*
explosión *f*, arranque *m*; **outcast** *n* paria
mf; **outcome** *n* resultado; **outcry** *n*
protestas *fpl*; **outdated** *adj* anticuado,
fuera de moda; **outdoor** *adj* exterior, de
aire libre; (*clothes*) de calle; **outdoors** *adv*
al aire libre
outer ['autə*] *adj* exterior, externo; **outer
space** *n* espacio exterior
outfit ['autfɪt] *n* (*clothes*) conjunto
out: **outgoing** *adj* (*character*) extrovertido;
(*retiring: president etc*) saliente; **outgoings**
(*BRIT*) *npl* gastos *mpl*; **outhouse** *n*
dependencia
outing ['autɪŋ] *n* excursión *f*, paseo
out: **outlaw** *n* proscrito ▷ *vt* proscribir;
outlay *n* inversión *f*; **outlet** *n* salida;
(*of pipe*) desagüe *m*; (*us Elec*) toma de
corriente; (*also*: **retail outlet**) punto de
venta; **outline** *n* (*shape*) contorno, perfil *m*;
(*sketch, plan*) esbozo ▷ *vt* (*plan etc*) esbozar;
in outline (*fig*) a grandes rasgos; **outlook**
n (*fig: prospects*) perspectivas *fpl*; (*: for weather*)
pronóstico; **outnumber** *vt* superar
en número; **out-of-date** *adj* (*passport*)
caducado; (*clothes*) pasado de moda; **out-of-
doors** *adv* al aire libre; **out-of-the-way** *adj*
apartado; **out-of-town** *adj* (*shopping centre
etc*) en las afueras; **outpatient** *n* paciente
mf externo/a; **outpost** *n* puesto avanzado;
output *n* (*volumen m de*) producción *m*,
rendimiento; (*Comput*) salida
outrage ['autreɪdʒ] *n* escándalo; (*atrocity*)
atrocidad *f* ▷ *vt* ultrajar; **outrageous**
[-'reɪdʒəs] *adj* monstruoso
outright [*adv* aut'raɪt, *adj* 'autraɪt]
adv (*ask, deny*) francamente; (*refuse*)
rotundamente; (*win*) de manera absoluta;
(*be killed*) en el acto ▷ *adj* franco; rotundo
outset ['autsɛt] *n* principio
outside [aut'saɪd] *n* exterior *m* ▷ *adj*
exterior, externo ▷ *adv* fuera ▷ *prep* fuera
de; (*beyond*) más allá de; **at the ~** (*fig*) a lo
sumo; **outside lane** *n* (*Aut: in Britain*) carril
m de la derecha; (*: in US, Europe etc*) carril *m*
de la izquierda; **outside line** *n* (*Tel*) línea
(exterior); **outsider** *n* (*stranger*) extraño,
forastero
out: **outsize** *adj* (*clothes*) de talla grande;
outskirts *npl* alrededores *mpl*, afueras *fpl*;
outspoken *adj* muy franco; **outstanding**
adj excepcional, destacado; (*remaining*)
pendiente
outward ['autwəd] *adj* externo; (*journey*)
de ida; **outwards** *adv* (*esp BRIT*) = **outward**
outweigh [aut'weɪ] *vt* pesar más que
oval ['əuvl] *adj* ovalado ▷ *n* óvalo
ovary ['əuvərɪ] *n* ovario
oven ['ʌvn] *n* horno; **oven glove** *n*
guante *m* para el horno, manopla para el
horno; **ovenproof** *adj* resistente al horno;
oven-ready *adj* listo para el horno
over ['əuvə*] *adv* encima, por encima
▷ *adj or adv* (*finished*) terminado; (*surplus*)

de sobra ▷ *prep* (por) encima de; (*above*)
sobre; (*on the other side of*) al otro lado de;
(*more than*) más de; (*during*) durante; **~
here** (por) aquí; **~ there** (por) allí or allá;
all ~ (*everywhere*) por todas partes; **~ and ~
(again)** una y otra vez; **~ and above** además
de; **to ask sb ~** invitar a algn a casa; **to bend
~** inclinarse

overall [*adj, n* 'əuvərɔ:l, *adv* əuvər'ɔ:l]
adj (*length etc*) total; (*study*) de conjunto
▷ *adv* en conjunto ▷ *n* (BRIT) guardapolvo;
overalls *npl* (*boiler suit*) mono (SP) or overol
m (LAM) (de trabajo)

overboard *adv* (Naut) por la borda

overcame [əuvə'keɪm] *pt of* **overcome**

overcast ['əuvəkɑːst] *adj* encapotado

overcharge [əuvə'tʃɑːdʒ] *vt*: **to ~ sb** cobrar
un precio excesivo a algn

overcoat ['əuvəkəut] *n* abrigo, sobretodo

overcome [əuvə'kʌm] *vt* vencer;
(*difficulty*) superar

over: overcrowded *adj* atestado de gente;
(*city, country*) superpoblado; **overdo** (*irreg*)
vt exagerar; (*overcook*) cocer demasiado; **to
overdo it** (*work etc*) pasarse; **overdone**
[əuvə'dʌn] *adj* (*vegetables*) recocido; (*steak*)
demasiado hecho; **overdose** *n* sobredosis
f inv; **overdraft** *n* saldo deudor; **overdrawn**
adj (*account*) en descubierto; **overdue** *adj*
retrasado; **overestimate** *vt* sobreestimar

overflow [*vb* əuvə'fləu, *n* 'əuvəfləu] *vi*
desbordarse ▷ *n* (*also*: **~ pipe**) (cañería de)
desagüe *m*

overgrown [əuvə'grəun] *adj* (*garden*)
invadido por la vegetación

overhaul [*vb* əuvə'hɔːl, *n* 'əuvəhɔːl] *vt*
revisar, repasar ▷ *n* revisión *f*

overhead [*adv* əuvə'hɛd, *adj, n* 'əuvəhɛd]
adv por arriba or encima ▷ *adj* (*cable*) aéreo
▷ *n* (US) = **overheads**; **overhead projector**
n retroproyector; **overheads** *npl* (*expenses*)
gastos *mpl* generales

over: overhear (*irreg*) *vt* oír por casualidad;
overheat *vi* (*engine*) recalentarse;
overland *adj, adv* por tierra; **overlap**
[əuvə'læp] *vi* traslaparse; **overleaf** *adv* al
dorso; **overload** *vt* sobrecargar; **overlook**
vt (*have view of*) dar a, tener vistas a; (*miss: by
mistake*) pasar por alto; (*excuse*) perdonar

overnight [əuvə'naɪt] *adv* durante la
noche; (*fig*) de la noche a la mañana ▷ *adj* de
noche; **to stay ~** pasar la noche; **overnight
bag** *n* fin *m* de semana, neceser *m* de viaje

overpass (US) ['əuvəpɑːs] *n* paso superior

overpower [əuvə'pauə*] *vt* dominar;
(*fig*) embargar; **overpowering** *adj* (*heat*)
agobiante; (*smell*) penetrante

over: overreact [əuvərɪ'ækt] *vi* reaccionar

de manera exagerada; **overrule** *vt*
(*decision*) anular; (*claim*) denegar; **overrun**
(*irreg*) *vt* (*country*) invadir; (*time limit*)
rebasar, exceder

overseas [əuvə'siːz] *adv* (*abroad: live*) en el
extranjero; (*travel*) al extranjero ▷ *adj* (*trade*)
exterior; (*visitor*) extranjero

oversee [əuvə'siː] (*irreg*) *vt* supervisar

overshadow [əuvə'ʃædəu] *vt*: **to be ~ed
by** estar a la sombra de

oversight ['əuvəsaɪt] *n* descuido

oversleep [əuvə'sliːp] (*irreg*) *vi* quedarse
dormido

overspend [əuvə'spɛnd] (*irreg*) *vi* gastar
más de la cuenta; **we have overspent by
5 pounds** hemos excedido el presupuesto
en 5 libras

overt [əu'vəːt] *adj* abierto

overtake [əuvə'teɪk] (*irreg*) *vt* sobrepasar;
(BRIT Aut) adelantar

over: overthrow (*irreg*) *vt* (*government*)
derrocar; **overtime** *n* horas *fpl*
extraordinarias

overtook [əuvə'tuk] *pt of* **overtake**

over: overturn *vt* volcar; (*fig: plan*)
desbaratar; (*: government*) derrocar ▷ *vi*
volcar; **overweight** *adj* demasiado gordo or
pesado; **overwhelm** *vt* aplastar; (*emotion*)
sobrecoger; **overwhelming** *adj* (*victory,
defeat*) arrollador(a); (*feeling*) irresistible

ow [au] *excl* ¡ay!

owe [əu] *vt*: **to ~ sb sth, to ~ sth to sb**
deber algo a algn; **owing to** *prep* debido a,
por causa de

owl [aul] *n* búho, lechuza

own [əun] *vt* tener, poseer ▷ *adj* propio; **a
room of my ~** una habitación propia; **to get
one's ~ back** tomar revancha; **on one's ~**
solo, a solas; **own up** *vi* confesar; **owner** *n*
dueño/a; **ownership** *n* posesión *f*

ox [ɔks] (*pl* **~en**) *n* buey *m*

Oxbridge ['ɔksbrɪdʒ] *n* universidades de
Oxford y Cambridge

oxen ['ɔksən] *npl of* **ox**

oxygen ['ɔksɪdʒən] *n* oxígeno

oyster ['ɔɪstə*] *n* ostra

oz. *abbr* = **ounce(s)**

ozone ['əuzəun] *n* ozono; **ozone friendly**
adj que no daña la capa de ozono; **ozone
layer** *n* capa *f* de ozono

p

p [piː] abbr = **penny; pence**

P.A. n abbr = **personal assistant; public address system**

p.a. abbr = **per annum**

pace [peɪs] n paso ▷ vi: **to ~ up and down** pasearse de un lado a otro; **to keep ~ with** llevar el mismo paso que; **pacemaker** n (Med) regulador m cardíaco, marcapasos m inv; (Sport: also: **pacesetter**) liebre f

Pacific [pə'sɪfɪk] n: **the ~ (Ocean)** el (Océano) Pacífico

pacifier ['pæsɪfaɪə*] (US) n (dummy) chupete m

pack [pæk] n (packet) paquete m; (of hounds) jauría; (of people) manada, bando; (of cards) baraja; (bundle) fardo; (US: of cigarettes) paquete m; (back pack) mochila ▷ vt (fill) llenar; (in suitcase etc) meter, poner; (cram) llenar, atestar; **to ~ (one's bags)** hacerse la maleta; **to ~ sb off** despachar a algn; **pack in** vi (watch, car) estropearse ▷ vt (inf) dejar; **pack it in!** ¡para!, ¡basta ya!; **pack up** vi (inf: machine) estropearse; (person) irse ▷ vt (belongings, clothes) recoger; (goods, presents) empaquetar, envolver

package ['pækɪdʒ] n paquete m; (bulky) bulto; (also: **~ deal**) acuerdo global; **package holiday** n vacaciones fpl organizadas; **package tour** n viaje m organizado

packaging ['pækɪdʒɪŋ] n envase m

packed [pækt] adj abarrotado; **packed lunch** n almuerzo frío

packet ['pækɪt] n paquete m

packing ['pækɪŋ] n embalaje m

pact [pækt] n pacto

pad [pæd] n (of paper) bloc m; (cushion) cojinete m; (inf: home) casa ▷ vt rellenar; **padded** adj (jacket) acolchado; (bra) reforzado

paddle ['pædl] n (oar) canalete m; (US: for table tennis) paleta ▷ vt impulsar con canalete ▷ vi (with feet) chapotear; **paddling pool** (BRIT) n estanque m de juegos

paddock ['pædək] n corral m

padlock ['pædlɔk] n candado

paedophile ['piːdəʊfaɪl] (US **pedophile**) adj de pedófilos ▷ n pedófilo/a

page [peɪdʒ] n (of book) página; (of newspaper) plana; (also: **~ boy**) paje m ▷ vt (in hotel etc) llamar por altavoz a

pager ['peɪdʒə*] n (Tel) busca m

paid [peɪd] pt, pp of **pay** ▷ adj (work) remunerado; (holiday) pagado; (official etc) a sueldo; **to put ~ to** (BRIT) acabar con

pain [peɪn] n dolor m; **to be in ~** sufrir; **to take ~s to do sth** tomarse grandes molestias en hacer algo; **painful** adj doloroso; (difficult) penoso; (disagreeable) desagradable; **painkiller** n analgésico; **painstaking** ['peɪnzteɪkɪŋ] adj (person) concienzudo, esmerado

paint [peɪnt] n pintura ▷ vt pintar; **to ~ the door blue** pintar la puerta de azul; **paintbrush** n (of artist) pincel m; (of decorator) brocha; **painter** n pintor(a) m/f; **painting** n pintura

pair [pɛə*] n (of shoes, gloves etc) par m; (of people) pareja; **a ~ of scissors** unas tijeras; **a ~ of trousers** unos pantalones, un pantalón

pajamas [pə'dʒɑːməz] (US) npl pijama m

Pakistan [pɑːkɪ'stɑːn] n Paquistán m; **Pakistani** adj, n paquistaní mf

pal [pæl] (inf) n compinche mf, compañero/a

palace ['pæləs] n palacio

pale [peɪl] adj (gen) pálido; (colour) claro ▷ n: **to be beyond the ~** pasarse de la raya

Palestine ['pælɪstaɪn] n Palestina; **Palestinian** [-'tɪnɪən] adj, n palestino/a m/f

palm [pɑːm] n (Anat) palma; (also: **~ tree**) palmera, palma ▷ vt: **to ~ sth off on sb** (inf) encajar algo a algn

pamper ['pæmpə*] vt mimar

pamphlet ['pæmflət] n folleto

pan [pæn] n (also: **sauce~**) cacerola, cazuela, olla; (also: **frying ~**) sartén f

pancake ['pænkeɪk] n crepe f

panda ['pændə] n panda m

pane [peɪn] n cristal m

panel ['pænl] n (of wood etc) panel m; (Radio, TV) panel m de invitados

panhandler ['pænhændlə*] (US) n (inf) mendigo/a

panic ['pænɪk] n terror m pánico ▷ vi dejarse llevar por el pánico

panorama [pænə'rɑːmə] n panorama m

pansy ['pænzɪ] n (Bot) pensamiento; (inf,

pej) maricón *m*
pant [pænt] *vi* jadear
panther ['pænθə*] *n* pantera
panties ['pæntɪz] *npl* bragas *fpl*, pantis *mpl*
pantomime ['pæntəmaɪm] (BRIT) *n*
revista musical representada en Navidad, basada
en cuentos dehadas

● **PANTOMIME**
●
●
● En época navideña se ponen en escena
● en los teatros británicos las llamadas
● **pantomimes**, que son versiones libres
● de cuentos tradicionales como Aladino
● o El gato con botas. En ella nunca faltan
● personajes como la dama ("dame"),
● papel que siempre interpreta un actor,
● el protagonista joven ("principal boy"),
● normalmente interpretado por una
● actriz, y el malvado ("villain"). Es un
● espectáculo familiar en el que se anima
● al público a participar y aunque va
● dirigido principalmente a los niños,
● cuenta con grandes dosis de humor para
● adultos.

pants [pænts] *n* (BRIT: *underwear: woman's*)
bragas *fpl*, (: *man's*) calzoncillos *mpl*;
(US: *trousers*) pantalones *mpl*
paper ['peɪpə*] *n* papel *m*; (*also:* **news~**)
periódico, diario; (*academic essay*) ensayo;
(*exam*) examen *m* ▷ *adj* de papel ▷ *vt*
empapelar, tapizar (MEX); **papers** *npl*
(*also:* **identity ~s**) papeles *mpl*, documentos
mpl; **paperback** *n* libro en rústica; **paper
bag** *n* bolsa de papel; **paper clip** *n* clip *m*;
paper shop (BRIT) *n* tienda de periódicos;
paperwork *n* trabajo administrativo
paprika ['pæprɪkə] *n* pimentón *m*
par [pɑ:*] *n* par *f*; (*Golf*) par *m*; **to be on a ~
with** estar a la par con
paracetamol [pærə'si:təmɔl] (BRIT) *n*
paracetamol *m*
parachute ['pærəʃu:t] *n* paracaídas *m inv*
parade [pə'reɪd] *n* desfile *m* ▷ *vt* (*show*)
hacer alarde de ▷ *vi* desfilar; (*Mil*) pasar
revista
paradise ['pærədaɪs] *n* paraíso
paradox ['pærədɔks] *n* paradoja
paraffin ['pærəfɪn] (BRIT) *n* (*also:* **~ oil**)
parafina
paragraph ['pærəgrɑ:f] *n* párrafo
parallel ['pærəlɛl] *adj* en paralelo; (*fig*)
semejante ▷ *n* (*line*) paralela; (*fig, Geo*)
paralelo
paralysed ['pærəlaɪzd] *adj* paralizado
paralysis [pə'rælɪsɪs] *n* parálisis *f inv*
paramedic [pærə'mɛdɪk] *n* auxiliar *m/f*

sanitario/a
paranoid ['pærənɔɪd] *adj* (*person, feeling*)
paranoico
parasite ['pærəsaɪt] *n* parásito/a
parcel ['pɑ:sl] *n* paquete *m* ▷ *vt* (*also:* **~
up**) empaquetar, embalar
pardon ['pɑ:dn] *n* (*Law*) indulto ▷ *vt*
perdonar; **~ me!, I beg your ~!** (*I'm sorry!*)
¡perdone usted!; **(I beg your) ~?, ~ me?**
(*US: what did you say?*) ¿cómo?
parent ['pɛərənt] *n* (*mother*) madre *f*;
(*father*) padre *m*; **parents** *npl* padres *mpl*
❚ Be careful not to translate **parent** by the
Spanish word *pariente*.
parental [pə'rɛntl] *adj* paternal/maternal
Paris ['pærɪs] *n* París
parish ['pærɪʃ] *n* parroquia
Parisian [pə'rɪzɪən] *adj, n* parisiense *mf*
park [pɑ:k] *n* parque *m* ▷ *vt* aparcar,
estacionar ▷ *vi* aparcar, estacionarse
parking ['pɑ:kɪŋ] *n* aparcamiento,
estacionamiento; **"no ~"** "prohibido
estacionarse"; **parking lot** (US) *n* parking
m; **parking meter** *n* parquímetro; **parking
ticket** *n* multa de aparcamiento
parkway ['pɑ:kweɪ] (US) *n* alameda
parliament ['pɑ:ləmənt] *n* parlamento;
(*Spanish*) Cortes *fpl*; **parliamentary**
[-'mɛntərɪ] *adj* parlamentario

● **PARLIAMENT**
●
● El Parlamento británico (**Parliament**)
● tiene como sede el palacio de
● Westminster, también llamado "Houses
● of Parliament" y consta de dos cámaras.
● La Cámara de los Comunes ("House
● of Commons"), compuesta por 650
● diputados (**Members of Parliament**)
● elegidos por sufragio universal en su
● respectiva circunscripción electoral
● (constituency), se reúne 175 días al año
● y sus sesiones son moderadas por el
● Presidente de la Cámara (**Speaker**). La
● cámara alta es la Cámara de los Lores
● ("House of Lords") y está formada por
● miembros que han sido nombrados
● por el monarca o que han heredado su
● escaño. Su poder es limitado, aunque
● actúa como tribunal supremo de
● apelación, excepto en Escocia.

Parmesan [pɑ:mɪ'zæn] *n* (*also:* **~ cheese**)
queso parmesano
parole [pə'rəul] *n*: **on ~** libre bajo palabra
parrot ['pærət] *n* loro, papagayo
parsley ['pɑ:slɪ] *n* perejil *m*
parsnip ['pɑ:snɪp] *n* chirivía

parson ['pɑːsn] n cura m
part [pɑːt] n (gen, Mus) parte f; (bit) trozo; (of machine) pieza; (Theatre etc) papel m; (of serial) entrega; (US: in hair) raya ▷ adv = **partly** ▷ vt separar ▷ vi (people) separarse; (crowd) apartarse; **to take ~ in** tomar parte or participar en; **to take sth in good ~** tomar algo en buena parte; **to take sb's ~** defender a algn; **for my ~** por mi parte; **for the most ~** en su mayor parte; **to ~ one's hair** hacerse la raya; **part with** vt fus ceder, entregar; (money) pagar; **part of speech** n parte f de la oración, categoría f gramatical
partial ['pɑːʃl] adj parcial; **to be ~ to** ser aficionado a
participant [pɑːˈtɪsɪpənt] n (in competition) concursante mf; (in campaign etc) participante mf
participate [pɑːˈtɪsɪpeɪt] vi: **to ~ in** participar en
particle ['pɑːtɪkl] n partícula; (of dust) grano
particular [pəˈtɪkjulə*] adj (special) particular; (concrete) concreto; (given) determinado; (fussy) quisquilloso; (demanding) exigente; **in ~** en particular; **particularly** adv (in particular) sobre todo; (difficult, good etc) especialmente; **particulars** npl (information) datos mpl; (details) pormenores mpl
parting ['pɑːtɪŋ] n (act) separación f; (farewell) despedida; (BRIT: in hair) raya ▷ adj de despedida
partition [pɑːˈtɪʃən] n (Pol) división f; (wall) tabique m
partly ['pɑːtlɪ] adv en parte
partner ['pɑːtnə*] n (Comm) socio/a; (Sport, at dance) pareja; (spouse) cónyuge mf; (lover) compañero/a; **partnership** n asociación f; (Comm) sociedad f
partridge ['pɑːtrɪdʒ] n perdiz f
part-time ['pɑːtˈtaɪm] adj, adv a tiempo parcial
party ['pɑːtɪ] n (Pol) partido; (celebration) fiesta; (group) grupo; (Law) parte f interesada ▷ cpd (Pol) de partido
pass [pɑːs] vt (time, object) pasar; (place) pasar por; (overtake) rebasar; (exam) aprobar; (approve) aprobar ▷ vi pasar; (Scol) aprobar, ser aprobado ▷ n (permit) permiso; (membership card) carnet m; (in mountains) puerto, desfiladero; (Sport) pase m; (Scol: also: ~ mark): **to get a ~ in** aprobar en; **to ~ sth through sth** pasar algo por algo; **to make a ~ at sb** (inf) hacer proposiciones a algn; **pass away** vi fallecer; **pass by** vi pasar ▷ vt (ignore) pasar por alto; **pass on** vt transmitir; **pass out** vi desmayarse;

pass over vi, vt omitir, pasar por alto; **pass up** vt (opportunity) renunciar a; **passable** adj (road) transitable; (tolerable) pasable
passage ['pæsɪdʒ] n (also: ~way) pasillo; (act of passing) tránsito; (fare, in book) pasaje m; (by boat) travesía; (Anat) tubo
passenger ['pæsɪndʒə*] n pasajero/a, viajero/a
passer-by [pɑːsəˈbaɪ] n transeúnte mf
passing place n (Aut) apartadero
passion ['pæʃən] n pasión f; **passionate** adj apasionado; **passion fruit** n fruta de la pasión, granadilla
passive ['pæsɪv] adj (gen, also Ling) pasivo
passport ['pɑːspɔːt] n pasaporte m; **passport control** n control m de pasaporte; **passport office** n oficina de pasaportes
password ['pɑːswɜːd] n contraseña
past [pɑːst] prep (in front of) por delante de; (further than) más allá de; (later than) después de ▷ adj pasado; (president etc) antiguo ▷ n (time) pasado; (of person) antecedentes mpl; **he's ~ forty** tiene más de cuarenta años; **ten/quarter ~ eight** las ocho y diez/cuarto; **for the ~ few/3 days** durante los últimos días/últimos 3 días; **to run ~ sb** pasar a algn corriendo
pasta ['pæstə] n pasta
paste [peɪst] n pasta; (glue) engrudo ▷ vt pegar
pastel ['pæstl] adj pastel; (painting) al pastel
pasteurized ['pæstəraɪzd] adj pasteurizado
pastime ['pɑːstaɪm] n pasatiempo
pastor ['pɑːstə*] n pastor m
past participle [-ˈpɑːtɪsɪpl] n (Ling) participio m (de) pasado or (de) pretérito or pasivo
pastry ['peɪstrɪ] n (dough) pasta; (cake) pastel m
pasture ['pɑːstʃə*] n pasto
pasty¹ ['pæstɪ] n empanada
pasty² ['peɪstɪ] adj (complexion) pálido
pat [pæt] vt dar una palmadita a; (dog etc) acariciar
patch [pætʃ] n (of material; eye patch) parche m; (mended part) remiendo; (of land) terreno ▷ vt remendar; **(to go through) a bad ~** (pasar por) una mala racha; **patchy** adj desigual
pâté ['pæteɪ] n paté m
patent ['peɪtnt] n patente f ▷ vt patentar ▷ adj patente, evidente
paternal [pəˈtɜːnl] adj paternal; (relation) paterno
paternity leave [pəˈtɜːnɪtɪ-] n permiso m

por paternidad, licencia por paternidad
path [pɑ:θ] *n* camino, sendero; (*trail, track*)
pista; (*of missile*) trayectoria
pathetic [pə'θεtɪk] *adj* patético,
lastimoso; (*very bad*) malísimo
pathway ['pɑ:θweɪ] *n* sendero, vereda
patience ['peɪʃns] *n* paciencia; (*BRIT Cards*)
solitario
patient ['peɪʃnt] *n* paciente *mf* ▷ *adj*
paciente, sufrido
patio ['pætɪəʊ] *n* patio
patriotic [pætrɪ'ɒtɪk] *adj* patriótico
patrol [pə'trəʊl] *n* patrulla ▷ *vt* patrullar
por; **patrol car** *n* coche *m* patrulla
patron ['peɪtrən] *n* (*in shop*) cliente *mf*; (*of
charity*) patrocinador(a) *m/f*; **~ of the arts**
mecenas *m*
patronizing ['pætrənaɪzɪŋ] *adj*
condescendiente
pattern ['pætən] *n* (*Sewing*) patrón *m*;
(*design*) dibujo; **patterned** *adj* (*material*)
estampado
pause [pɔ:z] *n* pausa ▷ *vi* hacer una pausa
pave [peɪv] *vt* pavimentar; **to ~ the way
for** preparar el terreno para
pavement ['peɪvmənt] (*BRIT*) *n* acera,
banqueta (*MEX*), andén *m* (*CAM*), vereda (*SC*)
pavilion [pə'vɪlɪən] *n* (*Sport*) caseta
paving ['peɪvɪŋ] *n* pavimento, enlosado
paw [pɔ:] *n* pata
pawn [pɔ:n] *n* (*Chess*) peón *m*; (*fig*)
instrumento ▷ *vt* empeñar; **pawn broker**
n prestamista *mf*
pay [peɪ] (*pt, pp* **paid**) *n* (*wage etc*) sueldo,
salario ▷ *vt* pagar ▷ *vi* (*be profitable*) rendir;
to ~ attention (to) prestar atención (a);
to ~ sb a visit hacer una visita a algn; **to ~
one's respects to sb** presentar sus respetos
a algn; **pay back** *vt* (*money*) reembolsar;
(*person*) pagar; **pay for** *vt fus* pagar; **pay in**
vt ingresar; **pay off** *vt* saldar ▷ *vi* (*scheme,
decision*) dar resultado; **pay out** *vt* (*money*)
gastar, desembolsar; **pay up** *vt* pagar
(de mala gana); **payable** *adj*: **payable to**
pagadero a; **pay day** *n* día *m* de paga; **pay
envelope** (*US*) *n* = **pay packet**; **payment**
n pago; **monthly payment** mensualidad
f; **payout** *n* pago; (*in competition*) premio
en metálico; **pay packet** (*BRIT*) *n* sobre *m*
(de paga); **pay phone** *n* teléfono público;
payroll *n* nómina; **pay slip** *n* recibo de
sueldo; **pay television** *n* televisión *f* de
pago
PC *n abbr* = **personal computer**; (*BRIT*)
(= *police constable*) policía *mf* ▷ *adv abbr*
= **politically correct**
p.c. *abbr* = **per cent**
PDA *n abbr* (= *personal digital assistant*)

agenda electrónica
PE *n abbr* (= *physical education*) ed. física
pea [pi:] *n* guisante *m* (*SP*), arveja (*LAM*),
chícharo (*MEX, CAM*)
peace [pi:s] *n* paz *f*; (*calm*) paz *f*,
tranquilidad *f*; **peaceful** *adj* (*gentle*)
pacífico; (*calm*) tranquilo, sosegado
peach [pi:tʃ] *n* melocotón *m* (*SP*), durazno
(*LAM*)
peacock ['pi:kɔk] *n* pavo real
peak [pi:k] *n* (*of mountain*) cumbre *f*, cima;
(*of cap*) visera; (*fig*) cumbre *f*; **peak hours** *npl*
horas *fpl* punta
peanut ['pi:nʌt] *n* cacahuete *m* (*SP*), maní
m (*LAM*), cacahuate *m* (*MEX*); **peanut butter**
n manteca de cacahuete *or* maní
pear [pεə*] *n* pera
pearl [pə:l] *n* perla
peasant ['pεznt] *n* campesino/a
peat [pi:t] *n* turba
pebble ['pεbl] *n* guijarro
peck [pεk] *vt* (*also:* **~ at**) picotear ▷ *n*
picotazo; (*kiss*) besito; **peckish** (*BRIT: inf*)
adj: **I feel peckish** tengo ganas de picar algo
peculiar [pɪ'kju:lɪə*] *adj* (*odd*) extraño,
raro; (*typical*) propio, característico; **~ to**
propio de
pedal ['pεdl] *n* pedal *m* ▷ *vi* pedalear
pedalo ['pεdələʊ] *n* patín *m* a pedal
pedestal ['pεdəstl] *n* pedestal *m*
pedestrian [pɪ'dεstrɪən] *n* peatón/ona
m/f ▷ *adj* pedestre; **pedestrian crossing**
(*BRIT*) *n* paso de peatones; **pedestrianized**
adj: **a pedestrianized street** una calle
peatonal; **pedestrian precinct** (*US*
pedestrian zone) *n* zona peatonal
pedigree ['pεdɪgri:] *n* genealogía; (*of
animal*) raza, pedigrí *m* ▷ *cpd* (*animal*) de
raza, de casta
pedophile ['pi:dəʊfaɪl] (*US*) *n* =
paedophile
pee [pi:] (*inf*) *vi* mear
peek [pi:k] *vi* mirar a hurtadillas
peel [pi:l] *n* piel *f*; (*of orange, lemon*)
cáscara; (: *removed*) peladuras *fpl* ▷ *vt* pelar
▷ *vi* (*paint etc*) desconcharse; (*wallpaper*)
despegarse, desprenderse; (*skin*) pelar
peep [pi:p] *n* (*BRIT: look*) mirada
furtiva; (*sound*) pío ▷ *vi* (*BRIT: look*) mirar
furtivamente
peer [pɪə*] *vi*: **to ~ at** esudriñar ▷ *n* (*noble*)
par *m*; (*equal*) igual *m*; (*contemporary*)
contemporáneo/a
peg [pεg] *n* (*for coat etc*) gancho, colgadero;
(*BRIT: also:* **clothes ~**) pinza
pelican ['pεlɪkən] *n* pelícano; **pelican
crossing** (*BRIT*) *n* (*Aut*) paso de peatones
señalizado

pelt [pɛlt] *vt*: **to ~ sb with sth** arrojarle algo a algn ▷ *vi* (*rain*) llover a cántaros; (*inf*: *run*) correr ▷ *n* pellejo
pelvis ['pɛlvɪs] *n* pelvis *f*
pen [pɛn] *n* (*fountain pen*) pluma; (*ballpoint pen*) bolígrafo; (*for sheep*) redil *m*
penalty ['pɛnltɪ] *n* (*gen*) pena; (*fine*) multa
pence [pɛns] *npl of* **penny**
pencil ['pɛnsl] *n* lápiz *m*; **pencil in** *vt* (*appointment*) apuntar con carácter provisional; **pencil case** *n* estuche *m*; **pencil sharpener** *n* sacapuntas *m inv*
pendant ['pɛndnt] *n* pendiente *m*
pending ['pɛndɪŋ] *prep* antes de ▷ *adj* pendiente
penetrate ['pɛnɪtreɪt] *vt* penetrar
penfriend ['pɛnfrɛnd] (*BRIT*) *n* amigo/a por carta
penguin ['pɛŋgwɪn] *n* pingüino
penicillin [pɛnɪ'sɪlɪn] *n* penicilina
peninsula [pə'nɪnsjulə] *n* península
penis ['piːnɪs] *h* pene *m*
penitentiary [pɛnɪ'tɛnʃərɪ] (*US*) *n* cárcel *f*, presidio
penknife ['pɛnnaɪf] *n* navaja
penniless ['pɛnɪlɪs] *adj* sin dinero
penny ['pɛnɪ] (*pl* **pennies** *or* **pence**) (*BRIT*) *n* penique *m*; (*US*) centavo
penpal ['pɛnpæl] *n* amigo/a por carta
pension ['pɛnʃən] *n* (*state benefit*) jubilación *f*; **pensioner** (*BRIT*) *n* jubilado/a
pentagon ['pɛntəgən] (*US*) *n*: **the P~** (*Pol*) el Pentágono

● **PENTAGON**
●
● Se conoce como **Pentagon** al edificio
● de planta pentagonal que acoge las
● dependencias del Ministerio de Defensa
● estadounidense ("Department of
● Defense") en Arlington, Virginia. En
● lenguaje periodístico se aplica también
● a la dirección militar del país.

penthouse ['pɛnthaus] *n* ático de lujo
penultimate [pɛ'nʌltɪmət] *adj* penúltimo
people ['piːpl] *npl* gente *f*; (*citizens*) pueblo, ciudadanos *mpl*; (*Pol*): **the ~** el pueblo ▷ *n* (*nation*, *race*) pueblo, nación *f*; **several ~ came** vinieron varias personas; **~ say that ...** dice la gente que ...
pepper ['pɛpə*] *n* (*spice*) pimienta; (*vegetable*) pimiento ▷ *vt*: **to ~ with** (*fig*) salpicar de; **peppermint** *n* (*sweet*) pastilla de menta
per [pɜː*] *prep* por; **~ day/~son** por día/persona; **~ annum** al año

perceive [pə'siːv] *vt* percibir; (*realize*) darse cuenta de
per cent *n* por ciento
percentage [pə'sɛntɪdʒ] *n* porcentaje *m*
perception [pə'sɛpʃən] *n* percepción *f*; (*insight*) perspicacia; (*opinion etc*) opinión *f*
perch [pɜːtʃ] *n* (*fish*) perca; (*for bird*) percha ▷ *vi*: **to ~ (on)** (*bird*) posarse (en); (*person*) encaramarse (en)
percussion [pə'kʌʃən] *n* percusión *f*
perfect [*adj*, *n* 'pɜːfɪkt, *vb* pə'fɛkt] *adj* perfecto ▷ *n* (*also*: **~ tense**) perfecto ▷ *vt* perfeccionar; **perfection** [pə'fɛkʃən] *n* perfección *f*; **perfectly** ['pɜːfɪktlɪ] *adv* perfectamente
perform [pə'fɔːm] *vt* (*carry out*) realizar, llevar a cabo; (*Theatre*) representar; (*piece of music*) interpretar ▷ *vi* (*well*, *badly*) funcionar; **performance** *n* (*of a play*) representación *f*; (*of actor*, *athlete etc*) actuación *f*; (*of car*, *engine*, *company*) rendimiento; (*of economy*) resultados *mpl*; **performer** *n* (*actor*) actor *m*, actriz *f*
perfume ['pɜːfjuːm] *n* perfume *m*
perhaps [pə'hæps] *adv* quizá(s), tal vez
perimeter [pə'rɪmɪtə*] *n* perímetro
period ['pɪərɪəd] *n* período; (*Scol*) clase *f*; (*full stop*) punto; (*Med*) regla ▷ *adj* (*costume*, *furniture*) de época; **periodical** [pɪərɪ'ɔdɪkl] *n* periódico; **periodically** *adv* de vez en cuando, cada cierto tiempo
perish ['pɛrɪʃ] *vi* perecer; (*decay*) echarse a perder
perjury ['pɜːdʒərɪ] *n* (*Law*) perjurio
perk [pɜːk] *n* extra *m*
perm [pɜːm] *n* permanente *f*
permanent ['pɜːmənənt] *adj* permanente; **permanently** *adv* (*lastingly*) para siempre, de modo definitivo; (*all the time*) permanentemente
permission [pə'mɪʃən] *n* permiso
permit [*n* 'pɜːmɪt, *vt* pə'mɪt] *n* permiso, licencia ▷ *vt* permitir
perplex [pə'plɛks] *vt* dejar perplejo
persecute ['pɜːsɪkjuːt] *vt* perseguir
persecution [pɜːsɪ'kjuːʃən] *n* persecución *f*
persevere [pɜːsɪ'vɪə*] *vi* persistir
Persian ['pɜːʃən] *adj*, *n* persa *mf*; **the ~ Gulf** el Golfo Pérsico
persist [pə'sɪst] *vi*: **to ~ (in doing sth)** persistir (en hacer algo); **persistent** *adj* persistente; (*determined*) porfiado
person ['pɜːsn] *n* persona; **in ~** en persona; **personal** *adj* personal; individual; (*visit*) en persona; **personal assistant** *n* ayudante *mf* personal; **personal computer** *n* ordenador *m* personal; **personality**

[-'nælɪtɪ] n personalidad f; **personally** adv
personalmente; (in person) en persona; **to
take sth personally** tomarse algo a mal;
personal organizer n agenda; **personal
stereo** n Walkman® m
personnel [pə:sə'nɛl] n personal m
perspective [pə'spɛktɪv] n perspectiva
perspiration [pə:spɪ'reɪʃən] n
transpiración f
persuade [pə'sweɪd] vt: **to ~ sb to do sth**
persuadir a algn para que haga algo
persuasion [pə'sweɪʒən] n persuasión f;
(persuasiveness) persuasiva
persuasive [pə'sweɪsɪv] adj persuasivo
perverse [pə'və:s] adj perverso; (wayward)
travieso
pervert [n 'pə:və:t, vb pə'və:t] n
pervertido/a ▷ vt pervertir; (truth, sb's
words) tergiversar
pessimism ['pɛsɪmɪzəm] n pesimismo
pessimist ['pɛsɪmɪst] n pesimista mf;
pessimistic [-'mɪstɪk] adj pesimista
pest [pɛst] n (insect) insecto nocivo; (fig)
lata, molestia
pester ['pɛstə*] vt molestar, acosar
pesticide ['pɛstɪsaɪd] n pesticida m
pet [pɛt] n animal m doméstico ▷ cpd
favorito ▷ vt acariciar; **teacher's ~**
favorito/a (del profesor); **~ hate** manía
petal ['pɛtl] n pétalo
petite [pə'ti:t] adj chiquita
petition [pə'tɪʃən] n petición f
petrified ['pɛtrɪfaɪd] adj horrorizado
petrol ['pɛtrəl] (BRIT) n gasolina
petroleum [pə'trəulɪəm] n petróleo
petrol: petrol pump (BRIT) n (in garage)
surtidor m de gasolina; **petrol station** (BRIT)
n gasolinera; **petrol tank** (BRIT) n depósito
(de gasolina)
petticoat ['pɛtɪkəut] n enaguas fpl
petty ['pɛtɪ] adj (mean) mezquino;
(unimportant) insignificante
pew [pju:] n banco
pewter ['pju:tə*] n peltre m
phantom ['fæntəm] n fantasma m
pharmacist ['fɑ:məsɪst] n
farmacéutico/a
pharmacy ['fɑ:məsɪ] n farmacia
phase [feɪz] n fase f; **phase in** vt
introducir progresivamente; **phase out** vt
(machinery, product) retirar progresivamente;
(job, subsidy) eliminar por etapas
Ph.D. abbr = **Doctor of Philosophy**
pheasant ['fɛznt] n faisán m
phenomena [fə'nɔmɪnə] npl of
phenomenon
phenomenal [fɪ'nɔmɪnl] adj fenomenal,
extraordinario

phenomenon [fə'nɔmɪnən] (pl
phenomena) n fenómeno
Philippines ['fɪlɪpi:nz] npl: **the ~** las
Filipinas
philosopher [fɪ'lɔsəfə*] n filósofo/a
philosophical [fɪlə'sɔfɪkl] adj filosófico
philosophy [fɪ'lɔsəfɪ] n filosofía
phlegm [flɛm] n flema
phobia ['fəubjə] n fobia
phone [fəun] n teléfono ▷ vt telefonear,
llamar por teléfono; **to be on the ~** tener
teléfono; (be calling) estar hablando por
teléfono; **phone back** vt, vi volver a llamar;
phone up vt, vi llamar por teléfono; **phone
book** n guía telefónica; **phone booth** n
cabina telefónica; **phone box** (BRIT) n =
phone booth; **phone call** n llamada
(telefónica); **phonecard** n teletarjeta;
phone number n número de teléfono
phonetics [fə'nɛtɪks] n fonética
phoney ['fəunɪ] adj falso
photo ['fəutəu] n foto f; **photo album**
n álbum m de fotos; **photocopier** n
fotocopiadora; **photocopy** n fotocopia
▷ vt fotocopiar
photograph ['fəutəgrɑ:f] n fotografía
▷ vt fotografiar; **photographer**
[fə'tɔgrəfə*] n fotógrafo; **photography**
[fə'tɔgrəfɪ] n fotografía
phrase [freɪz] n frase f ▷ vt expresar;
phrase book n libro de frases
physical ['fɪzɪkl] adj físico; **physical
education** n educación f física; **physically**
adv físicamente
physician [fɪ'zɪʃən] n médico/a
physicist ['fɪzɪsɪst] n físico/a
physics ['fɪzɪks] n física
physiotherapist [fɪzɪəu'θɛrəpɪst] n
fisioterapeuta
physiotherapy [fɪzɪəu'θɛrəpɪ] n
fisioterapia
physique [fɪ'zi:k] n físico
pianist ['pi:ənɪst] n pianista mf
piano [pɪ'ænəu] n piano
pick [pɪk] n (tool: also: **~-axe**) pico, piqueta
▷ vt (select) elegir, escoger; (gather) coger
(SP), recoger; (remove, take out) sacar,
quitar; (lock) abrir con ganzúa; **take your
~** escoja lo que quiera; **the ~ of** lo mejor
de; **to ~ one's nose/teeth** hurgarse las
narices/limpiarse los dientes; **to ~ a
quarrel with sb** meterse con algn; **pick
on** vt fus (person) meterse con; **pick out** vt
escoger; (distinguish) identificar; **pick up** vi
(improve: sales) ir mejor; (: patient) reponerse;
(Finance) recobrarse ▷ vt recoger; (learn)
aprender; (Police: arrest) detener; (person: for
sex) ligar; (Radio) captar; **to pick up speed**

acelerarse; **to pick o.s. up** levantarse

pickle ['pɪkl] n (also: **~s**: as condiment) escabeche m; (fig: mess) apuro ▷ vt encurtir

pickpocket ['pɪkpɔkɪt] n carterista mf

pick-up ['pɪkʌp] n (also: **~ truck**) furgoneta, camioneta

picnic ['pɪknɪk] n merienda ▷ vi ir de merienda; **picnic area** n zona de picnic; (Aut) área de descanso

picture ['pɪktʃə*] n cuadro; (painting) pintura; (photograph) fotografía; (TV) imagen f; (film) película; (fig: description) descripción f; (: situation) situación f ▷ vt (imagine) imaginar; **pictures** npl: **the ~s** (BRIT) el cine; **picture frame** n marco; **picture messaging** n (envío de) mensajes con imágenes

picturesque [pɪktʃə'rɛsk] adj pintoresco

pie [paɪ] n pastel m; (open) tarta; (small: of meat) empanada

piece [piːs] n pedazo, trozo; (of cake) trozo; (item): **a ~ of clothing/furniture/advice** una prenda (de vestir)/un mueble/un consejo ▷ vt: **to ~ together** juntar; (Tech) armar; **to take to ~s** desmontar

pie chart n gráfico de sectores or tarta

pier [pɪə*] n muelle m, embarcadero

pierce [pɪəs] vt perforar; **pierced** adj: **I've got pierced ears** tengo los agujeros hechos en las orejas

pig [pɪg] n cerdo, chancho (LAM); (pej: unkind person) asqueroso; (: greedy person) glotón/ona m/f

pigeon ['pɪdʒən] n paloma; (as food) pichón m

piggy bank ['pɪgɪ-] n hucha (en forma de cerdito)

pigsty ['pɪgstaɪ] n pocilga

pigtail n (girl's) trenza

pike [paɪk] n (fish) lucio

pilchard ['pɪltʃəd] n sardina

pile [paɪl] n montón m; (of carpet, cloth) pelo; **pile up** vi +adv (accumulate: work) amontonarse, acumularse ▷ vt +adv (put in a heap: books, clothes) apilar, amontonar; (accumulate) acumular; **piles** npl (Med) almorranas fpl, hemorroides mpl; **pile-up** n (Aut) accidente m múltiple

pilgrimage ['pɪlgrɪmɪdʒ] n peregrinación f, romería

pill [pɪl] n píldora; **the ~** la píldora

pillar ['pɪlə*] n pilar m

pillow ['pɪləu] n almohada; **pillowcase** n funda

pilot ['paɪlət] n piloto ▷ cpd (scheme etc) piloto ▷ vt pilotar; **pilot light** n piloto

pimple ['pɪmpl] n grano

PIN n abbr (= personal identification number) número personal

pin [pɪn] n alfiler m ▷ vt prender (con alfiler); **~s and needles** hormigueo; **to ~ sb down** (fig) hacer que algn concrete; **to ~ sth on sb** (fig) colgarle a algn el sambenito de algo

pinafore ['pɪnəfɔ:*] n delantal m

pinch [pɪntʃ] n (of salt etc) pizca ▷ vt pellizcar; (inf: steal) birlar; **at a ~** en caso de apuro

pine [paɪn] n (also: **~ tree**) pino ▷ vi: **to ~ for** suspirar por

pineapple ['paɪnæpl] n piña, ananás m

ping [pɪŋ] n (noise) sonido agudo; **ping-pong**® n pingpong® m

pink [pɪŋk] adj rosado, (color de) rosa ▷ n (colour) rosa; (Bot) clavel m, clavellina

pinpoint ['pɪnpɔɪnt] vt precisar

pint [paɪnt] n pinta (BRIT = 568cc, US = 473cc); (BRIT: inf: of beer) pinta de cerveza ≈ jarra (SP)

pioneer [paɪə'nɪə*] n pionero/a

pious ['paɪəs] adj piadoso, devoto

pip [pɪp] n (seed) pepita; **the ~s** (BRIT) la señal

pipe [paɪp] n tubo, caño; (for smoking) pipa ▷ vt conducir en cañerías; **pipeline** n (for oil) oleoducto; (for gas) gasoducto; **piper** n gaitero/a

pirate ['paɪərət] n pirata mf ▷ vt (cassette, book) piratear

Pisces ['paɪsiːz] n Piscis m

piss [pɪs] (inf!) vi mear; **pissed** (inf!) adj (drunk) borracho

pistol ['pɪstl] n pistola

piston ['pɪstən] n pistón m, émbolo

pit [pɪt] n hoyo; (also: **coal ~**) mina; (in garage) foso de inspección; (also: **orchestra ~**) platea ▷ vt: **to ~ one's wits against sb** medir fuerzas con algn

pitch [pɪtʃ] n (Mus) tono; (BRIT Sport) campo, terreno; (fig) punto; (tar) brea ▷ vt (throw) arrojar, lanzar ▷ vi (fall) caer(se); **to ~ a tent** montar una tienda (de campaña); **pitch-black** adj negro como boca de lobo

pitfall ['pɪtfɔːl] n riesgo

pith [pɪθ] n (of orange) médula

pitiful ['pɪtɪful] adj (touching) lastimoso, conmovedor(a)

pity ['pɪtɪ] n compasión f, piedad f ▷ vt compadecer(se de); **what a ~!** ¡qué pena!

pizza ['piːtsə] n pizza

placard ['plækɑːd] n letrero; (in march etc) pancarta

place [pleɪs] n lugar m, sitio; (seat) plaza, asiento; (post) puesto; (home): **at/to his ~** en/a su casa; (role: in society etc) papel m ▷ vt (object) poner, colocar; (identify) reconocer;

p

to take ~ tener lugar; **to be ~d** (in race, exam) colocarse; **out of ~** (not suitable) fuera de lugar; **in the first ~** en primer lugar; **to change ~s with sb** cambiarse de sitio con algn; **~ of birth** lugar *m* de nacimiento; **place mat** *n* (wooden etc) salvamanteles *m inv;* (linen etc) mantel *m* individual; **placement** *n* (positioning) colocación *f;* (at work) emplazamiento

placid ['plæsɪd] *adj* apacible

plague [pleɪg] *n* plaga; (Med) peste *f* ▷ *vt* (fig) acosar, atormentar

plaice [pleɪs] *n inv* platija

plain [pleɪn] *adj* (unpatterned) liso; (clear) claro, evidente; (simple) sencillo; (not handsome) poco atractivo ▷ *adv* claramente ▷ *n* llano, llanura; **plain chocolate** *n* chocolate *m* amargo; **plainly** *adv* claramente

plaintiff ['pleɪntɪf] *n* demandante *mf*

plait [plæt] *n* trenza

plan [plæn] *n* (drawing) plano; (scheme) plan *m*, proyecto ▷ *vt* proyectar, planificar ▷ *vi* hacer proyectos; **to ~ to do** pensar hacer

plane [pleɪn] *n* (Aviat) avión *m;* (Math, fig) plano; (also: **~ tree**) plátano; (tool) cepillo

planet ['plænɪt] *n* planeta *m*

plank [plæŋk] *n* tabla

planning ['plænɪŋ] *n* planificación *f;* **family ~** planificación familiar

plant [plɑːnt] *n* planta; (machinery) maquinaria; (factory) fábrica ▷ *vt* plantar; (field) sembrar; (bomb) colocar

plantation [plæn'teɪʃən] *n* plantación *f;* (estate) hacienda

plaque [plæk] *n* placa

plaster ['plɑːstə*] *n* (for walls) yeso; (also: **~ of Paris**) yeso mate, escayola (SP); (BRIT: also: **sticking ~**) tirita (SP), curita (LAM) ▷ *vt* enyesar; (cover): **to ~ with** llenar or cubrir de; **plaster cast** *n* (Med) escayola; (model, statue) vaciado de yeso

plastic ['plæstɪk] *n* plástico ▷ *adj* de plástico; **plastic bag** *n* bolsa de plástico; **plastic surgery** *n* cirujía plástica

plate [pleɪt] *n* (dish) plato; (metal, in book) lámina; (dental plate) placa de dentadura postiza

plateau ['plætəu] (pl **~s** or **~x**) *n* meseta, altiplanicie *f*

platform ['plætfɔːm] *n* (Rail) andén *m;* (stage, BRIT: on bus) plataforma; (at meeting) tribuna; (Pol) programa *m* (electoral)

platinum ['plætɪnəm] *adj, n* platino

platoon [plə'tuːn] *n* pelotón *m*

platter ['plætə*] *n* fuente *f*

plausible ['plɔːzɪbl] *adj* verosímil; (person) convincente

play [pleɪ] *n* (Theatre) obra, comedia ▷ *vt* (game) jugar; (compete against) jugar contra; (instrument) tocar; (part: in play etc) hacer el papel de; (tape, record) poner ▷ *vi* jugar; (band) tocar; (tape, record) sonar; **to ~ safe** ir a lo seguro; **play back** *vt* (tape) poner; **play up** *vi* (cause trouble to) dar guerra; **player** *n* jugador(a) *m/f;* (Theatre) actor(actriz) *m/f;* (Mus) músico/a; **playful** *adj* juguetón/ona; **playground** *n* (in school) patio de recreo; (in park) parque *m* infantil; **playgroup** *n* jardín *m* de niños; **playing card** *n* naipe *m*, carta; **playing field** *n* campo de deportes; **playschool** *n* = **playgroup**; **playtime** *n* (Scol) recreo; **playwright** *n* dramaturgo/a

plc *abbr* (= public limited company) ≈ S.A.

plea [pliː] *n* súplica, petición *f;* (Law) alegato, defensa

plead [pliːd] *vt* (Law): **to ~ sb's case** defender a algn; (give as excuse) poner como pretexto ▷ *vi* (Law) declararse; (beg): **to ~ with sb** suplicar or rogar a algn

pleasant ['plɛznt] *adj* agradable

please [pliːz] *excl* ¡por favor! ▷ *vt* (give pleasure to) dar gusto a, agradar ▷ *vi* (think fit): **do as you ~** haz lo que quieras; **~ yourself!** (inf) ¡haz lo que quieras!, ¡como quieras!; **pleased** *adj* (happy) alegre, contento; **pleased (with)** satisfecho (de); **pleased to meet you** ¡encantado!, ¡tanto gusto!

pleasure ['plɛʒə*] *n* placer *m*, gusto; **"it's a ~"** "el gusto es mío"

pleat [pliːt] *n* pliegue *m*

pledge [plɛdʒ] *n* (promise) promesa, voto ▷ *vt* prometer

plentiful ['plɛntɪful] *adj* copioso, abundante

plenty ['plɛntɪ] *n:* **~ of** mucho(s)/a(s)

pliers ['plaɪəz] *npl* alicates *mpl*, tenazas *fpl*

plight [plaɪt] *n* situación *f* difícil

plod [plɔd] *vi* caminar con paso pesado; (fig) trabajar laboriosamente

plonk [plɔŋk] (inf) *n* (BRIT: wine) vino peleón ▷ *vt:* **to ~ sth down** dejar caer algo

plot [plɔt] *n* (scheme) complot *m*, conjura; (of story, play) argumento; (of land) terreno ▷ *vt* (mark out) trazar; (conspire) tramar, urdir ▷ *vi* conspirar

plough [plau] (US **plow**) *n* arado ▷ *vt* (earth) arar; **to ~ money into** invertir dinero en; **ploughman's lunch** (BRIT) *n* almuerzo de pub a base de pan, queso y encurtidos

plow [plau] (US) = **plough**

ploy [plɔɪ] *n* truco, estratagema

pluck [plʌk] *vt* (fruit) coger (SP), recoger (LAM); (musical instrument) puntear; (bird) desplumar; (*eyebrows*) depilar; **to ~ up courage** hacer de tripas corazón

plug [plʌg] *n* tapón *m*; (*Elec*) enchufe *m*, clavija; (*Aut: also:* **spark(ing) ~**) bujía ▷ *vt* (*hole*) tapar; (*inf: advertise*) dar publicidad a; **plug in** *vt* (*Elec*) enchufar; **plughole** *n* desagüe *m*

plum [plʌm] *n* (*fruit*) ciruela

plumber ['plʌmə*] *n* fontanero/a (SP, CAM), plomero/a (LAM)

plumbing ['plʌmɪŋ] *n* (*trade*) fontanería, plomería; (*piping*) cañería

plummet ['plʌmɪt] *vi:* **to ~ (down)** caer a plomo

plump [plʌmp] *adj* rechoncho, rollizo ▷ *vi:* **to ~ for** (*inf: choose*) optar por

plunge [plʌndʒ] *n* zambullida ▷ *vt* sumergir, hundir ▷ *vi* (*fall*) caer; (*dive*) saltar; (*person*) arrojarse; **to take the ~** lanzarse

plural ['pluərl] *adj* plural ▷ *n* plural *m*

plus [plʌs] *n* (*also:* **~ sign**) signo más ▷ *prep* más, y, además de; **ten/twenty ~** más de diez/veinte

ply [plaɪ] *vt* (*a trade*) ejercer ▷ *vi* (*ship*) ir y venir ▷ *n* (*of wool, rope*) cabo; **to ~ sb with drink** insistir en ofrecer a algn muchas copas; **plywood** *n* madera contrachapada

P.M. *n abbr* = **Prime Minister**

p.m. *adv abbr* (= *post meridiem*) de la tarde *or* noche

PMS *n abbr* (= *premenstrual syndrome*) SPM *m*

PMT *n abbr* (= *premenstrual tension*) SPM *m*

pneumatic drill [njuː'mætɪk-] *n* martillo neumático

pneumonia [njuː'məunɪə] *n* pulmonía

poach [pəutʃ] *vt* (*cook*) escalfar; (*steal*) cazar (*or* pescar) en vedado ▷ *vi* cazar (*or* pescar) en vedado; **poached** *adj* escalfado

P.O. Box *n abbr* (= *Post Office Box*) apdo., aptdo.

pocket ['pɔkɪt] *n* bolsillo; (*fig: small area*) bolsa ▷ *vt* meter en el bolsillo; (*steal*) embolsar; **to be out of ~** (BRIT) salir perdiendo; **pocketbook** (US) *n* cartera; **pocket money** *n* asignación *f*

pod [pɔd] *n* vaina

podiatrist [pɔ'diːətrɪst] (US) *n* pedicuro/a

podium ['pəudɪəm] *n* podio

poem ['pəuɪm] *n* poema *m*

poet ['pəuɪt] *n* poeta *m/f*; **poetic** [-'ɛtɪk] *adj* poético; **poetry** *n* poesía

poignant ['pɔɪnjənt] *adj* conmovedor(a)

point [pɔɪnt] *n* punto; (*tip*) punta; (*purpose*) fin *m*, propósito; (*use*) utilidad *f*; (*significant part*) lo significativo; (*moment*) momento; (*Elec*) toma (de corriente); (*also:* **decimal ~**): **2 ~ 3 (2.3)** dos coma tres (2,3) ▷ *vt* señalar; (*gun etc*): **to ~ sth at sb** apuntar

algo a algn ▷ *vi:* **to ~ at** señalar; **points** *npl* (*Aut*) contactos *mpl*; (*Rail*) agujas *fpl*; **to be on the ~ of doing sth** estar a punto de hacer algo; **to make a ~ of** poner empeño en; **to get/miss the ~** comprender/no comprender; **to come to the ~** ir al meollo; **there's no ~ (in doing)** no tiene sentido (hacer); **point out** *vt* señalar; **point-blank** *adv* (*say, refuse*) sin más hablar; (*also:* **at point-blank range**) a quemarropa; **pointed** *adj* (*shape*) puntiagudo, afilado; (*remark*) intencionado; **pointer** *n* (*needle*) aguja, indicador *m*; **pointless** *adj* sin sentido; **point of view** *n* punto de vista

poison ['pɔɪzn] *n* veneno ▷ *vt* envenenar; **poisonous** *adj* venenoso; (*fumes etc*) tóxico

poke [pəuk] *vt* (*jab with finger, stick etc*) empujar; (*put*): **to ~ sth in(to)** introducir algo en; **poke about** *or* **around** *vi* fisgonear; **poke out** *vi* (*stick out*) salir

poker ['pəukə*] *n* atizador *m*; (*Cards*) póker *m*

Poland ['pəulənd] *n* Polonia

polar ['pəulə*] *adj* polar; **polar bear** *n* oso polar

Pole [pəul] *n* polaco/a

pole [pəul] *n* palo; (*fixed*) poste *m*; (*Geo*) polo; **pole bean** (US) *n* ≈ judía verde; **pole vault** *n* salto con pértiga

police [pə'liːs] *n* policía ▷ *vt* vigilar; **police car** *n* coche-patrulla *m*; **police constable** (BRIT) *n* guardia *m*, policía *m*; **police force** *n* cuerpo de policía; **policeman** (*irreg*) *n* policía *m*, guardia *m*; **police officer** *n* guardia *m*, policía *m*; **police station** *n* comisaría; **policewoman** (*irreg*) *n* mujer *f* policía

policy ['pɔlɪsɪ] *n* política; (*also:* **insurance ~**) póliza

polio ['pəulɪəu] *n* polio *f*

Polish ['pəulɪʃ] *adj* polaco ▷ *n* (*Ling*) polaco

polish ['pɔlɪʃ] *n* (*for shoes*) betún *m*; (*for floor*) cera (de lustrar); (*shine*) brillo, lustre *m*; (*fig: refinement*) educación *f* ▷ *vt* (*shoes*) limpiar; (*make shiny*) pulir, sacar brillo a; **polish off** *vt* (*food*) despachar; **polished** *adj* (*fig: person*) elegante

polite [pə'laɪt] *adj* cortés, atento; **politeness** *n* cortesía

political [pə'lɪtɪkl] *adj* político; **politically** *adv* políticamente; **politically correct** políticamente correcto

politician [pɔlɪ'tɪʃən] *n* político/a

politics ['pɔlɪtɪks] *n* política

poll [pəul] *n* (*election*) votación *f*; (*also:* **opinion ~**) sondeo, encuesta ▷ *vt* encuestar; (*votes*) obtener

pollen ['pɔlən] n´ polen m

polling station ['pəulɪŋ-] n centro electoral

pollute [pə'luːt] vt contaminar

pollution [pə'luːʃən] n polución f, contaminación f del medio ambiente

polo ['pəuləu] n (sport) polo; **polo-neck** adj de cuello vuelto ▷ n (sweater) suéter m de cuello vuelto; **polo shirt** n polo, niqui m

polyester [pɔlɪ'ɛstə*] n poliéster m

polystyrene [pɔlɪ'staɪriːn] n poliestireno

polythene ['pɔlɪθiːn] (BRIT) n politeno; **polythene bag** n bolsa de plástico

pomegranate ['pɔmɪgrænɪt] n granada

pompous ['pɔmpəs] adj pomposo

pond [pɔnd] n (natural) charca; (artificial) estanque m

ponder ['pɔndə*] vt meditar

pony ['pəunɪ] n poni m; **ponytail** n coleta; **pony trekking** (BRIT) n excursión f a caballo

poodle ['puːdl] n caniche m

pool [puːl] n (natural) charca; (also: swimming ~) piscina, alberca (MEX), pileta (RPL); (fig: of light etc) charco; (Sport) chapolín m ▷ vt juntar; **pools** npl quinielas fpl

poor [puə*] adj pobre; (bad) de mala calidad ▷ npl: **the ~** los pobres; **poorly** adj mal, enfermo ▷ adv mal

pop [pɔp] n (sound) ruido seco; (Mus) (música) pop m; (inf: father) papá m; (drink) gaseosa ▷ vt (put quickly) meter (de prisa) ▷ vi reventar; (cork) saltar; **pop in** vi entrar un momento; **pop out** vi salir un momento; **popcorn** n palomitas fpl

poplar ['pɔplə*] n álamo

popper ['pɔpə*] (BRIT) n automático

poppy ['pɔpɪ] n amapola

Popsicle® ['pɔpsɪkl] (US) n polo

pop star n estrella del pop

popular ['pɔpjulə*] adj popular; **popularity** [pɔpju'lærɪtɪ] n popularidad f

population [pɔpju'leɪʃən] n población f

pop-up ['pɔpʌp] (Comput) adj (menu, window) emergente ▷ n ventana emergente, (ventana f) pop-up f

porcelain ['pɔːslɪn] n porcelana

porch [pɔːtʃ] n pórtico, entrada; (US) veranda

pore [pɔː*] n poro ▷ vi: **to ~ over** engolfarse en

pork [pɔːk] n carne f de cerdo or (LAM) chancho; **pork chop** n chuleta de cerdo; **pork pie** n (BRIT: Culin) empanada de carne de cerdo

porn [pɔːn] adj (inf) porno inv ▷ n porno; **pornographic** [pɔːnə'græfɪk] adj pornográfico; **pornography** [pɔː'nɔgrəfɪ] n pornografía

porridge ['pɔrɪdʒ] n gachas fpl de avena

port [pɔːt] n puerto; (Naut: left side) babor m; (wine) vino de Oporto; **~ of call** puerto de escala

portable ['pɔːtəbl] adj portátil

porter ['pɔːtə*] n (for luggage) maletero; (doorkeeper) portero/a, conserje m/f

portfolio [pɔːt'fəuliəu] n cartera

portion ['pɔːʃən] n porción f; (of food) ración f

portrait ['pɔːtreɪt] n retrato

portray [pɔː'treɪ] vt retratar; (actor) representar

Portugal ['pɔːtjugl] n Portugal m

Portuguese [pɔːtju'giːz] adj portugués/esa ▷ n inv portugués/esa m/f; (Ling) portugués m

pose [pəuz] n postura, actitud f ▷ vi (pretend): **to ~ as** hacerse pasar por ▷ vt (question) plantear; **to ~ for** posar para

posh [pɔʃ] (inf) adj elegante, de lujo

position [pə'zɪʃən] n posición f; (job) puesto; (situation) situación f ▷ vt colocar

positive ['pɔzɪtɪv] adj positivo; (certain) seguro; (definite) definitivo; **positively** adv (affirmatively, enthusiastically) de forma positiva; (inf: really) absolutamente

possess [pə'zɛs] vt poseer; **possession** [pə'zɛʃən] n posesión f; **possessions** npl (belongings) pertenencias fpl; **possessive** adj posesivo

possibility [pɔsɪ'bɪlɪtɪ] n posibilidad f

possible ['pɔsɪbl] adj posible; **as big as ~** lo más grande posible; **possibly** adv posiblemente; **I cannot possibly come** me es imposible venir

post [pəust] n (BRIT: system) correos mpl; (BRIT: letters, delivery) correo; (job, situation) puesto; (pole) poste m ▷ vt (BRIT: send by post) echar al correo; (BRIT: appoint): **to ~ to** enviar a; **postage** n porte m, franqueo; **postal** adj postal, de correos; **postal order** n giro postal; **postbox** (BRIT) n buzón m; **postcard** n tarjeta postal; **postcode** (BRIT) n código postal

poster ['pəustə*] n cartel m

postgraduate ['pəust'grædjuət] n posgraduado/a

postman ['pəustmən] (BRIT: irreg) n cartero

postmark ['pəustmɑːk] n matasellos m inv

post-mortem [-'mɔːtəm] n autopsia

post office n (building) (oficina de) correos m; (organization): **the Post Office** Correos inv (SP), Dirección f General de Correos (LAM)

postpone [pəs'pəun] vt aplazar

posture ['pɔstʃə*] n postura, actitud f
postwoman ['pəustwumən] (BRIT: irreg) n cartera
pot [pɔt] n (for cooking) olla; (teapot) tetera; (coffeepot) cafetera; (for flowers) maceta; (for jam) tarro, pote m; (inf: marijuana) chocolate m ▷ vt (plant) poner en tiesto; **to go to ~** (inf) irse al traste
potato [pə'teɪtəu] (pl **~es**) n patata (SP), papa (LAM); **potato peeler** n pelapatatas m inv
potent ['pəutnt] adj potente, poderoso; (drink) fuerte
potential [pə'tɛnʃl] adj potencial, posible ▷ n potencial m
pothole ['pɔthəul] n (in road) bache m; (BRIT: underground) gruta
pot plant ['pɔtplɑːnt] n planta de interior
potter ['pɔtə*] n alfarero/a ▷ vi: **to ~ around** or **about** (BRIT) hacer trabajitos; **pottery** n cerámica; (factory) alfarería
potty ['pɔtɪ] n orinal m de niño
pouch [pautʃ] n (Zool) bolsa; (for tobacco) petaca
poultry ['pəultrɪ] n aves fpl de corral; (meat) pollo
pounce [pauns] vi: **to ~ on** precipitarse sobre
pound [paund] n libra (weight = 453g or 16oz; money = 100 pence) ▷ vt (beat) golpear; (crush) machacar ▷ vi (heart) latir; **pound sterling** n libra esterlina
pour [pɔː*] vt echar; (tea etc) servir ▷ vi correr, fluir; **to ~ sb a drink** servirle a algn una copa; **pour in** vi (people) entrar en tropel; **pour out** vi salir en tropel ▷ vt (drink) echar, servir; (fig): **to pour out one's feelings** desahogarse; **pouring** adj: **pouring rain** lluvia torrencial
pout [paut] vi hacer pucheros
poverty ['pɔvətɪ] n pobreza, miseria
powder ['paudə*] n polvo; (also: **face ~**) polvos mpl ▷ vt polvorear; **to ~ one's face** empolvarse la cara; **powdered milk** n leche f en polvo
power ['pauə*] n poder m; (strength) fuerza; (nation, Tech) potencia; (drive) empuje m; (Elec) fuerza, energía ▷ vt impulsar; **to be in ~** (Pol) estar en el poder; **power cut** (BRIT) n apagón m; **power failure** n = **power cut**; **powerful** adj poderoso; (engine) potente; (speech etc) convincente; **powerless** adj: **powerless (to do)** incapaz (de hacer); **power point** (BRIT) n enchufe m; **power station** n central f eléctrica
p.p. abbr (= per procurationem); **p.p. J. Smith** p.p. (por poder de) J. Smith; (= pages) págs
PR n abbr = **public relations**

practical ['præktɪkl] adj práctico; **practical joke** n broma pesada; **practically** adv (almost) casi
practice ['præktɪs] n (habit) costumbre f; (exercise) práctica, ejercicio; (training) adiestramiento; (Med: of profession) práctica, ejercicio; (Med, Law: business) consulta ▷ vt, vi (US) = **practise**; **in ~** (in reality) en la práctica; **out of ~** desentrenado
practise ['præktɪs] (US **practice**) vt (carry out) practicar; (profession) ejercer; (train at) practicar ▷ vi ejercer; (train) practicar; **practising** adj (Christian etc) practicante; (lawyer) en ejercicio
practitioner [præk'tɪʃənə*] n (Med) médico/a
pragmatic [præg'mætɪk] adj pragmático
prairie ['prɛərɪ] n pampa
praise [preɪz] n alabanza(s) f(pl), elogio(s) m(pl) ▷ vt alabar, elogiar
pram [præm] (BRIT) n cochecito de niño
prank [præŋk] n travesura
prawn [prɔːn] n gamba; **prawn cocktail** n cóctel m de gambas
pray [preɪ] vi rezar; **prayer** [prɛə*] n oración f, rezo; (entreaty) ruego, súplica
preach [priːtʃ] vi predicar; **preacher** n predicador(a) m/f
precarious [prɪ'kɛərɪəs] adj precario
precaution [prɪ'kɔːʃən] n precaución f
precede [prɪ'siːd] vt, vi preceder; **precedent** ['prɛsɪdənt] n precedente m; **preceding** [prɪ'siːdɪŋ] adj anterior
precinct ['priːsɪŋkt] n recinto
precious ['prɛʃəs] adj precioso
precise [prɪ'saɪs] adj preciso, exacto; **precisely** adv precisamente, exactamente
precision [prɪ'sɪʒən] n precisión f
predator ['prɛdətə*] n depredador m
predecessor ['priːdɪsɛsə*] n antecesor(a) m/f
predicament [prɪ'dɪkəmənt] n apuro
predict [prɪ'dɪkt] vt pronosticar; **predictable** adj previsible; **prediction** [-'dɪkʃən] n predicción f
predominantly [prɪ'dɔmɪnəntlɪ] adv en su mayoría
preface ['prɛfəs] n prefacio
prefect ['priːfɛkt] (BRIT) n (in school) monitor(a) m/f
prefer [prɪ'fəː*] vt preferir; **to ~ doing** or **to do** preferir hacer; **preferable** ['prɛfrəbl] adj preferible; **preferably** ['prɛfrəblɪ] adv de preferencia; **preference** ['prɛfrəns] n preferencia; (priority) prioridad f
prefix ['priːfɪks] n prefijo
pregnancy ['prɛgnənsɪ] n (of woman) embarazo; (of animal) preñez f

pregnant ['prɛgnənt] adj (woman)
embarazada; (animal) preñada
prehistoric ['pri:hɪs'tɔrɪk] adj
prehistórico
prejudice ['prɛdʒudɪs] n prejuicio;
prejudiced adj (person) predispuesto
preliminary [prɪ'lɪmɪnərɪ] adj preliminar
prelude ['prɛlju:d] n preludio
premature ['prɛmətʃuə*] adj prematuro
premier ['prɛmɪə*] adj primero, principal
▷ n (Pol) primer(a) ministro/a
première ['prɛmɪɛə*] n estreno
Premier League [prɛmɪə'li:g] n primera
división
premises ['prɛmɪsɪz] npl (of business etc)
local m; **on the ~** en el lugar mismo
premium ['pri:mɪəm] n premio;
(insurance) prima; **to be at a ~** ser muy
solicitado
premonition [prɛmə'nɪʃən] n
presentimiento
preoccupied [pri:'ɔkjupaɪd] adj
ensimismado
prepaid [pri:'peɪd] adj porte pagado
preparation [prɛpə'reɪʃən] n preparación
f; **preparations** npl preparativos mpl
preparatory school [prɪ'pærətərɪ-] n
escuela preparatoria
prepare [prɪ'pɛə*] vt preparar, disponer;
(Culin) preparar ▷ vi: **to ~ for** (action)
prepararse or disponerse para; (event) hacer
preparativos para; **~d to** dispuesto a; **~d for**
listo para
preposition [prɛpə'zɪʃən] n preposición f
prep school [prɛp-] n = **preparatory
school**
prerequisite [pri:'rɛkwɪzɪt] n requisito
preschool ['pri:'sku:l] adj preescolar
prescribe [prɪ'skraɪb] vt (Med) recetar
prescription [prɪ'skrɪpʃən] n (Med) receta
presence ['prɛzns] n presencia; **in sb's ~**
en presencia de algn; **~ of mind** aplomo
present [adj, n 'prɛznt, vb prɪ'zɛnt]
adj (in attendance) presente; (current)
actual ▷ n (gift) regalo; (actuality): **the ~**
la actualidad, el presente ▷ vt (introduce,
describe) presentar; (expound) exponer; (give)
presentar, dar, ofrecer; (Theatre) representar;
to give sb a ~ regalar algo a algn; **at ~**
actualmente; **presentable** [prɪ'zɛntəbl]
adj: **to make o.s. presentable** arreglarse;
presentation [-'teɪʃən] n presentación f;
(of report etc) exposición f; (formal ceremony)
entrega de un regalo; **present-day** adj
actual; **presenter** [prɪ'zɛntə*] n (Radio, TV)
locutor(a) m/f; **presently** adv (soon) dentro
de poco; (now) ahora; **present participle** n
participio (de) presente

preservation [prɛzə'veɪʃən] n
conservación f
preservative [prɪ'zə:vətɪv] n
conservante m
preserve [prɪ'zə:v] vt (keep safe) preservar,
proteger; (maintain) mantener; (food)
conservar ▷ n (for game) coto, vedado; (often
pl: jam) conserva, confitura
preside [prɪ'zaɪd] vi presidir
president ['prɛzɪdənt] n presidente m/f;
presidential [-'dɛnʃl] adj presidencial
press [prɛs] n (newspapers): **the P~** la
prensa; (printer's) imprenta; (of button)
pulsación f ▷ vt empujar; (button etc)
apretar; (clothes: iron) planchar; (put
pressure on: person) presionar; (insist): **to ~
sth on sb** insistir en que algn acepte algo
▷ vi (squeeze) apretar; (pressurize): **to ~ for**
presionar por; **we are ~ed for time/money**
estamos apurados de tiempo/dinero; **press
conference** n rueda de prensa; **pressing**
adj apremiante; **press stud** (BRIT) n botón
m de presión; **press-up** (BRIT) n plancha
pressure ['prɛʃə*] n presión f; **to put ~
on sb** presionar a algn; **pressure cooker**
n olla a presión; **pressure group** n grupo
de presión
prestige [prɛs'ti:ʒ] n prestigio
prestigious [prɛs'tɪdʒəs] adj prestigioso
presumably [prɪ'zju:məblɪ] adv es de
suponer que, cabe presumir que
presume [prɪ'zju:m] vt: **to ~ (that)**
presumir (que), suponer (que)
pretence [prɪ'tɛns] (US **pretense**) n
fingimiento; **under false ~s** con engaños
pretend [prɪ'tɛnd] vt, vi (feign) fingir

▎Be careful not to translate **pretend** by the
▎Spanish word pretender.

pretense [prɪ'tɛns] (US) n = **pretence**
pretentious [prɪ'tɛnʃəs] adj presumido;
(ostentatious) ostentoso, aparatoso
pretext ['pri:tɛkst] n pretexto
pretty ['prɪtɪ] adj bonito, lindo (LAM) ▷ adv
bastante
prevail [prɪ'veɪl] vi (gain mastery)
prevalecer; (be current) predominar;
prevailing adj (dominant) predominante
prevalent ['prɛvələnt] adj (widespread)
extendido
prevent [prɪ'vɛnt] vt: **to ~ sb from doing
sth** impedir a algn hacer algo; **to ~ sth
from happening** evitar que ocurra algo;
prevention [prɪ'vɛnʃən] n prevención f;
preventive adj preventivo
preview ['pri:vju:] n (of film) preestreno
previous ['pri:vɪəs] adj previo, anterior;
previously adv antes
prey [preɪ] n presa ▷ vi: **to ~ on** (feed on)

alimentarse de; **it was ~ing on his mind** le preocupaba

price [praɪs] n precio ▷ vt (goods) fijar el precio de; **priceless** adj que no tiene precio; **price list** n tarifa

prick [prɪk] n (sting) picadura ▷ vt pinchar; (hurt) picar; **to ~ up one's ears** aguzar el oído

prickly ['prɪklɪ] adj espinoso; (fig: person) enojadizo

pride [praɪd] n orgullo; (pej) soberbia ▷ vt: **to ~ o.s. on** enorgullecerse de

priest [priːst] n sacerdote m

primarily ['praɪmərɪlɪ] adv ante todo

primary ['praɪmərɪ] adj (first in importance) principal ▷ n (us Pol) elección f primaria; **primary school** (BRIT) n escuela primaria

prime [praɪm] adj primero, principal; (excellent) selecto, de primera clase ▷ n: **in the ~ of life** en la flor de la vida ▷ vt (wood: fig) preparar; **~ example** ejemplo típico; **Prime Minister** n primer(a) ministro/a

primitive ['prɪmɪtɪv] adj primitivo; (crude) rudimentario

primrose ['prɪmrəuz] n primavera, prímula

prince [prɪns] n príncipe m

princess [prɪn'sɛs] n princesa

principal ['prɪnsɪpl] adj principal, mayor ▷ n director(a) m/f; **principally** adv principalmente

principle ['prɪnsɪpl] n principio; **in ~** en principio; **on ~** por principio

print [prɪnt] n (footprint) huella; (fingerprint) huella dactilar; (letters) letra de molde; (fabric) estampado; (Art) grabado; (Phot) impresión f ▷ vt imprimir; (cloth) estampar; (write in capitals) escribir en letras de molde; **out of ~** agotado; **print out** vt (Comput) imprimir; **printer** n (person) impresor(a) m/f; (machine) impresora; **printout** n (Comput) impresión f

prior ['praɪə*] adj anterior, previo; (more important) más importante; **~ to** antes de

priority [praɪ'ɔrɪtɪ] n prioridad f; **to have ~ (over)** tener prioridad (sobre)

prison ['prɪzn] n cárcel f, prisión f ▷ cpd carcelario; **prisoner** n (in prison) preso/a; (captured person) prisionero; **prisoner-of-war** n prisionero de guerra

pristine ['prɪstiːn] adj pristino

privacy ['prɪvəsɪ] n intimidad f

private ['praɪvɪt] adj (personal) particular; (property, industry, discussion etc) privado; (person) reservado; (place) tranquilo ▷ n soldado raso; **"~"** (on envelope) "confidencial"; (on door) "prohibido el paso";

in ~ en privado; **privately** adv en privado; (in o.s.) en secreto; **private property** n propiedad f privada; **private school** n colegio particular

privatize ['praɪvɪtaɪz] vt privatizar

privilege ['prɪvɪlɪdʒ] n privilegio; (prerogative) prerrogativa

prize [praɪz] n premio ▷ adj de primera clase ▷ vt apreciar, estimar; **prize-giving** n distribución f de premios; **prizewinner** n premiado/a

pro [prəu] n (Sport) profesional mf ▷ prep a favor de; **the ~s and cons** los pros y los contras

probability [prɔbə'bɪlɪtɪ] n probabilidad f; **in all ~** con toda probabilidad

probable ['prɔbəbl] adj probable

probably ['prɔbəblɪ] adv probablemente

probation [prə'beɪʃən] n: **on ~** (employee) a prueba; (Law) en libertad condicional

probe [prəub] n (Med, Space) sonda; (enquiry) encuesta, investigación f ▷ vt sondar; (investigate) investigar

problem ['prɔbləm] n problema m

procedure [prə'siːdʒə*] n procedimiento; (bureaucratic) trámites mpl

proceed [prə'siːd] vi (do afterwards): **to ~ to do sth** proceder a hacer algo; (continue): **to ~ (with)** continuar or seguir (con); **proceedings** npl acto(s) (pl) (Law) proceso; **proceeds** ['prəusiːdz] npl (money) ganancias fpl, ingresos mpl

process ['prəusɛs] n proceso ▷ vt tratar, elaborar

procession [prə'sɛʃən] n desfile m; **funeral ~** cortejo fúnebre

proclaim [prə'kleɪm] vt (announce) anunciar

prod [prɔd] vt empujar ▷ n empujón m

produce [n 'prɔdjuːs, vt prə'djuːs] n (Agr) productos mpl agrícolas ▷ vt producir; (play, film, programme) presentar; **producer** n productor(a) m/f; (of film, programme) director(a) m/f; (of record) productor(a) m/f

product ['prɔdʌkt] n producto; **production** [prə'dʌkʃən] n producción f; (Theatre) presentación f; **productive** [prə'dʌktɪv] adj productivo; **productivity** [prɔdʌk'tɪvɪtɪ] n productividad f

Prof. [prɔf] abbr (= professor) Prof

profession [prə'fɛʃən] n profesión f; **professional** adj profesional ▷ n profesional mf; (skilled person) perito

professor [prə'fɛsə*] n (BRIT) catedrático/a; (us, CANADA) profesor(a) m/f

profile ['prəufaɪl] n perfil m

profit ['prɔfɪt] n (Comm) ganancia ▷ vi: **to ~ by or from** aprovechar or sacar provecho

de; **profitable** adj (Econ) rentable
profound [prə'faund] adj profundo
programme ['prəugræm] (US **program**) n
programa m ▷ vt programar; **programmer**
(US **programer**) n programador(a)
m/f; **programming** (US **programing**) n
programación f
progress [n 'prəugrɛs, vi prə'grɛs]
n progreso; (development) desarrollo
▷ vi progresar, avanzar; **in ~** en curso;
progressive [-'grɛsɪv] adj progresivo;
(person) progresista
prohibit [prə'hɪbɪt] vt prohibir; **to ~ sb
from doing sth** prohibir a algn hacer algo
project [n 'prɔdʒɛkt, vb prə'dʒɛkt] n
proyecto ▷ vt proyectar ▷ vi (stick out) salir,
sobresalir; **projection** [prə'dʒɛkʃən]
n proyección f; (overhang) saliente m;
projector [prə'dʒɛktə*] n proyector m
prolific [prə'lɪfɪk] adj prolífico
prolong [prə'lɔŋ] vt prolongar, extender
prom [prɔm] n abbr = **promenade** (US: ball)
baile m de gala; **the P~s** ver abajo

● **PROM**
●
● El ciclo de conciertos de música clásica
● más conocido de Londres es el llamado
● **the Proms** (promenade concerts),
● que se celebra anualmente en el Royal
● Albert Hall. Su nombre se debe a que
● originalmente el público paseaba
● durante las actuaciones, costumbre que
● en la actualidad se mantiene de forma
● simbólica, permitiendo que parte de
● los asistentes permanezcan de pie. En
● Estados Unidos se llama **prom** a un
● baile de gala en un centro de educación
● secundaria o universitaria.

promenade [prɔmə'nɑːd] n (by sea) paseo
marítimo
prominent ['prɔmɪnənt] adj (standing out)
saliente; (important) eminente, importante
promiscuous [prə'mɪskjuəs] adj
(sexually) promiscuo
promise ['prɔmɪs] n promesa ▷ vt, vi
prometer; **promising** adj prometedor(a)
promote [prə'məut] vt (employee)
ascender; (product, pop star) hacer
propaganda por; (ideas) fomentar;
promotion [-'məuʃən] n (advertising
campaign) campaña f de promoción; (in rank)
ascenso
prompt [prɔmpt] adj rápido ▷ adv: **at 6
o'clock ~** a las seis en punto ▷ n (Comput)
aviso ▷ vt (urge) mover, incitar; (when
talking) instar; (Theatre) apuntar; **to ~ sb to**

do sth instar a algn a hacer algo; **promptly**
adv rápidamente; (exactly) puntualmente
prone [prəun] adj (lying) postrado; **~ to**
propenso a
prong [prɔŋ] n diente m, punta
pronoun ['prəunaun] n pronombre m
pronounce [prə'nauns] vt pronunciar
pronunciation [prənʌnsɪ'eɪʃən] n
pronunciación f
proof [pruːf] n prueba ▷ adj: **~ against** a
prueba de
prop [prɔp] n apoyo; (fig) sostén m
accesorios mpl, at(t)rezzo msg; **prop up**
vt (roof, structure) apuntalar; (economy)
respaldar
propaganda [prɔpə'gændə] n
propaganda
propeller [prə'pɛlə*] n hélice f
proper ['prɔpə*] adj (suited, right) propio;
(exact) justo; (seemly) correcto, decente;
(authentic) verdadero; (referring to place): **the
village ~** el pueblo mismo; **properly** adv
(adequately) correctamente; (decently)
decentemente; **proper noun** n nombre
m propio
property ['prɔpətɪ] n propiedad f;
(personal) bienes mpl muebles
prophecy ['prɔfɪsɪ] n profecía
prophet ['prɔfɪt] n profeta m
proportion [prə'pɔːʃən] n proporción
f; (share) parte f; **proportions** npl
(size) dimensiones fpl; **proportional**
adj: **proportional (to)** en proporción (con)
proposal [prə'pəuzl] n (offer of marriage)
oferta de matrimonio; (plan) proyecto
propose [prə'pəuz] vt proponer ▷ vi
declararse; **to ~ to do** tener intención de
hacer
proposition [prɔpə'zɪʃən] n propuesta
proprietor [prə'praɪətə*] n propietario/a,
dueño/a
prose [prəuz] n prosa
prosecute ['prɔsɪkjuːt] vt (Law) procesar;
prosecution [-'kjuːʃən] n proceso, causa;
(accusing side) acusación f; **prosecutor** n
acusador(a) m/f; (also: **public prosecutor**)
fiscal mf
prospect [n 'prɔspɛkt, vb prə'spɛkt]
n (possibility) posibilidad f; (outlook)
perspectiva ▷ vi: **to ~ for** buscar; **prospects**
npl (for work etc) perspectivas fpl;
prospective [prə'spɛktɪv] adj futuro
prospectus [prə'spɛktəs] n prospecto
prosper ['prɔspə*] vi prosperar;
prosperity [-'spɛrɪtɪ] n prosperidad f;
prosperous adj próspero
prostitute ['prɔstɪtjuːt] n prostituta;
(male) hombre que se dedica a la prostitución

protect [prə'tɛkt] *vt* proteger; **protection** [-'tɛkʃən] *n* protección *f*; **protective** *adj* protector(a)

protein ['prəuti:n] *n* proteína

protest [*n* 'prəutɛst, *vb* prə'tɛst] *n* protesta ▷ *vi*: **to ~ about** *or* **at/against** protestar de/contra ▷ *vt* (*insist*): **to ~ (that)** insistir en (que)

Protestant ['prɔtɪstənt] *adj, n* protestante *mf*

protester [prə'tɛstə*] *n* manifestante *mf*

protractor [prə'træktə*] *n* (*Geom*) transportador *m*

proud [praud] *adj* orgulloso; (*pej*) soberbio, altanero

prove [pru:v] *vt* probar; (*show*) demostrar ▷ *vi*: **to ~ (to be) correct** resultar correcto; **to ~ o.s.** probar su valía

proverb ['prɔvə:b] *n* refrán *m*

provide [prə'vaɪd] *vt* proporcionar, dar; **to ~ sb with sth** proveer a algn de algo; **provide for** *vt fus* (*person*) mantener a; (*problem etc*) tener en cuenta; **provided** *conj*: **provided (that)** con tal de que, a condición de que; **providing** [prə'vaɪdɪŋ] *conj*: **providing (that)** a condición de que, con tal de que

province ['prɔvɪns] *n* provincia; (*fig*) esfera; **provincial** [prə'vɪnʃəl] *adj* provincial; (*pej*) provinciano

provision [prə'vɪʒən] *n* (*supplying*) suministro, abastecimiento; (*of contract etc*) disposición *f*; **provisions** *npl* (*food*) comestibles *mpl*; **provisional** *adj* provisional

provocative [prə'vɔkətɪv] *adj* provocativo

provoke [prə'vəuk] *vt* (*cause*) provocar, incitar; (*anger*) enojar

prowl [praul] *vi* (*also*: **~ about, ~ around**) merodear ▷ *n*: **on the ~** de merodeo

proximity [prɔk'sɪmɪtɪ] *n* proximidad *f*

proxy ['prɔksɪ] *n*: **by ~** por poderes

prudent ['pru:dənt] *adj* prudente

prune [pru:n] *n* ciruela pasa ▷ *vt* podar

pry [praɪ] *vi*: **to ~ (into)** entrometerse (en)

PS *n abbr* (= *postscript*) P.D.

pseudonym ['sju:dənɪm] *n* seudónimo

PSHE (*BRIT: Scol*) *n abbr* (= *personal, social and health education*) formación social y sanitaria

psychiatric [saɪkɪ'ætrɪk] *adj* psiquiátrico

psychiatrist [saɪ'kaɪətrɪst] *n* psiquiatra *mf*

psychic ['saɪkɪk] *adj* (*also*: **~al**) psíquico

psychoanalysis [saɪkəuə'nælɪsɪs] *n* psicoanálisis *m inv*

psychological [saɪkə'lɔdʒɪkl] *adj* psicológico

psychologist [saɪ'kɔlədʒɪst] *n* psicólogo/a

psychology [saɪ'kɔlədʒɪ] *n* psicología

psychotherapy [saɪkəu'θɛrəpɪ] *n* psicoterapia

pt *abbr* = **pint(s); point(s)**

PTO *abbr* (= *please turn over*) sigue

pub [pʌb] *n abbr* (= *public house*) pub *m*, bar *m*

puberty ['pju:bətɪ] *n* pubertad *f*

public ['pʌblɪk] *adj* público ▷ *n*: **the ~** el público; **in ~** en público; **to make ~** hacer público

publication [pʌblɪ'keɪʃən] *n* publicación *f*

public: public company *n* sociedad *f* anónima; **public convenience** (*BRIT*) *n* aseos *mpl* públicos (*SP*), sanitarios *mpl* (*LAM*); **public holiday** *n* (día *m* de) fiesta (*SP*), (día *m*) feriado (*LAM*); **public house** (*BRIT*) *n* bar *m*, pub *m*

publicity [pʌb'lɪsɪtɪ] *n* publicidad *f*

publicize ['pʌblɪsaɪz] *vt* publicitar

public: public limited company *n* sociedad *f* anónima (S.A.); **publicly** *adv* públicamente, en público; **public opinion** *n* opinión *f* pública; **public relations** *n* relaciones *fpl* públicas; **public school** *n* (*BRIT*) escuela privada; (*US*) instituto; **public transport** *n* transporte *m* público

publish ['pʌblɪʃ] *vt* publicar; **publisher** *n* (*person*) editor/a *m/f*; (*firm*) editorial *f*; **publishing** *n* (*industry*) industria del libro

pub lunch *n* almuerzo que se sirve en un pub; **to go for a ~** almorzar o comer en un pub

pudding ['pudɪŋ] *n* pudín *m*; (*BRIT: dessert*) postre *m*; **black ~** morcilla

puddle ['pʌdl] *n* charco

Puerto Rico [pwɛ:təu'ri:kəu] *n* Puerto Rico

puff [pʌf] *n* soplo; (*of smoke, air*) bocanada; (*of breathing*) resoplido ▷ *vt*: **to ~ one's pipe** chupar la pipa ▷ *vi* (*pant*) jadear; **puff pastry** *n* hojaldre *m*

pull [pul] *n* (*tug*): **to give sth a ~** dar un tirón a algo ▷ *vt* tirar de; (*press: trigger*) apretar; (*haul*) tirar, arrastrar; (*close: curtain*) echar ▷ *vi* tirar; **to ~ to pieces** hacer pedazos; **not to ~ one's punches** no andarse con bromas; **to ~ one's weight** hacer su parte; **to ~ o.s. together** sobreponerse; **to ~ sb's leg** tomar el pelo a algn; **pull apart** *vt* (*break*) romper; **pull away** *vi* (*vehicle: move off*) salir, arrancar; (*draw back*) apartarse bruscamente; **pull back** *vt* (*lever etc*) tirar hacia sí; (*curtains*) descorrer ▷ *vi* (*refrain*) contenerse; (*Mil: withdraw*) retirarse; **pull down** *vt* (building) derribar; **pull in** vi (car etc) parar (junto a la acera); (train) llegar a la estación; **pull off** vt (deal etc) cerrar; **pull out** vi (car, train etc) salir ▷ vt sacar, arrancar; **pull over** vi (Aut) hacerse a un lado; **pull up** vi (stop) parar ▷ vt (raise) levantar; (uproot) arrancar, desarraigar

pulley ['pulɪ] n polea

pullover ['puləuvə*] n jersey m, suéter m

pulp [pʌlp] n (of fruit) pulpa

pulpit ['pulpɪt] n púlpito

pulse [pʌls] n (Anat) pulso; (rhythm) pulsación f; (Bot) legumbre f; **pulses** pl n legumbres

puma ['pju:mə] n puma m

pump [pʌmp] n bomba; (shoe) zapatilla ▷ vt sacar con una bomba; **pump up** vt inflar

pumpkin ['pʌmpkɪn] n calabaza

pun [pʌn] n juego de palabras

punch [pʌntʃ] n (blow) golpe m, puñetazo; (tool) punzón m; (drink) ponche m ▷ vt (hit): **to ~ sb/sth** dar un puñetazo or golpear a algn/algo; **punch-up** (BRIT: inf) n riña

punctual ['pʌŋktjuəl] adj puntual

punctuation [pʌŋktju'eɪʃən] n puntuación f

puncture ['pʌŋktʃə*] (BRIT) n pinchazo ▷ vt pinchar

punish ['pʌnɪʃ] vt castigar; **punishment** n castigo

punk [pʌŋk] n (also: ~ rocker) punki mf; (also: ~ rock) música punk; (US: inf: hoodlum) rufián m

pup [pʌp] n cachorro

pupil ['pju:pl] n alumno/a; (of eye) pupila

puppet ['pʌpɪt] n títere m

puppy ['pʌpɪ] n cachorro, perrito

purchase ['pə:tʃɪs] n compra ▷ vt comprar

pure [pjuə*] adj puro; **purely** adv puramente

purify ['pjuərɪfaɪ] vt purificar, depurar

purity ['pjuərɪtɪ] n pureza

purple ['pə:pl] adj purpúreo; morado

purpose ['pə:pəs] n propósito; **on ~** a propósito, adrede

purr [pə:*] vi ronronear

purse [pə:s] n monedero; (US: handbag) bolso (SP), cartera (LAM), bolsa (MEX) ▷ vt fruncir

pursue [pə'sju:] vt seguir

pursuit [pə'sju:t] n (chase) caza; (occupation) actividad f

pus [pʌs] n pus m

push [puʃ] n empuje m, empujón m; (of button) presión f; (drive) empuje m ▷ vt empujar; (button) apretar; (promote) promover ▷ vi empujar; (demand): **to ~ for** luchar por; **push in** vi colarse; **push off** (inf) vi largarse; **push on** vi seguir adelante; **push over** vt (cause to fall) hacer caer, derribar; (knock over) volcar; **push through** vi (crowd) abrirse paso a empujones ▷ vt (measure) despachar; **pushchair** (BRIT) n sillita de ruedas; **pusher** n (drug pusher) traficante mf de drogas; **push-up** (US) n plancha

pussy(-cat) ['pusɪ-] (inf) n minino (inf)

put [put] (pt, pp ~) vt (place) poner, colocar; (put into) meter; (say) expresar; (a question) hacer; (estimate) estimar; **put aside** vt (lay down: book etc) dejar or poner a un lado; (save) ahorrar; (in shop) guardar; **put away** vt (store) guardar; **put back** vt (replace) devolver a su lugar; (postpone) aplazar; **put by** vt (money) guardar; **put down** vt (on ground) poner en el suelo; (animal) sacrificar; (in writing) apuntar; (revolt etc) sofocar; (attribute): **to put sth down to** atribuir algo a; **put forward** vt (ideas) presentar, proponer; **put in** vt (complaint) presentar; (time) dedicar; **put off** vt (postpone) aplazar; (discourage) desanimar; **put on** vt ponerse; (light etc) encender; (play etc) presentar; (gain): **to put on weight** engordar; (brake) echar; (record, kettle etc) poner; (assume) adoptar; **put out** vt (fire, light) apagar; (rubbish etc) sacar; (cat etc) echar; (one's hand) alargar; (inf: person): **to be put out** alterarse; **put through** vt (Tel) poner; (plan etc) hacer aprobar; **put together** vt unir, reunir; (assemble: furniture) armar, montar; (meal) preparar; **put up** vt (raise) levantar, alzar; (hang) colgar; (build) construir; (increase) aumentar; (accommodate) alojar; **put up with** vt fus aguantar

putt [pʌt] n putt m, golpe m corto; **putting green** n green m; minigolf m

puzzle ['pʌzl] n rompecabezas m inv; (also: **crossword ~**) crucigrama m; (mystery) misterio ▷ vt dejar perplejo, confundir ▷ vi: **to ~ over sth** devanarse los sesos con algo; **puzzled** adj perplejo; **puzzling** adj misterioso, extraño

pyjamas [pɪ'dʒɑ:məz] (BRIT) npl pijama m

pylon ['paɪlən] n torre f de conducción eléctrica

pyramid ['pɪrəmɪd] n pirámide f

q

quack [kwæk] n graznido; (pej: doctor) curandero/a

quadruple [kwɔ'drupl] vt, vi cuadruplicar

quail [kweɪl] n codorniz f ▷ vi: **to ~ at** or **before** amedrentarse ante

quaint [kweɪnt] adj extraño; (picturesque) pintoresco

quake [kweɪk] vi temblar ▷ n abbr = **earthquake**

qualification [kwɔlɪfɪ'keɪʃən] n (ability) capacidad f; (often pl: diploma etc) título; (reservation) salvedad f

qualified ['kwɔlɪfaɪd] adj capacitado; (professionally) titulado; (limited) limitado

qualify ['kwɔlɪfaɪ] vt (make competent) capacitar; (modify) modificar ▷ vi (in competition): **to ~ (for)** calificarse (para); (pass examination(s): **to ~ (as)** calificarse (de), graduarse (en); (be eligible): **to ~ (for)** reunir los requisitos (para)

quality ['kwɔlɪtɪ] n calidad f; (of person) cualidad f

qualm [kwɑːm] n escrúpulo

quantify ['kwɔntɪfaɪ] vt cuantificar

quantity ['kwɔntɪtɪ] n cantidad f; **in ~** en grandes cantidades

quarantine ['kwɔrntiːn] n cuarentena

quarrel ['kwɔrl] n riña, pelea ▷ vi reñir, pelearse

quarry ['kwɔrɪ] n cantera

quart [kwɔːt] n ≈ litro

quarter ['kwɔːtə*] n cuarto, cuarta parte f; (US: coin) moneda de 25 centavos; (of year) trimestre m; (district) barrio ▷ vt dividir en cuartos; (Mil: lodge) alojar; **quarters** npl (barracks) cuartel m; (living quarters) alojamiento; **a ~ of an hour** un cuarto de hora; **quarter final** n cuarto de final; **quarterly** adj trimestral ▷ adv cada 3 meses, trimestralmente

quartet(te) [kwɔː'tɛt] n cuarteto

quartz [kwɔːts] n cuarzo

quay [kiː] n (also: **~side**) muelle m

queasy ['kwiːzɪ] adj: **to feel ~** tener náuseas

queen [kwiːn] n reina; (Cards etc) dama

queer [kwɪə*] adj raro, extraño ▷ n (inf: highly offensive) maricón m

quench [kwɛntʃ] vt: **to ~ one's thirst** apagar la sed

query ['kwɪərɪ] n (question) pregunta ▷ vt dudar de

quest [kwɛst] n busca, búsqueda

question ['kwɛstʃən] n pregunta; (doubt) duda; (matter) asunto, cuestión f ▷ vt (doubt) dudar de; (interrogate) interrogar, hacer preguntas a; **beyond ~** fuera de toda duda; **out of the ~** imposible; ni hablar; **questionable** adj dudoso; **question mark** n punto de interrogación; **questionnaire** [-'nɛə*] n cuestionario

queue [kjuː] (BRIT) n cola ▷ vi (also: **~ up**) hacer cola

quiche [kiːʃ] n quiche m

quick [kwɪk] adj rápido; (agile) ágil; (mind) listo ▷ n: **cut to the ~** (fig) herido en lo vivo; **be ~!** ¡date prisa!; **quickly** adv rápidamente, de prisa

quid [kwɪd] (BRIT: inf) n inv libra

quiet ['kwaɪət] adj (voice, music etc) bajo; (person, place) tranquilo; (ceremony) íntimo ▷ n silencio; (calm) tranquilidad f ▷ vt, vi (US) = **quieten**

> Be careful not to translate **quiet** by the Spanish word *quieto*.

quietly adv tranquilamente; (silently) silenciosamente

quilt [kwɪlt] n edredón m

quirky ['kwˊːkɪ] adj raro, estrafalario

quit [kwɪt] (pt, pp **~** or **~ted**) vt dejar, abandonar; (premises) desocupar ▷ vi (give up) renunciar; (resign) dimitir

quite [kwaɪt] adv (rather) bastante; (entirely) completamente; **that's not ~ big enough** no acaba de ser lo bastante grande; **~ a few of them** un buen número de ellos; **~ (so)!** ¡así es!, ¡exactamente!

quits [kwɪts] adj: **~ (with)** en paz (con); **let's call it ~** dejémoslo en tablas

quiver ['kwɪvə*] vi estremecerse

quiz [kwɪz] n concurso ▷ vt interrogar

quota ['kwəʊtə] n cuota

quotation [kwəʊ'teɪʃən] n cita; (estimate) presupuesto; **quotation marks** npl comillas fpl

quote [kwəʊt] n cita; (estimate) presupuesto ▷ vt citar; (price) cotizar ▷ vi: **to ~ from** citar de; **quotes** npl (inverted commas) comillas fpl

r

rabbi ['ræbaɪ] *n* rabino
rabbit ['ræbɪt] *n* conejo
rabies ['reɪbiːz] *n* rabia
RAC (BRIT) *n abbr* (= *Royal Automobile Club*) ≈ RACE *m*
rac(c)oon [rə'kuːn] *n* mapache *m*
race [reɪs] *n* carrera; (*species*) raza ▷ *vt* (*horse*) hacer correr; (*engine*) acelerar ▷ *vi* (*compete*) competir; (*run*) correr; (*pulse*) latir a ritmo acelerado; **race car** (US) *n* = **racing car**; **racecourse** *n* hipódromo; **racehorse** *n* caballo de carreras; **racetrack** *n* pista; (*for cars*) autódromo
racial ['reɪʃl] *adj* racial
racing ['reɪsɪŋ] *n* carreras *fpl*; **racing car** (BRIT) *n* coche *m* de carreras; **racing driver** (BRIT) *n* piloto *mf* de carreras
racism ['reɪsɪzəm] *n* racismo; **racist** [-sɪst] *adj, n* racista *mf*
rack [ræk] *n* (*also:* **luggage ~**) rejilla; (*shelf*) estante *m*; (*also:* **roof ~**) baca, portaequipajes *m inv*; (*dish rack*) escurreplatos *m inv*; (*clothes rack*) percha ▷ *vt* atormentar; **to ~ one's brains** devanarse los sesos
racket ['rækɪt] *n* (*for tennis*) raqueta; (*noise*) ruido, estrépito; (*swindle*) estafa, timo
racquet ['rækɪt] *n* raqueta
radar ['reɪdɑː*] *n* radar *m*
radiation [reɪdɪ'eɪʃən] *n* radiación *f*
radiator ['reɪdɪeɪtə*] *n* radiador *m*
radical ['rædɪkl] *adj* radical
radio ['reɪdɪəu] *n* radio *f*; **on the ~** por radio; **radioactive** *adj* radioactivo; **radio station** *n* emisora
radish ['rædɪʃ] *n* rábano
RAF *n abbr* (= *Royal Air Force*) las Fuerzas Aéreas Británicas
raffle ['ræfl] *n* rifa, sorteo
raft [rɑːft] *n* balsa; (*also:* **life ~**) balsa salvavidas

rag [ræg] *n* (*piece of cloth*) trapo; (*torn cloth*) harapo; (*pej: newspaper*) periodicucho; (*for charity*) actividades estudiantiles benéficas; **rags** *npl* (*torn clothes*) harapos *mpl*
rage [reɪdʒ] *n* rabia, furor *m* ▷ *vi* (*person*) rabiar, estar furioso; (*storm*) bramar; **it's all the ~** (*very fashionable*) está muy de moda
ragged ['rægɪd] *adj* (*edge*) desigual, mellado; (*appearance*) andrajoso, harapiento
raid [reɪd] *n* (*Mil*) incursión *f*; (*criminal*) asalto; (*by police*) redada ▷ *vt* invadir, atacar; asaltar
rail [reɪl] *n* (*on stair*) barandilla, pasamanos *m inv*; (*on bridge, balcony*) pretil *m*; (*of ship*) barandilla; (*also:* **towel ~**) toallero; **railcard** *n* (BRIT) tarjeta para obtener descuentos en el tren; **railing(s)** *n(pl)* vallado; **railroad** (US) *n* = **railway**; **railway** (BRIT) *n* ferrocarril *m*, vía férrea; **railway line** (BRIT) *n* línea (de ferrocarril); **railway station** (BRIT) *n* estación *f* de ferrocarril
rain [reɪn] *n* lluvia ▷ *vi* llover; **in the ~** bajo la lluvia; **it's ~ing** llueve, está lloviendo; **rainbow** *n* arco iris; **raincoat** *n* impermeable *m*; **raindrop** *n* gota de lluvia; **rainfall** *n* lluvia; **rainforest** *n* selvas *fpl* tropicales; **rainy** *adj* lluvioso
raise [reɪz] *n* aumento ▷ *vt* levantar; (*increase*) aumentar; (*improve: morale*) subir; (*: standards*) mejorar; (*doubts*) suscitar; (*a question*) plantear; (*cattle, family*) criar; (*crop*) cultivar; (*army*) reclutar; (*loan*) obtener; **to ~ one's voice** alzar la voz
raisin ['reɪzn] *n* pasa de Corinto
rake [reɪk] *n* (*tool*) rastrillo; (*person*) libertino ▷ *vt* (*garden*) rastrillar
rally ['rælɪ] *n* (*Pol etc*) reunión *f*, mitin *m*; (*Aut*) rallye *m*; (*Tennis*) peloteo ▷ *vt* reunir ▷ *vi* recuperarse
RAM [ræm] *n abbr* (= *random access memory*) RAM *f*
ram [ræm] *n* carnero; (*also:* **battering ~**) ariete *m* ▷ *vt* (*crash into*) dar contra, chocar con; (*push: fist etc*) empujar con fuerza
Ramadan [ræmə'dæn] *n* ramadán *m*
ramble ['ræmbl] *n* caminata, excursión *f* en el campo ▷ *vi* (*pej: also:* **~ on**) divagar; **rambler** *n* excursionista *mf*; (*Bot*) trepadora; **rambling** *adj* (*speech*) inconexo; (*house*) laberíntico; (*Bot*) trepador(a)
ramp [ræmp] *n* rampa; **on/off ~** (US Aut) vía de acceso/salida
rampage [ræm'peɪdʒ] *n*: **to be on the ~** desmandarse ▷ *vi*: **they went rampaging through the town** recorrieron la ciudad armando alboroto
ran [ræn] *pt of* **run**
ranch [rɑːntʃ] *n* hacienda, estancia

random ['rændəm] *adj* fortuito, sin
orden; (*Comput, Math*) aleatorio ▷ *n*: **at ~**
al azar

rang [ræŋ] *pt of* **ring**

range [reɪndʒ] *n* (*of mountains*) cadena de
montañas, cordillera; (*of missile*) alcance *m*;
(*of voice*) registro; (*series*) serie *f*; (*of products*)
surtido; (*Mil: also*: **shooting ~**) campo de
tiro; (*also*: **kitchen ~**) fogón *m* ▷ *vt* (*place*)
colocar; (*arrange*) arreglar ▷ *vi*: **to ~ over**
(*extend*) extenderse por; **to ~ from ... to ...**
oscilar entre ... y ...

ranger [reɪndʒə*] *n* guardabosques *mf inv*

rank [ræŋk] *n* (*row*) fila; (*Mil*) rango;
(*status*) categoría; (*BRIT: also*: **taxi ~**) parada
de taxis ▷ *vi*: **to ~ among** figurar entre ▷ *adj*
fétido, rancio; **the ~ and file** (*fig*) la base

ransom ['rænsəm] *n* rescate *m*; **to hold to**
~ (*fig*) hacer chantaje a

rant [rænt] *vi* divagar, desvariar

rap [ræp] *vt* golpear, dar un golpecito en
▷ *n* (*music*) rap *m*

rape [reɪp] *n* violación *f*; (*Bot*) colza ▷ *vt*
violar

rapid ['ræpɪd] *adj* rápido; **rapidly** *adv*
rápidamente; **rapids** *npl* (*Geo*) rápidos *mpl*

rapist ['reɪpɪst] *n* violador *m*

rapport [ræ'pɔ:*] *n* simpatía

rare [rɛə*] *adj* raro, poco común;
(*Culin: steak*) poco hecho; **rarely** *adv* pocas
veces

rash [ræʃ] *adj* imprudente, precipitado ▷ *n*
(*Med*) sarpullido, erupción *f* (cutánea); (*of*
events) serie *f*

rasher ['ræʃə*] *n* lonja

raspberry ['rɑːzbərɪ] *n* frambuesa

rat [ræt] *n* rata

rate [reɪt] *n* (*ratio*) razón *f*; (*price*) precio;
(: *of hotel etc*) tarifa; (*of interest*) tipo; (*speed*)
velocidad *f* ▷ *vt* (*value*) tasar; (*estimate*)
estimar; **rates** *npl* (*BRIT: property tax*)
impuesto municipal; (*fees*) tarifa; **to ~ sth/**
sb as considerar algo/a algn como

rather ['rɑːðə*] *adv*: **it's ~ expensive** es
algo caro; (*too much*) es demasiado caro; (*to*
some extent) más bien; **there's ~ a lot** hay
bastante; **I would** *or* **I'd ~ go** preferiría ir; **or**
~ mejor dicho

rating ['reɪtɪŋ] *n* tasación *f*; (*score*) índice
m; (*of ship*) clase *f*; **ratings** *npl* (*Radio, TV*)
niveles *mpl* de audiencia

ratio ['reɪʃɪəu] *n* razón *f*; **in the ~ of 100 to**
1 a razón de 100 a 1

ration ['ræʃən] *n* ración *f* ▷ *vt* racionar;
rations *npl* víveres *mpl*

rational ['ræʃənl] *adj* (*solution, reasoning*)
lógico, razonable; (*person*) cuerdo, sensato

rattle ['rætl] *n* golpeteo; (*of train etc*)
traqueteo; (*for baby*) sonaja, sonajero
▷ *vi* castañetear; (*car, bus*): **to ~ along**
traquetear ▷ *vt* hacer sonar agitando

rave [reɪv] *vi* (*in anger*) encolerizarse; (*with*
enthusiasm) entusiasmarse; (*Med*) delirar,
desvariar ▷ *n* (*inf: party*) rave *m*

raven ['reɪvən] *n* cuervo

ravine [rə'viːn] *n* barranco

raw [rɔ:] *adj* crudo; (*not processed*) bruto;
(*sore*) vivo; (*inexperienced*) novato, inexperto;
~ materials materias primas

ray [reɪ] *n* rayo; **~ of hope** (rayo de)
esperanza

razor ['reɪzə*] *n* (*open*) navaja; (*safety razor*)
máquina de afeitar; (*electric razor*) máquina
(eléctrica) de afeitar; **razor blade** *n* hoja
de afeitar

Rd *abbr* = **road**

RE *n abbr* (*BRIT*) = **religious education**

re [riː] *prep* con referencia a

reach [riːtʃ] *n* alcance *m*; (*of river etc*)
extensión *f* entre dos recodos ▷ *vt* alcanzar,
llegar a; (*achieve*) lograr ▷ *vi* extenderse;
within ~ al alcance (de la mano); **out of**
~ fuera del alcance; **reach out** *vt* (*hand*)
tender ▷ *vi*: **to reach out for sth** alargar *or*
tender la mano para tomar algo

react [riː'ækt] *vi* reaccionar; **reaction**
[-'ækʃən] *n* reacción *f*; **reactor** [riː'æktə*]
n (*also*: **nuclear reactor**) reactor *m* (nuclear)

read [riːd, *pt, pp* red] (*pt, pp* **~**) *vi* leer ▷ *vt*
leer; (*understand*) entender; (*study*) estudiar;
read out *vt* leer en alta voz; **reader** *n*
lector(a) *m/f*; (*BRIT: at university*) profesor(a)
m/f adjunto/a

readily ['redɪlɪ] *adv* (*willingly*) de buena
gana; (*easily*) fácilmente; (*quickly*) en seguida

reading ['riːdɪŋ] *n* lectura; (*on instrument*)
indicación *f*

ready ['redɪ] *adj* listo, preparado;
(*willing*) dispuesto; (*available*) disponible
▷ *adv*: **~-cooked** listo para comer ▷ *n*: **at**
the ~ (*Mil*) listo para tirar ▷ **to get ~** *vi*
prepararse ▷ **to get ~** *vt* preparar; **ready-**
made *adj* confeccionado

real [rɪəl] *adj* verdadero, auténtico; **in**
~ terms en términos reales; **real ale** *n*
cerveza elaborada tradicionalmente;
real estate *n* bienes *mpl* raíces; **realistic**
[-'lɪstɪk] *adj* realista; **reality** [riː'ælɪtɪ] *n*
realidad *f*; **reality TV** *n* telerrealidad *f*

realization [rɪəlaɪ'zeɪʃən] *n* comprensión
f; (*fulfilment, Comm*) realización *f*

realize ['rɪəlaɪz] *vt* (*understand*) darse
cuenta de

really ['rɪəlɪ] *adv* realmente; (*for emphasis*)
verdaderamente; (*actually*): **what ~**
happened lo que pasó en realidad; **~?** ¿de

r

veras?; **~!** (*annoyance*) ¡vamos!, ¡por favor!
realm [rɛlm] *n* reino; (*fig*) esfera
realtor ['rɪəltɔ:*] (*US*) *n* agente *mf*
inmobiliario/a
reappear [ri:ə'pɪə*] *vi* reaparecer
rear [rɪə*] *adj* trasero ▷ *n* parte *f* trasera
▷ *vt* (*cattle, family*) criar ▷ *vi* (*also:* **~
up**: *animal*) encabritarse
rearrange [ri:ə'reɪndʒ] *vt* ordenar *or*
arreglar de nuevo
rear: rear-view mirror *n* (*Aut*) (espejo)
retrovisor *m*; **rear-wheel drive** *n* tracción
f trasera
reason ['ri:zn] *n* razón *f* ▷ *vi*: **to ~ with sb**
tratar de que algn entre en razón; **it stands
to ~ that ...** es lógico que ...; **reasonable** *adj*
razonable; (*sensible*) sensato; **reasonably**
adv razonablemente; **reasoning** *n*
razonamiento, argumentos *mpl*
reassurance [ri:ə'ʃuərəns] *n* consuelo
reassure [ri:ə'ʃuə*] *vt* tranquilizar,
alentar; **to ~ sb that ...** tranquilizar a algn
asegurando que ...
rebate ['ri:beɪt] *n* (*on tax etc*) desgravación
f
rebel [*n* 'rɛbl, *vi* rɪ'bɛl] *n* rebelde *mf* ▷ *vi*
rebelarse, sublevarse; **rebellion** [rɪ'bɛljən]
n rebelión *f*, sublevación *f*; **rebellious**
[rɪ'bɛljəs] *adj* rebelde; (*child*) revoltoso
rebuild [ri:'bɪld] *vt* reconstruir
recall [*vb* rɪ'kɔ:l, *n* 'ri:kɔl] *vt* (*remember*)
recordar; (*ambassador etc*) retirar ▷ *n*
recuerdo; retirada
rec'd *abbr* (= *received*) rbdo
receipt [rɪ'si:t] *n* (*document*) recibo; (*for
parcel etc*) acuse *m* de recibo; (*act of receiving*)
recepción *f*; **receipts** *npl* (*Comm*) ingresos
mpl

▌Be careful not to translate **receipt** by the
Spanish word *receta*.

receive [rɪ'si:v] *vt* recibir; (*guest*) acoger;
(*wound*) sufrir; **receiver** *n* (*Tel*) auricular *m*;
(*Radio*) receptor *m*; (*of stolen goods*) perista
mf; (*Comm*) administrador *m* jurídico
recent ['ri:snt] *adj* reciente; **recently** *adv*
recientemente; **recently arrived** recién
llegado
reception [rɪ'sɛpʃən] *n* recepción *f*;
(*welcome*) acogida; **reception desk** *n*
recepción *f*; **receptionist** *n* recepcionista
mf
recession [rɪ'sɛʃən] *n* recesión *f*
recharge [ri:'tʃɑ:dʒ] *vt* (*battery*) recargar
recipe ['rɛsɪpɪ] *n* receta; (*for disaster,
success*) fórmula
recipient [rɪ'sɪpɪənt] *n* recibidor(a) *m/f*;
(*of letter*) destinatario/a
recital [rɪ'saɪtl] *n* recital *m*

recite [rɪ'saɪt] *vt* (*poem*) recitar
reckless ['rɛkləs] *adj* temerario,
imprudente; (*driving, driver*) peligroso
reckon ['rɛkən] *vt* calcular; (*consider*)
considerar; (*think*): **I ~ that ...** me parece
que ...
reclaim [rɪ'kleɪm] *vt* (*land, waste*)
recuperar; (*land: from sea*) rescatar; (*demand
back*) reclamar
recline [rɪ'klaɪn] *vi* reclinarse
recognition [rɛkəg'nɪʃən] *n*
reconocimiento; **transformed beyond ~**
irreconocible
recognize ['rɛkəgnaɪz] *vt*: **to ~ (by/as)**
reconocer (por/como)
recollection [rɛkə'lɛkʃən] *n* recuerdo
recommend [rɛkə'mɛnd] *vt* recomendar;
recommendation [rɛkəmɛn'deɪʃən] *n*
recomendación *f*
reconcile ['rɛkənsaɪl] *vt* (*two people*)
reconciliar; (*two facts*) compaginar; **to ~ o.s.
to sth** conformarse a algo
reconsider [ri:kən'sɪdə*] *vt* repensar
reconstruct [ri:kən'strʌkt] *vt* reconstruir
record [*n, adj* 'rɛkɔ:d, *vt* rɪ'kɔ:d] *n* (*Mus*)
disco; (*of meeting etc*) acta; (*register*) registro,
partida; (*file*) archivo; (*also:* **criminal ~**)
antecedentes *mpl*; (*written*) expediente
m; (*Sport, Comput*) récord *m* ▷ *adj* récord,
sin precedentes ▷ *vt* registrar; (*Mus: song
etc*) grabar; **in ~ time** en un tiempo
récord; **off the ~** *adj* no oficial ▷ *adv*
confidencialmente; **recorded delivery**
(*BRIT*) *n* (*Post*) entrega con acuse de recibo;
recorder *n* (*Mus*) flauta de pico; **recording**
n (*Mus*) grabación *f*; **record player** *n*
tocadiscos *m inv*
recount [rɪ'kaunt] *vt* contar
recover [rɪ'kʌvə*] *vt* recuperar ▷ *vi* (*from
illness, shock*) recuperarse; **recovery** *n*
recuperación *f*
recreate [ri:krɪ'eɪt] *vt* recrear
recreation [rɛkrɪ'eɪʃən] *n* recreo;
recreational vehicle (*US*) *n* caravan *or*
rulota pequeña; **recreational drug** droga
recreativa
recruit [rɪ'kru:t] *n* recluta *mf* ▷ *vt*
reclutar; (*staff*) contratar; **recruitment** *n*
reclutamiento
rectangle ['rɛktæŋgl] *n* rectángulo;
rectangular [-'tæŋgjulə*] *adj* rectangular
rectify ['rɛktɪfaɪ] *vt* rectificar
rector ['rɛktə*] *n* (*Rel*) párroco
recur [rɪ'kə:*] *vi* repetirse; (*pain, illness*)
producirse de nuevo; **recurring** *adj*
(*problem*) repetido, constante
recyclable [ri:'saɪkləbl] *adj* reciclable
recycle [ri:'saɪkl] *vt* reciclar

recycling [riːˈsaɪklɪŋ] *n* reciclaje

red [rɛd] *n* rojo ▷ *adj* rojo; (*hair*) pelirrojo; (*wine*) tinto; **to be in the ~** (*account*) estar en números rojos; (*business*) tener un saldo negativo; **to give sb the ~ carpet treatment** recibir a algn con todos los honores; **Red Cross** *n* Cruz *f* Roja; **redcurrant** *n* grosella roja

redeem [rɪˈdiːm] *vt* redimir; (*promises*) cumplir; (*sth in pawn*) desempeñar; (*fig. also Rel*) rescatar

red: red-haired *adj* pelirrojo; **redhead** *n* pelirrojo/a; **red-hot** *adj* candente; **red light** *n*: **to go through a red light** (*Aut*) pasar la luz roja; **red-light district** *n* barrio chino

red meat *n* carne *f* roja

reduce [rɪˈdjuːs] *vt* reducir; **to ~ sb to tears** hacer llorar a algn; **"~ speed now"** (*Aut*) "reduzca la velocidad"; **reduced** *adj* (*decreased*) reducido, rebajado; **at a reduced price** con rebaja *or* descuento; **"greatly reduced prices"** "grandes rebajas"; **reduction** [rɪˈdʌkʃən] *n* reducción *f*; (*of price*) rebaja; (*discount*) descuento; (*smaller-scale copy*) copia reducida

redundancy [rɪˈdʌndənsɪ] *n* (*dismissal*) despido; (*unemployment*) desempleo

redundant [rɪˈdʌndnt] *adj* (BRIT: *worker*) parado, sin trabajo; (*detail, object*) superfluo; **to be made ~** quedar(se) sin trabajo

reed [riːd] *n* (*Bot*) junco, caña; (*Mus*) lengüeta

reef [riːf] *n* (*at sea*) arrecife *m*

reel [riːl] *n* carrete *m*, bobina; (*of film*) rollo; (*dance*) baile escocés ▷ *vt* (*also*: **~ up**) devanar; (*also*: **~ in**) sacar ▷ *vi* (*sway*) tambalear(se)

ref [rɛf] (*inf*) *n abbr* = **referee**

refectory [rɪˈfɛktərɪ] *n* comedor *m*

refer [rɪˈfəː*] *vt* (*send: patient*) referir; (: *matter*) remitir ▷ *vi*: **to ~ to** (*allude to*) referirse a, aludir a; (*apply to*) relacionarse con; (*consult*) consultar

referee [rɛfəˈriː] *n* árbitro; (BRIT: *for job application*): **to be a ~ for sb** proporcionar referencias a algn ▷ *vt* (*match*) arbitrar en

reference [ˈrɛfrəns] *n* referencia; (*for job application*: *letter*) carta de recomendación; **with ~ to** (*Comm*: *in letter*) me remito a; **reference number** *n* número de referencia

refill [*vt* riːˈfɪl, *n* ˈriːfɪl] *vt* rellenar ▷ *n* repuesto, recambio

refine [rɪˈfaɪn] *vt* refinar; **refined** *adj* (*person*) fino; **refinery** *n* refinería

reflect [rɪˈflɛkt] *vt* reflejar ▷ *vi* (*think*) reflexionar, pensar; **it ~s badly/well on him** le perjudica/le hace honor; **reflection** [-ˈflɛkʃən] *n* (*act*) reflexión *f*; (*image*) reflejo; (*criticism*) crítica; **on reflection** pensándolo bien

reflex [ˈriːflɛks] *adj, n* reflejo

reform [rɪˈfɔːm] *n* reforma ▷ *vt* reformar

refrain [rɪˈfreɪn] *vi*: **to ~ from doing** abstenerse de hacer ▷ *n* estribillo

refresh [rɪˈfrɛʃ] *vt* refrescar; **refreshing** *adj* refrescante; **refreshments** *npl* refrescos *mpl*

refrigerator [rɪˈfrɪdʒəreɪtə*] *n* frigorífico (SP), nevera (SP), refrigerador *m* (LAM), heladera (RPL)

refuel [riːˈfjuəl] *vi* repostar (combustible)

refuge [ˈrɛfjuːdʒ] *n* refugio, asilo; **to take ~ in** refugiarse en; **refugee** [rɛfjuˈdʒiː] *n* refugiado/a

refund [*n* ˈriːfʌnd, *vb* rɪˈfʌnd] *n* reembolso ▷ *vt* devolver, reembolsar

refurbish [riːˈfəːbɪʃ] *vt* restaurar, renovar

refusal [rɪˈfjuːzəl] *n* negativa; **to have first ~ on** tener la primera opción a

refuse¹ [ˈrɛfjuːs] *n* basura

refuse² [rɪˈfjuːz] *vt* rechazar; (*invitation*) declinar; (*permission*) denegar ▷ *vi*: **to ~ to do sth** negarse a hacer algo; (*horse*) rehusar

regain [rɪˈgeɪn] *vt* recobrar, recuperar

regard [rɪˈgɑːd] *n* mirada; (*esteem*) respeto; (*attention*) consideración *f* ▷ *vt* (*consider*) considerar; **to give one's ~s to** saludar de su parte a; **"with kindest ~s"** "con muchos recuerdos"; **as ~s, with ~ to** con respecto a, en cuanto a; **regarding** *prep* con respecto a, en cuanto a; **regardless** *adv* a pesar de todo; **regardless of** sin reparar en

regenerate [rɪˈdʒɛnəreɪt] *vt* regenerar

reggae [ˈrɛgeɪ] *n* reggae *m*

regiment [ˈrɛdʒɪmənt] *n* regimiento

region [ˈriːdʒən] *n* región *f*; **in the ~ of** (*fig*) alrededor de; **regional** *adj* regional

register [ˈrɛdʒɪstə*] *n* registro ▷ *vt* registrar; (*birth*) declarar; (*car*) matricular; (*letter*) certificar; (*instrument*) marcar, indicar ▷ *vi* (*at hotel*) registrarse; (*as student*) matricularse; (*make impression*) producir impresión; **registered** *adj* (*letter, parcel*) certificado

registrar [ˈrɛdʒɪstrɑː*] *n* secretario/a (del registro civil)

registration [rɛdʒɪsˈtreɪʃən] *n* (*act*) declaración *f*; (*Aut*: *also*: **~ number**) matrícula

registry office [ˈrɛdʒɪstrɪ-] (BRIT) *n* registro civil; **to get married in a ~** casarse por lo civil

regret [rɪˈgrɛt] *n* sentimiento, pesar *m* ▷ *vt* sentir, lamentar; **regrettable** *adj* lamentable

regular [ˈrɛgjulə*] *adj* regular; (*soldier*)

profesional; (*usual*) habitual; (: *doctor*) de cabecera ▷ *n* (*client etc*) cliente/a *m/f* habitual; **regularly** *adv* con regularidad; (*often*) repetidas veces

regulate ['rɛgjuleɪt] *vt* controlar; **regulation** [-'leɪʃən] *n* (*rule*) regla, reglamento

rehabilitation ['riːəbɪlɪ'teɪʃən] *n* rehabilitación *f*

rehearsal [rɪ'həːsəl] *n* ensayo

rehearse [rɪ'həːs] *vt* ensayar

reign [reɪn] *n* reinado; (*fig*) predominio ▷ *vi* reinar; (*fig*) imperar

reimburse [riːɪm'bəːs] *vt* reembolsar

rein [reɪn] *n* (*for horse*) rienda

reincarnation [riːɪnkɑː'neɪʃən] *n* reencarnación *f*

reindeer ['reɪndɪə*] *n inv* reno

reinforce [riːɪn'fɔːs] *vt* reforzar; **reinforcements** *npl* (*Mil*) refuerzos *mpl*

reinstate [riːɪn'steɪt] *vt* reintegrar; (*tax, law*) reinstaurar

reject [*n* 'riːdʒɛkt, *vb* rɪ'dʒɛkt] *n* (*thing*) desecho ▷ *vt* rechazar; (*suggestion*) descartar; (*coin*) expulsar; **rejection** [rɪ'dʒɛkʃən] *n* rechazo

rejoice [rɪ'dʒɔɪs] *vi*: **to ~ at** *or* **over** regocijarse *or* alegrarse de

relate [rɪ'leɪt] *vt* (*tell*) contar, relatar; (*connect*) relacionar ▷ *vi* relacionarse; **related** *adj* afín; (*person*) emparentado; **related to** (*subject*) relacionado con; **relating to** *prep* referente a

relation [rɪ'leɪʃən] *n* (*person*) familiar *mf*, pariente *mf*; (*link*) relación *f*; **relations** *npl* (*relatives*) familiares *mpl*; **relationship** *n* relación *f*; (*personal*) relaciones *fpl*; (*also*: **family relationship**) parentesco

relative ['rɛlətɪv] *n* pariente *mf*, familiar *mf* ▷ *adj* relativo; **relatively** *adv* (*comparatively*) relativamente

relax [rɪ'læks] *vi* descansar; (*unwind*) relajarse ▷ *vt* (*one's grip*) soltar, aflojar; (*control*) relajar; (*mind, person*) descansar; **relaxation** [riːlæk'seɪʃən] *n* descanso; (*of rule, control*) relajamiento; (*entertainment*) diversión *f*; **relaxed** *adj* relajado; (*tranquil*) tranquilo; **relaxing** *adj* relajante

relay ['riːleɪ] *n* (*race*) carrera de relevos ▷ *vt* (*Radio, TV*) retransmitir

release [rɪ'liːs] *n* (*liberation*) liberación *f*; (*from prison*) puesta en libertad; (*of gas etc*) escape *m*; (*of film etc*) estreno; (*of record*) lanzamiento ▷ *vt* (*prisoner*) poner en libertad; (*gas*) despedir, arrojar; (*from wreckage*) soltar; (*catch, spring etc*) desenganchar; (*film*) estrenar; (*book*) publicar; (*news*) difundir

relegate ['rɛləgeɪt] *vt* relegar; (BRIT *Sport*): **to be ~d to** bajar a

relent [rɪ'lɛnt] *vi* ablandarse; **relentless** *adj* implacable

relevant ['rɛləvənt] *adj* (*fact*) pertinente; **~ to** relacionado con

reliable [rɪ'laɪəbl] *adj* (*person, firm*) de confianza, de fiar; (*method, machine*) seguro; (*source*) fidedigno

relic ['rɛlɪk] *n* (*Rel*) reliquia; (*of the past*) vestigio

relief [rɪ'liːf] *n* (*from pain, anxiety*) alivio; (*help, supplies*) socorro, ayuda; (*Art, Geo*) relieve *m*

relieve [rɪ'liːv] *vt* (*pain*) aliviar; (*bring help to*) ayudar, socorrer; (*take over from*) sustituir; (: *guard*) relevar; **to ~ sb of sth** quitar algo a algn; **to ~ o.s.** hacer sus necesidades; **relieved** *adj*: **to be relieved** sentir un gran alivio

religion [rɪ'lɪdʒən] *n* religión *f*

religious [rɪ'lɪdʒəs] *adj* religioso; **religious education** *n* educación *f* religiosa

relish ['rɛlɪʃ] *n* (*Culin*) salsa; (*enjoyment*) entusiasmo ▷ *vt* (*food etc*) saborear; (*enjoy*): **to ~ sth** hacerle mucha ilusión a algn algo

relocate [riːləu'keɪt] *vt* cambiar de lugar, mudar ▷ *vi* mudarse

reluctance [rɪ'lʌktəns] *n* renuencia

reluctant [rɪ'lʌktənt] *adj* renuente; **reluctantly** *adv* de mala gana

rely on [rɪ'laɪ-] *vt fus* depender de; (*trust*) contar con

remain [rɪ'meɪn] *vi* (*survive*) quedar; (*be left*) sobrar; (*continue*) quedar(se), permanecer; **remainder** *n* resto; **remaining** *adj* que queda(n); (*surviving*) restante(s); **remains** *npl* restos *mpl*

remand [rɪ'mɑːnd] *n*: **on ~** detenido (bajo custodia) ▷ *vt*: **to be ~ed in custody** quedar detenido bajo custodia

remark [rɪ'mɑːk] *n* comentario ▷ *vt* comentar; **remarkable** *adj* (*outstanding*) extraordinario

remarry [riː'mærɪ] *vi* volver a casarse

remedy ['rɛmədɪ] *n* remedio ▷ *vt* remediar, curar

remember [rɪ'mɛmbə*] *vt* recordar, acordarse de; (*bear in mind*) tener presente; (*send greetings to*): **~ me to him** dale recuerdos de mi parte; **Remembrance Day** *n* ≈ día en el que se recuerda a los caídos en las dos guerras mundiales

● **REMEMBRANCE DAY**

● En el Reino Unido el domingo más

próximo al 11 de noviembre se conoce como **Remembrance Sunday** o **Remembrance Day**, aniversario de la firma del armisticio de 1918 que puso fin a la Primera Guerra Mundial. Ese día, a las once de la mañana (hora en que se firmó el armisticio), se recuerda a los que murieron en las dos guerras mundiales con dos minutos de silencio ante los monumentos a los caídos. Allí se colocan coronas de amapolas, flor que también se suele llevar prendida en el pecho tras pagar un donativo destinado a los inválidos de guerra.

remind [rɪ'maɪnd] vt: **to ~ sb to do sth** recordar a algn que haga algo; **to ~ sb of sth** (of fact) recordar algo a algn; **she ~s me of her mother** me recuerda a su madre; **reminder** n notificación f; (memento) recuerdo

reminiscent [remɪ'nɪsnt] adj: **to be ~ of sth** recordar algo

remnant ['remnənt] n resto; (of cloth) retal m

remorse [rɪ'mɔːs] n remordimientos mpl

remote [rɪ'məut] adj (distant) lejano; (person) distante; **remote control** n telecontrol m; **remotely** adv remotamente; (slightly) levemente

removal [rɪ'muːvəl] n (taking away) el quitar; (BRIT: from house) mudanza; (from office: dismissal) destitución f; (Med) extirpación f; **removal man** (irreg) n (BRIT) mozo de mudanzas; **removal van** (BRIT) n camión m de mudanzas

remove [rɪ'muːv] vt quitar; (employee) destituir; (name: from list) tachar, borrar; (doubt) disipar; (abuse) suprimir, acabar con; (Med) extirpar

Renaissance [rɪ'neɪsãs] n: **the ~** el Renacimiento

rename [riː'neɪm] vt poner nuevo nombre a

render ['rendə*] vt (thanks) dar; (aid) proporcionar, prestar; (make): **to ~ sth useless** hacer algo inútil

rendezvous ['rɔndɪvuː] n cita

renew [rɪ'njuː] vt renovar; (resume) reanudar; (loan etc) prorrogar

renovate ['renəveɪt] vt renovar

renowned [rɪ'naund] adj renombrado

rent [rent] n (for house) arriendo, renta ▷ vt alquilar; **rental** n (for television, car) alquiler m

reorganize [riː'ɔːgənaɪz] vt reorganizar

rep [rep] n abbr = **representative**

repair [rɪ'peə*] n reparación f, compostura ▷ vt reparar, componer; (shoes) remendar; **in good/bad ~** en buen/mal estado; **repair kit** n caja de herramientas

repay [riː'peɪ] vt (money) devolver, reembolsar; (person) pagar; (debt) liquidar; (sb's efforts) devolver, corresponder a; **repayment** n reembolso, devolución f; (sum of money) recompensa

repeat [rɪ'piːt] n (Radio, TV) reposición f ▷ vt repetir ▷ vi repetirse; **repeatedly** adv repetidas veces; **repeat prescription** n (BRIT) receta renovada

repellent [rɪ'pelənt] adj repugnante ▷ n: **insect ~** crema or loción f anti-insectos

repercussions [riːpə'kʌʃənz] npl consecuencias fpl

repetition [repɪ'tɪʃən] n repetición f

repetitive [rɪ'petɪtɪv] adj repetitivo

replace [rɪ'pleɪs] vt (put back) devolver a su sitio; (take the place) reemplazar, sustituir; **replacement** n (act) reposición f; (thing) recambio; (person) suplente m

replay ['riːpleɪ] n (Sport) desempate m; (of tape, film) repetición f

replica ['replɪkə] n copia, reproducción f (exacta)

reply [rɪ'plaɪ] n respuesta, contestación f ▷ vi contestar, responder

report [rɪ'pɔːt] n informe m; (Press etc) reportaje m; (BRIT: also: **school ~**) boletín m escolar; (of gun) estallido ▷ vt informar de; (Press etc) hacer un reportaje sobre; (notify: accident, culprit) denunciar ▷ vi (make a report) presentar un informe; (present o.s.): **to ~ (to sb)** presentarse (ante algn); **report card** n (US, SCOTTISH) cartilla escolar; **reportedly** adv según se dice; **reporter** n periodista mf

represent [reprɪ'zent] vt representar; (Comm) ser agente de; (describe): **to ~ sth as** describir algo como; **representation** [-'teɪʃən] n representación f; **representative** n representante mf; (US Pol) diputado/a m/f ▷ adj representativo

repress [rɪ'pres] vt reprimir; **repression** [-'preʃən] n represión f

reprimand ['reprɪmɑːnd] n reprimenda ▷ vt reprender

reproduce [riːprə'djuːs] vt reproducir ▷ vi reproducirse; **reproduction** [-'dʌkʃən] n reproducción f

reptile ['reptaɪl] n reptil m

republic [rɪ'pʌblɪk] n república; **republican** adj, n republicano/a m/f

reputable ['repjutəbl] adj (make etc) de renombre

reputation [repju'teɪʃən] n reputación f

request [rɪ'kwest] n petición f; (formal)

solicitud f ▷ vt: **to ~ sth of** or **from sb**
solicitar algo a algn; **request stop** (BRIT) n
parada discrecional
require [rɪ'kwaɪə*] vt (need: person)
necesitar, tener necesidad de; (: thing,
situation) exigir; (want) pedir; **to ~ sb
to do sth** pedir a algn que haga algo;
requirement n requisito; (need) necesidad
f
resat [riː'sæt] pt, pp of **resit**
rescue ['rɛskjuː] n rescate m ▷ vt rescatar
research [rɪ'səːtʃ] n investigaciones fpl
▷ vt investigar
resemblance [rɪ'zɛmbləns] n parecido
resemble [rɪ'zɛmbl] vt parecerse a
resent [rɪ'zɛnt] vt tomar a mal;
resentful adj resentido; **resentment** n
resentimiento
reservation [rɛzə'veɪʃən] n reserva;
reservation desk (US) n (in hotel) recepción
f
reserve [rɪ'zəːv] n reserva; (Sport) suplente
mf ▷ vt (seats etc) reservar; **reserved** adj
reservado
reservoir ['rɛzəvwɑː*] n (artificial lake)
embalse m, tank; (small) depósito
residence ['rɛzɪdəns] n (formal: home)
domicilio; (length of stay) permanencia;
residence permit (BRIT) n permiso de
permanencia
resident ['rɛzɪdənt] n (of area) vecino/a;
(in hotel) huésped mf ▷ adj (population)
permanente; (doctor) residente; **residential**
[-'dɛnʃəl] adj residencial
residue ['rɛzɪdjuː] n resto
resign [rɪ'zaɪn] vt renunciar a ▷ vi
dimitir; **to ~ o.s. to** (situation) resignarse a;
resignation [rɛzɪg'neɪʃən] n dimisión f;
(state of mind) resignación f
resin ['rɛzɪn] n resina
resist [rɪ'zɪst] vt resistir, oponerse a;
resistance n resistencia
resit ['riːsɪt] (BRIT) (pt, pp **resat**) vt (exam)
volver a presentarse a; (subject) recuperar,
volver a examinarse de (SP)
resolution [rɛzə'luːʃən] n resolución f
resolve [rɪ'zɒlv] n resolución f ▷ vt
resolver ▷ vi: **to ~ to do** resolver hacer
resort [rɪ'zɔːt] n (town) centro turístico;
(recourse) recurso ▷ vi: **to ~ to** recurrir a; **in
the last ~** como último recurso
resource [rɪ'sɔːs] n recurso; **resourceful**
adj despabilado, ingenioso
respect [rɪs'pɛkt] n respeto ▷ vt respetar;
respectable adj respetable; (large: amount)
apreciable; (passable) tolerable; **respectful**
adj respetuoso; **respective** adj respectivo;
respectively adv respectivamente

respite ['rɛspaɪt] n respiro
respond [rɪs'pɒnd] vi responder; (react)
reaccionar; **response** [-'pɒns] n respuesta;
reacción f
responsibility [rɪspɒnsɪ'bɪlɪtɪ] n
responsabilidad f
responsible [rɪs'pɒnsɪbl] adj (character)
serio, formal; (job) de confianza; (liable): **~
(for)** responsable (de); **responsibly** adv con
seriedad
responsive [rɪs'pɒnsɪv] adj sensible
rest [rɛst] n descanso, reposo; (Mus, pause)
pausa, silencio; (support) apoyo; (remainder)
resto ▷ vi descansar; (be supported): **to ~ on**
descansar sobre ▷ vt: **to ~ sth on/against**
apoyar algo en or sobre/contra; **the ~ of
them** (people, objects) los demás; **it ~s with
him to ...** depende de él el que ...
restaurant ['rɛstərɒŋ] n restaurante m;
restaurant car (BRIT) n (Rail) coche-
comedor m
restless ['rɛstlɪs] adj inquieto
restoration [rɛstə'reɪʃən] n restauración
f; devolución f
restore [rɪ'stɔː*] vt (building) restaurar;
(sth stolen) devolver; (health) restablecer; (to
power) volver a poner a
restrain [rɪs'treɪn] vt (feeling) contener,
refrenar; (person): **to ~ (from doing)**
disuadir (de hacer); **restraint** n (restriction)
restricción f; (moderation) moderación f; (of
manner) reserva
restrict [rɪs'trɪkt] vt restringir, limitar;
restriction [-kʃən] n restricción f,
limitación f
rest room (US) n aseos mpl
restructure [riː'strʌktʃə*] vt
reestructurar
result [rɪ'zʌlt] n resultado ▷ vi: **to ~ in**
terminar en, tener por resultado; **as a ~ of** a
consecuencia de
resume [rɪ'zjuːm] vt reanudar ▷ vi
comenzar de nuevo

Be careful not to translate **resume** by the
Spanish word resumir.

résumé ['reɪzjuːmeɪ] n resumen m; (US)
currículum m
resuscitate [rɪ'sʌsɪteɪt] vt (Med) resucitar
retail ['riːteɪl] adj, adv al por menor;
retailer n detallista mf
retain [rɪ'teɪn] vt (keep) retener, conservar
retaliation [rɪtælɪ'eɪʃən] n represalias fpl
retarded [rɪ'tɑːdɪd] adj retrasado
retire [rɪ'taɪə*] vi (give up work) jubilarse;
(withdraw) retirarse; (go to bed) acostarse;
retired adj (person) jubilado; **retirement** n
(giving up work: state) retiro; (: act) jubilación
f

retort [rɪ'tɔːt] vi contestar

retreat [rɪ'triːt] n (place) retiro; (Mil) retirada ▷ vi retirarse

retrieve [rɪ'triːv] vt recobrar; (situation, honour) salvar; (Comput) recuperar; (error) reparar

retrospect ['rɛtrəspɛkt] n: **in ~** retrospectivamente; **retrospective** [-'spɛktɪv] adj retrospectivo; (law) retroactivo

return [rɪ'tɜːn] n (going or coming back) vuelta, regreso; (of sth stolen etc) devolución f; (Finance: from land, shares) ganancia, ingresos mpl ▷ cpd (journey) de regreso; (BRIT: ticket) de ida y vuelta; (match) de vuelta ▷ vi (person etc: come or go back) volver, regresar; (symptoms etc) reaparecer; (regain): **to ~ to** recuperar ▷ vt devolver; (favour, love etc) corresponder a; (verdict) pronunciar; (Pol: candidate) elegir; **returns** npl (Comm) ingresos mpl; **in ~ (for)** a cambio (de); **by ~ of post** a vuelta de correo; **many happy ~s (of the day)!** ¡feliz cumpleaños!; **return ticket** n (esp BRIT) billete m (SP) or boleto m (LAM) de ida y vuelta, billete m redondo (MEX)

reunion [riː'juːnɪən] n (of family) reunión f; (of two people, school) reencuentro

reunite [riːjuː'naɪt] vt reunir; (reconcile) reconciliar

revamp [riː'væmp] vt renovar

reveal [rɪ'viːl] vt revelar; **revealing** adj revelador(a)

revel ['rɛvl] vi: **to ~ in sth/in doing sth** gozar de algo/con hacer algo

revelation [rɛvə'leɪʃən] n revelación f

revenge [rɪ'vɛndʒ] n venganza; **to take ~ on** vengarse de

revenue ['rɛvənjuː] n ingresos mpl, rentas fpl

Reverend ['rɛvərənd] adj (in titles): **the ~ John Smith** (Anglican) el Reverendo John Smith; (Catholic) el Padre John Smith; (Protestant) el Pastor John Smith

reversal [rɪ'vɜːsl] n (of order) inversión f; (of direction, policy) cambio; (of decision) revocación f

reverse [rɪ'vɜːs] n (opposite) contrario; (back: of cloth) revés m; (: of coin) reverso; (: of paper) dorso; (Aut: also: **~ gear**) marcha atrás, revés m ▷ adj (order) inverso; (direction) contrario; (process) opuesto ▷ vt (decision, Aut) dar marcha atrás a; (position, function) invertir ▷ vi (BRIT Aut) dar marcha atrás; **reverse-charge call** (BRIT) n llamada a cobro revertido; **reversing lights** (BRIT) npl (Aut) luces fpl de retroceso

revert [rɪ'vɜːt] vi: **to ~ to** volver a

review [rɪ'vjuː] n (magazine, Mil) revista; (of book, film) reseña; (US: examination) repaso, examen m ▷ vt repasar, examinar; (Mil) pasar revista a; (book, film) reseñar

revise [rɪ'vaɪz] vt (manuscript) corregir; (opinion) modificar; (price, procedure) revisar ▷ vi (study) repasar; **revision** [rɪ'vɪʒən] n corrección f; modificación f; (for exam) repaso

revival [rɪ'vaɪvəl] n (recovery) reanimación f; (of interest) renacimiento; (Theatre) reestreno; (of faith) despertar m

revive [rɪ'vaɪv] vt resucitar; (custom) restablecer; (hope) despertar; (play) reestrenar ▷ vi (person) volver en sí; (business) reactivarse

revolt [rɪ'vəult] n rebelión f ▷ vi rebelarse, sublevarse ▷ vt dar asco a, repugnar; **revolting** adj asqueroso, repugnante

revolution [rɛvə'luːʃən] n revolución f; **revolutionary** adj, n revolucionario/a m/f

revolve [rɪ'vɔlv] vi dar vueltas, girar; (life, discussion): **to ~ (a)round** girar en torno a

revolver [rɪ'vɔlvə*] n revólver m

reward [rɪ'wɔːd] n premio, recompensa ▷ vt: **to ~ (for)** recompensar or premiar (por); **rewarding** adj (fig) valioso

rewind [riː'waɪnd] vt rebobinar

rewritable [riː'raɪtəbl] adj (CD, DVD) reescribible

rewrite [riː'raɪt] (pt **rewrote**, pp **rewritten**) vt reescribir

rheumatism ['ruːmətɪzəm] n reumatismo, reúma m

rhinoceros [raɪ'nɔsərəs] n rinoceronte m

rhubarb ['ruːbɑːb] n ruibarbo

rhyme [raɪm] n rima; (verse) poesía

rhythm ['rɪðm] n ritmo

rib [rɪb] n (Anat) costilla ▷ vt (mock) tomar el pelo a

ribbon ['rɪbən] n cinta; **in ~s** (torn) hecho trizas

rice [raɪs] n arroz m; **rice pudding** n arroz m con leche

rich [rɪtʃ] adj rico; (soil) fértil; (food) pesado; (: sweet) empalagoso; (abundant): **~ in** (minerals etc) rico en

rid [rɪd] (pt, pp **~**) vt: **to ~ sb of sth** librar a algn de algo; **to get ~ of** deshacerse or desembarazarse de

riddle ['rɪdl] n (puzzle) acertijo; (mystery) enigma m, misterio ▷ vt: **to be ~d with** ser lleno or plagado de

ride [raɪd] (pt **rode**, pp **ridden**) n paseo; (distance covered) viaje m, recorrido ▷ vi (as sport) montar; (go somewhere: on horse, bicycle) dar un paseo, pasearse; (travel: on bicycle, motorcycle, bus) viajar ▷ vt (a horse)

r

montar a; (*a bicycle, motorcycle*) andar en;
(*distance*) recorrer; **to take sb for a ~** (*fig*)
engañar a algn; **rider** *n* (*on horse*) jinete
mf; (*on bicycle*) ciclista *mf*; (*on motorcycle*)
motociclista *mf*
ridge [rɪdʒ] *n* (*of hill*) cresta; (*of roof*)
caballete *m*; (*wrinkle*) arruga
ridicule ['rɪdɪkjuːl] *n* irrisión *f*, burla ▷ *vt*
poner en ridículo, burlarse de; **ridiculous**
[-'dɪkjuləs] *adj* ridículo
riding ['raɪdɪŋ] *n* equitación *f*; **I like ~** me
gusta montar a caballo; **riding school** *n*
escuela de equitación
rife [raɪf] *adj*: **to be ~** ser muy común; **to be
~ with** abundar en
rifle ['raɪfl] *n* rifle *m*, fusil *m* ▷ *vt* saquear
rift [rɪft] *n* (*in clouds*) claro;
(*fig: disagreement*) desavenencia
rig [rɪg] *n* (*also*: **oil ~**: *at sea*) plataforma
petrolera ▷ *vt* (*election etc*) amañar
right [raɪt] *adj* (*correct*) correcto, exacto;
(*suitable*) indicado, debido; (*proper*)
apropiado; (*just*) justo; (*morally good*)
bueno; (*not left*) derecho ▷ *n* bueno;
(*title, claim*) derecho; (*not left*) derecha
▷ *adv* bien, correctamente; (*not left*) a la
derecha; (*exactly*): **~ now** ahora mismo ▷ *vt*
enderezar; (*correct*) corregir ▷ *excl* ¡bueno!,
¡está bien!; **to be ~** (*person*) tener razón;
(*answer*) ser correcto; **is that the ~ time?**
(*of clock*) ¿es esa la hora buena?; **by ~s** en
justicia; **on the ~** a la derecha; **to be in
the ~** tener razón; **~ away** en seguida; **~
in the middle** exactamente en el centro;
right angle *n* ángulo recto; **rightful** *adj*
legítimo; **right-hand** *adj*: **right-hand drive**
conducción *f* por la derecha; **the right-hand
side** derecha; **right-handed** *adj* diestro;
rightly *adv* correctamente, debidamente;
(*with reason*) con razón; **right of way** *n* (*on
path etc*) derecho de paso; (*Aut*) prioridad *f*;
right-wing *adj* (*Pol*) derechista
rigid ['rɪdʒɪd] *adj* rígido; (*person, ideas*)
inflexible
rigorous ['rɪgərəs] *adj* riguroso
rim [rɪm] *n* borde *m*; (*of spectacles*) aro; (*of
wheel*) llanta
rind [raɪnd] *n* (*of bacon*) corteza; (*of lemon
etc*) cáscara; (*of cheese*) costra
ring [rɪŋ] (*pt* **rang**, *pp* **rung**) *n* (*of metal*)
aro; (*on finger*) anillo; (*of people*) corro; (*of
objects*) círculo; (*gang*) banda; (*for boxing*)
cuadrilátero; (*of circus*) pista; (*bull ring*)
ruedo, plaza; (*sound of bell*) toque *m* ▷ *vi*
(*on telephone*) llamar por teléfono; (*bell*)
repicar; (*doorbell, phone*) sonar; (*also*: **~ out**)
sonar; (*ears*) zumbar ▷ *vt* (*BRITTel*) llamar,
telefonear; (*bell etc*) hacer sonar; (*doorbell*)

tocar; **to give sb a ~** (*BRITTel*) llamar or
telefonear a algn; **ring back** (*BRIT*) *vt, vi*
(*Tel*) devolver la llamada; **ring off** (*BRIT*) *vi*
(*Tel*) colgar, cortar la comunicación; **ring up**
(*BRIT*) *vt* (*Tel*) llamar, telefonear; **ringing
tone** *n* (*Tel*) tono de llamada; **ringleader**
n (*of gang*) cabecilla *m*; **ring road** (*BRIT*) *n*
carretera periférica or de circunvalación;
ringtone *n* (*on mobile*) tono de llamada
rink [rɪŋk] *n* (*also*: **ice ~**) pista de hielo
rinse [rɪns] *n* aclarado; (*dye*) tinte *m* ▷ *vt*
aclarar; (*mouth*) enjuagar
riot ['raɪət] *n* motín *m*, disturbio ▷ *vi*
amotinarse; **to run ~** desmandarse
rip [rɪp] *n* rasgón *m*, rasgadura ▷ *vt* rasgar,
desgarrar ▷ *vi* rasgarse, desgarrarse; **rip
off** *vt* (*inf: cheat*) estafar; **rip up** *vt* hacer
pedazos
ripe [raɪp] *adj* maduro
rip-off ['rɪpɔf] *n* (*inf*): **it's a ~!** ¡es una
estafa!, ¡es un timo!
ripple ['rɪpl] *n* onda, rizo; (*sound*)
murmullo ▷ *vi* rizarse
rise [raɪz] (*pt* **rose**, *pp* **risen**) *n* (*slope*)
cuesta, pendiente *f*; (*hill*) altura; (*BRIT: in
wages*) aumento; (*in prices, temperature*)
subida; (*fig: to power etc*) ascenso ▷ *vi*
subir; (*waters*) crecer; (*sun, moon*) salir;
(*person: from bed etc*) levantarse; (*also*: **~
up**: *rebel*) sublevarse; (*in rank*) ascender;
to give ~ to dar lugar or origen a; **to ~ to
the occasion** ponerse a la altura de las
circunstancias; **risen** ['rɪzn] *pp of* **rise**;
rising *adj* (*increasing: number*) creciente;
(*: prices*) en aumento or alza; (*tide*) creciente;
(*sun, moon*) naciente
risk [rɪsk] *n* riesgo, peligro ▷ *vt* arriesgar;
(*run the risk of*) exponerse a; **to take** or **run
the ~ of doing** correr el riesgo de hacer; **at
~** en peligro; **at one's own ~** bajo su propia
responsabilidad; **risky** *adj* arriesgado,
peligroso
rite [raɪt] *n* rito; **last ~s** exequias *fpl*
ritual ['rɪtjuəl] *adj* ritual ▷ *n* ritual *m*, rito
rival ['raɪvl] *n* rival *mf*; (*in business*)
competidor(a) *m/f* ▷ *adj* rival, opuesto ▷ *vt*
competir con; **rivalry** *n* competencia
river ['rɪvə*] *n* río ▷ *cpd* (*port*) de río;
(*traffic*) fluvial; **up/down ~** río arriba/abajo;
riverbank *n* orilla (del río)
rivet ['rɪvɪt] *n* roblón *m*, remache *m* ▷ *vt*
(*fig*) captar
road [rəud] *n* camino; (*motorway etc*)
carretera; (*in town*) calle *f* ▷ *cpd* (*accident*) de
tráfico; **major/minor ~** carretera principal/
secundaria; **roadblock** *n* barricada; **road
map** *n* mapa *m* de carreteras; **road rage**
n agresividad en la carretera; **road safety** *n*

seguridad f vial; **roadside** n borde m (del camino); **roadsign** n señal f de tráfico; **road tax** n (BRIT) impuesto de rodaje; **roadworks** npl obras fpl

roam [rəum] vi vagar

roar [rɔː*] n rugido; (of vehicle, storm) estruendo; (of laughter) carcajada ▷ vi rugir; hacer estruendo; **to ~ with laughter** reírse a carcajadas; **to do a ~ing trade** hacer buen negocio

roast [rəust] n carne f asada, asado ▷ vt asar; (coffee) tostar; **roast beef** n rosbif m

rob [rɔb] vt robar; **to ~ sb of sth** robar algo a algn; (fig: deprive) quitar algo a algn; **robber** n ladrón/ona m/f; **robbery** n robo

robe [rəub] n (for ceremony etc) toga; (also: **bath~**) albornoz m

robin ['rɔbɪn] n petirrojo

robot ['rəubɔt] n robot m

robust [rəu'bʌst] adj robusto, fuerte

rock [rɔk] n roca; (boulder) peña, peñasco; (US: small stone) piedrecita; (BRIT: sweet) ≈ pirulí ▷ vt (swing gently: cradle) balancear, mecer; (: child) arrullar; (shake) sacudir ▷ vi mecerse, balancearse; sacudirse; **on the ~s** (drink) con hielo; (marriage etc) en ruinas; **rock and roll** n rocanrol m; **rock climbing** n (Sport) escalada

rocket ['rɔkɪt] n cohete m; **rocking chair** ['rɔkɪŋ-] n mecedora

rocky ['rɔkɪ] adj rocoso

rod [rɔd] n vara, varilla; (also: **fishing ~**) caña

rode [rəud] pt of **ride**

rodent ['rəudnt] n roedor m

rogue [rəug] n pícaro, pillo

role [rəul] n papel m; **role-model** n modelo a imitar

roll [rəul] n rollo; (of bank notes) fajo; (also: **bread ~**) panecillo; (register, list) lista, nómina; (sound of drums etc) redoble m ▷ vt hacer rodar; (also: **~ up**: string) enrollar; (cigarette) liar; (also: **~ out**: pastry) aplanar; (flatten: road, lawn) apisonar ▷ vi rodar; (drum) redoblar; (ship) balancearse; **roll over** vi dar una vuelta; **roll up** vi (inf: arrive) aparecer ▷ vt (carpet) arrollar; (: sleeves) arremangar; **roller** n rodillo; (wheel) rueda; (for road) apisonadora; (for hair) rulo; **Rollerblades®** npl patines mpl en línea; **roller coaster** n montaña rusa; **roller skates** npl patines mpl de rueda; **roller-skating** n patinaje sobre ruedas; **to go roller-skating** ir a patinar (sobre ruedas); **rolling pin** n rodillo (de cocina)

ROM [rɔm] n abbr (Comput: = read only memory) ROM f

Roman ['rəumən] (irreg) adj romano/a;

Roman Catholic (irreg) adj, n católico/a m/f (romano/a)

romance [rə'mæns] n (love affair) amor m; (charm) lo romántico; (novel) novela de amor

Romania etc [ruː'meɪnɪə] n = **Rumania** etc

Roman numeral n número romano

romantic [rə'mæntɪk] adj romántico

Rome [rəum] n Roma

roof [ruːf] (pl **~s**) n techo; (of house) techo, tejado ▷ vt techar, poner techo a; **the ~ of the mouth** el paladar; **roof rack** n (Aut) baca, portaequipajes m inv

rook [ruk] n (bird) graja; (Chess) torre f

room [ruːm] n cuarto, habitación f; (also: **bed~**) dormitorio, recámara (MEX), pieza (SC); (in school etc) sala; (space, scope) sitio, cabida; **roommate** n compañero/a de cuarto; **room service** n servicio de habitaciones; **roomy** adj espacioso; (garment) amplio

rooster ['ruːstə*] n gallo

root [ruːt] n raíz f ▷ vi arraigarse

rope [rəup] n cuerda; (Naut) cable m ▷ vt (tie) atar or amarrar con (una) cuerda; (climbers: also: **~ together**) encordarse; (an area: also: **~ off**) acordonar; **to know the ~s** (fig) conocer los trucos (del oficio)

rose [rəuz] pt of **rise** ▷ n rosa; (shrub) rosal m; (on watering can) roseta

rosé ['rəuzeɪ] n vino rosado

rosemary ['rəuzmərɪ] n romero

rosy ['rəuzɪ] adj rosado, sonrosado; **a ~ future** un futuro prometedor

rot [rɔt] n podredumbre f; (fig: pej) tonterías fpl ▷ vt pudrir ▷ vi pudrirse

rota ['rəutə] n (sistema m de) turnos m

rotate [rəu'teɪt] vt (revolve) hacer girar, dar vueltas a; (jobs) alternar ▷ vi girar, dar vueltas

rotten ['rɔtn] adj podrido; (dishonest) corrompido; (inf: bad) pocho; **to feel ~** (ill) sentirse fatal

rough [rʌf] adj (skin, surface) áspero; (terrain) quebrado; (road) desigual; (voice) bronco; (person, manner) tosco, grosero; (weather) borrascoso; (treatment) brutal; (sea) picado; (town, area) peligroso; (cloth) basto; (plan) preliminar; (guess) aproximado ▷ n (Golf): **in the ~** en las hierbas altas; **to ~ it** vivir sin comodidades; **to sleep ~** (BRIT) pasar la noche al raso; **roughly** adv (handle) torpemente; (make) toscamente; (speak) groseramente; (approximately) aproximadamente

roulette [ruː'let] n ruleta

round [raund] adj redondo ▷ n círculo; (BRIT: of toast) rebanada; (of policeman) ronda; (of milkman) recorrido; (of doctor)

visitas *fpl*; (*game: of cards, in competition*)
partida; (*of ammunition*) cartucho; (*Boxing*)
asalto; (*of talks*) ronda ▷ *vt* (*corner*) doblar
▷ *prep* alrededor de; (*surrounding*): **~ his
neck/the table** en su cuello/alrededor de
la mesa; (*in a circular movement*): **to move ~
the room/sail ~ the world** dar una vuelta a
la habitación/circunnavegar el mundo; (*in
various directions*): **to move ~ a room/house**
moverse por toda la habitación/casa;
(*approximately*) alrededor de ▷ *adv*: **all ~** por
todos lados; **the long way ~** por el camino
menos directo; **all (the) year ~** durante
todo el año; **it's just ~ the corner** (*fig*) está
a la vuelta de la esquina; **~ the clock** *adv* las
24 horas; **to go ~ to sb's (house)** ir a casa
de algn; **to go ~ the back** pasar por atrás;
enough to go ~ bastante (para todos); **a ~
of applause** una salva de aplausos; **a ~ of
drinks/sandwiches** una ronda de bebidas/
bocadillos; **round off** *vt* (*speech etc*) acabar,
poner término a; **round up** *vt* (*cattle*)
acorralar; (*people*) reunir; (*price*) redondear;
roundabout (*BRIT*) *n* (*Aut*) isleta; (*at fair*)
tiovivo ▷ *adj* (*route, means*) indirecto; **round
trip** *n* viaje *m* de ida y vuelta; **roundup**
n rodeo; (*of criminals*) redada; (*of news*)
resumen *m*

rouse [raʊz] *vt* (*wake up*) despertar; (*stir
up*) suscitar

route [ruːt] *n* ruta, camino; (*of bus*)
recorrido; (*of shipping*) derrota

routine [ruːˈtiːn] *adj* rutinario ▷ *n* rutina;
(*Theatre*) número

row¹ [rəʊ] *n* (*line*) fila, hilera; (*Knitting*)
pasada ▷ *vi* (*in boat*) remar ▷ *vt* conducir
remando; **4 days in a ~** 4 días seguidos

row² [raʊ] *n* (*racket*) escándalo; (*dispute*)
bronca, pelea; (*scolding*) regaño ▷ *vi*
pelear(se)

rowboat [ˈrəʊbəʊt] (*US*) = **rowing boat**

rowing [ˈrəʊɪŋ] *n* remo; **rowing boat**
(*BRIT*) *n* bote *m* de remos

royal [ˈrɔɪəl] *adj* real; **royalty** *n* (*royal
persons*) familia real; (*payment to author*)
derechos *mpl* de autor

rpm *abbr* (= *revs per minute*) r.p.m.

R.S.V.P. *abbr* (= *répondez s'il vous plaôt*) SRC

Rt. Hon. *abbr* (*BRIT*) (= *Right Honourable*)
título honorífico de diputado

rub [rʌb] *vt* frotar; (*scrub*) restregar ▷ *n*: **to
give sth a ~** frotar algo; **to ~ sb up** *or* **~ sb**
(*US*) **the wrong way** entrarle algn por mal
ojo; **rub in** *vt* (*ointment*) aplicar frotando;
rub off *vi* borrarse; **rub out** *vt* borrar

rubber [ˈrʌbə*] *n* caucho, goma;
(*BRIT: eraser*) goma de borrar; **rubber band** *n*
goma, gomita; **rubber gloves** *npl* guantes

mpl de goma

rubbish [ˈrʌbɪʃ] (*BRIT*) *n* basura; (*waste*)
desperdicios *mpl*; (*fig: pej*) tonterías *fpl*; (*junk*)
pacotilla; **rubbish bin** (*BRIT*) *n* cubo o bote
m (*MEX*) o tacho (*SC*) de la basura; **rubbish
dump** (*BRIT*) *n* vertedero, basurero

rubble [ˈrʌbl] *n* escombros *mpl*

ruby [ˈruːbɪ] *n* rubí *m*

rucksack [ˈrʌksæk] *n* mochila

rudder [ˈrʌdə*] *n* timón *m*

rude [ruːd] *adj* (*impolite: person*) mal
educado; (: *word, manners*) grosero; (*crude*)
crudo; (*indecent*) indecente

ruffle [ˈrʌfl] *vt* (*hair*) despeinar; (*clothes*)
arrugar; **to get ~d** (*fig: person*) alterarse

rug [rʌg] *n* alfombra; (*BRIT: blanket*) manta

rugby [ˈrʌgbɪ] *n* rugby *m*

rugged [ˈrʌgɪd] *adj* (*landscape*)
accidentado; (*features*) robusto

ruin [ˈruːɪn] *n* ruina ▷ *vt* arruinar; (*spoil*)
estropear; **ruins** *npl* ruinas *fpl*, restos *mpl*

rule [ruːl] *n* (*norm*) norma, costumbre
f; (*regulation, ruler*) regla; (*government*)
dominio ▷ *vt* (*country, person*) gobernar
▷ *vi* gobernar; (*Law*) fallar; **as a ~** por
regla general; **rule out** *vt* excluir; **ruler** *n*
(*sovereign*) soberano; (*for measuring*) regla;
ruling *adj* (*party*) gobernante; (*class*)
dirigente ▷ *n* (*Law*) fallo, decisión *f*

rum [rʌm] *n* ron *m*

Rumania [ruːˈmeɪnɪə] *n* Rumanía;
Rumanian *adj* rumano/a ▷ *n* rumano/a
m/f; (*Ling*) rumano

rumble [ˈrʌmbl] *n* (*noise*) ruido sordo ▷ *vi*
retumbar, hacer un ruido sordo; (*stomach,
pipe*) sonar

rumour [ˈruːmə*] (*US* **rumor**) *n* rumor *m*
▷ *vt*: **it is ~ed that ...** se rumorea que ...

rump steak *n* filete *m* de lomo

run [rʌn] (*pt* **ran**, *pp* **run**) *n* (*fast pace*): **at
a ~** corriendo; (*Sport, in tights*) carrera;
(*outing*) paseo, excursión *f*; (*distance travelled*)
trayecto; (*series*) serie *f*; (*Theatre*) temporada;
(*Ski*) pista ▷ *vt* correr; (*operate: business*)
dirigir; (: *competition, course*) organizar;
(: *hotel, house*) administrar, llevar; (*Comput*)
ejecutar; (*pass: hand*) pasar; (*Press: feature*)
publicar ▷ *vi* correr; (*work: machine*)
funcionar, marchar; (*bus, train: operate*)
circular, ir; (: *travel*) ir; (*continue: play*)
seguir; (*contract*) ser válido; (*flow: river*) fluir;
(*colours, washing*) desteñirse; (*in election*)
ser candidato; **there was a ~ on** (*meat,
tickets*) hubo mucha demanda de; **in the
long ~** a la larga; **on the ~** en fuga; **I'll ~ you
to the station** te llevaré a la estación (en
coche); **to ~ a risk** correr un riesgo; **to ~ a
bath** llenar la bañera; **run after** *vt fus* (*to*

catch up) correr tras; (*chase*) perseguir; **run away** vi huir; **run down** vt (*production*) ir reduciendo; (*factory*) ir restringiendo la producción en; (*car*) atropellar; (*criticize*) criticar; **to be run down** (*person: tired*) estar debilitado; **run into** vt fus (*meet: person, trouble*) tropezar con; (*collide with*) chocar con; **run off** vt (*water*) dejar correr; (*copies*) sacar ▷ vi huir corriendo; **run out** vi (*person*) salir corriendo; (*liquid*) irse; (*lease*) caducar, vencer; (*money etc*) acabarse; **run out of** vt fus quedar sin; **run over** vt (*Aut*) atropellar ▷ vt fus (*revise*) repasar; **run through** vt fus (*instructions*) repasar; **run up** vt (*debt*) contraer; **to run up against** (*difficulties*) tropezar con; **runaway** adj (*horse*) desbocado; (*truck*) sin frenos; (*child*) escapado de casa

rung [rʌŋ] pp of **ring** ▷ n (*of ladder*) escalón m, peldaño

runner ['rʌnə*] n (*in race: person*) corredor(a) m/f; (*: horse*) caballo; (*on sledge*) patín m; **runner bean** (BRIT) n ≈ judía verde; **runner-up** n subcampeón/ona m/f

running ['rʌnɪŋ] n (*sport*) atletismo; (*of business*) administración f ▷ adj (*water, costs*) corriente; (*commentary*) continuo; **to be in/out of the ~ for sth** tener/no tener posibilidades de ganar algo; **6 days ~** 6 días seguidos

runny ['rʌnɪ] adj fluido; (*nose, eyes*) gastante

run-up ['rʌnʌp] n: **~ to** (*election etc*) período previo a

runway ['rʌnweɪ] n (*Aviat*) pista de aterrizaje

rupture ['rʌptʃə*] n (*Med*) hernia ▷ vt: **to ~ o.s** causarse una hernia

rural ['ruərl] adj rural

rush [rʌʃ] n ímpetu m; (*hurry*) prisa; (*Comm*) demanda repentina; (*current*) corriente f fuerte; (*of feeling*) torrente m; (*Bot*) junco ▷ vt apresurar; (*work*) hacer de prisa ▷ vi correr, precipitarse; **rush hour** n horas fpl punta

Russia ['rʌʃə] n Rusia; **Russian** adj ruso/a ▷ n ruso/a m/f; (*Ling*) ruso

rust [rʌst] n herrumbre f, moho ▷ vi oxidarse

rusty ['rʌstɪ] adj oxidado

ruthless ['ru:θlɪs] adj despiadado

RV (US) n abbr = **recreational vehicle**

rye [raɪ] n centeno

S

Sabbath ['sæbəθ] n domingo; (*Jewish*) sábado

sabotage ['sæbətɑːʒ] n sabotaje m ▷ vt sabotear

saccharin(e) ['sækərɪn] n sacarina

sachet ['sæʃeɪ] n sobrecito

sack [sæk] n (*bag*) saco, costal m ▷ vt (*dismiss*) despedir; (*plunder*) saquear; **to get the ~** ser despedido

sacred ['seɪkrɪd] adj sagrado, santo

sacrifice ['sækrɪfaɪs] n sacrificio ▷ vt sacrificar

sad [sæd] adj (*unhappy*) triste; (*deplorable*) lamentable

saddle ['sædl] n silla (de montar); (*of cycle*) sillín m ▷ vt (*horse*) ensillar; **to be ~d with sth** (*inf*) quedar cargado con algo

sadistic [sə'dɪstɪk] adj sádico

sadly ['sædlɪ] adv lamentablemente; **to be ~ lacking in** estar por desgracia carente de

sadness ['sædnɪs] n tristeza

s.a.e. abbr (= *stamped addressed envelope*) sobre con las propias señas de uno y con sello

safari [sə'fɑːrɪ] n safari m

safe [seɪf] adj (*out of danger*) fuera de peligro; (*not dangerous, sure*) seguro; (*unharmed*) ileso ▷ n caja de caudales, caja fuerte; **~ and sound** sano y salvo; **(just) to be on the ~ side** para mayor seguridad; **safely** adv seguramente, con seguridad; **to arrive safely** llegar bien; **safe sex** n sexo seguro or sin riesgo

safety ['seɪftɪ] n seguridad f; **safety belt** n cinturón m (de seguridad); **safety pin** n imperdible m, seguro (MEX), alfiler m de gancho (SC)

saffron ['sæfrən] n azafrán m

sag [sæg] vi aflojarse

sage [seɪdʒ] n (*herb*) salvia; (*man*) sabio

Sagittarius [sædʒɪ'tɛərɪəs] n Sagitario

Sahara [sə'hɑːrə] n: **the ~ (Desert)** el

(desierto del) Sáhara

said [sɛd] *pt*, *pp of* **say**

sail [seɪl] *n* (*on boat*) vela; (*trip*): **to go for a ~** dar un paseo en barco ▷ *vt* (*boat*) gobernar ▷ *vi* (*travel: ship*) navegar; (*Sport*) hacer vela; (*begin voyage*) salir; **they ~ed into Copenhagen** arribaron a Copenhague; **sailboat** (*US*) *n* = **sailing boat**; **sailing** *n* (*Sport*) vela; **to go sailing** hacer vela; **sailing boat** *n* barco de vela; **sailor** *n* marinero, marino

saint [seɪnt] *n* santo

sake [seɪk] *n*: **for the ~ of** por

salad ['sæləd] *n* ensalada; **salad cream** (*BRIT*) *n* (especie f de) mayonesa; **salad dressing** *n* aliño

salami [sə'lɑːmɪ] *n* salami *m*, salchichón *m*

salary ['sælərɪ] *n* sueldo

sale [seɪl] *n* venta; (*at reduced prices*) liquidación f, saldo; (*auction*) subasta; **sales** *npl* (*total amount sold*) ventas *fpl*, facturación f; **"for ~"** "se vende"; **on ~** en venta; **on ~ or return** (*goods*) venta por reposición; **sales assistant** (*US*), **sales clerk** *n* dependiente/a *m/f*; **salesman/woman** (*irreg*) *n* (*in shop*) dependiente/a *m/f*; **salesperson** (*irreg*) *n* vendedor(a) *m/f*, dependiente/a *m/f*; **sales rep** *n* representante *mf*, agente *mf* comercial

saline ['seɪlaɪn] *adj* salino

saliva [sə'laɪvə] *n* saliva

salmon ['sæmən] *n inv* salmón *m*

salon ['sælɔn] *n* (*hairdressing salon*) peluquería; (*beauty salon*) salón *m* de belleza

saloon [sə'luːn] *n* (*US*) bar *m*, taberna; (*BRIT Aut*) coche *m* (de) turismo; (*ship's lounge*) cámara, salón *m*

salt [sɔlt] *n* sal f ▷ *vt* salar; (*put salt on*) poner sal en; **saltwater** *adj* de agua salada; **salty** *adj* salado

salute [sə'luːt] *n* saludo; (*of guns*) salva ▷ *vt* saludar

salvage ['sælvɪdʒ] *n* (*saving*) salvamento, recuperación f; (*things saved*) objetos *mpl* salvados ▷ *vt* salvar

Salvation Army [sæl'veɪʃən-] *n* Ejército de Salvación

same [seɪm] *adj* mismo ▷ *pron*: **the ~** el(la) mismo/a, los(las) mismos/as; **the ~ book as** el mismo libro que; **at the ~ time** (*at the same moment*) al mismo tiempo; (*yet*) sin embargo; **all** *or* **just the ~** sin embargo, aun así; **to do the ~ (as sb)** hacer lo mismo (que algn); **the ~ to you!** ¡igualmente!

sample ['sɑːmpl] *n* muestra ▷ *vt* (*food*) probar; (*wine*) catar

sanction ['sæŋkʃən] *n* aprobación f ▷ *vt* sancionar; aprobar; **sanctions** *npl* (*Pol*)

sanciones *fpl*

sanctuary ['sæŋktjuərɪ] *n* santuario; (*refuge*) asilo, refugio; (*for wildlife*) reserva

sand [sænd] *n* arena; (*beach*) playa ▷ *vt* (*also*: **~ down**) lijar

sandal ['sændl] *n* sandalia

sand: sandbox (*US*) *n* = **sandpit**; **sandcastle** *n* castillo de arena; **sand dune** *n* duna; **sandpaper** *n* papel *m* de lija; **sandpit** *n* (*for children*) cajón *m* de arena; **sands** *npl* playa *sg* de arena; **sandstone** ['sændstəun] *n* piedra arenisca

sandwich ['sændwɪtʃ] *n* sandwich *m* ▷ *vt* intercalar; **~ed between** apretujado entre; **cheese/ham ~** sandwich de queso/jamón

sandy ['sændɪ] *adj* arenoso; (*colour*) rojizo

sane [seɪn] *adj* cuerdo; (*sensible*) sensato

▌ Be careful not to translate **sane** by the Spanish word *sano*.

sang [sæŋ] *pt of* **sing**

sanitary towel (*US* **sanitary napkin**) *n* paño higiénico, compresa

sanity ['sænɪtɪ] *n* cordura; (*of judgment*) sensatez f

sank [sæŋk] *pt of* **sink**

Santa Claus [sæntə'klɔːz] *n* San Nicolás, Papá Noel

sap [sæp] *n* (*of plants*) savia ▷ *vt* (*strength*) minar, agotar

sapphire ['sæfaɪə*] *n* zafiro

sarcasm ['sɑːkæzm] *n* sarcasmo

sarcastic [sɑː'kæstɪk] *adj* sarcástico

sardine [sɑː'diːn] *n* sardina

SASE (*US*) *n abbr* (= *self-addressed stamped envelope*) *sobre con las propias señas de uno y con sello*

Sat. *abbr* (= *Saturday*) sáb

sat [sæt] *pt*, *pp of* **sit**

satchel ['sætʃl] *n* (*child's*) mochila, cartera (*SP*)

satellite ['sætəlaɪt] *n* satélite *m*; **satellite dish** *n* antena de televisión por satélite; **satellite television** *n* televisión f vía satélite

satin ['sætɪn] *n* raso ▷ *adj* de raso

satire ['sætaɪə*] *n* sátira

satisfaction [sætɪs'fækʃən] *n* satisfacción f

satisfactory [sætɪs'fæktərɪ] *adj* satisfactorio

satisfied ['sætɪsfaɪd] *adj* satisfecho; **to be ~ (with sth)** estar satisfecho (de algo)

satisfy ['sætɪsfaɪ] *vt* satisfacer; (*convince*) convencer

Saturday ['sætədɪ] *n* sábado

sauce [sɔːs] *n* salsa; (*sweet*) crema; jarabe *m*; **saucepan** *n* cacerola, olla

saucer ['sɔːsə*] *n* platillo; **Saudi Arabia** *n*

Arabia Saudí or Saudita

sauna ['sɔːnə] n sauna

sausage ['sɔsɪdʒ] n salchicha; **sausage roll** n empanadita de salchicha

sautéed ['səuteɪd] adj salteado

savage ['sævɪdʒ] adj (cruel, fierce) feroz, furioso; (primitive) salvaje ▷ n salvaje mf ▷ vt (attack) embestir

save [seɪv] vt (rescue) salvar, rescatar; (money, time) ahorrar; (put by, keep: seat) guardar; (Comput) salvar (y guardar); (avoid: trouble) evitar; (Sport) parar ▷ vi (also: ~ **up**) ahorrar ▷ n (Sport) parada ▷ prep salvo, excepto

savings ['seɪvɪŋz] npl ahorros mpl; **savings account** n cuenta de ahorros; **savings and loan association** (US) n sociedad f de ahorro y préstamo

savoury ['seɪvərɪ] (US **savory**) adj sabroso; (dish: not sweet) salado

saw [sɔː] (pt ~**ed**, pp ~**ed** or ~**n**) pt of **see** ▷ n (tool) sierra ▷ vt serrar; **sawdust** n (a) serrín m

sawn [sɔːn] pp of **saw**

saxophone ['sæksəfəun] n saxófono

say [seɪ] (pt, pp **said**) n: **to have one's ~** expresar su opinión ▷ vt decir; **to have a** or **some ~ in sth** tener voz or tener que ver en algo; **to ~ yes/no** decir que sí/no; **could you ~ that again?** ¿podría repetir eso?; **that is to ~** es decir; **that goes without ~ing** ni que decir tiene; **saying** n dicho, refrán m

scab [skæb] n costra; (pej) esquirol m

scaffolding ['skæfəldɪŋ] n andamio, andamiaje m

scald [skɔːld] n escaldadura ▷ vt escaldar

scale [skeɪl] n (gen, Mus) escala; (of fish) escama; (of salaries, fees etc) escalafón m ▷ vt (mountain) escalar; (tree) trepar; **scales** npl (for weighing: small) balanza; (: large) báscula; **on a large ~** en gran escala; **~ of charges** tarifa, lista de precios

scallion ['skæljən] (US) n cebolleta

scallop ['skɔləp] n (Zool) venera; (Sewing) festón m

scalp [skælp] n cabellera ▷ vt escalpar

scalpel ['skælpl] n bisturí m

scam [skæm] n (inf) estafa, timo

scampi ['skæmpɪ] npl gambas fpl

scan [skæn] vt (examine) escudriñar; (glance at quickly) dar un vistazo a; (TV, Radar) explorar, registrar ▷ n (Med): **to have a ~** pasar por el escáner

scandal ['skændl] n escándalo; (gossip) chismes mpl

Scandinavia [skændɪ'neɪvɪə] n Escandinavia; **Scandinavian** adj, n escandinavo/a m/f

scanner ['skænə*] n (Radar, Med) escáner m

scapegoat ['skeɪpgəut] n cabeza de turco, chivo expiatorio

scar [skɑː] n cicatriz f; (fig) señal f ▷ vt dejar señales en

scarce [skɛəs] adj escaso; **to make o.s. ~** (inf) esfumarse; **scarcely** adv apenas

scare [skɛə*] n susto, sobresalto; (panic) pánico ▷ vt asustar, espantar; **to ~ sb stiff** dar a algn un susto de muerte; **bomb ~** amenaza de bomba; **scarecrow** n espantapájaros m inv; **scared** adj: **to be scared** estar asustado

scarf [skɑːf] (pl ~**s** or **scarves**) n (long) bufanda; (square) pañuelo

scarlet ['skɑːlɪt] adj escarlata

scarves [skɑːvz] npl of **scarf**

scary ['skɛərɪ] (inf) adj espeluznante

scatter ['skætə*] vt (spread) esparcir, desparramar; (put to flight) dispersar ▷ vi desparramarse; dispersarse

scenario [sɪ'nɑːrɪəu] n (Theatre) argumento; (Cinema) guión m; (fig) escenario

scene [siːn] n (Theatre, fig etc) escena; (of crime etc) escenario; (view) panorama m; (fuss) escándalo; **scenery** n (Theatre) decorado; (landscape) paisaje m

▌ Be careful not to translate **scenery** by the Spanish word escenario.

scenic adj pintoresco

scent [sɛnt] n perfume m, olor m; (fig: track) rastro, pista

sceptical ['skɛptɪkl] adj escéptico

schedule ['ʃɛdjuːl] (US) ['skɛdjuːl] n (timetable) horario; (of events) programa m; (list) lista ▷ vt (visit) fijar la hora de; **to arrive on ~** llegar a la hora debida; **to be ahead of/behind ~** estar adelantado/en retraso; **scheduled flight** n vuelo regular

scheme [skiːm] n (plan) plan m, proyecto; (plot) intriga; (arrangement) disposición f; (pension scheme etc) sistema m ▷ vi (intrigue) intrigar

schizophrenic [skɪtzə'frɛnɪk] adj esquizofrénico

scholar ['skɔlə*] n (pupil) alumno/a; (learned person) sabio/a, erudito/a; **scholarship** n erudición f; (grant) beca

school [skuːl] n escuela, colegio; (in university) facultad f ▷ cpd escolar; **schoolbook** n libro de texto; **schoolboy** n alumno; **school children** npl alumnos mpl; **schoolgirl** n alumna; **schooling** n enseñanza; **schoolteacher** n (primary) maestro/a; (secondary) profesor(a) m/f

science ['saɪəns] n ciencia; **science**

fiction n ciencia-ficción f; **scientific**
[-'tɪfɪk] adj científico; **scientist** n
científico/a
sci-fi ['saɪfaɪ] n abbr (inf) = **science fiction**
scissors ['sɪzəz] npl tijeras fpl; **a pair of ~**
unas tijeras
scold [skəʊld] vt regañar
scone [skɔn] n pastel de pan
scoop [sku:p] n (for flour etc) pala; (Press)
exclusiva
scooter ['sku:tə*] n moto f; (toy) patinete
m
scope [skəʊp] n (of plan) ámbito; (of
person) competencia; (opportunity) libertad
f (de acción)
scorching ['skɔ:tʃɪŋ] adj (heat, sun)
abrasador(a)
score [skɔ:*] n (points etc) puntuación f;
(Mus) partitura; (twenty) veintena ▷ vt (goal,
point) ganar; (mark) rayar; (achieve: success)
conseguir ▷ vi marcar un tanto; (Football)
marcar (un) gol; (keep score) llevar el tanteo;
~s of (lots of) decenas de; **on that ~** en lo
que se refiere a eso; **to ~ 6 out of 10** obtener
una puntuación de 6 sobre 10; **score out** vt
tachar; **scoreboard** n marcador m; **scorer**
n marcador m; (keeping score) encargado/a
del marcador
scorn [skɔ:n] n desprecio
Scorpio ['skɔ:pɪəʊ] n Escorpión m
scorpion ['skɔ:pɪən] n alacrán m
Scot [skɔt] n escocés/esa m/f
Scotch tape® (us) n cinta adhesiva, celo,
scotch® m
Scotland ['skɔtlənd] n Escocia
Scots [skɔts] adj escocés/esa; **Scotsman**
(irreg) n escocés; **Scotswoman** (irreg) n
escocésa; **Scottish** ['skɔtɪʃ] adj escocés/
esa; **Scottish Parliament** n Parlamento
escocés
scout [skaʊt] n (Mil: also: **boy ~**)
explorador m; **girl ~** (us) niña exploradora
scowl [skaʊl] vi fruncir el ceño; **to ~ at sb**
mirar con ceño a algn
scramble ['skræmbl] n (climb) subida
(difícil); (struggle) pelea ▷ vi: **to ~ through/
out** abrirse paso/salir con dificultad; **to ~
for** pelear por; **scrambled eggs** npl huevos
mpl revueltos
scrap [skræp] n (bit) pedacito; (fig) pizca;
(fight) riña, bronca; (also: **~ iron**) chatarra,
hierro viejo ▷ vt (discard) desechar,
descartar ▷ vi reñir, armar una bronca;
scraps npl (waste) sobras fpl, desperdicios
mpl; **scrapbook** n álbum m de recortes
scrape [skreɪp] n: **to get into a ~** meterse
en un lío ▷ vt raspar; (skin etc) rasguñar;
(scrape against) rozar ▷ vi: **to ~ through**

(exam) aprobar por los pelos; **scrap paper** n
pedazos mpl de papel
scratch [skrætʃ] n rasguño; (from claw)
arañazo ▷ vt (paint, car) rayar; (with claw,
nail) rasguñar, arañar; (rub: nose etc) rascarse
▷ vi rascarse; **to start from ~** partir de cero;
to be up to ~ cumplir con los requisitos;
scratch card n (BRIT) tarjeta f de "rasque
y gane"
scream [skri:m] n chillido ▷ vi chillar
screen [skri:n] n (Cinema, TV) pantalla;
(movable barrier) biombo ▷ vt (conceal)
tapar; (from the wind etc) proteger; (film)
proyectar; (candidates etc) investigar a;
screening n (Med) investigación f médica;
screenplay n guión m; **screen saver** n
(Comput) protector m de pantalla
screw [skru:] n tornillo ▷ vt (also: **~
in**) atornillar; **screw up** vt (paper etc)
arrugar; **to screw up one's eyes** arrugar el
entrecejo; **screwdriver** n destornillador m
scribble ['skrɪbl] n garabatos mpl ▷ vt, vi
garabatear
script [skrɪpt] n (Cinema etc) guión m;
(writing) escritura, letra
scroll [skrəʊl] n rollo
scrub [skrʌb] n (land) maleza ▷ vt fregar,
restregar; (inf: reject) cancelar, anular
scruffy ['skrʌfɪ] adj desaliñado, piojoso
scrum(mage) ['skrʌm(mɪdʒ)] n (Rugby)
melée f
scrutiny ['skru:tɪnɪ] n escrutinio, examen
m
scuba diving ['sku:bə'daɪvɪŋ] n
submarinismo
sculptor ['skʌlptə*] n escultor(a) m/f
sculpture ['skʌlptʃə*] n escultura
scum [skʌm] n (on liquid) espuma;
(pej: people) escoria
scurry ['skʌrɪ] vi correr; **to ~ off**
escabullirse
sea [si:] n mar m ▷ cpd de mar, marítimo;
by ~ (travel) en barco; **on the ~** (boat) en el
mar; (town) junto al mar; **to be all at ~** (fig)
estar despistado; **out to ~**, **at ~** en alta
mar; **seafood** n mariscos mpl; **sea front** n
paseo marítimo; **seagull** n gaviota
seal [si:l] n (animal) foca; (stamp) sello ▷ vt
(close) cerrar; **seal off** vt (area) acordonar
sea level n nivel m del mar
seam [si:m] n costura; (of metal) juntura;
(of coal) veta, filón m
search [sə:tʃ] n (for person, thing) busca,
búsqueda; (Comput) búsqueda; (inspection: of
sb's home) registro ▷ vt (look in) buscar en;
(examine) examinar; (person, place) registrar
▷ vi: **to ~ for** buscar; **in ~ of** en busca de;
search engine n (Comput) buscador m;

search party n pelotón m de salvamento
sea: seashore n playa, orilla del mar;
seasick adj mareado; **seaside** n playa,
orilla del mar; **seaside resort** n centro
turístico costero

season ['siːzn] n (of year) estación f;
(sporting etc) temporada; (of films etc)
ciclo ▷ vt (food) sazonar; **in/out of ~** en
sazón/fuera de temporada; **seasonal** adj
estacional; **seasoning** n condimento,
aderezo; **season ticket** n abono

seat [siːt] n (in bus, train) asiento; (chair)
silla; (Parliament) escaño; (buttocks) culo,
trasero; (of trousers) culera ▷ vt sentar;
(have room for) tener cabida para; **to be
~ed** sentarse; **seat belt** n cinturón m de
seguridad; **seating** n asientos mpl

sea: sea water n agua del mar; **seaweed** n
alga marina

sec. abbr = **second(s)**

secluded [sɪ'kluːdɪd] adj retirado

second ['sɛkənd] adj segundo ▷ adv en
segundo lugar ▷ n segundo; (Aut: also:
~ gear) segunda; (Comm) artículo con
algún desperfecto; (BRIT Scol: degree) título
de licenciado con calificación de notable
▷ vt (motion) apoyar; **secondary** adj
secundario; **secondary school** n escuela
secundaria; **second-class** adj de segunda
clase ▷ adv (Rail) en segunda; **secondhand**
adj de segunda mano, usado; **secondly**
adv en segundo lugar; **second-rate** adj de
segunda categoría; **second thoughts: to
have second thoughts** cambiar de
opinión; **on second thoughts** or **thought**
(US) pensándolo bien

secrecy ['siːkrəsɪ] n secreto

secret ['siːkrɪt] adj, n secreto; **in ~** en
secreto

secretary ['sɛkrətərɪ] n secretario/a; **S~
of State (for)** (BRIT Pol) Ministro (de)

secretive ['siːkrətɪv] adj reservado,
sigiloso

secret service n servicio secreto

sect [sɛkt] n secta

section ['sɛkʃən] n sección f; (part) parte f;
(of document) artículo; (of opinion) sector m;
(cross-section) corte m transversal

sector ['sɛktə*] n sector m

secular ['sɛkjulə*] adj secular, seglar

secure [sɪ'kjuə*] adj seguro; (firmly fixed)
firme, fijo ▷ vt (fix) asegurar, afianzar; (get)
conseguir

security [sɪ'kjuərɪtɪ] n seguridad f; (for
loan) fianza; (: object) prenda; **securities** npl
(Comm) valores mpl, títulos mpl; **security
guard** n guardia m/f de seguridad

sedan [sɪ'dæn] (US) n (Aut) sedán m

sedate [sɪ'deɪt] adj tranquilo ▷ vt tratar
con sedantes

sedative ['sɛdɪtɪv] n sedante m, sedativo

seduce [sɪ'djuːs] vt seducir; **seductive**
[-'dʌktɪv] adj seductor(a)

see [siː] (pt **saw**, pp **seen**) vt ver;
(accompany): **to ~ sb to the door** acompañar
a algn a la puerta; (understand) ver,
comprender ▷ vi ver ▷ n (arz)obispado; **to
~ that** (ensure) asegurar que; **~ you soon!**
¡hasta pronto!; **see off** vt despedir; **see
out** vt (take to the door) acompañar hasta la
puerta; **see through** vt fus (fig) calar ▷ vt
(plan) llevar a cabo; **see to** vt fus atender a,
encargarse de

seed [siːd] n semilla; (in fruit) pepita;
(fig: gen pl) germen m; (Tennis etc)
preseleccionado/a; **to go to ~** (plant)
granar; (fig) descuidarse

seeing ['siːɪŋ] conj: **~ (that)** visto que, en
vista de que

seek [siːk] (pt, pp **sought**) vt buscar; (post)
solicitar

seem [siːm] vi parecer; **there ~s to
be ...** parece que hay ...; **seemingly** adv
aparentemente, según parece

seen [siːn] pp of **see**

seesaw ['siːsɔː] n subibaja

segment ['sɛgmənt] n (part) sección f; (of
orange) gajo

segregate ['sɛgrɪgeɪt] vt segregar

seize [siːz] vt (grasp) agarrar, asir;
(take possession of) secuestrar; (: territory)
apoderarse de; (opportunity) aprovecharse de

seizure ['siːʒə*] n (Med) ataque m; (Law. of
power) incautación f

seldom ['sɛldəm] adv rara vez

select [sɪ'lɛkt] adj selecto, escogido
▷ vt escoger, elegir; (Sport) seleccionar;
selection n selección f, elección f; (Comm)
surtido; **selective** adj selectivo

self [sɛlf] (pl **selves**) n uno mismo; **the
~** el yo ▷ prefix auto...; **self-assured** adj
seguro de sí mismo; **self-catering** (BRIT)
adj (flat etc) con cocina; **self-centred** (US
self-centered) adj egocéntrico; **self-
confidence** n confianza en sí mismo;
self-confident adj seguro de sí (mismo),
lleno de confianza en sí mismo; **self-
conscious** adj cohibido; **self-contained**
(BRIT) adj (flat) con entrada particular;
self-control n autodominio; **self-defence**
(US **self-defense**) n defensa propia; **self-
drive** adj (BRIT) sin chofer or (SP) chófer;
self-employed adj que trabaja por cuenta
propia; **self-esteem** n amor m propio;
self-indulgent adj autocomplaciente;
self-interest n egoísmo; **selfish** adj

egoísta; **self-pity** n lástima de sí mismo;
self-raising [sɛlfˈreɪzɪŋ] (US **self-rising**)
adj: **self-raising flour** harina con levadura;
self-respect n amor m propio; **self-service**
adj de autoservicio

sell [sɛl] (pt, pp **sold**) vt vender ▷ vi
venderse; to ~ **at** or **for £10** venderse a 10
libras; **sell off** vt liquidar; **sell out** vi: **to
sell out of tickets/milk** vender todas las
entradas/toda la leche; **sell-by date** n
fecha de caducidad; **seller** n vendedor(a)
m/f

Sellotape® [ˈsɛləʊteɪp] (BRIT) n celo (SP),
cinta Scotch® (LAM) or Dúrex® (MEX, ARG)

selves [sɛlvz] npl of **self**

semester [sɪˈmɛstə*] (US) n semestre m

semi... [ˈsɛmɪ] prefix semi..., medio...;
semicircle n semicírculo; **semidetached
(house)** n (casa) semiseparada; **semi-final**
n semi-final m

seminar [ˈsɛmɪnɑː*] n seminario

semi-skimmed [sɛmɪˈskɪmd] adj
semidesnatado; **semi-skimmed (milk)** n
leche semidesnatada

senate [ˈsɛnɪt] n senado; **the S~** (US) el
Senado; **senator** n senador(a) m/f

send [sɛnd] (pt, pp **sent**) vt mandar, enviar;
(signal) transmitir; **send back** vt devolver;
send for vt fus mandar traer; **send in** vt
(report, application, resignation) mandar; **send
off** vt (goods) despachar; (BRIT Sport: player)
expulsar; **send on** vt (letter, luggage)
remitir; (person) mandar; **send out** vt
(invitation) mandar; (signal) emitir; **send up**
vt (person, price) hacer subir; (BRIT: parody)
parodiar; **sender** n remitente mf; **send-off**
n: **a good send-off** una buena despedida

senile [ˈsiːnaɪl] adj senil

senior [ˈsiːnɪə*] adj (older) mayor, más
viejo; (: on staff) de más antigüedad; (of
higher rank) superior; **senior citizen** n
persona de la tercera edad; **senior high
school** (US) n ≈ instituto de enseñanza
media; see also **high school**

sensation [sɛnˈseɪʃən] n sensación f;
sensational adj sensacional

sense [sɛns] n (faculty, meaning) sentido;
(feeling) sensación f; (good sense) sentido
común, juicio ▷ vt sentir, percibir; **it
makes ~** tiene sentido; **senseless** adj
estúpido, insensato; (unconscious) sin
conocimiento; **sense of humour** (BRIT) n
sentido del humor

sensible [ˈsɛnsɪbl] adj sensato; (reasonable)
razonable, lógico

▌Be careful not to translate **sensible** by
the Spanish word sensible.

sensitive [ˈsɛnsɪtɪv] adj sensible; (touchy)
susceptible

sensual [ˈsɛnsjuəl] adj sensual

sensuous [ˈsɛnsjuəs] adj sensual

sent [sɛnt] pt, pp of **send**

sentence [ˈsɛntns] n (Ling) oración f; (Law)
sentencia, fallo ▷ vt: **to ~ sb to death/
to 5 years (in prison)** condenar a algn a
muerte/a 5 años de cárcel

sentiment [ˈsɛntɪmənt] n sentimiento;
(opinion) opinión f; **sentimental** [-ˈmɛntl]
adj sentimental

Sep. abbr (= September) sep., set.

separate [adj ˈsɛprɪt, vb ˈsɛpəreɪt] adj
separado; (distinct) distinto ▷ vt separar;
(part) dividir ▷ vi separarse; **separately**
adv por separado; **separates** npl (clothes)
coordinados mpl; **separation** [-ˈreɪʃən] n
separación f

September [sɛpˈtɛmbə*] n se(p)tiembre
m

septic [ˈsɛptɪk] adj séptico; **septic tank** n
fosa séptica

sequel [ˈsiːkwl] n consecuencia,
resultado; (of story) continuación f

sequence [ˈsiːkwəns] n sucesión f, serie f;
(Cinema) secuencia

sequin [ˈsiːkwɪn] n lentejuela

Serb [sɜːb] adj, n = **Serbian**

Serbian [ˈsɜːbɪən] adj serbio ▷ n serbio/a;
(Ling) serbio

sergeant [ˈsɑːdʒənt] n sargento

serial [ˈsɪərɪəl] n (TV) telenovela, serie
f televisiva; (Book) serie f; **serial killer** n
asesino/a múltiple; **serial number** n
número de serie

series [ˈsɪərɪːs] n inv serie f

serious [ˈsɪərɪəs] adj serio; (grave) grave;
seriously adv en serio; (ill, wounded etc)
gravemente

sermon [ˈsɜːmən] n sermón m

servant [ˈsɜːvənt] n servidor(a) m/f; (house
servant) criado/a

serve [sɜːv] vt servir; (customer) atender;
(train) pasar por; (apprenticeship) hacer;
(prison term) cumplir ▷ vi (at table) servir;
(Tennis) sacar; **to ~ as/for/to do** servir de/
para/para hacer ▷ n (Tennis) saque m; **it ~s
him right** se lo tiene merecido; **server** n
(Comput) servidor m

service [ˈsɜːvɪs] n servicio; (Rel) misa;
(Aut) mantenimiento; (dishes etc) juego
▷ vt (car etc) revisar; (: repair) reparar; **to be
of ~ to sb** ser útil a algn; **~ included/not
included** servicio incluido/no incluido
(Econ: tertiary sector) sector m terciario or
(de) servicios; (BRIT: on motorway) área de
servicio; (Mil): **the S~s** las fuerzas armadas;
service area n (on motorway) área de

servicio; **service charge** (BRIT) n servicio;
serviceman (irreg) n militar m; **service
station** n estación f de servicio
serviette [sə:vɪˈɛt] (BRIT) n servilleta
session [ˈsɛʃən] n sesión f; **to be in ~** estar
en sesión
set [sɛt] (pt, pp **~**) n juego; (Radio) aparato;
(TV) televisor m; (of utensils) batería; (of
cutlery) cubierto; (of books) colección f;
(Tennis) set m; (group of people) grupo;
(Cinema) plató m; (Theatre) decorado;
(Hairdressing) marcado ⊳ adj (fixed) fijo;
(ready) listo ⊳ vt (place) poner, colocar; (fix)
fijar; (adjust) ajustar, arreglar; (decide: rules
etc) establecer, decidir ⊳ vi (sun) ponerse;
(jam, jelly) cuajarse; (concrete) fraguar;
(bone) componerse; **to be ~ on doing
sth** estar empeñado en hacer algo; **to
~ to music** poner música a; **to ~ on fire**
incendiar, poner fuego a; **to ~ free** poner
en libertad; **to ~ sth going** poner algo en
marcha; **to ~ sail** zarpar, hacerse a la vela;
set aside vt poner aparte, dejar de lado;
(money, time) reservar; **set down** vt (bus,
train) dejar; **set in** vi (infection) declararse;
(complications) comenzar; **the rain has set
in for the day** parece que va a llover todo
el día; **set off** vi partir ⊳ vt (bomb) hacer
estallar; (events) poner en marcha; (show
up well) hacer resaltar; **set out** vi partir
⊳ vt (arrange) disponer; (state) exponer; **to
set out to do sth** proponerse hacer algo;
set up vt establecer; **setback** n revés m,
contratiempo; **set menu** n menú m
settee [sɛˈtiː] n sofá m
setting [ˈsɛtɪŋ] n (scenery) marco; (position)
disposición f; (of sun) puesta; (of jewel)
engaste m, montadura
settle [ˈsɛtl] vt (argument) resolver;
(accounts) ajustar, liquidar; (Med: calm)
calmar, sosegar ⊳ vi (dust etc) depositarse;
(weather) serenarse; **to ~ for sth** convenir
en aceptar algo; **to ~ on sth** decidirse por
algo; **settle down** vi (get comfortable)
ponerse cómodo, acomodarse; (calm down)
calmarse, tranquilizarse; (live quietly) echar
raíces; **settle in** vi instalarse; **settle up**
vi: **to settle up with sb** ajustar cuentas con
algn; **settlement** n (payment) liquidación
f; (agreement) acuerdo, convenio; (village
etc) pueblo
setup [ˈsɛtʌp] n sistema m; (situation)
situación f
seven [ˈsɛvn] num siete; **seventeen**
num diez y siete, diecisiete; **seventeenth**
[sevnˈtiːnθ] adj decimoséptimo; **seventh**
num séptimo; **seventieth** [ˈsɛvntɪɪθ] adj
septuagésimo; **seventy** num setenta

sever [ˈsɛvə*] vt cortar; (relations) romper
several [ˈsɛvərl] adj, pron varios/as m/fpl,
algunos/as m/fpl; **~ of us** varios de nosotros
severe [sɪˈvɪə*] adj severo; (serious) grave;
(hard) duro; (pain) intenso
sew [səu] (pt **~ed**, pp **~n**) vt, vi coser
sewage [ˈsuːɪdʒ] n aguas fpl residuales
sewer [ˈsuːə*] n alcantarilla, cloaca
sewing [ˈsəuɪŋ] n costura; **sewing
machine** n máquina de coser
sewn [səun] pp of **sew**
sex [sɛks] n sexo; (lovemaking): **to have
~** hacer el amor; **sexism** [ˈsɛksɪzəm] n
sexismo; **sexist** adj, n sexista mf; **sexual**
[ˈsɛksjuəl] adj sexual; **sexual intercourse**
n relaciones fpl sexuales; **sexuality**
[seksjuˈælɪtɪ] n sexualidad f; **sexy** adj sexy
shabby [ˈʃæbɪ] adj (person) desharrapado;
(clothes) raído, gastado; (behaviour) ruin inv
shack [ʃæk] n choza, chabola
shade [ʃeɪd] n sombra; (for lamp) pantalla;
(for eyes) visera; (of colour) matiz m, tonalidad
f; (small quantity): **a ~ (too big/more)** un
poquitín (grande/más) ⊳ vt dar sombra a;
(eyes) proteger del sol; **in the ~** en la sombra;
shades npl (sunglasses) gafas fpl de sol
shadow [ˈʃædəu] n sombra ⊳ vt (follow)
seguir y vigilar; **shadow cabinet** (BRIT) n
(Pol) gabinete paralelo formado por el partido
de oposición
shady [ˈʃeɪdɪ] adj sombreado;
(fig: dishonest) sospechoso; (: deal) turbio
shaft [ʃɑːft] n (of arrow, spear) astil m; (Aut,
Tech) eje m, árbol m; (of mine) pozo; (of lift)
hueco, caja; (of light) rayo
shake [ʃeɪk] (pt **shook**, pp **shaken**) vt
sacudir; (building) hacer temblar; (bottle,
cocktail) agitar ⊳ vi (tremble) temblar; **to ~
one's head** (in refusal) negar con la cabeza;
(in dismay) mover o menear la cabeza,
incrédulo; **to ~ hands with sb** estrechar
la mano a algn; **shake off** vt sacudirse;
(fig) deshacerse de; **shake up** vt agitar;
(fig) reorganizar; **shaky** adj (hand, voice)
trémulo; (building) inestable
shall [ʃæl] aux vb: **~ I help you?** ¿quieres que
te ayude?; **I'll buy three, ~ I?** compro tres,
¿no te parece?
shallow [ˈʃæləu] adj poco profundo; (fig)
superficial
sham [ʃæm] n fraude m, engaño
shambles [ˈʃæmblz] n confusión f
shame [ʃeɪm] n vergüenza ⊳ vt
avergonzar; **it is a ~ that/to do** es una
lástima que/hacer; **what a ~!** ¡qué lástima!;
shameful adj vergonzoso; **shameless** adj
desvergonzado
shampoo [ʃæmˈpuː] n champú m ⊳ vt

lavar con champú

shandy ['ʃændɪ] n mezcla de cerveza con gaseosa

shan't [ʃɑ:nt] = **shall not**

shape [ʃeɪp] n forma ▷ vt formar, dar forma a; (sb's ideas) formar; (sb's life) determinar; **to take ~** tomar forma

share [ʃeə*] n (part) parte f, porción f; (contribution) cuota; (Comm) acción f ▷ vt dividir; (have in common) compartir; **to ~ out (among or between)** repartir (entre); **shareholder** (BRIT) n accionista mf

shark [ʃɑ:k] n tiburón m

sharp [ʃɑ:p] adj (blade, nose) afilado; (point) puntiagudo; (outline) definido; (pain) intenso; (Mus) desafinado; (contrast) marcado; (voice) agudo; (person: quick-witted) astuto; (: dishonest) poco escrupuloso ▷ n (Mus) sostenido ▷ adv: **at 2 o'clock ~** a las 2 en punto; **sharpen** vt afilar; (pencil) sacar punta a; (fig) agudizar; **sharpener** n (also: **pencil sharpener**) sacapuntas m inv; **sharply** adv (turn, stop) bruscamente; (stand out, contrast) claramente; (criticize, retort) severamente

shatter ['ʃætə*] vt hacer añicos or pedazos; (fig: ruin) destruir, acabar con ▷ vi hacerse añicos; **shattered** adj (grief-stricken) destrozado, deshecho; (exhausted) agotado, hecho polvo

shave [ʃeɪv] vt afeitar, rasurar ▷ vi afeitarse, rasurarse ▷ n: **to have a ~** afeitarse; **shaver** n (also: **electric shaver**) máquina de afeitar (eléctrica)

shavings ['ʃeɪvɪŋz] npl (of wood etc) virutas fpl

shaving cream ['ʃeɪvɪŋ-] n crema de afeitar

shaving foam n espuma de afeitar

shawl [ʃɔ:l] n chal m

she [ʃi:] pron ella

sheath [ʃi:θ] n vaina; (contraceptive) preservativo

shed [ʃed] (pt, pp ~) n cobertizo ▷ vt (skin) mudar; (tears, blood) derramar; (load) derramar; (workers) despedir

she'd [ʃi:d] = **she had; she would**

sheep [ʃi:p] n inv oveja; **sheepdog** n perro pastor; **sheepskin** n piel f de carnero

sheer [ʃɪə*] adj (utter) puro, completo; (steep) escarpado; (material) diáfano ▷ adv verticalmente

sheet [ʃi:t] n (on bed) sábana; (of paper) hoja; (of glass, metal) lámina; (of ice) capa

sheik(h) [ʃeɪk] n jeque m

shelf [ʃelf] (pl **shelves**) n estante m

shell [ʃel] n (on beach) concha; (of egg, nut etc) cáscara; (explosive) proyectil m,

obús m; (of building) armazón f ▷ vt (peas) desenvainar; (Mil) bombardear

she'll [ʃi:l] = **she will; she shall**

shellfish ['ʃelfɪʃ] n inv crustáceo; (as food) mariscos mpl

shelter ['ʃeltə*] n abrigo, refugio ▷ vt (aid) amparar, proteger; (give lodging to) abrigar ▷ vi abrigarse, refugiarse; **sheltered** adj (life) protegido; (spot) abrigado

shelves [ʃelvz] npl of **shelf**

shelving ['ʃelvɪŋ] n estantería

shepherd ['ʃepəd] n pastor m ▷ vt (guide) guiar, conducir; **shepherd's pie** (BRIT) n pastel de carne y patatas

sheriff ['ʃerɪf] (US) n sheriff m

sherry ['ʃerɪ] n jerez m

she's [ʃi:z] = **she is; she has**

Shetland ['ʃetlənd] n (also: **the ~s, the ~ Isles**) las Islas de Zetlandia

shield [ʃi:ld] n escudo; (protection) blindaje m ▷ vt: **to ~ (from)** proteger (de)

shift [ʃɪft] n (change) cambio; (at work) turno ▷ vt trasladar; (remove) quitar ▷ vi moverse

shin [ʃɪn] n espinilla

shine [ʃaɪn] (pt, pp **shone**) n brillo, lustre m ▷ vi brillar, relucir ▷ vt (shoes) lustrar, sacar brillo a; **to ~ a torch on sth** dirigir una linterna hacia algo

shingles ['ʃɪŋglz] n (Med) herpes mpl or fpl

shiny ['ʃaɪnɪ] adj brillante, lustroso

ship [ʃɪp] n buque m, barco ▷ vt (goods) embarcar; (send) transportar or enviar por vía marítima; **shipment** n (goods) envío; **shipping** n (act) embarque m; (traffic) buques mpl; **shipwreck** n naufragio ▷ vt: **to be shipwrecked** naufragar; **shipyard** n astillero

shirt [ʃə:t] n camisa; **in (one's) ~ sleeves** en mangas de camisa

shit [ʃɪt] (inf!) excl ¡mierda! (!)

shiver ['ʃɪvə*] n escalofrío ▷ vi temblar, estremecerse; (with cold) tiritar

shock [ʃɔk] n (impact) choque m; (Elec) descarga (eléctrica); (emotional) conmoción f; (start) sobresalto, susto; (Med) postración f nerviosa ▷ vt dar un susto a; (offend) escandalizar; **shocking** adj (awful) espantoso; (outrageous) escandaloso

shoe [ʃu:] (pt, pp **shod**) n zapato; (for horse) herradura ▷ vt (horse) herrar; **shoelace** n cordón m; **shoe polish** n betún m; **shoeshop** n zapatería

shone [ʃɔn] pt, pp of **shine**

shook [ʃuk] pt of **shake**

shoot [ʃu:t] (pt, pp **shot**) n (on branch, seedling) retoño, vástago ▷ vt disparar; (kill) matar a tiros; (wound) pegar un tiro; (execute) fusilar; (*film*) rodar, filmar ▷ *vi* (*Football*) chutar; **shoot down** *vt* (*plane*) derribar; **shoot up** *vi* (*prices*) dispararse; **shooting** *n* (*shots*) tiros *mpl*; (*Hunting*) caza con escopeta

shop [ʃɔp] *n* tienda; (*workshop*) taller *m* ▷ *vi* (*also*: **go ~ping**) ir de compras; **shop assistant** (BRIT) *n* dependiente/a *m/f*; **shopkeeper** *n* tendero/a; **shoplifting** *n* mechería; **shopping** *n* (*goods*) compras *fpl*; **shopping bag** *n* bolsa (de compras); **shopping centre** (US **shopping center**) *n* centro comercial; **shopping mall** *n* centro comercial; **shopping trolley** *n* (BRIT) carrito de la compra; **shop window** *n* escaparate *m* (SP), vidriera (LAM)

shore [ʃɔ:*] *n* orilla ▷ *vt*: **to ~ (up)** reforzar; **on ~** en tierra

short [ʃɔ:t] *adj* corto; (*in time*) breve, de corta duración; (*person*) bajo; (*curt*) brusco, seco; (*insufficient*) insuficiente; **(a pair of) ~s** (unos) pantalones *mpl* cortos; **to be ~ of sth** estar falto de algo; **in ~** en pocas palabras; **~ of doing ...** fuera de hacer ...; **it is ~ for** es la forma abreviada de; **to cut ~** (*speech, visit*) interrumpir, terminar inesperadamente; **everything ~ of ...** todo menos ...; **to fall ~ of** no alcanzar; **to run ~ of** quedarle a algn poco; **to stop ~** parar en seco; **to stop ~ of** detenerse antes de; **shortage** *n*: **a shortage of** una falta de; **shortbread** *n* especie de mantecada; **shortcoming** *n* defecto, deficiencia; **short(crust) pastry** (BRIT) *n* pasta quebradiza; **shortcut** *n* atajo; **shorten** *vt* acortar; (*visit*) interrumpir; **shortfall** *n* déficit *m*; **shorthand** (BRIT) *n* taquigrafía; **short-lived** *adj* efímero; **shortly** *adv* en breve, dentro de poco; **shorts** *npl* pantalones *mpl* cortos; (US) calzoncillos *mpl*; **short-sighted** (BRIT) *adj* miope; (*fig*) imprudente; **short-sleeved** *adj* de manga corta; **short story** *n* cuento; **short-tempered** *adj* enojadizo; **short-term** *adj* (*effect*) a corto plazo

shot [ʃɔt] *pt, pp of* **shoot** ▷ *n* (*sound*) tiro, disparo; (*try*) tentativa; (*injection*) inyección *f*; (*Phot*) toma, fotografía; **to be a good/poor ~** (*person*) tener buena/mala puntería; **like a ~** (*without any delay*) como un rayo; **shotgun** *n* escopeta

should [ʃud] *aux vb*: **I ~ go now** debo irme ahora; **he ~ be there now** debe de haber llegado (ya); **I ~ go if I were you** yo en tu lugar me iría; **I ~ like to** me gustaría

shoulder [ˈʃəuldə*] *n* hombro ▷ *vt* (*fig*) cargar con; **shoulder blade** *n* omóplato

shouldn't [ˈʃudnt] = **should not**

shout [ʃaut] *n* grito ▷ *vt* gritar ▷ *vi* gritar, dar voces

shove [ʃʌv] *n* empujón *m* ▷ *vt* empujar; (*inf: put*) **to ~ sth in** meter algo a empellones

shovel [ˈʃʌvl] *n* pala; (*mechanical*) excavadora ▷ *vt* mover con pala

show [ʃəu] (*pt* **~ed**, *pp* **~n**) *n* (*of emotion*) demostración *f*; (*semblance*) apariencia; (*exhibition*) exposición *f*; (*Theatre*) función *f*, espectáculo; (*TV*) show *m* ▷ *vt* mostrar, enseñar; (*courage etc*) mostrar, manifestar; (*exhibit*) exponer; (*film*) proyectar ▷ *vi* mostrarse; (*appear*) aparecer; **for ~** para impresionar; **on ~** (*exhibits etc*) expuesto; **show in** *vt* (*person*) hacer pasar; **show off** (*pej*) *vi* presumir ▷ *vt* (*display*) lucir; **show out** *vt*: **to show sb out** acompañar a algn a la puerta; **show up** *vi* (*stand out*) destacar; (*inf: turn up*) aparecer ▷ *vt* (*unmask*) desenmascarar; **show business** *n* mundo del espectáculo

shower [ˈʃauə*] *n* (*rain*) chaparrón *m*, chubasco; (*of stones etc*) lluvia; (*for bathing*) ducha, regadera (MEX) ▷ *vi* llover ▷ *vt* (*fig*): **to ~ sb with sth** colmar a algn de algo; **to have a ~** ducharse; **shower cap** *n* gorro de baño; **shower gel** *n* gel *m* de ducha

showing [ˈʃəuɪŋ] *n* (*of film*) proyección *f*

show jumping *n* hípica

shown [ʃəun] *pp of* **show**

show: show-off (*inf*) *n* (*person*) presumido/a; **showroom** *n* sala de muestras

shrank [ʃræŋk] *pt of* **shrink**

shred [ʃred] *n* (*gen pl*) triza, jirón *m* ▷ *vt* hacer trizas; (*Culin*) desmenuzar

shrewd [ʃru:d] *adj* astuto

shriek [ʃri:k] *n* chillido ▷ *vi* chillar

shrimp [ʃrɪmp] *n* camarón *m*

shrine [ʃraɪn] *n* santuario, sepulcro

shrink [ʃrɪŋk] (*pt* **shrank**, *pp* **shrunk**) *vi* encogerse; (*be reduced*) reducirse; (*also*: **~ away**) retroceder ▷ *vt* encoger ▷ *n* (*inf, pej*) loquero/a; **to ~ from (doing) sth** no atreverse a hacer algo

shrivel [ˈʃrɪvl] (*also*: **~ up**) *vt* (*dry*) secar ▷ *vi* secarse

shroud [ʃraud] *n* sudario ▷ *vt*: **~ed in mystery** envuelto en el misterio

Shrove Tuesday [ˈʃrəuv-] *n* martes *m* de carnaval

shrub [ʃrʌb] *n* arbusto

shrug [ʃrʌg] *n* encogimiento de hombros ▷ *vt*, *vi*: **to ~ (one's shoulders)** encogerse de hombros; **shrug off** *vt* negar importancia a

shrunk [ʃrʌŋk] *pp of* **shrink**

shudder [ˈʃʌdə*] *n* estremecimiento, escalofrío ▷ *vi* estremecerse

shuffle [ˈʃʌfl] *vt* (*cards*) barajar ▷ *vi*: **to ~**

(one's feet) arrastrar los pies

shun [ʃʌn] vt rehuir, esquivar

shut [ʃʌt] (pt, pp **~**) vt cerrar ▷ vi
cerrarse; **shut down** vt, vi cerrar; **shut
up** vi (inf: keep quiet) callarse ▷ vt (close)
cerrar; (silence) hacer callar; **shutter** n
contraventana; (Phot) obturador m

shuttle [ʃʌtl] n lanzadera; (also: **~ service**)
servicio rápido y continuo entre dos puntos;
(Aviat) puente m aéreo; **shuttlecock** n
volante m

shy [ʃaɪ] adj tímido

sibling [ˈsɪblɪŋ] n (formal) hermano/a

Sicily [ˈsɪsɪlɪ] n Sicilia

sick [sɪk] adj (ill) enfermo; (nauseated)
mareado; (humour) negro; (vomiting): **to be
~** (BRIT) vomitar; **to feel ~** tener náuseas;
to be ~ of (fig) estar harto de; **sickening**
adj (fig) asqueroso; **sick leave** n baja por
enfermedad; **sickly** adj enfermizo; (smell)
nauseabundo; **sickness** n enfermedad f,
mal m; (vomiting) náuseas fpl

side [saɪd] n (gen) lado; (of body) costado;
(of lake) orilla; (of hill) ladera; (team) equipo
▷ adj (door, entrance) lateral ▷ vi: **to ~ with
sb** tomar el partido de algn; **by the ~ of** al
lado de; **~ by ~** juntos/as; **from ~ to ~** de un
lado para otro; **from all ~s** de todos lados;
to take ~s (with) tomar partido (con);
sideboard n aparador m; **sideboards**
(BRIT) npl = **sideburns**; **sideburns** npl
patillas fpl; **sidelight** n (Aut) luz f lateral;
sideline n (Sport) línea de banda; (fig)
empleo suplementario; **side order** n plato
de acompañamiento; **side road** n (BRIT)
calle f lateral; **side street** n calle f lateral;
sidetrack vt (fig) desviar (de su propósito);
sidewalk (US) n acera; **sideways** adv de
lado

siege [siːdʒ] n cerco, sitio

sieve [sɪv] n colador m ▷ vt cribar

sift [sɪft] vt cribar; (fig: information)
escudriñar

sigh [saɪ] n suspiro ▷ vi suspirar

sight [saɪt] n (faculty) vista; (spectacle)
espectáculo; (on gun) mira, alza ▷ vt divisar;
in ~ a la vista; **out of ~** fuera de (la) vista;
on ~ (shoot) sin previo aviso; **sightseeing** n
excursionismo, turismo; **to go sightseeing**
hacer turismo

sign [saɪn] n (with hand) señal f, seña;
(trace) huella, rastro; (notice) letrero; (written)
signo ▷ vt firmar; (Sport) fichar; **to ~ sth
over to sb** firmar el traspaso de algo a algn;
sign for vt fus (item) firmar el recibo de;
sign in vi firmar el registro (al entrar); **sign
on** vi (BRIT: as unemployed) registrarse como
desempleado; (for course) inscribirse ▷ vt

(Mil) alistar; (employee) contratar; **sign up**
vi (Mil) alistarse; (for course) inscribirse ▷ vt
(player) fichar

signal [ˈsɪɡnl] n señal f ▷ vi señalizar ▷ vt
(person) hacer señas a; (message) comunicar
por señales

signature [ˈsɪɡnətʃə*] n firma

significance [sɪɡˈnɪfɪkəns] n (importance)
trascendencia

significant [sɪɡˈnɪfɪkənt] adj
significativo; (important) trascendente

signify [ˈsɪɡnɪfaɪ] vt significar

sign language n lenguaje m para
sordomudos

signpost [ˈsaɪnpəʊst] n indicador m

Sikh [siːk] adj, n sij mf

silence [ˈsaɪlns] n silencio ▷ vt acallar;
(guns) reducir al silencio

silent [ˈsaɪlnt] adj silencioso; (not speaking)
callado; (film) mudo; **to remain ~** guardar
silencio

silhouette [sɪluːˈɛt] n silueta

silicon chip [ˈsɪlɪkən-] n plaqueta de
silicio

silk [sɪlk] n seda ▷ adj de seda

silly [ˈsɪlɪ] adj (person) tonto; (idea) absurdo

silver [ˈsɪlvə*] n plata; (money) moneda
suelta ▷ adj de plata; (colour) plateado;
silver-plated adj plateado

similar [ˈsɪmɪlə*] adj: **~ (to)** parecido
or semejante (a); **similarity** [-ˈlærɪtɪ] n
semejanza; **similarly** adv del mismo modo

simmer [ˈsɪmə*] vi hervir a fuego lento

simple [ˈsɪmpl] adj (easy) sencillo;
(foolish, Comm: interest) simple; **simplicity**
[-ˈplɪsɪtɪ] n sencillez f; **simplify** [ˈsɪmplɪfaɪ]
vt simplificar; **simply** adv (live, talk)
sencillamente; (just, merely) sólo

simulate [ˈsɪmjuːleɪt] vt fingir, simular

simultaneous [sɪməlˈteɪnɪəs] adj
simultáneo; **simultaneously** adv
simultáneamente

sin [sɪn] n pecado ▷ vi pecar

since [sɪns] adv desde entonces, después
▷ prep desde ▷ conj (time) desde que;
(because) ya que, puesto que; **~ then, ever ~**
desde entonces

sincere [sɪnˈsɪə*] adj sincero; **sincerely**
adv: **yours sincerely** (in letters) le saluda
atentamente

sing [sɪŋ] (pt **sang**, pp **sung**) vt, vi cantar

Singapore [sɪŋəˈpɔː*] n Singapur m

singer [ˈsɪŋə*] n cantante mf

singing [ˈsɪŋɪŋ] n canto

single [ˈsɪŋɡl] adj único, solo; (unmarried)
soltero; (not double) simple, sencillo ▷ n
(BRIT: also: **~ ticket**) billete m sencillo;
(record) sencillo, single m; **singles** npl

(*Tennis*) individual *m*; **single out** *vt* (*choose*) escoger; **single bed** *n* cama individual; **single file** *n*: **in single file** en fila de uno; **single-handed** *adv* sin ayuda; **single-minded** *adj* resuelto, firme; **single parent** *n* padre *m* soltero, madre *f* soltera (*o divorciado etc*); **single parent family** familia monoparental; **single room** *n* cuarto individual

singular ['sɪŋgjulə*] *adj* (*odd*) raro, extraño; (*outstanding*) excepcional ▷ *n* (*Ling*) singular *m*

sinister ['sɪnɪstə*] *adj* siniestro

sink [sɪŋk] (*pt* **sank**, *pp* **sunk**) *n* fregadero ▷ *vt* (*ship*) hundir, echar a pique; (*foundations*) excavar ▷ *vi* hundirse; **to ~ sth into** hundir algo en; **sink in** *vi* (*fig*) penetrar, calar

sinus ['saɪnəs] *n* (*Anat*) seno

sip [sɪp] *n* sorbo ▷ *vt* sorber, beber a sorbitos

sir [sə*] *n* señor *m*; **S~ John Smith** Sir John Smith; **yes ~** sí, señor

siren ['saɪərn] *n* sirena

sirloin ['sə:lɔɪn] *n* (*also*: **~ steak**) solomillo

sister ['sɪstə*] *n* hermana; (*BRIT*: *nurse*) enfermera jefe; **sister-in-law** *n* cuñada

sit [sɪt] (*pt*, *pp* **sat**) *vi* sentarse; (*be sitting*) estar sentado; (*assembly*) reunirse; (*for painter*) posar ▷ *vt* (*exam*) presentarse a; **sit back** *vi* (*in seat*) recostarse; **sit down** *vi* sentarse; **sit on** *vt fus* (*jury, committee*) ser miembro de, formar parte de; **sit up** *vi* incorporarse; (*not go to bed*) velar

sitcom ['sɪtkɔm] *n abbr* (= *situation comedy*) comedia de situación

site [saɪt] *n* sitio; (*also*: **building ~**) solar *m* ▷ *vt* situar

sitting ['sɪtɪŋ] *n* (*of assembly etc*) sesión *f*; (*in canteen*) turno; **sitting room** *n* sala de estar

situated ['sɪtjueɪtɪd] *adj* situado

situation [sɪtju'eɪʃən] *n* situación *f*; **"~s vacant"** (*BRIT*) "ofrecen trabajo"

six [sɪks] *num* seis; **sixteen** *num* diez y seis, dieciséis; **sixteenth** [sɪks'ti:nθ] *adj* decimosexto; **sixth** [sɪksθ] *num* sexto; **sixth form** *n* (*BRIT*) clase *f* de alumnos del sexto año (*de 16 a 18 años de edad*); **sixth-form college** *n* instituto *m* para alumnos de 16 a 18 años; **sixtieth** ['sɪkstɪɪθ] *adj* sexagésimo; **sixty** *num* sesenta

size [saɪz] *n* tamaño; (*extent*) extensión *f*; (*of clothing*) talla; (*of shoes*) número; **sizeable** *adj* importante, considerable

sizzle ['sɪzl] *vi* crepitar

skate [skeɪt] *n* patín *m*; (*fish*: *pl inv*) raya ▷ *vi* patinar; **skateboard** *n* monopatín *m*;

skateboarding *n* monopatín *m*; **skater** *n* patinador(a) *m/f*; **skating** *n* patinaje *m*; **skating rink** *n* pista de patinaje

skeleton ['skelɪtn] *n* esqueleto; (*Tech*) armazón *f*; (*outline*) esquema *m*

skeptical ['skeptɪkl] (*US*) = **sceptical**

sketch [sketʃ] *n* (*drawing*) dibujo; (*outline*) esbozo, bosquejo; (*Theatre*) sketch *m* ▷ *vt* dibujar; (*plan etc*: *also*: **~ out**) esbozar

skewer ['skju:ə*] *n* broqueta

ski: [ski:] *n* esquí *m* ▷ *vi* esquiar; **ski boot** *n* bota de esquí

skid [skɪd] *n* patinazo ▷ *vi* patinar

ski: skier *n* esquiador(a) *m/f*; **skiing** *n* esquí *m*

skilful ['skɪlful] (*US* **skillful**) *adj* diestro, experto

ski lift *n* telesilla *m*, telesquí *m*

skill [skɪl] *n* destreza, pericia; técnica; **skilled** *adj* hábil, diestro; (*worker*) cualificado

skim [skɪm] *vt* (*milk*) desnatar; (*glide over*) rozar, rasar ▷ *vi*: **to ~ through** (*book*) hojear; **skimmed milk** (*US* **skim milk**) *n* leche *f* desnatada

skin [skɪn] *n* piel *f*; (*complexion*) cutis *m* ▷ *vt* (*fruit etc*) pelar; (*animal*) despellejar; **skinhead** *n* cabeza *m/f* rapada, skin(head) *m/f*; **skinny** *adj* flaco

skip [skɪp] *n* brinco, salto; (*BRIT*: *container*) contenedor *m* ▷ *vi* brincar; (*with rope*) saltar a la comba ▷ *vt* saltarse

ski: ski pass *n* forfait *m* (de esquí); **ski pole** *n* bastón *m* de esquiar

skipper ['skɪpə*] *n* (*Naut, Sport*) capitán *m*

skipping rope ['skɪpɪŋ-] (*US* **skip rope**) *n* comba

skirt [skə:t] *n* falda, pollera (*sc*) ▷ *vt* (*go round*) ladear

skirting board ['skə:tɪŋ-] (*BRIT*) *n* rodapié *m*

ski slope *n* pista de esquí

ski suit *n* traje *m* de esquiar

skull [skʌl] *n* calavera; (*Anat*) cráneo

skunk [skʌŋk] *n* mofeta

sky [skaɪ] *n* cielo; **skyscraper** *n* rascacielos *m inv*

slab [slæb] *n* (*stone*) bloque *m*; (*flat*) losa; (*of cake*) trozo

slack [slæk] *adj* (*loose*) flojo; (*slow*) de poca actividad; (*careless*) descuidado; **slacks** *npl* pantalones *mpl*

slain [sleɪn] *pp of* **slay**

slam [slæm] *vt* (*throw*) arrojar (violentamente); (*criticize*) criticar duramente ▷ *vi* (*door*) cerrarse de golpe; **to ~ the door** dar un portazo

slander ['slɑ:ndə*] *n* calumnia,

difamación f

slang [slæŋ] n argot m; (jargon) jerga

slant [slɑːnt] n sesgo, inclinación f; (fig) interpretación f

slap [slæp] n palmada; (in face) bofetada ▷ vt dar una palmada or bofetada a; (paint etc): **to ~ sth on sth** embadurnar algo con algo ▷ adv (directly) exactamente, directamente

slash [slæʃ] vt acuchillar; (fig: prices) fulminar

slate [sleɪt] n pizarra ▷ vt (fig: criticize) criticar duramente

slaughter ['slɔːtə*] n (of animals) matanza; (of people) carnicería ▷ vt matar; **slaughterhouse** n matadero

Slav [slɑːv] adj eslavo

slave [sleɪv] n esclavo/a ▷ vi (also: ~ away) sudar tinta; **slavery** n esclavitud f

slay [sleɪ] (pt slew, pp slain) vt matar

sleazy ['sliːzɪ] adj de mala fama

sled [slɛd] (US) = **sledge**

sledge [slɛdʒ] n trineo

sleek [sliːk] adj (shiny) lustroso; (car etc) elegante

sleep [sliːp] (pt, pp slept) n sueño ▷ vi dormir; **to go to ~** quedarse dormido; **sleep in** vi (oversleep) quedarse dormido; **sleep together** vi (have sex) acostarse juntos; **sleeper** n (person) durmiente mf; (BRIT Rail: on track) traviesa; (: train) coche-cama m; **sleeping bag** n saco de dormir; **sleeping car** n coche-cama m; **sleeping pill** n somnífero; **sleepover** n: **we're having a sleepover at Jo's** nos vamos a quedar a dormir en casa de Jo; **sleepwalk** vi caminar dormido; (habitually) ser sonámbulo; **sleepy** adj soñoliento; (place) soporífero

sleet [sliːt] n aguanieve f

sleeve [sliːv] n manga; (Tech) manguito; (of record) portada; **sleeveless** adj sin mangas

sleigh [sleɪ] n trineo

slender ['slɛndə*] adj delgado; (means) escaso

slept [slɛpt] pt, pp of **sleep**

slew [sluː] pt of **slay** ▷ vi (BRIT: veer) torcerse

slice [slaɪs] n (of meat) tajada; (of bread) rebanada; (of lemon) rodaja; (utensil) pala ▷ vt cortar (en tajos), rebanar

slick [slɪk] adj (skilful) hábil, diestro; (clever) astuto ▷ n (also: **oil ~**) marea negra

slide [slaɪd] (pt, pp slid) n (movement) descenso, desprendimiento; (in playground) tobogán m; (Phot) diapositiva; (BRIT: also: **hair ~**) pasador m ▷ vt correr, deslizar ▷ vi

(slip) resbalarse; (glide) deslizarse; **sliding** adj (door) corredizo

slight [slaɪt] adj (slim) delgado; (frail) delicado; (pain etc) leve; (trivial) insignificante; (small) pequeño ▷ n desaire m ▷ vt (insult) ofender, desairar; **not in the ~est** en absoluto; **slightly** adv ligeramente, un poco

slim [slɪm] adj delgado, esbelto; (fig: chance) remoto ▷ vi adelgazar; **slimming** n adelgazamiento

slimy ['slaɪmɪ] adj cenagoso

sling [slɪŋ] (pt, pp slung) n (Med) cabestrillo; (weapon) honda ▷ vt tirar, arrojar

slip [slɪp] n (slide) resbalón m; (mistake) descuido; (underskirt) combinación f; (of paper) papelito ▷ vt (slide) deslizar ▷ vi deslizarse; (stumble) resbalar(se); (decline) decaer; (move smoothly): **to ~ into/out of** (room etc) introducirse en/salirse de; **to give sb the ~** eludir a algn; **a ~ of the tongue** un lapsus; **to ~ sth on/off** ponerse/quitarse algo; **slip up** vi (make mistake) equivocarse; meter la pata

slipper ['slɪpə*] n zapatilla, pantufla

slippery ['slɪpərɪ] adj resbaladizo; **slip road** (BRIT) n carretera de acceso

slit [slɪt] (pt, pp ~) n raja; (cut) corte m ▷ vt rajar; cortar

slog [slɒg] (BRIT) vi sudar tinta; **it was a ~** costó trabajo (hacerlo)

slogan ['sləʊgən] n eslogan m, lema m

slope [sləʊp] n (up) cuesta, pendiente f; (down) declive m; (side of mountain) falda, vertiente m ▷ vi: **to ~ down** estar en declive; **to ~ up** inclinarse; **sloping** adj en pendiente; en declive; (writing) inclinado

sloppy ['slɒpɪ] adj (work) descuidado; (appearance) desaliñado

slot [slɒt] n ranura ▷ vt: **to ~ into** encajar en; **slot machine** n (BRIT: vending machine) distribuidor m automático; (for gambling) tragaperras m inv

Slovakia [sləʊˈvækɪə] n Eslovaquia

Slovene [sləʊˈviːn] adj esloveno ▷ n esloveno/a; (Ling) esloveno; **Slovenia** [sləʊˈviːnɪə] n Eslovenia; **Slovenian** adj, n = **Slovene**

slow [sləʊ] adj lento; (not clever) lerdo; (watch): **to be ~** atrasar ▷ adv lentamente, despacio ▷ vt, vi retardar; **"~"** (road sign) "disminuir velocidad"; **slow down** vi reducir la marcha; **slowly** adv lentamente, despacio; **slow motion** n: **in slow motion** a cámara lenta

slug [slʌg] n babosa; (bullet) posta; **sluggish** adj lento; (person) perezoso

slum [slʌm] n casucha

slump [slʌmp] n (economic) depresión f
▷ vi hundirse; (prices) caer en picado

slung [slʌŋ] pt, pp of **sling**

slur [slə:*] n: **to cast a ~ on** insultar ▷ vt
(speech) pronunciar mal

sly [slaɪ] adj astuto; (smile) taimado

smack [smæk] n bofetada ▷ vt dar con la
mano a; (child, on face) abofetear ▷ vi: **to ~ of**
saber a, oler a

small [smɔ:l] adj pequeño; **small ads**
(BRIT) npl anuncios mpl por palabras; **small
change** n suelto, cambio

smart [smɑ:t] adj elegante; (clever) listo,
inteligente; (quick) rápido, vivo ▷ vi escocer,
picar; **smartcard** n tarjeta inteligente

smash [smæʃ] n (also: **~-up**) choque m;
(Mus) exitazo ▷ vt (break) hacer pedazos;
(car etc) estrellar; (Sport: record) batir
▷ vi hacerse pedazos; (against wall etc)
estrellarse; **smashing** (inf) adj estupendo

smear [smɪə*] n mancha; (Med) frotis m inv
▷ vt untar; **smear test** n (Med) citología,
frotis m inv (cervical)

smell [smɛl] (pt, pp **smelt** or **~ed**) n olor
m; (sense) olfato ▷ vt, vi oler; **smelly** adj
maloliente

smelt [smɛlt] pt, pp of **smell**

smile [smaɪl] n sonrisa ▷ vi sonreír

smirk [smə:k] n sonrisa falsa or afectada

smog [smɔg] n esmog m

smoke [sməuk] n humo ▷ vi fumar;
(chimney) echar humo ▷ vt (cigarettes)
fumar; **smoke alarm** n detector m de
humo, alarma contra incendios; **smoked**
adj (bacon, glass) ahumado; **smoker** n
fumador(a) m/f; (Rail) coche m fumador;
smoking n: **"no smoking"** "prohibido
fumar"

▌ Be careful not to translate **smoking** by
the Spanish word smoking.

smoky adj (room) lleno de humo; (taste)
ahumado

smooth [smu:ð] adj liso; (sea) tranquilo;
(flavour, movement) suave; (sauce) fino;
(person: pej) meloso ▷ vt (also: **~ out**) alisar;
(creases, difficulties) allanar

smother ['smʌðə*] vt sofocar; (repress)
contener

SMS n abbr (= short message service) (servicio)
SMS; **SMS message** n (mensaje m) SMS

smudge [smʌdʒ] n mancha ▷ vt manchar

smug [smʌg] adj presumido; orondo

smuggle ['smʌgl] vt pasar de
contrabando; **smuggling** n contrabando

snack [snæk] n bocado; **snack bar** n
cafetería

snag [snæg] n problema m

snail [sneɪl] n caracol m

snake [sneɪk] n serpiente f

snap [snæp] n (sound) chasquido;
(photograph) foto f ▷ adj (decision)
instantáneo ▷ vt (break) quebrar; (fingers)
castañetear ▷ vi quebrarse; (fig: speak
sharply) contestar bruscamente; **to ~ shut**
cerrarse de golpe; **snap at** vt fus (dog)
intentar morder; **snap up** vt agarrar;
snapshot n foto f (instantánea)

snarl [snɑ:l] vi gruñir

snatch [snætʃ] n (small piece) fragmento
▷ vt (snatch away) arrebatar; (fig) agarrar; **to
~ some sleep** encontrar tiempo para dormir

sneak [sni:k] (pt (US) **snuck**) vi: **to ~ in/out**
entrar/salir a hurtadillas ▷ n (inf) soplón/
ona m/f; **to ~ up on sb** aparecérsele de
improviso a algn; **sneakers** npl zapatos
mpl de lona

sneer [snɪə*] vi reír con sarcasmo;
(mock): **to ~ at** burlarse de

sneeze [sni:z] vi estornudar

sniff [snɪf] vi sollozar ▷ vt husmear, oler;
(drugs) esnifar

snigger ['snɪgə*] vi reírse con disimulo

snip [snɪp] n tijeretazo; (BRIT: inf: bargain)
ganga ▷ vt tijeretear

sniper ['snaɪpə*] n francotirador(a) m/f

snob [snɔb] n (e)snob mf

snooker ['snu:kə*] n especie de billar

snoop [snu:p] vi: **to ~ about** fisgonear

snooze [snu:z] n siesta ▷ vi echar una
siesta

snore [snɔ:*] n ronquido ▷ vi roncar

snorkel ['snɔ:kl] n (tubo) respirador m

snort [snɔ:t] n bufido ▷ vi bufar

snow [snəu] n nieve f ▷ vi nevar;
snowball n bola de nieve ▷ vi (fig)
agrandarse, ampliarse; **snowstorm** n
nevada, nevasca

snub [snʌb] vt (person) desairar ▷ n
desaire m, repulsa

snug [snʌg] adj (cosy) cómodo; (fitted)
ajustado

s

○ KEYWORD

so [səu] adv **1** (thus, likewise) así, de este
modo; **if so** de ser así; **I like swimming – so
do I** a mí me gusta nadar – a mí también;
I've got work to do – so has Paul tengo
trabajo que hacer – Paul también; **it's 5
o'clock – so it is!** son las cinco – ¡pues es
verdad!; **I hope/think so** espero/creo que
sí; **so far** hasta ahora; (in past) hasta este
momento

2 (in comparisons etc: to such a degree) tan;
so quickly (that) tan rápido (que); **so big**

(that) tan grande (que); **she's not so clever as her brother** no es tan lista como su hermano; **we were so worried** estábamos preocupadísimos
3: **so much** adj, adv tanto; **so many** tantos/as
4 (phrases): **10 or so** unos 10, 10 o así; **so long!** (inf: goodbye) ¡hasta luego!
▷ conj **1** (expressing purpose): **so as to do** para hacer; **so (that)** para que +subjun
2 (expressing result) así que; **so you see, I could have gone** así que ya ves, (yo) podría haber ido

soak [səuk] vt (drench) empapar; (steep in water) remojar ▷ vi remojarse, estar a remojo; **soak up** vt absorber; **soaking** adj (also: **soaking wet**) calado or empapado (hasta los huesos or el tuétano)
so-and-so ['səuənsəu] n (somebody) fulano/a de tal
soap [səup] n jabón m; **soap opera** n telenovela; **soap powder** n jabón m en polvo
soar [sɔ:*] vi (on wings) remontarse; (rocket: prices) dispararse; (building etc) elevarse
sob [sɔb] n sollozo ▷ vi sollozar
sober ['səubə*] adj (serious) serio; (not drunk) sobrio; (colour, style) discreto; **sober up** vt quitar la borrachera
so-called ['səu'kɔ:ld] adj así llamado
soccer ['sɔkə*] n fútbol m
sociable ['səuʃəbl] adj sociable
social ['səuʃl] adj social ▷ n velada, fiesta; **socialism** n socialismo; **socialist** adj, n socialista mf; **socialize** vi: **to socialize (with)** alternar (con); **social life** n vida social; **socially** adv socialmente; **social security** n seguridad f social; **social services** npl servicios mpl sociales; **social work** n asistencia social; **social worker** n asistente/a m/f social
society [sə'saɪətɪ] n sociedad f; (club) asociación f; (also: **high ~**) alta sociedad
sociology [səusɪ'ɔlədʒi] n sociología
sock [sɔk] n calcetín m
socket ['sɔkɪt] n cavidad f; (BRIT Elec) enchufe m
soda ['səudə] n (Chem) sosa; (also: **~ water**) soda; (us: also: **~ pop**) gaseosa
sodium ['səudɪəm] n sodio
sofa ['səufə] n sofá m; **sofa bed** n sofácama m
soft [sɔft] adj (lenient, not hard) blando; (gentle, not bright) suave; **soft drink** n bebida no alcohólica; **soft drugs** npl drogas fpl blandas; **soften** ['sɔfn] vt

ablandar; suavizar; (effect) amortiguar
▷ vi ablandarse; suavizarse; **softly** adv suavemente; (gently) delicadamente, con delicadeza; **software** n (Comput) software m
soggy ['sɔgɪ] adj empapado
soil [sɔɪl] n (earth) tierra, suelo ▷ vt ensuciar
solar ['səulə*] adj solar; **solar power** n energía solar; **solar system** n sistema m solar
sold [səuld] pt, pp of **sell**
soldier ['səuldʒə*] n soldado; (army man) militar m
sold out adj (Comm) agotado
sole [səul] n (of foot) planta; (of shoe) suela; (fish: pl inv) lenguado ▷ adj único; **solely** adv únicamente, sólo, solamente; **I will hold you solely responsible** le consideraré el único responsable
solemn ['sɔləm] adj solemne
solicitor [sə'lɪsɪtə*] (BRIT) n (for wills etc) ≈ notario/a; (in court) ≈ abogado/a
solid ['sɔlɪd] adj sólido; (gold etc) macizo ▷ n sólido
solitary ['sɔlɪtərɪ] adj solitario, solo
solitude ['sɔlɪtju:d] n soledad f
solo ['səuləu] n solo ▷ adv (fly) en solitario; **soloist** n solista m/f
soluble ['sɔlju:bl] adj soluble
solution [sə'lu:ʃən] n solución f
solve [sɔlv] vt resolver, solucionar
solvent ['sɔlvənt] adj (Comm) solvente ▷ n (Chem) solvente m
sombre ['sɔmbə*] (US **somber**) adj sombrío

○ **KEYWORD**

some [sʌm] adj **1** (a certain amount or number): **some tea/water/biscuits** té/agua/(unas) galletas; **there's some milk in the fridge** hay leche en el frigo; **there were some people outside** había algunas personas fuera; **I've got some money, but not much** tengo algo de dinero, pero no mucho
2 (certain: in contrasts) algunos/as; **some people say that ...** hay quien dice que ...; **some films were excellent, but most were mediocre** hubo películas excelentes, pero la mayoría fueron mediocres
3 (unspecified): **some woman was asking for you** una mujer estuvo preguntando por ti; **he was asking for some book (or other)** pedía un libro; **some day** algún día; **some day next week** un día de la semana que viene

▷ *pron* **1** (*a certain number*): **I've got some** (*books etc*) tengo algunos/as **2** (*a certain amount*) algo; **I've got some** (*money, milk*) tengo algo; **could I have some of that cheese?** ¿me puede dar un poco de ese queso?; **I've read some of the book** he leído parte del libro
▷ *adv*: **some 10 people** unas 10 personas, una decena de personas

some: somebody ['sʌmbədɪ] *pron* = **someone**; **somehow** *adv* de alguna manera; (*for some reason*) por una u otra razón; **someone** *pron* alguien; **someplace** (*US*) *adv* = **somewhere**; **something** *pron* algo; **would you like something to eat/drink?** ¿te gustaría cenar/tomar algo?; **sometime** *adv* (*in future*) algún día, en algún momento; (*in past*): **sometime last month** durante el mes pasado; **sometimes** *adv* a veces; **somewhat** *adv* algo; **somewhere** *adv* (*be*) en alguna parte; (*go*) a alguna parte; **somewhere else** (*be*) en otra parte; (*go*) a otra parte
son [sʌn] *n* hijo
song [sɔŋ] *n* canción *f*
son-in-law ['sʌnɪnlɔː] *n* yerno
soon [suːn] *adv* pronto, dentro de poco; **~ afterwards** poco después; *see also* **as**; **sooner** *adv* (*time*) antes, más temprano; (*preference: rather*): **I would sooner do that** preferiría hacer eso; **sooner or later** tarde o temprano
soothe [suːð] *vt* tranquilizar; (*pain*) aliviar
sophisticated [səˈfɪstɪkeɪtɪd] *adj* sofisticado
sophomore ['sɔfəmɔː*] (*US*) *n* estudiante *mf* de segundo año
soprano [səˈprɑːnəʊ] *n* soprano *f*
sorbet ['sɔːbeɪ] *n* sorbete *m*
sordid ['sɔːdɪd] *adj* (*place etc*) sórdido; (*motive etc*) mezquino
sore [sɔː*] *adj* (*painful*) doloroso, que duele ▷ *n* llaga
sorrow ['sɔrəʊ] *n* pena, dolor *m*
sorry ['sɔrɪ] *adj* (*regretful*) arrepentido; (*condition, excuse*) lastimoso; **~!** ¡perdón!, ¡perdone!; **~?** ¿cómo?; **to feel ~ for sb** tener lástima a algn; **I feel ~ for him** me da lástima
sort [sɔːt] *n* clase *f*, género, tipo; **sort out** *vt* (*papers*) clasificar; (*organize*) ordenar, organizar; (*resolve: problem, situation etc*) arreglar, solucionar
SOS *n* SOS *m*
so-so ['səʊsəʊ] *adv* regular, así así
sought [sɔːt] *pt, pp of* **seek**
soul [səʊl] *n* alma

sound [saʊnd] *n* (*noise*) sonido, ruido; (*volume: on TV etc*) volumen *m*; (*Geo*) estrecho ▷ *adj* (*healthy*) sano; (*safe, not damaged*) en buen estado; (*reliable: person*) digno de confianza; (*sensible*) sensato, razonable; (*secure: investment*) seguro ▷ *adv*: **~ asleep** profundamente dormido ▷ *vt* (*alarm*) sonar ▷ *vi* sonar, resonar; (*fig: seem*) parecer; **to ~ like** sonar a; **soundtrack** *n* (*of film*) banda sonora
soup [suːp] *n* (*thick*) sopa; (*thin*) caldo
sour ['saʊə*] *adj* agrio; (*milk*) cortado; **it's ~ grapes** (*fig*) están verdes
source [sɔːs] *n* fuente *f*
south [saʊθ] *n* sur *m* ▷ *adj* del sur, sureño ▷ *adv* al sur, hacia el sur; **South Africa** *n* África del Sur; **South African** *adj, n* sudafricano/a *m/f*; **South America** *n* América del Sur, Sudamérica; **South American** *adj, n* sudamericano/a *m/f*; **southbound** *adj* (*con*) rumbo al sur; **southeastern** [saʊθ'iːstən] *adj* sureste, del sureste; **southern** ['sʌðən] *adj* del sur, meridional; **South Korea** *n* Corea del Sur; **South Pole** *n* Polo Sur; **southward(s)** *adv* hacia el sur; **south-west** *n* suroeste *m*; **southwestern** [saʊθ'westən] *adj* suroeste
souvenir [suːvəˈnɪə*] *n* recuerdo
sovereign ['sɔvrɪn] *adj, n* soberano/a *m/f*
sow[1] [səʊ] (*pt* **~ed**, *pp* **sown**) *vt* sembrar
sow[2] [saʊ] *n* cerda, puerca
soya ['sɔɪə] (*BRIT*) *n* soja
spa [spɑː] *n* balneario
space [speɪs] *n* espacio; (*room*) sitio ▷ *cpd* espacial ▷ *vt* (*also: ~ out*) espaciar; **spacecraft** *n* nave *f* espacial; **spaceship** *n* = **spacecraft**
spacious ['speɪʃəs] *adj* amplio
spade [speɪd] *n* (*tool*) pala, laya; **spades** *npl* (*Cards: British*) picas *fpl*; (*: Spanish*) espadas *fpl*
spaghetti [spə'ɡetɪ] *n* espaguetis *mpl*, fideos *mpl*
Spain [speɪn] *n* España
spam [spæm] *n* (*junk e-mail*) spam *m*
span [spæn] *n* (*of bird, plane*) envergadura; (*of arch*) luz *f*; (*in time*) lapso ▷ *vt* extenderse sobre, cruzar; (*fig*) abarcar
Spaniard ['spænjəd] *n* español(a) *m/f*
Spanish ['spænɪʃ] *adj* español(a) ▷ *n* (*Ling*) español *m*, castellano; **the Spanish** *npl* los españoles
spank [spæŋk] *vt* zurrar
spanner ['spænə*] (*BRIT*) *n* llave *f* (inglesa)
spare [speə*] *adj* de reserva; (*surplus*) sobrante, de más ▷ *n* = **spare part** ▷ *vt* (*do without*) pasarse sin; (*refrain from hurting*) perdonar; **to ~** (*surplus*) sobrante, de sobra; **spare part** *n* pieza de repuesto; **spare**

S

room n cuarto de los invitados; **spare time** n tiempo libre; **spare tyre** (US **spare tire**) n (Aut) neumático or llanta (LAM) de recambio; **spare wheel** n (Aut) rueda de recambio

spark [spɑːk] n chispa; (fig) chispazo; **spark(ing) plug** n bujía

sparkle ['spɑːkl] n centelleo, destello ▷ vi (shine) relucir, brillar

sparrow ['spærəu] n gorrión m

sparse [spɑːs] adj esparcido, escaso

spasm ['spæzəm] n (Med) espasmo

spat [spæt] pt, pp of **spit**

spate [speɪt] n (fig): **a ~ of** un torrente de

spatula ['spætjulə] n espátula

speak [spiːk] (pt **spoke**, pp **spoken**) vt (language) hablar; (truth) decir ▷ vi hablar; (make a speech) intervenir; **to ~ to sb/of** or **about sth** hablar con algn/de or sobre algo; **~ up!** ¡habla fuerte!; **speaker** n (in public) orador(a) m/f; (also: **loudspeaker**) altavoz m; (for stereo etc) bafle m; (Pol): **the Speaker** (BRIT) el Presidente de la Cámara de los Comunes; (US) el Presidente del Congreso

spear [spɪə*] n lanza ▷ vt alancear

special ['spɛʃl] adj especial; (edition etc) extraordinario; (delivery) urgente; **special delivery** n (Post): **by special delivery** por entrega urgente; **special effects** npl (Cine) efectos mpl especiales; **specialist** n especialista mf; **speciality** [spɛʃɪ'ælɪtɪ] (BRIT) n especialidad f; **specialize** vi: **to specialize (in)** especializarse (en); **specially** adv sobre todo, en particular; **special needs** npl (BRIT): **children with special needs** niños que requieren una atención diferenciada; **special offer** n (Comm) oferta especial; **special school** n (BRIT) colegio m de educación especial; **specialty** (US) n = **speciality**

species ['spiːʃiːz] n inv especie f

specific [spə'sɪfɪk] adj específico; **specifically** adv específicamente

specify ['spɛsɪfaɪ] vt, vi especificar, precisar

specimen ['spɛsɪmən] n ejemplar m; (Med: of urine) espécimen m; (: of blood) muestra

speck [spɛk] n grano, mota

spectacle ['spɛktəkl] n espectáculo; **spectacles** npl (BRIT: glasses) gafas fpl (SP), anteojos mpl; **spectacular** [-'tækjulə*] adj espectacular; (success) impresionante

spectator [spɛk'teɪtə*] n espectador(a) m/f

spectrum ['spɛktrəm] (pl **spectra**) n espectro

speculate ['spɛkjuleɪt] vi: **to ~ (on)** especular (en)

sped [spɛd] pt, pp of **speed**

speech [spiːtʃ] n (faculty) habla; (formal talk) discurso; (spoken language) lenguaje m; **speechless** adj mudo, estupefacto

speed [spiːd] n velocidad f; (haste) prisa; (promptness) rapidez f; **at full** or **top ~** a máxima velocidad; **speed up** vi acelerarse ▷ vt acelerar; **speedboat** n lancha motora; **speeding** n (Aut) exceso de velocidad; **speed limit** n límite m de velocidad, velocidad f máxima; **speedometer** [spɪ'dɔmɪtə*] n velocímetro; **speedy** adj (fast) veloz, rápido; (prompt) pronto

spell [spɛl] (pt, pp **spelt** (BRIT) or **~ed**) n (also: **magic ~**) encanto, hechizo; (period of time) rato, período ▷ vt deletrear; (fig) anunciar, presagiar; **to cast a ~ on sb** hechizar a algn; **he can't ~** pone faltas de ortografía; **spell out** vt (explain): **to spell sth out for sb** explicar algo a algn en detalle; **spellchecker** ['spɛltʃekə*] n corrector m ortográfico; **spelling** n ortografía

spelt [spɛlt] pt, pp of **spell**

spend [spɛnd] (pt, pp **spent**) vt (money) gastar; (time) pasar; (life) dedicar; **spending** n: **government spending** gastos mpl del gobierno

spent [spɛnt] pt, pp of **spend** ▷ adj (cartridge, bullets, match) usado

sperm [spəːm] n esperma

sphere [sfɪə*] n esfera

spice [spaɪs] n especia ▷ vt condimentar

spicy ['spaɪsɪ] adj picante

spider ['spaɪdə*] n araña

spike [spaɪk] n (point) punta; (Bot) espiga

spill [spɪl] (pt, pp **spilt** or **~ed**) vt derramar, verter ▷ vi derramarse; **to ~ over** desbordarse

spin [spɪn] (pt, pp **spun**) n (Aviat) barrena; (trip in car) paseo (en coche); (on ball) efecto ▷ vt (wool etc) hilar; (ball etc) hacer girar ▷ vi girar, dar vueltas

spinach ['spɪnɪtʃ] n espinaca; (as food) espinacas fpl

spinal ['spaɪnl] adj espinal

spin doctor n informador(a) parcial al servicio de un partido político etc

spin-dryer (BRIT) n secador m centrífugo

spine [spaɪn] n espinazo, columna vertebral; (thorn) espina

spiral ['spaɪərl] n espiral f ▷ vi (fig: prices) subir desorbitadamente

spire ['spaɪə*] n aguja, chapitel m

spirit ['spɪrɪt] n (soul) alma; (ghost) fantasma m; (attitude, sense) espíritu m; (courage) valor m, ánimo; **spirits** npl (drink) licor(es) m(pl); **in good ~s** alegre, de buen ánimo

spiritual ['spɪrɪtjuəl] *adj* espiritual ▷ *n* espiritual *m*

spit [spɪt] (*pt, pp* **spat**) *n* (*for roasting*) asador *m*, espetón *m*; (*saliva*) saliva ▷ *vi* escupir; (*sound*) chisporrotear; (*rain*) lloviznar

spite [spaɪt] *n* rencor *m*, ojeriza ▷ *vt* causar pena a, mortificar; **in ~ of** a pesar de, pese a; **spiteful** *adj* rencoroso, malévolo

splash [splæʃ] *n* (*sound*) chapoteo; (*of colour*) mancha ▷ *vt* salpicar ▷ *vi* (*also: ~ about*) chapotear; **splash out** (*inf*) *vi* (BRIT) derrochar dinero

splendid ['splɛndɪd] *adj* espléndido

splinter ['splɪntə*] *n* (*of wood etc*) astilla; (*in finger*) espigón *m* ▷ *vi* astillarse, hacer astillas

split [splɪt] (*pt, pp* **~**) *n* hendedura, raja; (*fig*) división *f*; (*Pol*) escisión *f* ▷ *vt* partir, rajar; (*party*) dividir; (*share*) repartir ▷ *vi* dividirse, escindirse; **split up** *vi* (*couple*) separarse; (*meeting*) acabarse

spoil [spɔɪl] (*pt, pp* **~t** *or* **~ed**) *vt* (*damage*) dañar; (*mar*) estropear; (*child*) mimar, consentir

spoilt [spɔɪlt] *pt, pp of* **spoil** ▷ *adj* (*child*) mimado, consentido; (*ballot paper*) invalidado

spoke [spəʊk] *pt of* **speak** ▷ *n* rayo, radio

spoken ['spəʊkn] *pp of* **speak**

spokesman ['spəʊksmən] (*irreg*) *n* portavoz *m*

spokesperson ['spəʊkspə:sn] (*irreg*) *n* portavoz *m/f*, vocero/a (LAM)

spokeswoman ['spəʊkswumən] (*irreg*) *n* portavoz *f*

sponge [spʌndʒ] *n* esponja; (*also: ~ cake*) bizcocho ▷ *vt* (*wash*) lavar con esponja ▷ *vi*: **to ~ off** *or* **on sb** vivir a costa de algn; **sponge bag** (BRIT) *n* esponjera

sponsor ['spɔnsə*] *n* patrocinador(a) *m/f* ▷ *vt* (*applicant, proposal etc*) proponer; **sponsorship** *n* patrocinio

spontaneous [spɔn'teɪnɪəs] *adj* espontáneo

spooky ['spu:kɪ] (*inf*) *adj* espeluznante, horripilante

spoon [spu:n] *n* cuchara; **spoonful** *n* cucharada

sport [spɔ:t] *n* deporte *m*; (*person*): **to be a good ~** ser muy majo ▷ *vt* (*wear*) lucir, ostentar; **sport jacket** (US) *n* = **sports jacket**; **sports car** *n* coche *m* deportivo; **sports centre** (BRIT) *n* polideportivo; **sports jacket** (BRIT) *n* chaqueta deportiva; **sportsman** (*irreg*) *n* deportista *m*; **sports utility vehicle** *n* todoterreno *m inv*;

sportswear *n* trajes *mpl* de deporte *or* sport; **sportswoman** (*irreg*) *n* deportista; **sporty** *adj* deportista

spot [spɔt] *n* sitio, lugar *m*; (*dot: on pattern*) punto, mancha; (*pimple*) grano; (*Radio*) cuña publicitaria; (*TV*) espacio publicitario; (*small amount*): **a ~ of** un poquito de ▷ *vt* (*notice*) notar, observar; **on the ~** allí mismo; **spotless** *adj* perfectamente limpio; **spotlight** *n* foco, reflector *m*; (*Aut*) faro auxiliar

spouse [spauz] *n* cónyuge *mf*

sprain [spreɪn] *n* torcedura ▷ *vt*: **to ~ one's ankle/wrist** torcerse el tobillo/la muñeca

sprang [spræŋ] *pt of* **spring**

sprawl [sprɔ:l] *vi* tumbarse

spray [spreɪ] *n* rociada; (*of sea*) espuma; (*container*) atomizador *m*; (*for paint etc*) pistola rociadora; (*of flowers*) ramita ▷ *vt* rociar; (*crops*) regar

spread [sprɛd] (*pt, pp* **~**) *n* extensión *f*; (*for bread etc*) pasta para untar; (*inf: food*) comilona ▷ *vt* extender; (*butter*) untar; (*wings, sails*) desplegar; (*work, wealth*) repartir; (*scatter*) esparcir ▷ *vi* (*also: ~ out: stain*) extenderse; (*news*) diseminarse; **spread out** *vi* (*move apart*) separarse; **spreadsheet** *n* hoja electrónica *or* de cálculo

spree [spri:] *n*: **to go on a ~** ir de juerga

spring [sprɪŋ] (*pt* **sprang**, *pp* **sprung**) *n* (*season*) primavera; (*leap*) salto, brinco; (*coiled metal*) resorte *m*; (*of water*) fuente *f*, manantial *m* ▷ *vi* saltar, brincar; **spring up** *vi* (*thing: appear*) aparecer; (*problem*) surgir; **spring onion** *n* cebolleta

sprinkle ['sprɪŋkl] *vt* (*pour: liquid*) rociar; (*: salt, sugar*) espolvorear; **to ~ water etc on, ~ with water** *etc* rociar *or* salpicar de agua *etc*

sprint [sprɪnt] *n* esprint *m* ▷ *vi* esprintar

sprung [sprʌŋ] *pp of* **spring**

spun [spʌn] *pt, pp of* **spin**

spur [spə:*] *n* espuela; (*fig*) estímulo, aguijón *m* ▷ *vt* (*also: ~ on*) estimular, incitar; **on the ~ of the moment** de improviso

spurt [spə:t] *n* chorro; (*of energy*) arrebato ▷ *vi* chorrear

spy [spaɪ] *n* espía *mf* ▷ *vi*: **to ~ on** espiar a ▷ *vt* (*see*) divisar, lograr ver

sq. *abbr* = **square**

squabble ['skwɔbl] *vi* reñir, pelear

squad [skwɔd] *n* (*Mil*) pelotón *m*; (*Police*) brigada; (*Sport*) equipo

squadron ['skwɔdrn] *n* (*Mil*) escuadrón *m*; (*Aviat, Naut*) escuadra

S

squander ['skwɔndə*] vt (money) derrochar, despilfarrar; (chances) desperdiciar

square [skwɛə*] n cuadro; (in town) plaza; (inf: person) carca m/f ▷ adj cuadrado; (inf: ideas, tastes) trasnochado ▷ vt (arrange) arreglar; (Math) cuadrar; (reconcile) compaginar; **all ~** igual(es); **to have a ~ meal** comer caliente; **2 metres ~** 2 metros en cuadro; **2 ~ metres** 2 metros cuadrados; **square root** n raíz f cuadrada

squash [skwɔʃ] n (BRIT: drink): **lemon/orange ~** zumo (SP) or jugo (LAM) de limón/naranja; (US Bot) calabacín m; (Sport) squash m ▷ vt aplastar

squat [skwɔt] adj achaparrado ▷ vi (also: ~ **down**) agacharse, sentarse en cuclillas; **squatter** n okupa mf (SP)

squeak [skwiːk] vi (hinge) chirriar, rechinar; (mouse) chillar

squeal [skwiːl] vi chillar, dar gritos agudos

squeeze [skwiːz] n presión f; (of hand) apretón m; (Comm) restricción f ▷ vt (hand, arm) apretar

squid [skwɪd] n inv calamar m; (Culin) calamares mpl

squint [skwɪnt] vi bizquear, ser bizco ▷ n (Med) estrabismo

squirm [skwəːm] vi retorcerse, revolverse

squirrel ['skwɪrəl] n ardilla

squirt [skwəːt] vi salir a chorros ▷ vt chiscar

Sr abbr = **senior**

Sri Lanka [srɪ'læŋkə] n Sri Lanka m

St abbr = **saint; street**

stab [stæb] n (with knife) puñalada; (of pain) pinchazo; (inf: try): **to have a ~ at (doing) sth** intentar (hacer) algo ▷ vt apuñalar

stability [stə'bɪlɪtɪ] n estabilidad f

stable ['steɪbl] adj estable ▷ n cuadra, caballeriza

stack [stæk] n montón m, pila ▷ vt amontonar, apilar

stadium ['steɪdɪəm] n estadio

staff [stɑːf] n (work force) personal m, plantilla; (BRIT Scol) cuerpo docente ▷ vt proveer de personal

stag [stæg] n ciervo, venado

stage [steɪdʒ] n escena; (point) etapa; (platform) plataforma; (profession): **the ~** el teatro ▷ vt (play) poner en escena, representar; (organize) montar, organizar; **in ~s** por etapas

stagger ['stægə*] vi tambalearse ▷ vt (amaze) asombrar; (hours, holidays) escalonar; **staggering** adj asombroso

stagnant ['stægnənt] adj estancado

stag night, stag party n despedida de soltero

stain [steɪn] n mancha; (colouring) tintura ▷ vt manchar; (wood) teñir; **stained glass** n vidrio m de color; **stainless steel** n acero inoxidable

staircase ['stɛəkeɪs] n = **stairway**

stairs [stɛəz] npl escaleras fpl

stairway ['stɛəweɪ] n escalera

stake [steɪk] n estaca, poste m; (Comm) interés m; (Betting) apuesta ▷ vt (money) apostar; (life) arriesgar; (reputation) poner en juego; (claim) presentar una reclamación; **to be at ~** estar en juego

stale [steɪl] adj (bread) duro; (food) pasado; (smell) rancio; (beer) agrio

stalk [stɔːk] n tallo, caña ▷ vt acechar, cazar al acecho

stall [stɔːl] n (in market) puesto; (in stable) casilla (de establo) ▷ vt (Aut) calar; (fig) dar largas a ▷ vi (Aut) calarse; (fig) andarse con rodeos

stamina ['stæmɪnə] n resistencia

stammer ['stæmə*] n tartamudeo ▷ vi tartamudear

stamp [stæmp] n sello (SP), estampilla (LAM), timbre m (MEX); (mark) marca, huella; (on document) timbre ▷ vi (also: ~ **one's foot**) patear ▷ vt (mark) marcar; (letter) franquear; (with rubber stamp) sellar; **stamp out** vt (fire) apagar con el pie; (crime, opposition) acabar con; **stamped addressed envelope** n (BRIT) sobre m sellado con las señas propias

stampede [stæm'piːd] n estampida

stance [stæns] n postura

stand [stænd] (pt, pp **stood**) n (position) posición f, postura; (for taxis) parada; (hall stand) perchero; (music stand) atril m; (Sport) tribuna; (at exhibition) stand m ▷ vi (be) estar, encontrarse; (be on foot) estar de pie; (rise) levantarse; (remain) quedar en pie; (in election) presentar candidatura ▷ vt (place) poner, colocar; (withstand) aguantar, soportar; (invite to) invitar; **to make a ~** (fig) mantener una postura firme; **to ~ for parliament** (BRIT) presentarse (como candidato) a las elecciones; **stand back** vi retirarse; **stand by** vi (be ready) estar listo ▷ vt fus (opinion) aferrarse a; (person) apoyar; **stand down** vi (withdraw) ceder el puesto; **stand for** vt fus (signify) significar; (tolerate) aguantar, permitir; **stand in for** vt fus suplir a; **stand out** vi destacarse; **stand up** vi levantarse, ponerse de pie; **stand up for** vt fus defender; **stand up to** vt fus hacer frente a

standard ['stændəd] n patrón m, norma; (level) nivel m; (flag) estandarte m ▷ adj

(size etc) normal, corriente; (text) básico;
standards npl (morals) valores mpl morales;
standard of living n nivel m de vida
standing ['stændɪŋ] adj (on foot) de
pie, en pie; (permanent) permanente ▷ n
reputación f; **of many years' ~** que lleva
muchos años; **standing order** (BRIT) n (at
bank) orden f de pago permanente
stand: standpoint n punto de vista;
standstill n: **at a standstill** (industry, traffic)
paralizado; (car) parado; **to come to a
standstill** quedar paralizado; pararse
stank [stæŋk] pt of **stink**
staple ['steɪpl] n (for papers) grapa ▷ adj
(food etc) básico ▷ vt grapar
star [stɑː*] n estrella; (celebrity) estrella,
astro ▷ vt (Theatre, Cinema) ser el/la
protagonista de; **the stars** npl (Astrology)
el horóscopo
starboard ['stɑːbəd] n estribor m
starch [stɑːtʃ] n almidón m
stardom ['stɑːdəm] n estrellato
stare [stɛə*] n mirada fija ▷ vi: **to ~ at**
mirar fijo
stark [stɑːk] adj (bleak) severo, escueto
▷ adv: **~ naked** en cueros
start [stɑːt] n principio, comienzo;
(departure) salida; (sudden movement)
salto, sobresalto; (advantage) ventaja ▷ vt
empezar, comenzar; (cause) causar; (found)
fundar; (engine) poner en marcha ▷ vi
comenzar, empezar; (with fright) asustarse,
sobresaltarse; (train etc) salir; **to ~ doing** or
to do sth empezar a hacer algo; **start off**
vi empezar, comenzar; (leave) salir, ponerse
en camino; **start out** vi (begin) empezar;
(set out) partir, salir; **start up** vi comenzar;
(car) ponerse en marcha ▷ vt comenzar;
poner en marcha; **starter** n (Aut) botón m
de arranque; (Sport: official) juez mf de salida;
(BRIT Culin) entrante m; **starting point** n
punto de partida
startle ['stɑːtl] vt asustar, sobrecoger;
startling adj alarmante
starvation [stɑːˈveɪʃən] n hambre f
starve [stɑːv] vi tener mucha hambre; (to
death) morir de hambre ▷ vt hacer pasar
hambre
state [steɪt] n estado ▷ vt (say, declare)
afirmar; **the S~s** los Estados Unidos; **to
be in a ~** estar agitado; **statement** n
afirmación f; **state school** n escuela
or colegio estatal; **statesman** (irreg) n
estadista m
static ['stætɪk] n (Radio) parásitos mpl
▷ adj estático
station ['steɪʃən] n estación f; (Radio)
emisora; (rank) posición f social ▷ vt

colocar, situar; (Mil) apostar
stationary ['steɪʃnərɪ] adj estacionario,
fijo
stationer's (shop) (BRIT) n papelería
stationery [-nərɪ] n papel m de escribir,
artículos mpl de escritorio
station wagon (US) n ranchera
statistic [stəˈtɪstɪk] n estadística;
statistics n (science) estadística
statue ['stætjuː] n estatua
stature ['stætʃə*] n estatura; (fig) talla
status ['steɪtəs] n estado; (reputation)
estatus m; **status quo** n (e)statu quo m
statutory ['stætjutrɪ] adj estatutario
staunch [stɔːntʃ] adj leal, incondicional
stay [steɪ] n estancia ▷ vi quedar(se);
(as guest) hospedarse; **to ~ put** seguir en el
mismo sitio; **to ~ the night/5 days** pasar
la noche/estar 5 días; **stay away** vi (from
person, building) no acercarse; (from event)
no acudir; **stay behind** vi quedar atrás;
stay in vi quedarse en casa; **stay on** vi
quedarse; **stay out** vi (of house) no volver a
casa; (on strike) permanecer en huelga; **stay
up** vi (at night) velar, no acostarse
steadily ['stedɪlɪ] adv constantemente;
(firmly) firmemente; (work, walk) sin parar;
(gaze) fijamente
steady ['stedɪ] adj (firm) firme; (regular)
regular; (person, character) sensato, juicioso;
(boyfriend) formal; (look, voice) tranquilo ▷ vt
(stabilize) estabilizar; (nerves) calmar
steak [steɪk] n filete m; (beef) bistec m
steal [stiːl] (pt **stole**, pp **stolen**) vt robar
▷ vi robar; (move secretly) andar a hurtadillas
steam [stiːm] n vapor m; (mist) vaho,
humo ▷ vt (Culin) cocer al vapor ▷ vi echar
vapor; **steam up** vi (window) empañarse;
to get steamed up about sth (fig) ponerse
negro por algo; **steamy** adj (room) lleno
de vapor; (window) empañado; (heat,
atmosphere) bochornoso
steel [stiːl] n acero ▷ adj de acero
steep [stiːp] adj escarpado, abrupto; (stair)
empinado; (price) exorbitante, excesivo ▷ vt
empapar, remojar
steeple ['stiːpl] n aguja
steer [stɪə*] vt (car) conducir (SP), manejar
(LAM); (person) dirigir ▷ vi conducir,
manejar; **steering** n (Aut) dirección f;
steering wheel n volante m
stem [stɛm] n (of plant) tallo; (of glass) pie
m ▷ vt detener; (blood) restañar
step [stɛp] n paso; (on stair) peldaño,
escalón m ▷ vi: **to ~ forward/back** dar
un paso adelante/hacia atrás; **steps** npl
(BRIT) = **stepladder**; **in/out of ~ (with)**
acorde/en disonancia (con); **step down**

vi (fig) retirarse; **step in** *vi* entrar; *(fig)* intervenir; **step up** *vt (increase)* aumentar; **stepbrother** *n* hermanastro; **stepchild** *(pl* **stepchildren**) *n* hijastro/a *m/f*; **stepdaughter** *n* hijastra; **stepfather** *n* padrastro; **stepladder** *n* escalera doble *or* de tijera; **stepmother** *n* madrastra; **stepsister** *n* hermanastra; **stepson** *n* hijastro

stereo ['stɛrɪəu] *n* estéreo ▷ *adj (also:* **~phonic**) estéreo, estereofónico

stereotype ['stɪərɪətaɪp] *n* estereotipo ▷ *vt* estereotipar

sterile ['stɛraɪl] *adj* estéril; **sterilize** ['stɛrɪlaɪz] *vt* esterilizar

sterling ['stə:lɪŋ] *adj (silver)* de ley ▷ *n (Econ)* libras *fpl* esterlinas *fpl*; **one pound ~** una libra esterlina

stern [stə:n] *adj* severo, austero ▷ *n (Naut)* popa

steroid ['stɪərɔɪd] *n* esteroide *m*

stew [stju:] *n* estofado, guiso ▷ *vt* estofar, guisar; *(fruit)* cocer

steward ['stju:əd] *n* camarero; **stewardess** *n (esp on plane)* azafata

stick [stɪk] *(pt, pp* **stuck**) *n* palo; *(of dynamite)* barreno; *(as weapon)* porra; *(also:* **walking ~**) bastón *m* ▷ *vt (glue)* pegar; *(inf: put)* meter; *(: tolerate)* aguantar, soportar; *(thrust):* **to ~ sth into** clavar or hincar algo en ▷ *vi* pegarse; *(be unmoveable)* quedarse parado; *(in mind)* quedarse grabado; **stick out** *vi* sobresalir; **stick up** *vi* sobresalir; **stick up for** *vt fus* defender; **sticker** *n (label)* etiqueta engomada; *(with slogan)* pegatina; **sticking plaster** *n* esparadrapo; **stick shift** *(US) n (Aut)* palanca de cambios

sticky ['stɪkɪ] *adj* pegajoso; *(label)* engomado; *(fig)* difícil

stiff [stɪf] *adj* rígido, tieso; *(hard)* duro; *(manner)* estirado; *(difficult)* difícil; *(person)* inflexible; *(price)* exorbitante ▷ *adv:* **scared/ bored ~** muerto de miedo/aburrimiento

stifling ['staɪflɪŋ] *adj (heat)* sofocante; bochornoso

stigma ['stɪgmə] *n (fig)* estigma *m*

stiletto [stɪ'lɛtəu] *(BRIT) n (also:* **~ heel**) tacón *m* de aguja

still [stɪl] *adj* inmóvil, quieto ▷ *adv* todavía; *(even)* aun; *(nonetheless)* sin embargo, aun así

stimulate ['stɪmjuleɪt] *vt* estimular

stimulus ['stɪmjuləs] *(pl* **stimuli**) *n* estímulo, incentivo

sting [stɪŋ] *(pt, pp* **stung**) *n* picadura; *(pain)* escozor *m*, picazón *f*; *(organ)* aguijón *m* ▷ *vt, vi* picar

stink [stɪŋk] *(pt* **stank**, *pp* **stunk**) *n* hedor *m*, tufo ▷ *vi* heder, apestar

stir [stə:*] *n (fig: agitation)* conmoción *f* ▷ *vt (tea etc)* remover; *(fig: emotions)* provocar ▷ *vi* moverse; **stir up** *vt (trouble)* fomentar; **stir-fry** *vt* sofreír removiendo ▷ *n plato preparado sofriendo y removiendo los ingredientes*

stitch [stɪtʃ] *n (Sewing)* puntada; *(Knitting)* punto; *(Med)* punto (de sutura); *(pain)* punzada ▷ *vt (Med)* suturar

stock [stɔk] *n (Comm: reserves)* existencias *fpl*, stock *m*; *(: selection)* surtido; *(Agr)* ganado, ganadería; *(Culin)* caldo; *(descent)* raza, estirpe *f*; *(Finance)* capital *m* ▷ *adj (fig: reply etc)* clásico ▷ *vt (have in stock)* tener existencias de; **~s and shares** acciones y valores; **in ~** en existencia *or* almacén; **out of ~** agotado; **to take ~ of** *(fig)* asesorar, examinar; **stockbroker** ['stɔkbrəukə*] *n* agente *mf or* corredor *mf* de bolsa(a); **stock cube** *(BRIT) n* pastilla de caldo; **stock exchange** *n* bolsa; **stockholder** ['stɔk-həuldə*] *(US) n* accionista *m/f*

stocking ['stɔkɪŋ] *n* media

stock market *n* bolsa (de valores)

stole [stəul] *pt of* **steal** ▷ *n* estola

stolen ['stəuln] *pp of* **steal**

stomach ['stʌmək] *n (Anat)* estómago; *(belly)* vientre *m* ▷ *vt* tragar, aguantar; **stomachache** *n* dolor *m* de estómago

stone [stəun] *n* piedra; *(in fruit)* hueso *(= 6.348 kg; 14 libras)* ▷ *adj* de piedra ▷ *vt* apedrear; *(fruit)* deshuesar

stood [stud] *pt, pp of* **stand**

stool [stu:l] *n* taburete *m*

stoop [stu:p] *vi (also:* **~ down**) doblarse, agacharse; *(also:* **have a ~**) ser cargado de espaldas

stop [stɔp] *n* parada; *(in punctuation)* punto ▷ *vt* parar, detener; *(break)* suspender; *(block: pay)* suspender; *(: cheque)* invalidar; *(also:* **put a ~ to**) poner término a ▷ *vi* pararse, detenerse; *(end)* acabarse; **to ~ doing sth** dejar de hacer algo; **stop by** *vi* pasar por; **stop off** *vi* interrumpir el viaje; **stopover** *n* parada; *(Aviat)* escala; **stoppage** *n (strike)* paro; *(blockage)* obstrucción *f*

storage ['stɔ:rɪdʒ] *n* almacenaje *m*

store [stɔ:*] *n (stock)* provisión *f*; *(depot (BRIT: large shop)* almacén *m*; *(US)* tienda; *(reserve)* reserva, repuesto ▷ *vt* almacenar; **stores** *npl* víveres *mpl*; **to be in ~ for sb** *(fig)* esperarle a algn; **storekeeper** *(US) n* tendero/a

storey ['stɔ:rɪ] *(US* **story**) *n* piso

storm [stɔ:m] *n* tormenta; *(fig: of*

applause) salva; (: *of criticism*) nube f ▷ vi (*fig*)
rabiar ▷ vt tomar por asalto; **stormy** *adj*
tempestuoso

story ['stɔːrɪ] *n* historia; (*lie*) mentira; (*us*)
= **storey**

stout [staut] *adj* (*strong*) sólido; (*fat*)
gordo, corpulento; (*resolute*) resuelto ▷ *n*
cerveza negra

stove [stəuv] *n* (*for cooking*) cocina; (*for
heating*) estufa

straight [streɪt] *adj* recto, derecho;
(*frank*) franco, directo; (*simple*) sencillo
▷ *adv* derecho, directamente; (*drink*) sin
mezcla; **to put** *or* **get sth ~** dejar algo en
claro; **~ away, ~ off** en seguida; **straighten**
vt (*also:* **straighten out**) enderezar,
poner derecho ▷ vi (*also:* **straighten
up**) enderezarse, ponerse derecho;
straightforward *adj* (*simple*) sencillo;
(*honest*) honrado, franco

strain [streɪn] *n* tensión f; (*Tech*) presión
f; (*Med*) torcedura; (*breed*) tipo, variedad f
▷ vt (*back etc*) torcerse; (*resources*) agotar;
(*stretch*) estirar; (*food, tea*) colar; **strained**
adj (*muscle*) torcido; (*laugh*) forzado;
(*relations*) tenso; **strainer** *n* colador m

strait [streɪt] *n* (*Geo*) estrecho (*fig*): **to be
in dire ~s** estar en un gran apuro

strand [strænd] *n* (*of thread*) hebra; (*of
hair*) trenza; (*of rope*) ramal m; **stranded**
adj (*person: without money*) desamparado;
(: *without transport*) colgado

strange [streɪndʒ] *adj* (*not known*)
desconocido; (*odd*) extraño, raro;
strangely *adv* de un modo raro; **stranger**
n desconocido/a; (*from another area*)
forastero/a

▌ Be careful not to translate **stranger** by
the Spanish word *extranjero*.

strangle ['stræŋɡl] *vt* estrangular

strap [stræp] *n* correa; (*of slip, dress*)
tirante m

strategic [strə'tiːdʒɪk] *adj* estratégico

strategy ['strætɪdʒɪ] *n* estrategia

straw [strɔː] *n* paja; (*drinking straw*) caña,
pajita; **that's the last ~!** ¡eso es el colmo!

strawberry ['strɔːbərɪ] *n* fresa, frutilla
(*sc*)

stray [streɪ] *adj* (*animal*) extraviado;
(*bullet*) perdido; (*scattered*) disperso ▷ vi
extraviarse, perderse

streak [striːk] *n* raya; (*in hair*) raya ▷ vt
rayar ▷ vi: **to ~ past** pasar como un rayo

stream [striːm] *n* riachuelo, arroyo; (*of
people, vehicles*) riada, caravana; (*of smoke,
insults etc*) chorro ▷ vt (*Scol*) dividir en
grupos por habilidad ▷ vi correr, fluir; **to ~
in/out** (*people*) entrar/salir en tropel

street [striːt] *n* calle f; **streetcar** (*us*) *n*
tranvía m; **street light** *n* farol m (*LAM*),
farola (*SP*); **street map** *n* plano (de la
ciudad); **street plan** *n* plano

strength [strɛŋθ] *n* fuerza; (*of girder,
knot etc*) resistencia; (*fig: power*) poder m;
strengthen *vt* fortalecer, reforzar

strenuous ['strɛnjuəs] *adj* (*energetic,
determined*) enérgico

stress [strɛs] *n* presión f; (*mental strain*)
estrés m; (*accent*) acento ▷ vt subrayar,
recalcar; (*syllable*) acentuar; **stressed**
adj (*tense* estresado, agobiado; (*syllable*)
acentuado; **stressful** *adj* (*job*) estresante

stretch [strɛtʃ] *n* (*of sand etc*) trecho
▷ vi estirarse; (*extend*) **to ~ to** *or* **as far as**
extenderse hasta ▷ vt extender, estirar;
(*make demands*) exigir el máximo esfuerzo
a; **stretch out** vi tenderse ▷ vt (*arm etc*)
extender; (*spread*) estirar

stretcher ['strɛtʃə*] *n* camilla

strict [strɪkt] *adj* severo; (*exact*) estricto;
strictly *adv* severamente; estrictamente

stride [straɪd] (*pt* **strode**, *pp* **stridden**) *n*
zancada, tranco ▷ vi dar zancadas, andar
a trancos

strike [straɪk] (*pt, pp* **struck**) *n* huelga;
(*of oil etc*) descubrimiento; (*attack*) ataque
m ▷ vt golpear, pegar; (*oil etc*) descubrir;
(*bargain, deal*) cerrar ▷ vi declarar la huelga;
(*attack*) atacar; (*clock*) dar la hora; **on ~**
(*workers*) en huelga; **to ~ a match** encender
un fósforo; **striker** *n* huelguista mf; (*Sport*)
delantero; **striking** *adj* llamativo

string [strɪŋ] (*pt, pp* **strung**) *n* cuerda;
(*row*) hilera ▷ vt: **to ~ together** ensartar;
to ~ out extenderse; **the strings** npl (*Mus*)
los instrumentos de cuerda; **to pull ~s** (*fig*)
mover palancas

strip [strɪp] *n* tira; (*of land*) franja; (*of metal*)
cinta, lámina ▷ vt desnudar; (*paint*) quitar;
(*also:* **~ down**: *machine*) desmontar ▷ vi
desnudarse; **strip off** vt (*paint etc*) quitar
▷ vi (*person*) desnudarse

stripe [straɪp] *n* raya; (*Mil*) galón m;
striped *adj* a rayas, rayado

stripper ['strɪpə*] *n* artista mf de
striptease

strip-search ['strɪpsəːtʃ] *vt*: **to ~ sb**
desnudar y registrar a algn

strive [straɪv] (*pt* **strove**, *pp* **striven**) *vi*: **to
~ for sth/to do sth** luchar por conseguir/
hacer algo

strode [strəud] *pt of* **stride**

stroke [strəuk] *n* (*blow*) golpe m;
(*Swimming*) brazada; (*Med*) apoplejía; (*of
paintbrush*) toque m ▷ vt acariciar; **at a ~** de
un solo golpe

S

stroll [strəul] n paseo, vuelta ▷ vi dar un paseo or una vuelta; **stroller** (us) n (for child) sillita de ruedas

strong [strɔŋ] adj fuerte; **they are 50 ~** son 50; **stronghold** n fortaleza; (fig) baluarte m; (believe) adv fuertemente, con fuerza; (believe) firmemente

strove [strəuv] pt of **strive**

struck [strʌk] pt, pp of **strike**

structure [ˈstrʌktʃə*] n estructura; (building) construcción f

struggle [ˈstrʌgl] n lucha ▷ vi luchar

strung [strʌŋ] pt, pp of **string**

stub [stʌb] n (of ticket etc) talón m; (of cigarette) colilla; **to ~ one's toe on sth** dar con el dedo (del pie) contra algo; **stub out** vt apagar

stubble [ˈstʌbl] n rastrojo; (on chin) barba (incipiente)

stubborn [ˈstʌbən] adj terco, testarudo

stuck [stʌk] pt, pp of **stick** ▷ adj (jammed) atascado

stud [stʌd] n (shirt stud) corchete m; (of boot) taco; (earring) pendiente m (de bolita); (also: **~ farm**) caballeriza; (also: **~ horse**) caballo semental ▷ vt (fig): **~ded with** salpicado de

student [ˈstjuːdənt] n estudiante mf ▷ adj estudiantil; **student driver** (us) n conductor(a) mf en prácticas; **students' union** n (building) centro de estudiantes; (BRIT: association) federación f de estudiantes

studio [ˈstjuːdɪəu] n estudio; (artist's) taller m; **studio flat** n estudio

study [ˈstʌdɪ] n estudio ▷ vt estudiar; (examine) examinar, investigar ▷ vi estudiar

stuff [stʌf] n materia; (substance) material m, sustancia; (things) cosas fpl ▷ vt llenar; (Culin) rellenar; (animals) disecar; (inf: push) meter; **stuffing** n relleno; **stuffy** adj (room) mal ventilado; (person) de miras estrechas

stumble [ˈstʌmbl] vi tropezar, dar un traspié; **to ~ across, ~ on** (fig) tropezar con

stump [stʌmp] n (of tree) tocón m; (of limb) muñón m ▷ vt: **to be ~ed for an answer** no saber qué contestar

stun [stʌn] vt dejar sin sentido

stung [stʌŋ] pt, pp of **sting**

stunk [stʌŋk] pp of **stink**

stunned [stʌnd] adj (dazed) aturdido, atontado; (amazed) pasmado; (shocked) anonadado

stunning [ˈstʌnɪŋ] adj (fig: news) pasmoso; (: outfit etc) sensacional

stunt [stʌnt] n (in film) escena peligrosa; (publicity stunt) truco publicitario

stupid [ˈstjuːpɪd] adj estúpido, tonto; **stupidity** [-ˈpɪdɪtɪ] n estupidez f

sturdy [ˈstəːdɪ] adj robusto, fuerte

stutter [ˈstʌtə*] n tartamudeo ▷ vi tartamudear

style [staɪl] n estilo; **stylish** adj elegante, a la moda; **stylist** n (hair stylist) peluquero/a

sub... [sʌb] prefix sub...; **subconscious** adj subconsciente

subdued [səbˈdjuːd] adj (light) tenue; (person) sumiso, manso

subject [n ˈsʌbdʒɪkt, vb səbˈdʒɛkt] n súbdito; (Scol) asignatura; (matter) tema m; (Grammar) sujeto ▷ vt: **to ~ sb to sth** someter a algn a algo; **to be ~ to** (law) estar sujeto a; (person) ser propenso a; **subjective** [-ˈdʒɛktɪv] adj subjetivo; **subject matter** n (content) contenido

subjunctive [səbˈdʒʌŋktɪv] adj, n subjuntivo

submarine [sʌbməˈriːn] n submarino

submission [səbˈmɪʃən] n sumisión f

submit [səbˈmɪt] vt someter ▷ vi: **to ~ to sth** someterse a algo

subordinate [səˈbɔːdɪnət] adj, n subordinado/a m/f

subscribe [səbˈskraɪb] vi suscribir; **to ~ to** (opinion, fund) suscribir, aprobar; (newspaper) suscribirse a

subscription [səbˈskrɪpʃən] n abono; (to magazine) subscripción f

subsequent [ˈsʌbsɪkwənt] adj subsiguiente, posterior; **subsequently** adv posteriormente, más tarde

subside [səbˈsaɪd] vi hundirse; (flood) bajar; (wind) amainar

subsidiary [səbˈsɪdɪərɪ] adj secundario ▷ n sucursal f, filial f

subsidize [ˈsʌbsɪdaɪz] vt subvencionar

subsidy [ˈsʌbsɪdɪ] n subvención f

substance [ˈsʌbstəns] n sustancia

substantial [səbˈstænʃl] adj sustancial, sustancioso; (fig) importante

substitute [ˈsʌbstɪtjuːt] n (person) suplente mf; (thing) sustituto ▷ vt: **to ~ A for B** sustituir A por B, reemplazar B por A; **substitution** n sustitución f

subtle [ˈsʌtl] adj sutil

subtract [səbˈtrækt] vt restar, sustraer

suburb [ˈsʌbəːb] n barrio residencial; **the ~s** las afueras (de la ciudad); **suburban** [səˈbəːbən] adj suburbano; (train etc) de cercanías

subway [ˈsʌbweɪ] n (BRIT) paso subterráneo or inferior; (us) metro

succeed [səkˈsiːd] vi (person) tener éxito; (plan) salir bien ▷ vt suceder a; **to ~ in**

doing lograr hacer
success [sək'sɛs] n éxito

▌Be careful not to translate **success** by the Spanish word *suceso*.

successful adj exitoso; (business) próspero; **to be successful (in doing)** lograr (hacer); **successfully** adv con éxito
succession [sək'sɛʃən] n sucesión f, serie f
successive [sək'sɛsɪv] adj sucesivo, consecutivo
successor [sək'sɛsə*] n sucesor(a) m/f
succumb [sə'kʌm] vi sucumbir
such [sʌtʃ] adj tal, semejante; (of that kind): **~ a book** tal libro; (so much): **~ courage** tanto valor ▷ adv tan; **~ a long trip** un viaje tan largo; **~ a lot of** tanto(s)/a(s); **~ as** (like) tal como; **as ~** como tal; **such-and-such** adj tal o cual
suck [sʌk] vt chupar; (bottle) sorber; (breast) mamar
Sudan [su'dæn] n Sudán m
sudden ['sʌdn] adj (rapid) repentino, súbito; (unexpected) imprevisto; **all of a ~** de repente; **suddenly** adv de repente
sue [su:] vt demandar
suede [sweɪd] n ante m, gamuza
suffer ['sʌfə*] vt sufrir, padecer; (tolerate) aguantar, soportar ▷ vi sufrir; **to ~ from** (illness etc) padecer; **suffering** n sufrimiento
suffice [sə'faɪs] vi bastar, ser suficiente
sufficient [sə'fɪʃənt] adj suficiente, bastante
suffocate ['sʌfəkeɪt] vi ahogarse, asfixiarse
sugar ['ʃugə*] n azúcar m ▷ vt echar azúcar a, azucarar
suggest [sə'dʒɛst] vt sugerir; **suggestion** [-'dʒɛstʃən] n sugerencia
suicide ['suɪsaɪd] n suicidio; (person) suicida mf; see also **commit**; **suicide attack** n atentado suicida; **suicide bomber** n terrorista mf suicida; **suicide bombing** n atentado suicida
suit [su:t] n (man's) traje m; (woman's) conjunto; (Law) pleito; (Cards) palo ▷ vt convenir; (clothes) sentar a, ir bien a; (adapt): **to ~ sth to** adaptar or ajustar algo a; **well ~ed** (well matched: couple) hecho el uno para el otro; **suitable** adj conveniente; (apt) indicado; **suitcase** n maleta, valija (RPL)
suite [swi:t] n (of rooms, Mus) suite f; (furniture): **bedroom/dining room ~** (juego de) dormitorio/comedor; see also **three-piece suite**
sulfur ['sʌlfə*] (US) n = **sulphur**
sulk [sʌlk] vi estar de mal humor
sulphur ['sʌlfə*] (US **sulfur**) n azufre m

sultana [sʌl'tɑ:nə] n (fruit) pasa de Esmirna
sum [sʌm] n suma; (total) total m; **sum up** vt resumir ▷ vi hacer un resumen
summarize ['sʌmaraɪz] vt resumir
summary ['sʌmarɪ] n resumen m ▷ adj (justice) sumario
summer ['sʌmə*] n verano ▷ cpd de verano; **in ~** en verano; **summer holidays** npl vacaciones fpl de verano; **summertime** n (season) verano
summit ['sʌmɪt] n cima, cumbre f; (also: **~ conference, ~ meeting**) (conferencia) cumbre f
summon ['sʌmən] vt (person) llamar; (meeting) convocar; (Law) citar
Sun. abbr (= Sunday) dom
sun [sʌn] n sol m; **sunbathe** vi tomar el sol; **sunbed** n cama solar; **sunblock** n filtro solar; **sunburn** n (painful) quemadura; (tan) bronceado; **sunburned, sunburnt** adj (painfully) quemado por el sol; (tanned) bronceado
Sunday ['sʌndɪ] n domingo
sunflower ['sʌnflauə*] n girasol m
sung [sʌŋ] pp of **sing**
sunglasses ['sʌnɡlɑ:sɪz] npl gafas fpl (SP) or anteojos fpl (LAM) de sol
sunk [sʌŋk] pp of **sink**
sun: sunlight n luz f del sol; **sun lounger** n tumbona, perezosa (LAM); **sunny** adj soleado; (day) de sol; (fig) alegre; **sunrise** n salida del sol; **sun roof** n (Aut) techo corredizo; **sunscreen** n protector m solar; **sunset** n puesta del sol; **sunshade** n (over table) sombrilla; **sunshine** n sol m; **sunstroke** n insolación f; **suntan** n bronceado; **suntan lotion** n bronceador m; **suntan oil** n aceite m bronceador
super ['su:pə*] (inf) adj genial
superb [su:'pə:b] adj magnífico, espléndido
superficial [su:pə'fɪʃəl] adj superficial
superintendent [su:pərɪn'tɛndənt] n director(a) m/f; (Police) subjefe/a m/f
superior [su:'pɪərɪə*] adj superior; (smug) desdeñoso ▷ n superior m
superlative [su'pə:lətɪv] n superlativo
supermarket ['su:pəmɑ:kɪt] n supermercado
supernatural [su:pə'nætʃərəl] adj sobrenatural ▷ n: **the ~** lo sobrenatural
superpower ['su:pəpauə*] n (Pol) superpotencia
superstition [su:pə'stɪʃən] n superstición f
superstitious [su:pə'stɪʃəs] adj supersticioso

superstore ['su:pəstɔ:*] n (BRIT)
hipermercado
supervise ['su:pəvaɪz] vt supervisar;
supervision [-'vɪʒən] n supervisión f;
supervisor n supervisor(a) m/f
supper ['sʌpə*] n cena
supple ['sʌpl] adj flexible
supplement [n 'sʌplɪmənt, vb sʌplɪ'mɛnt]
n suplemento ▷ vt suplir
supplier [sə'plaɪə*] n (Comm)
distribuidor(a) m/f
supply [sə'plaɪ] vt (provide) suministrar;
(equip): **to ~ (with)** proveer (de) ▷ n
provisión f; (of gas, water etc) suministro;
supplies npl (food) víveres mpl; (Mil)
pertrechos mpl
support [sə'pɔ:t] n apoyo; (Tech) soporte
m ▷ vt apoyar; (financially) mantener;
(uphold, Tech) sostener

Be careful not to translate **support** by
the Spanish word soportar.

supporter n (Pol etc) partidario/a; (Sport)
aficionado/a
suppose [sə'pəuz] vt suponer; (imagine)
imaginarse; (duty): **to be ~d to do sth** deber
hacer algo; **supposedly** [sə'pəuzɪdlɪ] adv
según cabe suponer; **supposing** conj en
caso de que
suppress [sə'prɛs] vt suprimir; (yawn)
ahogar
supreme [su'pri:m] adj supremo
surcharge ['sə:tʃɑ:dʒ] n sobretasa,
recargo
sure [ʃuə*] adj seguro; (definite, convinced)
cierto; **to make ~ of sth/that** asegurarse
de algo/asegurar que; **~!** (of course) ¡claro!,
¡por supuesto!; **~ enough** efectivamente;
surely adv (certainly) seguramente
surf [sə:f] n olas fpl ▷ vt: **to ~ the Net**
navegar por Internet
surface ['sə:fɪs] n superficie f ▷ vt (road)
revestir ▷ vi salir a la superficie; **by ~ mail**
por vía terrestre
surfboard ['sə:fbɔ:d] n tabla (de surf)
surfer ['sə:fə*] n (in sea) surfista mf; **web** or
net ~ internauta mf
surfing ['sə:fɪŋ] n surf m
surge [sə:dʒ] n oleada, oleaje m ▷ vi (wave)
romper; (people) avanzar en tropel
surgeon ['sə:dʒən] n cirujano/a
surgery ['sə:dʒərɪ] n cirugía; (BRIT: room)
consultorio
surname ['sə:neɪm] n apellido
surpass [sə:'pɑ:s] vt superar, exceder
surplus ['sə:pləs] n excedente m; (Comm)
superávit m ▷ adj excedente, sobrante
surprise [sə'praɪz] n sorpresa ▷ vt
sorprender; **surprised** adj (look, smile) de

sorpresa; **to be surprised** sorprenderse;
surprising adj sorprendente; **surprisingly**
adv: **it was surprisingly easy** me etc
sorprendió lo fácil que fue
surrender [sə'rɛndə*] n rendición f,
entrega ▷ vi rendirse, entregarse
surround [sə'raund] vt rodear,
circundar; (Mil etc) cercar; **surrounding**
adj circundante; **surroundings** npl
alrededores mpl, cercanías fpl
surveillance [sə:'veɪləns] n vigilancia
survey [n 'sə:veɪ, vb sə:'veɪ] n inspección
f, reconocimiento; (inquiry) encuesta ▷ vt
examinar, inspeccionar; (look at) mirar,
contemplar; **surveyor** n agrimensor(a) m/f
survival [sə'vaɪvl] n supervivencia
survive [sə'vaɪv] vi sobrevivir; (custom
etc) perdurar ▷ vt sobrevivir a; **survivor** n
superviviente mf
suspect [adj, n 'sʌspɛkt, vb səs'pɛkt] adj, n
sospechoso/a m/f ▷ vt (person) sospechar
de; (think) sospechar
suspend [səs'pɛnd] vt suspender;
suspended sentence n (Law) libertad f
condicional; **suspenders** npl (BRIT) ligas
fpl; (US) tirantes mpl
suspense [səs'pɛns] n incertidumbre f,
duda; (in film etc) suspense m; **to keep sb in
~** mantener a algn en suspense
suspension [səs'pɛnʃən] n (gen, Aut)
suspensión f; (of driving licence) privación f;
suspension bridge n puente m colgante
suspicion [səs'pɪʃən] n sospecha; (distrust)
recelo; **suspicious** adj receloso; (causing
suspicion) sospechoso
sustain [səs'teɪn] vt sostener, apoyar;
(suffer) sufrir, padecer
SUV [esp US] n abbr (= sports utility vehicle)
todoterreno m inv, 4x4 m
swallow ['swɒləu] n (bird) golondrina ▷ vt
tragar; (fig.: pride) tragarse
swam [swæm] pt of **swim**
swamp [swɒmp] n pantano, ciénaga
▷ vt (with water etc) inundar; (fig) abrumar,
agobiar
swan [swɒn] n cisne m
swap [swɒp] n canje m, intercambio
▷ vt: **to ~ (for)** cambiar (por)
swarm [swɔ:m] n (of bees) enjambre
m; (fig) multitud f ▷ vi (bees) formar un
enjambre; (people) pulular; **to be ~ing with**
ser un hervidero de
sway [sweɪ] vi mecerse, balancearse ▷ vt
(influence) mover, influir en
swear [sweə*] (pt **swore**, pp **sworn**) vi
(curse) maldecir; (promise) jurar ▷ vt jurar;
swear in vt: **to be sworn in** prestar
juramento; **swearword** n taco, palabrota

403 | **system**

sweat [swɛt] *n* sudor *m* ▷ *vi* sudar
sweater ['swɛtə*] *n* suéter *m*
sweatshirt ['swɛtʃəːt] *n* suéter *m*
sweaty ['swɛtɪ] *adj* sudoroso
Swede [swiːd] *n* sueco/a
swede [swiːd] *n* nabo
Sweden ['swiːdn] *n* Suecia; **Swedish**
['swiːdɪʃ] *adj* sueco ▷ *n* (*Ling*) sueco
sweep [swiːp] (*pt, pp* **swept**) *n* (*act*)
barrido; (*also:* **chimney ~**) deshollinador(a)
m/f ▷ *vt* barrer; (*with arm*) empujar; (*current*)
arrastrar ▷ *vi* barrer; (*arm etc*) moverse
rápidamente; (*wind*) soplar con violencia
sweet [swiːt] *n* (*candy*) dulce *m*, caramelo;
(*BRIT: pudding*) postre *m* ▷ *adj* dulce;
(*fig: kind*) dulce, amable; (*: attractive*) mono;
sweetcorn *n* maíz *m*; **sweetener**
['swiːtnə*] *n* (*Culin*) edulcorante *m*;
sweetheart *n* novio/a; **sweetshop** *n*
(*BRIT*) confitería, bombonería
swell [swɛl] (*pt* **~ed**, *pp* **swollen** *or*
~ed) *n* (*of sea*) marejada, oleaje *m* ▷ *adj*
(*US: inf: excellent*) estupendo, fenomenal ▷ *vt*
hinchar, inflar ▷ *vi* (*also:* **~ up**) hincharse;
(*numbers*) aumentar; (*sound, feeling*) ir
aumentando; **swelling** *n* (*Med*) hinchazón *f*
swept [swɛpt] *pt, pp* of **sweep**
swerve [swəːv] *vi* desviarse bruscamente
swift [swɪft] *n* (*bird*) vencejo ▷ *adj* rápido,
veloz
swim [swɪm] (*pt* **swam**, *pp* **swum**) *n:* **to go
for a ~** ir a nadar or a bañarse ▷ *vi* nadar;
(*head, room*) dar vueltas ▷ *vt* nadar; (*the
Channel etc*) cruzar a nado; **swimmer** *n*
nadador(a) *m/f*; **swimming** *n* natación *f*;
swimming costume (*BRIT*) *n* bañador *m*,
traje *m* de baño; **swimming pool** *n* piscina,
alberca (*MEX*), pileta (*RPL*); **swimming
trunks** *npl* bañador *m* (de hombre);
swimsuit *n* = **swimming costume**
swing [swɪŋ] (*pt, pp* **swung**) *n* (*in
playground*) columpio; (*movement*) balanceo,
vaivén *m*; (*change of direction*) viraje *m*;
(*rhythm*) ritmo ▷ *vt* balancear; (*also:* **~
round**) voltear, girar ▷ *vi* balancearse,
columpiarse; (*also:* **~ round**) dar media
vuelta; **to be in full ~** estar en plena marcha
swipe card [swaɪp-] *n* tarjeta magnética
deslizante, tarjeta swipe
swirl [swəːl] *vi* arremolinarse
Swiss [swɪs] *adj, n inv* suizo/a *m/f*
switch [swɪtʃ] *n* (*for light etc*) interruptor
m; (*change*) cambio ▷ *vt* (*change*) cambiar
de; **switch off** *vt* apagar; (*engine*) parar;
switch on *vt* encender (*SP*), prender (*LAM*);
(*engine, machine*) arrancar; **switchboard** *n*
(*Tel*) centralita (*SP*), conmutador *m* (*LAM*)
Switzerland ['swɪtsələnd] *n* Suiza

swivel ['swɪvl] *vi* (*also:* **~ round**) girar
swollen ['swəulən] *pp of* **swell**
swoop [swuːp] *n* (*by police etc*) redada ▷ *vi*
(*also:* **~ down**) calarse
swop [swɔp] = **swap**
sword [sɔːd] *n* espada; **swordfish** *n* pez
m espada
swore [swɔː*] *pt of* **swear**
sworn [swɔːn] *pp of* **swear** ▷ *adj*
(*statement*) bajo juramento; (*enemy*)
implacable
swum [swʌm] *pp of* **swim**
swung [swʌŋ] *pt, pp of* **swing**
syllable ['sɪləbl] *n* sílaba
syllabus ['sɪləbəs] *n* programa *m* de
estudios
symbol ['sɪmbl] *n* símbolo; **symbolic(al)**
[sɪm'bɔlɪk(l)] *adj* simbólico; **to be
symbolic(al) of sth** simbolizar algo
symmetrical [sɪ'mɛtrɪkl] *adj* simétrico
symmetry ['sɪmɪtrɪ] *n* simetría
sympathetic [sɪmpə'θɛtɪk] *adj*
(*understanding*) comprensivo; (*showing
support*): **~ to(wards)** bien dispuesto hacia
| Be careful not to translate **sympathetic**
| by the Spanish word *simpático*.
sympathize ['sɪmpəθaɪz] *vi:* **to ~ with**
(*person*) compadecerse de; (*feelings*)
comprender; (*cause*) apoyar
sympathy ['sɪmpəθɪ] *n* (*pity*) compasión *f*
symphony ['sɪmfənɪ] *n* sinfonía
symptom ['sɪmptəm] *n* síntoma *m*,
indicio
synagogue ['sɪnəgɔg] *n* sinagoga
syndicate ['sɪndɪkɪt] *n* sindicato; (*of
newspapers*) agencia (de noticias)
syndrome ['sɪndrəum] *n* síndrome *m*
synonym ['sɪnənɪm] *n* sinónimo
synthetic [sɪn'θɛtɪk] *adj* sintético
Syria ['sɪrɪə] *n* Siria
syringe [sɪ'rɪndʒ] *n* jeringa
syrup ['sɪrəp] *n* jarabe *m*; (*also:* **golden ~**)
almíbar *m*
system ['sɪstəm] *n* sistema *m*; (*Anat*)
organismo; **systematic** [-'mætɪk] *adj*
sistemático, metódico; **systems analyst** *n*
analista *mf* de sistemas

ta [tɑː] (BRIT: inf) excl ¡gracias!

tab [tæb] n lengüeta; (label) etiqueta; **to keep ~s on** (fig) vigilar

table ['teɪbl] n mesa; (of statistics etc) cuadro, tabla ▷ vt (BRIT: motion etc) presentar; **to lay** or **set the ~** poner la mesa; **tablecloth** n mantel m; **table d'hôte** [tɑːbl'dəut] adj del menú; **table lamp** n lámpara de mesa; **tablemat** n (for plate) posaplatos m inv; (for hot dish) salvamantel m; **tablespoon** n cuchara de servir; (also: **tablespoonful**: as measurement) cucharada

tablet ['tæblɪt] n (Med) pastilla, comprimido; (of stone) lápida

table tennis n ping-pong m, tenis m de mesa

tabloid ['tæblɔɪd] n periódico popular sensacionalista

taboo [tə'buː] adj, n tabú m

tack [tæk] n (nail) tachuela; (fig) rumbo ▷ vt (nail) clavar con tachuelas; (stitch) hilvanar ▷ vi virar

tackle ['tækl] n (fishing tackle) aparejo (de pescar); (for lifting) aparejo ▷ vt (difficulty) enfrentarse con; (challenge: person) hacer frente a; (grapple with) agarrar; (Football) cargar; (Rugby) placar

tacky ['tækɪ] adj pegajoso; (pej) cutre

tact [tækt] n tacto, discreción f; **tactful** adj discreto, diplomático

tactics ['tæktɪks] npl táctica

tactless ['tæktlɪs] adj indiscreto

tadpole ['tædpəul] n renacuajo

taffy ['tæfɪ] (US) n melcocha

tag [tæg] n (label) etiqueta

tail [teɪl] n cola; (of shirt, coat) faldón m ▷ vt (follow) vigilar a; **tails** npl (formal suit) levita

tailor ['teɪlə*] n sastre m

Taiwan [taɪ'wɑːn] n Taiwán m; **Taiwanese** [taɪwə'niːz] adj, n taiwanés/esa m/f

take [teɪk] (pt **took**, pp **taken**) vt tomar; (grab) coger (SP), agarrar (LAM); (gain: prize) ganar; (require: effort, courage) exigir; (tolerate: pain etc) aguantar; (hold: passengers etc) tener cabida para; (accompany, bring, carry) llevar; (exam) presentarse a; **to ~ sth from** (drawer etc) sacar algo de; (person) quitar algo a; **I ~ it that ...** supongo que ...; **take after** vt fus parecerse a; **take apart** vt desmontar; **take away** vt (remove) quitar; (carry) llevar; (Math) restar; **take back** vt (return) devolver; (one's words) retractarse de; **take down** vt (building) derribar; (letter etc) apuntar; **take in** vt (deceive) engañar; (understand) entender; (include) abarcar; (lodger) acoger, recibir; **take off** vi (Aviat) despegar ▷ vt (remove) quitar; **take on** vt (work) aceptar; (employee) contratar; (opponent) desafiar; **take out** vt sacar; **take over** vt (business) tomar posesión de; (country) tomar el poder ▷ vi: **to take over from sb** reemplazar a algn; **take up** vt (a dress) acortar; (occupy: time, space) ocupar; (engage in: hobby etc) dedicarse a; (accept): **to take sb up on** aceptar algo de algn; **takeaway** (BRIT) adj (food) para llevar ▷ n tienda or restaurante m de comida para llevar; **taken** pp of **take**; **takeoff** n (Aviat) despegue m; **takeout** (US) n = **takeaway**; **takeover** n (Comm) absorción f; **takings** npl (Comm) ingresos mpl

talc [tælk] n (also: **~um powder**) (polvos de) talco

tale [teɪl] n (story) cuento; (account) relación f; **to tell ~s** (fig) chivarse

talent ['tælnt] n talento; **talented** adj de talento

talk [tɔːk] n charla; (conversation) conversación f; (gossip) habladurías fpl, chismes mpl ▷ vi hablar; **talks** npl (Pol etc) conversaciones fpl; **to ~ about** hablar de; **to ~ sb into doing sth** convencer a algn para que haga algo; **to ~ sb out of doing sth**

disuadir a algn de que haga algo; **to ~ shop** hablar del trabajo; **talk over** vt discutir; **talk show** n programa m de entrevistas

tall [tɔ:l] adj alto; (object) grande; **to be 6 feet ~** (person) ≈ medir 1 metro 80

tambourine [tæmbə'ri:n] n pandereta

tame [teɪm] adj domesticado; (fig) mediocre

tamper ['tæmpə*] vi: **to ~ with** tocar, andar con

tampon ['tæmpən] n tampón m

tan [tæn] n (also: **sun~**) bronceado ▷ vi ponerse moreno ▷ adj (colour) marrón

tandem ['tændəm] n tándem m

tangerine [tændʒə'ri:n] n mandarina

tangle ['tæŋgl] n enredo; **to get in(to) a ~** enredarse

tank [tæŋk] n (water tank) depósito, tanque m; (for fish) acuario; (Mil) tanque m

tanker ['tæŋkə*] n (ship) buque m, cisterna; (truck) camión m cisterna

tanned [tænd] adj (skin) moreno

tantrum ['tæntrəm] n rabieta

Tanzania [tænzə'nɪə] n Tanzania

tap [tæp] n (BRIT: on sink etc) grifo (SP), llave f, canilla (RPL); (gas tap) llave f; (gentle blow) golpecito ▷ vt (hit gently) dar golpecitos en; (resources) utilizar, explotar; (telephone) intervenir; **on ~** (fig: resources) a mano; **tap dancing** n claqué m

tape [teɪp] n (also: **magnetic ~**) cinta magnética; (cassette) cassette f, cinta; (sticky tape) cinta adhesiva; (for tying) cinta ▷ vt (record) grabar (en cinta); (stick with tape) pegar con cinta adhesiva; **tape measure** n cinta métrica, metro; **tape recorder** n grabadora

tapestry ['tæpɪstrɪ] n (object) tapiz m; (art) tapicería

tar [tɑ:] n alquitrán m, brea

target ['tɑ:gɪt] n blanco

tariff ['tærɪf] n (on goods) arancel m; (BRIT: in hotels etc) tarifa

tarmac ['tɑ:mæk] n (BRIT: on road) asfaltado; (Aviat) pista (de aterrizaje)

tarpaulin [tɑ:'pɔ:lɪn] n lona impermeabilizada

tarragon ['tærəgən] n estragón m

tart [tɑ:t] n (Culin) tarta; (BRIT: inf: prostitute) puta ▷ adj agrio, ácido

tartan ['tɑ:tn] n tejido escocés m

tartar(e) sauce ['tɑ:tə-] n salsa tártara

task [tɑ:sk] n tarea; **to take to ~** reprender

taste [teɪst] n (sense) gusto; (flavour) sabor m; (sample): **have a ~!** ¡prueba un poquito!; (fig) muestra, idea ▷ vt probar ▷ vi: **to ~ of** or **like** (fish, garlic etc) saber a; **you can ~ the garlic (in it)** se nota el sabor a ajo; **in**

good/bad ~ de buen/mal gusto; **tasteful** adj de buen gusto; **tasteless** adj (food) soso; (remark etc) de mal gusto; **tasty** adj sabroso, rico

tatters ['tætəz] npl: **in ~** hecho jirones

tattoo [tə'tu:] n tatuaje m; (spectacle) espectáculo militar ▷ vt tatuar

taught [tɔ:t] pt, pp of **teach**

taunt [tɔ:nt] n burla ▷ vt burlarse de

Taurus ['tɔ:rəs] n Tauro

taut [tɔ:t] adj tirante, tenso

tax [tæks] n impuesto ▷ vt gravar (con un impuesto); (fig: memory) poner a prueba; (: patience) agotar; **tax-free** adj libre de impuestos

taxi ['tæksɪ] n taxi m ▷ vi (Aviat) rodar por la pista; **taxi driver** n taxista mf; **taxi rank** (BRIT) n = **taxi stand**; **taxi stand** n parada de taxis

tax payer n contribuyente mf

TB n abbr = **tuberculosis**

tea [ti:] n té m; (BRIT: meal) ≈ merienda (SP); cena; **high ~** (BRIT) merienda-cena (SP); **tea bag** n bolsita de té; **tea break** (BRIT) n descanso para el té

teach [ti:tʃ] (pt, pp **taught**) vt: **to ~ sb sth, ~ sth to sb** enseñar algo a algn ▷ vi (be a teacher) ser profesor(a), enseñar; **teacher** n (in secondary school) profesor(a) m/f; (in primary school) maestro/a, profesor(a) de EGB; **teaching** n enseñanza

tea: tea cloth n (BRIT) paño de cocina, trapo de cocina (LAM); **teacup** n taza para el té

tea leaves npl hojas de té

team [ti:m] n equipo; (of horses) tiro; **team up** vi asociarse

teapot ['ti:pɔt] n tetera

tear¹ [tɪə*] n lágrima; **in ~s** llorando

tear² [tɛə*] (pt **tore**, pp **torn**) n rasgón m, desgarrón m ▷ vt romper, rasgar ▷ vi rasgarse; **tear apart** vt (also fig) hacer pedazos; **tear down** vt +adv (building, statue) derribar; (poster, flag) arrancar; **tear off** vt (sheet of paper etc) arrancar; (one's clothes) quitarse a tirones; **tear up** vt (sheet of paper etc) romper

tearful ['tɪəfəl] adj lloroso

tear gas ['tɪə-] n gas m lacrimógeno

tearoom ['ti:ru:m] n salón m de té

tease [ti:z] vt tomar el pelo a

tea: teaspoon n cucharita; (also: **teaspoonful**: as measurement) cucharadita; **teatime** n hora del té; **tea towel** (BRIT) n paño de cocina

technical ['tɛknɪkl] adj técnico

technician [tɛk'nɪʃn] n técnico/a

technique [tɛk'ni:k] n técnica

technology [tɛk'nɔlədʒɪ] n tecnología

teddy (bear) ['tɛdɪ-] n osito de felpa
tedious ['tiːdɪəs] adj pesado, aburrido
tee [tiː] n (Golf) tee m
teen [tiːn] adj =**teenage** ▷ n (US) =
  teenager
teenage ['tiːneɪdʒ] adj (fashions etc)
  juvenil; (children) quinceañero; **teenager** n
  adolescente mf
teens [tiːnz] npl: **to be in one's ~** ser
  adolescente
teeth [tiːθ] npl of **tooth**
teetotal ['tiː'təʊtl] adj abstemio
telecommunications
  [tɛlɪkəmjuːnɪ'keɪʃənz] n
  telecomunicaciones fpl
telegram ['tɛlɪɡræm] n telegrama m
telegraph pole ['tɛlɪɡrɑːf-] n poste m
  telegráfico
telephone ['tɛlɪfəun] n teléfono ▷ vt
  llamar por teléfono, telefonear; (message)
  dar por teléfono; **to be on the ~** (talking)
  hablar por teléfono; (possessing telephone)
  tener teléfono; **telephone book** n guía f
  telefónica; **telephone booth, telephone
  box** (BRIT) n cabina telefónica; **telephone
  call** n llamada (telefónica); **telephone
  directory** n guía (telefónica); **telephone
  number** n número de teléfono
telesales ['tɛlɪseɪlz] npl televenta(s) (f(pl))
telescope ['tɛlɪskəup] n telescopio
televise ['tɛlɪvaɪz] vt televisar
television ['tɛlɪvɪʒən] n televisión f; **on ~**
  en la televisión; **television programme** n
  programa m de televisión
tell [tɛl] (pt, pp **told**) vt decir; (relate: story)
  contar; (distinguish): **to ~ sth from**
  distinguir algo de ▷ vi (talk): **to ~ (of)**
  contar; (have effect) tener efecto; **to ~ sb to
  do sth** mandar a algn hacer algo; **tell off**
  vt: **to tell sb off** regañar a algn; **teller** n (in
  bank) cajero/a
telly ['tɛlɪ] (BRIT: inf) n abbr (= television)
  tele f
temp [tɛmp] n abbr (BRIT) (= temporary)
  temporero/a
temper ['tɛmpə*] n (nature) carácter m;
  (mood) humor m; (bad temper) (mal) genio;
  (fit of anger) acceso de ira ▷ vt (moderate)
  moderar; **to be in a ~** estar furioso; **to lose
  one's ~** enfadarse, enojarse
temperament ['tɛmprəmənt] n
  (nature) temperamento; **temperamental**
  [tɛmprə'mɛntl] adj temperamental
temperature ['tɛmprətʃə*] n
  temperatura; **to have** or **run a ~** tener fiebre
temple ['tɛmpl] n (building) templo; (Anat)
  sien f
temporary ['tɛmpərərɪ] adj provisional;

(passing) transitorio; (worker) temporero;
  (job) temporal
tempt [tɛmpt] vt tentar; **to ~ sb into
  doing sth** tentar or inducir a algn a hacer
  algo; **temptation** n tentación f; **tempting**
  adj tentador(a); (food) apetitoso/a
ten [tɛn] num diez
tenant ['tɛnənt] n inquilino/a
tend [tɛnd] vt cuidar ▷ vi: **to ~ to do sth**
  tener tendencia a hacer algo; **tendency**
  ['tɛndənsɪ] n tendencia
tender ['tɛndə*] adj (person, care) tierno,
  cariñoso; (meat) tierno; (sore) sensible ▷ n
  (Comm: offer) oferta; (money): **legal ~** moneda
  de curso legal ▷ vt ofrecer
tendon ['tɛndən] n tendón m
tenner ['tɛnə*] n (inf) (billete m de) diez
  libras m
tennis ['tɛnɪs] n tenis m; **tennis ball** n
  pelota de tenis; **tennis court** n cancha de
  tenis; **tennis match** n partido de tenis;
  tennis player n tenista mf; **tennis racket**
  n raqueta de tenis
tenor ['tɛnə*] n (Mus) tenor m
tenpin bowling ['tɛnpɪn-] n (juego de
  los) bolos
tense [tɛns] adj (person) nervioso; (moment,
  atmosphere) tenso; (muscle) tenso, en tensión
  ▷ n (Ling) tiempo
tension ['tɛnʃən] n tensión f
tent [tɛnt] n tienda (de campaña) (SP),
  carpa (LAM)
tentative ['tɛntətɪv] adj (person, smile)
  indeciso; (conclusion, plans) provisional
tenth [tɛnθ] num décimo
tent: tent peg n clavija, estaca; **tent pole**
  n mástil m
tepid ['tɛpɪd] adj tibio
term [təːm] n (word) término; (period)
  período; (Scol) trimestre m ▷ vt llamar;
  terms npl (conditions, Comm) condiciones
  fpl; **in the short/long ~** a corto/largo plazo;
  to be on good ~s with sb llevarse bien con
  algn; **to come to ~s with** (problem) aceptar
terminal ['təːmɪnl] adj (disease) mortal;
  (patient) terminal ▷ n (Elec) borne m;
  (Comput) terminal m; (also: **air ~**) terminal f;
  (BRIT: also: **coach ~**) estación f terminal f
terminate ['təːmɪneɪt] vt terminar
termini ['təːmɪnaɪ] npl of **terminus**
terminology [təːmɪ'nɔlədʒɪ] n
  terminología
terminus ['təːmɪnəs] n (pl **termini**) n
  término, (estación f) terminal f
terrace ['tɛrəs] n terraza; (BRIT: row of
  houses) hilera de casas adosadas; **the ~s**
  (BRIT Sport) las gradas fpl; **terraced** adj
  (garden) en terrazas; (house) adosado

terrain [tɛˈreɪn] *n* terreno
terrestrial [tɪˈrɛstrɪəl] *adj* (*life*) terrestre; (BRIT: *channel*) de transmisión (por) vía terrestre
terrible [ˈtɛrɪbl] *adj* terrible, horrible; (*inf*) atroz; **terribly** *adv* terriblemente; (*very badly*) malísimamente
terrier [ˈtɛrɪə*] *n* terrier *m*
terrific [təˈrɪfɪk] *adj* (*very great*) tremendo; (*wonderful*) fantástico, fenomenal
terrified [ˈtɛrɪfaɪd] *adj* aterrorizado
terrify [ˈtɛrɪfaɪ] *vt* aterrorizar; **terrifying** *adj* aterrador(a)
territorial [tɛrɪˈtɔːrɪəl] *adj* territorial
territory [ˈtɛrɪtərɪ] *n* territorio
terror [ˈtɛrə*] *n* terror *m*; **terrorism** *n* terrorismo; **terrorist** *n* terrorista *mf*; **terrorist attack** *n* atentado (terrorista)
test [tɛst] *n* (*gen, Chem*) prueba; (*Med*) examen *m*; (*Scol*) examen *m*, test *m*; (*also*: **driving ~**) examen *m* de conducir ▷ *vt* probar, poner a prueba; (*Med, Scol*) examinar
testicle [ˈtɛstɪkl] *n* testículo
testify [ˈtɛstɪfaɪ] *vi* (*Law*) prestar declaración; **to ~ to sth** atestiguar algo
testimony [ˈtɛstɪmənɪ] *n* (*Law*) testimonio
test: test match *n* (*Cricket, Rugby*) partido internacional; **test tube** *n* probeta
tetanus [ˈtɛtənəs] *n* tétano
text [tɛkst] *n* texto; (*on mobile phone*) mensaje *m* de texto ▷ *vt*: **to ~ sb** (*inf*) enviar un mensaje (de texto) *or* un SMS a algn; **textbook** *n* libro de texto
textile [ˈtɛkstaɪl] *n* textil *m*, tejido
text message *n* mensaje *m* de texto
text messaging [-ˈmɛsɪdʒɪŋ] *n* (envío de) mensajes *mpl* de texto
texture [ˈtɛkstʃə*] *n* textura
Thai [taɪ] *adj, n* tailandés/esa *m/f*
Thailand [ˈtaɪlænd] *n* Tailandia
than [ðæn] *conj* (*in comparisons*): **more ~ 10/once** más de 10/una vez; **I have more/less ~ you/Paul** tengo más/menos que tú/Paul; **she is older ~ you think** es mayor de lo que piensas
thank [θæŋk] *vt* dar las gracias a, agradecer; **~ you (very much)** muchas gracias; **~ God!** ¡gracias a Dios! ▷ *excl* (*also*: **many ~s, ~s a lot**) ¡gracias! ▷ **~s** *to prep* gracias a; **thanks** *npl* gracias *fpl*; **thankfully** *adv* (*fortunately*) afortunadamente; **Thanksgiving (Day)** *n* día *m* de Acción de Gracias

● **THANKSGIVING (DAY)**

● En Estados Unidos el cuarto jueves

● de noviembre es **Thanksgiving Day**,
● fiesta oficial en la que se recuerda la
● celebración que hicieron los primeros
● colonos norteamericanos ("Pilgrims"
● o "Pilgrim Fathers") tras la estupenda
● cosecha de 1621, por la que se dan gracias
● a Dios. En Canadá se celebra una fiesta
● semejante el segundo lunes de octubre,
● aunque no está relacionada con dicha
● fecha histórica.

○ **KEYWORD**

that [ðæt] (*pl* **those**) *adj* (*demonstrative*) ese/a; (*pl*) esos/as; (*more remote*) aquel(aquella); (*pl*) aquellos/as; **leave those books on the table** deja esos libros sobre la mesa; **that one** ése(ésa); (*more remote*) aquél(aquélla); **that one over there** ése(ésa) de ahí; aquél(aquélla) de allí
▷ *pron* **1** (*demonstrative*) ése/a; (*pl*) ésos/as; (*neuter*) eso; (*more remote*) aquél(aquélla); (*pl*) aquéllos/as; (*neuter*) aquello; **what's that?** ¿qué es eso (*or* aquello)?; **who's that?** ¿quién es ése/a (*or* aquél (aquélla))?; **is that you?** ¿eres tú?; **will you eat all that?** ¿vas a comer todo eso?; **that's my house** ésa es mi casa; **that's what he said** eso es lo que dijo; **that is (to say)** es decir
2 (*relative: subject, object*) que; (*with preposition*) (el (la)) que *etc*, (el (la) cual *etc*; **the book (that) I read** el libro que leí; **the books that are in the library** los libros que están en la biblioteca; **all (that) I have** todo lo que tengo; **the box (that) I put it in** la caja en la que *or* donde lo puse; **the people (that) I spoke to** la gente con la que hablé
3 (*relative: of time*) que; **the day (that) he came** el día (en) que vino
▷ *conj* que; **he thought that I was ill** creyó que yo estaba enfermo
▷ *adv* (*demonstrative*): **I can't work that much** no puedo trabajar tanto; **I didn't realise it was that bad** no creí que fuera tan malo; **that high** así de alto

thatched [θætʃt] *adj* (*roof*) de paja; (*cottage*) con tejado de paja
thaw [θɔː] *n* deshielo ▷ *vi* (*ice*) derretirse; (*food*) descongelarse ▷ *vt* (*food*) descongelar

○ **KEYWORD**

the [ðiː, ðə] *def art* **1** (*gen*) el *f*, la *pl*, los *fpl*, las (*NB 'el' immediately before f n beginning with stressed (h)a; a+ el =al; de + el = del*); **the boy/girl** el chico/la chica; **the books/flowers**

theatre | 408

los libros/las flores; **to the postman/from the drawer** al cartero/del cajón; **I haven't the time/money** no tengo tiempo/dinero **2** (+adj to form n) los; lo; **the rich and the poor** los ricos y los pobres; **to attempt the impossible** intentar lo imposible **3** (in titles): **Elizabeth the First** Isabel primera; **Peter the Great** Pedro el Grande **4** (in comparisons): **the more he works the more he earns** cuanto más trabaja más gana

theatre ['θɪətə*] (US **theater**) n teatro; (also: **lecture ~**) aula; (Med: also: **operating ~**) quirófano
theft [θɛft] n robo
their [ðɛə*] adj su; **theirs** pron (el) suyo((la) suya etc); see also **my; mine¹**
them [ðɛm, ðəm] pron (direct) los/las; (indirect) les; (stressed, after prep) ellos(ellas); see also **me**
theme [θiːm] n tema m; **theme park** n parque de atracciones (en torno a un tema central)
themselves [ðəm'sɛlvz] pl pron (subject) ellos mismos(ellas mismas); (complement) se; (after prep) sí (mismos(as)); see also **oneself**
then [ðɛn] adv (at that time) entonces; (next) después; (later) luego, después; (and also) además ▷ conj (therefore) en ese caso, entonces ▷ adj: **the ~ president** el entonces presidente; **by ~** para entonces; **from ~ on** desde entonces
theology [θɪ'ɔlədʒɪ] n teología
theory ['θɪərɪ] n teoría
therapist ['θɛrəpɪst] n terapeuta mf
therapy ['θɛrəpɪ] n terapia

○ **KEYWORD**

there ['ðɛə*] adv **1** **there is, there are** hay; **there is no-one here/no bread left** no hay nadie aquí/no queda pan; **there has been an accident** ha habido un accidente **2** (referring to place) ahí; (distant) allí; **it's there** está ahí; **put it in/on/up/down there** ponlo ahí dentro/encima/arriba/abajo; **I want that book there** quiero ese libro de ahí; **there he is!** ¡ahí está! **3** **there, there** (esp to child) ea, ea

there: thereabouts adv por ahí; **thereafter** adv después; **thereby** adv así, de ese modo; **therefore** adv por lo tanto; **there's** =there is; there has
thermal ['θəːml] adj termal; (paper) térmico

thermometer [θə'mɔmɪtə*] n termómetro
thermostat ['θəːməustæt] n termostato
these [ðiːz] pl adj estos/as ▷ pl pron éstos/as
thesis ['θiːsɪs] (pl **theses**) n tesis f inv
they [ðeɪ] pl pron ellos(ellas); (stressed) ellos (mismos)(ellas (mismas)); **~ say that ...** (it is said that) se dice que ...; **they'd** =they had; they would; **they'll** =they shall; they will; **they're** =they are; **they've** =they have
thick [θɪk] adj (in consistency) espeso; (in size) grueso; (stupid) torpe ▷ n: **in the ~ of the battle** en lo más reñido de la batalla; **it's 20 cm ~** tiene 20 cm de espesor; **thicken** vi espesarse ▷ vt (sauce etc) espesar; **thickness** n espesor m; grueso
thief [θiːf] (pl **thieves**) n ladrón/ona m/f
thigh [θaɪ] n muslo
thin [θɪn] adj (person, animal) flaco; (in size) delgado; (in consistency) poco espeso; (hair, crowd) escaso ▷ vt: **to ~ (down)** diluir
thing [θɪŋ] n cosa; (object) objeto, artículo; (matter) asunto; (mania): **to have a ~ about sb/sth** estar obsesionado con algn/algo; **things** npl (belongings) efectos mpl (personales); **the best ~ would be to ...** lo mejor sería ...; **how are ~s?** ¿qué tal?
think [θɪŋk] (pt, pp **thought**) vi pensar ▷ vt pensar, creer; **what did you ~ of them?** ¿qué te parecieron?; **to ~ about sth/sb** pensar en algo/algn; **I'll ~ about it** lo pensaré; **to ~ of doing sth** pensar en hacer algo; **I ~ so/not** creo que sí/no; **to ~ well of sb** tener buen concepto de algn; **think over** vt reflexionar sobre, meditar; **think up** vt (plan etc) idear
third [θəːd] adj (before n) tercer(a); (following n) tercero/a ▷ n tercero/a; (fraction) tercio; (BRIT Scol: degree) título de licenciado con calificación de aprobado; **thirdly** adv en tercer lugar; **third party insurance** (BRIT) n seguro contra terceros; **Third World** n Tercer Mundo
thirst [θəːst] n sed f; **thirsty** adj (person, animal) sediento; (work) que da sed; **to be thirsty** tener sed
thirteen ['θəː'tiːn] num trece; **thirteenth** [-'tiːnθ] adj decimotercero
thirtieth ['θəːtɪəθ] adj trigésimo
thirty ['θəːtɪ] num treinta

○ **KEYWORD**

this [ðɪs] (pl **these**) adj (demonstrative) este/a pl; estos/as; (neuter) esto; **this man/woman** este hombre(esta mujer); **these children/flowers** estos chicos/estas flores;

this one (here) éste/a, esto (de aquí)
▷ pron (demonstrative) éste/a pl, éstos/as;
(neuter) esto; **who is this?** ¿quién es
éste/ésta?; **what is this?** ¿qué es esto?; **this
is where I live** aquí vivo; **this is what he
said** esto es lo que dijo; **this is Mr Brown**
(in introductions) le presento al Sr. Brown;
(photo) éste es el Sr. Brown; (on telephone)
habla el Sr. Brown
▷ adv (demonstrative): **this high/long** etc así
de alto/largo etc; **this far** hasta aquí

thistle ['θɪsl] n cardo
thorn [θɔːn] n espina
thorough ['θʌrə] adj (search) minucioso;
(wash) a fondo; (knowledge, research)
profundo; (person) meticuloso; **thoroughly**
adv (search) minuciosamente; (study)
profundamente; (wash) a fondo; (utterly: bad,
wet etc) completamente, totalmente
those [ðəuz] pl adj esos(esas); (more
remote) aquellos/as
though [ðəu] conj aunque ▷ adv sin
embargo
thought [θɔːt] pt, pp of **think** ▷ n
pensamiento; (opinion) opinión f;
thoughtful adj pensativo; (serious) serio;
(considerate) atento; **thoughtless** adj
desconsiderado
thousand ['θauzənd] num mil; **two ~**
dos mil; **~s of** miles de; **thousandth** num
milésimo
thrash [θræʃ] vt azotar; (defeat) derrotar
thread [θrɛd] n hilo; (of screw) rosca ▷ vt
(needle) enhebrar
threat [θrɛt] n amenaza; **threaten** vi
amenazar ▷ vt: **to threaten sb with/
to do** amenazar a algn con/con hacer;
threatening adj amenazador(a),
amenazante
three [θriː] num tres; **three-dimensional**
adj tridimensional; **three-piece suite** n
tresillo; **three-quarters** npl tres cuartas
partes; **three-quarters full** tres cuartas
partes lleno
threshold ['θrɛʃhəuld] n umbral m
threw [θruː] pt of **throw**
thrill [θrɪl] n (excitement) emoción f;
(shudder) estremecimiento ▷ vt emocionar;
to be ~ed (with gift etc) estar encantado;
thrilled adj: **I was thrilled** Estaba
emocionada; **thriller** n novela (or obra
or película) de suspense; **thrilling** adj
emocionante
thriving ['θraɪvɪŋ] adj próspero
throat [θrəut] n garganta; **to have a sore
~** tener dolor de garganta
throb [θrɔb] vi latir; dar punzadas; vibrar

throne [θrəun] n trono
through [θruː] prep por, a través de;
(time) durante; (by means of) por medio de,
mediante; (owing to) gracias a ▷ adj (ticket,
train) directo ▷ adv completamente, de
parte a parte; de principio a fin; **to be ~
to sb** (Tel) poner or pasar a algn con algn; **to
be ~** (Tel) tener comunicación; (have finished)
haber terminado; **"no ~ road"** (BRIT) "calle
sin salida"; **throughout** prep (place) por
todas partes de, por todo; (time) durante
todo ▷ adv por or en todas partes
throw [θrəu] (pt **threw**, pp **thrown**) n tiro;
(Sport) lanzamiento ▷ vt tirar, echar; (Sport)
lanzar; (rider) derribar; (fig) desconcertar;
to ~ a party dar una fiesta; **throw away**
vt tirar; (money) derrochar; **throw in** vt
(Sport: ball) sacar; (include) incluir; **throw
off** vt deshacerse de; **throw out** vt tirar;
(person) echar; expulsar; **throw up** vi
vomitar
thru [θruː] n (us) = **through**
thrush [θrʌʃ] n zorzal m, tordo
thrust [θrʌst] (pt, pp **~**) vt empujar con
fuerza
thud [θʌd] n golpe m sordo
thug [θʌg] n gamberro/a
thumb [θʌm] n (Anat) pulgar m; **to ~ a
lift** hacer autostop; **thumbtack** (us) n
chincheta (SP)
thump [θʌmp] n golpe m; (sound) ruido
seco or sordo ▷ vt golpear ▷ vi (heart etc)
palpitar
thunder ['θʌndə*] n trueno ▷ vi tronar;
(train etc): **to ~ past** pasar como un trueno;
thunderstorm n tormenta
Thur(s). abbr (= Thursday) juev
Thursday ['θəːzdɪ] n jueves m inv
thus [ðʌs] adv así, de este modo
thwart [θwɔːt] vt frustrar
thyme [taɪm] n tomillo
Tibet [tɪˈbɛt] n el Tibet
tick [tɪk] n (sound: of clock) tictac m; (mark)
palomita; (Zool) garrapata; (BRIT: inf): **in
a ~** en un instante ▷ vi hacer tictac ▷ vt
marcar; **tick off** vt marcar; (person) reñir
ticket ['tɪkɪt] n billete m (SP), boleto
(LAM); (for cinema etc) entrada; (in shop: on
goods) etiqueta; (for raffle) papeleta; (for
library) tarjeta; (parking ticket) multa de
aparcamiento (SP) or estacionamiento
(indebido) (LAM); **ticket barrier** n
(BRIT: Rail) barrera más allá de la cual se
necesita billete/boleto; **ticket collector**
n revisor(a) m/f; **ticket inspector** n
revisor(a) m/f, inspector(a) m/f de boletos
(LAM); **ticket machine** n máquina de
billetes (SP) or boletos (LAM); **ticket office** n

t

(*Theatre*) taquilla (*SP*), boletería (*LAM*); (*Rail*) mostrador *m* de billetes (*SP*) or boletos (*LAM*)

tickle ['tɪkl] *vt* hacer cosquillas a ▷ *vi* hacer cosquillas; **ticklish** *adj* (*person*) cosquilloso; (*problem*) delicado

tide [taɪd] *n* marea; (*fig: of events etc*) curso, marcha

tidy ['taɪdɪ] *adj* (*room etc*) ordenado; (*dress, work*) limpio; (*person*) (bien) arreglado ▷ *vt* (*also:* ~ **up**) poner en orden

tie [taɪ] *n* (*string etc*) atadura; (*BRIT: also:* **neck~**) corbata; (*fig: link*) vínculo, lazo; (*Sport etc: draw*) empate *m* ▷ *vt* atar ▷ *vi* (*Sport etc*) empatar; **to ~ in a bow** atar con un lazo; **to ~ a knot in sth** hacer un nudo en algo; **tie down** *vt* (*fig: person: restrict*) atar; (: *to price, date etc*) obligar a; **tie up** *vt* (*dog, person*) atar; (*arrangements*) concluir; **to be tied up** (*busy*) estar ocupado

tier [tɪə*] *n* grada; (*of cake*) piso

tiger ['taɪɡə*] *n* tigre *m*

tight [taɪt] *adj* (*rope*) tirante; (*money*) escaso; (*clothes*) ajustado; (*bend*) cerrado; (*shoes, schedule*) apretado; (*budget*) ajustado; (*security*) estricto; (*inf: drunk*) borracho ▷ *adv* (*squeeze*) muy fuerte; (*shut*) bien; **tighten** *vt* (*rope*) estirar; (*screw, grip*) apretar; (*security*) reforzar ▷ *vi* estirarse; apretarse; **tightly** *adv* (*grasp*) muy fuerte; **tights** (*BRIT*) *npl* panti *mpl*

tile [taɪl] *n* (*on roof*) teja; (*on floor*) baldosa; (*on wall*) azulejo

till [tɪl] *n* caja (registradora) ▷ *vt* (*land*) cultivar ▷ *prep, conj* = **until**

tilt [tɪlt] *vt* inclinar ▷ *vi* inclinarse

timber ['tɪmbə*] *n* (*material*) madera

time [taɪm] *n* tiempo; (*epoch: often pl*) época; (*by clock*) hora; (*moment*) momento; (*occasion*) vez *f*; (*Mus*) compás *m* ▷ *vt* calcular or medir el tiempo de; (*race*) cronometrar; (*remark, visit etc*) elegir el momento para; **a long ~** mucho tiempo; **4 at a ~** de 4 en 4; 4 a la vez; **for the ~ being** de momento, por ahora; **from ~ to ~** de vez en cuando; **at ~s** a veces; **in ~** (*soon enough*) a tiempo; (*after some time*) con el tiempo; (*Mus*) al compás; **in a week's ~** dentro de una semana; **in no ~** en un abrir y cerrar de ojos; **any ~** cuando sea; **on ~** a la hora; **5 ~s 5** 5 por 5; **what ~ is it?** ¿qué hora es?; **to have a good ~** pasarlo bien, divertirse; **time limit** *n* plazo; **timely** *adj* oportuno; **timer** *n* (*in kitchen etc*) programador *m* horario; **time-share** *n* apartamento (*or* casa) a tiempo compartido; **timetable** *n* horario; **time zone** *n* huso horario

timid ['tɪmɪd] *adj* tímido

timing ['taɪmɪŋ] *n* (*Sport*) cronometraje *m*;

the ~ of his resignation el momento que eligió para dimitir

tin [tɪn] *n* estaño; (*also:* ~ **plate**) hojalata; (*BRIT: can*) lata; **tinfoil** *n* papel *m* de estaño

tingle ['tɪŋɡl] *vi* (*person*): **to ~ (with)** estremecerse (de); (*hands etc*) hormiguear

tinker ['tɪŋkə*]: ~ **with** *vt fus* jugar con, tocar

tinned [tɪnd] (*BRIT*) *adj* (*food*) en lata, en conserva

tin opener [-əupnə*] (*BRIT*) *n* abrelatas *m inv*

tint [tɪnt] *n* matiz *m*; (*for hair*) tinte *m*; **tinted** *adj* (*hair*) teñido; (*glass, spectacles*) ahumado

tiny ['taɪnɪ] *adj* minúsculo, pequeñito

tip [tɪp] *n* (*end*) punta; (*gratuity*) propina; (*BRIT: for rubbish*) vertedero; (*advice*) consejo ▷ *vt* (*waiter*) dar una propina a; (*tilt*) inclinar; (*empty: also:* ~ **out**) vaciar, echar; (*overturn: also:* ~ **over**) volcar; **tip off** *vt* avisar, poner sobre aviso a

tiptoe ['tɪptəu] *n*: **on ~** de puntillas

tire ['taɪə*] *n* (*US*) = **tyre** ▷ *vt* cansar ▷ *vi* cansarse; (*become bored*) aburrirse; **tired** *adj* cansado; **to be tired of sth** estar harto de algo; **tire pressure** (*US*) = **tyre pressure**; **tiring** *adj* cansado

tissue ['tɪʃuː] *n* tejido; (*paper handkerchief*) pañuelo de papel, kleenex® *m*; **tissue paper** *n* papel *m* de seda

tit [tɪt] *n* (*bird*) herrerillo común; **to give ~ for tat** dar ojo por ojo

title ['taɪtl] *n* título

T-junction ['tiːdʒʌŋkʃən] *n* cruce *m* en T

TM *abbr* = **trademark**

○ **KEYWORD**

to [tuː, tə] *prep* **1** (*direction*) a; **to go to France/London/school/the station** ir a Francia/Londres/al colegio/a la estación; **to go to Claude's/the doctor's** ir a casa de Claude/al médico; **the road to Edinburgh** la carretera de Edimburgo

2 (*as far as*) hasta, a; **from here to London** de aquí a *or* hasta Londres; **to count to 10** contar hasta 10; **from 40 to 50 people** entre 40 y 50 personas

3 (*with expressions of time*): **a quarter/twenty to 5** las 5 menos cuarto/veinte

4 (*for, of*): **the key to the front door** la llave de la puerta principal; **she is secretary to the director** es la secretaría del director; **a letter to his wife** una carta a *or* para su mujer

5 (*expressing indirect object*) a; **to give sth to sb** darle algo a algn; **to talk to sb** hablar con

algn; **to be a danger to sb** ser un peligro para algn; **to carry out repairs to sth** hacer reparaciones en algo
6 (*in relation to*): **3 goals to 2** 3 goles a 2; **30 miles to the gallon** ≈ 94 litros a los cien (kms)
7 (*purpose, result*): **to come to sb's aid** venir en auxilio *or* ayuda de algn; **to sentence sb to death** condenar a algn a muerte; **to my great surprise** con gran sorpresa mía
▷ *with vb* **1** (*simple infin*): **to go/eat** ir/comer **2** (*following another vb*): **to want/try/start to do** querer/intentar/empezar a hacer
3 (*with vb omitted*): **I don't want to** no quiero **4** (*purpose, result*) para; **I did it to help you** lo hice para ayudarte; **he came to see you** vino a verte
5 (*equivalent to relative clause*): **I have things to do** tengo cosas que hacer; **the main thing is to try** lo principal es intentarlo
6 (*after adj etc*): **ready to go** listo para irse; **too old to ...** demasiado viejo (como) para ...
▷ *adv*: **pull/push the door to** tirar de/empujar la puerta

toad [təud] *n* sapo; **toadstool** *n* hongo venenoso
toast [təust] *n* (*Culin*) tostada; (*drink, speech*) brindis *m* ▷ *vt* (*Culin*) tostar; (*drink to*) brindar por; **toaster** *n* tostador *m*
tobacco [tə'bækəu] *n* tabaco
toboggan [tə'bɔgən] *n* tobogán *m*
today [tə'deɪ] *adv, n* (*also fig*) hoy *m*
toddler ['tɔdlə*] *n* niño/a (que empieza a andar)
toe [təu] *n* dedo (del pie); (*of shoe*) punta; **to ~ the line** (*fig*) conformarse; **toenail** *n* uña del pie
toffee ['tɔfɪ] *n* toffee *m*
together [tə'gɛðə*] *adv* juntos; (*at same time*) al mismo tiempo, a la vez; **~ with** junto con
toilet ['tɔɪlət] *n* inodoro; (*BRIT: room*) (cuarto de) baño, servicio ▷ *cpd* (*soap etc*) de aseo; **toilet bag** *n* neceser *m*, bolsa de aseo; **toilet paper** *n* papel *m* higiénico; **toiletries** *npl* artículos *mpl* de tocador; **toilet roll** *n* rollo de papel higiénico
token ['təukən] *n* (*sign*) señal *f*, muestra; (*souvenir*) recuerdo; (*disc*) ficha ▷ *adj* (*strike, payment etc*) simbólico; **book/record ~** (*BRIT*) vale *m* para comprar libros/discos; **gift ~** (*BRIT*) vale-regalo
Tokyo ['təukjəu] *n* Tokio, Tokío
told [təuld] *pt, pp of* **tell**
tolerant ['tɔlərnt] *adj*: **~ of** tolerante con
tolerate ['tɔləreɪt] *vt* tolerar

toll [təul] *n* (*of casualties*) número de víctimas; (*tax, charge*) peaje *m* ▷ *vi* (*bell*) doblar; **toll call** *n* (*US Tel*) conferencia, llamada interurbana; **toll-free** (*US*) *adj, adv* gratis
tomato [tə'mɑ:təu] (*pl* **~es**) *n* tomate *m*; **tomato sauce** *n* salsa de tomate
tomb [tu:m] *n* tumba; **tombstone** *n* lápida
tomorrow [tə'mɔrəu] *adv, n* (*also: fig*) mañana; **the day after ~** pasado mañana; **~ morning** mañana por la mañana
ton [tʌn] *n* tonelada (*BRIT* = 1016 kg; *US* = 907 kg); (*metric ton*) tonelada métrica; **~s of** (*inf*) montones de
tone [təun] *n* tono ▷ *vi* (*also: ~ in*) armonizar; **tone down** *vt* (*criticism*) suavizar; (*colour*) atenuar
tongs [tɔŋz] *npl* (*for coal*) tenazas *fpl*; (*curling tongs*) tenacillas *fpl*
tongue [tʌŋ] *n* lengua; **~ in cheek** irónicamente
tonic ['tɔnɪk] *n* (*Med*) tónico; (*also: ~ water*) (agua) tónica
tonight [tə'naɪt] *adv, n* esta noche; esta tarde
tonne [tʌn] *n* tonelada (métrica) (1.000kg)
tonsil ['tɔnsl] *n* amígdala; **tonsillitis** [-'laɪtɪs] *n* amigdalitis *f*
too [tu:] *adv* (*excessively*) demasiado; (*also*) también; **~ much** demasiado; **~ many** demasiados/as
took [tuk] *pt of* **take**
tool [tu:l] *n* herramienta; **tool box** *n* caja de herramientas; **tool kit** *n* juego de herramientas
tooth [tu:θ] (*pl* **teeth**) *n* (*Anat, Tech*) diente *m*; (*molar*) muela; **toothache** *n* dolor *m* de muelas; **toothbrush** *n* cepillo de dientes; **toothpaste** *n* pasta de dientes; **toothpick** *n* palillo
top [tɔp] *n* (*of mountain*) cumbre *f*, cima; (*of tree*) copa; (*of head*) coronilla; (*of ladder, page*) lo alto; (*of table*) superficie *f*; (*of cupboard*) parte *f* de arriba; (*of box*) tapa; (: *of bottle, jar*) tapón *m*; (*of list etc*) cabeza; (*toy*) peonza; (*garment*) blusa; camiseta ▷ *adj* de arriba; (*in rank*) principal, primero; (*best*) mejor ▷ *vt* (*exceed*) exceder; (*be first in*) encabezar; **on ~ of** (*above*) sobre, encima de; (*in addition to*) además de; **from ~ to bottom** de pies a cabeza; **top up** *vt* llenar; (*mobile phone*) recargar (el saldo de); **top floor** *n* último piso; **top hat** *n* sombrero de copa
topic ['tɔpɪk] *n* tema *m*; **topical** *adj* actual
topless ['tɔplɪs] *adj* (*bather, bikini*) topless *inv*
topping ['tɔpɪŋ] *n* (*Culin*): **with a ~ of**

cream con nata por encima
topple ['tɒpl] vt derribar ▷ vi caerse
top-up card n (for mobile phone) tarjeta prepago
torch [tɔːtʃ] n antorcha; (BRIT: electric) linterna
tore [tɔː*] pt of **tear²**
torment [n 'tɔːmɛnt, vt tɔː'mɛnt] n tormento ▷ vt atormentar; (fig: annoy) fastidiar
torn [tɔːn] pp of **tear²**
tornado [tɔː'neɪdəʊ] (pl ~es) n tornado
torpedo [tɔː'piːdəʊ] (pl ~es) n torpedo
torrent ['tɔrnt] n torrente m; **torrential** [tɔ'rɛnʃl] adj torrencial
tortoise ['tɔːtəs] n tortuga
torture ['tɔːtʃə*] n tortura ▷ vt torturar; (fig) atormentar
Tory ['tɔːrɪ] (BRIT) adj, n (Pol) conservador(a) m/f
toss [tɒs] vt tirar, echar; (one's head) sacudir; **to ~ a coin** echar a cara o cruz; **to ~ up for sth** jugar a cara o cruz algo; **to ~ and turn** (in bed) dar vueltas
total ['təʊtl] adj total, entero; (emphatic: failure etc) completo, total ▷ n total m, suma ▷ vt (add up) sumar; (amount to) ascender a
totalitarian [təʊtælɪ'tɛərɪən] adj totalitario
totally ['təʊtəlɪ] adv totalmente
touch [tʌtʃ] n tacto; (contact) contacto ▷ vt tocar; (emotionally) conmover; **a ~ of** (fig) un poquito de; **to get in ~ with sb** ponerse en contacto con algn; **to lose ~** (friends) perder contacto; **touch down** vi (on land) aterrizar; **touchdown** n aterrizaje m; (on sea) amerizaje m; (us Football) ensayo; **touched** adj (moved) conmovido; **touching** adj (moving) conmovedor(a); **touchline** n (Sport) línea de banda; **touch-sensitive** adj sensible al tacto
tough [tʌf] adj (material) resistente; (meat) duro; (problem etc) difícil; (policy, stance) inflexible; (person) fuerte
tour ['tʊə*] n viaje m, vuelta; (also: **package ~**) viaje m todo comprendido; (of town, museum) visita; (by band etc) gira ▷ vt recorrer, visitar; **tour guide** n guía mf turístico/a
tourism ['tʊərɪzm] n turismo
tourist ['tʊərɪst] n turista mf ▷ cpd turístico; **tourist office** n oficina de turismo
tournament ['tʊənəmənt] n torneo
tour operator n touroperador(a) m/f, operador(a) m/f turístico/a
tow [təʊ] vt remolcar; **"on** or **in** (us) **~"**

(Aut) "a remolque"; **tow away** vt llevarse a remolque
toward(s) [tə'wɔːd(z)] prep hacia; (attitude) respecto a, con; (purpose) para
towel ['taʊəl] n toalla; **towelling** n (fabric) felpa
tower ['taʊə*] n torre f; **tower block** (BRIT) n torre f (de pisos)
town [taʊn] n ciudad f; **to go to ~** ir a la ciudad; (fig) echar la casa por la ventana; **town centre** (BRIT) n centro de la ciudad; **town hall** n ayuntamiento
tow truck (us) n camión m grúa
toxic ['tɒksɪk] adj tóxico
toy [tɔɪ] n juguete m; **toy with** vt fus jugar con; (idea) acariciar; **toyshop** n juguetería
trace [treɪs] n rastro ▷ vt (draw) trazar, delinear; (locate) encontrar; (follow) seguir la pista de
track [træk] n (mark) huella, pista; (path: gen) camino, senda; (: of bullet etc) trayectoria; (: of suspect, animal) pista, rastro; (Rail) vía; (Sport) pista; (on tape, record) canción f ▷ vt seguir la pista de; **to keep ~ of** mantenerse al tanto de, seguir; **track down** vt (prey) seguir el rastro de; (sth lost) encontrar; **tracksuit** n chándal m
tractor ['træktə*] n tractor m
trade [treɪd] n comercio; (skill, job) oficio ▷ vi negociar, comerciar ▷ vt (exchange): **to ~ sth (for sth)** cambiar algo (por algo); **trade in** vt (old car etc) ofrecer como parte del pago; **trademark** n marca de fábrica; **trader** n comerciante mf; **tradesman** (irreg) n (shopkeeper) tendero; **trade union** n sindicato
trading ['treɪdɪŋ] n comercio
tradition [trə'dɪʃən] n tradición f; **traditional** adj tradicional
traffic ['træfɪk] n (gen, Aut) tráfico, circulación f ▷ vi: **to ~ in** (pej: liquor, drugs) traficar en; **traffic circle** (us) n isleta; **traffic island** n refugio, isleta; **traffic jam** n embotellamiento; **traffic lights** npl semáforo; **traffic warden** n guardia mf de tráfico
tragedy ['trædʒədɪ] n tragedia
tragic ['trædʒɪk] adj trágico
trail [treɪl] n (tracks) rastro, pista; (path) camino, sendero; (dust, smoke) estela ▷ vt (drag) arrastrar; (follow) seguir la pista de ▷ vi arrastrar; (in contest etc) ir perdiendo; **trailer** n (Aut) remolque m; (caravan) caravana; (Cinema) trailer m, avance m
train [treɪn] n tren m; (of dress) cola; (series) serie f ▷ vt (educate, teach skills to) formar; (sportsman) entrenar; (dog) adiestrar; (point: gun etc): **to ~ on** apuntar

a ▷ vi (Sport) entrenarse; (learn a skill): **to ~ as a teacher** etc estudiar para profesor etc; **one's ~ of thought** el razonamiento de algn; **trainee** [treɪ'niː] n aprendiz(a) m/f; **trainer** n (Sport: coach) entrenador(a) m/f; (of animals) domador(a) m/f; **trainers** npl (shoes) zapatillas fpl (de deporte); **training** n formación f; entrenamiento f; **to be in training** (Sport) estar entrenando; **training course** n curso de formación; **training shoes** npl zapatillas fpl (de deporte)

trait [treɪt] n rasgo

traitor ['treɪtə*] n traidor(a) m/f

tram [træm] (BRIT) n (also: **~car**) tranvía m

tramp [træmp] n (person) vagabundo/a; (inf: pej: woman) puta

trample ['træmpl] vt: **to ~ (underfoot)** pisotear

trampoline ['træmpəliːn] n trampolín m

tranquil ['træŋkwɪl] adj tranquilo; **tranquillizer** (us **tranquilizer**) n (Med) tranquilizante m

transaction [træn'zækʃən] n transacción f, operación f

transatlantic ['trænzət'læntɪk] adj transatlántico

transcript ['trænskrɪpt] n copia

transfer [n 'trænsfə:*, vb træns'fə:*] n (of employees) traslado; (of money, power) transferencia; (Sport) traspaso; (picture, design) calcomanía ▷ vt trasladar; transferir; **to ~ the charges** (BRIT Tel) llamar a cobro revertido

transform [træns'fɔ:m] vt transformar; **transformation** n transformación f

transfusion [træns'fju:ʒən] n transfusión f

transit ['trænzɪt] n: **in ~** en tránsito

transition [træn'zɪʃən] n transición f

transitive ['trænzɪtɪv] adj (Ling) transitivo

translate [trænz'leɪt] vt traducir; **translation** [-'leɪʃən] n traducción f; **translator** n traductor(a) m/f

transmission [trænz'mɪʃən] n transmisión f

transmit [trænz'mɪt] vt transmitir; **transmitter** n transmisor m

transparent [træns'pærnt] adj transparente

transplant ['trænspla:nt] n (Med) transplante m

transport [n 'trænspɔ:t, vt træns'pɔ:t] n transporte m; (car) coche m (SP), carro (LAM), automóvil m ▷ vt transportar; **transportation** [-'teɪʃən] n transporte m

transvestite [trænz'vɛstaɪt] n travestí mf

trap [træp] n (snare, trick) trampa; (carriage) cabriolé m ▷ vt coger (SP) or agarrar (LAM) (en una trampa); (trick) engañar; (confine) atrapar

trash [træʃ] n (rubbish) basura; (nonsense) tonterías fpl; (pej): **the book/film is ~** el libro/la película no vale nada; **trash can** (US) n cubo or bote m (MEX) or tacho (SC) de la basura

trauma ['trɔːmə] n trauma m; **traumatic** [trɔː'mætɪk] adj traumático

travel ['trævl] n el viajar ▷ vi viajar ▷ vt (distance) recorrer; **travel agency** n agencia de viajes; **travel agent** n agente mf de viajes; **travel insurance** n seguro de viaje; **traveller** (US **traveler**) n viajero/a; **traveller's cheque** (US **traveler's check**) n cheque m de viajero; **travelling** (US **traveling**) n los viajes, el viajar; **travel-sick** adj: **to get travel-sick** marearse al viajar; **travel sickness** n mareo

tray [treɪ] n bandeja; (on desk) cajón m

treacherous ['trɛtʃərəs] adj traidor, traicionero; (dangerous) peligroso

treacle ['triːkl] (BRIT) n melaza

tread [trɛd] (pt **trod**, pp **trodden**) n (step) paso, pisada; (sound) ruido de pasos; (of stair) escalón m; (of tyre) banda de rodadura ▷ vi pisar; **tread on** vt fus pisar

treasure ['trɛʒə*] n tesoro ▷ vt (value: object, friendship) guardar; (: memory) guardar; **treasurer** n tesorero/a

treasury ['trɛʒərɪ] n: **the T~** el Ministerio de Hacienda

treat [triːt] n (present) regalo ▷ vt tratar; **to ~ sb to sth** invitar a algn a algo; **treatment** n tratamiento

treaty ['triːtɪ] n tratado

treble ['trɛbl] adj triple ▷ vt triplicar ▷ vi triplicarse

tree [triː] n árbol m; **~ trunk** tronco (de árbol)

trek [trɛk] n (long journey) viaje m largo y difícil; (tiring walk) caminata

tremble ['trɛmbl] vi temblar

tremendous [trɪ'mɛndəs] adj tremendo, enorme; (excellent) estupendo

trench [trɛntʃ] n zanja

trend [trɛnd] n (tendency) tendencia; (of events) curso; (fashion) moda; **trendy** adj de moda

trespass ['trɛspəs] vi: **to ~ on** entrar sin permiso en; **"no ~ing"** "prohibido el paso"

trial ['traɪəl] n (Law) juicio, proceso; (test: of machine etc) prueba; **trial period** n periodo de prueba

triangle ['traɪæŋgl] n (Math, Mus) triángulo

triangular [traɪˈæŋɡjulə*] *adj* triangular
tribe [traɪb] *n* tribu *f*
tribunal [traɪˈbjuːnl] *n* tribunal *m*
tribute [ˈtrɪbjuːt] *n* homenaje *m*, tributo;
to pay ~ to rendir homenaje a
trick [trɪk] *n* (*skill, knack*) tino, truco;
(*conjuring trick*) truco; (*joke*) broma; (*Cards*)
baza ▷ *vt* engañar; **to play a ~ on sb** gastar
una broma a algn; **that should do the ~** a
ver si funciona así
trickle [ˈtrɪkl] *n* (*of water etc*) goteo ▷ *vi*
gotear
tricky [ˈtrɪkɪ] *adj* difícil; delicado
tricycle [ˈtraɪsɪkl] *n* triciclo
trifle [ˈtraɪfl] *n* bagatela; (*Culin*) *dulce de
bizcocho borracho, gelatina, fruta y natillas*
▷ *adv*: **a ~ long** un poquito largo
trigger [ˈtrɪɡə*] *n* (*of gun*) gatillo
trim [trɪm] *adj* (*house, garden*) en buen
estado; (*person, figure*) esbelto ▷ *n* (*haircut
etc*) recorte *m*; (*on car*) guarnición *f* ▷ *vt*
(*neaten*) arreglar; (*cut*) recortar; (*decorate*)
adornar; (*Naut: a sail*) orientar
trio [ˈtriːəu] *n* trío
trip [trɪp] *n* viaje *m*; (*excursion*) excursión *f*;
(*stumble*) traspié *m* ▷ *vi* (*stumble*) tropezar;
(*go lightly*) andar a paso ligero; **on a ~** de
viaje; **trip up** *vi* tropezar, caerse ▷ *vt* hacer
tropezar *or* caer
triple [ˈtrɪpl] *adj* triple
triplets [ˈtrɪplɪts] *npl* trillizos/as *mpl/fpl*
tripod [ˈtraɪpɔd] *n* trípode *m*
triumph [ˈtraɪʌmf] *n* triunfo ▷ *vi*: **to ~
(over)** vencer; **triumphant** [traɪˈʌmfənt]
adj (*team etc*) vencedor(a); (*wave, return*)
triunfal
trivial [ˈtrɪvɪəl] *adj* insignificante;
(*commonplace*) banal
trod [trɔd] *pt of* **tread**
trodden [ˈtrɔdn] *pp of* **tread**
trolley [ˈtrɔlɪ] *n* carrito; (*also*: **~ bus**)
trolebús *m*
trombone [trɔmˈbəun] *n* trombón *m*
troop [truːp] *n* grupo, banda; **troops** *npl*
(*Mil*) tropas *fpl*
trophy [ˈtrəufɪ] *n* trofeo
tropical [ˈtrɔpɪkl] *adj* tropical
trot [trɔt] *n* trote *m* ▷ *vi* trotar; **on the ~**
(*BRIT: fig*) seguidos/as
trouble [ˈtrʌbl] *n* problema *m*, dificultad
f; (*worry*) preocupación *f*; (*bother, effort*)
molestia, esfuerzo; (*unrest*) inquietud
f; (*Med*): **stomach** *etc* **~** problemas *mpl*
gástricos *etc* ▷ *vt* (*disturb*) molestar; (*worry*)
preocupar, inquietar ▷ *vi*: **to ~ to do sth**
molestarse en hacer algo; **troubles** *npl* (*Pol
etc*) conflictos *mpl*; (*personal*) problemas *mpl*;
to be in ~ estar en un apuro; **it's no ~!** ¡no

es molestia (ninguna)!; **what's the ~?** (*with
broken TV etc*) ¿cuál es el problema?; (*doctor
to patient*) ¿qué pasa?; **troubled** *adj* (*person*)
preocupado; (*country, epoch, life*) agitado;
troublemaker *n* agitador(a) *m/f*; (*child*)
alborotador *m*; **troublesome** *adj* molesto
trough [trɔf] *n* (*also*: **drinking ~**)
abrevadero; (*also*: **feeding ~**) comedero;
(*depression*) depresión *f*
trousers [ˈtrauzəz] *npl* pantalones *mpl*;
short ~ pantalones *mpl* cortos
trout [traut] *n inv* trucha
trowel [ˈtrauəl] *n* (*of gardener*) palita; (*of
builder*) paleta
truant [ˈtruənt] *n*: **to play ~** (*BRIT*) hacer
novillos
truce [truːs] *n* tregua
truck [trʌk] *n* (*lorry*) camión *m*; (*Rail*) vagón
m; **truck driver** *n* camionero
true [truː] *adj* verdadero; (*accurate*) exacto;
(*genuine*) auténtico; (*faithful*) fiel; **to come
~** realizarse
truly [ˈtruːlɪ] *adv* (*really*) realmente;
(*truthfully*) verdaderamente;
(*faithfully*): **yours ~** (*in letter*) le saluda
atentamente
trumpet [ˈtrʌmpɪt] *n* trompeta
trunk [trʌŋk] *n* (*of tree, person*) tronco;
(*of elephant*) trompa; (*case*) baúl *m*; (*US Aut*)
maletero; **trunks** *npl* (*also*: **swimming ~s**)
bañador *m* (de hombre)
trust [trʌst] *n* confianza; (*responsibility*)
responsabilidad *f*; (*Law*) fideicomiso ▷ *vt*
(*rely on*) tener confianza en; (*hope*) esperar;
(*entrust*): **to ~ sth to sb** confiar algo a algn;
to take sth on ~ fiarse de algo; **trusted** *adj*
de confianza; **trustworthy** *adj* digno de
confianza
truth [truːθ, *pl* truːðz] *n* verdad *f*; **truthful**
adj veraz
try [traɪ] *n* tentativa, intento; (*Rugby*)
ensayo ▷ *vt* (*attempt*) intentar; (*test: also*: **~
out**) probar, someter a prueba; (*Law*) juzgar,
procesar; (*strain: patience*) hacer perder ▷ *vi*
probar; **to have a ~** probar suerte; **to ~ to
do sth** intentar hacer algo; **~ again!** ¡vuelve
a probar!; **~ harder!** ¡esfuérzate más!; **well, I
tried** al menos lo intenté; **try on** *vt* (*clothes*)
probarse; **trying** *adj* (*experience*) cansado;
(*person*) pesado
T-shirt [ˈtiːʃəːt] *n* camiseta
tub [tʌb] *n* cubo (*SP*), cubeta (*SP, MEX*),
balde *m* (*LAM*); (*bath*) bañera (*SP*), tina (*LAM*),
bañadera (*RPL*)
tube [tjuːb] *n* tubo; (*BRIT: underground*)
metro; (*for tyre*) cámara de aire
tuberculosis [tjubəːkjuˈləusɪs] *n*
tuberculosis *f inv*

tube station (BRIT) n estación f de metro
tuck [tʌk] vt (put) poner; **tuck away** vt (money) guardar; (building): **to be tucked away** esconderse, ocultarse; **tuck in** vt meter dentro; (child) arropar ▷ vi (eat) comer con apetito; **tuck shop** n (Scol) tienda ≈ bar m (del colegio) (SP)
Tue(s). abbr (= Tuesday) mart
Tuesday ['tjuːzdɪ] n martes m inv
tug [tʌg] n (ship) remolcador m ▷ vt tirar de
tuition [tjuː'ɪʃən] n (BRIT) enseñanza; (: private tuition) clases fpl particulares; (US: school fees) matrícula
tulip ['tjuːlɪp] n tulipán m
tumble ['tʌmbl] n (fall) caída ▷ vi caer; **to ~ to sth** (inf) caer en la cuenta de algo; **tumble dryer** (BRIT) n secadora
tumbler ['tʌmblə*] n (glass) vaso
tummy ['tʌmɪ] (inf) n barriga, tripa
tumour ['tjuːmə*] (US **tumor**) n tumor m
tuna ['tjuːnə] n inv (also: **~ fish**) atún m
tune [tjuːn] n melodía ▷ vt (Mus) afinar; (Radio, TV, Aut) sintonizar; **to be in/out of ~** (instrument) estar afinado/desafinado; (singer) cantar afinadamente/desafinar; **to be in/out of ~ with** (fig) estar de acuerdo/en desacuerdo con; **tune in** vi: **to tune in (to)** (Radio, TV) sintonizar (con); **tune up** vi (musician) afinar (su instrumento)
tunic ['tjuːnɪk] n túnica
Tunisia [tjuːˈnɪzɪə] n Túnez m
tunnel ['tʌnl] n túnel m; (in mine) galería ▷ vi construir un túnel/una galería
turbulence ['təːbjuləns] n (Aviat) turbulencia
turf [təːf] n césped m; (clod) tepe m ▷ vt cubrir con césped
Turk [təːk] n turco/a
Turkey ['təːkɪ] n Turquía
turkey ['təːkɪ] n pavo
Turkish ['təːkɪʃ] adj, n turco; (Ling) turco
turmoil ['təːmɔɪl] n: **in ~** revuelto
turn [təːn] n turno; (in road) curva; (of mind, events) rumbo; (Theatre) número; (Med) ataque m ▷ vt girar, volver; (collar, steak) dar la vuelta a; (page) pasar; (change): **to ~ sth into** convertir algo en ▷ vi volver; (person: look back) volverse; (reverse direction) dar la vuelta; (milk) cortarse; (become): **to ~ nasty/forty** ponerse feo/cumplir los cuarenta; **a good ~** un favor; **it gave me quite a ~** me dio un susto; **"no left ~"** (Aut) "prohibido girar a la izquierda"; **it's your ~** te toca a ti; **in ~** por turnos; **to take ~s (at)** turnarse (en); **turn around** vi (person) volverse, darse la vuelta ▷ vt (object) dar la vuelta a, voltear (LAM); **turn away** vi

apartar la vista ▷ vi rechazar; **turn back** vi volverse atrás ▷ vt hacer retroceder; (clock) retrasar; **turn down** vt (refuse) rechazar; (reduce) bajar; (fold) doblar; **turn in** vi (inf: go to bed) acostarse ▷ vt (fold) doblar hacia dentro; **turn off** vi (from road) desviarse ▷ vt (light, radio etc) apagar; (tap) cerrar; (engine) parar; **turn on** vt (light, radio etc) encender (SP), prender (LAM); (tap) abrir; (engine) poner en marcha; **turn out** vt (light, gas) apagar; (produce) producir ▷ vi (voters) concurrir; **to turn out to be ...** resultar ser ...; **turn over** vi (person) volverse ▷ vt (object) dar la vuelta a; (page) volver; **turn round** vi volverse; (rotate) girar; **turn to** vt fus: **to turn to sb** acudir a algn; **turn up** vi (person) llegar, presentarse; (lost object) aparecer ▷ vt (gen) subir; **turning** n (in road) vuelta; **turning point** n (fig) momento decisivo
turnip ['təːnɪp] n nabo
turn: **turnout** n concurrencia; **turnover** n (Comm: amount of money) volumen m de ventas; (: of goods) movimiento; **turnstile** n torniquete m; **turn-up** (BRIT) n (on trousers) vuelta
turquoise ['təːkwɔɪz] n (stone) turquesa ▷ adj color turquesa
turtle ['təːtl] n galápago; **turtleneck (sweater)** n jersey m de cuello vuelto
tusk [tʌsk] n colmillo
tutor ['tjuːtə*] n profesor(a) m/f; **tutorial** [-'tɔːrɪəl] n (Scol) seminario
tuxedo [tʌk'siːdəu] (US) n smóking m, esmoquin m
TV [tiːˈviː] n abbr (= television) tele f
tweed [twiːd] n tweed m
tweezers ['twiːzəz] npl pinzas fpl (de depilar)
twelfth [twelfθ] num duodécimo
twelve [twelv] num doce; **at ~ o'clock** (midday) a mediodía; (midnight) a medianoche
twentieth ['twentɪɪθ] adj vigésimo
twenty ['twentɪ] num veinte
twice [twaɪs] adv dos veces; **~ as much** dos veces más
twig [twɪg] n ramita
twilight ['twaɪlaɪt] n crepúsculo
twin [twɪn] adj, n gemelo/a m/f ▷ vt hermanar; **twin(-bedded) room** n habitación f doble; **twin beds** npl camas fpl gemelas
twinkle ['twɪŋkl] vi centellear; (eyes) brillar
twist [twɪst] n (action) torsión f; (in road, coil) vuelta; (in wire, flex) doblez f; (in story) giro ▷ vt torcer; (weave) trenzar; (roll around) enrollar; (fig) deformar ▷ vi serpentear

twit [twɪt] (inf) n tonto
twitch [twɪtʃ] n (pull) tirón m; (nervous) tic m ▷ vi crisparse
two [tu:] num dos; **to put ~ and ~ together** (fig) atar cabos
type [taɪp] n (category) tipo, género; (model) tipo; (Typ) tipo, letra ▷ vt (letter etc) escribir a máquina; **typewriter** n máquina de escribir
typhoid ['taɪfɔɪd] n tifoidea
typhoon [taɪ'fu:n] n tifón m
typical ['tɪpɪkl] adj típico; **typically** adv típicamente
typing ['taɪpɪŋ] n mecanografía
typist ['taɪpɪst] n mecanógrafo/a
tyre ['taɪə*] (us **tire**) n neumático, llanta (LAM); **tyre pressure** (BRIT) n presión f de los neumáticos

UFO ['ju:fəu] n abbr (= unidentified flying object) OVNI m
Uganda [ju:'gændə] n Uganda
ugly ['ʌglɪ] adj feo; (dangerous) peligroso
UHT abbr (= UHT milk) leche f UHT, leche f uperizada
UK n abbr = **United Kingdom**
ulcer ['ʌlsə*] n úlcera; (mouth ulcer) llaga
ultimate ['ʌltɪmət] adj último, final; (greatest) máximo; **ultimately** adv (in the end) por último, al final; (fundamentally) a or en fin de cuentas
ultimatum [ʌltɪ'meɪtəm] (pl **~s** or **ultimata**) n ultimátum m
ultrasound ['ʌltrəsaund] n (Med) ultrasonido
ultraviolet ['ʌltrə'vaɪəlɪt] adj ultravioleta
umbrella [ʌm'brɛlə] n paraguas m inv; (for sun) sombrilla
umpire ['ʌmpaɪə*] n árbitro
UN n abbr (= United Nations) NN. UU.
unable [ʌn'eɪbl] adj: **to be ~ to do sth** no poder hacer algo
unacceptable [ʌnək'sɛptəbl] adj (proposal, behaviour, price) inaceptable; **it's ~ that** no se puede aceptar que
unanimous [ju:'nænɪməs] adj unánime
unarmed [ʌn'ɑ:md] adj (defenceless) inerme; (without weapon) desarmado
unattended [ʌnə'tɛndɪd] adj desatendido
unattractive [ʌnə'træktɪv] adj poco atractivo
unavailable [ʌnə'veɪləbl] adj (article, room, book) no disponible; (person) ocupado
unavoidable [ʌnə'vɔɪdəbl] adj inevitable
unaware [ʌnə'wɛə*] adj: **to be ~ of** ignorar; **unawares** adv: **to catch sb unawares** pillar a algn desprevenido
unbearable [ʌn'bɛərəbl] adj insoportable
unbeatable [ʌn'bi:təbl] adj (team)

invencible; (*price*) inmejorable; (*quality*) insuperable

unbelievable [ʌnbɪ'liːvəbl] *adj* increíble

unborn [ʌn'bɔːn] *adj* que va a nacer

unbutton [ʌn'bʌtn] *vt* desabrochar

uncalled-for [ʌn'kɔːldfɔː*] *adj* gratuito, inmerecido

uncanny [ʌn'kænɪ] *adj* extraño

uncertain [ʌn'səːtn] *adj* incierto; (*indecisive*) indeciso; **uncertainty** *n* incertidumbre *f*

unchanged [ʌn'tʃeɪndʒd] *adj* igual, sin cambios

uncle ['ʌŋkl] *n* tío

unclear [ʌn'klɪə*] *adj* poco claro; **I'm still ~ about what I'm supposed to do** todavía no tengo muy claro lo que tengo que hacer

uncomfortable [ʌn'kʌmfətəbl] *adj* incómodo; (*uneasy*) inquieto

uncommon [ʌn'kɔmən] *adj* poco común, raro

unconditional [ʌnkən'dɪʃənl] *adj* incondicional

unconscious [ʌn'kɔnʃəs] *adj* sin sentido; (*unaware*): **to be ~ of** no darse cuenta de ▷ *n*: **the ~** el inconsciente

uncontrollable [ʌnkən'trəuləbl] *adj* (*child etc*) incontrolable; (*temper*) indomable; (*laughter*) incontenible

unconventional [ʌnkən'venʃənl] *adj* poco convencional

uncover [ʌn'kʌvə*] *vt* descubrir; (*take lid off*) destapar

undecided [ʌndɪ'saɪdɪd] *adj* (*character*) indeciso; (*question*) no resuelto

undeniable [ʌndɪ'naɪəbl] *adj* innegable

under ['ʌndə*] *prep* debajo de; (*less than*) menos de; (*according to*) según, de acuerdo con; (*sb's leadership*) bajo ▷ *adv* debajo, abajo; **~ there** allí abajo; **~ repair** en reparación; **undercover** *adj* clandestino; **underdone** *adj* (*Culin*) poco hecho; **underestimate** *vt* subestimar; **undergo** (*irreg*) *vt* sufrir; (*treatment*) recibir; **undergraduate** *n* estudiante *mf*; **underground** *n* (BRIT: *railway*) metro; (*Pol*) movimiento clandestino ▷ *adj* (*car park*) subterráneo ▷ *adv* (*work*) en la clandestinidad; **undergrowth** *n* maleza; **underline** *vt* subrayar; **undermine** *vt* socavar, minar; **underneath** [ʌndə'niːθ] *adv* debajo ▷ *prep* debajo de, bajo; **underpants** *npl* calzoncillos *mpl*; **underpass** (BRIT) *n* paso subterráneo; **underprivileged** *adj* desposeído; **underscore** *vt* subrayar; **undershirt** (US) *n* camiseta; **underskirt** (BRIT) *n* enaguas *fpl*

understand [ʌndə'stænd] *vt, vi* entender, comprender; (*assume*) tener entendido;

understandable *adj* comprensible;

understanding *adj* comprensivo ▷ *n* comprensión *f*, entendimiento; (*agreement*) acuerdo

understatement ['ʌndəsteɪtmənt] *n* modestia (excesiva); **that's an ~!** ¡eso es decir poco!

understood [ʌndə'stud] *pt, pp of* **understand** ▷ *adj* (*agreed*) acordado; (*implied*): **it is ~ that** se sobreentiende que

undertake [ʌndə'teɪk] (*irreg*) *vt* emprender; **to ~ to do sth** comprometerse a hacer algo

undertaker ['ʌndəteɪkə*] *n* director(a) *m/f* de pompas fúnebres

undertaking ['ʌndəteɪkɪŋ] *n* empresa; (*promise*) promesa

under: underwater *adv* bajo el agua ▷ *adj* submarino; **underway** *adj*: **to be underway** (*meeting*) estar en marcha; (*investigation*) estar llevándose a cabo; **underwear** *n* ropa interior; **underwent** *vb see* **undergo**; **underworld** *n* (*of crime*) hampa, inframundo

undesirable [ʌndɪ'zaɪrəbl] *adj* (*person*) indeseable; (*thing*) poco aconsejable

undisputed [ʌndɪ'spjuːtɪd] *adj* incontestable

undo [ʌn'duː] (*irreg*) *vt* (*laces*) desatar; (*button etc*) desabrochar; (*spoil*) deshacer

undone [ʌn'dʌn] *pp of* **undo** ▷ *adj*: **to come ~** (*clothes*) desabrocharse; (*parcel*) desatarse

undoubtedly [ʌn'dautɪdlɪ] *adv* indudablemente, sin duda

undress [ʌn'dres] *vi* desnudarse

unearth [ʌn'əːθ] *vt* desenterrar

uneasy [ʌn'iːzɪ] *adj* intranquilo, preocupado; (*feeling*) desagradable; (*peace*) inseguro

unemployed [ʌnɪm'plɔɪd] *adj* parado, sin trabajo ▷ *npl*: **the ~** los parados

unemployment [ʌnɪm'plɔɪmənt] *n* paro, desempleo; **unemployment benefit** *n* (BRIT) subsidio de desempleo or paro

unequal [ʌn'iːkwəl] *adj* (*unfair*) desigual; (*size, length*) distinto

uneven [ʌn'iːvn] *adj* desigual; (*road etc*) lleno de baches

unexpected [ʌnɪk'spektɪd] *adj* inesperado; **unexpectedly** *adv* inesperadamente

unfair [ʌn'feə*] *adj*: **~ (to sb)** injusto (con algn)

unfaithful [ʌn'feɪθful] *adj* infiel

unfamiliar [ʌnfə'mɪlɪə*] *adj* extraño, desconocido; **to be ~ with** desconocer

unfashionable [ʌnˈfæʃnəbl] *adj* pasado
or fuera de moda
unfasten [ʌnˈfɑːsn] *vt* (*knot*) desatar;
(*dress*) desabrochar; (*open*) abrir
unfavourable [ʌnˈfeɪvərəbl] (*us*
unfavorable) *adj* desfavorable
unfinished [ʌnˈfɪnɪʃt] *adj* inacabado, sin
terminar
unfit [ʌnˈfɪt] *adj* bajo de forma;
(*incompetent*): ~ **(for)** incapaz (de); ~ **for
work** no apto para trabajar
unfold [ʌnˈfəʊld] *vt* desdoblar ▷ *vi* abrirse
unforgettable [ʌnfəˈɡetəbl] *adj*
inolvidable
unfortunate [ʌnˈfɔːtʃnət] *adj*
desgraciado; (*event, remark*) inoportuno;
unfortunately *adv* desgraciadamente
unfriendly [ʌnˈfrendlɪ] *adj* antipático;
(*behaviour, remark*) hostil, poco amigable
unfurnished [ʌnˈfəːnɪʃt] *adj* sin amueblar
unhappiness [ʌnˈhæpɪnɪs] *n* tristeza,
desdicha
unhappy [ʌnˈhæpɪ] *adj* (*sad*) triste;
(*unfortunate*) desgraciado; (*childhood*) infeliz;
~ **about/with** (*arrangements etc*) poco
contento con, descontento de
unhealthy [ʌnˈhelθɪ] *adj* (*place*) malsano;
(*person*) enfermizo; (*fig: interest*) morboso
unheard-of [ʌnˈhəːdɔv] *adj* inaudito, sin
precedente
unhelpful [ʌnˈhelpful] *adj* (*person*) poco
servicial; (*advice*) inútil
unhurt [ʌnˈhəːt] *adj* ileso
unidentified [ʌnaɪˈdentɪfaɪd] *adj* no
identificado, sin identificar; *see also* **UFO**
uniform [ˈjuːnɪfɔːm] *n* uniforme *m* ▷ *adj*
uniforme
unify [ˈjuːnɪfaɪ] *vt* unificar, unir
unimportant [ʌnɪmˈpɔːtənt] *adj* sin
importancia
uninhabited [ʌnɪnˈhæbɪtɪd] *adj* desierto
unintentional [ʌnɪnˈtenʃənəl] *adj*
involuntario
union [ˈjuːnjən] *n* unión *f*; (*also:* **trade
~**) sindicato ▷ *cpd* sindical; **Union Jack** *n*
bandera del Reino Unido
unique [juːˈniːk] *adj* único
unisex [ˈjuːnɪseks] *adj* unisex
unit [ˈjuːnɪt] *n* unidad *f*; (*section: of furniture
etc*) elemento; (*team*) grupo; **kitchen ~**
módulo de cocina
unite [juːˈnaɪt] *vt* unir ▷ *vi* unirse;
united *adj* unido; (*effort*) conjunto; **United
Kingdom** *n* Reino Unido; **United Nations
(Organization)** *n* Naciones *fpl* Unidas;
United States (of America) *n* Estados
mpl Unidos
unity [ˈjuːnɪtɪ] *n* unidad *f*

universal [juːnɪˈvəːsl] *adj* universal
universe [ˈjuːnɪvəːs] *n* universo
university [juːnɪˈvəːsɪtɪ] *n* universidad *f*
unjust [ʌnˈdʒʌst] *adj* injusto
unkind [ʌnˈkaɪnd] *adj* poco amable;
(*behaviour, comment*) cruel
unknown [ʌnˈnəʊn] *adj* desconocido
unlawful [ʌnˈlɔːful] *adj* ilegal, ilícito
unleaded [ʌnˈledɪd] *adj* (*petrol, fuel*) sin
plombo
unleash [ʌnˈliːʃ] *vt* desatar
unless [ʌnˈles] *conj* a menos que; ~ **he
comes** a menos que venga; ~ **otherwise
stated** salvo indicación contraria
unlike [ʌnˈlaɪk] *adj* (*not alike*) distinto
de or a; (*not like*) poco propio de ▷ *prep* a
diferencia de
unlikely [ʌnˈlaɪklɪ] *adj* improbable;
(*unexpected*) inverosímil
unlimited [ʌnˈlɪmɪtɪd] *adj* ilimitado
unlisted [ʌnˈlɪstɪd] (*us*) *adj* (*Tel*) que no
consta en la guía
unload [ʌnˈləʊd] *vt* descargar
unlock [ʌnˈlɔk] *vt* abrir (con llave)
unlucky [ʌnˈlʌkɪ] *adj* desgraciado; (*object,
number*) que da mala suerte; **to be ~** tener
mala suerte
unmarried [ʌnˈmærɪd] *adj* soltero
unmistak(e)able [ʌnmɪsˈteɪkəbl] *adj*
inconfundible
unnatural [ʌnˈnætʃrəl] *adj* (*gen*)
antinatural; (*manner*) afectado; (*habit*)
perverso
unnecessary [ʌnˈnesəsərɪ] *adj*
innecesario, inútil
UNO [ˈjuːnəʊ] *n abbr* (= *United Nations
Organization*) ONU *f*
unofficial [ʌnəˈfɪʃl] *adj* no oficial; (*news*)
sin confirmar
unpack [ʌnˈpæk] *vi* deshacer las maletas
▷ *vt* deshacer
unpaid [ʌnˈpeɪd] *adj* (*bill, debt*) sin pagar,
impagado; (*Comm*) pendiente; (*holiday*) sin
sueldo; (*work*) sin pago, voluntario
unpleasant [ʌnˈpleznt] *adj* (*disagreeable*)
desagradable; (*person, manner*) antipático
unplug [ʌnˈplʌɡ] *vt* desenchufar,
desconectar
unpopular [ʌnˈpɔpjulə*] *adj* impopular,
poco popular
unprecedented [ʌnˈpresɪdəntɪd] *adj* sin
precedentes
unpredictable [ʌnprɪˈdɪktəbl] *adj*
imprevisible
unprotected [ˈʌnprəˈtektɪd] *adj* (*sex*) sin
protección
unqualified [ʌnˈkwɔlɪfaɪd] *adj* sin título,
no cualificado; (*success*) total

unravel [ʌn'rævl] vt desenmarañar
unreal [ʌn'rɪəl] adj irreal; (*extraordinary*) increíble
unrealistic [ʌnrɪə'lɪstɪk] adj poco realista
unreasonable [ʌn'riːznəbl] adj irrazonable; (*demand*) excesivo
unrelated [ʌnrɪ'leɪtɪd] adj sin relación; (*family*) no emparentado
unreliable [ʌnrɪ'laɪəbl] adj (*person*) informal; (*machine*) poco fiable
unrest [ʌn'rest] n inquietud f, malestar m; (*Pol*) disturbios mpl
unroll [ʌn'rəul] vt desenrollar
unruly [ʌn'ruːlɪ] adj indisciplinado
unsafe [ʌn'seɪf] adj peligroso
unsatisfactory ['ʌnsætɪs'fæktərɪ] adj poco satisfactorio
unscrew [ʌn'skruː] vt destornillar
unsettled [ʌn'setld] adj inquieto, intranquilo; (*weather*) variable
unsettling [ʌn'setlɪŋ] adj perturbador(a), inquietante
unsightly [ʌn'saɪtlɪ] adj feo
unskilled [ʌn'skɪld] adj (*work*) no especializado; (*worker*) no cualificado
unspoiled ['ʌn'spɔɪld], **unspoilt** ['ʌn'spɔɪlt] adj (*place*) que no ha perdido su belleza natural
unstable [ʌn'steɪbl] adj inestable
unsteady [ʌn'stedɪ] adj inestable
unsuccessful [ʌnsək'sesful] adj (*attempt*) infructuoso; (*writer, proposal*) sin éxito; **to be ~** (*in attempting sth*) no tener éxito, fracasar
unsuitable [ʌn'suːtəbl] adj inapropiado; (*time*) inoportuno
unsure [ʌn'fuə*] adj inseguro, poco seguro
untidy [ʌn'taɪdɪ] adj (*room*) desordenado; (*appearance*) desaliñado
untie [ʌn'taɪ] vt desatar
until [ən'tɪl] prep hasta ▷ conj hasta que; **~ he comes** hasta que venga; **~ now** hasta ahora; **~ then** hasta entonces
untrue [ʌn'truː] adj (*statement*) falso
unused [ʌn'juːzd] adj sin usar
unusual [ʌn'juːʒuəl] adj insólito, poco común; (*exceptional*) inusitado; **unusually** adv (*exceptionally*) excepcionalmente; **he arrived unusually early** llegó más temprano que de costumbre
unveil [ʌn'veɪl] vt (*statue*) descubrir
unwanted [ʌn'wɒntɪd] adj (*clothing*) viejo; (*pregnancy*) no deseado
unwell [ʌn'wel] adj: **to be/feel ~** estar indispuesto/sentirse mal
unwilling [ʌn'wɪlɪŋ] adj: **to be ~ to do sth** estar poco dispuesto a hacer algo
unwind [ʌn'waɪnd] (*irreg*) vt desenvolver ▷ vi (*relax*) relajarse

unwise [ʌn'waɪz] adj imprudente
unwittingly [ʌn'wɪtɪŋlɪ] adv inconscientemente, sin darse cuenta
unwrap [ʌn'ræp] vt desenvolver
unzip [ʌn'zɪp] vt abrir la cremallera de; (*Comput*) descomprimir

○ **KEYWORD**

up [ʌp] prep: **to go/be up sth** subir/estar subido en algo; **he went up the stairs/ the hill** subió las escaleras/la colina; **we walked/climbed up the hill** subimos la colina; **they live further up the street** viven más arriba en la calle; **go up that road and turn left** sigue por esa calle y gira a la izquierda
▷ adv 1 (*upwards, higher*) más arriba; **up in the mountains** en lo alto (de la montaña); **put it a bit higher up** ponlo un poco más arriba or alto; **up there** ahí or allí arriba; **up above** en lo alto, por encima, arriba
2: **to be up** (*out of bed*) estar levantado; (*prices, level*) haber subido
3: **up to** (*as far as*) hasta; **up to now** hasta ahora or la fecha
4: **to be up to: it's up to you** (*depending on*) depende de ti; **he's not up to it** (*job, task etc*) no es capaz de hacerlo; **his work is not up to the required standard** su trabajo no da la talla; (*inf: be doing*): **what is he up to?** ¿que estará tramando?
▷ n: **ups and downs** altibajos mpl

up-and-coming [ʌpənd'kʌmɪŋ] adj prometedor(a)
upbringing ['ʌpbrɪŋɪŋ] n educación f
update [ʌp'deɪt] vt poner al día
upfront [ʌp'frʌnt] adj claro, directo ▷ adv a las claras; (*pay*) por adelantado; **to be ~ about sth** admitir algo claramente
upgrade [ʌp'greɪd] vt (*house*) modernizar; (*employee*) ascender
upheaval [ʌp'hiːvl] n trastornos mpl; (*Pol*) agitación f
uphill [ʌp'hɪl] adj cuesta arriba; (*fig: task*) penoso, difícil ▷ adv: **to go ~** ir cuesta arriba
upholstery [ʌp'həulstərɪ] n tapicería
upmarket [ʌp'mɑːkɪt] adj (*product*) de categoría
upon [ə'pɒn] prep sobre
upper ['ʌpə*] adj superior, de arriba ▷ n (*of shoe: also:* **~s**) empeine m; **upper-class** adj de clase alta
upright ['ʌpraɪt] adj derecho; (*vertical*) vertical; (*fig*) honrado
uprising ['ʌpraɪzɪŋ] n sublevación f
uproar ['ʌprɔː*] n escándalo

u

upset [n 'ʌpsɛt, vb, adj ʌp'sɛt] n (to plan etc) revés m, contratiempo; (Med) trastorno ▷ vt irreg (glass etc) volcar; (plan) alterar; (person) molestar, disgustar ▷ adj molesto, disgustado; (stomach) revuelto
upside-down [ʌpsaɪd'daun] adv al revés; **to turn a place ~** (fig) revolverlo todo
upstairs [ʌp'stɛəz] adv arriba ▷ adj (room) de arriba ▷ n el piso superior
up-to-date ['ʌptə'deɪt] adj al día
uptown ['ʌptaun] (US) adv hacia las afueras ▷ adj exterior, de las afueras
upward ['ʌpwəd] adj ascendente; **upward(s)** adv hacia arriba; (more than): **upward(s) of** más de
uranium [juə'reɪnɪəm] n uranio
Uranus [juə'reɪnəs] n Urano
urban ['əːbən] adj urbano
urge [əːdʒ] n (desire) deseo ▷ vt: **to ~ sb to do sth** animar a algn a hacer algo
urgency ['əːdʒənsɪ] n urgencia
urgent ['əːdʒənt] adj urgente; (voice) perentorio
urinal ['juərɪnl] n (building) urinario; (vessel) orinal m
urinate ['juərɪneɪt] vi orinar
urine ['juərɪn] n orina, orines mpl
US n abbr (= United States) EE. UU.
us [ʌs] pron nos; (after prep) nosotros/as; see also **me**
USA n abbr (= United States (of America)) EE.UU.
use [n juːs, vb juːz] n uso, empleo; (usefulness) utilidad f ▷ vt usar, emplear; **she ~d to do it** (ella) solía or acostumbraba hacerlo; **in ~** en uso; **out of ~** en desuso; **to be of ~** servir; **it's no ~** (pointless) es inútil; (not useful) no sirve; **to be ~d to** estar acostumbrado a, acostumbrar; **use up** vt (food) consumir; (money) gastar; **used** [juːzd] adj (car) usado; **useful** adj útil; **useless** adj (unusable) inservible; (pointless) inútil; (person) inepto; **user** n usuario/a; **user-friendly** adj (computer) amistoso
usual ['juːʒuəl] adj normal, corriente; **as ~** como de costumbre; **usually** adv normalmente
utensil [juː'tɛnsl] n utensilio; **kitchen ~s** batería de cocina
utility [juː'tɪlɪtɪ] n utilidad f; (public utility) (empresa de) servicio público
utilize ['juːtɪlaɪz] vt utilizar
utmost ['ʌtməust] adj mayor ▷ n: **to do one's ~** hacer todo lo posible
utter ['ʌtə*] adj total, completo ▷ vt pronunciar, proferir; **utterly** adv completamente, totalmente
U-turn ['juː'təːn] n viraje m en redondo

v. abbr = **verse; versus**; (= volt) v; (= vide) véase
vacancy ['veɪkənsɪ] n (BRIT: job) vacante f; (room) habitación f libre; **"no vacancies"** "completo"
vacant ['veɪkənt] adj desocupado, libre; (expression) distraído
vacate [və'keɪt] vt (house, room) desocupar; (job) dejar (vacante)
vacation [və'keɪʃən] n vacaciones fpl; **vacationer** (US **vacationist**) n turista m/f
vaccination [væksɪ'neɪʃən] n vacunación f
vaccine ['væksiːn] n vacuna
vacuum ['vækjum] n vacío; **vacuum cleaner** n aspiradora
vagina [və'dʒaɪnə] n vagina
vague [veɪg] adj vago; (memory) borroso; (ambiguous) impreciso; (person: absent-minded) distraído; (: evasive): **to be ~** no decir las cosas claramente
vain [veɪn] adj (conceited) presumido; (useless) vano, inútil; **in ~** en vano
Valentine's Day ['væləntaɪnzdeɪ] n día de los enamorados
valid ['vælɪd] adj válido; (ticket) valedero; (law) vigente
valley ['vælɪ] n valle m
valuable ['væljuəbl] adj (jewel) de valor; (time) valioso; **valuables** npl objetos mpl de valor
value ['væljuː] n valor m; (importance) importancia ▷ vt (fix price of) tasar, valorar; (esteem) apreciar; **values** npl (principles) principios mpl
valve [vælv] n válvula
vampire ['væmpaɪə*] n vampiro
van [væn] n (Aut) furgoneta, camioneta
vandal ['vændl] n vándalo/a; **vandalism** n vandalismo; **vandalize** vt dañar, destruir
vanilla [və'nɪlə] n vainilla

vanish ['vænɪʃ] *vi* desaparecer
vanity ['vænɪtɪ] *n* vanidad *f*
vapour ['veɪpə*] (*US* **vapor**) *n* vapor *m*; (*on breath, window*) vaho
variable ['vɛərɪəbl] *adj* variable
variant ['vɛərɪənt] *n* variante *f*
variation [vɛərɪ'eɪʃən] *n* variación *f*
varied ['vɛərɪd] *adj* variado
variety [və'raɪətɪ] *n* (*diversity*) diversidad *f*; (*type*) variedad *f*
various ['vɛərɪəs] *adj* (*several: people*) varios/as; (*reasons*) diversos/as
varnish ['vɑːnɪʃ] *n* barniz *m*; (*nail varnish*) esmalte *m* ⊳ *vt* barnizar; (*nails*) pintar (con esmalte)
vary ['vɛərɪ] *vt* variar; (*change*) cambiar ⊳ *vi* variar
vase [vɑːz] *n* jarrón *m*
┃ Be careful not to translate **vase** by the Spanish word *vaso*.
Vaseline® ['væsɪliːn] *n* vaselina®
vast [vɑːst] *adj* enorme
VAT [væt] (*BRIT*) *n abbr* (= *value added tax*) IVA *m*
vault [vɔːlt] *n* (*of roof*) bóveda; (*tomb*) panteón *m*; (*in bank*) cámara acorazada ⊳ *vt* (*also:* **~ over**) saltar (por encima de)
VCR *n abbr* = **video cassette recorder**
VDU *n abbr* (= *visual display unit*) UPV *f*
veal [viːl] *n* ternera
veer [vɪə*] *vi* (*vehicle*) virar; (*wind*) girar
vegan ['viːgən] *n* vegetariano/a estricto/a, vegetaliano/a
vegetable ['vɛdʒtəbl] *n* (*Bot*) vegetal *m*; (*edible plant*) legumbre *f*, hortaliza ⊳ *adj* vegetal
vegetarian [vɛdʒɪ'tɛərɪən] *adj, n* vegetariano/a *m/f*
vegetation [vɛdʒɪ'teɪʃən] *n* vegetación *f*
vehicle ['viːɪkl] *n* vehículo; (*fig*) medio
veil [veɪl] *n* velo ⊳ *vt* velar
vein [veɪn] *n* vena; (*of ore etc*) veta
Velcro® ['vɛlkrəu] *n* velcro® *m*
velvet ['vɛlvɪt] *n* terciopelo
vending machine ['vɛndɪŋ-] *n* distribuidor *m* automático
vendor ['vɛndə*] *n* vendedor(a) *m/f*; **street ~** vendedor(a) *m/f* callejero/a
vengeance ['vɛndʒəns] *n* venganza; **with a ~** (*fig*) con creces
venison ['vɛnɪsn] *n* carne *f* de venado
venom ['vɛnəm] *n* veneno; (*bitterness*) odio
vent [vɛnt] *n* (*in jacket*) respiradero; (*in wall*) rejilla (de ventilación) ⊳ *vt* (*fig: feelings*) desahogar
ventilation [vɛntɪ'leɪʃən] *n* ventilación *f*
venture ['vɛntʃə*] *n* empresa ⊳ *vt*

(*opinion*) ofrecer ⊳ *vi* arriesgarse, lanzarse; **business ~** empresa comercial
venue ['vɛnjuː] *n* lugar *m*
Venus ['viːnəs] *n* Venus *m*
verb [vəːb] *n* verbo; **verbal** *adj* verbal
verdict ['vəːdɪkt] *n* veredicto, fallo; (*fig*) opinión *f*, juicio
verge [vəːdʒ] (*BRIT*) *n* borde *m*; **"soft ~s"** (*Aut*) "arcén *m* no asfaltado"; **to be on the ~ of doing sth** estar a punto de hacer algo
verify ['vɛrɪfaɪ] *vt* comprobar, verificar
versatile ['vəːsətaɪl] *adj* (*person*) polifacético; (*machine, tool etc*) versátil
verse [vəːs] *n* poesía; (*stanza*) estrofa; (*in bible*) versículo
version ['vəːʃən] *n* versión *f*
versus ['vəːsəs] *prep* contra
vertical ['vəːtɪkl] *adj* vertical
very ['vɛrɪ] *adv* muy ⊳ *adj*: **the ~ book which** el mismo libro que; **the ~ last** el último de todos; **at the ~ least** al menos; **~ much** muchísimo
vessel ['vɛsl] *n* (*ship*) barco; (*container*) vasija; *see* **blood**
vest [vɛst] *n* (*BRIT*) camiseta; (*US: waistcoat*) chaleco
vet [vɛt] *vt* (*candidate*) investigar ⊳ *n abbr* (*BRIT*) = **veterinary surgeon**
veteran ['vɛtərn] *n* excombatiente *mf*, veterano/a
veterinary surgeon ['vɛtrɪnərɪ-] (*US* **veterinarian**) *n* veterinario/a *m/f*
veto ['viːtəu] (*pl* **~es**) *n* veto ⊳ *vt* prohibir, poner el veto a
via ['vaɪə] *prep* por, por medio de
viable ['vaɪəbl] *adj* viable
vibrate [vaɪ'breɪt] *vi* vibrar
vibration [vaɪ'breɪʃən] *n* vibración *f*
vicar ['vɪkə*] *n* párroco (de la Iglesia Anglicana)
vice [vaɪs] *n* (*evil*) vicio; (*Tech*) torno de banco; **vice-chairman** (*irreg*) *n* vicepresidente *m*
vice versa ['vaɪsɪ'vəːsə] *adv* viceversa
vicinity [vɪ'sɪnɪtɪ] *n*: **in the ~ (of)** cercano (a)
vicious ['vɪʃəs] *adj* (*attack*) violento; (*words*) cruel; (*horse, dog*) resabido
victim ['vɪktɪm] *n* víctima
victor ['vɪktə*] *n* vencedor(a) *m/f*
Victorian [vɪk'tɔːrɪən] *adj* victoriano
victorious [vɪk'tɔːrɪəs] *adj* vencedor(a)
victory ['vɪktərɪ] *n* victoria
video ['vɪdɪəu] *n* vídeo (*SP*), video (*LAM*); **video call** *n* videollamada; **video camera** *n* videocámara, cámara de vídeo; **video (cassette) recorder** *n* vídeo (*SP*), video (*LAM*); **video game** *n* videojuego;

videophone n videoteléfono; **video shop** n videoclub m; **video tape** n cinta de vídeo
vie [vaɪ] vi: **to ~ (with sb for sth)** competir (con algn por algo)
Vienna [vɪ'ɛnə] n Viena
Vietnam [vjɛt'næm] n Vietnam m; **Vietnamese** [-nə'miːz] n inv, adj vietnamita mf
view [vjuː] n vista; (outlook) perspectiva; (opinion) opinión f, criterio ▷ vt (look at) mirar; (fig) considerar; **on ~** (in museum etc) expuesto; **in full ~ (of)** en plena vista (de); **in ~ of the weather/the fact that** en vista del tiempo/del hecho de que; **in my ~** en mi opinión; **viewer** n espectador(a) m/f; (TV) telespectador(a) m/f; **viewpoint** n (attitude) punto de vista; (place) mirador m
vigilant ['vɪdʒɪlənt] adj vigilante
vigorous ['vɪgərəs] adj enérgico, vigoroso
vile [vaɪl] adj vil, infame; (smell) asqueroso; (temper) endemoniado
villa ['vɪlə] n (country house) casa de campo; (suburban house) chalet m
village ['vɪlɪdʒ] n aldea; **villager** n aldeano/a
villain ['vɪlən] n (scoundrel) malvado/a; (in novel) malo; (BRIT: criminal) maleante mf
vinaigrette [vɪneɪ'grɛt] n vinagreta
vine [vaɪn] n vid f
vinegar ['vɪnɪgə*] n vinagre m
vineyard ['vɪnjɑːd] n viña, viñedo
vintage ['vɪntɪdʒ] n (year) vendimia, cosecha ▷ cpd de época
vinyl ['vaɪnl] n vinilo
viola [vɪ'əulə] n (Mus) viola
violate ['vaɪəleɪt] vt violar
violation [vaɪə'leɪʃən] n violación f; **in ~ of sth** en violación de algo
violence ['vaɪələns] n violencia
violent ['vaɪələnt] adj violento; (intense) intenso
violet ['vaɪələt] adj violado, violeta ▷ n (plant) violeta
violin [vaɪə'lɪn] n violín m
VIP n abbr (= very important person) VIP m
virgin ['vəːdʒɪn] n virgen f
Virgo ['vəːgəu] n Virgo
virtual ['vəːtjuəl] adj virtual; **virtually** adv prácticamente; **virtual reality** n (Comput) mundo or realidad f virtual
virtue ['vəːtjuː] n virtud f; (advantage) ventaja; **by ~ of** en virtud de
virus ['vaɪərəs] n (also Comput) virus m inv
visa ['viːzə] n visado (SP), visa (LAM)
vise [vaɪs] (US) n (Tech) = **vice**
visibility [vɪzɪ'bɪlɪtɪ] n visibilidad f
visible ['vɪzəbl] adj visible
vision ['vɪʒən] n (sight) vista; (foresight, in dream) visión f

visit ['vɪzɪt] n visita ▷ vt (person (US: also: ~ with)) visitar, hacer una visita a; (place) ir a, (ir a) conocer; **visiting hours** npl (in hospital etc) horas fpl de visita; **visitor** n (in museum) visitante mf; (invited to house) visita; (tourist) turista mf; **visitor centre** (US **visitor center**) n centro m de información
visual ['vɪzjuəl] adj visual; **visualize** vt imaginarse
vital ['vaɪtl] adj (essential) esencial; (dynamic) dinámico; (organ) vital
vitality [vaɪ'tælɪtɪ] n energía, vitalidad f
vitamin ['vɪtəmɪn] n vitamina
vivid ['vɪvɪd] adj (account) gráfico; (light) intenso; (imagination, memory) vivo
V-neck ['viːnɛk] n cuello de pico
vocabulary [vəu'kæbjulərɪ] n vocabulario
vocal ['vəukl] adj vocal; (articulate) elocuente
vocational [vəu'keɪʃənl] adj profesional
vodka ['vɔdkə] n vodka m
vogue [vəug] n: **in ~** en boga
voice [vɔɪs] n voz f ▷ vt expresar; **voice mail** n fonobuzón m
void [vɔɪd] n vacío; (hole) hueco ▷ adj (invalid) nulo, inválido; (empty): **~ of** carente or desprovisto de
volatile ['vɔlətaɪl] adj (situation) inestable; (person) voluble; (liquid) volátil
volcano [vɔl'keɪnəu] (pl **~es**) n volcán m
volleyball ['vɔlɪbɔːl] n vol(e)ibol m
volt [vəult] n voltio; **voltage** n voltaje m
volume ['vɔljuːm] n (gen) volumen m; (book) tomo
voluntarily ['vɔləntrɪlɪ] adv libremente, voluntariamente
voluntary ['vɔləntərɪ] adj voluntario
volunteer [vɔlən'tɪə*] n voluntario/a ▷ vt (information) ofrecer ▷ vi ofrecerse (de voluntario); **to ~ to do** ofrecerse a hacer
vomit ['vɔmɪt] n vómito ▷ vt, vi vomitar
vote [vəut] n voto; (votes cast) votación f; (right to vote) derecho de votar; (franchise) sufragio ▷ vt (chairman) elegir; (propose): **to ~ that** proponer que ▷ vi votar, ir a votar; **~ of thanks** voto de gracias; **voter** n votante mf; **voting** n votación f
voucher ['vautʃə*] n (for meal etc) vale m
vow [vau] n voto ▷ vt: **to ~ to do/that** jurar hacer/que
vowel ['vauəl] n vocal f
voyage ['vɔɪɪdʒ] n viaje m
vulgar ['vʌlgə*] adj (rude) ordinario, grosero; (in bad taste) de mal gusto
vulnerable ['vʌlnərəbl] adj vulnerable
vulture ['vʌltʃə*] n buitre m

W

waddle ['wɔdl] vi anadear
wade [weɪd] vi: **to ~ through** (water) vadear; (fig: book) leer con dificultad
wafer ['weɪfə*] n galleta, barquillo
waffle ['wɔfl] n (Culin) gofre m ▷ vi dar el rollo
wag [wæg] vt menear, agitar ▷ vi moverse, menearse
wage [weɪdʒ] n (also: **~s**) sueldo, salario ▷ vt: **to ~ war** hacer la guerra
wag(g)on ['wægən] n (horse-drawn) carro; (BRIT Rail) vagón m
wail [weɪl] n gemido ▷ vi gemir
waist [weɪst] n cintura, talle m; **waistcoat** (BRIT) n chaleco
wait [weɪt] n (interval) pausa ▷ vi esperar; **to lie in ~ for** acechar a; **I can't ~ to** (fig) estoy deseando; **to ~ for** esperar (a); **wait on** vt fus servir a; **waiter** n camarero; **waiting list** n lista de espera; **waiting room** n sala de espera; **waitress** ['weɪtrɪs] n camarera
waive [weɪv] vt suspender
wake [weɪk] (pt **woke** or **~d**, pp **woken** or **~d**) vt (also: **~ up**) despertar ▷ vi (also: **~ up**) despertarse ▷ n (for dead person) vela, velatorio; (Naut) estela
Wales [weɪlz] n País m de Gales; **the Prince of ~** el príncipe de Gales
walk [wɔːk] n (stroll) paseo; (hike) excursión f a pie, caminata; (gait) paso, andar m; (in park etc) paseo, alameda ▷ vi andar, caminar; (for pleasure, exercise) pasear ▷ vt (distance) recorrer a pie, andar; (dog) pasear; **10 minutes' ~ from here** a 10 minutos de aquí andando; **people from all ~s of life** gente de todas las esferas; **walk out** vi (audience) salir; (workers) declararse en huelga; **walker** n (person) paseante mf, caminante mf; **walkie-talkie** ['wɔːkɪ'tɔːkɪ] n walkie-talkie m; **walking**
n el andar; **walking shoes** npl zapatos mpl para andar; **walking stick** n bastón m; **Walkman®** n Walkman® m; **walkway** n paseo
wall [wɔːl] n pared f; (exterior) muro; (city wall etc) muralla
wallet ['wɔlɪt] n cartera, billetera
wallpaper ['wɔːlpeɪpə*] n papel m pintado ▷ vt empapelar
walnut ['wɔːlnʌt] n nuez f; (tree) nogal m
walrus ['wɔːlrəs] (pl **~** or **~es**) n morsa
waltz [wɔːlts] n vals m ▷ vi bailar el vals
wand [wɔnd] n (also: **magic ~**) varita (mágica)
wander ['wɔndə*] vi (person) vagar; deambular; (thoughts) divagar ▷ vt recorrer, vagar por
want [wɔnt] vt querer, desear; (need) necesitar ▷ n: **for ~ of** por falta de; **wanted** adj (criminal) buscado; **"wanted"** (in advertisements) "se busca"
war [wɔː*] n guerra; **to make ~ (on)** declarar la guerra (a)
ward [wɔːd] n (in hospital) sala; (Pol) distrito electoral; (Law: child: also: **~ of court**) pupilo/a
warden ['wɔːdn] n (BRIT: of institution) director(a) m/f; (of park, game reserve) guardián/ana m/f; (BRIT: also: **traffic ~**) guardia mf
wardrobe ['wɔːdrəub] n armario, ropero; (clothes) vestuario
warehouse ['wɛəhaus] n almacén m, depósito
warfare ['wɔːfɛə*] n guerra
warhead ['wɔːhɛd] n cabeza armada
warm [wɔːm] adj caliente; (thanks) efusivo; (clothes etc) abrigado; (welcome, day) caluroso; **it's ~** hace calor; **I'm ~** tengo calor; **warm up** vi (room) calentarse; (person) entrar en calor; (athlete) hacer ejercicios de calentamiento ▷ vt calentar; **warmly** adv afectuosamente; **warmth** n calor m
warn [wɔːn] vt avisar, advertir; **warning** n aviso, advertencia; **warning light** n luz f de advertencia
warrant ['wɔrnt] n autorización f; (Law: to arrest) orden f de detención; (: to search) mandamiento de registro
warranty ['wɔrəntɪ] n garantía
warrior ['wɔrɪə*] n guerrero/a
Warsaw ['wɔːsɔː] n Varsovia
warship ['wɔːʃɪp] n buque m or barco de guerra
wart [wɔːt] n verruga
wartime ['wɔːtaɪm] n: **in ~** en tiempos de guerra, en la guerra
wary ['wɛərɪ] adj cauteloso

was [wɒz] *pt of* **be**
wash [wɒʃ] *vt* lavar ▷ *vi* lavarse; (*sea etc*): **to ~ against/over sth** llegar hasta/cubrir algo ▷ *n* (*clothes etc*) lavado; (*of ship*) estela; **to have a ~** lavarse; **wash up** *vi* (*BRIT*) fregar los platos; (*US*) lavarse; **washbasin** (*US*) *n* lavabo; **wash cloth** (*US*) *n* manopla; **washer** *n* (*Tech*) arandela; **washing** *n* (*dirty*) ropa sucia; (*clean*) colada; **washing line** *n* cuerda de (colgar) la ropa; **washing machine** *n* lavadora; **washing powder** (*BRIT*) *n* detergente *m* (en polvo)
Washington ['wɒʃɪŋtən] *n* Washington *m*
wash: washing-up (*BRIT*) *n* fregado, platos *mpl* (para fregar); **washing-up liquid** (*BRIT*) *n* líquido lavavajillas; **washroom** (*US*) *n* servicios *mpl*
wasn't ['wɒznt] = **was not**
wasp [wɒsp] *n* avispa
waste [weɪst] *n* derroche *m*, despilfarro; (*of time*) pérdida; (*food*) sobras *fpl*; (*rubbish*) basura, desperdicios *mpl* ▷ *adj* (*material*) de desecho; (*left over*) sobrante; (*land*) baldío, descampado ▷ *vt* malgastar, derrochar; (*time*) perder; (*opportunity*) desperdiciar; **waste ground** (*BRIT*) *n* terreno baldío; **wastepaper basket** *n* papelera
watch [wɒtʃ] *n* (*also:* **wrist ~**) reloj *m*; (*Mil: group of guards*) centinela *m*; (*act*) vigilancia; (*Naut: spell of duty*) guardia ▷ *vt* (*look at*) mirar, observar; (: *match, programme*) ver; (*spy on, guard*) vigilar; (*be careful of*) cuidarse de, tener cuidado de ▷ *vi* ver, mirar; (*keep guard*) montar guardia; **watch out** *vi* cuidarse, tener cuidado; **watchdog** *n* perro guardián; (*fig*) *persona u organismo encargado de asegurarse de que las empresas actúan dentro de la legalidad*; **watch strap** *n* pulsera (de reloj)
water ['wɔːtə*] *n* agua ▷ *vt* (*plant*) regar ▷ *vi* (*eyes*) llorar; (*mouth*) hacerse la boca agua; **water down** *vt* (*milk etc*) aguar; (*fig: story*) dulcificar, diluir; **watercolour** (*US* **watercolor**) *n* acuarela; **watercress** *n* berro; **waterfall** *n* cascada, salto de agua; **watering can** *n* regadera; **watermelon** *n* sandía; **waterproof** *adj* impermeable; **water-skiing** *n* esquí *m* acuático
watt [wɒt] *n* vatio
wave [weɪv] *n* (*of hand*) señal *f* con la mano; (*on water*) ola; (*Radio, in hair*) onda; (*fig*) oleada ▷ *vi* agitar la mano; (*flag etc*) ondear ▷ *vt* (*handkerchief, gun*) agitar; **wavelength** *n* longitud *f* de onda
waver ['weɪvə*] *vi* (*voice, love etc*) flaquear; (*person*) vacilar
wavy ['weɪvɪ] *adj* ondulado
wax [wæks] *n* cera ▷ *vt* encerar ▷ *vi*

(*moon*) crecer
way [weɪ] *n* camino; (*distance*) trayecto, recorrido; (*direction*) dirección *f*, sentido; (*manner*) modo, manera; (*habit*) costumbre *f*; **which ~? - this ~** ¿por dónde? *or* ¿en qué dirección? - por aquí; **on the ~** (*en route*) en (el) camino; **to be on one's ~** estar en camino; **to be in the ~** bloquear el camino; (*fig*) estorbar; **to go out of one's ~ to do sth** desvivirse por hacer algo; **under ~** en marcha; **to lose one's ~** extraviarse; **in a ~** en cierto modo *or* sentido; **no ~!** (*inf*) ¡de eso nada!; **by the ~ ...** a propósito ...; **"~ in"** (*BRIT*) "entrada"; **"~ out"** (*BRIT*) "salida"; **the ~ back** el camino de vuelta; **"give ~"** (*BRIT Aut*) "ceda el paso"
W.C. *n* (*BRIT*) wáter *m*
we [wiː] *pl pron* nosotros/as
weak [wiːk] *adj* débil, flojo; (*tea etc*) claro; **weaken** *vi* debilitarse; (*give way*) ceder ▷ *vt* debilitar; **weakness** *n* debilidad *f*; (*fault*) punto débil; **to have a weakness for** tener debilidad por
wealth [wɛlθ] *n* riqueza; (*of details*) abundancia; **wealthy** *adj* rico
weapon ['wɛpən] *n* arma; **~s of mass destruction** armas de destrucción masiva
wear [weə*] (*pt* **wore**, *pp* **worn**) *n* (*use*) uso; (*deterioration through use*) desgaste *m* ▷ *vt* (*clothes*) llevar; (*shoes*) calzar; (*damage: through use*) gastar, usar ▷ *vi* (*last*) durar; (*rub through etc*) desgastarse; **evening ~** ropa de etiqueta; **sports~/baby~** ropa de deportes/de niños; **wear off** *vi* (*pain etc*) pasar, desaparecer; **wear out** *vt* desgastar; (*person, strength*) agotar
weary ['wɪərɪ] *adj* cansado; (*dispirited*) abatido ▷ *vi*: **to ~ of** cansarse de
weasel ['wiːzl] *n* (*Zool*) comadreja
weather ['wɛðə*] *n* tiempo ▷ *vt* (*storm, crisis*) hacer frente a; **under the ~** (*fig: ill*) indispuesto, pachucho; **weather forecast** *n* boletín *m* meteorológico
weave [wiːv] (*pt* **wove**, *pp* **woven**) *vt* (*cloth*) tejer; (*fig*) entretejer
web [wɛb] *n* (*of spider*) telaraña; (*on duck's foot*) membrana; (*network*) red *f*; **the (World Wide) W~** la Red; **web address** *n* dirección *f* de Internet; **webcam** *n* webcam *f*; **web page** *n* (página) web *m or f*; **website** *n* sitio web
Wed. *abbr* (= *Wednesday*) miérc
wed [wɛd] (*pt, pp* **~ded**) *vt* casar ▷ *vi* casarse
we'd [wiːd] = **we had; we would**
wedding ['wɛdɪŋ] *n* boda, casamiento; **silver/golden ~ (anniversary)** bodas *fpl* de plata/de oro; **wedding anniversary** *n*

aniversario de boda; **wedding day** n día
m de la boda; **wedding dress** n traje m de
novia; **wedding ring** n alianza
wedge [wɛdʒ] n (of wood etc) cuña; (of cake)
trozo ▷ vt acuñar; (push) apretar
Wednesday ['wɛnzdɪ] n miércoles m inv
wee [wi:] (SCOTTISH) adj pequeñito
weed [wi:d] n mala hierba, maleza
▷ vt escardar, desherbar; **weedkiller** n
herbicida m
week [wi:k] n semana; **a ~ today/
on Friday** de hoy/del viernes en ocho
días; **weekday** n día m laborable;
weekend n fin m de semana; **weekly**
adv semanalmente, cada semana ▷ adj
semanal ▷ n semanario
weep [wi:p] (pt, pp **wept**) vi, vt llorar
weigh [weɪ] vt, vi pesar; **to ~ anchor** levar
anclas; **weigh up** vt sopesar
weight [weɪt] n peso; (metal weight) pesa;
to lose/put on ~ adelgazar/engordar;
weightlifting n levantamiento de pesas
weir [wɪə*] n presa
weird [wɪəd] adj raro, extraño
welcome ['wɛlkəm] adj bienvenido ▷ n
bienvenida ▷ vt dar la bienvenida a; (be
glad of) alegrarse de; **thank you – you're ~**
gracias – de nada
weld [wɛld] n soldadura ▷ vt soldar
welfare ['wɛlfɛə*] n bienestar m; (social
aid) asistencia social; **welfare state** n
estado del bienestar
well [wɛl] n fuente f, pozo ▷ adv bien
▷ adj: **to be ~** estar bien (de salud) ▷ excl
¡vaya!, ¡bueno!; **as ~** también; **as ~ as**
además de; **~ done!** ¡bien hecho!; **get ~
soon!** ¡que te mejores pronto!; **to do ~**
(business) ir bien; (person) tener éxito
we'll [wi:l] = we will; we shall
well: well-behaved adj bueno; **well-built**
adj (person) fornido; **well-dressed** adj bien
vestido
wellies ['wɛlɪz] (inf) npl (BRIT) botas de
goma
well: well-known adj (person) conocido;
well-off adj acomodado; **well-paid**
[wel'peɪd] adj bien pagado, bien retribuido
Welsh [wɛlʃ] adj galés/esa ▷ n (Ling)
galés m; **Welshman** (irreg) n galés m;
Welshwoman (irreg) n galesa
went [wɛnt] pt of **go**
wept [wɛpt] pt, pp of **weep**
were [wə:*] pt of **be**
we're [wɪə*] = we are
weren't [wə:nt] = were not
west [wɛst] n oeste m ▷ adj occidental,
del oeste ▷ adv al or hacia el oeste; **the
W~** el Oeste, el Occidente; **westbound**

['wɛstbaund] adj (traffic, carriageway) con
rumbo al oeste; **western** adj occidental
▷ n (Cinema) película del oeste; **West Indian**
adj, n antillano/a m/f
wet [wɛt] adj (damp) húmedo; (soaked): **~
through** mojado; (rainy) lluvioso ▷ n
(BRIT: Pol) conservador(a) m/f moderado/a;
to get ~ mojarse; **"~ paint"** "recién
pintado"; **wetsuit** n traje m térmico
we've [wi:v] = we have
whack [wæk] vt dar un buen golpe a
whale [weɪl] n (Zool) ballena
wharf [wɔ:f] (pl **wharves**) n muelle m

○ **KEYWORD**

what [wɔt] adj 1 (in direct/indirect questions)
qué; **what size is he?** ¿qué talla usa?; **what
colour/shape is it?** ¿de qué color/forma es?
2 (in exclamations): **what a mess!** ¡qué
desastre!; **what a fool I am!** ¡qué tonto soy!
▷ pron 1 (interrogative) qué; **what are you
doing?** ¿qué haces or estás haciendo?; **what
is happening?** ¿qué pasa or está pasando?;
what is it called? ¿cómo se llama?; **what
about me?** ¿y yo qué?; **what about doing
...?** ¿qué tal si hacemos ...?
2 (relative) lo que; **I saw what you did/was
on the table** vi lo que hiciste/había en la
mesa
▷ excl (disbelieving) ¡cómo!; **what, no coffee!**
¡que no hay café!

whatever [wɔt'ɛvə*] adj: **~ book you
choose** cualquier libro que elijas ▷ pron: **do
~ is necessary** haga lo que sea necesario; **~
happens** pase lo que pase; **no reason ~** or
whatsoever ninguna razón sea la que sea;
nothing ~ nada en absoluto
whatsoever [wɔtsəu'ɛvə*] adj see
whatever
wheat [wi:t] n trigo
wheel [wi:l] n rueda; (Aut: also: **steering
~**) volante m; (Naut) timón m ▷ vt (pram
etc) empujar ▷ vi (also: **~ round**) dar la
vuelta, girar; **wheelbarrow** n carretilla;
wheelchair n silla de ruedas; **wheel clamp**
n (Aut) cepo
wheeze [wi:z] vi resollar

○ **KEYWORD**

when [wɛn] adv cuando; **when did it
happen?** ¿cuándo ocurrió?; **I know when it
happened** sé cuándo ocurrió
▷ conj 1 (at, during, after the time that)
cuando; **be careful when you cross the
road** ten cuidado al cruzar la calle; **that**

W

was when I needed you fue entonces que te necesité
2 (on, at which): **on the day when I met him** el día en qué le conocí
3 (whereas) cuando

whenever [wɛn'ɛvə*] conj cuando; (every time that) cada vez que ▷ adv cuando sea
where [wɛə*] adv dónde ▷ conj donde; **this is ~** aquí es donde; **whereabouts** adv dónde ▷ n: **nobody knows his whereabouts** nadie conoce su paradero; **whereas** conj visto que, mientras; **whereby** pron por lo cual; **wherever** conj dondequiera que; (interrogative) dónde
whether [wɛðə*] conj si; **I don't know ~ to accept or not** no sé si aceptar o no; **~ you go or not** vayas o no vayas

○ **KEYWORD**

which [wɪtʃ] adj **1** (interrogative: direct, indirect) qué; **which picture(s) do you want?** ¿qué cuadro(s) quieres?; **which one?** ¿cuál?
2 **in which case** en cuyo caso; **we got there at 8 pm, by which time the cinema was full** llegamos allí a las 8, cuando el cine estaba lleno
▷ pron **1** (interrogative) cual; **I don't mind which** el/la que sea
2 (relative: replacing noun) que; (: replacing clause) lo que; (: after preposition) (el(la)) que etc el/la cual etc; **the apple which you ate/which is on the table** la manzana que comiste/que está en la mesa; **the chair on which you are sitting** la silla en la que estás sentado; **he said he knew, which is true/I feared** dijo que lo sabía, lo cual or lo que es cierto/me temía

whichever [wɪtʃ'ɛvə*] adj: **take ~ book you prefer** coja (SP) el libro que prefiera; **~ book you take** cualquier libro que coja
while [waɪl] n rato, momento ▷ conj mientras; (although) aunque; **for a ~** durante algún tiempo
whilst [waɪlst] conj = **while**
whim [wɪm] n capricho
whine [waɪn] n (of pain) gemido; (of engine) zumbido; (of siren) aullido ▷ vi gemir; zumbar; (fig: complain) gimotear
whip [wɪp] n látigo; (Pol: person) encargado de la disciplina partidaria en el parlamento ▷ vt azotar; (Culin) batir; (move quickly): **to ~ sth out/off** sacar/quitar algo de un tirón; **whipped cream** n nata or crema montada
whirl [wə:l] vt hacer girar, dar vueltas

a ▷ vi girar, dar vueltas; (leaves etc) arremolinarse
whisk [wɪsk] n (Culin) batidor m ▷ vt (Culin) batir; **to ~ sb away** or **off** llevar volando a algn
whiskers [ˈwɪskəz] npl (of animal) bigotes mpl; (of man) patillas fpl
whiskey [ˈwɪskɪ] (US, IRELAND) n = **whisky**
whisky [ˈwɪskɪ] n whisky m
whisper [ˈwɪspə*] n susurro ▷ vi, vt susurrar
whistle [ˈwɪsl] n (sound) silbido; (object) silbato ▷ vi silbar
white [waɪt] adj blanco; (pale) pálido ▷ n blanco; (of egg) clara; **whiteboard** n pizarra blanca; **interactive whiteboard** pizarra interactiva; **White House** (US) n Casa Blanca; **whitewash** n (paint) jalbegue m, cal f ▷ vt blanquear
whiting [ˈwaɪtɪŋ] n inv (fish) pescadilla
Whitsun [ˈwɪtsn] n pentecostés m
whittle [ˈwɪtl] vt: **to ~ away, ~ down** ir reduciendo
whizz [wɪz] vi: **to ~ past** or **by** pasar a toda velocidad

○ **KEYWORD**

who [hu:] pron **1** (interrogative) quién; **who is it?, who's there?** ¿quién es?; **who are you looking for?** ¿a quién buscas?; **I told her who I was** le dije quién era yo
2 (relative) que; **the man/woman who spoke to me** el hombre/la mujer que habló conmigo; **those who can swim** los que saben or sepan nadar

whoever [hu:'ɛvə*] pron: **~ finds it** cualquiera or quienquiera que lo encuentre; **ask ~ you like** pregunta a quien quieras; **~ he marries** no importa con quién se case
whole [həʊl] adj (entire) todo, entero; (not broken) intacto ▷ n todo; (all): **the ~ of the town** toda la ciudad, la ciudad entera ▷ n (total) total m; (sum) conjunto; **on the ~, as a ~** en general; **wholefood(s)** n(pl) alimento(s) m(pl) integral(es); **wholeheartedly** [həʊl'hɑ:tɪdlɪ] adv con entusiasmo; **wholemeal** adj integral; **wholesale** n venta al por mayor ▷ adj al por mayor; (fig: destruction) sistemático; **wholewheat** adj = **wholemeal**; **wholly** adv totalmente, enteramente

○ **KEYWORD**

whom [hu:m] pron **1** (interrogative): **whom did you see?** ¿a quién viste?; **to**

whom did you give it? ¿a quién se lo diste?; **tell me from whom you received it** dígame de quién lo recibió **2** (*relative*) que; **to whom** a quien(es); **of whom** de quien(es), del/de la que *etc*; **the man whom I saw/to whom I wrote** el hombre que vi/a quien escribí; **the lady about/with whom I was talking** la señora de (la) que/con quien *or* (la) que hablaba

whore [hɔ:*] (*inf, pej*) *n* puta

○ KEYWORD

whose [hu:z] *adj*
1 (*possessive: interrogative*): **whose book is this?**, **whose is this book?** ¿de quién es este libro?; **whose pencil have you taken?** ¿de quién es el lápiz que has cogido?; **whose daughter are you?** ¿de quién eres hija? **2** (*possessive: relative*) cuyo/a, *pl* cuyos/as; **the man whose son you rescued** el hombre cuyo hijo rescataste; **those whose passports I have** aquellas personas cuyos pasaportes tengo; **the woman whose car was stolen** la mujer a quien le robaron el coche ▷ *pron* de quién; **whose is this?** ¿de quién es esto?; **I know whose it is** sé de quién es

○ KEYWORD

why [waɪ] *adv* por qué; **why not?** ¿por qué no?; **why not do it now?** ¿por qué no lo haces (*or* hacemos *etc*) ahora? ▷ *conj*: **I wonder why he said that** me pregunto por qué dijo eso; **that's not why I'm here** no es por eso (por lo) que estoy aquí; **the reason why** la razón por la que
▷ *excl* (*expressing surprise, shock, annoyance*) ¡hombre!, ¡vaya!; (*explaining*): **why, it's you!** ¡hombre, eres tú!; **why, that's impossible** ¡pero sí eso es imposible!

wicked ['wɪkɪd] *adj* malvado, cruel
wicket ['wɪkɪt] *n* (*Cricket: stumps*) palos *mpl*; (: *grass area*) terreno de juego
wide [waɪd] *adj* ancho; (*area, knowledge*) vasto, grande; (*choice*) amplio ▷ *adv*: **to open ~** abrir de par en par; **to shoot ~** errar el tiro; **widely** *adv* (*travelled*) mucho; (*spaced*) muy; **it is widely believed/known that ...** mucha gente piensa/sabe que ...; **widen** *vt* ensanchar; (*experience*) ampliar ▷ *vi* ensancharse; **wide open** *adj* abierto de par en par; **widespread** *adj* extendido, general

widow ['wɪdəu] *n* viuda; **widower** *n* viudo
width [wɪdθ] *n* anchura; (*of cloth*) ancho
wield [wi:ld] *vt* (*sword*) blandir; (*power*) ejercer
wife [waɪf] (*pl* **wives**) *n* mujer *f*, esposa
wig [wɪg] *n* peluca
wild [waɪld] *adj* (*animal*) salvaje; (*plant*) silvestre; (*person*) furioso, violento; (*idea*) descabellado; (*rough: sea*) bravo; (: *land*) agreste; (: *weather*) muy revuelto; **wilderness** ['wɪldənɪs] *n* desierto; **wildlife** *n* fauna; **wildly** *adv* (*behave*) locamente; (*lash out*) a diestro y siniestro; (*guess*) a lo loco; (*happy*) a más no poder

○ KEYWORD

will [wɪl] *aux vb* **1** (*forming future tense*): **I will finish it tomorrow** lo terminaré *or* voy a terminar mañana; **I will have finished it by tomorrow** lo habré terminado para mañana; **will you do it? – yes I will/no I won't** ¿lo harás? – sí/no
2 (*in conjectures, predictions*): **he will** *or* **he'll be there by now** ya habrá *or* debe (de) haber llegado; **that will be the postman** será *or* debe ser el cartero
3 (*in commands, requests, offers*): **will you be quiet!** ¿quieres callarte?; **will you help me?** ¿quieres ayudarme?; **will you have a cup of tea?** ¿te apetece un té?; **I won't put up with it!** ¡no lo soporto! ▷ *vt* (*pt, pp* **willed**): **to will sb to do sth** desear que algn haga algo; **he willed himself to go on** con gran fuerza de voluntad, continuó
▷ *n* voluntad *f*; (*testament*) testamento

willing ['wɪlɪŋ] *adj* (*with goodwill*) de buena voluntad; (*enthusiastic*) entusiasta; **he's ~ to do it** está dispuesto a hacerlo; **willingly** *adv* con mucho gusto
willow ['wɪləu] *n* sauce *m*
willpower ['wɪlpauə*] *n* fuerza de voluntad
wilt [wɪlt] *vi* marchitarse
win [wɪn] (*pt, pp* **won**) *n* victoria, triunfo ▷ *vt* ganar; (*obtain*) conseguir, lograr ▷ *vi* ganar; **win over** *vt* convencer a
wince [wɪns] *vi* encogerse
wind¹ [wɪnd] *n* viento; (*Med*) gases *mpl* ▷ *vt* (*take breath away from*) dejar sin aliento a
wind² [waɪnd] (*pt, pp* **wound**) *vt* enrollar; (*wrap*) envolver; (*clock, toy*) dar cuerda a ▷ *vi* (*road, river*) serpentear; **wind down** *vt* (*car window*) bajar; (*fig: production, business*) disminuir; **wind up** *vt* (*clock*) dar cuerda a; (*debate, meeting*) concluir, terminar

windfall ['wɪndfɔːl] n golpe m de
suerte

winding ['waɪndɪŋ] adj (road) tortuoso;
(staircase) de caracol

windmill ['wɪndmɪl] n molino de viento

window ['wɪndəu] n ventana; (in car, train)
ventanilla; (in shop etc) escaparate m (SP);
vidriera (LAM); **window box** n jardinera
de ventana; **window cleaner** n (person)
limpiacristales mf inv; **window pane** n
cristal m; **window seat** n asiento junto a la
ventana; **windowsill** n alféizar m, repisa

windscreen ['wɪndskriːn] (us **windshield**)
n parabrisas m inv; **windscreen wiper** (us
windshield wiper) n limpiaparabrisas
m inv

windsurfing ['wɪndsəːfɪŋ] n windsurf m

windy ['wɪndɪ] adj de mucho viento; **it's
~** hace viento

wine [waɪn] n vino; **wine bar** n enoteca;
wine glass n copa (para vino); **wine list** n
lista de vinos; **wine tasting** n degustación
f de vinos

wing [wɪŋ] n ala; (Aut) aleta; **wing mirror**
n (espejo) retrovisor m

wink [wɪŋk] n guiño, pestañeo ▷ vi
guiñar, pestañear

winner ['wɪnə*] n ganador(a) m/f

winning ['wɪnɪŋ] adj (team) ganador(a);
(goal) decisivo; (smile) encantador(a)

winter ['wɪntə*] n invierno ▷ vi invernar;
winter sports npl deportes mpl de
invierno; **wintertime** n invierno

wipe [waɪp] n: **to give sth a ~** pasar un
trapo sobre algo ▷ vt limpiar; (tape) borrar;
wipe out vt (debt) liquidar; (memory) borrar;
(destroy) destruir; **wipe up** vt limpiar

wire ['waɪə*] n alambre m; (Elec) cable m
(eléctrico); (Tel) telegrama m ▷ vt (house)
poner la instalación eléctrica en;
(also: **~ up**) conectar; (person: telegram)
telegrafiar

wiring ['waɪərɪŋ] n instalación f
eléctrica

wisdom ['wɪzdəm] n sabiduría, saber
m; (good sense) cordura; **wisdom tooth** n
muela del juicio

wise [waɪz] adj sabio; (sensible) juicioso

wish [wɪʃ] n deseo ▷ vt querer; **best ~es**
(on birthday etc) felicidades fpl; **with best
~es** (in letter) saludos mpl, recuerdos mpl; **to
~ sb goodbye** despedirse de algn; **he ~ed
me well** me deseó mucha suerte; **to ~ to
do/sb to do sth** querer hacer/que algn haga
algo; **to ~ for** desear

wistful ['wɪstful] adj pensativo

wit [wɪt] n ingenio, gracia; (also: **~s**)
inteligencia; (person) chistoso/a

witch [wɪtʃ] n bruja

○ **KEYWORD**

with [wɪð, wɪθ] prep **1** (accompanying, in
the company of) con (con +mí, ti, sí = conmigo,
contigo, consigo); **I was with him** estaba con
él; **we stayed with friends** nos quedamos
en casa de unos amigos; **I'm (not) with you**
(don't understand) (no) te entiendo; **to be
with it** (inf: person: up-to-date) estar al tanto;
(: alert) ser despabilado

2 (descriptive, indicating manner etc) con; de;
a room with a view una habitación con
vistas; **the man with blue eyes** el hombre
de los ojos azules; **red with anger** rojo de
ira; **to shake with fear** temblar de miedo;
to fill sth with water llenar algo de agua

withdraw [wɪθ'drɔː] vt retirar, sacar ▷ vi
retirarse; **to ~ money (from the bank)**
retirar fondos (del banco); **withdrawal** n
retirada; (of money) reintegro; **withdrawn**
pp of **withdraw** ▷ adj (person) reservado,
introvertido

withdrew [wɪθ'druː] pt of **withdraw**

wither ['wɪðə*] vi marchitarse

withhold [wɪθ'həuld] vt (money) retener;
(decision) aplazar; (permission) negar;
(information) ocultar

within [wɪð'ɪn] prep dentro de ▷ adv
dentro; **~ reach (of)** al alcance (de); **~ sight
(of)** a la vista (de); **~ the week** antes de
acabar la semana; **~ a mile (of)** a menos de
una milla (de)

without [wɪð'aut] prep sin; **to go ~ sth**
pasar sin algo

withstand [wɪθ'stænd] vt resistir a

witness ['wɪtnɪs] n testigo mf ▷ vt
(event) presenciar; (document) atestiguar
la veracidad de; **to bear ~ to** (fig) ser
testimonio de

witty ['wɪtɪ] adj ingenioso

wives [waɪvz] npl of **wife**

wizard ['wɪzəd] n hechicero

wk abbr = **week**

wobble ['wɔbl] vi temblar; (chair) cojear

woe [wəu] n desgracia

woke [wəuk] pt of **wake**

woken ['wəukən] pp of **wake**

wolf [wulf] n lobo

woman ['wumən] (pl **women**) n mujer f

womb [wuːm] n matriz f, útero

won [wʌn] pt, pp of **win**

wonder ['wʌndə*] n maravilla, prodigio;
(feeling) asombro ▷ vi: **to ~ whether/why**
preguntarse si/por qué; **to ~ at** asombrarse
de; **to ~ about** pensar sobre or en; **it's no**

~ (that) no es de extrañarse (que +*subjun*);
wonderful *adj* maravilloso
won't [wəunt] = **will not**
wood [wud] *n* (*timber*) madera; (*forest*)
bosque *m*; **wooden** *adj* de madera;
woodwind *n* (*Mus*) instrumentos *mpl*
de viento de madera; **woodwork** *n*
carpintería
wool [wul] *n* lana; **to pull the ~ over sb's**
eyes (*fig*) engatusar a algn; **woollen** (*us*
woolen) *adj* de lana; **woolly** (*us* **wooly**) *adj*
lanudo, de lana; (*fig*: *ideas*) confuso
word [wə:d] *n* palabra; (*news*) noticia;
(*promise*) palabra (de honor) ▷ *vt* redactar;
in other ~s en otras palabras; **to break/**
keep one's ~ faltar a la palabra/cumplir la
promesa; **to have ~s with sb** reñir con algn;
word processing *n* proceso de textos;
word processor *n* procesador *m* de textos
wore [wɔ:*] *pt of* **wear**
work [wə:k] *n* trabajo; (*job*) empleo,
trabajo; (*Art, Literature*) obra ▷ *vi* trabajar;
(*mechanism*) funcionar, marchar; (*medicine*)
ser eficaz, surtir efecto ▷ *vt* (*shape*)
trabajar; (*stone etc*) tallar; (*mine etc*) explotar;
(*machine*) manejar, hacer funcionar ▷ *npl*
(*of clock, machine*) mecanismo; **to be out**
of ~ estar parado, no tener trabajo; **to ~**
loose (*part*) desprenderse; (*knot*) aflojarse;
works *n* (*BRIT*: *factory*) fábrica; **work out**
vi (*plans etc*) salir bien, funcionar; **works**
vt (*problem*) resolver; (*plan*) elaborar;
it works out at £100 suma 100 libras;
worker *n* trabajador(a) *m/f*, obrero/a;
work experience *n*: **I'm going to do my**
work experience in a factory voy a hacer
las prácticas en una fábrica; **workforce**
n mano de obra; **working class** *n* clase
f obrera ▷ *adj*: **working-class** obrero;
working week *n* semana laboral;
workman (*irreg*) *n* obrero; **work of art** *n*
obra de arte; **workout** *n* (*Sport*) sesión *f*
de ejercicios; **work permit** *n* permiso de
trabajo; **workplace** *n* lugar *m* de trabajo;
worksheet *n* (*Scol*) hoja de ejercicios;
workshop *n* taller *m*; **work station** *n*
puesto *or* estación *f* de trabajo; **work**
surface *n* encimera; **worktop** *n* encimera
world [wə:ld] *n* mundo ▷ *cpd* (*champion*)
del mundo; (*power, war*) mundial; **to think**
the ~ of sb (*fig*) tener un concepto muy alto
de algn; **World Cup** *n* (*Football*): **the World**
Cup el Mundial, los Mundiales; **world-wide**
adj mundial, universal; **World-Wide Web**
n: **the World-Wide Web** el World Wide Web
worm [wə:m] *n* (*also*: **earth ~**) lombriz *f*
worn [wɔ:n] *pp of* **wear** ▷ *adj* usado;
worn-out *adj* (*object*) gastado; (*person*)
rendido, agotado
worried ['wʌrɪd] *adj* preocupado
worry ['wʌrɪ] *n* preocupación *f* ▷ *vt*
preocupar, inquietar ▷ *vi* preocuparse;
worrying *adj* inquietante
worse [wə:s] *adj, adv* peor ▷ *n* lo peor;
a change for the ~ un empeoramiento;
worsen *vt, vi* empeorar; **worse off** *adj*
(*financially*): **to be worse off** tener menos
dinero; (*fig*): **you'll be worse off this way**
de esta forma estarás peor que nunca
worship ['wə:ʃɪp] *n* adoración *f* ▷ *vt*
adorar; **Your W~** (*BRIT*: *to mayor*) señor
alcalde; (: *to judge*) señor juez
worst [wə:st] *adj, adv* peor ▷ *n* lo peor; **at**
~ en lo peor de los casos
worth [wə:θ] *n* valor *m* ▷ *adj*: **to be ~**
valer; **it's ~ it** vale *or* merece la pena; **to be ~**
one's while (to do) merecer la pena (hacer);
worthless *adj* sin valor; (*useless*) inútil;
worthwhile *adj* (*activity*) que merece la
pena; (*cause*) loable
worthy ['wə:ðɪ] *adj* respetable; (*motive*)
honesto; **~ of** digno de

⊙ **KEYWORD**

would [wud] *aux vb* **1** (*conditional tense*): **if**
you asked him he would do it si se lo
pidieras, lo haría; **if you had asked him**
he would have done it si se lo hubieras
pedido, lo habría *or* hubiera hecho
2 (*in offers, invitations, requests*): **would you**
like a biscuit? ¿quieres una galleta?; (*formal*)
¿querría una galleta?; **would you ask him**
to come in? ¿quiere hacerle pasar?; **would**
you open the window please? ¿quiere *or*
podría abrir la ventana, por favor?
3 (*in indirect speech*): **I said I would do it** dije
que lo haría
4 (*emphatic*): **it WOULD have to snow today!**
¡tenía que nevar precisamente hoy!
5 (*insistence*): **she wouldn't behave** no
quiso comportarse bien
6 (*conjecture*): **it would have been midnight**
sería medianoche; **it would seem so** parece
ser que sí
7 (*indicating habit*): **he would go there on**
Mondays iba allí los lunes

wouldn't ['wudnt] = **would not**
wound¹ [wu:nd] *n* herida ▷ *vt* herir
wound² [waund] *pt, pp of* **wind²**
wove [wəuv] *pt of* **weave**
woven ['wəuvən] *pp of* **weave**
wrap [ræp] *vt* (*also*: **~ up**) envolver;
(*gift*) envolver, abrigar ▷ *vi* (*dress warmly*)
abrigarse; **wrapper** *n* (*on chocolate*) papel

w

m; (BRIT: *of book*) sobrecubierta; **wrapping** *n* envoltura, envase *m*; **wrapping paper** *n* papel *m* de envolver; (*fancy*) papel *m* de regalo

wreath [riːð, *pl* riːðz] *n* (*funeral wreath*) corona

wreck [rɛk] *n* (*ship: destruction*) naufragio; (: *remains*) restos *mpl* del barco; (*pej: person*) ruina ▷ *vt* (*car etc*) destrozar; (*chances*) arruinar; **wreckage** *n* restos *mpl*; (*of building*) escombros *mpl*

wren [rɛn] *n* (*Zool*) reyezuelo

wrench [rɛntʃ] *n* (*Tech*) llave *f* inglesa; (*tug*) tirón *m*; (*fig*) dolor *m* ▷ *vt* arrancar; **to ~ sth from sb** arrebatar algo violentamente a algn

wrestle ['rɛsl] *vi*: **to ~ (with sb)** luchar (con or contra algn); **wrestler** *n* luchador(a) *m/f* (de lucha libre); **wrestling** *n* lucha libre

wretched ['rɛtʃɪd] *adj* miserable

wriggle ['rɪgl] *vi* (*also*: **~ about**) menearse, retorcerse

wring [rɪŋ] (*pt, pp* **wrung**) *vt* retorcer; (*wet clothes*) escurrir; (*fig*): **to ~ sth out of sb** sacar algo por la fuerza a algn

wrinkle ['rɪŋkl] *n* arruga ▷ *vt* arrugar ▷ *vi* arrugarse

wrist [rɪst] *n* muñeca

writable ['raɪtəbl] *adj* (CD, DVD) escribible

write [raɪt] (*pt* **wrote**, *pp* **written**) *vt* escribir; (*cheque*) extender ▷ *vi* escribir; **write down** *vt* escribir; (*note*) apuntar; **write off** *vt* (*debt*) borrar (como incobrable); (*fig*) desechar por inútil; **write out** *vt* escribir; **write-off** *n* siniestro total; **writer** *n* escritor(a) *m/f*

writing ['raɪtɪŋ] *n* escritura; (*hand-writing*) letra; (*of author*) obras *fpl*; **in ~** por escrito; **writing paper** *n* papel *m* de escribir

written ['rɪtn] *pp of* **write**

wrong [rɔŋ] *adj* (*wicked*) malo; (*unfair*) injusto; (*incorrect*) equivocado, incorrecto; (*not suitable*) inoportuno, inconveniente; (*reverse*) del revés ▷ *adv* equivocadamente ▷ *n* injusticia ▷ *vt* ser injusto con; **you are ~ to do it** haces mal en hacerlo; **you are ~ about that, you've got it ~** en eso estás equivocado; **to be in the ~** no tener razón, tener la culpa; **what's ~?** ¿qué pasa?; **to go ~** (*person*) equivocarse; (*plan*) salir mal; (*machine*) estropearse; **wrongly** *adv* mal, incorrectamente; (*by mistake*) por error; **wrong number** *n* (Tel): **you've got the wrong number** se ha equivocado de número

wrote [rəʊt] *pt of* **write**

wrung [rʌŋ] *pt, pp of* **wring**

WWW *n abbr* (= *World Wide Web*) WWW *m*

XL *abbr* = **extra large**

Xmas ['ɛksməs] *n abbr* = **Christmas**

X-ray ['ɛksreɪ] *n* radiografía ▷ *vt* radiografiar, sacar radiografías de

xylophone ['zaɪləfəʊn] *n* xilófono

yacht [jɔt] *n* yate *m*; **yachting** *n* (*sport*) balandrismo

yard [jɑːd] *n* patio; (*measure*) yarda; **yard sale** (*US*) *n* venta de objetos usados (*en el jardín de una casa particular*)

yarn [jɑːn] *n* hilo; (*tale*) cuento, historia

yawn [jɔːn] *n* bostezo ▷ *vi* bostezar

yd. *abbr* (=yard) yda

yeah [jɛə] (*inf*) *adv* sí

year [jɪə*] *n* año; **to be 8 ~s old** tener 8 años; **an eight-~-old child** un niño de ocho años (de edad); **yearly** *adj* anual ▷ *adv* anualmente, cada año

yearn [jəːn] *vi*: **to ~ for sth** añorar algo, suspirar por algo

yeast [jiːst] *n* levadura

yell [jɛl] *n* grito, alarido ▷ *vi* gritar

yellow ['jɛləu] *adj* amarillo; **Yellow Pages®** *npl* páginas *fpl* amarillas

yes [jɛs] *adv* sí ▷ *n* sí *m*; **to say/answer ~** decir/contestar que sí

yesterday ['jɛstədɪ] *adv* ayer ▷ *n* ayer *m*; **~ morning/evening** ayer por la mañana/tarde; **all day ~** todo el día de ayer

yet [jɛt] *adv* ya; (*negative*) todavía ▷ *conj* sin embargo, a pesar de todo; **it is not finished ~** todavía no está acabado; **the best ~** el/la mejor hasta ahora; **as ~** hasta ahora, todavía

yew [juː] *n* tejo

Yiddish ['jɪdɪʃ] *n* yiddish *m*

yield [jiːld] *n* (*Agr*) cosecha; (*Comm*) rendimiento ▷ *vt* ceder; (*results*) producir, dar; (*profit*) rendir ▷ *vi* rendirse, ceder; (*US Aut*) ceder el paso

yob(bo) ['jɔb(bəu)] *n* (*BRIT inf*) gamberro

yoga ['jəugə] *n* yoga *m*

yog(h)ourt ['jəugət] *n* yogur *m*

yog(h)urt ['jəugət] *n* =**yog(h)ourt**

yolk [jəuk] *n* yema (de huevo)

○ **KEYWORD**

you [juː] *pron* **1** (*subject: familiar*) tú; (*pl*) vosotros/as (*SP*), ustedes (*LAM*); (*polite*) usted; (*pl*) ustedes; **you are very kind** eres/es *etc* muy amable; **you Spanish enjoy your food** a vosotros (*or* ustedes) los españoles os (*or* les) gusta la comida; **you and I will go** iremos tú y yo

2 (*object: direct: familiar*) te; (*pl*) os (*SP*), les (*LAM*); (*polite*) le; (*pl*) les; (*f*) la; (*pl*) las; **I know you** te/le *etc* conozco

3 (*object: indirect: familiar*) te; (*pl*) os (*SP*), les (*LAM*); (*polite*) le; (*pl*) les; **I gave the letter to you yesterday** te/os *etc* di la carta ayer

4 (*stressed*): **I told you to do it** te dije a ti que lo hicieras, es a ti a quien dije que lo hicieras; *see also* **3; 5**

5 (*after prep: NB: con +ti = contigo: familiar*) ti; (*pl*) vosotros/as (*SP*), ustedes (*LAM*); (: *polite*) usted; (*pl*) ustedes; **it's for you** es para ti/vosotros *etc*

6 (*comparisons: familiar*) tú; (*pl*) vosotros/as (*SP*), ustedes (*LAM*); (: *polite*) usted; (*pl*) ustedes; **she's younger than you** es más joven que tú/vosotros *etc*

7 (*impersonal one*): **fresh air does you good** el aire puro (te) hace bien; **you never know** nunca se sabe; **you can't do that!** ¡eso no se hace!

you'd [juːd] = **you had; you would**

you'll [juːl] = **you will; you shall**

young [jʌŋ] *adj* joven ▷ *npl* (*of animal*) cría; (*people*): **the ~** los jóvenes, la juventud; **youngster** *n* joven *mf*

your [jɔː*] *adj* tu; (*pl*) vuestro; (*formal*) su; *see also* **my**

you're [juə*] = **you are**

yours [jɔːz] *pron* tuyo (*pl*), vuestro; (*formal*) suyo; *see also* **faithfully; mine¹** *see also* **sincerely**

yourself [jɔːˈsɛlf] *pron* tú mismo; (*complement*) te; (*after prep*) tí (mismo); (*formal*) usted mismo; (: *complement*) se; (: *after prep*) sí (mismo); **yourselves** *pl pron* vosotros mismos; (*after prep*) vosotros (mismos); (*formal*) ustedes (mismos); (: *complement*) se; (: *after prep*) sí mismos; *see also* **oneself**

youth [*pl* juːðz *n* juventud *f*; (*young man*) joven *m*; **youth club** *n* club *m* juvenil; **youthful** *adj* juvenil; **youth hostel** *n* albergue *m* de juventud

you've [juːv] = **you have**

Z

zeal [ziːl] *n* celo, entusiasmo
zebra ['ziːbrə] *n* cebra; **zebra crossing**
 (BRIT) *n* paso de peatones
zero ['zɪərəu] *n* cero
zest [zɛst] *n* ánimo, vivacidad *f*; (*of orange*)
 piel *f*
zigzag ['zɪgzæg] *n* zigzag *m* ▷ *vi*
 zigzaguear, hacer eses
Zimbabwe [zɪm'bɑːbwɪ] *n* Zimbabwe *m*
zinc [zɪŋk] *n* cinc *m*, zinc *m*
zip [zɪp] *n* (*also:* ~ **fastener,** (US) ~**per**)
 cremallera (SP), cierre (AM) *m*, zíper *m* (MEX,
 CAM) ▷ *vt* (*also:* ~ **up**) cerrar la cremallera
 de; (*file*) comprimir; **zip code** (US) *n*
 código postal; **zip file** *n* (*Comput*) archivo
 comprimido; **zipper** (US) *n* cremallera
zit [zɪt] *n* grano
zodiac ['zəudɪæk] *n* zodíaco
zone [zəun] *n* zona
zoo [zuː] *n* (jardín *m*) zoo *m*
zoology [zu'ɔlədʒɪ] *n* zoología
zoom [zuːm] *vi*: **to ~ past** pasar zumbando;
 zoom lens *n* zoom *m*
zucchini [zuː'kiːnɪ] (US) *n(pl)*
 calabacín(ines) *m(pl)*